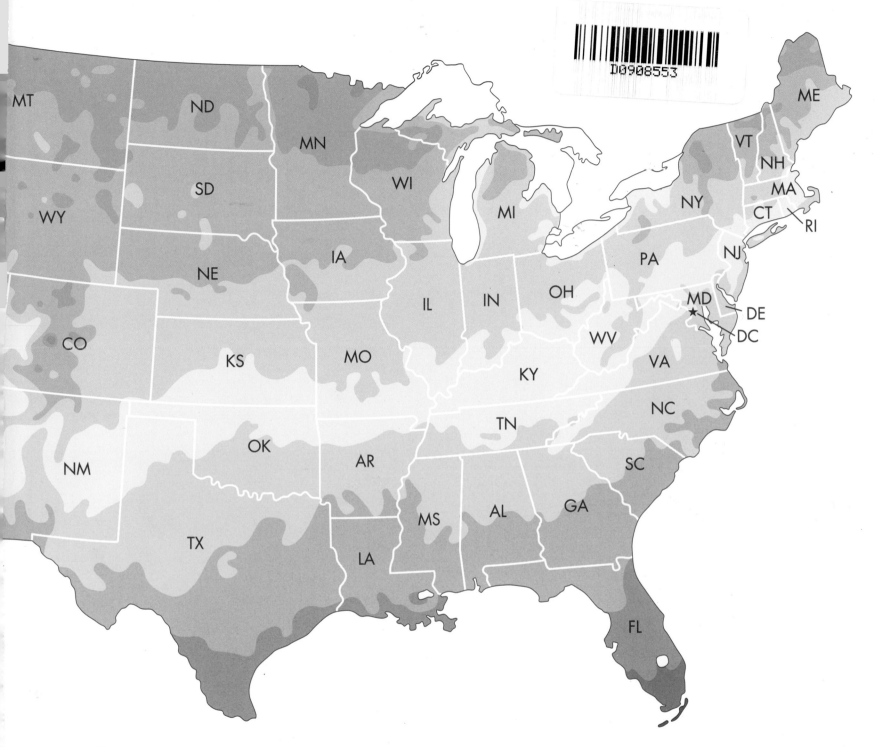

This system for rating hardiness has some obvious limitations. Microclimates are likely to make a particular garden warmer or colder than temperatures in the surrounding area. As a result, your yard may not entirely agree with the zone assigned to it by this map. In addition, this map does not take into account the threat that summer heat, humidity, and climate change may pose to a plant's survival, especially in the south-ern states. Overall, however, the zone system of rating plant hardiness does provide a simple and fairly reliable guide to the adaptation of plants to the climate in your region. Because the USDA map has been accepted as the standard hardiness index by the U.S. nursery industry, it is a convenient shopping guide; generally zones of hardiness are listed in nursery catalogs. When in doubt, check with nursery staff before planting.

For Canada's hardiness zones, see inside back cover.

THE ALL-NEW
ILLUSTRATED GUIDE TO
Gardening

THE ALL-NEW ILLUSTRATED GUIDE TO

Gardening

PLANNING • SELECTION • PROPAGATION • ORGANIC SOLUTIONS

EDITED BY

Fern Marshall Bradley
Trevor Cole

The Reader's Digest Association, Inc.
New York, NY / Montreal

The All-New Illustrated Guide to Gardening

Published by World Publications Group, Inc.
140 Laurel Street
East Bridgewater, MA 02333
www.wrldpub.com

Reader's Digest Project Staff

Project Editor: Robert Ronald
Senior Designer: Andrée Payette
Senior Editor: Pamela Johnson
Assistant Editors: Jesse Corbeil, John David Gravenor
Assistant Designers: Ann Devoe, Solange Laberge
Copy Editor: Anita Winterberg
Photo Researcher: Rachel Irwin
Cover Designer: Jennifer Tokarski
Senior Art Director: George McKeon
Indexer: Patricia Buchanan

Reader's Digest Trade Publishing

Executive Editor, Trade Publishing: Dolores York
Manufacturing Manager: Elizabeth Dinda
Associate Publisher, Trade Publishing: Rosanne McManus
President and Publisher, Trade Publishing: Harold Clarke

Library of Congress Cataloging-in-Publication Data

The all-new illustrated guide to gardening : planning, selection, propogation, organic solutions.
    p. cm.
  "Consultants: Fern Marshall Bradley, Trevor Cole"
  Includes index.
  ISBN 978-1-4643-0028-8
 1. Gardening. I. Bradley, Fern Marshall. II. Cole, Trevor J. (Trevor Jack)
III. Reader's Digest Association.

SB453.A613 2009
635--dc22

                  2008038499

Note to Our Readers

This publication is designed to provide useful information to the reader.
Products or active ingredients, treatments, and the names of organizations that appear in this publication
are included for informational purposes only; the inclusion of commercial products in the book
does not imply endorsement by Reader's Digest, nor does the omission of any product or active ingredient
or treatment advice indicate disapproval by Reader's Digest. When using any commercial product,
readers should read and follow all label directions carefully.

We are committed to both the quality of our products and the service we provide to our customers.
We value your comments, so please feel free to contact us.
The Reader's Digest Association, Inc.
Adult Trade Publishing
44 S. Broadway
White Plains, NY 10601

For more Reader's Digest products and information, visit our website:
www.rd.com

Printed and bound in China

1 3 5 7 9 10 8 6 4 2

Contents

Introduction

This new edition of an old favorite has been completely revised, enlarged, and updated with the latest plant introductions and more than 500 new photographs and color illustrations. As many municipalities have now banned the use of chemical pest and weed controls, this new edition has been made ecologically friendly by replacing chemicals with organically safe methods to deal with these problems.

The new opening chapter explores garden planning, including environmentally friendly topics such as wildflower gardens, xeriscaping, rain gardens, and methods of encouraging wildlife. The book's content has been completely reorganized and expanded. For example, all the perennial plants are in one chapter, and new features on daylilies, hostas, ornamental grasses, and peonies have been added. The line drawings at the top of the pages giving cultural details have been redrawn in color to give a better representation of the plants.

The chapters on annuals, bulbs, perennials, trees, and shrubs now end with lists of plants suitable for specific locations or purposes, such as "Fragrant Bulbs" or "Trees for Acidic Soils." In addition, there is a list of plants that should be planted with caution, since they may become invasive under certain conditions.

The chapter on plant disorders has been completely revised and now gives organic methods to combat pests and diseases that may attack plants, as well as suggestions on how to control the weeds.

The All-New Illustrated Guide to Gardening answers the call for those who want to create and maintain a garden of beauty using safe organic methods, with the added assurance of getting great results.

A GUIDE TO PLANT NAMES

In *The All-New Illustrated Guide to Gardening* charts, plants are listed by their botanical, or scientific, names, with common names in parentheses. All known plants have a botanical name, usually two or three words. The first word, always capitalized, identifies the genus, a group marked by one or more common characteristics. This word, used with a second one—the specific epithet—provides the botanical name of the species, a division of genus. Third or fourth words are sometimes used to designate species' subdivisions (subspecies and varieties).

In the genus Magnolia, *M. grandiflora* is a magnolia species with, as the epithet suggests, large white flowers, and *M. g.* 'Saint Mary' is a variety of this. Unlike most plants, magnolias have the same botanical and common names. However, *M. grandiflora* is known both as southern magnolia and bull bay, and *M. acuminata* as cucumber tree. Buddleias' botanical and common names sound alike but are spelled differently—*Buddleja* is the genus.

Rose of Sharon is a good example of why plants are not readily identifiable by common name alone. This hardy shrub belongs to the genus *Hibiscus*, not—as one might expect—to the rose genus, *Rosa*. Rose of Sharon (*H. syriacus*) is related to the Chinese hibiscus (*H. rosa-sinensis*) but you would never know this from its common name.

Consider, too, that such well-known plants as myrtle, laurel, bluebell, and daisy refer to one plant in some localities and other, quite different, plants elsewhere. Only botanical names can be depended upon everywhere.

Naturally occurring varieties of plants are shown in italics, as in *Euonymus fortunei radicans*, for example; those that arose as horticultural selections are enclosed in single quotation marks, as in *E. f.* 'Emerald Gaiety'. Note that the word "variety" indicates not only species variations that have developed in the wild but also those that have occurred under cultivation, or have been hybridized.

The word "cultivar" (from cultivated variety) is used to distinguish horticultural selections and man-made hybrids from natural varieties.

A well-planned garden provides a place to relax and enjoy the flowers with a minimal amount of work once the initial construction and planting has been done.

Planning Your Garden

Whether it is a small town-house lot, or part of a large suburban yard, a garden should be a reflection of the owner's tastes and requirements. The plantings may be minimal or complex, but every plant should have a reason for being included.

Few of us are fortunate enough to plan our landscape from scratch. When we purchase a house, we inherit what someone else started. Whatever the state of the inherited landscape, be it simply a few shrubs or a planting of many different species, you, as the new owner, can do much to make it an ecologically friendly place. When deciding on plants to include, try and choose ones that will encourage birds and butterflies to visit, rather than ones that are attractive but have no food value for native fauna. Also try to incorporate an area of wildflowers that will provide food and shelter for the many predatory insects that feed on garden pests.

Landscapes start with planning and the first step is to make a rough plan of the existing landscape. This should show the location of the house on the lot, any fixed objects, such as driveways or utility poles, and the location of existing trees and shrubs. Do not be overly concerned with beds of annuals or perennials; they are relatively easy to move at a later date. It pays to spend the first year observing your property, and doing little actual work, except for mowing the lawn and general maintenance. During this time, keep careful notes on what is in flower on a weekly basis, try to identify the plants as they come into bloom (ask around the neighborhood—there may be a local keen gardener who could give advice on this), and if

they are worth the space they occupy. Keep a check on which parts of the garden receive sunlight at different times of the day and month, and just as important, which parts do not receive sunlight; these places will need shade-loving plants. Look at the trees and shrubs and decide if they are worth keeping. Most likely are, unless they are very weedy species. Trees may need a professional arborist to prune out crossing or diseased branches, but most shrubs can be safely pruned by the home owner following the illustrations shown in the chapter on shrubs. Also record the birds, animals, and obvious butterflies that come to feed. Most will be welcome, but some are not. For example, if you find that deer are a regular visitor, you will need to concentrate your new plantings on plants that deer do not like to eat (see list on p. 68).

The next decision involves thinking about what purpose you want your yard to serve. The needs of a family with young children are considerably different from those of a family whose children have grown. You may need to plan a play area, or make room for a swing set or climbing frame. You may want to include a vegetable or fruit garden to grow pesticide-free food for the family. Keep in mind also the amount of time you are able to devote to this hobby. The best gardening plan in the world is of little use without the

time to put it into practice and maintain the resulting landscape.

This is also the time to decide whether the character of the landscape will tend toward the formal or the informal. Formal design is mostly symmetrical, with virtually identical plantings on either side of an imaginary line running through the center. Although this line can be on a diagonal from corner to corner, it is more often a central walkway. The plantings are mirror images on either side of the line, edges are usually straight, and the plants are trimmed and formal looking. In an informal landscape the beds are often curved, plants are allowed to grow to their natural shape, and there is little or no repetition of design or plants. This is the type of landscape most home gardeners enjoy, since formal design is more difficult to achieve and more time consuming to keep up if it is done well.

Whatever style is your final choice, start small. Gradually implement the features drawn on the master plan so the work involved is spread over time and you find the level of involvement for which you have time and inclination to maintain. This will lead to a much more attractive and rewarding garden. We live in a time of instant everything, but trying to achieve too much, too soon, can lead to frustration and discouragement.

The Design Process

Make a list of the things you want in your landscape and gardens: vegetables, a sandbox, flowers for arrangements, roses, a pool or waterfall, a putting green. Trying to fit them all in is probably impossible, but here are some good ideas for trying out, on paper at least.

Garden shape. What shape is your property? The average city lot is about 50 x 100 feet with the house situated toward the front of the lot, giving a more-or-less square backyard. Many modern subdivisions, however, have moved away from the grid system of roads, and the resulting curved streets means that yards come in quite a wide range of shapes, from square to triangular to pie-shaped. Modern in-filling in cities has resulted in narrow houses with long narrow lots—avoid hedges or borders along the sides of such spaces, they make them look even more narrow. Instead, use borders across the area to divide it into a series of smaller spaces.

Three-part garden. When planning your garden, think of the property as being composed of three distinct areas. First, there is the welcome area where guests arrive. This is the area seen by passersby and where you make the first impression. This is the part of a private yard that is fairly public, unless shut off from view by a tall hedge or fence.

Next is the utility area where you keep necessary items such as garbage cans, bicycle racks, a tool shed; things you need, but do not want very visible to you or any guests.

Finally comes the living area where you relax and spend your free time, have space for a barbeque, maybe a lawn, flower gardens, and so on. This is your own private space, visitors come only when invited, and it is here that you lavish a lot of the time available for gardening.

Hardscaping. The first thing to consider and plan is what is known as hardscaping, specifically the layout of paths and walkways you will need to get around your property. It is paramount to think seriously about these details. What parts of the landscape you will need to access depends on the layout of your yard, but, while winding paths look good on paper, in practice people move in straight lines—look at the lawns on almost any high school, the students take the direct route, no matter where the walkways go. The main entrance should be wide enough for two people to walk side-by-side. Unless the soil is very well drained, it might pay to have this professionally installed so that it does not become uneven in time and cause someone to trip. Think also about moving soil and compost around your landscape. A wheelbarrow needs only a narrow path, but a two-wheeled cart needs a much wider one.

If you are planning to add a swimming pool at some later date, remember to leave access for the machinery that will be needed to dig the hole or transport an aboveground one. This includes, of course, a gate or door that allows entry into the yard and enough space to maneuver through it.

Sketch the locations of the hardscaping onto the rough plan and then find the list of features you wanted to have. Prioritize these and then try to fit them into the open spaces. It is rather like doing a jigsaw and some will have to be left out, but you should end up with a design that, in time, will give you a rewarding garden.

Another route is to buy one of the many garden design software programs. These vary considerably in price and complexity, but can help to ease the design process; although the more complex ones can have a steep learning curve. They generally require you to enter your zip code and then show a list of plants suitable for your area. The number of plants available increases with the price of the software and some allow you to add more plants. Some will allow you to peek into the future and can generate a picture of what various aspects of the garden will look like in 5, 10, or 20 years time as the plants grow. The more expensive programs allow you to zoom in to a specific part of the garden and enlarge it to plan an individual area, such as a perennial bed, in greater detail. When the planning is finished, the program will print out a list of the plants needed that you can take to the garden center and, if applicable, a list of the construction material needed to install the hardscaping.

Go vertical. In small town-house or condominium gardens, space can be limited. For best results, use trellises to grow annual climbers, train cucumbers upward, and support cherry tomatoes. Grow plants in containers that can be moved into prominence when at their peak. For more information on container plants, see Growing Shrubs in Containers on p. 256.

Patios. A patio does not have to be directly behind the house, providing it is linked to the house by a wide path. If there is a mature shade tree close by, the patio could go under that—grass will not thrive there anyway. From a visual point, interlocking bricks are better than cement slabs, but they need to be installed properly by a professional, and, to have them as a patio, vehicle access to the back garden may be necessary. Interlock comes in a wide range of patterns and is fairly flexible, removing the need for patios to be rectangular.

Right: An attractive entrance welcomes your guests. The annuals shown here, follow a spring display of tulips and forget-me-nots.

Making New Plantings

Always think about how the garden will look in the future. This requires considering the ultimate size of a shrub or tree before planting. Look up the height and spread as you make the plan and space plants far enough apart that the tips of the branches will not overlap at maturity. The plantings will look a bit sparse at first, but this is preferable to having to dig out well-rooted shrubs in a few years time because you did not realize how big they were going to grow. Set the plants far enough from the house that, when mature, they will not block windows, hide views, or make it difficult to wash windows. It is always best to select plants that will grow well in the type of soil and location you have, rather than trying to change things to suit the plant. And of course, some conditions, such as the weather, are beyond your control. If you live in a part of the country that is arid, it is wise to avoid raising plants that need moist growing conditions.

A lawn is generally considered an essential part of most suburban yards, but with increasing water shortages and restrictions on water use, it is well worth considering alternatives. Some of the plants listed in the section on ground covers will make good lawn substitutes, standing up to a reasonable amount of foot traffic, and as a result you may be able to reduce mowing time for good and use it for something more productive. If a lawn is desired, make sure it receives enough light to thrive, and has soil deep enough to be able to grow properly. Lawns on shallow soil seldom grow well and need frequent watering and fertilizing. When designing the lawn area, make curves gentle; wider than the minimum turning circle of a riding mower to eliminate maneuvering. Even with a push mower tight turns are difficult. For more information on ground covers, turn to Lawns and Ground Covers, starting on page 21.

Top left: Thyme and alyssum will take light foot traffic.
Left: Even a small courtyard garden can be an oasis of beauty and tranquility.
Above: Every garden needs a place to rest, if only to please the cat.

Hedges or Fences?

If there is a need to define the property line and provide privacy, there are two choices: hedges or fences. Initially, hedges are probably cheaper, but in the long run they are more time consuming, requiring clipping at least once a year. Like all live plants, they are not "instant," needing time to make a good visual barrier, and, even with regular clipping, they may eventually become too large. There is a large choice of hedging plants (see Hedges on p. 346) and this governs the size and texture of a hedge. They act as a wind filter and provide a relatively sheltered area on the lee side. In snowy locations, the denseness of the hedge has a large influence on the way the snow lays on the downwind side. Deciduous hedges that allow the wind to pass easily in winter will spread a snowfall across a wide area, while evergreen ones will tend to cause it to fall closer to the hedge.

Unlike hedges, which require time to mature, solid fences are instant and give the desired privacy from the start, but they are more expensive to install and will eventually rot and need replacing. Remember that if you are tempted to paint them, maintenance will be required and it could become almost as time consuming as the maintenance on a hedge. They act as a wind block and give an area of turbulence on the lee side, so plants grown close to a fence may need extra support in summer. In snowy locations, the snow piles up close to the downwind side, which could leave a deep snow cover where it is not wanted. A lattice fence, covered with annual vines, may give enough of a visual barrier and does not give the same snow problems since it offers little wind resistance.

This unusual fence of tree stumps provides a home for several different climbers. The wooden fence (right) makes a good support for a climbing rose.

The hedges provides privacy and act as a wind-break. They also hide some of the garden, giving a sense on mystery.

Sun and Shade

Almost every house has a shaded side, and this is obviously the place to grow shade-loving plants. But, the amount of shade varies by the season. In summer, when the sun is high, the band of shade may be fairly narrow, while in winter, when the sun is closer to the horizon, the band will be much wider. Make notes on this when evaluating the yard initially because a shrub with bright winter bark planted close to the house, for example, will be in shade during the winter and the bark will not stand out. When looking at the shaded area in spring to decide how many shade-loving plants to buy, remember that by July, this area will be much smaller and some of those shade plants will be in full sun.

Ideas for Saving Labor

Lawns set off flower beds nicely, but they also tend to spread into them. If the lawn is edged with concrete pavers, or bricks set in concrete, one wheel of the mower can run on this, limiting the amount of edging needed. Also available is plastic or aluminum lawn edging, which will prevent the lawn from growing into the flower bed. The grass, however, will still need to be trimmed along the edging to maintain a tidy appearance.

When planning borders and beds, especially for growing vegetables, be sure to make them narrow enough that you can reach the center without stepping on the bed itself. This way crops can be gathered, or flowers cut, soon after rain without compacting the soil. If a wide flower border is needed, remember to put stepping stones across it to give access to the back for deadheading, staking, etc. Also, it is a very good idea to keep high maintenance areas, such as rock gardens for example, small enough that they can be kept weeded in the time available.

Massed plantings, like those above, are easy to maintain as there is no space for weeds to grow. The raised bed edged with logs (top right) makes a very attractive feature that will add depth to the garden. The ground cover and shrubs in the garden shown at bottom right are time-savers because very little maintenance is required.

Wildlife Gardening

An ecologically friendly garden should be a haven for wildlife. Birds are a constant source of pleasure in the yard. Even if you are not a bird watcher, their bright colors, movement, and song adds much to the enjoyment. They also eat seeds and insects. To reap the benefits of these flying visitors in winter make food available, and provide water when it will not freeze. Evergreen trees and shrubs give shelter from winter winds and are used as nesting sites by many species of birds in summer. Offer a choice of other nesting sites. Simple bird boxes, purple martin houses, or hedges. The website http://library.fws.gov/Bird_Publications/house.html has information about nesting boxes and charts showing the size of the boxes and entrance holes for different species of birds.

Hummingbirds are always welcome and can be attracted to the garden by planting nectar-rich flowers and by making available feeders filled with sugar syrup (¼ cup of sugar dissolved in 1 cup of water, but add no food coloring. Either boil the water briefly or leave overnight to allow the chlorine to evaporate). They also eat small insects and spiders and help in the pollination of many of the plants they feed on.

Butterflies and moths can be encouraged to visit by growing nectar-rich plants. They prefer small fragrant flowers and rarely visit those with trumpet-shaped blooms like lilies, or those with large showy flowers like roses, even though they are scented. They are also attracted to water sources, such as a small mud puddle, or flat rocks sloping into the water of a garden pool. The butterflies will congregate there to drink.

Smaller still are the many beneficial insects that feed on some of the pests. Best known are the ladybird beetles that feed on aphids. There are many different species of ladybirds, with colors ranging from pale yellow to dark orange, along with different numbers of spots.

Praying mantises hide on the stems of plants and snatch passing insects out of the air, but eat the good ones along with the bad. Ground beetles, the black or brown ones that scurry away when you turn over a piece of wood or a stone, prey on many pests that live in the soil, such as cutworms and root maggots. In addition, there are hundreds of other species of hoverflies, parasitic wasps, lacewings, beetles, and bugs that are beneficial. They can be encouraged to take up residence by planting an area of nectar-producing plants with small flowers, including clover, goldenrod, alfalfa, yarrow, or by planting these in a flower border or as edging. Many of these beneficial insects are available from mail-order sources. For more information on pests, turn to the section on plant disorders on page 506. For more information on control methods, turn to page 542.

Far left: Birds and butterflies, naturally attracted to water, will be regular visitors in this garden.
Left: Adding a bird feeder in the garden can attract cardinals, songbirds that are likely to visit regularly.
Below: Majestic sunflowers will attract birds that feed on unwanted insects.

Some Wildlife Challenges

In general, larger animals are not welcome in the yard. Rabbits, groundhogs, gophers, deer, moose, and elk are too partial to home grown flowers and vegetables. Even the cute ones, squirrels and chipmunks, do a lot of damage by digging up bulbs and chewing shoots on trees and shrubs. Opossum, raccoons, and skunks are beneficial in that they eat beetles, grasshoppers, and other insects, but they also have a thing about garbage, opening bags and strewing the contents, or about digging holes in lawns to find grubs. Mice and voles are generally tolerated, providing they do not get indoors. They are difficult to control outdoors. Bats are now accepted as being beneficial and are encouraged to take up residence. They sleep all day and are active at dusk, feeding on the many nocturnal flying insects, such as mosquitoes. They can be given shelter in special bat houses, similar to a bird

house, but with the opening at the base. Visit www.wildaboutgardening.org and click on Bats under Attracting Wildlife for information about bats and plans for making a bat house.

The only other animal commonly found in the yard is the toad. Because they need water only for a short time during the spring mating season, toads are found in places that do not have a pond or permanent source of water. They live in damp areas, often near the house foundations, and come out at dusk to hunt. They will sit still and, with a flick of their sticky tongue, snatch an insect out of the air. They also eat cutworms, armyworms, slugs, snails, and sow bugs. Reward them by placing a shallow basin of water with the top sunk to ground level so that the toad can crawl in, absorb water through its skin, and then crawl out again.

Butterflies and moths, who are usually welcome visitors to a garden, do have a downside. Their young are caterpillars. While it is true they feed on plants, only a few, like the gypsy moth and the cabbage white butterfly, are so troublesome that they need to be controlled. Most plants can stand a few chewed leaves without any problems. The majority of moths are night flying and a walk around the garden at night with a flashlight reveals the numbers that are present.

A pile of small logs and rough sticks in an out-of-the-way corner of the garden provides a refuge for species, such as the mourning cloak, that overwinter as adults and are the first butterflies to appear in spring. You can also build your own special box where butterflies can overwinter in safety. To see the plans for making a box, go to www.igs.net/~wyliecoyote/butterfl.htm.

Top left: Toads like to soak in water, but live on land.
Top center: A scare crow will keep some birds away, but needs to be moved every few days to remain effective.
Top right: Berried shrubs and trees provide food for wintering birds as well as color in the winter garden.
Above: This garden wants everyone to know it is ecologically friendly.
Left: Adding a pathway and decorative features creates a connection between a garden and a bordering natural area.

Friendly Insects

Not all insects are garden pests. Many visitors are beneficial and can be encouraged by planting nectar-rich flowers, such as clover, goldenrod, alfalfa, and yarrow, which give a change of diet.

Ladybugs (ladybird beetles) may be red, orange, or yellow and the number of spots differs depending on the species. Both the adults and the (rather ugly) nymphs eat aphids, leafhoppers, mealybugs, and scale insects.

Hover flies look like small wasps but do not sting. As their name suggests, they tend to hover in one place. They eat aphids and mealybugs, as well as nectar and decaying fruit. They are also important as pollinators.

Lacewings may be green or brown, depending on the species, and are identified by their large, almost transparent wings, held vertically when at rest. They, and their larvae (called aphid-lions), feed on aphids, mealybugs, scale insects, thrips, and mites.

Chalcid, braconid, and ichneumon wasps are very small wasps that prey on a wide range of other insects (including a few beneficial ones). They generally lay an egg in the body of the prey, which hatches and feeds on the host. Insects attacked include aphids, armyworms, chinch bugs, corn borers, gypsy moths, long-horned beetles, mealybugs, sawflies, and scale insects.

Ground beetles are brown or black beetles that shelter under stones or pieces of wood during the day and hunt at night. They feed on armyworms, chinch bugs, cutworms, gypsy moths, and tent caterpillars.

Wheel bug is mainly a tree dweller and is recognized by a semi-circular crest on its head. It feeds on cutworms, hornworms, Japanese beetles, and other caterpillars.

Praying mantis are related to grasshoppers. They wait on a stem with their front legs in a "praying" position and snatch any passing insect out of the air.

Wildflower Gardens

A wildflower garden does not have to be huge. Even a modest area can be converted into a stand of wildflowers, which will be a magnet for butterflies and home for many of the insects that prey on garden pests. It does have to be in an open location with good air circulation (to minimize disease) and have full sun for at least half the day. Establishing a wildflower garden calls for careful preparation if the wildflowers are not to be crowded out by less desirable species. All perennial weeds need to be removed and the area should then be dug over or tilled. A rich soil is not needed because these plants are not heavy feeders. There is no need to add compost when digging.

To grow trouble-free wildflowers, the next requirement is patience. The area should be left for the weed seeds on the surface of the soil to germinate. As soon as there are a number of green shoots, shallowly hoe the entire bed. Repeat. Each time you hoe you bring to the surface more weed seeds, which can be killed, and which will not crowd out the desirable wildflower seedlings later. Make sure the hoeing is only shallow or deeper buried seeds will be brought to the surface. Ideally, the area should be left for a year to control weeds that germinate at different times. Alternatively, the soil can be solarized by covering it with black plastic, burying the edges, and allowing the sun to heat and sterilize the soil. The hotter the summer, the better this works, and a greater number of the deeper weed seeds will be killed.

Wildflower seed mixes are available from several different seed companies and they have mixtures to suit most climates where this type of garden is feasible. Look at the website www.prairienursery.com for information on various seed mixes or ask your local nurseryperson for more details.

Sow the seeds in early spring, as soon as the soil is dry enough to walk on and rake it just into the soil surface. If the weed control was done properly, there should be very few weed seedlings germinating to compete with the wildflowers.

Most mixes contain seeds of both annual and perennial plants. The annuals will bloom the first summer and set seed. The second year again will be mostly annuals, but the perennials will be getting larger and one or two varieties may flower. As the years progress, the perennials will gradually take over and the annuals will virtually disappear.

Top: Shallow steps are planted with a mix of wildflowers and lead to a meadow where the butterfly weed (*Asclepias*) is in flower.
Far right: Annual poppies put on a brilliant display in this patch of wildflowers.
Right: Butterfly weed lives up to its name and provides nectar for a monarch butterfly.

Rain Gardens

A rain garden is a planted area that collects the run-off water from a house roof or paved area and holds it until it percolates down into the ground water or is evaporated into the air by plants. By diverting water away from storm sewers and drainage ditches, more rain is returned to the ground water and contaminants are filtered out by the soil, rather than being flushed into the rivers. A rain garden should not have standing water, except immediately following heavy rain, and then for not more than 48 hours.

The size of the rain garden is determined by the drainage rate of the soil and the area that will capture the rain. Sandy soils that drain freely are ideal, but most other soils, except heavy clay, are suitable. If the drainage rate is slow, it may be necessary to excavate the soil and put a layer of coarse drainage material at the bottom. Test the permeability by digging a small hole, filling it with water and noting how long it takes to drain.

Locate the garden in full sun and at least 12 feet away from the house to prevent any chance of damage to the foundation. If the ground is sloping, it may be necessary to build a berm at the downslope side to retain the water. Also make sure that there is no chance of water flooding a neighbor's property following very heavy rain.

An extension to a downspout can lead water from the roof to a rain garden, or, if this would be impractical, an underground pipe can be installed to take the water from the downspout to the garden. If an above-ground extension is used, it should empty onto a pile of stones or a concrete pad to prevent soil erosion. For further construction details go to www.watershedactivities.com.

As previously mentioned, much of the water from a rain garden is evaporated into the air by the plants growing there. These are generally native plants that are able to withstand periodic flooding and also occasional periods of drought during summer. In many ways, this mimics the wildflower garden, and makes a good home for many beneficial insects, but the range of plants grown is smaller and will often include some woody plants whose deep root system helps to open channels into the subsoil so water can percolate away (see Shrubs For Specific Locations/Purposes on p. 340 for shrubs that can adapt to wet soils). Unlike the wildflower garden, the plants in a rain garden are not grown from seed sown on the site, but are nursery-grown young plants. This makes the initial cost greater, but the garden will reach maturity sooner. The transplants will need to be kept watered for the first summer, when rain does not do the job, but subsequently should be sufficiently well established to grow without additional water except in prolonged periods of drought. For an idea of the range of plants that will thrive in these conditions, visit www.infinetivity.com/~stack/rain.

Top left: A stone pathway is a central feature of the rain garden.
Top right: Overflow from the roof and barrel will generously water the surrounding plants.
Above: Native plants are subject to both dry conditions and occasional flooding following a storm.

Xeriscaping

This is the complete opposite of rain gardens, and may call for a complete change in attitude for someone moving from a water-rich region. Originating in Denver, Colorado, it is a water-conserving method of gardening for very dry areas, for places that do not have access to fresh water, or for regions where rainfall is limited to a certain period of the year. Although it may take more thought and time to implement than a conventional garden, it is easier to maintain, there is little or no mowing, and the water bill is smaller.

Native plants that are adapted to the local region are used where possible, together with summer-dormant bulbs, and other plants that tolerate arid conditions, such as deep-rooted perennials and plants with thick or hairy leaves that use less water. Lawns are reduced to a minimum and composed of drought-tolerant grass species, or are eliminated entirely. Even drought-resistant plants need water to get established and this is applied through drip irrigation—individual emitters that trickle water directly to the plant, rather than covering the entire area.

Plants with similar water requirements are grouped together so that watering, when needed, is applied only to a limited area. Where area watering is needed, on a vegetable patch for example, it should be given in early morning or late afternoon when the evaporation rate is least. Even then the area should be carefully watched so that water is not wasted on paved areas or other places where it is not needed.

The soil should be improved by the addition of organic materials so it will hold more water, but still be well aerated. Soils in some regions tend to be alkaline and low in phosphorous. A soil test, using a home kit, will indicate this. Add bone meal or rock phosphate if this is the case. Where possible, drought-tolerant trees and shrubs (see lists on p. 245 and p. 340) should be planted to block the prevailing wind and reduce evaporation from the soil.

Stop soil evaporation by covering all bare areas with a heavy mulch, which also helps limit soil temperature and smothers weed seedlings. Leaves, coarse compost, wood chips, shredded bark, pine needles, or coarse gravel are all suitable. Use whatever is available locally. Organic mulches will slowly decompose and need renewing from time to time. Wood chips or bark may also deplete the nitrogen in the soil as they break down. If plants start to turn yellow, add a source of nitrogen like blood meal or fish meal. The layer of mulch also serves to hide the main irrigation pipes that feed the emitters for the individual plants.

For more information, including resources to help promote and facilitate using water more efficiently, go to the Colorado Water Wise Council website at www.coloradowaterwise.org.

Top: The plants are grown as individuals with the soil between them mulched to conserve moisture in this xeriscape garden.
Middle left: Some cactus, like this *Opuntia humifusa*, are surprisingly hardy and will survive cold and deep snow.
Bottom left: The round boulders help to keep the soil moist and plant roots will grow under them.
Right: The annual rock rose (*Portulaca*) and perennial spurge (*Euphorbia*) will both grow well with minimal watering.

A well-maintained lawn makes the ideal recreation and play area. It is also the perfect complement to a colorful garden. Where water shortages occur in summer, an attractive and practical ground cover is a great alternative.

LAWNS AND GROUND COVERS

A lawn is an ideal setting for a home. It also provides a pleasing background for ornamental plants and a useful area for leisure-time activities.

Lawns not only beautify an open space; they also freshen the air, insulate the ground in winter, and reduce temperatures in summer. In very hot weather they can be substantially cooler than artificial grass or paving. (Tall grass is somewhat cooler than short grass, short grass appreciably cooler than bare soil.)

It is for good reason that well-tended lawns along residential streets have become classics of the North American landscape. A well-kept lawn forms an attractive setting for a house and is the perfect background for trees, shrubs, and flower beds.

Wherever lawns are grown extensively there is a tendency to take them for granted. We expect them to perform consistently under all kinds of stress, to make a mud-proof cover the year round, and to thrive on all types of soil, even in areas where the topsoil was stripped off before the lawn was planted.

Often, lawns are not given the appropriate and properly timed care. They are frequently overwatered or underwatered. They may be cut too low, rolled when it is unnecessary, or subjected to other mistreatment.

It is a tribute to the flexibility of lawn grasses that in spite of such handling they are durable enough under average conditions to keep on growing and even to withstand games and foot traffic.

Grass. Grasses are ideal because they have meristematic (growing point) tissue nestled near the soil surface and at the base of expanding leaves. Because these growth points are so low to the ground, mowing does them no harm. By contrast, other plants tend to grow from the tip, and if cut, they require a longer time to recover.

Grass is basically a crop, whether it grows as a lawn or a meadow. The harvesting is the mowing, which must be done regularly. If this activity, which is the most time-consuming requirement of lawn maintenance, is neglected, weed grasses become dominant and can sometimes smother the finer grasses completely.

Experience has shown which grasses are especially suited for lawns. Mostly these grasses evolved as pasture species, and with few exceptions they came from the Old World. They have adapted to North American climatic peculiarities, and special strains have evolved from which many of our most useful varieties have been developed.

For lawns in the southern states, warm-season grasses, including Bermuda, zoysia, and St. Augustine grass, flourish in hot summers and go dormant in winter. Be sure to overseed with annual grass in fall for winter color.

Cool-season grasses, like Kentucky bluegrass, flourish in cool spring and fall temperatures, and in mild climates in winter.

Other ground covers can be used: pachysandra, bearberry, and cotoneaster are just a few of the many choices available.

Requirements for a lawn. Given reasonable attention to watering and feeding when the grass is obviously in need, lawns will almost take care of themselves. The major requirement on the part of the homeowner is, of course, consistent mowing, which helps to maintain a tight turf and eliminate tall-growing weeds. Regular mowing keeps the lawn usable and attractive. When cut frequently, the clippings are short and can be left on the lawn.

Sunlight. Most lawn grasses do best if they have from four to six hours of sunlight a day. One reason for this requirement is that shade is usually created by trees and, in shady situations, there is direct competition between the surface-feeding roots of the trees and the roots of lawn grass.

The grasses that do best in the shade, such as *Poa trivialis*, are deep rooted. Heavier fertilization in shady places is advisable to provide plant food for the tree roots and for those of the lawn grass as well.

Fertilizer. Except on naturally fertile soils, feeding a lawn is necessary to maintain its quality. Although lawns can survive without feeding, fertilized lawns wear better, fight weeds better, and look better. Many organic fertilizers are available.

Watering. Depending on where you live, watering may be needed. Grasses are equipped to endure some drought and actually may be healthier for it. But during long dry periods they will look better if irrigated regularly.

Weeds and pests. A consideration that cannot be overlooked is weed and pest control. Weeds can be controlled without herbicides. Insects, fortunately, are a less prevalent problem. Suggested controls for weeds and pests are given on pages 25–27 and 548.

Diseases. Diseases ebb and flow in response to weather, seasonal activity, and physiological changes. Controlling them is discussed on pages 26, 27, and 542. The best way to approach the problem is to plant disease-tolerant grasses (which most of the newer varieties are).

Other treatments. There may be an occasional need for soil aerifying, thatch removing, liming, or acidifying the soil. On some soils, compaction is a major problem, and the lawn will need aerating every couple of years. Details on these procedures are included on the pages that follow.

In most cases, however, a lawn will get along nicely with no more than regular mowing and well-planned fertilizing, supplemented when necessary by irrigation and aerating.

Types of lawn. Some homeowners want a perfect lawn, meticulously kept; others are contented with an informal lawn of grasses and clover.

The former will devote much time and money to the lawn and may choose elegant grasses, such as those used for golf greens, which require a great deal of care. The latter will not mind a mix of grasses and even a few weeds, so long as the lawn remains dense and green overall.

Most homeowners choose a lawn somewhere in between. They want a nice-looking lawn that is serviceable and requires little care.

A wide selection of grasses to meet all these requirements is available. In the North, named varieties of Kentucky bluegrasses, fine fescues, and perennial ryegrasses, as well as some varieties of bent grass are among the most suitable choices.

In the South, Bermuda, zoysia, and Bahia grasses grow well. These are grown vegetatively and are sold as small plants, or as "plugs," or as short pieces of stems with several shoots, or "sprigs." Named varieties of these grasses do not come from seed.

Best timing. In most northern regions, lawns can be started at any time during the growing season if you are laying sod. From seed, lawns are best begun in early spring (as soon as the soil is dry enough to work), or in early fall, six weeks before the first-frost date.

Seed. Use the best seed mix you can afford. In most cases, cheaper mixes contain a small percentage of the good grasses of the Kentucky bluegrass type and a large percentage of the large-seeded and less desirable coarse grasses.

Regional differences. Start southern gardens in late winter or early spring, while weather is relatively cool. In the transition zone, neither type of grass is fully satisfactory, but a tall fescue is probably the best choice.

Ground preparation

Spreader with application adjuster

Before laying sod, prepare the ground as you would for seeding. The spreader shown distributes fertilizer in a strip the same width as the hopper.

How to Make a New Lawn

Depending on where you live, new lawns can be started from seed, from live stems (sprigs), small pieces of sod, or full sod. Seed, while slower, is less costly, and it allows you to vary the seed mixture to take into account the varying shade areas in the garden. Sod gives an instant lawn and you are far less restricted on timing. But try to schedule the work so that you avoid hot, muggy summer days.

Reputable sod growers offer choice varieties that are free of weeds and pests. Many buyers assume that sod is an easy (though expensive) road to success, needing little attention. However, sod laid on compact, infertile soil will be no more successful than a seeding would be.

Sodding avoids the early inconvenience of getting a new lawn laid down and established; it does not diminish the requirements for maintaining grass.

The Soil Bed

To ensure good drainage, grade soil to slope slightly away from the house in all directions. If you add topsoil, spread it over the surface evenly. You can buy topsoil or mix in organic material such as compost. The cost and effort are worth it for a long-lasting lawn that will thrive with less need for supplemental fertilizer and water.

Soil-Bed Preparation

Loosening compacted soil is essential. Remove all foreign materials. Do not bury them, since that may alter the chemical balance of the soil.

Cultivate to loosen the soil uniformly a few inches deep. Mix in compost, and if desired, a balanced organic fertilizer blend. Grass seeds themselves contain only enough nourishment to form the first sprout and roots, so added nutrients are necessary for further growth.

For best results, apply a mix of 2 parts blood meal and 3 parts bone meal to the area before digging, as these need to be broken down by bacteria in the soil. Apply at a rate of 11 pounds per 1,000 square feet.

Cultivation

Cultivate to loosen the soil and break up large clods, but avoid excessive cultivation. Take special care to not whip the soil bed into a fluffy texture by repeated passes with a rotary tiller. This will break down the soil particles to such a small size that the surface will "melt" when heavily watered, sealing the pores of the soil and keeping the water from soaking in.

Lawn seeds are best situated for quick, effective sprouting if they sift into the crevices between soil lumps about as big as the tip of a finger.

Rolling

If the soil has not been unduly fluffed, rolling may not be needed. In some cases, rolling can undo the benefits of cultivation by mashing down the soil particles, making the surface less permeable. Rolling will not damage sandy soils, and in some cases it is the only way to reestablish capillary action to transport water from deeper levels. It may also be necessary on heavy soils that have become unduly fluffy during preparation.

Planting

Southern, heat-tolerant grasses are often grown from small plants, either plugs or sprigs. Plant plugs with a trowel, level with the soil surface. Sprigs are planted on an angle with one end of the rhizome about 1 inch below the surface and the other end at, or slightly above, the soil.

Sodding

Sod is laid down in strips like pieces of carpet, and may arrive in strips or rolls, depending on the time between cutting and delivery. In all cases, the soil must be prepared as thoroughly as it would be for a new lawn.

If possible, lay the first strip of sod against a straight edge. Butt each sod flush against the previous one, and lay the rows in a staggered pattern. Keep a bucket of fine soil handy, for filling in gaps between sod, where they may have been damaged.

Seeding

Usually approximately 3 pounds of seeds are used per 1,000 square feet (less with bent grass, more with perennial ryegrass). Use a lawn spreader to avoid possible misses. Spread half the seeds in one direction, then spread the remainder at right angles to the first.

Spreaders that drop the seeds from a hopper have the advantage of cutting off the coverage exactly at borders. The centrifugal cyclone type, which throws seeds from a whirling disk, feathers the edges of the successive passes of seeds better, and it also covers the ground more quickly.

Rake the seeds lightly with the back of a bamboo rake, barely covering them with soil. After seeds are sown, keep the soil bed thoroughly moist for about two weeks, or until the grass is well established. Be sure to avoid light sprinklings. The water should penetrate the soil to a depth of several inches. If it dries out, the seedlings will die. In warm weather ryegrass should sprout in one week, bluegrass and fescue in two weeks.

Mulching

A mulch over the seeding will help prevent rapid drying out. Even with a mulch, light watering daily, after an initial thorough soaking, is often necessary to encourage the quickest possible germination.

Mulch also helps protect a new seeding against heavy rains. As long as the soil remains somewhat rough, rain is likely to soak in.

Possible kinds of mulch include straw (laid down no more than a few straws deep), excelsior, shredded twigs, pine boughs, crop or garden stems, moistened newsprint, and woven burlap. Twigs and other debris should be removed before the first mowing.

1. Open out each sod and press it firmly into position.

2. Stand or kneel on a plank on one row to lay the next.

3. Trim the edges with a half-moon edging tool, making a sloping cut.

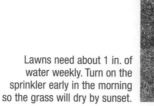

Lawns need about 1 in. of water weekly. Turn on the sprinkler early in the morning so the grass will dry by sunset.

Oscillating sprinkler

Maintaining the Lawn

Mowing

Plants require the green tissue that contains chlorophyll to manufacture the food they need for proper growth. So mowing can be counterproductive, particularly if the grass is cut too low.

Rooting depth is related to the height of the foliage above ground; thus, turf that is constantly cut too low becomes inhibited in its reach for moisture and nutrients in the soil. To avoid shallow rooting, cut away no more than one-third the foliage at a time. Mowing high is especially helpful in shade conditions in summer, or if the soil and habitat are problematic.

Mowing height will vary with the kind of grass, its use, and the season. Golf-green grasses, especially creeping bent grasses, are mowed when about a quarter inch tall. Most lawn grasses, including Kentucky bluegrasses, fine fescues, and most southern grasses are mowed at a height of 2½–3 inches. Bermuda grass, however, is usually mowed shorter. Weekly mowing is usually adequate. Longer intervals between mowings may suffice when growth slows down.

In areas with hot summers, it is a good practice to increase mowing height to 3 inches. This shades the soil, keeping it cooler and reduces water loss. Reduce the height as the weather cools in fall.

Mowers

Lawn-mowing equipment ranges from manual push reel mowers to self-propelled machines capable of mowing acres of grass. Gas-, diesel-, and battery-powered riding mowers are all popular. Some garden tractors have attachments for mowing, tilling, aerating, and other tasks.

Reel mowers generally do a neater job than rotary mowers. They work best on lawns that are cut relatively low—on bent grass, some low-growing Kentucky bluegrasses, and perennial ryegrasses. Hard to use in tall grasses, they usually need professional sharpening and adjustment.

Rotary and flail mowers cut by the impact of a fast-moving blade. This tends to fray the ends of the grass, especially if the blade is dull. Rotary blades can be sharpened at home. Simply disconnect the spark plug lead, so the engine cannot fire, remove the blade, put it in a vise, and sharpen to the original cutting angle. To keep the blade in balance, file equal amounts from each end.

For general use, whenever grass can be cut fairly high, gasoline or electric rotary mowers are more versatile, more easily maintained, and less expensive than reel mowers.

Mulching rotary mowers have a deck designed to swirl the clippings around so that they are cut into small pieces. These decompose faster than large pieces, feeding the lawn and reducing the risk of thatch buildup.

Watering

In hot, dry weather, lawns need an inch or more of water per week. Where rain does not provide it, irrigation should. Watering is essential in arid climates, such as in parts of the Prairies. In addition to supplying moisture for the roots, watering draws air into the pores of the soil so that the roots can breathe. As water percolates down, fresh air follows.

Bent grasses, which are adapted to humid conditions, need more watering than species such as fescue grasses that are not adversely affected by periods of drought. Fescue is

A bamboo fan rake will remove clippings and lift flattened grass.

often planted in sandy soils and under shade trees, where dryness is likely to develop. Wheat grass, a native prairie grass, can also withstand periods of drought.

Heavy soils. Clays and other heavy soils are slow to soak up moisture and slow to dry out. Clay has relatively few drainage pores but many small capillary pores that retain moisture. Heavy soils must be watered slowly for a fairly long time to soak the root zone. They can then go about two weeks without watering.

Dense or compacted soil can be made more porous by aerating the ground—punching holes in it with an engine-powered coring machine. Hand-driven aerators can also do the job. However, a mechanical core aerator is the best choice for most lawns. You can hire a lawn professional to do the job, or you can rent a machine. For tiny lawns, or small problem patches, you can aerate with a garden fork (see photo at top of page 26).

Sandy soils. By and large, sandy soils tend to be overly porous and therefore have limited water-holding capacity. They soak up water quickly but drain it equally fast. For that reason they should be watered more often than clays. They usually need watering about every three or four days in the absence of rain, but for shorter periods of time.

Sprinklers. Lawn-watering regulations as well as water pressure varies with municipalities, so check before installing an underground sprinkling system. The pressure will influence the distance that the spray heads can be set apart. With surface sprinklers, it is a good idea to match the spray pattern to the shape of the area to be watered. To check that all parts of your lawn receive the same amount of water, place cans or jars within the spraying radius and compare their contents.

Wasteful runoff occurs when sprinklers apply water faster than it can soak into the ground.

Fertilization

An adequately fed lawn is denser, more weed free, and more attractive. A well-fertilized lawn withstands wear better and is more resistant to pests and diseases. One great way to naturally fertilize your lawn is by using a mulching mower and leaving clippings in place.

Applying too much fertilizer, on the other hand, can create problems. Standard recommendations for feeding lawns with chemical fertilizers do not apply to organic lawn care.

One of the best ways to ensure that your lawn gets the nutrients it needs is to top-dress it with screened compost. Or, you can use an organic fertilizer blend especially formulated for lawns.

Nitrogen promotes leaf formation and a deep color. Some phosphorus and potassium should accompany it to maintain a proper balance and to avoid overstimulation that might encourage disease. The three major nutrients of a complete fertilizer—nitrogen (N), phosphorus (P), and potassium (K)—can be in such ratios as 3–1–1, 5–2–3, and so on.

There are many companies producing organic fertilizers and the exact formulation depends on the specific brand, but they will be somewhere close to these ratios. A lawn properly maintained, and cut with a mulching mower, will not need a lot of additional fertilizer. The clippings left by the mower will break down and supply much of the lawn's requirements. The various varieties of Kentucky bluegrass may need additional fertilization, while a lawn made with a variety of tall fescue probably would not.

Bare spots, poor, thin growth, new weed seedlings, moss, or the presence of diseased grass, all indicate a lawn in need of additional fertilizer. Kentucky bluegrass, the commonest lawn grass in much of the northern states, is especially prone to disease when it is lacking nutrients.

Dandelion digger

Dandelions

Fungi

Dandelions and other weeds not only look unsightly but steal nutrients from the lawn and serve as hosts for pests, fungal infestations, and other diseases.

Organic lawn fertilizers are a combination of various substances such as blood meal, fish meal, bone meal, seaweed, alfalfa meal, granite dust, greensand, manure, or rock phosphate, in differing proportions to achieve the desired formulation. They break down slowly and provide the much needed nutrients over a period of time and also add organic material to the soil, helping to improve its texture.

Homemade compost can also be used as a lawn fertilizer. The nutrient value will not be known but the humus content will be high and will help improve the soil so the grass will grow better and stronger, crowding out weeds. It should be put through a screen first to remove any material that has not decomposed, and to break up the lumps. It can either be broadcast onto the lawn with a shovel, or, for a more uniform coverage, be applied with a fertilizer spreader. The compost can also be used to make a compost tea, which can be sprayed onto the lawn using a hose-end or a backpack sprayer, and gives a fast acting, low-level feed to green-up a yellowing lawn. Fish emulsion or liquid seaweed can also be used.

How to Apply

Where only a small area is involved, such as the gardens of many town houses, fertilizer can be applied by hand. Be sure to wear heavy-duty rubber gloves and a painter's dust mask.

For larger areas, the rotary spreader has a drum to hold the fertilizer, which drops through a hole onto a plate that spins as the spreader is pushed along. The faster it is pushed, the faster the plate spins and the wider the swath that is covered. But if the lawn is irregularly shaped, some of the fertilizer will spread onto adjacent flower or vegetable beds. For smaller gardens, a drop-type spreader is preferable. It has a rectangular hopper with a slot in the base. As it is pushed over the lawn, the fertilizer drops through the slot at a controlled rate. The amount of lawn covered on each pass is less than with the broadcast spreader, but the application rate is more accurate. The width of the slot is controlled by a lever. Many fertilizer companies have a chart (sometimes on their website) that gives the correct setting numbers for different makes of spreaders. Apply half the fertilizer in bands running up and down the lawn and the other half in bands at right angles.

When to Apply

In spring, northern grasses use the food stored in their roots to start growth, pushing out new stolons, which thicken the lawn. You may need to mow every five days or so during this time. Growth then slows and the grass may go dormant during the summer heat. With fall's cooler weather, the grass resumes growth and starts to store food in the roots for the following spring. This is the best time to fertilize the lawn. Where the autumn season is long, give two applications at half the recommended rate: one in early fall and the second just before the cold weather. If not taken up by the grass, this second application will be available in the spring. If the lawn is thin and in poor condition, give another feeding in spring, as soon as the lawn has dried sufficiently. This will give the boost needed to produce new shoots and thicken the lawn.

Southern grasses need feeding in spring. If the soil is poor, zoysia and Bermuda grass could need a second feeding in late summer. Do not feed any of the warm-season grasses in late fall as this could encourage new growth just as the grass should be going dormant.

Weeds

Weeds pop up in even the best kept grass. But you can do a number

Push a fork or trowel vertically into the soil to get at a weed's rootstock.

of things to minimize their spread. Lawn weeds will sprout in any uncovered piece of soil, but cannot compete with a dense stand of grass. Growing a good lawn will do much to prevent their intrusion. Mowing at the correct time to the correct height—so that you don't take off more than one-third of the leaf length—will help build a healthy lawn. Fertilize in the fall as the grass resumes active growth. Summer fertilization feeds the weeds more than the grass. Water during periods of drought, adding at least 1 inch of water each time, so that it soaks down into the soil to encourage deep rooting. The occasional weed can be removed by hand (see above).

Hardest to control are grass weeds, which are often not noticed until mature. Crabgrass germinates from seed each spring. One overlooked plant can shed thousands of seeds to grow the following year. It is easy to identify but tough to pull by hand, so use a small fork. Bad infestations are best controlled by using corn gluten applied in early spring; It kills the weed seedlings as they germinate. It is active in the soil for several weeks, so don't overseed with desirable lawn grass seed after using it.

The weeds that are present in the lawn can tell a lot about the soil type and how to correct it. Ox-eyed daisy, foxtail grass, and yellow dock indicate a soil that needs improved drainage. Mosses and wild strawberries thrive on acidic soils, indicating the need for lime, while plantain and knotweed will be found growing on soils that need aerating.

Perennial broad-leaved weeds, like dandelion and plantain can be dug by hand, but this is time consuming. The aim is to grow a lawn that is deep rooted so it can withstand drought, and that has a dense texture that will crowd out existing weeds and not allow seedlings to become established. With a neglected lawn, it may be necessary to spend some time digging out the worst of the broad-leaved weeds. Plantain, in particular, spreads across the grass and leaves a big bare patch when it is removed. Dandelions dig out easiest in early spring before they grow feeder roots off the main taproot. They are much less likely to break off at this time. The worst time to remove plantains

1. If lawn beside a path is bare, cut out a section beside the bald spot.

2. Lift and rotate the section. Fill the hole with soil, and sprinkle on grass seed.

Before reseeding a bare patch of lawn, aerate the problem area with a fork, then fill the holes with sand.

Aeration   Reseeding

is just as dandelions go to seed. It is asking for a dandelion seedling to take the plantain's place because the grass will not have had time to grow and fill the hole.

Weed control really comes down to growing a good lawn by fertilizing at the right time, cutting to the best height for the time of year so that the grass blades shade out the weeds, and watering when required.

1. If there is a bump on your lawn that you need to level out, make parallel cuts with a spade, as shown, then slice down the middle of the cut area.

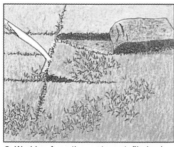

2. Working from the center cut, flip back all the sod.

3. Use a fork to loosen the earth and remove the excess.

4. When the ground is level, replace the sod, and tamp them into place.

5. Finish by sprinkling a mixture of sand and soil along the cut lines.

Moss and Algae Control

Moss is most likely to develop in shady places, particularly on under-fed grass or where the soil has been compacted. To eliminate, add fertilizer, improve the surface drainage, and aerate the soil. Algae usually occur only where there is standing water. They can usually be eliminated by improving the drainage.

Thatch

Thatch is the layer of dead grass clippings resting on the soil beneath the grass blades. In a good organic lawn this should not be a problem, as it breaks down and feeds the grass as part of the nutrition cycle. A deep layer on a neglected lawn can be removed with a de-thatching machine or hand raking with a fan-type rake.

Renovation

Tilling and reseeding or resodding a lawn that has deteriorated may expose the soil to a number of problems, including erosion and enabling buried weed seeds to germinate. Besides, less drastic measures may suffice. For bald patches or salt-damaged sections along sidewalks, follow the steps illustrated at lower right on page 25. Often fertilizing and weeding may be more than enough. If not, you can also sow new seeds.

Before reseeding, mow grass almost to ground level. If there is much thatch, scarify the surface with a thatch-removing machine set low enough for the blades to slice lightly into the soil. When the soil is partially bared and the thatch is removed, sow a seed mixture containing the varieties you want.

Keep the lawn moist until the grass becomes established. When the area is watered and fertilized, the old vegetation is likely to revive and compete for nutrients and water. Renovation will not necessarily relieve the lawn of unwanted grasses.

Acid-Alkaline Balance

Lawn grasses tolerate a wide range of pH in the soil but respond best to the 5.5–7.5 span. This means moderately acid to mildly alkaline, 7 being neutral on the scale.

If a soil with an extreme pH was not limed or acidified before the lawn was planted, liming to increase alka-linity or sulfur treatment to lower it may be needed. Repeated use of certain fertilizers may have an acidifying influence. A soil test will indicate the pH and whether it is changing. Kits are available for home use, or commercial laboratories will do a complete test, including nutrient contents, for a fee. Look under "Soil Testing" in the Yellow Pages.

Bent grasses thrive under moderately acid conditions. Bluegrass generally does best under neutral or mildly acid conditions. Other species normally grow vigorously on mildly acid soils.

The amount of lime needed to reduce an acid condition depends on the kind of soil and the degree of acidity. From 20–50 pounds of ground limestone per 1,000 square feet will bring a mildly acid soil close to neutral. Strongly acid soils (especially heavy types) may need 100 pounds per 1,000 square feet annually for several years.

Acidifying alkaline soils may require the application of 10–50 pounds of elemental sulfur per 1,000 square feet, depending on the degree of alkalinity.

What Can Go Wrong With Lawns

A healthy, well-tended lawn will be resistant to most of the ills listed here, particularly if disease-resistant grass is used. It also pays to plant a mixture of grasses instead of just one strain. The lawn will thus show less damage should one strain succumb.

Lawns made from commercially grown sod will probably contain only one type of grass. Check with the source (if possible) to discover which. Overseed with a different grass when needed.

For information on symptoms not included on page 27, and for illustrations on some of the problems listed, see the section on plant disorders, starting on page 506.

If you want a meadowlike lawn, plant wildflowers. But don't expect quick results. It may take years before your work looks like the natural setting shown here.

Wild daisies and knapweed add to this meadow's charm.

SYMPTOMS AND SIGNS	CAUSE	CONTROL
Mounds of sand and soil on lawn.	Ants	Use borax bait.
Tiny (¼ in.) pests suck juices from leaves and crowns. Patches of grass are discolored and die.	Chinch bugs	Keep lawns well-watered. Apply insecticidal soap as a soil drench.
Grubs chew roots off grass plants; grass is yellowed and often can be rolled up like carpet. Moles and skunks damage lawns, but eat grubs. Once grubs are controlled, moles and skunks will go elsewhere.	Grubs (larvae of chafers, Asiatic, and June beetles)	Drench the area with insecticidal soap or apply beneficial nematodes.
Holes in leaves; chewed shoots; some entire plants destroyed.	Armyworms, cutworms, or sod webworms	Spray with insecticidal soap.
Large heaps of loose soil; tunnels under turf.	Moles	Use mole trap, or place smoke pellets in runs. Control grubs.
Cup-size or larger holes dug in lawn in late summer or fall.	Skunks	Fill holes. Control grubs that skunks are digging for.
Slippery gelatinous layer develops over grass.	Algae or gelatinous lichens (slime molds)	Drain and aerate soil. Apply copper sulfate (1 rounded tsp. to 10 gal. of water). Top-dress with compost.
Leaf blades with orange-red spots on pustules. Leaves often pale yellow.	Bluegrass rust	Fertilize. Water only in mornings. Overseed with a resistant variety.
In summer, very dark green circular areas, 2–4 ft. in diameter, appear on lawn. Later, these areas turn lighter in color; small mushrooms appear.	Fairy ring (mushrooms)	Seldom serious. Fungus feeds on decaying wood in soil. Ring expands and will eventually go. If several rings, water with mix of 2–3 tsp. of copper sulfate in 10 gal. of water.
Patches of yellow, dying grass, which later become brown or covered with cottony white mold. Often seen after long-lasting snow cover has melted or when nitrogen has been applied later than August.	Fusarium snow mold	Keep lawn mowed short in fall. In spring, break up snow mold webs with a fan rake. Spray with a copper-based fungicide if serious.
Small straw-colored spots on lawn. Later, large crusty mats. Mats can suffocate and kill grass. Fungus may develop when snow cover is more than 4 in. deep; shows up as snow melts.	Gray snow mold (Typhula)	Break up crusty masses with rake. Spray with a copper-based fungicide if raking doesn't control. Long grass is more likely to be attacked.

SYMPTOMS AND SIGNS	CAUSE	CONTROL
Oval to round brown spots on foliage, especially in spring and fall.	Leaf spots (melting out)	Usually disappears when weather warms. Spray with fish emulsion. Occurs mainly on Kentucky bluegrass.
Leaves show white powdery deposit during periods of high humidity in summer.	Powdery mildew	Generally disappears with the return of cooler weather. Spray with a potassium bicarbonate product.
Pink or reddish gelatinous growths, particularly on fine-leaved grasses in coastal regions.	Red thread (fungus)	Aerate lawn and plant a variety such as 'Eclipse'. Improve drainage if problem occurs frequently.
Black stripes of fungal spores split grass blades open.	Striped smut	Difficult to control. If severe, remove grass and reseed with a resistant strain.

Modern Turf Grasses

Many varieties of lawn grasses are available. Some were discovered as superior clones in established turf, others are the result of highly involved breeding procedures.

Buy seeds in mixtures developed for specific uses, such as show lawns.

NORTHERN SPECIES

Kentucky bluegrass (*Poa pratensis*). Kentucky bluegrass and its varieties are outstanding lawn grasses, and spread by underground stems, take well to mowing, and are an excellent choice, except where the soil is poor.

Varieties developed at Rutgers University—'Adelphi', 'Glade', and 'Plush'—tend to be low, dark green, resistant to many diseases, and outstanding in winter.

Perennial ryegrass (*Lolium perenne*). Improved ryegrasses are as attractive as bluegrass, although they do not spread or mow quite so neatly or tolerate extreme climates. No other fine turf grass establishes itself so fast.

Fescues (*Festuca rubra*). Fine fescues are adapted to dry habitats, poor soils, and shade. Chewings fescues are prized for density. Tall fescues are coarser, but very hard wearing.

Bent grass (*Agrostis* species). These grasses have exacting requirements, especially frequent mowing. They do well in humid areas.

SOUTHERN SPECIES

Bermuda Grass (*Cynodon dactylon*). An aggressive grass, it spreads by runners, needs frequent mowing and full sun. Hybrids are available as sprigs, and soon will make a lush lawn. Look for the Tifton varieties, 'Tifway', Tifdwarf', etc.

Zoysia (*Zoysia matrella*). Slow growing, it makes an excellent lawn once established. Normally started by plugs, it does well in sun or light shade. 'Emerald' is the best variety for the South.

Centipede (*Eremochloa ophiuroides*). The best choice for poor soils, it spreads by stolons and is usually propagated by sprigs. 'Oaklawn' and 'Tennessee' are popular varieties.

St. Augustine (*Stenotaphrum secundatum*). Probably the most used grass in Florida and the Gulf Coast. It does well in sun or part shade.

Bahia (*Paspulum notatum*). A tough grass that is useful in the Deep South. While not as attractive as Bermuda, it needs less maintenance and can be grown from seed.

Ground Covers

Pulmonaria
officinalis
➡

Plants suitable for ground covers are listed here alphabetically according to their botanical names. Others are noted in the chapters on shrubs, rock and water gardens, and perennials.

These plants are all particularly adaptable to steep slopes or rocky terrains, where a lawn is not practical; some thrive in deep shade and can be used under trees. Established ground covers shade out most weeds. To determine whether a plant will survive the lowest average temperatures in your area, check the Hardiness column, then refer to the Hardiness Zone Map at the front of the book. Recommended propagation methods are described in the chapter on perennials (see pp. 39–40).

Ajuga reptans

Ajuga reptans
(carpet bugleweed)

Arctostaphylos uva-ursi
(bearberry)

Ceratostigma plumba-ginoides (leadwort)

Convallaria majalis
(lily-of-the-valley)

Cotoneaster dammeri
(bearberry)

Euonymus fortunei
(wintercreeper)

Fragaria chiloensis
(wild strawberry)

BOTANICAL AND COMMON NAMES	HARDINESS	SOIL	LIGHT	DECORATIVE CHARACTERISTICS, SPECIAL REQUIREMENTS, AND REMARKS	PROPAGATION
Aegopodium (goutweed, or bishop's-weed) *A. podagraria*	Zones 3–9	☐	◑	A deciduous plant that grows to about 1 ft. in height. Small white blossoms open in early summer. An invasive spreader, it can be controlled by up to 3 mowings each year. The variegated form is more attractive.	Divide root in spring or fall.
Ajuga (ajuga, or bugleweed) *A. reptans* (carpet bugleweed)	Zones 3–9	☐	●-●	Shiny leaves form tight mat. From late spring into early summer small spikes of blue blooms appear. Foliage may die back to crowns in cold winters, but plants recover in spring. Carpet bugleweed can be invasive.	Divide clumps in spring or fall.
Arctostaphylos (bearberry) *A. uva-ursi*	Zones 2–6	☐	●	Shiny, dark green leaves turn bronze in fall but remain on the plant. Pink flowers and bright red berries. 'Vancouver Jade' has the best winter color.	Semi-hardwood cuttings in early spring or early fall.
Ceratostigma (leadwort, plumbago) *C. plumbaginoides*	Zones 6–9	▣	●	Long lasting blue flowers in late summer. Foliage turns bright red in fall. Good city plant that is pollution-tolerant.	Take softwood cuttings in summer or divide established plants.
Convallaria (lily-of-the-valley) *C. majalis*	Zones 2–7	☐	●	A rather aggressive plant that can become invasive in cold areas. Dark green, lance-shaped leaves that die down in winter. White, very fragrant bell-like flowers in spring.	Divide and transplant while dormant.
Cotoneaster (cotoneaster) *C. dammeri* (bearberry)	Zones 4–8	■	●	Evergreen leaves are about 1 in. long. Fruits are bright red and are eaten by birds. A useful prostrate plant. Susceptible to fire blight.	Take semi-hardwood cuttings in summer.
Euonymus (euonymus) *E. fortunei* varieties (wintercreeper)	Zones 4–9	☐	●	The 1-in. evergreen leaves are dark purple from fall through winter. Oval leaves are handsomely highlighted by rounded light pink fruits. Runners will cling to rough surfaces. Good variegated forms. Can be invasive.	Take semi-hardwood cuttings in summer or firm-wood cuttings later.
Fragaria (wild strawberry) *F. chiloensis*	Zones 4–8	☐	◑	Evergreen leaves are shiny above, bluish white beneath. Large dark red fruits form after white blossoms fade. Spreads slowly by runners.	Transplant rooted runners.
Gaultheria (wintergreen) *G. procumbens*	Zones 4–8	▣	●	The foliage is fragrant when crushed and small flowers give rise to red fruits. Wintergreen oil is extracted from both leaves and and fruits.	Seeds, sown as soon as the fruit are ripe.
Geranium (big-root geranium) *G. macrorrhiza*	Zones 4–8	☐	●	Spicy fragrant when crushed, the foliage turns a copper tone in fall. Mauve-pink flowers over a long period in summer.	Divide and replant in spring or fall.
Hedera (ivy) *H. helix* varieties (English)	Zones 5–11	☐	●-●	Evergreen leaves form dense carpet. Runners climb rough masonry surfaces. Can become very invasive.	Take semi-hardwood cuttings in summer or late summer.

■ well drained to sandy ■ moist ■ wet ▪ acidic ▪ alkaline ☐ regular soil ● full sun ◑ partial shade ● shade

The variegated form of goutweed (*Aegopodium*) is invasive but will take foot traffic, unlike the creeping juniper (*Juniperus procumbens nana*).

Aegopodium podagraria 'variegatum'

Juniperus procumbens nana

Hypericum calycinum (St. John's wort)

Lamium maculatum (spotted deadnettle)

Mukdenia rossii (mukdenia)

Ophiopogon japonicus (lilyturf)

Pachysandra termi-nalis (pachysandra)

Paxistima canbyi (ratstripper)

Thymus serphyllum (thyme)

Vinca minor (periwinkle)

BOTANICAL AND COMMON NAMES	HARDINESS	SOIL	LIGHT	DECORATIVE CHARACTERISTICS, SPECIAL REQUIREMENTS, AND REMARKS	PROPAGATION
Hypericum (Aaron's beard, St. John's wort) H. calycinum	Zone 5–9	▦	●	Bright yellow flowers in late summer. Plants are deciduous in the North, evergreen where winters are mild. Does not grow well where summers are humid.	Seed sown as soon as ripe or softwood cutting in summer.
Juniperus (juniper) J. procumbens nana (creeping)	Zone 4–9	□	●	Bluish-green needles are borne on branches that seldom grow taller than 1 ft. Branches grow in horizontal tiers. Plant slowly develops tight, rounded profile. Evergreen.	Make soil layers or take firm-wood cuttings in late summer.
Lamium (spotted deadnettle) L. maculatum	Zone 3–8	□	● ◐	Leaves may be pale green edged with a darker band or be dotted with white spots, depending on the variety. Flowers also vary from white to pink to mauve. Some varieties can be invasive.	Divide and replant in spring or fall. Often self-seeds.
Lysimachia (moneywort, creeping Jenny) L. nummularia	Zone 4–8	□	●	A vigorous plant with rooting stems that will take light foot traffic. Yellow flowers in summer are a bonus. The golden-leaved form 'Aurea' is more attractive. Very invasive in natural areas and more so in home gardens.	Dig up a piece and transplant almost any time during the summer.
Microbiata (Russian arborvitae) M. decussata	Zone 3–7	□	●	A low, wide-spreading evergreen (up to 10 ft.) similar to junipers but turning a purple shade in winter. It does not grow well where summers are very hot.	Take mature wood cuttings in late summer.
Mukdenia (red-leaved mukdenia) M. rossii 'Crimson Fans'	Zone 4–9	■	●	The foliage emerges green, becomes tinged with bronze-red and turns bright red in fall. Sprays of white flowers in spring. A good woodland plant.	Divide and replant in spring.
Ophiopogon (lilyturf) O. japonicus (dwarf)	Zone 6–10	□	●-●	Deep green, grassy leaves are evergreen. Purplish flowers are followed by small blue fruits. Variegated forms are best in sun.	Divide and transplant.
Pachysandra (pachysandra or Japanese spurge) P. terminalis	Zone 4–8	■	●	Has handsome, shiny, evergreen foliage. Creamy white blooms open in late spring. Initial close planting encourages rapid coverage. Useful under maples, where little else will grow.	Transplant clumps and take semi-hardwood cuttings in summer.
Paxistima (paxistima, ratstripper) P. canbyi	Zone 3–7	□	●	This quickly makes a dense mat that crowds out weeds. The evergreen leaves turn bronze in fall.	Take cuttings in summer or divide in fall.
Phlox (moss phlox) P. subulata	Zone 3	□	●	Dense mats of evergreen foliage become covered with bright flowers in late spring. There are many named forms with red, pink, white, or two-toned flowers. Often self-seeds.	Sow seed as soon as ripe or take cuttings in summer.
Stephanandra (cut-leaved stephanandra) S. incisa 'Crispa'	Zone 4–9	□	●	This spreads by underground runners and is a good choice for controling erosion on banks. This variety is shorter (3 ft.) than the species. White flowers in late summer and reddish foliage in fall.	Take cuttings in summer.
Thymus (thyme) T. serphyllum	Zone 4–9	■	●	A fragrant carpet that can withstand foot traffic. The species has purple flowers in summer, but named forms have pink, white, or red flowers.	Divide and replant in spring or fall.
Vinca (periwinkle) V. minor	Zone 3–9	■	◐	Shiny ovate leaves are up to 2 in. long. In midspring lilac-blue blossoms appear. Varieties are available with white or pink blooms. A rapid spreader, this evergreen may be invasive.	Divide root in spring or fall.

■ well drained to sandy ■ moist ■ wet ▨ acidic ▦ alkaline □ regular soil ● full sun ◐ partial shade ● shade

The blanketflower (Gaillardia), *an excellent cut flower that adds color to the garden all summer long, does best in a sunny spot. 'Goblin' has velvety red, golden-tipped flowers. Although this miniature form grows only to about 10 in., other varieties reach heights of 2½ ft.*

PERENNIALS

Many of our best-loved flowers are herbaceous perennials that spring up afresh year after year and make outstanding features in borders.

Whether your garden is a small backyard or a generous plot of land around a country house, there are always places to use perennials for the varied color and character of their flowers and foliage.

The terms "perennial" and "herbaceous perennial" are often used interchangeably to mean a plant that comes up year after year and in most cases dies down to dormant roots each winter, leaving only lifeless stems. The lupine, delphinium, phlox, and monarda are some popular examples. A few, such as the yucca and dianthus, are termed and treated as herbaceous plants even though their leaves remain green all year. Tolerance to cold depends on the species or cultivar.

Some perennials, such as hollyhock and delphinium, are short-lived, dying out only four or five years after planting. But others, such as asters, tickseed, and anthemis, will live for many years, and will respond with renewed vigor each time you dig and divide them. A few perennials, such as peony and meadow rue, will continue to thrive for decades with no special care needed.

Once upon a time, perennial gardens were grand affairs called borders, which could easily stretch 30 feet long and 10 feet deep, often backed by stately evergreens. Needless to say, these huge gardens required a crew of workers to maintain them. Fortunately, there are plenty of terrific ways to plant and enjoy perennials without planting a large border. One great option is to plant a mixed bed or border that combines perennials with annuals, biennials, roses, bulbs, and shrubs. This type of border is easier to maintain than a garden of perennials only, plus it will provide a long season of interest. But do not stop there with planting perennials. You can also use small combinations of perennials for a pathway garden bed or as a decorative accent beside a wall or fence.

Convert a section of your lawn to a wildlife garden featuring perennials for birds and butterflies (see page 68).

Island beds are convenient alternatives to a long border, and they offer plenty of design opportunities while being simpler to maintain. An island garden, accessible from all sides, is far easier to plant, cultivate, and weed than a wide one-sided border. The taller plants should be set toward the center, with the shorter ones toward the edges. Free-form shapes are usually more effective than circles or ovals. Avoid star or diamond shapes because their angles are awkward to plant and difficult to maintain.

Another popular style of perennial garden is one in which three to five different perennials make up the entire border. The perennials are chosen according to color and blooming time to provide the longest possible period of color. For example, by selecting the early-, mid-season-, and late-blooming varieties from among irises, day lilies, peonies, and asters, there will be flowers for many months with minimal care.

Perennials can also be used to good advantage as ground cover, in which vigorous, spreading, and fairly short types are planted close togeth-er to form a dense, continuous mass, concealing the bare ground. Such plantings are often useful for covering banks or, if the plants are shade-lovers, for carpeting the ground beneath shrubs, perhaps interplant-ed with naturalized bulbs (planted informally). Theoretically, ground-cover plants smother weeds, but in the initial stages careful weeding is required, and afterward some hand weeding is always needed, as hoeing is not practical. For a list of ground-cover plants, see page 28.

A pleasing variation of a solid planting is a checkerboard area of pavement and soil, with the open squares planted with specimens chosen for both foliage and flowers, such as the bergenia and day lily. This can often be done on a terrace with as few as one or two planted squares.

Informal plantings of herbaceous perennials are a great accent for almost any location. Around the edges of garden pools and streams, they complement aquatic plants. On the edges of woodlands and in open fields, they can be planted in drifts. Beside steps and over the edges of paths, wispy or spreading plants, such as baby's breath or dianthus, spill out to soften straight edges. And as single accents in strategic places—by a lamppost, a garden gate, or a birdbath—just one handsome perennial, such as a day lily, peony, or yarrow, will add interest.

On balconies, decks, and roofs of apartments favorite perennials can be grown in containers.

Add perennials with attractive foliage to your design palette, too. You'll love their textural qualities and long-season effect—among them the ornamental grasses, artemisias, hostas, lungworts, stonecrops, and yuccas. Silver-, gold-, and purple-leaved types are particularly interesting. Seed heads of Chinese lantern and Oriental poppy and the flowers of plants such as globe thistle, yarrow, and many species, including sea lavender, are often dried for indoor decoration.

An attractive border greatly depends on how plants are arranged. Late-flowering or foliage plants should conceal gaps left by earlier flowers; colors should be pleasing, all plants should be in scale.

Carefully kept notes can be an asset. No book or catalog will provide the exact flowering dates for your garden. But by recording your own bloom dates, you can recombine plants that flower at the same time.

A traditional perennial border (below) has the lowest plants in front and the tallest toward the rear. A modern island bed has the tallest perennials in the center.

Kniphofia uvaria 'Primrose Beauty'

Doronicum 'Miss Mason'

Lupinus 'Russell Hybrids'

Delphinium elatum hybrid

Monarda didyma 'Croftway Pink'

Acanthus mollis

Sidalcea malviflora 'Brilliant'

Veronica spicata 'Alba'

Helleborus orientalis

Achillea 'Moonshine'

Sedum spectabile 'Meteor'

Pulmonaria angustifolia

Stokesia laevis 'Blue Danube'

Potentilla nepalensis 'Miss Willmott'

Aster 'Eventide'

Hosta hybrid

Achillea filipendulina 'Coronation Gold'

Eryngium bourgatii

Brunnera macrophylla

Heuchera 'Chatterbox'

Sedum spectabile 'Brilliant'

Bergenia cordifolia

The wooly yarrow (*Achillea tomentosa*) is good for the front of a border. In windy places the prairie mallow (*Sidalcea*) should have some protection.

Achillea tomentosa

Sidalcea 'Elsie Heugh'

Giving Perennials the Right Start

Preparing the Perennial Border for Planting

Spade or rototill the bed two or three weeks prior to planting to give the soil time to settle. Remove all perennial weeds. Incorporate a bucketful of compost per square yard, or alternatively spread about 1–3 inches of it over the area first. Also, sprinkle a complete fertilizer (a mix of equal parts blood meal, bone meal, and kelp meal) over the area prior to spading. Apply a small handful per square yard.

Just before planting, rake the area to break up any large clumps of soil and to level the surface.

Drawing a plan to show the approximate location of each perennial is a good idea. A large piece of graph paper works well for this. Outdoors, use label stakes to mark the location of plants before setting them out.

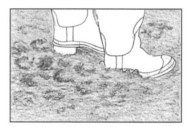

1. Add fertilizer, then tread on soil to eliminate air pockets.

2. Level the soil surface with a rake just prior to setting out plants.

Setting Out the New Perennials

Perennials can be planted almost any time the soil can be worked. Spring is the most popular season, but fall is also excellent. In cold regions spring planting is probably safer; fall planting must be done early so that plants become established before winter. Apply mulch after the ground has frozen, to prevent alternate freezing and thawing, which heaves plants up out of the soil and exposes roots.

Container-grown plants establish themselves readily even when in bloom and can be planted in summer if they are kept well watered.

Dormant perennials, either bare rooted or in small pots, may arrive by mail several days before it is convenient to plant them. Open the package, water if necessary, and keep in a cool place indoors or in a shaded place outdoors away from drying winds. The sooner they are planted, the better are their chances of survival. Water well after planting.

Take care to set the plants at the proper depth. In most cases this means that the point at which roots and stems meet should be at the established soil level. If planted too shallowly, the roots will be exposed; if too deeply, the crowns can rot.

Following the planting plan, draw guidelines on the bed with the corner of a hoe. In a large bed the guidelines are easier to follow if they are marked out with sand. These will remain even if rain should postpone planting. Work on one section at a time; or do the back first, and work toward the front. Space the plants to allow for the eventual spread of the foliage. The best effects are obtained when three or more of one kind of plant are set together.

For plants with small root systems, use a trowel to make holes; for large root systems, use a spade. Make holes large enough to accommodate the spread-out roots. Set the plant upright in the center, and fill the hole with soil. Firm the soil around each plant and water.

1. Space out a few plants at a time within a marked-off section of bed.

2. Use a trowel to dig planting holes deep and wide enough for the roots.

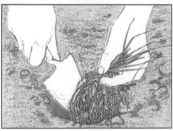

3. Set the plant in the hole, spread the roots, and return soil.

4. Firm in the plant with your fingers and the back of a trowel.

PLANTING BIG ROOTS

Large-rooted plants. Use a spade to dig out a deep hole wide enough to accommodate roots. Set the root ball in the center, and fill the hole with soil. Firm in with your heel.

PLANTING DIVISIONS

Well-developed clumps. These can be divided. Gently pull them apart so that each piece has crown and roots. Plant divisions immediately to keep them from drying out.

Monarda didyma 'Croftway Pink'

Sedum spectabile 'Brilliant'

The blooms of the bergamot (*Monarda*) attract butterflies. Seed heads of the showy stonecrop (*Sedum spectabile*) give interest long after the flowers have faded.

Jobs to Be Done When Spring Arrives

Keeping the Ground Clear of Weeds

Begin weeding as soon as growth appears. Neglecting the job only leads to more work later on if the weeds are allowed to mature and disperse their seeds. Also, weeds flourish in well-prepared soil and deprive the perennials of both nutrients and moisture. Keep a basket nearby, and drop weeds into it as you remove them. If left on moist soil, many of them will reroot. Add the weeds to the compost pile. Once the ground has been cleared of weeds, a mulch can be applied to deter further growth. Another benefit of a mulch is that it conserves soil moisture during dry spells.

In small beds weeding can be done with a short-handled cultivator. But for larger areas, to eliminate prolonged stooping, a long-handled tool is preferable.

To remove weeds with a standard hoe, cut them off with a chopping motion, drawing the hoe toward you and taking care not to injure any of the desirable plants. The flat side of a Warren hoe is used the same way; the two-pronged side is used for larger weeds.

The scuffle, or Dutch, hoe is pushed backward and forward through the soil, just below the surface, to cut off the weeds.

Cultivators break up the surface soil and uproot weeds at the same time. When such persistent, deep-rooted weeds as quack grass are growing around the base of a plant, it may be necessary to dig up the plant, split it apart, and replant it in order to remove weeds in the center of the clump or entangled with the roots.

REMOVING SURFACE AND DEEP-ROOTED WEEDS

Around plants. Chop off weeds among close-growing plants with a short-handled cultivator.

Between rows. For surface weeding and between rows of plants, use a long-handled hoe.

In matted clumps. Use a spading fork to loosen matted weeds growing through clumps.

Loosening the Soil in Established Beds

At the start of the growing season, and again in late autumn, the soil in established beds should be loosened. This is particularly important on heavy or unmulched soil that has become compacted. Loosening allows air and moisture to penetrate to the roots of plants and at the same time eliminates any weed seedlings. A fork can be used, but a long-handled, tined cultivator is ideal.

Cultivators have three or five hooked tines; use a three-tined one in restricted areas.

Supplying Plant Food and Constant Moisture

The health of plants can be maintained or improved, and their growth encouraged, by the application of a complete fertilizer containing the three most important plant nutrients—nitrogen, phosphorus, and potash—in varying proportions.

Organic fertilizers are particularly suited to perennials, since the nutrients are released slowly over the full period of growth. In early spring, just as growth becomes apparent and before mulching, apply fertilizer by hand. Avoid letting it come in contact with foliage. Use a complete organic fertilizer with an analysis such as 4–12–4. Always apply fertilizers according to directions.

Between late spring and early summer feed the plants once with a fast-acting liquid foliar spray such as liquid seaweed.

Watering should not be necessary if the bed has been mulched, except during prolonged dry spells. The mulch, which is a layer of organic material over the soil, conserves moisture by reducing evaporation. If watering is needed, the most effective method is to use a watering wand that will direct the water to the soil surface.

Clay soils, which compact under heavy rain, should have their surfaces loosened before watering, feeding, or mulching. A mulch also serves some other worthwhile purposes. It prevents compacting. It improves the quality of both clay and sandy soils. It helps to keep water from spattering the undersides of leaves and thus lessens the spread of soil-borne fungous disease. It helps to suppress weed seedlings. And as the organic materials break down, they add nutrients to the soil.

Apply mulch in late spring after the ground has been weeded but before growth is advanced. In dry weather soak soil before mulching.

It is best to cover the planting bed completely. But if this is not possible, it is better to apply a thick mulch around some plants than to spread it thinly over the whole bed.

MULCHING

Spread mulch, 2–3 in. deep, over the root area of the plants. Use rotted garden compost or manure, leaf mold, cocoa shells, or other materials. In dry weather always water soil before applying mulch.

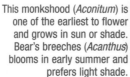
This monkshood (*Aconitum*) is one of the earliest to flower and grows in sun or shade. Bear's breeches (*Acanthus*) blooms in early summer and prefers light shade.

Aconitum napellus   *Acanthus spinosus*

How to Support Top-heavy Perennials

Perennials need support if they have a floppy habit of growth, are top-heavy when in flower, or are likely to suffer from wind or storm damage. Use bamboo stakes, galvanized wire hoops or mesh, or twiggy brushwood. Lightweight individual plants and clumps can be supported by brushwood, but heavier plants are best staked with canes or wire mesh. Put supports in place before growth has become too advanced and difficult to handle.

The supports should reach to just below the flower spikes; so one must know in advance the eventual approximate height of a plant (p. 44).

Plants supported by brushwood, hoops, or wire mesh need no tying in, but tall stems should be attached to their cane supports with strong raffia or garden twine or with one of the commercially available ties. These are usually made of thin wire covered with plastic or paper, cut to length or in rolls, or Velcro.

Wire-Mesh Supports for Tall-Growing Plants

A plant that grows exceptionally tall (5–6 feet)—such as certain meadow-sweets, some heliopsis, rudbeckias, Solomon's seals, and tall delphiniums—can be supported with wire-mesh cylinders. Once the support is in position, no tying in is necessary. Use 4-inch-square galvanized mesh (also available in green) to make a cylinder that is wide enough to just enclose the whole group of plants. If the cylinder is smaller than the diameter of the mature plants, it will not show.

Insert three tall bamboo canes upright in the ground inside the cylinder. Tie each cane to the wire mesh, first just above ground level, then halfway up, and again at the top.

For taller plants it may be necessary to fit a second cylinder on top of the first. Overlap the two cylinders, and tie them together with twine.

1. Push canes into the soil inside the mesh, and fasten with soft twine.

2. For taller plants, overlap mesh cylinder with another one above.

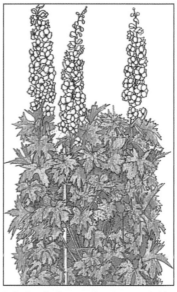
3. As the plants grow, the stems are held securely within the framework.

Supporting Plants With Stakes and Twine

Use bamboo cane stakes or other available slender wood or metal stakes to support single stems or groups of plants, such as delphiniums, phlox, and meadow rues, that are more than 2 feet and up to 4–5 feet in height.

For a single-stemmed plant firmly insert one bamboo cane in the ground close to the plant, and attach the stem with raffia, twine, or plastic-covered wire. As the stem grows, add more ties at approximately 1-foot intervals or as needed.

For a group of plants or a large clump, firmly insert three stakes in the ground close to the plant at equidistant intervals. These will be hidden when the plant fills out.

Knot the twine to one cane, 6–9 inches aboveground; then loop the twine around the other two canes and secure. Tie again as plant grows.

1. Support a clump of delphiniums with bamboo canes and twine.

2. As the plants grow, add another piece of twine, 9 in. above the first.

3. When mature, plants will be supported by several circles of twine.

RING SUPPORT

A homemade galvanized-wire ring support can be raised as the plant increases in height. Insert three bamboo canes around the plant, and place the ring over them, tying it to each of the canes.

The giant scabious (*Cephalaria*) is suitable only for large gardens. Growing up to 6 ft., this perennial is very effective when grown through shrubs.

Cephalaria gigantea

Seasonal Care of Perennials

Keeping Floppy Plants Up With Twiggy Brushwood

To support plants up to 2 feet in height that tend to become floppy, use strong twiggy brushwood similar to that used for peas.

When pruning small trees or trimming hedges, save little twiggy branches (sometimes called peasticks) for this purpose. Almost any tree or shrub provides good material, particularly spirea, birch, and oak.

Before inserting the brushwood in the ground, carefully sharpen the lower ends, and make sure that the soil is soft. Because it is branched, too much pressure will break the brushwood. If the soil is compacted, make a hole first.

Push in each piece of brushwood deeply enough so that it will hold firmly under the weight of the growing plant. Two or three pieces for each group of plants are usually sufficient. If the plants are known to sprawl badly after heavy rains, or to form especially large spreading clumps, use more brushwood.

Break the tops of the brushwood inward and interlace them to form a loose roof framework that will help support the flowering stems as they grow.

1. Push twiggy brushwood into the center of a clump of plants.

2. Break the tops of the sticks, turning them to the center of the plants.

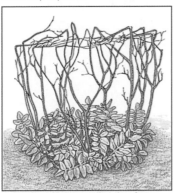

3. Interlace the tops so that they form a framework over the plants.

4. As the plants grow, stems and leaves will hide the supports.

Removing Faded Flowers and Stems

As soon as the flowers fade, cut them back. On some plants, such as delphinium, phlox, and low-growing achillea, you may then get a second period of bloom. Continue to remove all faded flowers into the fall. This procedure, known as deadheading, improves appearance and prevents self-sown seedlings, which may be inferior plants, from taking hold.

Cut back single, bare flower stems as close as possible to the base.

Where the lower parts of flower stems have foliage, cut the stems just above the top leaves.

The seed heads on some plants are worth retaining for fall decorating.

CUTTING STEMS

Bare flower stems should be cut to ground level (left). Trim stems with foliage to just above the top leaves (right).

Cutting Back Straggly Plants After Flowering

Often used as edging in perennial borders, mat-forming plants grow straggly after blooming. Plants such as aubrieta and candytuft need hard pruning when flowering is over. Cut back by about one-half to two-thirds of their original height. This hard pruning promotes new growth and may encourage reblooming. If not pruned, plants grow woody and straggly, and bloom less.

Plants, such as anthemis and pyrethrum, that have one profuse bloom, make little new growth. To keep them tidy, cut back by one-third after they flower. Plants grown mainly for their foliage effect, lamb's ears and lady's mantle for example, can either have their flowers removed as soon as they appear, or be allowed to bloom normally.

MAT-FORMING PLANTS

Mat-forming edging plants are cut back hard, with scissors or hedge shears, as soon as flowers fade.

Asters come in many colors and sizes. The Italian aster (*Aster amellus*) comes in different shades of violet and grows up to 2 ft. The Michaelmas daisy (*A. novi-belgii*) grows to 4 ft. or more.

Aster amellus 'King George'

Aster novi-belgii 'Fellowship'

Tending to Perennials Before Winter

Perennial borders should be tidied up when growth ceases in the fall. Continue flower removal as necessary, and in cold regions remove the foliage of plants that normally die down to the ground.

Divide and replant overgrown clumps (see p. 39). Before replanting, fork over the soil; then rake in ½ cup of bone meal per square yard.

In very cold areas, mulch perennials after the ground freezes to prevent alternate freezing and thawing of soil, which can tear roots and lift crowns above soil level, resulting in the death of plants. Use a light mulch that will not smother plants: pine branches, oak leaves, salt hay. Remove the mulch gradually in spring.

1. Cut the dead stems of perennials to just above ground level.

2. Cover the plants with a layer of salt hay or evergreen boughs.

Lifting Tender Tubers; Interplanting Hardy Bulbs

In cold regions, tender bulbs or tubers such as gladiolus or dahlias, that have been interplanted among the perennials for summer color, should be lifted in late fall and stored until spring in a cool, dry place.

At the same time spring-flowering bulbs, such as daffodils and tulips, can be interplanted among the perennials. These bulbs will provide the garden with considerable color in spring, a time when most perennials have not started to flower. Daffodils will continue to flower for many years without any attention, but tulips are best replaced when they no longer bloom well. When planting, remember that bulb foliage must be left to ripen after flowering. However, it can be well hidden by taller perennials.

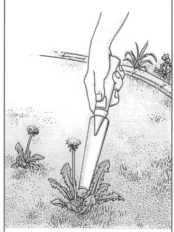

Stray dandelions pop up even in the best-kept gardens, but can be dug out easily with a trowel.

What Can Go Wrong With Perennials

Properly positioned perennials growing in good soil seldom develop any serious pest or disease problems. If your plants show symptoms that are not described here, turn to the section on plant disorders beginning on page 506.

SYMPTOMS AND SIGNS	CAUSE	CONTROL
Stem tips and flower spikes are covered with sticky insects. In severe cases growth may be distorted, flowers fail to open.	Aphids	Spray with a strong stream of water from a hose. If problem persists, apply insecticidal soap.
Leaves are chewed.	Caterpillars	Spray with *Bacillus thuringiensis.*
Young stems, chewed through at ground level, wilt and fall over.	Cutworms	Cultivate in spring to expose cutworms to birds, or hand-pick at night.
Leaves have silvery spots. Leaves, buds, and flowers are webbed together or severely distorted.	Mites (two-spotted or cyclamen)	Spray with a strong jet of water or apply insecticidal soap, especially on the undersides of the leaves.
Young leaves, flower buds, or stem tips are distorted. Leaves may have small, irregular holes.	Plant bugs (four-lined, harlequin, phlox, or tarnished)	Spray with insecticidal soap.
Young shoots are eaten and slime trails present.	Slugs or snails	Use an iron phosphate slug bait, or trap with beer.
Leaves, young shoots, and sometimes flowers are covered with waxy white powder; may become withered or distorted.	Powdery mildew (fungus)	Spray with sulfur or a potassium bicarbonate product.
Leaves (occasionally young stems) have brown or red pustules, which erupt and show powdery spores. Leaves may yellow and die.	Rust (fungus)	Spray with summer oil or sulfur. May be difficult to control.
Leaves and soft stem tips wither, yellow, and hang down; entire plant may be infected (particularly Michaelmas daisies).	Verticillium wilt (fungus)	Remove infected shoots and spray with sulfur.
Flower buds fail to develop properly, withering or dropping before they open.	Drought	Soak with 2 gal. of water per sq. yd.; repeat at least weekly during dry spells. Mulch with garden compost, shredded leaves, or wood chips.
Stems are thin and often crowded; flowers are small. Leaves wilt, especially on hot days; lower ones yellow and die prematurely.	Starvation or drought	Spray plants with foliar feed, soak thoroughly with water, and mulch with decayed manure or garden compost. Divide clumps as required.

The graceful astilbe (*Astilbe*) needs damp soil and looks especially good beside ponds. The lupinelike wild indigo (*Baptisia*) has attractive seedpods that dry well.

Astilbe 'Feuer'

Baptisia australis

Increasing Your Stock by Dividing Perennials

Lifting Overgrown Plants From the Soil

An overgrown perennial that has outgrown its allotted space in the garden likely does not produce as much bloom as it did formerly. Some plants, phlox and iris are two such examples, reach this state in a few years. Others such as helenium and day lily, take five or more years. Yet others seldom require division, gas

plant and peony being notable examples.

Lifting overgrown perennials for division (the methods are described here and on the next page) should be done before growth begins or when it slows, after flowering. Plants that flower very early are best divided in autumn, while those that flower very late are best tended to in spring. Most others can be divided in spring or fall. However, these rules are flex-

ible, and division can often be done when it is most convenient if special aftercare is given.

Since perennials remain in the same spot for many years, it pays to improve the soil prior to replanting. Incorporate compost plus bone meal.

Choose a day for lifting when the soil is neither frozen nor sticky. In very cold regions, division in late summer or fall should be done well

in advance of very cold weather to allow roots to become established before the ground freezes. Also keep in mind that the sooner the plants are divided and reset after lifting, the less setback will occur.

Always protect lifted plants from sun or drying winds while they await your attention, and water if unavoidable delays occur. Plants divided in fall should first have their foliage cut back to make division easier.

Dividing Rhizomatous-Rooted Plants

Plants that grow from rhizomes are easily lifted, since the rhizome (which is really a swollen underground stem) grows at, or just below, the surface of the soil. Bergenias, bearded iris, and Solomon's seal are all rhizomatous, and each plant can be separated into several new ones.

Ideally, this should be done in the early spring, just as the new growth buds begin to emerge. For iris division, see page 74.

After lifting the plant, carefully remove all the soil, so that the old rhizomes can be seen, together with the younger rhizomes growing from it. If the soil clings, making it difficult to see all the rhizomes, wash it away with a stream of water.

In separating the side growths from the old rhizomes, cut the new divisions off with a sharp knife to avoid damaging the tissues. To prevent drying, plant the young rhizomes at once.

In planting, make sure that the rhizomes are completely covered and well anchored in the soil and are at about the same depth as the original plant. Rhizomes of bearded irises are

an exception and are generally planted horizontally with the upper third of the rhizome above soil level (see p. 74). Deeper planting may rot the rhizome.

If you are unable to plant the divisions immediately, do not let them dry out. Store them in a box, and cover them with moist sand or peat moss. Never leave them unplanted for more than a day or two.

1. Bergenias may need dividing every three years, preferably just as growth commences in spring. Choose healthy young rhizomes having at least two buds or young shoots and undamaged fibrous roots. Carefully cut off the young rhizomes, which should be at least 3 in. long.

2. Cut off the side growths flush with the old rhizome, and discard it.

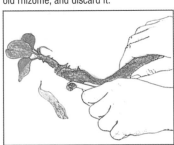

4. Remove any stumps or pieces of rotten stem and any dead leaves.

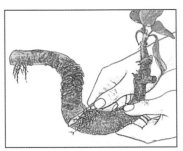

3. Trim cut pieces to just below a cluster of fine, healthy roots.

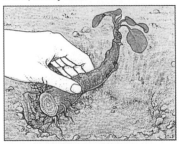

5. The young trimmed rhizome is now ready for planting in the garden.

Both mountain bluet (*Centaurea montana*) and clustered bellflower (*Campanula glomerata*) flower from midsummer onward and make good cut flowers.

Centaurea montana

Campanula glomerata 'Superba'

Division of Young Perennials

Two- or three-year-old perennials that have fibrous roots, such as heleniums, rudbeckia, and perennial asters, are easily divided in spring if more plants are needed.

The larger divisions—those with three or more shoots—can be set out immediately in their permanent locations, where they can be expected to make a good show of bloom that same season. Smaller divisions are best planted in an out-of-the-way bed until the following spring or summer, when they can be moved to their permanent places.

1. Divide plants with small root systems by gently pulling them apart.

2. Trim off with a knife any roots that are rotten, dead, or damaged.

3. Use pieces with several shoots to replant in the garden.

Division of Older, Large Perennials

Large, overgrown, fibrous-rooted perennials, such as heleniums and phlox, are sometimes difficult to divide, since the crown is a solid mass of shoots and roots. After lifting the clump, force the prongs of two garden forks into the center of the clump, back to back, and pry apart as shown at right.

After making the major divisions, use a sharp knife to cut away the older, woodier portions toward the center. Then separate the pieces into sections. Try to have at least six buds or shoots on each. When planting, be sure to firm the soil around the roots; then water thoroughly to settle the soil and eliminate air pockets.

Plants that have extremely tough woody crowns—for instance baptisias—cannot usually be split with forks. In such cases, cut through the crown with a strong, sharp knife, so that each severed portion has both roots and growth buds. Replant the divisions at once and water them.

Fleshy-rooted plants, such as hostas, also are best divided by prying apart with two garden forks. Work carefully to avoid damaging the fleshy roots.

1. Separate overgrown, matted plants with two forks, back to back.

2. Press handles of the forks together; then force them apart to lever and split the clump in two. Split the two sections in half the same way.

3. Cut away any woody shoots and dead roots from the divisions.

4. On fleshy rooted plants trim rotten or damaged roots to healthy tissue.

5. Plant out divisions at once in their permanent location.

The golden sunflower (*Heliopsis*) blooms in different shades of yellow. Single, semi-double, and fully double forms are available.

Heliopsis helianthoides 'Hohlspiegel'

How to Grow New Perennials From Cuttings

New Perennials From Layers

Many perennials that have an arching habit of growth can be propagated from layers. Layering is a good choice when you need only a few additional plants, and it works well when the parent plant is still too small to lift and divide. Propagating by layers also doesn't require the special facilities—like a greenhouse or cold frame—needed for rooted cuttings. This method works particularly well with garden pinks (*Dianthus*) but is also worth trying with any species that has thin individual shoots, rather than a solid crown bearing the leaves and flowering stems.

Once the plant has started growing in spring, but before the stems start to get woody, carefully bend a stem toward the soil. Where the stem touches the ground, slice off a little of the skin. Bend the tip back more or less upright and peg the wounded area down with a small metal hook, a tent peg, or a flat stone and cover it with soil, leaving the shoot tip exposed.

By fall, the stem should be rooted and can be dug up and moved to a new location.

Taking Tip Cuttings in Summer and Autumn

Some perennials, notably low-growing shrubby plants—phlox, penstemons, and sedums—and foliage perennials—anthemis and rues—are best increased from tip cuttings.

Take tip cuttings from the ends of nonflowering lateral shoots. This can be done whenever the stems are semi-firm. In cold areas, protect rooted cuttings by placing them in a cold frame during their first winter.

Take the cuttings, 3–4 inches long, from the tips of healthy, leafy stems, ensuring that each cutting has at least three leaf joints (nodes).

Fill a pot to just below its rim with equal parts of peat moss and coarse sand or perlite, or use a commercial seed-starter mixture. A 4-inch pot will hold about six cuttings, but avoid overcrowding.

Trim each cutting just below the lowest leaf node, using a sharp knife or a razor blade. Pull off or cut away the lowest pair of leaves.

Make shallow holes in the rooting mixture with a pencil. Insert each cutting so that the base of its stem touches the bottom of the hole without burying any of the leaves. Firm in with the fingers.

Water the pot thoroughly and label. Cover the pot with a plastic bag that has a few small holes poked in for ventilation; secure with a rubber band. To keep the bag from touching the cuttings, make a framework of sticks or wires before putting on the plastic. Set pots of cuttings in a shaded spot or cold frame for five to six weeks to root.

If cuttings are taken in cool weather, keep in mind that a propagating case with bottom heat of 60°F will hasten rooting.

To check to see if the cuttings have rooted, tug them gently. If they do not yield, they have rooted and can be removed from the plastic covering or propagator. Leave the pot of cuttings uncovered for four or five days. Then remove the cuttings by turning the pot upside down and carefully dislodging the contents all in one piece. The cuttings can also be pried out, but this tends to damage many of the roots.

Separate the cuttings gently, and pot again as shown. Firm the soil, water thoroughly, and drain.

In mild regions put the pots in a shaded spot or cold frame for about a week before setting them out in the garden. Pinching out the growing tip at this time will encourage the plants to develop strong roots before making top growth.

In cold regions, winter the cuttings in a closed cold frame. Plunge pots in sand or peat moss. Plant outside where you want them in spring after there is no danger of frost.

LAYERING

Pegged down in spring, this layer is now ready to be moved to a new location.

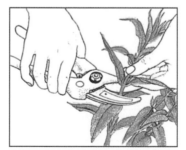

1. Snip off nonflowering side shoots 3–4 in. long when semi-firm.

2. Trim the cuttings just below a leaf node, and remove lower leaves.

3. Make planting holes in a 4-in. pot of rooting mixture; insert the cuttings.

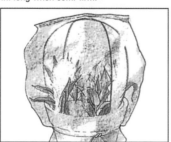

4. Crisscross two wire loops to make a framework, and cover with plastic.

5. When each cutting is rooted, plant it in a 3-in. pot of soil.

6. Pinch out the tip of each cutting. In cold areas, winter in a cold frame.

Wild bergamot (*Monarda fistulosa*) with its long-lasting blooms can be used for perennial beds or for wild gardens. Cupid's dart (*Catananche*) needs dividing every few years.

Monarda fistulosa

Catananche caerulea 'Alba'

Taking Basal Cuttings in Spring

Most clump-forming perennials—anchusa, achillea, delphinium, baptisia, and scabiosa among others—can be propagated not only by division but also from the young shoots that grow at the base of the plants in spring.

When the shoots are 3–4 inches long, scrape the soil from around the crown of the plant and cut some off, just below soil level, with pruners or a sharp knife. Insert cuttings into porous soil in a cold frame, or put them in 4- to 5-inch pots filled with equal parts of peat moss and sand (or perlite), before putting the pots into a cold frame. By putting cuttings into pots in a shaded cold frame, rather than directly into the soil, you can move them from the frame at any time—perhaps for hardening off after rooting—without transplanting.

Water cuttings well by spraying them from overhead, and keep the frame closed. As new growth starts to show, increase ventilation by gradually opening the frame during the warmer hours. When cuttings are rooted, pot them singly into 3- or 4-inch pots of soil. Plant them outside in summer as soon as they are established, or hold them over the winter in a cold frame.

1. Scrape soil from the crown and cut off young shoots below soil level.

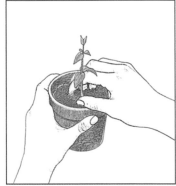

2. Insert cuttings in rooting mixture and place in a cold frame.

Growing Perennials From Pieces of Root

Many perennials with fleshy roots lend themselves to rapid multiplication via root cuttings. When a plant has no well-defined vegetative shoots—Oriental poppies, for instance—this is the most practical means of propagation to increase a plant.

Root cuttings can be taken from mature plants at any time but are most often made during periods of less active growth—as in the late summer, fall, or very early spring.

Cut thick or fleshy roots, such as those of dicentras and Oriental poppies, into 2- to 3-inch pieces. Cut thin roots, such as those of phlox, to about 2 inches.

Fill large pots or flats with equal parts of peat moss and sand (or perlite). Make holes 2 inches apart, 2–3 inches deep. Insert thick cuttings vertically, and cover their tops with ¼ inch of the mixture. Place thin roots horizontally and cover as above. Keep moist.

When cuttings have two or three sets of leaves, transplant them to individual pots, and later into the garden. In cold regions keep the plants over the winter in a cold frame.

1. In late summer, fall, or early spring, cut thick roots into 2–3-in. lengths.

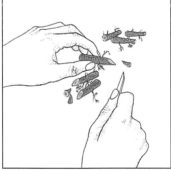

2. Cut lower end of cutting at a slant to distinguish base from top.

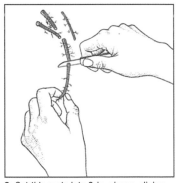

3. Cut thin roots into 2-in. pieces, slicing them straight across.

4. Insert thick roots in mixture, slanted end down; cover tops ¼ in.

5. Lay thin-root cuttings flat on the rooting mixture, and cover ¼ in.

6. When cuttings have formed leaves, pot them up individually.

Papaver orientale 'Prinzessin Victoria Louise'   *Hemerocallis* 'Ice Carnaval'   *Paeonia* 'Fairy Princess'

Oriental poppies (*Papaver*), day lilies (*Hemerocallis*), and peonies (*Paeonia*) all have fleshy roots.

Growing New Plants From Seeds

Buying Versus Gathering Seeds

In nature all flowering plants reproduce themselves from seeds that fall to the ground when ripe. These seeds usually spend time under the cover of dead leaves and germinate when conditions are suitable.

Cultivated plants can also be propagated from seeds, but the offspring often vary. Although most of our garden plants originated from species growing in the wild, they have been hybridized to produce different and often improved forms. Plants grown from these hybrid seeds will differ and usually be inferior to the parent. Note that collected seeds should always be stored in a closed container and kept in a cool place until they are sown.

Consider growing seedlings in a nursery bed, saving only the most attractive ones. Of course, in order to perpetuate a seed-raised strain, subsequent plants must be propagated by cuttings or division.

Commercial seeds can usually be relied upon to produce true to type seedlings (or variable seedlings having desirable characteristics), and they provide an inexpensive means of raising plants.

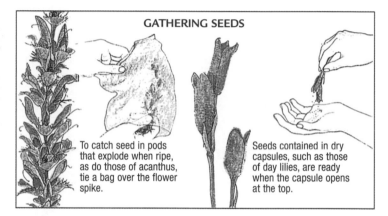

GATHERING SEEDS

To catch seed in pods that explode when ripe, as do those of acanthus, tie a bag over the flower spike.

Seeds contained in dry capsules, such as those of day lilies, are ready when the capsule opens at the top.

Sowing Seeds and Transplanting Seedlings

Sow seeds in mid to late winter in a greenhouse or under lights. Window light is seldom adequate. In mild climates, sow seeds in a cold frame or sheltered bed.

When sowing small quantities of seeds indoors, the simplest method is to plant only one kind in a pot. Fill the pot to about ½ inch below its rim with a commercial seed-starting mixture or your own sterilized formula (equal parts of soil, peat moss, and perlite). Level, firm gently, water with a fine spray, and let drain.

Sprinkle the seeds evenly but thinly over the surface; cover with ⅛-inch layer of starting medium. Leave fine seeds uncovered.

Cover the seed container with a pane of glass or a plastic bag to retain necessary moisture and warmth for germination. Keep the container out of the sun to avoid excessive heat. Most seeds germinate at 66°–70°F. Depending on the kind, seedlings should appear in about one to three weeks. When they do, remove the glass or plastic covering.

When seedlings are large enough to handle easily, transplant to a flat pot filled with sterilized soil, and space 1–2 inches apart. Give them all the sun and light available to prevent weak, spindly growth. As seedlings become crowded, pot individually.

Before setting the seedlings out, acclimate them to outdoor conditions by putting them in a cold frame or sheltered spot in the garden. Set pots or flats on the surface of the soil, and lightly shade for a few days; then gradually admit more air and light. Later transplant to an out-of-the-way bed for further growth. In late summer of the same year, plant in permanent positions, or wait until the following spring.

For an early start in cold climates, outdoor seed sowing is best done in a heated frame. A soil-heating cable set for 65°F is satisfactory. In an unheated frame, sow about six weeks prior to the last spring frost. Prepare soil in frame by adding peat moss or perlite, so that it will not crust over and deter the emergence of the seedlings.

Sow seeds shallowly in rows or in pots as previously described. Shade the frame with burlap until seeds germinate; then give full light, ventilation, and moisture. Transplant as needed into well-spaced rows or pots in the cold frame, and then later to the garden.

1. In late winter, sprinkle seeds on moist potting mix; cover thinly.

2. Cover with plastic, which must be removed when seedlings appear.

3. When seedlings have two pairs of leaves, move to another container.

4. One or two months later, move vigorous plants to individual pots.

Perennials for Your Garden

Most of the widely grown plants described in the chart that follows are long-lived and suitable for growing in herbaceous or mixed borders. The plants are listed according to their botanical names. Also included are recommended species and varieties.

Height is measured to the tip of the flower stem; spread applies to the area covered by the foliage after several years. The height of each individual species or variety is listed in the Species and Varieties column. Size, of course, is influenced by soil and climate.

Appropriate soil and light conditions for each individual plant are listed using pictograms. A key, detailing all the soil and light condition pictograms, is found at the bottom of every left-hand page.

There are, of course, many more perennials grown than would fit into this chart, and some of these are illustrated in the color photographs.

Aconitum cammarum 'Bicolor'

Acanthus spinosus
(bear's-breeches)

Achillea filipendulina
'Gold Plate' (yarrow)

Aconitum napellus
(monkshood)

Agapanthus africanus
(African lily)

BOTANICAL AND COMMON NAMES	HEIGHT	SPREAD	SOIL	LIGHT	SPECIES AND VARIETIES	SPECIAL REQUIREMENTS AND REMARKS	PROPAGATION (See p. 39)
Acanthus (acanthus, or bear's-breeches) Basal clusters of handsome, deeply lobed, shiny leaves often 2 ft. long and 1 ft. wide; spikes of tubular flowers open in early summer.	2–3 ft.	2½ ft.	■	◑ ●	*A. hungaricus*, white to pink, 3–5 ft. *A. mollis*, whitish, lilac, or rose, 2–3 ft. *A. m.* 'Latifolius', as above, larger leaves, 2–3 ft. *A. spinosus*, pure white with purple bracts, 4–5 ft. The hardiest species.	Locate in shade except in coastal areas where it will withstand sun. Plants can be cut back to ground after bloom for complete renewal of growth. In summer wash leaves with stream from hose to keep clean. Roots are invasive, plants difficult to eradicate.	Divide plants in spring; take root cuttings in spring; sow seeds in spring.
Achillea (milfoil, or yarrow) Showy plants, some with attractive, pungent, fernlike leaves. Flowers in broad flat heads or loose clusters, all can be dried.	1½–3 ft.	1–3 ft.	□	●	*A. filipendulina* 'Gold Plate', mustard-yellow, 3–4 ft. *A. f.* 'Cloth of Gold', bright yellow, 5 ft. *A. millefolium* 'Cerise Queen', bright magenta-pink, 1–1½ ft. *A.* 'Moonshine', yellow, 1½ ft. *A. ptarmica* 'The Pearl', double, white, 1½ ft. *A. tomentosa*, grayish foliage, yellow, 1–1½ ft.	Very hardy, withstands drought well. *A. ptarmica* may be invasive but can be dug out. Mature clump of *A. filipendulina* often has 100 or more flower heads that last many weeks in dry weather. All are virtually trouble-free.	Divide in early fall; or sow seeds of *A. millefolium* and *A. ptarmica* in spring.
Aconitum (aconite, or monkshood) Long spikes of hooded flowers mostly in late summer above deeply cut leaves. Poisonous if eaten.	2½–8 ft.	1–2 ft.	□	◑	*A. cammarum* 'Bicolor', blue and white, 4–4½ ft. *A. carmichaelii*, pale blue, 2½–3½ ft. *A. c.* 'Barker's Variety', dark violet-blue, 4–5 ft. *A.* 'Ivorine', pale yellow in early summer, 3 ft. *A. napellus*, blue to violet, earliest, 3½–4 ft. *A.* 'Spark's Variety', deep violet-blue, 3–4 ft.	Grows best in soil enriched with compost. Tall varieties may need staking. Plants never invasive. Excellent for cut flowers and good substitute for delphinium; blooms late in season when few other perennials bloom. Tuberous roots.	Divide in early spring or sow seeds in spring. Do not disturb unless crowding reduces bloom.
Agapanthus (agapanthus, or African lily) Evergreen and deciduous tuberous-rooted plants with handsome strap-shaped leaves, clusters of blue or white funnel-shaped flowers.	1½ ft.	1–2 ft.	■	◑	*A. africanus* (lily of the Nile), blue, 3 ft. *A. a.* 'Peter Pan', a dwarf form, 1½ ft. *A.* 'Bressingham White', pure white, 3 ft. *A.* 'Headbourne Hybrids', blue to deep violet, hardier, 3–4 ft. *A. praecox orientalis*, mid-blue, 2–3 ft. More tender. Many new cultivars becoming available.	Does best as a cool greenhouse plant in the north. It can be grown outside without winter protection in zones 8–11 only. Fertilizing and watering increase bloom.	Divide evergreen forms in spring or fall, deciduous in fall; or sow seeds in spring to bloom in 3–4 yr.

■ well drained to sandy ■ moist ■ wet ■ acidic ■ alkaline □ regular soil ● full sun ◑ partial shade ● shade

Lady's mantle (*Alchemilla*), pearly everlasting (*Anaphalis*), and alkanet (*Anchusa*), all need well-drained soil.

Alchemilla mollis

Anaphalis triplinervis

Anchusa azurea 'Loddon Royalist'

Alchemilla mollis (lady's mantle)

Althaea officinalis (marshmallow)

Amsonia tabernaemontana (amsonia, or bluestar)

Anaphalis margaritacea (pearly everlasting)

Anchusa azurea (anchusa, or alkanet)

Anemone sylvestris (snowdrop anemone)

BOTANICAL AND COMMON NAMES	HEIGHT	SPREAD	SOIL	LIGHT	SPECIES AND VARIETIES	SPECIAL REQUIREMENTS AND REMARKS	PROPAGATION (See p. 39)
Alchemilla (alchemilla, or lady's mantle) Distinguished but not spectacular, with spring to midsummer fluffy flower sprays above handsome, rounded, lobed, plaited leaves.	6 in.–1½ ft.	1 ft.	■	●◐	*A. alpina* (mountain lady's mantle), sulfur-yellow, grayish leaves, 6 in. *A. erythropoda*, blue-green leaves, 8–12 in. *A. mollis* (common lady's mantle), yellow-green, 1½ ft.	Flowers last up to 2 wk. in water. An especially handsome plant for all-green border, wildflower garden, edging, or shaded rock garden.	Divide plants in early spring; or sow seeds.
Althaea (marshmallow) Upright plant with slightly hairy, lobed leaves.	4–6 ft.	3–5 ft.	■	●	*A. officinalis*, soft pink, late summer. *A. o.* 'Alba' is white-flowered.	Needs support in windy locations. Once used medicinally and gave its name to candy—marshmallow.	Sow seeds in summer, or use spring cuttings.
Amsonia (amsonia, or bluestar) Clusters of small soft blue flowers in late spring and shiny willowlike leaves that cover the entire stem. Long tapering seedpods also add interest.	2–3 ft.	1–2 ft.	■	◐	*A. hubrichtii*, pale blue with feathery foliage, 2–3 ft. *A. orientalis* (oriental bluestar), violet-blue, 2–3 ft. *A. tabernaemontana* (willow bluestar), light blue, 2–3 ft.	Generally trouble-free. Clumps grow in beauty and seldom require division. A rather late starter in spring; so take care not to injure when cultivating.	Divide deeply rooted plants in spring; or sow seeds in spring. Often self-sows but not invasive.
Anaphalis (pearly everlasting) Spreading plants with grayish foliage and round heads of small papery flowers that dry well (and are popular in winter arrangements).	1½–2 ft.	S 2 ft.	■	●◐	*A. margaritacea*, white heads with yellow centers, 2 ft. *A. m.* 'Neuschnee' (New Snow), pure white flower heads, 1½ ft.	Do not allow to become very dry in summer. Good border plants that are effective for a long time.	Sow seeds in spring; divide in spring or use soft spring cuttings.
Anchusa (anchusa, or alkanet) Clusters of small blue flowers like forget-me-nots in early to mid summer. For *A. myosotidiflora*, see Brunnera.	1–5 ft.	1–1½ ft.	□	●	*A. azurea* 'Dropmore', blue, 4–5 ft. *A. a.* 'Little John', brilliant blue, 1 ft. *A. a.* 'Royal Blue', royal blue in pyramidal clusters, 3 ft. (similar to, and often listed as, 'Loddon Royalist'). *A. capensis* 'Blue Angel', blue, short-lived, 1 ft.	Plants may bloom again if they are cut back after flowering. Tall varieties may require staking. Their self-sowing habit can be a nuisance in small garden, but plants can be pulled easily. Somewhat coarse foliage.	Divide plants or sow seeds in spring. Often self-sows in garden. Take root cuttings.
Anemone (anemone) Fall blooming, single to double flowers up to 3 in. across above foliage that is similar to grape leaves.	8 in.–3 ft.	1–2 ft.	■	◐	*A. hupehensis japonica* selections (Japanese anemone), including single-flowered, white or pink. 'Prinz Heinrich' is bright pink, 2½–3 ft. *A. hybrida* selections include 'Honorine Jobert', white, and 'Konigin Charlotte', semi-double, pink, 3–4 ft. *A. sylvestris*, (snowdrop anemone), 1–1½ ft.	Hardy only under good snow cover. Plants take several years to become established and multiply slowly. *A. vitifolia robustissima* hardier than *A.* hybrid forms.	Divide plants or sow seeds in spring. No need for division for many years.

The gleaming gold-yellow blossoms of the golden marguerite (*Anthemis tinctoria*) grow singly on long stems. Blooms of the attractive columbine (*Aquilegia*) appear from the middle of spring until early summer.

Anthemis tinctoria 'Beauty of Grallagh'

Aquilegia flabellata

Anthemis tinctoria 'Moonlight'
(chamomile)

Aquilegia vulgaris
(columbine)

Artemisia schmidtiana
(silver mound)

Aruncus sylvester
(goatsbeard)

Asclepias tuberosa
(butterfly weed)

BOTANICAL AND COMMON NAMES	HEIGHT	SPREAD	SOIL	LIGHT	SPECIES AND VARIETIES	SPECIAL REQUIREMENTS AND REMARKS	PROPAGATION (See p. 39)
Anthemis (anthemis, or chamomile) Deeply cut leaves and 2½-in. yellow daisylike flowers from midsummer until early fall. Flowers are long lasting when cut for indoor decoration.	1–3 ft.	1 ft.	▪	●	*A. marschalliana*, bright yellow, 1 ft. *A. nobilis*, or *Chamaemelum* nobile (garden chamomile), white and yellow, 1 ft., grown as ground cover or as herb. *A. tinctoria* (golden marguerite), yellow or gold, 2–3 ft. *A. t.* 'Beauty of Grallagh', deep yellow. *A. t.* 'E. C. Buxton', lemon-yellow. *A. t.* 'Kelwayi', dark yellow. *A. t.* 'Moonlight', pale yellow.	Excellent choice for hot, dry areas with sandy soil. Since somewhat weak stemmed, plants may need staking. Divide frequently to avoid dead centers in plants, and remove faded flowers to extend period of bloom and prevent self-sowing. The foliage is aromatic when it is bruised.	Divide in early spring or fall; take cuttings of basal shoots in same season. Seeds of *A. t.* 'Kelwayi' sometimes available.
Aquilegia (columbine) Graceful plant that in late spring bears funnel-shaped flowers with prominent spurs above basal cluster of segmented leaves. Many varieties available.	15 in.–3 ft.	6 in.–1ft.	▪	● ◐	*A. caerulea* (Colorado colombine), blue and white, 2½ ft. *A. chrysantha* 'Yellow Queen', white, long blooming, 2–2½ ft. *A.* 'Dragonfly Hybrids', lavender, red, yellow, white, 18 in. *A.* 'McKana Hybrids', mixed colors, long spurs, 3 ft. *A. vulgaris* 'Nora Barlow', double, pale green and red, spurless flowers, 3 ft.	Remove faded flowers to prevent self-sowing, which may produce inferior colors and blooms. Leaf miners may disfigure leaves with white streaks; control by removing infected leaves, or squash insects. Old clumps tend to die; so renew occasionally.	Propagated by seeds sown in early spring; occasionally by division in very early spring.
Artemisia (artemisia, or wormwood) Prized for aromatic, feathery gray-green or silver foliage. Small flowers are of secondary value.	6 in.–5 ft.	1–1½ ft.	▪	●	*A. abrotanum* (southernwood), woody stemmed, 3–5 ft. *A. lactiflora* (white mugwort), white flowers in fall, 4 ft. *A. ludoviciana* 'Silver King', silver foliage, 2–3 ft. *A. l.* 'Silver Queen', glistening silver foliage, 2–3 ft. *A.* 'Powis Castle', feathery silver foliage, 2 ft. *A. schmidtiana* 'Nana' (silver mound), makes a mound of silvery foliage, 6 in. *A. stelleriana* (dusty miller), East Coast native, 3 ft.	Preferably not too rich soil. Low forms can be sheared back if they become sprawly, although in full sun they seldom do. Plants generally trouble-free with proper culture. Gray foliage excellent transition between other garden colors.	Divide in spring or late summer; take cuttings or layer in late summer.
Aruncus (aruncus, or goatsbeard) A dramatic plant with attractive compound foliage and tall plumes of white flowers in early summer that resemble astilbe.	4–5 ft.	3 ft.	▪	● ◐	*A. aethusifolius*, cream, good for edging, 1 ft. *A. dioicus*, white, 3–5 ft. *A. sylvester* 'Kneiffii', similar to *A. dioicus* but finer cut foliage, 4–5 ft.	Although tall, it seldom needs to be staked. Often planted near a pond or other water feature, where it is very effective.	Divide in spring or early fall.
Asclepias (butterfly weed) Familiar wild flower, but its clusters of flowers in midsummer make it choice plant for perennial garden. Attractive foliage and seedpods.	2 ft.	1 ft.	▪	●	*A. incarnata*, magenta, good in wet soils, 3 ft. *A. tuberosa*, brilliant orange, attracts butterfiles, 2 ft.	A trouble-free perennial that can remain in same place for years and not outgrow its allotted space. Shoots are slow to appear in spring; so mark plant's location. Attractive before, during, and after bloom.	Sow seeds in spring. Division not recommended, as plant has easily broken taproot.

■ well drained to sandy   ■ moist   ■ wet   ■ acidic   ■ alkaline   □ regular soil   ● full sun   ◐ partial shade   ● shade

Michaelmas daisy (*Aster*), a flower of late summer or autumn, needs full sun and well-drained soil. Astilbe (*Astilbe*), a worthwhile plant for shaded areas and that also grows in sun, does best in moist locations.

Aster novi-belgii 'Helen Ballard'

Astilbe chinensis var. *pumila*

Aster novi-belgii
(Michaelmas daisy)

Astilbe chinensis
(false spirea)

Baptisia australis
(wild indigo)

Bergenia 'Silberlicht'
(bergenia 'Silver Light')

Boltonia latisquama
(boltonia)

Brunnera macrophylla
(Siberian bugloss)

BOTANICAL AND COMMON NAMES	HEIGHT	SPREAD	SOIL	LIGHT	SPECIES AND VARIETIES	SPECIAL REQUIREMENTS AND REMARKS	PROPAGATION (See p. 39)
Aster (aster, or Michaelmas daisy) Hybrids have popularized these familiar fall-blooming plants with profuse daisy-like flowers. Make good companions for chrysanthemums.	10 in.–4 ft.	1–3 ft.	☐	●	Several species with mostly single hybrids and a few doubles. *A. amellus* 'King George', purple-blue, 2 ft. *A. ericoides* 'Monte Casino', white, 4 ft. *A. frikartii* 'Moench', violet-blue, 3 ft. *A. novae-angliae* 'Harrington's Pink', rose-pink, 4 ft. *A. novi-belgii* 'Eventide', violet-blue, 3½ ft. *A. n.-b.* 'Professor Anton Kippenberg', lavender, 14 in. *A. n.-b.* 'Winston S. Churchill', deep red, 2 ft.	Pinch to induce branching, water frequently, and stake tall varieties. In humid regions plants are subject to mildew and rust; prevent problems by providing excellent drainage; control with organic fungicide. Rabbits have fondness for these plants.	Divide in early spring, saving outer shoots and discarding older center portion.
Astilbe (astilbe, or false spirea) Graceful plant with deeply cut, dark green or copper-tinted foliage. Large plumes of dainty flowers in early summer suitable for cutting.	12 in.– 3½ ft.	15 in.	■	●◐	*A. arendsii* 'Bridal Veil', pure white, 2½ ft. *A. a.* 'Cattleya', bright pink, 3 ft. *A. a.* 'Fanal', dark crimson, 2 ft. *A. chinensis* 'Finale', pink arching plumes, late, 15 in. *A. japonica* 'Deutschland', creamy white, 1½ ft. *A. j.* 'Rheinland', mid-pink, 1½ ft. *A. simplicifolia* 'Snowdrift', white, late, 1 ft.	Divide every 3 yr. for best blooms. Plants are heavy feeders; so apply fertilizer each spring. Water liberally during dry spells. Cut back faded flowers; foliage remains attractive all summer if well watered.	Divide plants in early spring or early fall. Be sure to work in plenty of compost or peat moss.
Baptisia (baptisia, or wild indigo) Grown for its deep blue flowers that bloom on tall spikes in early summer, followed by attractive black seedpods.	3–4 ft.	2–4 ft.	☐	●◐	*B. australis*, deep blue, 3–4 ft.	Vigorous plants grow very large, but are not invasive. Plants are very winter hardy. Seed pods dry well	Divide thick roots in early fall or very early spring; or sow seeds in spring.
Bergenia (bergenia, or pigsqueak) Grown primarily for striking, 8- to 10-in., glossy green, round leaves that are evergreen, reddish in winter. Flowers in midspring on short stems.	10 in.– 1½ ft.	1½– 3 ft.	■ ■	● ●	*B.* 'Bressingham White', pure white, 12–18 in. *B. cordifolia*, reddish pink, most readily available, 1 ft. *B.* 'Morgenrot' ('Morning Red'), bright reddish pink, 12–18 in. *B.* 'Silberlicht' ('Silver Light'), white becoming pink, 12–18 in.	Foliar feeding tends to increase vigor. In cold regions flowers may not appear. Most effective planted in groups. Spreading but not invasive.	Divide frequently after flowering or in early fall to prevent dead centers.
Boltonia (boltonia) Mostly tall-growing plants bearing in mid to late summer small starlike flowers that resemble wild asters. Found wild in many regions.	2–6 ft.	2–3 ft.	☐	●	*B. asteroides*, white and shades of purple, 4–6 ft. *B. a. latisquama*, pink to purple, 4–6 ft. *B. a. l.* 'Nana', pink, 2 ft. *B. a.* 'Snowbank', pure white, 4–5 ft.	Useful for wildflower garden or as background plant in perennial border.	Divide plants in spring; or sow seeds in spring.
Brunnera (brunnera, or Siberian bugloss) In mid to late spring loose clusters of blue, starlike flowers rise above large, dark green, heart-shaped leaves.	1–1½ ft.	1½ ft.	■	● ●	*B. macrophylla* (often listed as *Anchusa myosotidiflora*), blue flowers, some varieties are grown for their attractive variegated foliage, ¼ in. across, 1–1½ ft.	Multiplies slowly and needs to be divided only when centers of clumps look vacant. Makes interesting ground cover during summer.	Divide in early spring; or take root cuttings in late summer.

Varieties of the milky bellflower (*Campanula lactiflora*) have white, rose, or blue flowers. The black snakeroot (*Cimicifuga racemosa*) is a stately, long-flowering perennial.

Campanula lactiflora 'Prichard's Variety'

Cimicifuga racemosa

Campanula persicifolia (bellflower)

Catananche caerulea (cupid's dart)

Centaurea montana (centaurea)

Centranthus ruber (centranthus)

Chelone obliqua (turtlehead)

Cimicifuga simplex (bugbane)

BOTANICAL AND COMMON NAMES	HEIGHT	SPREAD	SOIL	LIGHT	SPECIES AND VARIETIES	SPECIAL REQUIREMENTS AND REMARKS	PROPAGATION (See p. 39)
Campanula (campanula, or bellflower) Diverse group of plants with small, neat foliage and mostly cup-shaped flowers. Taller varieties listed here; for shorter forms, see p. 311.	2–3 ft.	1–2 ft.	☐	●	C. glomerata (clustered bellflower), blue, white, 2 ft. C. lactiflora (milky bellflower) 'Prichard's Variety', violet-blue, 3 ft. C. latifolia (great bellflower), violet, 3 ft. C. l. macrantha, deep violet, 3 ft. C. persicifolia and hybrids (peach-leaved bellflower), in various shades of blue or white, 2–2½ ft.	Tall varieties seldom need staking. Removing faded flower spikes helps to prolong flowering. Valuable border plants suitable for cutting.	Divide or take basal cuttings in spring; or sow seeds in spring.
Catananche (catananche, or cupid's dart) Blue or white flowers resembling wild chicory appear in midsummer on slender-stemmed plants with narrow, silvery leaves. Good for cutting.	2 ft.	1 ft.	■	●	C. caerulea, blue with deeper blue center, 2 ft. C. c. 'Alba', white, 2 ft. C. c. 'Major', lilac-blue with dark center, 2 ft.	Plants must be divided frequently to ensure survival. Grow in groups for best effect. Flowers dry well for winter use.	Sow seeds in spring or divide plants; take root cuttings in early summer.
Centaurea (centaurea, or knapweed) Tufted flowers on long stems bloom in mid to late summer, some with rather coarse leaves. The blue ones are particularly valued.	2–4 ft.	1–2 ft.	■	●	C. dealbata (Persian centaurea), lilac to purple, 2 ft. C. d. 'Steenbergii', bright purple, 2 ft. C. hypoleuca 'John Coutts', bright pink, 2 ft. C. macrocephala (globe centaurea), yellow, thistle-like, 4 ft. C. montana (mountain bluet), blue, one of the best, 2 ft.	Easily grown. Plants withstand drought. C. montana most commonly seen; a rapid spreader. It self-sows, which may prove a nuisance. All hardy if soil is well drained.	Divide plants in very early spring. Seeds can be sown in spring but are rarely available.
Centranthus (centranthus, or valerian) Bushy plants with 3–4 in. gray-green leaves, fragrant crimson or white flowers in dense clusters along stems. Blooms early to mid summer.	2–3 ft.	1–2 ft.	☐	●	C. ruber (red valerian), crimson, 2–3 ft. Not to be confused with true valerian (*Valeriana officinalis*). C. r. 'Albus', white, 2–3 ft.	Plants multiply rapidly, less so in poor soil. Plants attractive over long period.	Sow seeds in spring; or divide plants in spring.
Chelone (chelone, or turtlehead) Short spikes of flowers like penstemon are borne in late summer on tall, unbranched stems. Alternate dark green leaves are broad and strongly veined.	2–4 ft.	2–4 ft.	■	◖	C. glabra, white or tinged pink, 2 ft. C. lyonii, pink to rose-purple, 3–4 ft. C. obliqua, rose-pink, 2 ft.	Plant in rich soil. Plants spread rapidly; so will need to be divided every few years. Generally insect-free. Most often listed in wildflower catalogs, as plants usually grow in moist woodland.	Divide plants in early spring. Plants spread by underground runners.
Cimicifuga (bugbane or snakeroot) Tall plumelike flower spikes top a basal cluster of fernlike leaves in early to mid fall. Useful at back of border or in wildflower garden.	3–8 ft.	1½–2 ft.	☐	● ◖ ●	C. dahurica (dahurian bugbane), white, late summer, 5 ft. C. racemosa (black snakeroot), white, midsummer, 5–8 ft. C. simplex (autumn snakeroot), early to mid fall, 4–4½ ft. C. s. 'White Pearl', white, early to mid fall, 3–4 ft.	When grown in sun, it is especially important to mix plenty of compost into soil before planting to help retain moisture. Flower spikes make excellent cut flowers, although some people find aroma objectionable.	Divide in early spring. Plants not generally invasive.

■ well drained to sandy   ■ moist   ■ wet   ■ acidic   ■ alkaline   ☐ regular soil   ● full sun   ◖ partial shade   ● shade

Lily of the valley (*Convallaria*) spreads quickly and makes a good ground cover under trees and shrubs.

Convallaria majalis

Clematis integrifolia
(clematis)

Convallaria majalis
(lily of the valley)

Coreopsis verticellata
(tickseed)

Corydalis flexuosa
(corydalis)

Cynoglossum nervosum
(Chinese forget-me-not)

BOTANICAL AND COMMON NAMES	HEIGHT	SPREAD	SOIL	LIGHT	SPECIES AND VARIETIES	SPECIAL REQUIREMENTS AND REMARKS	PROPAGATION (See p. 39)
Clematis (clematis) Not as well known as clematis vines, these herbaceous forms make interesting border plants. Long blooming. Some are fragrant.	2–6 ft.	2–3 ft.	■ ■	◑ ◑	*C. durandii*, indigo blue flowers, all summer, 3–6 ft. *C. heracleaefolia davidiana*, deep blue, late summer, 3 ft. *C. integrifolia*, blue, summer, 2 ft. *C. recta*, white, early to mid summer, 3–4 ft. *C. r.* 'Purpurea', young foliage is purple, 4 ft.	Mulch to keep soil cool. Avoid cultivating around plants; roots are shallow. Support plants with wire-mesh cylinders or twiggy brush in spring. Fluffy seedpods add interest and remain on plants for some time.	Take stem cuttings in midsummer for bloom following year. Protect over first winter.
Convallaria (lily of the valley) Sprays of fragrant, waxy, white or pinkish, bell-shaped flowers bloom in spring; old favorite of gardeners. Best as shady ground cover. Fruit poisonous.	6–8 in.	2 ft.	□	●	*C. majalis*, white, 6–8 in. *C. m. rosea*, pink, 6–8 in. The following are only rarely available: *C. m.* 'Albostriata', white, variegated leaves, 6–8 in. *C. m.* 'Flore Pleno', double, white, 6–8 in. *C. m.* 'Fortin's Giant', white, 1 ft.	Plants respond to fertilizer by producing more and larger flowers; apply after tops die down.	Divide into single crowns in early fall; division seldom needed and only after flowering deteriorates.
Coreopsis (coreopsis, or tickseed) Daisylike flowers bloom in profusion over long period in summer. Leaves are neat and unobtrusive, broader in some kinds than in others. Excellent cut flower.	1–3 ft.	1–2 ft.	■	●	*C. auriculata* 'Nana', (dwarf-eared), orange-yellow, 6 in. *C. lanceolata*, yellow, 2 ft. *C. l.* 'Baby Sun', hybrid usually raised from seeds, yellow, 20 in. *C. l.* 'Sunburst', semi-double, bright yellow, 2 ft. *C. grandiflora* 'Mayfield Giant', yellow, 3 ft. *C. verticillata* 'Golden Shower', yellow, 2 ft. *C. v.* 'Moonbeam', paler than 'Golden Shower', 1½ ft.	Keep flowers or seed heads picked to prolong flowering. *C. verticillata* withstands drought particularly well and has narrow, almost threadlike leaves. Divide every few years except *C. lanceolata*, which seldom needs this.	Divide plants in spring; or sow seeds of available varieties in spring.
Corydalis (corydalis) Spring flowers in white, pink, blue, or yellow above fernlike foliage. Flowers are two lipped with conspicuous spurs. Most species form a slow spreading mat that grow well beneath shrubs, but one species grows from corms.	8 in.–2½ ft.	6–12 in.	■	◑ ●	*C. elata*, almost evergreen with bright green foliage and deep blue flowers, 2 ft.. *C. flexuosa* 'Blue Panda', long flowering, mid-blue, several similar cultivars, 8–12 in. *C. lutea*, bright yellow flowers from spring to early fall, 12–16 in. *C. nobilis*, golden yellow tipped black, dies down after flowering, 2½ ft. *C. ochroleuca*, white flowers, tipped yellow, takes more sun, 12 in.	Grow in humus-rich soil. Locate plants that die down after flowering where they will not leave a hole in the border. Some will self-sow profusely.	Division in early fall, or in late spring for those that die back quickly. Sow seeds as soon as ripe.
Cynoglossum (cynoglossum, or Chinese forget-me-not) Small flowers like forget-me-nots borne on branching stems above rough, hairy leaves for several weeks in mid to late summer.	2–3 ft.	1–1½ ft.	■	● ◑	*C. grande*, blue or purple, 2–3 ft. *C. nervosum*, gentian-blue, 2½ ft. Not to be confused with annual cynoglossum, p. 201.	May need staking. Spreads rapidly; so best divided every 2 or 3 yr. Plants branch well and are covered with small blue flowers.	Divide in very early spring or early fall; or sow seeds in early spring. Plants often self-sow.

Short-lived *Delphinium grandiflorum* has cone-shaped blooms in blue, violet, or white. It is often treated like a biennial. Long-lived gas plant (*Dictamnus*) has flowers of white or pink and attractive seedpods.

Delphinium grandiflorum

Dictamnus albus

Delphinium hybrid
(delphinium)

Diascia integerrima
(twinspur)

Dianthus plumarius
(garden carnation)

Dicentra spectabilis
(bleeding heart)

Dictamnus albus
(gas plant)

BOTANICAL AND COMMON NAMES	HEIGHT	SPREAD	SOIL	LIGHT	SPECIES AND VARIETIES	SPECIAL REQUIREMENTS AND REMARKS	PROPAGATION (See p. 39)
Delphinium (delphinium) Tall spikes of closely spaced flowers (*D. elatum* types) or shorter spikes of loosely spaced flowers (*D. belladonna*) bloom in early to late summer. Each of the flowers consists of 5 showy sepals, 1 with a spur. True petals are smaller, often crowded in throat, and are called the "eye" or "bee." Flowers that are bicolored are the showiest.	2½–8 ft.	1–3 ft.	☐ ■	●	*D. belladonna* hybrids, white and shades of blue, 3–5 ft. *D.* 'Connecticut Yankee', blue, purple, lavender, white, 2½ ft. *D. elatum* hybrids, many in shades of blue, purple, pink, and white, often with contrasting "eye" or "bee," 6–8 ft. *D.* Pacific hybrids, similar to elatum in habit, but raised from seed and short-lived, 6 ft.	Locate in soil well mixed with humus. Fertilize heavily, supply ample water, and stake tall varieties early, before they topple. Check frequently for mildew, cyclamen mites, and black spot. Mulch over winter in cold regions, or carry them over in cold frame.	Divide in early spring; or take basal cuttings; sow seeds early indoors for bloom same season.
Diascia (twinspur) Upright to sprawling plants that bloom for a long time in a wide range of colors. Flowers have two spurs and are carried in clusters just above the foliage. Many new hybrids are being introduced and are becoming increasingly popular.	6–18 in.	6–24 in	■	●	*D. barbarae*, low mats of foliage with salmon pink flowers, 8 in. *D. integerrima*, spikes of deep pink flowers over toothed leaves, 18 in. *D.* Sun Chimes Series, flowers in pinks, reds, and lavender, 18 in.	Good choice for containers and will grow in part shade but with reduced flowering. Cut back hard when flowering finishes and fertilize to promote repeat blooming.	Take cuttings of new growth in spring or early summer.
Dianthus (dianthus, pink, or garden carnation) Single to double flowers—some fringed, most fragrant—bloom over long period. Narrow leaves. Colors: pink, red, salmon, yellow, or white.	1–2 ft.	1 ft.	■ ■	●	*D. allwoodii* hybrids, double or single, 1–1½ ft. *D. caryophyllus* hybrids (garden carnation), 1–1½ ft. (Here belong the grenadin carnations and related large-flowered florist types listed in catalogs.) *D. plumarius* hybrids (cottage or grass pink), 1–1½ ft.	Dianthus bloom best in cool weather and should be planted in full sun. *D. caryophyllus* hybrids need richer soil than others. Keep faded flowers picked to prolong bloom. Remove side buds as soon as they appear on *D. caryophyllus* types to obtain larger flowers.	Sow seeds in spring; take cuttings of vigorous nonflowering side shoots in midsummer.
Dicentra (dicentra, or bleeding heart) Graceful plants with pendulous heart-shaped flowers blooming on arching stems in late spring, some intermittently all summer. Fernlike leaves for all or part of season.	1–2½ ft.	1–2 ft.	☐	● ◖ ●	*D.* 'Bacchanal', gray-green leaved, dark red, 1½ ft. *D. eximia* (fringed bleeding heart), pink, 1–1½ ft. (Many hybrids of *D. eximia* with *D. formosa* or *D. oregana* range from pink to red.) *D. formosa* (western bleeding heart), deep pink. H 1–2½ ft./S 1–2 ft. *D.* 'Luxuriant', free-blooming, red, 1 ft. *D. spectabilis* (common bleeding heart), large, pink, 2½ ft.	All bleeding hearts like humus-rich soil. *D. formosa* and *D. eximia* self-sow freely. Locate *D. spectabilis* so that bare spaces left after leaves die back in late summer will be hidden by other foliage. Be sure to mark spot with a label so that area will not be disturbed during fall or spring cleanup.	Divide brittle fleshy roots in very early spring; or take root cuttings of *D. spectabilis* in spring. *D. eximia* self-sows freely.
Dictamnus (gas plant, or burning bush) Handsome, usually long-lived plant with pink or white flower spikes, blooming in early to mid summer. Aromatic, leathery, rich green leaves and attractive, persistent seedpods good for drying.	2–3 ft.	2–2½ ft.	☐	● ◖	*D. albus* (often listed as *D. fraxinella*), white, 2–3 ft. *D. a. purpureus*, pink with darker veins, 2–3 ft.	Grow in moderately rich soil. Staking not necessary. Common name derives from resin on leaves and upper part of stems, which is said to ignite if lighted after still, warm day. Leaves and pods poisonous, can cause dermatitis.	Plants best left undisturbed. Sow seeds where plants are to grow, as they resent transplanting.

■ well drained to sandy ■ moist ■ wet ■ acidic ■ alkaline ☐ regular soil ● full sun ◖ partial shade ● shade

Attractive to bees and butterflies, the globe thistle (*Echinops*) makes a good cut flower.

Echinops ritro

Doronicum 'Miss Mason' (leopard's-bane)

Dracocephalum ruyschianum (Siberian dragon's head)

Echinacea purpurea (purple coneflower)

Echinops bannaticus (echinops, or globe thistle)

Epimedium youngianum 'Niveum' (barrenwort)

BOTANICAL AND COMMON NAMES	HEIGHT	SPREAD	SOIL	LIGHT	SPECIES AND VARIETIES	SPECIAL REQUIREMENTS AND REMARKS	PROPAGATION (See p. 39)
Doronicum (doronicum, or leopard's-bane) Mid- to late-spring flowering with single, large, yellow daisylike flowers above mass of rich green heart-shaped leaves. Makes a good cut flower.	1½–2 ft.	1–1½ ft.	☐	◉ ◐	D. 'Miss Mason', yellow, 2 ft. D. orientale magnificum, yellow, 2 ft. D. o. 'Finesse', cactus flowered, yellow, 1½ ft. D. plantagineum, very large, yellow, 2½ ft., not widely available.	Plants may require staking. They go dormant in summer (except 'Miss Mason'), and foliage disappears; so plan to have other plants hide them.	Sow seeds in spring; or divide plants in late summer. Germination may be erratic.
Dracocephalum (dragon's head) Bushy plants with lance-shaped leaves in pairs and with toothed margins. Flowers are in spikes and are similar to *Nepeta*, only larger.	1–2 ft.	8–12 in.	▪	◉	D. grandiflorum, only basal leaves are stalked, hooded dark blue flower from midsummer, 12 in. D. ruyschianum (Siberian dragon's head), blue-purple flowers in late summer, 2 ft.	Good in dry locations but may need water during drought. In hot climates give midday shade.	Sow seed in spring or fall. Take cuttings from new growth in spring.
Echinacea (purple coneflower) Long-lasting, large daisylike flowers with rounded cone-shaped centers on long stiff stems bloom in mid to late summer. Excellent for cutting.	2½–4 ft.	1–1½ ft.	▪	◉	E. 'Art's Pride', bright orange, strap-like petals, 24–32 in. E. Harvest Moon™, slightly reflexed bright yellow, fragrant, 2½ ft. E. pallida, narrow, pink petals, 3–4 ft. E. purpurea 'Fragrant Angel', white with overlapping petals, 20 in. E. p. 'Little Giant', 2 in. bright pink flowers, 12 in. E. p. 'Sparkler' rose pink, cream variegated foliage, 2 ft.	Care-free plant with stiff stems that make staking unnecessary. Not reliably hardy on the Great Plains. Flowers are long lasting, well suited for drying. Dried centers can be used for making artificial flowers. Has a tendency to self-sow; flowers of self-sown seedlings are not showy.	Divide plants in early spring. 'Bright Star' seeds are available and can be sown in spring.
Echinops (echinops, or globe thistle) Globular flower heads are borne in late summer above dark green thistlelike foliage that is whitish beneath. Flowers excellent for drying.	3–5 ft.	1½–2 ft.	▪	◉	E. bannaticus 'Taplow Blue', deep blue, 4 ft. E. ritro (steel globe thistle), shades of blue, 3–5 ft. E. sphaerocephalus (common globe thistle), silver-gray, 5 ft.	Long-lived, easy-care plants that withstand considerable drought. Plants somewhat difficult to divide, as roots extend a foot or more deep. Small pieces of root left in ground when digging will generally sprout and make new plant. Leaves are prickly.	Divide plants or take root cuttings in spring; sow seeds in spring.
Epimedium (barrenwort) Spring flowering woodland plants that form large clumps in time. Leaves are divided into (mostly) three uneven parts and are often tinged or marked with bronzy-red when young. Flowers are in small sprays and often have spurs behind the petals.	10–16 in.	1–2 ft.	▪	◉	E. grandiflorum 'Lilafee', deep violet with white spurs, 10 in. E. parralchicum 'Frohnleiten', copper-red young foliage, yellow flowers, 16 in. E. rubrum, evergreen, sprays of up to 25 red and yellow blooms, 16 in. E. versicolor 'Sulphureum', pale yellow, good ground cover, 14 in E. youngianum 'Niveum', purple young leaves, white flowers, 12 in.	Grow in a woodland type soil with lots of humus. Drought resistant when established, water regularly in early years. Mulch with decayed leaves or bark in spring.	Division in early fall every 3–4 years or when flowering becomes poor.

The sea holly (*Eryngium*) thrives in full sun. The distinctive, silvery blue blooms appear in mid to late summer, and can be cut for drying.

Eryngium bourgatii

Eremurus robustus
(foxtail lily or desert candle)

Erigeron aurantiacus
(erigeron, or fleabane)

Eryngium bourgatii
(eryngium, or sea holly)

Euphorbia polychroma
(euphorbia, or spurge)

Filipendula purpurea
(filipendula, or meadowsweet)

BOTANICAL AND COMMON NAMES	HEIGHT	SPREAD	SOIL	LIGHT	SPECIES AND VARIETIES	SPECIAL REQUIREMENTS AND REMARKS	PROPAGATION (See p. 39)
Eremurus (foxtail lily or desert candle) Imposing spikes of yellow, pale pink, apricot, or white flowers grow from a yucca-like rosette of foliage in early summer. The roots are fleshy and radiate out from the crown, rather like an octopus. There are several named hybrids.	5–10 ft.	2–3½ ft.	■	●	*E. robustus*, several hundred pale pink 1½ in. flowers on the top 3 ft. of the tall stem, 8–10 ft. *E. stenophyllus*, smaller, bright yellow spikes of ¾ in. blooms, 3–5 ft.	Plant in a shallow hole on top of coarse sand with the crown at soil level. Protect emerging crown from late frosts in spring. Tolerates alkaline soil. Does not like competition from bushy plants close by.	When flowering becomes poor, lift plant in fall after foliage starts to die down. Shake apart gently so as to not damage the brittle roots. Can be grown from seed; takes 3–5 years to flower.
Erigeron (erigeron, or fleabane) Daisylike flowers with narrow petals are borne in clusters from early to late summer.	9 in.–2 ft.	1–1½ ft.	■	●	*E. aurantiacus*, semi-double, orange, 9 in. *E. speciosus*, single, blue, 1½–2 ft. *E. s.* 'Azure Fairy', semi-double, lavender, 2½ ft. *E. s.* 'Foerster's Liebling', semi-double, pink, 1½ ft. *E. s.* 'Pink Jewel', single, baby-pink, 2 ft. *E. s.* 'Prosperity', semi-double, mauve, 1½ ft.	Select location in full sun where soil is well drained and of average fertility; plants tolerate dry soil. Remove faded blooms to encourage more flowering. Plants spread slowly.	Divide plants in spring; sow seeds in spring.
Eryngium (eryngium, or sea holly) Steel-gray to blue thistlelike flowers blooming in mid to late summer. Foliage is also thistlelike and prickly.	1½–3 ft.	1–2 ft.	■	●	*E. alpinum* (blue-top sea holly), silvery blue, 1½ ft. *E. amethystinum* (amethyst sea holly), grayish blue, 2 ft. *E. bourgatii* (Mediterranean sea holly), steel-blue, 1½ ft. *E. giganteum* (Miss Willmott's ghost), silvery, 3 ft. *E. planum* (flat sea holly), blue, 3 ft. *E. yuccifolium* (rattlesnake master), pale blue, 4 ft.	Since plant is very long-lived and resents disturbance, locate in soil that is not soggy in winter. Generally trouble-free. Flowers retain their color when dried if picked when fully open.	Divide fleshy roots or take root cuttings in spring; sow seeds in spring.
Euphorbia (euphorbia, or spurge) Relatively inconspicuous flowers are surrounded by showy petallike white, orange, or yellow bracts in late spring or midsummer.	1–2½ ft.	1½–2 ft.	■	●	*E. amygdaloides robbiae* (wood spurge), yellow, 2½ ft. *E. characias* (frog spawn), yellow, 4 ft. *E. corollata* (flowering spurge), white, midsummer, 2 ft. *E. griffithii* 'Fireglow', orange-red, 2½ ft. *E. myrsinites* (myrtle spurge), greenish yellow, 1 ft. *E. polychroma*, chartreuse-yellow, 1½ ft.	Long-lived plants that resent disturbance. Plants prefer average soil. All euphorbias have milky sap that can cause skin irritation. If used as cut flowers, sear bottom of stems in flame before putting in water.	Divide plants or take basal cuttings in spring.
Filipendula (filipendula, or meadowsweet) Feathery terminal clusters of small flowers bloom in early or mid summer. Some have finely divided fernlike foliage; others are coarser. Roots of *F. vulgaris* are tuberous.	1½–4 ft.	1–1½ ft.	□	●	*F. palmata* 'Nana', deep rose pink, 2 ft. *F. purpurea* (Japanese meadowsweet), carmine, 4 ft. *F. rubra* (queen of the prairie), pink, early, 4–6 ft. *F. ulmaria* (queen of the meadow), creamy white, 2–3 ft. *F. vulgaris* (dropwort), white, tinged red, 2 ft. *F. v.* 'Multiplex', double white, midsummer, 2 ft.	Tall types especially well suited for back of border, along stream, or in woodland planting. *F. vulgaris* and its double form prefer moist soil; others tolerate more dryness. All are long-lived plants that seldom require division.	Divide plants in spring; sow seeds in spring

■ well drained to sandy ■ moist ■ wet ■ acidic ■ alkaline □ regular soil ● full sun ◑ partial shade ● shade

Gaillardia 'Dazzler'

Gaura lindheimeri

Geum chiloense 'Mrs. Bradshaw'

The lively colored blossoms of the blanketflower (*Gaillardia*) last well, but the plants are short-lived. Gaura (*Gaura*) needs a warm climate to be a perennial. Geum, or avens (*Geum*), blooms from late spring to midsummer.

Gaillardia 'Dazzler' (gaillardia, or blanketflower)

Galium odoratum (sweet woodruff)

Gaura lindheimeri (gaura)

Geranium macrorrhizum (geranium, or cranesbill)

Gerbera jamesonii (gerbera, or Transvaal daisy)

Geum (geum, or avens)

BOTANICAL AND COMMON NAMES	HEIGHT	SPREAD	SOIL	LIGHT	SPECIES AND VARIETIES	SPECIAL REQUIREMENTS AND REMARKS	PROPAGATION (See p. 39)
Gaillardia (gaillardia, or blanketflower) Large, single, daisylike flowers with varied contrasting markings on petal tips or near center bloom from mid summer to early fall or hard frost. For annual gaillardias, see p. 203.	6 in.–3 ft.	6 in.–1½ ft.	■	●	*G. aristata*, yellow, often with purple or red, 2 ft. *G.* 'Baby Cole', red with yellow petal tips, 6 in. *G.* 'Burgundy', wine-red, 2½ ft. *G.* 'Dazzler', yellow with maroon center, 2–3 ft. *G.* 'Goblin', red with yellow petal tips, 1 ft. *G.* 'Portola', combinations of red and yellow, 2½ ft.	Require very well-drained soil if they are to survive cold winters. Often need staking, as plants tend to sprawl. Remove faded blooms for further flowering. Good cut flower.	Divide plants or sow seeds in spring; make root cuttings in summer.
Galium (bedstraw) Small white scented flowers in clusters in late spring to summer. Foliage is hay-scented and was used to stuff mattresses.	1½ ft.	3 ft.	□	◐	*G. odoratum* (sweet woodruff), whorls of 6–9 bright green leaves, 1½ ft.	Does best in moist, humus-rich soil. A good plant for bees. Makes a good ground cover.	Seed in early spring or as soon as ripe. Division of rhizomes in fall or spring.
Gaura (gaura) Slender, wiry stems have pink buds that open to white, 1-in. starry flowers that fade to pink. Flowers for most of the summer.	5 ft.	3 ft.	□ ■	● ◐	*G. lindheimeri* (white gaura), flowers open at dawn, 5 ft. *G. l.* 'Whirling Butterflies', red sepals, free-flowering, 5 ft.	May be a self-sowing annual in cold climates, but is not invasive.	Seed, sown in spring, division in spring or soft-wood cuttings.
Geranium (geranium, or cranesbill) These dainty, mostly single-flowered plants bloom from early to late summer. Not to be confused with the common geranium (*Pelargonium*), p. 209.	1–3 ft.	1–2 ft.	□	● ◐	Only taller types listed here. For low forms, see p. 163. *G.* 'Johnson's Blue', light blue, 1½ ft. *G. macrorrhizum* 'Ingwersen's Variety', soft pink, 1½ ft. *G. maculatum*, magenta pink, 2–2½ ft. *G. oxonianum* 'Claridge Druce', pink, veined red, 1½–2½ ft. *G. phaeum* 'Samobor', maroon, leaves marked with brown, 3 ft. *G. pratense*, blue with red veins, 3 ft.	Overly rich soil may produce rampant growth. Plants seldom need division unless flowering is poor. Not good cut flower.	Divide plants in spring; or sow seeds of available kinds.
Gerbera (gerbera, or Transvaal daisy) Large daisylike flowers with very long, graceful petals; single and double forms. Blooms all summer. Excellent cut flower.	1–1½ ft.	1–1½ ft.	■	●	*G. jamesonii*, white through cream, yellow, orange, pink, salmon, rose to red, 1–1½ ft.	Locate in full sun. Add compost to well-drained soil. Plants respond well to periodic fertilizing during summer. In colder regions lift in fall; keep in sunny window for winter bloom.	Sow seeds in early spring; divide plants in spring.
Geum (geum, or avens) Mostly double flowers up to 3 in. across. Attractive basal leaves are evergreen in warm areas. Blooms late spring to midsummer. Good cut flower. Generally short-lived.	1–2 ft.	1–1½ ft.	■	● ◐	Hybrids derived mostly from *G. chiloense*. *G.* 'Lady Stratheden', semi-double, yellow, 2 ft. *G.* 'Mrs. Bradshaw', semi-double, scarlet, 2 ft. *G.* 'Princess Juliana', semi-double, bronzy orange, 2 ft. *G.* 'Starker's Magnificent', double, apricot-orange, 1 ft.	Soil should be well drained but moisture retentive. May need support. Cut flower stems back after flowering.	Divide plants in spring; sow seeds in spring. Fresh seeds germinate best.

To reach full flower, baby's breath (*Gypsophila*), and helenium, or sneezeweed (*Helenium*), all require full sun and moist, well-drained soil.

Gypsophila repens 'Rosy Veil'

Helenium 'Golden Youth'

Gypsophila paniculata (baby's breath)

Helenium 'Moerheim Beauty' (helenium, or sneezeweed)

Helianthus decapetalus (sunflower)

Heliopsis helianthoides scabra (ox-eye, or golden sunflower)

Helleborus niger (Christmas rose)

BOTANICAL AND COMMON NAMES	HEIGHT	SPREAD	SOIL	LIGHT	SPECIES AND VARIETIES	SPECIAL REQUIREMENTS AND REMARKS	PROPAGATION (See p. 39)
Gypsophila (baby's breath) Prized for clusters of many small flowers in midsummer that give airy effect. Good cut flower, fresh or dried. Can be invasive in the Midwest and West.	1–4 ft.	2–3 ft.	■ ■	●	*G. paniculata*, single, white, 3–3½ ft. *G. p.* 'Bristol Fairy', double, white, 4 ft. *G. p.* 'Perfecta', largest flowers, double, white, 3–4 ft. *G. p.* 'Pink Fairy', double, pink, 1½ ft. *G. p.* 'Viette's Dwarf', light pink, 16 in. *G. repens* 'Rosy Veil', double, soft pink to white, 1½ ft.	Mulch in cold climates. Some varieties of *G. paniculata* grafted; set union 1 in. below soil level.	Sow seeds of available kinds in spring. Or take basal cuttings in spring.
Helenium (helenium, or sneezeweed) Prized for its mostly late summer to fall bloom of long-lasting daisylike single flowers and neat foliage. A good cut flower.	1½–4 ft.	1–2 ft.	□	●	Most varieties are hybrids of *H. autumnale.* *H.* 'Butterpat', yellow, 3–4 ft. *H. hoopesii*, orange, blooms earlier than others, 2 ft. *H.* 'Moerheim Beauty', deep bronze-red, 2½ ft. *H.* 'Rotgold' (Red and Gold), range of color combinations from seed, 3–4 ft.	Add compost to soil before planting. Plants respond to ample moisture with improved growth. Most need no support. Rabbit proof.	Divide plants in spring. Seeds can be sown in spring.
Helianthus (sunflower) Showy but somewhat coarse plants. Multitude of single or double flowers resembling dahlias bloom in late summer or early fall.	4 ft.	2–3 ft.	□	●	*H.* 'Capenoch Star', quilled petals, yellow, 5 ft. Hybrids mostly derived from *H. decapetalus.* *H.* 'Flore Pleno', large, double, yellow, 4 ft. *H.* 'Loddon Gold', double, yellow, 4 ft.	Plants multiply rapidly and will need frequent division. Generally trouble-free. For annual sunflowers, see p. 203.	Divide plants in spring. Seeds not widely available but can be sown in spring.
Heliopsis (ox-eye, or golden sunflower) Valued for late-summer bloom. Double or semi-double flowers 3–4 in. across with long stems are excellent for cutting.	2–5 ft.	1½–2 ft.	□	●	*H. helianthoides*, single to double, deep yellow, 3–6 ft. *H. h.* Loraine Sunshine™, yellow, variegated leaves, 3 ft. *H. h.* 'Prairie Sunset', golden orange, 5 ft. Following hybrids derived mostly from *H. h. scabra*: *H. h.* 'Hohlspiegel', semi-double, yellow, serrated tips, 3 ft. *H. h. s.* 'Ballerina', dark yellow, semi-double, 4 ft. *H. h. s.* 'Sommersonne', single to semi-double, bright yellow, 3 ft.	Plants will perform better when watered during dry spells, but excessive rain may cause marred flowers and broken stems. Staking not generally required; plants are trouble-free.	Divide plants in spring; sow seeds of available kinds in spring.
Helleborus (Christmas rose, and lenten rose) Lustrous evergreen leaves. Stunning, waxy, cup-shaped flowers bloom in late winter or early spring. Leaves and roots of *H. niger* poisonous if eaten. Increasingly popular with many new named hybrids.	1–1½ ft.	1½–2 ft.	□	●	*H. foetidus* (bear's foot), green tipped purple, 2 ft. *H. hybridus*, single or double flowers, white, cream, pink, or red, 1½–2 ft. *H. niger* (Christmas rose), white, early winter, 1 ft. *H. n.* 'Potter's Wheel', white, larger flowers than above, 1 ft. *H. orientalis* (lenten rose), purple shades, midspring, 1½ ft. *H. o.* 'Millet Hybrids', white, pink, red, chocolate, some speckled and striped, 1½ ft.	Grow where readily seen when in bloom and where there is winter sun, summer shade. Provide nearly neutral soil (pH 6.5–7). Cover crown with 1 in. of soil. Use plastic- or glass-covered frame, open at side, to protect flowers from severe weather.	Sow fresh seeds in early summer. Late-sown seeds need freezing to break dormancy. Divide plants in late summer.

■ well drained to sandy ■ moist ■ wet ■ acidic ■ alkaline □ regular soil ● full sun ◐ partial shade ● shade

Heuchera 'Pewter Moon'

Heucherella alba 'Bridget Bloom'

Inula magnifica

An ideal border plant, *Heuchera* 'Pewter Moon' has pink flowers and dark-purple leaves. *Heucherella alba* 'Bridget Bloom' has heart-shaped leaves and pink bell-shaped flowers. Elecampane (*Inula*) produces sunflowerlike flowerheads from July to September.

Heuchera 'Palace Purple' (coralbells)

Heucherella tiarelloides (heucherella)

Hibiscus 'Disco Belle' (hibiscus, or rose mallow)

Incarvillea delavayi (incarvillea)

Inula royleana (inula, or elecampane)

BOTANICAL AND COMMON NAMES	HEIGHT	SPREAD	SOIL	LIGHT	SPECIES AND VARIETIES	SPECIAL REQUIREMENTS AND REMARKS	PROPAGATION (See p. 39)
Heuchera (coralbells) Slender stems carry small bell-shaped flowers in early summer and often again later. Dainty cut flower. Attractive evergreen leaves. Many new varieties grown for attractive mottled or colored foliage.	1–2 ft.	1–1½ ft.	■	◐	Hybrids of *H. sanguinea*, grown for their flowers: *H.* 'Bressingham Hybrids', mixed in white, pink, red, 2 ft. *H.* 'Chatterbox', deep rose-pink, 1½ ft. *H.* 'Pluie de Feu', cherry-red, 1½ ft. Hybrids grown for their colored foliage: *H.* 'Amber Wave', ruffled leaves, yellow above, bronze beneath, 12 in. *H.* 'Palace Purple', bronzy-red leaves, 1½ ft. *H.* 'Pewter Moon', silvery pink with green veins, 1½ ft.	Plant in spring in soil with ample humus. Set crowns 1 in. below soil level. Remove faded flower stems to encourage later bloom. In cold regions, light mulch helps keep plants from heaving.	Divide in spring; root leaf cutting with small piece of leaf stalk attached in summer; sow seeds in spring.
Heucherella (heucherella) Resembling related coralbells, with panicles of small bell-shaped flowers above tufts of leaves in summer. They are hybrids of *Heuchera* and *Tiarella*.	1–1½ ft.	9–12 in.	■	◐	*H. alba* 'Bridget Bloom', white, 1½–1¾ ft. *H.* 'Pink Frost', pink, spring to fall, 2 ft. *H. tiarelloides*, carmine, 1–1½ ft.	Grow plants in soil with ample compost. Cut flower stems almost to ground level after flowering. Leaves often mottled brown when young; do not mistake mottling for disease. Plants do not set seeds.	Divide plants in spring.
Hibiscus (hibiscus, or rose mallow) A spectacular tall plant with enormous flowers up to 10 in. across with five or more petals. Bloom period is mid to late summer.	4–6 ft.	2–4 ft.	■	●	Hybrids are mostly derived from *H. moscheutos*: *H.* 'Disco Belle', mixed colors, from seed, 1½–2 ft. *H.* 'Lady Baltimore', pink with red eye, 4 ft. *H.* 'Lord Baltimore', bright red, 4 ft. *H.* 'Mallow Marvels', mixed colors, seed-grown, 5 ft. *H.* 'Southern Belle', mixed colors, seed-grown, 4–5 ft.	Incorporate compost with soil; plants need plenty of moisture. When seeds are sown indoors in early spring, plants flower same season. Easily grown but difficult to transplant. In cold areas mulch roots in fall.	Divide plants in spring; sow seeds in spring.
Incarvillea (incarvillea) Two-lipped tubular flowers bloom in late spring or early summer in clusters held well above deeply cut leaves.	1½–2 ft.	1 ft.	■	●	*I. delavayi*, rose-red with yellow throat, 1½–2 ft. *I. d.* 'Bee's Pink', pale pink, 1–1½ ft. *I. mairei grandiflora*, crimson, 1½ ft.	Water standing in soil over winter can be fatal. In cold climates mulch in late fall, or lift and store roots in soil in cool place.	Divide fleshy roots in fall (often difficult). Sow seeds in spring; takes 2–3 yr. to bloom.
Inula (inula, or elecampane) Flowers resemble 4- or 5-in. sunflower but with narrower and more graceful petals. Coarse leaves.	1½–6 ft.	1–3 ft.	■	●	*I. ensifolia*, yellow, 1½–2 ft. *I. helenium*, yellow, leaves hairy beneath, 3–6 ft. *I. magnifica*, yellow, narrow petals, 6 ft. *I. orientalis*, yellow, 2–3 ft. *I. royleana*, yellow, 10 in.; leaves 2 ft.	Set out plants in spring in moisture-retentive soil (clay acceptable). Divide and replant about every 3 yr. to contain spreading habit. Remove faded flowers.	Divide plants in spring; or sow seeds (when available) in spring. Not widely available.

Iris See p. 69.

Sweet pea (*Lathyrus*) thrives in sunny locations with well-drained soil.

Lathyrus latifolius 'Albus'

Kirengeshoma palmata (kirengeshoma)

Kniphofia (red-hot poker)

Lamium galeobdolon 'Herman's Pride' (lamium, or dead nettle)

Lathyrus vernus (pea)

Lavandula angustifolia (lavender)

Lavatera 'Burgundy Wine' (mallow)

Leucanthemum (shasta daisy)

BOTANICAL AND COMMON NAMES	HEIGHT	SPREAD	SOIL	LIGHT	SPECIES AND VARIETIES	SPECIAL REQUIREMENTS AND REMARKS	PROPAGATION (See p. 39)
Kirengeshoma (kirengeshoma) Clump-forming plant with dark stems and tubular yellow flowers in late summer. Plant is upright with arching stems, a good woodland plant.	3–4 ft.	2–3 ft.	■	◑	*K. palmata*, flowers are in open sprays on shoot tips, 3–4 ft.	Soil should be rich in humus for best growth, may need staking as it is a small plant with only a few stems.	Sow seeds as soon as ripe, or divide in spring.
Kniphofia (red-hot poker) Dense spikes of closely set drooping flowers bloom in mid to late summer. Grasslike foliage. Long-lasting flowers attract hummingbirds.	2–4 ft.	2–3 ft.	■	●	*K.* 'Alcazar', salmon pink, 3½ ft. *K.* 'Pfitzeri', orange-red, 3 ft. *K. uvaria* 'Primrose Beauty', primrose-yellow, 2–3 ft.	Rich soil and excellent drainage are essential. Where not hardy, mulch in fall or lift and store in cool place.	Sow seeds in spring. Divide plants in spring.
Lamium (lamium, or dead nettle) Spikes of small hooded flowers bloom in spring for many weeks. Leaves often variegated. Best in wildflower garden or as ground cover.	9 in.–2 ft.	3 ft.	□	◑ ○	*L. galeobdolon* (yellow archangel), yellow, 1–1½ ft. *L. g.* 'Herman's Pride', silver-streaked leaves, 1 ft. *L. maculatum*, purple, 9 in.–1 ft. *L. m.* 'Beacon Silver', pink, silvery leaves, 9 in. *L. m.* 'White Nancy', white, 6 in.	*L. galeobdolon* grows in alkaline or slightly acid soil. Only occasionally planted in borders because of tendency to spread rapidly.	Divide plants in spring; or take cuttings in summer.
Lathyrus (pea) Climbing or trailing plants with clusters of long-lasting flowers. Useful to cover fences or as ground cover. Good cut flower. For annual sweet pea, see p. 205.	6–9 ft.	2 ft.	□	●	*L. latifolius* 'White Pearl', white, 6–9 ft. *L. l.* 'Pink Pearl', rose, 6–9 ft. *L. vernus*, clump-forming, pink, spring, 1½ ft.	Provide some means of support unless plants are grown on slopes or over rocks. Keep faded flowers picked to encourage further flowering. Easily grown.	Sow seeds in spring. Soak seeds overnight before sowing to hasten germination.
Lavandula (lavender) Flowers open in early summer. Scented flowers are dried and used in sachets.	1–4 ft.	1–1½ ft.	■ ■	●	*L. angustifolia*, or *L. spica* (English lavender), gray-blue, 3–4 ft. *L. a.* 'Hidcote', deep violet-blue, 1½ ft. *L. a.* 'Munstead Dwarf', deep lavender, 1 ft. *L. dentata* (French lavender), lavender-purple, 3 ft. *L. stoechas* (Spanish lavender), dark purple, 1½–3 ft.	Technically a subshrub but grown in perennial gardens, particularly dwarfed forms. Tall kinds often clipped to make low hedge.	Take cuttings in summer of half-ripened shoots with heel. Or sow seeds.
Lavatera (mallow) Showy plants with hibiscuslike flowers, often with scalloped petals, in mid to late summer. Usually needs support. Named hybrids give best display.	3–6 ft.	6 ft.	■	●	*L.* 'Barnsley', pale pink with notched petals, 6 ft. *L.* 'Bredon Springs', magenta with darker veins, 6 ft. *L.* 'Burgundy Wine', purple-red, 6 ft. *L.* 'Shorty', white to pale pink, 3 ft.	Not reliably hardy in colder regions, so mulch in fall.	Softwood cuttings in spring, or semi-ripe later on.
Leucanthemum (shasta daisy) Single or double flowers grow on long stems, bloom in early summer and intermittently thereafter, especially when picked. Neat foliage. Suitable for cutting.	1–3 ft.	1–2½ ft.	■	●	*L. superbum* 'Aglaya', double, white, fringed petals, 2 ft. *L. s.* 'Alaska', single, white with yellow center, 2 ft. *L. s.* 'Esther Read', double, white, 1½ ft. *L. s.* 'Little Miss Muffet', semi-double, white, 14 in. *L. s.* 'Marconi', very large double, white, 3 ft. *L. s.* 'T. E. Killin', double, white, crested center, 2 ft.	Doubles may do better in partial shade. Soggy winter soil can kill plant. Inspect frequently for aphids and other bugs in spring. Not reliably hardy in cold regions.	Divide plants or make basal cuttings in spring; or sow seeds in spring.

■ well drained to sandy ■ moist ■ wet ■ acidic ■ alkaline □ regular soil ● full sun ◑ partial shade ○ shade

Liatris spicata

Linum narbonense 'Heavenly Blue'

Gayfeather (*Liatris*) is native to eastern and central North America. Flax (*Linum*) blooms freely in warm, dry soil from early summer until September.

Liatris scariosa 'White Spire' (liatris, or gayfeather)

Ligularia (ligularia, or senecio)

Limonium (sea lavender, or hardy statice)

Linum flavum (linum, or flax)

Liriope muscari (lilyturf, or liriope)

Lobelia cardinalis (lobelia)

BOTANICAL AND COMMON NAMES	HEIGHT	SPREAD	SOIL	LIGHT	SPECIES AND VARIETIES	SPECIAL REQUIREMENTS AND REMARKS	PROPAGATION (See p. 39)
Liatris (liatris, or gayfeather) Tufted plants with tall spikes of fluffy flowers that bloom above grasslike foliage in late summer. In most kinds, flowers open from top of spike downward.	2–5 ft.	1½ ft.	■	●◑	*L. pycnostachya* (Kansas gayfeather), pinkish lavender, 5 ft. *L. scariosa* (tall gayfeather), purple, 2–3 ft. *L. s.* 'September Glory', purple, opens all at once, 5 ft. *L. s.* 'White Spire', white, opens all at once, 5 ft. *L. spicata* (spike gayfeather), purple, 3 ft. *L. s.* 'Kobold', dark purple, compact, 1½–2 ft.	Soggy winter soils prove fatal. Tall kinds may require staking. Division may be needed after 4–5 yr. Very adaptable plants. Good cut flower; dries well. Favorite of bees.	Divide tuberous-rooted plants in spring; sow seeds in spring.
Ligularia (ligularia, or senecio) Bold plant with large roundish leaves. Towering spikes of small flowers bloom in midsummer. Good ground cover or large container plant.	2½–6 ft.	4 ft.	■	◑	*L. clivorum* 'Desdemona', orange-yellow, leaves green with purple tinge, 4–5 ft. *L. przewalskii*, dark stems, yellow, 6 ft. *L. stenocephata* 'The Rocket', slender, yellow, 6 ft. *L. wilsoniana*, golden-yellow, dense spikes, 5–6 ft.	Incorporate generous amounts of compost prior to planting, and water during dry spells.	Divide plants in spring.
Limonium (sea lavender, or hardy statice) Valued for its fine sprays of small flowers in mid to late summer.	1½–2 ft.	2–3 ft.	■	●	*L. latifolium*, bright lavender, 1½–2 ft. *L. l.* 'Violetta', deep violet-blue, 1½ ft.	Excellent seaside plant. Best left undisturbed for years.	Sow seeds in spring. Divide in spring.
Linum (linum, or flax) Dainty 5-petaled flowers are borne in profusion intermittently from early to late summer on fine stems. Blue-green leaves are needlelike except broad in *L. flavum*.	1–2 ft.	1–2 ft.	■	●	*L. flavum* (golden flax), yellow, 1½ ft. *L. narbonense*, azure blue with white centers, 1½–2 ft. *L. n.* 'Heavenly Blue', deep blue, 1–1½ ft. *L. perenne*, pale blue, 2 ft. *L. p. album*, white, 2 ft. *L. p.* 'Blau Saphir', sky-blue, 1 ft.	Winter sogginess can prove fatal. Unobtrusive seedpods, but removal of faded flowers will help to keep plants blooming. Dainty plants that look best at the front or edge of a bed. Not good for cutting, as flowers last only a day.	Sow seeds in spring. Take basal cuttings in spring; stem cuttings in summer. Plants difficult to divide.
Liriope (lilyturf, or liriope) Graceful, recurving, grasslike leaves with leathery texture. Spikes of flowers in midsummer to fall that are good for cutting. Blue-black berries follow flowers.	1–1½ ft.	1–2 ft.	■	◑	*L. muscari*, dark violet, 1½ ft. *L. m.* 'Big Blue', violet-blue, 9 in. *L. m.* 'Majestic', dark violet, cockscomblike, 20 in. *L. m.* 'Variegata', lilac, yellow-edged leaves, 1 ft. *L. spicata*, pale violet to white, 9 in. *L. s.* 'Silver Dragon', leaves striped white, 9 in.	Plant in sun in coastal areas, *L. spicata* (hardiest form), Zone 6; others, Zone 7. Withstands short periods of drought. In cold areas leaves may brown in late winter and should be cut back in spring. Makes good edging or accent plant as well as ground cover.	Divide tufted or rhizomatous plants in early spring before new growth starts. *L. spicata* spreads by underground stems
Lobelia (lobelia) Spikes of small tubular 2-lipped flowers bloom over long period from midsummer to early fall. Especially good woodland or streamside plant.	2–4 ft.	1–1½ ft.	■	◑●	*L. cardinalis* (cardinal flower), scarlet red, 3–4 ft. *L. c. alba*, white, rare, propagated from cuttings, 3–4 ft. *L.* 'Queen Victoria', purplish leaves, scarlet, 3 ft. *L. siphilitica* (great blue lobelia), deep blue, 2–3 ft. *L. speciosa*, named hybrids, pink to dark purple, 2–4 ft.	Grow in light to medium shade. Mulch in summer to retain moisture. Where snow cover cannot be counted on all winter, mulch after soil has frozen. May be short-lived but often self-sows. Makes long-lasting cut flower.	Divide plants immediately after flowering or in early spring; sow seeds in spring.

Spikes of lupine (*Lupinus*) blooms in early to mid summer. The moisture-loving yellow loosestrife (*Lysimachia*) grows well beside water. The plume poppy (*Macleaya cordata*), which grows up to 8 ft. high and 4 ft. wide, needs plenty of room.

Lupinus 'Kayleigh Ann Savage'

Lysimachia punctata

Macleaya cordata

Lupinus arboreus
(lupine)

Lychnis chalcedonica
(lychnis, or campion)

Lysimachia punctata
(lysimachia, or loosestrife)

Macleaya cordata
(plume poppy)

Mertensia virginica
(mertensia, or Virginia bluebell)

BOTANICAL AND COMMON NAMES	HEIGHT	SPREAD	SOIL	LIGHT	SPECIES AND VARIETIES	SPECIAL REQUIREMENTS AND REMARKS	PROPAGATION (See p. 39)
Lupinus (lupine) Towering spikes of pealike flowers bloom in mid to late spring above deeply divided leaves. Dwarf types are recent introductions.	1½–3 ft.	6 in.–1½ ft.	■	●	Almost all popular garden lupines have been derived from crosses of *L. polyphyllus* with *L. arboreus*, and recrosses between hybrids. Known as 'Russell Hybrids', they grow to 3 ft. and come in shades of red, pink, blue, yellow, salmon, and purple; often bicolor. Dwarfs that grow 1½ ft. tall include 'Little Lulu' and 'Minarette'.	Provide soil that contains plenty of compost. Grows best in cool regions. Soak seeds overnight in water to hasten germination.	Sow seeds in spring; treat as for peas with nitrifying powder. Take basal cuttings in spring.
Lychnis (lychnis, or campion) As a group these have widely divergent flower forms, ranging in shape from upright spikes to rounded heads or loose clusters. Blooms mid to late summer, depending on kind.	1½–3 ft.	6 in.–1 ft.	■	●	*L. chalcedonica* (Maltese cross), true red, 2½–3 ft. *L. c. alba*, white, less showy than above, 2½–3 ft. *L. coronaria* (rose campion, mullein pink), red-purple, 2 ft. *L. haageana* (hybrid of *L. fulgens* and *L. sieboldii*), orange-red, 2 ft. *L. viscaria* (German catchfly), reddish purple, 1–1½ ft. *L. v.* 'Splendens Pleno', double, rose-pink, 1–1½ ft.	Some varieties tend to be short-lived but can be easily replenished from seeds.	Sow seeds in spring. Divide plants in spring.
Lysimachia (lysimachia, or loosestrife) Showy plants. The two listed are quite different in flower form and bloom at different times. Reasonably good cut flower.	2½–3 ft.	1 ft.	■	● ◐	*L. clethroides* (gooseneck loosestrife), white flower spikes curved like a goose's neck in late summer, 3 ft. *L. punctata*, small yellow flowers arranged in tiers around stem bloom in early summer, 2½–3 ft.	Add compost, and water during dry spells. May need some support. Plants spread rapidly and can become invasive; should be planted inside a barrier.	Divide plants in spring. Roots are rhizomatous.
Macleaya (plume poppy) Statuesque plants suitable for large gardens. Tall plumes of tiny flowers appear in midsummer or early fall. Handsome, large, deeply lobed leaves.	5–8 ft.	3–4 ft.	■	●	*M. cordata*, creamy white, mid to late summer, 6–8 ft.	Provide a humus-rich soil. Invasive; control by cutting outside growth yearly. Best grown by itself so that sculptured gray-green leaves can be seen. Flowers and seedpods dry well.	Sow seeds in spring. Divide plants in spring. Root suckers in summer.
Mertensia (mertensia, or Virginia bluebell) Unusual late-spring flowering plant with pink buds and nodding sapphire-blue bell-shaped flowers above smooth light green leaves.	1½ ft.	1–1½ ft.	■	◐	*M. virginica*, blue, 1½ ft.	Grow in soil well fortified with compost. Foliage dies down soon after flowering; mark area with a stake so that plants will not be disturbed later.	Sow seeds as soon as ripe in early summer. Divide plants in early fall.

■ well drained to sandy ■ moist ■ wet ■ acidic ■ alkaline □ regular soil ● full sun ◐ partial shade ● shade

The aromatic leaves of bergamot (*Monarda*) have a distinctive scent and can be used for herbal tea.

Monarda didyma

Monarda didyma
(bergamot, or bee balm)

Musa basjoo
(banana)

Nepeta 'Six Hills Giant'
(nepeta, or catmint)

Oenothera speciosa
(evening primrose, or sundrops)

Ophiopogon planiscarpus
(mondo grass)

BOTANICAL AND COMMON NAMES	HEIGHT	SPREAD	SOIL	LIGHT	SPECIES AND VARIETIES	SPECIAL REQUIREMENTS AND REMARKS	PROPAGATION (See p. 39)
Monarda (bergamot, or bee balm) Tubular flowers in crowded clusters bloom in mid to late summer. Square stems, scented foliage. Good cut flower.	2–3 ft.	2 ft.	■	◐	*M. didyma* (Oswego tea). *M. d.* 'Blue Stocking', violet-purple, 3 ft. *M. d.* 'Cambridge Scarlet', dark scarlet, 3 ft. *M. d.* 'Croftway Pink', rose pink, 3 ft. *M. d.* 'Gardenview Scarlet', bright scarlet, large heads, very mildew resistant, 2–3 ft. *M. d.* 'Marshall's Delight', mid-pink, mildew resistant, 2½–3 ft. *M. d.* 'Snow White', pure white, 3 ft. *M. fistulosa* (wild bergamot), lavender, white, 3 ft., the hardiest species.	Wild bergamot tolerates drier soil than hybrids, but all benefit from plenty of moisture during summer. Divide every 3 yr. for maximum bloom.	Sow seeds in spring. Divide plants in spring.
Musa (banana) Grown for their very large leaves these provide a spectacular focal point. Pendulous spikes of small yellow flowers give rise to the well known fruit. Shoots die after flowering but plant sends up new suckers from the base.	15–20 ft.	8–10 ft.	■	◐	*M. basjoo*, very large leaves, cream flowers and inedible fruits, 15 ft. There are many other named varieties.	Protect from strong winds which shred the leaves. Worth trying in protected sites in Zone 7 or even lower, the top will be killed but roots may survive.	Dig up suckers as they emerge in spring and replant. Seeds needs soaking in warm water for 24 hours before sowing.
Nepeta (nepeta, or catmint) Somewhat sprawling plants with small gray-green leaves; 5-in. spikes of small lavender flowers bloom in early summer, often into fall.	9 in.–3 ft.	1½ ft.	■	●	*N. cataria* (catnip), favorite of cats, is best grown in herb garden. *N. faassenii*, a hybrid, pale lavender, 1½ ft. *N. f.* 'Dropmore', large flowers, 1½–2 ft. *N.* 'Six Hills Giant', lavender-blue, 3 ft.	Grow in sandy soil. This is excellent seaside plant. Shear plants back after first bloom to encourage further flowering. Seldom needs support if grown in a not-too-rich soil.	Divide plants in spring. Take stem cuttings in summer. Sow seeds of *N. cataria*; *N. faassenii* sets no seeds.
Oenothera (evening primrose, or sundrops) Showy single flowers 1½ in. or more across appear in early to mid summer over period of several weeks. Foliage is relatively inconspicuous.	8 in.–2 ft.	1–1½ ft.	■	●	*O. fruticosa* 'Fireworks', yellow with red buds, 1½ ft. *O. f.* 'Highlight', golden yellow, 1½ ft. *O. f.* 'Yellow River', canary-yellow, 1–1½ ft. *O. f.* 'Youngii' (common sundrop), yellow, 2 ft. *O. macrocarpa* (Ozark sundrop), yellow, 8 in.–1 ft. *O. speciosa* 'Rosea', pale pink, 1 ft.	*O. macrocarpa* is late to appear in spring; mark position so that it will not be disturbed. All tend to spread, and *O. macrocarpa* may be invasive. Water freely during dry spells.	Divide plants in early spring.
Ophiopogon (mondo grass) Clump-forming plants with grasslike foliage and sprays of white or lilac flowers followed by dark fruits. Varieties with variegated or colored foliage are particularly striking.	12 in.	8 in.	□ ■	◐	*O. japonicus*, very narrow foliage, spreads slowly, white flowers in late summer, 8–12 in. *O. j.* 'Nanus', similar but smaller, with darker green foliage, 4–5 in. *O. planiscapus* 'Nigrescens', almost black leaves, dark purple flowers and black berries, 6–8 in.	Good edging plants for the front of a bed or as ground cover. Very adaptable to light and soil conditions.	Division in spring. Species can be grown from seed but forms with colored foliage will not come true this way.

This poppy, whose single red flower has an eye-catching black center, thrives in full sun or part shade.

Papaver orientale 'Allegro'

Papaver orientale
(Oriental poppy)

Penstemon
(penstemon, or beardtongue)

Perovskia atriplicifolia
(Russian sage)

Persicaria
(bistort or knotweed)

Phlomis
(Jerusalem sage)

Phlox paniculata
(phlox)

BOTANICAL AND COMMON NAMES	HEIGHT	SPREAD	SOIL	LIGHT	SPECIES AND VARIETIES	SPECIAL REQUIREMENTS AND REMARKS	PROPAGATION (See p. 39)
Papaver (Oriental poppy) Impressive, mostly single flowers, many with black centers, bloom for short period in early summer. Basal foliage, fleshy roots.	2–4 ft.	1½ ft.	■	●	*P. orientale* hybrids—only a few of the dozens available listed here. *P. o.* 'Allegro', orange-scarlet, black markings, 3 ft. *P. o.* 'Beauty of Livermore', crimson, 3–4 ft. *P. o.* 'Helen Elizabeth', salmon-pink, 3–4 ft. *P. o.* 'Maiden's Blush', white edged pink, 2–2½ ft. *P. o.* 'Pinnacle', white and scarlet, 2½ ft.	Plants may need staking. For cut flower, sear basal end of stem in flame; put in water immediately. Foliage dies down soon after flowering, reappears in late summer. New plants usually set out in late summer as roots without leaves.	Divide in early spring. Sow seeds in spring. Take root cuttings in summer.
Penstemon (penstemon, or beardtongue) Semi-evergreen, often short-lived plants. Spikes of foxglove-shaped flowers in mid to late summer. Excellent cut flower.	1–3 ft.	1–2 ft.	■	●	*P. barbatus*, pink to red, 1½ ft. *P. b.* 'Elfin Pink', good pink, 1 ft. *P. digitalis* 'Husker Red', reddish foliage, white, 2½ ft. *P.* 'Garnet', wine-red, prolific, 2½ ft. *P. pinifolius*, scarlet, narrow leaves, 1½ ft. *P.* 'Prairie Fire', orange-red, 1½ ft. *P. strictus*, dark blue to violet, 2½ ft.	Some varieties are not hardy; so check locally. Remove faded flower stems, and plants may bloom again. An interesting plant, and many fine hybrids are being developed and made available.	Sow seeds in spring. Divide in spring. Take softwood stem cuttings in summer.
Perovskia (Russian sage) From mid to late summer violet-blue flowers are borne above small, silvery gray leaves with a sage scent.	2½–3 ft.	1–2 ft.	■ ■	●	*P. atriplicifolia*, lavender-blue, 2½–3 ft. *P. a.* 'Filagran', finer foliage, 2½ ft. *P. a.* 'Longin', more upright, 3 ft.	Shrublike stems may die back to ground but usually come back from roots. Withstands drought.	Take stem cuttings in summer.
Persicaria (bistort or knotweed) Upright clumps with showy spikes or sprays of small individual flowers from midsummer on, often turning pink or brown and lasting well. Some have patterns of color on their foliage. Other species may be invasive.	1½–6½ ft.	1½–5 ft.	■	● ◐	*P. amplexicaulis* 'Firetail' (red bistort), long bright red spikes, 3–4 ft. *P. polymorpha* (great white fleece flower), large heads of creamy flowers in summer, turn color and last to fall, 6½ ft. *P. virginiana* 'Painter's Palette' (jumpseed), variegated leaves with maroon chevron, 1½–2 ft.	Several species are invasive but can make good ground covers with care and annual pruning.	Seed sown in spring, soft cuttings of nonflowering shoots, or division in spring or fall.
Phlomis (Jerusalem sage) Large leaves, woolly underneath are attractive all summer. Hooded flowers are in whorls surrounding the stem in summer.	3–5 ft.	2–3 ft.	■	●	*P. russeliana*, yellow flowers dry well, bright green leaves, 3 ft. *P. tuberose*, dark leaves, pink flowers, dark red stems, 4–5 ft.	Intolerant of wet conditions, especially in winter. Slow to emerge in spring, mark location well.	Division in fall or soft cuttings in spring.
Phlox (phlox) Valuable group for spring or summer bloom. Best show from large heads of *P. paniculata* that bloom once in midsummer and then intermittently until frost.	5 in.– 3½ ft.	1–2 ft.	□	● ●	*P. carolina* 'Miss Lingard', white, early summer, 2½ ft. *P. divaricata*, blue, mid to late spring, 15 in. *P. maculata* hybrids, early summer, white to pink, 3 ft. *P. paniculata* hybrids, all colors but yellow and orange, midsummer to early fall, 2–3½ ft. *P. stolonifera* 'Blue Ridge', light blue, late spring, 6 in.	Provide sunny location except for *P. divaricata* and *P. stolonifera*, which need shade. *P. paniculata* needs rich soil, plenty of water in summer, frequent division. Check regularly for two-spotted mites and mildew, and remove spent flowers to prevent self-seeding.	Divide plants in spring. Take tip cuttings in summer, also root cuttings of *P. paniculata*.

■ well drained to sandy   ■ moist   ■ wet   ■ acidic   ■ alkaline   □ regular soil   ● full sun   ◐ partial shade   ● shade

The Chinese lantern (*Physalis*) is valued for its red calyxes and orange-red berries. Lanternlike too are the buds of the balloonflower (*Platycodon*), which blooms for several weeks in summer.

Physalis alkekengi var. franchetii

Platycodon grandiflorus

Phygelius capensis
(phygelius, or Cape fuchsia)

Physalis alkekengi
(Chinese lantern)

Physostegia virginiana
(obedient plant, or false dragonhead)

Platycodon grandiflorus
(balloonflower)

Podophyllum peltatum
(mayapple)

Polemonium caeruleum
(Jacob's ladder)

Polygonatum biflorum
(Solomon's seal)

BOTANICAL AND COMMON NAMES	HEIGHT	SPREAD	SOIL	LIGHT	SPECIES AND VARIETIES	SPECIAL REQUIREMENTS AND REMARKS	PROPAGATION (See p. 39)
Phygelius (phygelius, or Cape fuchsia) Shrubby, somewhat weedy plant in mild climates with pendent tubular flowers in loose clusters from midsummer to early fall.	1½–4 ft.	1½–3 ft.	■	●	*P. capensis*, red with yellow throat, 3–4 ft. *P. rectus*, named forms in pink, red, orange, and yellow, 1½-4 ft.	Locate plants in rich soil with ample humus. Cut stems back to near ground level in spring. Prune in summer for neatness. Plants not dependably hardy.	Sow seeds in spring. Divide plants in spring. Take basal cuttings in spring.
Physalis (Chinese lantern) Valued primarily for colorful, papery, inflated calyx (lantern) that is dried and used for winter decoration. Flowers not ornamental.	8 in.– 2½ ft.	1–3 ft.	□	● ◑	*P. alkekengi*, obscure small white flowers, fruit surrounded by inflated orange-red calyx, 2–2½ ft. *P. a.* 'Pygmy', flowers and fruit as above, 8 in. (Often grown as pot plant.)	Plants spread by creeping rhizomes. To control spread, cut off with sharp spade and remove. To dry fruits, pick when they show color, strip leaves, hang in dark, airy location.	Sow seeds in spring (often grown as annual); divide or take root cuttings in spring.
Physostegia (obedient plant, or false dragonhead) From midsummer to early fall spikes of small tubular flowers appear in profusion. Small, neat leaves. Good cut flower.	2–3 ft.	1½–2 ft.	■	● ◑	*P. virginiana*, purplish red, 3 ft. *P. v.* 'Bouquet Rose', lilac-pink, 2½–3 ft. *P. v.* 'Summer Snow', white, 1½–2 ft. *P. v.* 'Variegata', pink, green, and white leaves, 2½ ft. *P. v.* 'Vivid', deep rose-pink, 2 ft.	Divide every 2 or 3 yr., saving only outer portions of clump. Water during dry spells. Called obedient plant because flowers stay put when pushed left or right.	Sow seeds in spring. Divide plants in spring, replanting outer portions, discarding others.
Platycodon (balloonflower) Spikes of large, cup-shaped flowers open from inflated balloonlike buds in midsummer and bloom for many weeks. Attractive leaves. Long lasting when cut.	8 in.–3 ft.	1 ft.	■	● ◑	*P. grandiflorus*, blue, 2–3 ft. *P. g. albus*, white, 2–3 ft. *P. g. apoyama*, violet-blue, dwarf, 8 in. *P. g.* 'Double Blue', deep blue, 2 ft. *P. g. mariesii*, bright blue, 1½ ft. *P. g.* 'Shell Pink', light pink, 1½–2 ft.	Long-lived, provided soil drains well. Grow in sun or partial shade. Plant appears in late spring. Cut flowers in evening; put in deep water. Next day strip lower leaves; cut ½ in. off stems before arranging.	Sow seeds in spring. Divide in spring (difficult due to fleshy taproot; resents disturbance).
Podophyllum (mayapple) Broad, toothed leaves. Large nodding saucer-shaped flowers appear in late spring, followed by lemon-shaped fruits, edible when ripe. Poisonous leaves and roots.	1½ ft.	1 ft.	■	●	*P. hexandrum* (Himalayan mayapple), mottled leaves, white, 1½ ft. *P. peltatum* (American mandrake), white, 1½ ft.	Provide moist soil where possible, but will grow under less-than-ideal conditions. Good in wildflower garden or wherever deciduous ground cover is needed. Spreads rapidly; thick, fibrous roots.	Divide plants in early fall. Sow seeds in fall.
Polemonium (Jacob's ladder) Chief assets are attractive, finely divided leaves and small, clear blue, loosely arranged flowers blooming in spring or early summer.	8 in.–3 ft.	1–2 ft.	□	◑	*P. caeruleum*, blue, 1–3 ft. *P. c. album*, white, 14 in. *P. c.* 'Brise d'Anjou', leaflets edged cream, 2 ft. *P. reptans*, blue, sprawling, 8 in. *P. r.* 'Blue Pearl', light blue with yellow center, 8–10 in.	In full sun, leaves will probably yellow in midsummer, especially if water is scant. The low forms show to best advantage in rock gardens.	Sow seeds in spring. Divide in spring (except for *P. caeruleum* and its hybrids in fall).
Polygonatum (Solomon's seal) Blue-green leaves on arching stems with small flowers that hang from stalks in late spring. Greatest asset is foliage.	1½–4 ft.	2–3 ft.	■	◑	*P. biflorum* (small Solomon's seal), white, 1½–3 ft. *P. odoratum* (fragrant Solomon's seal), white, 3½ ft. *P. o.* 'Variegatum', white-edged leaves, 3 ft.	Locate in rich soil. Plants multiply by creeping rhizomes but are not invasive. Ideal for woodland garden.	Divide plants in very early spring or late summer.

The cinquefoil (*Potentilla*) is a low, bushy perennial that does well as a front edging or as a ground cover. Coneflower (*Rudbeckia*) blooms from mid to late summer.

Potentilla atrosanguinea

Rudbeckia 'Herbstsonne'

Potentilla 'Gibson's Scarlet'
(potentilla, or cinquefoil)

Primula sieboldii
(primrose)

Pulmonaria officinalis
(pulmonaria, or lungwort)

Pulsatilla vulgaris
(pasqueflower)

Ranunculus aconitifolius
(ranunculus, or buttercup)

Romneya coulteri
(romneya)

Rudbeckia 'Goldquelle'
(rudbeckia, or coneflower)

BOTANICAL AND COMMON NAMES	HEIGHT	SPREAD	SOIL	LIGHT	SPECIES AND VARIETIES	SPECIAL REQUIREMENTS AND REMARKS	PROPAGATION (See p. 39)
Potentilla (potentilla, or cinquefoil) Single flowers that appear all summer. Leaves with 3–5 leaflets. For lower-growing types, see p. 167. Better known are the shrubby potentillas (p. 322).	6 in.–1½ ft.	1–2 ft.	□	● ◑	*P.* 'Gibson's Scarlet', bright scarlet, 1½ ft. *P. nepalensis* hybrids. *P. n.* 'Miss Willmott', bright rosy crimson, 1 ft. *P. recta* 'Warrenii', yellow, 1 ft. *P. tonguei* (staghorn), yellow, 6 in.	Water during periods of extreme dryness. Plants tend to sprawl and may need support. Divide every 3 or 4 yr. for best results.	Sow seeds in spring. Divide plants in spring. Take cuttings in summer.
Primula (primrose) Delightful plants valued for spring bloom in wide assortment of colors, patterns, and forms. Clustered flowers are long lasting when cut.	8 in.–3 ft.	1 ft.	■ ■	◑	A diverse group of plants with varying characteristics. Best known are hybrid *P. polyanthus* and other hybrids of *P. vulgaris*. Others available include hybrids of *P. auricula, P. beesiana, P. bulleyana, P. cortusoides, P. denticulata, P. japonica, P. sieboldii,* and *P. veris.*	Locate plants in soil fortified with compost to help retain moisture. Divide plants when they get crowded. Grow best where spring is cool.	Divide plants immediately after flowering in late spring or summer. Sow seeds in spring or fall.
Pulmonaria (pulmonaria, or lungwort) Dainty drooping clusters of small flowers in mid to late spring. Often valued more for leaves that remain attractive all season. Many new and established hybrids available.	8 in.–1½ ft.	1–2 ft.	■	●	*P. angustifolia* (blue cowslip), bright blue, 8–10 in. *P. longifolia*, lancelike leaves, spotted white, 1 ft. *P. officinalis*, pink then violet, plain leaves, 10 in. *P. rubra*, red to salmon, plain leaves, 1½ ft. *P. saccharata* (Bethlehem sage), pink turning to blue, white-spotted leaves, 1 ft.	Grow where soil will remain moist and cool. Plants spread quite rapidly. They need to be divided only when vigor wanes. Water well after dividing. Makes excellent ground cover or border plant.	Divide plants in late summer.
Pulsatilla (pasqueflower) Spring flowers, finely divided foliage, and attractive seed heads.	4–8 in.	8 in.	■	●	*P. vulgaris*, pink to purple or white, 4–8 in.	Does not transplant easily, but will self-sow.	Seeds as soon as ripe.
Ranunculus (ranunculus, or buttercup) Showy, glistening, waxen double flowers bloom on slender stems in late spring or early summer.	6 in.–2 ft.	1½ ft.	■	● ◑	*R. aconitifolius* 'Flore Pleno' (fair maids of France), double, white, 1½ ft. *R. acris* 'Flore Pleno', double, yellow, 1½–2 ft. *R. repens* 'Pleniflorus', double, yellow, 1–1½ ft.	A moist soil is essential; so mix compost with soil before planting and mulch in spring. Plants may need support.	Divide plants in spring.
Romneya (romneya) Spectacular plants have deeply cut gray-green leaves. Towering stems bear fragrant 6-petaled flowers to 9 in. across. Blooms in early to mid summer.	8 ft.	4 ft.	■	●	*R. coulteri* (matilija poppy), glistening white, crinkled petals, center of clustered yellow stamens, 8 ft. *R. c. tricocalyx*, white, 3–6 ft.	Provide a soil with plenty of compost. Water sparingly in summer to restrain growth. Plants are invasive; so best located where they can spread undisturbed. Plants hardy in Zone 8.	Remove and replant suckers in spring or fall. Take root cuttings in spring or summer.
Rudbeckia (rudbeckia, or coneflower) Showy, single or double, daisylike flowers bloom over long period in mid to late summer. 'Goldsturm' blooms are particularly weather resistant. Good cut flower. For annual rudbeckia, see p. 210.	2½–7 ft.	2–4 ft.	■	● ◑	*R. fulgida sullivantii* 'Goldsturm', deep yellow, black conelike center, 2½ ft. *R.* 'Herbstsonne', bright yellow with green cone, 6 ft. *R. laciniata* 'Golden Glow', double, yellow, 7 ft. *R. l.* 'Goldquelle', double, yellow, 2½ ft. *R. maxima*, tall brown cone, drooping petals, 6 ft.	Grow in soil fortified with liberal amounts of compost. Division required every 4–5 yr. Remove faded flowers on 'Goldsturm' to prevent self-sowing if this is not desired.	Sow seeds in spring. Divide plants in spring.

■ well drained to sandy ■ moist ■ wet ■ acidic ■ alkaline □ regular soil ● full sun ◑ partial shade ● shade

Salvia nemorosa 'Ostfriesland'

Sedum telephium 'Herbstfreude'

Sage (*Salvia*) is long-blooming. It is also a good perennial for cut flowers or for drying. *Sedum* 'Herbstfreude' gives color to gardens late in the year.

Ruta graveolens (rue)

Salvia argentea (salvia, or sage)

Santolina chamaecyparissus (santolina, or lavender cotton)

Scabiosa columbaria (scabiosa, or pincushion flower)

Sedum spectabile (sedum, or stonecrop)

BOTANICAL AND COMMON NAMES	HEIGHT	SPREAD	SOIL	LIGHT	SPECIES AND VARIETIES	SPECIAL REQUIREMENTS AND REMARKS	PROPAGATION (See p. 39)
Ruta (rue) Shrublike, with aromatic blue-green leaves, evergreen in Zone 8. Small flowers and decorative brown seed capsules.	1½–3 ft.	1 ft.	▪	●	R. graveolens, greenish yellow, 2–3 ft. R. g. 'Blue Mound', greenish yellow, 1½–2 ft.	Cut plants back in spring. Some gardeners remove flowers to emphasize blue-green leaves. Often grown in herb gardens. May cause dermatitis	Sow seeds in spring. Take cuttings in summer.
Salvia (salvia, or sage) Slender spikes of small flowers bloom over long period at various times in summer according to variety. Excellent cut flower; good dried.	1½–4 ft.	1½–2 ft.	▫	●	S. argentea (silver sage), woolly-leaved, pinkish, 3 ft. S. azurea pitcheri, sky-blue, 3–4 ft. S. greggii (autumn sage), red, pink, violet, or yellow, 1½ ft. S. guaranitica (anise sage), blue shades, tender in North, 4 ft. S. nemorosa 'Ostfriesland' ('East Friesland'), deep blue, 1½ ft. S. sclarea (clary sage), lilac to pink, short-lived, 3 ft. S. sylvestris 'Mainacht' ('May Night'), indigo, 2½ ft. S. s. 'Rose Queen', rose-pink, grayish leaves, 2½ ft.	Best when soil contains ample humus. Plants may need to be staked. Remove faded blooms to promote further flowering. Hardiness varies.	Sow seeds in spring. Divide plants in spring.
Santolina (santolina, or lavender cotton) Technically a shrub, but often planted as a low edging for perennial beds and herb gardens. Small flowers and aromatic gray or green foliage.	6 in.–2 ft.	1½–3 ft.	▫	●	S. chamaecyparissus, silver-gray foliage can be trimmed to 6 in. or left to grow to 2½ ft. S. c. 'Nana', silver-gray foliage, 8–10 in. S. rosmarinifolia, emerald-green foliage, 1½ ft.	Locate in soil that does not remain very wet. If desired, trim to control size. Not for cold regions.	Take cuttings in summer.
Scabiosa (scabiosa, or pincushion flower) Globular heads of flowers with protruding stamens give plant its common name. Fowers from early summer into fall.	1½–2½ ft.	1 ft.	▪ ▪	●	S. caucasica (Caucasian scabiosa), blue, 2½ ft. S. c. alba, white, 2½ ft. S. c. House Hybrids, lavender-blue shades, 2½ ft. S. columbaria, blue, pink, and white varieties, 2½ ft. S. c. 'Butterfly Blue', lavender-blue, gray-green leaves, 1½ ft. S. c. 'Pink Mist', pink to lavender, 1½ ft.	Keep flowers cut to prolong bloom; divide as needed to maintain vigor. May require staking.	Divide plants in spring. Sow seeds in summer.
Sedum (sedum, or stonecrop) Fleshy-leaved plants with large clusters of small flowers in late summer or early fall. Attractive even when not in bloom.	15 in.	12–15 in.	▪	●	S. spectabile (showy stonecrop), rosy pink, 15 in. S. s. 'Brilliant', carmine, 15 in. S. s. 'Meteor', wine-red, 15 in. S. s. 'Star Dust', ivory-white, blue-green leaves, 15 in. S. telephium 'Herbstfreude' ('Autumn Joy'), rust-brown, 15 in. S. 'Vera Jameson', pink, spreading, late summer, 1 ft.	Wet soils, especially in winter, will cause rot at the crown. Plants are very tolerant of drought and generally pest-free. Division necessary only to maintain good flowering.	Divide in spring. Even small rootless pieces take root quickly.

The magenta-pink flowers of *Sidalcea* 'Elsie Heugh' bloom in mid to late summer. *Stachys byzantina* has pink flowers and hairy leaves.

Sidalcea 'Elsie Heugh'

Stachys byzantina

Sidalcea 'Elsie Heugh' (sidalcea)

Solidago (goldenrod)

Stachys byzantina (stachys, or betony)

Stokesia laevis (stokesia, or Stokes' aster)

Symphytum uplandicum (comfrey)

Tanacetum coccineum (pyrethrum, or painted daisy)

BOTANICAL AND COMMON NAMES	HEIGHT	SPREAD	SOIL	LIGHT	SPECIES AND VARIETIES	SPECIAL REQUIREMENTS AND REMARKS	PROPAGATION (See p. 39)
Sidalcea (sidalcea) Slender spikes with 5-petaled flowers resembling small hollyhocks appear mid to late summer. Lower leaves differ in appearance from upper leaves.	1½–5 ft.	1½ ft.	◾	●	*S. malviflora* and other species have been crossed to produce hybrids commonly offered. *S.* 'Brilliant', carmine red, 2½ ft. *S.* 'Elsie Heugh', magenta pink, 3 ft. *S.* 'Party Girl', bright pink, 2–3 ft. *S.* Stark's hybrids, rose to red, 5 ft.	Locate in moisture-retentive soil. Cut back after first flowering period to encourage later bloom. Less showy than hollyhocks; rarely suffers from rust fungus that attacks hollyhocks.	Divide plants in spring. Seeds are occasionally available; sow in spring.
Solidago (goldenrod) Good for late-summer color. The hybrids of the common goldenrod have improved compact form. Goldenrod pollen does not cause hay fever.	2½–6 ft.	1–3 ft.	◾	●	Most garden varieties are hybrids derived from *S. canadensis* and *S. virgaurea*. *S.* 'Crown of Rays', upright, horizontal flower spikes, 2 ft. *S.* 'Fireworks', slender, arching sprays, 6½ ft. *S.* 'Golden Baby', yellow plumes, 1–1½ ft. *S.* 'Golden Fleece', much branched, 2 ft.	Divide every 3 or 4 yr. Remove faded flowers to prevent inferior self-sown seedlings.	Divide plants in spring.
Stachys (stachys, or betony) The species listed are quite different in appearance and use. The first is grown more for its gray leaves, the others for their flowers.	1–2 ft.	1½–2 ft.	☐ ◾	●	*S. byzantina* (lamb's ears), gray, hairy leaves, pinkish flowers in summer are not showy, 1 ft. *S. b.* 'Primrose Heron', yellowish leaves that hold their color, 1 ft. *S. b.* 'Silver Carpet', silver-gray, nonflowering, 1 ft. *S. macrantha* 'Superba', pinkish purple, summer, 2 ft. *S. officinalis* (wood betony), pink, purple, or white, summer, 2 ft.	*S. macrantha* will tolerate partial shade and is good cut flower. *S. byzantina* can be invasive, especially in rich soil, but is still one of more valuable gray-leaved perennials.	Divide plants in spring
Stokesia (stokesia, or Stokes' aster) Cornflowerlike flowers appear in mid to late summer; on slender stems. Foliage is evergreen in mild areas. Good cut flower. The only species in this genus.	1–1½ ft.	1 ft.	◾	●	*S. laevis*, or *S. cyanea*, hybrids are generally available. *S. l.* 'Blue Danube', deep blue, 1–1½ ft. *S. l.* 'Blue Moon', silvery blue to lilac, 1–1½ ft. *S. l.* 'Blue Star', light blue, 1–1½ ft. *S. l.* 'Silver Moon', white, 1–1½ ft.	Well-drained soil in winter is essential to survival. Divide plants when they appear crowded—generally not until the third or fourth year.	Sow seeds in spring. Divide plants in spring. Make root cuttings in summer.
Symphytum (comfrey) Rather sprawling plants with rough, hairy leaves that make a good ground cover but can be highly invasive. The bell-like flowers are in terminal clusters in spring or summer.	6 in.–4 ft.	1–2 ft.	◾	● ●	*S. ibericum* 'Goldsmith', leaves edged in yellow, flowers blue, pink, and white, 6–12 in. *S. uplandicum* 'Variegatum' (Russian comfrey), narrow leaves edged with cream, flowers mauve, 2–3 ft.	Best in light shade, but adaptable. The herb comfrey (*S. officinale*) is rich in nutrients and can be used as fertilizer. Do not allow flowers to set seed.	Division in spring or fall. Nonvariegated varieties by root cuttings in early winter.
Tanacetum (pyrethrum, or painted daisy) Large single or double flowers on long stems above finely divided leaves bloom In late spring and early summer. Excellent long-lasting cut flower.	2–3½ ft.	1½ ft.	◾	●	*T. coccineum* hybrids. *T. c.* 'Eileen May Robinson', pale pink, 2½ ft. *T. c.* 'James Kelway', crimson-pink, 2 ft. *T. c.* 'Robinson's Hybrids', many colors, hardiest, 1½ ft. *T. c.* 'Snow Cloud', white, 2 ft.	Plants grow best in fairly rich soil. Not reliably hardy unless soil is well drained. Needs warm weather for best performance. Cut back after flowering to encourage further blooming.	Sow seeds in spring. Divide plants in spring.

◾ well drained to sandy   ◾ moist   ◾ wet   ◾ acidic   ◾ alkaline   ☐ regular soil   ● full sun   ◐ partial shade   ● shade

Trillium rivale

Trilliums (*Trillium*) are woodland plants that prefer shade and damp soil in spring.

Thalictrum aquilegifolium
(thalictrum, or meadow rue)

Thermopsis villosa
(thermopsis, or false lupine)

Tiarella cordifolia
(foamflower)

Tradescantia
(tradescantia, or spiderwort)

Tricyrtis formosana
(toad lily)

Trillium ovatum
(trillium)

BOTANICAL AND COMMON NAMES	HEIGHT	SPREAD	SOIL	LIGHT	SPECIES AND VARIETIES	SPECIAL REQUIREMENTS AND REMARKS	PROPAGATION (See p. 39)
Thalictrum (thalictrum, or meadow rue) Attractive gray-green or blue-green leaves that resemble maidenhair fern. Loose sprays of tiny flowers in late spring or summer.	2–6 ft.	1½–2 ft.	■	● ◐	*T. aquilegifolium*, cream, early summer, 2–3 ft. *T. a.* 'Thundercloud', purple stamens, early summer, 2–3 ft. *T. delavayi* 'Hewitt's Double', tiny mauve powder puffs, 4–6 ft. *T. flavum glaucum* (dusty meadow rue), yellow, midsummer, 3–4 ft. *T. rochebrunianum*, pale purple, midsummer, 3–4 ft. *T. r.* 'Lavender Mist', darker flowers and stems, 5 ft.	Grow in moisture-retentive soil. May be difficult to transplant. Plants gradually increase in size but are not invasive. Rabbit proof. Easily grown plants with airy appearance found in few other plants.	Sow seeds as soon as ripe or in spring. Divide plants in spring.
Thermopsis (thermopsis, or false lupine) Spikes of lupinelike flowers tower above attractive pealike foliage in early to mid summer. Foliage remains effective after flowering.	2–5 ft.	2–3 ft.	□	● ◐	*T. rhombifolia*, sulfur-yellow, early summer, 3 ft. *T. villosa*, yellow, late spring, 3–5 ft.	Avoid very rich soil. Transplanting difficult because deep rooted. Plants may need staking. Generally trouble-free. Seed spikes dry well.	Divide (difficult) in spring. Sow seeds in late summer using pea and bean inoculant.
Tiarella (foamflower) Basal heart-shaped leaves with slender spikes of small white or pink-tinged flowers blooming in late spring.	8–12 in.	12 in.	■ ■	◐	*T. cordifolia* (Allegheny foamflower), white, 1 ft. *T.* 'Mint Chocolate', brown-striped leaves, 14 in. *T.* 'Spring Symphony', pink flowers, 10 in. *T. wherryi*, white, more compact than above, 1 ft. *T. w.* 'Oakleaf', larger lobes on foliage, pink, 8 in.	Particularly good ground cover in wildflower garden and rock garden.	Divide plants in spring or early fall.
Tradescantia (tradescantia, or spiderwort) Clusters of 3-petaled flowers rise above long narrow leaves from midsummer to early fall. Flowers close on sunny afternoons.	1½–2½ ft.	2–3 ft.	■	● ◐	*T. virginiana* 'Iris Prichard', white, violet flush, 2–2½ ft. *T. v.* 'J. C. Weguelin', porcelain-blue, 2–2½ ft. *T. v.* 'Pauline', rose-mauve, 2–2½ ft. *T. v.* 'Purple Dome', rose-purple, 2–2½ ft. *T. v.* 'Red Cloud', rose-red, 1½ ft. *T. v.* 'Snowcap', pure white, 2–2½ ft.	Plant tends to be very invasive and difficult to eradicate; so may best be grown in isolated areas. Can be cultivated easily, but is not reliably hardy on the Great Plains.	Divide plants in spring. Occasionally grown from seeds or cuttings.
Tricyrtis (toad lily) Arching stems carry prettily-marked flowers in fall. Flowers have 6 petals and a colored, three-parted center. There are several species and many hybrids in a range of colors.	2½–3½ ft.	1½–2 ft.	■	● ●	*T. formosana*, pale purple with darker spots, mild climates only, 3½ ft. *T. hirta*, white or pale pink with purple markings, several named varieties, 3 ft. *T.* 'Lightning Strike', leaves streaked with yellow, lavender flowers with darker spots, 2½ ft.	Grow in humus-rich soil and water during drought to ensure good flowering in fall. Does well near water gardens where soil is always moist.	Take cuttings in summer or divide in spring as growth starts.
Trillium (trillium) Choice spring-blooming wildflower with showy petals and sepals mostly in white or shades of pink or red above a whorl of 3 leaves.	6 in.–1½ ft.	1 ft.	■	◐	Many species offered, usually by wildflower specialists. *T. grandiflorum* (snow trillium), white, one of showiest, 1 ft. Others available include *T. chloropetalum*, *T. erectum*, *T. nivale*, *T. ovatum*, *T. recurvatum*, *T. sessile*, and *T. undulatum*.	Grow in soil well mixed with compost. Some species require greater acidity than others. Plants go dormant in summer and leaves disappear.	Sow seeds when ripe in early summer. Divide in early fall, but best left undisturbed.

Globeflowers (*Trollius*) are native to wet meadows and so grow best in moist locations, in full sun. Mullein (*Verbascum*), which grows up to 8 ft. tall, is among the tallest perennials. Speedwell (*Veronica*) is a mid-border plant that flowers for much of the summer.

Trollius chinensis 'Golden Queen'

Verbascum bombyciferum

Veronica austriaca 'Crater Lake Blue'

Trollius europaeus (globeflower)

Valeriana officinalis (valerian)

Verbascum (verbascum, or mullein)

Verbena bipinnatifida (verbena, or vervain)

Veronica (veronica, or speedwell)

Viola odorata (viola, or violet)

Yucca (yucca)

BOTANICAL AND COMMON NAMES	HEIGHT	SPREAD	SOIL	LIGHT	SPECIES AND VARIETIES	SPECIAL REQUIREMENTS AND REMARKS	PROPAGATION (See p. 39)
Trollius (globeflower) Divided, shiny dark green leaves set off large single or double flowers like buttercups that bloom in late spring. Long-lasting cut flower.	1½–4 ft.	1–1½ ft.	■	◐	*T. chinensis* 'Golden Queen', bright yellow, 4 ft. *T. cultorum* 'Canary Bird', pale lemon, long flowering, 2 ft. *T. c.* 'Earliest of All', yellow, midspring, 1½ ft. *T. c.* 'Feuertroll' ('Fireglobe'), orange-yellow, 2 ft. *T. c.* 'Lemon Queen', pale lemon, large, 2 ft. *T. c.* 'Orange Princess', golden orange, late spring, 2 ft. *T. europaeus*, yellow, early to mid summer, 2½ ft.	Grows best where soil is very moist, even swampy; and where soil contains plenty of compost. Plants will multiply, but division not generally necessary for at least 5 or 6 yr.	Divide plants in spring. Sow seeds in spring or fall. May take more than a year to germinate.
Valeriana (valerian) Tall straight stems bear loose clusters of fragrant flowers in mid to late summer above finely divided leaves. Effective cut flower.	4 ft.	2 ft.	□	● ◑	*V. officinalis* (garden heliotrope), white, lavender, or pink, 4 ft., often sold by herb growers. See also the true heliotrope, an annual, p. 204. Another plant, the perennial *Centranthus*, p. 48, is often sold under the common name valerian.	Tolerates fairly moist soil. Plants spread by underground runners and tend to be invasive and somewhat weedy.	Sow seeds in spring. Divide plants in spring.
Verbascum (verbascum, or mullein) The flowers are borne on tall spikes above basal rosettes of silver-gray or green leaves in mid to late summer.	2–8 ft.	1–2 ft.	■ ■	●	*V. bombyciferum* 'Arctic Summer', yellow, silver leaves, 8 ft. *V. hybridum* 'Cotswold Queen', yellow, purple center, 3–4 ft. *V. h.* 'Pink Domino', rose-pink, maroon center, 4 ft. *V. nigrum*, yellow, purple center, 2–3 ft. *V. phoeniceum* (purple mullein), violet to purple, 2½–3 ft.	Remove faded flowers and side spikes may develop. Cutting also encourages new basal rosettes of leaves. May self-sow. Often behaves like biennial (see p. 196).	Sow seeds in spring. Divide plants in spring.
Verbena (verbena, or vervain) Clusters of small flowers over long period in summer and small, very divided leaves.	3 in.–6 ft.	1–2 ft.	■	●	*V. bipinnatifida* (Dakota verbena), light purple, 3 in. *V. bonariensis*, slender open habit, pale mauve, 6 ft. *V. rigida*, or *V. venosa*, purplish to sky-blue, 1 ft.; neither is reliably hardy in the colder states.	*V. bonariensis* can reseed itself prolifically, so it is important to cut back flowers before they go to seed.	Sow seeds in spring. Take cuttings in summer.
Veronica (veronica, or speedwell) Widely grown for spikes of closely set, small flowers from mid to late summer. Neat, often attractive foliage.	15 in.–2 ft.	1–1½ ft.	■	● ◑	*V. austriaca* 'Crater Lake Blue', gentian-blue, 1½ ft. *V. spicata* 'Goodness Grows', dark blue, all summer, 1–1½ ft. *V. s.* 'Icicle', white, 2 ft. *V. s.* 'Rotfuchs' ('Red Fox'), dark pink, long flowering, 1 ft. *V. s. incana*, blue, silvery foliage, 1 ft. *V.* 'Sunny Border Blue', violet-blue, all summer, 1½ ft.	Water in dry weather. Stake as needed. Divide when plants no longer bloom well. Easily grown plants that provide color over long period, especially if faded spikes are removed.	Divide plants in spring. Sow seeds of available kinds in spring or early summer. Take cuttings in spring.
Viola (viola, or violet) Fragrant flowers are borne in profusion; mostly solid colors. Rich green, oval or heart-shaped leaves. Useful for bedding or as ground cover.	6–8 in.	9 in.–1 ft.	■	● ◑	*V. cornuta* hybrids (tufted pansy) often grown as annuals, 6–8 in.: 'Avalanche', white; 'Jersey Gem', purple; 'Yellow Perfection', yellow; 'Chantryland', apricot; 'Arkwright Ruby', crimson. *V. odorata* hybrids (sweet violet), 6 in.: 'White Czar', white; 'The Czar', blue; 'Royal Robe', deep purple.	Grow in soil that has been mixed with plenty of compost. Water in dry weather. Keep flowers picked to prolong bloom, which is heaviest in spring but continues intermittently until fall.	Sow seeds in spring or late summer. Divide plants or take basal cuttings in spring.
Yucca (yucca) Basal evergreen swordlike leaves, fragrant, close-set flowers rise in midsummer.	3–6 ft.	3–4 ft.	■	●	*Y. filamentosa* (Adam's needle), creamy white, 3–6 ft. *Y. flaccida* 'Ivory Tower', creamy white, 5–6 ft. For larger species, *Y. glauca*, see p. 339.	Tolerates drought. Aphids may attack flowers; control with insecticidal soap. Generally grown from plants set out in spring.	Take root cuttings in spring.

■ well drained to sandy ■ moist ■ wet ■ acidic ■ alkaline □ regular soil ● full sun ◑ partial shade ● shade

PERENNIALS FOR SPECIFIC LOCATIONS/PURPOSES

Perennials for Dry, Poor Soils

Acanthus spinosus

Echinops ritro

Gaura lindheimeri

Acanthus spinosus (bear's breeches)
Achillea—most (yarrow)
Anaphalis margaritacea
 (pearly everlasting)
Anthemis tinctoria (chamomile)
Campanula persicifolia
 (peachleaved bellflower)
Centranthus ruber (red valerian)
Diascia rigescens (twinspur)
Dictamnus albus (gas plant)
Echinops ritro (globe thistle)
Eryngium planum (sea holly)
Euphorbia myrsinites (spurge)

Gaillardia grandiflora (blanketflower)
Gaura lindheimeri (gaura)
Gypsophila paniculata (baby's breath)
Knautia macedonica (knautia)
Linum flavum (yellow flax)
Lychnis coronaria (rose campion)
Nepeta faassenii (catmint)
Oenothera speciosa
 (evening primrose)
Penstemon—most (beardstongue)
Sedum–most (stonecrop)
Stachys byzantina (betony)
Veronica spicata (speedwell)

Drought-resistant Perennials (when established)

Baptisia australis

Kniphofia hybrids

Oenothera fruticosa

Achillea—most (yarrow)
Anthemis tinctoria (chamomile)
Artemisia—most (wormwood)
Baptisia australis (wild indigo)
Centranthus ruber (valerian)
Coreopsis grandiflora (tickseed)
Corydalis lutea (yellow corydalis)
Euphorbia polychrome (spurge)
Gaillardia aristata (blanketflower)
Gaura lindheimeri (gaura)
Kniphofia hybrids (red-hot poker)

Liatris—most (gayfeather)
Lychnis coronaria (rose campion)
Oenothera fruticosa (sundrops)
Penstemon species (beardstongue)
Perovskia atriciplicifolia
 (Russian sage)
Phormium tenax (New Zealand flax)
Santolina chamaecyparissus
 (lavender cotton)
Sedum spectabile (stonecrop)
Yucca filamentosa (yucca)

Perennials with Flowers/Seed Heads for Drying

Catananche caerulea

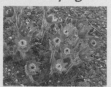
Eryngium giganteum

Pulsatilla vulgaris

Achillea filipendula (yarrow)
Alchemilla mollis (lady's mantle)
Anaphalis margaritacea
 (pearly everlasting)
Anemone pulsatilla (Pasqueflower)
Astilbe—most (astilbe)
Baptisia australis (wild indigo)
Catananche caerulea (Cupid's dart)
Centaurea macrocephala
 (globe centaurea)

Cimicifuga racemosa (bugbane)
Dictamnus albus (gas plant)
Echinops—all (globe thistle)
Eryngium—all (sea holly)
Lavendula angustifolia (lavender)
Limonium latifolium (sea lavender)
Macleaya cordata (plume poppy)
Physalis alkekengi (Chinese lantern)
Pulsatilla vulgaris (Pasqueflower)
Sedum telephium (stonecrop)

Salt-tolerant (coastal sites) Perennials

Achillea millefolium

Bergenia hybrid

Perovskia atriplicifolia

Achillea—most (yarrow)
Aconitum cammarum (monkshood)
Agapanthus–most (lily of the Nile)
Anthemis tinctoria (chamomile)
Artemisia—most (wormwood)
Bergenia cordifolia and hybrids
 (bergenia)
Campanula persicifolia
 (peachleaved bellflower)
Catananche caerulea (Cupid's dart)
Centranthus ruber (red valerian)
Echinops—all (globe thistle)
Erigeron speciosus (fleabane)
Eryngium—all (sea holly)
Filipendula vulgaris (dropwort)

Gaillardia grandiflora (blanketflower)
Hemerocallis hybrids (daylily)
Lavatera hybrids (mallow)
Mertensia virginica
 (Virginia bluebells)
Monarda didyma (Oswego tea)
Nepeta cataria (catnip)
Perovskia atriplicifolia (Russian sage)
Phormium hybrids (New Zealand flax)
Physostegia virginiana
 (obedient plant)
Scabiosa—most (pincushion flower)
Sedum telephium (stonecrop)
Stachys byzantina (betony)
Veronica spicata (speedwell)

Perennials for Dry Shade

Convallaria majalis

Epimedium grandiflorum

Polygonatum odoratum

Aquilegia vulgaris (columbine)
Convallaria majalis (lily of the valley)
Corydalis lutea (yellow corydalis)
Dicentra Formosa (bleeding heart)
Epimedium—most (barrenwort)
Galium odoratum (bedstraw)
Geranium macrorrhizum
 (bigroot geranium)

Helleborus orientalis (lenten rose)
Hosta—some (hosta)
Lamium maculatum
 (spotted deadnettle)
Liriope muscari (lilyturf)
Phlox divaricata (blue phlox)
Polygonatum odoratum
 (Solomon's seal)

Perennials for Acidic Soils

Aruncus dioicus

Dicentra spectabilis

Trillium erectum

Aruncus dioicus (goatsbeard)
Asclepias tuberosus (butterfly weed)
Chelone lyonii (turtlehead)
Cimicifuga racemosa (snakeroot)
Dicentra spectabilis (bleeding heart)
Iris ensata (Japanese iris)

Kirengeshoma palmata (kirengeshoma)
Lobelia cardinalis (cardinal flower)
Mertensia virginica (Virginia bluebell)
Phlox divaricata (woodland phlox)
Tricyrtis formosana (toad lily)
Trillium—most (trillium)

Perennials for Alkaline Soils

Acanthus mollis

Amsonia tabernaemontana

Platycodon grandiflorus

Acanthus mollis (bear's breeches)
Amsonia tabernaemontana (bluestar)
Bergenia cordifolia (bergenia)
Centaurea dealbata (knapweed)
Coreopsis verticillata
 (threadleaf tickseed)
Echinacea purpurea (coneflower)
Echinops ritro (globe thistle)
Euphorbia polychrome (spurge)
Gaura lindheimeri (gaura)
Geranium macrorrhizum
 (bigroot geranium)
Helleborus orientalis (lenten rose)
Hemerocallis hybrids (daylily)

Kniphofia hybrids (red-hot poker)
Liatris spicata (spike gayfeather)
Oenothera speciosa
 (evening primrose)
Perovskia atriplicifolia (Russian sage)
Physostegia virginiana
 (obedient plant)
Platycodon grandiflorus
 (balloon flower)
Liatris spicata (spike gayfeather)
Sedum telephium (stonecrop)
Sidalcea malviflora (sidalcea)
Thalictrum flavum glaucum
 (dusty meadow rue)

Perennials That Attract Hummingbirds* and Butterflies

Agastache foeniculum

Centranthus ruber

Phlox paniculata

Agastache—most (hyssop)*
Aguilegia—most (columbine)*
Asclepias tuberosus (butterfly weed)*
Aster—most (aster)
Baptisia australis (wild indigo)
Centaurea macrocephala
 (globe centaurea)
Centranthus ruber (red valerian)*
Chelone lyonii (turtlehead)*
Coreopsis verticillata
 (threadleaf tickseed)
Dicentra spectabilis (bleeding heart)*
Echinacea purpurea (coneflower)
Hemerocallis citrina (lemon daylily)
Heuchera sanguinea (coralbells)*
Hosta plantaginea (hosta)*

Lavendula angustifolia (lavender)
Liatris spicata (spike gayfeather)
Lilium—most (lily)*
Lobelia cardinalis (cardinal flower)*
Lychnis coronaria (rose campion)*
Monarda didyma (Oswego tea)*
Nepeta faassenii (catmint)
Oenothera macrocarpa
 (Ozark sundrops)
Perovskia atriplicifolia (Russian sage)
Phlox paniculata (summer phlox)*
Rudbeckia fulgida (coneflower)
Salvia guaranitica (anise sage)*
Solidago—most (goldenrod)
Verbena bonariensis (vervain)*

Rabbit-proof Perennials

Aconitum napellus

Geranium macrorrhizum

Helleborus orientalis

Acanthus mollis (bear's breeches)
Aconitum species (monkshood)
Anemone hybrida (anemone)
Aguilegia—most (columbine)
Astilbe hybrids (astilbe)
Bergenia cordifolia (bergenia)
Convallaria majalis (lily of the valley)
Epimedium species (barrenwort)
Eryngium—all (sea holly)

Geranium—most (cranesbill)
Helleborus orientalis (lenten rose)
Lamium maculatum (deadnettle)
Nepeta faassenii (catmint)
Paeonia species & hybrids (peony)
Pulmonaria species (lungwort)
Tradescantia hybrids (spiderwort)
Trollius cultorum (globeflower)

Perennials That Deer Avoid

Ajuga reptans

Astilbe chinensis

Paeonia lactiflora

Achillea—most (yarrow)
Aconitum species (monkshood)
Ajuga pyramidalis (bugleweed)
Alchemilla mollis (lady's mantle)
Amsonia tabernaemontana (bluestar)
Anemone hybrida (anemone)
Aguilegia—most (columbine)
Asclepias tuberosus (butterfly weed)
Astilbe hybrids (astilbe)
Baptisia australis (wild indigo)
Centranthus ruber (red valerian)
Chelone lyonii (turtlehead)
Cimicifuga racemosa (snakeroot)
Convallaria majalis (lily of the valley)

Echinacea purpurea (coneflower)
Epimedium species (barrenwort)
Geranium macrorrhizum
 (bigroot geranium)
Liriope muscari (lilyturf)
Lobelia cardinalis (cardinal flower)
Monarda didyma (Oswego tea)
Nepeta faassenii (catmint)
Paeonia species & hybrids (peony)
Pulmonaria species (lungwort)
Solidago—most (goldenrod)
Tradescantia hybrids (spiderwort)
Trillium—most (trillium)
Veronica spicata (speedwell)

Perennials for City Gardens–Pollution Tolerant

Anaphalis margaritacea

Aster novae-angliae

Potentilla 'Gibson's Scarlet'

Achillea–most (yarrow)
Anaphalis margaritacea
 (pearly everlasting)
Aster frikartii (Frikart's aster)
Astrantia major (masterwort)
Centaurea montana (mountain bluet)
Coreopsis grandiflora (tickseed)
Dicentra eximea
 (fringed bleeding heart)
Geranium species–most (cranesbill)
Geum hybrids (avens)
Hemerocallis hybrids (daylily)
Lamium maculatum (deadnettle)

Leucanthemum superbum
 (Shasta daisy)
Liatris spicata (spike gayfeather)
Lychnis chalcedonica (Maltese cross)
Malva moschata (musk mallow)
Monarda didyma (Oswego tea)
Nepeta faassenii (catmint)
Persicaria polymorpha
 (white fleece flower)
Potentilla 'Gibson's Scarlet'
 (cinquefoil)
Rudbeckia fulgida (coneflower)
Veronica spicata (speedwell)

IRISES

From the stately bearded iris—long known as the flag iris—down to the tiny plants that grow from bulbs, these flowers provide a delicate beauty in any garden.

Irises are garden plants that were cultivated in Asia long before the birth of Christ.

There are two groups: those that grow from rhizomes (thick underground stems) and those that grow from bulbs.

The rhizomatous types develop pointed, straplike leaves that grow in fans from the ends of the rhizomes and produce stalks that bear one or more flowers. Colors include white, pink, blue, purple-black, gold, red, and combinations of these hues.

The most popular of these types are the bearded irises, which have fleshy hairs like a beard on the outer petals, or "falls."

Botanically, the rhizomatous types are divided into two categories: Eupogons, which include the popular tall bearded iris, and Arils.

Both Eupogons and Arils are true bearded irises and are grown in the same way. Both include wild species as well as many hybrids developed from them. The more exotic and difficult Arils differ from other bearded irises in flower forms and patterns. Their beards are somewhat narrow but conspicuous, frequently in vivid colors, on flowers that are veined, stippled, and more closely clustered than Eupogon irises. Leaves are short and sickle shaped.

The numerous hybrids of the Eupogons, called bearded irises, are classified further by height, starting with the standard tall forms (at least 28 inches high). These are followed by five classes of median irises in the following descending order of height: border, miniature tall, intermediate, and standard dwarf. The smallest bearded irises, the miniature dwarfs, vary from 3 to 10 inches.

Eupogons bloom from early spring to early summer in height sequence—smallest first. Reblooming irises—varieties of tall bearded forms—may also bloom in fall, depending on the climate.

Aril irises, which range in height from about 5 to 18 inches, begin blooming as much as a month earlier than most Eupogons.

Ideally, the taller bearded irises should be planted in their own beds or in groups in front of perennial or shrub borders. The lower-growing types look best in the foreground of beds or borders, or in rock gardens.

Dwarf bearded irises do not tolerate strong competition and are best used only in rock gardens or grouped in front of small plants.

In addition to the bearded irises, there are the equally beautiful Eurasian beardless (Spathula) types. Among them are *Iris dichotoma,* a lavender-flowered August bloomer, and *I. foetidissima,* which has brilliant vermilion seeds: these more than make up for its plain gray flowers and the unpleasant odor of its leaves when crushed.

The Apogons, an important section of the beardless group, consist of the following distinct series, or subsections, which vary in height from 4 inches to 5 feet.

The Laevigata series encompasses the Japanese and some American species plus the familiar tall Eurasian yellow flag (*I. pseudacorus*). All are known as water irises because of their preference for growing on the banks of streams and ponds. The American species, *I. versicolor* and *I. virginica,* also are close relatives.

The sun-loving Longipetalae species, *I. longipetala* and *I. missouriensis,* are American natives not often grown in gardens. They share a liking for dampness in the spring but prefer to have drier conditions in summer. The former is distinguished by violet-veined white blooms and nearly evergreen leaves; the latter by flowers in white or shades of purple.

The Louisiana irises, which are native to the southern United States, will also grow in areas farther north with winter protection.

The Siberian irises survive cold weather especially well and are

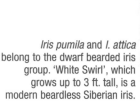

Iris pumila and *I. attica* belong to the dwarf bearded iris group. 'White Swirl', which grows up to 3 ft. tall, is a modern beardless Siberian iris.

Iris pumila

Iris attica

Iris sibirica 'White Swirl'

widely grown in much of the country. They include many hybrids of *I. sibirica* and the Manchurian *I. sanguinea,* or *I. orientalis,* both of which produce flowers in purple, blue, or white.

The Pacific Coast irises, though available in a wide range of colors and easily grown from seed, are seldom seen outside the moist, mild region for which they are named, since they are extremely difficult to transplant in other climates.

Two other excellent Apogons are the spurias, members of a widely varied and much hybridized species, and the miniature kinds, with origins from Japan to Romania.

Crested irises, or evansias (technically, bearded Apogons), look somewhat like orchids. Their 3- to 10-inch blooms have crests on the falls that resemble a rooster's comb. The broad, glossy leaves are evergreen.

Beardless irises should be planted with the same attention to height as the bearded types, with the tall forms in the background of a bed and the miniatures in the foreground or in rock gardens.

The bulbous irises, which must be grown in full sun, are the only types that are sometimes forced in pots indoors. In the garden they provide a welcome continuity of flowers for borders. They are divided into three subgenera, only two of which—*Scorpiris* (the junos) and *Xiphium*—have importance for home gardeners.

The junos (9–15 inches tall) have leaves that give these irises a strong resemblance to tiny corn plants. Their storage roots are fleshy and easily injured. Otherwise they are easy to grow in full sun. The yellow *I. bucharica* is the most readily available of the group. All junos bloom in midspring and are crested, except for *I. tubergeniana.* Both the subgenus *Xiphium* (18–24 inches), which includes the well-known Dutch, Spanish, and English irises,

and the reticulata group (4–12 inches) demand little care and offer much.

Dutch irises—noted for their large, long-lasting blooms, which are ideal for indoor arrangements—are the tallest of the bulbous group. They flower in early summer, about two weeks before Spanish irises.

Both Dutch and Spanish irises produce new foliage in the fall, and must be given a protective mulch wherever winters are cold. Their flowers come in white and shades of blue and yellow.

Blooming from early to mid summer, English irises prefer the moist climate of the Pacific Northwest. But they sometimes bloom in other regions if they are planted where they will have partial shade and somewhat acid soil that is moist but well drained. English irises produce new leaves during the spring only.

Reticulatas are quite distinctive, with their four-sided leaf spikes. They bloom in late winter or early spring, and the flowers of some varieties are sweetly perfumed.

Reticulatas are well suited to the rock garden or any sheltered area in full sun, since their height seldom exceeds 4 inches. Like the little species crocuses, they multiply rapidly and lend themselves well to informal, naturalistic plantings.

In addition to the rich violet *I. reticulata* and its named forms, which vary in color from red-violet to light blue, other outstanding reticulatas include *I. histrioides major* and *I. bakeriana.* Native, respectively, to the Caucasus and Asia Minor, the former is blue, and the latter has blue standards, bluish-purple falls, and dark-speckled yellow and white centers. Also in this group is the bright yellow *I. danfordiae,* which contrasts well with some of the purple varieties of *I. reticulata.*

For more information on iris culture, including links to other iris sites, visit the American Iris Society at www.irises.org.

IRIS TYPES

Rhizomatous irises are divided into three groups: bearded, beardless, and crested. *I. germanica* (above), of the bearded group, is further classified as an intermediate bearded (IB), comes in many colors, and is parent to many garden hybrids.

Beardless irises, such as the flowerhead above, are divided into five main sections, one of which is the Sibiricae or Siberian group, which is native to Siberia, Manchuria, and Japan. These hardy plants do well in herbaceous borders or beside pools.

Plants in the crested iris group are evergreen with slender rhizomes. At first glance, crested irises appear bearded but a closer look shows that what appears to be a beard is actually a raised band of tissue. Orchidlike in how the bloom opens, crested irises do best in a greenhouse.

Irises that flourish in or near water belong to the *Laevigatae* group, a subsection of beardless irises. Many originate from the Japanese water iris (*I. ensata*). *I. laevigatae* is the only one that must be grown in water. Other so-called water irises can be grown in soil that is kept moist.

Bulbous irises are divided into three groups, *Reticulata,* the smallest, one of which is shown here, *Juno,* and *Xiphium.*

Dutch, Spanish, and English irises, all from the *Xiphium* group, are among the most easily grown of the bulbous irises in mild climates.

Iris sibirica

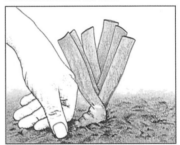

Iris sibirica 'Anniversary'

Modern Siberian irises are a big improvement on the original species, and offer a rich variety of colors. Siberian iris do well at a pond's edge, but will not survive in the water.

Irises That Grow From Rhizomes

Preparing a Well-Drained, Fertile Soil

Most rhizomatous irises can be planted in the same manner, and all share the need for proper soil preparation if plants are to bloom and multiply through the years. Good drainage is essential, and full sun is generally best, although a few varieties prefer a little shade.

Almost any soil is suitable for irises, but heavy clay and light sand demand more preparation than loam and clay loam, which are the best mediums for these perennials. Heavy clay soils can be encouraged to drain better if generous amounts of sharp sand and humus are added. Conversely, very sandy soils will retain moisture longer if humus is mixed in.

If drainage is poor, or you find a layer of impervious hardpan, double dig the bed. Excavate a wide trench, putting the topsoil to one side, and fork in at least 3 inches of compost or well-rotted manure into the subsoil. Turn the next block of topsoil onto this and fork more compost or manure into the base. Repeat until the entire bed has been dug. Then fill the final trench with the topsoil from the start.

Most soils will need to have a 1- to 2-inch layer of old manure or compost worked into the top 10 inches. Spread a low-nitrogen fertilizer, such as blood meal, over the soil—about 10 pounds per 1,000 square feet—and work into the top few inches with a cultivator. Let the soil settle for a few weeks before planting.

If a soil test indicates a need for lime, apply it with a lawn spreader a few weeks before preparing the beds. Most irises do best in slightly acid to neutral (pH 6.0–7.2 or so) soil. Japanese irises, however, cannot tolerate lime or bone meal. They need acid soil with a pH of 5.0–6.0. Lime improves the structure of heavy clay soils, but do not add more than is needed to establish the proper pH.

Planting Bearded Irises Near the Surface

Bearded iris rhizomes should be planted between midsummer and early fall. Where midsummers are extremely dry and hot, early-fall planting can help reduce stress on the plants.

Inspect the rhizomes carefully for evidence of damage by borers or rot. With a sharp knife, gently cut away decayed parts and broken roots. Dust all cut surfaces with sulfur, or you could sterilize the rhizomes with antibacterial hand soap to discourage recurring disease.

For best effect, plant three to seven rhizomes of the same variety in a clump. Plant them with the roots down either side of a ridge of soil so that the top of the rhizome is just showing. Face the fans away from the center of the clump.

Press the soil firmly around the rhizomes to drive out air pockets, which cause soil to dry out and also impede anchoring. Label clumps.

Watering and Feeding Bearded Irises

Immediately after planting, water the soil thoroughly, using a fine spray to prevent washing the soil away from the rhizomes and exposing the roots to the sun.

Irises should be watered often for up to three weeks after planting, particularly if the weather is dry.

Bearded irises, especially the tall varieties, feed heavily. Apply a blood meal and bone meal blend in early spring and again about one month after the blooms fade. Put on a handful for each large clump in spring and about half this amount for the second feeding. Scatter the meal blend near the rhizomes, but not on them, and water it in. Use about half this rate for dwarf varieties. This blend of blood meal and bone meal will provide both nitrogen and phosphorus.

1. Before planting use a knife to trim the long leaves to a neat fan shape.

2. Dig each planting hole so that rhizomes will be at soil level.

3. See that all leaf fans face outward. Spread roots down evenly.

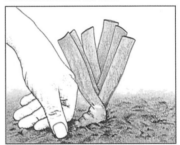

4. Firm soil to eliminate air pockets, hasten anchoring, and deter heaving.

FROST HAZARD

If frost lifts the rhizomes, do not press them back, since this can damage or break roots and weaken plants. Instead, bank up sand or soil around the rhizomes.

SPRING TRIMMING

Trim foliage in the early spring. This will reduce each plant's exposure to wind, which can loosen or break roots. Destroy dead leaves that may shelter slugs.

Bearded irises such as 'Jane Phillips' and 'Maui Moonlight' are so named because of the hairy center to their lower petals.

Iris 'Jane Phillips'

Iris 'Maui Moonlight'

Planting Beardless Irises Below the Surface

Before planting beardless irises, take the same precautions regarding borers and rot as you would with bearded types.

In general, beardless irises do best in well-drained soils, although Japanese, Louisiana, and American irises will live in wet soils where they can be grown.

Japanese and American irises can use plenty of humus. They also need more nutrients than other types do. Being acid lovers, they prefer acid fertilizers, such as those that are used for azaleas and rhododendrons.

Begin planting in early fall, except with Pacific Coast irises. These respond better to midspring planting, which takes less energy from the rhizomes. Spurias should be planted in mid to late fall, since early-fall weather is often too dry.

Rhizomes of all varieties should be planted 15–18 inches apart and about 2 inches deep, with two excep-

tions: Louisiana irises do best at a depth of 1½ inches, while the long, narrow rhizomes of the crested irises should be covered with no more than a very thin layer of soil.

When planting more than one variety in the same bed, make certain that flower colors will complement each other if bloom dates coincide. Color clashes can be further avoided by planting early- and late-flowering types together.

Water new plantings well, and keep them moist until rhizomes are well established.

Apply a mulch to conserve moisture and diminish the unavoidable shock of transplanting. This is especially important with crested irises, which are planted close to the soil surface and are vulnerable to drying out. A mulch is also useful for discouraging the growth of weeds. Use any mulch that will not pack down and get soggy. However, do not use oat or wheat straw over Japanese iris beds, since wheat rust disease may be transmitted to the plants.

1. Before transplanting, cut leaves off beardless and crested irises to 9 in.

2. Dig a hole large enough to take the roots of the variety being planted.

3. Mix humus into the hole. Even roots out and cover. Firm the soil.

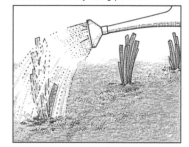

4. Water well. Keep soil moist until plants are established. Label groups.

Keeping Beardless Irises Vigorous and Healthy

In cold winter areas the leaves of many beardless irises shrivel up and die down to the ground.

Unless slugs or other pests are active, this dead foliage can remain on plants as a means of reducing damage to roots caused by alternate thawing and freezing.

In spring, however, all dead leaves should be removed and destroyed. Do not add them to the compost pile, since they may carry diseases or insect eggs that can pose problems elsewhere in the garden.

Avoid cultivating the soil around the plants, since their roots are near the surface and are easily injured. Remove weeds by hand, or better still, add a thick mulch in early spring. This will discourage weeds and help conserve moisture. It will also pre-

vent soil surface temperatures from becoming too high on hot days.

After blooms fade, break them off. If left on the plants, they will form seeds that use energy needed for the further development of roots, rhizomes, and leaves. Seed heads can also choke the surrounding soil with seedlings.

If spring weather is dry, water the beds thoroughly, keeping in mind that one deep watering is better than several shallow sprinklings.

Apply fertilizer as soon as the surface soil can be worked in spring, and give a second feeding after flowering is over. Read the directions on the container of a balanced organic fertilizer before applying.

Do not worry if spurias fail to bloom, or bloom only sparsely, for as long as two years after planting. This kind of iris often takes considerable time to begin producing well.

SPRING MULCHING

Add to mulch scattered by winter winds. This cover helps suppress weeds and retain moisture.

SEEDPOD REMOVAL

Seedpods develop after blooms have faded. Break them off to keep seedlings from choking beds.

Modern iris hybrids have large blossoms in clear colors. The bearded iris 'Stepping Out' won top award of the American Iris Society.

Iris 'Stepping Out'

Staking and Cutting Bearded Iris Flower Stems

The few tall bearded-iris varieties that have weak stems should be staked in late spring when the flower spikes first appear. Use 3-foot canes, and loosely secure the flower stems to them with soft string. Lower-growing irises need not be staked.

Some foliage may turn brown or may develop withered tips before flowering. Remove any unsightly leaves, either by peeling them away or by cutting off the brown tips.

After bearded irises have flowered, the parent rhizomes may have produced offset rhizomes with small fans. If so, cut off the flower spikes close to the rhizomes. This will prevent water from collecting in the stems and causing rhizome rot.

If no offset rhizomes have formed, cut the spikes back to a point just below where the lowest flowers have bloomed. This will prevent further weakening of already weak rhizomes. It will also promote offsets.

SUPPORTING TALL FLOWERS

In late spring, weak-stemmed tall bearded-iris varieties should be staked. Loop soft string around stems and fasten it to stakes.

REMOVING OLD FLOWER STEMS

After flowers have faded, their stems should be removed before seed heads form. If offset rhizomes are present (left), cut stems close to the rhizome to prevent water from collecting and rotting it. If no offsets have developed, cut off stems below the lowest flower (right).

What Can Go Wrong With Irises

To ensure that your irises are healthy, check foliage and rhizomes often for pests or disease. Weeds should be controlled so plants get sufficient light, nutrients, and air circulation. See page 506 for symptoms not listed below.

SYPTOMS AND SIGNS	CAUSE	CONTROL
Leaf and flower stems are distorted.	Aphids	Apply insecticidal soap or pyrethrum to foliage at weekly intervals.
In midspring, edges of young leaves appear saw-toothed. Later, larvae tunnel into rhizomes.	Iris borers	Remove old foliage in fall; monitor new growth and remove infected leaves as they appear.
In wet weather large irregular spots appear on leaves; thick liquid seeps out. Rhizomes are not attacked.	Bacterial leaf blight	Remove and destroy affected foliage and all debris in beds. Drench plants and surrounding soil with antibacterial soap at 1 tbsp/gal.
Rhizomes are pulpy and smell; bloom points are often destroyed. Damage is most likely from early spring through midsummer, or when iris borers are present.	Bacterial soft rot	Cut away soft areas and destroy. Treat cut surfaces with half-strength liquid chlorine bleach, then dust with powdered sulfur.
Dry rot at base of leaves; dead leaf tips. Rot spreads into rhizomes. Thin webs may occur on soil, later becoming brown and seedlike.	Crown (or sclerotium) rot	Cut away and destroy affected parts of rhizomes. If rhizome of bearded iris not showing, scrape away some soil.
In early summer, leaves have oval, yellow blotches. Affected foliage often turns brown and dies.	Leaf spot (fungus)	Remove and destroy dead foliage. Cut off green leaves below lowest blotches. Avoid overhead watering.
Pale yellowish-green stripes on foliage. In wet weather petals may be mottled.	Mosaic (virus)	Plant only resistant varieties. Control aphids, which spread this disease (see above).
Affects tall bearded irises only. Rhizomes and leaves turn reddish brown. Leaves are stunted and look burned. Scorch is usually associated with nematode damage.	Scorch	No known control. Dig up and destroy affected plants.
Rot is visible in rhizomes and roots. Disease enters through cuts in rhizomes; occurs only in cool weather.	Winter rot (fungus)	Cut away and destroy affected growth. Protect with winter mulch.

Dividing the Rhizomes of Bearded Irises

Clumps of bearded irises should be divided and replanted before they become overcrowded.

A single rhizome will branch many times over the years, developing into a heavy crisscross clump, choked with old leafless rhizomes. If it is not divided, it will exhaust the surrounding soil, and the mass of leaves will exclude sun and air from the roots. This leads to poor flowering or no flowering and also weakens the plants, making them more susceptible to insects and disease.

Dividing is best done at the same time of year that initial plantings should be made. Lift each clump by gently prying it loose from the soil. A spading fork is better for this than a shovel because it is less likely to cut roots and rhizomes.

Use a sharp, strong-bladed knife to trim younger rhizomes into sections that include healthy-looking roots and one or two strong leaf fans. Carefully wash all soil off the roots under low pressure from a hose. Finally, discard the old rhizomes from the center sections.

Prepare the leaves as shown and replant the rhizomes (see p. 71).

1. When clumps of bearded irises become crowded, they cease to flower.

2. Loosen soil around clumps. Pry them out with gentle rocking motion.

3. Cut young rhizomes—each with one or two fans—from clump edges.

4. Peel withered leaves from rhizomes, retaining only healthy foliage.

5. Trim foliage to a fan shape. Remove damaged roots. Replant rhizomes.

6. Fill in soil around each rhizome; leave tops exposed. Water thoroughly.

Dividing the Rhizomes of Beardless Irises

Beardless irises also need periodic dividing to maintain their flowering vigor. Sparse growth in the center of large clumps is a sure sign that the soil has been exhausted. Make divisions in the same season in which each variety should originally have been planted.

The rhizomes of certain beardless irises need considerable care because they are very much smaller and thinner than the bearded ones.

Trim back the foliage to about 9 inches to make the clumps easier to handle. Then remove all the dead leaves from the center of each clump and destroy them.

Loosen the soil around the clumps with a spading fork, and carefully lever them from the soil. Separate them with a spading fork into sections with five to nine shoots.

Then gently wash the soil from each section, and cut away any damaged or rotted roots. Be sure to use a sharp knife.

Do not allow the divisions to dry out. If delays in replanting are unavoidable, put the sections into plastic bags, with the leaves exposed to the air, and place them in a shady, wind-free spot. Replant according to the directions on page 72.

1. Before lifting beardless irises, cut back foliage and remove it from beds.

2. Separate clumps. Cut roots. Then replant divisions.

Iris forrestii

Iris sibirica 'Butter & Sugar'

Iris chrysographes

These are all in the Siberian iris group. *I. forrestii* grows 18 in. tall, 'Butter & Sugar' may grow more than 3 ft. tall, and the black-purple *I. chrysographes* can reach a height of 20 in.

How to Breed Your Own Hybrid Irises

Although any interested amateur can produce new hybrid irises by cross-pollination, beginners should limit themselves to plants of the same general type and color. Bearded varieties are the easiest to handle.

As soon as the blooms on the selected plants open, remove a pollen-covered anther from one of them with tweezers. Expose all three stigmas in a flower on a second plant, and wipe the pollen onto the lip or outer edge. Use only dry pollen.

Remove the falls from the second flower to prevent chance insect pollination from taking place.

Label each pollinated bloom, indicating the names of both parents (female first) and the date of pollination.

When the seedpod starts swelling, remove any leafy bracts on the stem to keep moisture from rotting it. Support each pod with a stake.

After about eight weeks the seedpod will have ripened, changing from green to brown. When it begins to split, the seed is ripe.

Ripened seeds should be planted in a mixture of screened topsoil, peat moss, and sharp sand. A cold frame offers good protection, but seeds can also be planted in beds, provided they can be left undisturbed for up to three years in cases of slow germination. The soil should not be allowed to dry out.

Transplant in late spring when seedlings are 1–2 inches tall. Allow 8–10 inches between tall bearded irises, 3 inches between miniature dwarfs. Space rows at least 15 inches apart. Water and feed with a weak dose of compost tea.

When young plants begin to bloom, examine them closely to evaluate their good and bad points. Look for adequate leaf-fan production. Flower stems should not be too thick or too thin. Stems should support three branches plus a terminal with six to eight flower buds.

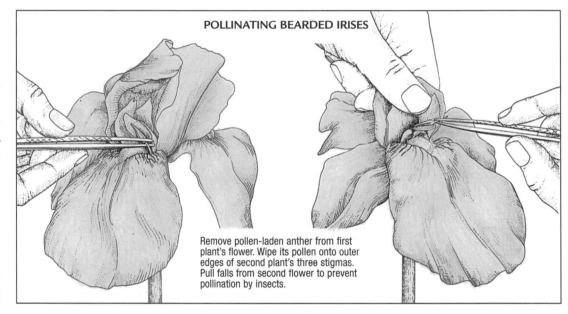

POLLINATING BEARDED IRISES

Remove pollen-laden anther from first plant's flower. Wipe its pollen onto outer edges of second plant's three stigmas. Pull falls from second flower to prevent pollination by insects.

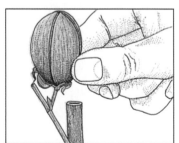

1. When seedpod starts to swell, pull bracts from stem and fasten to stake.

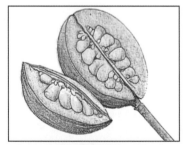

2. Pod turns brown as it ripens. When it splits open, seeds are ready to plant.

3. Fill pots with moistened potting mix. Plant seeds no deeper than ½ in.

4. Frequent light waterings are vital, especially while seeds are germinating.

5. Cold frames give seedlings protection from low temperatures and rains.

6. Transplant 2- to 3-in. seedlings in late spring. Feed later. Water well.

Iris 'Harmony' and *I. danfordiae* belong to the *reticulata* group, which are well suited to rock gardens. They blossom in spring.

Iris 'Harmony'

Iris danfordiae

Irises That Grow From Bulbs

Bulbous irises make valuable additions to the garden by providing a continuity of attractive flowers.

The reticulatas often bloom in late winter and last into midspring. They overlap the blooming period of junos, which flower in midspring. The vivid flowers and unique flower form of the reticulatas seldom fail to attract attention.

Setting and Planting Bulbous Irises

With only minor variations, as noted below, all bulbous irises like a well-drained soil and a spot in full sun where they can soak up plenty of summer heat.

Good drainage is a key factor in growing junos. They generally require raised beds containing nearly neutral (pH 6.5–7.0) soil with a high clay content. Plant them singly or in clumps in early fall at a depth of 2 inches. Allow 6–9 inches between the bulbs. Handle them carefully to avoid breaking off the long, brittle storage roots, from which the vitally essential feeding roots develop during the growing season.

Periodic Maintenance of Bulbous Irises

During the growing season watch the iris beds closely for signs of attack by pests and disease. Serious trouble is often easy to stop, if it is identified in time.

Remove any flowers that have faded. After the blooming season has ended for each variety, dust the beds with a low nitrogen organic fertilizer, and scratch it into the soil. Give the planting bed a watering at this time, if rainfall is inadequate, but do not water during the summer months.

Add to the mulch as needed. If weeds penetrate it, pull them out and place on the compost pile.

Dutch, Spanish, and English irises provide color in early and mid summer, which is a time when most other bulbs have faded and annuals have only just begun to reach their peak.

Flowering periods vary with climates. In West Coast gardens, for instance, bulbous irises may bloom earlier than indicated here.

Bulbs of the reticulata iris should be planted in early to mid fall. Set them 3 inches deep and 3 inches apart in raised beds. Their soil should contain plenty of sharp sand, since poor drainage can be fatal.

Dutch and Spanish irises can be treated alike. Plant them in midfall at a depth of 4 inches where winters are cold; in milder climates plant at about 2½ inches.

Do not expect too much from these bulbs. Even under the most favorable circumstances, they may have to be replaced every two years.

English irises usually have a longer life than their Dutch and Spanish relatives. They need a mildly acid soil and semi-shade. Plant them 6 inches deep in early fall.

Allow foliage to ripen undisturbed. Do not remove it until after it has turned brown, or the bulbs will not perform well the following year.

To help screen the ripening foliage, you can sow annual seeds in the bulb beds. Do not do this where bulbs must be divided after their leaves have withered, however.

When division is necessary, Dutch and Spanish irises should be dug up after their foliage has died. Leave them in a shaded, airy spot to dry out for three weeks. They can then be separated, stored in a dry place, and replanted in midfall.

Since the foliage of Dutch and Spanish irises develops in the fall, their bulbs must be mulched for protection in cold regions.

Propagating Bulbous Irises by Division

All bulbous irises can be increased by separation of the offset bulbs. This can be done any time after their foliage has ripened and died.

Carefully remove the bulbs from the ground with a spading fork. Gently shake off the soil, and dry them on the surface for a few weeks. Divide the clump into single bulbs, discarding any that show signs of rot. Be sure that each separated bulb has a segment of root attached to it.

Store in a cool, dry place, out of direct sunlight. Replant in the season recommended for each variety. Provide proper drainage, soil type, exposure, and depth of planting.

Large bulbs will flower the following year. Small offsets, however, may need up to two years to reach maturity and begin flowering. Plant offsets 1 inch deep in rows in a seedbed containing light, well-worked soil. Spread a handful of bone meal evenly over each square yard of this soil and mix it in.

When junos are divided, each bulb should have at least one storage root attached. As with initial planting, do not break off this growth, since bulbs will be weakened and will not flower until new roots have developed. It may take two seasons for them to flower.

Never allow the roots of junos to dry out. Replant them immediately after lifting and dividing.

If the bulbs of Dutch and Spanish irises fail to flower after being divided, discard them and order fresh stock from a grower.

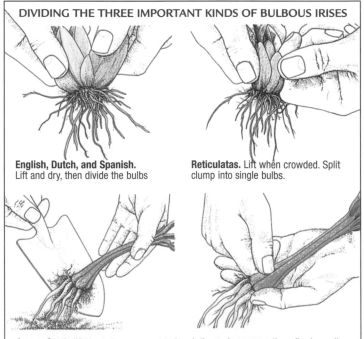

DIVIDING THE THREE IMPORTANT KINDS OF BULBOUS IRISES

English, Dutch, and Spanish. Lift and dry, then divide the bulbs

Reticulatas. Lift when crowded. Split clump into single bulbs.

Junos. Gently lift the bulbs so as not to break the roots; remove the adhering soil. Divide so that each bulb retains a thick storage root; then replant.

PEONIES

Cultivated for more than 2,000 years as ornamental and medicinal plants, long-lived and low-maintenance peonies add a fabulous splash of color to the spring landscape.

Peonies can be divided into two distinct groups, the popular herbaceous ones that die down to the ground each fall, and the less common tree peonies that have a wood stem, often quite short, but still remaining above ground all winter. It is the herbaceous type that most people think of when they hear the word "peony"; tree peonies are neither as hardy nor as readily available.

Herbaceous Peonies

Modern herbaceous peonies are derived mainly from two different species that originated in quite distinct parts of the globe. From southern Europe comes the peony of mythology, *Paeonia officinalis*, which has been in cultivation for centuries, and was long used by apothecaries

as a cure for epilepsy. Peony is named after Paeon, the physician of the Greek gods. Single and double forms of this, in both red and white, were described in literature almost 400 years ago. The other main parent of today's peony is the Asian *P. lactiflora*, or milky flowered peony. This is found in the wild from central Siberia to mid-China, and it was cultivated in China and Japan long before its introduction to Europe in 1656. It has large, single pure white flowers, although occasionally a form with the petals tinged with pink is available as *P. a.* 'Rosea'. While several other species of peony have also been used in producing the peonies we now grow, these two were the main source of modern hybrids.

There are several hundred named

varieties of these peonies in a wide range of colors, many of the most popular ones, like 'Monsieur Jules Elie', were first introduced over 100 years ago. Any good peony catalog will give you a great choice of varieties in a range of flower forms. They also differ in the strength of their perfume, nearly all are scented to some degree, but some are much more fragrant than others. Peony cultivars bloom at different times and are listed as early, mid-season, or late varieties. If planting several new varieties, select ones from different blooming periods to extend the season of flower. Check out www.peonygarden.com and www.songsparrow.com for online pictures of a selection of varieties.

Herbaceous peonies make good

cut flowers and last for a week or more at normal room temperatures. In addition, they can be cut at the bud stage, placed in a refrigerator and be held for up to a month, opening normally when brought into the warmth. They also make ideal dried flowers. Although there is a large commercial trade to supply dried peony flowers to florists, it is easy to dry them at home. Simply cut flowers as soon as they are fully open and hang them upside-down in a dark, airy place for a couple of weeks. Dark colors dry best, pale ones tend to dry a pale brown. In addition to the flowers, the foliage can also be dried to add to winter arrangements. Store in the dark when not being used in arrangements.

Tree Peonies

There are three main parents of the many named forms of tree peony. *P. suffruticosa*, commonly known as the moutan peony, comes in many forms, and the plants that we grow under this name were mostly collected in gardens in China by the early plant explorers. Recent work by Chinese botanists, who searched for species in the wild, has resulted in a reclassification of this single species into four new ones, but these changes will probably take several years to come into common use. They make shrubs up to 5 feet tall with flowers up to 10 inches across in a wide range of colors, including red, pink, white, salmon, and purple. It is native to western China and the first plants reached Europe in 1787, although they had made their way to Japan by 724.

The yellow tones in modern tree peonies come from breeders using *P. lutea* in their work. This species, from southern China, can grow to 6 feet tall with smaller lemon-yellow flowers that are often hidden by the leaves. The third species is also from southern China. *P. delavayi* grows to 5 feet, has its leaves in clusters of three and has dark red

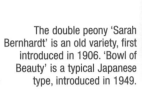
The double peony 'Sarah Bernhardt' is an old variety, first introduced in 1906. 'Bowl of Beauty' is a typical Japanese type, introduced in 1949.

Paeonia lactiflora 'Sarah Bernhardt'

Paeonia lactiflora 'Bowl of Beauty'

nodding flowers, almost black in some plants. It has added maroon tints to modern hybrids.

The foliage on most tree peony hybrids is a pale green and more dissected than that of the herbaceous type. Flowers can be single or double and are generally larger than those of herbaceous peonies. They come in a wide range of colors, often flushed with a different shade, and with pleated petals. Flowers are often on slightly curved stems, so they arch out from the plant, rather than being on top of the stems like herbaceous peony flowers. They are equally good as cut flowers, lasting several days in water.

Dividing tree peonies is difficult because of their wood stem. Until recently they were increased by grafting, a slow and labor-intensive job, resulting in expensive plants. In recent years, they have been reproduced by tissue culture, and the price has dropped considerably.

Toichi Itoh in Japan was the first person to successfully produce a hybrid peony between these distinct groups in 1948. It was not until these seedlings bloomed that the success of this cross was realized. There were only four seedlings but they all had bright yellow petals flushed with red at the base. After his death, an American peony grower brought these plants to North America and since that time many other hybrids have been introduced in apricot, pink, and red tones as well as the original yellows. These hybrids are known as Itoh Hybrids and they have the added advantage of being shorter than regular tree peonies and thus better suited to smaller gardens.

In general, herbaceous peonies are much hardier than the tree types and will survive on the prairies in Zone 2, while tree peonies are only hardy to Zone 5. Tree peonies at the limits of hardiness may be killed back almost to the ground by the cold, and never develop characteristic woody stems. They usually flower every year.

Other Species

There are about 30 species of herbaceous peonies, including two native to North America, but most of these are rarely available. There are some that can be found in specialist nurseries, and occasionally at a local garden center. *P. officinalis* and *P. lactiflora*, the main parents of modern peonies, are not difficult to find and are worth growing.

One of the first peonies to bloom in spring is the cut-leaved peony, *P. anomala*, which has leaves deeply divided into nine finger-width leaflets. The flowers are blood-red with bright yellow stamens in the center. It is native from Russia's Ural Mountains to Siberia and grows 25 inches high and wide.

The most readily available species is probably the fern-leaved peony, *P. tenuifolia*, native to central Europe. This has foliage that is divided into very narrow, almost grasslike leaflets on a smaller plant growing only 20 inches tall. It spreads slowly by thin roots that run just below the soil surface. The flowers are a bright red, slightly cupped and open a few days after those of the cut-leaved peony. There is also a double form, 'Plena', with globe-shaped flowers, and a hard-to-find single pink variety.

The only yellow peony in the herbaceous group is *P. mlokosewitschii*, commonly known as Molly-the-witch. This is also an early bloomer with the round flower buds appearing on the top of the shoots almost as soon as they emerge in spring. The flowers last well on plants that grow 25 inches tall. Foliage turns a bronze-red in fall. It is native to the southeast Caucasus and has been used in hybridizing to produce some of the pale yellow varieties such as 'Claire de Lune'. All these species are hardy to at least Zone 5.

There are many good pictures of almost all the species peonies at www.peonies.org.

FLOWER FORMS

Peony flowers are made up of an outer ring of petals, known as guard petals, and a central group of stamens. These stamens are often modified to resemble narrow petals, although they still produce pollen, and are then known as staminodes. Peony flowers come in several distinctive shapes which have been classified as follows:

Single. A ring of eight to ten petals and central stamens. All the species have single flowers.

Japanese. Similar to single, but the stamens are enlarged and more prominent, and are now called staminodes.

Semi-double. More than one row of petals and twice as many staminodes, but are still open or cup-shaped like the single group.

Crown. A raised crown of frilly petallike staminodes in the center, surrounded by almost flat guard petals.

Bombs. Similar central staminodes, but they are much wider and more closely resemble true petals.

Double. Almost spherical and are made up of petals with the stamens not visible. They are generally infertile.

Paeonia lactiflora 'White Wings'

Paeonia delavayi

'White Wings' is a *P. lactiflora* hybrid with flowers up to 12 in. across and dark green foliage. *P. delavayi* has pale gereen leaves and can reach 5 ft. in height.

Before Planting

Peonies are one of the least demanding perennials known. Provided they receive sunlight, sufficient water, and a winter rest long enough to ensure spring growth, peonies can be left undisturbed for 40 years or more. It is therefore wise to make sure that their planting site is well prepared first. Deeply dig the area, working in plenty of well-rotted manure or compost. Add well-rotted manure or a balanced organic fertilizer blend, at the rate recommended. Avoid lawn fertilizers with a high nitrogen content (first number) as they will promote soft, leafy growth at the expense of good root formation.

Where to Grow

Plant peonies in full sun for best flowering. Growth is best with at least 6 hours sunlight each day. They will grow in part shade but will not flower nearly as freely. Plant well away from competing tree and shrub roots and not too close to paved areas that would shield their roots from rainfall. Tree peonies should be located where they will be protected from cold north and east winds.

They are ideal plants for a perennial border where their lush green foliage acts as a foil for later flowering plants, and, in many varieties, turns a copper color in fall. The height of peony cultivars ranges from about 30 inches to close to 4 feet, so be aware of the final height when locating new plants in an existing bed. Some are good plants for the front, others need to be in the center. Taller varieties are also good choices for foundation plantings. Their foliage shades the foundation in summer, but allows the winter sun to warm it. Plant them at last 25 inches away from the wall, and outside an overhanging roof line so rain can fall on them.

Remove all traces of perennial weeds such as Canada thistle or couch grass. If possible, prepare the site well ahead of planting time so that any missed perennial weed will have time to grow and be removed. In heavy, clay soil, add coarse sand or fine gravel to improve the drainage. Avoid regular builder's sand, which is mostly fine particles and will make the soil set like concrete. In poor, sandy soils, add as much humus as possible, preferably compost. If your only source of organic matter is peat moss, be sure to moisten it first. Soil should be slightly acidic to just alkaline, pH 6.0-7.5, and peonies will grow well with both rhododendrons and most other perennials.

When to Plant

Peony roots have an unusual growth pattern. They develop new feeding roots in autumn, which continue to grow even after the leaves have fallen. This provides the stored energy for the plants to grow the following year. In the spring, as the soil starts to warm, the roots put on another growth spurt which gives the energy for summer growth and flowering.

It follows, therefore, that the time to plant is before these periods of root growth, i.e., in late summer or early fall. In the North, this will be from early September to mid October, but as you move south this could be from late October into late November. If you are ordering plants from a specialist nursery, this is when they will be delivered, bare root. Local nurseries may sell potted peonies in spring, but in most cases they have not been potted for long. If you try to remove them from the pot, most of the soil will fall off. It is preferable to leave the plants in their pots, plunge them in a spare part of the garden to keep the soil from overheating, keep them well watered, and plant them at the correct time, in late summer.

PLANTING PEONIES

Plant peonies with the crown buds 2–3 in. below the soil. Planted deeper, they may not start to flower for several years.

How to Plant

Dig a hole large enough to take the roots without crowding, allowing about 6 inches space all around and beneath the roots. Add some compost or well-rotted manure and a handful of bone meal to the soil removed from the hole. Also work a little more compost into the base of the hole with a small handful of bone meal. It is a good source of potassium, which promotes root growth, but it is slow acting, needing to be broken down by bacteria in the soil. Adding it at planting time will make it available to the plant the following spring. If the plants have come by mail, they will be dry. Soak them in water while you prepare the hole, or preferably overnight.

Place the bare root plant in the hole, holding so that the buds on the crown (where the base of the leaves arise) are 2-3 inches below the soil level. Fill in the hole with the prepared soil, taking care to work it down around the fleshy roots and firming it down well so as not to leave any air pockets. Then water well. Plants set deeper than this will still grow, but likely won't flower for several years. This probably accounts for the old tale that peonies took five years to flower after moving. Most species are less vigorous than the hybrids and should be planted 1 inch deep.

Do not expect a tremendous show of flowers the following spring. There may not be any at all, while the plant is busy recovering from being dug up and divided. The second year should see a few blooms and by year three the plant should be fully recovered and from then on will put on an increasingly impressive floral display.

General Care

Apply a general, all purpose fertilizer in early fall to coincide with the renewed root activity. Use a fertilizer with a low first number, or at least no larger that the remaining two. Apply a mulch of well-rotted manure or compost in late fall, after the leaves have fallen, taking care not to cover the crowns. Once plants are well established, they also benefit from a second fertilizing in early summer as the plants come into flower.

The flowers on many peony hybrids are large and heavy. Left unsupported, they can bend the flowering stems to the ground. Peony

RING SUPPORT

Ring supports can be fixed to several bamboo canes pushed in around the plant.

Often listed as a variety of *Paeonia suffruticosa*, *P. rockii* is the parent of many tree peonies. 'Fairy Princess' is an early flowering variety with a fairly dwarf habit of growth.

Paeonia rockii

Paeonia 'Fairy Princess'

rings of heavy gauge metal on one or two stakes are available, but are expensive. The cages sold for tomatoes are rather flimsy for the weight of a large peony flower and the bases are too small to fit over a mature clump without running the risk of damaging the roots when pushing the rods into the soil. The simplest solution is to use several bamboo canes, pushed in around the plant, with a circle of green horticultural twine tied around them. A single circle about 8 inches below the developing blooms is often enough, but very heavy blooms would benefit from a second circle about 8 inches below this. If green canes are used they are hardly noticed.

As the buds develop, they exude a sticky nectar, usually in the few days before the flowers start to open. The buds often get several ants running over them at this time. They are not doing any damage, simply collecting this sweet nectar and taking it back to their nest. Once the flowers open, the ants disappear.

When flowering is finished, go over the plants and remove the old flower heads, cutting just above the top set of leaves. This removes the seed pods and sends energy that would have gone into seed production into forming the following year's flowers.

The fleshy roots of peonies hold a considerable amount of water, making peonies drought resistant. In arid climates watering may be needed in summer. If so, use an irrigation system that delivers the water at soil level, rather than as an overhead spray. Evaporation is much less and the risk of disease is greatly reduced with dry foliage. Newly planted peonies should be watered regularly during their first summer.

In fall, once the foliage has changed color, it should be removed. As the leaves can carry peony blight, (see What Can Go Wrong With Peonies) they should be disposed of in the garbage.

Dividing Herbaceous Peonies

Although these peonies can be left in one place for many years, if the quality and quantity of blooms starts to decrease, and regular fertilizing doesn't improve things, it may be time to lift and divide your plant. This should be done in late summer or very early fall so that the plant has time to make new roots before winter. A day or two before lifting the plant, and if the soil is dry, give it a good soaking. Then, before digging, cut the foliage 2-4 inches above soil level. If possible, use a spading fork (one with wide tines) rather than a spade to lift the plant. Remember, it has fleshy roots that are the food reserve for future growth. Start digging well away from the crown and gradually remove soil to expose the roots.

Once the plant is out of the soil leave it for several hours to allow the roots to become less brittle, then remove as much soil as possible by hand, eventually washing away any that remains to expose the crown and root system. Trim back any broken roots, the thin ends on the remaining plump storage ones, and the fibrous feeder roots. Close to the old stems, pointed buds (usually either white or pink) will be next years growth. With a sharp knife, divide the crown into pieces, each having three or four of these buds. Replant as shown on p. 79.

Peonies From Seed

Peonies are easy to raise from seed, although the resulting plants may not have flowers of the same color or form. Many hybrids, especially those with double flowers, have their stamens and pistils transformed into petals and are incapable of forming seed; but most of the other flower types will produce seed if the old flowers are not removed. Collect the seed as soon as the seed pod starts to open and sow it in a light, sandy soil, outdoors. Some will germinate

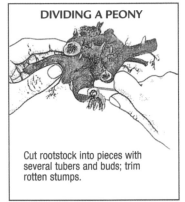

DIVIDING A PEONY

Cut rootstock into pieces with several tubers and buds; trim rotten stumps.

the following spring, and more the one after. Line out into rows once the plants are large enough to handle. It will take at least three years before

What Can Go Wrong With Peonies

While peonies are relatively trouble-free if properly positioned and grow-

flowers appear, and the first ones may not be typical of the flowers that will be produced in the years following. Be selective, and prepared to discard the majority of the seedlings, as most of the plants will not be improvements on their parents. Both herbaceous and tree peonies can be grown in this way.

Peonies From Layers

Where tree peonies can be grown without too much winter dieback, it is possible to propagate them by layering; by bending a low-growing shoot down to the soil, wounding it, and holding it in place with a peg. See Layering—New Plants From a Growing Shoot on page 262.

For more information go to the American Peony Society's website at www.americanpeonysociety.org.

ing in good soil, they do have occasional problems. If plants show symptoms that are not described below, turn to the section on plant disorders on page 506.

SYMPTOMS AND SIGNS	CAUSE	CONTROL
Flower buds fail to develop and rarely get above pea size.	Immaturity, cold, or insufficient nutrients	In new transplants there may not be enough energy to support flowers the first year. With mature plants, it could be caused by late spring frosts after growth has begun, or by a lack of potassium in the soil.
Stems turn black and leaves wilt.	Peony blight	Remove below infection, do not allow to contact healthy foliage, dispose of in garbage. Sterilize pruners with rubbing alcohol. If problem persists, spray with Bordeaux mixture.
Plants become weak, stunted, and fail to bloom.	Root-knot nematodes	No control. Dig out, discard, and do not plant peonies in same location for 10 years.
Holes in leaves, or leaves almost eaten entirely.	Japanese or rose-chafer beetles	Hand pick if the infestation is slight, spray with neem if heavy.

DAYLILIES

Probably North America's favorite perennial,
there are more new daylilies introduced each year
than in any other single genus.

Although native to Japan, and often wrongly called tiger lilies, the common tawny daylily has become so well entrenched in this continent that it has become a common roadside weed. In part, this is due to its toughness. Plants that are dug up from a garden and discarded along a roadway rarely die, they put down roots and thrive. They are known as daylilies because in many of the species the flowers open in late afternoon and die the following day.

The first daylilies were sent to Europe from Korea, China, and Japan before 1600, but were not thought to be very important. It was not until 1892 that an English schoolteacher crossbred some of the species and introduced a named variety, 'Apricot'. His work was soon reinforced by other European breeders and before long there were well over a hundred cultivars, some of which are still available.

This work was soon duplicated in North America and the first hybrid was described here in 1899. It was in the 1920's that the Curator of Education at the New York Botanical Garden began his life's work on daylily hybridizing. Dr. Arlow Stout was the first person to introduce pink shades into hybrids and eventually registered nearly 100 cultivars from the many thousands of seedlings he raised. Some, like 'Mikado', are still available commercially, while others have been used to produce more modern hybrids. The Stout Silver Medal, the highest award of the American Hemerocallis Society, is named in his honor.

In recent years, many others have taken up the challenge and have introduced daylilies in a wide range of heights, colors, and blooming times. Flowers may be single or double, or occasionally even triple. They can be almost white or so dark a red that they appear nearly black, and any shade in between. The one exception is blue, although breeders are getting closer to unearthing blue. Some of the modern varieties bloom almost continually from late spring until fall, but most have a more limited season.

The Species

In total, there are about 30 different species of daylily, although only about half of these are used in hybridizing and four are quite often grown in gardens.

The citron daylily, *Hemerocallis citrina*, has lemon-scented, bright yellow flowers in midsummer. It grows 40 inches tall and flowers prolifically. The flowers open in late afternoon and last until about noon the next day. It has been used by breeders to bring fragrance into hybrids.

Hemerocallis dumortieri is known as the early daylily and has pale orange flowers in early spring. Widely grown, it makes a good ground cover, especially on banks. The fleshy roots are edible, as are the buds and flowers. It is a smaller plant, 12–24 inches tall, and both the height and earliness have been incorporated in some modern hybrids.

The common roadside lily is *H. fulva*, which spreads by underground roots and can be invasive. Like all daylilies it grows best in full sun but can also be grown in part shade. The double form, 'Kwanso', is also widely grown and has naturalized itself. There is a form with single flowers and variegated foliage, but this is not nearly as vigorous.

The first daylily to open in spring is *H. lilioasphodelus* (which may be called *H. flava* in catalogs), the lemon daylily. Growing almost 4 feet tall, this has very fragrant lemon yellow flowers on an upright plant. Blooms open in the morning, last overnight, and into the next day. Plant this near a patio where it will scent the air.

'Catherine Woodbery' has slightly ruffled tepals with a lavender sheen overlaying the orchid pink. The tepals on 'Pink Damask' recurve slightly and the throat is pale yellow.

Hemerocallis 'Catherine Woodbery'

Hemerocallis 'Pink Damask'

FLOWER TYPES

Trumpet. Traditional lily shape.

Flaring. Unusually open with rather flat petals and sepals.

Recurved. Petals and sepals stretch back from throat.

Circular. Flower appears quite round because of the shape of petals and sepals.

Double. In addition to three petals and three sepals, extra flower segments result in blooms.

Star. Long, pointed petals and sepals with spaces between.

Spider. Petals and sepals are quite narrow throughout their length.

Dormant or Evergreen?

Most nursery catalogs add a designation on a daylily's type of growth. On dormant plants, foliage turns brown in the fall and the plant rests for the winter like most other perennials. On evergreen plants the leaves remain green over winter. Those classified as semi-evergreen will remain green where the climate is mild—although the foliage may brown at the top—but go dormant where it is cold.

In general, dormant varieties are hardier and better suited to northern climates. Many will not survive where winters are warm because they require a period of cold. Evergreen varieties are better suited to mild regions, but a surprising number will survive where winters are cold, even if they are covered in snow. Because many daylily breeders live in the South, a large percentage of modern hybrids, with their bright colors and interesting flower forms, are evergreen. Northern gardeners should give them a try, especially if you can obtain them from a specialist nursery nearby, rather than from a distant catalog source.

Diploids and Tetraploids

The species of daylily contain 22 chromosomes in each cell, as do many modern hybrids. These are known as "diploids." In the late 1930's it was found that treating sprouting seeds or seedlings with colchicines, a chemical extracted from the autumn crocus, *Colchicum*, would sometimes double the number of chromosomes in each cell. This has been done to a considerable number of varieties, which have since been crossed to produce new cultivars which are known as "tetraploids" or tets.

There is no obvious difference in the plant, although it may be more vigorous. At flowering time the flowers are generally larger, with thicker petals, more individual blooms, and more side branches on each flower stem. However, many of the modern

diploids also have large flowers and improved growth habits, and it is often difficult to tell if a plant is diploid or tetraploid, even in bloom.

Types of Flowers

Modern plant breeders have produced daylilies with a range of flower shapes and color patterns. In most plants in the lily family, where the outer sepals and inner petals are almost identical, they are collectively known as tepals. In each of the following descriptions (left), the flowers can be almost flat, cupped, or trumpet-shaped, and the tips of the tepals may lie flat or be recurved. Flowers are composed of two rings of three tepals each, offset so that each ring is visible. The tepals in each circle may be the same size, or the upper set may be larger.

A daylily is said to be a miniature when the flowers are less than 3 inches in diameter. These are generally found on low growing varieties, but not always.

In addition to the flower forms shown at left, blooms are often marked with a contrasting band of color, known as an eyezone or halo. This depends on how close the band is to the throat, and whether there is a different color in the throat. Some have a flush of a different shade of the base color spreading from the throat, while others have darker veins adding contrast. Tepals may be flat or pleated, with edges that resemble crumpled paper. In addition, the two rings of tepals may be different shades of the same color or entirely different colors. See Color Markings on page 83.

FLOWER PATTERNS

Self. Petals and sepals are same color.

Bitone. Both petals and sepals are of a different shade of same color.

Blend. Petals and sepals are a blend of two colors.

Bicolor. Petals and sepals are of totally different colors.

Hemerocallis 'Stella de Oro'

Hemerocallis 'Eenie Weenie'

Two miniature daylilies. 'Stella de Oro' flowers from late spring to fall. 'Eenie Weenie' has even smaller flowers and is also an extended bloomer.

COLOR MARKINGS

Band. A different or darker colored band on the petals only at the point where the flower segments join the throat.

Eyezone. A different or darker colored band on both petals and sepals at the point where the flower segments join the throat.

Halo. A very faint, or only slightly visible, band of a different or darker color.

Watermark. A wide stripe of a very light shade where the color of the petals and sepals joins the throat.

Preparing the Site

Daylilies are long lived and can remain in the same place for several years, so soil preparation before planting is important. If planting in a new area, or renovating an existing bed, take the time to remove all perennial weeds by carefully forking them out. Never use a tiller on this type of weed because that would chop them into small pieces, each of which grows. Having removed the weeds, if possible, wait a few weeks to see if missed pieces start to grow, and remove them.

Lighten very heavy soils by adding humus in some form, such as compost or well-rotted manure. If planting a new bed, spread a layer about 3 inches deep over the bed and dig it in. If adding individual plants to an existing bed, work extra humus into each planting hole. The same applies to light, sandy soils, which need the humus to help retain moisture. Daylilies are known for being heavy feeders and have a deep root system. For these reasons, the addition of humus is very beneficial, and the soil should be dug as deeply as possible, rather than being tilled since most home tillers only work the soil relatively shallowly. They will grow in almost all types of soil and in a wide range of acidic and alkaline conditions, from pH 5.5 to 7.5, so there is seldom need to amend the soil pH to accommodate them.

How to Plant Daylilies

If new plants arrive by mail, soak them for an hour before planting. This is not needed if the plants are pieces off old clumps in your own garden. Space the plants about 24 inches apart, more for vigorous varieties and slightly less for miniature ones.

Dig a hole large enough to take the roots without crowding and work some compost into the soil you remove. Fill the hole with water and allow it to soak away to ensure the surrounding soil is moist. Put some of the prepared soil in the hole and adjust the amount so that the crown of the plant—where the roots and shoots meet—is at soil level. Fill in around the plant, working the soil between the roots with your fingers. Firm the soil well in place, leaving a very slight depression to retain water. Unless your memory is excellent, label the new plant with the variety name, then you will know what color it is when not in bloom.

Immediately after planting, water thoroughly. Then water every other day for the first two weeks—unless it rains heavily—to help the plants become established.

After planting and watering, mulch around the plants with any available material, including shredded bark, compost, partly decomposed leaves, hay, cocoa hulls, etc. Apply a generous layer to conserve moisture, but keep it clear of the plant crowns.

Watering, Feeding, and General Cultivation

In many parts of the country, natural rainfall will be enough to keep established daylilies growing well because of their deep root system. Where summers are dry, watering will be needed if the plants are to produce blooms over a long period. Overhead watering tends to leave marks on the tepals, especially on red and orange varieties. It is therfore advisable to apply water by soaker hoses laid along the soil, or by watering systems that wind between the plants and have an individual emitter for each plant. Where summers are hot, evening watering is preferable since less is lost by evaporation.

Feed new plants in spring the first year after planting, using an organic slow-release fertilizer such as alfalfa pellets (available from farm supply stores). Apply a small handful around each plant and water with a diluted liquid manure tea a couple of times the first summer. Once they are established, do not apply fertilizer as this will promote foliage at the expense of flowers. Instead, add a further layer of a mulch, such as well-rotted manure. After a few years, if blooming is poor and few new growth fans are producing, feed in spring with an organic fertilizer at about half the recommended rate.

Daylilies have strong flower stalks and rarely need staking. The main summer jobs are weed control and removing old blooms. This is not essential, but adds to the appearance of the plants. Some varieties shed their old flowers readily and will need little attention, while on others, the old flowers remain for several days and can even hinder the opening of new buds. Also, remove any seedpods that form—they snap off easily—so that energy goes into flowering rather than seed production. Once flowering is over, remove the old flower stalks by cutting them at the base.

In fall, leave the dead foliage in place in harsh climates, it helps protect the crown and is easy to pull off in spring. Where winters are mild, it is immaterial if the foliage of dormant varieties is removed in fall or spring.

The 3 in. flowers of 'Pardon Me' are typical lily-shaped, while those of 'Bonanza', are star-shaped and 4 in. across.

Hemerocallis 'Pardon Me'

Hemerocallis 'Bonanza'

Propagating Daylilies

Unlike many perennials, daylilies can be left in place for several years, but eventually the plants will be old, the soil will become depleted of nutrients, and flowering will be poor. It is then time to lift and divide the plants. This is done in the same way as other perennials (see below). Do not try to divide the plants into very small pieces because they will take longer to establish and bloom well. Aim for divisions with at least three fans, and preferably four or five.

A very large clump can be split into sections with a spade before lifting, this makes it easier to dig out as the individual pieces are more manageable. The individual pieces can then be divided into planting size using a knife to cut the crown into sections. If you just want a piece of a clump to give to a friend, this can be cut out of the side of a clump in the same way, without lifting the entire plant.

Dividing daylilies is normally done in spring, and this is the best time in colder regions; the plants then have all summer to recover before the stress of winter. In warmer climates they can be split at almost any time, even when in flower if necessary, providing they will be replanted very quickly.

Daylilies are easy to grow from seed and take two to three years to produce their first bloom. Collect seeds from the pods as soon as they turn brown and start to open. The seeds need a cold treatment to germinate well, several weeks below 41°F is required. Either store the seeds in a refrigerator until midwinter and then sow indoors under fluorescent light, or keep them in the refrigerator all winter and sow outside in spring. In warm regions sow directly outside in fall and let winter give the cold, but this is not recommended where winters are harsh.

The resulting seedlings will vary greatly in desirability and many will be no improvement on your existing varieties, but keep them for a couple of years, sometimes the flowers show hidden charms as they mature. Be prepared to discard a very large percentage of open pollinated seedlings—those that were pollinated by bees, rather than as controlled crosses. For information on how to cross-pollinate daylilies, go to the American Hemerocallis Society website at daylilies.org. A very good site for pictures, where you can see the different flower types and markings, and access numerous links to other daylily sites, is abacom.comchacha/garden.htm.

DIVIDING A DAYLILY

1. A large healthy clump can be split in several parts with a sharp spade.

2. The entire clump may be dug up and the fans cut apart with a knife

What Can Go Wrong With Daylilies

Daylilies are fairly trouble-free and the few problems they have are seldom serious. Check the foliage often for the first signs of trouble, during flowering check the flowers also for signs of damage or spotting. See page 506 for symptoms not listed in the box at right.

SYMPTOMS AND SIGNS	CAUSE	CONTROL
Plant wilts, crown becomes soft and smells bad.	Bacterial soft rot	Lift plant immediately, scrape off all diseased material, soak in a 50% bleach solution for 10 minutes. Replant in a different location. Most common on sites with a high water table.
Small insects in clusters on foliage and buds. Leaves become sticky and may turn yellowish.	Aphids	Spray with a strong stream of water or apply insecticidal soap.
In spring, a healthy plant turns yellowish and stops growing, or leaves become twisted and crinkled.	Spring sickness	Cause is unknown, some varieties are more prone than others. Plants generally recover when weather warms up.
White cottonlike threads appear in the crown, bearing small black fruiting bodies. Plant may turn yellow.	Mustard seed fungus also known as southern blight. More likely in warm climates.	Spray with Bordeaux mixture if slight. If serious, dig up plant, soak in Bordeaux mixture and replant in a different location.
Holes in leaves and flowers, beetles often present on foliage.	Japanese beetles (large) or cucumber beetles (small) or several others.	Spray with neem or handpick if infestation is only small.
Flowers either fail to open properly or have small pale spots when they do open.	Thrips	Very small insects that feed on the developing buds by sucking their sap. Spray with insecticidal soap. It may be necessary to start spraying in spring, following a bad infestation the previous year.
Foliage has a bronzy sheen, very fine webs on underside of leaves and on flower stems.	Spider mites	Almost invisible to the naked eye, their presents is only seen by the damage, spray with insecticidal soap, especially the undersides of the leaves.
Holes in flowers, insects hiding in flower throat by day.	Earwigs	More of a nuisance unless numerous. Put out traps of short lengths of pipe, pots filled with straw, etc., and empty daily into containers of soapy water.

HOSTAS

Once known as Funkia and plantain lily, hostas are deservedly popular as the perfect shade plant. Although grown mainly for their patterned foliage, some varieties have attractive, fragrant flowers.

Cultivated in China and Japan for centuries, hostas made their way to North America from plants sent to Europe around 1780 when the French consul to Macao in southern China sent seeds to the Jardin des Plantes in Paris. This was germinated and described in 1789 as *Hemerocallis plantaginea*. Now called *Hosta plantaginea*, this is still grown for its late flowering and fragrant blooms.

Soon after the 1789 germination, an English nurseryman imported live plants of two hosta species, which were initially grown in greenhouses. It was about another 50 years before the German, Philipp von Siebold, working for the Dutch East India Company in Nagasaki, Japan, started to send back many different forms of hosta collected in Japanese gardens. Some of these eventually made their way to North America.

Thomas Hogg, who was a nurseryman on Manhattan Island, was sent to Japan by President Lincoln to fill the post of U.S. Marshall. During his stay he collected and purchased many different hostas, as well as other species, that he shipped back to the family nursery. From there they went to gardens across the nation, and to Europe. Two different variegated hostas that he introduced became known as *Funkia* 'Thomas Hogg', and his name is still used in descriptions occasionally.

By the early 1920's hostas were well established and widely grown, initially as ground covers in cemeteries, but increasingly in private gardens. The number of hostas available from nurseries grew slowly and by the 1940's several nurseries across the northern United States and in Canada were offering a wide selection. The introduction of a chance mutation in a nursery row, noticed by Frances Williams, brought hostas to the forefront of popularity and sparked the rapid growth of hybridizing and the introduction of several hundred new varieties over the years. This mutation differed from the regular gray-green form of *H. sieboldiana* by having the leaves edged in yellow. It was eventually grown by several other nurseries who sold it under different names, such as 'Yellow Edge' and *Aureus marginatus*, but eventually was registered as *H.* 'Frances Williams' and is probably the most popular of the named forms of hosta. This hosta sparked the rise in popularity of the plant and encouraged others to develop new hybrids. Today there are well over 1,000 named varieties of hostas.

Which Hostas Should You Grow?

Hostas vary greatly in size, from the very small, like 'Tiny Tears' that grows only 2 inches high, to the huge, like 'Sum and Substance' that grows 30 inches tall and 5 feet across. Leaf color varies from a very glaucous blue, through dark, mid, and light green to shades of yellow, depending on the variety. The most popular forms of hostas are those with variegated foliage. They can have green margins with a central area of white, yellow, or a different green; or the reverse: a green center and a colored edging. In some forms there are irregular bands of different shades around the leaf.

The leaf color determines to an extent where to locate a specific variety. Forms with blue foliage need shade and will burn badly if planted in full sun, even in the North. Yellow foliage, on the other hand, is more sun tolerant and these varieties can take a considerable amount of sunshine—all day in the North and only needing midday shade in warmer regions. Variegated forms differ in their tolerance to sun. Look at similar plants in local gardens to see how well they stand up to direct sunlight.

Leaf shape and substance also varies. Some varieties have narrow, lance-shaped leaves that are soft, while others have almost circular foliage that can be dinner-plate size and stiff. In some forms the leaves are smooth and almost flat, while others have foliage that is puckered and corrugated with wavy edges.

Although they are grown chiefly for their foliage, many varieties have attractive flowers. These vary from white, through shades of lilac, to a red-tinged mauve and purple. They also vary in shape from starlike to tubular. A few, like 'Honeybells' and 'Sugar and Cream' even have fragrant flowers. Depending on the

Both of these hostas have white flowers in midsummer, those of 'Royal Standard' are fragrant. The blue foliage of *H. sieboldiana* 'Elegans' will burn in bright sunlight.

Hosta sieboldiana 'Elegans'

Hosta 'Royal Standard'

FLOWER TYPES

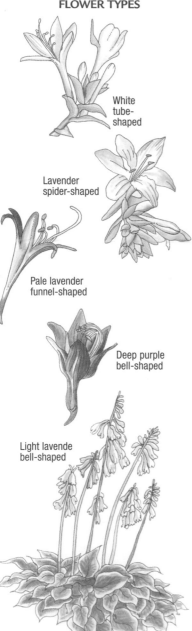

White tube-shaped

Lavender spider-shaped

Pale lavender funnel-shaped

Deep purple bell-shaped

Light lavende bell-shaped

variety, they bloom from midsummer onward, with the fragrant *H. plantaginea* being the last to bloom in early fall.

A great number of hosta pictures can be found online. Several hundred varieties are shown at www.hostalibrary.org, often with several pictures of each showing both foliage and flowers. For general information on culture, visit the American Hosta Society website at www.hosta.org.

Where to Plant Hostas

Variegated hostas do a wonderful job of brightening up shady areas, either on the north side of the house or under shrubs. There are so many different varieties available that a planting can be a feature on its own, but they blend well with other shade-loving plants. Adding the occasional blue-leaved variety will give contrast. For small townhouse gardens, there is a hosta to fit any available space, either a miniature form or a stately specimen plant.

Hostas make good ground cover and varieties such as 'Groundmaster' and 'Francee' spread slowly by underground runners. Even in quite sunny locations the green lance-leaved hosta, *H. lancifolia* will quickly make a dense carpet. The readily available *H. undulata* 'Univittata', which has mid-green leaves with a large irregular white middle, will also take considerable sun and makes a good ground cover or edging plant.

Providing they are given adequate water until well established, some

LEAF SHAPES

Lance-shaped

Twisted, curly leaf

Heart-shaped

Dinner-plate, stiff and puckered

varieties of hosta will grow well in dry shade. This may be shaded areas in regions where the summers are arid, or in locations, such as under a large tree that sheds rainfall and has roots close to the surface. Variegated forms, such as undulate 'Albo-marginata', 'Francee', and 'Ginko Craig' will do well as will blue forms like 'Blue Boy' and 'Blue Angel', and green ones like 'Candy Hearts', *H. lancifolia*, and *H. tokudama*.

Other varieties will definitely grow well in moist locations, not actually with their roots in water, but close to a pond or stream where the soil is always moist. Try *H. fortunei* 'Aureo-marginata', 'Tall Boy', or the yellow 'Sum and Substance' in this sort of situation. These varieties will grow equally well in normal garden soil.

Hostas grow well in containers and can be used in this way on patios, beside doorways, or even as an indoor foliage plant in winter. One advantage of growing them in containers is that they are less prone to

slug damage. They are hardy to about -40°F and can survive being left outside in a container over winter. Grow them in a soil-based mix, rather than in a soilless, peat based mix as these dry out too quickly and are difficult to rehydrate.

There are a number of varieties suitable for growing in a shaded rock garden, or in a small trough garden. All of the following are under 10 inches in height. 'Blue Moon' is blue-green with bell-shaped white flowers; 'Chartreuse Wiggles' has bright green leaves with wavy edges and purple flowers; 'Elfin Power' is a mid-green with the leaves edged with white, and lavender flowers; the leaves on 'Lemon Lime' are a bright lime green to yellow, with bell-shaped purple flowers; 'Saishu Jima' is named for an island off the Korean peninsula and has mid-green leaves and purple flowers; 'Vanilla Cream' is yellow with wavy-edged leaves and lavender flowers. There are many other small varieties available from specialist growers.

Preparing the Site and Planting

Hostas are almost permanent residents of the garden and need to be left in one location for several years to develop their full potential. It is therefore wise to spend time enriching and improving the soil so that

they will grow to mature size. Clean the site of all perennial weeds and cultivate as deeply as possible, at least to a full spade depth. If time allows, wait a few weeks before planting to give any missed pieces of weed time to root and grow and be removed. If the soil is either very heavy or very sandy, dig in a good

layer (at least 3 inches) of compost, old manure, or other source of humus. If the soil is in fairly good condition, a thinner layer will suffice, but the plants will be there for several years so the better the soil the longer they will go on growing well.

Hostas grow best in a slightly acidic soil with a pH of around 6.0,

'Golden Tiara' is a medium-sized hosta that does well in dappled shade and has lilac flowers in mid-summer. The taller 'Francee' can take a little more sun and has paler flowers in late summer.

Hosta 'Golden Tiara'   *Hosta* 'Francee'

HOSTA VARIEGATIONS

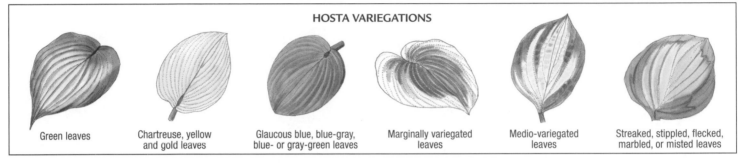

Green leaves

Chartreuse, yellow and gold leaves

Glaucous blue, blue-gray, blue- or gray-green leaves

Marginally variegated leaves

Medio-variegated leaves

Streaked, stippled, flecked, marbled, or misted leaves

but seem to survive in more alkaline soils, around 7.5, just as well A pH that is too high will make the leaves on blue-leaved varieties look dull and slightly brown.

The best time to plant hostas is in the early spring, just as the new shoots are emerging, and if you are buying by mail order, this is when they should arrive. Many local nurseries pot their plants in early spring

Growing Hostas in the Garden

One of the least demanding plants, hostas can be left to take care of themselves once established; however they perform better with a little care and attention. In fall, once the foliage has died down and been cleared away, surround the plants with a mulch of compost or rotted leaf mold, taking care not to cover the crown of the plant. In spring, check the new growth to make sure the mulch is not touching the shoots and add organic fertilizer. Where slugs and snails are especially troublesome, remove the mulch in spring since it attracts even more of them. (see box on page 88)

Hostas, especially the large varieties are very demanding of nutrients and can quickly deplete the soil. For best growth, add an organic fertilizer, such as alfalfa pellets, in spring once the foliage starts to unfurl. The amount required depends on the size

and sell them as container grown well into summer. These can be planted any time the weather is not too hot if you protect the new plants from drying winds and give adequate water.

For hostas that will eventually grow large, like 'Krossa Regal' and 'Sum and Substance', dig a hole large enough to plant a shrub, about 40 inches wide by 18 inches deep. Add

and age of the individual plant; a light sprinkle may be enough for small varieties, while two handfuls may be needed for an established large-leaved one. Let plant growth be your guide, you can always add more pellets if growth is poor.

Newly planted hostas will need regular watering for the first year. Large varieties will only need watering in prolonged periods of drought. If varieties with shiny leaves start to look dull, they need watering. Small varieties will need watering more often because their roots are not deep. The best way to water is to apply it close to the crown of the plant, under the foliage, using a hose with a wand or a watering can. Overhead watering is not as effective because the foliage tends to shed the water away from the root zone. In a mixed border, where it is necessary to use an oscillating sprinkler, water in early morning or late afternoon, water droplets on hosta leaves in bright sunlight can burn them.

compost or well-rotted manure and work into the bottom of the hole and cover this with a layer of the excavated soil. Plant the hosta on a mound of soil in the middle of the hole with the roots spread down the sides of the mound, making sure the roots do not come into contact with any manure. Fill in around the roots, and firm well. Use the same technique for smaller varieties with an appropriate sized

If you are growing hostas in containers, remember the amount of soil is very limited and the plants will need additional feeding during the summer. Since they will require watering as well, the easiest way to apply a feed, such as fish emulsion, is with the water. Either use at full strength once a month or use at one-quarter strength with every watering.

Hostas are the ideal plant to associate with a Japanese-style garden. Their form blends well with the Japanese image and they look completely in place with the bamboo fencing and dwarf maples or carefully pruned pines that one finds in this type of garden. Even if the garden is small, there is a hosta of a suitable size to complement it. A Japanese stone lantern can look intrusive out on its own, but partly cover the base with hosta foliage and it seems a natural part of the landscape. The edges of a small reflective pool can be softened by using hostas with foliage in varying shades of green.

hole but add more humus to the surrounding soil close to the surface. For container-grown hostas, prepare the soil as previously mentioned and set the plants in the hole with the crown just at soil level. When you remove the plant from its pot, if the roots form a solid ball, gently tease some of the outer ones free before planting. Water well with compost tea and add a mulch of compost.

New Plants From Old

Hostas produce abundant seed which germinates very readily, but the resulting seedlings are probably not an improvement on the parent plant. Unless you are making controlled crosses and are prepared to discard 99 percent of the seedlings, growing them from seed is not worth the effort and time involved.

The best way to increase your plants is by division. If you want only one extra plant of a particular variety, cut a slice from the mature clump with a spade, as though you were slicing a cake. Fill the hole with fresh soil and the clump will soon grow back to fill the gap. This is best done in early spring when the new shoots are just showing, if left until the leaves have unfurled, they may be severely damaged.

Large established clumps can also be lifted and divided like other perennials (see page 40) but the rootstock is very woody and will need cutting,

The foliage of 'Halcyon' is narrow when young, becoming wider with age. In hot climates *H. fortunei* 'Albopicta' fades in color and loses its distinctive variegation as summer progresses.

Hosta 'Halcyon'

Hosta f. 'Albopicta'

or even chopping, apart. Discard the woody center and replant pieces from the outside. Some varieties spread by runners and underground shoots, these are easy to divide and will readily break up into small plants. This can be done in spring or early fall.

Varieties that are slow to increase—ones that grow slowly and take several years to become large enough to divide—can be induced to produce more basal buds. In spring or early summer, at the time when the leaf buds are just starting to unfurl, carefully scrape the soil away around the crown of the plant to expose the basal plate where the roots arise. Push a thin sharp knife into the stem, just above the plate, and cut down through it. Further cuts can be made at right angles. Repack

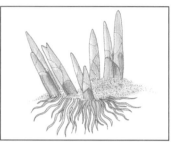

1. In spring, carefully scrape the soil away around the crown of the plant to expose the basal plate where the roots arise.

2. Push a thin sharp knife into the stem just above the plate and cut down through it.

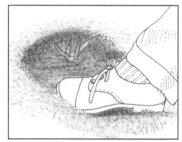

3. Repack the soil around the stem and water well.

the soil around the stem and water well (see steps 1, 2, and 3, above). By the time fall arrives, each wounded area should have produced growth buds and the plant can then be dug up, divided into four pieces and replanted.

Controlling Slugs and Snails

The chief enemy of hostas are slugs and snails, especially the small ones that are hard to find. They come out at night and eat holes in the foliage, leaving it lacelike after a few weeks. Some varieties are more resistant to damage than others and those with thick, crinkled leaves are less likely to be damaged than those with thin soft foliage.

Control is difficult. Hand pick slugs and snails at night with a flashlight, dropping them into a can of insecticidal soap or light oil. Shallow containers, buried to their rims in the soil and filled with beer attract and kill both pests. Small plants can be protected by putting a ring of diatomaceous earth around them, but it needs to be replenished after rain or watering. If only a few plants are involved, a copper tape barrier will keep the slugs and snails at bay. These pests are repelled by a mild electric reaction which occurs as they try to cross the barrier. If copper tape is not readily available, empty a jar of pennies to make the barrier.

What Can Go Wrong With Hostas

Hostas are relatively trouble-free, but they do have occasional problems and should be checked regularly for the first signs of trouble. If plants show symptoms that are not described below, turn to the section on plant disorders on page 506.

SYMPTOMS AND SIGNS	CAUSE	CONTROL
Holes in leaves, silver trails on foliage	Slugs and snails	Difficult to control completely, see left.
Sudden wilting, especially with potted plants, or semi-circular holes in leaf edge.	Vine weevils	Re-pot into fresh soil, look for white grubs in old soil and kill them. Adults eat foliage, spray with insecticidal soap.
Leaves completely eaten, often overnight.	Deer or rabbits	Other than surrounding the garden with a tall fence, deer control is very difficult. For rabbits, surround plants with a fine wire mesh buried into the soil and 3 ft. high.
Foliage yellows and pulls away from crown easily.	Crown rot (fungus)	Dig up plant, scrape away all diseased tissue, dust with sulfur and replant in fresh location. More common where summers are hot and humid or in poorly drained sites.
Brown spots on leaves.	Leaf spot (fungus) or frost or sun damage	Spray with fungicidal soap. Protect new growth in spring from late frosts. Don't water overhead in bright sunlight.
Leaves distorted, often with irregular pale and thinner areas.	Virus	Slow to appear, it can take several years for a plant to show symptoms. Spreads easily when dividing, removing blooms, etc., from hands or knife blade. Dig up infected plants and destroy. Don't plant hostas on same site for 2 years.

HOSTAS LEAST LIKELY TO SHOW DAMAGE FROM SLUGS AND SNAILS

'Big Daddy'	'Green Sheen'
'Blue Angel'	'Green Wedge'
'Blue Cadet'	'Krossa Regal'
'Blue Umbrellas'	'Midas Touch'
'Bold Ruffles'	'Pizzazz'
'Christmas Tree'	'Sea Drift'
'Frances Williams'	'Spritzer'
	'Sum and
'Fringe Benefit'	Substance'
'Gold Edger'	*tokudama* (and
'Gold Regal'	forms)
'Green Fountain'	'Zounds'
'Green Piecrust'	

CHRYSANTHEMUMS

Varied colors, shapes, and sizes help make chrysanthemums some of the most versatile and popular plants in the world.

Reflexing incurve

Intermediate incurve

Semi-double

Spider

Irregular incurve

Spray

Regular incurve

Chrysanthemums are unequaled for their late-summer and fall blooms. They flower for three to eight weeks with blossoms that range from tiny buttons to immense globes 8 or more inches across. Blossoming periods are triggered by the shortening days of late summer. It is then that the plants' energies switch from vegetative growth to flower production.

Chrysanthemums are often categorized by their response time, the elapsed time from when buds appear until flowers bloom. This can be six to seven weeks for low-growing bushy types or up to 12 weeks for other varieties. Catalogs often provide approximate flowering times.

Used to describe the low, cushion types, the term "hardy chrysanthemums" is somewhat misleading. Roots of all perennial chrysanthemums can withstand temperatures slightly below freezing. It is alternate freezing and thawing that causes most winterkill by lifting these shallow-rooted plants out of the ground.

One way to prevent this is to dig up the plants after they have bloomed and store them in a cold frame. Another is to store them on the ground along the north side of a building and cover them with straw. Plants in very well drained soil may be left there and covered with 2–4 inches of loose mulch after the ground freezes.

For more information on chrysanthemum culture visit the National Chrysanthemum Society website at www.mums.org.

Purchasing Plants by Mail

Snow may still be on the ground when the first chrysanthemum catalogs arrive. It is then that the gardener's imagination takes flight, envisioning the colorful flowers in the catalog blooming in the garden. Bear in mind that too many varieties will lessen the overall effect when the plants flower. Also, it may cost less to order three plants of one variety than one each of three types.

The plants are shipped with their roots carefully packed in material that maintains their moisture. Even if they should appear dry upon arrival, the plants will probably recover if they stand overnight in water. Next, transfer them to containers or, weather permitting, to their permanent locations.

Making Softwood Cuttings

Because new basal growth around an old chrysanthemum clump is pliable, the term "softwood" is used. To make a cutting, remove a new 2½- to 3-inch long stem growing from the base of the old clump in late spring.

Since chrysanthemum stolons spread out, trace each growth back to its parent before removal. This way you can avoid mix-ups with other plants. Carefully pinch off the lower leaves of the new growth, but do not strip skin from the stem. Using a razor blade, sever the plant stem just below a leaf joint.

Insert cuttings into 1-inch-deep holes set 2 inches apart in a rooting medium—washed sand, or mixtures containing peat moss, perlite, and vermiculite; the proportions are not critical as long as the mixture is kept moist but not soggy.

To protect the cuttings from infestation, dip them in a combination insecticidal and fungicidal soap before planting. For extra-fast rooting, dip the bottom ends of the cuttings in a rooting hormone powder. Place cuttings in a bottom-heated propagator or in a cold frame.

A week after the cuttings have been set out, carefully lift one and examine it for roots. When the roots are half an inch long, remove the cuttings from the rooting medium, and transplant them to pots or boxes, or directly into the ground.

'Clara Curtis,' with its simple rose-colored blossoms, is a good garden form. *Chrysanthemum weyrichii*, a carpet-forming species, is an ideal edging plant.

Chrysanthemum 'Clara Curtis'

Chrysanthemum weyrichii

Chrysanthemums in the Garden

Preparing Beds for Garden Mums

Once established, chrysanthemums need a predominantly sunny exposure, an evenly sustained food supply, and plenty of space around them to develop properly. Their roots require a soil that is loose and drains well after a heavy rain. A soil that is too soggy during either the growing season or the winter resting period will adversely affect growth and subsequent survival.

To overcome the difficulties imposed by compacted clay soil and poor drainage, try planting chrysanthemums in raised beds. Such beds can be made by using a 6- to 8-inch-high wood frame or a 4-inch-high cinder-block enclosure.

A growing medium of compost and leaf mold combined with a sandy or clayey soil is ideal for supplying the organic material and slightly acid conditions under which chrysanthemum plants thrive.

Though chrysanthemums can be planted at any time after the last frost date, the bloom date will be approximately the same for all plants in a particular response group, whether they are planted early or late. Early planting, therefore, offers no significant advantage. On the contrary, it may result in plants taller than the gardener desires.

Planting Out and Spacing

Left to themselves, cushion mums can spread several feet in all directions from the main stem within three or four years. By controlling growth, the gardener can direct some of this tremendous plant energy into producing fewer but bigger and better flowers.

These early bloomers are normally grown for mass effect, but some can be induced to yield terminal sprays and flowers large enough to enter in a flower show. When grown for maximum bloom, chrysanthemum plants should be spaced at least 24 inches apart. A well-grown plant will form a mound and cover itself with flowers. Some garden varieties can be grown as single stem plants and be used to produce flowers suitable for cutting.

Mound chrysanthemums can be grown in a spare bed away from the main display part of the garden—the vegetable plot, for instance. Just as the flowers start to show color, the plants can be lifted with a good ball of soil and transplanted into the main garden. If early frost threatens, a piece of floating row cover thrown over the plants is usually enough to protect the blooms.

Plants started in clay or plastic pots should be moistened before planting.

Then you can remove them easily by tapping the rim of the pot while holding the plant upside down with the stem between your fingers. All plants should be placed in a hole no deeper than the ball of soil that was removed from the pot. After the root ball is planted, the ground should be firmed.

Controlling Weeds With Mulch

Chrysanthemums do best when the root area is covered with a mulch to keep down weeds and conserve moisture. Partially composted leaves, cocoa-bean hulls, or other locally available humus can be used. A combination of leaves with an overlay of no more than an inch of cocoa hulls is adequate. Avoid peat moss becomes it can become compacted and prevent moisture from seeping down to the roots.

Growing Chrysanthemums in Flats

The same type of container used to root cuttings can be employed to grow plants until it is time to place them in the garden. When you set plants in flats, you give them an opportunity to establish their roots in soil while eliminating problems that develop when soil is too wet or too dry—conditions prevalent in many gardens in the spring. When in the flats the plants will do best in a loose, nutritious growing medium—either a commercial potting mix or one consisting of equal parts of rich soil (or compost), peat moss, and washed sand (or perlite).

For potting chrysanthemum cuttings, use 3-inch-deep pots made of clay, plastic, or peat. The first two kinds of pots are reusable, but peat pots are designed to be placed in the soil with their plants.

If the soil is kept moist after planting, the plant's roots will penetrate the peat, and the pot will disintegrate.

Generally, most chrysanthemums should be kept in pots for two or three weeks before being planted in their permanent locations. Though starting chrysanthemums in pots requires more work than placing them directly in the garden, the extra effort usually pays off by producing plants that are stronger than those exposed to the vagaries of the elements at an earlier age.

Planting in the Garden

Rooted cuttings can be planted directly in the garden. Bear in mind, too, that plants removed from a rooting mix for transplantation are like rooted cuttings bought from the nursery, and their subsequent treatment is the same. Both types of cuttings will need a great deal of care to keep them from drying out in the sun; and to protect them from the ravages of insects, beating rains, and strong winds. Also, it would be wise to provide some form of temporary shade to shield the plants until they have become firmly established.

1. Rooted cuttings can be grown in flats or pots until they are large enough to plant out in the garden.

2. Do not allow cuttings to dry out, but do not overwater either.

3. When established, pinch the tip out of each plant to make it bush out.

The garden chrysanthemum 'Debonair' develops thick branches, with flower clusters 12 in. wide. It will grow 20 in. tall.

Chrysanthemum 'Debonair'

Supporting Chrysanthemum Plants

Ingenious gardeners have developed a variety of methods for supporting chrysanthemums. Plants with only a few blooms are generally supported by a steel or bamboo stake for each branch (see below). Plastic- or paper-covered wire ties are used to fasten the stems of the plants to the stakes.

Another way to support chrysanthemum plants is to use metal hoops with three or four wire legs. These types of hoop are sold in most garden centers and are often used to support peonies. They are long-last-

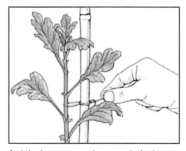

A stake is necessary to support plants grown for large blooms.

Care During the Summer

Feeding. Slow-release organic fertilizers like bone meal and blood meal, incorporated when planting, will nourish the soil for several months. Too much fertilizer promotes foliage at the expense of flowers; so diluted feeding once a week is usually best. For a diluted solution of liquid fertilizer such as liquid seaweed or manure tea, mix it at one-half the recommended strength. **Watering.** In dry spells, a thorough weekly watering is required. Chrysanthemums seldom need watering after the blooms show color. Overhead watering is fine in summer, but may spread mildew in fall.

ing and convenient to store because they can be folded flat. Such hoops work reasonably well if the plants grow no taller than 3 feet.

If an entire bed is planted with chrysanthemums, a checkerboard of strings can be stretched between supporting wires to form squares about 8–10 inches across. The first row of strings can be positioned when the plants are about 1 foot high. As the plants grow, additional strings can be added, so that each plant is enclosed in its own square, several tiers high.

Pinching, or Stopping

A technique that North Americans call pinching and Britons stopping involves cutting or breaking off the top half inch of growth. This forces the chrysanthemum plant to produce side shoots, called breaks, directly below the point of the pinch. All plants should be pinched when they are 6–8 inches high.

Three breaks are usually formed after each pinch. Each break can itself be pinched after it has grown about 6 inches, and it may even be possible to pinch it once more. However, no pinching should take place once the plant is within 90 days of its normal bloom time.

FERTILIZING

Sprinkle dry fertilizer, or add liquid manure, around the plant before watering.

What Can Go Wrong With Chrysanthemums

The chart below describes the commonest problems that are likely to occur in growing chrysanthemums. Symptoms and signs of common plant disorders appear in the first column; their cause is stated in column two; measures to control the problem are in column three. If plants show symptoms that are not described below, turn to the section on plant disorders on page 506.

SYMPTOMS AND SIGNS	CAUSE	CONTROL
Sinuous whitish lines in leaf tissue.	Leaf miners	Remove mined leaves as soon as noticed.
Distorted buds and flowers. Leaves crippled or with small holes.	Four-lined, harlequin, or tarnished plant bugs	Spray young nymphs with insecticidal soap, neem, or *Beauveria bassiana*.
Leaves flecked with brown. Webs at end of new growths.	Two-spotted mites (red spider mites)	Spray with insecticidal soap. Use strong jets of water to wash pests off underside of leaves
Young shoots eaten off, especially on stolons.	Slugs (if slimy trails present) or caterpillars	Treat with saucers of beer placed flush with soil for slugs. For caterpillars use *Bacillus thuringiensis*.
V-shaped or triangular patches between leaf veins.	Foliar nematodes (eelworms)	Burn damaged leaves.
Plants yellowed and often stunted. Leaves and shoots wilt during warm, sunny weather. Thin stems; small, pale leaves.	Root knot nematodes or symphilids in soil	Dig out plants and put in garbage. Do not replant in this location.
	Lack of water	Check for dryness.
	Starvation or chlorosis	Check feeding program; add several tablespoons of magnesium sulfate.
Petals (ray flowers) show brown spots. Flowers deformed.	Ascochyta ray blight (fungus)	Spray with fungicidal soap.
Powdery gray or brown masses on buds and petals.	Botrytis, or gray mold (fungus)	Spray with Bordeaux mixture.
Whitish coating over leaves and shoots, which may be deformed.	Powdery mildew (fungus)	Spray with potassium bicarbonate fungicide or sulfur.
Brown or black spots on leaves.	Rust disease or septoria leaf spot (fungus)	Dust with sulfur when seen.
General wilting of entire plant. Leaves turn brown at base of plant and die progressively upward. Dead brown leaves hang on for a long time.	Verticillium wilt or Seidewitz disease (fungus)	Destroy infected leaves and stems. Spray with Bordeaux mixture.

Among the early-blooming garden chrysanthemums such as 'Crimson Yvonne Arnaud' (decorative) and 'Enbee Wedding' (single), flowering starts in late summer or early fall. Most varieties should be protected for the winter.

Chrysanthemum 'Crimson Yvonne Arnaud'   *Chrysanthemum* 'Enbee Wedding'

Growing for Exhibition

Bolder in form and often with larger flowers and longer stems than early garden chrysanthemums, these late bloomers are highly prized. These are the plants proudly displayed on flower-show tables, and their growers go to great lengths to nurture them to the absolute peak of their bloom potential. They are usually grown in those gardens where protection from frost can be provided, or in pots that can be moved to sheltered areas.

Two especially popular classes of chrysanthemums for exhibition are the incurves and the spiders. The incurves can produce the largest of all chrysanthemum flowers, and the spiders are considered the most unusual and interesting. But many other classes are grown for display in flower shows.

Growing in the open ground. Late bloomers need all the care that is lavished on the earlier bloomers, and more. Provide maximum practical spacing between plants, and restrict each plant of the large-bloom type to two stems. Bush types are normally trained to produce from three to six sprays. Many growers install a frame of galvanized pipe or redwood two-by-fours around this type of chrysanthemum; when needed, the frame can support a frost cover or a shading cloth for the summer.

Growing in pots. Many growers of the late bloomers prefer to concentrate on a small number of plants and to cultivate them in pots—sometimes kept above the ground, sometimes below. Aboveground pots should be supported to prevent them blowing over in the wind. Pots give the grower greater control because they can be turned to prevent blooms from leaning to one side or another, and during rainy spells they can be carried to a sheltered area. If pots are belowground, they can easily be lifted out for moving.

Normally, each potted plant is transplanted twice as it grows to maturity—first from its 2- to 3-inch pot to a 4-inch model and finally to a 7- or 8-inch pot. However, a plant can be transplanted directly from a 2- to 3-inch pot to a 7- or 8-inch pot if care is taken to prevent the larger pot from becoming waterlogged. An organic mulch in the large pot deters weeds and conserves moisture. Many flower shows accept only potted plants for display, and these, of course, must be grown for the full season in pots.

Aboveground potting. Chrysanthemum enthusiasts often grow their plants in pots set on rows of tiles or bricks and use a double wire for support. Though this method discourages soil-borne insect infestation, watering may become something of a problem, particularly in hot, dry weather. Since a 4-foot chrysanthemum requires a large amount of water, close attention must be paid to its watering needs when it is potted in this manner.

The installation of an irrigation line, with an emitter in each pot, reduces the amount of work and makes feeding easier as well.

Plunge pit. The plunge pit is a variation of aboveground potting in which pots are buried up to their rims in moist sand or soil. Watering is less of a problem, particularly if clay pots are used. The clay lets some moisture through the wall of the pot. Plastic, however, does not. But if heavy rains bring an overabundance of water, the plants may have difficulty absorbing the moisture.

Making a Time Pinch to Produce Large Blooms

The 9- to 12-week response group varieties are pinched in the same way as the earlier bloomers except that a final pinch—the time pinch—is made toward the end of the growing season to generate the largest possible blossoms. A final pinch 90 to 110 days before the bloom date will produce a terminal bud cluster on stems of adequate length to qualify the chrysanthemums as entries in competitive shows. If the last pinch is made late in the growing season, a terminal bud cluster will form. (The word "terminal" here means the last flowering effort in the sequence.) Had there been no pinching, the plant would branch by itself to produce many blooms on short stems.

The grower who looks forward to winning show honors is primarily interested in concentrating the energies of the plant on producing large blooms. Ideally, these flowers will form a superb terminal spray in which a central crown bloom is surrounded by smaller satellite blossoms. In addition, top show honors require that the terminal bloom be set on an underpinning of chrysanthemum leaves. After the final pinch has been made, the rest is largely up to the inherent qualities of the plant itself as well as the weather.

Plants grown to produce sprays should be pinched 90 days before bloom date. Those designed for large blooms in competitions should be time-pinched 100 days before the plant is expected to flower.

The time pinch usually generates three lateral growths, or breaks, just as other pinches do. If show entries are the goal, only two breaks should be allowed to grow, and these will yield two large blooms per plant. For sprays, three breaks can be retained.

After the plants are well established, and throughout the growing season, lateral growth will occur at the junction of each leaf below the terminal bud. These shoots must be removed as soon as they are about half an inch long, or they will rob the terminal bud of needed strength. Just use your thumb to rub off the unwanted bud stems. This must be done on a regular basis when the buds are young.

In September a change occurs in the terminal growth of each stem: a central bud appears, surrounded by side buds. For plants that are intended to have one large bloom per stem, the central buds should be retained and the others removed.

Remove side buds as early as possible, but not until they have grown distinct stems that can be rubbed off without disturbing the center bud.

In the case of prospective sprays, the central bud and all side buds should be left to develop untouched. The central bud will become the primary bloom.

1. Flower buds grow in groups—a central bud surrounded by side buds.

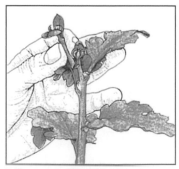

2. If you want only one large bloom per stem, pinch out the side buds.

Chrysanthemum 'Mei-kyo'

Colorful in the garden and superb cut flowers, those hardy early garden mums are small-flowered spray varieties with anemone-type blossoms.

Making a Frame for Shading and Frost Cover

Many of the chrysanthemum varieties bloom after the first frost, which often comes too late for autumn shows. Growers can force early blooming by using the black-cloth shading method.

A frame of galvanized pipe or redwood two-by-fours is needed to support the shading cloth. The frame should be high enough to keep the cloth from touching the plants and should provide a roof slope so that rain will run off.

The cloth itself should be dense enough to screen out almost all light. Attach it to the frame in such a way that it can easily be installed and removed daily. Position the cloth on the north end of the structure so that it can be pulled to the south end late in the day and back to provide full sun the following morning.

Since chrysanthemums remain at peak bloom for a long period, a plant that is scheduled to bloom on October 15, for example, can be entered in shows as much as a week before or after that date. Because each response group requires a designated number of short-day weeks, subtract that number from October 15 to decide when to begin the shading process. If different response groups are grown together, pick an average date. This will usually be around August 6. Shade should be applied each afternoon at a time that will ensure 12 hours of darkness. Shading should continue until bud clusters are visible on the terminals.

Chrysanthemum plants can withstand temperatures as low as 28°F. But when the temperature drops below freezing, moisture may damage the petals. A frost cover will prevent this kind of injury. The shading frame can be used to support the frost cover, which should be made of a 6-mil vinyl material.

A 500- to 1,000-watt heater will prevent damage on a cold night.

PINCHING

Both garden and exhibition mums require pinching.

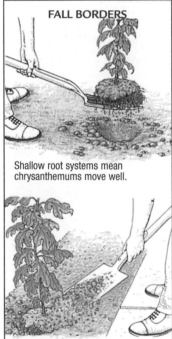

FALL BORDERS

Shallow root systems mean chrysanthemums move well.

Dig them in bud, replant in a new location, and water well.

Using Chrysanthemums and Growing Them Well

Chrysanthemums are hardy garden plants. The ease with which they can be moved to make instant borders eliminates problems caused by spacing or height differences. And as show plants, mums have few peers.

When you enter chrysanthemums in a show, check the schedule well to make sure that your entries are placed in the proper class. Groom your show flowers carefully. If you enter a competition for three-bloom or spray classes, be sure the blossoms have a uniform configuration.

In beds where chrysanthemums have been grown for many years, nematodes or verticillium wilt disease may be present. This may necessitate solarizing; place a sheet of clear plastic over the bed before planting for four to six weeks to heat the soil enough to kill most diseases.

A high clay content presents problems for the chrysanthemum grower. Avoid digging in damp weather. Mixing the soil with washed sand, gravel, or perlite makes it more friable. If the soil breaks up easily when turned over in the spring, its clay content is probably not too high.

Slightly acid soil (pH 6–7) is best for chrysanthemums. If the soil has a pH of 5–6, the excess acidity can be corrected by adding ground limestone. If the pH is 7–8, the soil is too alkaline, and sulfur should be worked in. See page 498 for information on changing pH levels of the soil.

Mums sold as house plants are seldom suitable for the garden. Mostly, they are tall varieties that have been kept dwarf by chemicals. After several months the effects of these wear off and the plants grow taller. Also, they are usually in the 8- to 12-week response group and will not bloom outside until after frosts have arrived.

1. After blooming, cut plant down to about 1 ft.

2. Lift the root ball and shake off surplus soil.

3. Cut back any soft new growth at the base.

4. Pack into flats or a cold frame and fill gaps with soil.

CARNATIONS

To many people, this word conjures up the florist's flower, available year-round. But there are other forms that are not as demanding to grow.

Carnations have been cultivated since the mid-15th century. They are mentioned in *Turner's Herbal* of 1550, and *Gerard's Herbal* of 1597 describes great double carnations with a sweet smell. In 1629, John Parkinson referred to those with large flowers as carnations and those with smaller flowers as gilliflowers. By the early 18th century, amateur breeders were introducing flowers with flakes of a different color on a white background, flowers edged in a different color (picotee), and flowers with two different colors on each petal.

The modern florists', or perpetually flowering, carnation was first bred in the United States in the 1900's. Developed by Scottish nurseryman William Sim, the large, mostly scentless flowers became a staple of the cut-flower trade.

Florists' and border carnations are forms of *Dianthus caryophyllus,* which is native to Europe's Pyrenee Mountains. The name carnation is now reserved for perpetual-blooming greenhouse varieties, hardy border forms, and old-fashioned Malmaison carnations. See Perennials (p. 50) for the closely related border pinks *(D. plumarius);* Annuals and Biennials (p. 202), for sweet Williams *(D. barbatus)* and China pinks *(D. chinensis);* and Rock and Water Gardens (p. 161), for other dwarf species.

Perpetual-flowering carnations. Although they will withstand short periods below freezing, perpetual-flowering carnations are not hardy. They are grown commercially in greenhouses that are heated to a minimum temperature of 45–50°F. Keen gardeners in mild parts of the United States, where greenhouse heating is not too expensive, often grow a few plants to provide cut flowers for the house. It has been mainly due to gifted amateurs crossing the older perpetuals with border carnations that modern varieties of perpetual-flowering carnations are fragrant again. Since these carnations are susceptible to soil-borne diseases, they are best grown in pots of sterilized soil or commercial soilless mix. Sit pots on pea gravel on a bench rather than on the floor, where worms could introduce disease.

Small plants, potted into 5-inch pots, should be pinched back, and will start to flower about five months later. The most popular varieties are grown and disbudded (see p. 95) to produce one large flower per stem. Some varieties have been developed to produce spray carnations; in such cases the terminal bud is removed to promote growth on the side buds.

Border carnations. All border carnations flower prolifically from midsummer until frost. Grown in the open garden, either in a massed bed or in a border with other plants, they grow best in a slightly alkaline soil. Plant in spring or fall, where they are to flower, in soil that has been well worked, enriched with compost or old manure, and allowed to settle. Do not protect before the ground is frozen, as this may give rise to stem rot. In early winter, evergreen boughs can be laid over the plants to help trap snow. In spring, as the stems start to grow, tie them to thin bamboo canes, but don't pinch out the growing tip, as you would for perpetual-flowering carnations.

Plants can be disbudded to give larger flowers. If this is done, remove only the bud beside the terminal one the first year or all buds may abort.

Malmaison carnations. These are of historic interest only, and are rarely grown. Cultivation is similar to that of perpetual-flowering types, but they do better in cooler temperatures during the fall and winter.

Dianthus 'Devon Cream'

Dianthus 'Laced Monarch'

Dianthus 'Devon Cream' and 'Laced Monarch' show the range of colors and forms available in border carnations.

1. Dig a hole and add a little sulfur dust to reduce likelihood of wilt.

2. Place the plant in the hole and fill around it.

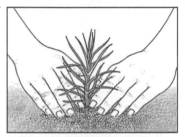

3. Firm well with the fingers, leaving a slight depression, then water.

4. As border carnations grow, tie to thin bamboo canes.

How to Plant Border Carnations

Make sure the plants have been fully hardened off (see p. 195). Water all potted plants at least an hour before planting. Dig a hole deep enough to take the root ball, and dust a little general purpose fungicide into the hole. Set the plant in place and fill the hole. Firm with the fingers, leaving a slight depression, and water well. Space plants 15–18 inches apart in the border. In a cutting garden, they can go 12 inches apart in rows. As they grow, tie them to thin canes.

Growing Border Carnations from Seed

Annual varieties will bloom in July if sown indoors about 10 weeks before the last frost. Freeze the seed for one week, then sow on a sterilized seed mix. Germination is fastest if seeds can be given warm days (70°F) and cooler nights (60°F). When seedlings have two true leaves, transplant into small pots and grow in a sunny window or under fluorescent lights. Seed can be sown directly outside one week or so before the average last frost date, but will not begin to bloom as early. Germination is improved if the seed is frozen first.

Biennial varieties can be sown indoors in late winter. Germination should take less than a week if the seed is kept cool (50°F) after sowing. After germination, grow seedlings on in pots for hardening off and planting outdoors in early spring. After flowering, cut them back.

Alternatively, seed can be sown outside in June and will overwinter and bloom the following year. Sow thinly where you want them to flower or in a nursery bed and transplant in early fall.

Obtaining Larger Flowers

Left alone to flower, border carnations will give a pleasing display of small flowers. Flower size increases as the number of blooms produced goes down. This is achieved by carefully removing side buds to channel energy into the terminal one (see below). By the third year, all the side buds can be removed, to give a show-size terminal bloom. If you try disbudding the first year before the plant is strong enough, the terminal bud will not develop properly, and you will most likely end up with no bud at all. If you prefer a spray-type of flower truss, remove just the tip buds, and the energy that would have gone into what is normally the largest flower will be shared among the remaining buds.

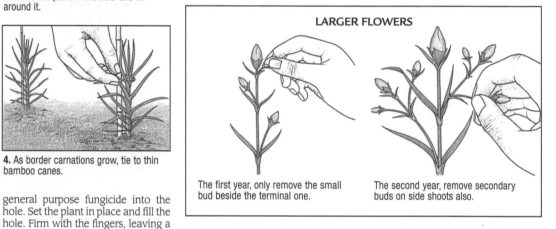

LARGER FLOWERS

The first year, only remove the small bud beside the terminal one.

The second year, remove secondary buds on side shoots also.

What Can Go Wrong With Carnations

Properly positioned carnations growing in good soil seldom develop any serious pest or disease problems. If your plants show symptoms that are not described here, turn to the section on plant disorders beginning on page 506.

SYMPTOMS AND SIGNS	CAUSE	CONTROL
Growing tips have small, slow-moving green pests (may also be pink or black).	Aphids (greenfly)	Spray with insecticidal soap.
Leaves are pale or yellowish, fine webs run between them. Plants are stunted.	Mites	Spray with insecticidal soap.
Leaves are yellow, stems are soft and brown at the base. Plants wilt.	Wilt (fungus)	Dispose of plant in the garbage. Do not plant carnations in that place for several years
Leaves are grayish first, then yellow. Yellow streaks appear on the stem. Plants wilt.	Wilt (bacterial)	Dispose of plant in the garbage. Do not plant carnations in that place for several years.
Young plants chewed through at soil level. Flowering plants have chewed buds that may be cut off.	Cutworm	Put tinfoil collars around plants. Apply *Steinernema* nematodes to soil.

ORNAMENTAL GRASSES

Since the 1980s grasses have become increasingly prominent in home landscapes, and the number of available species and varieties has grown enormously. Many of the plants that we think of as grass are really sedges, rushes, or bamboos, but their role in the garden remains unchanged. They provide a different texture and pleasing contrast to regular broad-leaved plants.

As a group, grasses are the most versatile of plants. Species can be found that will thrive in wet or dry locations, in full sun or dense shade, in acid or alkaline soils. Within a single genus grasses can be found with greatly differing foliage. *Miscanthus sinensis* 'Zebrinus' (right) is the opposite of 'Goldfeder', which has stripes running vertically. Many are excellent ground covers (after all Kentucky Blue is a grass), some make good container specimens, while others add stature and height to a mixed border where their stately plumes bend and sway in the slightest breeze.

The color of their foliage varies greatly and there are varieties that can be used to provide foliage contrast in monochrome borders, such as one growing only silver-leaved plants, or in a border with a limited palette range, like yellow and green. Some variegated forms blend well with hostas and can be difficult to tell apart from narrow-leaved hosta varieties—until they flower.

Attractive as their foliage is, most ornamental grasses are grown for their interesting, and usually decorative, flower spikes and the resulting seed heads; whether it is the white woolly stems of cotton grass (*Eriophorum*), only 18 inches tall, or the towering 10 feet spikes of pampas grass (*Cortaderia*), it is the seed heads that are important. As well as the tall plumes of seed heads that are so prominent in the fall garden, many grasses have interesting pendulous seeds. Wild oats (*Chasmanthium*), have diamond-shaped, flattened seed heads in hanging clusters, while those of Job's tears (*Coix*) are so hard they can be strung and used as beads.

Clump-forming or Spreading

All grasses spread slowly and gradually increase in size, but some are more aggressive and spread rapidly. In most catalogs grasses are listed as clumping or running. Clumping grasses stay in one place and will not suddenly appear some distance away; ones that increase very slowly are referred to as bunch grasses.

Running grasses spread rapidly by underground roots (stolons) or stems (rhizomes) and can become a major problem if left unchecked. They make excellent ground covers and are an ideal choice for planting on a bank to stabilize the soil. In the border, they can be planted in a tough container, such as half a garbage can or a concrete sewer pipe, although some varieties of bamboo will eventually force their way through even a tough plastic garbage can. They can also be kept under control by chopping around them with a spade in late spring and again in fall and removing the outside shoots. Climate plays a part in the spread of these running grasses, and a species that is aggressive in warm climates may be well behaved in a cool one. Check with local sources before planting to determine the rate of growth.

A few grasses, like the Japanese Hakone grass, (*Hakonechloa*), actually spread by rhizomes, but so slowly that they can be treated as a clump grass in most situations. Even within the same species, some varieties may be clump-forming and others spreading. Most of the cultivars of the Japanese silver grass (*Miscanthus sinensis*) are clump forming but the variety 'Silberfeder' (silver feather) is a quite rampant spreader.

Hakonechloa macra 'Aureola'

Calamagrostis acutiflora 'Karl Foerster'

'Aureola' is one form of the Japanese Hakone grass, others are green and white, or all yellow. 'Karl Foerster' keeps its feathery plumes well into winter and withstands wind well.

Cool or Warm?

Grasses can be divided into cool and warm season ones. This is not an indication of their hardiness, but of their season of growth, and many species native to the cool north are actually warm season plants.

Cool season grasses come into growth early, flower in early summer and go semi-dormant during the summer heat. They thrive in temperatures from just above freezing up to around 75°F. They often have a second period of growth in late summer and only go dormant with the onset of winter. This growth cycle corresponds with the availability of moisture in spring and fall, and they should be moved at the start of their growth cycle in spring. In the garden, the tendency toward summer dormancy can be offset in part by watering and growing them where they will get summer shade. In cool climates these grasses may be semi-evergreen. Common examples of cool season grasses include feather reed grass (*Calamagrostis*); moor grass (*Molina*); blue oat grass (*Helictotrichon*); melic (*Melica*); and needle grass (*Stipa*).

Warm season grasses revel in hot temperatures, 80-95°F. Many species still grow well in northern gardens but are slower to come into growth in spring and go dormant in fall. It is then that grasses like the Japanese silver grass (*Miscanthus*) take on their wonderful fall colors. In addition to the silver grass, moor grass (*Molina*), Japanese Hakone grass (*Hakonechloa*), switch grass (*Panicum*), and fountain grass (*Pennisetum*) are examples of warm season grasses.

Non-grass Grasses

True grasses belong to the family *Poaceae*, but gardeners also consider sedges (*Cyperaceae*) and rushes (*Juncaceae*) as ornamental grasses. Sedges are easy to identify by their triangular stems and leaves that come in threes, with their bases wrapped around the stem, and no leaf stalk. The most commonly grown sedges belong to the genus *Carex*, but other include papyrus and bullrush. Many sedges grow best in moist to wet locations and full sun, but some do well in normal soils and a few in part shade. Rushes are a much smaller group and there are only two species commonly grown. *Juncus*, the common rush found in moist, sunny locations, and *Luzula*, the wood rush, with quite broad leaves, growing in shady woodland.

Preparing the Site

As mentioned above, there are grass species for all types of soils, but most of the commonly grown species are very adaptable and will grow in soils ranging from quite heavy clay to fast-draining and infertile sands, although their performance will differ greatly. Winter survival in cold climates may depend on good drainage and species like blue fescue (*Festuca glauca*) may die if planted in a poorly drained soil. Grasses that spread underground can be overly aggressive in a rich soil, but quite manageable in a poor one.

Most soils benefit from the addition of compost to increase their moisture holding capacity, but the use of nutrient-rich manures should be avoided. Grasses are very efficient plants and can survive well in regular to poor soils, but may become overlarge and floppy if given a rich soil.

The most important consideration in preparing a soil for grasses is the removal of perennial weeds, especially perennial grasses, such as couch grass (also known as twitch). This grass spreads by underground stolons, which can grow into the middle of clump-forming ornamental grasses and be almost impossible to remove. It can grow from small pieces left in the soil and areas containing couch grass should be dug over carefully with a fork, rather than with a spade, and never with a rototiller which just chops it into small pieces. After digging, leave the area unplanted for several weeks so any perennial weed roots have time to sprout and be removed.

Buying and Planting

Most nurseries, either local or mail-order, sell their grasses in pots, but some of the larger mail-order nurseries also ship their plants bare-root. Most often, these will be shipped in spring and arrive while still dormant, but occasionally, in mild climates, they may be shipped in fall as well. Potted plants can be planted any time the soil is not frozen, but again early spring is best. Avoid buying plants that are in full growth, they do not transplant as well and have probably become root-bound in the container.

Stand potted grasses in a container of water for an hour or two before planting to ensure their root balls are soaked all the way through. Dig a hole large enough to take the root ball and work a little bone meal into the base of the hole to stimulate root production. Fill in around the roots and firm the soil in place with your fingers to leave no air pockets. Leave the top of the root ball just slightly below soil level so that the plant sits in a slight depression to retain water. Give the area a good soaking and be prepared to water frequently for the first few weeks. Grasses are very drought tolerant but they need a little pampering at first. Small potted plants are preferable to large ones in big containers. They establish better and often outgrow a larger plant.

GRASSES SPIKES

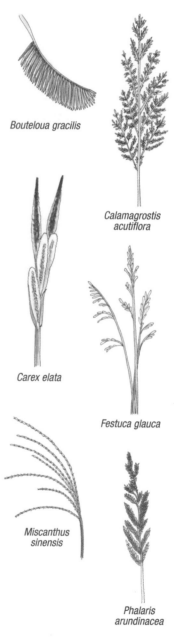

Bouteloua gracilis

Calamagrostis acutiflora

Carex elata

Festuca glauca

Miscanthus sinensis

Phalaris arundinacea

A somewhat rampant bamboo, *Pleioblastus auricomus*, known as golden-striped bamboo, is excellent for containers. Silver fescue (*Festuca glauca*) is more refined and makes a good edging.

Pleioblastus auricomus

Festuca glauca

Summer Care and Cutting Back

Mulch around the clumps in early spring, using garden compost or a commercial sterilized manure that is low in nitrogen, taking care not to cover the crowns. In regions with hot, dry summers watering will be necessary, but in most of the country the grasses will be able to survive on their own once established. Where watering is required, it is best to use a drip irrigation system that puts the water at each individual plant rather than overhead sprinklers that lose a lot of water by evaporation.

Many grasses need cutting back in late winter or early spring, in nature they would have either been grazed or had the old stems burned off in a prairie fire. Do not cut too close to the crown, 6-12 inches is plenty, and wear heavy-duty gloves, since the leaves can have serrated edges. Cut the cool season grasses back in early spring and the warm season grasses a few weeks later. Evergreen grasses and small growing ones like blue fescue will not need cutting back at all, simply comb through them with your fingers to remove any dead stems.

Dividing Plants

Once clumps get old, their centers die out and it is time to divide them. For best results, lift clumps in early spring, after cutting back the old stems, and cut them into pieces. You will need a sharp spade to cut through large clumps, but a knife will be enough for smaller species. Replant young material from the outside of the clump and discard the old middle. Running varieties are easy to propagate once they age. When you chop around the plant in fall and dig up the runners, remember to pot a few and keep them watered while you dig up and throw away the old middle.

Grasses for Arrangements and Drying

Many ornamental grasses can be cut fresh for use in flower arrangements or dried for use in winter arrangements. Cut them before they fully open when using fresh spikes. The color of the flowers will intensify as they open, and they last well in fresh

What Can Go Wrong With Grasses

Properly positioned grasses growing in good soil seldom develop any serious pest or disease problems. If your plants show symptoms that are not described here, turn to the section on plant disorders beginning on page 506.

SYMPTOMS AND SIGNS	CAUSE	CONTROL
Plants stunted, grayish insects in leaf bases.	Miscanthus mealybug	None known. Dig out and put in garbage. Inspect new plants carefully before planting.
Reddish spots on leaves.	Rust	Plant far enough apart to allow good air circulation, spray with wettable sulfur.
Plant collapses.	Crown rot	Don't plant too deep or cover crown with mulch.
Plants eaten to ground level.	Deer, rabbits, or gophers	Usually only a problem on soft-leaved species. Protect with wire cage or fence.

water. The variegated foliage of some varieties can add interest to arrangements and complement the more flamboyant flowers.

To use as dried flowers, cut the spikes as soon as they are fully open and hang upside-down in a well ventilated place out of direct sunlight. Keep the bunches small so air can circulate freely through the stems.

Once fully dry, store them flat in a box, indoors. Handled carefully they can last for several years.

The following will dry well: *Bouteloua gracilis* (blue grama), *Calamagrostis acutiflora* (feather reed grass), *Chasmanthium latifolium* (wild oats), *Luzula sylvatica* (wood rush), *Panicum virgatum* (switch grass) *Pennisetum alopecuroides* (fountain grass).

ANNUAL GRASSES

The grasses in the chart on pp. 99–100 are all perennial, but there are also some good annual grasses, easy to grow from seed, that make good additions to the border. Most are comparatively small and are useful as edging or for planters where you don't want towering spikes.

Briza (quaking grass) comes in two forms; little quaking grass (*B. minor*) which grows 18 in. tall, and big quaking grass (*B. maxima*) which grows to 3 ft. high. Both have small heads of seed on the end of thin stalks that move in the slightest breeze. Both can be dried for winter arrangements. Sow indoors

about six weeks before last frost and plant outside once the soil is warm 10 in. apart.

Coix lachryma-jobi (Job's tears) grows 3 ft. tall with cornlike leaves. Flowers are in clusters at the tips of the shoots, with individual seed heads arching downward, and make good dried flowers. Seeds are hard, white, shiny, full of protein, and make a rich flour. They are often found in rosaries. Sow indoors eight weeks before planting time and space them 12 in. apart.

Lagurus ovatus (hare's tail) is a charming little grass that grows about 12 in. tall and has fluffy seed heads

3 in. long that start green and turn whitish with age. They make good dried flowers and can be attractive when dyed garish colors. Sow 3–4 weeks before last frost and space the seedlings out in well-drained soil about 6 in. apart.

Pennisetum setaceum (fountain grass) is an annual version of the perennial one described in the chart. It will grow to 5 ft. tall and has plumes tinged with pink or purple. The variety 'Burgundy Giant' is a bit taller and has leaves of a deep burgundy shade and dark red flower spikes. Both may be hardy in warm climates. Start seeds 6

weeks before last frost and plant out 15-18 in. apart.

Triticum 'Black Tip' is a variety of wheat that has black bristles on the tips of the white seed and makes very attractive dried flowers. Another form has black seeds and bristles. The many varieties of wheat can be dried in fall for use in attractive dried arrangements.

Seeds should be started indoors where growing seasons are short, but can be sown directly in the garden in more moderate climates. They don't make very attractive plants and are best grown in a cutting garden.

Recommended Grasses

The number of grasses available from specialist nurseries continues to grow. The ones listed here should be readily available, often from a local garden center. Information on whether they are clumping or spreading, and on if they are cool or warm season, is included as an aid in locating the plants and knowing when to cut back. Appropriate soil and light conditions for each individual plant are listed using pictograms. A key, detailing all the soil and light condition pictograms, is found at the bottom of the page.

Imperata cylindrica 'Red Baron'

| *Arrhenatherum elatius* (tuber oat grass) | *Arundo donax* (striped giant reed) | *Bouteloua gracilis* (mosquito grass) | *Calamagrostis acutiflora* (feather reed grass) | *Carex* (sedge) | *Cortaderia selloana* (pampas grass) | *Cyperus alternifolius* (umbrella palm) | *Eriophorum angustifolia* (cotton grass) | *Festuca glauca* (blue fescue) |

BOTANICAL AND COMMON NAMES	HEIGHT	SPREAD	SOIL	LIGHT	CHARACTERISTICS AND REQUIREMENTS	CLUMPING OR SPREADING	COOL OR WARM SEASON
Arrhenatherum elatius bulbosum (tuber oat grass)	1 ft.	3 ft.	□	◖	Needs frequent division. Give shade where summers are hot. Varigated form is most attractive with white-striped leaves.	Spreading	Cool
Arundo donax 'variegata' (striped giant reed)	14 ft.	10 ft.	▪▪	●	Cream and green in spring, becoming yellow and green in time. Best in warm climate. Good container plant. Can escape by seed in warm climates and invade natural settings.	Spreading	Warm
Bouteloua gracilis (blue grama, or mosquito grass)	1–2 ft.	12 in.	▪	●	Native prairie grass with brown, horizontal seed heads in summer and early fall. Can be kept mown as a lawn in dry regions.	Clumping	Warm
Calamagrostis acutiflora (feather reed grass)	6 ft.	2 ft.	□	●	Very upright with attractive seed heads in summer. 'Karl Foester' is bright green, 'Overdam' striped with white.	Clumping	Cool
Carex (sedge)	4 in.– 2½ ft.	6–12 in.	□ ▪	● ●	*C. elata* 'Aurea' (Bowle's golden sedge) to 2½ ft. with yellow striped leaves. *C. morrowii* 'Ice Dance' leaves edged in white, best in shade. Many other species and varieties.	Clumping or spreading	—
Cortaderia selloana (pampas grass)	10 ft.	8 ft.	▪	●	Striking white seed heads that last well into winter. Also variegated and smaller forms. Needs a warm climate.	Clumping	Warm
Cymbopogon citratus (lemon grass)	2–3 ft.	3 ft.	▪	●	Lemon scented foliage much used in Asian cooking. Makes a good pot plant but is tender.	Clumping	Warm
Cyperus alternifolius (umbrella palm, or umbrella sedge)	3 ft.	3 ft.	▪ ▪	● ◖	A good waterside or container plant with leaves like umbrella ribs on top of a long stalk. Tender.	Clumping	—
Deschampsia cespitosa (tufted hair grass)	2 ft.	3 ft.	□ ▪	● ◖	Very airy flower spikes that can double the plant's height. Several named forms.	Spreading	Cool
Eriophorum angustifolium (cotton grass)	2½ ft.	indefinite	▪ ▪	●	Native to bogs and wet areas, actually a sedge. Fluffy white seed heads.	Spreading	—
Festuca glauca (blue fescue)	6–10 in.	12–18 in.	▪	● ◖	Mound-forming, makes a good edging. Named forms brighter blue to silver. Cut off flower spikes after blooming to improve look.	Clumping	Cool

● full sun ◖ partial shade ● shade ▪ well drained to sandy ▪ moist ▪ wet ▪ acidic ▪ alkaline □ regular soil

These three grasses are grown for their showy fall seed heads that last into winter.

Panicum virgatum

Miscanthus sinensis

Pennisetum alopecuroides

Hakonechloa macra (Japanese forest grass)

Imperata cylindrica 'Red Baron' (Japanese blood grass)

Leymus arenarius (blue lyme grass)

Luzula sylvatica (wood rush)

Molina caerulea (purple moor grass)

Panicum virgatum (panic grass)

Pennisetum alopecuroides (fountain grass)

Pleioblastus auriocomus (golden striped bamboo)

BOTANICAL AND COMMON NAMES	HEIGHT	SPREAD	SOIL	LIGHT	CHARACTERISTICS AND REQUIREMENTS	CLUMPING OR SPREADING	COOL OR WARM SEASON
Hakonechloa macra (Hakone grass, or Japanese forest grass)	1–3 ft.	2–4 ft.	■	◑ ◕	Arching foliage, but named forms edged white or yellow, or all yellow are more attractive.	Spreading (slowly)	Warm
Imperata cylindrica 'Red Baron' (Japanese blood grass)	20 in.	6 in.	■	● ◑	The species is invasive in warm regions, 'Red Baron' is not. Leaves have green bases, red tops in spring, red tint spreads down the leaf during summer.	Spreading (slowly in cultivar)	Warm
Juncus effusus (soft rush, or common rush)	4 ft.	12 in.	■ ■	●	An upright species with dark green foliage. 'Spiralis' has spreading, twisted stems and is only 14 in. tall.	Clumping	—
Leymus arenearius (blue lyme grass)	3–4 ft.	indefinite	■ □	●	Steel-blue foliage. Good for slopes or stabilizing dunes, but invasive.	Spreading	Cool
Luzula sylvatica (wood rush)	1 ft.	3 ft. or more	□ ■	◑ ◕	Good under shrubs, flowers double the height in early summer. Leaves ¾ in. wide. 'Marginata' has cream-edged leaves.	Spreading	—
Miscanthus sinensis (Japanese silver grass, or eulalia)	5–7 ft.	3–4 ft.	■ □	●	Probably the most popular grass in its many forms. Outstanding for tall fall color and winter interest. Spreading varieties can be quite invasive in some regions.	Most clumping, but some varieties spreading	Warm
Molina caerulea (purple moor grass)	3 ft.	5 ft.	■	● ◕	Slender spikes of purple-tinted flowers. Best in cool regions. Does well in poor, acid soils. 'Rotschopf' has red-tinted leaves.	Clumping	Cool
Panicum virgatum (switch grass, or panic grass)	4–8 ft.	2 ft.	■ ■	●	Green, blue, or reddish foliage in summer and good fall color. Several named varieties. Native species.	Spreading (slowly)	Warm
Pennisetum alopecuroides (fountain grass)	2–3 ft.	3–4 ft.	■ ■	● ◑	Fountains of white flowers, turning tan with age. 'Little Honey' is only 12 in. tall. Some species are annuals.	Clumping	Warm
Phalaris arundinacea (reed canary grass, or gardener's garters)	5 ft.	indefinite	□ ■	● ◑	The green form is invasive but the variegated 'Feesey', with green-edged white leaves, is more refined.	Spreading (rapidly)	Cool
Pleioblastus auriocomus (golden striped bamboo)	3 ft.	indefinite	□ ■	● ◑	Bright yellow leaves with thin green stripes. Needs to be contained. *P. variegatus* is green and white and equally vigorous.	Spreading (rapidly)	Warm

● full sun ◑ partial shade ● shade ■ well drained to sandy ■ moist ■ wet ■ acidic ■ alkaline □ regular soil

FERNS

In places with open or partial shade, ferns form delicate patterns of green. And they mix well with other shade-loving plants, such as primroses and columbines.

Ferns are among the most ancient plants on earth, first appearing about 400 million years ago, long before any plants bore flowers. The surviving species, with their arching fronds and cool green colors, are ideal for parts of the garden where there is little sun. They can transform a difficult corner, where few other plants will thrive, into an oasis of delicate foliage.

There are more than 12,000 species of ferns throughout the world. The vast majority are found in tropical countries. Of the 360 species that grow naturally in North America, many are concentrated in the North and East, where the higher humidity ensures the moisture necessary for fertilization. Some species from other temperate parts of the world are also available here.

Most of the native ferns can be successfully transplanted into home gardens. A real enthusiast may use ferns alone in a shady border, mixing species of different sizes, shapes of frond, and shades of green. They also make a good foil for shade-loving flowering plants, which thrive in similar conditions as ferns.

Bleeding hearts (*Dicentra spectabilis*) and astilbes blend well with the larger ferns, such as the shield ferns (*Dryopteris*) and the osmundas. Wild flowers, such as wild geraniums and violets, add a touch of color to the ferns' varying shades of green. Columbines and primroses come in a variety of colors and can be interspersed effectively. Some flowering shrubs, such as azaleas, add a mass of color in springtime.

Some of the best foliage plants to grow with ferns are the hostas, some with variegated leaves striped with green and white or yellow. Other types are plain green or blue-green. The pale green and white leaves of the goutweed (*Aegopodium*) also contrast well with the darker green of the ferns, but the goutweed spreads rapidly and may prove too invasive.

To look their best, ferns should be grown far enough apart to prevent the fronds from intermingling. The spaces between the plants or at the front near the border can be filled in with low-growing perennials, such as lady's mantle or lilies of the valley. The latter are very invasive, however, and should be fenced in with slates, tiles, or corrugated plastic or aluminum edging, sunk into the ground to keep the roots within reasonable bounds.

Torenias and the wax begonias also make good edging plants in a fern garden. And tuberous begonias, hardy begonias (*Begonia evansiana*), with their red stems and leaves, and impatiens scattered throughout the garden combine with the ferns to give a very pleasing effect.

Daffodils should be used only with large ferns, which will cover the flowers' untidy leaves after they have finished blooming. When planted among a group of ferns, tall woodland lilies look very elegant, rising above the arching fronds.

Ferns, however, need not be restricted to a shady corner. Some, for example, the hay-scented fern (*Dennstaedtia punctiloba*), which can be aggressive, grow well in nearly full sun. They can be used to cast interesting shadows.

Many ferns are evergreen and are invaluable for brightening up a garden in winter. The shield ferns and the polypodies (*Polypodium*) are particularly delightful, especially when their fronds are edged with frost. In a rock garden the evergreen spleenworts (*Asplenium*) remain bright when most other plants have faded.

The hardy ostrich fern (*Matteuccia struthiopteris*) grows up to 5 ft. tall and thrives almost anywhere there is acid to neutral humus-rich soil.

Matteuccia struthiopteris

Planting Hardy Ferns

Most ferns will grow in any soil except one where drainage is poor. A few will grow in a bog. They need a position that is shaded from midday sun and protected from wind.

The north side of a house or fence will provide the right kind of shade, protecting the plants from prolonged sunlight but leaving them open to the sky. Shade cast by trees is also excellent for ferns if it is not too dense. Ferns prefer open shade with patches of sunlight passing over them.

Ferns are best planted in fall or spring. Summer planting is all right as long as the soil is kept moist while the plants become established. If ferns are bought and delivered some time before they can be planted, do not allow their roots to dry out.

Before planting, dig over the planting bed to a depth of 1 foot, and break up the soil. Sprinkle bone meal over the surface at the rate of a scant cupful per square yard. Add a 3-inch layer of leaf mold or garden compost on top of the bone meal, and then fork it all in.

Ferns can be divided into three types: crown forming, those with rhizomatous roots, and rock ferns.

A crown-forming fern is one whose fronds emerge from a stout rhizome in the form of a vase or a crown. The shield ferns (*Dryopteris*) and the ostrich ferns (*Matteuccia*) are examples of this type.

When planting crown-forming ferns, first snap off or cut away any old woody frond bases. This will enable the new roots to emerge more quickly.

Dig a hole to the depth of the fern's root system, place the fern in the hole, and fill with soil so that the crown is flush with the surface, not below. Firm the roots in well by treading with your feet.

Rhizomatous ferns, among them the hay-scented fern (*Dennstaedtia punctiloba*) and the polypodies (*Polypodium*), produce fronds along the rhizome without forming a crown. To plant, make a shallow depression in the soil with a fork. Place the rhizome in the hole, fill in with soil, and firm with the fingers.

Rock ferns grow best tucked tightly among rocks, often horizontally. They are ideal for rock gardens or dry-stone walls, especially if lightly shaded. The maidenhair spleenwort (*Asplenium trichomanes*) and the woodsias (*Woodsia*) are examples of rock ferns. To plant, remove a stone from the wall or rock garden. Place the fern on its side in the resulting gap, and generously cover its roots with leaf mold. Replace the stone.

Water liberally immediately after planting, and keep moist (but not waterlogged) for the rest of the first summer. After this they need watering only during prolonged droughts.

THREE PLANTING TECHNIQUES

Crown-forming ferns. Remove old frond bases, and plant with the crown flush with the surface. Examples: shield ferns and the ostrich fern.

Rhizomatous ferns. Lay the rhizome in a shallow hole, cover with soil, and firm. Examples: the hay-scented fern and polypodies.

Rock ferns. Remove a stone, plant the fern on its side with leaf mold, and replace the stone. Examples: maidenhair, spleenwort, and woodsia.

PREPARING THE SOIL BEFORE PLANTING

1. Dig the soil in fall or spring, and sprinkle bone meal over it.

2. Add a 3-in. layer of leaf mold, and fork it into the soil.

Fronds of the splendid royal fern (*Osmunda regalis*) are brown at first, then green, and fade into yellow tones in autumn.

Osmunda regalis

Keeping Ferns Healthy

Watering, Feeding, and General Care

Once ferns are established, they need watering only during hot periods, when the soil may dry out.

After planting, cover the entire surface around the ferns with a 3-inch-deep mulch of garden compost or leaf mold. This will help to conserve moisture during dry spells.

Reapply this mulch each autumn and spring. Also in spring, before spreading the mulch on the bed, scatter bone meal around the plants, using about a cupful per square yard.

Weed ferns by hand, since forking or hoeing can damage the root system, which in established ferns is near the surface of the soil.

Each spring remove dead fronds with a knife, as near to the crown as possible. This will encourage new shoots to form. Do not remove in fall as they help protect the crown.

MULCHING

Mulch ferns in spring and fall with leaf mold or compost.
In spring apply bone meal first.

What Can Go Wrong With Ferns

Properly positioned ferns growing in good soil seldom develop any serious pest or disease problems. If your plants show symptoms that are not described here, turn to the section on plant disorders beginning on page 506.

SYMPTOMS AND SIGNS	CAUSE	CONTROL
Sticky patches, sometimes covered with sooty mold. Fronds may be distorted.	Aphids or plant bugs	Spray with insecticidal soap for aphids. Use neem for plant bugs.
Fronds collapse or wilt during warm or dry spells.	Vine weevil larvae	Very difficult to control. Water in parasitic nematodes.
Blackish-brown streaks or narrow blotches across fronds. Severe attack causes death of fronds.	Foliar nematodes (eelworms)	No effective control for these pests; badly infected plants should be lifted and destroyed.
Fronds are eaten off.	Slugs or snails	Put out saucers of beer set flush with soil. Apply iron phosphate baits around the plants.
Young fronds are chewed around edges.	Wood lice (sow bugs)	Sprinkle diatomaceous earth around plants.

Division—The Easiest Method of Propagation

The easiest way to propagate the crown-forming ferns, such as shield fern and ostrich fern, is by dividing the crowns in midspring.

Carefully dig up a clump of ferns with a fork, and cut off the fronds.

With a small clump it may be possible to pull the crowns apart with the hands. If the clump is large, use two garden forks. Push them back to back into the center of the clump. Taking care not to damage the actual crowns, push the forks into the clumps between the crowns, not through them. Gently push the handles together; then pull them apart until the clump is broken into two parts. It may sometimes be best to make the final division with a sharp knife to minimize possible damage.

Subdivide the two new clumps by the same method to produce several new plants, each with its own root system. Plant these by the method described for crown-forming ferns on page 102.

Rhizomatous ferns can also be propagated by division. In midspring dig up a clump of ferns, and cut off the fronds. With a sharp knife cut the rhizome into sections, each with at least one growing point (the point from which new shoots are emerging). Plant these individual sections by the method described for rhizomatous-rooted ferns on page 102. Each of these will form a new fern.

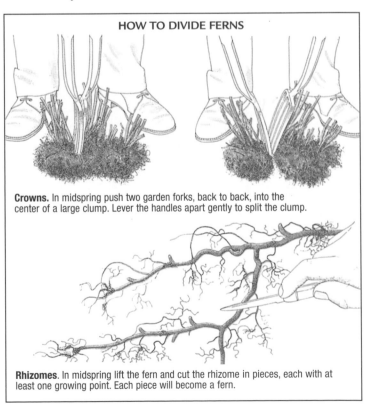

HOW TO DIVIDE FERNS

Crowns. In midspring push two garden forks, back to back, into the center of a large clump. Lever the handles apart gently to split the clump.

Rhizomes. In midspring lift the fern and cut the rhizome in pieces, each with at least one growing point. Each piece will become a fern.

The deer fern (*Blechnum spicant*) can easily be cultivated in any lime-free soil. The graceful maidenhair fern (*Adiantum pedatum*) is good in a shaded rock garden or a wall.

Blechnum spicant

Adiantum pedatum

How to Increase Your Ferns

Mass-producing New Ferns From Spores

To raise large numbers of new ferns rapidly, sow the spores found on the underside of each fertile frond.

Choose only perfect plants, as deformities can be passed on.

Between early summer and early fall, cut a frond off your chosen fern, and lay it on half a piece of clean white tissue paper. Fold the other half of the paper over the frond, and put it in a dry place.

A day or two later the spores, which resemble fine dust, will have fallen from their capsules.

Tap the paper to shift the spores into the crease. Then fold the tissue, and carefully place it in an envelope. Label the envelope.

The collected spores can be sown immediately or the following spring; many species remain viable for several years.

Sowing the spores. Sterilize a seed flat or pan or a 3½- to 4-inch pot, either in a chlorine-based disinfecting solution (1 part disinfectant to 10 parts water) or by pouring boiling water over it.

Put a ½- to ¾-inch-deep layer of gravel or crock fragments in the pan. The pan should have drainage holes.

Sift some potting soil or commercial African violet soil through a ¼-inch-mesh sieve. Put the rough part in the pan first, about 1 inch deep. Then add the fine soil, about ½ inch deep, and firm the mixture with the base of a pot.

Put a piece of paper on the soil, and pour boiling water over it into the pan. As the water subsides, add more. Continue this process until the pan is too hot to handle.

As soon as the pan has cooled, remove the paper and place a sheet of glass on top.

When the soil is cold, lift a few spores from the envelope on the tip of a penknife.

Remove the glass from the pan. Gently tap the knife with your forefin-ger so that the spores are sprinkled evenly over the surface of the soil.

Insert a label giving the name of the fern and the date of sowing.

Replace the glass. Put the pan in a shady greenhouse, indoors on a shady windowsill, or under fluorescent lights. Do not remove the glass.

If the soil shows signs of drying out, water it by placing the pan in a bowl filled with previously boiled water that has been allowed to cool. This kills any organisms in the water.

The prothallia. About one or two months later a green film will indicate development of prothallia, the structures that are the intermediate sexual stage in the life cycle of ferns. Three months after sowing, the prothallia should have become small, flat, heart-shaped growths.

Five to six months after sowing, tiny new ferns should be growing from the prothallia. When these are 1–1½ inches high, they will need pricking out into a larger seed tray or flat. A 6- by 8½-inch tray will hold about 35 young ferns.

Place a shallow layer of gravel on the bottom of the tray, covering the drainage holes.

Cover the gravel with sterilized soil (put the soil in a container with drainage holes in the base, and pour boiling water over it). The soil should fill the tray to ½ inch from the rim. Settle the soil by tapping the tray on a firm surface.

Dig out a small clump of ferns from the pan with a penknife and separate them.

Plant each fern in the soil, making sure that the root system is covered. Firm gently.

Stand the newly planted tray in a container of water that reaches halfway up its side. When the surface of the soil darkens perceptibly, it has received enough water.

Put the tray in a box, and place a clean sheet of glass over it. An alternative container to the glass-covered box is a clear plastic shoe box or a one-loaf bread box with a clear plas-tic cover. These boxes are inexpensive and excellent for this purpose as well as for propagating cuttings taken from house plants.

Keep the tray in a cool, shady place—a greenhouse, a windowsill, or under lights. Whenever the soil shows signs of drying out, water moderately from above.

After the young ferns have produced new fronds (this will probably occur in about six weeks), they need hardening off.

To accomplish this, 10 to 14 days after the new growth appears, gradually raise the cover, inserting progressively thicker wedges between the box and the cover. Two or three

GATHERING THE SPORES

Spores, which grow in clusters on the undersides of fronds, can be collected by folding a frond carefully in white tissue paper. After a day or two the spores will appear on the paper as fine dust.

The prickly shield fern (*Polystichum aculeatum*) brings fresh green to a wintry garden.

Polystichum aculeatum

weeks later remove the cover altogether. A few days later the plants will be hardened off.

Potting the ferns. Once hardened off, the young ferns will need to be transferred to individual pots.

Fill a 2½-inch pot with a light soil mixture to within ½ inch of the rim. Ease a young fern from the tray with a small trowel, and plant it in the pot.

Firm the soil around the plant with your fingers.

Sprinkle a layer of gravel over the soil. This helps to stop the soil from caking when it is watered and keeps the surface cool.

Water thoroughly, and place the pot in a shady greenhouse or indoors on a shady windowsill or under fluorescent lights.

About two months later you will need to examine the soil ball for roots. Remove by inverting the pot and tapping its rim on the edge of a table. Remember to hold the fern between your fingers throughout.

If the roots have reached the outside of the ball, loosen up the base of the root ball, and plant in a 3-inch pot. Put in a shady place.

When the 3-inch pot is filled with roots, repot into a 4-inch pot, and then into progressively larger pots as the plant continues to grow.

Set the pot outdoors when the fern is established and the weather is suitable. Depending on the time of year and local climate, you may even be able to set the young plants out in a cold frame.

FROM SPORE TO FERN IN 12 STEPS

1. Sieve soil mixture and place in a seed pan, with the fine soil on top.

2. Sterilize soil with boiling water. Paper protects the fine surface.

3. Sprinkle the spores on the soil, and cover with a sheet of glass.

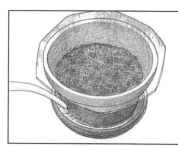

4. Water dry soil by standing it in a saucer of water.

5. In a month or two, prothallia (first stages of a fern) will have developed.

6. When they are 1–1½ in. high, the ferns will be too crowded in the pan.

7. Separate the ferns and plant in a seed flat, firming with the fingers.

8. Put on a propagating cover; keep in a cool, shady place for six weeks.

9. When the ferns grow new fronds, lift from the tray with a small trowel.

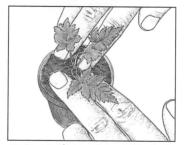

10. Plant in 2½-in. pots in a light soil mixture. Firm with the fingers.

11. Cover the surface with gravel to keep soil from caking when watered.

12. In two months, examine roots. Move fern to a larger pot if necessary.

Ferns to Brighten a Shady Place

The following chart provides a wide selection of ferns that can be grown outdoors in North America. Sizes range from the tiny maidenhair spleenwort (*Asplenium trichomanes*), often only 5 inches high, to the royal fern (*Osmunda regalis*), which can reach 6 feet in height.

Appropriate soil and light conditions for each individual plant are listed using pictograms. A key, detailing all the soil and light condition pictograms, is found at the bottom of the page.

The term "dimorphic" used in the Remarks column means that fertile and sterile fronds that occur on the same plant are different in form.

Asplenium trichomanes

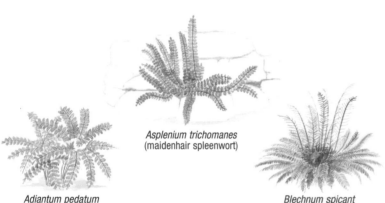

Adiantum pedatum
(maidenhair fern)

Asplenium trichomanes
(maidenhair spleenwort)

Blechnum spicant
(deer fern)

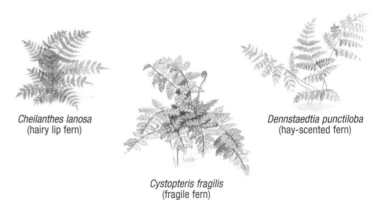

Cheilanthes lanosa
(hairy lip fern)

Cystopteris fragilis
(fragile fern)

Dennstaedtia punctiloba
(hay-scented fern)

BOTANICAL AND COMMON NAME	HEIGHT	SPREAD	SOIL	LIGHT	TYPE	HARDINESS	PROPAGATION	REMARKS
Adiantum								
A. capillus-veneris (southern maidenhair fern)	18 in.	18 in.	■	◐	Deciduous	Semi-hardy	Division or spores	Good on limestone in mild climate.
A. pedatum (maidenhair fern)	18 in.	18 in.	☐	◐	Deciduous	Very hardy	Division or spores	Attractive texture.
Asplenium								
A. platyneuron (ebony spleenwort)	12 in.	12 in.	▩	◐	Evergreen	Hardy	Division or spores	Good on soil or among rocks.
A. trichomanes (maidenhair spleenwort)	5 in.	8 in.	☐■	●	Evergreen	Hardy	Division or spores	Best in rock crevices.
Blechnum								
B. spicant (deer fern)	12 in.	18 in.	■■	●	Evergreen	Very hardy	Division	Suitable anywhere free of lime.
Cheilanthes								
C. lanosa (hairy lip fern)	8 in.	10 in.	▩	●◐	Deciduous	Semi-hardy	Division	Grows among rocks.
Cystopteris								
C. fragilis (fragile fern)	8 in.	8 in.	☐	●	Deciduous	Very hardy	Division or spores	Grows on soil or among rocks.
Dennstaedtia								
D. punctiloba (hay-scented fern)	2 ft.	2 ft.	☐■	●◐	Deciduous	Hardy	Division	Spreads rapidly and can become weedy.

■ well drained to sandy ■ moist ■ wet ■ acidic ■ alkaline ☐ regular soil ● full sun ◐ partial shade ● shade

The sensitive fern (*Onoclea sensibilis*), whose fronds turn dark brown at the first frost, has fruiting spikes that are very striking in winter.

Onoclea sensibilis

Gymnocarpium dryopteris
(oak fern)

Onoclea sensibilis
(sensitive fern)

Dryopteris cristata
(crested shield fern)

Matteuccia struthiopteris
(ostrich fern)

Osmunda regalis
(royal fern)

BOTANICAL AND COMMON NAME	HEIGHT	SPREAD	SOIL	LIGHT	TYPE	HARDINESS	PROPAGATION	REMARKS
Dryopteris								
D. cristata (crested shield fern)	2–3 ft.	2 ft.	■ ■	●	Evergreen	Hardy	Division or spores	Leaflets turn horizontally in steplike fashion.
D. goldiana (Goldie's shield fern)	4 ft.	4 ft.	□	●	Evergreen	Hardy	Division or spores	Large, impressive plant.
D. intermedia (fancy fern)	2 ft.	2 ft.	□ ■	●	Evergreen	Very hardy	Division or spores	Desirable for dark bluish-green leaves.
D. marginalis (marginal shield fern)	2–3 ft.	2 ½ ft.	□	◐	Evergreen	Very hardy	Division or spores	Easily established. Grayish-green fronds.
Gymnocarpium								
G. dryopteris (oak fern)	9 in.	9 in.	■	●	Deciduous	Hardy	Division	One of loveliest ferns. Suitable for humus-rich garden.
Matteuccia								
M. struthiopteris (ostrich fern)	3–5 ft.	4–8 ft.	□ ■	◐	Deciduous	Hardy	Division	Most suitable for foundation planting. Dimorphic fronds.
Onoclea								
O. sensibilis (sensitive fern)	2–3 ft.	2 ft.	■ ■	●◐	Deciduous	Hardy	Division	Suitable anywhere. Dimorphic fronds. Green fronds shrivel at first frost.
Osmunda								
O. cinnamomea (cinnamon fern)	4–6 ft.	2–3 ft.	■ ■	◐	Deciduous	Very hardy	Division or spores	First fern up in spring. White woolly crosiers.
O. regalis (royal fern)	4–6 ft.	4–8 ft.	■ ■	◐	Deciduous	Hardy	Division or spores	Golden terminal spore cases resemble blooms.

Fortune's hollyfern (*Cyrtomium*) and the Asian chain fern (*Woodwardia*) are both evergreen ferns that need a protected location in shade. They are hardy only in warmer parts of North America.

Cyrtomium fortunei

Woodwardia unigemmata

Phyllitis scolopendrium
(hart's-tongue fern)

Polypodium virginianum
(polypody fern)

Polystichum braunii
(Braun's holly fern)

Thelypteris phegopteris
(narrow beech fern)

Woodsia ilvensis
(rusty woodsia)

Woodwardia fimbriata
(western chain fern)

BOTANICAL AND COMMON NAME	HEIGHT	SPREAD	SOIL	LIGHT	TYPE	HARDINESS	PROPAGATION	REMARKS
Phyllitis P. scolopendrium (hart's-tongue fern)	15 in.	18 in.	■	◑	Evergreen	Hardy	Division or spores	Many crested and frilled varieties.
Polypodium P. virginianum (polypody fern)	6–8 in.	12 in.	□	◑	Evergreen	Hardy	Division	Grows best on mossy rocks.
Polystichum P. braunii (Braun's holly fern)	2 ft.	2 ft.	■	●	Evergreen	Hardy	Division or spores	Striking glossy, dark green leaves.
P. munitum (western sword fern)	3 ft.	3–4 ft.	■	●	Evergreen	Hardy	Division or spores	Handsome plant. Grows well in humus-rich soil.
Thelypteris T. noveboracensis (New York fern)	18–24 in.	24 in.	■	◑	Deciduous	Hardy	Division	Spreads very rapidly.
T. phegopteris (narrow beech fern)	6–12 in.	12–18 in.	■	◑	Deciduous	Hardy	Division	Excellent for shady rock garden.
Woodsia W. ilvensis (rusty woodsia)	6 in.	8 in.	□	◑	Deciduous	Hardy	Division or spores	Good in rock garden. Crosiers that appear in spring have silver scales.
Woodwardia W. areolata (netted chain fern)	2 ft.	18 in.	■■	●	Deciduous	Hardy	Division	Dimorphic fronds.
W. fimbriata (western chain fern)	4–8 ft.	4–8 ft.	■	●	Evergreen	Semi-hardy	Division or spores	Grows well in humus-rich soil.

■ well drained to sandy   ■ moist   ■ wet   ■ acidic   ■ alkaline   □ regular soil   ● full sun   ◑ partial shade   ● shade

The flowers of Colchicum, or false autumn crocus, push up through the soil in early fall. The large dull-green leaves appear in spring and die down by midsummer.

BULBS, CORMS, AND TUBERS

From the first snowdrop in spring to the last fall-flowering crocus, bulbs, corms, and tubers provide color throughout the year, and most need little attention.

The wide range of bulbs, corms, and tubers readily available from catalogs and garden centers is a great aid to a colorful garden. On the pages that follow, the group as a whole will be referred to as bulbs or bulbous plants—except where it is necessary to identify the plants specifically as corms or tubers. Once planted, many bulbs will maintain themselves for years with minimum care.

Although the large majority of herbaceous perennials, annuals, and bedding plants flower only during the summer months, the outdoor flowering season for bulbs extends from late winter right through the following fall. Another advantage of growing bulbs is the ease with which these plants adapt to varied habitats. Most bulbs grow well in average soil and full sun, and a few will do well in partial shade.

In every garden, however small, there is room for bulbs. The spring-flowering bulbs, in particular, flourish in a large number of settings.

Where space allows, they can be "naturalized"—planted at random for an informal effect—in lawns and wild-flower gardens.

Clumps of bulbs will brighten beds and borders before other perennials reawaken. They bloom beneath trees and shrubs, in perennial borders, and fill out nooks of rock gardens and paved areas. In winter they can fill the house with fragrance and color.

The finest displays result if plans for planting and proposed locations of the bulbs are first roughed out on paper. Indicate the kind and quantity that you will need.

Before planting it can be useful to study displays in existing gardens, public and private. Also, do not hesitate to experiment. Although some mistakes may occur at first, through experience you will gradually learn which are the best types of groupings, which soils in your garden are best suited to bulb culture, which colors of flowers harmonize and which clash, where a splash of contrasting color is needed, and so on.

Most specialist bulb suppliers offer species, horticultural varieties, and hybrids. Species are those that grow in the wild.

Hybrids and horticultural varieties are obtained by crossbreeding, through pollination, two species or varieties, usually of the same genus, and by selecting spontaneous variants from large plantings. Such improvements are then reproduced in ways other than by seeds so that offspring will be identical.

The popular hybrids often have larger, more vividly colored blooms than the species. Occasionally, new hybrids are sold at high prices for the first few years.

Although some bulbous plants seem costly, many kinds will reproduce themselves each year without any special attention, and eventually need to be lifted and divided in order to continue flowering well. A few will deteriorate and disappear.

Bulbs fall into four main categories according to bloom time: late-winter and early-spring flowering, spring flowering, summer flowering, and autumn flowering.

Earliest flowers of the year. The snowdrop is one of the first flowers to make its appearance each year, opening its delicate white bell-shaped flowers in mid to late winter. Soon afterward comes the blue glory-of-the-snow, followed by the early yellow and purple crocuses, pink and white cyclamens, and blue scillas.

Another forerunner of spring is the small winter aconite (*Eranthis hyemalis*), with its golden flowers rising above a collar of green leaves. All these plants associate well with one another, planted in groups beneath deciduous trees or in rock gardens. For an indoor display these winter-flowering bulbs can also be grown in pots and taken indoors after a prescribed period of cold. After flowering plant them out in the garden.

Heralds of spring. March, April, and May are the months when most spring-flowering bulbs appear. First come the Dutch crocuses, their green-tipped shoots pushing through earth and grass to reveal their goblet-shaped blooms of yellow, lavender, white, mauve, or violet. Some are striped or heavily marked with a contrasting hue, and in bright sunshine they all open wide, revealing deep golden or orange anthers.

The large narcissus group flowers from early to mid spring. Many catalogs list the trumpet-shaped types under their common name of daffodil and those with short-cupped flowers under narcissus; but botanically they all belong to the genus *Narcissus*. They can be left undisturbed for several years in perennial borders or can be naturalized in grass; the smaller types provide an effective display in rock gardens. Many of them are sweetly scented.

Other heralds of spring are the hyacinths and muscari, the early tulips, and the spring snowflakes (*Leucojum vernum*), with flowers like rounded snowdrops, their white petals tipped with pale green.

Crocuses and narcissi look best naturalized or planted in groups beneath trees or among perennials. But some spring-flowering bulbs, such as tulips, adapt well to formal schemes where one or more beds are devoted to them. In warm areas where winters are mild, muscaris and the larger crocuses can be grown in containers on a patio or deck, or placed near a window or glass door so that they are visible from indoors.

Hyacinths are well suited for window boxes. For garden planting it is advisable to use moderate-size bulbs—those with a circumference of about 5½–6 inches (14–16 centimeters: bulbs are frequently advertised and sold in metric units)—instead of the large bulbs used for indoor flowering. The flower spikes are relatively small but can withstand wind and rain better. Named varieties of hyacinths are available with flowers of white, pink, yellow, salmon, red, and many shades of blue.

The first tulip species, perfect in rock gardens and raised beds, appear in early spring; the larger-flowered hybrids bloom in mid to late spring. The single late tulips and Darwin Hybrids are probably the most popular, with their strong stems, each of which carries the typical cup-shaped flower. They are majestic when grown in clusters and in formal bedding schemes. They can also be grown in rows for cutting. The Darwin Hybrids and Triumphs flower a few weeks before the single late tulips appear.

Among other bulbs that will flower in late spring, less familiar but decidedly worthwhile are the handsome fritillarias, many of the anemones, the hardy, bright blue Spanish bluebells (*Hyacinthoides hispanica*), which naturalize well, the summer snowflake (*Leucojum aestivum*), delicate camassias, ranunculus, and several kinds of ornamental onion (*Allium*).

Vivid summer displays. Ixias and sparaxis brighten warm, sunny borders, followed by the species of gladioli, with their delicate flower spikes.

High summer brings the stately gladiolus hybrids (see pp. 143–144) and the shade-tolerant tuberous begonias, as well as dahlias and lilies (see pp. 134–142 and pp. 145–150). These can be grown as accents or in massed displays; tuberous begonias are particularly attractive in containers. Gladioli for cutting can be planted in rows in the vegetable garden.

Modern cannas have more to offer than just brilliant flowers, many have leaves striped in bright yellow or red that add a tropical look to the border. Their spikes of bloom, often in vivid shades, are long-lasting.

Equally showy are the many varieties of *Crocosmia* (montbretia), which come in a wide range of colors. They

bloom from midsummer onward and modern varieties have branched spikes that increase the display.

Color in autumn and winter. Autumn crocuses (*Colchicum*) and fall-flowering crocuses (*Crocus*) follow the late gladioli in early fall. Like the spring-flowering crocuses, these are best grown in bold groups beneath deciduous trees, in pockets in a rock garden, or, in the case of colchicums, naturalized among low-growing ground covers, where they make an effective splash of color and can be left undisturbed for many years.

In mild areas autumn also brings *Amaryllis belladonna*, with its massive pink or white trumpet-shaped flowers. Then there are the hardy cyclamens, with their crimson, pink, or white flowers and handsome foliage, and the low sternbergias, whose bright yellow, crocus-shaped flowers appear from early to late fall.

In winter, hyacinths, crocuses, tulips, and daffodils, all potted three months or so beforehand for indoor flowering, can brighten dark days. There are also exotic "house plant" bulbs, some of which have been specially treated to produce earlier indoor bloom—the amaryllis is a notable example.

Inner petals of crocus 'Blue Bird' are white; the outer ones are blue-gray. The jonquil group of narcissus, to which 'Suzy' belongs, have up to five flowers per stalk.

Crocus chrysanthus 'Blue Bird'

Narcissus 'Suzy'

Favorite Flowers from Bulbs and Corms

Narcissus 'Unsurpassable' (Trumpet daffodil)

Narcissus 'Barrett Browning' (Small-cupped narcissus)

Crocus 'Remembrance' (Spring flowering)

The snowdrop is one of the earliest of the spring bulbs, with pearlike buds that push up through the snow in late winter. In very cold weather, the buds stay closed but will open during the day when the sun shines.

Snowdrops (*Galanthus*) are very often confused with snowflakes (*Leucojum*), which in cold climates flower later. Snowdrops have three long petals and three short ones, whereas the six green-tipped petals of snowflakes are all the same size. Also, two or more flowers are carried on each snowflake stem, compared with the snowdrop's one.

Snowdrops look best in informal woodland settings, in rough grass, under deciduous trees or shrubs, or among low ground covers.

Snowdrop bulbs dry out quickly, so they must be replanted without delay if divided after flowering. Bulbs bought in the fall should be soaked for 24 hours before planting. They may not flower prolifically the first year, as they need time to become established; but after that they need little attention. Unlike many bulbs, they prefer a moist organic soil, with some shade.

Although they are rarely grown indoors, snowdrops can be raised in pots in the same way as crocuses or hyacinths. Keep them comparatively cool. A cold frame is useful until the flower buds are visible. Then they can be brought into a cool room.

Crocuses

Massed crocuses make a brilliant show of color in late winter and early spring, when little else is in flower.

The white, yellow, blue, purple, and bicolored blooms open before the daffodils. They, too, can be naturalized in grass or planted in groups beneath shrubs and trees.

In addition to the spring-flowering crocuses, there are those that flower in autumn and late winter. They all grow from small, flattish corms. The winter and spring crocuses produce their leaves and flowers at the same time, but the autumn-flowering types develop their leaves the following spring. All multiply freely.

The crocus flower, 3–5 inches high, has six petals, which are rounded in the hybrids and named cultivars and pointed in the species. In bright sun the petals open out flat, revealing conspicuous golden or orange anthers. The flowers close up at night.

The winter-flowering crocuses, which appear outdoors from midwinter onward (early spring in the north), were developed from *C. chrysanthus* and other species. The 3-inch-high flowers range through shades of yellow, blue, white, and purple. Many have contrasting stripes or have markings at the base of the petals; the inner color frequently differs from the outer one.

The large-flowered crocuses that bloom in early spring are Dutch cultivars of *C. vernus*. The largest of all the crocuses, they come in white, blue, lilac, red-purple, and golden yellow, or they are sometimes striped with different colors.

Fall-flowering crocuses appear from early to late fall. The flowers, which are 4–5 inches high, are pure white, lavender, or violet-blue. They are not as hardy as the winter- and spring-flowering types.

Daffodils and Other Narcissi

No garden is complete without clumps of golden yellow, trumpet-flowered daffodils dancing in the spring breezes. Daffodils are among the most reliable and versatile of all bulbs. Not only do the bulbs increase each year but their bitter taste repels rodents. Besides, the daffodil is one of the best bulbs for naturalizing in the garden, because it grows well under deciduous trees and in open woodlands.

Most garden varieties of the daffodil are descendants of the wild narcissus. There are now more than 30,000 cultivars of narcissi, divided into groups according to flower shape and parentage. The flower has a central trumpet or cup surrounded by six petals. Daffodil's trumpets are as long as, or longer than, the petals.

The trumpet is frilled or flared at the outer edge, and the six overlapping petals are usually pointed at the tips. Colors vary. In some cultivars, such as the old favorite 'King Alfred', trumpet and petals are clear yellow. In others, petals are a deeper or paler shade than the trumpets. Bicolored daffodils may have yellow or orange trumpets and white petals. Others, like 'Beersheba', are all white.

The word "narcissus" is popularly used to describe varieties with a short central cup, even though the large-cupped and trumpet daffodils are also botanically *Narcissus*. Between the large-cupped and the short-cupped narcissi are other varieties with many different cup sizes and great variations in color. Their cups and petals (sometimes contrasting) range from white through cream and yellow to pink, red, and orange. Cups are often ruffled.

The double-flowered varieties have cups that are indistinguishable from the petals. Most are all one color, such as the yellow 'Ingelescombe', but some of the newer ones are bicolored, like the orange and yellow 'Texas'.

Triandrus and cyclamineus narcissi have pendent, bell-shaped trumpets and backswept petals. Tazetta narcissi (for forcing and mild climates only) carry several blooms on each stem, and poeticus narcissi have frilled, colored centers and conspicuous, nonoverlapping petals. Many are fragrant.

Jonquils (*Narcissus jonquilla* hybrids) are also known for their sweet fragrance. Each stem bears a small cluster of flowers with shallow cream, yellow, or orange cups and contrasting petals.

For further details on daffodils and all the other narcissi see the chart on pages 127–128.

Galanthus nivalis

Hyacinthus 'Pink Pearl'

Tulipa 'Hamilton'

The snowdrop (*Galanthus*) is among the garden's earliest bloomers. Hyacinths and parrot tulips follow as the soil warms.

Hyacinths

In the drab days of winter, the scented blooms of hyacinths bring color and cheer into normally flowerless rooms. Although hyacinths are widely used for indoor forcing, they are very suitable for the garden and for planters in mild areas.

Some dealers offer specially treated bulbs, which, if planted in autumn, will flower indoors in early winter, instead of from midwinter onward. The technique of forcing bulbs into early flower is described on pages 119–120.

Most hyacinths are derived from a single species—*Hyacinthus orientalis*—and most of the modern varieties have the characteristic large, single-spike flowers. These are known as Dutch hyacinths.

Top-size bulbs with large flower heads are ideal for indoors, but in the garden smaller bulbs with smaller stalks and flower heads withstand the rain and wind better. After several years in the garden, the bulbs and spikes increase in number but are smaller in size. The sweetly scented flowers are available in white, cream, yellow, salmon, pink, red, light and dark blue, and purple.

The Roman hyacinths (*H. orientalis albulus*) have smaller flower spikes than the Dutch hybrids, and they produce several to each bulb. The flowers are more loosely set on the spike than those of the Dutch hyacinths. Less hardy than their Dutch counterparts, they are often grown indoors. They come in white, pink, and blue.

Tulips

More than 300 years ago the tulip was brought from Turkey to other European countries and then to Holland. In the intervening centuries Dutch bulb growers have bred, cross-bred, and altered the original varieties to such an extent that they have been divided into groups according to their different characteristics.

Tulips, like many other bulbs, produce a dramatic effect with little attention. They almost never fail to flower the first year after planting.

The tulip grows from a pointed, thin-skinned bulb that produces a single erect flower stem (branched on bouquet tulips). One or two large, lance-shaped leaves appear near ground level, and two or three smaller ones grow higher up on the stem.

The typical flower is goblet shaped, with six petals, but it varies considerably in overall size and from a short to a long goblet. Some tulip flowers have very pointed petals, and some are double. Still others open flat into star-shaped blooms (*Tulipa kaufmanniana*) or into twisted and fringed shapes (parrot tulips).

The so-called bouquet tulips, which produce five or six flowers per bulb on a branching stem, provide a spectacular garden accent. Lily-flowered tulips have long pointed petals and a goblet shape, slightly constricted toward the top.

Tulips come in every color except true blue and in many bicolors as well. They grow best in regions with long winters and should be planted in early to mid fall. Southerners can purchase prechilled bulbs to plant in late fall and grow as spring flowering annuals.

Species, or botanical, tulips, available from mail-order bulb specialists and in the better garden centers, are ideal for rock gardens. They are exquisite, with short, sturdy stems and goblet-shaped flowers of exceptionally brilliant colors.

Unlike their large-flowered relatives that gradually deteriorate, many of the species tulips will multiply year by year. Some, like *T. tarda*, can be naturalized in the lawn with crocuses and will self-seed.

Ornamental Onions

Onions can be divided into those we eat, such as garlic, leeks, scallions, and storage onions, and those we enjoy in flower. These come in a range of heights, from species suitable for the rock garden, to ones that fit in well at the back of a border.

Flowers can be in loose trusses or tight globular heads and come in almost every color except brilliant red, although some species are bright pink.

The tallest is *Allium giganteum*, which can reach 6 feet tall and has 50 or more lilac flowers on a ball-shaped head. Other, slightly shorter varieties, with this type of flower head that are suitable for the back of the border include *A. aflatunense*, pink; 'Lucy Ball', dark lilac; 'Purple Sensation', dark purple; and 'Globemaster', dark violet. These all flower in early summer and their foliage dies down soon after flowering. Remove the seed heads when flowering is done to stop them seeding, but leave the green stems to help feed the bulb for the following year.

For the middle of the border, plant the drumstick onion (*A. sphaerocephalon*) with oval heads of dark red flowers on a 2-foot stem. It tones well with the blue *A. caeruleum*, which is the same height and flowers at the same time, midsummer, but with more open heads of bloom.

Probably the most eye-catching onion is the star of Persia, (*A. cristophii*) with 8-inch heads of star-shaped flowers in early summer. The pink flowers are on long individual stalks and form a slightly flattened globe. The seed heads can be used in dried arrangements later.

Chives (*A. schoenoprasum*) are usually grown in the herb garden, but they make a good front of the border edging even when their early summer pink flowers are not present. The plant known as Chinese or garlic chives (*A. tuberosum*) can also be used in this way. It has white flowers in late summer. Both grow about 15 inches tall and should be deadheaded regularly to prevent the spread of unwanted seedlings.

Galanthus nivalis (Snowdrop)

Gladiolus 'Land o' Lakes' (Large flowered)

Hyacinthus orientalis 'Jan Bos' (Dutch)

Tulipa 'Bellona' (Single early)

'White Parrot' is a particularly attractive tulip for floral arrangements. The richly rose-colored 'Peach Blossom' is an early double-flowered variety.

Tulipa 'White Parrot'

Tulipa 'Peach Blossom'

How to Plant Bulbs and Corms

Choosing the Sites and Preparing the Ground

Provided they are protected from strong winds, and given reasonably fertile garden soil, sufficiently well drained to prevent rot, most bulbs will thrive in any part of the garden. They can be grown in beds, borders, and tubs (some kinds in rock gardens), and some of the small ones, such as snowdrops, winter aconites, and crocuses, can be planted beneath shrubs and trees or ground cover. Bulbs that naturalize well in grass, such as crocuses, can be left undisturbed for years.

Most bulbs do best in a sunny location, but a few—cyclamens, bluebells, dog's-tooth violets, snowdrops, and winter aconites—do well in shaded spots. Some bulbs, including the acidanthera, amaryllis, nerine, and sparaxis, are sensitive to cold weather and are best grown where they can get maximum sun and pro-tection from strong winds, such as at the foot of a south-facing wall.

If you plant spring-flowering bulbs under grass, remember that the area above them must not be mowed until the foliage has turned yellow.

Plant spring-flowering bulbs from early to late fall and most summer-flowering bulbs in early spring (mid to late spring for the less hardy ones). Plant autumn-flowering bulbs in late spring to late summer.

Whatever the time of year, the planting site must first be carefully prepared. Dig the ground to a depth of about 10 inches.

Mix mature compost (preferable to peat moss) into the soil (one 2-gallon bucket per square yard), and let it settle for a few days before planting. Also mix bone meal into the planting area at a rate of about 5 pounds per 100 square feet, or add a balanced organic fertilizer at the same rate. If preferred, mix a small quantity in each planting hole.

Bulbs in Rock Gardens and Between Paved Areas

Many of the low-growing bulbs—spring, summer, or autumn flowering—easily establish themselves in rock gardens and in small spaces between paving stones on terraces.

Remove any covering of mulch from the site, and dig holes with a trowel to the depths indicated for each kind (pp. 121–131). Plant the bulbs in small groups of at least three or four. After planting, level the soil with the trowel, replace the mulch, and label the site. If the soil is dry, water thoroughly after planting and again when there is little rain.

Good bulbs that provide a welcome show of color in the rock garden early in the year include snowdrops (*Galanthus*), the winter-flowering crocuses, glory-of-the-snow (*Chionodoxa luciliae*), winter aconite (*Eranthis hyemalis*), dwarf narcissi, and spring squill (*Scilla*).

After the spring bulbs there are dwarf alliums to give summer color. These are not as widely available as many other bulbs but are listed in the catalogs of some bulb specialists. These can be followed by sternbergias, colchicums, and the fall and winter crocuses.

Low-growing bulbs look particularly attractive growing through such mat-forming plants as the creeping thyme and *Dianthus*. The green or gray-green foliage provides a striking background for the flowering bulbs when they are in bloom, and then it remains attractive all year, long after the bulb flowers fade.

Where the mat-forming plant is firmly rooted in, loosen it slightly with a hand fork, and then plant the bulbs with a blunt dibble.

If the plant has only a central root—for instance, *Gypsophila repens*—simply roll the matted stems aside, and plant the bulbs beneath them with a narrow trowel.

Planting Bulbs in Groups for Formal Display

Before planting large bulbs for a formal display, place the bulbs over the area, spacing them at regular intervals. With a trowel, dig holes to the recommended depth (the chart on pp. 121–131 gives planting depth and eventual spread, for spacing).

For large numbers of bulbs, it may be easier to dig out the entire bed to the proper depth before planting. Cover the bulbs with soil, and water thoroughly if it is dry.

When the whole area has been planted, set a label stake in the center for identification, and remember to mark the edges of the planting area in some way to ensure that other plants will not later be put in there by mistake.

If certain plants, such as forget-me-nots, pansies, or polyanthus primroses, are to be grown between the bulbs to provide additional spring color, space the bulbs a few inches farther apart. Set out the plants before planting the bulbs or in spring as shoots of bulbs show above ground.

Growing Bulbs for Cut Flowers

When picking flowers for indoor decoration, it is advisable to cut as few leaves as possible, so as not to exhaust the bulbs. If cut flowers are of prime importance, grow bulbs in a special area where the garden's future appearance is not critical. Prepare the soil in the normal way, and plant the bulbs slightly closer together than the eventual spread of the plant (see pp. 121–131). Allow 1½–2 feet between the rows.

When you are cutting bulb flowers for arrangements, it is preferable to do so in the early morning or the late evening, using a pair of sharp scissors or a sharp knife. Immediately place the flowers in deep, warm water in a cool, dark place for several hours or overnight. Allowing them to soak up plenty of water will prolong their life when they are placed in the warmth of an indoor room.

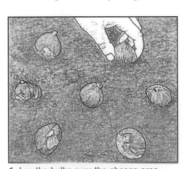

1. Lay the bulbs over the chosen area, spacing them at regular intervals.

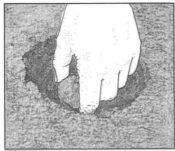

2. Place each bulb, point uppermost, in a hole at least twice its depth.

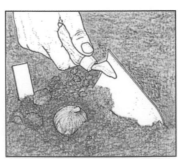

3. Cover the bulbs with soil removed from the planting holes. Label area.

Tulipa 'Spring Green'

Tulipa aucheriana

'Spring Green' belongs to the group of tulips called *Viridiflora*, whose blossoms are mottled, or streaked with green. They are effective at the front of shrub beds. *Tulipa aucheriana* is a rewarding early bloomer for sunlit rock gardens.

Climate and Spring Bulbs

Naturalizing Bulbs

When planting bulbs for naturalizing, they look more attractive scattered than placed in formal groups.

Narcissi and crocuses can be naturalized in any convenient lawn area with well-drained soil. The bulbs will not need fertilizing—the materials you apply to feed your lawn will feed the bulbs, too. Scatter handfuls of the bulbs and, for an informal effect, plant them where they land.

For individual bulbs, dig the holes with a trowel. Or use a special bulb planter, which consists of an open-ended, slightly tapered metal cylinder attached to a handle. The cylinder is forced into the ground to the proper planting depth and then pulled up with a plug of soil and turf. Replace the turf plug after planting the bulb, and water.

When you set out groups of bulbs in a lawn area, first cut a figure H in the grass with an edging tool or a spade. Then cut back under each half, and fold the turf back.

Loosen the soil with a garden fork, and dig the planting holes with a trowel. Place the bulbs in their positions; then cover them with soil, and level it. Roll back the turf, firm it down, and water thoroughly.

Many spring-flowering bulbs and corms, if planted and cared for correctly, can be grown in the coldest regions of the U.S. as well as in the more temperate zones.

In the northern parts of the country and in high mountain regions such as the Rockies, hardy spring-flowering bulbs should be planted at least three weeks before the ground is expected to freeze, to allow sufficient time for root development. (This is particularly important with narcissi.) In mountain areas especially, where extremes of temperature between day and night are the rule, a partly shaded site and a winter mulch are advisable.

Planting depths in cold climates are the same as they are for more temperate regions. The bulbs, of course, will flower somewhat later, although the sequence of bloom will be the same as it is elsewhere.

In the warmer parts of the South and West, where a winter freeze is either unlikely or nonexistent, spring-flowering bulbs need not be planted until very late fall, since the early to mid autumn months are likely to be quite hot.

Dealers in these regions often have spring-flowering bulbs available in early fall, at the same time as dealers in cold climates. In this event, they can be bought as soon as they become available and then stored in a refrigerator, where they can be "precooled" until a suitable planting time.

The bulbs can be placed in the bottom of the refrigerator, preferably in a vegetable crisper, in the paper bags in which they were purchased. They should not be allowed to freeze; the best temperature is about 40°F. Keep them there for up to eight weeks or until the ground is cool enough—in late fall or in early winter.

In warm climates it is advisable to add compost or other organic material to the soil before planting to improve drainage and moisture retention. Be sure to plant the bulbs in a lightly shaded site rather than in full sun, and mulch them after shoots appear.

Among the spring-flowering bulbs that do well in warm climates are hyacinths, many of the smaller narcissi, and mid- to late-season tulips, such as Triumphs and Darwins.

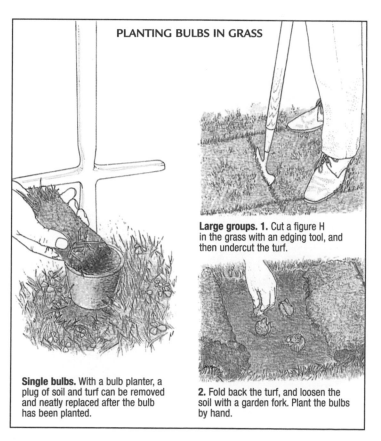

PLANTING BULBS IN GRASS

Single bulbs. With a bulb planter, a plug of soil and turf can be removed and neatly replaced after the bulb has been planted.

Large groups. 1. Cut a figure H in the grass with an edging tool, and then undercut the turf.

2. Fold back the turf, and loosen the soil with a garden fork. Plant the bulbs by hand.

Some Pointers on Buying Quality Bulbs and Corms

How can you tell a good bulb or corm? Basically it should be firm, not shriveled, and free of soft spots.

Because most spring-flowering bulbs come from the Netherlands, where growers exercise strict control over the quality of their exports, they arrive in North America in good condition. How they are handled after that, however, can spell the difference between good and bad bulbs. Left in a hot store or subjected to rough handling by customers, they lose quality rapidly. Even when you buy good bulbs, they can deteriorate if you leave them in an airless bag in a hot place.

What about size? The top-size bulbs and corms are the most expensive and generally produce the biggest flowers. The newer varieties will also cost more than the older ones. But the smaller sizes may be perfectly adequate for a good garden display. After a couple of years, you will not know the difference anyway. If you are inexperienced in buying bulbs, purchase a dozen of both sizes and compare their performance over time.

If you are buying bulbs in considerable numbers, you will find that many mail-order bulb specialists offer a discount for early orders—generally those received by July or August. This may seem early to think about bulbs to be planted in fall, but it is a good way to make sure that you order before the stocks of your favorite varieties are gone.

Narcissus 'Salome' is an excellent garden variety and can also be used for forcing. 'Geranium', a vigorous hybrid with a flat cup and several blossoms per stem is especially recommended.

Narcissus 'Salome'

Narcissus 'Geranium'

Care of Bulbs After Planting

Care of Established Bulbs in Borders and Grass

Most hardy bulbs and corms need relatively little attention during the growing season, and many will thrive for several years.

Remove weeds, by hand or with a hoe, as soon as the bulbs' shoots show clearly. Take special care not to damage the shoots, and avoid using weed killers.

Feeding is generally recommended for bulbs that are to be left in the ground for several years. Use a mix of bone and blood meals on these bulbs, raking it lightly into the soil during the fall cultivation.

During prolonged dry spells in spring and summer, thorough watering will improve growth. If the plants are in bloom, water around the base rather than from above. Continue watering in dry spells even after the flowers have faded. The growing cycle does not end until the leaves turn yellow and die.

Unless you must lift bulbs that have finished flowering to make room for other plants, the bulb foliage should be allowed to ripen naturally because it manufactures all the nutrients needed for the plant's future growth.

One exception is snowdrops. If the bulbs are crowded, these are best transplanted while still growing. Lift after flowering, divide, replant them immediately and water.

Some gardeners tidy bulb foliage by knotting or otherwise fastening the leaves together. However, this technique should be avoided because it reduces the amount of leaf surface exposed to the sun, with a subsequent diminishing of nourishment to the bulbs.

Bulbs that are grown to provide cut flowers for the house in summer, gladioli for example, produce larger flowers if fed with a manure tea. This should be done every three weeks after the buds form and until they open.

Deadheading. As soon as spring bulbs—daffodils and other narcissi, tulips, and hyacinths—finish flowering, remove their faded blooms. (This is called deadheading.) Cut off only the dead flower heads, but not the stem. The stems and leaves are needed to build up nourishment in the bulbs.

On a hyacinth remove the small flowers that make up the spike by running your hand from below the flower cluster up to the tip. Leave the flower stem, since it will provide nourishment for the bulb.

On a faded gladiolus cut off the flower spike, but leave at least four pairs of leaves.

Some bulbs and corms multiply freely from self-sown seeds. Snowdrops, scillas, winter aconites, muscaris, chionodoxas, and cyclamens should be deadheaded only if no more plants are wanted.

Supporting tall plants. Few bulbs need supporting if they have been planted deeply enough. In windy, exposed positions, however, the taller cultivars of gladioli, acidantheras, and alliums may need to be tied to bamboo canes.

Gladioli grown in rows for cutting are usually self-supporting. If necessary, however, insert a stake at both ends of each row, and tie strong string tautly between the stakes to the front and rear of the row for extra support.

Frost protection. Although certain types of bulbs are usually lifted and stored for the winter, gladioli, ixias, and nerines can be left in the ground in mild areas of the country. Protect these bulbs with a mulch, however, in frosty weather.

For mulching, some gardeners use a layer of salt hay, straw, or leaves kept in place with evergreen branches. Others prefer bark, buckwheat hulls, or pine needles. Do not use peat moss as a mulch because it blows away when dry and holds too much water when wet. Mulch bulbs after freeze-up.

Increasing Your Stock of Bulbs

By producing offsets, many hardy bulbs and corms increase steadily when they are left in the ground. Eventually, a clump will become congested, producing fewer flowers of poorer quality. Division then becomes necessary. At this stage the offsets can be separated and grown on in nursery rows until they reach flowering size. Some offsets can take as long as seven years to reach maturity, but others, including some crocuses, lilies, and gladioli, will flower in only two years. The time from offset to bloom also depends on the size of the offset and the general cultural conditions that are provided.

Propagation by seeds is possible, but the seedlings take years to bloom, and the hybrid plants—especially narcissi, hyacinths, gladioli, and tulips—will usually be inferior to, and different from, the parent, unless a controlled cross was made.

Dividing and Replanting Overgrown Plants

Some bulbs and corms must be lifted and divided every three or four years; those naturalized in grass can be left for many years. When bulbs flourish, they may increase, causing overcrowding and reduced bloom. This is the time to divide.

It is best to dig up an entire clump of bulbs or corms soon after the foliage has withered but while it is still firmly attached to the bulb. After lifting the clump out of the ground, brush the soil away. Then separate the bulbs or corms.

Daffodils and other narcissi, tulips, and crocuses can be replanted immediately or dried, cleaned, and stored until fall. But certain bulbs, such as snowdrops and winter aconites, should be divided just after flowering and replanted at once. It is best to replant all bulbs, especially tulips, in a new location.

When you divide and replant, separate small bulbs and corms for propagation (as shown on p. 117), planting only large ones in permanent sites.

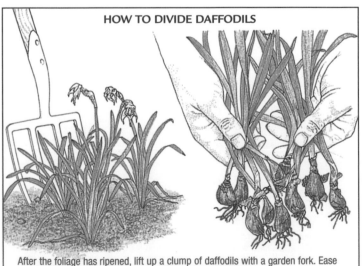

HOW TO DIVIDE DAFFODILS

After the foliage has ripened, lift up a clump of daffodils with a garden fork. Ease the soil away from the bulbs, and separate them carefully.

The fragrant 'Carnegie', a late-blossoming hyacinth, has a compact flower spike that makes it a good choice for exposed locations.

Hyacinthus 'Carnegie'

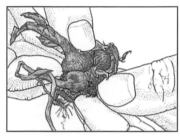

1. Pull away the cormels or bulblets from the parent bulb.

3. Space the cormels or bulblets at a distance twice their width.

2. Dig out a narrow trench, and put ½–1 in. of sand in the base.

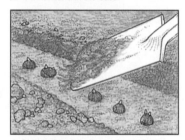

4. Put another 1-in. layer of sand in the trench; then fill with soil.

Growing Bulblets and Cormels to Blooming Size

Established bulbs and corms that are lifted from the ground will have offsets attached. These can be used to raise new bulbs or corms identical to the parent variety.

Bulblets are produced on either side of the parent bulb, while cormels appear at the base and alongside the corm. After the parent bulb or corm has dried, break off the offsets with your fingers.

Small bulbs can be used for propagation and naturalizing, especially crocus, chionodoxa, galanthus, and scilla. Bear in mind that very small offsets will take a couple of years to produce flowers.

Offsets from hardy bulbs and corms can be planted in a new place during summer and early autumn. In cold areas, the offsets from less hardy bulbs or corms should be stored in a frost-free place over the winter and planted the following spring. Plant in sun or partial shade, by digging narrow trenches, varying in depth to suit the size of the offsets (see illustrations above).

Large bulblets (about half the size of the parent bulb) should be planted two to three times their own depth; the smaller ones, like crocus cormels, 2 inches deep; tiny cormels, 1 inch deep.

Unless the soil has excellent drainage, put a ½- to 1-inch layer of sand at the bottom of the trench before planting the offsets. The distance between them should be twice their width.

Cover them with another inch of sand before filling in with soil. Sand improves drainage and makes lifting easier later on.

The bulblets and cormels will develop leaves but no flowers the first year. Once they have flowered, they can be moved to their permanent locations.

What Can Go Wrong With Bulbs

If any of your bulbs show symptoms that are not described in the chart below, turn to the section on plant disorders that starts on page 506. A list of organic controls for use in the garden can be found on page 542.

SYMPTOMS AND SIGNS	CAUSE	CONTROL
Stems, leaves, or flower buds are covered with small green or black insects; growth is often malformed.	Aphids (greenflies or blackflies)	Spray plants with a strong stream of water; if flower buds are present, spray with insecticidal soap.
Rust-colored streaks on leaves and flowers, especially those of potted narcissi. Leaves and flowers stunted.	Bulb scales or bulb mites	Destroy severely infested bulbs. Expose dormant bulbs to frost for 2 or 3 nights; or dip in hot water (110°–115°F) for 3 hr. Before planting, treat bulbs with sulfur.
If squeezed gently, bulbs (particularly those of daffodils and other narcissi) feel soft at neck end and base. If planted, bulbs fail to grow.	Narcissus bulb flies or lesser bulb flies	Test bulbs at planting time; discard soft ones. Do not plant in warm, sheltered places that attract the flies.
Leaves of hyacinths, narcissi, and tulips have pale stripes. Leaves may become distorted and stunted, may eventually die.	Stem or bulb eelworms	Destroy infected bulbs and move healthy ones to new location.
Flowers and foliage of gladioli have silvery streaks and patches, which eventually turn brown.	Thrips	Destroy infested flowers and foliage. Spray affected plants early with *Beauveria bassiana*. Insecticidal soap and neem may be effective.
Plants are stunted, foliage is normal in color but small. Flowers fail to open normally or open and droop.	Shallow planting (especially tulips)	When foliage starts to turn yellow, lift bulbs and either store until next fall or replant at proper depth.
Anemone leaves have patches of whitish powder; leaves may be distorted.	Downy mildew (fungus)	Apply potassium bicarbonate spray.
Leaves of gladioli turn yellow and topple over, usually before flowers appear. Corms show black spots or lesions; later, corm shrivels.	Dry rot (fungus)	Remove and destroy infected plants; dust remaining bulbs with sulfur before storing. Replant in new location.
Foliage of tulips shows water-soaked specks and streaks, which turn brown. Petals are often spotted. Brown rot may attack stems, which topple over.	Tulip fire, or botrytis (fungus)	Destroy diseased plants. Dust remaining bulbs with sulfur after lifting from soil. Replant in another location.

Dutch crocus (*C. vernus*) has larger flowers than the snow crocus (*C. chrysanthus*), but both are excellent for planting in lawns and under shrubs.

Crocus vernus

Crocus chrysanthus 'Ladykiller'

Lifting, Drying, and Storing Bulbs

Bulbs may be lifted from the ground if room is needed for other plants, if they are not hardy enough to spend the winter outdoors, or if they are crowded and blooming poorly.

Ideally, hyacinths, narcissi, tulips, and other spring-flowering bulbs should be left until the foliage has ripened. Foliage is often prematurely removed to improve the garden's appearance, but this can jeopardize future performance of the bulbs. Where space is needed for summer plants, bulbs can be transferred to an unused area to complete their growing.

To transfer, insert a spading fork straight down into the ground, well clear of the plants and deep enough to avoid damaging the bulbs. Carefully lever up the bulbs, complete with soil, leaves, and stems. Discard any pulpy or rotting bulbs.

Dig a trench about 5–6 inches deep, 12 inches wide, and long enough to take all the lifted bulbs. Lay a piece of fine wire or plastic netting at the bottom of the trench, and place the bulbs on it at a slight angle. They can be set so that they almost touch each other, but at least half the length of the stems and leaves must be above soil level. Let some netting protrude above the trench to make lifting the bulbs easier later on.

Fill the trench halfway with soil, and water thoroughly (repeat during dry spells). After the leaves and stems have withered, the bulbs can be taken up for storing. Just pull up the netting, and lift the bulbs out.

If only a few bulbs are involved, it may be easier to lay them in deep trays of damp peat moss. Cover the bulbs with more peat moss, and place the trays in a lightly shaded place. Keep the peat moss moist.

When the leaves have ripened fully, remove the bulbs from the trays (or trench). Pull off the dead leaves, roots, and shriveled skins. The bulblets attached to the parent bulb can be used for propagation; otherwise discard them. Place the cleaned bulbs, uncovered, in single layers in labeled flats, and store in a cool, dry place (safe from rodents) until fall replanting. Do not enclose the bulbs in a way that prevents air circulation, which is needed to prevent mold.

If garden space is not a problem, leave most hardy bulbs in the ground until just after the foliage has ripened; then divide and replant them (p. 116). This is much simpler than the trenching method and is preferred by most gardeners.

In very mild climates tender bulbs can be left undisturbed in the ground all year. Elsewhere, they should be lifted when the leaves begin to turn brown in the fall. Lift them with a spading fork. For gladioli, cut off the top stems and leaves an inch above the corm. Let the corms dry, uncovered, in trays in a cool, airy shed, for 7 to 10 days. If necessary, they can be left longer before cleaning.

Break away the shriveled corms, and separate the small cormels that surround the new corm. Cormels can be discarded or saved for replanting.

Remove tough outer skins from the large corms, and destroy any that show signs of lesions or rotting. Dust the remaining corms with diatomaceous earth to control thrips, with sulfur to prevent dry rot and scab. This will pay dividends the next year in the corms. Store the corms in flats or mesh bags in a cool but frost-free place with good air circulation until spring. Some gardeners store corms in old nylon stockings.

In cold regions all tender bulbs must be lifted in the fall and dried and stored like gladioli. Label to avoid mistakes when you plant next year.

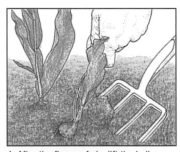

1. After the flowers fade, lift the bulbs with a fork and remove the soil.

2. If only a few bulbs are lifted, lay them in deep flats of damp peat moss. Set large numbers of bulbs on netting in the trench; cover with soil.

3. When all the leaves and stems have shriveled, remove the bulbs.

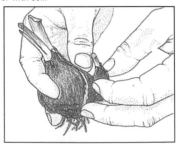

4. Before storing, remove dead foliage and loose skins.

5. Clean off soil and the old roots.

6. Break clumps into individual bulbs ready for replanting.

7. Put bulbs in labeled boxes. Store in a cool, dry place until planting time.

Double forms of narcissus, such as 'White Lion', do not have a trumpet. Tender acidantheras (*Gladiolus callianthus*) are very fragrant. Plant them near a sitting area.

Narcissus 'White Lion'

Gladiolus callianthus

How to Grow Bulbs for Indoor Flowering

Crocus 'Golden Yellow'
(Spring flowering)

Many of the hardy bulbs that bloom outdoors during spring can be had in flower indoors weeks or months earlier. If you pot them in early fall and allow sufficient time in cool conditions for root growth, you can then "force" flowers by placing pots in a warm room.

Among the most popular spring-flowering bulbs for indoor use are hyacinths, crocuses, daffodils and other narcissi, irises, and tulips. Most require storage for 10 to 13 weeks or more at temperatures of 40°F or less before forcing.

Bulb catalogs often indicate which cultivars do best indoors. Good trumpet daffodils are 'Dutch Master' (yellow), 'Mount Hood' (white), and 'Salome' (white with a soft pink trumpet). Fragrant, small-flowered *Narcissus tazetta* 'Paperwhite' and

'Soleil d'Or' need no cold treatment. Among the tulips, the Early Singles, Triumphs, and some Darwin Hybrids and Parrots are easiest to force. Also popular are large-flowered Dutch hyacinths, and crocuses such as *Crocus chrysanthus* 'Blue Pearl' and large-flowered *C. vernus* varieties like 'Remembrance' and 'Pickwick'.

There are many different potting mixtures available, or you can make your own by mixing equal parts of sifted garden soil, sifted compost, and pulverized peat moss. (Heavy clay soil can be lightened by adding sand and vermiculite.) It is not necessary to add fertilizer to the medium in order to obtain good bloom.

Large bulbs can be planted singly in 3- to 4-inch pots, but they are more effective when several are set close together in bigger pots.

Potting Bulbs for Forcing

When bulbs are potted for indoor flowering, it is best to plant them in pots or bulb containers that have drainage holes so that you will be able to check these holes later for evidence of root growth.

Clay or plastic containers can be used, but tall species, such as tulips and narcissi, tend to get top-heavy and fall over when growing in plastic pots. Also, because plastic pots are not porous, they do not dry out as quickly as clay pots, something to keep in mind when watering.

Cover drainage holes with pebbles or shards of clay pots (to stop the soil blocking them), then put a layer of moist potting mixture into the pot. The amount used depends on the size of the container and bulbs; when set in place, the tops of the bulbs should be about even with, or slightly above, the top of the pot. Place bulbs touching each other, putting in as many bulbs as the pot can hold. With tulips, the first leaf emerging from the bulb folds out on the flat side of the bulb. To ensure a more symmetrical display, place each bulb with its flat side facing out from the pot's center. Then finish filling the pot. Level the soil about ½ inch below the pot's rim. Plant only one kind of bulb in a pot. Label each container, indicating the kind and variety of the bulb and the date. Water well and let drain.

FORCING IN A SHALLOW DISH

Trim off any old roots, cover drainage holes, and put a thin layer of mix in the base. Space bulbs and cover.

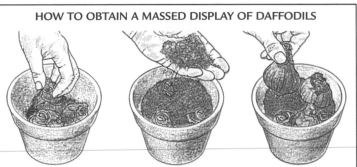

HOW TO OBTAIN A MASSED DISPLAY OF DAFFODILS

Place three bulbs on a 2-in. layer of moist potting soil in a 5- to 6-in. pot. Cover to the necks; then set three more bulbs between them, and fill.

The hardy cyclamen (*Cyclamen coum*) should be planted in small clusters under trees and shrubs. It blooms as early as February. 'Album' has dark green leaves that may have silvery markings.

Cyclamen coum 'Album'

Storing Spring-Flowering Bulbs After Potting

Three months of cool temperatures and darkness are essential for the proper rooting of bulbs grown for bloom ahead of their normal outdoor flowering time. You will need a storage area where temperatures remain at 45°–50°F or lower, but where bulbs will not freeze. A spare home refrigerator is ideal, but fruit must not be stored in the refrigerator at the same time. Keep the pots well watered.

The outdoor method of storage, in a trench or a cold frame, is probably the most reliable, since it duplicates natural conditions. The object is to keep bulbs from freezing, yet ensure that the pots can be removed easily when it is time to bring them indoors.

Dig a trench at least 6 inches deeper than the deepest pot. Place a plank of wood in the bottom of the trench to prevent the bulbs from rooting in the soil, and set the pots on it. (If rodents are a problem, cover the pots with screening.) Cover the pots with 3 inches of perlite, sand, or shredded polystyrene "popcorn." Add a 3- to 6-inch layer of dry leaves, hay, or other mulch, then cover with evergreen boughs. Because the mulch keeps the ground from freezing, the pots can be removed easily.

In very cold climates, extra precautions are needed to prevent the bulbs from freezing. You will have to line and cover the trench with polystyrene sheets, then mulch.

When storing pots in a cold frame, bury them in the same manner as in a trench. Put the cold frame cover on during severe weather or very cold nights; open the cover or remove it entirely on warm days. Where there is space to put a cold frame on the north side of a building, there will probably be little need for opening it.

A dark area in an unheated garage is also suitable for storing potted bulbs. The temperature must be warm enough to prevent the bulbs from freezing, yet cool enough for proper root development. (An attic is usually too warm.) If the area is open to the outdoors, you will need to protect the bulbs from mice and squirrels. An enclosure made from ½-inch hardware cloth or window screening should be adequate. Make the cover large enough to surround the pots, and allow about 6 inches above the bulbs for air circulation.

Except for bulbs set in garden trenches, check frequently for watering requirements. This may be especially necessary for bulbs in clay pots which dry out faster.

Once the roots have formed, the soil dries out even more rapidly and may even require daily watering. However, care must be taken not to overwater, as this may rot the bulbs. **Aftercare.** Bulbs cannot be forced two years in succession, although they can be planted in the garden to add to the existing display. Once the flowers are faded, pick them off to stop the plant trying to produce seed. Keep the pots in a sunny window and water as needed. Feed with half-strength kelp solution or other soluble fertilizer every third watering. Wait until the danger of frost is past before putting the pots outside.

Once the foliage starts to die, stop watering and allow the soil to dry. Then clean the bulbs and store them ready to plant the following autumn.

Growing Hyacinths in Glass Jars

Hyacinths are well suited to growing in water. It is not surprising then that some garden centers sell glass hyacinth jars with constricted necks that have been specially designed for this purpose.

Begin by filling the jar up to its neck with water, and then insert a small lump of charcoal into the jar to keep the water fresh.

Root end down, carefully place a hyacinth bulb in the top portion of the jar, in such a way that the water is just touching the base of the bulb.

Repeat this procedure with whatever number of bulbs and hyacinth jars you have. When all the bulbs are set in place, put each jar in a cool, dark place until the roots growing into the water are about 4 inches long and the shoots are showing. Then move the jars to a warmer, well-lighted place. Add more water to the jars as the level falls.

After the flowers have faded, discard the bulbs. They will not produce any more flowers.

Growing Crocuses in Special Pots

Special glazed clay pots, with holes around the sides, can be bought for growing crocuses. The corms are planted in such a way that the tip of each one, and later on the flower, will protrude through a hole.

Fill such a pot to the first row of holes with moist potting soil; then place crocus corms with their necks showing through the holes. Add more soil and set more corms in position. Finally, set a group of corms in the top opening, and fill around them with mix.

Like other bulb containers, crocus bowls should be kept in a cool, dark place for at least 13 weeks. Then the bowls can be brought into a warmer, well-lighted room.

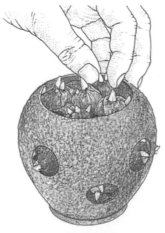

Crocuses can be planted to flower through holes in special pots.

Bringing Bulb Containers Indoors for Forcing

After the rooting and cooling period of about 13 weeks, move potted bulbs from their cold bed to a well-lighted location indoors. Temperature at the new site should be about 55°–60°F.

In this environment, the flowers will begin to develop. Keep the soil moist at all times.

Place a cone of dark paper over the shoot of a hyacinth for two weeks to elongate the flower spike above the foliage.

For a succession of flowers, bring out one container a week into its new location.

If you want to display them in a warm room, return the pots to a cool room each night.

Hyacinth bulbs grow well in water, in glass jars with constricted necks.

Bulbous Plants for All Seasons

All bulbs, corms, and tubers in the chart that follows can be grown outdoors. Some, however, such as the amaryllis, cannot survive a winter in the open and should be lifted after flowering and stored in a frost-free location. The remarks column gives this information when pertinent.

All the botanical names are listed alphabetically. In instances where a botanical name has changed recently, the old name is given as a cross-reference. This may be helpful since most nurseries, garden centers, and catalogs are sometimes slow to use the new name.

Included here are some of the outstanding species and varieties that are usually widely available.

Flowering times will be later where it is colder, and earlier where warmer. For more information and pictures, visit www.bulb.com.

Amaryllis belladonna

BOTANICAL AND COMMON NAMES	HEIGHT	SPREAD	SOIL	LIGHT	DECORATIVE CHARACTERISTICS AND REMARKS	PLANTING AND PROPAGATION
Allium (allium, or ornamental onion)			■	●	Easily grown bulbs. Low growers best in rock gardens; taller kinds may need staking and are best in groups among other plants. Many kinds dry well for indoor arrangements. Alliums listed grow well from Zone 4 southward except as noted.	Plant all large alliums 8 in. deep in early to mid fall or as soon as available. Lift and divide in autumn or early spring when crowded.
Allium aflatunense	2½–3 ft.	9 in.	■	●	Lilac-pink flowers in ball-like heads in early summer. *A. aflatunense* is somewhat less hardy than other varieties.	
A. bulgaricum					See *Nectaroscordum siculum*.	
A. caeruleum (blue allium)	24 in.	6 in.	■	●	Round heads of bright blue flowers on wiry stems in summer. Hardy in Zones 3–8. May be called *A. azureum* in catalogs.	Plant 2 in. deep in early fall.
A. cristophii (star of Persia)	2½–3 ft.	1 ft.	■	●	Deep lilac flower heads 8–10 in. in diameter with star-shaped flowers appear in early summer. Excellent for drying.	
A. 'Globemaster'	32 in.	18 in.	■	●	Large globe-shaped heads of dark lilac flowers above straplike leaves in early summer.	
A. moly (golden garlic)	6–10 in.	6 in.	■	●	Yellow flower heads to 3 in. wide appear in early summer. Hardy in Zones 3–9.	Plant 2 in. deep.
A. 'Mount Everest'	40 in.	18 in	■	●	Similar to 'Globemaster' but taller and white.	
A. neapolitanum	8–18 in.	6 in.	■	●	Fragrant white flowes. Good cut flower. Hardy to Zone 5. Also known as *A. cowanii*.	Plant 2 in. deep in early fall.
A. oreophilum	2–6 in.	3 in.	■	●	Rose-pink flowers in early summer. Excellent in rock gardens. Extremely hardy.	Plant 1½–2 in. deep.
A. 'Purple Sensation'	3 ft.	18 in.	■	●	Similar to 'Globemaster' but slightly taller and dark purple, with a larger flower head.	
A. sphaerocephalon (drumstick allium)	2–3 ft.	14 in.	■	●	Dense, egg-shaped heads of dark red flowers in midsummer. Hardy in Zones 4–11.	Plant 3–4 in. deep.
Amaryllis (amaryllis) *Amaryllis belladonna* (magic lily, or naked ladies)	2 ft.	1 ft.	■	●	Fragrant pink blooms in early to mid fall. Leaves appear before flowers. Can be grown indoors in pots in cold regions by potting in late summer. Hardy to Zone 7–10.	Plant 6 in. deep in mid to late summer. In cool climates plant deeper and against south-facing wall. Divide bulbs when they become crowded.

Allium moly (golden garlic)

Amaryllis belladonna (magic lily)

■ well drained to sandy   ■ moist   ■ wet   ■ acidic   ■ alkaline   □ regular soil   ● full sun   ◑ partial shade   ● shade

The hardy camass (*Camassia*) is not well known but makes a welcome addition to the garden.

Camassia leichtlinii

BOTANICAL AND COMMON NAMES	HEIGHT	SPREAD	SOIL	LIGHT	DECORATIVE CHARACTERISTICS AND REMARKS	PLANTING AND PROPAGATION
Anemone (anemone, or windflower) *Anemone blanda* (Grecian windflower)	6 in.	4 in.	■	●◑	White as well as many shades of blue and mauve-pink flowers in late winter to midspring. Plant in small groups. Good in rock gardens. Grow from Zone 4 southward. Farther north, mulch heavily.	*A. blanda:* Plant tuberous roots 2–3 in. deep in early to mid fall. Take offsets or divide tuberous roots in late summer; replant at once.
A. coronaria (poppy anemone)	6–12 in.	4–6 in.	■	●◑	White, lavender, mauve, pink, crimson, and scarlet blooms in early spring or early summer. Excellent cut flower. Nitrogen fertilizer, such as blood meal, applied as buds appear helps to lengthen stems. Grows best in the Pacific Northwest. Tuberous roots not hardy beyond southern portions of Zones 7–12.	*A. coronaria:* Plant tuberous roots 1½–2 in. deep, in late fall (far South, early spring in North).
A. ranunculoides (buttercup windflower)	2–4 in.	18 in. or more	■	●◑	Bright yellow flowers above lacy dark green leaves that die down soon after flowering. Spreads slowly by underground runners.	Plant 1 in. deep while dormant. Divide rhizomes after foliage dies. Will self-seed but is not invasive.
Begonia (begonia) *Begonia evansiana*	1½–2 ft.	1 ft.	□	◑	White or pink flowers in midsummer to fall. Good flowering plant for shady places. Not reliably hardy if left outside in any zone; store over winter at 45°–50°F.	*B. evansiana:* Plant tubers 2 in. deep in spring in partial shade. Remove bulblets from axil of leafstalk. Place in pot on soil surface; cover with glass until young plants form. Set out in spring.
B. tuberhybrida (tuberous begonia)	2 ft.	1 ft.	□	◑	White, pink, yellow, orange, and red blooms from midsummer to fall. Often sold according to form of flower, such as camellia flowered or carnation flowered. Particularly useful in containers. Tubers must be dug before frost or when flowering slows and stored over winter in peat moss at 45°–50°F. For earliest bloom, start tubers indoors 2–3 mo. prior to outdoor planting time. Keep barely moist in a well-lighted window or greenhouse until top growth appears. Many hybrid strains offered with various flower forms. See Annuals (p. 198) for seed-raised forms.	*B. tuberhybrida:* Plant tubers 1–2 in. deep in spring in partial shade. Take cuttings of shoots growing from tubers in spring. Plant outside when rooted.
Brodiaea (brodiaea) *Brodiaea coronaria*	18 in.	3–6 in.	■	●	Blue-purple, star-shaped flowers in late spring and early summer. Plant in groups of 5 or 6 in sun. Avoid summer watering. West Coast native, hardy Zones 8–10 without winter protection.	Plant 2–3 in. deep in fall; in cold regions plant in spring. Remove offsets from corms at lifting time; replant.
B. laxa (grass nut)					see *Triteleia laxa,* p. 130.	
Bulbocodium (bulbocodium) *Bulbocodium vernum*	1½–3 in.	4 in.	□	●	Bright pink flowers in very early spring, one of the first to flower. A pair of leaves emerge later and grow 6 in. tall. Hardy in Zones 4–8.	Plant 4 in. deep in late summer. Lift and divide every few years. Sow seeds as soon as ripe.
Caladium (caladium) *Caladium bicolor* (elephant's ears)	1 ft.	1 ft.	■	●◑	Valued for attractive leaves in solid colors or patterned with white, green, pink, or red, according to variety. Effective from midsummer until cold weather. Grow in shade or sun. Dig in fall; let dry for 1 wk. Store in dry peat moss or perlite at 70°–75°F.	Plant 2 in. deep directly outdoors after temperatures reach 70°F, or start earlier in pots indoors. In spring cut tubers into pieces with one or more eyes each. Dust with sulfur before planting.

Anemone blanda
(Grecian windflower)

Begonia evansiana
(begonia)

Brodiaea coronaria
(brodiaea)

Bulbocodium vernum
(bulbocodium)

Caladium bicolor
(elephant's ears)

■ well drained to sandy　■ moist　■ wet　■ acidic　■ alkaline　□ regular soil　● full sun　◑ partial shade　● shade

The showy Indian shot (*Canna generalis*) is widely grown but will not survive frost. Tropical *Crinum* is a late-summer bloomer.

Canna generalis 'Wyoming'

Crinum powellii 'Album'

Camassia leichtlinii
(camass)

Canna generalis
(Indian shot)

Chionodoxa sardensis
(glory-of-the-snow)

*Colchicum
speciosum*
(autumn crocus)

Corydalis
(fumitary)

Crinum powellii
(crinum)

BOTANICAL AND COMMON NAMES	HEIGHT	SPREAD	SOIL	LIGHT	DECORATIVE CHARACTERISTICS AND REMARKS	PLANTING AND PROPAGATION
Camassia (camassia, or camass) *Camassia cusickii*	2½–3 ft.	1½–2 ft.	☐	◐	Pale blue flowers in late spring. Good in wildflower gardens or by pools or bogs. Long-lived bulbs that increase slowly.	Plant 6 in. deep in early to mid fall. Remove offsets in fall; replant at once.
C. leichtlinii	2–3 ft.	1½ ft.	■	◐	White to deep blue flowers in late spring.	
Canna (canna) *Canna generalis* (Indian shot)	1½–4 ft.	1–1½ ft.	☐	●	Large flowers on spikes above very large leaves. Colors range from white to shades of pink, yellow, and scarlet. Many new varieties have color-striped foliage. Blooms in midsummer until cold weather. Does best in long, hot summers. Grow in gardens, or in pots or large tubs on terraces. Dig up in fall after blackened by frost, dry a few days, store upside down in dry peat moss or vermiculite at 50°–60°F. Hardy Zones 8–11.	Plant rhizomes in spring, after night temperatures stay above 50°F; cover with 3 in. of soil. Divide rhizomes in spring. 'Tropical Rose' and 'Seven Dwarfs' strains can be grown from seeds.
Chionodoxa (chionodoxa, or glory-of-the-snow) *Chionodoxa luciliae*	6 in.	4 in.	☐	● ◐	White, light blue, or pink blooms in midspring. Plant in large groups in rock gardens and at front of borders. Hardy in almost all parts of North America. 'Pink Giant' has larger rose-pink flowers.	Plant bulbs 2 in. deep in early fall, in open, sunny site. Propagates freely from self-sown seeds. Lift and divide the bulbs when crowded.
C. sardensis	8 in.	4 in.	☐	● ◑	Star-shaped, bright blue flowers with a white eye in early spring. Good for naturalizing.	Plant 2 in. deep in early fall. Sow seed as soon as ripe.
Colchicum (autumn crocus) *Colchicum autumnale* (meadow saffron)	6 in.	9 in.	☐	● ◑	White or rose-lilac, single or double flowers bloom in early fall. Flowers resemble crocuses but are larger and are produced in fall before leaves. Leaves appear in spring, then die. Plant in groups under trees or shrubs. Hardy in Zone 4–9.	Plant corms 3–4 in. deep in late summer, in sun or partial shade.
C. speciosum	6–10 in.	9–12 in.	☐	● ◑	White or rose-purple blooms in mid to late fall. Many hybrids between this and *C. autumnale*.	Plant *C. speciosum* 4–6 in. deep. Separate cormlets in midsummer, and replant at once.
Corydalis (fumitary) *Corydalis flexuosa* (blue fumitary)	12 in.	8 in.	☐	◑	Dense clusters of slim, bright blue flowers with white throats in late spring and early summer. Best in a soil rich in humus. 'Blue Panda' is darker, shorter, and flowers more. Zones 4–8.	Plant 2 in. deep in fall. Lift and divide occasionally, sow seeds as soon as ripe.
C. solida (fumewort)	6 in.	8 in.	☐	◑	Pale lilac to light purple flowers above grayish foliage. Seeds freely but never becomes weedy. Considerable variation in flower color. 'George Baker' is a bright red. Zones 4–9.	Soak store-bought tubers for 24 hours before planting in early fall. Lift established clumps after flowering, divide and replant immediately.
Crinum (crinum) *Crinum longifolium*	3 ft.	1½–2 ft.	☐	●	White or pink blooms in late summer. Hardiest of the crinums and can be grown in sheltered locations in climates as severe as Zone 6.	Plant bulbs 6 in. deep or more, in spring or fall in warm areas, spring in colder parts. Remove offsets in early spring; pot singly in 3- to 4-in. pots. Will flower in 3 yr.
C. powellii	5 ft.	1½–2 ft.	☐	●	White to pink flowers in late summer. In Zone 8 or warmer, try outdoors against south-facing wall with heavy winter mulch. Pots can be wintered in frost-free place.	

Cyclamen (*Cyclamen hederifolium*) is a late-summer bloomer that does well in the shade.

Cyclamen hederifolium

Crocus chrysanthus
(winter-flowering crocus)

Cyclamen purpurascens
(cyclamen)

Dichelostemma ida-maia
(Firecracker flower)

Eranthis hyemalis
(winter aconite)

Eremurus robustus
(desert candle)

Erythronium
(trout lily)

BOTANICAL AND COMMON NAMES	HEIGHT	SPREAD	SOIL	LIGHT	DECORATIVE CHARACTERISTICS AND REMARKS	PLANTING AND PROPAGATION
Crocus (crocus) WINTER-FLOWERING CROCUS *Crocus chrysanthus* and other species	3 in.	3 in.	☐	●	White, blue, mauve, yellow, or bronze flowers, some striped with contrasting colors, bloom in late winter and early spring. Best in rock gardens, under trees or shrubs, in front of beds or borders, and naturalized in lawns. Large-flowered varieties, such as 'E. A. Bowles', good for forcing in indoor pots. All hardy in Zone 4 and often into Zone 3.	Plant 3 in. deep in sunny position. Plant in early fall as soon as obtainable. Early planting is especially important for fall-flowering varieties. After 3 or 4 years, lift when leaves turn brown, and remove cormlets. Replant at once; put smallest ones in unused spot until they grow to flowering size.
SPRING-FLOWERING CROCUS *C. vernus*	4–5 in.	4 in.	☐	●	Same colors as winter-flowering varieties but bloom from early to mid spring. Locate as winter-flowering types. Largest flowers are in this most widely planted class.	
AUTUMN-FLOWERING CROCUS *C. speciosus*, etc.	4–5 in.	3–4 in.	☐	●	White, lilac-blue, lavender, rose, or yellow flowers in midfall. Not recommended for forcing indoors, or for climates colder than Zone 4.	
Cyclamen (hardy cyclamen) *Cyclamen coum*	3 in.	6 in.	☐	◑	Pink to carmine, sometimes white flowers bloom midwinter and midspring. Plant in small clusters beneath trees and shrubs or at base of north-facing wall. Mulch in spring. Hardy in Zones 4–9.	Plant 1–2 in. deep, in mid to late summer. Cyclamen corms (tuberous roots) do not divide or produce offsets; sow seeds in summer. May take a year or more to bloom.
C. hederifolium (baby cyclamen)	4 in.	6 in.	☐	◑	Rose to white flowers bloom in late summer. The most tender species, Zones 7–9.	
C. purpurascens	4 in.	6 in.	☐	◑	Fragrant crimson flowers bloom in late summer, early fall. Hardy in Zones 5–9.	
Dichelostemma (Firecracker flower) *Dichelostemma ida-maia*	12 in.	6 in.	■	●	Slender stalks of red tubular flowers with green tips over grasslike foliage. Lasts well when cut. 'Pink Diamond' has bright pink blooms. Hardy in Zones 4–8.	Plant 2 in. deep in very well drained soil. Corms need to bake in summer to ripen. Divide in late summer.
Eranthis (eranthis) *Eranthis hyemalis* (winter aconite)	4 in.	3 in.	■	● ◑	Buttercup-yellow flowers bloom in late winter, early spring. Set in groups beneath deciduous trees and shrubs. Combine with snowdrops (*Galanthus*) for extended bloom period. Keep well watered in spring. Hardy in all but coldest regions.	Plant tuberous roots 1 in. deep, in late summer or early fall. Soak for 24 hrs. first. Lift and divide tubers in late spring; replant at once. Self-sows.
Eremurus (foxtail lily, desert candle) *Eremurus* Ruiter Hybrids	6 ft.	2 ft.	■	●	Tall spikes of several hundred small individual flowers in a range of colors from orange to yellow and white in early summer. Fleshy roots look like an octopus. Hardy in Zones 4–8.	Plant in a shallow hole, on a layer of sand, with the crown 2 in. below soil level. When flowering becomes poor, lift carefully in late summer, shake apart, and replant immediately. See Ruiter Hybrids (above)
E. robustus	10 ft.	3 ft.	■	●	Towering spikes of pink flowers with yellow stamens. Leaves are gray-green. Zones 4–8.	
E. stenophyllus	5 ft.	2 ft.	■	●	Bright yellow becoming darker with age. Zones 4–9.	
Erythronium species and varieties (erythronium, or trout lily)	6 in.	4–6 in.	■ ☐	◑	White, purple, pink, rose, or yellow flowers bloom in mid and late spring. Plant in groups in woodland or partially shaded areas. Once established, leave undisturbed; but if necessary, lift and replant after leaves wither. Many species and varieties offered. Some are hardy in southern portions of Zone 4.	Plant corms 2–3 in. deep, in late summer or as soon as available. Provide mulch. Offsets can be removed in summer, planted immediately in unused piece of ground for several years to increase size.

■ well drained to sandy ■ moist ■ wet ■ acidic ■ alkaline ☐ regular soil ● full sun ◑ partial shade ● shade

Dog's-tooth violet (*Erythronium*), a spring bloomer, is well suited to planting under trees. The checkered lily (*Fritillaria meleagris*) takes its name from its petal patterns, which look like a checkerboard. It can be planted in clusters in beds or in short grass.

Erythronium dens-canis

Fritillaria meleagris

Fritillaria imperialis
(crown imperial)

Galanthus nivalis
(common snowdrop)

Galtonia candicans
(summer hyacinth)

Gloriosa superba
'Rothschildiana'
(glory-lily)

Hippeastrum hybrid
(amaryllis)

BOTANICAL AND COMMON NAMES	HEIGHT	SPREAD	SOIL	LIGHT	DECORATIVE CHARACTERISTICS AND REMARKS	PLANTING AND PROPAGATION
Fritillaria (fritillary) *Fritillaria imperialis* (crown imperial)	2–3 ft.	9–15 in.	☐	●◑	Yellow, orange, or red flowers bloom in mid and late spring. Plant in groups in borders. Sometimes difficult to establish, but forms clumps in right site. Divide when crowded. Grows in southernmost parts of Zone 4.	Plant bulbs on sides, 8 in. deep, in midfall, in sun or partial shade. Plant *F. meleagris* 4 in. deep. Remove offsets in late summer; grow in cold frame or pots. Seeds sown in summer take 4–6 yr. to bloom. Plant *F. michailovskyi* 3 in. deep. Plant *F. pallidiflora* 3 in. deep. Plant *F. persica* bulbs 6 in. deep.
F. meleagris (snake's-head, or checkered lily)	1 ft.	6 in.	☐	●◑	Pure white or purple and white flowers bloom in mid and late spring. Treat like *F. imperialis*; can be grown also in short grass. Hardy in Zone 3.	
F. michailovskyi	4–8 in.	4 in.	■		Pendent, blood-red bells edged with yellow on slender stems in early summer. May be called *F. michailowski*. Hardy in Zones 3–9.	
F. pallidiflora	12 in.	6 in.	☐ ■	●	About 6 cream to pale yellow, nodding flowers, with green bases, on leafy stems in early summer. Hardy in Zones 4–8.	
F. persica	3 ft.	9 in.	☐ ■	●	Long spikes of purple-brown bells. *F. persica* 'Adiyaman' is freer flowering.	
Galanthus (snowdrop) *Galanthus elwesii* (giant snowdrop)	6–10 in.	4–6 in.	☐	◑	White flowers with green-tipped inner petals appear in late winter, early spring. Plant in groups under trees or shrubs, among low ground covers, and with other small-flowering spring bulbs, such as *Chionodoxa* and *Eranthis*. Sometimes difficult to establish but afterward multiplies freely. Hardy in Zones 4–9.	Plant bulbs 3–4 in. deep, in early fall or immediately after flowering, in area that is partially shaded in summer. Lift and divide after flowering; replant at once.
G. nivalis (common snowdrop)	4–10 in.	4–6 in.	☐	◑	Flowers are similar to *G. elwesii*. Excellent in rock gardens. 'S. Arnott' is 10 in. tall, large-flowered, and fragrant. There is also a double form. Zones 3–8.	
Galtonia (galtonia) *Galtonia candicans* (summer hyacinth)	3–4 ft.	9 in.	☐	●	White flowers tipped with green bloom in mid and late summer. Plant in groups in perennial or shrub borders. Lift and store as for gladiolus. Zones 7–10.	Plant bulbs 4–6 in. deep in late spring, except in mildest regions, where they can be set out in fall in sunny site. A few offsets are produced. These can be stored over winter and planted again in spring.
Gloriosa (gloriosa, or glory-lily) *Gloriosa superba* 'Rothschildiana'	3–4 ft.	1 ft.	☐	●	Red flowers with yellow-edged petals bloom in early summer, also at other times in mild areas. Attractive vines that can be grown against trellises or in pots with support. Dig in fall, store in dry peat moss at 55°–60°F.	Separate tubers in spring, and plant at once. Plant horizontally 4 in. deep, in spring. Locate in sun, and provide some support. Seeds usually take 2–3 yr. to reach flowering size. Species can also be grown year-round in a cool greenhouse.
Hippeastrum hybrids (hippeastrum, or amaryllis)	2 ft.	1–1½ ft.	■	◑	White, pink, salmon, or red flowers, some with striping, bloom in spring outdoors, winter or spring indoors. Flowers usually precede leaves. Most often grown as house plants, but can be cultivated outside in mildest regions. Popular hybrids include 'Apple Blossom' (blush-pink), 'Jeanne d'Arc' (white), 'Belinda' (red). See also *Amaryllis*.	Plant bulbs outdoors 6–8 in. deep, in midfall, in partial shade. In pots, plant from fall to spring. Leave top third of bulb uncovered and remove offsets from around bulb in fall before replanting. Seeds normally take 3–4 yr. to flower.

As its name suggests, the spring snowflake (*Leucojum vernum*) is in bloom as early as March. By midsummer, fragrant blooms appear on the white spider lily (*Hymenocallis festalis*).

Hymenocallis festalis

Leucojum vernum

Hyacinthoides hispanica
(Spanish bluebell)

Hyacinthus orientalis
(hyacinth)

Hymenocallis narcissiflora
(spider lily)

Ipheion uniflorum
(spring starflower)

Ixia maculata hybrid
(corn lily)

Leucojum vernum
(spring snowflake)

Lycoris radiata
(red spider lily)

BOTANICAL AND COMMON NAMES	HEIGHT	SPREAD	SOIL	LIGHT	DECORATIVE CHARACTERISTICS AND REMARKS	PLANTING AND PROPAGATION
Hyacinthoides (or Scilla) *Hyacinthoides hispanica,* or *Scilla campanulata* (Spanish bluebell)	1 ft.	6 in.	☐	◐	White, blue, or pink blooms in late spring. Good under trees, shrubs, and in woodland. Can be grown in shade. Good cut flower.	Plant 4 in. deep, in early fall. Propagation by self-sown seedlings or by division of crowded bulbs after leaves have withered.
H. non-scripta (English bluebell)	1–1½ in.	6 in.	☐	◐	Rich blue bell-shaped flowers. Not quite as hardy as Spanish bluebell.	
Hyacinthus (hyacinth) LARGE-FLOWERED HYBRID, or DUTCH HYACINTH *Hyacinthus orientalis* hybrids	8–9 in.	6–8 in.	☐	◐	White, blue, mauve, yellow, pink, red, or orange flowers bloom in early to late spring. Plant in groups and near house, where fragrance can be enjoyed. May need staking. Hardy to Zone 4. Varieties include 'L'Innocence' (white), 'Delft Blue' (blue), 'City of Haarlem' (yellow), 'Pink Pearl' (pink), 'Jan Bos' (crimson).	Plant bulbs 5–6 in. deep, in midfall except in mild climates, where late-fall or early-winter planting is best. Dig up old bulbs when leaves turn yellow; separate and replant.
ROMAN HYACINTH *H. o. albulus*	6 in.	6–9 in.	☐	◐	White flowers, smaller than above, appear in early to late spring. Extremely fragrant. Best for forcing. Not hardy in northern half of Zone 4.	
Hymenocallis (spider lily, or ismene) *Hymenocallis narcissiflora,* or *Ismene calathina* (Peruvian daffodil)	1½–2 ft.	10–12 in.	☐	◐	White blooms appear in midsummer. Hardy in southern half of Zone 7; in colder regions dig in fall and store upside down in vermiculite or peat moss at 64°F. Varieties include 'Advance' and 'Festalis' (white) and 'Sulfur Queen' (yellow).	Plant bulbs 6–8 in. deep, in spring when night temperatures average 60°F. Lift in fall, and separate offsets. Should be replanted in spring.
Ipheion (spring starflower) *Ipheion uniflorum,* or *Brodiaea uniflora,* or *Triteleia uniflora*	6–8 in.	4 in.	☐	◐	Up-facing white flowers tinged with blue bloom in early spring; have minty scent. Foliage appears in fall. Plant in large groups under shrubs or in rock garden. Hardy in southernmost parts of Zone 4 and southward.	Plant bulbs 3–4 in. deep, in early fall. Remove offsets when foliage dies in summer; replant immediately. Multiplies rapidly.
Ixia (corn lily) *Ixia maculata*	1½ ft.	4 in.	■	●	Hybrids with cream, pink, yellow, orange, or red flowers bloom in late spring, early summer. Soil must be dry in summer for corms to ripen. Grow in groups. Can be grown in pots. Hardy in southern parts of Zone 6.	Plant corms 3–4 in. deep. Plant in early to late fall in southern part of Zone 6 and southward; in spring, north of Zone 6. Remove offsets after foliage dries in summer.
Leucojum (leucojum, or snowflake) *Leucojum aestivum* (summer snowflake)	1½ ft.	6 in.	☐	◐	White flowers tipped with green, 4–8 per stem, bloom in mid to late spring. Plant in groups in rock gardens or sunny nooks. Hardy in all of Zone 2.	Plant bulbs 3–4 in. deep, in early fall. Remove offsets when foliage dies; replant at once.
L. vernum (spring snowflake)	6–8 in.	4 in.	☐	◐ ●	Smaller white flowers, 1 per stem, are tipped with green, bloom early to mid spring. This and summer snowflake do better in mild climates than *Galanthus*, or snowdrop.	
Lycoris (lycoris, or spider lily) *Lycoris radiata* (red spider lily)	1½ ft.	10–12 in.	☐	◐	Deep pink to red blooms in late summer, early fall. Leaves precede flowers, then die; keep fairly dry until flowers appear. Bulbs bloom best when crowded. Makes excellent container plant for late bloom. Hardy from southern half of Zone 7.	Plant bulbs 6–8 in. deep in garden in midsummer; set bulbs in containers with tips exposed. In borderline areas of hardiness, *L. squamigera* should be planted deeper. To propagate, dig after foliage dies (before flowering); remove offsets; replant.
L. squamigera (autumn amaryllis, or resurrection lily)	2 ft.	10–12 in.	☐	◐	Fragrant lilac-rose flowers bloom in late summer, early fall. Hardier than *L. radiata*. Can be grown outdoors from southern parts of Zone 4.	

■ well drained to sandy　■ moist　■ wet　■ acidic　■ alkaline　☐ regular soil　● full sun　◐ partial shade　● shade

'Ice Follies' is one of the large-cupped narcissi. It multiplies quickly and forms large clumps.

Narcissus 'Ice Follies'

Muscari armeniacum
(grape hyacinth)

Narcissus
(trumpet narcissus)

Narcissus
(large-cupped narcissus)

Narcissus (double-flowered narcissus)

Narcissus cyclamineus
(narcissus)

BOTANICAL AND COMMON NAMES	HEIGHT	SPREAD	SOIL	LIGHT	DECORATIVE CHARACTERISTICS AND REMARKS	PLANTING AND PROPAGATION
Muscari (muscari, or grape hyacinth) *Muscari armeniacum*	8 in.	4 in.	☐	●	Deep blue flowers edged with white appear in mid and late spring. Best in groups at front of borders and rock gardens. One of hardiest bulbs; grows from Zone 2 southward. 'Valerie Finnis' has very pale blue, almost white flowers.	Plant bulbs 3 in. deep, in early to late fall. Seeds freely where it blooms well. Divide every 3 yr. when leaves yellow; replant immediately, or store until fall.
M. aucheri 'Tuberginianum'	6 in.	4 in.	☐	●	Sky-blue flowers bloom from early to mid spring. White form also available.	
M. botryoides	7 in.	4 in.	☐	●	Light blue sterile flowers top the spikes, while the lower flowers are a dark blue. Multiplies rapidly.	
M. comosum (tassel grape hyacinth)	1 in.	4–6 in.	☐	●	Upper flowers blue to mauve, sterile; lower flowers olive-colored, fertile. Petals finely cut. Bloom in late spring to early summer. 'Plumosum' has feathery heads.	
Narcissus TRUMPET NARCISSUS, or DAFFODIL Trumpet is as long or longer than petals. One flower borne per stem.	14–18 in.	6–8 in.	☐	● ◐	Flowers are all yellow or white, or with trumpets one color, petals another; bloom in early to late spring in Zone 4. Plant in groups in shrub or perennial borders or under trees. Excellent cut flower. Popular cultivars include 'Dutch Master', 'King Alfred', 'Unsurpassable' (yellow); 'Beersheba', 'Mount Hood' (white); 'Spellbinder' (yellow and ivory); and 'Pink Glory' (white and pink).	Plant bulbs 6–8 in. deep and 6 in. apart, in mid to late fall. After a few years, lift in early summer after foliage yellows; remove offsets and replant at once or store until early fall.
LARGE-CUPPED NARCISSUS Cup, or corona, is more than one-third length of petals and may be frilled. One flower per stem.	14–22 in.	6–8 in.	☐	● ◐	Trumpets and petals often different colors. Combinations of yellow, pink, and white. Good varieties include 'Gigantic Star' (yellow), 'Ice Follies' (white), 'Flower Record' (yellow and white), 'Mrs. R. O. Backhouse' (pink and white), and 'Professor Einstein' (white and orange).	See trumpet narcissus (above).
SMALL-CUPPED NARCISSUS Cup, or corona, is not more than one-third length of petals. One flower per stem.	14–18 in.	6 in.	☐	● ◐	Flowers are all white or combinations of yellow, white, or other colors; bloom from early to late spring. Varieties include 'Barrett Browning' (white and orange), 'Verger' (white and red), and 'Angel' (white).	See trumpet narcissus (above).
DOUBLE-FLOWERED NARCISSUS All types with more than 1 layer of petals. One or more flowers per stem.	1–1½ ft.	6 in.	☐	● ◐	White, yellow, or bicolored flowers bloom from early to late spring. Varieties include 'Ice King' (white and yellow), 'Petit Four' (cream and apricot), and 'Sir Winston Churchill' (cream, ivory, and orange, fragrant).	See trumpet narcissus (above).
TRIANDRUS NARCISSUS Cup is about two-thirds as long as the petals are. One to 6 flowers per stem; may be pendulous.	6–18 in.	6 in.	☐	● ◐	Varieties include 'Hawara' (yellow), 'Thalia', 'Tresamble' (white), and 'Tuesday's Child' (white and yellow).	See trumpet narcissus (above).
CYCLAMINEUS NARCISSUS Long pendent cup with petals curving back from it. One flower is borne per stem.	8–15 in.	3–6 in.	☐	● ◐	White, yellow, or bicolored. Varieties include 'February Gold' (yellow), 'Jack Snipe' (white and yellow), and 'Jenny' (white).	See trumpet narcissus (above).
JONQUILLA, or JONQUIL Cup longer or shorter than petals. Two to 6 fragrant flowers are borne per stem. Tubular leaves.	7–14 in.	4–6 in.	☐	● ◐	Yellow or bicolored, often with red, pink, or orange cup. Blooms in late spring. Varieties include 'Trevithian' (pale yellow), 'Suzy' (yellow and orange-red), and 'Lintie' (white and pale pink).	See trumpet narcissus (above).

Star of Bethlehem (*Ornithogalum*) looks good in a woodland setting. Nerine, usually grown in pots, can be an excellent cut flower.

Nerine bowdenii

Ornithogalum nutans

Narcissus tazetta (tazetta narcissus)

Narcissus poeticus (poet's narcissus)

Narcissus (dwarf narcissus)

Nectaroscordum (Bulgarian onion)

Nerine bowdenii (nerine)

Ornithogalum thyrsoides (chincherinchee)

Oxalis adenophylla (sorrel)

BOTANICAL AND COMMON NAMES	HEIGHT	SPREAD	SOIL	LIGHT	DECORATIVE CHARACTERISTICS AND REMARKS	PLANTING AND PROPAGATION
TAZETTA NARCISSUS (includes poetaz) Four to 8 fragrant short-cupped flowers are borne per stem.	14 in.	6–8 in.	☐	● ◐	White or yellow, usually with colored cup, single or double. Outdoors, blooms in early to late spring; forced bulbs can bloom from early winter into spring. Except in mildest regions grow tazettas in pots (p. 119); poetaz can be grown as for trumpet narcissus. Tazettas include 'Paper-white' (white) and 'Soleil d'Or' (yellow). Poetaz include 'Geranium' (white and orange-red) and 'Cheerfulness' (yellow, double).	Suitable only for pot culture except in southern part of Zone 7 and southward. Treat poetaz as for trumpet narcissus. Bulbs grown indoors in pebbles and water should be discarded after blooming.
POETICUS NARCISSUS Petals white, short cup is contrasting color; fragrant. Usually 1 flower is borne per stem.	17–20 in.	6 in.	☐	● ◐	White flower has yellow cup edged with red, blooms from mid to late spring. Very fragrant and good cut flower. Excellent in cold climates. Most popular variety is 'Actaea' (white with yellow cup edged with red).	See trumpet narcissus, p. 127.
DWARF NARCISSUS Includes true species and some hybrids. Most are small flowered and short; 1 or more flowers are borne per stem.	3–6 in.	2–3 in.	☐	● ◐	White or yellow flowers from late winter to midspring. Best planted in small groups in rock garden or where readily seen. Some in this group not hardy north of Zone 7. Popular are *Narcissus bulbocodium* (yellow) and *N. triandrus* albus, or angel's tears (cream-white); *N.* 'Tête-à-Tête' (yellow and orange); *N.* 'Jumblie' (golden).	Plant at least 3 times the depth of bulb, in early to mid fall. Propagate as for daffodils; but also by seeds collected when ripe and sown in early summer. Takes 3–7 yr. to bloom.
Nectaroscordum (Bulgarian onion) *Nectaroscordum siculum*	4 ft.	18 in.	☐	● ◐	Up to 30 pendulous pink-tinged cream flowers at the top of an upright stem, like a bursting firework. Upright tan seed heads are attractive later and can be dried. Zones 4–10. May be listed as *Allium bulgaricum* in catalogs.	Plant 4 in. deep in fall. Lift and divide in late summer when clumps get large. Sow seed as soon as ripe. May self-seed.
Nerine (nerine) *Nerine bowdenii*	2 ft.	6 in.	☐	●	Pink flowers bloom in late fall, early winter. After potting grow indoors at 50°F over winter. Do not water until growth commences; then keep moist and fertilize monthly with diluted manure tea. Leaves grow during winter and spring. Gradually dry off and withhold water when leaves start to yellow until growth resumes. Hardy Zones 8–10.	Usually grown in pots except in mildest regions. In pots, bury lower half of bulbs; in ground, set 4–6 in. deep. Plant in early fall. Lift and divide overgrown clumps after flowering or in spring. Repot offsets from pot plants.
Ornithogalum (star of Bethlehem) *Ornithogalum nutans* (nodding star of Bethlehem)	1 ft.	6 in.	☐	● ◐	White and pale green flowers bloom from mid to late spring. Plant in groups at front of borders, or woodland. Hardy in Zone 4.	Plant 2–3 in. deep, in midfall. Large bulbs can be set 4–6 in. deep. *O. thyrsoides* is planted 2–3 in. deep, in fall, in mild climates. To grow in pots indoors, barely cover bulb. Lift and remove bulblets after leaves yellow; replant at once.
O. thyrsoides (chincherinchee)	1½ ft.	4 in.	☐	● ◐ ●	White to cream flowers bloom in late spring, midsummer. Can be grown as pot plant in cool greenhouse (50°F at night) to flower in spring. Also easily grown in window. Cut flowers last well. Hardy in southern parts of Zone 6.	
O. umbellatum (star of Bethlehem)	9–12 in.	6 in.	☐	◐	White flowers from late spring to early summer. Multiplies rapidly, may become a nuisance. Hardy in most of Zone 2.	
Oxalis (sorrel) *Oxalis adenophylla*	3–4 in.	2–3 in.	■	●	Small 1½-in. bell-shaped flowers are lavender-pink, petals veined in deeper shade; bloom in late spring, midsummer. Commonly grown in rock gardens.	Plant tuberous roots 2–3 in. deep and 4–5 in. apart, in midfall. Hardy in Zone 4. North of this, lift in fall; store as gladiolus until planting time.

■ well drained to sandy   ■ moist   ■ wet   ■ acidic   ■ alkaline   ☐ regular soil   ● full sun   ◐ partial shade   ● shade

Striped squill (*Puschkinia*) and spring squill (*Scilla*) are good choices for a rock garden or for naturalizing in a lawn. Each tiger flower (*Tigridia*) blossom lasts only one day.

Puschkinia scilloides

Scilla sibirica 'Spring Beauty'

Tigridia pavonia

Puschkinia scilloides libanotica
(striped squill)

Ranunculus asiaticus
(Persian buttercup)

Scilla tubergeniana
(spring squill)

Sparaxis tricolor
(harlequin flower)

Sternbergia lutea
(winter daffodil)

Tigridia pavonia
(peacock flower)

BOTANICAL AND COMMON NAMES	HEIGHT	SPREAD	SOIL	LIGHT	DECORATIVE CHARACTERISTICS AND REMARKS	PLANTING AND PROPAGATION
Puschkinia (puschkinia, or striped squill) *Puschkinia scilloides libanotica*	4–6 in.	2–3 in.	☐	● ◑	Fragrant pale blue flowers with darker blue stripes; sometimes an exquisite white form is available. Blooms from early to mid spring. Grow in groups in rock gardens, in front of shrubs, or in short grass; leave undisturbed if possible.	Plant bulbs 3 in. deep, in early to midfall. Remove offsets after foliage dies; replant at once or store in cool place until fall. They bloom in a couple of years.
Ranunculus (ranunculus, or buttercup) *Ranunculus asiaticus* (Persian buttercup)	1–1½ ft.	6 in.	●	■	Mixed shades of white, pink, gold, orange, or crimson flowers in late winter, late spring, early summer. Plant in groups in borders, or in rows for cut flowers. Keep roots moist, crown dry. Does best where spring is long and cool. May need staking. Hardy Zones 7–11.	Plant clawlike tubers with claws down, 2 in. deep, around first week of May. Tubers should be soaked in water overnight prior to planting to accelerate root formation. Separate tubers when lifted in autumn; store in frost-free location.
Scilla (scilla, or spring squill) *Scilla scilloides* (Chinese squill)	6–8 in.	4 in.	☐	● ◑	Spikes of dusky pink flowers in late summer and early fall. Can be invasive if not dead-headed regularly. Hardy to Zone 5.	Plant 3 in. deep while dormant.
Scilla sibirica (Siberian squill)	6 in.	4 in.	☐	● ◑	Brilliant blue flowers appear from early to mid spring. Plant in informal groups at edges of borders, beneath trees and shrubs, in rock gardens, or in short grass. White form is available.	Plant bulbs 4 in. deep, in early fall. Multiplies readily by self-sown seeds; also by division. Replant offsets at once; will bloom in 2–3 yr.
S. tubergeniana	4 in.	3 in.	☐	● ◑	Silvery blue flowers appear in late winter, early spring. Associates well with *eranthis* and *galanthus*. For *S. hispanica*, see *Hyacinthoides hispanica*.	
Sparaxis (sparaxis, or harlequin flower) *Sparaxis tricolor*	1–1½ ft.	4 in.	■	●	Flowers of varieties are white, blue, purple, yellow, or red, usually with contrasting markings; appear in late spring. Foliage appears in fall and remains over winter. Plant in groups, or in rows for cut flowers. After foliage dies back in summer, corms should remain dry; in wet regions dig and store until fall. Can also be planted in pots in cool greenhouse for even earlier flowers. Not suitable where spring is short or hot. Does best in southern states and Pacific Northwest.	Plant corms 3–4 in. deep, in midfall. To propagate, lift corms after foliage dies back in summer and remove cormels; replant at once.
Sternbergia (sternbergia) *Sternbergia lutea* (winter daffodil)	6–9 in.	4 in.	■	●	Shiny yellow flowers, 1½ in. long, appear in early fall, as do leaves, which are narrow and often 1 ft. long. Plant in groups at edge of borders or in rock gardens. Sometimes takes a year to become established and should not be disturbed unless overcrowded. Hardy in Zones 6–9. Give winter mulch in colder areas.	Plant bulbs 5–6 in. deep, where soil is quite dry. Separate offsets in late summer after leaves die down; replant at once.
Tigridia (tigridia, or tiger flower) *Tigridia pavonia* (peacock flower)	1–1½ ft.	4 in.	■	●	Flowers, in white, yellow, orange, and red with spots of a contrasting color, bloom in mid to late summer. Plant in groups in mixed borders. Lift after flowering and store bulbs until spring.	Plant bulbs 3–4 in. deep, in spring when night temperatures remain above 60°F. Requires sunny position. To propagate, lift in late summer and remove bulblets; store over winter.

Greigii hybrid tulips, such as 'Zampa', are ideal for sunlit rock gardens.

Tulipa 'Zampa'

Triteleia
(grass nut)

Tulipa
(double early tulip)

Tulipa Triumph
(tulip)

Tulipa
(Darwin hybrid)

Tulipa
(lily-flowered tulip)

Tulipa viridiflora
(tulip)

BOTANICAL AND COMMON NAMES	HEIGHT	SPREAD	SOIL	LIGHT	DECORATIVE CHARACTERISTICS AND REMARKS	PLANTING AND PROPAGATION
Triteleia *Triteleia laxa* (grass nut)	2 ft.	6 in.	☐	●	Blue-purple, rarely white, blooms in early spring and early summer. Hardy to Zones 6–10. 'Konigin Fabiola' has brighter flowers.	Plant 2–3 in. deep in fall; in cold regions plant in spring. Remove offsets from corms at lifting time; replant.
Tulipa (tulipa, or tulip) SINGLE EARLY TULIP Lower growing than late-flowering tulips; flowers open wide, nearly flat.	8–14 in.	4–6 in.	☐	●	Flowers are white, violet, pink, yellow, red, or bicolored; bloom in midspring. Plant in beds, mixed borders, or in groups in front of shrubs. Does well in all areas, if planted before frost. Varieties include 'Christmas Marvel' (pink), 'Bellona' (yellow), and 'Keizerskroon' (red and yellow).	Plant bulbs 8–10 in. deep, in mid to late fall, in sun. Sheltered site is preferable, to protect against variable spring weather. When bulbs become crowded after several years, dig after leaves have withered, and store dry in well-ventilated place until planting time. Smallest bulbs are best planted in an out-of-the-way spot until they are of flowering size, which usually takes several years.
DOUBLE EARLY TULIP Resemble double peonies.	12–15 in.	6 in.	☐	●	White, pink, yellow, orange, and scarlet flowers appear in midspring. Varieties include 'Peach Blossom' (rose), 'Electra' (red), 'Monte Carlo' (yellow), and 'Schoonoord' (scarlet).	
TRIUMPH TULIP Angular flowers on sturdy stems of medium height.	16–26 in.	6 in.	☐	●	White, lavender, pink, yellow, orange, red, and bicolored flowers appear from mid to late spring. Excellent for massed planting; can be forced. Foliage ripens early. Varieties include 'Peerless Pink' (satin-pink), 'Golden Melody' (yellow), and 'Albury' (cherry-red).	
DARWIN HYBRID Largest of all tulips, and the most popular.	2–2½ ft.	6–8 in.	☐	●	Flowers are cream, yellow, orange, red, and appear in midspring. Large flowers with strong stems. Varieties include 'Golden Oxford' (yellow), 'Apeldoorn' (scarlet), 'Pink Impression' (rose-pink), and 'Gudoshnik' (yellow shaded red).	See single early tulip (above).
SINGLE LATE TULIP Rounded flowers but variable in form.	24–28 in.	6–8 in.	☐	●	Flowers are white, green, lilac, pink, yellow, orange, red, or bicolored and appear in mid to late spring. Slightly recurved petals and graceful stems. Varieties include 'Modern Style' (pink shades), 'Queen of the Night' (near black), and 'Renown' (carmine-red).	See single early tulip (above).
LILY-FLOWERED TULIP Elongated flowers with pointed petals that bend outward at tips.	1½–2 ft.	6 in.	☐	●	White, lavender, pink, yellow, red, or bicolored flowers appear from mid to late spring. Very graceful flowers with strong stems. Popular varieties include 'White Triumphator' (white), 'Maytime' (reddish violet, cream edge), 'China Pink' (pink), 'West Point' (yellow), 'Red Shine' (red), and 'Queen of Sheba' (scarlet-brown, edged in yellow).	See single early tulip (above).
FRINGED TULIP Cup-shaped flowers with fringed edges to the petals.	1½–2 ft.	6–8 in.	☐	●	White, yellow, pink, red, or violet flowers a little after the Darwin hybrids. (Interesting form grabs attention.) Varieties include 'Blue Heron' (lilac), 'Burgundy Lace' (wine-red), and 'Fancy Frills' (rose-pink).	See single early tulip (above).
VIRIDIFLORA TULIP Bowl-shaped blooms are either all green or another color marked with green.	1½–2 ft.	6–8 in.	☐	●	Most unusual coloring that stands out against more conventional colors. Later flowering. Varieties include 'Groenland' (green with a pink edge), 'Artist' (salmon flushed with green), and 'Spring Green' (pale green fading to white, long blooming).	See single early tulip (above).

■ well drained to sandy   ■ moist   ■ wet   ▨ acidic   ■ alkaline   ☐ regular soil   ● full sun   ◖ partial shade   ◗ shade

Tulipa 'Princeps'

Zantedeschia aethiopica

The common calla lily (*Zantedeschia aethiopica*), which thrives in wet conditions, blooms from early to mid summer. Kaufmanniana hybrids, like 'Princeps' shown here, are spring's first tulips.

Tulipa
(parrot tulip)

Tulipa
(Kaufmanniana hybrid)

Tulipa
(greigii tulip)

Zantedeschia aethiopica
(common calla lily)

BOTANICAL AND COMMON NAMES	HEIGHT	SPREAD	SOIL	LIGHT	DECORATIVE CHARACTERISTICS AND REMARKS	PLANTING AND PROPAGATION
PARROT TULIP Large flowers often with twisted or irregular bicolored petals.	2 ft.	8 in.	□	●	White, lavender, pink, yellow, orange, red, or bicolored flowers with wavy petals appear from mid to late spring. Varieties include 'Flaming Parrot' (red and yellow) and 'Estella Rijnveld' (red and white).	See single early tulip, p. 130.
DOUBLE LATE TULIP Resemble peonies, and flowers are long-lasting.	18–22 in.	6–8 in.	□	●	White, pink, yellow, or red flowers appear in late spring. Plant in protected spot, as heavy flowers are easily toppled by wind. Varieties include 'Mount Tacoma' (white), 'Angélique' (pink), and 'Carnaval de Nice' (white striped red).	See single early tulip, p. 130.
KAUFMANNIANA HYBRID Flowers open into 6-pointed star.	6–10 in.	5 in.	□	●	Some solid-colored flowers but mostly bicolored as red and yellow or red and white appear in early spring. Leaves sometimes mottled. Varieties include 'Ancilla' (white to pink), 'Yellow Dawn' (yellow with pink blush), and 'Shakespeare' (salmon).	See single early tulip, p. 130.
FOSTERIANA HYBRID Very large flowers; foliage sometimes mottled.	1–1½ ft.	6 in.	□	●	Very large pink, yellow, orange, red, and bicolored flowers appear in midspring. Varieties include 'Purissima' (white), 'Candela' (yellow), and 'Red Emperor' (red).	See single early tulip, p. 130.
GREIGII TULIP Very large flowers; leaves mottled or striped.	7–14 in.	6 in.	□	●	Flowers in shades of red, some bicolored with yellow, appear from mid to late spring. Beautiful mottled leaves. Varieties include 'Cape Cod' (apricot edged with yellow), 'Red Riding Hood' (red), and 'Plaisir' (red and yellow).	See single early tulip, p. 130.
SPECIES (OR BOTANICAL) TULIP Mostly small flowers on dwarf plants.	3–18 in.	3–9 in.	■	●	Many species are ideal for rock gardens or for planting in lawns. Given the right conditions, they will often self-seed. Species include *T. tarda* (yellow and white, 4 in.), *T. pulchella* (violet, 10 in.), *T. praestans* (scarlet, 8 in.), *T. batalinii* (pale yellow, 8 in.), and *T. clusiana* (lady tulip, red and white with pointed petals, 12 in.).	Plant in well-drained soil about 4 times the bulb's size deep.
Zantedeschia (zantedeschia, or calla) *Zantedeschia aethiopica* (common calla lily)	3 ft.	1½–2 ft.	■	● ◐	White flowers appear from early to mid summer. Keep faded flowers picked, but leave some leaves if rhizomes are to be kept for another year. This species can also be grown as aquatic plant in mild regions. Lift rhizomes after first frost. Dry for a few days; store covered in dry peat moss or vermiculite at 40°–50°F. Hardy Zones 8–10.	Start indoors in pots in early spring, and set outdoors after frost danger is past. *Z. elliottiana* is planted 2 in. deep. Does best in mild regions. In cold regions, grown mostly in greenhouses. To propagate (except *Z. elliottiana*) divide clumps in fall when they become crowded (mild climates only). Because this species thrives in wet conditions, it is a good choice for aquatic or bog gardens. Sow seeds in spring. Will flower in 1–2 yr.
Z. albomaculata (spotted calla)	2 ft.	1½–2 ft.	■	● ◐	White flowers with purple mark appear in early to mid summer. Leaves are spotted with white.	
Z. elliottiana (golden calla)	1½–2 ft.	1½–2 ft.	■	● ◐	Yellow flowers appear from early to mid summer. Can take more sun than the white forms. Dwarf variety sometimes available.	
Z. rehmannii (pink, or red calla)	1–1½ ft.	1½–2 ft.	■	● ◐	Pink or red flowers appear from late spring to early summer. Leaves are green or spotted with white. Can take more sun than white forms without flowers burning. Hybrids come in lavender, purple, and orange.	

Tulipa
(greigii tulip)

Zantedeschia aethiopica
(common calla lily)

BULBS FOR SPECIFIC LOCATIONS/PURPOSES

Bulbs to Naturalize in Grass

Allium moly

Anemone blanda

Puschkinia scilloides

Be sure not to mow until the bulb foliage turns brown.

Allium moly (golden garlic)
Allium oreophyllum
Anemone blanda
  (Grecian windflower)
Chionodoxa luciliae (glory-of-the-snow)
Chionodoxa sardensis
Corydalis solida (fumewort)
Crocus—all spring flowering crocus

Eranthis hyemalis (winter aconite)
Galanthus nivalis (snowdrop)
Ornithogalum umbellatum
  (star of Bethlehem)
Puschkinia scilloides (Siberian squill)
Scilla sibirica (spring squill)
Tulipa tarda and other dwarf
  species tulips

Bulbs to Grow Under Deciduous Trees

Fritillaria meleagris

Hyacinthoides hispanica

Leucojum

Anemone blanda (Grecian windflower)
Anemone ranunculoides
  (buttercup windflower)
Camassia cusickii (camass)
Corydalis flexuosa (blue fumitary)
Corydalis solida (fumewort)
Cyclamen coum (hardy cyclamen)
Eranthis hyemalis (winter aconite)
Fritillaria meleagris
  (snake's-head lily)

Galanthus nivalis (snowdrop)
Hyacinthoides hispanica
  (Spanish bluebell)
Leucojum aestivum (summer snowflake)
Lilium—most (lily)
Narcissus—most, providing the shade
  is not too dense in summer
Puschkinia scilloides (striped squill)
Scilla sibirica (Siberian squill)
Trillium—most (trillium)

Bulbs to Cut for Flower Arrangements

Canna generalis

Crinum powellii

Nerine bowdenii

The majority of bulb flowers are good as cut flowers but many only last a few days. The following should last for a week or more.

Allium cowanii (Cowan's allium)
Anemone coronaria (poppy anemone)
Canna generalis (Indian shot)
Crinum powellii (crinum)
Crocosmia hybrids (montbretia)
Dahlia hybrids (dahlia)
Dichelostemma ida-maia
  (firecracker flower)
Fritillaria meleagris
  (snake's head lily)
Galtonia candicans
  (summer hyacinth)
Gladiolus hybrids (gladiolus)
Gladiolus murieliae (acidanthera)

Leucojum aestivum
  (summer snowflake)
Lilium hybrids (lily)
Narcissus—most
  (daffodils and narcissi)
Nectaroscordum siculum
  (Bulgarian onion)
Nerine bowdenii (nerine)
Ornithogalum thyrsoides
  (chincherinchee)
Ranunculus asiaticus
  (Persian buttercup)
Tulipa—most (tulip)
Zantedeschia aethiopica (calla lily)

Bulbs With Fragrant Flowers

Crocus chrysanthus

Hyacinthus 'Pink Pearl'

Lilium regale

Allium moly (golden garlic)
Allium neapolitanum
Crocus chrysanthus (crocus)
Eranthis hyemalis (winter aconite)
Galanthus nivalis (snowdrop)
Galtonia candicans
  (summer hyacinth)
Gladiolus murieliae (acidanthera)
Gladiolus hybrids—many (gladiolus)
Hyacinthoides hispanica
  (Spanish bluebell)
Hyacinthoides non-scripta
  (English bluebell)
Hyacinthus hybrids—most (hyacinth)
Iris danfordiae (Danforts iris)
Iris histrioides
Iris reticulate (netted iris)
Iris xiphium (Dutch iris)
Leucojum vernum (spring snowflake)

Lilium longiflorum (Easter lily)
Lilium hybrids—most—especially
  the oriental hybrids
Lycoris squamigera (resurrection lily)
Muscari armeniacum
  (grape hyacinth)
Narcissus jonquilla hybrids–
  especially 'Trevithian'
Narcissus poeticus hybrids
  (poet's daffodil)
Narcissus trumpet hybrids—most
  (daffodils)
Puschkinia scilloides (striped squill)
Scilla sibirica (Siberian squill)
Trillium sessile (toadshade)
Tulipa hybrids—several (tulip)
Tulipa saxatilis (species tulip)
Tulipa sylvestris (wood tulip)

Seed Heads to Dry for Winter Arrangements

Lilium

Muscari

Scilla scilloides

Allium cristophii (star of Persia)
Anemone coronaria (poppy anemone)
Camassia leichtlinii (camass)
Fritillaria meleagris
  (snake's head lily)
Lilium—some (lily)

Hyacinthoides hispanica
  (Spanish bluebell)
Muscari—all (grape hyacinth)
Nectaroscordum siculum
  (Bulgarian onion)
Scilla scilloides (Chinese squill)

DAHLIAS

The brightness of the flowers, their complex shapes, and their rich foliage make a glorious addition to the garden from mid to late summer.

The dahlia originated in Mexico, where it was known to the Aztecs and recorded by Europeans in the late 16th century. Two centuries later the Spanish introduced it to Europe. It was, however, a very different plant from the dahlia we know today.

One of the original species, *Dahlia imperialis*, had single lilac-colored or reddish flowers and grew in a tree-like form to a height of 6–18 feet. Smaller species were also discovered, including *D. coccinea*, which had single red flowers. From several of these single-flowered species, the modern plants with their large, complex blooms were developed. The plant was called dahlia in honor of the eminent Swedish botanist Dr. Andreas Dahl.

As a native of Mexico, the dahlia is a subtropical plant that needs humus-rich soil, constant watering, and regular feeding. It has tuberous roots, hollow stems, bright green to bronze-green leaves, and flowers ranging from pure white through attractive shades of yellow to the deepest maroon. Some dahlias are bicolored. There are two plant types: bedding dahlias, most commonly grown annually from seeds but also available as tubers; and exhibition, or show, dahlias, which are almost always grown from tubers.

The most popular ones for mixed borders are the bedding dahlias, which grow to about 2 feet tall. Catalogs offer 'Harlequin' and 'Figaro' dwarfs 12–15 inches high with double or semi-double flowers about 2½ inches across. You can also buy seeds for taller kinds such as 'Dandy', about 24 inches high. All these have green leaves. 'Diablo Mix' has similar flowers, grows 16 inches tall, and has dull red foliage. Seed packets are of mixed colors, since the hue of dahlias grown from seeds

cannot be predicted. Tubers are available in specific colors as named varieties. If you grow plants from seeds, you can lift and store the tubers of favorite colors for use the following year.

Exhibition dahlias are propagated by taking stem cuttings from growing tubers or by division of the tubers. The color of flowers that have been grown from a tuber will be true to the parent plant.

Dahlias are classified into groups

according to flower form and size. More than a dozen are recognized by the American Dahlia Society, dealers, and hybridizers.

Singles may be as much as 4 inches across and have one row of petals and open centers.

Mignons are singles that grow on plants less than 18 inches tall.

Duplexes are like singles, but there are two rows of outer, or ray, petals and an open center.

Orchid-flowering dahlias resemble

singles except that the rays curve up and in.

Anemones are similar to singles, but the petals in the center are rolled or tubular.

Collarettes have flowers with yellow centers made up of stamens and a single row of petals around the edge. An inner collar of smaller petals surrounds the stamens, lying between them and the petals. This inner ring of petals is the reason for the name collarette.

Dahlia 'David Howard'

Dahlia 'Ellen Houston'

Leaves of the small-flowered formal decorative dahlia 'David Howard' are strikingly deep green. Equally extraordinary is the purple foliage of the dwarf dahlia 'Ellen Houston'.

Peony dahlias can be 4 inches across; they have open centers with twisted petaloids (sepals or stamens that look like petals) and up to four rows of flat ray petals.

Incurved cacti have fully double flowers with narrow, quilled rays, or outer petals, that curve in at the tips, toward the center of the flower. The blooms of cactus dahlias can be as much as 10 inches wide.

Recurved, or straight, cacti are like incurved cacti, but all the rays are straight or recurve outward.

Semi-cacti are similar to cacti, except the petals are broader and quilled for half their length or less.

Formal decorative dahlias have a symmetrical shape and are fully double with no central disk. The petals are broad and rounded at the ends and slightly curved in. The blooms of these dahlias can measure more than 10 inches wide.

Informal decorative dahlias are similar to the above, but, as the name implies, the arrangement of the petals is less regular.

Ball dahlias are rounded but sometimes flattened on top. Petals are blunt or rounded at the tip and arranged spirally. Each petal is rolled for more than half its length. The flowers are more than 4 inches wide.

Miniatures are ball dahlias with flowers that are no more than 4 inches in diameter. Pompons are ball dahlias that are less than 2 inches across.

The leaf color of dahlias ranges from rich green to deep bronze or greenish red. Variegated foliage occasionally appears on young plants, but leaves revert to solid color at maturity. The shape of the leaves is generally oval, but there are also decorative dahlias that have deeply cut, fernlike foliage.

Exhibition dahlias are best grown alone in a bed where there is plenty of sun. They should not be in the shade of buildings or of overhanging trees. They can, however, be used in a perennial border: the yellow, scar-let, and bronze varieties contrast well with white flowers or those with cool colors.

Wherever they are used, the striking flowers of the dahlia bring a richness, splendor, variety, and warmth of hue to the late-summer garden that few other flower species in North America can equal.

Plant bedding dahlias, either of one color or a variety of colors chosen to blend well together, in groups of three or five along the edge of a border or in a bed by themselves.

Decorative, cactus, semi-cactus, collarette, ball, and pompon dahlias should be planted singly or in groups of three of one variety.

It is essential to reach the tall kinds for tying, disbudding, fertilizing, and weeding; so leave an access path when planting.

At the end of the season there is usually no urgent need to clear the bed and lift the tubers if the dahlias have been grown for garden display. They can be left in the ground until autumn frosts blacken the leaves.

With exhibition plants, however, there is little point in leaving them in the ground after the tubers have ripened. A spell of cold, wet weather can encourage the growth of fungi and bacteria, and valuable plants can be destroyed.

As soon as the tubers are ripe, lift them. The evidence of ripeness is when the leaves begin to turn yellow, blooms are poorly colored and somewhat daisy eyed, and bud production is slowing down.

Do not lift the tubers before they are ripe, because they must absorb enough nourishment from the leaves to carry them through the winter and to produce strong new growth the next season. In short-season climates this will probably mean leaving them in the ground until after the first heavy frost.

Dahlias grown from seeds form tuberous roots, but most gardeners discard the tubers and plant new seeds the next year.

Anemone. Flat ray petals surround tightly packed, tubular disk petals.

Ball. The spherical flowers have blunt, quilled petals, set in a spiral pattern.

Single. One row of petals (two if duplex) encircles a central disk of stamens.

Peony. Two to four rows of flat ray petals surround a disk of twisted petaloids.

Collarette. A collar of small petals grows between the ray petals and the yellow disk.

Cactus. Fully double flowers have narrow, pointed ray of quilled petals, either recurved (above) or incurved.

Semi-cactus. Similar to cactus, but petals are broader and quilled for half their length or less.

Pompon. The flower is a ball type, but less than 2 in. wide. Those 2–4-in. plants are called miniatures.

Decorative. The double flowers have no central disk. Petals are broad and rounded at the ends.

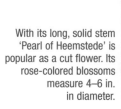

With its long, solid stem 'Pearl of Heemstede' is popular as a cut flower. Its rose-colored blossoms measure 4–6 in. in diameter.

Dahlia 'Pearl of Heemstede'

When, Where, and How to Plant Dahlias

Sun and Rich Soil for Better Blooms

Dahlias need full sun and a rich, porous soil that retains moisture well but drains easily. Ideal soil pH is neutral to slightly acid.

Locate dahlias in a warm, sunny spot where there is good air circulation. A site with some shade from the afternoon sun will do.

Since dahlias are heavy feeders, in the fall you will need to dig into the bed a rich dressing of dried or well-rotted manure, compost, or other suitable organic material.

Sprinkle on a topdressing of 4 ounces of bone meal for each square yard. You want to allow frost and air to penetrate and break down the added materials, therefore it is best to not smooth down the ground.

The soil may not be very rich. If this is the case, apply a balanced organic fertilizer (such as 3–1–5), according to package directions.

How to Plant and Space Dahlia Tubers

Plant tubers as soon as the danger of frost no longer exists—mid to late spring in most areas. Allow 2–3 feet between tubers for tall dahlias (4–5 feet), 2 feet between for medium plants (3–4 feet), and 15 inches between for shorter ones.

New growth comes from eyes at the base of the previous year's stem. Each stem has several tuberous roots. These can be planted as a clump or divided into single tubers (see p. 142).

In the planting bed insert a 1-inch-square stake long enough to support tall plants. In front of it dig a 6-inch-deep hole. Prepare a mixture of half peat moss and half soil, and incorporate about a handful of bone meal. Fill the hole with this mixture to a level that will bring the tuber's eye to about 2 inches below the surface. Place the tuber in front of the stake with the eye against it. Cover the tuber to ground level with the soil and peat moss mixture. Firm the soil gently over the tuber. Except in extremely arid regions, do not water until new growth begins. Label the stake with the variety name.

Tubers can also be started into growth indoors ahead of time. If more plants are needed, divide tubers when the new shoots are about ¾ inch tall. Harden the plants (see p. 195) before planting out.

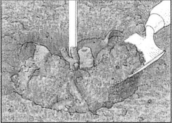
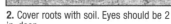

1. Partly fill hole with enriched soil. Plant with tuber's eye against stake.

2. Cover roots with soil. Eyes should be 2 in. deep.

3. Firm down soil over tuber. Label the stake with variety name.

Setting Out Young Pot-Grown Plants

Young plants in pots can be bought from mail-order growers, local nurseries, and garden-supply centers. Mail-order houses generally ship when it is the appropriate time for planting in your area—after the last frost has occurred.

Pot-grown plants are planted in much the same way as tubers (see above). Before you plant, set out stakes; space according to ultimate size. Water the plants lightly. Prepare a mixture of half soil and half peat moss; work a handful of bone meal thoroughly into the mixture so that it is evenly distributed.

Next to the stake dig a hole 2–3 inches deeper than the root ball and wide enough to fit it. Add a few handfuls of the mixture. Remove the plant from the pot with soil ball intact. If the roots appear twined, do not try to get them loose.

Set the ball in the hole with its top 2 inches below soil surface. Make sure the stem is straight and close to the stake. Fill the hole with the soil and peat moss mixture and firm it down, leaving a shallow depression around the stem in which moisture can collect to give plants a good start. After about two days water well. When the plant begins to show signs of top growth, fill up the depression around the stem with soil, and firm it down level with the surrounding soil.

Dahlias are very frost sensitive and a late frost can kill newly set-out plants. Be sure to cover them if a frost is forecast. Bottomless soft drink bottles make good mini-greenhouses.

1. An hour before planting, water plant lightly. Prepare enriched soil.

2. Set in stake, and dig hole beside it. Remove plant from pot.

3. Put plant in hole, and fill in with soil mixture.

4. Firm soil around the plant, leaving a depression to collect water.

Dahlias are classified according to flower shape and size. The examples at right are semi-cactus dahlias.

Dahlia 'Wootton Impact'

Dahlia 'Hillcrest Albino'

Caring for Dahlias Throughout the Year

Water Thoroughly As the Buds Develop

When potted plants or tubers are first planted, watering represents a danger to them—it can cause the tubers to rot. It does the roots no harm to search for moisture.

For the best results, give dahlias a great deal of moisture as they approach their flowering season. In dry spells the plants should be watered freely, whether or not they are coming into bloom.

When weather is hot and sunny, water every five days or so on heavy clay soils. Lighter soils dry out more quickly, and the plants should be watered about every three days.

Use an automatic sprinkler that throws a fine spray up high enough for the water to fall vertically on the plants, or a soaker hose laid through the plants. Either one will ensure that the area around the dahlias receives the required thorough soaking.

If you use a can or hose, give about 3 gallons of water to each plant when they are 2–3 feet apart; use less if they are set closer together.

Use a sprinkler so that a fine spray will fall on the plants.

Mulch Plants to Keep Down Weeds

When the plant is about 1 foot high, put a 1-inch layer of mulch around the base but not against the stem. This helps keep down weeds and retain moisture. Use materials such as wood chips, buckwheat hulls, cocoa shells, or clean, dry straw.

If you mulch with grass clippings, do not use grass from a lawn that has been treated with a selective weed killer. Apply in thin layers, and allow each to dry before applying more. Do not mulch too early. Wait until the plants have grown to a height of 1 foot. The ground should be moist when mulch is applied and well soaked immediately after.

If weeds appear before mulching, remove them by hoeing, which will also keep the soil aerated. Do not cultivate more than 1 inch deep.

Dampen the ground and apply a 1-in. layer of mulch. Water well.

Remove early weeds with a hoe. Do not hoe more than 1 in. deep.

Add Supports As the Dahlias Grow

Dahlias need support to prevent wind damage. Two or three weeks after planting, loop string around each stake 4–8 inches above the ground. Tie every plant, taking the string around the stem in a figure-eight pattern. Fasten the knot against the stake.

As the plants grow, make further ties higher up the stem. Be sure the lower ties have not become too tight around the main stem.

To prevent damage to the side growths, insert thin canes firmly in the ground—three in a triangular pattern around the main stake and about 9 inches from it—sloping out. Loop soft string around these canes to support the side growths.

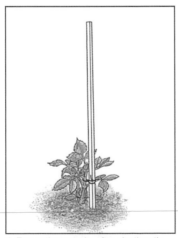

1. Two or three weeks after planting, tie plants to stakes with soft string.

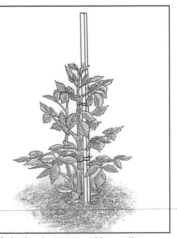

2. As the plants grow, add more ties. Check that lower ties are not too tight.

3. Support side shoots with soft string tied around three thin stakes.

Dahlia 'Yellow hammer' ➡

The splendid yellow blossoms of the semi-cactus *dahlia* 'Hamari Accord' can be 4 in. in diameter. The petals are slightly curled.

Dahlia 'Hamari Accord'

Pinching Out and Disbudding the Big Dahlias

Most exhibition or large-flowered dahlias send up strong center shoots but develop little side growth until the center shoots have flower buds.

To encourage side growth and more flowers, pinch out the center shoots two or three weeks after planting. The center shoot is the growing tip of the stem. Usually, this is done in late spring or early summer for tuber-grown plants and somewhat later for pot-grown plants.

In two weeks or so half a dozen side shoots should have developed in the leaf axils. Remove the top pair of shoots to promote growth in the lower side shoots. These will each produce a terminal bud and several side buds.

To encourage big flowers, remove the side buds as soon as they are large enough to be removed without harming the tip buds.

To promote longer-stemmed side shoots and to encourage more growth in the upper part of the dahlias, cut off all the leaves that develop on the main stem a few inches from the ground.

1. Two or three weeks after planting, pinch out growing point of main stem.

2. Two weeks later remove the top pair of side shoots from leaf axils.

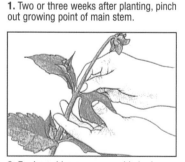

3. For large blooms remove side buds from remaining side shoots later on.

4. Cut off leaves growing on main stem within a few inches of ground.

An Extra Feeding for Healthy Growth

Soil that has been well fed before planting will not need much additional fertilizer during the growing season. Mulching with rotted manure or rich compost will help to develop the growth of the plants if the soil is poor or if extraordinary blooms are the objective.

An additional feeding can be given when bedding dahlias show their first buds or, in the case of exhibition dahlias, after they have been pinched out for the second time.

For quick results, use a seaweed or fish-oil liquid fertilizer. For a slower response, scatter a handful of dried organic fertilizer around the plant.

Too much nitrogen at this time of year will encourage an overabundance of foliage rather than flowers and can reduce the winter storage quality of the tubers as well. After feeding the dahlias with any dry fertilizer, water them well to make sure that the plants are able to take up nutrients as they become available.

It can be helpful to feed the plants every two to three weeks until the end of summer. If you plan to store the tubers, top-dress the soil in late summer or very early fall with a mixture of equal parts of bone meal and green sand.

What Can Go Wrong With Dahlias

On the chart below are listed the pests and diseases that can afflict dahlias. If your plants show symptoms not described, consult the section on plant disorders on page 506. Also look up the section on organic controls on page 542.

SYMPTOMS AND SIGNS	CAUSE	CONTROL
Young shoots (particularly ones with flower buds) are stunted or malformed and sticky, and covered with small, black or green insects.	Aphids	Spray with a strong stream of water or apply insecticidal soap.
Buds, flowers, and new leaves are eaten; tips die. Stems and stalks tunneled; plants later wilt.	Borers (European corn or stalk)	Apply *Bacillus thuringiensis* as soon as the borers begin to feed.
Petals are eaten; flowers look ragged.	Earwigs	Spray with insecticidal soap. Alternatively, invert 3-in. pot on stake after loosely packing pot with straw; earwigs will crawl up into container. Shake out pot daily over bowl of hot water.
Flower buds and opening flowers are deformed. Leaves develop irregular holes and are spotted, ragged, or malformed.	Plant bugs, or leaf bugs	Spray with neem.
Leaves are finely mottled, with overall silvery look.	Thrips	Destroy infested flowers and foliage. Spray affected plants early with *Beauveria bassiana*. Insecticidal soap and neem may be effective.
Leaves and shoots of young plants are eaten. Silvery slime trails may be apparent.	Slugs or snails	Put out iron phosphate slug baits and use beer traps.
Leaves develop yellow or brown rings or spots and may be distorted. Plants are stunted.	Virus disease	To prevent spread of disease, remove and destroy affected plants immediately.
Plants are dwarfed, with thin stems and relatively small yellowish leaves.	Nutrient deficiency	Apply dressing of rotted compost or manure; feed with balanced organic fertilizer.

Cactus dahlias have blossoms with narrow, pointed petals. 'Glorie van Heemstede' is an example of a water-lily dahlia.

Dahlia 'Hillcrest Royal'

Dahlia 'Glorie van Heemstede'

Use a sharp knife to prevent bruising. Cut stems and immediately plunge them into warm water up to the blossoms.

Cutting Flowers for Indoor Display

The best time to cut dahlia blooms is in the evening or early morning, when the air is cool and the stems are full of moisture. Cut the stems with a sharp knife rather than scissors or pruning shears, which might bruise the stems and reduce their ability to take up water. Make the cut at a 45-degree angle to expose more of the stem. The length of the stem should be in proportion to the size of the flower. Giant blooms will probably need stems about 2 feet long; smaller blooms can be cut proportionately shorter.

Take a container of warm water with you when cutting the blooms. Plunge them into it immediately, and when you take them indoors, transfer them to a bucket of cold water up to the top of the stems. Hold them underwater, and cut another inch off the stems. Leave in a cool place for a few hours before arranging them.

Storing Tubers to Survive the Winter

At the end of the growing season, exhibition dahlias should be lifted and stored for the winter in a frost-free place. The following spring they can be used for stem cuttings, or be divided and replanted.

In some mild parts of the country, where the soil is sandy and the water table is low, tubers can be left in the ground through the winter, but there is always the danger that in a particularly severe winter they will be killed. The damage to the tubers is caused by a combination of cold and damp soil.

Immediately after the first frosts in autumn have blackened the foliage, cut the stems back to about 6 inches above the ground. The roots can be left in the ground for two or three more weeks if light frosts come early in your area, but they should be lifted immediately if there happens to be a hard frost.

With a fork loosen the soil around the tubers, being careful not to damage them, and lift them by pressing back on the handle. Using a blunt-ended stick, gently remove surplus soil from between the tubers. Take care not to break off any of the old stems. Fasten labels to the stumps of the stems for easy identification in the spring.

Place the tubers upside down in a dry, airy place for about two weeks to allow the moisture to drain out of the stems. If it collects there, it will cause the necks to rot, and although the tubers may not be damaged, the area of new growth will be lost. The tubers must be completely dry before they are stored for the winter.

Dust the tubers with sulfur to prevent fungus attack, and store them in a cool, dry, frost-free place away from drafts.

Where winter temperatures stay above 16°F, a simple and easy way to store tubers is to place 6 inches of dry leaves or peat moss in the bottom of a 2-foot-deep cold frame. Space out the tubers on the leaves, keeping them 9 inches from the sides of the frame. Cover tubers with another layer of dry leaves or peat moss at least 12 inches deep. Finally, cover with a piece of burlap or similar material to absorb condensation. The leaves will insulate the roots against heavy frosts. Replace the frame top.

Alternatively, you can store the tubers in trays of dry sand or peat moss beneath the benches in a cool greenhouse or in a dry cellar or cupboard at 40°–45°F. Never store them in a warm cupboard, however; they will simply dry out and shrivel rapidly under such conditions.

When only a few tubers are to be stored, netting or sealing the roots will provide adequate protection. For netting, first wrap the roots in straw. Place tubers inside garden netting drawn tightly into a hammock shape; hang from the ceiling of a frost-free building until spring.

The tubers can also be placed in a box lined with ½-inch-thick sheets of Styrofoam (sold by hardware stores and home centers for insulation).

Alternatively, store tubers by placing them in a heavy-grade, black plastic bag without additional packing material, and seal the bag tightly with wire. This will prevent the roots from dehydrating; however, there is a danger that they will sweat and rot.

You can also keep the tubers in a frost-free shed or indoors underneath the basement stairs if you have such a space. In spring new shoots will have developed on the crowns.

It is advisable to inspect the tubers every few weeks during the winter to check for disease or shriveling. Diseased parts can be cut off and the wounds dusted with sulfur.

Place shriveled tubers in a bucket of water overnight to plump them up. Allow them to dry thoroughly before returning them to storage.

1. As soon as frost has blackened the foliage, cut stems back to about 6 in.

2. Lift tubers and, with a blunt stick, remove loose soil from between them.

3. Place tubers on a 6-in. layer of peat moss or dry leaves, in a box.

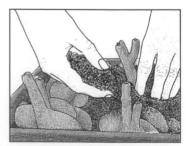

4. Cover with another layer of peat moss or dry leaves, about 12 in. deep.

Single dahlias have a ring of petals surrounding a sharply defined disk.

Dahlia 'Preston Park'

How to Grow New Dahlias From Existing Stock

Taking Cuttings for the Greatest Number of Plants

New plants can be raised from cuttings or by division of tubers in spring. Tubers deteriorate if they are not separated at regular intervals; so replanting the parent clump indefinitely is not recommended. Only exhibition or big dahlias are grown from cuttings or by tuber division. Small bedding types are usually started from seeds each season.

Seeds collected from exhibition plants will not run true to parent color or form, but plants grown from cuttings or division reproduce the parent plants exactly.

In late winter or early spring, take the tubers from storage, clean away any old soil, cut out diseased parts, and dust the wounds with sulfur.

To start new plants from cuttings, place the tubers in a flat or on a layer of loamy soil, peat moss, or compost. Cover them with this material to just below the old stems. Water moderately. Place the flat in a greenhouse or cool (between 60° and 65°F), sunny window; keep the soil moist.

In two or three weeks, when shoots are 3–4 inches long, cut them off a little above their bases with a sharp knife or razor blade. Do not cut out any of the tuber itself, since doing so will prevent more new shoots from forming.

The first shoots may be hollow. Discard these, since they are hard to root. Subsidiary stems will develop after the first shoots, and these are usually normal and more suitable for propagation.

Trim back shoots to just below the lowest leaf joint. Remove the lowest pair of leaves, taking special care neither to injure the buds that will have developed in the leaf axils nor to leave stem stubs.

For each four shoots fill a 3-inch clay pot with equal parts of peat moss and sand. Make four holes about 1 inch deep around the edge.

Dip the base of each cutting in water and then into hormone rooting powder. Place cuttings in the holes, and firm the mixture around the cuttings. Water the pots, label them, and mark the date.

Place pots in an unheated propagating case in the greenhouse; or tent them with plastic, and set them in a cool, well-lighted window. Keep soil moderately moist. Ventilate to avoid excessive humidity and condensation, which will encourage the growth of fungus. Keep cuttings shaded from direct sun.

After two or three weeks, when cuttings have roots—indicated by the growth of new leaves—put them singly into 3-inch clay pots. Use any sterile potting soil that drains well, and keep it uniformly moist.

After potting, shade the plants for two days. Then until late spring keep them in a well-ventilated greenhouse or in an airy place indoors where there is sun. Later move them to a cold frame for hardening off. The frame need not be closed unless there is danger of frost.

If you have no cold frame, harden off the plants in a warm, sunny, sheltered corner outdoors for one week before planting. In cold climates postpone the hardening-off process until after the last frost.

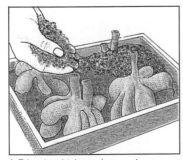

1. Take stored tubers, clean, and cover with damp soil or peat moss.

2. Keep in a greenhouse or window. Sever shoots when 3–4 in. high.

3. Trim shoots with a sharp knife, and remove the lowest pair of leaves.

4. Dip cuttings in rooting powder, and plant in pots of peat moss and sand.

5. Water well. Label the pots and set in a cool, well-lighted, protected spot.

6. After two or three weeks pot the cuttings individually in 3-in. pots.

7. Shade plants for two days; then move to greenhouse or windowsill.

8. After the last frost, harden off in a cold frame for a week; then plant out.

When in full bloom, ball dahlias such as 'Jeanette Carter', as well as the small pompon dahlias, are completely round.

Dahlia 'Jeanette Carter'

Dividing Tubers: The Easy Way to Propagate

Propagating by taking cuttings produces more new plants, but propagating by dividing tubers is easy—so if the need is for only a few new plants, divide the old tubers in mid or late spring.

For each new plant you will need one section of the tuberous root and a piece of the stem with an eye in it. New growth comes from this eye.

Each plant needs only enough tuber to keep the plant growing until new roots form. A single piece of tuber with a single piece of stem attached is best. Too large a section of the tuberous root will delay formation of new roots, and the plant will produce a mass of leafy growth, which will further result in few and inferior blooms.

Before cutting the clump of tubers, examine each stem to locate the eyes. If they prove difficult to locate, place the tubers in damp peat moss or soil, and keep them in a warm place for a few days to give the buds time to develop.

As soon as the eyes or buds are visible, use a sharp knife to cut down through the stem, doing your best not to damage any of the eyes in the process. Dust raw cuts thoroughly with sulfur to prevent rot.

Plant the divisions of the tubers following the techniques described on page 136. The best time for planting in most areas is late spring or early summer—or as soon as all danger of frost is past.

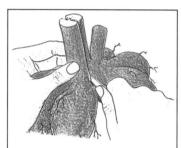

Cut tubers into clumps so that each has a piece of stem with an eye.

Growing Annual Dahlias From Seeds

Seeds are sold for both small bedding dahlias and tall exhibition kinds, but they will not run true in color or form. To start a collection of exhibition dahlias from seeds, plant them one year, and save the tubers of the best plants for the next year.

Start seeds in early spring if an indoor space or a warm greenhouse is available. In a cold frame plant four to six weeks before the safe outdoor planting date.

Prepare pots or flats of sterilized soil or seed-starting mixture, level the surface, and firm it. Water thoroughly. Thinly sprinkle the seeds over the surface, and cover them with about ¼ inch of coarse sand.

Cover the pots or flats with glass shaded by brown paper or with plastic bag. Set in a warm place in a greenhouse or in a dim, warm room to germinate—in 10 to 21 days.

When the seedlings are up, remove the glass or plastic. If you are growing them indoors, set them on a sunny sill. When the seedlings are sturdy, transplant them to individual 3-inch peat pots filled with potting soil. Once established, they can take full light and sun.

If the plants are being grown in a cold frame, harden them there several weeks before setting them out. If there is no cold frame, set them in a dependably warm, sunny spot outdoors for a week before planting.

For instructions on planting potted dahlias outdoors, see page 136.

COLLECTING YOUR OWN SEEDS

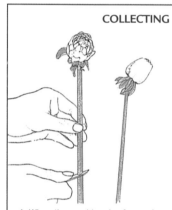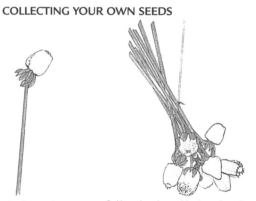

1. When the seed heads of annual dahlias begin to go dry, remove them with 9-in.-long stems.

2. Hang heads upside down in a dry place until the heads are dry. Remove seeds and store them.

1. In spring, sprinkle seeds in 5-in. pot. Lightly cover with vermiculite.

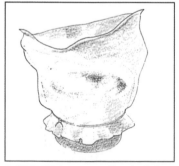

2. After watering, cover with a plastic bag. Keep warm, out of direct sun.

3. As soon as seedlings are sturdy, transplant into individual 3-in. pots.

4. After the last frost, harden off the plants in a cold frame.

GLADIOLI

Easy to grow in almost any garden, gladioli make a splash of summer color in a border, are long-lasting cut flowers, and are inexpensive enough that you don't have to store them over winter if you don't want to. They have a dazzling range of colors and a range of sizes to fit any garden.

The name "gladiolus" comes from the Latin word for sword (*gladius*) which describes the shape of the leaves, but it is the spectacular flowers that have made this bulb so popular. Like tulips, the range of flower colors is very wide, but unlike tulips, flowers can be enjoyed for many weeks, by planting early to late varieties, and by staggering the planting times.

Gladioli make a superb cut flower that lasts in water for a week or more and are wonderful in flower arrangements since the individual flowers all face in the same direction, set on either side of the stem. A flower spike can contain up to 26 trumpet-shaped flowers composed of six petals each. Flowers may be of a single color, but are more commonly a blend of two or three colors, often with a conspicuous marking in the throat.

Gladiolus grow from corms, which are swollen stem bases. The corm provides the energy to produce the shoot and flower. During the growing season, the new stem base swells with stored food and becomes a new corm sitting on top of the shrivelled old one.

Horticulturally gladiolus is divided into three groups. The Grandiflorus group is the best known and contains most of the varieties grown in gardens. It is further subdivided into five classes, ranging from Giant to Miniature depending on flower size. Giant varieties can have spikes up to 6 feet long with flowers 5½ inches across. The Primulinus group has spikes up to 24 inches long with flowers 2½–3½ inches wide. The flowers are staggered up the stem so that green shows between the flowers. The Nanus group has small spikes up to 14 inches long with flowers 2½ inches or less wide and generally seven buds per stem. They are all tender in most of the country, needing lifting before winter and storing indoors. Only in Zones 8-10 can gladioli be left in the ground over winter.

In addition to these well known hybrids there are several species occasionally available from seed exchanges, two of which are often listed in specialist bulb catalogs. *Gladiolus murieliae* was known for many years as *Acidanthera*, which is still its common name. It has spikes of up to 10 pure white, very fragrant flowers, with a dark purple marking in the throat. The individual flowers are on slender, tubular stems and arch downward away from the main stalk. Occasionally available is the European species, *G. imbricatus*. This grows only 12-16 inches tall and has pink to purplish flowers on small spikes. It is the hardiest species and will survive winters in the southern parts of Zone 4.

There are several thousand named varieties of gladiolus, with new ones being introduced each year. Corms are graded by size and the biggest flower spikes come from the top sized corms, 1½ inches or more in diameter, although corms of the Nanus and Primulinus groups rarely get this large. Unless you plant to exhibit gladioli in a flower show, medium sized corms (¾-1¼ inches) will give a good display in the garden and their flower spikes are still large enough to cut for indoors, but will flower several days later than large corms of the same variety. Small corms, (under ¾ inch) will still flower but take even longer. Different varieties take different lengths of time from planting to flowering, so they are also classified as early (70-74 days), early-mid (75-79 days), midseason (80-84 days), late-mid (85-90 days), and late (91-99 days). By planting some of each type, flowering can be extended over several weeks.

Visit the North American Gladiolus Council website at www.gladworld.org for more information, pictures of modern varieties, show locations and dates, and the addresses of gladiolus specialists near you.

'Nova-Lux' and 'Seraphin' are hybrid gladioli that grow about 40 in. tall; the fragrant *G. callianthus*, which may be called *Acidanthera* in some catalogs, is slightly shorter. All make excellent cut flowers.

Gladiolus 'Nova-Lux'

Gladiolus callianthus

Gladiolus 'Seraphin'

Soil and Site

Gladioli are not fussy about the soil, provided it is well drained. A heavy, clay soil should be lightened by adding compost or sharp sand. Groups planted in a border need little special preparation ahead of time, but for those to be planted in a cutting garden, the soil should be dug the previous fall to at least 8 inches deep. Rake the area level in spring as soon as the soil is dry enough to work. Gladioli grow best in a soil with a pH of 6.5—slightly acidic, but they will still grow and flower where the pH is 7.5. The only stipulation on the site is that it must be in full sun. Gladioli do not grow well in even part shade.

Planting

Plant gladioli from spring to early summer, keeping in mind the days to flowering and the local average first frost date for later plantings. The first plantings can be made about 10 days before the average last frost date, with successive plantings every 10-14 days after that. If the first plantings are through the soil and there is a frost warning, the small shoots are easy to protect.

Small groups, planted in an existing border, can be planted with a

Harvesting and Storing

Approximately six weeks after flowering the new corms will be mature and can be lifted and cured. If a frost comes before the six weeks is up, lift them anyway as growth has come to a halt. Dig the corms and immediately cut off the stems as close to the corm as possible (to prevent the spread of thrips—see What Can Go Wrong) and put in the garbage. If the weather is warm and sunny, spread the corms out in the sun to start drying, covering them with a tarp or

Summer Care

Mulch with chopped straw or well rotted leaves to suppress weed growth and conserve moisture. Water as needed since gladioli need adequate moisture. In a border, surrounded by other plants, staking is seldom necessary, but if grown in rows for cutting, support will probably be needed. A stake at each end of the row, with a string run down each side of the plants will be sufficient. Alternatively, each individual plant can be tied to a single bamboo cane.

Plants not used for cut flowers should have their old spikes removed once they fade so that energy is not used for seed production that should go into forming next years corm.

trowel, but in a cutting garden, where a quantity of corms will be planted, it is easier to make a narrow trench and plant them in a row. In both cases, add a little bone meal to the base of the hole or trench and scratch it into the soil. For large corms, plant them 6 inches deep; plant medium sized corms 4½ inches deep and small ones 3 inches deep, measured from the bottom of the hole to soil level. If planted in rows, leave at least 12 inches between the rows for easy of cutting later.

other waterproof cover at night. If the weather is rainy, spread the corms out in seed trays and dry them indoors. To dry properly, they need the warmth of the house, rather than being left in a cool garage. After a couple of weeks, the old corm and roots should come away easily from the new corm; if not, wait a few more days. Store the bulbs in mesh-bottomed trays or in net bags, at temperatures just above freezing. Check the corms every few weeks during the winter and discard any that are becoming soft.

Propagation

When you lift the corms in the fall, you will probably notice small cormels clustered around the base of the plant. These are small editions of the parent and can be saved and planted the following year to grow on. This is best done in a special area where you can keep a close eye on them to make sure they don't get smothered by weeds. Plant them in rows, carefully marked and labeled, about 2 inches deep with the rows about 6 inches apart.

What Can Go Wrong With Gladioli

Providing you practice crop rotation and don't grow gladioli in the same

They will need lifting, curing, and storing at the end of the year, just like large bulbs. Some may flower the second year if the corms are large enough, and they all should flower by year three.

Gladioli can also be grown from seed sown in spring and will take three or four years to produce a flower, but the resulting plants will probably be inferior to the seed parent and this is really only worth doing if you are growing hundreds of seedlings and are prepared to discard 99.9% of them.

place year after year, gladioli are not terribly affected by problems, but the following may occur, particularly where winters are mild and the soil doesn't freeze.

SYMPTOMS AND SIGNS	CAUSE	CONTROL
Holes in leaves.	Any of several loopers and caterpillars	Spray with insecticidal soap or *Bacillus thuringiensis kurstaki*.
Foliage and flowers badly chewed, metallic beetles present.	Japanese beetles	Hand pick or spray with neem or insecticidal soap.
Pale stripes on leaves, whitish spots and stripes on flowers.	Thrips	Spray with insecticidal soap. Remove tops immediately when lifting to prevent thrips migrating to bulbs. Dust bulbs with pyrethrin before storage.
Holes in corms and stem bases.	Wireworms	Common in soils with high organic content. Apply parasitic nematodes to soil.
Foliage dull and yellowish, often with a purple tint, fine webs between leaves.	Mites	Spray foliage with strong jets of water to wash off these very small spiderlike creatures that suck plant juices.
Brown spots on upper side of leaves, flowers rotting and not opening.	Botrytis (fungus)	Plant in sun, avoid low-lying locations or places without good air circulation.
Plants stop growing and become stunted and yellow. Corms have corky areas.	Fusarium (fungus)	Soil-born disease. Do not plant gladioli there again. Discard infected plants and corms.
Plants rot at the neck and fall over, brown to black spots on corms.	Stromatinia (fungus)	See above.

LILIES

Stately lily plants, with their exotic flower forms and their great variety in color and size, add a dramatic accent to the summer garden.

One of the oldest cultivated flowers, the lily has been cherished for at least 3,000 years—in ancient Egypt, Rome, Greece, China, and Japan. For centuries only a few species were known, the most famous being the pure white Madonna lily (*Lilium candidum*)—traditionally a symbol of purity—from the eastern Mediterranean. Another species fairly widespread in Europe was *L. martagon*, with nodding dark-spotted pink-mauve flowers.

Few plants are as versatile as the lily, a genus of mainly hardy bulbs with about 90 species. They vary widely in flower size and form, height, color, flowering period, planting schemes, and the growing conditions they need.

Like many other wild plants, lily species can be difficult to transfer to the cultivated garden. Their requirements are not always understood, and it is sometimes difficult to re-create a suitable situation for them. When transplanted, if they survive at all, these lilies often languish for a season or two. Nevertheless, wild lilies have caught the fancy of plant breeders, who have produced hybrids from them that are generally far superior to their parents.

For summer color in the garden, the hybrid lilies are a welcome addition. When most spring perennials have bloomed, lilies start to flower and provide continuing interest into late summer. As its many buds open each day, an established clump of lilies will bloom over an extended period. Coming in all colors but blue—some are in solid colors, others may be freckled, spotted, or flushed—and having a very wide range of sizes and forms, hybrid lilies can be used in a great number of ways.

After more than a half-century of hybridizing by professionals as well as amateurs around the world, named varieties now exist that are free flowering, robust, and disease resistant. Many outshine their parents in vigor and variety of color and form. Named varieties are propagated vegetatively from the bulbs' scales and are identical to the parent.

Some lilies are grown commercially from seeds from selected crosses, making them relatively inexpensive. They vary from one another only slightly, usually in color rather than form.

They are sold as strains, such as the Burgundy, Golden Splendor, and Imperial strains. They can be grown in a mixed border with evergreens and deciduous shrubs as a color accent, used among perennials, grown in pots, or for cut flowers.

Lilies have a variety of forms. Flowers may face upward, flare horizontally, or hang in inversed tiers. The trumpets, so called for the flaring trumpet shape of their flowers, are exemplified by the Sentinel strain and the Easter lily (*L. longiflorum*). Many lilies are shaped like saucers, which face either upward or outward. 'Enchantment' and 'Connecticut King' face upward; the Imperial strains face outward. The familiar Turk's cap form is represented by *L. lancifolium* and *L. davidii*, as well as most of their hybrids. 'Nutmegger' and the vari-colored Harlequin Hybrids have that shape too.

There are a number of other variations and combinations that many plant breeders find fascinating to work with in order to produce new lilies. Combining the different forms, colors, and seasons of bloom has become an unending challenge.

Many lilies are fragrant. The Trumpet, Aurelian, and Oriental hybrids are so heavily scented that they can be overpowering in a confined area.

The Madonna lily (*Lilium candidum*) is typical of the trumpet lilies. *L. davidii*, a Turk's cap lily, is hardier, but not as fragrant.

Lilium candidum

Lilium davidii

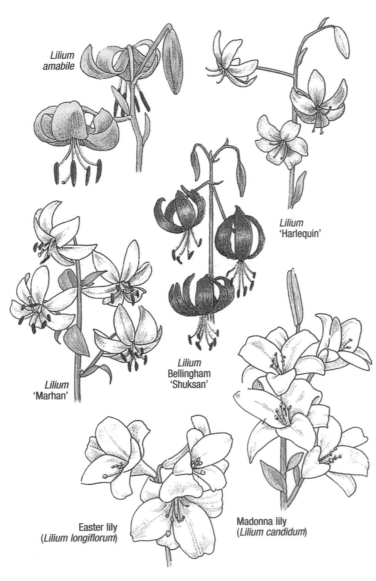

Lilium amabile

Lilium 'Harlequin'

Lilium Bellingham 'Shuksan'

Lilium 'Marhan'

Easter lily (*Lilium longiflorum*)

Madonna lily (*Lilium candidum*)

Flower shapes. Lilies are grouped into categories based on flower shape. Shown are Turk's cap and Trumpet. Turk's cap lilies—all those shown above except the Madonna lily and the Easter lily—have pendent flowers that are usually about 1½ in. long, the petals rolled and curved backward at the tips. The flowers of the Trumpet lilies range in form from narrow tubes with flared ends to large bowl-shaped blossoms.

Most of the species cross easily with only a few others. Over several decades, significant breakthroughs by breeders in the United States, Canada, New Zealand, and Japan have resulted in greater vigor, adaptability, and color range. Improved production methods greatly increased the availability of hybrid lilies to growers.

In a mixed border, lilies will make a good show as long as they are not crowded by other plants. Because they are not particularly attractive when out of bloom, lilies look best when grown with ground covers or low-growing companion plants that do not hinder lily roots.

A planting of lilies, such as the large Trumpet types, early-flowering Asiatics, or later-flowering Oriental hybrids, with low-growing annuals at their base, is a magnificent sight. A clump of lilies in bloom, between or in front of shrub plantings, also creates an attractive picture. For two or more weeks the added color complements the green foliage.

Hybrid lilies have been grouped under headings loosely based on species, origins, and flower forms, but there is overlapping. For instance, the Asiatics, most of whose parents originated in China, are usually lilies bred from *L. longifolium*, *L. davidii*, *L. cernuum*, and others that readily intercross.

The Asiatic hybrids are the most widely varied group in color and form. Some have upright flowers; blooms of others face outward; and some have backswept petals. An established clump of Asiatics has one of the longest blooming periods of all lilies—from early summer to midsummer. They are the hardiest and most reliable performers. Many breeders consider them to have the greatest hybridizing potential.

American hybrids are derived from native American species. Best known are Bellingham Hybrids. Non-native hybrids developed in the United States are not included in this group.

Martagon hybrids are most often used in natural settings at the edges of wooded areas. Among the first of the lilies to bloom, they should not be disturbed after being put into place. They may take two years to reappear after transplanting.

Backhouse hybrids originated before 1900 in England. They are the offsprings of *L. martagon*, a lily native to European mountains and western Asia to Mongolia, and *L. hansonii*, of Japan, Korea, and Siberia. Small flowered, they have many blooms, do well in shade, but are not widely available. The newer Paisley strain is similar.

Trumpet hybrids are the offsprings of four Chinese species: *L. regale*, *L. sargentiae*, *L. leucanthum*, and *L. sulphureum*. A clump of white, yellow, or pink Trumpets standing 4–6 feet tall is a spectacular sight in midsummer. They are less hardy than the Asiatics and have fragrant, usually outfacing or occasionally pendent flowers.

Aurelian hybrids result from crosses of the Trumpets with the Chinese *L. henryi*, which imparts adaptability and additional hardiness. Varying in form from reflexed stars to wide-flaring bowls and trumpets, they often have willowy stems that need support. They bloom from mid to late summer.

The most exotic and difficult hybrids are Orientals, with magnificent flowers in shades of white, pink, or red on sturdy stems. But they are susceptible to bulb rot and virus disease, and many lily growers settle for one season of colorful bloom and treat them as annuals or biennials. They are derived from *L. auratum* and *L. speciosum*. Jamboree hybrids are closer to *L. speciosum* and are among the most dependable of the Orientals. They bloom in late summer.

Among the true species, *L. candidum*, *L. longifolium*, *L. henryi*, *L. regale*, *L. martagon*, *L. superbum*, and *L. speciosum* are easy to obtain and among the most reliable.

The palette of the Bellingham Hybrids stretches from soft pink to orange. *Lilium henryi* is a deep orange. Both are recognizable as Turk's cap lilies by the backward bend of the petals.

Lilium Bellingham Hybrids

Lilium henryi

Planting and Caring for Lilies

Preparing the Soil and Selecting the Bulbs

Lilies will grow in almost any well-drained soil that has a pH slightly on the acid side. An exception is the Madonna lily, which does best in a neutral to slightly alkaline soil.

Full sun will provide the most vigorous growth, but lilies also perform well in partial shade.

Soil preparation before planting lilies is important, just as it is with other bulbs. In light soils, a generous addition of well-composted organic material or leaf mold will improve moisture retention. Bear in mind that lily bulbs and roots will be damaged if fresh manure is applied.

Improve heavy soils by adding coarse sand or light gravel. Bone meal, well mixed in, will enrich and condition the soil for several seasons (see pp. 496–502).

The subsoil must also provide good drainage so that water will not accumulate around the bulbs. Where impervious subsoil prevails, raised beds with well-drained soil should be prepared. Planting on a gentle slope serves the same purpose.

Buy only plump, healthy-looking bulbs. They are available in late fall or early spring from mail-order and local nurseries, and from lily specialists. The bulbs should be firm, with closely packed scales and a dense root system. If you do purchase bargain lots of bulbs, which may be bruised or limp, remove the loose outer scales and put the bulbs into plastic bags with slightly moist peat moss, and add a pinch of sulfur as a fungicide. Close the bags and store in a cool, dark place for several days until the bulbs are plump. Then remove them from the bags and plant.

Medium-sized bulbs in a given category are best. They reestablish in a new location more dependably than large bulbs, which may perform well the first year but fail to repeat their initial showing. Also, the medium-sized bulbs are considerably less expensive than the large ones.

When and How to Plant Lily Bulbs

Lilies can be planted any time the ground can be dug, but fall planting is best. Madonna lilies, however, should be planted in late summer so that there will be enough time for them to grow leaves before winter.

If planting is delayed because of bad weather or late arrival of your bulbs, you can protect them through the winter in pots, as described on the next page. If planting will be delayed for only a short period, the bulbs can be held in a cool, dark place in a plastic bag with some slightly moist peat moss.

In cold climates the best procedure, when possible, is to anticipate probable late arrival and prepare the planting holes, mulch heavily to keep the ground from freezing, and plant the bulbs as soon as they arrive.

Planting depth should be at least three times as deep as the height of the bulb.

Most lilies grown in North America are stem rooting and put out a covering of roots on top of the bulb. These roots both feed the bulb and provide support for the plant against wind. Take care not to damage them by cultivating too deeply. Others root from the base, as do most bulbs.

When planting, spread the roots and set the bulb so that it will rest with its tip beneath 3 or 4 inches of soil. (Madonna lilies require only 1 inch of soil over the bulb.)

In climates where it does not freeze, dig up the bulbs in fall and provide 8 to 10 weeks of simulated winter in the refrigerator.

Staking, Watering, and Feeding

Unless they are sturdily staked, lilies more than 3 feet tall may be damaged by strong winds. Those with arching stems, such as *L. davidii*, *L. henryi*, and their hybrids, look better if supported. Use one stake for each bulb. When placing it, take care not to drive it through the bulb. As the plant grows, tie the stem to the stake with twist ties or other soft material.

Lilies need a steady supply of moisture during the growing season. A summer mulch is a good way to conserve moisture. Keep the stem roots cool during hot weather to help control weeds. Mulch to a depth of 3 or 4 inches with oak leaves, pine needles, salt hay, or any other loose material that will allow passage of water and air to the soil.

In early spring when the stems are emerging, a complete organic fertilizer should be applied. Another application when the buds are forming will be beneficial. And after the lily has bloomed, one more feeding will boost the bulb for the next season.

Cut-Flower Arrangements

Lilies make superb cut flowers. Each plant can be cut every second or third year. Cutting oftener may weaken the bulb. Leave as much stem as possible to nourish the bulb, and at least half of the foliage. Cut lilies just as the first buds on a stem begin to open so that you will have the enjoyment of seeing most buds opening indoors.

Plunge the fresh-cut stems into warm water and let stand for several hours before arranging them. Strip the lower leaves so that none will stand in water. Change the water every day. This will prolong the life of the flowers, and every bud on the stem should eventually open.

1. Spread the roots of the bulb in a deep hole in well-drained soil.

2. Spread soil over the roots, then fill the hole completely.

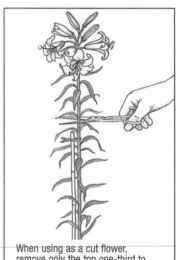

When using as a cut flower, remove only the top one-third to one-half of the stem.

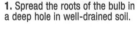

Lilium longiflorum

Lilium 'Connecticut King'

The milk-white Easter lily (*Lilium longiflorum*) has blossoms up to 8 in. long. 'Connecticut King', an Asiatic hybrid, is robust and suitable for the garden as well as for a container.

Deadheading to Stop Seeds From Forming

Pinching off flowers after they fade prevents seed formation, which tends to weaken the plant. As the stem dies down, trim off only the dry material and remove it from the garden. To prevent the spread of possible disease, do not put these trimmings into the compost heap.

To save seeds for growing new bulbs, leave one or two pods on each plant. Hybrid varieties do not come true from seeds, but seeds from the species' plants will produce lilies with only minor variations, unless you are growing several other forms nearby. Lilies can be hybridized by bees and you may get a surprise. Harvest the pods as soon as they turn yellow, and let them open indoors.

Unless you want the seed, pinch off lily's flowers as they fade.

What Can Go Wrong With Lilies

This chart describes the commonest problems encountered by lily growers. If your plants show symptoms that are not described here, turn to the full-color identification chart of pests and diseases that begins on page 506.

SYMPTOMS AND SIGNS	CAUSE	CONTROL
Shoot tips and buds covered with greenish or pinkish insects. Leaf undersides may be sticky. Buds and leaves may be malformed.	Aphids	Spray with insecticidal soap or neem.
Leaves and flowers are chewed.	Beetles or caterpillars	Spray plants with neem or *Bacillus thuringiensis*, depending on pest.
Leaves eaten entirely (often overnight). Bright red pests seen.	European lily beetles	Spray with neem.
Bulb scales are injured and roots destroyed.	Bulb mites	Destroy infested bulbs. Dust with sulfur before planting.
Leaves and shoots eaten; slime trails present.	Slugs or snails	Put out iron phosphate bait or trap with beer.
Water-soaked areas on leaves turn gray or white. Stems may rot and topple.	Botrytis, or gray mold (fungus)	Spray with copper fungicide.
Leaves have pale or yellow striping or mottling.	Virus disease	Destroy plants. Spray against insects that spread disease.

Growing Lilies in Pots and Other Containers

Lilies make excellent pot plants. They can be grown in pots to full bloom, or they can be started early indoors and set out when the weather warms up. Low-growing, early-blooming varieties, such as the Mid-Century hybrids 'Enchantment' and 'Cinnabar', are best.

In recent years many new varieties, having a wide range of colors, have been developed. Some of these are 'Connecticut King', 'Connecticut Lemon Glow', and the Sundrop strain. 'Red Carpet' is a fine, low-growing, spotless red lily that is hardy and easy to force at almost any time of year.

Bulbs available in the fall can be potted and put into a cold frame for two or three months and then brought indoors for forcing. Precooled bulbs are available from some lily dealers; these are ready to be started at any time. If you want good results in midwinter, supplementary light may be needed. Lily bulbs that are purchased in the spring should be potted immediately.

Use a 5-inch pot for a small to medium bulb, an 8- to 10-inch pot for a large bulb. Put drainage material in the bottom and over the hole.

The soil mixture should consist of 1 part coarse sand or perlite, 1 part peat moss, and 1 part good garden soil, well mixed together.

Water well upon planting. Thereafter, keep the soil barely moist until the lily is in active growth (to avoid bulb rot). Daytime temperatures should not exceed 68°F, nor night temperatures fall lower than 10°F.

Feed the plants every second week until the flowers have completed their blooming cycle. Afterward, plants grown indoors can be planted in the garden or kept in the same pots for another year. In either case, the foliage should be allowed to mature and turn yellow in order to nourish the bulb.

For good results the second season, keep bulbs in a protected cold frame over the winter or buried in the ground in a sheltered location.

Lilies can be grown in large containers outdoors. Plant them in the soil recommended for pots, and give them regular garden care. They also make stunning additions to a patio garden and are inexpensive enough to discard in the fall if you have no garden to plant them in.

Varieties to Grow

The most popular types of lily hybrids are the Asiatics (divisions I), Trumpets (division VI), and Orientals (division VII). There are many named forms of each, especially the Asiatics. These are subdivided according to the way the flowers are held on the stem, and good varieties include:

Division Ia (upward-facing flowers): 'Connecticut King' (yellow), 'Corina' (crimson); 'Enchantment' (orange-red with dark central spots), 'Red Carpet' (red), 'Sterling Star' (cream).
Division Ib (outward-facing flowers): 'Black Velvet' (dark red), 'Bold Knight' (red), 'Dawn Star' (pale yellow), 'Fire King' (orange-red),

'Moulin Rouge' (orange blotched brown).
Division Ic (pendent flowers): 'Citronella' (yellow), 'Katinka' (peach with brown spots), 'Nutmegger' (yellow flecked brown), 'Sally' (orange-pink with spotted centers), 'Viva' (red-orange, recurved).
Trumpet lily varieties: 'African Queen' (yellow), 'Black Dragon' (white with dark reverse), Pink Perfection Strain (rose pink).
Oriental lily varieties: 'Casa Blanca' (white), 'Imperial Gold' (yellow), 'Journey's End' (purple), 'Star Gazer' (red).

Visit the North American Lily Society's website at www.lilies.org for more information.

The brilliant yellow blossoms of the Turk's cap lily *Lilium pyrenaicum* are flecked with purple and have a rather unpleasant odor.

Lilium pyrenaicum

How to Propagate Your Own Lilies

Producing Plants From Scales

The easiest and most widely used method of increasing lilies is to propagate from the scales that make up the bulb. Flowering plants are produced from these scales in two or three years.

A bulb can be scaled at any time. Use only plump, healthy bulbs, because damaged or infected scales either will not produce new bulbs or will make new bulbs that do not grow properly. If the bulb that is used to supply scales has a viral disease, the new bulbs will have it too.

Remove any withered or damaged scales and discard them. Separate the plump, healthy scales by breaking them off as close to the base as possible, taking a bit of the basal plate with the scale. If only a few new bulbs are wanted, take two or three scales. If you want to develop a num-

ber of a given variety, a bulb can be scaled completely, leaving only its heart. Some varieties, however, do not produce good bulbs from scales. If you use a valuable lily, try just a few scales the first time. If you are successful with that bulb, it can be scaled again.

Wash the scales thoroughly; let them dry for several hours or overnight. Plant as shown, or place the scales in a plastic bag, with enough slightly moist peat moss to keep them separate. Add a pinch of sulfur as a fungicide. Seal the bag and label with the name of the variety and the date.

Put the bag in a warm place, such as a cupboard or closet. Check the bag every week or two to see that the moisture is maintained. If the scales show signs of mildew or other fungus, wash them and rebag.

In 8 to 10 weeks the miniature bulbs, called bulbils, should be

formed along the bottom edge of the scale. When the bulbils reach a quarter of an inch or more in diameter, they should be chilled in your refrigerator at about 40°F for six to eight weeks. The original bag with scales can be refrigerated for the cooling period, or the bulbils can be separated and put into a fresh bag with moistened peat moss and sulfur. Check the temperature in various sections of your refrigerator to determine the best location.

The alternate method is to separate the scales and plant them in seed flats as shown below. This can be done if the time of year permits you to put the flats into a cold frame for at least a six-week cooling period before the weather turns warm.

When the scale bulbils begin to show growth, treat them as you would seedlings (p. 150). By the end of the second or third season, the plants will be large enough to bloom.

Lifting and Dividing Lilies

Some lilies self-propagate quickly and need to be divided every third or fourth season. The best time to divide is in early fall when the stems are drying off. Lift the clump carefully with a garden fork or shovel; remove the soil; then wash with a gentle stream of water. Separate the bulbs carefully; replant in fresh soil.

Some of the offsets may be of blooming size. Those that are smaller can be planted in an area of the garden set aside to bring scale and seedling bulbs into bloom. Or let them develop in pots before planting them in the open garden.

A few lilies, such as Bellingham Hybrids, have rhizomatous bulbs (as illustrated below), which should be divided simply to keep them flowering well. Sever these bulbs with a sharp knife, dust with sulfur, and replant.

Lilies need a full season to settle into a new location after transplanting and may not perform at their best the first year. Therefore, divide only a few clumps each year.

1. Remove and discard the dried-up outer scales from bulbs.

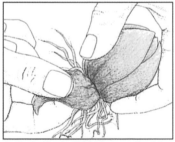

2. Gently break off the plump scales, taking some basal plate with each.

3. Plant each scale to half its depth and cover container with a plastic bag.

4. In 10 weeks bulbils should be formed. Refrigerate for six weeks.

5. Early in the spring, place each new plant in a 2½- to 3-in. pot.

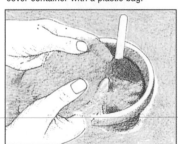

6. Sink the pots in sand or peat moss outdoors. Cover with 1 in. of sand.

DIVIDING BULBS

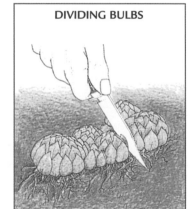

The rhizomatous bulbs formed by some vigorous lilies should be lifted every three or four years and separated with a sharp knife.

At 6 in., the regal (*Lilium regale*) has particularly large blossoms. This and the Pink Perfection Group have an exceptionally strong fragrance. These lilies are equally well suited to beds or containers.

Lilium regale

Lilium Pink Perfection Group

Increasing Lilies From Aerial Bulbils

Aerial bulbils are small green or purple-black bulbs that grow in the leaf axils of lilies like the tiger lily and several of its hybrids.

Detach the bulbils from the lily's stem in late summer or fall when they are loose and easy to remove. Plant them about 1 inch deep and 1 inch apart in seed flats. They will do well in a mixture of equal parts of soil, peat moss, and sand.

Grow them through the winter in a cold frame or in a sheltered location under a loose mulch. When the weather warms up in the spring, move the flats into partial shade, and water and feed the bulbils just as you would potted lilies. In fall plant the new lilies in the open garden.

Tiny bulbils growing in the leaf axils of some species can be taken in late summer to propagate new plants.

New Lilies From Bulblets

Many lilies form bulblets on top of the bulb. Some also form bulblets at the base of the mother bulb. Mounding the soil around the stem encourages this. If these offsets are small and do not have roots, plant them in the same way as bulbils. Larger bulblets with established roots can be planted directly in the ground.

In late summer remove the soil from around the stem of each plant and carefully detach the bulblets. Those that are less than ½ inch in diameter are best grown in seed flats for a season (as described for bulbils) before you plant them in the garden. The larger ones should be planted directly in the garden. Lightly spread 1–2 inches of soil over them, according to the size of the bulblets.

Bulblets, which grow among the stem roots or on the base of some lilies, can be detached and planted out in late summer.

Growing Lilies From Seeds

Sowing seeds is a good way to produce a large collection of lilies. Hybrid seeds will not produce plants identical to the parents, but most of the seedlings will be attractive, and a new lily of superior quality may even show up. Flowers first appear the second or third season after sowing, but plants take a year or two more to attain full bloom.

Young lily seedlings should be grown in a sterile soil (p. 504) during the early stages of development. Using pots or trays, sow the seeds an inch apart, covering them with about half an inch of soil. A cool greenhouse (or a windowsill that has some sun for part of the day) is a good location. A temperature range of 55°–75°F is best. Seeds germinate faster at warmer temperatures. A steady supply of moisture and nutrients is essential.

Seeds can be started at any time of the year indoors, and fluorescent lighting can be used with excellent results. Set the lights 2–3 inches above the flats; then raise the lights or lower the flats as the seedlings grow, always maintaining the same distance. When the seeds have germinated, give them from 14 to 16 hours of light per day.

Lily seeds are of two types: epigeal (which means close to the ground) and hypogeal (which means underground). Some of the former are among the easiest to grow. They germinate quickly and send up a leaf three to six weeks after sowing. Asiatics and most Trumpet types fall into this category. The hypogeal seeds do not show aboveground until they have had a warm period of three to four months, followed by two or three months of cool temperatures in the 34°–37°F range. A good example of this type is *L. speciosum*.

When leaves show, the seedlings can be transplanted 1–2 inches apart in a larger container or left to grow the first full season in the original flat. Seedlings with bulbs more than half an inch in diameter and good roots can be put into the open garden at the end of the first season, or they can be grown in a 3- to 4-inch pot for another year before being set out.

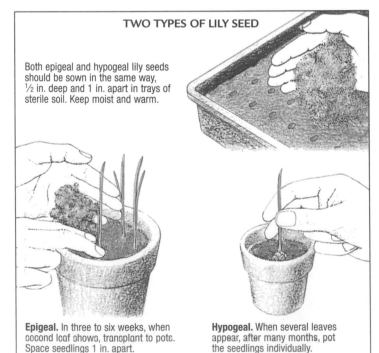

TWO TYPES OF LILY SEED

Both epigeal and hypogeal lily seeds should be sown in the same way, ½ in. deep and 1 in. apart in trays of sterile soil. Keep moist and warm.

Epigeal. In three to six weeks, when second leaf shows, transplant to pots. Space seedlings 1 in. apart.

Hypogeal. When several leaves appear, after many months, pot the seedlings individually.

Spherical flower heads of sea thrift (Armeria maritima) emerge from grasslike foliage. Rose-pink 'Dusseldorf Pride' grows about 8 in. tall.

ROCK GARDENS

A successful rock garden re-creates the natural rock outcrops on mountain slopes. Select only those plants that thrive in stony terrain.

With their delicate detail and exquisite form, alpines and other rock plants have a particular fascination—the wonder of the miniature.

Since the original habitats of many species are mountainous and rocky regions, they are for the most part hardy and can tolerate thin, stony soils, and some can survive drying winds. Provided their natural habitat's good drainage is imitated, many rock plants are easy to grow.

Their brilliant colors enhance any garden, and since their size allows them to grow well in troughs or containers, no garden, however small, need be without them. Once planted, they demand little attention, except to be kept clear of weeds.

In their natural habitats, nearly all mountain plants are covered by an insulating blanket of snow each year, have a short growing season, and do not suffer from the high temperatures and humid conditions they may have to endure under cultivation in many regions. Where there is little sustained snow cover, even if the winters are cold, plants will need the protection of a loose mulch. (Pine boughs are good.) This should be applied after the soil freezes.

Some high-altitude plants are best grown in pots in an "alpine house." This is simply a greenhouse with little or no heat. Most rock plants, however, grow best in the open and are commonly used in specially prepared rock gardens. Ideally, a rock garden should be on a slope, but a flat site is suitable if adequately drained.

The most practical way to construct a rock garden is by using the "outcrop" principle—that is, partially embedding a few large rocks in the soil to give the impression of more rocks beneath the surface. The outcrop system is possible with all types of rocks, although rounded stones require more effort and must be set deeper in the ground.

Other flat sites on which to grow rock plants are paved areas or "alpine lawns." To grow plants between paving, lay the slabs on sand, with gaps between to accommodate aromatic species that give off fragrance when they are walked on. An alpine lawn consists of low-growing rock plants with bulbs growing among them and can be located in the lower parts of your rock garden.

Alpines and rock plants also grow well in raised beds. In this manner plants with different requirements—lime lovers, lime haters, or sun lovers that require good drainage—can all be grown in separate beds filled with different soil mixtures. A system of raised beds can be constructed from several types of material. The best material is rocks, built up like a retaining wall, with soil between them. Plants can then be positioned to trail down the sides of the beds.

Bricks can also be used to build raised beds. They must be cemented in place, with holes left for drainage. Landscape ties, logs, and even boards can all serve as building material, as can pavers. However, they are likely to be unattractive unless used with skill.

The height of a raised bed may vary from 6 inches to about 3 feet. Tall beds are best for those who find it difficult to bend or stoop.

Before attempting to build a rock garden, you should have in mind (if not on paper) a plan of the basic design you wish to make. To get an idea of the possibilities, visit a rock garden in one of the many botanical gardens throughout the country. Smaller rock gardens that might be appropriate to a small plot can be seen in some private gardens that are open to the public on special occasions. Information regarding these can usually be obtained from local gardening clubs, horticultural societies, and garden sections of newspapers.

To build a successful, natural-looking rock garden, follow a few basic principles. Never attempt to copy an actual mountain in a garden; the scale would be quite out of proportion. Instead, try to simulate a natural outcrop of rock; this will be far more effective.

The relationship between height and width is also important. For every foot in height, a rock garden's planting area should be 4–5 feet wide at the base. A 4-foot mound, for example, should measure about 20 feet across at its base.

Once the basic rock garden has been built, other features can be added. Water is always an attractive feature; but if you construct a waterfall, take care to make it look as natural as possible.

Aquilegia alpina

Campanula cochlearifolia

Deep blue blossoms of *Aquilegia alpina*, the alpine columbine, begin appearing in spring. Fairies' thimbles (*Campanula cochlearifolia*), a charming miniature bellflower that grows amid rocks, does not blossom until midsummer.

How to Build a Rock Garden

You may be fortunate in having rocks and outcroppings on your property. If not, rocks can be purchased from a garden center or landscape contractor. Whenever possible, choose the pieces yourself, selecting for uniformity of color and texture. If you order from a supplier, ask for a variety of sizes.

Large rocks, although not always easy to move and put in place, are likely to provide the most natural effects, but smaller sizes will be needed, too.

An area roughly 10 feet by 15 feet will require about 1½–2 tons of rock. You will also need a supply of ¼-inch chips—gravel or crushed stone—to use as a mulch around the plants. Whatever kind of rock mulch you use, however, the material should blend, rather than contrast, with the surrounding rocks.

The ideal location is a gentle slope protected from strong winds. A sunny site is best for the majority of plants, but dappled sunshine coming through a tree several yards away is acceptable—and even beneficial during very sunny, hot weather. Do not build a rock garden beneath trees that cast heavy shade, or in other shady areas, unless you plan to grow only woodland plants. Too much shade from nearby trees can be reduced by cutting off lower branches and thinning upper growth.

Dig out or use an organic weed killer on all perennial weeds on the site. Good drainage is essential, too; most rock plants will not survive damp conditions. A light soil on a gravelly subsoil will have sufficient natural drainage. But a heavy claylike soil with a subsoil of clay may require a drainage system. This is particularly important if the site is flat.

To provide drainage, dig trenches that slope down to a lower level. Make them about 18 inches deep and 3–6 feet apart. Fill the bottom half of each trench with large stones, broken bricks, or rubble. Then place a layer of upturned sod (or several inches of gravel or crushed stone) on top. Finally, fill up with soil.

Sandy soil (or other types of soil that do not require drainage) needs to be dug over only lightly before the rocks are laid.

When the weeds are cleared and any required draining dug, place rocks along two sides of the prepared ground to form an L-shaped outcrop. Use the largest rock as the corner, or keystone, of the L. Employ progressively smaller rocks to form the two arms of the L, with the final rocks almost disappearing into the soil. The result should give the appearance of an outcrop of rock protruding from the earth, with a much larger mass of rock below.

A south-facing slope can be made on a north-facing slope by placing rocks on top of one another at the corner of the L to tilt the bed toward the south.

For good drainage place the rocks so that joints line up horizontally and vertically. All rocks have strata lines. Lay the rocks so that these lines run horizontally.

Take care to set the rocks firmly in position. When all have been properly placed, fill the space between the arms of the L with free-draining soil.

For this purpose, prepare a mixture of 2 parts ¼-inch rock chips, 1 part loam, and 1 part compost or leaf mold. Shovel this mixture inside the L until it is flush with the tops of the rocks. Then firm it by treading lightly. The mixture will settle; so keep some in reserve for adding later.

When this bed has been completed, further beds can be laid out if the rock garden is to be extended—either behind the first bed or to one side of it.

After about 10 days (earlier if there has been heavy rain), the soil will have subsided and can be brought to the proper level with the mixture that was held in reserve. Now, rake the surfaces flat. Finally, apply a mulch layer of ¼-inch rock chips, ½–1 inch deep. Rake the chips flat.

If the construction is on a slope, the stones should be positioned in such a way as to hold water in place, enabling it to soak into the soil rather than run off the slope.

A waterfall or pool for aquatic plants will enhance a garden's attractiveness. For specific details on how to construct your own water garden, see page 174.

1. Form an L by placing the largest rock at the corner and making the arms from progressively smaller rocks. Fill spaces with a free-draining soil mixture.

2. Additional outcrops can be built either behind or to one side of the first one. Small stones can be laid in a random arrangement on each outcrop.

3. Extra tiers can be added as far as space allows, but in its final form, the rock garden should be four to five times wider than it is high.

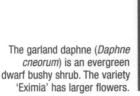

The garland daphne (*Daphne cneorum*) is an evergreen dwarf bushy shrub. The variety 'Eximia' has larger flowers.

Daphne cneorum 'Eximia'

Rock Plants Without a Rock Garden

Making a Raised Bed With Landscape Ties

A raised bed is ideal for dwarf rhododendrons, heathers, and other plants that flourish in an acid, humus-rich soil. The sides of a raised bed can be made with landscape ties, or even with logs or boards. Although sides can be as high or as low as desired, a height of about 2 feet is generally convenient. The bed should be in an open position, but near some trees that will give it dappled shade during hot summer months.

If beds are long enough to require more than one section of whatever material is used for the sides, the joints between the sections can be planted with ferns or other plants that thrive in crevices and need an acid soil, such as trailing arbutus, ramonda, or mountain cranberry.

Fill the beds with equal parts of loam and leaf mold. In spring topdress with moist, coarse peat or well-composted leaves—preferably oak—or composted pine needles. Both will supply nutrients. Remember to water the beds well during droughts.

A raised bed filled with acid, humus-rich soil is useful in alkaline soil regions for growing dwarf rhododendrons, heathers, ferns, and others plants.

Screes: Ideal for Rock Plants in Small Gardens

For the small garden, a scree—a bed of stone chips—provides a smaller, more easily constructed setting for rock plants than a full-scale rock garden. Many plants that do not live long in a rock garden do quite well in a scree because of its excellent drainage.

A slightly inclined site is best for a scree. Ideally, it should face south or west and should be located at the base of a rocky outcropping, as in nature. However, it is more important that the stones provide excellent drainage and sure moisture in spring and summer.

First, dig a hole about 2–3 feet deep. At the bottom of the hole place a 6-inch-deep layer of drainage material, such as rocks, bricks, or rubble. Cover this with a layer of inverted sod sections, if you have some; or use marsh hay, straw, coarse leaves, or some other kind of organic material.

Then fill in the hole with a mixture composed of 2 parts ¼-inch stone chips, 1 part leaf mold, and 1 part soil. If the soil has a high clay content, add some sand to the mixture to break it up.

PREPARING A SCREE

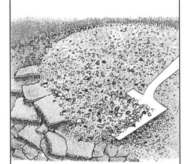

Dig a hole 2–3 ft. deep. Put in a 6-in. layer of drainage material. Cover with coarse compost or leaves. Fill the rest of the hole with a mix of stone chips, leaf mold, and soil.

Every year, in early spring, apply a ½-inch-deep topdressing of equal parts leaf mold and stone chips (or coarse sand), plus 2 ounces (about 2 tablespoons) of bone meal per bucketful.

Most of the plants suitable for troughs and sinks do well in a scree.

Suitable plants are listed in the chart beginning on page 156.

Paths, Patios, Retaining Walls, and Rock Plants

To relieve the starkness of a garden path, particularly a straight one, grow rock plants along the edges—or even directly in the path itself.

Rock plants can also add interest to a patio. When the patio is being constructed, leave spaces between the paving stones. In the spaces, position hardy "carpeting" plants, such as the mother of thyme, that can withstand trampling. (These plants also emit a pleasant scent.)

To provide a varied, three-dimensional look, put one or two taller plants in corners or borders where they are not likely to be trampled on.

Dwarf irises, conifers, and shrubs can help achieve this effect.

If the path or terrace is not often walked on in winter, dwarf bulbs such as the crocus and the muscari (grape hyacinth) can be planted to add a splash of bright color in spring.

A retaining wall that is lightly shaded from the midday sun is the ideal place for growing the really vigorous rock plants whose flowers and foliage provide the most striking color effects. With careful planning, the wall can be of interest throughout much of the year.

Some plants will grow well on a wall that is in a shady, perhaps even moist position. Among these are mossy saxifrages and ferns.

With proper planning, retaining walls, paths, and patios can have plants in flower for many months. For paths, choose plants that can withstand being walked on.

The maiden pink (*Dianthus deltoides*) is a mat-forming perennial, which grows well in partial shade. The evergreen mountain avens (*Dryas octopetala*) needs a sunlit location.

Dianthus deltoides 'Brilliant'

Dryas octopetala

Planting a Rock Garden

Rock plants do best if set in place in spring or early fall. If pot grown, they can be set out in summer, since they can be transplanted without unduly disturbing the roots. In mild-climate regions, rock plants can be set out any time the ground is workable.

To dislodge a plant from its pot, hold it upside down with the stem between two fingers, and gently pull away the pot if it is made of paper or other fiber. If the pot is plastic or clay, tap its rim sharply on a hard surface.

With a trowel dig a hole in the soil to the depth of the root ball and insert the plant. Fill the hole with soil, and firm the plant in position with your fingers or a trowel handle. Cover the area with stone chips, and water.

Homegrown seedlings and rooted cuttings that are ready for transplanting can be put directly into the rock garden. Upright shrubs or conifers look best when they are planted at the base of a rock. Prostrate shrubs or conifers are best planted at higher levels; lengthening branches will then cascade over the rocks.

Rosette-forming plants can be grown in a vertical crevice, where rain will not collect in the rosettes and cause rot. After taking such a plant from its pot and removing the drainage material from its soil ball, check that the plant fits into the crevice. If it does, tease its soil ball into the right shape.

Wedge the soil ball into the crevice, and firm in with soil beneath the plant. Finally, fill in the crevice from above the plant with a mixture of soil and stone chips. Ideally, crevice plants should be planted when the rocks are in position.

Large, well-established plants look good in the angles between rocks. Dig up the plant during wet weather in autumn or early spring, making sure that a generous ball of soil is taken up with the roots.

If necessary, use a crowbar to lift a rock temporarily so that the roots of the plant can be wedged beneath it. Firm the soil around the roots. Remember to water all newly set plants.

Locate fast-growing plants where they will not crowd others. Before planting, study the chart that begins on page 156 for detailed information on hundreds of rock plants.

THREE TYPES OF ROCK PLANTS

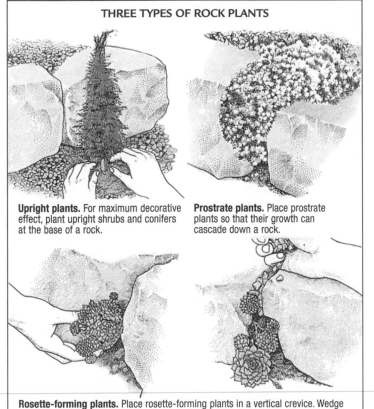

Upright plants. For maximum decorative effect, plant upright shrubs and conifers at the base of a rock.

Prostrate plants. Place prostrate plants so that their growth can cascade down a rock.

Rosette-forming plants. Place rosette-forming plants in a vertical crevice. Wedge the soil ball into the crevice. Firm the soil underneath the plant; then fill in from above with soil and stone chips.

What Can Go Wrong With Rock Plants

To deter snails and slugs, eliminate weeds. Other problems and their appropriate solutions are listed below. If plants show symptoms not described here, see the chart on page 506. More information on controls appears in the section starting on page 542.

SYMPTOMS AND SIGNS	CAUSE	CONTROL
Flowering stems or young growth stunted or distorted; covered with small, sticky, greenish, pink, or black insects.	Aphids	Spray with insecticidal soap.
Leaves eaten. No obvious slime trails.	Caterpillars	Spray with *Bacillus thuringiensis* or neem. Or locate and remove caterpillars by hand.
Stems bitten through at ground level or just beneath soil surface.	Cutworms (certain kinds of caterpillars)	Treat soil with *Steinernema* nematodes, and place a tinfoil collar around the plants.
Leaves and young shoots eaten. Slime trails often visible on or around plant.	Slugs or snails	Trap with saucers of beer. Put iron phosphate baits around plants.
Fluffy grayish patches atop brown patches when weather is damp.	Gray mold (botrytis)	Spray with potassium bicarbonate fungicide.
Cushionlike plants with brown patches.	Aging of plants	Propagate living parts.
	Ants' nests cause water to sink too rapidly into lower soil layers	Firm soil around plant. If brown patches are extensive, propagate living parts and discard remainder. Use borax traps or liquid for ant control.
	Drought conditions	Water regularly during dry spells.

Plants for Your Rock Garden

The plants listed in the chart are suitable for growing in rock gardens. Many can also be used between paving blocks and in containers, screes, retaining walls, and alpine lawns.

Many rock plants bloom in spring, but with careful selection it is possible to maintain some plants in flower throughout most of the growing season. To extend the flowering season, plant some early- and late-flowering dwarf bulbs.

The term "rock plant" refers to the natural habitat of the plants discussed here, but the rock plants are shrubs, perennials, or bulbs.

They all grow best in full sun and a gritty, well-drained soil unless otherwise noted. Visit the North American Rock Garden Society website at www.nargs.org for more information, including details on local chapters.

Alyssum wulfenianum

Acantholimon glumaceum (prickly thrift)

Achillea tomentosa (woolly yarrow)

Adonis amurensis (Amur adonis)

Aethionema grandiflorum (Persian stonecress)

Ajuga pyramidalis (pyramidal bugleweed)

Alchemilla alpina (alpine lady's mantle)

Allium senescens (ornamental onion)

BOTANICAL AND COMMON NAMES	HEIGHT	SPREAD	DECORATIVE CHARACTERISTICS, SPECIAL REQUIREMENTS, AND REMARKS	PROPAGATION
Acantholimon (prickly thrift) *A. glumaceum*	2–3 in.	8–12 in.	Mat to cushion perennials with spiny needlelike foliage and spikes of bright pink flowers in early to mid summer. Withstands cold, but not winter wet.	Cuttings from new growth in spring, or layer shoot tips. Sow seeds in spring.
Achillea (yarrow) *A. tomentosa* (woolly yarrow)	8–10 in.	18 in.	Low mats of very hairy, silvery foliage are attractive all year. Heads of yellow flowers on slender stems rise above the leaves in early summer.	Divide mats in spring or early fall.
Adonis (adonis) *A. amurensis* (Amur adonis) *A. vernalis* (pheasant's eye)	12 in. 12–18 in.	12 in. 12 in.	Perennial with ferny foliage. Buttercuplike flowers appear in early spring on short stems that elongate as flowers fade. Grow in sun or partial shade. Needs well-drained but moisture-retentive soil. Use in open woods, shrub foreground, paving.	Sow fresh seeds when ripe. Divide carefully in spring or after flowering.
Aethionema (aethionema, or stonecress) *A. grandiflorum* (Persian stonecress)	6–8 in.	15 in.	Shrubby perennial with small blue-green leaves. Heads of rose-colored flowers appear from late spring to early summer. *A hybrid, A.* 'Warley Rose', has deeper rose flowers. Add ground limestone to acid soils. Use for dry walls, screes, containers, alpine house.	Self-sows freely. Take cuttings from new growth in midsummer.
Ajuga (ajuga, or bugleweed) *A. pyramidalis* (pyramidal bugleweed)	6–10 in.	12–18 in.	Showy blue flowers are borne on spikes in midspring to early summer. Grow in sun or partial shade and in almost any soil. For ground cover ajuga, see p. 28. The variety 'Metallica Crispa' is smaller with crinkled foliage.	Easily increased by division of clumps.
Alchemilla (lady's mantle) *A. alpina* (alpine lady's mantle) *A. erythropoda*	6–8 in. 8–12 in.	8–10 in. 8 in.	Perennial with silvery green leaves, hairy underneath. Short sprays of small, green-tinged flowers in summer. Grow in sun or partial shade and in well-drained soil. Plant in crevices between rocks. Leaves of *A. alpina* are palmate, divided into leaflets. *A. erythropoda* has hairy, silvery, blue-green leaves.	Divide plants in early spring or fall.
Allium (allium, or ornamental onion) *A. cyaneum* *A. senescens*	6–8 in. 8–10 in.	4 in. 6–10 in.	Perennial with attractive straplike leaves, often twisted and gray tinged. Clear blue flowers above grasslike foliage in late summner. Pretty, long-lasting rose-lavender flowers borne in midsummer. Grow in partial shade and in well-drained soil. Use in dry walls, raised beds. See also p. 121.	Clumps are easily divided in spring or after flowering.

The tiny rock jasmine (*Androsace sarmentosa*), only 2 in. tall, requires well-drained soil. Rue anemone (*Anemonella*) needs a shaded humus-rich soil.

Androsace sarmentosa

Anemonella thalictroides 'Rosea Plena'

| *Alyssum wulfenianum* (alyssum) | *Andromeda polifolia* (bog rosemary) | *Androsace sarmentosa* (rock jasmine) | *Anemone sylvestris* (snowdrop anemone) | *Anemonella thalictroides* (rue anemone) | *Antennaria dioica* (pussytoes) | *Anthemis marschalliana* (camomile) | *Anthyllis vulneraria* (kidney vetch) |

BOTANICAL AND COMMON NAMES	HEIGHT	SPREAD	DECORATIVE CHARACTERISTICS, SPECIAL REQUIREMENTS, AND REMARKS	PROPAGATION
Alyssum (alyssum) A. spinosum (spiny alyssum)	6–8 in.	9–10 in.	Spreading woody perennial with small gray leaves. White or rose flowers form dense mounds in early summer. See also *Aurinia*.	Sow seeds in spring or fall. Take cuttings or layer after flowering.
A. wulfenianum	4–6 in.	18 in.	Prostrate plant with long-lasting bright yellow flowers in early summer and sometimes again in fall. Good on walls or walkways.	
Andromeda (andromeda) A. polifolia (bog rosemary)	12 in.	12 in.	Spreading dwarf shrub with blue-tinged evergreen foliage. Dainty white or pink flowers bloom in mid to late spring. Grow in sun or partial shade and in humus-rich soil. Fine with dwarf rhododendrons and azaleas in raised beds, bog gardens.	Sow seeds in sphagnum moss. Divide clumps in spring. Root hardwood cuttings in sand and leaf mold. Layer in spring.
Androsace (androsace, or rock jasmine) A. sarmentosa A. sempervivoides	4–6 in. 2–4 in.	24 in. 9–12 in.	Perennial rosettes of hairy leaves. Bears umbels of small pink flowers in mid to late spring. Mulch with stone chips. Use in dry walls, screes, containers.	Sever rosettes (formed after flowering) from parent plant and root in midsummer; transplant following spring.
Anemone (anemone, or windflower) A. lesseri A. sylvestris (snowdrop anemone)	8–10 in. 12–18 in.	6–8 in. 15–18 in.	Stiff, hairy, dark green foliage all summer. Slender stems of deep pink flowers in summer, followed by fluffy white seed heads. Clump-forming perennial. Fragrant, nodding, 2-in. white flowers appear in late spring. Grow in partial shade and in humus-rich soil. Looks best in groupings in woodlands or in large rock garden.	Divide clumps in early spring or early fall.
Anemonella (anemonella, or rue anemone) A. thalictroides	4–6 in.	6 in.	Tuberous-rooted perennial with delicate 3-lobed leaflets. Bears single, semi-double, or double white or rose flowers, ½ in. across, in late spring to early summer. Grow in partial shade and in humus-rich soil. Good choice for woodlands or shaded pockets of rock garden.	Gently divide tiny dahlialike tubers after flowering ceases. Foliage dies down in summer.
Antennaria (antennaria, or pussytoes) A. dioica	2–4 in.	18 in.	Mat-forming perennial with woolly gray leaves, white underneath. Heads of gray flowers, sometimes pink tinged, grow in close clusters in early to mid summer. Grow in full sun and in dry, lean soil. Attractive carpet for small spring bulbs; or use in paving, containers.	Easily divided in spring or fall.
Anthemis (camomile) A. marschalliana	6 in.	12–18 in.	Prostrate mats of silvery, fernlike foliage with bright yellow daisies on slender stems in early summer.	Division in early spring or seed sown as soon as ripe.
Anthyllis (anthyllis) A. vulneraria (kidney vetch)	3–6 in.	10 in.	Mat-forming perennial legume with gray compound leaves. Yellow and red cloverlike flower heads open in early summer. Grow in full sun and in well-drained soil. Use in retaining walls, paving, troughs.	Sow seeds or divide in early spring.

The astilbe (*Astilbe*) prefers damp, humus-rich soil. On a dry wall in full sun, cushions of aubrieta (*Aubrieta*) burst into bloom in early spring. 'Gurgedyke' has large single deep purple blossoms.

Astilbe chinensis pumila

Aubrieta 'Gurgedyke'

Aquilegia alpina (alpine columbine)

Arabis caucasica (wall rock cress)

Arctostaphylos uva-ursi (kinnikinnick)

Arenaria montana (mountain sandwort)

Armeria maritima (sea thrift)

Asarum europaeum (European wild ginger)

Aster alpinus (rock aster)

BOTANICAL AND COMMON NAMES	HEIGHT	SPREAD	DECORATIVE CHARACTERISTICS, SPECIAL REQUIREMENTS, AND REMARKS	PROPAGATION
Aquilegia (columbine, or aquilegia) A. alpina (alpine columbine) A. canadensis (common American columbine) A. flabellata alba A. saximontana	12 in. 12–24 in. 6–12 in. 3 in.	12 in. 18 in. 12 in. 2 in.	Perennial with mounds of attractive compound leaves, each leaflet deeply segmented and graceful. Showy flowers with prominent spurs in late spring and early summer. Grow in sun or partial shade; well-drained soil should be poor, but contain some leaf mold. Good plant for edges of woodlands, alpine lawns, raised beds, or foreground of shrub borders. *A. f. alba*, with white flowers and glaucous leaves, is outstanding, fairly long-lived rock plant. *A. alpina* has blue flowers; *A. canadensis*, red and yellow. *A. saximontana* is white with blue spurs over grayish foliage.	Sow seeds in spring or fall; germination may be slow. Most columbines self-sow freely. Some, such as *A. f. alba*, remain true to type.
Arabis (arabis, or rock cress) A. caucasica (wall rock cress) A. c. 'Flore Pleno'	6–10 in. 4–6 in.	24 in. 24 in.	Spreading perennial with soft-textured gray foliage. Racemes of fragrant white flowers appear in mid to late spring. *A. c.* 'Flore Pleno' has long-lasting double flowers. *A. c.* 'Variegata' has leaves mottled green and cream. Cut back after flowering. Use for dry walls, paving, screes.	From seeds. (Plants self-sow freely if not cut back after flowering.) Division or cuttings in midsummer.
Arctostaphylos (bearberry) A. uva-ursi (kinnikinnick)	2–4 in.	15 in.	Trailing shrub with beautiful, glossy evergreen leaves that turn reddish in winter. Small, urn-shaped pink flowers appear in late spring. Long-lasting red berries in fall and winter. Grow in sun or partial shade. Thrives in well-drained, acid, sandy or rocky soil. Useful ground cover for sandy dunes or rock-strewn slopes. 'Vancouver Jade' is slightly larger.	Transplants poorly from wild. Cuttings root easily in leaf mold and sand in plastic-enclosed flat. Set out rooted cuttings in spring or summer.
Arenaria (arenaria, or sandwort) A. montana (mountain sandwort)	2–4 in.	18 in.	Creeping or trailing perennial with small grasslike leaves. Starry white flowers, ½ in. across, in late spring to early summer. Grow in well-drained, humus-rich soil. Fine wall plant; also grows in screes and paving.	Seeds offer best success; more difficult are divisions in early fall and cuttings in midsummer.
Armeria (armeria, or thrift) A. juniperifolia A. maritima (sea pink, or sea thrift)	2–3 in. 6-12 in.	6 in. 12 in.	Mound-forming perennial with stiff, grasslike evergreen foliage. Papery-textured flower heads in pink, rose, or white appear from late spring to midsummer. Grow *A. juniperifolia* on top of dry walls, in screes, paving, or containers. *A. maritima* and its varieties are easier to grow. 'Bloodstone' (dark red), 'Dusseldorf Pride' (pink), and 'Vindictive' (pink, more compact), are good varieties.	*A. maritima* by division or fresh seeds. *A. juniperifolia* usually is more difficult; try rooting basal cuttings in leaf mold and sand mixture in early summer.
Asarum (wild ginger) A. europaeum (European wild ginger) A. shuttleworthii (mottled wild ginger) A. virginicum (Virginia wild ginger)	5 in. 8 in. 7 in.	10 in. 16 in. 14 in.	Mat-forming perennial with creeping ginger-flavored rhizomes. Handsome heart-shaped evergreen leaves, often mottled with silver, hide ground-hugging, tubular flowers of brown or maroon, which appear in early spring. Grow in shade and in well-drained, humus-rich soil. Choice but not spectacular for woodlands and shaded rock gardens.	Divide in spring by separating rhizomes and replanting in humus-rich soil. Keep well watered until established.
Aster (aster) A. alpinus (rock aster)	8–10 in.	π10–18 in.	Perennial with violet flowers (there are also white, lavender, and pinkish forms) in early summer. Fine plant for large rock gardens, alpine lawns, or between paving stones.	Divide clumps in late summer after flowering. Or sow seeds in early spring.

Cassiope lycopodioides

Chrysogonum virginianum

From mid to late spring, the mat-forming dwarf shrub cassiope (*Cassiope*) is covered in tiny bell-shaped flowers borne on delicate stems. Long-flowering golden star (*Chrysogonum virginianum*) thrives in full sun or partial shade.

Astilbe chinensis pumila (false spirea) • Aubrieta cultorum (purple rock cress) • Aurinia saxatilis (basket of gold) • Bellium minutum (bellium) • Bruckenthalia spiculifolia (spike heath) • Campanula portenschlagiana (Dalmatian bellflower) • Carlina acaulis (stemless thistle) • Cassiope tetragona (cassiope)

BOTANICAL AND COMMON NAMES	HEIGHT	SPREAD	DECORATIVE CHARACTERISTICS, SPECIAL REQUIREMENTS, AND REMARKS	PROPAGATION
Astilbe (astilbe, or false spirea) A. chinensis pumila A. crispa A. simplicifolia	10 in. 6–8 in. 12 in.	24 in. 8–12 in. 12 in.	Perennial with attractive clumps or mats of divided fernlike leaves. Leaves of *A. simplicifolia* are glossy and undivided. Showy spikes of pink, rose, or magenta flowers arise from mid to late summer. Grow in full sun or partial shade, in humus-rich soil. Valued as source of late color on top of dry walls, in raised beds, beside pools, or in bog gardens. *A. crispa* has crinkled foliage and spikes of pink flowers. Several named forms.	Easily divided in spring or early fall. *A. c. pumila* often self-sows.
Aubrieta (aubrieta, or purple rock cress) A. cultorum	6–8 in.	18 in.	Mat-forming perennial bears clusters of reddish-purple flowers from midspring to early summer. Grow in sun, but where summers are hot, provide midday shade. Cut back annually when flowers fade. Good for planting between paving stones and in dry walls. Many named forms.	Sow seeds in spring. Propagate by division, layers, or cuttings In midsummer.
Aurinia (basket of gold, or goldentuft) Aurinia saxatilis	6–8 in.	12–18 in.	Perennial with gray foliage. Bright yellow flower clusters appear in early spring. Cut back after flowering. Use in dry walls and between paving. *A. s.* 'Citrina' has flowers of lighter yellow.	From seeds in spring and summer (self-sows freely). Take cuttings in early summer.
Bellium (bellium) B. minutum	2 in.	12–4 in.	Tiny daisies with white flowers in summer. Will self-seed in warm climates, not reliably hardy in North.	Seed sown in spring where it is to flower.
Bruckenthalia (bruckenthalia, or spike heath) B. spiculifolia	9 in.	24 in.	Slow-spreading dwarf shrub with needlelike evergreen foliage. Short spikes of small pink bells appear from early to mid summer. Grow in sun or partial shade and in well-drained, acid soil; add leaf mold to sandy soil. Mulch with evergreen boughs over winter.	Cut off rooted divisions in spring or early summer and plant in moist, humusy soil. Water well.
Campanula (campanula, or bellflower) C. carpatica (tussock bellflower) C. cochleariifolia (fairies' thimbles) C. portenschlagiana (Dalmatian bellflower) C. poscharskyana (Serbian bellflower) C. pulla C. rotundifolia (harebell, or bluebells of Scotland)	9–12 in. 4–8 in. 6–9 in. 4 in. 3 in. 8–12 in.	12–15 in. 12 in. 10 in. 24 in. 8–12 in. 12 in.	Perennials that may be tufted, clump forming, or trailing in habit. Attractive bell-like or starry flowers in shades of blue or white appear from early to late summer. Most do best in full sun, but *C. rotundifolia*, one of easiest to grow, and *C. portenschlagiana* will tolerate partial shade. *C. pulla* forms rosettes with deep purple flowers on thin stalks. All do best in well-drained, gritty soil that retains moisture. Splendid wall plants; use also for screes, paving, in containers, and alpine houses. Many other species exist, some difficult to grow away from their alpine environment.	Sow seeds from spring through fall; some fall-sown seeds will germinate in spring. Seeds are very fine; mix with sand for better distribution. Most plants will self-sow unless fading flowers are cut off. Many kinds can be divided in spring or fall. Take cuttings of nonflowering shoots in late spring or early summer.
Carlina (stemless thistle) C. acaulis	4 in.	10 in.	Flat rosettes of spiny, dissected leaves with a central thistlelike lavender bloom in summer.	Seed sown as soon as ripe.
Cassiope (cassiope) C. lycopodioides C. tetragona	3 in. 10–12 in.	8–12 in. 6–8 in.	Mound-forming dwarf shrub. Small, narrow evergreen leaves on thin stems. Flowers are tiny white bells that develop in mid to late spring. Grow in sun or partial shade, in sandy, well-drained soil improved by leaf mold. Difficult to grow except where rock garden is blanketed with snow all winter long.	Take cuttings from nonblooming shoots in mid to late summer; root in sand and leaf mold mixture. Also by layering.

Showy flowers with distinctive "eyes" peek through the evergreen grasslike foliage of maiden pink (*Dianthus deltoides*) in spring: blooms of 'Brilliant' are a vivid red.

Dianthus deltoides 'Brilliant'

Cerastium alpinum
(alpine mouse-ear)

Ceratostigma plumbaginoides
(leadwort)

Chrysogonum virginianum
(golden star)

Coptis trifolia
(cankerroot)

Cornus canadensis
(bunchberry)

Corydalis flexuosa
(corydalis)

Cytisus kewensis
(Kew broom)

BOTANICAL AND COMMON NAMES	HEIGHT	SPREAD	DECORATIVE CHARACTERISTICS, SPECIAL REQUIREMENTS, AND REMARKS	PROPAGATION
Cerastium (cerastium, or mouse-ear) *C. alpinum lanatum* (alpine mouse-ear) *C. tomentosum* (snow-in-summer)	4 in. 6 in.	8 in. 4–5 ft.	Mat-forming perennial with woolly gray foliage. Clusters of small white flowers appear in early summer. *C. tomentosum* is fast-growing creeper that self-sows like a weed. *C. a. lanatum* is more refined. Grow in crevices or screes.	From seeds or division in spring or early fall. Rooted layers can be taken from *C. a. lanatum* in spring or early fall.
Ceratostigma (leadwort) *C. plumbaginoides*	6–12 in.	24 in.	Clump-forming perennial with glossy, semi-evergreen foliage that turns bronze in fall. Bright blue flowers open in late summer. Grow in full sun or partial shade, in average soil. Good wall plant.	Easily divided in late spring or after flowering in fall.
Chrysogonum (chrysogonum) *C. virginianum* (golden star)	8–12 in.	24 in.	Perennial with coarse, hairy foliage. Yellow, star-shaped flowers from midspring through midsummer. Grow in sun or partial shade. Grow in woodlands or among rocks.	Sow seeds in spring. Divide clumps in early spring or early fall.
Coptis (goldthread) *C. trifolia* (cankerroot)	4–6 in.	12–18 in.	Mat-forming stemless perennial with compound, scalloped evergreen leaves. White or yellow buttercuplike flowers are borne in early to mid summer. Grow in partial shade and in moist, humus-rich soil. Flourishes only where winters are cold. Attractive for use in woodlands or among shaded rocks.	Divide in early spring or late summer. Sow fresh seeds in mixture of leaf mold and sand; keep moist.
Cornus (dogwood) *C. canadensis* (bunchberry)	6–9 in.	1–3 ft.	Mat-forming shrublet with whorls of evergreen or semi-evergreen leaves. Showy white bracts appear around inconspicuous true flowers in late spring to early summer. Handsome bunches of edible red berries in late summer and fall. Grow in partial shade and in acid, humus-rich, moist soil. Use in woodland-type habitats.	Sow seeds in fall to germinate in spring. Plants collected from wild are difficult to establish. Potted plants available at nurseries.
Corydalis (corydalis) *C. cheilanthifolia* *C. flexuosa* *C. lutea* *C. wilsonii*	10–12 in. 6–9 in. 8–12 in. 4–6 in.	10 in. 6–8 in. 12 in. 4–6 in.	Perennial with fernlike foliage. Grow in partial to full shade, in well-drained soil. Fine plant for dry walls. *C. cheilanthifolia* has very finely cut foliage and spikes of pendent dark yellow flowers in spring. *C. flexuosa* has bright blue flowers from spring to summer. Plant then goes dormant. 'Blue Panda' is smaller with brighter flowers over a longer period. *C. lutea* bears short-spurred yellow flowers that arise from late spring through summer. *C. wilsonii* has blue-green foliage; the lemon-yellow flowers are tipped with green. Not quite as hardy as *C. lutea*, but a more refined plant.	Sow fresh seeds as soon as ripe. Self-sows freely. Transplant only in spring.
Cotoneaster horizontalis			see p. 298.	
Cytisus (Kew broom) *C. kewensis*	10 in.	24 in.	Trailing shrub with wiry green branches. Bears clusters of creamy white flowers, typical of pea family, in late spring. For large rock gardens or dry walls.	Take cuttings from nonflowering shoots in late spring or early summer.

see p. 298.

Dodecatheon meadia album

Epimedium grandiflorum 'Rose Queen'

Foliage growth on the white-flowered shooting star (*Dodecatheon meadia album*) ends once the plant's elegant blooms make their late-spring entrance. A good ground cover for the more spacious rock garden is the bishop's hat (*Epimedium grandiflorum*).

Daphne cneorum
(garland flower)

Delosperma cooperi
(ice plant)

Dianthus alpinus
(alpine pink)

Dicentra cucullaria
(Dutchman's breeches)

Dodecatheon meadia
(shooting star)

Douglasia vitaliana
(douglasia)

Draba aizoides
(yellow whitlow grass)

BOTANICAL AND COMMON NAMES	HEIGHT	SPREAD	DECORATIVE CHARACTERISTICS, SPECIAL REQUIREMENTS, AND REMARKS	PROPAGATION
Daphne (daphne) D. blagayana D. cneorum (garland flower) D. retusa	 6–12 in. 6 in. 3 in.	 6 ft. 24 in. 1½–3 in.	Small evergreen shrub. Fragrant flower clusters appear in late spring. Grow in sun or partial shade. Well-drained soil should be enriched with leaf mold. Useful plant for base of walls, deep soil pockets, raised beds. D. blagayana has creamy white flowers on nearly prostrate branches. D. cneorum has rose-pink flowers on trailing branches; requires full sun. D. retusa bears purple buds followed by pink flowers. Slow grower.	Buy pot-grown plants for best results. Root summer cuttings in leaf mold and sand for D. cneorum and D. retusa. Increase D. blagayana and D. cneorum by layering.
Delosperma (ice plant) D. cooperi (purple ice plant) D. nubigerum (yellow ice plant)	 2 in. 2 in.	 24 In. 24 in. or more	Mat-forming plants with fleshy leaves from South Africa, but surprisingly hardy. Flowers are produced in mid to late summer. In cold regions, pot in fall and grow indoors. D. cooperi has magenta flowers; D. nubigerum orange-red.	Take cuttings in spring or summer.
Dianthus (dianthus, or pink) D. alpinus (alpine pink) D. deltoides (maiden pink) D. neglectus (glacier pink)	 3–5 in. 4–15 in. 2–6 in.	 6 in. 12–18 in. 6 in.	Carpet- or cushion-forming perennials with grasslike evergreen foliage. Bears showy flowers of rose or pink, often with distinctive "eyes," in late spring to early summer. Useful for retaining walls, screes, paving, containers. There are many other fine pinks, both species and hybrids, that are useful for rock gardens. Many form tight cushions.	Divide or take cuttings after blooming. Sow seeds in late spring to early summer. Most pinks self-sow, but not all offspring come true.
Dicentra (dicentra) D. canadensis (squirrel corn) D. cucullaria (Dutchman's breeches) D. eximia (fringed bleeding heart)	 4–10 in. 10–12 in. 12–24 in.	 10 in. 12 in. 8–10 in.	Perennial with fernlike foliage. Racemes of dainty heart-shaped flowers appear from mid to late spring. Grow in partial shade, in humus-rich soil. (Add ground limestone to very acid soil.) Good for woodlands, shaded crannies of walls, or rock gardens. D. canadensis has short-spurred white flowers. D. cucullaria has long-spurred white or pinkish flowers. D. eximia has heart-shaped pink flowers borne on spikes. For other perennial dicentras, see p. 50.	Divide clumps by separating tubers after flowering. Seeds are slow to germinate; sow in fall for spring growth.
Dodecatheon (dodecatheon, or shooting star) D. dentatum D. meadia D. pulchellum	 7–10 in. 6–20 in. 6 in.	 10–12 in. 6–10 in. 5–6 in.	Perennial with foliage in basal rosettes. Graceful flowers of white, pink, rose, or purple are borne in clusters at end of bare stems in late spring; each flower has reflexed petals and prominent stamens. Foliage disappears after plant blooms. Grow in partial shade, in humus-rich, moisture-retentive soil. Use plant for woodlands or deep soil pockets among rocks.	Divide fleshy roots or take root cuttings after flowering. Seeds germinate quickly, but seedlings grow slowly; will flower in about 3 yr.
Douglasia (douglasia) D. vitaliana	 1–2 in.	 6 in.	Low mats of grayish-green foliage with clear yellow flowers in late spring. Good in troughs.	Seed sown in spring and give a cold treatment.
Draba (draba) D. aizoides (yellow whitlow grass) D. rigida D. sibirica	 4 in. 2–3 in. 2–6 in.	 6–9 in. 6–8 in. 12–24 in.	Mound-forming perennial with rosettes of hairy, often gray foliage. Small white or yellow flowers appear in racemes in early to mid spring. Grow in sun, with some noontime shade. Requires well-drained, gritty soil with added leaf mold. Most drabas are listed as alpines. Grow in screes, paving, alpine house, or in deep soil pockets of rock garden.	Divide by severing rosettes; or topdress with mixture of leaf mold and gritty soil to induce stem rooting of rosettes, and sever carefully. Also propagate by seeds.

The alpine liverwort (*Erinus alpinus*) is a dry wall climber. In September, the autumn gentian (*Gentiana sino-ornata*) begins to open azure-blue blossoms up to 2 in. long, with dark stripes.

Erinus alpinus

Gentiana sino-ornata

Dryas octopetala (mountain avens)   Edraianthus graminifolius (wheel bells)   Epigaea repens (trailing arbutus)   Epimedium youngianum (Niveum)   Erigeron compositus (flea bane)   Erinus alpinus (alpine liverwort)   Erodium reichardii (Erodium)   Euphorbia myrsinites (myrtle spurge)   Galax urceolata (galax)

BOTANICAL AND COMMON NAMES	HEIGHT	SPREAD	DECORATIVE CHARACTERISTICS, SPECIAL REQUIREMENTS, AND REMARKS	PROPAGATION
Dryas (dryas) D. octopetala (mountain avens)	3–4 in.	24 in.	Creeping shrub with rounded evergreen leaves. White flowers appear in early summer. Established plants transplant poorly; propagate or buy new plants.	Take hardwood cuttings in early to mid summer. Make layers in spring.
Edraianthus (wheel bells) E. graminifolius	3 in.	6–8 in.	Narrow leaves clothe branches that radiate from a central crown like spokes. Clusters of purple bells on the branch tips in summer.	Take cuttings of nonflowering shoots in summer or sow seed as soon as ripe.
Epigaea (trailing arbutus, or mayflower) E. repens	1–3 in.	12–24 in.	Mat-forming shrublet with evergreen leaves 3 in. long. Has clusters of fragrant bell-shaped flowers, pink or white, in midspring. Grow in partial to full shade and in acid, humus-rich soil. Mulch over winter; keep newly set plants moist until established. Good plant to use in woodlands or shaded pockets between rocks.	Buy pot-grown plants; mulch with leaf mold or pine needles. Root cuttings in summer in leaf mold and sand mixture.
Epimedium (epimedium) E. alpinum (alpine barrenwort) E. grandiflorum (bishop's hat) E. youngianum 'Niveum'	6–9 in. 9 in. 9–12 in.	12 in. 24 in. 10–12 in.	Spreading perennial with attractive evergreen foliage. Graceful racemes of spurred flowers in shades of white, pink, violet, or yellow, from midspring to early summer. Grow in sun to partial shade and in well-drained, humus-rich soil that retains moisture. Good plant to use for base of walls, woodlands, shrub foregrounds, and rock-strewn slopes. Several varieties and hybrids are available.	Easily divided in early spring, after flowering, or in early fall. Lift clumps and separate underground stems.
Erigeron (flea bane) E. compositus E. karvinskianus (for tall Erigerons see p. 50)	3–4 in. 6–8 in.	3–4 in. 6–8 in.	White daisies, tipped pink and with a golden center above dissected foliage in late spring. Similar to the above but smaller flowers are carried all summer. May be invasive in warm climates. Grow in screes, paving, and wall crevices.	Seed sown in early spring.
Erinus (fairy foxglove) E. alpinus (alpine liverwort)	3–6 in.	4–6 in.	Shrublike perennial with pink or white flowers in late spring. Often short-lived but usually self-seeds. Does well in walls and walkways.	Seed sown where it is to flower or root basal rosettes in spring.
Erodium (Erodium) E. manescaui E. reichardii	8–12 in. 2–3 in.	8 in. 8 in.	Closely related to *Geranium* these are attractive all summer because of their toothed, woolly foliage. *E. manescaui* has pink flowers, *E. reichardii*, white with pink veins, both in summer.	Divide in spring as growth starts or sow seed as soon as ripe.
Euphorbia (euphorbia, or spurge) E. myrsinites (myrtle spurge)	4–8 in.	12 in.	Prostrate perennial with attractive blue-gray foliage on fleshy stems. Sulfur-yellow floral bracts appear in late spring.	From seeds, division, or cuttings in mid to late spring.
Galax (galax) G. urceolata	6–12 in.	12–24 in.	Stemless perennial. Heart-shaped, evergreen leaves turn bronze in fall and winter. Bears wands of small white flowers in late spring. Grow in partial shade, in humus-rich, acid soil. Good for woodlands, shaded slopes, or among rocks.	Divide established plants in early spring or fall, separating rhizomatous roots. Growth from seeds is slow.

The deep blue blossoms of the summer gentian (*G. septemfida*) have dark stripes in their throats.
The creeping gypsophila (*Gypsophila repens*) can be white or pink. It trails nicely over a rock face.

Gentiana septemfida

Gypsophila repens 'Rosea'

Genista sagittalis
(broom)

Gentiana sino-ornata
(gentian)

Geranium sanguineum
(bloodred cranesbill)

Geum borisii
(avens)

Globularia cordifolia
(globe daisy)

Gypsophila repens
(creeping gypsophila)

BOTANICAL AND COMMON NAMES	HEIGHT	SPREAD	DECORATIVE CHARACTERISTICS, SPECIAL REQUIREMENTS, AND REMARKS	PROPAGATION
Genista (genista, or broom) G. pilosa G. sagittalis	4–12 in. 4–6 in.	2–3 in. 24 in.	Prostrate shrublets, usually with winged green stems that resemble evergreen foliage. Displays yellow pea-shaped flowers from late spring to early summer. Grow in deep, well-drained, sandy soil. Does not transplant well; buy container-grown plants or propagate new plants for new locations. Good for hot, dry climates and situations. Useful for banks and slopes, among large rocks, and in retaining walls.	Take cuttings of new growth in early summer, or sow seeds in fall or spring.
Gentiana (gentian) G. acaulis G. scabra G. septemfida G. sino-ornata	3–4 in. 12 in. 9–18 in. 2–3 in.	18 in. 12 in. 12 in. 8–12 in.	Perennials, some with evergreen foliage; handsome, intensely blue flowers. Grow in sun or partial shade. Requires well-drained but moist, humus-rich soil. Good for dry walls, shaded slopes, paving, and alpine houses. G. acaulis is evergreen, bears large blue trumpets in late spring; difficult to grow. G. scabra has large, deep blue flowers in mid to late fall; easy for gardens with partial shade. G. septemfida bears large, deep blue bells in midsummer. G. sino-ornata has solitary bright blue flowers with darker stripes.	Divide G. acaulis in early spring. Take cuttings for G. septemfida. All grow from seeds, especially G. scabra and G. septemfida.
Geranium (geranium, or cranesbill) G. cinereum 'Ballerina' G. c. subcaulescens G. dalmaticum G. macrorrhizum (bigroot geranium) G. renardii G. sanguineum (bloodred cranesbill) G. sessiliflorum novae-zelandiae 'Nigrescens'	6–9 in. 4–6 in. 3–6 in. 12–18 in. 8–10 in. 6–9 in. 3 in.	12 in. 12 in. 9–12 in. 18–24 in. 10 in. 30 in. 12 in.	Perennial with mounds of attractive, deeply cut leaves. Pretty flowers appear in early summer. Grow in sun or partial shade. Useful plants for ground cover, dry walls, paving, containers. G. c. 'Ballerina' has pink flowers. G. c. subcaulescens has small scalloped leaves and carmine flowers. G. dalmaticum has dark glossy foliage and pink or white flowers. G. macrorrhizum has scented light green foliage and pink to magenta flowers, depending on the variety. G. renardii has wrinkled gray leaves and white to pale pink flowers. G. sanguineum has pink flowers with rose veining, and many named forms. G. s. n. 'Nigrescens' has dark bronzy green foliage and pale flowers that nestle in the leaves. It is short-lived but seeds freely.	Divide clumps of most kinds in early spring or after flowering. Also propagated by root cuttings or seeds.
Geum (geum, or avens) G. borisii G. montanum G. reptans	10 in. 12 in. 6 in.	12 in. 12 in. 6–8 in.	Perennial with neat mounds of cut leaves. Roselike flowers appear from early to mid summer. Grow in sun or partial shade. Use for retaining walls, raised beds. G. borisii has orange-scarlet flowers; G. montanum, golden yellow. G. reptans, with ferny, bright green foliage, requires some midday shade and well-drained scree conditions. For perennial species, see p. 53.	Clumps are easily divided in early spring, or after flowering in late summer or early fall. Also grows from seeds.
Globularia (globe daisy) G. cordifolia	2 in.	8 in.	Mats of dark green spoon-shaped leaves with blue flowers in summer. Grows best in an alkaline soil, spreading over a rock.	Divide in spring or take cuttings in early summer.
Gypsophila (gypsophila) G. repens (creeping gypsophila)	4–5 in.	24 in.	Prostrate or trailing perennial with narrow gray-green leaves. Airy sprays of small white flowers appear from early to mid summer. Grow in a slightly alkaline soil. Versatile rock plant. G. r. 'Rosea' has pink flowers on 4-in. stems.	Best increased by seeds.

All varieties of rock rose (*Helianthemum*) need full sun if they are to thrive and flower well. The spreading perennial candytuft (*Iberis*) is a small evergreen shrub.

Helianthemum 'Wisley Primrose'

Iberis sempervirens

| *Helianthemum nummularium* (rock rose) | *Hepatica nobilis* (liverleaf) | *Houstonia caerulea* (bluets) | *Hypericum olympicum* (Saint-John's-wort) | *Iberis saxatilis* (evergreen candytuft) | *Iris cristata* (iris) | *Jeffersonia dubia* (twinleaf) | *Leiophyllum buxifolium* (box sand myrtle) |

BOTANICAL AND COMMON NAMES	HEIGHT	SPREAD	DECORATIVE CHARACTERISTICS, SPECIAL REQUIREMENTS, AND REMARKS	PROPAGATION
Helianthemum (helianthemum, sunrose, or rock rose) H. alpestre H. lunulatum H. nummularium	 3–6 in. 6–9 in. 4–12 in.	 12 in. 12 in. 24 in.	Shrublets with evergreen or semi-evergreen leaves. Roselike flowers from early to mid summer. Cut back after flowering. Buy pot-grown plants. Use for ground cover, retaining walls, raised beds, paving. *H. alpestre* has yellow flowers on twiggy plants. *H. lunulatum* has golden flowers. *H. nummularium* has single or double flowers of yellow, pink, or white, many named forms.	Propagate named varieties by cuttings taken in summer. Start others from cuttings taken in summer or seeds sown in spring.
Hepatica (hepatica, or liverleaf) H. acutiloba H nobilis H. transsilvanica	 6–9 in. 4–9 in. 4–6 in.	 6–10 in. 9–12 in. 10 in.	Perennial with 3-lobed leaves that persist over winter, new leaves appearing after flowers. Pretty violet-blue to near white flowers with showy stamens develop in early spring. Grow in shade and well-drained humus-rich soil. Use for woodlands, raised beds, retaining walls, rock-strewn slopes.	Divide clumps in early fall or after flowering. Fresh seeds can be sown in fall for germination in spring. Self-sows.
Houstonia (bluets, or Quaker ladies) H. caerulea (bluets) H. serpyllifolia (creeping bluets)	 3–6 in. 1 in.	 4 in. 3–4 in.	Perennial with mats of fragile foliage. Bears tiny, 4-petaled, starry blue flowers in late spring. *H. serpyllifolia* has deeper blue flowers. Grow in sun or partial shade and in moist soil. Good for retaining walls, paving, around pools.	Mats are easily divided after flowering. Also easily grown from seeds when available.
Hypericum (hypericum, or Saint-John's-wort) H. cerastioides H. coris H. olympicum	 5 in. 6–12 in. 9–12 in.	 8 in. 12 in. 12 in.	Procumbent shrublets, mostly evergreen in mild climates. Showy golden yellow flowers with prominent stamens appear in early to mid summer. Once planted, avoid disturbing roots. Use for crevices and deep soil pockets in walls and rock gardens; also good for use in paving, screes, and on sunny slopes. *H. o. minus* is smaller.	Take cuttings in early summer; root in sand-leaf mold mixture. Can also be grown from seeds, when available.
Iberis (candytuft) I. saxatilis (rock candytuft) I. sempervirens (evergreen, or edging, candytuft)	 6 in. 12 in.	 12 in. 24 in.	Spreading perennial or subshrub with narrow evergreen leaves. Umbels of long-lasting white flowers first appear in late spring. Good to use in paving, on retaining walls, or in foreground of shrub and flower borders. *I. sempervirens* 'Autumn Snow' blooms in both spring and fall.	Take cuttings after flowering; transplant following spring. Also by layering and division.
Iris (iris) I. cristata I. gracilipes I. pumila I. verna	 3–4 in. 8–10 in. 3 in. 10 in.	 12 in. 8 in. 6–8 in. 10 in.	Mat-forming perennials with grasslike foliage. Dainty flowers, miniature replicas of large garden irises, are displayed from early spring to early summer. Crested *I. cristata* and beardless *I. verna* have lilac-blue flowers; both grow well in partial shade and in humus-rich soil. *I. gracilipes*, an exquisite Japanese crested species, has 1-in. pinkish flowers with wavy orange crests. Tiny, bearded *I. pumila* blooms in early spring. See also Irises, p. 69.	Divide and transplant clumps after flowering. Water well until established. Iris species can be grown from seeds; plant in fall for spring germination.
Jeffersonia (jeffersonia, or twinleaf) J. diphylla J. dubia	 10 in. 6 in.	 8 in. 4–5 in.	Perennials with distinctive kidney- or heart-shaped leaves in pairs. Pretty anemonelike white flowers (blue in the rare Asiatic *J. dubia*) appear in midspring. Grow in partial shade and in humus-rich soil. Good plant for woodlands, shaded rock gardens.	Divide in early spring after foliage dies down, soon after flowering. Sow fresh seeds in late summer; germination slow.
Leiophyllum (sand myrtle) L. buxifolium (box sand myrtle)	 10–12 in.	 18 in.	Slow-growing shrub with small, shiny evergreen leaves that turn brownish green in autumn. Tight clusters of pink or white flowers are formed in late spring. Grow in sun or partial shade, in sandy loam enriched with leaf mold. Good plant for seaside areas. *L. b.* 'Nanum' is one-quarter the size given.	Sow seeds under glass in early spring. Take semi-hard-shoot cuttings in midsummer, or propagate by layering.

Leontopodium alpinum 'Mignon'

Linnaea borealis

'Mignon', shorter and with smaller blossoms and leaves than other varieties of edelweiss (*Leontopodium alpinum*), blooms profusely from June to August. Twinflower (*Linnaea borealis*) is named for fragrant delicate pink or white flowers that appear in pairs on slender stems in late spring.

| Leontopodium alpinum (edelweiss) | Lewisia cotyledon (lewisia) | Linaria alpina (alpine toadflax) | Linnaea borealis (twinflower) | Linum perenne alpinum (alpine flax) | Lithodora diffusa (lithospermum) | Lychnis alpina (alpine catchfly) | Mentha requienii (Corsican mint) | Mertensia maritima (oyster plant) |

BOTANICAL AND COMMON NAMES	HEIGHT	SPREAD	DECORATIVE CHARACTERISTICS, SPECIAL REQUIREMENTS, AND REMARKS	PROPAGATION
Leontopodium (edelweiss) *L. alpinum*	8 in.	9 in.	Creeping perennial with woolly gray leaves. Star-shaped white flowers with yellow centers appear in early summer. Protect from winter moisture. Grow in walls, paving, screes, or alpine house.	Divide clumps in early spring. Sow seeds in spring in light or sandy soil mixture.
Lewisia (lewisia) *L. brachycalyx* *L. cotyledon* *L. rediviva* (bitter root) *L. tweedyi*	 2–3 in. 8–10 in. 4–6 in. 4–6 in.	 6–9 in. 6 in. 4–8 in. 9 in.	Fleshy-rooted perennials with rosettes of succulent leaves. Beautiful wax-textured flowers of pink, apricot, or white are borne in late spring. Grow in sun or partial (midday) shade. Requires well-drained, deep soil (half sharp sand or fine gravel and half loam and leaf-mold mixture) and stone-chip mulch. Some species are difficult to grow outside their western North American habitat, but new hybrids of *L. cotyledon*, in a wide range of colors, are relatively easy, providing the soil is well drained. Grow in rock crevices, screes, any site that has spring moisture and dry, cool summers.	Root crown offsets in leaf mold and sand after flowering. Will grow from fresh seeds but may not germinate for a year.
Linaria (linaria, or toadflax) *L. alpina* (alpine toadflax)	3–9 in.	12 in.	Trailing perennial with blue-green leaves. Small purple and yellow flowers like snapdragons are displayed all summer. Grow in sun or partial shade. Use for walls.	Sow seeds in spring. Short-lived but established plants self-sow freely.
Linnaea (twinflower) *L. borealis*	2–3 in.	24 in.	Trailing shrublet with small evergreen leaves. Bears pairs of delicate pink bells on 2-in. stems in late spring. Grow in partially shaded rock pockets and in moist, humus-rich, acid soil.	Divide rooted sections or layers in spring; provide moisture until established.
Linum (linum, or flax) *L. perenne alpinum* (alpine flax)	4–10 in.	8 in.	Perennial with narrow gray-blue leaves. Pretty blue flowers are borne in early summer. For *L. flavum* and *L. narbonense*, see p. 57.	Easily increased by fresh seeds; plant in final position as seedlings.
Lithodora (lithospermum) *L. diffusa* *L. oleifolia*	 8–12 in. 6 in.	 12–15 in. 12 in.	Prostrate shrublet with clusters of trumpet-shaped flowers in late spring. Grow in well-drained, humus-rich soil with limestone chips. Use in dry walls, deep soil pockets. *L. diffusa* has evergreen leaves and deep blue flowers. *L. oleifolia* is deciduous, with whitish, silky leaves and violet flowers.	Root cuttings in summer in leaf mold and sand.
Lychnis (lychnis, or campion) *L. alpina* (alpine catchfly)	4 in.	4 in.	Perennials with tufts of narrow leaves. Rose-purple flower heads open in early summer. Grow in sun or partial shade. Good for screes, paving, containers, alpine houses.	Easy to grow from seeds sown in midsummer.
Mentha (mint) *M. requienii* (Corsican mint)	¼ in.	6–8 in.	Probably the smallest rock plant, this forms a green film in any soil that is not too dry. Tiny mauve flowers dot the carpet in summer. Good for pavings and moist screes. Grow in shade where summers are hot.	Division in spring.
Mertensia (mertensia) *M. maritima* (oyster plant)	4 in.	12 in.	Prostrate stems form a circle around the crown and bear spoon-shaped almost blue leaves. In summer, terminal pink buds open to bright blue flowers. Somewhat difficult, it needs a deep soil.	Cuttings in early summer or seed sown in spring.

Well-drained soil is essential for moss pink (*Phlox subulata*), an excellent plant for borders or rock gardens. Unlike most primroses, *Primula auricula* needs an alkaline soil.

Phlox subulata 'Amazing Grace'

Primula auricula 'Prince John'

| *Myosotis alpestris* (forget-me-not) | *Omphalodes verna* (blue-eyed Mary) | *Papaver alpinum* (alpine poppy) | *Penstemon rupicola* (beardtongue) | *Persicaria affinis* (Himalayan knotweed) | *Phlox subulata* (moss pink) | *Physoplexis comosa* (horned rampion) | *Polygala chamaebuxus* (milkwort) |

BOTANICAL AND COMMON NAMES	HEIGHT	SPREAD	DECORATIVE CHARACTERISTICS, SPECIAL REQUIREMENTS, AND REMARKS	PROPAGATION
Myosotis (myosotis, or forget-me-not) *M. alpestris*	2–6 in.	4–6 in.	Dainty perennial with short heads of bright blue flowers in early summer. Grow in sun or partial shade, in well-drained, gritty soil that retains moisture. Short-lived plants for use in screes, paving, containers, alpine houses.	Sow seeds in late summer for flowering plants in 2 yr. Also divide by separating foliage rosettes.
Omphalodes (omphalodes) *O. verna* (blue-eyed Mary)	8 in.	12 in.	Trailing perennial with fine-textured foliage, evergreen in the South. Bright blue flowers, ½ in. across, appear in early spring. Grow in partial shade and in humus-rich soil. Useful plant for ground cover, woodlands, dry walls.	Divide rooted stems in spring or after flowering. Will grow from seeds, but they are rarely offered.
Papaver (poppy) *P. alpinum* (alpine poppy) *P. miyabeanum*	4–10 in. 2–3 in.	4–10 in. 4 in.	Perennial with finely cut foliage. Delicate flowers in wide color range appear in early summer. *P. miyabeanum* has 1 in. bright yellow flowers above hairy foliage. Grow in soil with added humus. Mulch with stone chips. Use for retaining walls, paving, screes, or containers.	Scatter seeds in early spring or fall where they are to flower; roots are too fragile to move. Self-sows.
Penstemon (penstemon, or beardtongue) *P. davidsonii menziesii* *P. fruticosus* 'Purple Haze' *P. pinifolius* *P. rupicola*	4–6 in. 8 in. 8–12 in. 4–5 in.	15–20 in. 12 in. 12 in. 12 in.	Low or prostrate shrublets with evergreen foliage. Showy tubular flowers. Grow in sunny site protected from midday sun. Difficult plants; grow in walls, crevices, screes. *P. d. menziesii* has deep blue flowers in early summer; *P. f.* 'Purple Haze' has purple flowers in early summer; *P. pinifolius* has needlelike leaves, red flowers in midsummer; *P. rupicola* has rose-red flowers during summer.	Take cuttings in summer. Seeds are slow to germinate, sometimes requiring 1 yr. or longer.
Persicaria (knotweed) *P. affinis* (Himalayan knotweed) (For tall *Persicaria* see p. 60)	10 in.	24 in.	Spreading stems of lance-shaped leaves that turn coppery in fall. In late summer spikes of pink to red flowers rise above the foliage. Grow in paving or rock walls. Several named varieties.	Divide in spring or take cuttings in early summer.
Phlox (phlox) *P. douglasii* *P. pilosa* *P. stolonifera* (creeping phlox) *P. subulata* (moss pink, or ground pink)	8 in. 10–12 in. 8–10 in. 3–6 in.	10–12 in. 15 in. 15–20 in. 20 in.	Perennial with showy flowers from early to late spring. Forms loose cushion of woody stems; flowers of white to violet-blue in late spring. Many named varieties in a range of colors. White, pink, or rose-purple flowers borne in small clumps. Grow in partial shade or sun. Rose-pink to lavender flowers. Grow in partial shade and in humus-rich soil. Star-shaped flowers in many shades of pink, rose, red, purple, blue, or white. Evergreen. For perennial *P. divaricata*, see p. 61.	Divide by separating clumps or mats in early spring or after flowering. They can also be increased by layering.
Physoplexis (horned rampion) *P. comosa*	3 in.	4 in.	Terminal clusters of 10–20 bottle-shaped, pale purple flowers in summer above dark green toothed leaves. The flowers have a long, protruding stigma and are very distinctive. Grows best in a crevice where it forms a small cushion. May be listed as *Phyteuma comosum*.	Easy from seed but protect the seedlings from slugs.
Polygala (polygala, or milkwort) *P. chamaebuxus*	6–12 in.	9–12 in.	Spreading shrublet with small evergreen leaves. Pretty, two-toned yellow flowers are produced in early summer. Grow in partial shade and in humus-rich soil. Protect in winter. Useful plant for shrub foregrounds, rocky slopes.	Sow fresh seeds. Take stem or root cuttings in midsummer; root in leaf mold and sand mixture.

Saponaria ocymoides

Saxifraga 'Cranbourne'

Saxifraga 'Cranbourne' is just one of the many named hybrids available from specialist nurseries. The rock soapwort (Saponaria) will thrive in alkaline soil, providing it drains freely.

Potentilla nitida
(cinquefoil)

Primula auricula
(primrose)

Ramonda nathaliae
(ramonda)

Ranunculus montanus
(buttercup)

Sanguinaria canadensis
(bloodroot)

Saponaria ocymoides
(rock soapwort)

BOTANICAL AND COMMON NAMES	HEIGHT	SPREAD	DECORATIVE CHARACTERISTICS, SPECIAL REQUIREMENTS, AND REMARKS	PROPAGATION
Potentilla (potentilla, or cinquefoil) P. alba (white cinquefoil) P. aurea, or P. verna aurea P. nitida P. tonguei P. tridentata (wineleaf cinquefoil)	3 in. 4 in. 1–3 in. 8 in. 6–10 in.	12–15 in. 6–8 in. 12 in. 24 in. 12–24 in.	Annual or perennial with compound foliage of 3–5 leaflets. Single, 5-petaled flowers. Good for dry walls, paving, screes. P. alba has silky leaflets, bears white flowers in early summer. P. aurea has yellow flowers in early spring on cushions of dark green foliage. P. nitida has pale pink flowers in early summer above mats of silk-textured foliage. P. tonguei has trailing stems, apricot flowers in late summer. P. tridentata has glossy semi-evergreen foliage, which is red in fall; small white flowers in midsummer.	Divide mats or clumps in early spring or after flowering in late summer. Can also be grown from seeds. Many self-sow.
Primula (primrose) P. auricula P. juliae P. polyantha P. sieboldii P. vulgaris	6–8 in. 3 in. 10–12 in. 6–9 in. 6–9 in.	6–10 in. 6 in. 10–12 in. 9–10 in. 6–15 in.	Perennial with foliage in clumps, rosettes, or tufts. Handsome, bright flowers appear in spring. Grow in partial shade and in fertile, humus-rich soil. Good for woodlands, shrub foregrounds, dry walls, alpine houses, screes. P. auricula has richly colored flowers, some fragrant, many with contrasting "eyes." Needs an alkaline soil. P. juliae bears flowers of rose, red, or crimson on tufted dwarf plants; many hybrids. P. polyantha has vivid color range of flowers. P. sieboldii has white, pink, or rose flowers and soft-textured scalloped leaves. P. vulgaris has solitary yellow flowers; many strains and hybrids in shades of blue, pink, red, and white. See also pp. 62 and 107.	Plants require division every 3–4 yr. to maintain vitality. After flowering, lift plants and pull apart, replanting divisions in humus-enriched soil. Sow fresh seeds in midsummer, or sow in fall for spring germination, which may be uneven and slow.
Ramonda (ramonda) R. myconi R. nathaliae	4–6 in. 4 in.	9 in. 6–8 in.	Perennial with rosettes of hairy leaves. Clusters of lavender-blue flowers with gold stamens appear in early summer. Grow in shade and in moist, humus-rich soil. R. myconi has hairier leaves; flowers are 5-petaled rather than 4-petaled.	Separate multicrowned plants; take leaf-stem cuttings; sow seeds.
Ranunculus (buttercup, or ranunculus) R. alpestris R. gramineus R. montanus	6 in. 12 in. 6 in.	6 in. 8–12 in. 12 in.	Perennial that forms mats or clumps of divided foliage, gray-green in R. alpestris and R. gramineus. Yellow flowers (white in R. alpestris) are borne in midspring. Grow plant in sun or partial shade, in moist, well-drained soil. (R. alpestris does better in a humus-rich scree mix.)	Clumps are easily divided in early spring or after flowering season ends.
Sanguinaria (bloodroot) S. canadensis	4–9 in.	9–12 in.	Perennial with rhizomes and lobed gray leaves. Foliage usually dies by midsummer. Beautiful white flowers (double and longer lasting in S. c. 'Flore Pleno') in early spring. Grow in partial shade and humus-rich soil. Good in woodlands or on shaded slopes.	Rhizomes can be cut apart after flowering, allowing 1 or more eyes per division. Plants self-sow.
Saponaria (saponaria, or rock soapwort) S. ocymoides	3 in.	6–12 in.	Trailing perennial with sprays of small but showy pink flowers in late spring. Grow in soil that offers deep, cool haven to taproots. Cut back immediately after flowering. Traditional wall and rock plant; use also for paving, alpine houses.	Sow seeds in spring; transplant seedlings to permanent sites when young. Take cuttings to increase superior forms.

Moist shady conditions are essential for Nippon bells (*Shortia uniflora*), which is known for its bell-shaped flowers and heavily veined leaves. Campion (*Silene schafta*), which produces sprays of flowers from early to late summer, needs a well-drained sunny site.

Shortia uniflora

Silene schafta 'Shell Pink'

Saxifraga apiculata
(rockfoil)

Saxifraga umbrosa
(London pride)

Sedum sieboldii
(stonecrop)

Sempervivum tectorum
(hens and chicks)

Shortia galacifolia
(Oconee bells)

Silene acaulis
(moss campion)

BOTANICAL AND COMMON NAMES	HEIGHT	SPREAD	DECORATIVE CHARACTERISTICS, SPECIAL REQUIREMENTS, AND REMARKS	PROPAGATION
Saxifraga (saxifrage, or rockfoil) S. apiculata S. cotyledon S. grisebachii S. longifolia S. moschata S. stolonifera (strawberry geranium) S. umbrosa (London pride)	 4 in. 24 in. 6–9 in. 18 in. 1–3 in. 24 in. 12 in.	 12–18 in. 12–15 in. 9–12 in. 12 in. 12–18 in. 12–18 in. 12–18 in.	Creeping cushion- or rosette-forming perennial with silvery or variegated foliage, varying in form from mosslike to succulent. Flowers of white, pink, purple, or yellow appear from late spring to early summer. Grow in sun or partial shade and in well-drained, gritty soil (add leaf mold for *S. sarmentosa* and *S. umbrosa*). Versatile plants adaptable to retaining walls, rock cracks and crevices, paving, screes, containers, and alpine houses (especially *S. apiculata* and *S. grisebachii*). There are many other species and even more hybrids in a wide range of colors and forms. *S. sarmentosa* requires winter protection in most areas; useful in woodland gardens.	Separate and plant rooted rosettes after flowering; unrooted rosettes can be started earlier in moist sand. Divide some species after flowering, including *S. cotyledon*, *S. longifolia*, and *S. sarmentosa*. Sow seeds in pots of gritty soil containing some loam mixed with leaf mold; flowering plants should be produced in about 3 yr.
Sedum (sedum, or stonecrop) S. cauticola S. dasyphyllum S. ewersii S. sieboldii S. spurium	 3–10 in. 1–2 in. 4–12 in. 6–9 in. 4–6 in.	 10–24 in. 12 in. 12–15 in. 12 in. 12–18 in.	Spreading perennial with succulent foliage. Easy to grow. Useful for walls, paving, ground cover. *S. cauticola* has grayish foliage; bears rosy red flower clusters in midsummer. *S. dasyphyllum* forms mats of gray-blue foliage; has pink flowers in early summer. *S. ewersii* is neat and shrublike, with gray-green leaves; has pink flowers in late summer. *S. sieboldii* has gray leaves on arching branches; displays pink flowers in late summer and fall. *S. spurium* grows readily and forms tangled mats with pink flowers in summer. Several named forms in various shades.	Division in spring or summer is quickest method of increasing sedums.
Sempervivum (sempervivum, or houseleek) S. arachnoideum (cobweb houseleek) S. fauconnettii S. tectorum (hens and chicks) S. wulfenii	 1–4 in. 8 in. 2–3 in. 6–12 in.	 12 in. 10–12 in. 12 in. 10 in.	Spreading perennial forming small rosettes of succulent foliage. Panicles of star-shaped flowers appear in summer. Useful for planting between rock crevices, on ledges, walls, and paving. *S. arachnoideum* is outstanding rock plant, its rosettes connected by gray threads; bears showy rose-red flowers. *S. fauconnettii* has red- and purple-tinged foliage, bright red flowers. *S. tectorum* has gray leaves, pink flowers. *S. wulfenii* has pale yellow flowers. Many hybrids and varieties available.	Easily divided by detaching offshoot rosettes when they form. Seeds may or may not produce true to type.
Shortia (shortia) S. galacifolia (Oconee bells) S. uniflora (Nippon bells)	 6–8 in. 6–8 in.	 1–3 in. 12–14 in.	Creeping perennial with handsome evergreen foliage. Bell-shaped flowers of white, rose, or pink arise in midspring. Grow in shade, in moist, humus-rich soil. Mulch with oak leaves over winter. Good choice for shady gardens, foreground of shrubs.	Divide after flowering; keep moist until established. Treat sparse-rooted sections as cuttings in moist leaf mold and sand.
Silene (silene, or campion) S. acaulis (moss campion) S. alpestris (alpine catchfly) S. schafta	 2 in. 6–8in. 6–16 in.	 12–18 in. 8 in. 6–10 in.	Fleshy-rooted perennial forming cushions, tufts, or clumps of narrow, pointed leaves. Five-petaled, notched flowers of pink, red, or white are borne in early to late summer. *S. acaulis* has reddish-purple flowers, does best in tight rock crevices. White-flowered *S. alpestris* and pink-flowered *S. schafta* fairly easy to grow under most rock-garden conditions.	Divide clumps for *S. acaulis*, *S. alpestris*, and *S. schafta*. Root stem cuttings of *S. acaulis*, in sand and leaf mold in summer. Also sow seeds for all species.

Thymus serpyllum albus

Uvularia grandiflora

Blooms of *Thymus serpyllum*, a mat-forming variety of thyme, can be pink, crimson, red, or white. Merrybells (*Uvularia*) form dense clumps in part shade.

Soldanella alpina
(soldanella)

Thalictrum kiusianum
(meadow rue)

Thymus serpyllum
(mother of thyme)

Uvularia grandiflora
(merrybells)

Vaccinium vitis-idaea
minus (lingberry)

Vancouveria hexandra
(vancouveria)

Veronica prostrata
(speedwell)

Viola blanda
(sweet white violet)

BOTANICAL AND COMMON NAMES	HEIGHT	SPREAD	DECORATIVE CHARACTERISTICS, SPECIAL REQUIREMENTS, AND REMARKS	PROPAGATION
Soldanella (soldanella) S. alpina S. montana	3–6 in. 6 in.	9 in. 12 in.	Perennial with kidney-shaped or rounded leathery leaves. Pretty lavender-blue flowers, heavily fringed, appear in early spring. Rare, difficult alpines need light, humus-rich soil with underground moisture. Mulch with stone chips; give winter protection in snowless areas. For alpine houses.	Divide clumps after flowering, or sow fresh seeds as soon as they are ripe.
Thalictrum (thalictrum, or meadow rue) T. alpinum T. kiusianum	6–8 in. 2–8 in.	12–14 in. 10–12 in.	Perennial with graceful ferny foliage. Displays petalless flowers with yellow or rose stamens in midsummer. Grow in partial shade. Provide moist, rocky soil for *T. alpinum*; well-drained, humus-rich soil for *T. kiusianum*. Use for ground cover or in woodlands, raised beds, retaining walls. For tall perennial species, see page 65.	Clumps are easily divided in early spring or early fall.
Thymus (mother of thyme) T. serpyllum	1–3 in.	24 in.	Carpeting perennial or shrublet with small aromatic evergreen leaves. Rose-purple flowers bloom from early to late summer. Use for paving, dry walls. Named forms in other colors.	Divide clumps, or cut off rooted runners. Plants self-sow freely.
Uvularia (uvularia, or merrybells) U. grandiflora	12–18 in.	12 in.	Perennial with creeping rhizomes. Graceful, bell-like pale yellow flowers displayed in late spring. Grow in partial shade and in humus-rich soil. Use in raised beds among ferns, in woodlands, or along base of shaded walls.	Divide clumps after flowering by separating rhizomes.
Vaccinium (vaccinium) V. vitis-idaea minus (dwarf lingberry)	4–8 in.	18 in.	Creeping shrublet with small, glossy evergreen leaves. Clusters of bell-like pinkish-white flowers appear in late spring. Red berries appear in fall. Grow in sun or partial shade, in moist, humusy soil. Snow or other protection will prevent winter burn. Use for raised beds, heather gardens, shrub foregrounds.	Divide rooted layers or sections in spring; keep moist until well established.
Vancouveria (vancouveria) V. hexandra	8–12 in.	24 in.	Spreading perennial with delicate, ferny foliage. Sprays of tiny ivory flowers open in early summer. Grow in partial shade, in humus-rich soil. Use in woodlands, shrub foregrounds.	Divide clumps in early spring or late summer; replant in humus-rich soil.
Veronica (veronica, or speedwell) V. prostrata V. spicata incana (silver speedwell)	3–8 in. 12–18 in.	12–18 in. 12–18 in.	Carpeting perennial with green or grayish foliage. Tall flower spikes in shades of blue or rose arise in early summer. Grow in sun or partial shade. Easy, versatile plants for walls and rock gardens. *V. s. incana* has gray foliage and blue flowers; *V. s. i.* 'Rosea', pink flowers; *V. prostrata*, blue flowers.	Divide clumps after flowering, or sow seeds in spring or early summer.
Viola (viola, or violet) V. biflora (twin-flowered violet) V. blanda (sweet white violet) V. rupestris rosea	3–6 in. 2 in. 4 in.	3 in. 3 in. 4–5 in.	Perennial with mostly heart-shaped leaves. Has pretty blue, yellow, or white flowers in spring. Use in woodlands, paving, walls. Widespread and varied genus, some kinds choice, others weedlike, but all are popular. *V. biflora* has yellow flowers, the lip streaked with blackish purple; *V. blanda* has dainty white flowers; *V. r. rosea* has rose flowers, leaves that form flat rosettes. For perennial *V. cornuta*, see p. 66.	Divide clumps after flowering, or sow seeds. However, most, once acquired, self-sow prolifically.

WATER GARDENS

The sight and sound of water, the colorful fish and varied plants water can support, and the vitality of the birds that come to drink add welcome life to any garden. A water garden gives you the opportunity to grow plants that would not survive in regular soil.

Making a water garden is a fascinating adventure. Whether you live in a mansion surrounded by acres of land, or in a townhouse with a small yard, you can still enjoy the pleasures of water gardening. The smallest garden can have a pool or waterfall and even a city terrace can probably accommodate a container large enough to sustain a water lily, some smaller plants, and a few fish. Pygmy water lilies can be used for extra-small spaces, as they will thrive in a container only 2–3 feet across and equally deep.

Water is heavy, therefore pools large enough to contain plants and fish are not generally practical for apartment balconies. You can, however, still enjoy the sounds of moving water. Small fountains and waterfalls with a built-in pump are readily available and add sight and sound to the smallest space.

In small townhouse gardens, half wine barrels can be used, but, if new, should have a liner installed to prevent residues from the barrel—they could be toxic to plants and fish—leaching into the water. Half of a heavy-duty garbage can buried in the ground also makes a good small pool. Either use it for growing water plants in the normal way, or, with a small submersible pump feeding a bubbler-type fountain head and a grating over the top covered in rounded cobbles, you have an attractive feature at little expense.

In a city garden there will often be space to sink a preformed pool of fiberglass into the ground. Then, with the aid of a small submersible pump connected to an electrical outlet, a fountain or waterfall can be created. The same water is used over and over again; so the only running cost is for electricity—a small pump uses only about as much energy as one 75-watt lightbulb.

Larger gardens, of course, provide greater scope. Water can be used with rocks to form a pool. Or a cascading chain of pools connected by a running stream can be created with the aid of a pump. The same pump can be adapted to make a fountain or a decorative spray in a variety of patterns or even to handle several different features simultaneously.

Concrete pools are rarely built anymore. They tend to develop leaks as the soil settles beneath them and, in cold climates, to crack from alternate freezing and thawing. Most pools today are built with preformed fiberglass shells or heavy-duty plastic liners, designed specifically for the purpose. Plastic liners are also used to line existing concrete pools that have been damaged. Liner material is available from garden-supply mail-order catalogs and water-garden specialists in sizes suitable for pools of almost any dimension.

One of the great pleasures of water gardening is growing a wide variety of unusual plants. Elegant day-blooming and night-blooming water lilies—the undisputed aristocrats of water plants—can be cultivated in the deep water of a pool. So can the fascinating oxygenating plants, some of which float on the surface of the water and others of which grow completely underwater. Several interesting plants—including one of the most dramatic of all plants, the lotus—thrive in the shallow water around the edges of a pool. And finally, a large group of attractive bog plants do well in the moist soil adjacent to a pool or stream.

All water gardens need plenty of light if the plants are to flower. No more than two-thirds of the surface of a pool should be covered by lily pads or other plants. The patches of open water will reflect the sky, sparkle in the sunlight, ripple in the wind, and reveal the movement of the fish.

To keep the water in a pool clear, a balance between plant and animal life must be established and maintained. If this is not done, the pool will become murky and fish may die.

The cause is algae, microscopic plants that thrive in sunlight and feed on mineral salts in the water. Most of these salts are produced by the breakdown of organic material, such as leaves, twigs, and other debris. It is therefore essential to keep the pool free of leaves and to be quite sure that the soil on the bottom contains no humus.

It is impossible to keep all foreign organic material out of a pool, but the water can be kept clear by growing oxygenating plants. These plants starve out algae by taking up the mineral salts, and they create shady pockets that diminish the sunlight algae need.

In addition to controlling algae, oxygenating plants take in the carbon dioxide given off by animal life in the pool and—as their name implies—release oxygen into the water. Thus, an efficient cycle is established, plants and animals each making use of the other's waste.

Fish not only enhance the appearance of a water garden but they also keep down the mosquito population by feeding on the larvae. They consume small snail eggs, aphids, and caddisworms, and eat a certain amount of algae and submerged vegetable debris.

The most satisfactory fish for garden pools are the golden orfe, and varieties of goldfish, including comets and shubunkins. These fish are brightly colored, stay near the surface, and—with a little patience—can be trained to come for food.

Most pond-fish breeders also sell snails and tadpoles, which help keep a pool clean by eating algae. Tadpoles eat other debris as well, and they turn into frogs and toads—useful garden occupants that consume incredible numbers of insects.

The water lily (*Nymphaea*) comes in blue, red, pink, white, and yellow. The blooms shown at right are about 10 in. in diameter.

Nymphaea 'Madame Wilfon Gonnère'

Nymphaea 'Colonel A. J. Welch'

Planning and Installing a Garden Pool

Begin by selecting a sunny, open spot for your pool within reach of your garden hose. Then decide on the shape of the pool, and mark the outline with rope or flexible hose. Avoid narrow necks, dumbbell shapes, and crosses—all of which waste space. You may wish to have a ledge 6–8 inches below the surface for shallow-water plants.

The next step is to dig the pool and either install a preformed pool, or line the newly dug hole with plastic. Liners of polyvinyl chloride (PVC) of 32-mil thicknesses last 10–15 years. PVC liners do not stand up well where winter temperatures fall below –10°F. In such areas, a butyl rubber liner may be a better choice. It will not only withstand frigid temperatures but it will last up to 50 years.

Pools with flexible liners. To determine how much liner you will need, measure the maximum length and width of the pool (including the outside edge), and then add double the maximum depth to each of these figures. For a pool 12 feet long, 6 feet wide, and 3 feet deep, for example, you would need a piece of liner measuring 18 feet (12 plus 6) by 12 feet (6 plus 6). Always add a little to the dimensions to allow for errors and shrinkage. There is no need to make allowance for ledges or for overlap.

Dig a hole of the shape you have marked out, making the sides slope gradually. If your pool is to include a shallow-water ledge, make sure its surface is perfectly horizontal.

Span the pool with a plank, and use a spirit level on top of it to see that the ground is absolutely level all around the edges. If it is not, build it up with soil from the excavation. A pool whose edge is not perfectly level will look unbalanced when filled with water. Remove all sharp stones from the hole, spread an inch of sand over the bottom, and line the hole with an old carpet or foam rubber sheet for more protection.

Unfold the liner in the hole, placing it so that at least 6 inches of the material overlaps the edges. Weight this overlap down with bricks or smooth stones. Run water slowly into the pool, carefully pleating and tucking the liner for a neat finish. When the pool is filled up, the weights can be removed.

Trim off any excess liner with a sharp knife, leaving a 6-inch overlap

all around. Lay paving slabs or stones on the overlap so that they project 1–2 inches over the edges of the pool. Fill between them with mortar so they are bonded together and cannot tip to cause injury. When you are finished, no part of the liner should show.

Keep the pool filled. Direct sunlight can cause the liner to deteriorate in a relatively short time.

Preformed pools. Dig a hole the shape of the pool but a few inches wider. Remove all stones from the hole and pack the soil firmly.

Lower the preformed pool into position. Span the pool with a plank, and place a spirit level on it to be sure the pool is level. Fill in the gap around the pool, and tamp the soil down firmly.

MAKING A GARDEN POOL FROM PLASTIC LINER

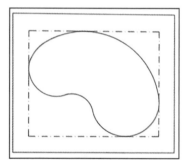

1. Measure dimensions; add double the maximum depth to each figure.

2. Dig the hole, make shelves, and level. Remove stones and put in sand.

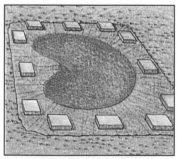

3. Unfold liner in the hole, and hold it down with bricks or paving blocks.

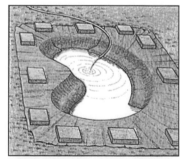

4. Fill the pool slowly, allowing the liner to adapt to the shape of the hole.

5. Pleat liner into shape. Many small tucks are better than a few large ones.

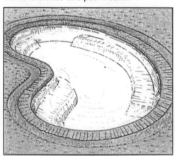

6. When pool is full, remove weights. Trim liner edges to a 6-in. overlap.

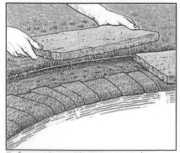

7. Cover edges with stones or paving blocks, slightly overlapping pool.

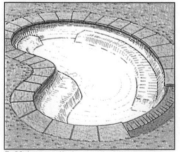

8. Make sure that no part of the liner is visible when the pool is finished.

Nymphaea 'Escarboucle'

Nymphaea 'Albida'

White petals of the water lily 'Albida' have a soft pink-tinted underside. Its aromatic blossoms have an 8-in. diameter. Tropical varieties of water lilies (*Nymphaea*) need protection in winter. 'Escarboucle' is winter hardy.

Running Water in the Garden

Recirculating Water for a Fountain

A fountain, waterfall, cascade, or stream creates a lively effect in the garden and improves the oxygen content of the water in a pool.

The running water should be supplied by recirculating the water from the pool itself. Not only would it be wasteful to make a steady draw upon the public water supply, but the use of cold tap water would inhibit the growth of plants and might destroy the pool's organic balance.

Two types of pump are available for recirculating water: submersible pumps and surface pumps. Both are usually powered by standard household current. For outdoor use, have electrical connections with ground-fault circuit interrupters (GFCI) installed by a licensed electrician.

Submersible pumps sit on the bottom of the pool. They may have attachments that power fountain jets, or that supply waterfalls or streams. Surface pumps are concealed near the pool. Water is drawn from the pool and delivered to various outlets through tubing. Surface pumps are more expensive than submersibles, and may need extra plumbing.

The capacity of a recirculating pump is expressed in gallons per hour (GPH) of flow. This figure decreases as the height to which the water is being raised increases.

Thus, a pump that delivers about 200 GPH through a ¼-inch tube to a height of 1 foot will pump only 120 GPH to a height of 5 feet, and 78 GPH to a 6-foot waterfall. If the same pump was used to power a fountain, it could provide a steady jet of water up to 4 feet in height, depending on the fountainhead. By limiting the height of a fountain jet to half the width of the pool, you can avoid splashing water out of the pool. The jet in a pool 4 feet wide, for example, should be about 24 inches high.

Building a Waterfall or Cascade

A waterfall is created by pumping water from the main pool to a small pool above it and then allowing the water to run down over a horizontal lip. A cascade is merely a series of small waterfall pools.

Preformed shells are available for making waterfall pools or cascades, or you can build your own shell from the same material that you use to line the pool.

For a cascade, cut out a series of steps approximately 4 inches deep, each of which will be a small pool. Cut shallow pouring lips in the appropriate places. Bury the tube from the pump beneath soil and rocks alongside this watercourse.

Cover the whole watercourse with a sheet of PVC, held in place with large stones along its edges. Use a large, flat rock to hide the vertical sheeting of each small waterfall. Lay a flat stone on the lip of each pool, slightly overhanging the drop, to produce a realistic waterfall effect. Fill in the watercourse with rounded pebbles or pea gravel to add to its natural appearance.

Do not try to grow rooted plants in waterfall pools; the running water will wash away the soil.

THE PUMP THAT POWERS THE FOUNTAIN

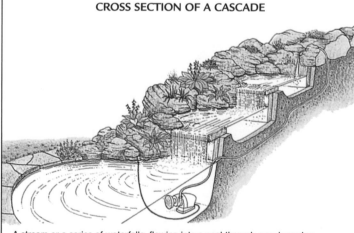

A fountain can easily be installed in a pool by using a submersible pump fitted with a fountain jet and driven by household electricity.

CURTAIN OF WATER

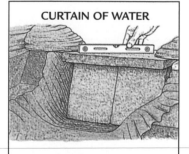

For an even fall of water, make the pouring lip absolutely level.

CROSS SECTION OF A CASCADE

A stream or a series of waterfalls, flowing into a pool through a rock garden, makes a lovely effect. For the most natural look, plan the cascade so that the water changes direction as it flows. Plastic sheeting lining the watercourse determines the available area for planning the shape. Water is recirculated from the pool to the top of the cascade by an electric pump.

'James Brydon,' a water lily with an apple aroma, needs a 3-ft.-deep pool. The wide-spreading, yellow pond lily (*Nuphar lutea*) is suitable only for large ponds. The water hawthorn (*Aponogeton distachyos*) has a vanilla fragrance and thrives in the sun.

Nymphaea 'James Brydon' *Nuphar lutea* *Aponogeton distachyos*

Introducing Water Plants Into a Pool

Planting Water Lilies in Containers

The water lily (*Nymphaea*) is the deep-water flowering plant most often used in pools. There are two types: hardy water lilies with rhizomatous roots, which survive year after year if the roots can be kept from freezing; and tuberous-rooted tropicals, which must be treated as annuals in all but the warmest sections of the country.

In warm areas you can put them into the pool at any time. In colder areas wait until late spring or early summer when the water is dependably warm.

It is less expensive to buy plants just starting into growth. The best time to plant hardy water lilies in the early stage of development is in mid-spring—if the weather is reasonably warm—or late spring. Tropicals should not be planted until you can be sure the water in the pool will not fall below 70°F.

Fill the pool at least one week before planting the hardy lilies and two weeks before planting tropicals. This will allow the water to dissipate the chlorine it may contain. If your water is treated with chloramine rather than chlorine, you will need to add a neutralizer before you can grow plants or add fish. Check with your local aquarium store.

It is a good idea to plant water lilies in containers that can be easily lifted in and out of the pool. You can buy plastic baskets designed specifically for the purpose, or you can drill several ¼-inch holes in 12-inch plastic pots to make your own.

Wooden boxes or tubs can also be used if several holes are drilled to allow water to circulate. All should be lined with clean, coarse burlap.

For planting soil, take some good, heavy loam from the garden and remove all obvious roots. Avoid organic materials, such as peat moss or compost, which will decompose in the water, clouding it, encouraging algae, and harming fish.

Soils with too much sand leach their nutrients too quickly. Use a soil that contains more clay, and into each bucket of soil, mix a double handful of bone meal.

Water lilies have sturdy roots that are used for anchorage, and finer hair roots that are used for feeding. In mid to late spring new leaf shoots, or growing points, will emerge from the rhizomes of hardy water lilies. Do not touch these shoots; they are easily damaged.

All parts of the water lily must be kept wet while out of water. Its delicate tissues desiccate rapidly. A spray bottle comes in handy.

If the nursery has not trimmed the rhizomes, or if they have been damaged in transit, use a sharp knife to cut off dead and broken leaves, and to remove other brown roots.

Place a rhizome horizontally into a container partly filled with the prepared soil mix. The rhizome should be placed with the growing tip pointing toward the center of the container. Top up with more moist soil so that the growing tip protrudes above the surface. Firm the soil with your fingers, adding more soil if necessary, but do not pack it down too tightly.

Plant tuberous-rooted tropicals vertically and centered in the container, with the roots going straight down; the soil should cover the base of the stems, but not the crowns of the plants. To reduce clouding of the pond water, cover the entire soil surface with paper towels. If there are to be fish in the pool, top-dress the container with a thin layer of coarse sand or pea gravel, to keep the fish from disturbing the roots of plants.

With hardy lilies, immerse the container in the pool until the soil surface is no more than 2 feet deep (18–24 inches is ideal; 6–12 inches for pygmies). In deeper pools place the container on stacked-up bricks. Lower it to the bottom (by removing bricks) at a rate of 1 foot every week.

With tropicals, immerse the container a few inches the first week or two. Then increase the depth to about 6 inches. Although this is the ideal depth, tropicals can survive at depths up to 12 inches. But if water lilies are to grow that deep, lower them gradually, at the rate of 2–3 inches per week.

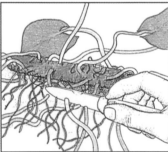

1. Cut off all old brown roots, and trim new white roots to 3½–4 in. long.

2. Plant in burlap-lined containers partly filled with moist, heavy soil.

3. Top-dress with coarse sand or pea gravel to protect plants from fish.

4. Submerge the container so that the soil surface is just below the water.

Feeding Water Lilies

Water lilies will not last indefinitely in containers without the help of supplementary feeding. This should be administered at least once a year. For best flowering after the first year, water lilies should also be fertilized once a month during summer.

Plants needing fertilizer lack vigor, have undersized, yellowing leaves, and the few blossoms produced are generally small. One tried method to provide fresh nutrients is to repot the plant using fresh heavy garden loam.

You can also make bone-meal pills by mixing a 3-inch flowerpotful of sterilized bone meal with enough clay to bind it firmly. Roll this into two round pills and wrap these in a paper towel. Lift the container, push the pills into the soil beneath the roots, and return the plant to the pool. For a large water lily, use two pills at each feeding. One pill at each feeding should have sufficient nourishment for a medium-size water lily.

Nymphoides peltata

Caltha palustris

The water fringe (*Nymphoides peltata*) spreads rapidly. It bears bright yellow blossoms up to 1 in. in diameter that are held above the surface of the water. In early spring, the marsh marigold (*Caltha*) gives a first splash of color.

Edging the Pool With Shallow-Water Plants

A constructed pool looks more natural with some shallow-water plants, such as cattails and flowering rush, growing around the edges. Pools can be designed with shelves to give these plants the 2–3 inches of water they need over their roots, or, failing that, the containers holding them can be raised on bricks.

Plants such as bog arum (*Calla palustris*), with creeping rhizomatous roots, should be planted in containers large enough to accommodate the rootstocks. First, remove dead leaves and old brown roots. Then place the rhizome horizontally on the soil, and use your fingers to pack the soil firmly, but not too tightly, around the roots. Leave the rhizome itself exposed. Cover the surface of the soil with coarse sand or pea gravel, and sink the container just deep enough so that the roots are completely covered by 2–3 inches of water.

In the case of shallow-water plants with tuberous root systems, such as pickerel weed (*Pontederia cordata*), begin by removing all dead or discolored leaves. Then trim back any large shoots with a sharp knife. Remove all of the old brown roots, and trim the remaining roots to a length of about 3 inches.

Make a hole in the soil just deep enough to insert the plant, with the roots going straight down and the soil rising to the base of the shoots. Pack the soil firmly around the plant, add coarse sand or pea gravel to the surface, and immerse it to a depth of 2–3 inches.

Keeping the Balance With Oxygenators

Oxygenating plants are essential in any water garden. They maintain an ecological balance by using up the carbon dioxide produced by fish and other animals and by giving off oxygen that these animals require. They also provide fish with shelter and spawning places, and by competing with algae in the pool for light and nourishment, they help keep the water clear and fresh. These submerged aquatics can also perform the useful function of masking the water lily container.

Most of these plants, such as anacharis (*Elodea canadensis*) and cabomba (*Cabomba caroliniana*), are sold in the form of bunches of unrooted cuttings. Since their rootstocks develop quickly, they need only be weighted down with lead sinkers, such as those used by fishermen, and dropped into pools with soil-covered bottoms. Oxygenating plants can also be placed in containers of their own and then installed in the pool.

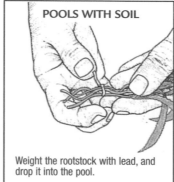

POOLS WITH SOIL

Weight the rootstock with lead, and drop it into the pool.

POOLS WITHOUT SOIL

Plant roots firmly in small soil-filled pots. Place in pool.

Floating Plants That Need No Soil

Some plants, such as water lettuce (*Pistia stratiotes*), float on the surface of the pool. Their trailing roots absorb from the water dissolved nutrients that have come from the soil in containers of other plants or from the droppings of fish. They are planted simply by putting them into the pool.

Some floating plants, such as duckweed (*Lemna minor*), water hyacinth (*Eichhornia*), and azolla (*Azolla caroliniana*), proliferate so quickly that they may cover the surface of the pool. Simply scoop out extra plants and compost them.

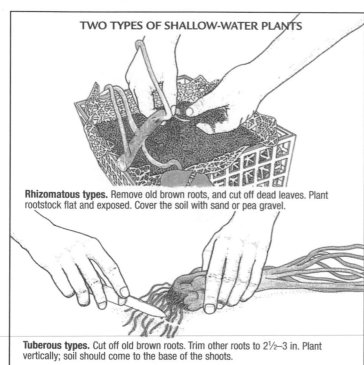

TWO TYPES OF SHALLOW-WATER PLANTS

Rhizomatous types. Remove old brown roots, and cut off dead leaves. Plant rootstock flat and exposed. Cover the soil with sand or pea gravel.

Tuberous types. Cut off old brown roots. Trim other roots to 2½–3 in. Plant vertically; soil should come to the base of the shoots.

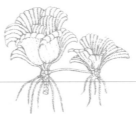

Pistia stratiotes (water lettuce)

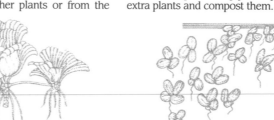

Lemna minor (duckweed)

The globeflower (*Trollius*) is suited to moist locations beside a pond.

Trollius cultorum 'Earliest of All'

Caring for the Garden Pool

Fish and Snails in the Pool

Animal life helps balance the ecology of a pool. Fish and snails exhale carbon dioxide, essential to photosynthesis, and plants return the favor by releasing oxygen into the water for the fish to breathe. In addition, fish eat mosquito larvae, and snails help keep the pool clean by eating algae and debris. Also, fish add a new dimension of life and color and can be considered as pets.

Do not introduce any animal life until the pool has settled—six to eight weeks after planting. If chlorinated water is used to fill the pool, a dechlorination agent must be used before adding fish. Your dealer will advise you on the type of fish to use in your pool. As a guide, allow 3 square feet of surface to each fish.

Fish are usually delivered in oxygenated plastic bags. Submerge the unopened bag in the pool for about 20 minutes so that it reaches pool temperature. Then hold the bag open, and let the fish swim out.

Artificial feeding is seldom necessary for fish living in an outdoor pool. Overfeeding, in fact, is often a problem. In any case, feeding must be stopped altogether from late fall until early spring because the water is too cold to allow the fish to digest food properly.

Feed fish in autumn, before the winter fast, and again in spring.

Protecting Fish and Plants in Winter

The best protection against winter damage to both fish and plants, in all but the coldest climates, is to keep the pool filled with water. As long as the water does not freeze solid, from top to bottom, both goldfish and hardy water plants should survive. If you live in an area where winters are long and severe, it is a good idea to make your pool at least 3 feet deep. In such a pool even a 1-foot-thick ice layer will leave 2 feet of water underneath for the fish.

During autumn prevent leaves from falling into the pool by covering it with fine-mesh screening or plastic netting stretched on a light wooden frame. Use a net or a rake to remove any debris that does get into the pool, or scoop it out with a garden fork covered with wire or plastic netting.

When frost begins, cut the old, dying growth from the shallow-water plants to prevent diseases and to keep pests from wintering among the leaves. Remove all dead leaves from hardy water lilies, and remove and discard all tropicals. Rotting old vegetation is the main reason for cloudiness in neglected pools.

You can control the thickness of the ice on your pool by insulating the surface. First, lay a covering of narrow wooden planks, leaving some gaps between them so that air can circulate. Spread burlap or plastic netting over this, and then a 3- to 4-inch layer of leaves, straw, or other coarse mulching material. Finally, cover this with another layer of burlap or netting, and stake it down for the winter. In areas where winters are only moderately severe, the surface of a pool thus protected may not freeze at all.

Alternatively, before your pool freezes, float a large rubber ball or a piece of wood on the surface. These will absorb the pressure of expanding ice, thus protecting the pool itself during the coldest weather. In a larger pool several of these objects may be needed.

From time to time throughout the winter, push down on the ball or piece of wood to break the ice and admit oxygen to the shallow layer of air beneath the ice. Do not break the ice with a hammer or other implement; this can injure the fish and do damage to the pool. Alternatively, a submersible heater can be used to keep a small area ice-free.

What Can Go Wrong With Water Plants

Use no controls in a pool that contains fish or other animal life. If your plants show symptoms that are not described below, consult the section on plant disorders beginning on page 506. For more information on controls, see page 542.

SYMPTOMS AND SIGNS	CAUSE	CONTROL
Young leaves and flowering stems are malformed; flowers are discolored and may fail to open properly.	Aphids	Hose leaves to dislodge insects, or use weighted wire mesh to keep leaves underwater for 24 hr. Introduce lacewings.
Water lily leaves have ragged holes that often rot around the edges. Grubs may be visible.	Water lily beetles	Destroy affected leaves. Apply *Bacillus thuringiensis* to grubs.
Water is green or cloudy.	Algae	Shade water with floating plants; remove rotting plant matter; introduce more oxygenating plants. If desired, use copper compound.
Leaves of water lilies have brown spots.	Water lily leaf spot	Destroy diseased leaves.
Water surface has dirty film.	Scum	Remove scum by drawing sheet of newspaper across water surface.
Leaves and flowers near top of plant are small and few. Leaves may be pale.	Starvation	Move plant into larger container with fresh soil, divide and replant in separate containers, or fertilize.

REMOVING INSECT PESTS

Use weighted chicken wire to force leaves under, so that insects drown or are eaten by fish.

CLEARING FLOATING LEAVES

Cover the tines of a garden fork with netting, or use a rake to scoop out leaves.

Nymphaea 'Froebelii'

Iris pseudacorus

The water lily 'Froebelii' grows best at a depth of 2 ft. Like other varieties of iris, yellow flag (*Iris pseudacorus*) is a marginal plant, but grows taller in water.

Growing Bog Plants Around the Pool

Taking Advantage of a Natural Bog Area

Some so-called bog plants require a plentiful supply of water although they do not actually grow immersed in water. These are ideal for growing around the edge of a pool, since they bridge the gap between the water plants and the rest of the garden.

A bog garden can also be an attractive feature by itself, without a pool. It may be the only choice to occupy an area where water collects to form a natural bog.

As both drought and excess water can be harmful to the various plants that prosper in a bog garden, it may take considerable attention to main-tain a precise balance of moisture during wet or dry spells.

Sufficient water is usually present in heavy clay soil. It can be con-served by a topdressing of compost-ed leaves in mid to late spring. If the bog garden is in a low-lying area, however, there is danger that the plants will be totally submerged dur-ing periods of heavy rainfall.

To successfully grow bog plants where soil drains well, it may be nec-essary to construct a special garden bed (see below) that will retain water, while allowing excess to escape.

Most bog plants are herbaceous perennials. The best time to plant them is in early autumn, while the soil is still warm from the summer.

Make the planting holes wide enough to allow for the roots to be fully spread out. Make the soil finger firm around the roots; if it is wet, however, take care not to compact it too much.

Do not space the plants far apart. Groups of plants of the same type are more striking than the same number of plants dotted about at wide intervals. Where the soil is moist and rich, many bog plants, such as primroses and irises, will add to this cluster effect by self-seeding to make drifts of blossoms in subse-quent seasons.

For more detailed planting sugges-tions, turn to the section on herba-ceous perennials, page 31.

AUTUMN PLANTING

Spread the roots of bog plants, and firm the soil around them.

How to Build a Bog Garden

The proper conditions for bog plants can be created, as shown below. Dig a hole 12 inches deep, the width and length you wish, and put an inch of sand on the bottom. Line the hole with heavy-duty plastic sheeting.

Cut holes in the plastic liner all around the sides, about 6 inches up, to drain surplus water. Cover the base of the sheeting with a layer of sod, laid grass side down.

Finally, overfill the hole with about 12 inches of garden soil, mixed with an equal amount of leaf mold, to make a raised soil bed. The plastic liner will hold water, and the sod will provide nutrition as it decomposes.

Caring for a Bog Garden

Make sure the soil in your bog gar-den remains damp at all times. This may require frequent watering in dry weather.

If the bog garden is located down-hill from a pool, you can flood it by allowing the pool to overflow as needed. Or you can install a pool-side sprinkler system, which will help aerate the pool as well as keep the bog garden moist.

In autumn, cut the dead foliage of herbaceous perennials down to the ground and clean up the debris. Then apply 1–2 inches of well-rotted com-post mixed with dehydrated cow manure. On top of this apply a 1–2 inch dressing of shredded leaves or bark. This will nourish the soil and help it retain moisture the fol-lowing year.

Propagation From Rootstocks and Seeds

Most bog-garden plants, including primulas, rodgersias, irises, lobelias, and skunk cabbages, can be easily propagated by division in the spring.

Seeds of the primula and skunk cabbage will germinate readily in a greenhouse or cold frame if they are sown as soon as they are ripe in par-tially shaded, rich, moist soil. For details on propagation methods, see pages 39–43 and 180.

CLEANING UP

Each autumn remove all dead foliage, and clean up any debris.

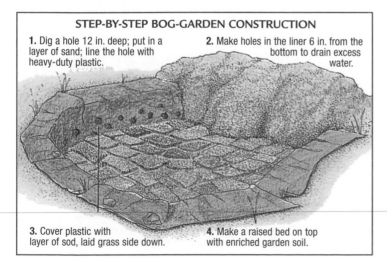

STEP-BY-STEP BOG-GARDEN CONSTRUCTION

1. Dig a hole 12 in. deep; put in a layer of sand; line the hole with heavy-duty plastic.

2. Make holes in the liner 6 in. from the bottom to drain excess water.

3. Cover plastic with layer of sod, laid grass side down.

4. Make a raised bed on top with enriched garden soil.

Star-shaped blossoms of the water lily 'Sioux' start out as yellow, then turn orange, and later crimson-red. These plants grow at a depth of 2 ft.

Nymphaea 'Sioux'

Growing New Water Plants From Old Ones

Dividing Overgrown Old Water Lilies

After two to four years water lilies will become overcrowded. Often growing shoots will produce an over-abundance of leaves that are heaved up out of the water and conceal the flowers. When this occurs, dividing is necessary.

This is best done in spring either before growth starts or while the new leaves are still small. In warm climates it can be done in fall.

First, remove the roots from their containers and wash them well. Keep the plants wet at all times.

With tuberous water lilies, carefully tear apart the rootstocks into sections, each with a growing tip. Before replanting, remove broken leaves, cut off old brown anchorage roots, and trim the new white roots. Plant the sections individually as described on page 176.

With rhizomatous water lilies, cut 6–8 inches from the growing tip and replant the tip. Discard the rest, unless you want to increase your water lily collection.

Growing Water Lilies From Offsets and Eyes

New water lilies can be grown from the eyes found on tuberous root-stocks and from the offset rhizomes found on rhizomatous ones.

To divide lilies of the tuberous type, search for the eyes on the roots and cut them out with a sharp knife. In pots of heavy soil, press the eyes to just below the surface of the soil. Immerse the pot in a container of water. Place this container in a greenhouse or cold frame, partially shaded, until strong young shoots appear in three to four weeks. Replant them in the pool, submerging the pots to a depth of 4–6 inches. If not done in spring, keep the pots in a greenhouse or cold frame, immersed in a container of water until the following spring.

Rhizomatous water lilies have small offsets on the main rhizome. Break these off and press each offset into the surface of a 3- to 4-inch pot full of rich soil.

Keep pots in a greenhouse or cold frame, immersed in water and partially shaded, until spring.

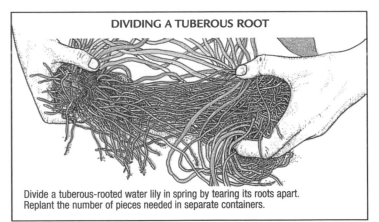

DIVIDING A TUBEROUS ROOT

Divide a tuberous-rooted water lily in spring by tearing its roots apart. Replant the number of pieces needed in separate containers.

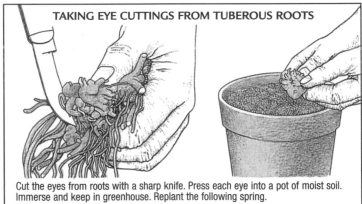

TAKING EYE CUTTINGS FROM TUBEROUS ROOTS

Cut the eyes from roots with a sharp knife. Press each eye into a pot of moist soil. Immerse and keep in greenhouse. Replant the following spring.

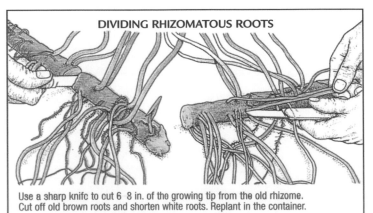

DIVIDING RHIZOMATOUS ROOTS

Use a sharp knife to cut 6–8 in. of the growing tip from the old rhizome. Cut off old brown roots and shorten white roots. Replant in the container.

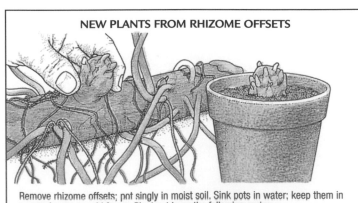

NEW PLANTS FROM RHIZOME OFFSETS

Remove rhizome offsets; pot singly in moist soil. Sink pots in water; keep them in a greenhouse or cold frame. Plant outdoors the following spring.

Water plantain (*Alisma plantago-aquatica*) has white blossoms that open on summer afternoons. The long blossom stems emerge from lance-shaped leaves held above the water.

Alisma plantago-aquatica

Dividing Shallow-Water Plants

Rhizomatous shallow-water plants, such as the bog arum (*Calla palustris*), are propagated by dividing the creeping rootstocks. Lift the roots in spring, and cut off a growing tip about 6–8 inches long. Remove all dead leaves and any brown roots and plant as described on page 177: even pieces a mere ½ inch long will grow. They will do best in a greenhouse with a temperature of about 60°F until they root. Plant outside in early to mid summer.

Shallow-water plants with fibrous roots growing from a thick, celery-like crown, such as arrowhead (*Sagittaria*) and pickerel weed (*Pontederia cordata*), are propagated simply by pulling the rootstocks apart.

Remove dead leaves and old brown roots. Trim the new white roots to 2½–3 inches, and plant as shown on page 177.

BOG ARUM

Divide the creeping rootstock of rhizomatous shallow-water plants. Cut off a 6- to 8-in. section of the growing tip, and replant it horizontally in a container of moist soil.

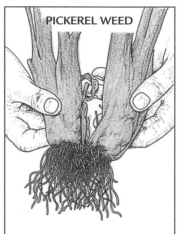

PICKEREL WEED

To propagate plants with tuberous or celerylike roots, pull rootstock apart, cut off dead leaves and old roots, and trim new roots to approximately 3 in. Then plant units separately.

Propagating Floaters and Oxygenators

Many hardy floaters can be increased by dividing their rootstocks in autumn. Simply pull them apart, and return the pieces to the pool—or discard them if the pool has become overcrowded. The water chestnut (*Trapa natans*)—which can be invasive—and duckweed (*Lemna minor*) are two plants that can be treated this way.

Taking soft cuttings in spring and summer is the usual way to increase such oxygenators as the anacharis (*Elodea canadensis*) and curled pondweed (*Potamogeton crispus*).

Cut off growing pieces 3–4 inches long, and plant them in deep, water-retentive containers with 2 inches of soil on the bottom. The containers should be deep enough to allow the cuttings to be covered by 6–9 inches of water. Keep the water temperature around 60°F to assist rapid rooting.

Growing Water Plants From Seeds

Though the easiest method of propagating most water plants is by division, some plants, such as water hawthorn (*Aponogeton distachyos*), can be grown from seeds.

Collect the seeds from the ripe seed heads after they have finished flowering. The best seeds will come from mature pods in late summer. Do not dry the seeds; keep them moist and cold or they will take longer to germinate.

Fill a shallow container with soil, and place the seeds on the surface. Put the container in a pan of water deep enough so that the surface of the soil will be covered by about an inch of water.

The seeds may float at first. This is natural. When all the air inside them has been released, they will lose their buoyancy and sink.

Leave the pan in a partially shaded spot in the greenhouse or cold frame.

The seeds should germinate the following spring.

When the first pair of true leaves appears, transplant the seedlings into individual pots or boxes. Grow them standing in water for that year.

When the pool warms up the following spring, transfer the plants to it.

1. Collect seeds from mature seed heads after flowering. Do not dry.

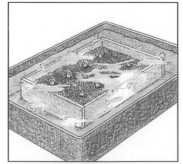

2. Fill a tray with heavy soil. Put seeds on top. Cover with 1 in. of water.

3. When first leaves appear in two or three weeks, transplant into pots.

4. Plant in spring, after keeping in water in a greenhouse or cold frame.

Selecting Plants for a Water Garden

A water garden and its environs offer the opportunity to cultivate a variety of fascinating plants. The most colorful of these plants are the water lilies.

Hardy water lilies will live outdoors year-round, provided the roots are covered sufficiently with water or soil that prevents them from freezing. On sunny days their flowers open in the morning and close in the middle of the afternoon. They are available in all colors except blue.

Tropical lilies, both day and night bloomers, are dependably hardy only in frost-free climates. In colder areas you can treat them as annuals, replacing them each year, or you can overwinter in a bucket of water in a basement, garage, or other cool place.

Some plants that float on the water and are not rooted in soil tend to propagate rapidly. They may have to be thinned.

The plants that grow in shallow water or boggy places provide a visual transition from the plants on the surface of the water to the rest of the garden.

The plants listed here are grouped by kind: plants for deep water, floating, bog plants, etc. Each is arranged alphabetically by botanical name. Common names are also given.

Butomus umbellatus

DEEP-WATER PLANTS WITH FLOATING LEAVES AND FLOWERS	BOTANICAL AND COMMON NAMES	DECORATIVE CHARACTERISTICS, SPECIAL REQUIREMENTS, AND REMARKS	PROPAGATION (See also p. 182)
Aponogeton distachyos (water hawthorn)	***Aponogeton*** (water hawthorn) *A. distachyos*	Green leaves up to 4 in. long. Small white flowers with tiny purple "antlers." Sweet vanilla fragrance. Not winter hardy.	Division or seeds
Nymphaea 'Sioux' (hardy water lily)	***Nymphaea*** (water lily) HARDY *N.* 'Attraction' *N.* 'Chromatella' *N.* 'Gladstone' *N.* 'Paul Hariot' *N.* 'Sioux'	Flowers float on water surface. Plant 18–24 in. deep. Dark red flowers with yellow stamens, to 10 in. across. Mottled foliage. Clear yellow, cup-shaped flowers. Large white flowers with yellow centers, 6–8 in. across. Opens apricot and turns pink with age. Yellow-bronze flowers change to copper-orange as they open.	Division
Nymphaea 'Missouri' (tropical water lily)	TROPICAL DAY BLOOMING *N.* 'Director George T. Moore' *N.* 'General Pershing' *N.* 'Green Smoke' *N.* 'Margaret Randig' *N.* 'Talisman' *N.* 'Yellow Dazzler'	Large flowers rise above water. Plant 6 in. deep. Rich purple flowers with yellow centers. Very fragrant. Large, orchid-pink double flowers open early and close late. Large, scalloped green leaves speckled with bronze. Distinctive greenish flowers with smoky blue overcast. Broad-petaled sky-blue flowers. Long growing season. Yellow flowers suffused with pink. Very fragrant. Vigorously viviparous (complete new plants develop on leaf surface). Showy, chrome-yellow flowers. Very fragrant. Blooms prolifically.	Division. A few varieties grow plantlets on the surface of their leaves. Detach these, pot up, and grow on in a greenhouse.
	TROPICAL NIGHT BLOOMING *N.* 'Emily Grant Hutchings' *N.* 'H. C. Haarstick' *N.* 'Missouri' *N.* 'Omarana'	Large flowers open at dusk, close following morning. Bright pink, cup-shaped flowers, almost luminous under night lighting. Fragrant and free blooming. Coppery foliage. Vivid red flowers to 12 in. across. Fragrant. Creamy white flowers up to 13 in. across, with broad, slightly textured petals. Shows up beautifully in moonlight. Deep orchid-pink, almost lavender flowers with orange-red centers, up to 12 in. across. Very fragrant.	Division
Nymphaea 'Aurora' (pygmy water lily)	PYGMY, OR MINIATURE *N.* 'Aurora' *N.* 'Colorata'	Plant 6–12 in. deep. Flowers open rosy yellow, turn reddish orange on second day, become deep red by third day. Hardy. Pale violet flowers are 2–3 in. across. Day-blooming tropical.	Division
Nymphoides peltata (water fringe, or floating heart)	***Nymphoides*** (floating heart) *N. indicum* (water snowflake) *N. peltata* (water fringe)	Heart-shaped green leaves sometimes mottled with yellow. Leaves to 8 in. across. Tiny, fuzzy-coated white flowers with yellow centers. Hardy only in warm climates. Leaves about 4 in. across. Bright yellow flowers. Hardy as long as rootstock does not freeze.	Division

The marsh marigold (*Caltha palustris*), a spring and early summer bloomer, thrives in very wet soil. The double variety 'Flore Pleno' is more attractive than the single-flowered form.

Caltha palustris 'Flore Pleno'

OXYGENATING PLANTS	BOTANICAL AND COMMON NAMES	DECORATIVE CHARACTERISTICS, SPECIAL REQUIREMENTS, AND REMARKS	PROPAGATION (See also p. 182)
	Cabomba (fanwort) C. caroliniana	Glossy green leaves, fan-shaped and finely divided. Stems red or green. Roots easily, grows entirely submerged.	Cuttings
	Elodea (Canadian pondweed) E. canadensis	Whorls of dark green leaves on long, lighter green stems. Grows vigorously, entirely submerged. Plant 12 in., or more, deep.	Cuttings
	Ludwigia (ludwigia) L. alternifolia (rattlebox) L. natans	Flat, rounded leaves, green on top, reddish beneath. Erect stems rise above water surface, bear flowers of yellow or white. Does best in water 6–8 in. deep. Leaves coppery on top, bright red beneath. Grow in water 4–6 in. deep.	Cuttings
	Myriophyllum (water milfoil) M. aquaticum (parrot feather) M. spicatum	Green feathery leaves like fanwort, but bushier. Bright yellow-green leaves, red tipped in autumn. Pushes out of water a few inches. Not hardy. Invasive in South. Green leaves in delicate, plumelike whorls. Very hardy. Invasive in South.	Cuttings
	Potamogeton (curled pondweed) P. crispus	Crisped green leaves are densely clustered on long stems. Tiny greenish flowers rise out of water in late spring and summer.	Cuttings
	Sagittaria (arrowhead) S. graminea S. subulata (miniature arrowhead)	Dark green, sword-shaped leaves grow directly from rootstock. Leaves grow to 3 ft. or more. Use in deep pools. Like *S. graminea* but only 12–14 in. high.	Separation of rooted runners
	Vallisneria (eelgrass) V. americana	Long, ribbonlike green leaves arrow directly from roots. Hardy, becomes dormant in winter.	Separation of rooted runners

Cabomba (fanwort)

Ludwigia natans

Elodea (Canadian pondweed)

Myriophyllum spicatum (water milfoil)

Potamogeton crispus (curled pondweed)

Vallisneria americana (eelgrass)

Sagittaria graminea (arrowhead)

PLANTS THAT FLOAT FREELY IN THE WATER	BOTANICAL AND COMMON NAMES	DECORATIVE CHARACTERISTICS AND REMARKS	PROPAGATION (See also p. 182)
	Azolla (azolla) A. filiculoides (fairy moss)	Tiny plants with crinkly, mosslike green leaves that turn russet-crimson in autumn. Proliferates rapidly. May become a pest in warm weather.	Separation of colonies of individual plants
	Ceratopteris (water fern) C. thalictroides	True ferns, with edible, lettucelike dark green leaves that stand up to 1 ft. above water surface. Not reliably hardy in winter.	Formation of new plants on edges of fronds
	Eichhornia (water hyacinth) E. crassipes	Clusters of heart-shaped, glossy green leaves. Showy, blue to purple flowers have yellow centers. Spreads rapidly. A pestiferous weed in warm waterways in Central America. Will not withstand frost.	Division
	Lemna (duckweed) L. minor	Tiny bright green leaves on many separate floating plants. Goldfish feed on tender young roots. Spreads rapidly by offshoots. May become a pest; scoop out extra plants and compost.	Separation of offshoots
	Pistia (water lettuce) P. stratiotes (shellflower)	Free-floating 6-in. rosettes, resembling pale green heads of lettuce, with velvety coats. Thrives in full sun or shade. Long, feathery roots trail in water, may anchor in wet soil if plant runs aground. Forms colonies of runnerlike offshoots. Bring indoors for winter.	Separation of offshoots from parent plant
	Trapa (water chestnut) T. natans	Clusters of small, hollylike green leaves are kept afloat by hollow stems. Small white flowers in summer. Large, spiny seeds are edible, taste similar to true chestnut.	Division or from nutlike seeds

Azolla filiculoides (fairy moss)

Ceratopteris thalictroides (water fern)

Lemna minor (duckweed)

Eichhornia crassipes (water hyacinth)

Pistia stratiotes (shellflower)

Trapa natans (water chestnut)

Golden club (*Orontium*) is a deep-rooted plant that needs at least 14 in. of soil. Species such as arrowhead (*Sagittaria*) and cattail (*Typha*) will grow in less soil than this.

Orontium aquaticum

Sagittaria sagittifolia

Typha latifolia

PLANTS FOR BOGS AND SHALLOW WATER	BOTANICAL AND COMMON NAMES	DECORATIVE CHARACTERISTICS, SPECIAL REQUIREMENTS, AND REMARKS	PROPAGATION (See also p. 182)
Acorus calamus (sweet flag)	**Acorus** (sweet flag) A. calamus A. c. 'Variegatus' (variegated sweet flag) A. gramineus 'Variegatus' (variegated Japanese rush)	Irislike green leaves rise 2–3 ft. out of water. Small brownish-green flowers bloom in midsummer. Grow in water 2–4 in. deep. Leaves are striped lengthwise with green and creamy white, fragrant when bruised or crushed. Narrow, grasslike foliage striped green and white. Grows 6–12 in. high. Not fragrant.	Division
Alisma lanceolatum (water plantain)	**Alisma** (water plantain) A. lanceolatum A. plantago-aquatica (mad-dog weed)	Whorls of small white or pink-tinted flowers bloom in candelabra sprays in midsummer. Grow in bog or water 2–6 in. deep. Hardy. Leaves sword-shaped, to 12 in. long. Large, almond-shaped, bright green leaves on 3-ft. stems.	Division or seeds
Butomus umbellatus (flowering rush)	**Butomus** (flowering rush) B. umbellatus	Slender dark green leaves, purple at base, and clusters of fragrant, rose-pink flowers in summer. Grow in bog or water up to 10 in. deep. Hardy.	Division or seeds
Calla palustris (water dragon)	**Calla** (bog, or water, arum) C. palustris (water dragon)	Heart-shaped, bright green leaves rise 6–9 in. high. Small, creamy white flowers with yellow hearts borne in showy clusters in early and mid summer, followed by bunches of red berries in fall. Grow in bog or shallow water to 6 in. deep. Hardy.	Division
Caltha (kingcup)	**Caltha** (marsh marigold, or kingcup) C. leptosepala (elkslip) C. palustris C. p. alba C. p. 'Flore Pleno'	Grows in small, rounded clumps, with attractive foliage. Very hardy bog plant. Rocky Mountain native, 6–12 in. high, with oval green leaves. Bluish-white flowers appear in early and mid summer. Heart-shaped green leaves. Covered with golden buttercuplike flowers in midspring to early summer. Dies back mid to late summer. Grows 1–3 ft. high. Flowers are white, long lasting. Golden yellow flowers are double, very large. Prolific.	Division or seeds
Colocasia esculenta (green taro)	**Colocasia** (taro, or elephant's ear) C. esculenta (green taro) C. e. 'Illustris' (imperial taro)	Huge leathery leaves, each on a 2- to 4-ft. stem, are edible, as are tuberous roots. Overwinter indoors. Hardy only in Deep South and on West Coast. Foliage is deep, rich green. Varieties are available with stems of red, purple, and violet. Green leaves blotched with dark brown and deep violet.	Division
Cyperus alternifolius (umbrella palm)	**Cyperus** (cyperus) C. alternifolius (umbrella palm, or umbrella plant) C. a. 'Gracilis' (dwarf umbrella) C. papyrus (papyrus) C. profiler (dwarf papyrus)	Clumps of round stems to 3 ft. high, each topped by umbrellalike tuft of leaves. Not hardy. Grow in containers in shallow water 2–6 in. deep. For winter, treat as houseplant. Dwarf form, to 12 in. high. Triangular stalks grow 5–8 ft. high, topped by tufts of threadlike leaves. Grow in containers in shallow water 2–6 in. deep. Not hardy in winter; take indoors or add to compost heap. Like C. papyrus, but only about 2 ft. high.	Division
Hosta sieboldiana (plantain lily)	**Hosta** (plantain lily) H. sieboldiana	Hardy bog plant with large, stiff, blue-green leaves 12–15 in. long and nearly as wide. Dense clusters of funnel-shaped lavender flowers appear in spring and early summer. Grow in partial shade. See also p. 55. Not all hostas will grow well in bog conditions.	Division

Native to northeastern North America, *Iris versicolor* thrives in very wet soil.

Iris versicolor

PLANTS FOR BOGS AND SHALLOW WATER *(Continued)*	BOTANICAL AND COMMON NAMES	DECORATIVE CHARACTERISTICS, SPECIAL REQUIREMENTS, AND REMARKS	PROPAGATION *(See also p. 182)*
Hydrocleys nymphoides (water poppy)	**Hydrocleys** (water poppy) *H. nymphoides*	Round, dark-green leaves float on surface of water. Poppylike, bright yellow flowers bloom freely from early summer on. New plants develop on runners. Grows best in water 2–4 in. deep, but will grow in deeper water. Not hardy in winter.	Division, or separation of runners
Iris versicolor (blue flag)	**Iris** (iris) *I. ensata* (Japanese iris) *I. laevigata* *I. pseudacorus* (yellow flag, or water iris) *I. sibirica* (Siberian iris) *I. versicolor* (blue flag, or water iris)	Named varieties have flowers of many colors; bloom in mid to late summer. Root area must be kept well drained in winter. Deep blue flowers in early to mid summer. Varieties available with flowers of white, pink, violet, and shades of blue. Bog plant. Will grow to 2 ft. high in water 2 in. deep. Bright golden blooms in late spring and early summer. Will grow 2–3 ft. high in water 2–18 in. deep (will grow higher in deeper water). Flowers of white, pink, mauve, or blue in early summer. Will grow 2–4 ft. high in bog or in water 2–4 in. deep. Like *I. pseudacorus*, but has blue or violet flowers. About 2 ft. high. Grow in water 2–12 in. deep.	Division or seeds (see p. 75)
Lobelia cardinalis (cardinal flower)	**Lobelia** (cardinal flower) *L. cardinalis*	Narrow, deep-green leaves. Flower spikes of bright cardinal-red are borne in late summer and early fall on sturdy stalks 3–4 ft. high. Grow in bog or shallow water 2–4 in. deep. *L. c. alba* has white flowers; *L. c. rosea* has rose-pink flowers.	Division or cuttings
Ludwigia longifolia (primrose willow)	**Ludwigia** (primrose willow) *L. longifolia* *L. peploides* (primrose creeper)	Willowlike foliage. Yellow primroselike flowers borne all summer. Grows 2–3 ft. high, with pointed leaves. Grow in bog or water 2–6 in. deep. Tropical plant; must be treated as annual throughout the country, and over-wintered in greenhouse pool or other protected container of water. Fast-spreading vine with small, shiny green leaves on reddish stems. Yellow flowers bloom just above surface of water. Grow in shallow water up to 12 in. deep. Moderately hardy. May survive in mildest areas of country.	Division or seeds
Lysimachia nummularia (moneywort)	**Lysimachia** (lysimachia) *L. nummularia* (moneywort, or creeping Jenny) *L. n.* 'Aurea'	Small, round green leaves on creeping vine. Bright yellow flowers appear profusely throughout summer. Grow in bog or in shallow water up to 2 in. deep. Hardy. Foliage is yellow. Spreads quickly.	Division
Mimulus luteus (golden monkey flower)	**Mimulus** (monkey flower) *M. luteus* (golden monkey flower) *M. ringens* (Allegheny monkey flower)	Bushy perennial bog plant. Flowers are odd-looking, monkey-faced, with 2 distinct lips. Grow in shade or partial shade and in humus-rich soil. Vinelike, 6–12 in. high. Covered all summer long with yellow flowers, spotted with red or purple. Grow in bog or shallow water to 4 in. deep. Not hardy below –18°C. Shrublike, to 18 in. high. Purple, soft lavender, or white flowers appear profusely in late summer and early autumn. Grow in bog or shallow water to 6 in. deep. Very hardy.	Division or cuttings
Nasturtium officinale (watercress)	**Nasturtium** (watercress) *N. officinale*	Edible, round green leaves cluster at edge of pools or running streams. Small white flowers appear all summer in sun or partial shade. Plant in water 4–6 in. deep. Hardy and fast growing.	Division or cuttings

At its best in bog gardens and alongside streams, primrose (*Primula*) also thrives in a wide range of habitats. *P. beesiana* bears whorls of lilac blooms on sturdy stems.

Primula beesiana

PLANTS FOR BOGS AND SHALLOW WATER *(Continued)*	BOTANICAL AND COMMON NAMES	DECORATIVE CHARACTERISTICS, SPECIAL REQUIREMENTS, AND REMARKS	PROPAGATION *(See also p. 182)*
Nelumbo nucifera 'Rosea Plena' (sacred lotus)	**Nelumbo** (lotus)	Large round leaves resemble parasols above water. Fragrant, beautiful flowers rise as high as 6–8 ft. on straight stems. Grow in water 6–9 in. deep. Hardy as long as rootstock does not freeze.	Division
	N. lutea (American lotus)	Large bluish-green leaves. Soft yellow flowers, 8–10 in. across, appear all summer long.	
	N. nucifera (sacred lotus)	Fragrant pink flowers arise all summer long. Larger than *N. lutea*.	
	N. n. 'Alba Grandiflora'	Deep green leaves. Pure white flowers are delicately scented.	
	N. n. 'Alba Striata'	White flowers are edged with carmine-red.	
	N. n. 'Rosea Plena'	Rich, rose-pink, fully double flowers are up to 12 in. across, extremely fragrant.	
Orontium aquaticum (golden club)	**Orontium** (golden club) *O. aquaticum*	Narrow, floating or aerial leaves and strange clublike yellow flowers in early summer. Grow in bog or shallow water and full sun. May need protection in North.	Division or seeds
Osmunda regalis (royal fern)	**Osmunda** (osmunda fern)	Hardy bog plant with long, feathery fronds from midspring to first frost. Grow in partial shade and in acid soil. For other ferns suited to boggy areas, see pp. 101–105.	Division or spores
	O. cinnamomea (cinnamon fern)	Fronds 2–4 ft. long and 6–8 in. wide, green when young, turning cinnamon colored when spores develop. Fronds emerge from ground in early to mid spring as edible, fiddlehead-shaped sprouts.	
	O. claytoniana (Interrupted fern)	Fronds 1–2 ft. long and 8–12 in. wide. Requires moist, highly acid soil.	
	O. regalis (royal, or flowering, fern)	Dramatically beautiful, with fronds up to 8 ft. long and 12–18 in. across, pale green and much divided. Brownish spore clusters at ends of fronds resemble flowers. Will grow in shallow water, to 4 in. deep. Varieties have reddish or bronze-colored fronds.	
Primula beesiana	**Pontederia** (pickerel weed) *P. cordata*	Stalk to about 2 ft. high, bearing spearhead-shaped, shiny olive-green leaves. Azure to violet-blue flower spikes last all summer. Grow in water 2–12 in. deep (start very shallow, increase depth gradually). Very hardy.	Division
Pontederia cordata (pickerel weed)	**Primula** (primrose) *P. beesiana*	Shade-loving bog plant. Hardy. Grows to 2 ft. high, with oblong green leaves. Stalks of yellow-eyed rose-lilac flowers bloom in early and mid summer.	Division or seeds
	P. florindae (Tibetan primrose)	Long, broad, glossy green leaves on reddish stems. Flat clusters of bright yellow flowers appear atop 2- to 3-ft. stems in late summer. Will grow in water 2–3 in. deep.	
	P. japonica (Japanese primrose)	Small green leaves. Flowers appear in whorls along 18- to 24-in. stalks, from late spring to midsummer. Available in shades of purple, rose, red, and white.	
Rodgersia pinnata (rodgersia)	**Rodgersia** (rodgersia) *R. aesculifolia*	Bog plant with large, hairy green leaves. White flowers appear all summer in thick clusters along 1½- to 3-ft. stalks.	Division
	R. pinnata	Stalks 3–4 ft. high, with reddish flowers. Varieties are available in shades of red, pink, rose, and white.	
Sagittaria sagittifolia (Japanese arrowhead)	**Sagittaria** (arrowhead) *S. latifolia* (giant arrowhead)	Large, arrowhead-shaped leaves rise 2–3 ft. above water. Hardy native plant with large white flowers borne on spikes in mid to late summer. Grow in water 2–6 in. deep.	Division
	S. sagittifolia (Japanese arrowhead)	Foliage sometimes variegated. Flowers smaller than *S. latifolia*, with purple spots at base of petals.	
	S. s. 'Flore Pleno'	Double flowers displayed all summer long.	
Symplocarpus foetidus (skunk cabbage)	**Symplocarpus** (skunk cabbage) *S. foetidus*	Hardy bog plant with large, oval leaves that emit unpleasant odor when crushed. Brownish-purple hoods with green mottling, 6–12 in. high, enclose true, club-shaped, blackish flowers. Blooms in very early spring.	Division or seeds

'Golden Queen' globeflower, with its orange-yellow blossoms, is one of the brightest flowers of early summer.

Trollius cultorum 'Golden Queen'

PLANTS FOR BOGS AND SHALLOW WATER *(Continued)*	BOTANICAL AND COMMON NAMES	DECORATIVE CHARACTERISTICS, SPECIAL REQUIREMENTS, AND REMARKS	PROPAGATION *(See also p. 182)*
Thalia dealbata (water canna)	**Thalia** (water canna) *T. dealbata*	Cannalike green leaves, maroon at base, covered with powdery white, on 3- to 4-ft. stems. Clusters of purple flowers appear in late summer atop 3- to 5-ft. stalks. Grow in water 4–6 in. deep. Not hardy in winter. Grow in submerged pot during summer; bring indoors in winter.	Division
Typha latifolia (common cattail)	**Trollius** (trollius, or globeflower) *T. cultorum*	Small palmlike or ferny green leaves. Big, round, buttercuplike flowers of orange and yellow bloom from late spring to midsummer. Grows to 3 ft. high. Many varieties. Hardy bog plant.	Division or seeds
	Typha (cattail, or bulrush) *T. angustifolia* (narrow-leaved, or graceful, cattail)	Flat, sword-shaped leaves rise from water. Brown flower heads are borne on stout, ramrod-stiff stalks. Hardy. Flowers appear in mid and late summer. Leaves very narrow. Flower stalks may grow 4–6 ft. high. Grow in shallow water 4–6 in. deep. Plant in containers to check invasive habit.	Division; or plant seeds in pots, put in shallow water in spring
Zantedeschia (calla lily)	*T. latifolia* (common cattail) *T. minima* (dwarf cattail)	Flower stalks may grow 10 ft. high. Flower heads purple-brown on stalks only 12–18 in. high. Plant in containers 2–6 in. deep.	
Trollius cultorum (globeflower)	**Zantedeschia** (calla lily) *Z. aethiopica*	Large, arrowhead-shaped, glossy green leaves grow 2–3 ft. high. Trumpet-shaped flowers appear from late spring to autumn. Bog plant. Can overwinter in mild climates. See also p. 131.	Division, or separation of offsets

GRASSES THAT REQUIRE MOISTURE AND GOOD DRAINAGE	BOTANICAL AND COMMON NAMES	DECORATIVE CHARACTERISTICS AND REMARKS	PROPAGATION *(See also p. 182)*
Fargesia nitida (bamboo)	**Arundo** (giant reed) *A. donax*	Long, arching, gray-green leaves on cornstalklike stems 12–15 ft. high. Plumelike reddish or white flowers appear in fall. Hardy to Zones 6–9. Can be invasive.	Division or seeds; root stems in water
	Bambusa (several genera) *Fargesia nitida* *Phyllostachys niger*	Graceful, arching stems with attractive, long, thin leaves. Canes 12–20 ft. high. Hardy to Zones 4–9. Arching canes, 8–15 ft. high, are green first year, then turn deep purple-black. Young shoots edible. Invasive in warm climate. Will not survive below 10°F.	Division
Arundo donax (giant reed)	*Sasa palmata*	Long green leaves with silvery undersides on canes up to 8 ft. high. May be evergreen in mild winters. Spreads by underground runners; must be kept in check. Hardy to southern part of Zones 7–11.	
Pennisetum setaceum (fountain grass)	**Miscanthus** (miscanthus) *M. sacchariflorus* (silver grass)	Long, grassy leaves on reedy stems. Flowers in late summer. Stems 6–8 ft. high. Foliage silky and silvery. Flowers are brown spikelets surrounded by long, silky hairs. Genus can be invasive.	Division or seeds
	M. sinensis (eulalia grass) *M. s.* 'Gracillimus' (maiden grass) *M. s.* 'Zebrinus' (zebra grass)	To 10 ft. high, with graceful, 2- to 3-ft.-long leaves. Fanlike, pinkish-white flower plumes in late summer and fall. Hardy. Miniature form, to 3 ft. high. Narrow leaves have center stripe of white or yellow. Foliage crossbanded in white or yellow.	
Miscanthus sinensis (eulalia grass)	**Pennisetum** (pennisetum) *P. alopecuroides* (fountain grass) *P. setaceum* (tender fountain grass)	Highly ornamental grasses. Not reliably hardy. Grow as annual. Narrow, 2-ft. leaves on stems 3–4 ft. high. Plumelike flowers of silvery purple in late summer followed by gaudy seed heads in fall. Very narrow, graceful leaves. Seed heads are 1 ft. long or more, nodding, and very showy, in shades of purple, coppery orange, red, rose, and pink.	Seeds

The hyacinth-flowered candytuft (Iberis amara) *makes a good cut flower, and when planted close to a patio or under a window, its fragrance will fill the air. There are also varieties with flowers in pastel shades of rose, purple, and lilac.*

ANNUALS AND BIENNIALS

A garden can be quickly filled with color by using annuals and biennials. These plants flower longer than many others and are ideal for filling gaps in a border.

Almost any patch of soil can be transformed into a blaze of color in a matter of weeks by planting nursery-grown annuals, or in two or three months with the plants you grow from direct-sown seeds.

Annuals are plants that grow, flower, produce seeds, and die in one growing season. The most popular kinds provide a longer-lasting display than perennials or bulbs, and they are invaluable for starting a new garden quickly. They can also be used to supply bright accents among shrubs or perennials, under trees, and in containers. Many of these plants provide excellent cut flowers as well.

Most annuals are inexpensive, easy to grow, and available in a broad range of colors and heights.

Plants that are similar in their general effect are biennials. They are started from seeds one year; they flower the next; and then they die.

In mild climates, however, some of the plants grown as annuals may survive the winter (they actually are tender perennials), and some biennials can be grown as annuals.

Annuals are classified in some books and catalogs, and on some seed packets, according to the British system, which divides them into two groups—hardy and half-hardy. Hardy annuals, which tolerate cold weather, can be sown earlier than half-hardy annuals. This terminology often proves more confusing than helpful, however, because it does not apply to all areas of North America. Therefore, it is not used in this book.

The quickest and easiest way to enjoy flowers in the garden is to purchase young annuals or biennials in plant form in spring (also in autumn in the South) and set them directly in the garden. A wide choice of plants is available, but seeds, especially those offered in catalogs, provide an even greater diversity.

Seeds can be given an extra early start (especially in cold regions) by sowing them in a protected and controlled environment. This is almost a necessity for very fine seeds, such as those of the wax begonia; for seeds that need high temperatures to germinate, such as those of the impatiens; and for those plants that are slow to bloom from seeds, such as the vinca, petunia, and ageratum. Seeds can be started indoors if sufficient light and proper temperature are provided (see p. 193), or outdoors if a cold frame or hotbed that protects them from the elements can be located conveniently.

Seeds can also be sown directly outdoors where they are to flower. This is a popular and practical method for plants that bloom quickly, as well as for those that have large seeds (see p. 191).

Biennials, although fewer in number than the annuals or perennials, have some of the showiest garden flowers. Particularly popular are sweet William, Canterbury bell, fox-glove, hollyhock, and pansy. They are usually sown in the late spring or early summer outdoors in a protected location.

When biennial seedlings are large enough to handle, they can be transplanted in rows to grow until late summer. By then they should be sturdy enough for transplantation to permanent positions or to spend the winter in a cold frame.

Many annuals and biennials have been garden favorites for centuries. A worthwhile advance in recent years has been the development of the F_1 first generation, and the F_2, second generation, hybrids (the F stands for filial). They are the result of selecting and inbreeding different parent lines of the same plant to get the most desirable characteristics and then cross-pollinating the plants to combine the best characteristics of each.

Several generations of this kind of breeding are required to produce plants of the desired quality. Some home gardeners may be deterred by the relatively high price of the seeds,

especially since seeds saved from such hybrid plants will not produce plants of equal vigor or identical color the next year.

But the first generation of flowers grown from F_1 hybrid seeds will demonstrate such superiority to the less expensive types that they are well worth the added cost. These hybrids offer clearer colors, more vigor, larger size, greater weather and disease resistance, and better, more uniform growth habits than their forebears.

F_2 hybrids are the results of the hybridizers' attempts to improve the quality without the high cost of the F_1 method. This is achieved by self-fertilizing the F_1's. In some cases it has worked. Generally, the F_2 hybrids are an improvement on standard seeds, though not so spectacular as the F_1's. Most seed catalogs do not mention the designations, but the difference in the price is usually an indication that the most expensive seeds are F_1 hybrids or a new variety.

Selecting varieties from a catalog or seed rack can be confusing. In an

attempt to simplify the choice, All-America Selections, founded in 1932, began growing new varieties submitted by hybridizers in official test gardens throughout the continent. Those awarded the highest number of points are designated as the All-America Selections, and every seed packet of those varieties is so labeled. The buyer can be assured that these varieties have proven to be superior to other plants under varied climatic and soil conditions.

Among most recent All-Americas are petunia 'Opera Supreme Pink Morn', a ground cover that flowers profusely; celosia 'Fresh Look Gold', free-branching and weather-tolerant; dianthus 'Supra Purple', long-flowering and heat-tolerant; cleome 'Sparkler Blush', with pink flowers that turn white with age; gaillardia 'Arizona Sun', with dark red flowers with petals tipped in yellow on a spreading plant; and zinnia 'Magellan Coral', with fully double flowers on a 12-inch plant. Other All-Americas are indicated by an asterisk on the chart beginning on page 197.

This planting scheme for a bed of annuals includes low-growing evergreen shrubs—some arborvitae, February daphne, and garland spirea—to give a backdrop of foliage and flowers before the annuals are dominant.

The undemanding pot marigold (*Calendula*) can be grown outdoors from seed. The annual love-in-a-mist (*Nigella*) thrive everywhere providing they are in full sun and well-drained soil.

Calendula officinalis

Nigella damascena

How to Succeed With Annuals Sown Outdoors

Clearing the Site and Preparing the Soil

Ideally, soil in which annuals are to be grown is best prepared in the fall or at least a few months before sowing seeds. However, if this cannot be done, you should still work in some organic matter before sowing seeds. This will help the seedlings to break through the soil, improve root growth, increase moisture retention, and make cultivation simpler by preventing caking of the soil.

Dig up any weeds and other vegetation, and consign them to the compost pile. Then put down a 1- or 2-inch layer of organic material, such as garden compost or manure (the latter should be well rotted if applied just before sowing). This helps to retain moisture in light sandy soil and breaks up heavy clay soil. If lime is required, it can be added at this time. Turn the added organic matter into the soil with a spading fork, or use a power tiller. If the soil is prepared in the fall ready for spring, leave it rough dug. The action of frost on the clods of soil will break them into crumbs, ideal for raking level into a seed bed or for setting out plants.

Slightly moist soil is easier to turn than dry soil, which falls through the spading fork. If the soil is too dry, water a day or so in advance. If rain makes the soil sticky, wait a few days. If the soil is low in fertility or lacking in humus, a green-manure cover crop can be sown in fall. For example, if annual rye is sown, it can be turned under in spring or any time after it grows to a foot or more in height. This adds humus and nutrients to the soil. Check locally for the recommended cover crops.

In spring (sometimes fall in mild areas) or a few weeks before sowing seeds, loosen the top 6–10 inches of soil with a spading fork or power tiller. The soil should be dry enough so that a handful squeezed into a ball will fall apart readily.

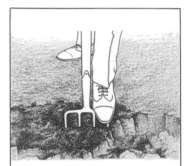

Before sowing seeds, use a fork to incorporate compost or other organic matter into the soil.

How to Sow Seeds Directly Outdoors

It is a good idea to prepare a planting plan in advance, indicating where each variety is to grow. Sowing seeds directly where they are to grow eliminates the need for special planting containers, as well as the work involved in transplanting the small seedlings.

Most seeds are sold loose in packets, but some are available as pellets, on tapes that can be cut to the desired length, or attached to sticks. A pellet is made by coating a seed with a decomposable material to increase its size and make spacing easier. Before buying pelleted seeds, check to make sure that coating does not also contain chemical fertilizers or fungicides.

Seeds on a tape are evenly spaced between two strips of decomposable material. Such tape can be cut to a specific length, laid in a furrow, and covered with soil.

A seed stick is a wooden label with a few seeds attached to the base. The label is stuck into the soil so that the seeds are planted at the proper depth. Although expensive, seed sticks are practical if only a few plants of a given variety are needed.

As a general rule, most seeds can be sown in the open after the last expected frost. In the mildest areas seeds can be sown much earlier in spring—or in late summer or fall for winter or early-spring bloom.

Water the soil the day before sowing unless it is already moist. If you have not yet added humus, lightly fork a pailful of slightly moist, compost per square yard into the top few inches of soil to keep it from caking. If the ground is too wet, add some dry compost.

Mark areas to be planted according to your plan. Within each area seeds can be sown in grooves, or rows, or scattered (broadcast) over the entire section and gently raked into the soil. The advantage of sowing in rows is that it is easier to hoe out weeds between seedlings grown in rows than between those growing at random. Allow ample space between the seeds to minimize thinning out later on.

The distance between rows should be determined by the eventual size of the plants. In general, tall, narrow plants should be spaced in rows that are the width of half their height. For bushy dwarf plants the rows should be the width of their full height. The expected height of a plant is indicated on the seed packet.

Keep the seedbed moist. Use the finest spray from a hose nozzle, and take care not to wash the seeds out or puddle the soil. In sunny weather seedlings may need watering every day. Excessive dryness delays germination and stunts growth.

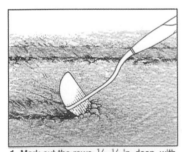

1. Mark out the rows, ¼–½ in. deep, with the edge, or handle, of a hoe.

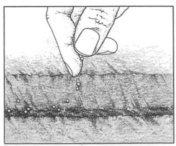

2. Sow the seeds sparingly to avoid the need for too much thinning later.

3. Thinly cover the seeds by drawing a rake lightly along the row.

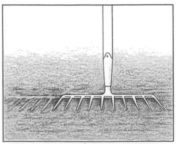

4. Use the back of the rake to firm the ground.

Cleome hassleriana

Tanacetum parthenium 'White Stars'

The tall bushlike spider flower (*Cleome*) gets its name from the shape of its fragrant blossoms. Feverfew (*Tanacetum*) is smaller and good for edging or containers.

Caring for Young Seedlings Outdoors

Planting Out Young Seedlings

Provided there is no danger of frost, young plants are ready to be set into their permanent places in the garden, once they have been hardened off (see p. 194). The latest possible planting date varies from region to region.

Prepare the site in the manner described on page 192.

Transplant only when the soil is moist. With a trowel or your fingers, lift a single plant or a row of plants from the container or directly from rows in the cold frame. (It sometimes helps to separate the plants in a container by running a knife between them.) Separate into individual plants, taking care that each retains as many roots as possible. With a trowel dig a planting hole that is wide enough and deep enough to accommodate the plant's root system and add about ½–1 tsp bone meal to each hole.

Insert the plant so that the base of its stem is level with the surface of the soil. Fill the hole and firm the soil with your fingers, leaving a slight depression that will collect water.

Water after planting to settle the soil around the roots and to minimize wilting. Shade if necessary.

Protecting Seedlings From Dogs, Cats, and Birds

Unfortunately, there is no foolproof way to keep animals out of flower beds. A specially treated rope to repel dogs can be strung around the bed's perimeter, and there are cat-repellent sprays of varying effectiveness. To deter birds, insert low stakes around the perimeter of the bed; tie black thread to one, and loop it crisscross over the bed. Or use netting sold for supporting pea vines.

Protect seedlings from birds with stake-supported netting.

The Best Way to Stake Tall Flowers

Some tall annuals need support. When twiggy branches pruned from shrubs are available, put them in position after thinning the seedlings. Place the branches at 1-foot intervals around each group of seedlings, with several more in the center of the group. Such branches should be about two-thirds the ultimate height of the plants so that they will eventually be hidden.

More readily available supports are plastic-covered metal or bamboo stakes. Use green twine, plastic tape, or covered-wire tape to tie each plant to a stake.

Support tall annuals with twiggy branches around groups of seedlings, or tie each one to a stake.

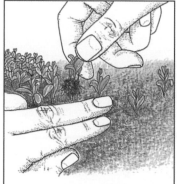

Thinning, the process of removing small, deformed, or overcrowded seedlings, gives the remaining plants a better chance for healthy, vigorous growth.

Deadheading Encourages Further Flowering

"Deadheading" is a descriptive term for removing faded flowers. If dead blooms are left, the plant's energy goes into producing seeds rather than more flowers. Deadheading is also essential if the appearance of the garden is to be maintained at its best. Cutting fresh blooms for indoor use will reduce the need for deadheading.

If you want to save some seeds for the next season (although they will probably be inferior to commercial seeds), allow one or two blooms to mature on each plant. Then harvest the seeds when ripe and store dry.

Cleaning Up the Garden in the Fall

After the annuals no longer have a pleasing appearance, or have been frosted, or have ceased flowering, pull them up and consign them to the compost pile. By not postponing this job until the following spring, you will not only have a better-looking garden all winter but you will also have an opportunity to improve the soil before the next planting season.

This is an excellent time to incorporate humus in the form of compost or shredded leaves, or to apply lime if it is needed. A green-manure crop such as annual rape or ryegrass can also be sown (see p. 498). However, it is usually only practical to do this in gardens where annuals are grown exclusively.

Pinching Seedlings to Encourage Branching

Encourage any plant that is not normally bushy to produce several stems and more blooms by pinching off its growing tip. Using your thumb and forefinger, pinch just above a set of leaves. Side shoots can be pinched later to make the plant bushier.

This can be done in the seedling stage, while the plants are indoors, or after setting out in the garden. Either way, give the seedling a few days to recover from being transplanted before pinching. Pinching plants set out in the garden delays blooming slightly—you probably pinched off the embryo buds—but ends up by giving you more flowers because the plants develop side shoots quicker.

Remove faded flowers by snapping them off between finger and thumb, or use pruning shears. This encourages more blooms and improves the plant's looks.

The plumed cockscomb (*Celosia*), which has blossoms like feathers, is an annual that needs starting inside. Century Series grows up to 18 in., and comes in several colors.

Celosia argentea var. *plumosa* 'Century Red'

Raising Annuals From Seeds Sown Indoors

Sowing Indoors or in a Greenhouse

The requirements for success in starting seeds and growing seedlings indoors are adequate light, a sterilized growing mixture, and the proper temperature. In the home, light is often the limiting factor. Even a window facing south does not have the intensity of a greenhouse's overhead light. However, where natural daylight is nonexistent or insufficient, two 40-watt fluorescent tubes (four are even better) set about 6 inches above the plants will provide adequate light.

An indoor temperature of 70°–75°F serves to germinate most seeds, but seedlings grow better at 50°–60°F. Too high a temperature, especially when coupled with insufficient light, results in weak, spindly seedlings that will be difficult to establish when transplanted to the garden.

Sow seeds in flats or pots, or use a presown container. It can be helpful to use a commercial seed-starting mix, which usually consists of peat moss, vermiculite, and/or perlite. To mix your own, use equal parts of peat moss, vermiculite, and perlite—none of which require sterilizing. This mixture lacks nutrients, however; so the seedlings will require transplanting to a compost-based soil mix once they have developed one or two sets of true leaves. If sterilized soil is used (see p. 502), feeding will be unnecessary.

Unless you have plenty of room, do not start seeds too early, since one pot of seeds can suddenly become many pots of seedlings.

For all but the slowest growers, six to eight weeks before the safe outdoor planting date is generally enough time. For really fast growers like dwarf marigolds, four weeks may suffice. The slowest growers, such as wax begonias, impatiens,

and vincas, need a three- or four-month advance start to ensure bloom in early summer.

Sow the seeds in rows, particularly when several kinds are grown in one container, or scatter them thinly. Sowing too thickly necessitates transplanting when seedlings are too small to handle easily. Barely cover the seeds with the growing mixture. Very fine seeds, such as those of wax begonia, need not be covered.

After sowing and covering, gently mist the flat with water. Cover the container with glass or clear plastic; inspect frequently. At the first sign of germination, remove the cover.

1. Fill a flat with moist seed-starting medium, level it, and tamp gently.

2. Sprinkle seeds over the surface or sow in rows. Space seeds evenly.

3. Cover the seeds with a very thin layer of sifted medium.

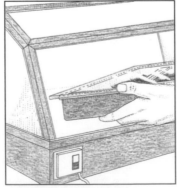

4. Water the flats and place them in a propagator, or cover with plastic.

SOWING IN A POT

1. Fill a 2- to 3-in. pot with seed-starting medium to within ¼ in. of the top; level and firm gently. Before seeding, water with a fine spray and allow to drain thoroughly. A clay pot can be watered by standing the base in water until the top of the medium is obviously moist.

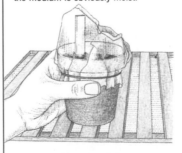

2. Sprinkle seeds thinly over the surface, and cover lightly with starting medium. Cover pot with a plastic bag to prevent soil mix from drying out.

3. Let seeds germinate in a dark, warm spot—about 70°–75°F. When seedlings appear, remove the plastic bag and move the pot into the light. Water as needed with a fine spray. When seedlings are large enough, transplant them into flats or individual pots to grow to planting size.

A fleshy-foliaged plant that grows some 6 in. high, moss rose (*Portulaca*) is a good ground cover for hot, dry locations. Its brilliant colored blossoms open in the sun.

Portulaca grandiflora

Thinning Out and Transplanting Seedlings

Seedlings need to be transplanted, either when they become crowded or when they reach the proper size. (Seedlings that remain crowded become weak and spindly.) Seedlings are large enough to be transplanted when they have grown three or four true leaves, not counting the first pair of seed leaves. Larger seedlings can be transplanted, and although they are easier to handle, wilting is apt to be severe, and growth slowed.

Make certain that the soil is moist so that the seedlings can be lifted out easily with some soil clinging to the roots. Avoid pulling them out, as this can damage the fine roots. First, loosen the seedlings with a label stake. After loosening them, hold those to be lifted with one hand; at the same time, use the fingers of your other hand to press the soil down on each side of the seedlings that are to remain, in order to disturb them as little as possible. Water the remaining seedlings to resettle the soil.

The distance to be left between the transplanted seedlings in the new container depends somewhat on the kind of plant being transplanted. Generally, 1–2 inches between seedlings at the first transplanting is adequate. If they should become crowded before they can be set in the garden, they can be transplanted again with more space between them. Where window areas are at a premium, it is often better to space them closely at first and then make a second transplanting later when they begin to crowd.

If you are unable to transplant all the seedlings you have dug out immediately, be sure to protect them from drying out in the meantime. One good way is to put them close together temporarily in a small pot of soil. Even if several days elapse before you can tend to them, they will suffer only a minimal setback.

As the plants grow, avoid any check in their growth by making sure that the soil stays moist. Remove any weeds that appear (few will if the soil is pasteurized).

Before seedlings are set out in the garden, they should be hardened to take outdoor conditions as described at the right. If this is not done, seedlings may suffer a setback, and flowering will be delayed. When you have surplus seedlings, always keep the strongest ones. Discarded seedlings should not be left lying on the soil, as they often attract fungi or pests—particularly in a greenhouse.

Hardening Off the Young Plants

Whenever seedlings or even mature plants are moved outdoors from the house or greenhouse, they need a short period of acclimatization because light intensity and outdoor temperatures are quite different from indoor conditions. If this is not done, the seedlings will be severely set back, and may even be killed.

A cold frame is the ideal place for this transition. The containers of seedlings can be set directly into the frame. Pay careful attention to watering and ventilating. On cool nights close the frame, but open it again as soon as the sun strikes it in the morning to prevent overheating. Gradually increase their exposure to cold and plant out after about 7–10 days.

If you don't have a cold frame, similar acclimatization is accomplished by setting the containers of seedlings outdoors for an increasing amount of sun each day and by taking them in at night whenever the night temperature falls below 50°F. After a week of hardening, seedlings can be transplanted into their permanent site.

Do not assume annuals you buy have been hardened off; do it yourself and be sure.

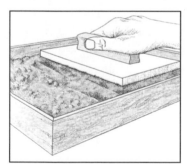

1. Fill a flat with slightly moist soil; then firm the soil gently and level.

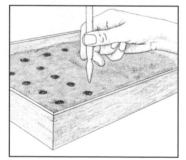

2. Make rows of planting holes with a dibble or pencil; space 1–2 in. apart.

3. Carefully lift out a small clump of seedlings with a plant label.

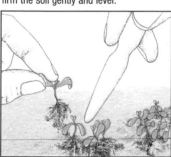

4. Hold a seedling by a leaf, and gently tease it away from the others.

5. Plant one seedling per hole, and firm surrounding soil.

6. Water the seedlings, and place in a cold frame or window.

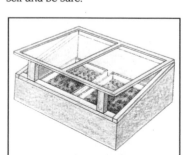

To harden mature seedlings, open the cold frame wider each day. Close in the evenings if the nights are cold, but make sure you open soon after sunup next morning to prevent overheating.

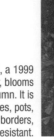

Verbena 'Quartz Burgundy', a 1999 All-America Selections winner, blooms from summer until autumn. It is suitable for window boxes, pots, hanging baskets, or borders, and is mildew-resistant.

Verbena 'Quartz Burgundy'

How to Grow Biennials

Biennials are plants that complete their life cycle in two growing seasons. They produce rosettes of leaves and sometimes stems the first year, but do not flower until the second, after which they die.

If given an early start, some biennials will flower the year they are sown. This can be a disadvantage, as they will then bloom later than they ordinarily would and at a time when temperatures may be too high for them to last well. This is particularly true of pansies, which produce sturdier plants and flower more prolifically when the weather is cool.

Certain biennials, honesty for example, tend to behave like perennials because they perpetuate themselves by self-sowing each year.

Also generally included among biennials are some plants that are actually perennials but are usually grown as biennials. This is because, after producing vigorous growth and plenty of blooms in their second year, these particular plants deteriorate to such an extent that they are not worth retaining. Examples include sweet Williams, some forget-me-nots, and wallflowers.

Seeds of biennials can be sown in early to mid summer in Zones 2–6, in early to mid autumn in Zones 7–8, and in late autumn in Zones 9–11.

Sow directly outdoors, as for annuals (see p. 192), in a lightly shaded area. Seeds can be sown in rows or broadcast. (If preferred, sow in a flat or in a large pot.) Water the seeds with a fine sprinkler. To keep them from drying out, you may find it helpful to cover the seeded area with a piece of burlap topped with a sheet of plastic.

After a week inspect daily for germination. Remove the covering as soon as the first seeds sprout; otherwise the seedlings will become spindly or die.

When the seedlings are well developed, lift them carefully and transplant them to a sunny or lightly shaded nursery bed.

If more convenient, plants can be raised in an unheated greenhouse or cold frame and then set out into flats or beds (as shown on p. 194). Sow them at the same time as when seeding directly outdoors, and take care not to allow the temperature to rise above 70°F. Some form of shading may be needed.

In cold regions it is essential that biennial plants be set in their flowering positions in time to become established—six to eight weeks before the first hard frost. This includes those that have been raised in a greenhouse or cold frame.

Before final planting, clear the bed, dig over the soil, and work in well-rotted manure or compost, together with bone meal at the rate of 40 pounds per 100 square feet.

Lift the plants from the site to which they had been transplanted, easing them out with a trowel and leaving as many roots as possible attached to each plant. If the soil is very dry, water it first to ease the lifting and to minimize the possibility of root damage.

After lifting, put the plants in their permanent positions as soon as possible, before their roots can dry out. Firm the soil around the plants and water. Wilting is seldom a problem at this time of year because the sun is not intense; if it is, provide shade.

In cold areas plants put out in exposed positions will need winter protection. Lay a few evergreen branches over them after the soil freezes, and then remove them gradually in spring. An alternative is to winter plants in a cold frame.

Although biennials are usually transplanted at least once, they can be sown in their permanent positions and later thinned.

Some so-called biennials, notably sweet Williams and foxgloves, will often survive an extra season if the stems are cut back to the basal rosette of leaves immediately after flowering.

What Can Go Wrong With Annuals and Biennials

Most annuals and biennials are remarkably free of pests. However, if your plants show any symptoms that are not described below, consult the section on plant disorders on page 506. Look up more information on controls on page 542.

SYMPTOMS AND SIGNS	CAUSE	CONTROL
Young stems appear distorted, flowers do not develop properly. Plant is sticky and covered with green or black insects.	Aphids	Spray plants with a strong stream of water; repeat at 5-day intervals. For severe infestations, use insecticidal soap.
Leaves and petals have irregular, ragged holes.	Earwigs	Use a hot pepper/garlic spray to repel earwigs.
Leaves have silvery spots. Leaves, buds, and flowers may be entangled with webs.	Mites	Spray plants with a strong stream of water; repeat at 5-day intervals. For severe infestations, apply insecticidal soap or neem.
Shoots and leaves are stunted and crippled. Leaves, especially younger ones, have spots and sometimes small, ragged holes. Flower buds are deformed or fail to develop.	Plant bugs (four-lined, harlequin, or tarnished)	Spray plants with garlic spray to repel the bugs. Spray young nymphs with *Beauveria bassiana*. As a last resort, use insecticidal soap.
Leaves are finely mottled and appear silvery, especially during hot, dry weather. No webbing.	Thrips	Use repellent garlic or hot pepper sprays; apply *Beauveria bassiana* or spinosad.
Young shoots are spun together with fine threads; growing points are eaten out of shoots by small greenish caterpillars.	Leaf-chewing caterpillar	Spray with *Bacillus thuringiensis kurstaki* or pick off infested shoots by hand.
Holes in foliage, silvery slime trails visible (young plants likeliest to be damaged).	Slugs and snails	Scatter iron phosphate baits on the soil around plants; reapply when eaten or every two weeks; set out shallow bowls of beer.
Small white flies dart about when plant is touched.	Whiteflies	Spray infested plants with *Beauveria bassiana* or neem.
Seedlings (particularly those thickly sown in pots, pans or boxes under glass) rot at ground level and topple over.	Damping-off (fungus)	Prevent disease by using sterilized medium, sowing thinly, not overwatering.
Leaves and young shoots are covered with fine white or gray powder; accompanied by stunting or slight crippling of plant.	Mildew (fungus)	Spray with potassium bicarbonate product or, near the end of the season, uproot and discard infected plants.
Plants are stunted, with small or malformed leaves showing yellow mottling or veins. Plants flower poorly.	Virus disease	Destroy plants as soon as symptoms are noticed. If viruses have been a past problem, spray to control viral insects.

Annuals and Biennials to Grow

In the chart that follows are popular and readily available annuals and biennials. Plants are listed according to their botanical names, with their best-known common names (as found in most catalogs and on seed packets) in parentheses. If you cannot find a particular plant, check the name you know in the Index.

Height and spread indicate the possible range, but note that the specific height will depend on the variety. Hence it is important to check this point before making a purchase.

Appropriate soil and light conditions for each individual plant are listed using pictograms. A key explaining the pictograms is found at the bottom of this page and every left-hand page.

Those variety names that are followed by an asterisk, such as Anchusa 'Blue Bird'*, are All-America Selections (see p. 191). They are generally superior in growth and bloom.

Amaranthus caudatus

Ageratum houstonianum
(flossflower)

Amaranthus caudatus
(love-lies-bleeding)

Amaranthus tricolor
(Joseph's coat)

Anchusa capensis
(summer forget-me-not)

Angelonia angustifolia
(angelonia)

BOTANICAL AND COMMON NAMES	HEIGHT	SPREAD	SOIL	LIGHT	SPECIES AND VARIETIES	SPECIAL REQUIREMENTS AND REMARKS
Ageratum houstonianum (ageratum, or flossflower) Mostly low-edging plants, with dense clusters of flowers like small powder puffs. Blooms over long period.	5 in.–2 ft.	6–9 in.	■	◑ ●	'Hawaii White', white; 'Adriatic', 'Bavaria', 'Blue Lagoon', 'Pacific', 'Blue Mink', many shades of blue; 'Royal Hawaii', royal purple; 'Swing Pink', pink.	Best started indoors from seeds; seeds germinate in 10 days. Plants tender when small. Pinching not usually necessary. Remove faded flowers. Seeds can be sown in late summer for fall bloom in mild-climate areas.
Amaranthus caudatus (love-lies-bleeding, or tassel flower) Somewhat coarse plants bear long, drooping tassels composed of very small flowers. Good dried flower.	2–2½ ft.	1½ ft.	□	●	*A. caudatus*, red. *A. c.* 'Viridis' has bright green tassels—good for dried flower arrangements.	Start seeds indoors about 6 wk. in advance of outdoor planting date, or sow directly outdoors after soil warms. Seedlings difficult to transplant, but will often self-seed.
Amaranthus tricolor (amaranthus, or Joseph's coat) Grown for brilliantly colored leaves.	3–4 ft.	1½–2 ft.	□	●	'Early Splendor', crimson top leaves, darker lower leaves; 'Illumination', red and gold top leaves, chocolate lower leaves; 'Joseph's Coat', red and gold top leaves, chocolate lower leaves.	Colors most brilliant in poor soil. Avoid excessive moisture. Start seeds indoors for large plants. Good background or accent plant, but use sparingly.
Anchusa capensis (anchusa, or summer forget-me-not) Biennial valued for its clusters of small blue flowers in summer. (Not to be confused with myosotis, true annual forget-me-not, or with perennial anchusa, p. 45).	9 in.–1½ ft.	10 in.	■	● ◑	'Blue Angel', ultramarine blue with white eyes, 9 in.; 'Blue Bird'*, clear gentian blue, 1½ ft.; 'Dawn', blue, pink, or white, 1½ ft.	Chill seeds 72 hr. before planting to speed germination. Sow seeds in full sun or partial shade, and provide plenty of moisture. Mass for best effect. Cut back by half after first bloom to encourage further flowering.
Angelonia angustifolia (angelonia) Tropical perennial treated as an annual in the north. Upright plants bear spikes of pink, mauve, white, or blue flowers; are heat and drought resistant; and flower over a long period.	10–12 in.	12–15 in.	■	●	Recent introductions that are rapidly becoming popular. Look for AngelMist®, Angelface® or Serina™ Series in a range of colors.	Buy plants and set out once the soil has warmed. Seed can be sown indoors 8–10 wk. before last frost and needs light to germinate. Grow the seedlings at 70°F.

■ well drained to sandy ■ moist ■ wet ▨ acidic ■ alkaline □ regular soil ● full sun ◑ partial shade ● shade

English daisies (*Bellis*) are a lawn weed in mild climates, but the cultivated forms are good for window boxes and planters everywhere. From May to September, the wax begonia has many small red, rose, or white blossoms. Depending on the variety, leaves are pale green, coppery, or reddish.

Bellis perennis 'Dresden China'

Begonia semperflorens

Antirrhinum majus
(snapdragon)

Arctotis
(African daisy)

Begonia semperflorens
(wax begonia)

Begonia tuberhybrida
(tuberous begonia)

Bellis perennis
(English daisy)

Bidens ferulifolia
(bidens)

Brachyscome iberidifolia
(Swan River daisy)

BOTANICAL AND COMMON NAMES	HEIGHT	SPREAD	SOIL	LIGHT	SPECIES AND VARIETIES	SPECIAL REQUIREMENTS AND REMARKS
Antirrhinum majus (snapdragon) Spikes of closely set individual flowers, mostly single, with unusual construction that enables them to be squeezed so that they snap open, hence common name. Tall kinds are excellent for cutting.	7 in.–4 ft.	9 in.–1½ ft.	■	●	Many varieties in mixed or separate colors: white, lavender, pink, rose, yellow, orange, red. Butterfly type has open-faced flowers with flaring petals. Check height of variety when buying, since there is wide range, from Chimes series at 6 in. to Rockets at 4 ft.	Sow seeds indoors 6–8 wk. before last spring frost; grow at 50°F. Sow outdoors in cold frame where winters are mild. Or buy plants in spring. May overwinter in warmer regions. Remove faded spikes of blooms for further flowering.
Arctotis species and hybrids (arctotis, or African daisy) Large single daisylike flowers that close at night.	10 in.	1 ft.	■	●	Hybrids come in colors that include white, pink, orange apricot, red, and terra-cotta, most with deeper color toward center.	Sow seeds early indoors, or sow outdoors when there is no danger of frost. Does best where summers are cool. Withstands drought.
Begonia semperflorens (wax begonia) A long-flowering plant with attractive, waxy leaves. Numerous small, usually single flowers.	6 in.–1 ft.	6 in.–15 ft.	■	●◐	A wide selection is available in white, white-tinged pink, and shades of pink and red. Green-leaved forms include Ambassador, Bayou, Olympia, and Varsity series. Hybrids with bronze leaves include Cocktail, Nightlife, and Senator series.	Buy plants or start dustlike seeds indoors at least 2 mo. in advance of outdoor planting time. Not easily started indoors. Plant in soil mixed with compost. Pot up in fall for growing indoors.
Begonia tuberhybrida (tuberous begonia) Seed-grown tuberous begonias make a tuber large enough to store only in regions with long frost-free periods. Normally treated as disposable annuals. Flowers much larger than those of wax begonias.	9–15 in.	8–12 in.	■	●●	Several different series are available, each in a range of colors; Pin Up have dark leaves and single flowers (Pin Up Flame was an All-America Selections winner); Non Stop are bright green with double flowers; Show Angel are pendulous and good for hanging baskets or window boxes.	Seed is very fine and slow to germinate and grow; start indoors about 12 wk. before last frost date. Not easy to grow indoors from seed, but make good pot plants.
Bellis perennis (English daisy) Flowers, usually double, 1–2 in. across, appear in spring and early summer on low, compact plants. Perennial, usually grown as biennial.	4–6 in.	3–6 in.	■	●◐	'Buttons Mixture', mixed-seed doubles of assorted colors including white, pink, red. Habanera Series, pink, white, or red, with large flowers.	Plants commonly sold in early spring, along with pansies, but can be started from seeds one year to bloom the next. Remove faded flowers. Will not overwinter below Zone 5.
Bidens ferulifolia (bidens) Free-flowering, spreading plant with fine leaves and bright yellow flowers all summer. Tender perennial normally grown from cuttings, but will self-seed.	8–12 in.	30 in.	■	●	'Gold Marie', spreading; 'Goldie', more compact; 'Solaire™ Yellow', compact, 8 in.	Ideal for edging, window boxes and hanging baskets. Cut back only if it grows out of bounds.
Brachyscome iberidifolia (Swan River daisy) Spreading, drought-tolerant plant with fragrant flowers. Good for borders, window boxes, and cut flowers.	18 in.	16 in.	□	●	Species has blue, mauve, or white flowers. Splendor Series is shorter (10 in.) and available in individual colors; flowers have a dark eye. *B. multifida* (rock daisy) has pink and yellow varieties, 'Break O'Day' and 'Lemon Mist'.	Sow seed indoors about one month before last frost. Pinch out tips of seedlings at 6 leaf stage to make plants branch out. Or sow outdoors after frost danger is past for later flowering.

■ well drained to sandy ■ moist ■ wet ■ acidic ■ alkaline □ regular soil ● full sun ◐ partial shade ● shade

Pot marigold (*Calendula*) is a good cut flower: the bushy 'Fiesta Gitana' is a dwarf form.

Calendula officinalis 'Fiesta Gitana'

Brassica oleracea
(ornamental cabbage)

Browallia speciosa
(browallia)

Calendula officinalis
(pot marigold)

Calibrachoa hybrida
(many bells)

Callistephus chinensis
(China aster)

Campanula medium
(Canterbury bell)

Capsicum annuum
(ornamental pepper)

BOTANICAL AND COMMON NAMES	HEIGHT	SPREAD	SOIL	LIGHT	SPECIES AND VARIETIES	SPECIAL REQUIREMENTS AND REMARKS
Brassica oleracea acephala (ornamental cabbage, and kale) Grown for ornamental leaves, which are tinged with cream, purple, pink, rose, or red, especially toward center of plant.	12–18 in.	1½ ft.	☐	●	Newer strains have made these increasingly popular. Look for 'Osaka' and 'Peacock' cabbage (the latter has feathery outer leaves), and 'Nagoya' or 'Sparrow' kale (both are edible, but tend to be coarse).	Can be started indoors or sown directly outdoors. Actually tender biennials that are killed by frost the first year before they can bloom the next. Flowers of no value. Leaves useful in flower arrangements. Good for color late in season.
Browallia (browallia species) Trumpet-shaped flowers up to 2 in. across on slender branched stems.	10 in.–2 ft.	10 in.	■	◐	*B. speciosa* (bush violet). Bells and Starlight Series have flowers of blue shades or white.	Sow seeds early indoors, or buy plants. Provide ample water. Pinch plants when 3 in. tall to force side shoots.
Calendula officinalis (calendula, or pot marigold) Flowers to 4 in. across, single or double. Light green leaves have pungent aroma. Good cut flower. Not to be confused with African or French marigolds.	6–20 in.	6 in.–1 ft.	■	●◐	'Golden Gem', dwarf, double, yellow; 'Pacific Beauty', double, yellow, orange, apricot; 'Orange Gem', double, medium orange; 'Sunny Boy', dwarf, mixed-seed packets of assorted colors. 'Bon Bon' is dwarf in yellow, apricot, and orange. 'Fiesta Gitana', bushy mix includes bicolors.	Seeds germinate readily outdoors; can be sown in fall or winter in frost-free areas. Tolerates low-fertility soil. Does best in cool weather; double flowers may be semi-double in extreme heat. Self-sows.
Calibrachoa hybrida (many bells) Similar to petunias but with hundreds of small bell-shaped flowers covering the plant. Excellent for hanging baskets and planters.	6–10 in.	12–18 in.	☐	●	Many different strains in a wide range of colors. Million Bells was the original, but Superbells, Spring Fling, Cabaret, and Colorburst are now available. MiniFamous™ has double flowers.	Buy plants for earliest bloom and set out when danger of frost is past. Sow seed indoors 10 wk. before last frost date. If flowering becomes less, cut back halfway and feed.
Callistephus chinensis (China aster) Attractive flowers, usually double, borne in late summer and through fall. Wide range in height—tall kinds make excellent cut flowers.	6 in.–2½ ft.	1–1½ ft.	☐	●	Many shades of white, blue, pink, rose, and scarlet. Varieties offered as extra early, midseason, or late flowering. Select according to height desired. Petals often curled, or quilled.	Best to grow in new location each year because of soil-borne diseases. Control leafhoppers that spread virus.
Campanula medium (Canterbury bell) Spikes of large, bell-shaped flowers, single or double. Usually grown as biennial.	2–2½ ft.	10 in.	■	●	Mixed-seed packets of white, blue, mauve, pink, or separate colors. *C. m.* 'Calycanthema' (cup and saucer) includes two types: in fully double flowers, one bell (or cup) fits closely within the other; in others, cup sits on a saucerlike outer bell.	Buy plants in spring to bloom in early summer, or sow seeds in summer to bloom the next year. Water freely in dry weather. May need staking.
Capsicum annuum (ornamental pepper) Short, bushy plants with edible fruits grown for their decorative value. Good as edging or in containers. Potted, they make good table centers.	8–20 in.	6–20 in.	■	●	'Chilly Chili'* has dark green foliage and 2 in. long, upright peppers that turn from yellow, through orange to red. 'Black Pearl'* has almost black leaves and round, shiny, black peppers that turn red when mature.	Ornamental peppers take up to 24 wk. from sowing to first flowers. Buy plants and set out once the soil is warm. Cold soil may cause flowers to drop off.

Pollution-resistant vinca, or periwinkle (*Catharanthus roseus*), is a good choice for city gardens or urban window boxes. Clarkia can be sown outside and is a good cut flower. The scented blooms of the long-flowering spider flower (*Cleome*) close in the afternoon.

Catharanthus roseus

Clarkia unguiculata

Cleome hassleriana

Catharanthus roseus (periwinkle)

Celosia argentea (cockscomb)

Centaurea cyanus (cornflower)

Chrysanthemum (chrysanthemum)

Clarkia (clarkia)

Cleome spinosa (spider flower)

BOTANICAL AND COMMON NAMES	HEIGHT	SPREAD	SOIL	LIGHT	SPECIES AND VARIETIES	SPECIAL REQUIREMENTS AND REMARKS
Catharanthus roseus (vinca, or periwinkle) Single 5-petaled flowers up to 1 in. across. Shiny green leaves are attractive throughout summer.	6–10 in	1–2 ft.	☐	●◑	Cooler Series, deep pink to white; Heatwave Series, mostly with contrasting eye; 'Parasol'*, white with red eye; 'Pretty in Rose'*, bright pink; 'Pacifica Burgundy Hale'* has larger flowers.	Sow seeds indoors at least 12 wk. in advance of outdoor planting season, or buy plants. Pinch to encourage branching. Withstands city conditions well.
Celosia argentea (celosia, or cockscomb) Showy plants with widely differing forms. Flowers of crested cockscomb are stiff, resemble rooster's comb; plumed cockscombs are feathery. Excellent dried flowers.	6 in.–3 ft.	9 in.–1 ft.	☐	●	*C. a. cristata* (crested): 'Big Chief', mixed; 'Gladiator', gold; 'Toreador'*, red; 'Fireglow'*, scarlet; 'Prestige Scarlet'*, bright red; *C. a. plumosa* (plumed): 'Red Fox'*, deep orange-red; 'Forest Fire'*, red; Century and Freshlook* Series in individual colors; 'Apricot Brandy'*, orange.	Sow seeds after soil warms outdoors. Does best in warm weather. Stake tall varieties. Plants usually available. To dry, pick in prime, strip off leaves, and hang upside down in airy, shaded place.
Centaurea cyanus (cornflower, or bachelor's button) Tall or dwarf plants with myriads of 2-in. flowers and small gray-green leaves. Good cut flower.	1–3 ft.	1 ft.	■	●	'Snowball'*, white; 'Jubilee Gem', blue, 1 ft. 'Polka Dot Mixed', white, blue, lavender, pink, and red, 16 in. 'Snow Man', white; 'Blue Boy', blue; 'Pinkie', light pink; 'Red Boy', red, 2½–3 ft.	When planting outdoors sow seeds early where plants are to grow, since they resent transplanting. Seeds can be sown in late fall for earlier bloom. Blooms best in cool weather. Often self-sows.
Chrysanthemum species and hybrids (annual chrysanthemum) Easily grown plants, with mostly single, daisylike flowers and finely divided foliage. Especially good for those who find perennial kinds difficult. Taller kinds good for cut flowers.	10 in.–2½ft.	9 in.–1 ft.	☐	●	'Paludosum', white with gold edge; 'Golden Raindrops', yellow; 'Golden Gem', yellow, double. Also available in mixes of yellow, orange, and red shades, often with a contrasting color ring. Many perennial types, notably 'Korean', will bloom first season if sown early; colors include white, yellow, and red.	Grows quickly from seeds started indoors or sown outdoors. Water in dry weather. Pinch to encourage branching. Plants transplant readily; can be moved at any time, even when in bud or bloom.
Clarkia unguiculata, C. pulchella, and C. amoena (clarkia) Varied group with single or double flowers carried in loose clusters or spikes. Good border plants.	1–2 ft.	6 in.–1 ft.	■	●	Offered in mixed-seed packets of assorted colors that include white, lavender, pink, creamy yellow, salmon, and crimson. *C. amoena* (godetia, or satinflower) is bushier than other clarkias.	Grows best in cool weather. Sow seeds early outdoors. Thrives in poor soil that can be relatively dry in summer. Do not grow where humidity is high. In frost-free regions seeds can be sown in fall. Does not transplant readily.
Cleome spinosa (cleome, or spider flower) Dramatic plants with airy, scented flower heads, each flower with long stamens that give spidery effect; long seedpods have similar appearance. Foliage palmlike.	3–4 ft.	1½–2 ft.	☐	●◑	'Helen Campbell', white; 'Purple Queen', lilac-purple; 'Pink Queen', pink; 'Cherry Queen', cherry-rose; 'Ruby Queen', ruby-rose; 'Rose Queen', salmon-pink; 'Sparkler Blush'*, pink and white.	Sow seeds outdoors, preferably where plants are to grow, after weather warms; or buy plants. Flowers close in afternoon. Stems have sharp thorns. Self-sows; generally trouble-free.
Coleus blumei (coleus)					See *Solenostemon scutellarioides* p. 211.	

■ well drained to sandy ■ moist ■ wet ■ acidic ■ alkaline ☐ regular soil ● full sun ◑ partial shade ● shade

Although sowing inside is usually recommended in the north, cosmos can be sown directly into the ground in spring in milder areas, and may self-seed.

Cosmos bipinnatus

Consolida ajacis
(larkspur)

Convolvulus tricolor
(dwarf morning glory)

Coreopsis tinctoria
(calliopsis)

Cosmos bipinnatus
(cosmos)

Lagenaria
(ornamental gourds)

Cynoglossum amabile
(cynoglossum)

BOTANICAL AND COMMON NAMES	HEIGHT	SPREAD	SOIL	LIGHT	SPECIES AND VARIETIES	SPECIAL REQUIREMENTS AND REMARKS
Consolida ajacis (larkspur) Single or double blooms densely set along tall, tapering spikes with feathery, finely cut, bright green leaves. Good cut flower that also dries well.	14 in.–4 ft.	1 ft.	☐	◐	Available in seed packets of mixed or separate colors that include shades of white, blue, lavender, pink, salmon, and red. Two types: base branching with long side spikes, and hyacinth flowered with single 14-in. spikes.	Sow seeds outdoors in very early spring or in fall. Where winters are mild, make fall sowing in time for seedlings to emerge before cold weather; in other regions sow just before soil freezes so that seeds will not germinate until spring. Flowers best in cool weather. Difficult to transplant.
Convolvulus tricolor (dwarf morning glory) Fairly large flowers resembling true morning glories are borne on low, bushy, somewhat trailing plants. Flowers stay open all day, unlike older varieties of more familiar vine.	9 in.–1½ ft.	6 in.–9 in.	☐	●	Seed packets of assorted colors including white, blue, rose, and red. 'Royal Ensign', royal blue. Offered by only a few seed companies. 'Dwarf Picotee', mixed colors edged in white.	Nick or file hard seeds before sowing to hasten germination. Sow after soil has warmed. Plants need warmth to prosper. Can be used in hanging baskets or as edging plant in tubs. Remove faded blooms for further flowering.
Coreopsis tinctoria (calliopsis) Multitudes of daisylike flowers are carried on wiry stems with fine foliage. Easily grown. Good cut flower.	8 in.–3 ft.	1 ft.	☐	●	'Golden Ray', yellow with crimson central zone, 8 in.; 'Tiger Star', crimson, striped and mottled with yellow; mixed-seed packets of bicolors: purple, yellow, red; mixed-seed packets of bicolors: yellow, orange, red, 3 ft.	Sow seeds early outdoors where plants are to grow. Cut back after first bloom to encourage further flowering. Low-growing kinds tend to cease flowering in very hot weather.
Cosmos bipinnatus and **C. sulphureus** (cosmos) Delightfully airy plants with large single or semi-double daisylike flowers on long, wiry stems. Very fine foliage. Excellent cut flower.	1½–4 ft.	1½–2 ft.	☐	●	Klondyke type (*C. sulphureus*), semi-double; 'Early Sunrise'*, yellow, 1½ ft.; Ladybird Series, reds and yellows; 'Sunny Gold'*, yellow; 'Diablo'*, red, 2–2½ ft. Sensation type (*C. bipinnatus*), single. 'Seashells Mix', pink and red shades; 'Daydream', pale pink, darker center; 'Radiance'*, rose, 3–4 ft.	Sow seeds outdoors or buy young plants. Very rich soils encourage more foliage than flowers. Tall types may need support. Remove faded flowers for further blooming. Put cut flowers in deep water immediately to prevent wilting.
Cucumis, Cucurbita, Lagenaria, Luffa, and others (ornamental gourds) Tropical vines grown for ornamental fruits in unusual shapes, some with showy flowers. Inedible fruits are dried and used for indoor decoration.	8–10 ft.	1–2 ft.	☐	●	Generally offered in mixed-seed packets of several genera or separately by common names descriptive of the fruit's shape: bottle, caveman's club, dolphin, Hercules' club, nest egg, penguin, serpent, spoon, striped pear, Turk's turban, warty.	Sow outdoors after soil warms where plants are to grow. Provide fence or trellis; fruits less perfect if they rest on ground. Let ripen on vine; harvest before frost. Do not bruise. Wash with disinfectant; dry in airy place. Apply floor wax; polish.
Cynoglossum amabile (cynoglossum, or Chinese forget-me-not) Clustered fragrant flowers and gray-green foliage. Biennial, usually grown as annual.	1½–2 ft.	1 ft.	☐	◐	'Firmament'*, sky-blue, 1½ ft. 'Blanche Burpee', white and various shades of blue; *C. amabile*, blue, 2 ft.	Best sown early outdoors where plants are to flower. Blooms quickly from seeds. Can also be sown in fall in warmer areas.

Excellent cut flowers, dahlias offer a tremendous choice of flower shape, size, and color. Foxglove (*Digitalis*) bears 3- to 5-ft. spikes of flowers.

Dahlia 'Redskin'

Digitalis purpurea f. *albiflora*

Dahlia
(dahlia)

Dianthus barbatus
(sweet William)

Dianthus caryophyllus
(carnation)

Dianthus chinensis
(China pink)

Digitalis purpurea
(foxglove)

Dorotheanthus bellidiformis
(Livingston daisy)

BOTANICAL AND COMMON NAMES	HEIGHT	SPREAD	SOIL	LIGHT	SPECIES AND VARIETIES	SPECIAL REQUIREMENTS AND REMARKS
Dahlia hybrids (dahlia) Neat and attractive bushy plants that bear single to double flowers over long period. Shiny green leaves. Makes excellent cut flower. See also p. 142.	1–2 ft.	1½–2 ft.	☐	●	Mixed-seed packets of assorted colors, including white, pink, yellow, orange, and red. Double and semi-double: double 'Figaro', mix or individual colors; 'Diablo Mixed', red foliage, 'Redskin'*. Single: 'Harlequin', two-toned; 'Dandy', dwarf. Taller kinds take longer to bloom.	Sow seeds early indoors, later outdoors, or buy young plants. Water during dry spells. Remove faded blooms for further flowering. Tubers can be dug after foliage has been killed by frost; store during winter months in cool, dry location.
Dianthus barbatus (sweet William) Densely packed heads of mildly fragrant, single or double flowers above neat basal foliage. Both annual and biennial varieties available; often perennial in Zone 6 and into Zone 4 if there is snow cover.	4 in.–1½ ft.	8–10 in.	☐	●	Annual: 'Red Monarch'*, red; 'Roundabout', shades of red, some patterned; 'Wee Willie', shades of red. Biennial: in mixed-seed packets of assorted colors: white, pink, salmon, crimson, scarlet; some bicolored. Dynasty Series has double flowers.	Sow seeds of annual kinds outdoors in early spring as soon as soil can be worked. Sow biennial kinds in spring or summer.
Dianthus caryophyllus (carnation) Garden-grown plants bear the familiar, fragrant florists' blossoms, but usually smaller. Wiry stems. Excellent cut flower.	1–2 ft.	1 ft.	■ ■	●	White and many shades of purple, pink, yellow, salmon, apricot, and red. Available in seed packets of separate or mixed colors. 'Scarlet Luminette'*, does especially well as annual. Lillipot Series are dwarf. 'Can Can Scarlet'* is very fragrant.	In cold regions grow as annual; start seeds early indoors. In warm areas can be grown as biennial or perennial. Plant in neutral or slightly alkaline soil. Stake tall varieties.
Dianthus chinensis (annual pink, or China pink) Scented, single to double flowers borne in great profusion. Good cut flower.	7 in.–1 ft.	6 in.–1 ft.	☐ ■	●	'Magic Charms'*, single, serrated, white, pink, red. 'Telstar Picotee'*, red, edged white; 'Ideal Violet'*, large flowers; 'Snowfire'*, white with red eye. 'Supra Purple'* is heat-tolerant.	Sow seeds outdoors as soon as soil can be worked or indoors 6–8 wk. earlier. Grow in slightly alkaline soil. Keep faded blooms picked to encourage further flowering.
Digitalis purpurea (foxglove) Tall spikes of closely set tubular flowers. Large, basal leaves. Generally grown as biennial unless started very early. Leaves poisonous if eaten.	3–5 ft.	1–1½ ft.	■	◐	In mixed-seed packets of white, purple, pink, rose, and yellow. 'Excelsior' and 'Shirley' have flowers all around stem, with 'Excelsior' more horizontal than pendant; 'Foxy'* blooms in 5 mo.	Sow early indoors for bloom same season or outdoors in late summer for bloom next year. Mulch with very light, airy material after ground freezes.
Dorotheanthus bellidiformis, or Mesembryanthemum criniflorum (Livingston daisy) Succulent with single 2-in. flowers resembling true daisies. Leaves are bright green and fleshy.	4 in.	1 ft.	■	●	'Magic Carpet' has assorted colors including buff, pink, rose, primrose, apricot, and crimson. Related to ice plant (*Mesembryanthemum crystallinum*, or *Cryophytum crystallinum*).	Sow seeds indoors at least 2 mo. prior to safe outdoor planting date, or sow directly outdoors after danger of frost is past. Plants sometimes available. Does best in hot, dry regions.

■ well drained to sandy ■ moist ■ wet ■ acidic ■ alkaline ☐ regular soil ● full sun ◐ partial shade ● shade

Daisylike gaillardia, or blanketflower, thrives in hot conditions and is self-sowing.

Gaillardia 'Kobold'

Erysimum cheiri
(English wallflower)

Eschscholzia californica
(California poppy)

Euphorbia marginata
(euphorbia)

Eustoma grandiflorum
(lisianthus)

Gaillardia pulchella
(blanketflower)

Gazania
(gazania)

BOTANICAL AND COMMON NAMES	HEIGHT	SPREAD	SOIL	LIGHT	SPECIES AND VARIETIES	SPECIAL REQUIREMENTS AND REMARKS
Erysimum cheiri (English wallflower) Flower spikes consist of fragrant, closely set, 4-petaled flowers up to 1 in. across. Does best in cool coastal areas.	15 in.–2 ft.	8 in.–1 ft.	☐	●	Listed in various ways in catalogs. *E. cheiri* comes in shades of purple, yellow, orange, red. Siberian wallflower, *E. allionii*, yellow and orange.	To grow as annual, sow seeds 8–10 wk. before last spring frost; to grow as biennial, sow in early summer. *E. cheiri* hardy only to Zone 5; *E. allionii* hardy to Zone 3.
Eschscholzia californica (California poppy) Masses of saucer-shaped flowers on low-spreading plants with finely cut leaves. Flowers close at night, reopen next day.	1 ft.	2 ft.	☐	●	'Ballerina', red, pink; semi-double or double, yellow; 'Mission Bells', semi-double or double, in shades of rose, yellow, orange, crimson; many two toned and with ruffled edges; 'Apricot Flambeau', yellow-edged coral; Thai Silk Series, compact, fluted, red shades.	Sow seeds in early spring where plants are to grow (difficult to transplant). Does well in dry areas. Flowers best in cool weather. When weather is hot, foliage yellows, and plants are best discarded. The California poppy often self-sows.
Euphorbia heterophylla and **E. marginata** (euphorbia) Both these euphorbias are grown for ornamental leaves and bracts that are attractively colored, give effect similar to flowers, and last over very long summer season. Latex sap of both kinds can cause skin irritation.	1½–3 ft.	1 ft.	■	●	*E. heterophylla* (Mexican fire plant, or annual poinsettia), green leaves turn bright red toward top in summer. *E. marginata* (snow-on-the-mountain), green leaves are edged or streaked in white. To 2 ft. high.	Sow seeds of *E. heterophylla* indoors early or outdoors after soil warms; sow *E. marginata* seeds very early outdoors (often self-sows). Grow both in sandy soil that is low in nutrients. Sear stem ends in flame or dip in boiling water to prevent loss of sap when using branches as cut flowers.
Eustoma grandiflorum (lisianthus or prairie gentian) Upright plants with gray-green leaves and upright, satiny, bell-shaped flowers, often with a darker center. A long lasting cut flower.	8–36 in.	12 in.	☐ ■	● ●	Flamenco, Heidi, and Yodel Series are tall, 18 in.; Lisa and Sapphire Series are short, 8 in., while Echo Series have double flowers. All come in shades of pink, cream, blue, and rose.	Sow seeds indoors 8 wk. before last frost, seedlings are slow growing. For an early display, buy plants and set out when frost is past. Taller varieties may need support in open locations.
Gaillardia pulchella (gaillardia, or blanketflower) Single or double daisylike flowers, often with contrasting color on tips of petals. Tall and short kinds. Good cut flower.	1–2 ft.	1–1½ ft.	☐	●	In mixed-seed packets of assorted colors or separate colors including rose, yellow, orange, scarlet, mahogany. 'Red Plume'*, fully double; 'Portola Giants', scarlet, tipped gold; 'Arizona Sun'*, red and yellow; 'Sundance Bicolor'* is double red-tipped yellow.	Start seeds early indoors or sow outdoors later. Thrives in heat. Drought-tolerant. Remove faded blooms to encourage further flowering. Self-sows.
Gazania (gazania) Spreading plants with lance shaped leaves and daisylike, brightly colored flowers on upright stalks all summer. May be hardy in mild climates.	8–10 in.	10 in.	■	● ●	Mostly available in mixed colors (yellow, pink, orange, red, and bronze) such as Daybreak or Sunshine Giants Series, but 'Mini-star Tangerine' and 'Mini-star Yellow' are single colored. Remove old flowers to extend flowering.	Sow indoors 10 wk. before last frost date and plant out once the soil is warm. Grow seedlings in a soil-based potting soil with added sharp sand, rather than a peat-based mix.

One of the tallest annuals, the sunflower (*Helianthus*) grows up to 15 ft. and develops plate-size blossoms. 'Moonwalker', a less common variety, reaches this size. Candytuft (*Iberis*) makes a good ground cover plant. It is fragrant and will self-seed in all but the harshest climates.

Helianthus 'Moonwalker'

Iberis amara

Gomphrena globosa
(globe amaranth)

Gypsophila elegans
(baby's breath)

Helianthus
(sunflower)

Heliotropium
(heliotrope)

Hibiscus moscheutos
(rose mallow)

Iberis
(candytuft)

BOTANICAL AND COMMON NAMES	HEIGHT	SPREAD	SOIL	LIGHT	SPECIES AND VARIETIES	SPECIAL REQUIREMENTS AND REMARKS
Gomphrena globosa (globe amaranth, or gomphrena) Small, round, papery flower heads on tall or dwarf plants. Long-lasting cut flower; dries well.	9 in.–1½ ft.	6–8 in.	☐	●	'Dwarf Buddy', rich purple; Gnome Series comes in several shades. 'Strawberry Fields' (*G. haageana*) is taller and a brilliant red. Woodcreek Series is good for cutting.	Sow seeds early indoors or directly outdoors after soil warms. Germinates in 2 wk. Best grown where summers are hot. To dry, pick when flowers open; hang them upside down in dry location.
Gypsophila elegans (gypsophila, or baby's breath) Masses of small, starry flowers lend airy effect to garden when intermixed with more substantial plants. Narrow leaves. Good filler for bouquets.	15 in.– 1½ ft.	8–10 in.	■	●	'Covent Garden', giant flowered, white; 'Snow Fountain', improved 'Covent Garden'; 'Rosea', pink; 'Gypsy'*, white with a pink flush. 'Gypsy Deep Rose'*, dark pink. For perennial gypsophila, or baby's breath, see p. 54.	Sow outdoors where plants are to grow; thin seedlings if necessary. Make repeated sowings at 4- to 5-wk. intervals to ensure continued bloom, since plants flower for relatively short time.
Helianthus species (sunflower, annual) Low-growing varieties of sunflower are best for general garden use; tall kinds for background plants. For perennial sunflower, see *Helianthus*, p. 54.	1½–10 ft.	1–2 ft.	☐	●	'Moonshadow', single, white to cream; 'Teddy Bear', double, yellow; 'Pacino Gold', bushy, orange, 1½–4 ft.; 'Amit', double, yellow; 'Moulin Rouge', dark red; 'Mammoth Russian', golden; 'Sunbright Supreme', lemon yellow, 6–10 ft.	Sow seeds outdoors, preferably where plants are to grow (difficult to transplant). Makes rapid growth; so no need to start early indoors. Birds eat seeds that follow flowers.
Heliotropium hybrids (heliotrope) Old-fashioned plants prized for fragrant heads of small flowers. Good container plant; often grown as standard.	15 in.–2 ft. taller in South	1–1½ ft.	☐	●	'Blue Opal', dark blue; 'Marine', rich violet; 'Mini Marine', dwarf.	Sow seeds indoors 2 mo. in advance of outdoor planting date. Wait until weather warms before setting out, since very sensitive to cold. Grow in rich soil, with not too much water. Plants occasionally sold.
Hibiscus moscheutos (hibiscus, or rose mallow) Huge, open bowl-shaped flowers, 10 in. across, on tall, fast-growing plants. Usually grown as perennial, but a recent variety that blooms first year from seeds justifies inclusion as annual.	5 ft.	2 ft.	☐	●	'Southern Belle'*, in mixed-seed packets of assorted colors or separate colors of white, white bicolor, and pink; 'Disco Belle' are dwarf (2 ft.), red, pink, white.	Sow indoors 6 mo. before outdoor planting date; takes 3 wk. to germinate. Grow in sunny window. Transplant to individual pots. When frost danger is past, plant outdoors in sunny location. Water in dry spells. In cold regions, mulching over winter may bring them through.
Iberis species (candytuft) Numerous small flowers in heads (globe flowered,) or spikes (hyacinth flowered).	8 in.–1½ ft.	6 in.–1 ft.	☐	●	*I. amara* (hyacinth flowered): 'Empress', giant, white; 'Iceberg', large, white. *I. umbellata* (globe flowered): 'Dwarf Fairy', white, lavender, purple, pink, rose, and red; 'Red Flash', red with yellow centers.	Sow seeds early, in a sunny location where plants are to bloom. Does best in cool weather; in frost-free areas, can be sown in fall for bloom in winter. Remove faded blooms to encourage further flowering unless self-sowing is desired. Withstands air pollution.

■ well drained to sandy ■ moist ■ wet ■ acidic ■ alkaline ☐ regular soil ● full sun ◐ partial shade ● shade

Individual blooms of the climbing morning glory (*Ipomoea*) only last a day, but the plant is in flower in midsummer.

Ipomoea purpurea

Impatiens balsamina
(garden balsam)

Impatiens New Guinea
New Guinea

Impatiens walleriana
(patience plant)

Ipomoea tricolor
(morning glory)

Lathyrus odoratus
(sweet pea)

Lavatera trimestris
(tree mallow)

BOTANICAL AND COMMON NAMES	HEIGHT	SPREAD	SOIL	LIGHT	SPECIES AND VARIETIES	SPECIAL REQUIREMENTS AND REMARKS
Impatiens balsamina (garden balsam) Waxy, usually double, camellialike flowers borne close to and toward top of stem. Not good for cutting.	10 in.– 2½ ft.	1–1½ ft.	■	◕	Many colors available, including white, purple, pink, salmon, and red, some with white markings on petals. Various heights available.	Sow seeds early indoors or outdoors after there is no danger of frost. Does not tolerate cold, wet weather.
Impatiens New Guinea hybrid Popular plants grown for their colored foliage and large flowers. They will withstand more sun than other impatiens. Most varieties grown from cuttings, but some from seed.	1–2 ft.	1½ ft.	□	●	Many named forms from cuttings. From seed, 'Spectra', dark green leaves, pink, red, salmon shades; 'Tango'*, bright orange; Infinity™ Series, in a range of colors, have green to purple foliage.	Sow seeds as below, buy plants of cutting varieties. Plant outside in a sunny location when danger of frost is passed.
Impatiens walleriana hybrids (busy Lizzie, or patience plant) Single or double flowers; waxy, deep green leaves. Superior plant for constant bloom all summer. Little or no care required.	6 in.–2 ft.	1–2 ft.	□	◑	Available in mixed or separate colors that include white, purple, pink, orange, salmon, carmine, and red, some with deeper-colored centers or striped or flecked petals. Blitz 2000 Series, 14 in.; Accent Series, 8 in.; Deco Series, 8 in., with dark leaves; Super Elfin Series, 10 in.; Tempo Series, 9 in., early; 'Victorian Rose'*, double, pink.	Buy plants or sow seeds indoors 8-10 wk. before safe outdoor planting time, when weather is warm. Grow in soil well mixed with compost. Water in dry spells. Not necessary to remove faded flowers. Perennial in frost-free areas. Cuttings root quickly.
Ipomoea purpurea and **I. tricolor** (morning glory) Popular vine with single or occasionally double flowers, some edged or striped with white, up to 8 in. across. Older varieties close in afternoon; some newer ones stay open most of day.	10 ft.	1 ft.	□	●	'Pearly Gates'*, white; 'Flying Saucers', white and blue striped; 'Early Call', blue, rose, or mixed; 'Heavenly Blue', sky-blue; 'Wedding Bells', rose-lavender; 'Scarlet O'Hara'*, crimson; 'Japanese Imperial', mixed colors, huge flowers; 'Tinkerbell's Petticoat', double. For dwarf forms, see *Convolvulus* p. 201.	Speed germination by enclosing seeds in wet paper towels for 48 hr. in warm (75°–80°F) place prior to sowing, or nick pointed end of seeds. Start early indoors in pots (resents root disturbance), or sow outdoors where plants are to grow, in not too rich soil. Provide support.
Lathyrus odoratus (sweet pea) Old-fashioned favorite with climbing and nonclimbing forms. Many varieties are fragrant. Good cut flower.	8 in.–10 ft.	3–6 ft.	□	●	Many varieties of tall climbers offered in mixed-seed packets or in individual colors: white, blue, lavender, orange-red, salmon, scarlet. Popular dwarf non-climbers in same colors: 'Bijou' and 'Little Sweetheart'. Intermediate in height are 'Jet Set', 28 in.; 'Knee-Hi', 2½ ft.	Sow seeds outdoors as soon as soil can be worked; soak seeds several hours prior to planting, and treat with bacterial inoculant. Does best in cool weather, but heat-resistant varieties now exist. Support tall varieties.
Lavatera trimestris (lavatera, or tree mallow) Bushy plants with single, satiny hollyhocklike flowers in mid to late summer. Leaves resemble those on maple tree.	2½–3 ft.	2 ft.	□	●	'Loveliness', deep rose; 'Tanagra', rose; 'Silver Cup', pale rose; 'Mont Blanc', pure white. For perennial lavatera, see p. 56.	Sow seeds in spring as soon as soil can be worked and where plants are to grow, since they are difficult to transplant. Remove faded flowers for further flowering. May need support.

Alyssum (*Lobularia*), a popular ground-cover plant, bears masses of colorful, fragrant flowers. Easily grown, it will self-seed in all but the harshest climates.

Lobularia maritima 'Oriental Night'

Limonium sinuatum
(statice)

Linaria maroccana
(toadflax)

Linum grandiflorum
(flowering flax)

Lobelia erinus
(lobelia)

Lobularia maritima
(sweet alyssum)

Lunaria annua
(honesty)

Lupinus
(annual lupine)

BOTANICAL AND COMMON NAMES	HEIGHT	SPREAD	SOIL	LIGHT	SPECIES AND VARIETIES	SPECIAL REQUIREMENTS AND REMARKS
Limonium sinuatum (statice) Clusters of little straw-textured flowers are borne on stiff, slender stems above basal leaves. Good seaside plant. Long-lasting flowers used fresh or dried.	1–2½ ft.	1 ft.	■	●	'Iceberg', white; 'Heavenly Blue', blue; 'Midnight Blue', dark blue; 'Gold Coast', yellow; 'American Beauty', rose; 'Apricot Beauty', peach and yellow bicolor. Forever Series, mixed or individual colors.	Sow seeds outdoors as soon as soil can be worked. If earlier flowers are desired, sow indoors 8 wk. before last spring frost. Seed packets often contain clusters of flower seed heads; separate before sowing.
Linaria maroccana (linaria, or toadflax) Flowers resemble miniature snapdragons and are borne along short spikes. Good cut flower.	9–24 in.	9–12 in.	□	●	'Fairy Bouquet'*, seed packets of assorted colors, including shades of chamois, lavender, purple, pink, gold, and crimson. 'Northern Lights' is similar but taller.	Sow seeds early outdoors in average soil (difficult to transplant). Best where summers are cool. Quick to flower. Good edging plant; mass for best effect.
Linum grandiflorum (linum, or flowering flax) Dainty 5-petaled flowers to 2 in. across atop slender stems. Narrow leaves. See also perennial linum, p. 57.	15 in.	8–10 in.	■	●	'Caeruleum', bluish purple; 'Rubrum', bright crimson-red. 'Bright Eyes', creamy white with dark eye.	Sow seeds in spring as soon as ground can be worked or in late fall. Make successive sowings, since flowering period is short. Best where summers are cool.
Lobelia erinus (lobelia) Small 5-petaled flowers, sometimes with white center (eye), are borne in abundance. Small green or bronze-green leaves. See also perennial lobelia, p. 57.	4–12 in.	12 in.	□	◑	'White Lady', white; 'Crystal Palace', dark blue; 'Blue Eyes', violet-blue with white eye; 'Rosamond', carmine-red with white eye, 4–6 in. 'Sapphire', azure-blue with white eye, 12 in. (trailing). 'Color Cascade', mix.	Sow seeds indoors 3 mo. in advance of outdoor planting season, or buy plants in spring. Shear plants back 1–2 in. after first bloom. Excellent edging and container plant.
Lobularia maritima (sweet alyssum) Small clusters of fragrant flowers appear all summer. Low, compact; one of best edging plants.	3–9 in.	1 ft.	□	●	'Carpet of Snow', 'Snow Crystals', white; 'Royal Carpet'*, 'Violet Queen', violet; 'Rosie O'Day'*, rose, 3–5 in. Basket Series are best for window boxes and hanging baskets.	Blooms quickly from seeds. Sow where plants are to bloom as soon as soil can be worked in spring. After first flowers fade, shear plants back for repeat bloom. May self-seed.
Lunaria annua (honesty, or money plant) Small, slightly fragrant flowers; coarse leaves. Called money plant because its seedpods have center partitions of white papery disks the size of silver dollars. Good in dried arrangements.	2 ft.	1 ft.	□	● ◑	'Alba Variegata', white, leaves edged white.	As annual, sow seeds in spring; as biennial, sow in summer. Sow outdoors in full sun or partial shade. To dry, gather as soon as seeds start to turn brown; rub off outer part of pod to expose papery disk. Self-sows; can be invasive.
Lupinus species and hybrids (annual lupine) Spikes of flowers above deeply divided leaves bloom for short period in summer. See also perennial lupine, p. 58.	1–3 ft.	1 ft.	■	● ◑	White, blue, lavender, pink, and yellow. Catalogs vary widely on how they list annual lupines. Look for word "annual" in descriptions. 'Pixie Delight', most common.	Sow seeds in spring as soon as ground can be worked. Grows best where springs and summers are cool.

■ well drained to sandy   ■ moist   ■ wet   ■ acidic   ■ alkaline   □ regular soil   ● full sun   ◑ partial shade   ● shade

Mimulus 'Highland Orange'

Mirabilis jalapa

Monkey flower (*Mimulus*) gets its name from flower patterns that are said to resemble grinning monkeys. Named for flowers that open late in the afternoon and fade the following morning, tall varieties of four o'clock plants (*Mirabilis jalapa*) make a good screen or hedge.

Malcolmia maritima
(Virginia stock)

Matthiola incana annua
(stock)

Mimulus luteus
(monkey flower)

Mirabilis jalapa
(four o'clock)

Molucella laevis
(bells of Ireland)

Myosotis alpestris
(forget-me-not)

Nemesia strumosa
(nemesia)

BOTANICAL AND COMMON NAMES	HEIGHT	SPREAD	SOIL	LIGHT	SPECIES AND VARIETIES	SPECIAL REQUIREMENTS AND REMARKS
Malcolmia maritima (Virginia stock) Loose racemes of fragrant 4-petaled flowers, gray-green leaves. See also *Matthiola*.	9 in.	6 in.	□	●	Sold in seed packets of assorted colors including white, lilac, pink, yellow (rare), and red. Not commonly sold in North America, but seeds can be found with a little searching.	Sow seeds as soon as soil can be worked in spring. Blooms quickly (in about 6 wk.) from seeds. Self-sows.
Matthiola bicornis and M. incana annua (stock) Fragrant flowers, single or double, are borne in spikes on bushy plant. Ten Week stock is a good cut flower.	1–1½ ft.	9 in.–1 ft.	■	●	*M. bicornis* (evening stock), single, in loose spikes, 12–18 in. high, lilac; *M. incana annua* (Ten Week stock), seed packets of assorted or separate colors including white, lilac, purple, pink, rose, yellow; 'Trysomic Seven Week' and 'Dwarf Ten Week' bloom most quickly.	Sow seeds outdoors as soon as soil can be worked, or buy plants. Difficult to start indoors unless 50°F temperature can be maintained. Also make good cool greenhouse pot plants. Evening stock self-seeds and grows better.
Mimulus luteus and hybrids (monkey flower, or mimulus) Showy flowers with speckled petals on low, compact plants. Tender perennial, but usually grown as annual.	1 ft.	9 in.	■	◑	Available in mixed-seed packets including various shades of yellow and red with contrasting spots. Large-flowered strain is sometimes available.	Sow seeds indoors 2 mo. in advance of safe outdoor planting date; set outdoors after danger of frost is past. Or sow outdoors for late bloom. Good in pots, hanging baskets, and in part shade.
Mirabilis jalapa (four o'clock) Trumpet-shaped flowers up to 1 in. across open in late afternoon, stay open until next morning.	1½–4 ft.	1–2 ft.	■	●	Usually sold in mixed-seed packets containing white, lavender, pink, yellow, and salmon. 'Jingles', striped flowers; 'Pygmy', 1½ ft.; 'Petticoat', gives flower-within-flower effect.	Sow seeds outdoors. Grows quickly. Dig up tubers after frost, store as for dahlia, p. 134. Makes good screen or hedge; withstands air pollution. Perennial in mild regions.
Molucella laevis (bells of Ireland) An unusual plant having long spikes covered with large, pale green, shell-like calyxes, each surrounding a small white flower. Good cut flower; fresh or dried.	2–3 ft.	9 in.	□	●	*M. laevis*, green calyxes surrounding inconspicuous white flowers. This is the only species widely offered.	Seeds are best sown where plants are to grow. Difficult to transplant. Sow seeds early but after there is no danger of frost; germination (4 wk.) best in cool weather. To dry flowers, remove leaves and hang in cool, dark place.
Myosotis species (myosotis, or forget-me-not) Small clustered flowers bloom at same time as tulips and are often planted with them. Best grown as biennial, but can be grown as annual.	7 in.–1 ft.	4–9 in.	□	● ◑	Commonly offered in mixed-seed packets of white, blue, and pink; also in separate colors, usually blue only. Some catalogs list biennial form (*M. alpestris*, or *M. rupicola*) and annual form (*M. sylvatica*, or *M. oblongata*).	To grow as biennial, sow in late summer; to grow as annual, sow as soon as soil can be worked. In very cold regions some protection may be needed in winter. Self-sows; discard plants after seeds fall.
Nemesia strumosa (nemesia) Clusters of small flowers on bushy, compact plants. Grow as edging plant or in containers. Good cut flower.	10 in.–1 ft.	6 in.	■	● ◑	Mixed-seed packets of assorted colors including white, pink, rose, yellow, orange, and crimson. Sunsatin™ Series is better able to withstand heat and forms cascading mounds.	Best where summers are cool. Start indoors or in cold frame 6–8 wk. before last spring frost. In mild regions sow in fall or winter for early spring bloom. Pinch to encourage branching.

Nicotiana, or ornamental tobacco, bears clusters of long-lasting, fragrant flowers: among the most fragrant are those of *Nicotiana sylvestris*. Ornamental forms of the opium poppy (*Papaver somniferum*) can grow more than 3 ft. tall, and usually have double blossoms.

Nicotiana sylvestris

Papaver somniferum

| *Nemophila menziesii* (baby blue-eyes) | *Nicotiana* (ornamental tobacco) | *Nierembergia* (cupflower) | *Nigella damascena* (love-in-a-mist) | *Ocimum basilicum* (ornamental basil) | *Osteospermum* (African daisy) | *Papaver rhoeas* (Shirley poppy) |

BOTANICAL AND COMMON NAMES	HEIGHT	SPREAD	SOIL	LIGHT	SPECIES AND VARIETIES	SPECIAL REQUIREMENTS AND REMARKS
Nemophila (five spot and baby blue-eyes) Small 5-petaled flowers above somewhat fleshy, downy leaves.	6–8 in.	6 in.	☐	●	*N. maculate* (five spot) white flowers on long stalks in summer. Each petal is tipped with a violet spot. *N. menziesii* (baby blue-eyes) has blue flowers with a white center in summer.	Best where summers are cool or in frost-free areas where grown for winter or spring bloom. Sow in spring as soon as soil can be worked, or in frost-free areas sow in fall. Sow where plants are to bloom (transplanting difficult).
Nicotiana alata and **sanderae** (nicotiana, or ornamental tobacco) Clusters of fragrant, trumpet-shaped flowers appear over long period above large, mostly basal leaves. *N. sylvestris* is most fragrant, but much taller (to 6 ft.).	10 in.– 2½ ft.	10 in.–2 ft.	☐	● ◑	*N. alata*, fragrant, 'Perfume Deep Purple'; Nicki Series, several colors, including green. *N. sanderae*, Domino Series; Havana Series; Metro Series; all dwarf in many shades or mixed seed. *N. sylvestris*, tubular white flowers, intensely fragrant, towering, much-branched plant.	Sow seeds indoors 4–6 wk. before last spring frost. Germinates best when exposed to light; so best not to cover seeds. Can take 2–3 wk. to come up. Plants can usually be bought in spring. Tolerant of heat.
Nierembergia species and hybrids (nierembergia, or cupflower) Five-petaled, cup-shaped flowers to 1 in. across are borne toward tops of slender stems. Flowers over long period.	6 in.–2 ft.	4–6 in.	■	●	*N. caerulea*, violet-blue, free-flowering. 'Purple Robe' widely available. 'Mont Blanc', white, 6 in.	Sow seeds indoors 8–10 wk. before last spring frost; set seedlings outdoors when frost danger is past. In very hot regions can be grown in partial shade. Often perennial in Zone 7. In cold areas may be possible to winter in cold frame.
Nigella damascena (nigella, or love-in-a-mist) Flowers to 1½ in. across resemble more familiar cornflower; borne on tips of dainty stems. Very finely cut leaves. Dried seedpods used in winter bouquets.	15 in.– 1½ ft.	9 in.–1 ft.	■	●	'Miss Jekyll', blue; 'Monarch Persian Rose', rose; 'Mulberry Rose', double rose and pink; 'Persian jewels', mixed-seed packets of assorted colors including white, purple, pink, rose, carmine.	Sow seeds outdoors where plants are to grow (difficult to transplant) as soon as soil can be worked in spring. Flowering period is short, but successive sowings will extend it.
Ocimum basilicum (ornamental, or sweet, basil) Grown primarily for ornamental leaves that are also used to flavor many foods. White or purple-tinged flowers are relatively inconspicuous.	1–1½ ft.	1 ft.	■	●	*O. basilicum*, green leaves; *O. b.* 'Dark Opal'*, dark purple leaves, variety most often grown as garden ornament. 'Siam Queen'*, narrow leaves and showy purple flowers, good for planters.	Start seeds indoors, 6–8 wk. in advance of outdoor planting season. Pinch to encourage branching. For drying, cut stems when in bloom, and hang upside down in cool, dry place. Can be cut back and potted up in fall for growing indoors.
Osteospermum hybrids (African daisy, or Cape marigold) Daisylike flowers in a range of colors often with a contrasting stripe or disk.	1–1½ ft.	1 ft.	■	●	'Passion Mix'*, rose, purple, or white; 'Whirligig', spoon-shaped petals, white with lavender backs. 'Asti White'*, Soprano™ Series.	Sow indoors at least 12 wk. before last frost or buy plants. Very drought-tolerant once established. Keeps flowering late in fall. Good for planters.
Papaver rhoeas (Shirley poppy) Satiny flowers, single or double, on wiry stems above divided leaves. Good cut flower.	1½ ft.	1 ft.	☐	●	Singles and doubles, often bicolored, in seed packets of assorted colors including pink, yellow, salmon, apricot, red, many shaded and edged with other colors. Garden forms of opium poppy (*P. somniferum*) are fully double, frilly, pink and red shades, or white. Self-seeds freely.	Sow seeds outdoors in late fall or as soon as soil can be worked in spring. Difficult to transplant.

■ well drained to sandy ■ moist ■ wet ■ acidic ■ alkaline ☐ regular soil ● full sun ◑ partial shade ● shade

Long-lasting, petunia's many types and varieties are extremely popular, especially for window boxes. The *multiflora* type has smaller flowers in larger quantity.

Petunia multiflora 'Fantasy Pink Morn'

Pelargonium hortorum
(common geranium)

Perilla frutescens crispa
(beefsteak plant)

Petunia hybrida
(petunia)

Phacelia campanularia
(California bluebell)

Phlox drummondii
(annual phlox)

Phygelius aequalis
(Cape fuchsia)

Portulaca grandiflora
(moss rose)

BOTANICAL AND COMMON NAMES	HEIGHT	SPREAD	SOIL	LIGHT	SPECIES AND VARIETIES	SPECIAL REQUIREMENTS AND REMARKS
Pelargonium hortorum (common, or zonal, geranium) Large clusters of flowers above handsome leaves with concentric markings. Good in containers. Widely grown as annual but perennial if overwintered indoors.	1–2 ft. except far South 3–6 ft.	1 ft.	■	●	Many varieties sold as plants. Colors include white, pink, salmon, and red. Forms with scented or colored foliage are grown from cuttings. Most flowering forms are now raised from seed. Multibloom, Americana, and Orbit Series, single flowers in range of colors; 'Black Magic Rose'* has chocolate-edged green leaves, rose flowers.	To grow from seeds, sow 4 mo. in advance of outdoor planting date. Plants readily increased from terminal cuttings that can be grown in sunny window indoors over winter.
Perilla frutescens crispa (perilla, or beefsteak plant) Grown for its reddish-purple leaves, which have metallic sheen.	1½–2½ ft.	1–1½ ft.	□	●	Reddish-purple leaves. On single plant flower colors can range from white to lavender-pink, but are tiny and of secondary interest.	Sow seeds indoors 6–8 wk. before last spring frost, or sow outdoors after last frost. In cold regions, root cuttings in fall and grow indoors until spring.
Petunia hybrida (petunia) Large single or double flowers up to 5 in. across; some fringed, bordered, or streaked. Compact or trailing plants are long blooming. Somewhat fragrant.	10–15 in.	1–2 ft.	□	●	Main types include P. h. grandiflora (large flowers) and P. h. multiflora (prolific bloomer). Cascade forms good for hanging baskets. Colors: white, violet-blue, deep violet, lavender, pink, rose, yellow, crimson. Hundreds of named forms including AAS winners such as 'Merlin Blue Morn', 'Limbo Violet', 'Opera Supreme Pink Morn'.	Buy plants for earliest bloom; set out after last spring frost. Sow seeds indoors or in heated frame, 8–10 wk. before last frost. Keep flowers picked for continued bloom. Air pollution can damage flowers.
Phacelia campanularia (phacelia, or California bluebell) Clusters of bell-shaped flowers. Not suited for cutting. Leaves can cause dermatitis.	8–9 in.	6 in.	■	●	Blue with white toward center. Other species occasionally offered include P. viscida (sticky phacelia), blue; P. tanacetifolia (fiddleneck), lavender-blue.	Sow seeds outdoors after last spring frost where plants are to grow (difficult to transplant). In frost-free areas sow in fall. Grows best in poor, sandy soil. Plants bloom longer when days are hot and dry, nights are cool.
Phlox drummondii (annual phlox) Dense heads of small 5-petaled flowers, some bicolored or fringed, are borne over long period above neat foliage. Good cut flower.	7–15 in.	9 in.	□	●	Diamond Series, seed packets of assorted or individual colors including white, blue, pink, salmon, crimson; 'Twinkle'*, fringed petals, seed packets of assorted or individual colors, 7 in. 'Glamour'*, salmon, white eye, 15 in.	Quick to flower from seeds sown outdoors after last spring frost. Sow where plants are to bloom (or inside, 6 wk. earlier). Cut plants back after first bloom to encourage further flowering.
Phygelius aequalis (Cape figwort, or Cape fuchsia) South African perennials that are now being grown as annuals in the North. Long stems of pendulous, fuchsialike flowers in yellow, orange, and pink shades.	3–5 ft.	5 ft.	■	●	P. aequalis has yellow flowers to 3 ft. P. capensis has orange-red flowers and grows to 4 ft. There are several hybrids such as 'African Queen', pale red, and 'Moonraker', cream.	Sow seeds of species in early spring. Pot hybrids and overwinter indoors then take cuttings in spring. Buy plants from a local garden center. Heat-loving and drought-tolerant.
Portulaca grandiflora (portulaca, or moss rose) Ground-hugging plant with succulent, narrow leaves and single to double flowers to 2½ in. across. Profuse blooms remain open only when sun shines.	5–7 in.	6 in.–2 ft.	■	●	Many varieties offered in singles and doubles. Seed packets of mixed or individual colors including white, lavender, rose, yellow, orange, coral, red. Sundial Series are bushier, such as 'Sundial Peach'*.	Sow seeds outdoors where plants are to grow or in cold frame, or start 6–8 wk. earlier indoors. Young seedlings transplant easily. Grows best in dry places and in not overly rich soil. Blooms quickly; often self-sows.

Strawflower (*Rhodanthe*), a long-flowering annual, can be cut and dried for winter arrangements. Painted tongue (*Salpiglossis*) is a good border plant and also makes an attractive pot plant.

Rhodanthe chlorocephala rosea

Salpiglossis 'Casino'

Reseda odorata
(mignonette)

Rhodanthe chlorocephala
(strawflower)

Ricinus communis
(castor bean)

Rudbeckia hirta strain
(gloriosa daisy)

Salpiglossis sinuata
(painted tongue)

Salvia splendens
(scarlet sage)

Sanvitalia procumbens
(creeping zinnia)

BOTANICAL AND COMMON NAMES	HEIGHT	SPREAD	SOIL	LIGHT	SPECIES AND VARIETIES	SPECIAL REQUIREMENTS AND REMARKS
Reseda odorata (mignonette) Grown primarily for fragrance of its yellowish-green flowers. Leaves are coarse, and plants tend to be sprawling. Good cut flower.	1 ft.	9 in.–1 ft.	☐	● ◐	Available in mixed-seed packets with flowers of varying colors from yellowish green to brownish red. Also as 'Machet Giant', pale red, a large-flowered variety.	Sow after danger of frost is past where plants are to grow, since seedlings are difficult to transplant. In frost-free areas can be sown in late fall or early winter. Grow as filler among showier plants. Grows best in cool weather.
Rhodanthe species (strawflower, or acroclinium) Attractive, long-lasting flowers resemble double daisies. Prized for drying.	15 in.–2 ft.	6–8 in.	☐	●	*R. manglesii*, rose-pink flowers. *R. chlorocephala roseum*, or *Acroclinium roseum*, mix of white, cream, pink, rose, cerise, salmon, and apricot.	After weather warms, sow seeds where they are to grow, since seedlings are difficult to transplant. To use dried, cut when flowers begin to open and hang upside down in cool, dry, airy place to harden stems.
Ricinus communis (castor bean) Quick-growing plants valued for large, sharply lobed leaves. Good background plant. Flowers insignificant. Seeds poisonous; leaves and seedpods may irritate skin.	8–10 ft.	3–5 ft.	■	●	*R. communis*, green leaves. *R. c.* 'Carmencita', red leaves. *R. c.* 'Zanzibarensis', extra large green leaves, sometimes variegated.	Soak seeds 24 hr. before sowing. In colder areas can be started early indoors. Protect from strong winds. Usually perennial and shrublike in very mild regions.
Rudbeckia hirta strain (rudbeckia, or gloriosa daisy) Large single or double daisylike flowers up to 5 in. across, with green or brown centers, long stems. Showy perennial, often grown as annual. Good cut flower.	8 in.–3 ft.	1–2 ft.	■	● ◐	'Becky Mixed', lemon to brown, 8–10 in.; Marmalade', golden yellow, 1½–2 ft. 'Irish Eyes', single, yellow, green center, 2–2½ ft. 'Double Gold'*, double, yellow; 'Cherokee Sunset'*, yellow to mahogany, double or semi-double, 2–2½ in. 'Indian Summer'*, bright yellow, large flowers, 3 ft.	Sow seeds outdoors as soon as soil can be worked in spring, or sow in fall. Grow in well-drained soil or even poor, dry soil. Plants usually survive winter in Zone 4 (with a mulch). Self-sows freely. Long blooming and trouble-free.
Salpiglossis sinuata (salpiglossis, or painted tongue) Funnel-shaped flowers up to 2½ in. across with velvety texture, delicately veined petals. Long-lasting cut flower.	2–2½ ft.	1 ft.	☐	●	Mixed-seed packets of assorted colors: purple, rose, gold, scarlet. 'Splash', first-generation hybrid, bushy; 'Bolero', second-generation hybrid, bushy. Both are more rugged than older strains.	Sow seeds indoors 8 wk. before last spring frost, or buy plants in spring. Seedlings grow slowly in early stages. Blooms best before weather turns hot; so early start is important.
Salvia splendens (salvia, or scarlet sage) Spikes of closely set flowers on bushy plants that bloom over long period. Popular and easily grown plant; extremely showy. Actually a tender shrub, but grown as annual. Not good for cutting.	7 in.–3 ft.	1 ft.	■	● ◐	Wide assortment of varieties in shades of red, some listed as early flowering. Check for height desired. Also offered in white, lavender, purple, rose, salmon. Also often listed: *S. farinacea*, blue; *S. horminum*, mixed-seed packets of assorted colors; *S. patens*, blue.	Sow seeds indoors 4–6 wk. before last spring frost, or sow outdoors when weather warms. Or buy plants in spring. To keep leaves dark green, apply light feedings of liquid fish emulsion but do not overfeed.
Sanvitalia procumbens (creeping zinnia) Creeping ground cover for edging paths or using in planters. Covered in small zinnialike flowers all summer.	2–4 in.	18 in.	■	● ●	'Golden Carpet' has small, bright yellow flowers and dark green leaves. 'Mandarin Orange'* is semidouble. 'Yellow Carpet' flowers have black centers.	Sow seeds indoors about a month before planting date, or in a cold frame 6 wk. before planting. In mild climates sow outside in fall or early spring

■ well drained to sandy ■ moist ■ wet ■ acidic ■ alkaline ☐ regular soil ● full sun ◐ partial shade ● shade

Scaevola aemula 'Blue Wonder'

Schizanthus 'Hit Parade'

A trailing habit makes the fairy fan-flower (*Scaevola aemula*) especially attractive in hanging baskets and window boxes. Often cultivated in greenhouses and good in groups, the butterfly flower (*Schizanthus*) also makes an attractive pot plant.

| *Scabiosa atropurpurea* (pincushion flower) | *Scaevola aemula* (fairy fan-flower) | *Schizanthus pinnatus* (butterfly flower) | *Senecio cineraria* (dusty miller) | *Solenostemon scutellarioides* (coleus) | *Sutera cordata* (bacopa) | *Tagetes erecta* (African marigold) |

BOTANICAL AND COMMON NAMES	HEIGHT	SPREAD	SOIL	LIGHT	SPECIES AND VARIETIES	SPECIAL REQUIREMENTS AND REMARKS
Scabiosa atropurpurea (scabiosa, or pincushion flower) Rounded flower heads up to 3 in. across give pincushion effect because of protruding silvery stamens. Delicate stems and leaves. Long-lasting, fragrant cut flower. For perennial scabiosa, see p. 63.	1½–3 ft.	9 in.	■	●	Offered in mixed-seed packets of assorted colors including white, blue, lavender, pink, rose, crimson, maroon; both dwarf and tall varieties.	Sow seeds indoors 4–6 wk. before last spring frost, or sow outdoors when weather warms. Can be sown in fall in areas with mild winters. Taller varieties tend to be floppy, often need staking. Flowers can be dried for bouquets.
Scaevola aemula (fairy fan-flower) Fanlike flowers with five petals in clusters over dark toothed leaves. Plants upright to creeping and very heat-tolerant. An Australian tender perennial, grown as an annual and increased by cuttings.	1–1½ ft.	1–1½ ft.	■	●	'Blue Wonder' (or 'New Wonder'), lilac-blue, long flowering; 'Mauve Clusters', more trailing. 'Whirlwind™ White' is more drought-tolerant.	Purchase plants in spring. Does not tolerate either very dry or very wet soil. Prefers slightly acidic soil so treat with chelated iron if foliage or flowers turn pale.
Schizanthus pinnatus (butterfly flower, or poor man's orchid) Dainty, loosely arranged flowers rising above lacy foliage. Somewhat resembles orchids. Often grown in containers.	1–1½ ft.	1 ft.	■	●◑	'Angel Wings' and 'Hit Parade' are two improved compact varieties offered in mixed-seed packets. Flowers are mostly bicolors of white, violet, purple, pink, or crimson.	Sow seeds indoors 6–8 wk. before last spring frost or outdoors when weather warms. Grows best where summers are cool. In greenhouse, sow in fall for flowers in late winter, early spring. Slow to germinate.
Senecio cineraria (dusty miller) Grown for its deeply cut silvery gray leaves. Plants shrublike, occasionally with tiny yellow flowers.	8 in.–2½ ft.	1–3 ft.	□	●	'Cirrus', finely cut white leaves; 'Silverdust', very finely cut silvery leaves. Other plants sold as dusty miller include *Centaurea cineraria* and *C. gymnocarpa*. All very similar.	In cold regions, buy plants, or sow seeds indoors 2 mo. in advance of outdoor planting date. Withstands drought and seaside conditions.
Solenostemon scutellarioides (coleus) Luxuriant foliage in many colors and patterns, some leaves edged in contrasting color, some with fringed or narrow leaves. Flowers insignificant.	8 in.–3 ft.	8 in.–1 ft.	□	●	Wizard Series, self-branching in a range of colors, 10 in.; Seven Dwarfs Series, smaller, 9 in.; Sabre Series have narrow leaves, 9 in.; Kong™ series, taller with larger leaves.	Start seeds indoors. Pinch to encourage branching. Plants easily propagated by tip cuttings. Can be grown over winter as house plants.
Sutera cordata (bacopa) Platter-shaped flowers with 5 petals and yellow stamens on a low-spreading plant with bright green leaves. Tender perennial grown from cuttings, not seed.	3 in.	1–1½ ft.	□	●◑	'Snowflake' has ½-in. white flowers; 'Snowstorm' (also called 'Snow Falls') has larger flowers; 'Pink Domino' has rose flowers and is slightly taller.	Plants available at local garden centers. Keep well watered. Shade is preferable where summers are hot. Good for planters and hanging baskets.
Tagetes erecta (African, or American, marigold), **T. patula** (French marigold) Long-flowering, plants with single, semi-double, or double flowers that are often bicolored; finely divided leaves are usually pungent. Good cut flowers. **T. tenuifolia** (signet marigold) has masses of small flowers on compact plants with lacy foliage.	7 in.–4 ft.	6 in.–1½ ft.	□	●	*T. erecta*: large double flowers in white, cream, yellow, and orange, usually borne on tall plants. 'Antigua Gold', yellow; 'First Lady'*, lemon; 'Orange Marvel', fully double. *T. patula*: smaller, usually double flowers in yellow, orange, and mahogany-red, on short plants. 'Queen Sophia'*, rusty red edged gold; 'Golden Gate'*, orange with reddish centers; 'Bonanza Bolero'*, bright orange. *T. tenuifolia*: single flowers. Gem Series in yellow and orange; 'Lulu', lemon yellow.	Sow seeds indoors 6 wk. in advance of outdoor planting season or directly outdoors after weather warms. *T. erecta* usually first to flower. Remove faded blooms for further flowering. *T. tenuifolia* has edible flowers.

Quick-growing ornamental vines such as black-eyed Susan (*Thunbergia alata*) provide attractive cover for fences and trellises.

Thunbergia alata

Eschscholzia (California poppies) ➡

Tanacetum parthenium
(feverfew)

Tithonia rotundifolia
(Mexican sunflower)

Torenia fournieri compacta
(wishbone flower)

Tropaeolum majus
(nasturtium)

Verbena canadensis
(verbena)

Thunbergia alata
(black-eyed Susan)

Viola hybrid
(pansy)

Zinnia elegans
(zinnia)

BOTANICAL AND COMMON NAMES	HEIGHT	SPREAD	SOIL	LIGHT	SPECIES AND VARIETIES	SPECIAL REQUIREMENTS AND REMARKS
Tanacetum parthenium (feverfew, or matricaria) Double, button-type flowers grow in clusters on tall or short plants. Pungent scent. Perennial, often grown as annual.	6 in.–2 ft.	9 in.	☐	◐ ◑	6–10 in.: 'Snowball', white; 'White Stars', white, yellow center; 'Golden Ball', yellow. 2 ft.: 'Ball's Double White', white; 'White Wonder', white.	For earliest bloom, sow seeds indoors 6–8 wk. in advance of outdoor planting season. Or sow outdoors for later bloom.
Tithonia rotundifolia (tithonia, or Mexican sunflower) Large daisylike flowers up to 3 in. across resemble zinnias. Flowers in late summer.	4–5 ft.	2 ft.	☐	●	'Torch'*, orange-red, yellow center; 'Goldfinger', orange, compact. 'Fiesta del Sol'*, orange, 2 ft.	Plants take 3–4 mo. to flower from seeds; so best started indoors 6–8 wk. in advance of last spring frost. Drought- and heat-resistant.
Torenia fournieri compacta (torenia, or wishbone flower) Bicolored tubular flowers have central yellow blotch. Particularly attractive plant to grow in partial shade.	8 in.–2 ft.	6 in–2 ft.	☐	◑	'Clown Mix'*, white, pink, purple, and lavender.	Sow seeds indoors 8–10 wk. before safe outdoor planting date; or set plants out when night temperatures will not drop below 61°F. In cool climates grow in full sun.
Tropaeolum majus (nasturtium) Plants are low and compact, climbing, or trailing with single or double flowers. Leaves can be used in salads and taste like watercress. Good cut flower.	8 in.–2 ft.	6 in–2 ft.	■	●	8 in. (dwarfs): Seed packets of assorted or separate colors including rose, yellow, orange, crimson, mahogany; 'Cherry Rose', cherry-rose, double; 'Whirlybird', single. 2 ft. (climbing or trailing): Seed packets of assorted or separate colors as above; 'Gleam'*, double.	Sow outdoors after weather warms. Transplanting is difficult. Needs not too rich nor too moist soil. Climbing types good for hiding fences or for use in hanging baskets.
***Verbena* hybrids** (verbena) Fragrant, small, single to semi-double flowers in large clusters up to 3 in. across. Mostly low, spreading plants.	8–10 in.	1 ft.	☐	●	*V. canadensis* 'Homestead Purple', spreading, good for planters. *V. hybrida*, assorted colors, many named forms, e.g., 'Quartz Burgundy'*; 'Peaches and Cream'*, apricot fading to cream; 'Imagination', violet, trailing. *V. bonariensis*, lilac-purple, airy to 6 ft., good accent plant.	Sow seeds 12 wk. before last spring frost or buy plants. Keep faded flowers picked to encourage more bloom and to keep plants from becoming lanky.
Vines (ornamental: various genera) Many annual vines grow quickly from seeds and provide good flowering cover for fences and trellises.	6–10 ft.	6–10 ft.	☐	●	*Thunbergia alata* (black-eyed Susan vine), cream, yellow, or orange, with purple throat; *Cobaea scandens* (cathedral bell), blue; *Tropaeolum peregrinum* (canary creeper), yellow; *Ipomoea* (*Quamoclit*) *lobata*.	Sow seeds indoors 8–10 wk. before last spring frost. All annual vines need some means of support. Canary creeper can only be grown where summers are cool.
***Viola* species and hybrids** (pansy and viola) Large-flowered pansy and related but smaller flowered viola bear fragrant 5-petaled flowers with or without "faces."	6–9 in.	9 in.–1 ft.	■	● ◑	Many varieties of both pansies and violas available in shades of white, blue, purple, yellow, and red. First-generation pansy hybrids are the most heat-tolerant. Pansies generally more heat-tolerant than violas.	Purchase plants in spring for immediate bloom. Or grow as annual from seeds started early indoors for spring bloom same year; grow as biennial by sowing seeds outdoors in midsummer.
***Zinnia elegans* hybrids** (zinnia) Single or double daisylike flowers with petals often quilled, sometimes bicolored. Wide range of plant sizes. Reliable, easily grown, long blooming. Excellent cut flower.	6 in.–1½ ft.	6 in.–1½ ft.	☐	●	Wide range of types and colors including white, chartreuse, purple, pink, yellow, orange; study catalogs to select types desired. 'Crystal White'* is a good edging plant, 8 in.; 'Profusion Orange'*, disease-resistant.	Sow seeds indoors 4–6 wk. in advance of outdoor planting time, or sow outdoors after last spring frost. Grows best in warm weather. Keep faded blooms picked for further flowering.

212 ■ ANNUALS AND BIENNIALS

■ well drained to sandy   ■ moist   ■ wet   ■ acidic   ■ alkaline   ☐ regular soil   ● full sun   ◑ partial shade   ● shade

ANNUALS FOR SPECIFIC LOCATIONS/PURPOSES

Annuals for Light or Dappled Shade

Begonia semperflorens

Myosotis

Schizanthus pinnatus

Begonia semperflorens (wax begonia)
Browallia speciosa (bush violet)
Calendula officinalis (pot marigold)
Catharanthus roseus (vinca)
Cleome spinosa (spider flower)
Cynoglossum amabile
  (Chinese forget-me-not)
Digitalis purpurea (foxglove)
Lobelia erinus (lobelia)
Lunaria annua (honesty)

Myosotis species (forget-me-not)
Nemesia strumosa (nemesia)
Nicotiana species (flowering tobacco)
Reseda odorata (mignonette)
Rudbeckia hirta (gloriosa daisy)
Salpiglossis sinuata (painted tongue)
Salvia splendens (scarlet sage)
Schizanthus pinnatus
  (butterfly flower)
Viola hybrids (violet and pansy)

Annuals as Cut Flowers

Antirrhinum majus

Lathyrus odoratus

Rudbeckia hirta

Antirrhinum majus (snapdragon)
Callistephus chinensis (China aster)
Centaurea cyanus (cornflower)
Coreopsis tinctoria (calliopsis)
Euphorbia marginata
  (snow-on-the-mountain)
Eustoma grandiflorum (lisianthus)
Gypsophila elegans (baby's breath)
Lathyrus odoratus (sweet pea)
Limonium sinuatum (statice)

Matthiola incana (ten week stock)
Molucella laevis (bells of Ireland)
Nigella damascena (love-in-a-mist)
Papaver nudicaule (Iceland poppy)
Rudbeckia hirta (gloriosa daisy)
Salvia farinacea (mealy-cup sage)
Scabiosa atropurpurea
  (pincushion flower)
Zinnia elegans (zinnia)

Fragrant Annuals

Heliotropium

Petunia

Scabiosa

Antirrhinum majus (snapdragon)
Dianthus caryophyllus (carnation)
Heliotropium hybrids (heliotrope)
Lathyrus odoratus (sweet pea)
Lobularia maritima (sweet alyssum)
Matthiola bicornis
  (evening-scented stock)

Matthiola incana (ten week stock)
Nicotiana sylvestris (only the lonely)
Petunia hybrids—some (petunia)
Reseda odorata (mignonette)
Scabiosa atropurpurea
  (pincushion flower)
Viola hybrids—some (pansy)

Annuals for Full Shade

Begonia tuberhybrida

Impatiens walleriana

Solenostemon

Begonia tuberhybrida
  (tuberous begonia)
Impatiens walleriana (busy Lizzie)

Mimulus luteus (monkey flower)
Solenostemon scutellarioides (coleus)
Torenia fournieri (wishbone flower)

Annuals That Attract Butterflies

Ageratum houstonianum

Gazania

Nicotiana sylvestris

Ageratum houstonianum (flossflower)
Cleome hassleriana (spider flower)
Cosmos bipinnatus (cosmos)
Dianthus species—most
  (pinks, carnation, sweet William)
Euphorbia marginata
  (snow-on-the-mountain)
Gaillardia pulchella (blanketflower)
Gazania hybrids (gazania)
Gomphrena globosa (globe amaranth)
Heliotropium hybrids (heliotrope)
Lathyrus odoratus (sweet pea)

Myosotis species (forget-me-not)
Nicotiana alata (flowering tobacco)
Nicotiana sylvestris (only the lonely)
Petunia hybrids (petunia)
Rudbeckia hirta (gloriosa daisy)
Salvia species—most (sage)
Scabiosa atropurpurea
  (pincushion flower)
Tagetes patula (French marigold)
Verbena sp. especially *V. bonariensis*
  (vervain)
Zinnia hybrids (zinnia)

Annuals for Drying

Dianthus

Tagetes

Verbena

Ageratum houstonianum (flossflower)
Calendula officinalis (pot marigold)
Callistephus chinensis (China aster)
Celosia cristata plumosa
  (plumed cockscomb)
Centaurea cyanus (cornflower)
Dianthus caryophyllus (carnation)
Euphorbia marginata
  (snow-on-the-mountain)
Gaillardia pulchella (blanketflower)
Gomphrena globosa (globe amaranth)

Limonium sinuatum (statice)
Lunaria annua (honesty)
Molucella laevis (bells of Ireland)
Nigella damascena (love-in-a-mist)
Papaver rhoeas (Shirley poppy)
Rudbeckia hirta (gloriosa daisy)
Salvia farinacea (mealy-cup sage)
Tagetes species (marigold)
Verbena hybrida (vervain)
Zinnia elegans (zinnia)

Splendid blossoms make ornamental trees of the multi-variety Prunus genus immensely popular. One of the lesser-known species, the Japanese cherry (P. 'Ukon') is shown here. Its spring crop of pink buds opens into magnificent clusters of double white flowers that are tinged on the outside with a hint of greenish-yellow. Its greenish-bronze leaves gradually turn dark green, then red and purple in fall.

Juniper

TREES

Few plants provide as much personal pleasure or make such a useful contribution to the immediate environment as the trees you plant in your yard.

Trees give an air of maturity and permanence to a landscape. They add height and depth to even simple garden designs and provide shelter and privacy. Deciduous trees give shade in summer, while in winter the naked branches have a stark beauty outlined against the sky. Evergreen trees, be they broad-leaved or coniferous, will maintain their attraction throughout the year and are especially appreciated in colder climates during the drab months when there is little landscape color.

Trees condition the air by taking in carbon dioxide and giving off oxygen. They also give off water. A large tree releases thousands of gallons a day through its leaves by the process of transpiration.

Most people select trees for their foliage, flowers, and forms, or for a specific purpose, such as to provide a windbreak. Since trees have to be lived with for many years, it is particularly important to choose, at the start, the right tree for the right purpose and place. In suburban residential areas, in particular, it is important that the height and scale of the trees be in keeping with the surrounding area.

This does not mean that your choice must be limited. But, if your neighbor has a weeping willow, rewarding as it is to grow, one is probably enough in that immediate area. And, while it is best not to follow the local pattern slavishly, it is not recommended that you seek out the most unusual or impressive tree you can possibly find. Study the setting to see which tree would best fit in.

The imposing beech tree, for example, equally attractive for its shape, leaves, and autumn colors, is as out of proportion in the small suburban garden as is an isolated crab apple in parkland. However, there are settings in the suburbs where good-size trees are appropriate and an oak tree or one of the large flowering cherries would be an excellent addition to the landscape.

One reason for planting trees is to create a shelterbelt against the wind. Dense evergreen or coniferous trees are best for this.

If shade is desired, do not plant erect and columnar trees, such as the columnar Siberian crab. Instead, grow wide-spreading or weeping trees, such as the maple, birch, and willow. If a tree is to be planted in the foreground, open shapes, such as the paper birch and honey locust, provide a frame for the rest of the garden. For a boundary the solid shape of a plane tree or an oak or the dark, pyramidal shape of a fir will give a feeling of privacy by obscuring the houses beyond.

The different shapes and sizes of the various leaves can also be chosen for specific effects. The fernlike leaves of honey locusts produce attractive patterns, and the small leaves of birches and many Japanese maples have interesting shapes.

Today's gardens are generally small, and nearly all the maintenance is carried out by the owner. The amount of work necessary can be greatly reduced by adopting informal layouts for the ornamental part of the garden. Once planted, trees and shrubs require little attention. They make an ideal setting for perennial and annual flowers and can often be used to provide the partial shade and shelter that some of these plants require.

If you intend to plant a single specimen tree—on a lawn, at the back of a wide border, or near a boundary—consider carefully the merits and disadvantages of your choice. If the prime consideration when choosing a tree is its shape —such as spreading, columnar, or weeping—only the soil, position, and eventual size need be evaluated.

On the other hand, if you choose a tree for a seasonal characteristic, such as its flowers or autumn colors, try to ascertain its appearance at other times of the year. When the massed display of blossoms in spring fades away, you may have a tree of no particular beauty for the rest of the year. Bear in mind that the vivid autumn color of the foliage of most trees is effective for little more than one month.

Evergreen trees are popular, not only for their screening and hedging value but also for their beautiful shapes. Many evergreens, and especially conifers, are both wind and drought resistant once established. They are ideal as specimen trees on lawns, and even the smallest garden can accommodate a dwarf conifer. It is during winter in northern gardens that evergreens are at their most impressive. The green foliage brings welcome color to a drab scene, and this can be made even more interesting by selecting evergreens with golden, silver, or blue-green foliage. A mixed grouping that includes plantings of all-green and variegated evergreens is particularly effective.

Fitting the tree to the site. As a general rule it is not advisable to plant trees close to your house. Not only can the roots eventually injure the foundation and drains but fast-growing trees can also quickly exclude light and air from the house. Avoid planting anything but dwarf evergreens or medium-size deciduous trees, such as flowering cherries or crab apples, in small gardens. Trees should be in harmony with the house; they should not overshadow it. A wide-spreading or very tall tree on a small front lawn can be quite out of proportion. Where trees overhang paths and driveways, there is both a nuisance and a danger from broken branches and, in autumn, from fallen leaves that are slippery underfoot in wet weather. For such

small areas, narrow, columnar conifers or similar types of deciduous trees fulfill the homeowner's aesthetic as well as the practical needs.

Wherever space allows, a group planting of three or five trees is usually more effective than a single specimen. By far the best effects come from letting one shape dominate the group—one tall tree, one thin tree, and one triangular-shaped tree will look awkward. No set pattern can be specified, but the trees should belong to the same genus and have roughly the same dimensions and shapes. Three hawthorns, say, or three crab apples, with different-colored flowers and fruit, make a handsome group, as do several Japanese maples of various leaf shapes and autumn tints. A group of variegated and green hollies is striking in winter, especially if the trees have berries of different hues. Conifers with silver or golden leaves are other obvious choices, while the blue-gray spruces are best as single specimens.

The spacing between trees in a group depends on the varieties to be planted. The idea is to put them close enough together so that they are obviously a grouping—but not so close that they touch or shade one another when they mature. The nurseryperson from whom you buy the trees can give you a good estimate as to their ultimate spread in your climate. Some judicious pruning can also be done if they tend to overgrow.

Trees for screens and shelterbelts should be planted close together, but the initial spacing could well allow for the removal of every other tree as they grow larger.

Such screens in their early stages are often made up of fast-growing deciduous trees and slower-growing conifers. As the conifers become effective, the deciduous trees are then removed, providing this was the ultimate goal when you set out. Most nurseries and garden centers will give advice on suitable trees.

The trees described in the chart beginning on page 225 provide a varied basis for selection (see also Trees for Specific Locations/Purposes on page 245). However, the choice is so vast that it is worth checking catalogs or, ideally, inspecting the trees at nurseries before making a decision.

Trees, more than anything else in the landscape, can create a particular atmosphere. For example, trees that have a formal appearance include the fir, horse chestnut, cedar, and yew; for a pastoral feeling choose a birch, oak, or weeping willow; more romantic are the magnolia, maple, or beech; and to complement an urban landscape, there are the flowering cherry, linden, honey locust, and some of the firs.

Popular trees are relatively inexpensive, but buying rare types can call for a substantial outlay. In such a case it is even more important to inspect the tree of your choice in a local nursery or an arboretum, and ideally at the time of year when it is at its best—either in flower, fruit, or autumn color.

It is possible to plant trees of almost any size; but after they get to be 15 feet or so high, the problems and the costs increase considerably, and the chances of success diminish. So it is usually best to buy a tree when it is small. There is also pleasure to be derived from watching it grow through its most vigorous, formative period, when you can enjoy the foliage at eye level.

Tree surgery. The wise gardener should check the condition of his established trees once a year, and if heavy pruning or repair is necessary, he should call for professional help. Overhanging branches can be a safety hazard—and a homeowner can be liable for any damage sustained by passersby. Treatment of splitting trunks, top pruning of tall trees, and felling of diseased or unwanted trees are best left to professional tree surgeons, who have the knowledge and equipment to deal efficiently and

safely with such difficult and potentially dangerous garden problems.

The homeowner and the law. A homeowner may be held responsible for any destruction of neighboring land by encroaching roots and overhanging branches. He may also be required to pay compensation for any damage to plants on adjoining land that is caused by spraying.

Prevent roots from harming your own and neighboring property by planting trees well away from buildings and walls. The main cause of cracks in walls can be traced to trees extracting moisture from the soil, especially in heavy clay; the dry soil subsides and brings about a settlement of the foundations. The poplar and ash are the worst offenders and should never be planted near houses. Roots of large maple trees can literally raise a concrete sidewalk. The distance to which roots will spread is assumed to equal the eventual height of the tree, although some extend much farther.

Roots cannot penetrate into the main drains of houses because the socketed joints are sealed, but they do sometimes find their way into the open joints of drainage tiles. If an area of your yard tends to become waterlogged after rain, any land drains should be examined and invading roots removed. There are professionals who do this job.

Overgrown hedges and trees that may be a hazard are yet another responsibility where they border on neighboring land or public roads. The homeowner may be required to trim the hedge back properly or remove any trees that are potential dangers. When damage has actually occurred, the person who owns the land on which the offending plant grows may have to pay for it.

These few restrictions are minor, however, when compared to the beauty of foliage and flowers, as well as the bounty of dappled shade, and the striking sculptural forms that only trees can bring.

Birch trees are grown for their ornamental bark and colorful autumn foliage. *Betula nigra*'s is dark brown. Glossy green leaves turn yellow in fall.

Betula nigra

How to Plant a Tree

When, Where, and How to Dig the Hole

The ideal planting time for deciduous trees is midautumn to early spring, providing the ground is neither waterlogged nor frozen. Broad-leaved evergreens and conifers are best planted earlier in the fall or later in spring, when the soil is warm and moist. Keep roots moist to prevent foliage from shedding.

Trees ordered from a nursery will probably arrive bare rooted, with their roots either contained in a ball of soil wrapped in burlap, or in a wire basket. If you pick the tree up from the nursery, it may already be growing in a container. In that case it can be planted at any time except when the soil is frozen. Where summers are hot, avoid planting during periods of extreme heat.

In the case of some soils, inadequate drainage may result in poor growth of newly planted trees; therefore, ensuring good drainage is a prime consideration. The first step is proper selection of the planting site. A spot that is swampy or where water tends to collect after a rainfall is not a good place to plant most trees.

For the average young tree, the planting hole should be about 3 feet across and 18 inches deep—large enough to give the roots plenty of room to spread in all directions.

If you are planting in grass, mark out a circle, remove the sod as shown below, break it up, and save it to incorporate with the soil you put around the roots. Begin digging from the center of the circle, saving the topsoil as you go. When you see the soil becoming more yellowish or lighter colored, it means you have

reached the less organic subsoil. Keep digging, but put this in a separate pile.

When the hole is dug, fill it with water to test drainage. If it takes longer than an hour or so to empty, you have a problem that might easily be solved or might require the installation of a whole drainage system (see "Taking Care of Your Garden," beginning on p. 495).

Sometimes a layer of impermeable soil will be fairly thin, and you can break through by thrusting your garden fork deeply into the bottom of the hole. If so, break up the base of the hole and proceed. If not, you might be well advised to pick another site.

All trees should be staked during their first two or three years. Stout wooden stakes treated with wood preservative are obtainable from most nurseries. They should be long

enough to hold the trunk upright but allow the crown and upper trunk to flex in the wind. With a bare-rooted tree, use a single stake driven in before planting; with a balled-and-burlapped tree, drive in two stakes after planting, one on either side of the root ball.

Make starting holes for the sharpened stakes, insert them, and hammer them in with a sledge.

Place a layer of rubble in the bottom of the hole to increase aeration. This is of value only if the hole already drains; it will not solve the problem of poor drainage.

Add sod (and compost or leaf mold) in the manner illustrated below. Mix the subsoil you have taken out with an equal amount of topsoil, and use to form a thin layer in the hole. Tread firmly, fill with water, and let drain.

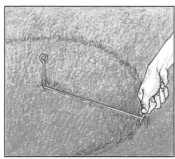

1. Use a peg, a knife, and a piece of string to mark a 3-ft. circle in grass.

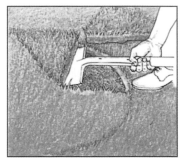

2. Remove sod from within the circle; stack it to one side for future use.

3. Dig 18-in.-deep hole; loosen bottom soil with a fork. Test drainage.

4. With heavy soils, use a garden fork to break down the sides of the hole.

5. Drive in a stout stake. Add heavy gravel or rubble to help aeration.

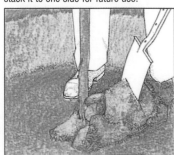

6. Chop sod into 3- to 4-in. pieces; place in hole, grass side down.

7. If available, add a little leaf mold or compost to act as a slow fertilizer.

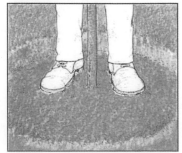

8. Add thin layer of subsoil to fertilizer. Tread firmly and water.

Acer pseudoplatanus 'Brilliantissimum'

Cercidiphyllum japonicum 'Pendulum'

The pollution-resistant sycamore maple (*Acer pseudoplatanus*) provides excellent wind protection. In its autumn foliage, the katsura tree (*Cercidiphyllum japonicum*) is a splendid sight.

Planting and Staking a Young Tree

Before planting a tree the top branches, and the roots if they are exposed, should be trimmed as shown. Remove container-grown trees from their containers, gently shake loose a little of the soil, and prune the roots. Remove roots that have grown around the circumference of the pot or they will continue to engirdle the tree; in effect the tree will still be pot-bound. If the root ball from the container has very little soil showing, make three or four vertical cuts down the roots to encourage them to develop new growth.

Planting is easier if done by two people. Let one hold the tree in position while the other places a flat piece of wood across the hole. The old soil mark on the stem should be level with the piece of wood; remove or add soil accordingly. If the tree is bare rooted, make a mound over which to spread the roots.

With a balled-root tree, now is the time to loosen the top of the burlap, but do not remove it. While one person holds the tree upright—or against the stake with a bare-rooted tree—the other should start filling the hole with the soil mix. Shake a bare-rooted tree from time to time to make sure that the soil is settling around the roots, and if the soil is sandy, tread it down as you go. In heavier soil, when the roots are covered, soak the area with water to settle the soil before filling the hole.

Fill in the hole and firm the soil down until it is level with the surrounding ground. The old soil mark on the trunk should be just visible.

Surround the bare-soil area with a small mound to form a kind of basin to catch and hold water in the root area. Keep the surface free of grass and weeds to reduce competition. The following spring, you can apply a layer of mulch.

The tree must now be tied to the stakes. The best ties are strong plastic or webbing straps with rubber buffers. With a bare-rooted tree, attach the tie as low as possible to keep the tree standing upright. This may be only 2 feet or so above ground level. If using burlap, wrap it in a figure eight and secure with strong cord as shown below, right.

The reason for using two stakes with a balled-root tree is to prevent the tree from rocking back and forth in the wind. Stretch rope or wire from the padded trunk to strong stakes on either side of the tree, keeping them as low as possible.

Inspect ties periodically, especially after strong winds, and retie if necessary. As the tree grows, loosen ties to prevent strangulation. Check in early spring and again in midsummer.

REMOVE DAMAGED ROOTS

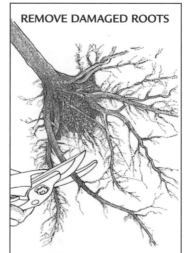

To prevent the onset of fungal diseases, prune dead or damaged roots back to healthy tissue.

1. On top branches, cut off any dead stumps of wood, flush with branch.

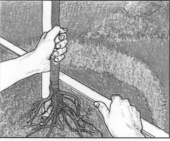

2. Trim any branches with damaged tips back to an outward-facing bud.

3. Line up the old soil mark on the trunk level with surrounding surface.

TYING A TREE TO A STAKE

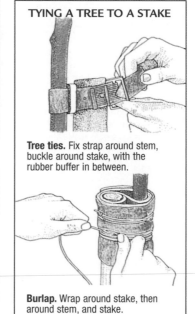

Tree ties. Fix strap around stem, buckle around stake, with the rubber buffer in between.

Burlap. Wrap around stake, then around stem, and stake.

4. Begin filling in hole with topsoil. Shake tree to avoid air pockets.

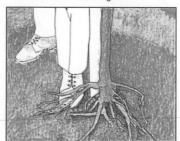

5. Continue to fill, firming soil down often, until the hole is filled in.

6. Level with a fork. Water well. Leave bare until next spring.

One outstanding characteristic of plane trees (*Platanus*) is their flaking bark, which exposes light-golden inner layers. With its silver-white bark, the European white birch (*Betula pendula*) is a beautiful specimen tree.

Platanus hispanica

Betula pendula

Taking Care of Trees

Mulching and Feeding After Planting

Mulching holds in moisture, inhibits weeds, and encourages organisms that aerate and enrich the soil. It also protects against overheating in summer and freezing and thawing in winter. As time passes, it will also provide a little nourishment.

Leaf mold, bark chips, peanut hulls, and other useful mulches can be bought from garden centers or nurseries. Apply in early autumn or spring when soil is moist and warm, mulching 3–4 inches deep over the root area.

Feeding is generally not needed for trees in their formative years. Later, small leaves or reduced growth may indicate a lack of nourishment.

Make nutrients available to the tiny feeder roots by boring a number of holes in the soil around the perimeter of the root area (roughly the same spread as the branches) and filling them with fertilizer as shown.

Use an organic fertilizer that provides its nutrients gradually over a period of a year or more.

Trees planted in a lawn area may never need special fertilizing—the fertilizer applied to the lawn will supply all the nutrients the trees need as well. If the tree is planted beside a paved area, such as a driveway, you'll need to concentrate the fertilizer (compost or a balanced organic fertilizer) on the side of the tree where you have access to the roots.

1. Use a soil auger to bore holes 12 in. deep, 18–24 in. apart over root area.

2. Funnel granular fertilizer into the holes. Fill with soil; tamp down.

Removing Suckers From Grafted and Budded Trees

A sucker is a shoot that appears near the base of a main stem. It diverts energy and must be removed—particularly from trees that have been grafted or budded onto the root stocks of related species. With these trees, suckers develop from below the graft, and if not removed, they will subvert the graft.

Trace the sucker to its point of origin belowground, grasp it firmly, and pull it cleanly away. Cutting encourages more suckers.

Never cut suckers off; always pull them away cleanly.

Selecting a New Leading Shoot After Damage

Trees that grow in columnar or pyramidal shapes are especially susceptible to damage by strong winds or ice. In such circumstances, the trees may be deformed, or it may be that the central leader, the upright stem from which side branches radiate, is snapped off.

If this happens, you can reestablish new growth by training another leading shoot. When making your selection, choose a leader that is growing upright, which is as near as possible to the damaged point of the old leader.

Fasten a stake to the lower trunk, and a bamboo cane long enough to reach 2 feet above the base of the new leader to this. Attach the new leader to the cane in several places, and cut off the old leader flush with the stem. Leave the cane in place for about two years, or until the new leading shoot has become self-supporting. Check the ties from time to time to be sure they are not hampering the young shoot's growth, or constricting the main stem.

Tie the chosen shoot upright to the cane; cut off the old leader.

Preventing a Young Tree From Drying Out

Established trees seldom need watering except in times of extreme drought. The foliage of young trees, however, may wilt; and evergreens, particularly conifers, may turn brown and scorched looking within a few weeks after planting. This condition may be caused by a lack of water or by drying winds.

To be sure young trees receive enough water, use a rain gauge. Give a 1-inch total of rain and watering per week.

Trees grown in containers must be watered regularly and thoroughly. In some areas, this may be a necessary chore even in winter, especially if the containers are sheltered from the rain.

If a young tree is being scorched by drying wind, which in some climates can happen in winter, make a shelter of burlap or thick sheet plastic around it as tall as the tree. To make the shelter, insert three or four stakes around the tree and secure the material to them. Leave the top of this windbreak open to the rain.

Oxydendrum arboreum

Native to the eastern part of the country, *Oxydendrum arboreum* has tubular white flowers that bloom in late summer and dark green leaves that turn red in early autumn.

Removing Unwanted Shoots

Good tree pruning principles call for the removal of all dead or straggly shoots. Two types of shoots may develop on trees. Water shoots are upright, rapidly growing shoots that occur mainly on branches, but occasionally on the trunk. They happen most frequently following hard pruning and should be removed flush with the branch in late summer, before they spoil the shape of the tree.

Remove side shoots that grow from the trunk of established trees.

Side shoots sometimes arise from the trunk, even on mature trees. These grow outward, rather than upright, and increase in size more slowly. Cut them off flush in fall or winter.

Cutting Off Unwanted Thick Branches

It may occasionally be necessary to remove a large, thick branch, either because it is damaged or because it is growing at an awkward angle or over a neighbor's land.

The danger here is that the weight of the branch may cause it to break away before the cut has been cleanly finished, thereby damaging the trunk.

To prevent this, first use a pruning saw to reduce the long branch to a convenient length, leaving about 18 inches to be dealt with in the final cut. (If this is impossible, support the offending branch by tying it to a higher one while you saw it off at the 18-inch mark.) Locate the branch collar, the region close to the base of the branch, where it merges into the

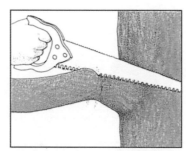
1. Undercut and shorten branch, leaving an 18-in. stub.

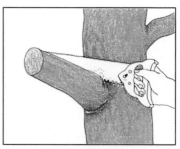
2. Saw off the stub just outside the branch collar.

trunk (see right), and prune the stub at that point, making an undercut first. Trim off any jagged edges with a sharp knife.

Some years ago, it was common practice to cover all tree cuts larger than one inch with wound paint, or some form of dressing, in the belief that this would prevent disease. Such actions are no longer considered appropriate. There is no evidence that they speed healing or prevent disease. If anything, wound paint merely serves to seal in disease.

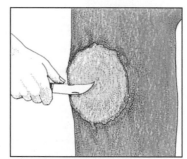
3. Smooth the surface by paring off all ragged edges with a knife.

Cutting a Long Branch to Shape

In most cases a tree will produce its branches to conform with its natural shape. Sometimes, however, one branch will grow too vigorously in a quest for light or in response to other conditions. When this happens, the

result is often a lopsided appearance and perhaps overall weakened growth.

During the tree's dormant period, you can restore overall symmetry by pruning such overeager branches to about one-third of their length. Cut back to a side shoot growing in the same direction.

Removing a Competing Leader From a Young Tree

Some trees, especially those with erect, conical, or pyramidal growth habits, will occasionally fork at the tip of the leading shoot. If allowed to grow, this secondary leader will spoil the tree's symmetrical shape.

A competing leader on a single-stemmed tree—commonest on conifers—must be completely removed at its point of origin. On trees that form side shoots, prune the second leader back to half its length, cutting diagonally just above an outward-facing bud. This will induce the competing leader to put out horizontal side shoots.

In mild climates this pruning can be done at any time the plant is not actively growing. Where winters are severe, trim in early spring.

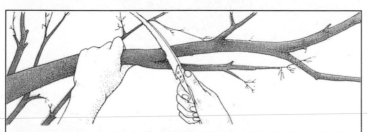
Maintain the outline of a tree by shortening, in winter, any branch that is growing too strongly. Cut to a side shoot about two-thirds of the way back.

Remove competing leaders from any single-stemmed tree.

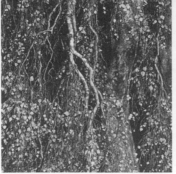

Trailing or weeping birches such as 'Tristis' or 'Youngii' have long branches that can hang down almost to the ground. *Betula jacquemontii* has a gleaming white bark that shreds into large pieces.

Betula pendula 'Tristis'

Betula pendula 'Youngii'

Betula jacquemontii

What Can Go Wrong With Trees

With trees, the most important pest control strategy is choosing the right tree. Consult a local nursery owner to ensure that you do not buy and plant trees that are prone to pests or diseases that are widespread in your area. Once a tree grows more than about 10 feet tall, it becomes very difficult to control pests or diseases by spraying control products. The controls recommended here will be useful for young trees, but if a tree suffers problems year after year, it is better to cut it down and replace it with a different species.

SYMPTOMS AND SIGNS	CAUSE	CONTROL
Needled evergreens		
Needles sticky or deformed; shoot tips may be swollen or deformed; may show sooty mold. Pests may be visible.	Aphids, mealy bugs, leaf hoppers, cottony scale, white flies	Spray with insecticidal soap to kill pest; with soapy water to remove sooty mold.
Needles are eaten, either entirely or in part.	Caterpillars, sawfly larvae, gall midges	Apply *Bacillus thuringiensis* for caterpillars, insecticidal soap or neem for other pests.
Needles are whitish to almost transparent.	Leaf miners	Spray with insecticidal soap.
Foliage turns yellow, then brown, may have a purplish tinge.	Spider mites	Spray forcefully with water, especially the undersides; also with insecticidal soap at 5-day intervals.
Shoots wilt, become crooked or stunted, die quickly.	Borers	Difficult. Prune out infected shoots and destroy.
Needles or stems have corky or waxy look.	Scale insects	Apply dormant oil in late winter, prune out badly infected branches, spray with insecticidal soap in May.
Needles turn yellow and fall; white resin on trunk and branches.	Cytospora canker (fungus)	Prune out infected branches. In spring, spray 3 times, at 10-day intervals, with copper-based fungicide.
Needles turn yellow in late summer, brown in winter, and eventually drop. Often starts at base and moves up.	Needle cast (fungus), common in spruce, pines	In summer, spray 3 times, at 21-day intervals, with Bordeaux mixture.
Shoot tips yellow in fall. Needles hang on for almost a year without falling. Black spots then appear on shoots.	Twig blight (fungus)	Prune out infected shoots. Spray 3 times with copper fungicide after needles fall.
Dead branches in crown, white resin on trunk, or yellow patches on needles may be fruiting bodies exuding orange jelly.	Several different rusts (fungus) attack conifers	Prune out infected branches, spray with wettable sulfur.

SYMPTOMS AND SIGNS	CAUSE	CONTROL
Broad-leaved trees		
Leaves distorted, twisted, and puckered: sooty mold may be present, pests visible.	Insects, such as aphids, lace bugs, whiteflies	Spray with dormant oil in winter or with insecticidal soap during growing season.
Leaves pale, whitish, or with a pinkish tinge; small white dots visible.	Mites	Use dormant oil in late winter. In summer, spray with a strong spray of water or insecticidal soap.
Leaves are eaten, maybe only veins left. Pests usually visible.	Caterpillars, sawfly larvae, beetles of many kinds	Apply *Bacillus thuringiensis* for the caterpillars, insecticidal soap or neem for the rest.
Leaves or leaf stalks have pimples or swellings.	Gall-forming midges and mites	Seldom serious. Good sanitation in fall—remove infected foliage as it falls.
Shoots wilt, holes visible in bark, sawdust may be present.	Wood borers and bark beetles	Difficult since the pests are inside the tree. If possible, prune off branch and destroy.
Branches have corky, raised areas, often black or brown.	Scale insects	Spray with dormant oil in winter, with insecticidal soap in May.
Leaves have brown patches and may fall early; shoots die.	Anthracnose (fungus)	Spray 3 times, at 10-day intervals, with dormant oil in late winter, with Bordeaux mixture in spring as leaves open.
Leaves have small spots (pale, yellow, or brown) that run together. Leaves may fall early.	Leaf spots (many different fungi)	Spray with a copper-based fungicide. Dispose of infected leaves as they fall.
Leaves have orange to yellow raised spots, mostly on the underside.	Rust (disease)	Prune orange galls from nearby cedars and junipers. Spray with wettable sulfur 5 times at 10-day intervals.
Leaves have olive-green patches, fruit has corky areas.	Scab (fungus)	Spray with lime sulfur while dormant. Spray with dilute lime sulfur during spring and early summer.
Dead branches in crown have sunken areas of bark.	Nectria canker (fungus)	Prune out infected branches. Take care not to injure trunk with mowers as this attacks from the soil.
Leaves turn brown quickly, hang down but do not fall.	Fire blight (bacterial)	Prune off infected branches and destroy. Sterilize pruners between cuts. Spray with lime sulfur in spring.
Tree dies slowly from top down, especially birch and maple.	Stress or pollution	Keep trees growing well by watering and feeding.
Vertical splits in bark on trunk or main branches, usually on west or south side.	Rapid winter temperature changes	Shade bark by wrapping or fixing a board to cover wounded area. It will heal.
Tree leafs out normally in spring, but later all leaves dry up.	Mouse or string trimmer	Plant a new tree and protect from mice with a tree wrap. Mulch around tree so there is no need to use trimmer.

Deciduous Trees

Deciduous trees are those that drop their leaves in the dormant season. In the chart that follows, they are listed alphabetically by their botanical names, with their common names in parentheses. Recommended species and varieties are also listed.

Although many factors influence a deciduous tree's survival, the most dependable indicator of its hardiness is the lowest temperature it can endure in winter. To determine whether a specific tree can reasonably be expected to survive the lowest average temperature in your particular area, check the zone designation for that tree in the Hardiness column. Then refer to the Hardiness Zone Map at the front of the book.

The figures in the second and third columns indicate the height and spread each tree can be expected to attain—contingent upon growing conditions and the care it receives over its lifetime. Knowing the mature size is an aid to deciding planting distance.

Acer palmatum

Acer japonicum
(full-moon maple)

Acer palmatum
(Japanese maple)

Accr platanoides 'Crimson King'
(Norway maple)

Acer saccharum
(sugar maple)

BOTANICAL AND COMMON NAMES	HEIGHT	SPREAD	HARDINESS	DECORATIVE CHARACTERISTICS, SPECIAL REQUIREMENTS, AND REMARKS
Acer (maple)				
Acer buergerianum (trident)	20–25 ft.	20–25 ft.	Zones 5–9	Outstanding shade tree for small gardens. Holds up well in dry spells.
A. davidii (snakebark)	20–45 ft.	15–25 ft.	Zones 6–8	This tree has interesting white-striped, glossy green bark. In spring 8-in.-long leaves are red but soon change to green, and yellow-green flowers put on a fine display. In autumn leaves turn to shades of yellow and purple.
A. freemanii (Freeman's)	60–70 ft.	50–60 ft.	Zone 4	A cross between the red and sugar maples that is faster growing and more pollution tolerant than red maple, but still has the good fall color. The varieties 'Morgan' and 'Autumn Blaze', often sold as red maples, really belong here.
A. griseum (paperbark)	20–25 ft.	15–20 ft.	Zones 4–8	Attractive reddish-brown bark peels like that of paper birch.
A. japonicum (full-moon)	20–30 ft.	20–30 ft.	Zones 5–7	Lobed leaves turn crimson in fall.
A. negundo (Manitoba)	30–50 ft.	40–50 ft.	Zones 2–8	No autumn color changes. Fast growing, weak wooded, prolific seeder. Good where summer drought and winter cold prohibit growing better maples.
A. palmatum (Japanese)	15–20 ft.	20–25 ft.	Zones 5–8	Somewhat similar to A. japonicum but with more intricately lobed leaves, which turn vivid red in autumn. Needs good soil. Does best in partial shade.
A. pensylvanicum (striped)	20–25 ft.	15–20 ft.	Zone 3	A native tree that grows well in the shade of other, larger trees. The bark is marked with vertical white stripes, giving winter interest.
A. platanoides (Norway)	50–60 ft.	40–50 ft.	Zones 4–7	Although widely planted in the past, self-sown trees are proving to be a serious threat to native woodlands, and its use is now discouraged. Forms with colored or variegated foliage, and narrow or globose shape are still available.
A. rubrum (red)	50–60 ft.	40–50 ft.	Zones 3–9	Plant this for its fall color. Named forms are the most consistent.
A. saccharinum (silver)	60–80 ft.	40–60 ft.	Zones 3–9	The white undersides of the leaves make this tree appear to change color in the breeze. Branches are often pendulous. Brittle wood makes it prone to damage in storms. 'Silver Cloud' is a more upright variety with an oval crown.
A. s. 'Wieri' (cutleaf)	50–60 ft.	35–50 ft.	Zones 3–9	The leaf blade is cut almost to the midrib, giving a distinctive appearance.
A. saccharum (sugar)	50–60 ft.	35–45 ft.	Zones 4–8	Bright green leaves have whitish undersides and turn bright yellow in fall. Sap is used for maple syrup.
A. tataricum ssp ginnala (Amur)	15–20 ft.	20–25 ft.	Zones 2–8	In late summer winged fruits turn red, while leaves remain green. In fall foliage becomes brilliant scarlet. A hardy species attracting few pests.

By late summer, clusters of pear-shaped nuts appear among the yellow-green leaves of the Indian horse chestnut (*Aesculus indica*).

Aesculus indica

Aesculus hippocastanum
'Baumannii' (horse chestnut)

Aesculus indica
(Indian horse chestnut)

Albizia julibrissin
(silk tree, or mimosa)

Alnus glutinosa
(black or common alder)

Amelanchier arborea
(apple shadblow)

BOTANICAL AND COMMON NAMES	HEIGHT	SPREAD	HARDINESS	DECORATIVE CHARACTERISTICS, SPECIAL REQUIREMENTS, AND REMARKS
Aesculus (horse chestnut, or buckeye) *Aesculus carnea* (red horse chestnut)	30–50 ft.	30–50 ft.	Zones 4–7	Pink to red flowers and reddish leaves. Although similar to *A. hippocastanum*, this hybrid is considered more ornamental.
A. flava (yellow, or sweet, buckeye)	40–50 ft.	30–40 ft.	Zones 3–8	Yellow flowers grow in upright clusters 4–6 in. long and bloom in late spring and early summer. Young leaves and fruits poisonous if eaten.
A. glabra (Ohio buckeye)	30–35 ft.	20–40 ft.	Zones 3–7	Rounded shape, orange fall color. Young leaves and seeds poisonous.
A. hippocastanum (common horse chestnut)	45–60 ft.	35–50 ft.	Zones 3–7	Clusters of large, red-spotted white flowers in late spring. Large leaves in uneven star pattern of 5–7 leaflets are poisonous in early spring and do not change color in autumn. Late summer blight may disfigure them. Chestnuts, poisonous unless processed, abundantly produced.
A. h. 'Baumannii' (double-flowered horse chestnut)	45–60 ft.	35–50 ft.	Zones 3–7	Since its double white flowers are sterile, it does not produce nuts. This eliminates considerable cleaning up under tree.
A. indica (Indian horse chestnut)	40–50 ft.	35–40 ft.	Zones 7–8	Long clusters of white flowers are marked with yellow at top, tinged rose at bottom. Lance-shaped leaflets grow as long as 9 in.
Albizia (silk tree, or mimosa) *Albizia julibrissin*	20–35 ft.	25–45 ft.	Zones 6–9	Fernlike compound leaves cast partial shade. From mid to late summer feathery pink and white flowers open from tight, round heads. It prefers dry, gravelly soil of low fertility. Can be invasive.
A. j. 'Ernest Wilson', or *A. j. rosea*	20–35 ft.	25–45 ft.	Zones 6–9	Summer flowering period lasts almost 6 wk. Recently transplanted young trees need winter protection. Hardiest of the mimosas. Can be invasive.
Alnus (alder) *Alnus glutinosa* (black or common)	30–40 ft.	25–30 ft.	Zones 3–7	A good choice for wet locations where few other trees will survive. The spring catkins are attractive and the summer foliage is dark, shiny green. It will grow well in part shade or sun, but not in dry sandy soils.
Amelanchier (serviceberry, shadblow, or Juneberry) *Amelanchier arborea* (downy)	15–25 ft.	10–15 ft.	Zones 3–9	Produces many white flowers in mid or late spring as leaves open or just before. Fruits are reddish purple. In fall foliage turns yellow to red. Grayish bark is handsome during winter. Easily grown in any good soil.
A. grandiflora (apple)	18–30 ft.	15–25 ft.	Zones 4–9	Has largest flowers of any shadblow. White or sometimes pale pink, they open in late spring before foliage appears. 'Autumn Brilliance' has exceptional fall color, and 'Ballerina' is more upright.
A. laevis (Allegheny)	25–35 ft.	15–25 ft.	Zones 4–8	In late spring drooping white flower clusters contrast with young leaves, which are purplish green before turning bright green. Fruits are purplish black. 'Cumulus' is slightly smaller and has an oval shape.

The rapid-growing *Betula pendula* has arched branches and drooping branchlets.

Betula pendula

Betula papyrifera
(paper birch)

Broussonetia papyrifera
(paper mulberry)

Caesalpinia gilliesii
(bird of paradise bush)

Carpinus betulus
(European hornbeam)

Carya pecan
(pecan)

Castanea mollissima
(Chinese chestnut)

BOTANICAL AND COMMON NAMES	HEIGHT	SPREAD	HARDINESS	DECORATIVE CHARACTERISTICS, SPECIAL REQUIREMENTS, AND REMARKS
Betula (birch)				
Betula lenta (sweet, or cherry)	40–50 ft.	40–60 ft.	Zones 3–7	Dark reddish-brown bark resembles that of cherry tree. Drooping catkins in spring and yellow foliage in fall are most attractive. Plant in rich, moist soil.
B. nigra (river)	40–60 ft.	40–60 ft.	Zones 4–9	Brown flaking bark, yellow fall foliage, good on moist soils. 'Heritage' has particularly attractive bark and is less subject to leaf miners and borers.
B. papyrifera (paper)	50–70 ft.	25–45 ft.	Zones 2–6	Bark is white, and leaves turn brilliant yellow in fall. Provides more shade and is less susceptible to borers than B. pendula.
B. pendula (European white)	30–40 ft.	25–35 ft.	Zones 2–6	Bark is white, and older branches are gracefully pendulous. Most attractive when planted near evergreens. Easily grown but is best transplanted while small. Can be invasive.
B. p. gracilis (weeping)	30–40 ft.	30–40 ft.	Zones 2–6	Recognizable by thin, pendulous branches and deeply cut leaves.
B. utilis jacquemontii (white bark Himalayan)	30–40 ft.	20–30 ft.	Zones 4–7	Brilliant white to cream bark. Color is variable, so try to choose one with whitest bark. A good choice if leaf miner is a problem in your area.
Broussonetia (paper mulberry)				
Broussonetia papyrifera	35–40 ft.	40–50 ft.	Zones 6–10	Irregularly lobed leaves. Female catkins that develop in late spring turn into orange to red fruits in mid to late summer. Trunk gnarled on old trees.
Caesalpinia (poinciana)				
Caesalpinia gilliesii (bird of paradise bush)	10–20 ft.	8–12 ft.	Zones 9–11	Feathery greenish-blue foliage and yellow flowers with prominent red stamens. Stays in bloom all summer.
Carpinus (hornbeam)				
Carpinus betulus (European)	35–45 ft.	35–40 ft.	Zones 4–7	Autumn leaf color is yellow. Upright forms available. Transplant when young. Young trees adapt well to shearing and can be used for hedging.
C. caroliniana (American)	20–30 ft.	20–30 ft.	Zones 3–9	Grayish, smooth bark. Develops fruiting catkins, like all hornbeams. Leaves turn reddish in fall. Grows slowly, forming a number of main branches. Needs some shade and wind protection. A fine tree for small gardens.
C. japonica (Japanese)	25–30 ft.	30–35 ft.	Zones 4–8	Toothed leaves turn bright red in fall. Slow grower; develops into fan shape.
Carya (hickory)				
Carya illinoinensis, or C. pecan (pecan)	60–80 ft.	40–50 ft.	Zones 4–9	Produces sweet nuts in easy-to-crack shells. Transplant when very young. Yields are reduced by shortened growing season in some areas.
C. ovata (shagbark hickory)	60–80 ft.	30–40 ft.	Zones 4–8	Light gray, shaggy bark and sweet, egg-shaped, edible nuts.
Castanea (Chinese chestnut)				
Castanea mollissima	40–50 ft.	40–60 ft.	Zones 4–8	Least susceptible to chestnut blight. For best results, set 2 trees, preferably different varieties, about 100 ft. apart. Improves cross-pollination, yields more nuts.

Few dogwoods are more impressive in spring than a *Cornus kousa* covered in creamy white blooms.

Cornus kousa

Catalpa bignonioides 'Nana' (umbrella catalpa)

Celtis occidentalis (common hackberry)

Cercidiphyllum japonicum (katsura tree)

Cercis (redbud)

Chionanthus virginicus (American fringe tree)

Cladrastis kentukea (American yellowwood)

Cornus florida (flowering dogwood)

BOTANICAL AND COMMON NAMES	HEIGHT	SPREAD	HARDINESS	DECORATIVE CHARACTERISTICS, SPECIAL REQUIREMENTS, AND REMARKS
Catalpa (catalpa)				
Catalpa bignonioides 'Nana' (umbrella)	15–20 ft.	10–15 ft.	Zones 4–9	The species has white showy flowers in erect spikes, but this dwarf form rarely flowers and is grown for its shape.
C. speciosa (northern)	40–60 ft.	20–35 ft.	Zones 4–8	Larger than *C. bignonioides* 'Nana'. Broad, dark, pendulous seed pods persist all winter. Very late to leaf out in spring.
Celtis (hackberry)				
Celtis laevigata (Mississippi hackberry, or sugarberry)	30–60 ft.	30–40 ft.	Zones 5–9	Orange-red fruit that turns purple furnishes winter color if not eaten by birds. This broad, roundheaded tree is resistant to witches' broom.
C. occidentalis (common)	30–50 ft.	30–40 ft.	Zones 2–9	Easily grown in most soils. Resistant to droughts, pests, and diseases. Makes good substitute for American elm. Casts dense shade.
Cercidiphyllum (katsura tree)				
Cercidiphyllum japonicum	25–60 ft.	20–30 ft.	Zones 4–8	Often forms several trunks at base and has spreading branches. Makes columnar specimen if grown with a single trunk. Blue-green leaves turn yellow to scarlet in fall and smell of caramel. Requires considerable moisture.
Cercis (redbud)				
Cercis canadensis (eastern)	15–25 ft.	20–30 ft.	Zones 4–9	Light pink or white blooms arise in clusters on trunk and branches in early spring.
Cercis chinensis (Chinese)	12–20 ft.	10–15 ft.	Zones 6–9	Rose-purple flowers appear in spring before leaves. Fall foliage is yellow.
Chionanthus (fringe tree)				
Chionanthus retusus (Chinese)	15–20 ft.	12–18 ft.	Zones 5–8	White flowers cover tree from early to mid summer. Leaves and flower clusters are about half as large as those of *C. virginicus*. Excellent small tree.
C. virginicus (American)	12–20 ft.	10–25 ft.	Zones 4–9	White flower panicles appear in early summer, just after late-developing leaves. These are followed by blue berries in grapelike clusters on female trees. In fall leaves turn yellow. Susceptible to scale infestations.
Cladrastis (yellowwood)				
Cladrastis kentukea (American)	30–45 ft.	30–40 ft.	Zones 4–8	Has bright green leaves and pendulous, fragrant white flowers in early summer. Develops attractive rounded shape with age.
Cornus (dogwood)				
Cornus alternifolia (pagoda)	15–25 ft.	20–30 ft.	Zones 3–7	Horizontal branches turn up at the ends. Clusters of white flowers held above branches in spring. Blue-black berries attract birds. Good fall color. Does best in light, dappled shade, but will take full sun, especially in the North.
C. florida (flowering)	20–40 ft.	10–40 ft.	Zones 5–9	In late spring tiny greenish flowers are surrounded by white or pink bracts that resemble the petals of a large flower. Leaves turn red in fall, and scarlet fruits attract birds. In winter large flower buds and twiggy horizontal branches make this tree attractive in the landscape. There are many named forms with flowers of different shades and sizes, and some with variegated foliage.
C. f. rubra (red-flowered)	10–20 ft.	15–35 ft.	Zones 6–9	Bracts range from pink to Not quite so hardy as *C. florida*.

Rich green foliage adorns the spreading branches of the dove tree (*Davidia involucrata*) from spring through fall. Creamy white bracts Around the tiny flowers resemble doves in flight and appear after a few years' growth.

Davidia involucrata

Davidia involucrata

Cornus mas
(cornelian cherry)

Corylus
(hazel)

Cotinus coggygria
(smoke tree)

Crataegus laevigata
(English hawthorn)

Davidia involucrata
(dove tree)

BOTANICAL AND COMMON NAMES	HEIGHT	SPREAD	HARDINESS	DECORATIVE CHARACTERISTICS, SPECIAL REQUIREMENTS, AND REMARKS
C. kousa (kousa dogwood)	20–30 ft.	20–35 ft.	Zones 5–8	Blooms in midsummer; more compact than *C. florida*. Showy, long-lasting, pointed bracts change from green to white to pink. Red fruits in autumn, which last several weeks, resemble large raspberries. 'Gold Star' has leaves with a central area of pale yellow.
C. mas (cornelian cherry)	15–25 ft.	20–25 ft.	Zones 4–8	Small, rounded tree with dense, dark green leaves and clusters of little yellow flowers in early spring. Foliage turns soft red in autumn. Useful as windbreak or screen. Tolerates shade and city conditions.
C. nuttallii (Pacific)	20–40 ft.	20–40 ft.	Zones 7–8	Blooms in midspring and often again in autumn. Showy bracts are white or pink, appearing in midspring; fruits are orange or red. Thrives on West Coast; seldom survives in the East.
Corylus (hazel) *Corylus colurna* (Turkish)	35–40 ft.	20–25 ft.	Zones 4–7	A tough tree that withstands city conditions and drought. It has dark green foliage and a pyramidal outline. Catkins give spring interest and provide nuts in fall.
Cotinus (smoke tree) *Cotinus coggygria*	12–15 ft.	15–20 ft.	Zones 4–8	Fluffy purplish flower clusters appear in summer. When they fade, hairy flower stalks continue "smoky" effect that gives this tree its common name. Rounded leaves, up to 3 in. long, are blue-green in summer, changing to yellow to orange-red in autumn. Named varieties are female, and these give best display.
Crataegus (hawthorn) *Crataegus crus-galli* (cockspur)	25–35 ft.	25–40 ft.	Zones 3–7	Hardy species with abundance of thorns and red fruit. Shiny leaves.
C. laevigata (English)	15–25 ft.	10–20 ft.	Zones 5–7	Clusters of 6–12 white flowers become scarlet fruits each fall. Leaves stay green in fall. Low-branched habit of growth forms round-topped outline.
C. lavallei (Lavalle)	15–25 ft.	15–20 ft.	Zones 4–7	Grown mainly for its orange-red fruit that remains on branches most of winter. Leaves become bronze-red in autumn. Flowers are white with red markings.
C. l. 'Crimson Cloud'	15–25 ft.	10–20 ft.	Zones 5–7	Deep red single blossoms.
C. l. 'Paul's Scarlet'	15–25 ft.	10–20 ft.	Zones 5–7	Bright scarlet double flowers make a fine show.
C. l. plena	15–25 ft.	10–20 ft.	Zones 5–7	Outstanding variety with double white flowers.
C. mordenensis 'Snowbird'	15–20 ft.	15–20 ft.	Zones 3–7	Has double white flowers, red fruit, and fewer thorns than most hawthorns. Double light pink flowers darkening with age. Also quite thorn-free.
C. m. 'Toba'	15–20 ft.	15–20 ft.	Zones 3–7	White flowers in early summer; red fruit lasts into winter. Shiny foliage turns scarlet in fall. Superior tree with dense branching, rounded top.
C. phaenopyrum (Washington)	20–30 ft.	15–25 ft.	Zones 4–8	
Davidia (dove tree) *Davidia involucrata*	25–40 ft.	25–40 ft.	Zones 6–8	This choice tree has showy creamy white bracts (resembling doves in flight) that accompany inconspicuous flowers. It may take a few years before this tree blossoms for the first time. Leaves remain green in autumn.

The weeping European ash (*Fraxinus excelsior pendula*) is a specimen tree. The flowering ash (*F. ornus*) blooms in early summer.

Fraxinus excelsior pendula

Fraxinus ornus

Delonix regia (flame tree)   *Ebenopsis ebano* (Texas ebony)   *Elaeagnus angustifolia* (Russian olive)   *Evodia daniellii* (Korean)   *Fagus sylvatica* (European beech)   *Franklinia alatamaha* (Franklin tree)   *Fraxinus americana* (white ash)

BOTANICAL AND COMMON NAMES	HEIGHT	SPREAD	HARDINESS	DECORATIVE CHARACTERISTICS, SPECIAL REQUIREMENTS, AND REMARKS
Delonix (poinciana) *Delonix regia* (royal, or flame tree)	25–30 ft.	15–30 ft.	Zone 11	Feathery foliage and scarlet and yellow flowers in summer. Shallow-rooted.
Ebenopsis (ebony) *Ebenopsis ebano* (Texas ebony)	25–30 ft.	18–20 ft.	Zones 7–9	A slow-growing native species with thorny branches and fragrant spikes of creamy flowers in summer. It may be partly evergreen in the southern part of its range.
Elaeagnus (Russian olive, or oleaster) *Elaeagnus angustifolia*	10–20 ft.	10–20 ft.	Zones 2–7	Narrow grayish-green leaves are silvery beneath. Small yellowish berries in fall follow inconspicuous, fragrant yellow flowers of summer. An invasive tree in the western United States.
Evodia (evodia) *Evodia daniellii* (Korean)	30–50 ft.	30–50 ft.	Zones 4–8	Flat heads of small white flowers cover this tree in midsummer when few other trees are in bloom. The fruits are red to black and give color in early fall. Most soils and sun.
Fagus (beech) *Fagus grandifolia* (American)	60–80 ft.	50–70 ft.	Zones 3–9	Attractive light gray bark and foliage that turns yellow-bronze in fall add distinction to this large tree. Casts dense shade. Requires space around it.
F. sylvatica (European)	50–70 ft.	30–50 ft.	Zones 5–7	Similar attractive bark. Dark green leaves are slightly toothed.
Franklinia (Franklin tree) *Franklinia alatamaha*	18–20 ft.	10–15 ft.	Zones 5–8	Blooms in fall after most other trees. White, camellialike flowers are enhanced by shiny 6-in. leaves that turn orange-red in fall. May not survive sustained sub-zero temperatures.
Fraxinus (ash) *Fraxinus americana* (white)	50–70 ft.	30–40 ft.	Zones 3–9	In autumn its compound leaves turn to colors ranging from yellow to purple. Seedless varieties that do not leave unsightly litter on ground are available.
F. excelsior pendula (weeping European)	40–60 ft.	40–70 ft.	Zones 4–7	Branches droop to form umbrella shape.
F. nigra (black)	30–40 ft.	25–35 ft.	Zones 2–5	A smaller tree that does well in both wet and dry soils.
F. n. 'Fallgold'	30–40 ft.	20–25 ft.	Zones 2–5	Better fall color and more upright.
F. ornus (flowering)	40–50 ft.	35–45 ft.	Zones 5–6	In late spring fragrant whitish flowers develop in terminal clusters.
F. pennsylvanica (green)	40–50 ft.	20–30 ft.	Zones 3–9	Bright green foliage turns vivid yellow in fall. This is excellent choice for windy sites. Seedless varieties such as 'Marshall's Seedless' are the best choice.

From late spring to early summer, *Laburnum* is spectacular with long trailing clusters of golden-yellow flowers.

Laburnum watereri 'Vossii'

| *Ginkgo biloba* (maidenhair tree) | *Gleditsia triacanthos* (honey locust) | *Gymnocladus dioica* (Kentucky coffee tree) | *Halesia monticola* (Carolina silver bell) | *Jacaranda mimosifolia* (jacaranda) | *Juglans nigra* (black walnut) | *Koelreuteria paniculata* (goldenrain tree) | *Laburnum watereri* (golden chain) |

BOTANICAL AND COMMON NAMES	HEIGHT	SPREAD	HARDINESS	DECORATIVE CHARACTERISTICS, SPECIAL REQUIREMENTS, AND REMARKS
Ginkgo (ginkgo, or maidenhair tree) *Ginkgo biloba*	35–60 ft.	20–30 ft.	Zones 3–8	Fan-shaped leaves turn yellow in fall. Plant only male trees (named forms), since fruit on female trees is unsightly and foul smelling when it falls. Although slow to establish and gawky when young, tree becomes handsome, shapely specimen. Virtually immune to diseases and pests and withstands city conditions.
Gleditsia (honey locust) *Gleditsia triacanthos Inermis* (thornless)	35–75 ft.	35–45 ft.	Zones 3–9	Fernlike leaves. Bears pods to 1½ ft. long that create litter when they fall. Easy to transplant. Good city tree.
Gymnocladus (Kentucky coffee tree) *Gymnocladus dioica*	40–50 ft.	35–45 ft.	Zones 4–8	Coarse tree with 1½-to-3-ft compound leaves that remain green in fall. Bears flat reddish-brown pods 8 in. long. Winter profile is picturesque.
Halesia (silver bell) *Halesia carolina* (Carolina)	20–30 ft.	25–35 ft.	Zones 4–8	White bell-shaped flowers in clusters open in early spring before leaves unfold. Needs well-drained soil and protection from wind. Persistent fruit are attractive.
H. diptera (two-winged)	20–30 ft.	20–30 ft.	Zones 5–8	Similar to but less profuse bloom than *H. carolina*.
H. monticola (mountain)	40–60 ft.	30–50 ft.	Zones 5–8	Pendulous large white flowers in late spring; yellow leaves in fall.
Jacaranda (jacaranda) *Jacaranda mimosifolia*	40–50 ft.	25–30 ft.	Zone 11	Spreading tree with clusters of purple flowers in spring.
Juglans (walnut) *Juglans cinerea* (butternut)	40–60 ft.	40–50 ft.	Zones 3–7	A well-shaped tree that needs a rich, well-drained soil. It may grow larger than the given size in native stands. The nuts are very hard and difficult to crack without smashing the meat.
J. nigra (black)	60–90 ft.	60–90 ft.	Zones 4–9	Edible nuts have very hard shells. Two trees ensure greater production of nuts. Tree requires fertile soil, considerable moisture. Attracts few pests. Secretions from roots inhibit growth of some plants.
J. regia (English, or Persian)	50–60 ft.	40–50 ft.	Zones 5–9	Leaves are dark green and glossy. Nuts have thinner shells, more meat than *J. nigra*, but cultural needs are the same. Variety 'Carpathian' hardy to Zone 3.
Koelreuteria (varnish tree) *Koelreuteria paniculata* (goldenrain tree)	20–30 ft.	20–30 ft.	Zones 5–9	In summer tan or yellow seedpods form after small, bright yellow blooms fade. No autumn color change. Grows in most soils. Does best in full sun.
Laburnum (golden chain) *Laburnum watereri*	15–20 ft.	12–15 ft.	Zones 5–7	In late spring yellow pealike flowers develop in long, hanging clusters, followed by 2-in. brown seedpods lasting into winter and containing poisonous seeds.
L. w. 'Vossii'	15–20 ft.	12–15 ft.	Zones 5–7	Leaves like clover. Good small garden tree. Longer flower trusses.

The American sweet gum (*Liquidambar*) has outstanding fall color.

Liquidambar styraciflua

| *Lagerstroemia indica* (crape myrtle) | *Liquidambar styraciflua* (American sweet gum) | *Liriodendron tulipifera* (tulip tree) | *Maackia amurensis* (Amur) | *Magnolia soulangiana* (saucer magnolia) | *Malus* (flowering crab apple) |

BOTANICAL AND COMMON NAMES	HEIGHT	SPREAD	HARDINESS	DECORATIVE CHARACTERISTICS, SPECIAL REQUIREMENTS, AND REMARKS
Lagerstroemia (crape myrtle) *Lagerstroemia indica*	20–25 ft.	20–25 ft.	Zones 7–9	Small tree with attractive bark and good fall color. Many named varieties in different colors have crinkled flowers in late summer.
Liquidambar (sweet gum) *Liquidambar styraciflua* (American)	50–70 ft.	35–45 ft.	Zones 5–9	Leaves are star shaped. A sweet-smelling gum exudes from crevices in trunk. Not easy to transplant. Grown mainly for its outstanding fall colors of yellow, red, and bronze. There are many named forms.
Liriodendron (tulip tree) *Liriodendron tulipifera*	50–65 ft.	20–25 ft.	Zones 4–9	Leaves turn golden yellow in autumn. Pale yellow-green and orange tuliplike flowers open in early summer. Good lawn specimen where soil is rich and moderately moist.
Maackia (maackia) *Maackia amurensis* (Amur)	20–25 ft.	25–30 ft.	Zones 3–7	The 12-in.-long leaves, with many smaller leaflets, give a light, filtered shade. Upright spikes of creamy-white flowers in summer have a pleasant fragrance, while the yellow-to-amber bark adds winter interest. Good in most soils.
Magnolia (magnolia) *Magnolia acuminata* (cucumber tree)	50–70 ft.	45–65 ft.	Zones 4–8	Flowers in late spring are small, greenish yellow, and not very noticeable. Fruits, 3–4 in. long, are pink to red in autumn and very showy. Attractive leaves have pale green downy undersides. Fast-growing, handsome tree.
M. denudata (Yulan magnolia)	35–50 ft.	35–50 ft.	Zones 5–8	Cup-shaped blossoms are creamy white and aromatic. They open in late spring before pale green leaves come out.
M. loebneri (Loebner magnolia)	20–30 ft.	15–20 ft.	Zones 4–8	White lily-shaped blossoms have pale purple line at base. They appear in midspring but do not last long.
M. l. 'Merrill'	25–30 ft.	30–35 ft.	Zones 4–8	Will bloom at younger age than other magnolias with fragrant 4-in. white flowers in mid to late spring before leaves appear.
M. salicifolia (anise magnolia)	18–30 ft.	15–25 ft.	Zones 5–8	In late spring soft hairy buds open into fragrant, handsome white blossoms. Leaves appear later and turn yellowish in fall. When crushed, they exude anise aroma. In winter watch out for magnolia scale on all species and varieties. Treat scale as recommended on p. 507.
M. soulangiana (saucer magnolia)	15–25 ft.	15–25 ft.	Zones 4–9	Showy, large purplish flowers even on young trees. Many varieties available, with flowers ranging from white to pink. Tree may have one or more trunks.
Malus (flowering crab apple) *Malus baccata* (Siberian)	25–30 ft.	25–30 ft.	Zones 3–7	White flowers develop into small yellow or red fruit that birds love. Columnar and weeping forms are also available.
M. 'Candied Apple'	15 ft.	20 ft.	Zones 4–8	A weeping variety with pink flowers and cherry-red fruits.
M. 'Centurion'	25 ft.	15–20 ft.	Zones 4–8	Rose-red flowers, even on young trees, and bright red persistent fruits.
M. 'Dolgo'	35–40 ft.	40 ft.	Zones 2–8	Aromatic white flowers appear in abundance only every other year, in late spring. Red fruits in late summer are good for jelly. This wide-spreading tree is very hardy and resistant to scab.

Parrotia persica

Parrotia persica 'Pendula'

The Persian parrotia (*Parrotia persica*) is a spreading tree that rather resembles an overhanging bush. 'Pendula' is a smaller weeping form.

Morus alba
(white mulberry)

Nyssa sylvatica
(sour gum)

Ostrya virginiana
(hop hornbeam)

Oxydendrum arboreum
(sourwood)

Parrotia persica
(Persian parrotia)

BOTANICAL AND COMMON NAMES	HEIGHT	SPREAD	HARDINESS	DECORATIVE CHARACTERISTICS, SPECIAL REQUIREMENTS, AND REMARKS
M. floribunda (Japanese)	25–30 ft.	15–20 ft.	Zones 4–8	In late spring this rounded tree has fragrant rose-red flowers that later fade to white. Fruits are red and yellow, showy each year from late summer to midfall.
M. 'Harvest Gold'	30 ft.	15 ft.	Zones 4–8	Pink buds open white. The golden fruits can persist until spring. Flowers after most other crab apples. Habit is more upright, almost columnar.
M. 'Molten Lava'	15 ft.	18 ft.	Zones 4–7	Pendulous branches. Single white flowers and persistent vivid red fruits.
M. 'Prairiefire'	20 ft.	20 ft.	Zones 4–8	Dark pink flowers and red-tinged new foliage. Fruits are dark red.
M. 'Profusion'	20 ft.	15–20 ft.	Zones 2–8	Red to purple flowers which fade to pink. Leaves open purple and turn bronze-green.
M. 'Robinson'	25 ft.	20 ft.	Zones 4–8	Buds are crimson, flowers dark pink, and fruits red.
M. 'Sugar Tyme'	20 ft.	15 ft.	Zones 4–8	Pale pink buds and white, fragrant flowers. Fruits are red and last well.
M. sargentii 'Tina'	5 ft.	10 ft.	Zones 4–8	A dwarf spreading variety with white flowers and red fruits.
Morus (mulberry) *Morus alba* (white)	20–45 ft.	25–35 ft.	Zones 4–8	White, pink, or purple fruit. Is a fast-growing tree. Withstands poor soil and drought. Attracts birds. Ripened fruits tend to drop and cause stains. The weeping form is widely available. Can be invasive.
Nyssa (sour or black gum, or tupelo) *Nyssa sylvatica*	30–60 ft.	25–30 ft.	Zones 4–9	Horizontal branches that droop at ends bear leathery, dark green leaves. Foliage turns vivid orange to scarlet in fall. This tree grows well even in very moist soil—for instance, bordering swamps and streams.
Ostrya (hop hornbeam, or ironwood) *Ostrya virginiana*	25–35 ft.	15–25 ft.	Zones 3–9	Inconspicuous greenish flowers develop into attractive, bladderlike fruits that are an asset all summer. Slow grower; difficult to transplant.
Oxydendrum (sourwood, or sorrel tree) *Oxydendrum arboreum*	15–35 ft.	15–25 ft.	Zones 5–9	Glossy, leathery leaves on drooping branches are dark green, turning to brilliant red in autumn. Hanging 6-to 8-in. clusters of fragrant, white bell-shaped flowers resemble lilies of the valley and are followed by gray fruits. Does best in acid soil.
Parrotia (parrotia) *Parrotia persica* (Persian)	15–20 ft.	10–15 ft.	Zones 5–8	Flowers with showy red stamens appear in spring. In fall foliage turns bright yellow, orange, or scarlet. Horizontal, wide-spreading branches. Attractive, flaking bark.

The phellodendron requires a lot of space and its leaves and tiny inedible fruits smell of turpentine if handled. One of the most vigorous of the fast-growing poplars, *Populus canadensis* 'Aurea' bears clear yellow leaves that turn gold in fall.

Phellodendron amurense

Populus canadensis 'Aurea'

Phellodendron amurense
(amur cork tree)

Pistacia chinensis
(Chinese pistachio)

Platanus hispanica
(London plane tree)

Populus deltoides
(cottonwood)

Prunus padus
(European bird cherry)

Prunus maackii
(amur)

BOTANICAL AND COMMON NAMES	HEIGHT	SPREAD	HARDINESS	DECORATIVE CHARACTERISTICS, SPECIAL REQUIREMENTS, AND REMARKS
Phellodendron (amur cork tree) *Phellodendron amurense*	30–45 ft.	30–45 ft.	Zones 3–7	Heavy-textured, soft, porous bark and shapely, wide-spreading form. Small ¼-in. black berries, borne only on female trees, may be a nuisance when they fall. Leaves and berries emit scent of turpentine when crushed. Grass grows easily beneath, as leaves cast light shade. Adapts to almost any soil. Resistant to pests and diseases. Withstands pollution well. In spite of common name, this does not produce cork. Source of cork is *Quercus suber*. Should not be planted in the Mid Atlantic and Midwest, where it is invasive.
Pistacia (pistachio) *Pistacia chinensis* (Chinese)	30–35 ft.	25–35 ft.	Zones 7–9	Leaves resemble those of sumac. Colorful foliage in fall, which is unusual in hot climates. Grows rapidly and tolerates heat, drought, and alkaline soil.
Platanus (plane tree, or sycamore) *Platanus hispanica* (London plane)	50–75 ft.	50–75 ft.	Zones 5–8	Cream-colored bark flakes to reveal yellow inner bark. Similar to *P. occidentalis*. Usually produces fruits in clusters of 2. Good for urban gardens.
P. occidentalis (buttonwood, or sycamore)	60–80 ft.	60–80 ft.	Zones 4–9	Flaking bark and clusters of ball-like fruits make this tree distinctive. Slow to establish after being moved.
Populus (poplar, aspen, or cottonwood) *Populus balsamifera* (balm of Gilead)	50–70 ft.	40–60 ft.	Zones 3–8	Toothed leaves with hairy undersides are often more than 6 in. long.
P. berolinensis (Berlin poplar)	40–50 ft.	25–35 ft.	Zones 3–7	A hardy species that is frequently used as a windbreak in severe regions of country.
P. canadensis 'Eugenei' (Carolina poplar)	60–85 ft.	20–25 ft.	Zones 3–8	Has shiny, coarse leaves and narrow, pyramidal shape. Do not plant near pipes or drains—roots are invasive.
P. canescens 'Tower' (tower poplar)	60–70 ft.	8–10 ft.	Zones 2–9	A narrow upright form that is seedless and doesn't sucker. Probably the best pyramidal poplar.
P. deltoides (cottonwood)	60–80 ft.	45–60 ft.	Zones 3–9	Capsules discharge annoying cotton. Cottonless kinds available.
P. nigra 'Italica' (Lombardy poplar)	60–70 ft.	10–15 ft.	Zones 3–9	A fast-growing, short-lived tree with branches parallel to the main trunk.
P. 'Northwest'	40–50 ft.	25–35 ft.	Zones 2–8	A good upright form, very hardy and useful on the prairies. Can be invasive in natural areas.
P. tremuloides (quaking aspen)	50–70 ft.	30–40 ft.	Zones 1–8	The 3-in. leaves stir in even gentlest breezes. In fall leaf color is dazzling yellow. Plant in groups for most striking effect.
Prunus (bird cherry, or Mayday) *Prunus padus* (European bird cherry)	25–35 ft.	20–30 ft.	Zones 3–6	Six-inch sprays of fragrant white flowers give black fruits that birds love.
	30–40 ft.	30–40 ft.	Zones 3–6	Foliage has a purple tinge and the flowers are pink. Gives a dense shade.
P. p. 'Colorata' (Swedish Mayday) P. p. commutata (Mayday tree)	30–40 ft.	30–40 ft.	Zones 3–6	Similar to the species, but comes into bloom at least a week earlier and with larger flowers. One of the very first trees to bloom.
Prunus (choke cherry) *Prunus maackii* (amur)	25–35 ft.	20–25 ft.	Zones 2–6	Pyramidal when young but widening with age. White flowers in late spring give black fruits that bring birds. Good fall color. Cinnamon-brown bark peels like that of birch.
P. virginiana (common)	25–30 ft.	15–20 ft.	Zones 2–6	White flowers in drooping clusters give purple fruits that are only good for cooking (with lots of sugar).
P. v. 'Shubert'	20–25 ft.	10–20 ft.	Zones 2–6	Leaves open green and turn purple as they age. Good for small spaces and poor soils.

Prunus padus

Prunus serrulata 'Kanzan'

In April the ornamental Japanese cherry tree (*Prunus serrulata* 'Kanzan') opens its dark rose blossoms. White blossoms of the bird cherry (*P. padus*) have a light almond scent.

Prunus triloba 'Multiplex'
(flowering almond)

Prunus mume
(Japanese flowering apricot)

Prunus avium plena
(Mazzard)

Prunus cerasifera
(purple-leaved flowering plum)

Pterocarya fraxinifolia
(Caucasian wing nut)

Pterostyrax hispida
(fragrant epaulette tree)

Pyrus calleryana
(Callery pear)

BOTANICAL AND COMMON NAMES	HEIGHT	SPREAD	HARDINESS	DECORATIVE CHARACTERISTICS, SPECIAL REQUIREMENTS, AND REMARKS
Prunus (flowering almond)				
Prunus triloba 'Multiplex'	15–20 ft.	20 ft.	Zones 3–6	Double, pale pink flowers on this fruitless shrub or small tree look like powder puffs.
Prunus (flowering apricot)				
Prunus mume (Japanese)	15–20 ft.	15–20 ft.	Zones 6–9	Fragrant pale pink flowers in early spring. Large green or yellow fruit.
Prunus (flowering cherry)				
Prunus avium plena (Mazzard)	40–50 ft.	40–50 ft.	Zones 3–8	Double white flowers open in late spring. Very hardy tall tree.
P. sargentii (Sargents)	30–35 ft.	20–25 ft.	Zones 4–7	Pink flowers open before the leaves. Good bronzy fall color and attractive reddish bark. The variety 'Rancho' is narrower.
P. serrulata 'Amanogawa' (Oriental)	15–20 ft.	10–15 ft.	Zones 5–8	Semi-double flowers are pale pink.
P. s. 'Kiku-shidare-zakura'	20–25 ft.	20–25 ft.	Zones 5–8	A weeping form with double pink flowers.
P. s. 'Kanzan'	20–25 ft.	15–20 ft.	Zones 5–8	Also known as P. s. 'Hisakura', this variety has dark pink double blossoms that hang downward. Young leaves bronze, turn green during summer.
P. s. 'Shirotae'	15–20 ft.	15–20 ft.	Zones 5–8	Excellent semi-double or double variety with pleasing fragrance.
P. subhirtella (Higan)	20–30 ft.	20–30 ft.	Zones 5–8	Pale pink blossoms cover tree in midspring; blue-black fruits develop in summer. Semi-double pink flowers opening in late fall and spring in some varieties.
P. yedoensis (Yoshina)	20–25 ft.	20–25 ft.	Zones 6–8	Grows fast and provides white flowers tinged with pink that have faint aroma.
Prunus (flowering plum)				
Prunus blireiana	20–30 ft.	15–20 ft.	Zones 5–8	In spring leaves open with copper color that lasts into summer. Double flowers are light pink; branches flower well indoors. Needs considerable pruning to thrive.
P. cerasifera 'Newport' (purple-leaved)	15–20 ft.	12–18 ft.	Zones 4–8	Reddish-purple leaf coloration, enhanced by full sun, lasts all summer. Light pink flowers survive only a few days. Purple autumn fruits, 1 in. in diameter, are edible.
P. nigra (Canada)	20–30 ft.	10–15 ft.	Zones 2–5	White flowers appear before the leaves and give yellowish fruits in small clusters.
Pterocarya (wing nut)				
Pterocarya fraxinifolia (Caucasian)	40–90 ft.	40–80 ft.	Zones 5–8	Bears 12- to 20-in. clusters of winged seeds that hang beneath branches and ripen in fall. Does best in full sun and moist soil.
P. stenoptera (Chinese)	40–100 ft.	40–90 ft.	Zones 6–8	Has shorter clusters of seeds than P. fraxinifolia. Both have broadly spreading branches and are good street trees. Will survive even in compacted soil.
Pterostyrax (epaulette tree)				
Pterostyrax hispida (fragrant)	20–30 ft.	20–35 ft.	Zones 4–8	Drooping clusters of white, very fragrant flowers in early summer, even on young trees. Leaves are silvery beneath and turn dull yellow in fall. Makes a roundheaded tree at maturity.
Pyrus (pear)				
Pyrus calleryana (Callery)	15–25 ft.	15–20 ft.	Zone 4–8	Clusters of white flowers open in late spring, followed by inedible, small rust-colored fruits that birds consume. Good street tree with glossy foliage. Many named forms.
P. ussuriensis (Ussurian)	30–40 ft.	25–30 ft.	Zone 3–7	White flowers in spring and good fall color.

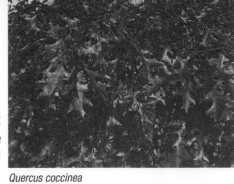

The long-lived scarlet oak (*Quercus coccinea*) is named for its splendid fall foliage. *Robinia pseudoacacia* 'Bessoniana' is a small variety of black locust.

Quercus coccinea

Robinia pseudoacacia 'Bessoniana'

Quercus alba
(white oak)

Robinia pseudoacacia
(black locust)

Salix babylonica
(weeping willow)

Sassafras albidum
(sassafras)

BOTANICAL AND COMMON NAMES	HEIGHT	SPREAD	HARDINESS	DECORATIVE CHARACTERISTICS, SPECIAL REQUIREMENTS, AND REMARKS
Quercus (oak)				
Quercus alba (white)	50–75 ft.	50–70 ft.	Zones 3–9	Spreading branches form stately, rounded head. In autumn foliage turns purplish red. This is a slow-growing species and extremely long-lived.
Q. bicolor (swamp white)	50–60 ft.	50–60 ft.	Zones 3–8	Similar to white oak but grows better in moist to wet soils. Needs an acidic soil or leaves become chlorotic.
Q. coccinea (scarlet)	50–60 ft.	35–40 ft.	Zones 4–9	Shiny green leaves become vivid scarlet in autumn. Needs an acidic soil.
Q. imbricaria (shingle)	40–50 ft.	40–50 ft.	Zones 4–8	Shiny deep green leaves turn russet in fall, and persists until spring. If allowed to grow freely, these trees will assume rounded shape with age. A row planting can be clipped to form high hedge.
Q. macrocarpa (burr or mossycup)	70–80 ft.	80–100 ft.	Zones 2–8	Slow growing but pollution tolerant. Acorn cup is fringed with hairs that gives common name.
Q. palustris (pin)	30–50 ft.	25–30 ft.	Zones 4–8	Lower branches droop downward. Leaves turn red in fall. Needs acid soil.
Q. phellos (willow)	40–60 ft.	30–40 ft.	Zones 6–9	Thin willowlike leaves, pointed at both ends, turn dull yellow in fall.
Q. robur 'Fastigiata' (upright English)	50–60 ft.	15–20 ft.	Zones 4–8	A good narrow tree for small gardens. Somewhat variable in size from seed.
Q. rubra (red)	50–60 ft.	50–60 ft.	Zones 4–8	Rich red leaves in fall. Easily transplanted; a rapid grower.
Q. shumardii (Shumard)	50–75 ft.	40–50 ft.	Zones 5–9	Imposing hardwood similar in characteristics to *Q. coccinea*.
Robinia (locust)				
Robinia 'Idaho' (Idaho)	35–40 ft.	15–30 ft.	Zones 3–8	Blossoms are deep reddish purple. Survives in poor soil and hot, dry climates.
R. pseudoacacia (black locust, or false acacia)	30–50 ft.	25–30 ft.	Zones 3–8	This tree has large compound leaves and aromatic white flowers in pendulous racemes. Reddish-brown pods, up to 4 in. long, stay on tree through winter. The variety 'Frisia' has yellow foliage that retains its color all summer. Can be invasive. Do not plant near prairies or woodland edges.
Salix (willow)				
Salix alba (white)	45–60 ft.	40–50 ft.	Zones 4–9	Delicately toothed leaves are silky on undersides. Handsome upright species with open habit of growth.
S. a. vitellina (yellowstem)	45–60 ft.	40–50 ft.	Zones 3–9	Twigs are vivid yellow, providing interesting accent during winter.
S. babylonica (weeping)	30–40 ft.	30–40 ft.	Zones 6–8	Pendulous branches bend to ground. Finely toothed leaves are grayish green on undersides. Roots likely to spread.
S. caprea (goat)	15–20 ft.	12–15 ft.	Zones 4–8	Nearly oblong 3- to 4-in. leaves are slightly toothed. Catkins are vivid yellow or silvery. Tree tolerates heavy clay soil. 'Kilmarnock' (often sold as 'Pendula') is a small weeping form.
S. discolor (pussy)	15–20 ft.	12–15 ft.	Zones 3–8	Oblong or elliptic leaves are up to 4 in. long and bluish green on undersides, some with toothed margins.
S. elegantissima (Thurlow weeping)	30–40 ft.	25–30 ft.	Zones 4–7	Better suited to cold-winter regions than *S. babylonica*, but leaves are not as lustrous.
S. matsudana 'Tortuosa' (corkscrew)	30–40 ft.	25–35 ft.	Zones 4–7	Spirally twisted olive-green twigs bear narrow lance-shaped leaves. Like most willows, this variety needs moisture to thrive.
Sassafras (sassafras)				
Sassafras albidum	40–60 ft.	25–40 ft.	Zones 5–9	Inconspicuous blooms. Fiery red and orange leaves in fall. Dark blue berries appear in autumn on vivid red stalks. Hard to transplant but thrives in poor soils. Suckers freely.

Sorbus aucuparia

Stewartia pseudocamellia

The rowan tree (*Sorbus aucuparia*) is distinguished by large clusters of brilliant red berries. Cup-shaped white flowers make the Japanese stewartia (*Stewartia pseudocamellia*) a delight all summer long. Its bright green leaves turn gold, purple, and red in fall.

Sophora japonica
(Chinese scholar tree)

Sorbus americana
(American ash)

Stewartia pseudocamellia
(Japanese stewartia)

Styrax obassia
(fragrant snowbell)

Syringa reticulata
(Japanese tree)

Tilia cordata
(little-leaved linden)

Zelkova serrata
(Japanese zelkova)

BOTANICAL AND COMMON NAMES	HEIGHT	SPREAD	HARDINESS	DECORATIVE CHARACTERISTICS, SPECIAL REQUIREMENTS, AND REMARKS
Sophora (scholar tree, or pagoda tree) Sophora japonica (Chinese)	30–40 ft.	40–50 ft.	Zones 4–8	Ascending and spreading branches form neat canopy of dark green leaves. Small, creamy white, pealike flowers appear in late summer. Good city tree.
Sorbus (mountain ash) Sorbus alnifolia (Korean)	25–35 ft.	20–25 ft.	Zones 3–7	Produces many flowers that measure up to 1 in. across. In fall leaves turn orange to scarlet; berry clusters assume same colors. Bark is dark gray and smooth.
S. americana (American)	20–30 ft.	20–25 ft.	Zones 2–7	Up to 15 leaflets form compound leaves. Late spring flowers are white. Bright red berries appear In autumn. Does best in acid soil.
S. aucuparia (European, or rowan tree)	20–30 ft.	20–25 ft.	Zones 3–7	Reddish leaves and vivid red fruit clusters in fall make this a handsome specimen for lawns. Do not plant if fire blight disease (see p. 525) is prevalent in your area.
S. thuringiaca (oakleaved)	20–30 ft.	15–20 ft.	Zones 4–8	Foliage is not as dissected as most mountain ash and turns a copper color in fall.
Stewartia (stewartia) Stewartia pseudocamellia (Japanese)	40–50 ft.	30–40 ft.	Zones 5–7	Red bark peels off in large pieces. White flowers and bright crimson leaves are attractive in autumn.
Styrax (snowbell) Styrax japonicus (Japanese)	20–30 ft.	25–35 ft.	Zones 4–8	In early and mid summer fragrant, white bell-shaped flowers appear on undersides of branches. Good lawn tree. Few insect or disease problems, but sometimes dies for no apparent reason.
S. obassia (fragrant)	20–30 ft.	20–30 ft.	Zones 5–8	Large oval or almost round leaves have hairy undersides. White flowers open in early summer and are partly hidden by leaves. Flowers are followed by egg-shaped seedpods up to 1 in. long.
Syringa (lilac) Syringa reticulata 'Ivory Silk' (Japanese tree)	25–30 ft.	20–25 ft.	Zones 3–7	In summer creamy white flowers stand out against the dark green foliage. A good street and city tree.
Tilia (linden) Tilia americana (American)	40–60 ft.	30–40 ft.	Zones 2–8	Coarse-textured leaves are often up to 8 in. long. In early summer small aromatic flowers attract bees. Leaves turn brown in late summer.
T. cordata (little-leaved)	30–50 ft.	30–40 ft.	Zones 3–8	Grows slowly, developing pyramidal form. Good street and city tree, but prone to borers.
T. c. 'Glenleven'	30–50 ft.	30–35 ft.	Zones 3–8	Young twigs, light yellowish green, are especially attractive in winter.
T. c. 'Greenspire'	30–50 ft.	20–25 ft.	Zones 3–8	An excellent, fast-growing city tree.
T. tomentosa (silver)	40–60 ft.	20–30 ft.	Zones 4–7	Leaf undersides are covered with whitish down, hence common name. Upright branches produce pleasing pyramidal shape. Less suitable for city planting than other lindens.
Ulmus (elm) Ulmus americana (American)	60–70 ft.	45–50 ft.	Zones 2–9	Although decimated by Dutch elm disease, resistant clones and resistant hybrids with the smooth-leaf elm (U. carpinifolia) are in nurseries. Look for 'Homestead', 'Jacan', 'Liberty', 'Morton', and 'Pioneer'.
Zelkova (zelkova) Zelkova serrata (Japanese)	50–60 ft.	50–60 ft.	Zones 5–8	Disease free and fairly fast growing. Good substitute for American elm. 'Green Vase' and 'Village Green' are good choices.

Broad-leaved Evergreen Trees

Most broad-leaved evergreens have wide leaves like those of most deciduous trees, but they do not drop their leaves in fall. In the chart below, they are listed alphabetically by their botanical names, with each tree's common name in parentheses. Recommended species and varieties are also listed.

Although many factors influence a tree's chance of survival, the most dependable indicator of its hardiness is the lowest temperature it can endure in winter. To determine whether a broad-leaved evergreen may reasonably be expected to survive the lowest average winter temperature in your area, check the zone designation for that tree in the Hardiness column. Then refer to the Hardiness Zone Map at the front of the book.

The figures in the second and third columns indicate the height and spread each tree can be expected to attain—contingent upon growing conditions and the care it receives in your garden. Some trees grow taller in the wild.

Arbutus unedo

Juniperus communis 'Hibernica' ➡

Acacia farnesiana
(sweet acacia)

Arbutus unedo
(strawberry tree)

Eriobotrya japonica
(Japanese loquat)

Ilex altaclarensis
(Altaclara holly)

Magnolia grandiflora
(Southern magnolia)

Prunus laurocerasus
(cherry laurel)

Washingtonia filifera
(California fan)

BOTANICAL AND COMMON NAMES	HEIGHT	SPREAD	HARDINESS	DECORATIVE CHARACTERISTICS, SPECIAL REQUIREMENTS, AND REMARKS
Acacia (acacia) *Acacia farnesiana* (sweet)	20–25 ft.	15–25 ft.	Zones 8–11	Bright yellow flowers in late winter on thorny branches.
Arbutus (strawberry tree) *Arbutus unedo*	10–25 ft.	10–25 ft.	Zones 7–9	Toothed leaves are a glossy dark green. White blooms in 2-in. clusters and strawberrylike fruits appear in autumn.
Eriobotrya (loquat) *Eriobotrya japonica* (Japanese)	15–20 ft	15–25 ft.	Zones 8–10	Leaves dark green above, tan below. White flowers in fall.

Ilex (holly)
Ilex altaclarensis (Altaclara)
   I. aquifolium (English)
 	
   I. opaca (American)
	35–45 ft.
	30–40 ft.
	
	15–30 ft
		20–30 ft.
		30–40 ft.
		
		10–20 ft.
			Zones 7–10
			Zones 7–9
			
			Zones 5–9
				A hybrid with shiny, toothed leaves and red berries.
				Spiny oblong to oval leaves are up to 4 in. long. Fruits are bright red or yellow. Used as Christmas decorations.
				Spiny leaves up to 3 in. long are yellowish green on undersides. Fruits are usually red.

Magnolia (magnolia) *Magnolia grandiflora* (southern, or bull bay)	60–80 ft.	30–50 ft.	Zones 6–9	Leathery oblong leaves up to 8 in. long have glossy upper surfaces and rusty undersides. Fragrant, large white flowers open in early and mid summer.
Prunus (prunus) *Prunus laurocerasus* (cherry, or English, laurel)	18–20 ft.	25–30 ft.	Zones 6–8	Glossy leaves to 6 in. long. Fragrant flowers in late spring; small purple-black fruits. Tolerates shearing. Makes handsome windbreak.
Quercus (oak) *Quercus virginiana* (southern live)	40–80 ft.	60–100 ft.	Zones 8–10	Wide-spreading tree with white-backed oval leaves.
Washingtonia (palm) *Washingtonia filifera* (California fan)	50–70 ft	10–20 ft.	Zone 11	Erect grayish-green leaves. Good in dry soil.

Coniferous Trees

Conifers are cone-bearing plants; most are evergreen with needlelike leaves. Most provide year-round foliage in shades of blue, bronze, gray, gold, green, and silver.

In the charts that follow, conifers are listed in alphabetical order according to their botanical names. Their common names are in parentheses. Recommended species and varieties are also listed.

Although many factors influence a tree's chances of survival, the most dependable indicator of its hardiness is the lowest temperature it can endure. To determine whether a conifer can reasonably be expected to survive the lowest average temperature in your area, check the zone designation for that conifer in the Hardiness column, then refer to the Hardiness Zone Map at the front of the book.

The figures in the second and third columns indicate the height and spread each tree can be expected to attain.

Cedrus deodara 'Kashmir'

Abies koreana
(Korean fir)

Araucaria araucana
(monkey puzzle)

Calocedrus decurrens
(incense cedar)

Cedrus libani 'Glauca'
(cedar of Lebanon)

BOTANICAL AND COMMON NAMES	HEIGHT	SPREAD	HARDINESS	DECORATIVE CHARACTERISTICS, SPECIAL REQUIREMENTS, AND REMARKS
Abies (fir)				
Abies balsamea (balsam)	30–60 ft.	20–25 ft.	Zones 3–5	Glossy green leaves rounded or notched at their apex. Tree has a narrow, spirelike form.
A. cephalonica (Greek)	75–90 ft.	40–50 ft.	Zones 6–7	Sharp-pointed needles, up to 1 in. long, spread widely around shoots.
A. concolor (white)	60–80 ft.	40–50 ft.	Zones 3–7	Needles are bluish or green, and large cones are greenish purple. Reasonably resistant to drought and heat. Best fir for city settings.
A. homolepis (Nikko)	60–80 ft.	20–30 ft.	Zones 4–6	Needles are 1 in. long with white bands beneath and purplish cones up to 4 in. long.
A. koreana (Korean)	45–50 ft.	30–40 ft.	Zones 4–6	A distinctively compact pyramidal tree with needles which are silver-white beneath.
A. veitchii (Veitch)	50–70 ft.	20–35 ft.	Zones 3–6	Needles point forward, curve upward, have white undersides. Blue-purple cones.
Araucaria (araucaria)				
Araucaria araucana (monkey puzzle)	55–60 ft.	20–30 ft.	Zones 7–10	Tiers of branches produce intricate, open tree with flat oval leaves.
A. heterophylla (A. excels) (Norfolk Island pine)	80–120 ft.	20–25 ft.	Zones 9–11	Branches in horizontal tiers with sharp-pointed leaves.
Calocedrus (incense cedar)				
Calocedrus decurrens	60–100 ft.	20–30 ft.	Zones 5–8	Small, shiny scalelike leaves are aromatic when crushed. Bark is reddish brown and furrowed. Few insects bother this tree.
Cedrus (cedar)				
Cedrus atlantica (Atlas)	70–80 ft.	60–70 ft.	Zones 6–9	Light green leaves less than 1 in. long have attractive silvery sheen. Pale brown cones are often 3 in. long. Forms flat top at maturity. Like all cedars, this species needs plenty of room and does best in moist but very well drained soil.
C. a. 'Fastigiata'	50–70 ft.	30–40 ft.	Zones 6–9	Bluish-gray needlelike leaves have silvery hue. Narrow upright form.
C. a. 'Glauca' (blue Atlas)	80–100 ft.	60–70 ft.	Zones 6–9	Foliage is beautiful bluish shade.
C. deodara (deodar)	70–80 ft.	40–50 ft.	Zones 6–8	Branches with pendulous ends are characteristic of this species. Deep blue-green leaves are about 2 in. long. Red-brown cones are often up to 5 in. long.
C. libani (cedar of Lebanon)	70–80 ft	70–80 ft.	Zones 5–7	Dark to bright green 1-in.-long leaves and brown cones up to 4 in. long.
C. l. 'Glauca'	75–100 ft.	50–60 ft.	Zones 6–8	Much like C. libani, but foliage has silvery cast.

Juniperus chinensis 'Plumosa Aurea'

Cryptomeria japonica 'Cristata'

Juniper is a welcome addition to any garden. Dense foliage of the Chinese juniper (*Juniperus chinensis*) becomes golden bronze in cold weather. Japanese cedar (*Cryptomeria japonica*) is an ideal single tree for smaller gardens. Tips of the variety 'Cristata' form cockscomblike crests.

Cephalotaxus harringtonia
(Japanese plum yew)

Chamaecyparis lawsoniana
(Lawson false cypress)

Cryptomeria japonica
(Japanese cedar)

Cupressocyparis leylandii
(Leyland cypress)

Cupressus macrocarpa
(Monterey cypress)

Juniperus chinensis 'Stricta'
(spiny Greek juniper)

BOTANICAL AND COMMON NAMES	HEIGHT	SPREAD	HARDINESS	DECORATIVE CHARACTERISTICS, SPECIAL REQUIREMENTS, AND REMARKS
Cephalotaxus (plum yew)				
Cephalotaxus harringtonia (Japanese)	15–20 ft.	20–25 ft.	Zones 6–9	Green needlelike leaves are borne on branches that are pendulous at tips. Fleshy egg-shaped fruits are purple, ripening in second season. Good near coast or in shade.
Chamaecyparis (false cypress)				
Chamaecyparis lawsoniana (Lawson)	75–80 ft.	25–30 ft.	Zones 5–7	Pendulous branches have reddish-brown bark. Scalelike leaves in sprays are usually green or blue-green, but there are varieties with silver, blue, yellow, and white-tipped leaves. Male cones are reddish; mature female cones, brown. Needs considerable moisture.
C. obtusa (Hinoki)	65–70 ft.	30–35 ft.	Zones 4–8	Scalelike leaves on branchlets hanging in flat sprays are shiny green and have pale white lines on undersides. Cones, ⅜ in. wide, are orange-brown. Bark is red-brown. Many varieties are slow growing. Some reach only 3–10 ft. Some have rich yellow foliage. Needs moist soil.
C. pisifera (Sawara)	15–60 ft.	5–20 ft.	Zones 4–8	Horizontal branches form narrow pyramidal shape. Brownish-red bark peels in older specimens. Some varieties have yellow branch tips or leaves that are pale blue or silver-gray. Has open habit of growth.
Cryptomeria (cryptomeria, or cedar)				
Cryptomeria japonica (Japanese cedar)	30–100 ft.	15–40 ft.	Zones 5–9	Abundant small leaves that curve inward at their ends, small cones, and shredding, reddish-brown bark make this an attractive tree. Foliage becomes brownish in winter. Cannot tolerate prolonged periods of heat, drought, cold winter wind.
C. j. 'Lobbii'	40–50 ft.	15–25 ft.	Zones 5–9	Similar to *C. japonica* but somewhat hardier.
Cupressocyparis (Leyland cypress)				
Cupressocyparis leylandii	60–70 ft.	10–15 ft.	Zones 6–10	Flat sprays of gray-green scalelike leaves. Adaptable to either dry or moist situations. Takes pruning well. Makes an excellent hedge or screen plant. A fast grower.
Cupressus (cypress)				
Cupressus macrocarpa (Monterey)	40–75 ft.	30–60 ft.	Zones 7–9	Scalelike leaves are in 4 rows. Female cones are longer than they are wide. When young, tree has pyramidal form; develops wide top with age. Shear to form hedges and windbreaks. Fine along seacoast. A fast grower.
Juniperus (juniper)				
Juniperus chinensis (Chinese)	20–35 ft.	15–20 ft.	Zones 3–9	Numerous varieties available, some with blue-green to steel-blue foliage.
J. c. 'Stricta' (spiny Greek)	20–35 ft.	10–15 ft.	Zones 3–9	This narrow, erect form is often sold as *J. excelsa stricta*.
J. communis (common)	20–25 ft.	10–15 ft.	Zones 2–6	Prickly foliage makes it hard to handle; good salt tolerance. Many varieties are prostrate, but several are treelike.
J. rigida (needle)	25–35 ft.	15–25 ft.	Zones 6–9	An excellent evergreen with drooping branches. Needlelike leaves.
J. scopulorum (Rocky Mountain)	25–35 ft.	variable	Zones 3–7	Often forks near base like *J. virginiana*. Blue fruit ripens during second year.
J. virginiana (eastern red cedar)	50–75 ft.	15–25 ft.	Zones 3–9	Like many junipers, this species has needlelike foliage on young branches and scalelike leaves on older wood. Fruit is dark blue. Reddish-brown bark peels off in strips. Grows well in rocky soil. Yellow-tipped and grayish-green-needled varieties are widely available.

The European larch (*Larix decidua*) requires deep soil. The Colorado spruce (*Picea pungens*) is impressive on the lawn: 'Globosa' is a shimmering blue.

Larix decidua

Picea pungens 'Globosa'

Larix decidua
(European larch)

Metasequoia glyptostroboides
(dawn redwood)

Picea glauca
(white spruce)

Pinus parviflora
(Japanese white pine)

BOTANICAL AND COMMON NAMES	HEIGHT	SPREAD	HARDINESS	DECORATIVE CHARACTERISTICS, SPECIAL REQUIREMENTS, AND REMARKS
Larix (larch)				
Larix decidua (European)	40–60 ft.	25–30 ft.	Zones 3–6	Like all the larches, loses its needlelike leaves in fall after turning bright yellow. Pyramidal shape later becomes irregular.
L. kaempferi (Japanese)	40–60 ft.	25–35 ft.	Zones 3–7	A fast-growing species with bluish-green leaves and egg-shaped cones.
Metasequoia (dawn redwood)				
Metasequoia glyptostroboides	80–100 ft.	25–35 ft.	Zones 4–8	Deciduous conifer. Needlelike leaves turn bronze in fall. In moist soils it may grow several feet taller each year. Trunks grow to 9 ft. in diameter.
Picea (spruce)				
Picea abies (Norway)	150–165 ft.	60–80 ft.	Zones 2–7	Branches are pendulous at ends. Foliage is handsome deep green. Numerous varieties exist, including a few dwarf forms and one with dark yellow foliage. Grows rapidly when young. Can be invasive.
P. asperata (dragon)	60–75 ft.	30–35 ft.	Zones 4–8	Pale green to bluish needles stay on branches as long as 7 yr., making attractively dense form. Grayish-brown bark peels off.
P. engelmannii (Engelmann)	75–150 ft.	40–70 ft.	Zones 3–5	Retains lower branches longer than many other spruces. Has bluish-green foliage. Needs great amount of room. Fine-looking, extremely hardy tree.
P. glauca (white)	70–90 ft	30–40 ft.	Zones 1–6	Moderately attractive evergreen with bluish-green foliage on ascending branches that droop at tips. Tolerates considerable drought and heat. Varieties encompass 1 dwarf and several compact growers.
P. omorika (Serbian)	90–115 ft.	20–25 ft.	Zones 3–7	Branches become pendulous with age. Shiny green needles are flat and have 2 white stripes on undersides.
P. pungens (Colorado)	70–100 ft.	20–30 ft.	Zones 2–7	Extremely hardy evergreen with sharp, bluish-green needles. The popular 'Koster' blue spruce is a selection of this species. Susceptible to spruce gall aphid attacks. One of few spruces that can survive city conditions.
Pinus (pine)				
Pinus bungeana (lacebark)	60–75 ft.	35–45 ft.	Zones 5–8	Dark green needles grow in clusters of 3. May have more than 1 trunk. Multicolored bark peels to reveal cream-colored inner bark.
P. cembra (Swiss stone)	50–75 ft.	30–35 ft.	Zones 2–7	Bluish-green needles in clusters of 5 are almost 5 in. long and abundantly produced. Forms dense, pyramidal shape. Seeds are edible.
P. contorta (shore)	25–30 ft	15–25 ft.	Zones 5–7	Develops many branches. Dark green needles are in pairs. Cones are 3 in. long. Forms rounded top. Grows in dry or wet soil.
P. c. latifolia (lodgepole)	50–80 ft	40–45 ft.	Zones 1–5	Distinguished by pairs of short, twisted needles and a vigorous habit.
P. densiflora (Japanese red)	80–90 ft	50–60 ft.	Zones 4–7	Easily recognized by orange-red color of trunk and older branches.
P. flexilis (limber)	50–70 ft.	40–60 ft.	Zones 4–7	Stiff, dark green needles in threes. Cones are egg shaped. A slow grower.
P. nigra (Austrian)	70–90 ft.	30–40 ft.	Zones 4–7	Dark green needles. Pyramidal shape. Lives in alkaline soils. A fast grower.
P. parviflora (Japanese white)	60–75 ft	60–70 ft.	Zones 4–7	Long needles in clusters of 5 are usually toward ends of twigs.
P. ponderosa (ponderosa)	100–150 ft.	25–30 ft.	Zones 2–6	Needles are in clusters of 2 or 3. A fast grower. Not for small gardens.
P. resinosa (red)	60–75 ft.	40–50 ft.	Zones 2–7	Green needles, in pairs, are shiny. Bark is reddish. Grows rapidly even in poor soil.
P. strobus (eastern white)	60–100 ft.	50–60 ft.	Zones 3–8	An elegant tree with soft needles in clusters of 5. Makes a good windbreak.
P. sylvestris (Scotch)	40–90 ft.	35–40 ft.	Zones 2–8	Particularly attractive in winter, when its reddish bark is very striking. Can be invasive.

Pinus sylvestris

Pseudolarix amabilis

Slow-growing Scotch pine (*Pinus sylvestris*) may need 40 years' growth to produce flowers and cones. Golden larch (*Pseudolarix amabilis*) on the other hand grows rapidly, especially in its early years.

Platycladus orientalis
(yew podocarpus)

Podocarpus macrophylla
(southern yew)

Pseudolarix
(golden larch)

Pseudotsuga menziesii
(Douglas fir)

Sciadopitys verticillata
(umbrella pine)

Sequoia sempervirens
(coast redwood)

Sequoiadendron
(giant sequoia)

Taxodium distichum
(bald cypress)

BOTANICAL AND COMMON NAMES	HEIGHT	SPREAD	HARDINESS	DECORATIVE CHARACTERISTICS, SPECIAL REQUIREMENTS, AND REMARKS
Platycladus (oriental arborvitae) *Platycladus orientalis*	20–50 ft.	15–20 ft.	Zones 6–9	Densely branched trees with bright green foliage. Egg-shaped cones have scales with hooklike tips. Varieties include pyramidal kinds and those with yellow, blue, and variegated foliage.
Podocarpus (podocarpus) *Podocarpus macrophylla* (southern yew)	40–60 ft.	30–40 ft.	Zones 8–10	Lance-shaped, 3- to 4-in. leaves are yewlike and have dark green upper surfaces with paler hue beneath. Greenish-purple, egg-shaped fruits are about ½ in. long.
Pseudolarix (golden larch) *Pseudolarix amabilis*	20–50 ft.	20–40 ft.	Zones 5–7	Needlelike leaves turn golden before dropping in fall. Light brown egg-shaped cones shatter. Not troubled by pests that generally attack true larches.
Pseudotsuga (Douglas fir) *Pseudotsuga menziesii*	90–100 ft.	15–25 ft.	Zones 6–8	Short flat needles have 2 light-colored bands on undersides. Egg-shaped cones are often over 4 in. long and hang down. Handsome tree.
P. m. glauca	80–90 ft.	20–25 ft.	Zones 4–6	Soft needles are blue-green. Grow in sheltered spot. Has shallow roots, can blow over in windstorm.
P. m. 'Pendula'	70–80 ft.	15–20 ft.	Zones 6–8	Resembles *P. menziesii* except that branches droop.
Sciadopitys (umbrella pine) *Sciadopitys verticillata*	25–30 ft.	15–20 ft.	Zones 5–8	Bears 2 types of leaves, some of which are scalelike and hardly recognizable as such. Other leaves are long, shiny green needles in umbrellalike clusters of up to 30. Does not do well in wind and dry soil. Very few pests. Slow grower.
Sequoia (coast redwood) *Sequoia sempervirens*	80–100 ft.	40–50 ft.	Zones 6–9	Evergreen needles about 1 in. long are in 2 rows. Cones are less than 1 in. Has straight, massive trunk. Does best in rainy, foggy areas.
Sequoiadendron (giant sequoia, or big tree) *Sequoiadendron giganteum*	100–150 ft.	30–50 ft.	Zones 5–8	Among tallest and most massive-trunked trees known; some are up to 40 ft. in diameter. Has short scalelike needles and cones 2–3 in. long. Needs considerable rain and fog.
Taxodium (bald, or swamp, cypress) *Taxodium distichum*	100–120 ft.	50–60 ft.	Zones 4–9	Feathery, light green, deciduous foliage turns orange in fall. Bark is pale brown and scaly. Mature trees develop unique upright "knees" near base of trunk. Grows best in ordinary wet or damp soil.
T. mucronatum (Montezuma)	40–75 ft.	30–40 ft.	Zones 8–11	Similar to *T. distichum* except for wider top, larger cones, shorter leaves. Generally evergreen, but may be partially deciduous toward northern limits of its hardiness zone.

The English yew (*Taxus baccata*) makes a good specimen tree, is excellent for topiary, and makes fine hedging. 'Dovastoniana' is a spreading variety.

Taxus baccata 'Dovastoniana'

Taxus baccata
(English yew)

Thuja
(American arborvitae)

Thujopsis dolobrata
(hiba arborvitae)

Torreya californica
(California nutmeg)

Tsuga heterophylla
(Western hemlock)

BOTANICAL AND COMMON NAMES	HEIGHT	SPREAD	HARDINESS	DECORATIVE CHARACTERISTICS, SPECIAL REQUIREMENTS, AND REMARKS
Taxus (yew) Taxus baccata (English)	20–40 ft.	20–30 ft.	Zones 5–7	Wide, rounded top. Will grow in shade or sun and can be sheared. Like all yews, susceptible to black vine weevils and other pests. Foliage and berries of all yews are poisonous if eaten.
T. cuspidata (Japanese)	30–40 ft.	20–40 ft.	Zones 4–7	Female bears bright scarlet berries. Faster growing and hardier than *T. baccata*. Some forms of *T. cuspidata* are also denser and spread more.
T. media	20 ft.	10 ft.	Zones 4–7	This hybrid between English and Japanese yews comes in a range of shapes, from spreading to upright.
Thuja (arborvitae) Thuja occidentalis (eastern white cedar)	15–45 ft.	10–15 ft.	Zones 3–8	Dark green to yellow-green foliage. Cones to ½ in. long. Varieties of different heights and shapes, some with yellow, blue-green, or variegated leaves. Reddish bark. This species needs more than average moisture.
T. plicata (western red cedar)	150–200 ft.	45–70 ft.	Zones 5–7	Flat sprays of shiny green leaves with white marks beneath are handsome bronze from late fall through winter.
Thujopsis (hiba, or false, arborvitae) Thujopsis dolobrata	30–50 ft.	10–20 ft.	Zones 5–7	Similar in appearance to the common arborvitae. Leaves are white banded beneath and grow in flat sprays. Bears small woody cones. Needs plenty of moisture.
Torreya (torreya) T. californica (California nutmeg)	50–75 ft.	40–50 ft.	Zones 7–10	Glossy green 2½-in.-long leaves are evergreen except in northernmost range, where they may drop in autumn. Green and purple fruits. Fissured bark.
T. nucifera (Japanese)	50–75 ft.	25–30 ft.	Zones 6–10	Similar to *T. californica*, but thin evergreen leaves are only about half as long. Assumes pleasing pyramidal shape.
Tsuga (hemlock) T. canadensis (Canada)	70–75 ft.	25–35 ft.	Zones 3–7	Leaves are shiny, dark green on upper sides, with 2 whitish lines underneath. Shallow rooted and easy to transplant in many soil types but may fail on windy sites and in city smog. Can be sheared to form hedges.
T. caroliniana (Carolina)	45–50 ft.	20–25 ft.	Zones 5–7	Resembles *T. canadensis*, but does better in city conditions.
T. diversifolia (Japanese)	50–70 ft.	40–50 ft.	Zones 6–8	Needles that cling to branches for up to 10 yr. produce dense effect.
T. heterophylla (Western)	90–120 ft.	40–50 ft.	Zones 5–8	Energy goes mainly into height since side branches tend to be pendulous and short. Thrives in moist summer environment. Not good choice for eastern gardens.
T. sieboldii (Siebold)	60–80 ft.	35–45 ft.	Zones 6–8	Slender horizontal branches with shiny, dark green leaves.

TREES FOR SPECIFIC LOCATIONS/PURPOSES

Trees That Tolerate Wet Soil

Betula nigra

Chamaecyparis lawsoniana

Quercus palustris

Acer rubrum (red maple)
Betula nigra (river birch)
Carya illinoiensis (pecan)
Celtis laevigata (sugar hackberry)
Celtis occidentalis (hackberry)
Chamaecyparis lawsoniana
   (Lawson false-cypress)
Chamaecyparis obtuse
   (Hinoki false-cypress)
Cryptomeria japonica
   (Japanese cedar)
Fraxinus americana (white ash)
Fraxinus nigra (black ash)

Larix decidua (European larch)
Liquidambar styraciflua (American
   sweet gum)
Metasequoia glyptostroboides
   (dawn redwood)
Nyssa sylvatica (black gum)
Populus ssp. (poplar—most)
Quercus bicolor (swamp white oak)
Quercus palustris (pin oak)
Quercus virginiana (southern live oak)
Salix ssp. (willow—most)
Taxodium distichum (bald cypress)
Thuja occidentalis (arborvitae)

Trees That Tolerate Dry Soil

Acer tataricum ssp. *ginnala*

Eucalyptus globulus

Koelreuteria paniculata

Acer tataricum ssp *ginnala*
   (Amur maple)
Acer negundo (Manitoba maple)
Aesculus glabra (Ohio buckeye)
Castanea molissima
   (Chinese chestnut)
Catalpa speciosa (northern catalpa)
Celtis occidentalis
   (common hackberry)
Eucalyptus globulus (blue gum)
Fagus sylvatica (European beech)
Ginkgo biloba (maidenhair tree)

Gymnocladus dioica
   (Kentucky coffee tree)
Juniperus ssp. (juniper—most)
Koelreuteria paniculata (varnish tree)
Maackii amurensis (Amur maackii)
Phellodendron amurensis
   (Amur cork tree)
Picea pungens (Colorado spruce)
Pistachia chinensis
   (Chinese pistachio)
Prunus nigra (Canada plum)
Quercus macrocarpa (burr oak)

Trees That Grow Well in Acidic Soil

Cryptomeria japonica

Liquidambar styraciflua

Quercus coccinea

Cladrastis kentukea (yellowwood)
Cornus alternifolia (pagoda dogwood)
Cryptomeria japonica
   (Japanese cedar)
Franklinia alatamaha (Franklin tree)
Halesia caroliniana
   (Carolina silver bell)
Ilex ssp. (holly—most)

Liquidambar styraciflua
   (American sweet gum)
Nyssa sylvatica (black gum)
Pseudolarix amabilis (golden larch)
Quercus coccinea (scarlet oak)
Quercus palustris (pin oak)
Sciadopitys verticillata
   (umbrella pine)
Styrax japonicus (Japanese snowbell)

Trees That Tolerate Roadside or Seaside Salt

Morus alba

Populus deltoids

Prunus virginiana

Carya ovata (shagbark hickory)
Cladrastis kentukea (yellowwood)
Fraxinus americana (white ash)
Morus alba (white mulberry)

Populus deltoides (cottonwood)
Prunus virginiana (chokecherry)
Quercus rubra (red oak)

Trees for Part* or Full Shade**

Catalpa speciosa

Taxus

Thujopsis dolobrata

Acer pensylvanicum (striped maple**)
Carpinus carolinianus
   (American hornbeam**)
Catalpa speciosa (northern catalpa*)
Cornus alternifolia
   (pagoda dogwood*)
Cornus mas (cornelian cherry*)

Laburnum watereri (golden chain*)
Ostrya virginiana (hop hornbeam**)
Styrax japonicus
   (Japanese snowbell*)
Taxus ssp. (yew—most*)
Thujopsis dolobrata (hiba arborvitae*)

Trees With Colored Foliage (often only on the cultivar)

Abies concolor

Cornus kousa

Gleditsia triacanthos

Abies concolor (white fir—SILVER)
Cercis canadensis
   (redbud—RED-PURPLE)
Cornus florida (flowering dogwood—
   GREEN & WHITE, GREEN & YELLOW,
   PURPLE)
Cornus kousa (kousa dogwood—
   GREEN & YELLOW)
Fagus sylvatica (European beech—
   PURPLE, MULTICOLORED)

Gleditsia triacanthos (honey locust—
   YELLOW, REDDISH)
Juniperus virginiana
   (red cedar—BLUISH)
Prunus cerasifera
   (flowering plum—PURPLE)
Prunus virginiana
   (chokecherry—PURPLE)
Pyrus salicifolia
   (willow-leaved pear—SILVER)

Trees With Showy Winter Fruit

Crataegus lavallei

Malus fruits

Ostrya virginiana

Catalpa speciosa (northern catalpa)
Crataegus ssp. (hawthorn—most)
Euonymus europaeus (spindle tree)
Gymnocladus dioica
 (Kentucky coffee tree)
Halesia caroliniana
 (Carolina silver bell)

Malus ssp. (crab apple—most)
Ostrya virginiana (hop hornbeam)
Phellodendron amurensis
 (Amur cork tree)
Sophora japonica (pagoda tree)
Sorbus ssp. (mountain ash—most)

Trees With Interesting Winter Bark or Shape

Acer griseum

Platanus hispanica

Prunus maackii

Acer griseum (paperbark maple)
Acer pensylvanicum (striped maple)
Betula nigra (river birch)
Betula papyrifera (paper birch)
Betula utilis (whitebark birch)
Carpinus carolinianus
 (American hornbeam)
Carya ovata (shagbark hickory)
Crataegus crus-galli
 (cockspur hawthorn)
Fagus ssp. (beech)
Laburnum watereri (golden chain)

Maackia amurensis (Amur maackia)
Ostrya virginiana (hop hornbeam)
Parrotia persica (Persian parrotia)
Phellodendron amurensis
 (Amur cork tree)
Pinus bungeana (lacebark pine)
Pinus sylvestris (Scots pine)
Platanus ssp. (plane tree)
Prunus maackii (Amur chokecherry)
Prunus sargentii (Sargent's cherry)
Tilia tomentosa (silver linden)

Weeping Trees (often only on the cultivar)

Cercidiphyllum japonicum

Larix decidua

Picea omorika

Cercidiphyllum japonicum
 (katsura tree)
Fagus sylvatica (European beech)
Larix decidua (European larch)
Malus baccata (Siberian crab apple)
Malus hybrids (hybrid crab apple)
Morus alba (white mulberry)

Picea abies (Norway spruce)
Pinus strobes (white pine)
Pinus omerika (Serbian spruce)
Prunus serrula
 (Japanese flowering cherry)
Salix alba (white willow)
Salix caprea (goat willow)

Trees for Fall Color

Euonymus europaeus

Prunus sargentii

Sorbus berries

Acer griseum (paperbark maple)
Acer rubrum (red maple)
Acer saccharum (sugar maple)
Amelanchier ssp. (serviceberry)
Carpinus carolinianus
 (American hornbeam)
Carya ovata (shagbark hickory)
Cercidiphyllum japonicum
 (katsura tree)
Cercis canadensis (redbud)
Chionanthus virginicus (fringe tree)
Cornus kousa (Japanese dogwood)
Crataegus crus-galli
 (cockspur hawthorn)
Crataegus phaenopyrum
 (Washington hawthorn)
Euonymus europaeus (spindle tree)
Fagus ssp. (beech)
Gleditsia triacanthos (honey locust)
Halesia caroliniana
 (Carolina silver bell)

Koelreuteria paniculata (varnish tree)
Larix decidua (European larch)
Liquidambar styraciflua
 (American sweet gum)
Nyssa sylvatica (black gum)
Ostrya virginiana (hop hornbeam)
Parrotia persica (Persian parrotia)
Populus tremuloides
 (trembling aspen)
Prunus sargentii (Sargent's cherry)
Pyrus ussuriensis (Ussurian pear)
Quercus coccinea (scarlet oak)
Quercus palustris (pin oak)
Sorbus alnifolia
 (Korean mountain ash)
Sorbus thuringiaca
 (oak-leaved mountain ash)
Styrax japonicus (Japanese snowbell)
Zelkova serrata (Japanese zelkova)

Upright Trees (often only on the cultivar)

Carpinus betulus

Ginkgo biloba

Thuja occidentalis

Abies concolor (silver fir)
Acer saccharum (sugar maple)
Carpinus betulus
 (European hornbeam)
Cryptomeria japonica
 (Japanese cedar)
Ginkgo biloba (maidenhair tree)
Juniperus ssp. (juniper—several)
Malus baccata (Siberian crab apple)
Malus hybrids (hybrid crab apple)

Metasequoia glyptostroboides
 (dawn redwood)
Picea omerika (Serbian spruce)
Pinus cembra (Swiss stone pine)
Pyrus calleryana (Callery pear)
Quercus robur (English oak)
Sorbus aucuparia
 (European mountain ash)
Thuja occidentalis (arborvitae)
Tilia cordata (little-leaved linden)

*S*hrubs play many roles in the garden. Some, like the mock orange (Philadelphus 'Innocence') shown here, are grown for their sweetly scented flowers, others for their ornamental fruits that brighten up the winter. There are shrubs with flowers that attract butterflies, and fruits that feed the birds. Then, of course, there are taller, dense shrubs that provide the perfect foil to displays of colorful annuals and perennials.

SHRUBS AND VINES

Shrubs are among the garden's most versatile plants, not only serving as a background to other displays but providing their own varying colors and textures.

The difference between a shrub and a tree is not just a matter of height. Both have stout, woody branches that stay alive the entire year, but a shrub initiates its branches at, near, or below ground level, while a tree usually has a single trunk with branches starting some distance up.

Thus, the common lilac (*Syringa vulgaris*) is a shrub even though it can reach 20 feet in height, and a 10-foot-tall flowering dogwood (*Cornus florida*) is still a tree.

Large shrubs can, of course, be pruned to look like small trees; and a large number of trees can be trained to grow like shrubs. Most vines are also technically shrubs in that they form structures of permanent woody branches.

Because shrubs are substantial and long-lived, they play a vital role in turning a patch of ground into a garden. Filling the middle ground between trees and flowers, they are the permanent framework around which showy annuals and perennials are interwoven year by year. Shrubs can be used for foundation plantings and borders, interplanted with flowers, used in their prostrate or creeping forms as ground covers, or encouraged to form their own striking silhouettes. A garden without them lacks emphasis and variety, and in the winter is reduced to a flat and lifeless plain.

With their showy berries, leaves, flowers—and sometimes even with their brightly colored bark—shrubs and vines provide visual interest in all seasons.

Deciduous or evergreen. A deciduous plant drops its leaves in the fall, often with a spectacular display of color prior to leaf-drop. It spends the winter in bare-framed dormancy and leafs out again each spring.

Compared with evergreens, which retain their foliage all winter, many deciduous shrubs make up for their wintry drabness with a spectacular spring or summer show of flowers, and perhaps with an autumnal display of colored leaves as well. Many gardeners value deciduous shrubs because they *do* change with the seasons. Also, most deciduous shrubs are less expensive than evergreens and grow more rapidly.

Evergreens provide winter color, of course, and offer certain other advantages: many kinds thrive in shady places; the tone and texture of their foliage make an interesting contrast to the more flamboyant deciduous shrubs and flowering annuals; and they give the landscape year-round stability.

There are broad-leaved evergreens, and there are those with needles. Generally speaking, the farther south you go, the wider choice of broad-leaved evergreens you will have. Most tropical and subtropical shrubs are evergreen, and in the deep South, Southwest, and Pacific Coast, they constitute the majority of garden shrubbery.

Magnolia stellata

Syringa vulgaris 'Charles Joly'

Lilacs, such as *Syringa vulgaris*, left, top the list of easy-to-grow deciduous shrubs that produce a great show of flowers. *Magnolia stellata* (star magnolia), far left, is named for its fragrant, star-shaped flowers.

Some kinds, like the magnolias, are represented in the southern states by evergreens but have deciduous species that grow well farther north. Others, such as the California privet (*Ligustrum ovalifolium*), lose their foliage only in regions where bitter winters denude their branches. And some, like the mountain laurel (*Kalmia latifolia*) and *Rhododendron maximum*, stay green all winter.

Needle or coniferous evergreens flourish throughout most of North America. They offer a wide range of shapes and colors and some variety in texture. They are often best planted along with deciduous shrubs.

The front endsheet zone map is a guide to choosing shrubs that will be winter hardy in your locale.

Other variables will affect which plants you choose, including the composition of the soil—whether it is sandy, loamy, or clayey, for example, and its acid-alkaline balance; the degree of humidity and amount of precipitation where you live; temperature extremes; the amount of sun the plant will receive; the elevation of your property; and if you live by the sea, the problems posed by salt spray.

For help with these questions, turn to the chart starting on page 288, which describes the characteristics and requirements of the most popular shrubs. Also, see the lists of shrubs for specific locations or with similar attributes starting on page 288. For more specific information, consult a reputable nursery in your area.

Uses of shrubs. A shrub may be upright, rounded, weeping, or spreading. The shape you choose depends largely on the use you plan to make of the plant in your garden.

If, for example, you need a hedge to act as a windbreak, the tough, upright bayberry (*Myrica pensylvanica*) makes sense. The English boxwood (*Buxus sempervirens*), rounded and quite tolerant of pruning, is a good choice for a low boundary hedge.

Spiny shrubs can deter intruders when planted as a hedge under first-floor windows.

If yours is a small garden, make sure the shrubs you choose are in keeping with the garden size and will not be over-large when they mature, or plant shrubs such as the red-twigged dogwood (*Cornus stolonifera*) that can be cut back almost to the ground every couple of years. If you have space, and you want to mask a compost heap or some other such eyesore, look for a large evergreen, such as an eastern white cedar (*Thuja occidentalis*), rhododendron, mountain laurel (*Kalmia latifolia*), holly (*Ilex*), yew (*Taxus*), or an upright form of juniper. Deciduous shrubs might do in summer but would be less effective in other seasons, when their branches are bare.

Shrubs serve to define and delineate space in a garden. They guide the eye toward what the gardener wants highlighted. In a small garden they can create the illusion of depth, and in an open space they can form cozy nooks. The effects depend on the imagination and skill with which the shrubs are planted.

Many shrubs, ground covers, and vines can be useful for disguising unattractive parts of a garden or home. A prostrate juniper will spread over a poorly-placed public utility cover and still allow for its removal. A chain-link fence will seem to disappear under a covering of Dropmore honeysuckle. This hardy and long-lived deciduous vine has red, tubelike flowers from midsummer to frost.

In mild climates, various climbing varieties of evergreen English ivy (*Hedera helix*) will do the same job of concealment, or will turn a dull cement-block wall into a living green backdrop for plants with flowers. An evergreen honeysuckle (*Lonicera nitida*) that is fan trained on a trellis will hide trash cans, a compost heap, tool shed, or whatever, and it will fill the air with its intoxicating fragrance as well.

Many shrubs have this bonus of sweet-scented flowers. Some give off their fragrance throughout the day, others at night, and a few only after rain. Often the aroma comes from the shrub's blooms or buds, although many shrubs have aromatic foliage and even bark. Therefore, to get maximum enjoyment from this aspect of your shrubbery, make it a point to plant beneath or around your windows.

Lilacs, mock oranges, and some viburnums are all good for this purpose. They will also do a great deal to add to the pleasure of your terrace, patio, or swimming-pool area.

Shady parts of a garden are no problem for shrubs if you use the right ones. Witch hazel (*Hamamelis virginiana*) and hydrangea are two that actually prefer partial shade. Many others, such as daphne, magnolia, skimmia, and many viburnums, do very well without the benefit of full sun.

Designing for color. Shrubs are a major part of a garden's color scheme, and because they are permanent fixtures, their placement must be carefully planned.

You must decide before planting whether adjacent shrubs should be in flower at the same time, and, if so, how well the colors of their blossoms will combine. You must choose among the coniferous evergreens—broad-leaved evergreens with flowers and berries—and the ever-changing deciduous shrubs. Furthermore, you must decide whether or not the types should be blended or planted in separate groupings.

The possible color combinations of garden shrubs are nearly infinite. In choosing one over another, the gardener comes into his or her own as a landscape artist. You can weave a striking tapestry by alternating colorful and plain shrubs, or ones with complementary foliage colors. Or you can combine masses of the same colorful shrub for a striking effect. You can even plan seasonally, using

color to enliven the winter landscape and suggest coolness on sweltering summer days. Your choice of color is a question of your own taste.

Still, certain combinations will always work and are worth considering. The association of gray foliage and white flowers, for instance, is particularly effective near water.

Gray-foliaged shrubs are also useful for separating brightly colored ones that might otherwise clash. One of the finest examples of these is silverberry (*Elaeagnus commutata*), whose silvery foliage seems to shimmer in the sun.

The combination of blue- and white-flowered shrubs against a brick wall makes a pleasant contrast. This effect could easily be achieved by grouping together one or more plants each of a blue- and a white-flowered variety of butterfly bush (*Buddleja davidii*), which blooms in late summer.

Rather than grouping shrubs in strong color contrasts, it is often better to choose a toning sequence of colors, using shades of silver, gray, and pink, or perhaps a blending of blue, mauve, rose, purple, and white.

However, bright effects should not be dismissed, and there is at least one such effect that only the right shrubs can provide. The combination of the spring heath (*Erica carnea*), with its dark green to bronze winter foliage, used as a ground cover beneath a witch hazel, with its bright yellow flowers, makes a spectacular splash of color late in the fall and even into winter, when there is little other color in the garden.

Clever use of color can mean more than appealing visual effects, however. It can also alter the perspective of your garden. Using soft colors near the end of the garden, for example, tends to disguise the boundary limits and to give the illusion of depth. This simple and easy effect is heightened by using brighter-colored foliage in the foreground and middle distance.

The snowberry (*Symphoricarpos albus*) is grown for its attractive winter fruits.

Symphoricarpos albus

Planting and Supporting Shrubs

How to Space and Plant Freestanding Shrubs

Shrubs are supplied by nurseries in three forms: container grown, with balled roots, or with bare roots.

Container shrubs are established plants growing in pots of soil or soil substitute. They can be planted outdoors at any time of year except in the dead of winter. If you plant in summer, keep the soil well watered until autumn. Newly planted shrubs may die if the soil dries out.

Balled and burlapped (sometimes called balled-root) shrubs have some soil around the roots, kept in place by burlap. Plants that have difficulty establishing themselves are sold this way to keep the root systems intact. Shrubs that develop easily after transplanting are sold with bare roots.

Shrubs are best planted in autumn or early winter after dormancy has set in but before the ground is frozen, or early spring. Evergreens can be set out earlier in the fall or later in the spring than can deciduous shrubs.

First, prepare the soil. Remove weeds from the bed with a garden fork. Dig over the soil to one spade's depth, and if possible, let it settle for about two weeks. If you must plant immediately, firm the whole bed thoroughly by treading it down.

If you are planting more than one shrub, work out the spacing beforehand and mark the planting positions. The space between shrubs should be at least half the total of their combined ultimate spread. For example, two shrubs expected to spread 4 feet and 6 feet, respectively, should be planted about 5 feet apart.

Remove the marker. Dig a hole slightly deeper and twice as wide as the container or root ball. If the plant is bare rooted, allow room for its roots to spread comfortably. Measure for depth against the plant itself.

If working with a container-grown shrub, the surface of the soil in the pot should be level with the surrounding ground. With balled- or bare- root shrubs, use the mark on the stem that indicates the former soil level. Do not remove natural burlap around a balled-root shrub; remove synthetic burlap and any rope.

Do not mix anything into the soil you remove, a rich soil stops the shrub sending roots out into the surrounding area. Break up the soil in the bottom of the hole and add some of the removed soil (backfill) to bring the base up to the correct planting level. Trim the top growth of the shrub as illustrated below if required.

If the shrub is container grown, water it well before removing the container. Make sure that the plant has an extensive root system. If it does not, return it to the nursery.

If your shrub is bare rooted, look for damaged or diseased roots and cut them back to healthy growth. Before putting the plant in the hole, make a small mound on the bottom over which to spread the roots.

When you set the shrub in the hole, hold it firmly by the base of the stem in order to keep it vertical while you fill in the hole with the prepared soil. With a container-grown or balled-root shrub, fill the hole halfway—balled-root plants should have the burlap untied and laid back across the hole at this point—then water thoroughly and let the water drain before adding more soil. Tread the soil firmly. Top with more soil, tread again, and build a small wall of soil around the hole to retain water. Soak well all around the base of the plant.

With a bare-root shrub, lift the plant up and down as you fill the hole, gently shaking the roots so that the soil will settle around them. Firm the soil with your feet several times to eliminate air pockets.

1. Dig hole twice as wide as shrub diameter. Top of roots should be at soil level.

2. Loosen soil at bottom. When refilling hole use unenriched backfill or new top soil.

3. Water well and remove container. Make sure roots are well developed.

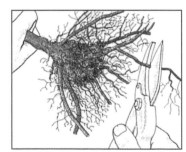

4. With a bare-root shrub, cut back all damaged and diseased roots.

5. With all shrubs, prune stumps of old wood flush with the stem.

6. Remove damaged or diseased wood. Always cut just above a bud.

7. Holding plant in place, fill the hole with soil until it is level all around.

8. Tread the soil, eliminating air pockets. Soak thoroughly.

Fragrant yellow spring blooms of *Ribes odoratum* (buffalo currant) give crops of inedible berries. *Clematis* 'Ville de Lyon' should be cut back hard in spring to bloom in summer.

Ribes odoratum

Clematis 'Ville de Lyon'

Planting a Climbing Vine Against a Wall or Fence

The soil at the foot of a wall or fence is often too dry for planting without some amount of preparation. This is particularly the case when the structure serves as a shield against prevailing winds, since the leeward side gets less rain. And because semihardy vines should never be planted in cold, exposed positions, the leeward side of wall or fence is the best location for them.

Except for clematis, you should plant vines as you do shrubs. Clematis, however, should be planted about 3 inches deeper than they were in the pot.

Most ivies, Virginia creepers, and climbing hydrangeas fasten themselves to walls with little or no assistance. Other vines may need the support of a trellis or horizontal wires.

Plastic snow fencing provides a good support. Choose netting with mesh sizes of 4–6 inches. The large mesh simplifies training and tying, and the plastic surface reduces the risk of damage to young growth from chafing.

Put supports in place before planting—about an inch from the wall so that the growing vine can twine around them.

Most plants tend to grow away from a wall; so attach young shoots to their supports as soon as possible after planting. Use string, strips of cloth, twist ties, or plant rings. Do not use bare wire, as it can cut and bruise stems. After this, shoots should start to twine themselves around the support without further help.

Staking Shrubs Vulnerable to Wind Damage

If a columnar shrub more than 3 feet tall is growing in an exposed, wind-buffeted position, it may require staking after planting. The stake should be stout and long enough to reach just below the head of the shrub.

You can buy preservative-treated stakes from garden centers. Do not use untreated stakes, which may rot.

At planting time, drive the stake in outside the root ball, or between the roots of a bare-root plant. Then, fasten the shrub with a tree tie or a strip of strong cloth. Tree ties have built-in pads of plastic or rubber to keep the stake from rubbing on the shrub stem.

You can accomplish the same purpose with cloth strips tied in a figure-eight pattern—around the stem, around the stake, and back again—until the tie is both firm and cushioned.

One tie near the top should be enough for a shrub less than 6 feet tall. Taller plants need another tie about halfway down the stake.

Inspect the ties in midsummer and autumn to see if they have become constrictive. If they are too tight, retie.

Stakes should be removed a year or so after planting. Once established, if the shrub cannot withstand winds, it is not the right choice for the site.

1. Dig the hole 12 in. from base of wall, and spread the roots outward.

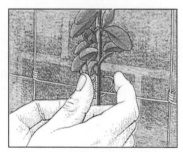

2. After planting, fasten each shoot to supports with string or vine clips.

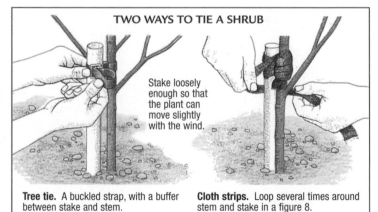

TWO WAYS TO TIE A SHRUB

Stake loosely enough so that the plant can move slightly with the wind.

Tree tie. A buckled strap, with a buffer between stake and stem.

Cloth strips. Loop several times around stem and stake in a figure 8.

Planting a Shrub in a Lawn

A shrub grown in a lawn looks best if its bed is cut neatly out of the sod. You can do this job by making a sort of compass out of a small bamboo or dowel stake, a piece of string, and a sharp knife.

Insert the stake into the grass at the center of the proposed bed, then tie the string to it. Mark off the radius of the bed on the string, and tie the knife at that point. Then, holding the string taut, score the circumference of the bed on the lawn. Cut through the sod on this mark with a spade or half-moon edger. Slice the sod into sections and remove it, stacking it to one side for later use in planting.

Dig the bed, and plant the shrub in the normal way. The sections of sod, placed grass-side-down in the bottom of the planting hole, add valuable humus to the soil.

The size of the bed should finally be about equal to the spread of the fully grown shrub, but you can start with a small bed and enlarge it a little at a time as the shrub grows.

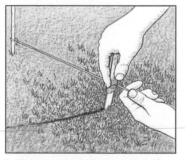

1. Mark out a circular bed, using a knife on a string attached to a peg.

2. Slice out the sod with a spade. Save sod for its value as plant food.

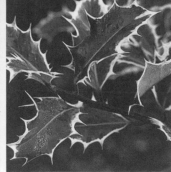

Berried shrubs add color in fall and winter. *Hippophae rhamnoides* (common sea buckthorn) produces a fall crop of showy orange fruit. Do not eat berries of the English hollies 'J. C. van Tol' and 'Handsworth New Silver'.

Hippophae rhamnoides

Ilex aquifolium 'J. C. van Tol'

Ilex aquifolium 'Handsworth New Silver'

Care and Protection of Shrubs All Year Round

Mulching, Watering, and Feeding New Shrubs

Soon after planting, while the soil is still moist, spread mulch about 2 inches thick between and around the shrubs. This will retain moisture in the soil and help to keep down weeds. If you use an organic mulch, such as leaf mold, straw, or bark chips, it will feed the plants in later years also, as it breaks down and is absorbed into the soil. Add a fresh layer of mulch each spring.

If a shrub is planted in autumn, winter, or early spring, watering after the first watering-in will probably be unnecessary, except during a long dry spell.

If you plant in late spring or summer, the shrub will need to be watered during the first few weeks to help it get established.

Late winter or very early in the spring is the time to add nutrition to the soil in the form of an all-purpose organic fertilizer. Rake back mulch around the plant. Sprinkle the fertilizer directly on the soil surface (about 1 cup per square yard). Rake mulch back into place and water well.

Whenever pests appear, hand pick if possible, wash them off using a hose with a strong stream of water, introduce natural enemies or, as a last resort, spray with environmentally friendly controls.

WATERING

Always water thoroughly after planting. Use a nozzle to break the flow of water.

MULCHING

Spread straw, leaf mold, or similar material to retain moisture after planting.

Protecting Tender Shrubs in Winter

The zone map on the front of this book defines regions in terms of average low temperatures. You can extend the range of some shrubs by sheltering them from extreme cold, especially from freezing winds, which do the most damage.

The first consideration is to choose a sheltered position at planting time—on the south side of a high wall or fence, for example, or behind a dense evergreen hedge. Shade-tolerant shrubs will also be protected from the worst winds if they are planted among trees.

But shelter is not always enough. During severe cold spells, tender shrubs will need to be blanketed with a material that will offer additional protection from wind and cold. Straw serves the purpose, as do boughs of needle evergreens; evergreen boughs from discarded Christmas trees can also be used in some regions.

With a large shrub, wrap the material around the branches, and bind with sheets of burlap tied with twine. Plants, such as roses, that regularly produce shoots from the base must also be protected in this vital area.

Toward the end of autumn, put a 6- to 9-inch layer of straw, peat moss, or even some coarse sand around the base of the plant, and leave it there until spring.

Wall shrubs and vines can be protected by removable mats made of chicken wire and straw. Simply sandwich the straw tightly in a 4- to 5-inch layer between two sheets of the chicken wire; then join the edges of the sheets by twisting the wires together. In bad weather stand the mats in front of the plants.

The same device can be used for small freestanding shrubs. Shape each mat into a cylinder, and stand it on end like a collar around the shrub. You can also top the cylinder with a lid of similar construction.

An alternative is to make a tepee from about six bamboo canes tied together at the top. Loop string around the tepee halfway down, and stuff with evergreen boughs or straw. For additional protection, cover the tepee with a sheet of burlap.

To prevent excessive moisture loss, spray evergreens with an antidesiccant in fall and winter. Strong slatted wooden frames over evergreens protect them from any snow that may slide off a roof.

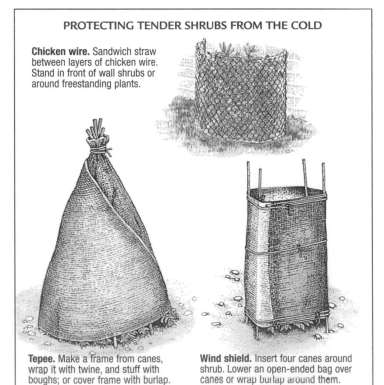

PROTECTING TENDER SHRUBS FROM THE COLD

Chicken wire. Sandwich straw between layers of chicken wire. Stand in front of wall shrubs or around freestanding plants.

Tepee. Make a frame from canes, wrap it with twine, and stuff with boughs; or cover frame with burlap.

Wind shield. Insert four canes around shrub. Lower an open-ended bag over canes or wrap burlap around them.

Buddleja weyeriana 'Sungold'   Buddleja davidii

Buddleia shrubs need a sunny location and fertile, well-drained soil. In return, they yield clusters of small fragrant flowers. The purple blooms of *Buddleja davidii* (butterfly bush) attract butterflies in late summer.

Removing Unwanted Suckers From Shrubs

A sucker is a shoot that grows from the plant base or below ground.

On most shrubs suckers are simply part of the plant and can be left in place. But a shrub that has been grafted onto a different rootstock can be weakened by the growth of suckers, and they should be removed. Shrubs likely to produce this sort of sucker include hollies, magnolias, camellias, rhododendrons, roses, and lilacs.

An unwanted sucker grows from the rootstock, and so it always appears below the union, the point where the graft has been made. In the case of shrubs, the union is usually planted below the surface; so suckers spring from below ground.

In all cases trace the sucker to its point of origin and wrench it off by hand. Do not cut it off above ground, as this will simply encourage the growth of more suckers.

Transplanting a Healthy, Established Shrub

An established shrub can be transplanted from early autumn to late spring provided the soil is neither frozen nor waterlogged.

The main danger in transplanting is that the roots can be badly damaged. To avoid this, dig deeply all the way around the shrub near the perimeter of the foliage. It is better to take too much soil than not enough.

Lever the shrub out with a shovel; then crumble away the surplus soil to lighten the load and reduce the size of the new planting hole.

Plant as though you were putting in a new balled-root shrub (see p. 250). Water thoroughly.

REMOVING SUCKERS

Dig to where the sucker joins the plant; then wrench it off.

1. Dig a trench around the shrub to avoid root damage, and pry it out.

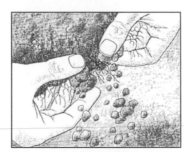

2. Expose some of the roots by crumbling soil before replanting.

Using Shrubs to Attract Birds to Your Garden

Many gardeners enjoy providing a natural haven for birds. Some shrubs and trees are grown for their attractive colored berries or fruit they produce in autumn or winter, and these are powerful draws for birds. Plant species with fruit that ripens sequentially to keep birds feeding in your garden. In return, birds will help to reduce annoying insect pests, as they have an enormous appetite for them. Birds can damage berry crops however. In the winter, finches may eat buds that would flower the following year. Thrushes and mourning doves may eat ripening fruits. If you wish to reserve and protect some of the berry crop, cover shrubs with bird netting. However, poor crops of berries can be caused by various factors.

Some varieties produce more abundant crops than others. The right growing conditions are important. A shrub's affinity for acid or alkaline soil should also be noted.

Some shrubs are dioecious—that is, the male and female flowers grow on separate plants—and cross-pollination has to occur before fruit will form. Plant dioecious shrubs—such as hollies—in groups of three or more females, with a male plant in the center of the group to ensure pollination.

Weather conditions can affect each year's crop. If a plant suffers drought at flowering time or as its berries are forming, either flowers or fruits can drop prematurely. Frost at flowering time can prevent the formation of fruit altogether. Practicing organic methods in your garden will have a beneficial effect on birds and other wildlife.

Shrubs encourage birds to visit your garden. The cotoneaster above—bright red in most species—persist from autumn well into winter. They will not only provide your garden with showy bunches of berries, they will feed the birds as well as.

Clematis
montana
'Elizabeth' ➡

Honeysuckle and clematis are favorite climbers that do well on walls and trellises but can also be grown into trees and shrubs. The common honeysuckle or woodbine (right) has a heady fragrance. 'Général Sikorski' (far right) is a summer flowering variety of clematis.

Lonicera periclymenum 'Serotina'

Clematis 'Général Sikorski'

Growing Evergreens Successfully

Evergreen shrubs are often less tolerant of intense cold and drought than deciduous shrubs. Unless a species is known to be wind tolerant, plant evergreens in sheltered places. Make sure that they are kept moist. If they are exposed to drying winds, spray with an antidesiccant in late fall or erect a burlap screen.

Watering is particularly important for both needle and broad-leaved evergreen shrubs. Lack of water shows first in the browning of the lower branches. Where the soil is frozen for long periods, make sure the soil is wet in late fall.

Container-grown specimens can also suffer from starvation. This usually shows as a general slowing down of growth, with smaller, yellow-green leaves. To maintain healthy growth, apply compost tea monthly from midspring until late in the summer. Add a cup of blood meal and bone meal to each container in late spring.

Keeping Weeds Down

Once a shrub has grown, it will probably cast too much shade for weeds to be much of a problem beneath its branches. Until then, however, any weeds that do appear must be regularly removed.

While they are still very small, use an oscillating hoe. But use it with care; many shrubs have shallow roots spreading near the surface.

Annual weeds can be smothered with a 1- to 2-inch mulch layer. This will still allow bulbs, such as daffodils and lilies, to grow between the shrubs. To eliminate weeds entirely, lay landscape fabric under the mulch.

Care should be taken to try and eliminate all perennial weeds before planting. Leave the soil bare for several weeks to give root pieces time to grow. Any that are missed, or perennial weeds that become established between the shrubs, can be killed by cutting them back repeatedly.

What Can Go Wrong With Shrubs

Properly positioned shrubs growing in good soil seldom develop any serious pest or disease problems. If your plants show symptoms that are not described here, turn to the section on plant disorders beginning on page 506.

SYMPTOMS AND SIGNS	CAUSE	CONTROL
Shrub is disfigured. Pests may be visible.	Aphids, lace bugs, leafhoppers, whiteflies, or mites	Use dormant oil in late winter. Spray with insecticidal soap.
Leaves distorted, pale, yellowed, or pinkish, with silvery dots.	Mites	Frequent sprays with water (forcefully) or insecticidal soap at 5-day intervals, especially undersides.
Leaves covered with sooty mold, pests may be visible.	Honeydew released by aphids, mealybugs, whiteflies	Control insects as above, wash off mold with soap and water spray.
Leaves have holes or ragged edges.	Caterpillars, inchworms, or beetles, usually visible	Spray caterpillars with *Bacillus thuringiensis,* inchworms and beetles with insecticidal soap or neem.
Leaves have semi-transparent blotches or lines.	Leaf miners	Spray with neem.
Leaves rolled or tied together.	Leaf rollers	Spray with insecticidal soap or *Bacillus thuringiensis.*
Leaves or leaf stalks have swellings or pimples.	Gall insects or mites	Seldom serious. In fall, rake up and dispose of fallen foliage.
Leaves wilt, stems chewed at base, or roots eaten.	Root weevils	Difficult, pest is resistant to most controls. A beneficial nematode is available commercially.

SYMPTOMS AND SIGNS	CAUSE	CONTROL
Branches and stems have rough, corky areas.	Scale insects	Prune out and destroy infected branches. Spray with dormant oil in winter, insecticidal soap in May.
Leaves, buds, or flowers are covered with a gray mold.	Botrytis (fungus)	Keep shrub growing well, spray with summer oil.
Leaves have brown blotches and fall early, shoots die.	Anthracnose (fungus)	Spray with dormant oil in late winter, with Bordeaux mixture in spring, starting as leaves unfurl. Repeat 3 times at 10-day intervals.
Leaves have circular spots that may run together.	Leafspot (several different fungi)	Spray with a copper-based fungicide or wettable sulfur.
Small brown spots on petals expand rapidly, flowers wilt and fall. Mostly on rhododendrons and azaleas.	Petal blight (fungus)	Pick off and remove infected flowers as soon as seen. Spray with Bordeaux mixture in spring.
Leaves, flowers, or buds have a white powdery coating and turn black eventually.	Powdery mildew (fungus)	Good sanitation. Dispose of leaves as they fall. Spray with potassium bicarbonate fungicide.
Leaves have rusty to orange spots; on conifers, irregular galls turn orange in spring.	Rust (fungus)	This alternates between two different host plants. On conifers, prune out as soon as seen. On other plants, spray with diluted lime sulfur.
Leaves and young fruits have sunken areas that turn corky.	Scab (fungus)	Spray with lime sulfur in late winter, with dilute lime sulfur several times in spring.
Leaves and flowers turn black, wilt, but don't fall.	Fire blight (bacterial)	Prune off and remove infected branches. Spray with lime sulfur in spring.
Spongy swellings develop on branches, stems, and roots.	Crown gall (bacterial)	Prune out, disinfect pruners between cuts with antibacterial hand soap. Avoid wounding stems when hoeing. If galls are on main stems, remove and destroy plant.

Growing Shrubs in Containers

Many of the most decorative shrubs can be grown in large pots or tubs to adorn your patio or terrace. The fact that the roots are restricted may actually improve flowering.

Not all shrubs respond well to container culture, however. In general avoid kinds with thick, fleshy roots.

Shrubs that grow well in containers include aucuba, camellia, clematis, deutzia, euonymus, fire thorn, flowering currant, forsythia, honeysuckle, kerria, mahonia, Saint John's-wort, spirea, tamarix, weigela, and wisteria.

In areas colder than Zone 6, containers should be wintered in an unheated building or put in the ground each fall to prevent undue frost penetration, which could kill the plants, even within their recommended hardiness zone.

Planting. A shrub expected to grow 4–5 feet tall and 3–4 feet wide will need a tub at least 2½ feet wide by 1½ feet deep. If there are no drainage holes in the bottom, you can make them with a drill. Add lightweight material to the bottom of the container so it won't be too heavy to move.

Add a layer of potting soil deep enough so that when the plant is placed on it the base of the stem will be slightly below the rim of the tub.

You can mix your own soil from 3 parts compost-based potting soil mix to 1 part coarse sand. Add 4 tablespoons of a blood meal and bone meal mix per bushel.

Make sure that the root ball is moist and the root system is good before setting the shrub in the container. Fill in around the shrub with more of the prepared planting mix.

Firm it down well; then fill with more soil mix to ½ inch below the rim. Water thoroughly, let the water settle, and soak the soil again.

Care and feeding. Confined roots cannot seek out water; so you must bring it to them. Water well whenever the soil surface dries out.

A year after planting—and again monthly or if the leaves seem small and discolored or when growth is meager—apply compost tea or a liquid organic fertilizer.

Shrubs that tend to grow large can be kept small and healthy by annual or biannual root pruning. In any case, maintaining a healthy shrub requires pruning both the top growth and the roots in autumn or early spring every four to six years. Remove the shrub from its pot and strip about 4 inches of roots and soil from the root ball. Scrub the container and repot with fresh soil mix.

PLANTING IN A TUB

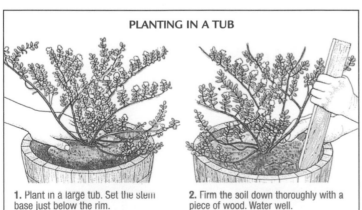

1. Plant in a large tub. Set the stem base just below the rim.

2. Firm the soil down thoroughly with a piece of wood. Water well.

PRUNING THE SHRUB

1. Prune stems as for the specific shrub (see chart, pp. 288–339).

2. Cut back roots periodically so that shrub will not be pot-bound.

The beauty-berry has clusters of very small lilac-colored flowers that are followed by bluish-violet berries. They last well into winter.

Callicarpa bodinieri 'Giraldii'

How to Grow New Shrubs From Cuttings

Hardwood Cuttings From Deciduous Shrubs

The simplest way to propagate many hardy deciduous shrubs is by taking hardwood cuttings in late fall or early winter. These are taken from vigorous stems that have just completed their first season's growth.

Hardwood cuttings are taken after the shrubs have dropped their leaves and begun a period of dormancy.

In mild regions, where the ground does not freeze to a depth of more than an inch or two, choose a site sheltered from winds and spade it thoroughly. In heavy soil incorporate coarse sand or perlite with old compost. The proportions are not critical, but use enough to lighten the soil, usually about 2 parts soil to 1 part of the mixture.

Make a narrow trench by pushing in a spade to its full blade depth and wiggling it back and forth for several inches. Place a 1- to 2-inch layer of sand or perlite in the bottom.

Choose a pencil-thick stem of the current season's growth and cut near the base. Make cuttings 9–12 inches long—a long shoot will supply two or more—but avoid using the soft tip as a cutting, since it is harder to root and may produce weak growth. Sever each cutting cleanly; cut just below a bud at the base and just above a bud at the top end, but at a slight angle.

Where frost may be a problem, cuttings are inserted vertically 3–4 inches apart in a trench, as shown; the lower half or two-thirds of the cutting is below ground when the trench is filled in. Fill in soil and firm it with your foot.

Vertically placed cuttings that become loosened by frost action should be pushed down until the base is embedded in the sand. Except for regular weeding and watering, this is the only care needed.

In still colder regions bury the cuttings horizontally under 6–8 inches of sand or sandy soil after first tying them together in bundles of six or more. In early spring dig up the cuttings, separate, and insert vertically in a trench as shown in Fig. 2.

The second spring the easily rooted cuttings will be ready to be moved to their permanent quarters. Shrubs that are slower to root or grow should be left for another year.

Firm-Wood Cuttings From Evergreens

The best time for taking firm-wood cuttings of many broad-leaved evergreens and conifers is in early to mid fall when new growth has hardened. For broad-leaved evergreens, make terminal cuttings 4–6 inches long. Trim the leaves from the lowest inch, and insert the cutting in a rooting mix—either sand or equal parts peat moss and perlite. In mild climates set directly into nursery rows when rooted; in cold climates leave in a cold frame the first winter.

Few conifers root readily from cuttings. In late summer take firm-wood cuttings from short side growths, with a heel (see p. 54) or without. Root in a greenhouse or cold frame.

Some shrubs, particularly among the broad-leaved evergreens and the conifers (needle evergreens), are difficult to root. Such cuttings often respond to wounding prior to rooting. To do this, remove a thin sliver of bark from one side or opposite sides near the base of the cutting.

Protecting with antidesiccant. Evergreen cuttings are subject to water loss from the leaves, which may retard rooting or even be fatal. This can be averted by spraying with a liquid antidesiccant, available from most garden centers.

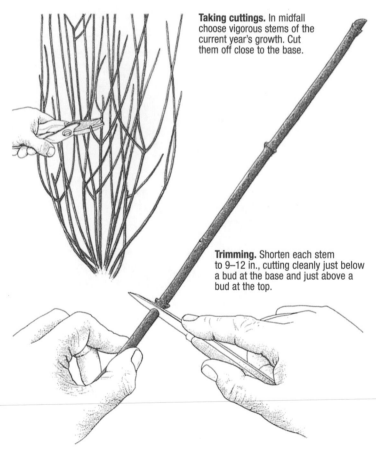

Taking cuttings. In midfall choose vigorous stems of the current year's growth. Cut them off close to the base.

Trimming. Shorten each stem to 9–12 in., cutting cleanly just below a bud at the base and just above a bud at the top.

ROOTING CUTTINGS

1. To aid rooting, remove a thin sliver of wood near the base.

2. Plant cuttings to about half their length in trenches.

3. In a year or two, cuttings are ready for transplanting.

Clusters of small, saucerlike flowers characterize potentilla, a bushy shrub that can make a good hedge or border. Dwarf potentillas are suitable for rock gardens.

Potentilla fruticosa 'Princess'

Semi-Hardwood Cuttings— Taking Them in Summer

There are a number of shrubs—the aucuba, bluebeard, and Mexican orange among them—that root poorly from hardwood cuttings, but that respond well if semi-hard material is used instead.

Semi-hard cuttings are from the current year's growth; they have become somewhat firm and woody toward the base but are still growing. The best time to take them is during the heat of mid to late summer; in a very hot year, however, they may be ready a bit earlier.

Semi-hard cuttings require some attention from the time they are taken until they have become well rooted. The essentials are: some sort of propagating frame (with or without bottom heat), regular watering, and shading from direct sun.

When the young plants have rooted, but are not yet fully established, they can either be potted or set outside in a nursery bed, where they can grow on. Either way, it will be at least a year or two before they are ready for planting in their permanent locations.

Take the cuttings by severing 6- to 8-inch side shoots from the current season's growth. These will be easy to identify—leaves will be growing on them. Cut each shoot off close to the main stem.

Strip the leaves from the bottom part of a shoot; then cut it straight across just below the lowest leaf node. Trim off the soft tip, cutting just above a leaf, to make a cutting that is 2–4 inches long.

Heeled cuttings. Semi-hard cuttings may root more surely if they include at the base a small wedge or portion of the parent stem. This is known as a heel, and it encourages roots to form by preventing the sap, as it flows down from the leaves, from draining away into the soil.

Some shrubs, such as the ceanothus and the firethorn, will root very poorly—or more likely not at all—if the heel is missing from a semi-hard cutting.

First, clip off a main shoot that carries several side shoots, but preferably without flowers. At the spots where the side shoots join the main stem, remove shoots by making V-shaped incisions into the wood of the parent.

Use a sharp knife for the task, and cut just deep enough to include some of the cambium layer (the tissue just beneath the bark).

Trim the tip back to make cuttings 2–3 inches long. Care for them as illustrated on the next page for all semi-hard cuttings.

Taking the cuttings. Late in the summer choose 6- to 8-in. side shoots of the current season's wood—any shoots with leaves on them. Cut them off close to the main stem.

Trimming. Remove the lower leaves and sever the shoots just below the longest leaf nodes, cutting straight across. Trim off the soft tips of the shoots so that the cuttings are 2–4 in. long.

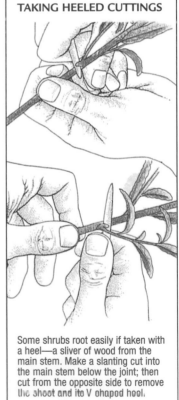

TAKING HEELED CUTTINGS

Some shrubs root easily if taken with a heel—a sliver of wood from the main stem. Make a slanting cut into the main stem below the joint; then cut from the opposite side to remove the shoot and its V-shaped heel.

Hydrangeas produce spectacular flowerheads containing masses of tiny blooms. Flowerheads may be flat (left), domed (far left), or conical.

Hydrangea macrophylla 'Alpenglühen'

Hydrangea anomala spp. *petiolaris*

Planting and Care of Semi-Hardwood Cuttings

Once the cuttings have been taken, fill a pot to just below its rim with a light soil mix meant for starting seeds, or mix your own from equal parts of peat moss and coarse sand.

The size of the pot used will depend on the length and number of cuttings. A 3-inch pot should be large enough for up to 5 cuttings, a 5-inch pot for as many as 10. For a really large number, a wooden box is best.

You may lose a few cuttings; it is therefore wise to start with more than you need so that you can select the strongest for repotting later on.

Make a hole in the soil about one-third the length of a cutting. Insert the cutting and firm the soil gently around it. Plant the other cuttings in the same way, spaced evenly, and water well with a fine spray from a mister or hose.

At this stage three things are criti-cal to successful rooting: humidity, warmth, and partial shade.

You can provide the first of these by turning the pot into a small green-house. All it takes is a clear plastic bag and two pieces of galvanized wire about 12–15 inches long. Bend the wires (coat-hanger wire will do nicely) into arcs and insert the ends into the soil so that the two arcs form a cross-shaped support. Slip the bag over this framework and secure it below the rim of the pot with string, tape, or a rubber band. The same device can be adapted for starting cuttings in a box.

If available, place the propagating container in a shaded greenhouse or cold frame. If you do not have either, place in a cool, dry area where it can-not be touched by frost. Beware of direct sunlight; it will cause over-heating in the closed atmosphere.

Ideal rooting conditions for most hardy plants exist when the soil tem-perature is maintained at a steady 61°–65°F. Although it is not absolute-ly essential, supplying the heat from beneath hastens the rooting of most plants. This can be done by using soil-warming cables or a small heat-ing mat. Propagating frames or units with similar cables built into them are also available.

If all the steps suggested here are followed carefully—the cuttings are taken at the right time and in the right way, suitable soil is used, tem-perature and humidity are main-tained—and if no fungus or other dis-ease intervenes in the process, root-ing should occur in two or three weeks. But the work is not over.

Hardening off. After cuttings have rooted, they need to be acclimatized slowly to the harsher conditions they will face outside their plastic tents. Keep them in the greenhouse or frame and raise the plastic half an inch or so, or poke a few holes in it to let in air. Keep the cuttings away from strong light. After a week, raise the plastic higher or increase the number of holes in it.

After yet another week, remove the covering. Water the cuttings, wait one more week, and they will be ready to go into individual pots.

Repotting cuttings. Shake rooted cuttings from the pot and gently sep-arate them. Prepare a 3½-inch pot for each cutting by putting in a little potting mix. Stand the young plant on this and fill it with the mix to just below the lowest pair of leaves.

Firm the soil to about ½ inch below the rim of the new container. Water generously. Keep the plant in a greenhouse or cold frame. Never let the soil dry out.

It should take the roots about three weeks to reach the limits of the pot. If the shrub is hardy in your climate, it can now be planted in the open, in a prepared bed, to become estab-lished. Tender plants should first go into larger pots and be protected until spring.

1. Insert cutting one-third of its length into a pot of peat moss and sand.

2. Water generously with sprayer or a watering can with a fine head.

3. Make a frame of galvanized wire; plastic cover retains humidity.

4. After rooting, harden off by raising the plastic a little at a time.

5. After about three weeks shake out and gently separate the cuttings.

6. Plant rooted cuttings singly in 3½-in. pots of potting soil.

7. When plant is established, it is ready for planting in the garden.

Dogwoods are cultivated for their rich foliage, summer blooms, and fall berries. In winter, the bare stems of *Cornus stolonifera* 'Flaviramea' are eye-catching in yellow-green.

Cornus stolonifera 'Flaviramea'

Softwood Cuttings Taken From Shoot Tips

Softwood cuttings are the current year's shoot tips, taken before they have become hard. Commonly used for hardy perennials and houseplants, they provide another means of propagating shrubs. Rooting potential varies greatly between species, but this method is always worth a try; if the cuttings die, you still have time to try semi-ripe or hardwood cuttings.

In the garden, prepare a site in the shade, amending the soil to make it free-draining. Create a mini-greenhouse by constructing a small polytunnel over hoops. The cuttings may be put in the soil or in pots. Indoors, a propagating case with heating cables, or a small mist unit sold by some nurseries will help ensure rooting. Since cuttings are small, they will need to be grown on in a nursery bed for a couple of years before they are large enough to plant out.

Softwood cuttings should be young and nonflowering, firm but not hard, and 2–6 inches long. Take them no later than midsummer. Cut off a shoot that has four or five pairs of leaves. Using a sharp knife or razor blade, and cutting cleanly and diagonally, sever the shoot just beneath the pair of leaves closest to the main stem. Remove the two pairs of leaves at the bottom, and dip the base of the stem in a hormone rooting powder.

Take about 10 cuttings for planting in a 5-inch pot. Fill the pot to just below its rim with a light soil mix or with a mixture of equal parts peat moss and coarse sand.

Make holes in the soil about one-third the length of the cuttings. Insert the cuttings and firm the soil. Continue propagation as for semi-hard cuttings, but allow more time for each step.

Growing Shrubs From Pieces of Root

Some plants, both herbaceous and woody, readily produce shoots directly from their roots, particularly at a point where damage has occurred. Consequently, pieces of root can be used as cuttings. Some shrubs likely to grow well from root cuttings are spireas, cotoneasters, and sumacs. One feature of root cuttings is that they require less attention than semi-hard or softwood cuttings.

In autumn, winter, or early spring, use a garden fork to lift the plant or, unearth part of the root system. Cut off some thick roots close to the main stem. With a sharp knife, cut 1½-inch-long pieces from these roots. (Thinner roots can be used, but they should be 2–3 inches long and planted horizontally about ½ inch deep.) Cut each piece of root straight across at the end nearest the stem, diagonally at the other end.

Fill a pot to just below its rim with a light soil mix or with equal parts peat moss and coarse sand. Make a hole in the soil mix to accommodate the full length of the cutting, using a dibble. Insert the cutting, straight end up, so that its top is flush with the soil surface. A 5-inch pot will hold about six cuttings.

Cover with ¼ inch of coarse sand and spray with water. Keep cuttings in a greenhouse or cold frame, and maintain warmth and moisture.

Six months later shake out the rooted cuttings from their pots and separate them gently. Pot them separately and give them the same care recommended for semi-hardwood cuttings (see p. 259).

TAKING A SOFTWOOD CUTTING

Cut off a shoot with four or five pairs of leaves. Use a sharp knife to cut the bottom of the shoot diagonally, just below the first leaves. Remove the first and second pair of leaves. Put 10 cuttings in a 5-in. pot filled with equal parts peat moss and coarse sand.

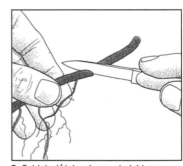

1. Use pruning shears to cut off a thick root close to shrub's main stem.

2. Cut into 1½-in. pieces, straight across at the top, angled at the base.

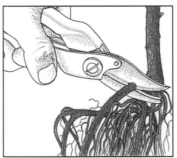

3. Use a dibble to make a hole in potting mix to accommodate each cutting.

4. In six months plants should be ready to move to 3½-in. pots.

Hibiscus syriacus

Hibiscus syriacus 'Red Heart'

Shrubby hibiscus bloom in late summer, when few other shrubs are in flower.

Leaf-Bud Cuttings for Quantity and Speed

If you want to propagate many plants from a limited amount of parent material, leaf-bud cuttings may be the best way to go. If you take these cuttings at the right time, they can root and break into growth more quickly than other types of cuttings. (But note that a year after rooting, hardwood or semi-hard cuttings will probably have grown into larger plants.)

In late summer or early fall, clip off some semi-hard lateral shoots—shoots that began growing the previous spring. Each shoot will have several leaves, and at the axil of each leaf—the spot where the leaf joins the stem—will be a growth bud.

About ¾ inch below the lowest leaf, cut through the shoot at an angle with a sharp knife. Then sever the shoot straight across just above the bud in the leaf axil. Do the same with the next leaf. You should get three or four cuttings from each shoot in this way.

Wound each cutting by scraping some bark off the ¾-inch stub. Dip the end, including the wounded part, in rooting hormone. Fill a pot to just below its rim with a light sandy soil or with equal parts peat moss and coarse sand or perlite. Insert the cuttings so that each bud barely shows above the surface. A 6- to 7-inch pot should hold about a dozen cuttings.

Water lightly with a small hand sprayer or by shaking water onto the buds with your fingertips. Cover the pot with a wire-and-plastic tent, as with semi-hard cuttings (see p. 259). Place it in a greenhouse or sheltered area, and make sure that it is protected from direct sun.

It may be up to six months before the cuttings are ready for hardening off and repotting in individual containers. Shake them from the pot and gently separate them.

Place drainage material, covered with a layer of porous soil, in the bottom of some 3½-inch pots. Stand a rooted cutting in each pot and fill with soil until the cutting is covered to just below the original leaf. Firm the soil to about ½ inch below the rim of the pot. Water generously. Keep the pots in a greenhouse or cold frame. Never allow the soil to dry out.

In three to six weeks the roots should have spread to the outside of the soil. If the shrub is hardy, it can then be planted out in the open, in a prepared bed. Tender plants should go into a larger pot and spend a year in a greenhouse or cold frame before being planted outdoors.

Gray Mold—The Main Enemy of Cuttings

The greatest threat to cuttings is botrytis, or gray mold. Appearing as a fluffy, grayish-white coating on stems, leaves, and flower buds, this fungus is at its worst from autumn to early spring. Thriving in cool, moist conditions, it requires dead or dying plant tissue to grow on.

If gray mold appears on a cutting, the plant should be destroyed—not composted. Getting rid of the infected plants is necessary because once it gets established, botrytis will kill the rest of the cuttings as well.

The best way to prevent mold is attentive care. Look carefully at your cuttings at least weekly, and remove dying or dead leaves. Take care that the soil mix does not become oversaturated—moist only.

1. Late in the summer cut off a shoot that has several leaves on it.

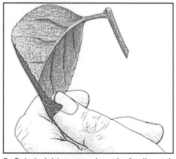

2. Cut straight across above leaf axils, and at an angle ¾ in. below them.

4. Plant cuttings so that the leaf axil just shows. Maintain humidity.

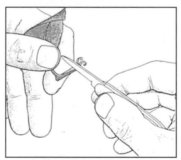

3. Scrape off some bark; then dip the wounded part in rooting hormone.

5. When well rooted, plant the cuttings in separate 3½-in. pots.

Using Rooting Hormones to Promote Growth

Rooting powders and rooting liquids contain hormones that, when applied to the base of a cutting, stimulate root formation.

These hormones are present in the plants themselves, but often in such minute quantities that natural rooting takes place very slowly. In most cases, the application of hormones can either speed up rooting or make it more certain for plants such as winter sweet (*Chimonanthus praecox*) that are difficult to root.

However, with English ivy (*Hedera helix*), and a few other plants that root easily on their own, the outcome is far less satisfactory. Hormone treatment in such instances can have a negative effect.

Rooting powders and liquids come in various strengths: weaker for softwood, stronger for hardwood cuttings. There are also general-purpose formulations.

For large-scale propagation, use the specific strength for the job.

Both *Cotinus* 'Flame' (smoke tree) and *Corylus maxima* (giant filbert) put on spectacular fall displays.

Cotinus 'Flame'

Corylus maxima 'Purpurea'

Layering—New Plants From a Growing Shoot

Ordinary Soil Layering—The Basic Method

Soil layering is a simple method of propagating shrubs without using a greenhouse or cold frame. It takes advantage of the fact that a plant that has been cut, lacerated, or fractured is likely to produce roots when the wound is in contact with the soil.

The best branches for soil layering are nonflowering ones that have grown in the current year. They provide the freshest shoots.

Deciduous plants are best layered in autumn or winter. Layer evergreens in autumn or spring.

First, fork over the surface of the soil around the plant. Then, choose a flexible branch and bend it down until it reaches the ground 9–12 inches from its tip. Strip the leaves from the branch as shown in the illustration.

Wound the underside with a knife by cutting a shallow tongue in the direction of the growing tip; or injure the surface tissue by twisting.

Dig a 3- to 4-inch hole at the spot where the wound touches the ground, and partly fill it with equal parts peat moss and coarse sand. Push the branch into the hole, forming a sharp angle at the wound.

Peg the branch to the ground with a bent piece of galvanized wire 6–8 inches long. Stake the upright tip. Fill the hole with soil.

Repeat the process with other branches. Water the whole area thoroughly, and make sure that it never dries out.

Most plants will have rooted 12 months later. You can determine whether they have done so by carefully scraping away the soil.

If roots are well established, sever the new plant from the parent branch, lift it out with a good root ball, and plant it where you want it.

If the roots have not grown well but the top growth seems healthy, replace the soil and wait a few more months before checking again.

Each branch of the current year's growth of a shrub can produce a rooted plant without first being severed from the parent plant.

1. First, bend the branch to the ground. Then, at a spot 9–12 in. from its tip, dig a hole 3–4 in. deep.

2. Strip the leaves from the part of the branch that is over the hole.

3. Cut a shallow tongue into the underside of the branch, cutting toward the growing tip. Alternatively, twist the branch sharply to break the surface tissue.

4. Bend branch upward at the wound, and peg into the hole with wire.

5. Stake the upright tip and fill in the hole with soil. Water well.

6. A year later, sever branch and transplant the young shrub.

Wisterias put on splendid fragrant floral displays against walls or fences but need strong supports.

Wisteria floribunda 'Alba'

Serpentine Soil Layering for Vines

Serpentine soil layering is a handy method of propagating vines and many shrubs with long, vinelike stems, such as honeysuckle and jasmine. It should be done at the same time as ordinary soil layering, using the long, trailing shoots that have grown during the current year.

Bend a shoot carefully to the ground and, where it touches, dig a hole 2 inches deep.

Wound the shoot on the underside, as with ordinary layering, and peg it into the hole with a bent piece of wire. A hairpin or paper clip can serve the purpose.

Fill the hole with equal parts peat moss and coarse sand. Cover with soil and firm down with your fingers.

Leave the next two pairs of leaves above ground; then repeat the layering operation. Continue along the entire length of the shoot. Water well and do not allow to dry out.

A year later each buried point should have rooted. (Check by scraping the soil away.) If roots are established, sever the sections between the exposed leaf pairs, and plant in the normal way. If not, rebury the shoot for a few months longer; then check again.

There is a technique that makes transplanting easier, although it involves more trouble at the beginning. Instead of pegging the shoots directly into the ground, prepare small pots of light soil mix, sink them into the ground, and peg into them. The layers can then be moved without disturbing the new roots.

1. Bend down a shoot, peg into a 2-in. hole, and fill hole with light soil.

2. Repeat the process, leaving two pairs of leaves above the ground.

Air Layering for Stiff or Upright Branches

Branches that cannot be layered at soil level can be layered in the air. This can be done anytime between late spring and midsummer.

Select a healthy branch of the current year's growth, and strip the leaves from the middle. Wound it by removing a slice of wood about an inch long, cutting well into the cambium layer. Apply rooting hormone.

Wrap a strip of plastic that is 4–5 inches wide around the cut, and tie it at the bottom as shown at right. Fill with a moist mixture of equal parts peat moss, coarse sand, and sphagnum moss, and tie at the top.

In about 10 weeks you should be able to see or feel roots. Remove the covering and cut off the branch below the layer. Put the new plant into a 4- to 6-inch pot of light soil, and keep it moist in a closed cold frame for about two weeks.

Harden the plant by gradually opening the frame, a little more each day, until the plant is fully exposed. Plant in the open in spring.

1. From a newly grown branch, strip off a pair of leaves.

2. Cut off a 1-in. slice of wood and dab rooting hormone onto the area.

3. Wrap cut area with plastic, tie at the bottom, and stuff with soil mix.

4. Tie the plastic tube at the top and leave it for at least 10 weeks.

5. When roots have formed, remove plastic and cut off the new plant.

6. Plant in a 4- to 6-in. pot. Keep moist and protected for two weeks.

Flowering quinces are easy to care for and make good wall shrubs. Masses of deep red flowers are replaced by yellow fall fruits. Extremely decorative, they are also very thorny shrubs.

Chaenomeles superba 'Crimson and Gold'

Chaenomeles speciosa 'Simonii'

New Shrubs From Seeds, Suckers, and Division

Collecting and Preparing Seeds for Sowing

Shrub seeds ripen at different times of the year. Since birds seem to know exactly when certain seeds are ripe, the appearance of birds is a fairly reliable signal as to when to harvest. The challenge, then, is to get there before the birds and before the dry seeds spill out.

Most shrub seeds ripen in the fall, but even in cold climates, seeds of some varieties, the honeysuckle is one example, are collected in late spring. Another shrub, beauty bush, ripens in late summer, and many kinds of rhododendron produce seeds in midfall.

The seeds of some shrubs will germinate without special treatment. Among these are the azalea, beauty bush, buddleia, deutzia, enkianthus, hypericum, hydrangea, mock orange, mountain laurel, pieris, potentilla, rhododendron, spirea, sweet pepper bush, and weigela.

Other seeds, such as those of the arborvitae, barberry, common lilac, and most of the spruces and pines, have a single dormant period requiring two or three months of cold to break dormancy and induce germination. This can be accomplished in cold climates by sowing seeds outdoors in the fall in a cold frame, where they will germinate the following spring.

Dried seeds can also be enclosed in a small plastic bag containing just enough moist peat moss or coarse sand to cover them. They can be stored this way in a household refrigerator (39°F) for two or three months prior to sowing.

A few shrubs, such as the cotoneaster, holly, and juniper, have double dormancy, which requires a warm period followed by a cold period before germination can occur.

If the seeds are sown outdoors, they can take two years to germinate. However, this time can be considerably shortened by putting the seeds in a plastic bag with slightly moist peat moss. Keep the bags at room temperature for about five months to break the first dormant period. Then store them in the same bags in a household refrigerator for three months to break the second period of dormancy. Following this cold treatment, sow the seeds.

Pulpy seeds, such as yew seeds, should have the pulp removed before storing or sowing. This can be done by soaking them in water to soften the pulp. The good seeds will sink and the bad ones will float.

Nonpulpy seeds should be cleaned of chaff (bits of the seed capsule or other extraneous material that could cause rot after sowing).

A few seeds, including those of genistas and wisterias, have the problem of seed-coat dormancy. This is difficult to control, but there is a solution. It must be overcome mechanically or with hot water. The hard covering of seeds large enough to hold can be broken through with a file or by scraping with a knife.

If hot water is used to soften the dormant coating, it should be at least 194°F. Pour it over the seeds and let them soak overnight. After treatment, sow them immediately in a cold frame or in pots indoors or in a greenhouse.

If seeds are sown in the fall in a cold frame, protect them from rodents, which find them inviting in winter when there is little other food. The most practical protection is to put fine wire mesh, such as household screening, over the pots or the soil in the cold frame.

For more on sowing seeds, see page 43.

Growing New Shrubs From Suckers

Several kinds of trees and shrubs propagate naturally by means of shoots from beneath the ground. Known as suckers, these shoots offer an easy way to grow new plants.

The method is useful only with plants growing from their own roots. Suckers from grafted plants, such as some lilacs, rhododendrons, roses, viburnums, and witch hazels, will reproduce the rootstock, not the top plant. Shrubs that produce true suckers include the deutzia, forsythia, mock orange, species roses, spirea, sumac, and some *Prunus* species.

Between midfall and early spring, remove soil from the base of a sucker to see if roots have formed. If so, trace the sucker to its point of origin (a stem or root), cut it off, and carefully lift it out.

Well-rooted plants can go into permanent sites. Put poorly rooted ones in special beds to develop.

PROPAGATION BY SUCKERS

In autumn or winter uncover the base of a sucker to check for roots. If any have formed, cut off the sucker near its point of origin, lift out, and plant.

Producing New Plants From Simple Division

Many shrubs produce their main branches from underground buds. The buried bases of these branches, therefore, produce roots. These shrubs resemble woody herbaceous perennials, and they can be divided in the same way as perennials, thus providing an easy method of getting large new plants instantly.

Shrubs that can be propagated by this method include the glorybower, indigo, kerria, and some dogwoods.

Simply lift an existing shrub and divide it at its base into two or more equal-size pieces, each with plenty of healthy roots attached. The separate pieces can be planted immediately.

This method works best when carried out in the spring, but it can be used with likelihood of success at any time between midautumn and midspring. A shrub should be at least three years old before being divided.

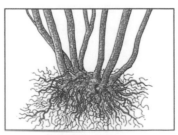

1. Plants that produce main branches from below ground can be divided.

2. Divide the plant into equal-size pieces with roots; then replant them.

The mock orange (*Philadelphus*) is covered with white blossoms in May and June. The drooping flower spikes of Japanese pieris (*Pieris japonica*) appear in early to mid spring.

Philadelphus coronarius　　　　*Pieris japonica*　　　　*Pieris japonica* 'Valley Valentine'

Basic Methods of Pruning Shrubs and Vines

A shrub will rarely die if it is left unpruned. However, it is often desirable to control its size, to improve the overall shape, or to remove dead or diseased branches. Such pruning is basic for all shrubs. On some shrubs growth may be improved if light is let into the center by cutting away old branches. And some shrubs will bear larger—but generally fewer—flowers if they are pruned each year. To sum up, prune selectively.

Three tools are used for pruning: pruning shears for removing shoots and small stems; long-handled lopping shears for larger stems; and a pruning saw for large branches. A sharp knife may also be needed for trimming around large wounds.

When shortening branches, cut just above an outward-facing bud or shoot. Cut diagonally, parallel with the angle of the bud or shoot and never straight across. The new branches will expand and open the shrub.

When removing entire side branches, cut a little away from the trunk or main branch. This minimizes the area of the cut (compared to cutting flush) and the wound heals faster. If the branches are large enough to need a pruning saw, rather than lopping shears, undercut the branch first (see p. 221) to avoid tearing the bark.

Shrubs that have been heavily pruned—especially those that receive such treatment annually—benefit from a 2-inch-thick mulch after pruning, plus a cupful per square yard of a balanced organic fertilizer.

Removing Dead, Straggly, and Weak Wood

Most shrubs need only to have their dead, straggly, and weak wood pruned as a matter of general upkeep. This can be done at any time of year. You might do it when a shrub develops a long straggly branch or to remove a branch that has been damaged by a storm or some other mishap. It is a good idea to examine all your garden shrubs each spring to determine their pruning needs.

Remove any dead or damaged wood, always cutting back to a healthy, outward-facing shoot or bud. Buds or branches facing inward will grow into the center and clutter up the plant.

Remove shoots that are obviously weak, cutting right back to a main branch. Prune any straggly branches by half to a strong shoot or bud facing outward. Do not remove any well-formed, healthy wood, or you are likely to do away with buds that would produce flowers later.

The following shrubs should not be pruned except to remove damaged wood: daphne, euonymus, hebe, potentilla, rockrose, *Viburnum burkwoodii*, and *V. carlesii*.

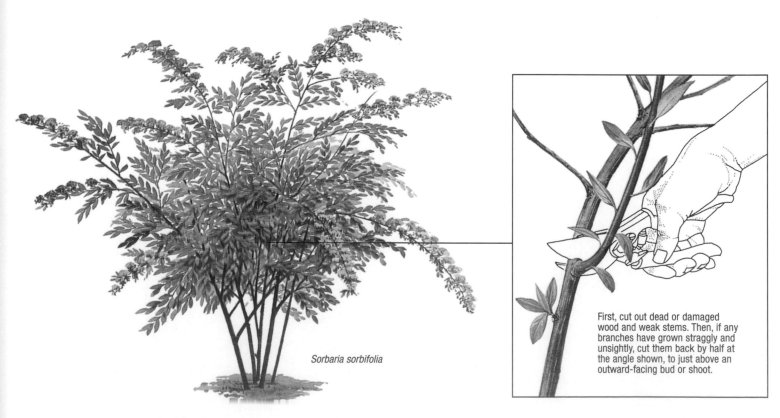

Sorbaria sorbifolia

First, cut out dead or damaged wood and weak stems. Then, if any branches have grown straggly and unsightly, cut them back by half at the angle shown, to just above an outward-facing bud or shoot.

Varieties of the European snowball are characterized by a profusion of flowers in spring and summer and most have ornamental fruits and colorful foliage in the fall.

Viburnum opulus 'Compactum'

Viburnum opulus 'Roseum'

Cutting Down Large, Overgrown Plants

Some shrubs, particularly evergreens, seldom need pruning unless they become overgrown or bare at the base, after many years. In spring use a pruning saw to cut down all the main branches to within a few inches of the ground. Apply a cupful of a balanced organic fertilizer per square yard. Apply a mulch, and water deeply during prolonged dry spells. The shrub will not flower the following summer, but within a few years its appearance should be improved.

SOME SHRUBS THAT MAY REQUIRE THIS TREATMENT

Aucuba (aucuba)
Caragana (peashrub)
Cornus (dogwood)
Elaeagnus (elaeagnus)

Ligustrum (privet)
Mahonia (mahonia)
Myrica (bayberry)
Olearia (daisybush)

Pieris (pieris)
Prunus laurocerasus
 (English and cherry laurels)
Viburnum (viburnum)

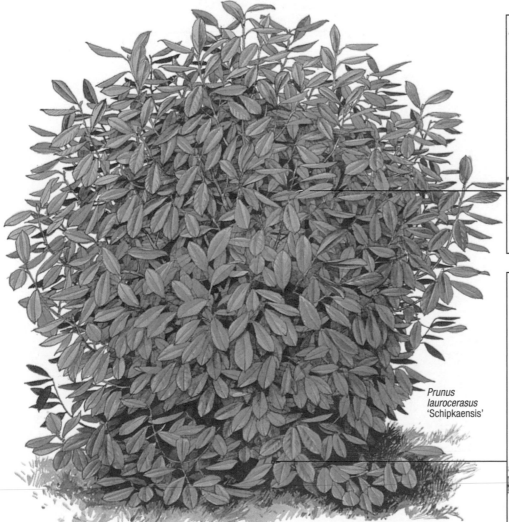

Prunus laurocerasus 'Schipkaensis'

Begin in spring by clearing away top growth with long-handled lopping shears.

Saw off branches a few inches from the ground, undercutting first.

The deutzia is a pleasing shrub that thrives in almost all soils. *Deutzia scabra* is particularly tough. *D. rosea* is quite dwarf with arching branches.

Deutzia scabra

Deutzia rosea

Pruning Shrubs Trained As Espaliers

Some shrubs that have particularly attractive foliage, flowers, or berries lend themselves to espaliering against fences or walls. During the formative years prune to develop a framework of well-placed, permanent branches. This is done by shortening the leader shoots that you have selected to make the basic framework. Cut them back to one-third or one-half their lengths each spring. When the shrub has filled its allotted space, cut back the leaders to within an inch or so of their established length every year. At the same time, cut back all of the shoots that grow outward from the wall.

On shrubs that bear flowers on growth that has developed within the current year, do all necessary pruning in early spring. If flowers are borne on the previous year's growth, prune immediately after they bloom.

<table>
<tr><th colspan="2">SOME SHRUBS THAT CAN BE TRAINED BY THIS METHOD</th></tr>
<tr><td>*Ceanothus* (ceanothus—evergreen varieties)
Chaenomeles (flowering quince)
Cotoneaster (cotoneaster)
Forsythia (forsythia)</td><td>*Fremontodendron* (flannel bush)
Jasminum (jasmine)
Pyracantha (firethorn)
Taxus (yew)
Viburnum (viburnum)</td></tr>
</table>

Train selected side shoots along wires, pruning back new leaders by about half in spring and cutting other shoots to 3–4 in. long in summer until the desired length is reached. Then remove all but 1–2 in. of each year's new growth.

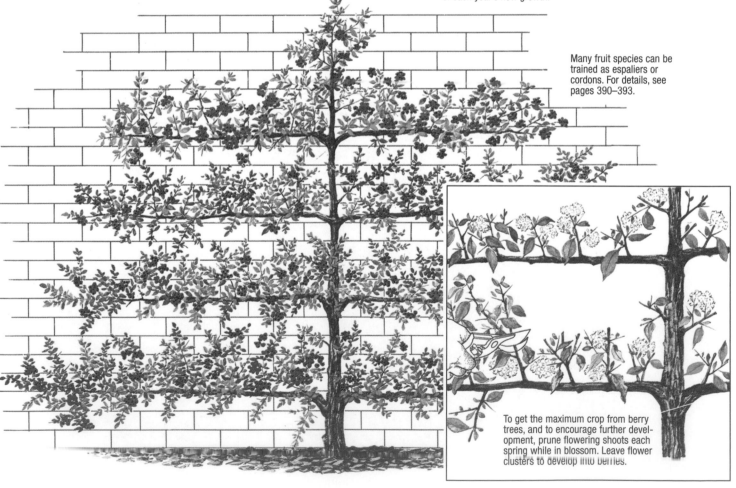

Many fruit species can be trained as espaliers or cordons. For details, see pages 390–393.

To get the maximum crop from berry trees, and to encourage further development, prune flowering shoots each spring while in blossom. Leave flower clusters to develop into berries.

Mahonia aquifolium

Colutea arborescens

The evergreen mahonia (*Mahonia aquifolium*) is dotted with yellow blossoms in spring; in summer, it bears blue-black berries, and its glossy leaves turn purplish red in late fall. From early summer onward, the bladder senna (*Colutea arborescens*) carries clusters of yellow flowers. Inflated pink-tinged seed pods are attractive in late summer.

Pruning Shrubs That Flower on New Shoots

Some shrubs flower on long shoots that have grown in the current season. To restrict their size or to encourage larger but fewer flowers, the shrubs can be pruned in late winter or spring as growth begins.

Cut all of last year's shoots back to two or three buds or shoots from their base. Unless you want to thin out or reduce the size of the permanent framework, do not cut back into the older wood.

After pruning, fortify the shrub by applying a cupful of a balanced organic fertilizer per square yard. Mulch with a 2-inch layer of peat moss, compost, or well-rotted manure.

SOME SHRUBS THAT CAN BE PRUNED BY THIS METHOD

Aloysia (lemon verbena)	(fuchsia)	(crape myrtle)
Buddleja davidii (butterfly bush)	*Hydrangea arborescens* 'Grandiflora' and *H. paniculata* 'Grandiflora' (hydrangea)	*Spartium* (Spanish broom)
Caryopteris (bluebeard)		*Spiraea bumalda* and *S. japonica* (Bumalda and Japanese spirea)
Ceanothus (ceanothus— deciduous varieties)		
Fuchsia magellanica	*Indigofera* (indigo)	*Tamarix ramosissima* (five-stamen tamarix)
	Lagerstroemia	

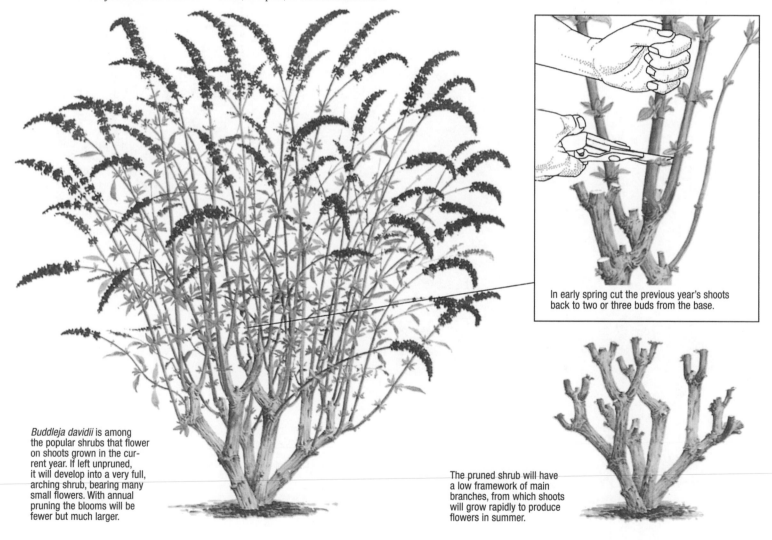

In early spring cut the previous year's shoots back to two or three buds from the base.

Buddleja davidii is among the popular shrubs that flower on shoots grown in the current year. If left unpruned, it will develop into a very full, arching shrub, bearing many small flowers. With annual pruning the blooms will be fewer but much larger.

The pruned shrub will have a low framework of main branches, from which shoots will grow rapidly to produce flowers in summer.

The graceful beauty bush (*Kolkwitzia amabilis*) is a lovely shrub for a sunny location.

Kolkwitzia amabilis

Pruning Shrubs That Flower on Last Year's Wood

Some shrubs, as they mature, have a tendency to lose their shape, to become too dense overall, and to produce fewer flowers than before.

The shrubs that do this and produce their flowers on shoots that were formed during the previous season can be pruned to good advantage immediately after blooming—each year if necessary.

First, cut out or shorten some of the oldest branches. Then, if the shrub is still crowded, thin out the weakest of the new shoots. Always cut just above a vigorous side branch.

SOME SHRUBS THAT CAN BE PRUNED BY THIS METHOD

Acacia (acacia)
Buddleja alternifolia (fountain buddleia)
Deutzia (deutzia)
Forsythia (forsythia)

Hydrangea macrophylla (florist's hydrangea)
Kolkwitzia (beauty bush)
Philadelphus (mock orange)

Prunus glandulosa 'Alba Plena', *P. triloba* (almond)
Ribes (flowering currant)
Stephanandra (stephanandra)
Weigela (weigela)

In midsummer, as soon as flowers fade, prune by one-third. Remove wood that has borne blossoms; keep young strong shoots.

To encourage extra large blooms, prune a florist's hydrangea after flowering. When growth begins the following spring, the pruned shrub will present a rounded silhouette of young shoots (see right) that will bear flowers in summer.

Clematis montana 'Mayleen'

Parthenocissus tricuspidata

'Mayleen' has strongly scented 2 in. pink mauve blooms with golden stamens. The rootlike tendrils of Boston ivy (*Parthenocissus tricuspidata*) cling to walls and its bright red leaves provide decorative cover in fall.

Restricting the Size of Climbing Plants

Leave most climbers and vines unpruned until they get too large; then prune them after they flower. Prune those grown for foliage, rather than for flowers, in spring or summer.

Self-clinging climbers, such as the climbing hydrangea or English ivy, can be trimmed on the wall.

Climbers on supports, such as the honeysuckle, should first be detached. Then remove lateral growths, leaving only main stems.

If the main stems look old and woody, remove some of them and keep some of the younger ones—either the shoots growing at ground level or those low on the old stems.

For clematis, see page 273; for wisteria, see page 284.

SOME VINES THAT CAN BE PRUNED BY THIS METHOD	

Actinidia (actinidia)
Bougainvillea (bougainvillea)
Campsis (trumpet creeper)
Clematis montana
  (anemone clematis)
	Hydrangea (climbing hydrangea)
	Lonicera (honeysuckle)
	Parthenocissus (Virginia creeper)
	Fallopia baldschuanica (silver-lace
	  vine)

A vine that clings by suckers can be trimmed after flowering as though it were a hedge; if it bears no flowers, trim in spring. Vines like this honeysuckle (*Lonicera*) that need support should be taken down before pruning.

Having taken the climber down from its supports, see if the main stems are very old. If so, cut them back to the vigorous young shoots near the bases of the stems. If the main stems are still only a few years old, retain them and remove all their lateral growth.

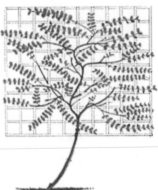

Then tie the pruned vine back into position on its supports. Flowering vines can be expected to bloom again the next year.

Aromatic leaves and purplish-blue umbels in August and September make the bluebeard (*Caryopteris*) a prized shrub for slopes and rock gardens.

Caryopteris clandonensis 'Heavenly Blue'

Pruning 26 Popular Shrubs, in Close-up

Buddleja alternifolia (fountain buddleia). After flowering, remove old shoots to encourage the growth of new ones.

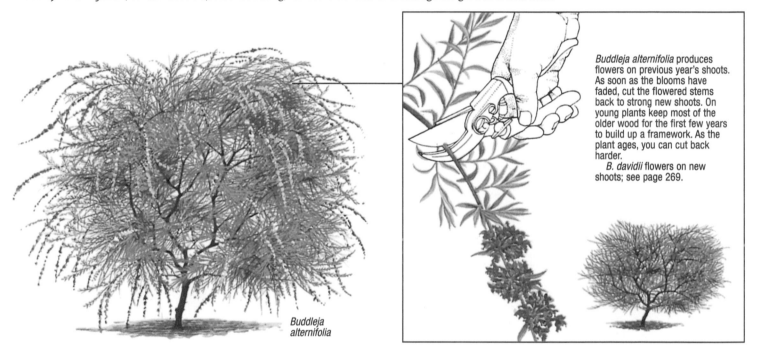

Buddleja alternifolia produces flowers on previous year's shoots. As soon as the blooms have faded, cut the flowered stems back to strong new shoots. On young plants keep most of the older wood for the first few years to build up a framework. As the plant ages, you can cut back harder.

B. davidii flowers on new shoots; see page 269.

Buddleja alternifolia

Caryopteris (bluebeard). Unless it is pruned each spring, the bush becomes twiggy and bears small flowers.

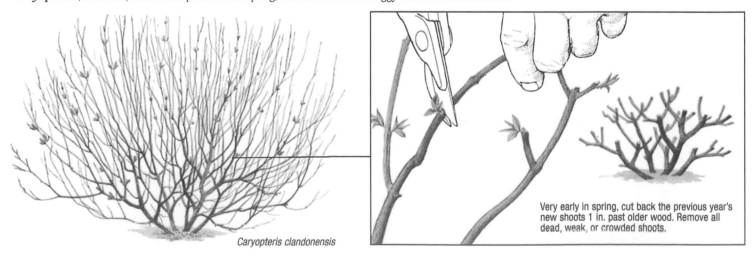

Caryopteris clandonensis

Very early in spring, cut back the previous year's new shoots 1 in. past older wood. Remove all dead, weak, or crowded shoots.

Clematis 'Ernest Markham'

Clematis 'The President'

Clematis pruning requirements depend on their flowering time. 'Ernest Markham' is an early-blooming hybrid; 'The President' should bloom twice.

Ceanothus delilianus (ceanothus). Prune deciduous ceanothus in midspring; new shoots will flower in late summer.

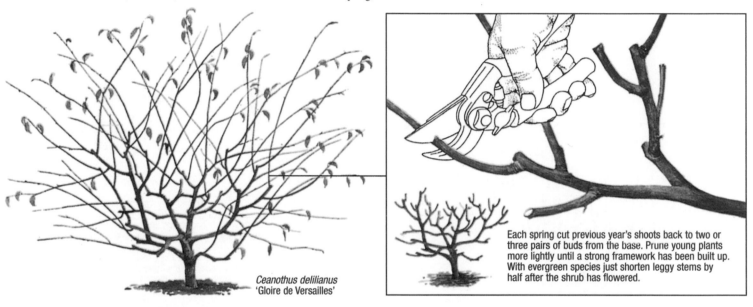

Ceanothus delilianus 'Gloire de Versailles'

Each spring cut previous year's shoots back to two or three pairs of buds from the base. Prune young plants more lightly until a strong framework has been built up. With evergreen species just shorten leggy stems by half after the shrub has flowered.

Clematis. Pruning depends mainly on the time and the type of flowering.

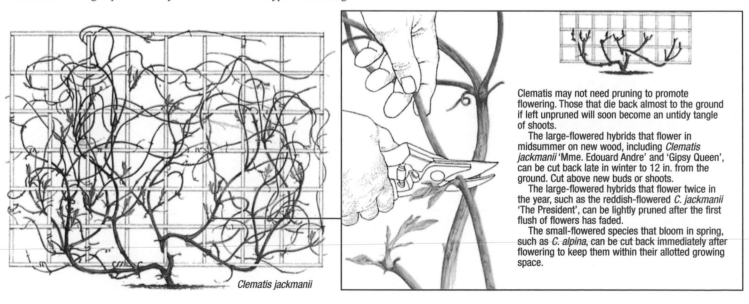

Clematis jackmanii

Clematis may not need pruning to promote flowering. Those that die back almost to the ground if left unpruned will soon become an untidy tangle of shoots.

The large-flowered hybrids that flower in midsummer on new wood, including *Clematis jackmanii* 'Mme. Edouard Andre' and 'Gipsy Queen', can be cut back late in winter to 12 in. from the ground. Cut above new buds or shoots.

The large-flowered hybrids that flower twice in the year, such as the reddish-flowered *C. jackmanii* 'The President', can be lightly pruned after the first flush of flowers has faded.

The small-flowered species that bloom in spring, such as *C. alpina*, can be cut back immediately after flowering to keep them within their allotted growing space.

The variegated Tatarian dogwood (*Cornus alba*) 'Elegantissima' has green and creamy white leaves on deep red stems. Cascading yellow flowers of broom (*Cytisus beanii*) are ideal for a rock garden.

Cornus alba 'Elegantissima'

Cytisus beanii

Cornus alba and **C. stolonifera** (dogwood). For colored stems in winter, prune hard early the previous spring.

Cornus alba

Cornus alba, with red bark, and *C. stolonifera* 'Flaviramea', with yellow bark, are valued for their colored stems in fall and winter. Young shoots are the brightest; so very early in the spring cut back the previous year's growth to a few inches tall.

To renovate an old bush, as shown at left, cut strong shoots back hard and remove dead or weak shoots completely, producing a framework about 12 in. high.

Cytisus scoparius (Scotch broom). Prune after the flowers fade to prevent the shrub from becoming leggy.

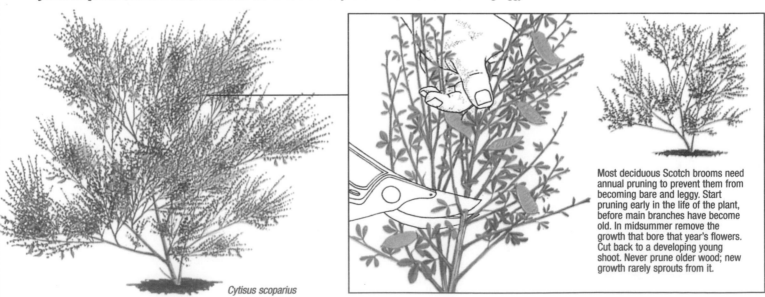

Cytisus scoparius

Most deciduous Scotch brooms need annual pruning to prevent them from becoming bare and leggy. Start pruning early in the life of the plant, before main branches have become old. In midsummer remove the growth that bore that year's flowers. Cut back to a developing young shoot. Never prune older wood; new growth rarely sprouts from it.

Forsythia displays its golden yellow floral splendor in spring when few other garden plants are in bloom. This hardy plant thrives in every soil and does well in sun or partial shade.

Forsythia intermedia 'Lynwood'

Deutzia. Remove the flowered stems in midsummer to prevent the shrub from becoming cluttered.

Deutzia gracilis

Left unpruned, a deutzia will become dense and untidy, bearing progressively fewer flowers. After the flowers have faded in midsummer, cut the flowering stems back to a point where new shoots are developing. Some deutzias have attractive flaking bark on the old wood; if you want this trait as a winter feature, leave some old shoots unpruned on the shrub.

Forsythia. Encourage fresh new wood by cutting out poor-flowering old wood regularly after spring flowers fade.

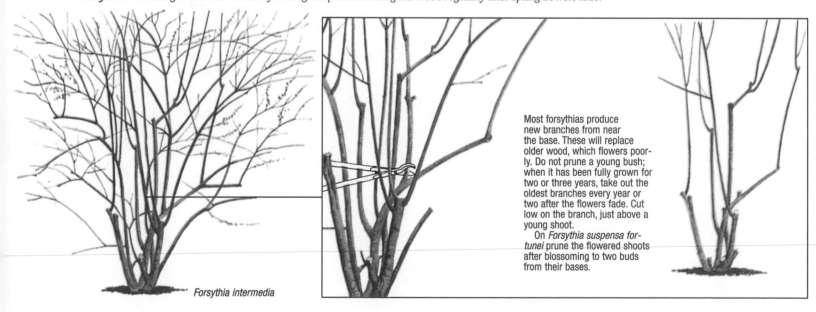

Forsythia intermedia

Most forsythias produce new branches from near the base. These will replace older wood, which flowers poorly. Do not prune a young bush; when it has been fully grown for two or three years, take out the oldest branches every year or two after the flowers fade. Cut low on the branch, just above a young shoot.

On *Forsythia suspensa fortunei* prune the flowered shoots after blossoming to two buds from their bases.

In bloom, the giant *Hydrangea paniculata* 'Grandiflora' (peegee hydrangea) and *H. macrophylla* 'Quadricolor' (florist's lacecap hydrangea) make striking displays.

Hydrangea paniculata 'Grandiflora'

Hydrangea macrophylla 'Quadricolor'

Hydrangea macrophylla (florist's hydrangea). Remove faded flowerheads. Cut back to a plump bud in spring; prune out thin growth.

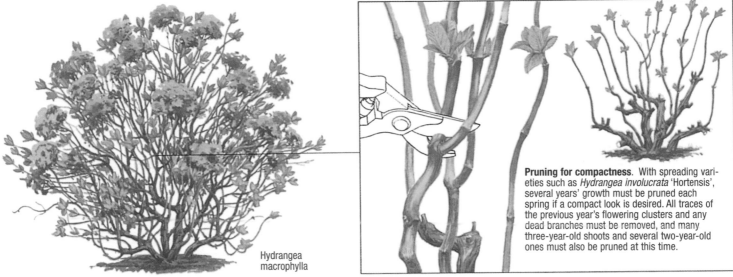

Hydrangea macrophylla

Pruning for compactness. With spreading varieties such as *Hydrangea involucrata* 'Hortensis', several years' growth must be pruned each spring if a compact look is desired. All traces of the previous year's flowering clusters and any dead branches must be removed, and many three-year-old shoots and several two-year-old ones must also be pruned at this time.

***Hydrangea paniculata* 'Grandiflora'** (peegee hydrangea). Prune the tall, white-flowered shrub back hard in spring.

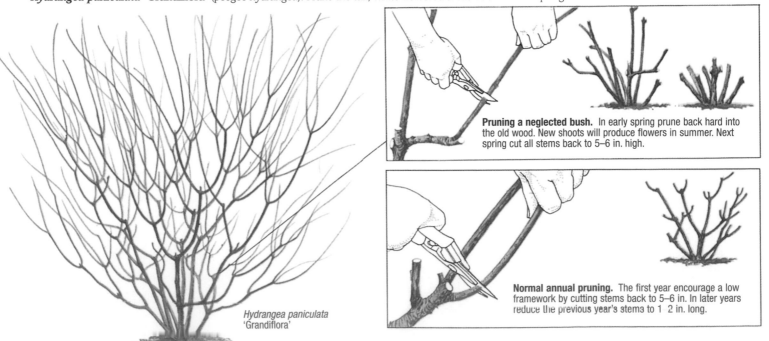

Hydrangea paniculata 'Grandiflora'

Pruning a neglected bush. In early spring prune back hard into the old wood. New shoots will produce flowers in summer. Next spring cut all stems back to 5–6 in. high.

Normal annual pruning. The first year encourage a low framework by cutting stems back to 5–6 in. In later years reduce the previous year's stems to 1–2 in. long.

Hypericum prolificum

Hypericum moserianum

Aaron's beard or Saint-John's-wort (*Hypericum*) bears its golden yellow flowers all summer long. *H. moserianum* will grow in shade but is best in a sheltered location. *H. prolificum* blooms a beautiful yellow between June and August.

Hypericum calycinum (Aaron's beard, or Saint-John's-wort). Cut back with shears in early spring for a dense, low cover.

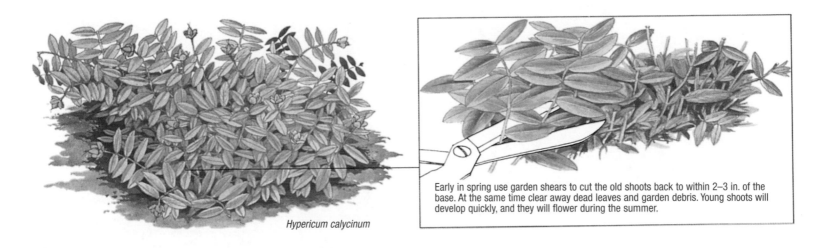

Hypericum calycinum

Early in spring use garden shears to cut the old shoots back to within 2–3 in. of the base. At the same time clear away dead leaves and garden debris. Young shoots will develop quickly, and they will flower during the summer.

Hypericum patulum (shrubby Saint-John's-wort). In early spring remove dead and spindly wood from the tall-growing Saint-John's-worts.

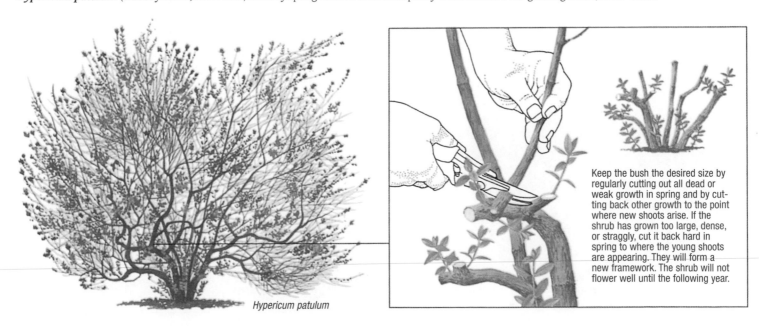

Hypericum patulum

Keep the bush the desired size by regularly cutting out all dead or weak growth in spring and by cutting back other growth to the point where new shoots arise. If the shrub has grown too large, dense, or straggly, cut it back hard in spring to where the young shoots are appearing. They will form a new framework. The shrub will not flower well until the following year.

Aromatic lavender (*Lavandula*) draws butterflies from July to September. Its flowers can be dried and used in sachets.

Lavandula angustifolia 'Hidcote'

Kerria (Japanese kerria). The best flowers appear on the young shoots; prune in late spring after the flowers have faded.

Kerria japonica

Kerrias produce new shoots each year near ground level, which flower the following season and then often die back. Encourage this habit by removing the flowering stems after the flowers have faded at the end of spring. Cut right back to the ground or, on stronger stems, to where new shoots are developing. *Kerria japonica* 'Plena' may need to have all its stems cut to the ground.

Lavandula (lavender). Prune in midspring to prevent this shrub from becoming leggy and sparse.

Lavandula officinalis

Without pruning, lavender will become leggy and bare stemmed. In midspring cut down the dead flower spikes from the year before, plus about 1 in. of top growth. Flowers can be removed in autumn if you wish to tidy the plant for winter, but trim it in spring anyway. When plants are young, prune hard to encourage a bushy shape; but do not cut into the old wood of older plants, or the trimmed branches may die back.

Japanese kerria is well suited for covering walls and fences. The double form, 'Pleniflora', blooms into September. The red seed heads on staghorn sumac (*Rhus*) are conspicuous until the foliage changes color in fall.

Kerria japonica 'Pleniflora'

Rhus typhina 'Dissecta'

Philadelphus (mock orange). Rejuvenate an aging plant by cutting out the oldest branches to make room for young ones.

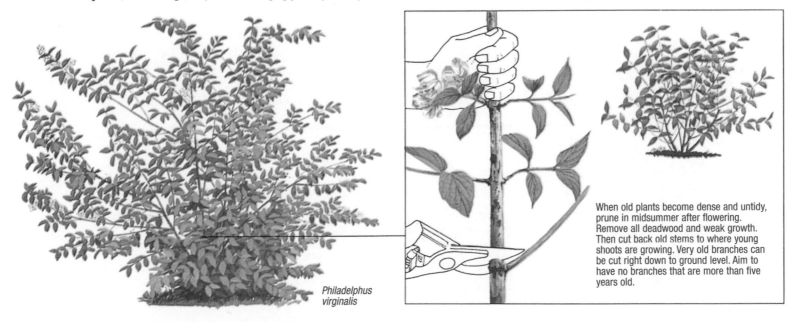

Philadelphus virginalis

When old plants become dense and untidy, prune in midsummer after flowering. Remove all deadwood and weak growth. Then cut back old stems to where young shoots are growing. Very old branches can be cut right down to ground level. Aim to have no branches that are more than five years old.

Rhus (sumac). Prune back previous year's growth in winter to produce large, attractive foliage for autumn display.

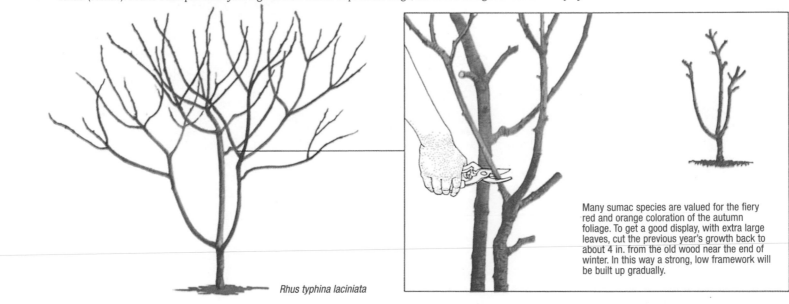

Rhus typhina laciniata

Many sumac species are valued for the fiery red and orange coloration of the autumn foliage. To get a good display, with extra large leaves, cut the previous year's growth back to about 4 in. from the old wood near the end of winter. In this way a strong, low framework will be built up gradually.

Where it is hardy, the flowering currant (*Ribes sanguineum*) blooms in early spring. Rubus is related to raspberries and blackberries.

Ribes sanguineum 'King Edward VII'

Rubus 'Benenden'

Ribes (flowering currant). Regularly replace old wood with new by pruning after the flowers fade.

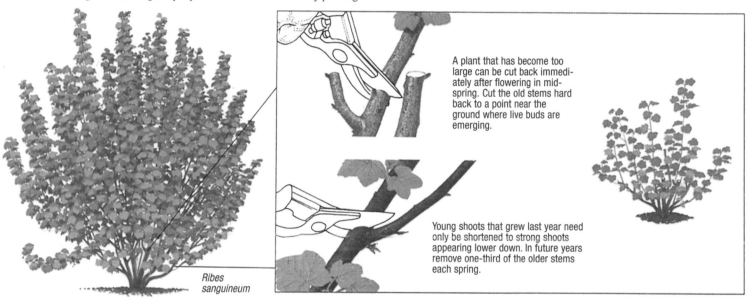

Ribes sanguineum

A plant that has become too large can be cut back immediately after flowering in mid-spring. Cut the old stems hard back to a point near the ground where live buds are emerging.

Young shoots that grew last year need only be shortened to strong shoots appearing lower down. In future years remove one-third of the older stems each spring.

Rubus cockburnianus (rubus). Cut out old stems after flowering to encourage new shoots to grow up from the base.

Rubus cockburnianus

Rubus cockburnianus is a raspberry that is grown for its white stems in winter. After the shrub has flowered in midsummer, cut out the stems that have borne flowers. Those that remain will be white in winter and will flower the next summer. Or you can forego flowers and ensure a good show of white stems by pruning the entire shrub back in late winter.

Plant Ural false spirea (*Sorbaria sorbifolia*) where it has sufficient room to spread. This shrub grows vigorously and forms thickets.

Sorbaria sorbifolia

Santolina (cotton lavender). Prune in midspring to produce larger flowers and to prevent the plant from becoming straggly and unkempt.

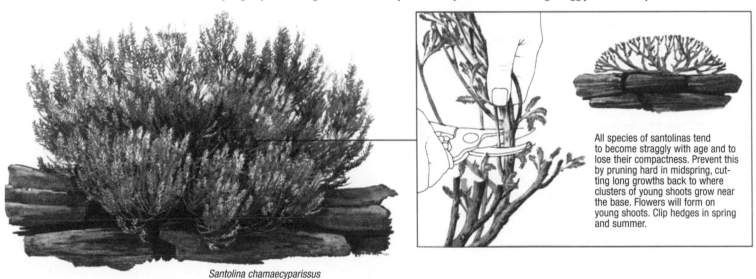

All species of santolinas tend to become straggly with age and to lose their compactness. Prevent this by pruning hard in midspring, cutting long growths back to where clusters of young shoots grow near the base. Flowers will form on young shoots. Clip hedges in spring and summer.

Santolina chamaecyparissus

Sorbaria (false spirea). For better foliage and larger flowers, cut down all the stems every winter.

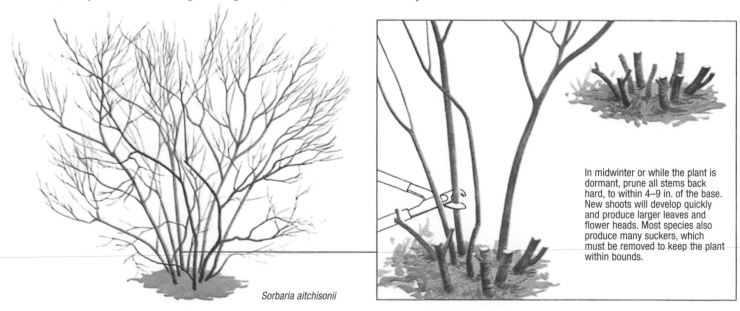

In midwinter or while the plant is dormant, prune all stems back hard, to within 4–9 in. of the base. New shoots will develop quickly and produce larger leaves and flower heads. Most species also produce many suckers, which must be removed to keep the plant within bounds.

Sorbaria aitchisonii

The many named forms of Japanese spirea (*Spiraea japonica*) come in a variety of heights and leaf colors.

Spiraea japonica

Spiraea arguta (garland spirea). When the plant has become overgrown, renovate it by cutting back the old stems after the flowers have faded.

Spiraea arguta

Some spireas, including *Spiraea arguta* and *S. thunbergii*, produce their flowers on stems that grew the previous year. An old, overcrowded plant can be renovated late in spring, immediately after the flowers have faded. Cut back old stems to the point where younger shoots are growing.

Both old and young plants require that their flowering shoots be shortened every year. Simply cut away the section of the stem that has borne flowers. The young lateral shoots already growing below that point will flower the following year.

Spiraea japonica (Japanese spirea). Prune almost to the ground in spring, and flat heads of pink flowers will develop in late summer.

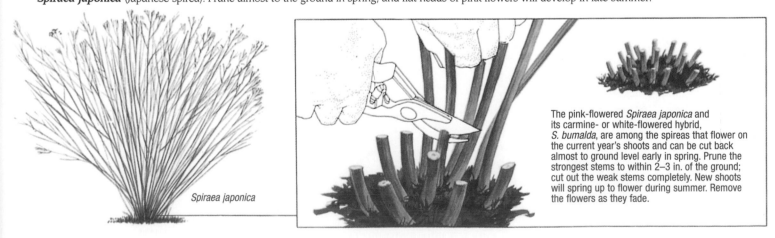

Spiraea japonica

The pink-flowered *Spiraea japonica* and its carmine- or white-flowered hybrid, *S. bumalda*, are among the spireas that flower on the current year's shoots and can be cut back almost to ground level early in spring. Prune the strongest stems to within 2–3 in. of the ground; cut out the weak stems completely. New shoots will spring up to flower during summer. Remove the flowers as they fade.

The star-shaped white blossoms of *Stephanandra tanakae* appear in June and July, and are followed by long-lasting fall color. Tolerant of dry, salty soil, *Tamarix ramosissima*, produces rosy flower spikes all summer.

Stephanandra tanakae

Tamarix ramosissima 'Pink Cascade'

Stephanandra. Prune hard after flowering in summer to encourage attractive colored leaves and stems.

Stephanandra is grown for the bright colors of its leaves in autumn and its stems in winter. Annual pruning will produce a new supply of stems and will let light into the center of the shrub to encourage strong, healthy growth. After the plant has flowered in early to mid summer, cut each flower-bearing stem down to where a strong, young shoot sprouts lower down, or cut it right to the ground. Remove completely all obviously weak stems.

Stephanandra incisa

Tamarix. To keep the plants compact, prune summer-flowering species hard late in winter, spring bloomers after flowering.

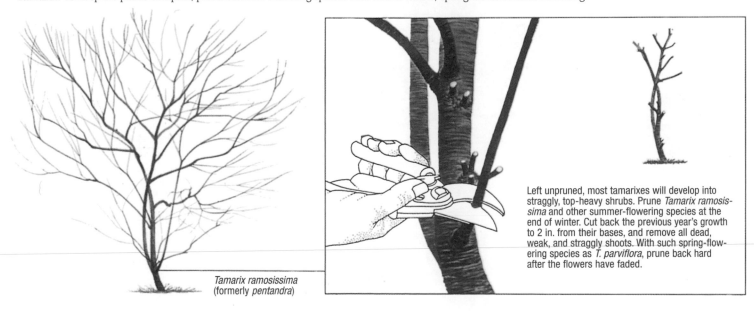

Left unpruned, most tamarixes will develop into straggly, top-heavy shrubs. Prune *Tamarix ramosissima* and other summer-flowering species at the end of winter. Cut back the previous year's growth to 2 in. from their bases, and remove all dead, weak, and straggly shoots. With such spring-flowering species as *T. parviflora*, prune back hard after the flowers have faded.

Tamarix ramosissima (formerly *pentandra*)

The popular weigela is a pretty summertime bloomer. It is hardy and stands up both to full sun and partial shade. Wisteria on the other hand is more sensitive, and needs warmth.

Weigela middendorffiana

Weigela 'Newport Red'

Wisteria sinensis

Weigela. To prevent plants from becoming overcrowded, prune away the flowered shoots after they have bloomed in summer.

Weigela florida

Weigela can quickly become dense and crowded, with fewer flowers. To prevent this, cut out dead and weak shoots after flowering in summer, and prune the flowered stems just above a point where young shoots are developing. With an old, neglected shrub, cut the oldest branches down to a few inches from the ground. If pure green leaves appear on *Weigela florida* 'Variegata,' remove the whole shoot.

Wisteria. To promote good flower clusters on this vine, cut back the fast-growing shoots in summer.

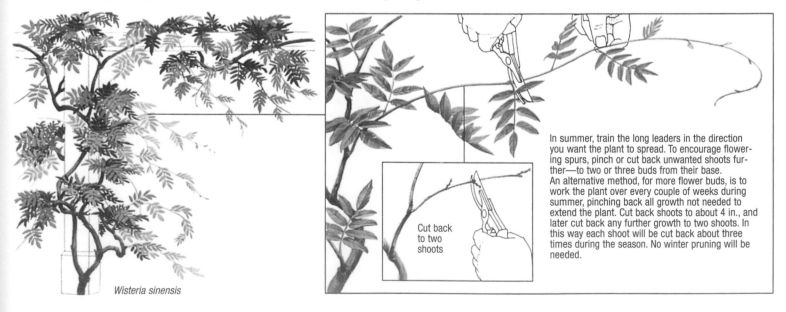
Wisteria sinensis

Cut back to two shoots

In summer, train the long leaders in the direction you want the plant to spread. To encourage flowering spurs, pinch or cut back unwanted shoots further—to two or three buds from their base.
An alternative method, for more flower buds, is to work the plant over every couple of weeks during summer, pinching back all growth not needed to extend the plant. Cut back shoots to about 4 in., and later cut back any further growth to two shoots. In this way each shoot will be cut back about three times during the season. No winter pruning will be needed.

Forsythia
'Beatrix
Farrand'
➡

Depending on the acidity of
the soil, florist's hydrangea
(*Hydrangea macrophylla*) can
be either pink or blue.

Hydrangea macrophylla

Shrubs for Your Garden

On the following pages you will find descriptions of and information about more than 120 different shrubs that will grow in North America. This information is presented in chart form to facilitate your finding what you need to know to keep shrubs healthy and productive. Vines are listed separately at the end of the section.

Names and Characteristics. Botanists classify all plants according to genus (general groupings of plants with similar characteristics) and species (specific plants within the genus). In the first column of each left-hand page that follows, you will find shrubs listed by genus, arranged alphabetically according to their botanical names.

In many cases, such as *Magnolia,* the botanical and common name is one and the same. With other shrubs, such as *Cornus* (dogwood), it is not. In either case, the name of the genus appears in italics, followed, in parentheses, by the common name.

The characteristics described in this column, and all information on the left-hand pages of the chart, apply to genuses specified in the left-hand column. On the right-hand chart pages, shrubs of each genus mentioned are subdivided into species, varieties, and hybrids. The illustration with each generic heading shows one specific species within that genus.

Uses and Requirements. Each shrub has its advantages and its limitations. Some are ideal for hedges; others make good windbreaks; still others need protection from the wind. In addition, many shrubs have rather specific needs in terms of water, drainage, pruning, feeding, general care, and pest control (to find the recommended treatment for control of pests or diseases, look up specific plant disorders in the Index).

If this information applies to all the species listed, it is incorporated under the heading Uses and Requirements on the chart. If it applies only to a single species, it is included

under the heading Decorative Characteristics and Remarks. Further details on planting and care of shrubs appear on pages 250–255. For pruning methods see pages 266–284.

Soil and **Light.** The pictograms used under these two headings refer to optimum soil conditions and intensity of sun for the growth of a particular shrub. A key detailing all the soil and light condition pictograms is found at the bottom of each left-hand page.

Propagation. An economical and satisfying way to obtain more shrubs is to propagate those you already have. With most shrubs the simplest propagation methods are to take hardwood cuttings or to soil-layer branches. But several other techniques are workable. The methods are illustrated on pages 257–264.

Under the heading Propagation on the following pages, you will find the appropriate method, or methods, for propagating each kind of shrub.

Species and Varieties. On the right-hand pages of the chart, you will find a selection of some widely planted shrubs. Each one's species name consists of the name of its genus, plus a second word (called a specific epithet). A third word indicates a subspecies variety or cultivated form. The genus name is written out and capitalized the first time it appears; for the related plants that follow, the genus name (and in many cases, the specific epithet) is abbreviated.

Both the genus name and the specific epithet (including any subspecies) are always italicized. Also italicized in the system followed throughout this book are naturally occurring varieties (*Euonymus fortunei vegetus,* for example). Varieties that have originated in gardens are known as cultivars—from cultivated varieties. Cultivars appear in roman type and in single quotation marks (*E. f.* 'Sarcoxie', for example).

A shrub that is listed by genus and species can be reproduced from seeds. The vast majority of cultivars,

however, can be duplicated only by vegetative propagation: via cuttings, division, layers, or grafts. There are a very few exceptions to this rule, but unfortunately, cultivar names do not indicate which varieties of shrubs will indeed "come true" from seeds.

In buying a shrub, it is important to ask for it by its full botanical name. There are wide differences among the species (and especially among the cultivars) in any genus, including whether they are evergreen or deciduous, as well as their size, hardiness, flower color, flowering time, and special requirements.

Hardiness. Before buying a shrub, your first consideration should be whether it will survive in the climate where you live. The U.S. Department of Agriculture has published a *Plant Hardiness Zone Map* as a general guide. On this map the continent is divided into 11 zones. On the front endsheet you will find a simplified map divided into the major zones, each zone representing about 10°F difference in average minimum winter temperature. Many plants, especially those adapted to cold weather, will not survive long at high temperatures. Summer heat can be as limiting as winter cold. In the following chart the range of hardiness zones in which the plant is expected to survive is indicated.

Bear in mind that the map is at best only a general indication of the climate where you are located. Higher altitudes in each area are likely to be colder than the zone map indicates; other topographical features create additional microclimates that can vary greatly from the average minimum temperatures listed.

Minimum winter temperature is not the only consideration affecting plant hardiness. Cold winds can do more damage than low temperatures. Therefore, a shrub that could be killed in an exposed site might survive unscathed on the lee side of a hedge or wall in the same yard.

Dates of the first and last frost are also important, as are the relative humidity and the amount of sunlight the shrub receives. The lowest temperature that a shrub can be expected to tolerate is still, however, the most useful and dependable single indicator of its likelihood of survival. In addition, some hardy plants *require* cold winters and cannot survive in warmer zones. Your local nurseryperson will know which these are.

Decorative Characteristics and Remarks. In this column on the chart, you will find a description of special qualities, most of which set a species or variety apart from other members of its genus. Such qualities may be decorative characteristics, such as the kind of foliage a shrub bears; its time of flowering; the size, color, or fragrance of its blossoms; or the nature of its fruit.

Northern winters can last five months or more, so the winter appearance of shrubs should be taken into account. Those with interesting bark are noted in the text.

Some shrub species require special growing conditions. Certain kinds cannot tolerate dry heat at anytime during the summer, while others are endangered by extreme humidity. Some must be planted in the sun, while others should be planted in the shade.

Soil requirements often vary among species. If a plant requires rapid drainage, or swampy conditions, the need is indicated here. If a species is tolerant of such special conditions as urban pollution or ocean or road salt spray, this, too, is noted.

Height and **Spread.** The dimensions given under these two headings are those that the particular species, variety, or hybrid reaches after several years in good growing conditions. The shrub's ultimate size, however, will vary according to the local climate, the degree of shelter, the amount of sunlight, the soil, and the care the shrub receives.

From midsummer to midfall, clusters of fragrant, pinkish, bell-shaped flowers grace the glossy abelia (*Abelia grandiflora*).

Abelia grandiflora

Abelia grandiflora
(abelia)

Abeliophyllum
(white forsythia)

Abies balsamea hudsonia (fir)

Abutilon
(flowering maple)

Acanthopanax
(five-leaved aralia)

Aesculus
(bottlebrush buckeye)

Aloysia triphylla
(lemon verbena)

BOTANICAL AND COMMON NAMES, GENERAL CHARACTERISTICS	USES AND REQUIREMENTS	SOIL	LIGHT	PROPAGATION (see also p. 257)
Abelia (abelia) Characterized by small tubular or bell-shaped summer flowers that range in color from white to shades of rosy pink. Leaves are small and on some kinds an interesting bronze-green color. Branches arch gracefully.	Some kinds have dense habit of growth and can be used for hedges. They are all strong growers and can be pruned in spring to any extent required for their specific situation in garden. Likes humusy soil.	■	● ◐	Take softwood cuttings in late spring or semi-hardwood cuttings in summer. Can be soil-layered in spring. Ripe seeds can be kept in closed containers for up to 1 yr.
Abeliophyllum (white forsythia) Resembles forsythia in habit of growth and prolific bloom, but flowers are smaller. They open on fingerlike racemes in midspring, pale pink but turn to white.	A single specimen adds interesting emphasis when planted in front of evergreen background.	□	● ◐	Sow seeds as soon as they ripen. Take leafy semi-hardwood cuttings in summer or leafless hardwood cuttings in fall.
Abies (fir) Coniferous evergreens with needlelike foliage that make a good contrast in form and texture to deciduous plants.	Mostly large trees but there are some dwarf, slow growing forms that are useful in the shrub border or on rock gardens. The sizes given are for mature plants and will not be reached for many years.	□	●	Seed sown as soon as ripe outdoors, or stratified for 3 months at 41°F. Commercially, most cultivars are grafted.
Abutilon (flowering maple) Leaves are maplelike, but flowers are usually pendulous bells.	Grow in a location sheltered from winds. Water well in droughts.	□	●	Take semi-hardwood cuttings in summer.
Acacia (acacia) Quick growing with tiny yellow flowers in early spring.	Transplant only when young and water well until established. Good for containers and heated sunrooms.	□	●	Give seeds a long soak in water to soften seed coat. Slow to germinate.
Acanthopanax (five-leaved aralia) Grown primarily for its handsome foliage. Inconspicuous summer flowers develop in multibranched clusters.	Excellent as border plant or as accent on lawns. Suitable for city use because it can tolerate soot and grime. Takes well to trimming and is sometimes used for hedges. Spines at base of leaves make it effective barrier plant. Is generally free of pests.	□	●	Sow seeds after stratifying or take root cuttings. Leafy semi-hardwood cuttings can also be taken in summer.
Aesculus (bottlebrush buckeye) Compound leaves consist of 5 to 7 elliptic leaflets. In midsummer flowers open in spikes up to 1 ft. long.	A good choice for a lawn specimen if there is adequate space around it. Spreads by underground suckers; so most plants are much wider than they are tall. Seldom needs pruning.	□	●	Sow seeds when ripe. Take root cuttings. Mound-layer in early spring by cutting stems to ground; cover with soil. Next spring remove and plant rooted shoots.
Aloysia (lemon verbena) Small blooms in clusters, but grown mainly for the fragrant foliage.	Excellent in tubs, but needs to be watered well. Makes a good houseplant where winters are too cold.	□	●	Take semi-ripe cuttings in summer or divide in spring or fall.

■ well drained to sandy　■ moist　■ wet　■ acidic　■ alkaline　□ regular soil　● full sun　◐ partial shade　● shade

Foot-long spikes of spidery-white flowers, appearing in midsummer on the bottlebrush buckeye (*Aesculus parviflora*), are followed by smooth, pear-shaped fruit in fall.

Aesculus parviflora

SPECIES AND VARIETIES	HARDINESS	DECORATIVE CHARACTERISTICS AND REMARKS	HEIGHT	SPREAD
Evergreen or semi-evergreen Abelia 'Edward Goucher' (pink)	Zones 6–9	Leaves are semi-evergreen. Lavender-pink blossoms open from midsummer to early fall. Even if killed to ground, usually recovers.	5 ft.	5 ft.
A. grandiflora (glossy)	Zones 5–9	Leaves that are semi-evergreen, or deciduous in cold climates, turn bronze-purple in fall. Pink flowers open in clusters of up to 4 from late summer until late fall and bloom until frost. A good hedge plant.	5 ft.	5 ft.
Deciduous Abeliophyllum distichum	Zones 5–8	Foliage is blue-green. Leaves are opposite and have short hairs on both sides. In cold winter regions dark purple flower buds may be damaged by frost unless plants are protected.	4 ft.	4 ft.
Evergreen Abies balsamea 'Hudsonia'	Zones 1–5	Rounded leaves are dark green, scented and about 1 in. long. Branches grow horizontally, giving a flat-topped profile. Will grow in alkaline soil.	1–2 ft.	1-2 ft.
A. koreana 'Prostrate Beauty'	Zones 4–6	Leaves are a glossy gray-green above, silvery beneath. Slow growing, at 14 yr. only 2 ft. high, 4 ft. wide.	6 ft.	10 ft.
A. lasiocarpa 'Compacta'	Zones 2–6	Silver-blue needles are 1½ in. long. Pale grayish branches are corky and give a wide, conical profile.	6 ft.	3 ft.
A. procera 'Prostrata'	Zones 5–6	Bluish foliage has a waxy sheen. Branches spread horizontally in asymmetrical pattern, giving pleasing informal effect.	2 ft.	3 ft.
Evergreen Abutilon hybridum	Zones 8–10	Many named forms with flowers in a range of colors from yellow to red.	10–15 ft.	12–15 ft.
Evergreen Acacia podalyraefolia (Queensland silver wattle)	Zones 10–11	One of the first to bloom with sprays of flowers. Foliage is silvery.	8–15 ft.	15 ft.
Acacia cultriformis	Zones 9–10	Fragrant flowers in spring. Leaf-like stems are small triangles that sprout from the branches.	15 ft.	15 ft.
Deciduous Acanthopanax sessiflorus	Zones 4–8	Where a plant of each sex can be cultivated, this is well worth growing for its shiny black fruit. Valuable for its glossy green foliage and ability to withstand shade.	12 ft.	8–10 ft.
A. sieboldianus	Zones 4–8	Glossy leaves are composed of up to 7 wedge-shaped leaflets. They are dark green and turn yellow before dropping. Plant blooms rather sparsely with greenish-white flowers; but is grown for its handsome leaves.	9 ft.	6–10 ft.
Deciduous Aesculus parviflora	Zones 4–8	Ornate pink stamens protrude from white flowers to make this a very showy plant when in bloom. Very attractive to butterflies, especially swallowtails.	12 ft.	36 ft.
Evergreen Aloysia triphylla	Zones 8–11	Narrow, lance-shaped leaves in circles of threes or fours around the stem. Often grown in herb gardens.	8 ft.	4–6 ft.

Prized for their glossy gold-splotched, pale green foliage and bright red berries, the varieties of Japanese laurel (*Aucuba japonica*) are well suited to seacoast gardens.

Aucuba japonica 'Crotonifolia'

Amorpha canescens
(leadplant)

Aralia
(angelica tree)

Arctostaphylos uva-ursi
(bearberry)

Aronia
(chokeberry)

Aucuba japonica
(aucuba)

Derberia thunborgii
(Japanese barberry)

BOTANICAL AND COMMON NAMES, GENERAL CHARACTERISTICS	USES AND REQUIREMENTS	SOIL	LIGHT	PROPAGATION (see also p. 257)
Amorpha (leadplant) Dependable but sometimes invasive plant. Its leaves are compound, and tiny, pealike blossoms form in terminal clusters that often branch. Slightly sticky pods follow flowers.	Use as single specimen plant or in borders, particularly where soil is poor and dry. May spread out of bounds unless restrained.	☐	●	Seeds can be sown immediately when ripe. Take leafy semi-hardwood cuttings in summer or leafless hardwood cuttings during autumn. Can also be increased quite easily by soil layering and suckers.
Aralia (angelica tree) Large shrub with long exotic-looking leaves. Stems have sharp spines.	Grow away from pathways where the spines may cause damage. A good specimen shrub.	☐	●	Sow seeds as soon as ripe, or watch for suckers which can be detached in spring.
Arctostaphylos (manzanita) Alternate leaves have smooth margins. Small, nodding, waxy, urn-shaped blossoms in racemes.	Not easy to transplant. Pot-grown plants from nursery are safest. Pinch tips during growing season to control growth. Protect from wind.	■	●	Ripened seeds can be stored in cool, dry place for up to 1 yr. prior to planting. Stratify seeds for 3 mo. at 41°F. Take semi-hardwood cuttings or firm-wood cuttings
Aronia (chokeberry) Upright shrubs with frothy white flowers in spring, good fall color and fruits that attract birds.	Named forms make good specimen plants. Basal suckers form a dense stand. An upright form is good for hedges. Mass plantings are very showy in fall and early winter.	☐	●	Seeds stratified for 90 days at 41°F or take softwood cuttings in early summer. Division also possible once plants have produced suckers.
Aucuba (aucuba) A handsome, densely leaved plant, with shiny, often variegated leaves. Minute male and female blossoms are on separate plants. Fruit is red or creamy white berry.	Useful in seacoast gardens, since it tolerates salt spray. Withstands smog. Foliage may burn in sun. Needs a great deal of water. For berry production, plant at least 4 females to every male.	☐	● ●	Sow seeds when ripe. Layer a branch into soil in spring. Take semi-hardwood cuttings in summer.
Berberis (barberry) Most barberries are known for yellow spring blooms. Branches are thorned. Foliage of some deciduous kinds turns attractive bright colors in fall. Some types also have remarkably showy display of berries in fall. Wide range of sizes makes these plants useful for many places in landscape.	The dense thorny kinds, of which there are a considerable number, make excellent barrier plantings in full sun or partial shade. Some of smaller kinds are useful for rock gardens, and those with showiest berries make interesting container plants for fall and early winter display. Deciduous types withstand poor, dry soil conditions. Barberries are seldom attacked by insects, but can act as an alternate host for wheat rust fungus. Varieties of the Japanese barberry may become invasive in warm climates and planting them is not recommended there.	☐	● ◑	Seeds can be sown when ripe or stored in cool place for up to 1 yr. Seeds can also be stratified for 2 mo. at 41°F. Root divisions can be made. Take leafy semi-hardwood cuttings in summer or hardwood cuttings in autumn.

■ well drained to sandy　■ moist　■ wet　■ acidic　■ alkaline　☐ regular soil　● full sun　◑ partial shade　● shade

Barberries include deciduous and evergreen shrubs, all with reddish-orange or yellow blossoms. Small red berries appear in fall amid the brilliant red foliage of the Japanese barberry (*Berberis thunbergii*).

Berberis thunbergii

SPECIES AND VARIETIES	HARDINESS	DECORATIVE CHARACTERISTICS AND REMARKS	HEIGHT	SPREAD
Deciduous *Amorpha canescens*	Zones 2–9	Densely hairy gray leaves often are made up of from 15 to more than 40 leaflets up to ¾ in. long; they remain attractive throughout growing season. In midsummer blue blossoms open on 4- to 6-in. spikes.	4 ft.	3–4 ft.
Deciduous *Aralia elata* (Japanese)	Zones 4–9	Flowers in terminal clusters in August.	5–15 ft.	5–10 ft.
Evergreen *Arctostaphylos alpina* (black bearberry)	Zones 6–10	Open form with strong, red-barked branches; hairy leaves and branches. White flowers from early to mid spring followed by red fruits in summer.	3–15 ft.	1½–10 ft.
A. uva-ursi (kinnikinnick)	Zones 1–6	A good ground cover for poor, rocky soils or sandy slopes. Red berries in fall.	1 ft.	4 ft.
Deciduous *Aronia arbutifolia* 'Brilliantissima' (red)	Zones 4–9	Dark green leaves turn scarlet in autumn and fall off to reveal the glossy red fruits.	6–8 ft.	5 ft.
A. melanocarpa 'Autumn Magic' (black)	Zones 4–9	Foliage turns red and purple in fall. Black berries are not a bitter as the red chokeberry. Grows well in moist soils.	6–8 ft.	5 ft.
Evergreen *Aucuba japonica*	Zones 7–10	Shiny oval leaves are deep green and up to 8 in. long. Panicles, 2–5 in. long, have small olive-colored blossoms in early spring. Bright red fruits (female only) last until spring. Both male and female plants available.	12 ft.	7 ft.
A. j. 'Crotonifolia'	Zones 7–10	Much the same as *A. japonica*, but foliage has golden yellow spots.	12 ft.	7 ft.
Deciduous *Berberis thunbergii* (Japanese)	Zones 4–8	Dense, thorny, and a profuse bloomer. Red fruit often lasts through winter. Grows well in poor soil. Will live in shade.	6 ft.	6 ft.
B. t. atropurpurea	Zones 4–8	Leaves are reddish purple from spring through autumn. Makes a good, dense hedge.	5 ft.	4 ft.
B. t. 'Concord'	Zones 4–8	Small, rounded shape with red foliage that turns purple.	2 ft.	3 ft.
B. t. 'Variegata'	Zones 4–8	Leaves have interesting pale gray, yellow, and white blotches. Not as good for hedging.	5 ft.	4 ft.
Evergreen *B. buxifolia* 'Nana'	Zones 5–8	Handsome foliage. Leaves about 1 in. long. Good for low hedging.	1½ ft.	1½ ft.
B. candidula (paleleaf)	Zones 5–8	Leaves are deep green above, white beneath. Fruit is pale gray. Dense habit of growth makes this especially useful in rock garden.	3 ft.	3 ft.
B. darwinii (Darwins berberis)	Zones 6–9	Oblong, 3-pointed, glossy green leaves. Densely blooming yellow-orange flowers and purple fruits. One of the most beautiful.	8 ft.	9 ft.
B. julianae (wintergreen)	Zones 5–8	Narrow toothed leaves are deep green on top, with light green undersides. Berries are bluish black. Develops heavy growth. This is one of the hardiest evergreen barberries.	6 ft.	4 ft.
B. sargentiana	Zones 6–9	Elliptic toothed leaves are dark green, 2–4 in. long. Thorns are often 1 in. long.	5 ft.	5 ft.
B. stenophylla (rosemary)	Zones 5–9	Hybrid with dark green leaves with whitish undersides. Berries are black. Makes fine sheared hedge.	8 ft.	12 ft.
B. verruculosa (warty)	Zones 4–7	Oval leathery leaves turn bronze in fall. Has very large flowers. Purplish-black fruit.	4 ft.	4 ft.

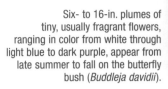

Six- to 16-in. plumes of tiny, usually fragrant flowers, ranging in color from white through light blue to dark purple, appear from late summer to fall on the butterfly bush (*Buddleja davidii*).

Buddleja davidii 'White Profusion'

Buddleja davidii (buddleia)

Buxus sempervirens 'Suffruticosa' (boxwood)

Callicarpa bodinieri (beauty-berry)

Callistemon (bottlebrush)

Calycanthus floridus (Carolina allspice)

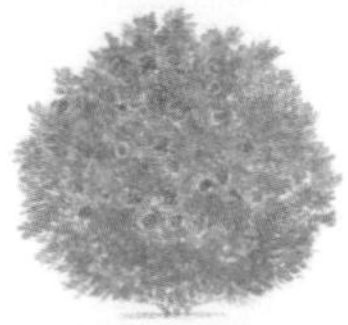

Camellia japonica (camellia)

Carissa macrocarpa (Natal plum)

BOTANICAL AND COMMON NAMES, GENERAL CHARACTERISTICS	USES AND REQUIREMENTS	SOIL	LIGHT	PROPAGATION (see also p. 257)
Buddleja (buddleia) Growth is characteristically very rapid, although slow to commence in spring. Known for its large clusters of tiny flowers. Leaves of *B. alternifolia* are alternate, those of all other kinds are opposite.	Fertilizing is almost never necessary unless soil is extremely low in nutrients. In cold winter areas branches of some species and varieties die back to the ground but develop new growth in spring. Prune *B. davidii* in early spring before growth begins; prune other sorts listed here after flowering. Butterfly bush is self-seeding and may become an invasive weed in warmer parts of the country.	■	●	Seeds can be planted as soon as ripe, or they can be stored for up to 1 yr. Softwood cuttings in early summer, firm-wood cuttings in late summer, or hardwood cuttings in fall root easily.
Buxus (boxwood) Grown mainly for pungent, deep green foliage that forms dense screen on mature plants. Tiny, inconspicuous flowers open in midspring.	Outstanding for hedges and topiary gardens. Protect from wind and sun in cold winter areas, as these may burn leaves.	■	●	As soon as seeds ripen, they can be sown, stratified, or stored in cool, dry place for up to 1 yr. Root divisions can also be made. Take leafy semi-hardwood cuttings in spring or autumn, or leafless hardwood cuttings in fall.
Callicarpa (beauty-berry) Tiny tubular flowers in clusters open during summer, but most are obscured by toothed foliage. In fall berry clusters put on good display after leaves turn yellow and drop.	In many areas plants may be killed to ground in winter, but new growth will appear in spring, flower, and bear fruit.	□	●	Seeds can be sown when ripe or can be stored in a dry, cool place for later use. Root divisions are easily made. Leafy semi-hardwood cuttings should be taken in summer, or leafless hardwood cuttings in fall.
Callistemon (bottlebrush) Dense brushlike spikes of flowers with protruding stamens. Narrow leaves give a feathery effect.	Fast growing and easily trained, but protect from strong winds. Good for coastal gardens.	□	●	Sow seeds in spring or take ripewood cuttings in late summer.
Calycanthus (Carolina allspice) A native shrub with dark green foliage that is spicy when crushed. The brownish-red flowers dry well for use in winter arrangements.	Plant close to a sitting area where the foliage can be appreciated.	□	● ◐	Seeds sown as soon as ripe (before seed pods turn all brown). Take leafy, firm-wood cuttings in mid to late summer.
Calluna (Scotch heather) See p. 376.				
Camellia (camellia) Decorative, dark green leaves are thick and leathery and arranged alternately on branches. Leaves are usually about 4 in. long. Bowl- or cup-shaped, single or double, showy flowers have waxy appearance.	A handsome plant for accents. Does not succeed in windy places. Spring planting is best in cold-winter regions. Feed in early spring and again in early summer. Mulch root area in spring to keep it cool and moist all summer.	■ ■	● ◐	Take semi-hardwood cuttings in summer.
Carissa (Natal plum) White or pink flowers borne year-round. Fruit varies in flavor depending on variety.	Does well near the coast. Makes a good hedge or specimen plant.	□	●	Seed, semi-hardwood or firm-wood cuttings.

■ well drained to sandy ■ moist ■ wet ■ acidic ■ alkaline □ regular soil ● full sun ◐ partial shade ● shade

Buxus sempervirens

Callicarpa bodinieri var. *giraldii*

Slow growth and long life characterize all species of boxwood (*Buxus*), a hardy evergreen that is ideal for hedging. The beauty-berry (*Callicarpa*) has lilac-colored flowers in summer but is grown mainly for its fruit.

SPECIES AND VARIETIES	HARDINESS	DECORATIVE CHARACTERISTICS AND REMARKS	HEIGHT	SPREAD
Deciduous *Buddleja alternifolia* (fountain)	Zones 4–8	Lance-shaped leaves have green undersides. The earliest buddleia to flower, its long garlands of tiny lavender-blue blossoms open in early summer on last year's wood. Branches are pendulous. A particularly hardy species.	10 ft.	15 ft.
B. davidii (butterfly bush)	Zones 4–9	Fragrant, pale purple flowers with orange throats develop on long, arching, spikelike clusters from late summer until frost. Many varieties are available, with colors ranging from white to purple and crimson. They attract butterflies.	12 ft.	8 ft.
B. weyeriana 'Honeycomb'	Zones 5–9	Creamy buds open yellow with an orange eye. Fragrant flowers attract butterflies. Cut back hard in spring.	4–6 ft.	4–6 ft.
Evergreen *Buxus microphylla japonica*	Zones 4–9	One of hardiest varieties, although leaves may turn brownish in winter.	2 ft.	2 ft.
B. sempervirens (English)	Zones 5–8	Shiny green leaves are rounded and paler green on undersides than tops.	20 ft.	10 ft.
B. s. 'Suffruticosa' (dwarf English)	Zones 5–8	Low habit of growth makes this a good candidate for edging, particularly in formal plantings.	3 ft.	3 ft.
Deciduous *Callicarpa bodinieri giraldii* (Giralds)	Zones 5–8	Elliptic leaves are 4 in. long and turn pink or purple before falling. Clusters of very small lilac-colored flowers are followed by attractive bluish-violet berries that last well into winter. Habit of growth is upright.	8 ft.	6 ft.
C. dichotoma (purple)	Zones 5–8	Leaves are coarsely toothed and 1–3 in. long. The little berries that follow the pink flowers, which measure only 1/2 in. across, are lilac to violet in color. In fall stems take on purplish color.	4 ft.	4 ft.
Evergreen *Callistemon citrinus* (crimson)	Zones 10–11	Arching shrub with crimson flowers in spikes in spring and summer.	20–25 ft	15–20 ft.
Deciduous *Calycanthus floridus*	Zones 4–9	Flowers open from spring to late summer and have marrow petals. Foliage turns yellow in fall.	6 ft.	6 ft.
Evergreen *Camellia japonica* (common camellia)	Zones 7–9	Bloom time differs by variety and climate. Varieties include several double and semi-double forms with white, red, or pink flowers.	30 ft.	15 ft.
C. j. 'Colonel Firey'	Zones 7–9	Large, formal, dark red flowers bloom mid to late season.	30 ft.	12 ft.
C. j. 'Debutante'	Zones 7–9	Large, light pink peony form. Early double blooms.	30 ft.	12 ft.
C. sasanqua	Zones 7–9	Leaves are only about 2 in. long, and flowers open earlier than those of *C. japonica* and its varieties. Flowers in white, pink, or purple; single, semi-double, and double. General habit of growth tends to be open and willowy.	15 ft.	10 ft.
Evergreen *Carissa macrocarpa* (grandiflora)	Zones 9–11	Branches have 1½-in. spines. Red fruit are egg-shaped about 2 in. long. Several named forms.	10–12 ft.	4–10 ft.

With five white petals and bright yellow stamens, *Carpentaria californica* is very fragrant and usually trouble-free.

Carpentaria californica

Carpenteria californica
(bush anemone)

Caryopteris clandonensis
(bluebeard)

Ceanothus delilianus
(California lilac)

Cedrus deodora
(cedar)

Cephalanthus occidentalis
(buttonbush)

Cestrum
(night flowering jasmine)

Chamaecyparis
(false cypress)

BOTANICAL AND COMMON NAMES, GENERAL CHARACTERISTICS	USES AND REQUIREMENTS	SOIL	LIGHT	PROPAGATION (see also p. 257)
Carpenteria (bush anemone) Clusters of saucer-shaped flowers are white, fragrant, and up to 3 in. across. Shiny leaves 3–4 in. long.	Intolerant of wet winters and must be screened from strong, cold winds. Not easy to transplant.	■	●◐	Increased by seeds or soil layers. Take semi-hardwood cuttings in summer.
Caryopteris (bluebeard) Heavy production of blue flowers with protruding stamens, borne in tight clusters. It develops winged nutlike fruits.	Effective because of its unusual cool blue flower color and season of bloom, which extends from late summer until frost sets in. Mulch root area heavily after soil freezes. In its northernmost range top growth is often killed by frost, but new branches will form in spring if all old growth is cut back to soil line.	■	●	Take firm-wood cuttings in late summer or leafless hardwood cuttings in autumn.
Ceanothus (ceanothus, or California lilac) Bears small flowers in attractive upright, branching, spikelike clusters. When ripe, fruit opens into 3 separate segments.	Water well during first year after transplanting. Plants are generally drought resistant; over-watering should be avoided since many species are liable to succumb to root rot. Occasionally the plants may be troubled by aphids and white flies but both can be controlled easily by spraying with insecticidal soap. Plants often have short life span.	■ ■	●	Soak seeds overnight in hot water, and stratify for 3 mo. at 41°F. Take softwood cuttings in spring or semi-hardwood cuttings in summer. Can also be soil-layered.
Cedrus (cedar) Low growing forms of what are normally tall trees.	The colored foliage makes these dwarf forms of cedar distinctive, and gives a good contrast in texture in addition.	□	●	Seed sown as soon as ripe will germinate erratically, giving a 2 week cold treatment, evens out the germination. Seed from these dwarf forms may not be true to type.
Cephalanthus (buttonbush) Native from New Brunswick to Florida, this gets its common name from the fruits, which look like round buttons. White flowers open in late summer on the ends of the branches.	The glossy green foliage makes a good backdrop for tall perennials. Fruits give winter interest.	■	●◐	Seed sown as soon as it is ripe will germinate readily. Take softwood cuttings in late spring.
Cestrum (cestrum) Many sweetly scented flowers followed by small berrylike fruit.	Grows best in well-drained soil with lots of humus. Cut out spindly branches in spring.	□	●	All three types of cuttings can be used at the appropriate time of year.
Chamaecyparis (false cypress) These grow best in cool, moist locations, protected from drying winds and are particularly suited to coastal areas.	Good for screens, hedges, foundations and as specimen plants. The smaller types are good in rock gardens and troughs.	■	●	Seed should be stratified for one month at room temperature followed by a month at 41°F. Cuttings taken in late fall and early winter will root indoors with bottom heat.

■ well drained to sandy   ■ moist   ■ wet   ■ acidic   ■ alkaline   □ regular soil   ● full sun   ◐ partial shade   ● shade

Early-flowering ornamental quinces (*Chaenomeles speciosa*) bear profuse clusters of five-petaled, cup-shaped, single or double flowers. These are followed by apple-shaped fragrant fruits.

Chaenomeles speciosa 'Geisha Girl'   *Chaenomeles speciosa* 'Nivalis'

SPECIES AND VARIETIES	HARDINESS	DECORATIVE CHARACTERISTICS AND REMARKS	HEIGHT	SPREAD
Evergreen *Carpenteria californica*	Zones 7–9	Leaves are oblong. Flowers develop individually or in clusters of 2–7.	8–10 ft.	8 ft.
Deciduous *Caryopteris clandonensis*	Zones 5–9	Vivid blue flowers open in late summer. This is hybrid between *C. incana* and *C. mongolica*.	4 ft.	4 ft.
C. c. 'Blue Mist'	Zones 5–9	Blossoms in autumn more profusely than *C. clandonensis*. Well suited to smaller gardens.	2 ft.	3 ft.
C. c. 'Longwood Blue'	Zones 6–9	Autumn flowers are darker blue than those of *C. c* 'Blue Mist'. Silvery foliage.	2 ft.	3 ft.
Deciduous *Ceanothus delilianus*	Zones 6–10	Leaves to 3 in. long. This hybrid has very tiny blue flowers that appear in great numbers in midspring.	6 ft.	3 ft.
C. d. 'Gloire de Versailles'	Zones 6–10	Fragrant powder-blue blossoms. Fine for espaliering. One of most popular varieties of *C. delilianus*.	8 ft.	5 ft.
Evergreen *C. arboreus* 'Ray Hartman'	Zones 8–10	Pale to bright blue flowers in early spring. Can be grown as shrub or small tree.	10–20 ft.	15 ft.
C. cyaneus 'Sierra Blue'	Zones 7–10	Dense, rich, and glossy green foliage to base of plant. Deep blue flowers bloom profusely in spring. Can be sheared to form hedge or trimmed to make informal screen.	6–12 ft.	5–8 ft.
Evergreen *Cedrus atlantica* 'Glauca Pendula'	Zones 6–9	Handsome bluish-green foliage hangs from gracefully drooping branches.	10–15 ft.	6–10 ft.
C. deodora 'Aurea Pendula'	Zones 6–8	Foliage is light yellow in spring, turning golden later in season. Almost prostrate. New shoots with upright habit of growth should be pruned out.	2 ft.	6 ft.
Deciduous *Cephalanthus occidentalis*	Zones 4–10	Flowers when few other shrubs are in bloom. Will grow readily in soggy soils.	10–12 ft.	12–15 ft.
Evergreen *Cestrum nocturnum* (night flowering jasmine)	Zones 10–11	Clusters of pale green to white fragrant flowers open at night.	10 ft.	6–8 ft.
Evergreen *Chamaecyparis lawsoniana* (Lawson's)	Zones 5–7	There are many named forms of this with foliage that varies from blue-green to yellow. Most are conical in shape and slow growing. The ultimate size depends on the variety.	50–60 ft.	10–15 ft.
C. obtuse (Hinoki)	Zones 4–8	Slow growing with dense foliage and many named forms. Generally conical in shape.	40–50 ft.	20–25 ft.
C. pisifera (Sawara)	Zones 4–8	Mostly conical but with a greater range of foliage colors, blue, gray, green or yellow.	40 ft.	30 ft.

Glory-bower (*Clerodendrum*) and sweet pepper bush (*Clethra*) produce fragrant flowers and thrive in sunny, sheltered locations.

Clerodendrum trichotomum

Clethra alnifolia

Chaenomeles speciosa
(flowering quince)

Chimonanthus praecox
(wintersweet)

Choisya ternata
(Mexican orange)

Clerodendrum trichotomum
(harlequin glory-bower)

Clethra alnifolia
(sweet pepper bush)

Colutea
(bladder senna)

Cornus alba sibirica
(dogwood)

BOTANICAL AND COMMON NAMES, GENERAL CHARACTERISTICS	USES AND REQUIREMENTS	SOIL	LIGHT	PROPAGATION (see also p. 257)
Chaenomeles, or Cydonia (flowering quince) Slightly angular branches. Flowers open before or just after leaves unfold. Aromatic green or yellow fruits used in preserves.	Tolerates both dry and wet conditions. In alkaline soil leaves may turn yellow. Needs only occasional pruning. Protect against scale (p. 521) and fire blight (p. 525).	☐	●	Divide roots or soil-layer lower branches. Take semi-hardwood cuttings in summer or leafless hardwood cuttings in fall.
Chimonanthus (wintersweet) Honey scented bowl-shaped blooms in early spring, before shiny leaves.	Protect from winter winds.	■	●	Seeds as soon as ripe or by layering in autumn.
Choisya (Mexican orange) Compound leaves are opposite. Flowers are displayed in clusters of up to 6.	Good border plant. Water in dry weather. Occasional pruning will help to maintain a good outline.	■	● ◖	Take semi-hardwood cuttings in summer.
Clerodendrum (glory-bower) Decorative blossoms develop in clusters and include calyxes that often display more color than tubelike corollas. Stamens protrude. Fleshy fruits develop in autumn.	Do not cultivate around roots, or many suckers will develop, spoiling overall contour.	☐	●	Stratify seeds for 3 mo. at 41°F. Take semi-hardwood cuttings in summer. Dig suckers in fall.
Clethra (sweet pepper bush, or summer sweet) Short-stalked, toothed leaves. Fragrant white flowers grow in terminal spikes.	Looks attractive on fringe of woodlands.	■	●	Take firm-wood cuttings in late summer. Responds well to root division and soil layering. Remove and plant rooted suckers in fall.
Colutea (bladder senna) Small, orange and yellow flowers are produced from midsummer to late fall and give bladder-like seed pods.	Grow as individual plant or as a screen or windbreak. Grows well in poor soils.	☐	●	Seeds have a hard coat and should be soaked for 2 hours in hot water before sowing. Semi-ripe cuttings in late summer root about 50% of the time.
Cornus (dogwood) Berries are decorative in fall. Some kinds have colorful twigs, which are particularly striking in cold climates, where they stand out against snowy backgrounds.	They need plenty of water in periods of heat and drought. Most dogwoods are resistant to pests and diseases. Easily grown and hardy.	☐	● ◖	Take semi-hardwood cuttings in summer or leafless hardwood cuttings in fall.

■ well drained to sandy　■ moist　■ wet　■ acidic　■ alkaline　☐ regular soil　● full sun　◖ partial shade　● shade

Yellow catkins appear on the hazelnut (*Corylus*) in early spring. The corkscrew hazel (*C. avellana* 'Contorta') gets its name from its oddly twisted branches.

Corylus avellana

Corylus avellana 'Contorta'

SPECIES AND VARIETIES	HARDINESS	DECORATIVE CHARACTERISTICS AND REMARKS	HEIGHT	SPREAD
Deciduous *Chaenomeles japonica* (Japanese)	Zones 4–8	Brick-red flowers are followed by yellow fruits almost 2 in. long. Low growing.	3 ft.	2–3 ft.
C. speciosa (common)	Zones 4–8	Single, semi-double, or double flowers range from white to pink, red, or orange. Fruits are pear shaped to rounded, 2–2½ in. long, and aromatic. Spreading habit of growth.	6–10 ft.	6 ft.
Deciduous *Chimonanthus praecox*	Zones 7–9	Pendant sulfur-yellow flowers have brownish-purple stripes inside.	9 ft.	9 ft.
Evergreen *Choisya ternata*	Zones 7–9	Fragrant leaflets are 3 in. long and have smooth edges. Orange-scented white flowers are up to 1 in. wide. 'Sundance' has bright yellow foliage, but rarely flowers.	8 ft.	6 ft.
Deciduous *Clerodendrum trichotomum* (harlequin)	Zones 6–9	Elliptic or oval leaves are often lobed and frequently up to 7 in. long. Ornate pale pink flower clusters are aromatic and have protruding stamens. Blue berries and prominent red calyxes put on handsome show in late summer and early fall, lasting through midfall or longer.	20 ft.	15 ft.
Deciduous *Clethra alnifolia*	Zones 4–9	Oblong leaves with pointed tips are up to 5 in. long. Foliage colors well in fall. Small blossoms begin to open in midsummer emitting strong scent.	6 ft.	5 ft.
C. a. 'Rosea'	Zones 4–9	In autumn foliage turns to shades of orange and yellow. Flowers are light pink. Needs plenty of moisture. Makes an excellent variety for seacoast settings.	6 ft.	5 ft.
C. a. 'September Beauty'	Zones 4–9	A late-flowering, compact form with good full color. The 6 in. long flower spikes are highly fragrant. Grows well in shade.	4–6 ft.	3–4 ft.
Deciduous *Colutea arborescens*	Zones 4–7	Strong growing with a bushy habit and small leaflets that allow light through.	6–8 ft.	4–6 ft.
Deciduous *Cornus alba* (Tatarian)	Zones 2–7	Oval leaves with bluish-green undersides turn red in fall. Vivid red twigs are spectacular in winter. Flowers appear in early summer. Pale blue fruits.	9 ft.	4–8 ft.
C. a. 'Elegantissima' (silverleaf)	Zones 2–7	One of the most useful of the variegated shrubs. Its leaves are bordered with white and retain excellent color all season long, even in shade.	6 ft.	4–6 ft.
C. a. 'Sibirica' (Siberian)	Zones 2–7	Autumn leaf color is red. Has creamy blossoms in late spring and tiny blue berries. Prune in early spring to promote plentiful new growth of red twigs in winter. Tolerates moisture.	8 ft.	4–8 ft.
C. a. 'Spaethii' (Spaeth's)	Zones 2–7	A yellow variegated selection which blends well with the silverleaf dogwood. Vivid red bark in winter.	6 ft.	4 ft.
C. sanguinea (bloodtwig)	Zones 4–7	Resembles *C. alba*, but twigs are usually darker red. Fruits are dark purple.	12 ft.	4–8 ft.
C. s. 'Winter Flame'	Zones 4–7	Long-lasting orange fall foliage and winter stems that shade from orange to red. Cut back hard in spring for best color.	3–5 ft.	3–5 ft.
C. stolonifera (red osier)	Zones 2–8	Underground stems produce heavy clumps. White flowers open in late spring or early summer. Suckers removed and planted in autumn will root readily. Used to help control erosion on sloping terrain.	6 ft.	4–8 ft.
C. s. 'Flaviramea' (yellowtwig)	Zones 2–7	Twigs are greenish yellow. Needs moisture.	6 ft.	4–8 ft.

Depending on the species, cotoneaster (*Cotoneaster*) can be a ground cover, can be used in rock gardens, or for covering an unsightly wall. *C. horizontalis* makes a good wall covering; *C. cochleatus*, which grows to only 8 in., makes an attractive ground cover.

Cotoneaster horizontalis

Cotoneaster cochleatus

Coryolpsis spicata
(spike hazel)

Corylus avellana 'Contorta'
(filbert)

Cotinus coggygria
(smoke tree)

Cotoneaster apiculatus
(cotoneaster)

Cryptomeria
(cryptomeria)

BOTANICAL AND COMMON NAMES, GENERAL CHARACTERISTICS	USES AND REQUIREMENTS	SOIL	LIGHT	PROPAGATION (see also p. 257)
Corylopsis (winter hazel) Lime-green leaves are toothed and display prominent veins. Yellow flowers open early in spring and may be damaged by late frosts.	Attractive in a woodland setting or with an evergreen background. Plant in sandy soil with generous amounts of peat moss. Does not tolerate alkalinity. Provide protection from cold winds.	◼	● ◐	Stratify seeds for 5 mo. at 70°F then for another 3 mo. at 41°F prior to sowing. Take semi-hardwood cuttings in summer.
Corylus (filbert, or hazelnut) Alternate, usually hairy, double toothed leaves. Minute flowers appear before leaves, the male flowers in catkins, the females in clusters, both on same plant. Edible egg-shaped nuts have smooth, hard shells covered by leafy growth.	Will live in heavy, wet clay. Grow several specimens for adequate cross-pollination and good nut crop.	☐	◐	Remove rooted suckers, and plant. Seeds usually should be stratified at 41°F for 3 mo. and then planted. Branches can be soil-layered. Take semi-hardwood cuttings in early summer.
Cotinus (smoke tree) A large shrub, sometimes grown as a tree, noted for its large clusters of minute fruits that suggest a cloud of smoke.	The species has brilliant yellow-to-orange fall color.	☐	●	Sow seed outside in the fall, or layer branches in September.
Cotoneaster (cotoneaster) Although small white or pinkish flowers appear in spring or summer, these hardy shrubs are grown mainly for their attractive branching pattern, foliage, and small red to black fruit that makes a showy display in fall and, in most types, remains through winter.	The lower-growing, more restrained kinds make fine additions to rock gardens. Borers (p. 540) and lace bugs (p. 511) sometimes attack plants. Susceptible to fire blight (p. 525), which causes cankers to form at base of shoots that have died back.	☐	● ◐	Seeds can be sown when ripe or stored for up to 1 yr. in cool, dry place and then planted. In some cases, germination may take 2 yr. All kinds can be soil-layered. Some can be increased by semi-hardwood cuttings in summer, others by leafless hardwood cuttings in fall.
Cryptomeria (cryptomeria) The species is a tree but there are several dwarf, and slow growing forms that are shrubs.	Easy to grow but needs shelter from winter winds.	◼ ◼	●	Soak seeds in cold water for 24 hours, then store at 41°F for 90 days. Named forms may not come true. Hardwood cutting, taken in early winter, root poorly.

◼ well drained to sandy ◼ moist ◼ wet ◼ acidic ◼ alkaline ☐ regular soil ● full sun ◐ partial shade ● shade

Thanks to its pretty flowers, fruit clusters, and colorful fall foliage, the smoke tree (*Cotinus*) looks splendid throughout most of the year.

Cotinus coggygria 'Royal Purple'

SPECIES AND VARIETIES	HARDINESS	DECORATIVE CHARACTERISTICS AND REMARKS	HEIGHT	SPREAD
Deciduous *Corylopsis pauciflora* (buttercup)	Zones 6–8	Oval, heart-shaped 2- to 3-in.-long leaves. Racemes have 2 or 3 blossoms.	6 ft.	10 ft.
C. spicata (spike)	Zones 5–8	Resembles *C. pauciflora*, but leaves are 3–5 in. long. Up to 12 flowers in each raceme.	6 ft.	10 ft.
Deciduous *Corylus americana* (American)	Zones 4–9	Alternate dark green leaves, 2–5 in. long, have hairy undersides. Bears round nuts about ½ in. in diameter, which grow in clusters of 2–6. A woodland shrub useful for its hardiness.	10 ft.	6–10 ft.
C. avellana 'Aurea' (European golden)	Zones 4–8	Yellowish leaves are about 3–4 in. long and heart shaped at base. Tips of nuts sometimes protrude through husks.	15 ft.	15 ft.
C. a. 'Contorta' (corkscrew)	Zones 4–8	Curiously twisted branches give this variety unusual gnarled look. Its bare branches are prized by flower arrangers.	15 ft.	15 ft.
Deciduous *Cotinus coggygria*	Zones 4–8	Pink hairs on the fruit stalks cause the unusual appearance.	12 ft.	15–20 ft.
C. c. 'Royal Purple'	Zones 4–8	A smaller selection with deep purple foliage that retains its color well into the season.	8 ft.	8–10 ft.
Deciduous *Cotoneaster acutifolius* (Peking)	Zones 2–8	Most often used as a hedge. A good addition to a shrub border. Has black fruit on arching branches.	4–10 ft.	3–12 ft.
C. adpressus (creeping)	Zones 4–8	Pinkish flowers open in early summer. Fruits are red. A prostrate species that grows slowly and is excellent for rock gardens.	6 in.	2–3 ft.
C. apiculatus (cranberry)	Zones 4–7	Leaves have pointed tips. A handsome species with pink blooms and scarlet fruits.	4 ft.	3–4 ft.
C. horizontalis (rock spray)	Zones 4–7	Its forked, wide-spreading branches bear rounded leaves; semi-evergreen in mild climates, deciduous in cold ones. Early summer flowers are pinkish, and fruits are brilliant red. It can easily be espaliered.	2 ft.	3–5 ft.
C. perpusillus	Zones 4–9	Has smaller leaves and is shorter than *C. horizontalis*.	1½ ft.	2–3 ft.
Evergreen *C. dammeri* (bearberry)	Zones 4–8	Flowers are white and fruits are red. If soil is loose, the prostrate branches of this species will root at joints, making it useful on slopes. Fruits often attract birds in early winter.	1 ft.	6 ft.
C. microphyllus (littleleaf)	Zones 4–8	Glossy leaves, white flowers, and profusion of scarlet berries make this an outstanding candidate for planting in foregrounds.	2 ft.	15 ft.
Evergreen *Cryptomeria japonica* 'Compressa' (Japanese cedar)	Zones 5–9	A mounded plant with dense ascending branches and branchlets. Leaves in juvenile form are small and fine; in adult form they are long and recurved.	3–4 ft.	3–4 ft.
C.j. 'Cristata'	Zones 5–9	Tips of new growth are contorted with thickly clustered leaves. Rounded cones are about 1 in. in diameter.	3–4 ft.	3–4 ft.
C.j. 'Globosa Nana'	Zones 5–9	Foliage is light green. When young, plant is cone-shaped, but with maturity shape becomes more rounded.	3–4 ft.	3–4 ft.
C.j. 'Vilmoriniana'	Zones 5–9	Foliage turns an attractive dark reddish bronze in winter. Slow growing with a dense, rounded shape.	3–4 ft.	3–4 ft.

Flowers of the broom (*Cytisus praecox*) appear in midspring all along the arching stems. The garland flower (*Daphne cneorum*) has very fragrant pink flowers in spring, brighter pink in the variety 'Eximia'.

Cytisus praecox 'Warminster'

Daphne cneorum 'Eximia'

	BOTANICAL AND COMMON NAMES, GENERAL CHARACTERISTICS	USES AND REQUIREMENTS	SOIL	LIGHT	PROPAGATION (see also p. 257)

Cytisus scoparius (broom)

Cytisus (broom)
Purple or white pealike blossoms are sometimes aromatic and always showy. Compound leaves consist of 3 leaflets. Green twigs are interesting feature in winter, especially in northern regions where color is scarce. The word "broom" probably derives from a name given centuries ago. It was descriptive of the upright dense growth of the Scotch broom, which was used for making brooms.

Good for borders, rock gardens, and informal plantings. Requires only average fertility but must have good drainage. Transplant young specimens only. Older plants are difficult to move. Needs judicious pruning after flowers fade. Has no particular disease or insect problems.

Seeds can be planted when ripe or stored in cool, dry place for up to 1 yr. prior to sowing. Soak in a commercially available sulfuric-acid concentrate for ½ hr., rinse carefully, then plant. Use glass container and avoid getting acid on skin, as it is highly corrosive. Take leafy semi-hardwood cuttings in early summer or firm-wood cuttings in late summer.

Daboecia (Irish heath) See p. 376.

Daphne cneorum (daphne)

Daphne (daphne)
Clusters of tiny flowers are handsome, and those of some kinds are fragrant. Although they resemble lilac blooms, they are not as large. Colorful fruit is fleshy or leathery. Leaves, fruit, and bark are poisonous.

An excellent choice for borders and rock gardens. Select a position that is well protected from wind. Does best in light, easily worked soil with considerable humus. Often hard to transplant. Move only young specimens. Aphids can cripple shoot tips by sucking sap from tissues. Virus diseases can stunt growth. There is no cure; dig up and destroy affected plants.

Can be increased by soil layers or root cuttings. Leafy semi-hardwood cuttings can also be taken in summer, or leafless hardwood cuttings in fall. Seeds should be stratified for 3 mo. at 41°F before planting.

■ well drained to sandy　■ moist　■ wet　■ acidic　■ alkaline　☐ regular soil　● full sun　◖ partial shade　● shade

From midspring into midsummer, abundant clusters of cup-shaped flowers, mostly white, but sometimes flushed pink, cover the branches of easily grown deutzia.

Deutzia scabra

SPECIES AND VARIETIES	HARDINESS	DECORATIVE CHARACTERISTICS AND REMARKS	HEIGHT	SPREAD
Deciduous *Cytisus battandieri* (Moroccan)	Zones 6–9	Silky, whitish hairs cover leaflets, which often grow more than 3 in. long. Cone-shaped racemes of pineapple-scented yellow flowers develop at ends of young shoots in early summer.	15 ft.	8 ft.
C. beanii (Beans)	Zones 4–8	In late spring vivid yellow flowers open in clusters of 1 to 5, often completely covering foliage. This is an outstanding semi-prostrate species.	2 ft.	3 ft.
C. multiflorus (Portuguese)	Zones 6–8	White or yellow-white flowers open in early summer. Leaflets are about 3 in. long.	1 ft.	2 ft.
C. praecox 'Warminster'	Zones 5–9	Noted for light yellow or yellowish-white flowers in spring. Its winter twig display is especially effective. Do not prune heavily.	6 ft.	5 ft.
C. purpureus (purple)	Zones 4–8	Low, sprawling habit of growth and heavy production of pale purple flowers in late spring make this a desirable species.	2 ft.	3 ft.
C. scoparius (Scotch)	Zones 6–8	Blossoms open a brilliant yellow in late spring. Twigs are particularly decorative in winter. There are several varieties, including one with red flowers and another with double blooms.	8 ft.	8 ft.
Deciduous *Daphne burkwoodii* 'Somerset'	Zones 4–8	Dark green foliage is boxwood and is semi-evergreen in mild climates. Pink blossoms are star shaped. They open in late spring and early summer. Does best in partial shade.	5 ft.	4 ft.
D. giraldii	Zones 3–8	Faintly aromatic yellow blossoms in early summer. Scarlet berries follow.	2 ft.	1–2 ft.
D. mezereum (February)	Zones 4–8	Highly scented rose-purple flower clusters unfold in early spring before alternate leaves open. In summer its scarlet berries attract birds. An upright grower, it prefers partial shade.	3 ft.	2 ft.
D. m. alba	Zones 4–8	Handsome variety. Has white blossoms and yellow fruits. Fine for limited space.	3 ft.	2 ft.
Evergreen *D. cneorum* (garland flower)	Zones 3–7	Oblong leaves to 1 in. long. Sweetly fragrant rose-pink flowers open in spring. Fruits are yellowish brown. Mulch in summer and protect from frost.	6 in.–1 ft.	2 ft.
D. collina	Zones 6–8	Terminal clusters of 10–15 sweetly scented, rose-purple blossoms in late spring.	3 ft.	3 ft.
D. laureola (spurge)	Zones 7–8	Leaves are 2–3 in. long. Yellowish-green blossoms open in early spring in short-stalked racemes and are usually scentless. Fruits are bluish black. Does best in partial shade and slightly acid soil.	2 ft.	1½–2 ft.
D. odora (winter)	Zones 6–9	Purplish-rose blossoms are very fragrant and abundantly produced in tight terminal clusters. It flowers in spring. Feed and prune lightly.	5 ft.	2–3 ft.
D. o. 'Albomarginata'	Zones 6–9	Similar to *D. odora*, but leaves have yellow borders.	4–6 ft.	3–4 ft.
D. retusa	Zones 6–9	Terminal clusters of fragrant, purplish-white flower clusters appear in late spring. Fruits are red. A tidy, compact species.	3 ft.	2–3 ft.

Elaeagnus is grown for its glossy green foliage. *E. pungens* 'Goldtrim', one of the more attractive varieties, is notable for gold-bordered rich green leaves and tiny fragrant flowers that are followed by colorful berries.

Elaeagnus pungens 'Goldtrim'

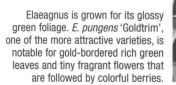

Deutzia
(deutzia)

Dirca palustris
(leatherwood)

Dodonea viscosa
(dodonea)

Elaeagnus pungens
(thorny elaeagnus)

Enkianthus campanulatus
(redvein enkianthus)

Escallonia rubra
(escallonia)

BOTANICAL AND COMMON NAMES, GENERAL CHARACTERISTICS	USES AND REQUIREMENTS	SOIL	LIGHT	PROPAGATION (see also p. 257)
Deutzia (deutzia) Growth rate is rapid. Plants bloom when still quite young. Flowers are usually white and develop in abundance on previous year's wood. Leaves are toothed. Bark shreds on most kinds, giving winter interest.	Mulch in spring. Flowers at times do not develop well due to poor light, lack of nutrients in soil, or too little water. Feed with general fertilizer, water more in dry spells. Prune just after blooming by thinning out old branches. Generally free of insects and diseases; tolerates polluted air.	□	● ◑	Sow seeds when ripe, or store them for up to 1 yr. in cool, dry place prior to planting. Root divisions can be made in spring. Take semi-hardwood cuttings in summer or leafless hardwood cuttings in fall.
Dirca (leatherwood) A native shrub with very pliable stems that were used for baskets and lashings. Pale yellow flowers in small spikes in early spring.	Best in a deep soil with plenty of organic matter. Good along banks of streams.	■	◑ ●	Seed need 90 days at 41°F before sowing. Or sow outdoors in fall where winters are cold.
Dodonea (dodonea) Narrow leaves with wavy margins. Flowers are green but fruit are colored.	Makes a good screen. Good city plant.	□	●	Semi-hardwood cuttings in summer or ripe cuttings later.
Elaeagnus (elaeagnus) Leaves are alternate, leathery, and often decorative. Fruit is often colorful.	Can be used singly as a specimen plant or in a row as a hedge. Ability to resist wind and survive in dry soil makes this an especially good selection for many areas of Prairies and along seacoast. Give new transplants a great amount of water during their first summer. Both Russian olive and autumn olive are invasive where winters are warm.	■	●	Stratify seeds for 3 mo. at 41°F, or store them for up to 1 yr. in a cool, dry place before stratifying. Take root cuttings in spring. Also soil-layer for new plants. Take leafy semi-hardwood cuttings in summer, hardwood cuttings in fall, or plant suckers.
Enkianthus (enkianthus) Most leaves are bunched at ends of twigs. Fall leaf color is showy. Heathlike flowers, in terminal clusters, open in late spring.	Useful in borders and attractive when planted with azaleas and rhododendrons. Does best in sheltered spot. Insect and disease resistant.	■ ■	◑	Sow seeds when ripe. Responds well to soil layering. In summer take semi-hardwood cuttings.
Erica (heath) See p. 376.				
Escallonia (escallonia) Arching branches bear flower clusters at terminals and sometimes in junctures of leaves and stems. Blossoms open in summer and often intermittently until fall. Flowers nearly all year in mild climates.	Good addition to seaside gardens, since its thick stems screen more sensitive plants from salt spray. Avoid highly alkaline soils. Feed in early spring.	■	●	Take firm-wood cuttings in late summer.

■ well drained to sandy ■ moist ■ wet ■ acidic ■ alkaline □ regular soil ● full sun ◑ partial shade ◆ shade

Erica tetralix 'Pink Star'

From midsummer to midautumn, the varieties of cross-leaved heath (*Erica tetralix*) bear masses of flowers.

SPECIES AND VARIETIES	HARDINESS	DECORATIVE CHARACTERISTICS AND REMARKS	HEIGHT	SPREAD
Deciduous *Deutzia crenata nakaiana* 'Nikko'	Zones 4–8	A compact shrub, suitable for small gardens, with lance-shaped leaves that have a good fall color, and sprays of starry white flowers in late spring.	2 ft.	4 ft.
D. gracilis (slender)	Zones 4–8	Oblong leaves are often more than 2 in. long. Flowers in upright clusters up to 4 in. long in late spring. Yellowish-gray bark shreds slightly.	5 ft.	3–4 ft.
D. lemoinei (Lemoine)	Zones 4–8	Leaves are often as long as 4 in. Flowers in late spring in flattened or pyramidal upright clusters up to 4 in. long. A hardy hybrid.	7 ft.	5–7 ft.
D. rosea 'Carminea'	Zones 5–8	Flowers that are pale pink and in clusters 2 in. across are handsome in late spring or early summer.	6 ft.	4–6 ft.
D. scabra 'Candidissima'	Zones 5–7	A fine variety with attractive double pure white blossoms.	8 ft.	5–8 ft.
D. s. 'Pride of Rochester'	Zones 5–7	Double blush-pink flowers that are pure white inside and about 1 in. across appear in large clusters in early summer.	8 ft.	5–8 ft.
Deciduous *Dirca palustris*	Zones 4–9	Bright green foliage turn a good yellow in fall, best color is in part shade.	3–5 ft.	3–5 ft.
Evergreen *Dodonea viscosa* 'Purpurea' (hop bush)	Zones 9–10	This variety has bronzy leaves that turn reddish purple in fall.	10–15 ft	12 ft.
Deciduous *Elaeagnus angustifolia* (Russian olive)	Zones 2–7	Can be grown as a tree or a shrub. Silver foliage, resists drought and has attractive shredding bark in winter. Fragrant yellow blooms.	20 ft.	10–12 ft.
E. commutata (silverberry)	Zones 2–6	Has erect habit of growth with oblong to oval silvery leaves up to 4 in. long. Yellow blossoms are tiny but heavily scented, appearing in late spring. Silvery fruits are egg shaped.	12 ft.	4–6 ft.
E. umbellata (autumn olive)	Zones 4–8	Elliptic or ovalish leaves with silvery undersides are borne on spreading branches with scaly bark. Aromatic flowers are yellowish white and open in late spring or early summer. Fruits are silvery, turning red with age.	15 ft.	6–10 ft.
Deciduous *Enkianthus campanulatus* (redvein)	Zones 4–7	Marginally toothed leaves are 1–3 in. long. Autumn leaf color is bright scarlet. Nodding bronze-yellow flowers have red veins. In fall small green pods develop, turning rust colored when mature.	25 ft.	4–12 ft.
Evergreen *Escallonia exoniensis*	Zones 7–9	Leaves ½-1½ in. long are lustrous green above, paler beneath. White or pink-tinged flowers about ½ in. long grow in terminal clusters. This is a hybrid.	10 ft.	6–8 ft.
E. rubra (red)	Zones 7–9	Branches are reddish brown. Lance-shaped leaves are up to 2 in. long and sticky. Flowers are red.	12 ft.	5–7 ft.

Euonymus (or spindle shrub) include deciduous and evergreen varieties. Foliage of the deciduous winged spindle shrub *Euonymus alatus* turns fiery red in fall. Evergreen leaves of some varieties of *E. fortunei* are bordered in white and cream.

Euonymus alatus

Euonymus fortunei 'Emerald Gaiety'

Euonymus fortunei 'Emerald 'n Gold'

Euonymus alatus
(winged euonymus)

Euonymus fortunei
(winter creeper)

Exochorda
(pearlbush)

Fatsia japonica
(Japanese aralia)

BOTANICAL AND COMMON NAMES, GENERAL CHARACTERISTICS	USES AND REQUIREMENTS	SOIL	LIGHT	PROPAGATION (see also p. 257)
Euonymus (euonymus) Tiny flowers in late spring and early summer are inconspicuous, but fruit and autumn leaf coloration is often attractive and sometimes spectacular. Fruits appear in midsummer and last until frost in cold climates.	The wide range of forms within the genus makes these useful plants for many garden situations. Give young transplants a great amount of water in dry spells. Young stems of almost all kinds are subject to attack by euonymus scale and aphids. If powdery mildew causes white patches on leaves, spray with baking soda or use a sulfur dust or spray.	☐	● ◑	Stratify seeds at 41°F for 4 mo. prior to planting. Germination is often poor. Evergreens can be increased by semi-hardwood cuttings in summer or hardwood cuttings in fall. Deciduous forms respond to softwood cuttings in spring.
Exochorda (pearlbush) Ovalish 1- to 3-in.-long leaves have smooth margins. Showy white flowers to 2 in. wide form profusely in racemes.	After flowers fade, prune out all old, weak wood to reduce crowding and maintain vigorous growth.	☐	◑	Seeds can be sown as soon as ripe or stored in cool, dry place for up to 1 yr. Take leafy softwood cuttings in spring. Lower branches can be soil-layered.
Fatsia (Japanese aralia) Leathery, glossy leaves up to 15 in. wide have 8- to 12-in. stalks and blades with up to 9 pointed oval lobes. Small whitish flowers are followed by blue-black berrylike fruits.	Grown as house plant in cold climates. Makes good tub plant. Does best in soil mixed with peat moss or other organic material. Older plants often sucker. Thin yearly to expose attractive branch structure.	■	● ●	Sow seeds when ripe. Transplant suckers in early or mid spring. Take leafy semi-hardwood cuttings in summer or air-layer.

■ well drained to sandy   ■ moist   ■ wet   ■ acidic   ■ alkaline   ☐ regular soil   ● full sun   ◑ partial shade   ● shade

Native to Japan, *Fatsia japonica* is a rounded evergreen that thrives in coastal gardens.

Fatsia japonica

SPECIES AND VARIETIES	HARDINESS	DECORATIVE CHARACTERISTICS AND REMARKS	HEIGHT	SPREAD
Deciduous *Euonymus alatus* (winged)	Zones 3–8	Young branches have interesting corklike fins. When 3-in. leaves turn fiery red in fall, this becomes one of showiest plants in garden.	8 ft.	6–8 ft.
E. a. 'Compactus' (dwarf winged)	Zones 3–8	Of particular merit where a dwarf shrub is needed. Makes an excellent hedge.	4 ft.	3–5 ft.
E. nanus (dwarf)	Zones 2–6	Grown chiefly for its vivid fall color, but has dark green leaves which are attractive all summer.	3 ft.	3 ft.
Evergreen *E. fortunei* (wintercreeper)	Zones 4–8	Mature plants often bear shiny leaves with several different shapes. Fruit is light pink. Spreading, vinelike habit of growth makes this useful species for rock gardens or near rough-surfaced walls, which it will readily climb.	6 in.–1 ft.	2–6 ft.
E. f. 'Canadale Gold'	Zones 4–8	Pale green leaves bordered with yellow on a mounding compact plant.	1 ft.	2–3 ft.
E. f. 'Coloratus' (purple leaf)	Zones 4–8	One-in. leaves have purplish cast from autumn through winter.	6 in.–1 ft.	3–6 ft.
E. f. 'Emerald Gaiety'	Zones 4–8	Rounded dark green leaves have a white edge that turns pink in winter.	2 ft.	3–4 ft.
E. f. 'Kewensis'	Zones 5–8	Miniature form with dark green leaves only about ¼ in. long. Ideal for rock gardens.	4 in.	2 ft.
E. f. radicans	Zones 5–8	Same habit of growth characteristics as *E. fortunei*, but leaves are often shorter and not quite so shiny.	6 in.–1 ft.	2–6 ft.
E. f. 'Sarcoxie'	Zones 4–8	Shiny semi-evergreen leaves are 1 in. long. Upright habit of growth.	4 ft.	2–3 ft.
E. f. 'Sun Spot'	Zones 4–8	Leaves have bright yellow centers and keep their color well. A rounded form.	3 ft.	6 ft.
E. f. vegetus (bigleaf wintercreeper)	Zones 4–8	Similar to *E. fortunei*, but less trailing in habit of growth.	2–4 ft.	3–5 ft.
Deciduous *Exochorda macrantha* 'The Bride'	Zones 4–8	In midspring tight, shiny, pearl-colored buds open into blossoms that last through late spring. Bushy and compact, this outstanding variety is good in limited space.	4 ft.	4 ft.
E. racemosa	Zones 4–8	Blooms less profusely than *E. macrantha* 'The Bride', but its flowers are larger, almost 2 in. wide; they open in mid to late spring.	10–12 ft.	6–10 ft.
Evergreen *Fatsia japonica*	Zones 7–10	Flowers appear in mid to late fall in distinctive branching clusters. Berries last into winter. Occasional pruning prevents leggy growth.	15 ft.	15 ft.
F. j. 'Moseri'	Zones 7–10	Lower and more compact than *F. japonica*.	6 ft.	6 ft.
F. j. 'Variegata'	Zones 7–10	Leaves are edged with creamy white. Needs some shade from strong sun.	10 ft.	10 ft.

Forsythia is one of spring's glories. Dwarf varieties develop into dense shrubs but grow no taller than 2 ft. Pale yellow flowers appear in spring before the leaves.

Forsythia viridissima 'Bronxensis'

Forsythia intermedia
(golden bell)

Fothergilla major
(fothergilla)

Fremontodendron californicum
(flannel bush)

Fuchsia magellanica
(fuchsia)

Garrya elliptica
(silk tassel)

Gaultheria procumbens
(salal)

BOTANICAL AND COMMON NAMES, GENERAL CHARACTERISTICS	USES AND REQUIREMENTS	SOIL	LIGHT	PROPAGATION (see also p. 257)
Forsythia (forsythia, or golden bell) Yellow flowers in clusters of up to 6 produce outstanding effect in early to mid spring, when few other shrubs are in bloom. Branches are often arching or pendulous, and in some kinds tips root where they touch ground.	Strong, fast grower that looks especially attractive when located in clumps in front of evergreens. As hedges, they can be sheared or left to develop natural informal shapes. Withstands air pollution and is suitable for city gardens. Mulch roots and water well during hot, dry spells. Prune after flowering, removing old wood low down to encourage formation of vigorous new shoots.	☐	● ◐	Stratify seeds for 2 mo. at 41°F. Separate rooted pieces from old plants. Many kinds respond readily to soil layering. Take semi-hardwood cuttings in summer or leafless hardwood cuttings in fall.
Fothergilla (fothergilla) A neat shrub noted for bottlebrushlike white flower spikes in mid to late spring that sometimes open before foliage appears. Alternate leaves are toothed and coarse. In autumn they turn into spectacular combinations of red, orange, and yellow. Fruit is a dried capsule.	Does best in cool, moist location with somewhat peaty soil.	■ ■	◐	Stratify seeds for 5 mo. at room temperature, and continue for another 3 mo. at 41°F prior to sowing. Take semi-hardwood cuttings in summer, or remove plant suckers. Responds well to soil layering.
Fremontodendron (flannel bush) Hollyhocklike blooms, 2 in. wide from late spring to midfall.	Grows best in a location sheltered from winds. A good wall shrub.	■	◐	Seeds as soon as ripe or semi-hardwood cuttings.
Fuchsia (fuchsia) Striking flowers begin to open in early to late summer in shades of purple, red, white, or blue, as well as in combinations of these colors. Blossoms form individually or in small clusters in junctures of leaves and stems.	Excellent as shrub, informal hedge, bedding plant, or trained in tree form; also good in hanging baskets and window boxes. Plant in partial shade. In cold climates delay pruning until spring.	■	● ◐	Sow seeds as soon as ripe, or store in cool, dry place for up to 1 yr. Take softwood cuttings in spring or semi-hardwood cuttings in summer.
Gardenia (gardenia) Glossy, leathery leaves and solitary white, sweetly perfumed flowers all summer long.	Good in containers, as a hedge or specimen plant.	■ ■	●	Semi-hardwood cuttings in summer or hardwood in winter.
Garrya (silk tassel) Grown mainly for its silver-gray catkins that form in midwinter on male plants; those of female specimens are less attractive.	Grows particularly well if planted close to a wall and then trained against it. Plant female and male plants near one another if purple-green fruits are to develop but flowers of either sex are attractive planted alone.	■	● ◐	Take semi-hardwood cuttings in summer. Soil-layer lower branches.
Gaultheria (salal) Low-growing shrub with toothed leaves and berrylike fruits. White flowers are bell shaped. Branches are often used in flower arrangements and are called lemon leaves by florists.	Good choice for rock gardens or woodland settings. Difficult to transplant. In poor soil plants grow to 1½ ft., but in fertile soil and shade they may reach 5 ft. or more.	■	● ◐	Sow ripened seeds in peat moss and sand. Take semi-hardwood cuttings in summer. Responds to soil layering and to root division.

■ well drained to sandy ■ moist ■ wet ■ acidic ■ alkaline ☐ regular soil ● full sun ◐ partial shade ● shade

Fothergilla gardenii

Garrya elliptica 'James Roof'

Fothergilla is known for its brilliant fall foliage and aromatic spring flowers. The evergreen silk tassel (*Garrya elliptica*) is so called for its catkins: in 'James Roof', these can be up to 8 in. long.

SPECIES AND VARIETIES	HARDINESS	DECORATIVE CHARACTERISTICS AND REMARKS	HEIGHT	SPREAD
Deciduous *Forsythia* 'Beatrix Farrand'	Zones 5–7	Abundant and spectacular display of vivid yellow blossoms, which are more than 2 in. wide. Habit of growth is generally upright, although outer branches are sometimes arching.	9 ft.	8 ft.
F. intermedia 'Lynwood'	Zones 5–7	Flowers are located all along stems rather than in clusters.	9 ft.	8 ft.
F. 'Meadowlark'	Zones 3–8	A very hardy variety developed to survive winter on the Northern Plains. Best in full sun.	8–10 ft.	6–10 ft.
F. ovata 'Ottawa'	Zones 4–7	An introduction from the Central Experimental Farm in Ottawa, Canada. The plant has hardy flower buds, and flowers above the snow line to the tops of its branches.	6 ft.	4–6 ft.
F. suspensa fortunei	Zones 5–7	Bright yellow flowers are more than 1 in. wide, opening on mainly upright branches that arch at ends.	12 ft.	9 ft.
F. viridissima 'Bronxensis'	Zones 5–7	Although restrained in habit of growth, this variety has masses of light yellow flowers that appear in midspring, even on young specimens. Stems are bright green.	1 ft.	2–3 ft.
Deciduous *Fothergilla gardenii* (dwarf)	Zones 4–8	Leaves are up to 2 in. long and wedge shaped. Their undersides are bluish white and covered with hairs. One-in.-long spikes of small white, fragrant flowers are borne at ends of branches.	3 ft.	3–4 ft.
F. major (large)	Zones 4–8	Oval or rounded leaves are 2–5 in. long and somewhat hairy underneath. Flowers are fragrant. Habit of growth is upright.	9 ft.	6 ft.
F. m. monticola (Alabama)	Zones 5–8	Oval leaves are up to 4 in. long. Spikes of fragrant blossoms are almost 3 in. long. More spreading than *F. major*. A good shrub that blends well with evergreens in open woodlands.	6 ft.	6 ft.
Evergreen *Fremontodendron californicum* (Californian)	Zones 8–10	Upright shrub with rounded dark green leaves and yellow flowers.	10–30 ft.	10–12 ft.
Evergreen *Fuchsia magellanica*	Zones 7–9	Lance-shaped leaves are up to 2 in. long, light green, and toothed. Flowers are red with splashes of blue or pale purple. May ramble for up to 20 ft. when trained on wall or trellis. Sometimes deciduous.	3 ft.	3 ft.
F. 'Riccartonii'	Zones 7–9	Abundant bloom of crimson blossoms. Top growth may winter-kill, plant will recover.	10 ft.	4 ft.
Evergreen *Gardenia augusta* (common)	Zones 8–10	Many named forms have larger and fully double flowers.	6 ft.	3–5 ft.
Evergreen *Garrya elliptica*	Zones 7–10	Has leathery oblong or elliptic leaves with hairy undersides. Male catkins up to 10 in. long, females up to 4 in., are seen from early to late winter. Sometimes a small tree.	8–20 ft.	6 ft.
G. fremontii	Zones 7–10	Shiny deep green leaves are up to 3 in. long. Catkins start to appear in midspring; males are up to 8 in. long, females up to 2 in.	6–15 ft.	6–7 ft.
Evergreen *Gaultheria procumbens* (wintergreen)	Zones 3–8	A native shrub, the source of wintergreen. Useful as a ground cover in shade.	6 in.–1 ft.	3–5 ft.
G. shallon (salal)	Zones 6–8	Leathery leaves are oval or round and up to 5 in. long. Small waxy flowers with white or pink corollas develop in 3- to 5-in. terminal clusters; they open in early summer. Purplish-black fruits are edible.	1½–5 ft.	2–3 ft.

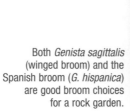

Both *Genista sagittalis* (winged broom) and the Spanish broom (*G. hispanica*) are good broom choices for a rock garden.

Genista sagittalis

Genista hispanica

Genista lydia (woadwaxen)

Hamamelis mollis (witch hazel)

Hebe (hebe)

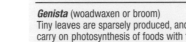

Heptacodium miconoides (seven-son flower)

Hibiscus syriacus 'Aphrodite' (hibiscus)

BOTANICAL AND COMMON NAMES, GENERAL CHARACTERISTICS	USES AND REQUIREMENTS	SOIL	LIGHT	PROPAGATION (see also p. 257)
Genista (woadwaxen or broom) Tiny leaves are sparsely produced, and plants carry on photosynthesis of foods with their green chlorophyll-containing stems. Pealike blossoms are usually yellow but sometimes white. They generally appear in racemes. Flat pods form later in season after flowering.	Will grow in poor, sandy soil. Does best in hot, dry place. Not easy to transplant. Plant with plenty of peat moss. After blooms fade, cut back flowering branches to prevent seed formation.	■	●	Sow seeds as soon as they are ripe, or store in cool, dry spot for up to 1 yr. before planting. Soak in hot water for 12 hr. prior to sowing. Take leafy semi-hardwood cuttings in summer or leafless hardwood cuttings in fall. Can also be soil-layered.
Hamamelis (witch hazel) Short-stalked leaves are alternate and generally turn yellow or sometimes red in autumn. Spidery-looking flowers are produced in shades of yellow or copper-red, or sometimes yellow with reddish centers. Most kinds bloom from late winter to early spring. Fruit capsules explode when ripe, ejecting 2 glossy black seeds.	Red-flowering kinds are more conspicuous than those that produce yellow flowers; so better suited for gardens to be viewed from distance. Needs moisture. Tolerates smog.	□	● ◐	Seeds should be stratified for 3 mo. at room temperature and then for another 3 mo. at 41°F prior to sowing. Germination may take 2 yr. Responds well to soil layering. Take semi-hardwood cuttings in summer.
Hebe (hebe) Leaves are opposite and leathery. Flowers are usually white or pinkish, developing in clusters at terminals or sometimes in junctures of leaves and stems.	Some kinds can be sheared to create informal hedges.	■	● ◐	Sow seeds when ripe. Take firm-wood cuttings in late summer.
Heptacodium (seven-son flower) The creamy flowers open in late summer and are followed by pinkish-red seed capsules crowned with five petallike sepals. The flowers are in bunches of seven.	Provides late summer interest. Can be grown as a small tree. Prune, if needed, in early spring.	□	●	Sow seed outside when ripe. Take soft-wood cuttings in late spring to early summer.
Hibiscus (hibiscus) Showy flowers are several inches across, either single or double, sometimes frilled or laciniated, in many colors, often with contrasting throat color. Deciduous forms flower when blooms on other shrubs are scarce—midsummer to early fall. Evergreen forms are limited to frost-free regions. They have shiny leaves and spectacular flowers produced throughout the summer. There are many named forms.	Young deciduous plants need protection during first few winters at limits of their hardiness. Prune established plants in early spring by removing about one-third of old wood. Protect the evergreen forms from strong winds, especially near the coast. They make a good container plant for indoor use.	■	●	Ripened seeds can be sown at once or stored in cool, dry place for up to 1 yr. and then planted. Lower branches can be soil-layered. Take softwood cuttings in spring or firm-wood cuttings in late summer. Responds to leafless hardwood cuttings taken in autumn.

■ well drained to sandy ■ moist ■ wet ■ acidic ■ alkaline □ regular soil ● full sun ◐ partial shade ● shade

Hamamelis intermedia 'Jelena'

Hamamelis mollis 'Pallida'

Early in February, even before the leaves appear, witch hazel (*Hamamelis*) opens its fragrant flowers.

SPECIES AND VARIETIES	HARDINESS	DECORATIVE CHARACTERISTICS AND REMARKS	HEIGHT	SPREAD
Deciduous *Genista hispanica* (Spanish)	Zones 6–9	Golden yellow blossoms cover this species in late spring to early summer. Pods are hairy. In winter big green spines and green twigs make plant look like an evergreen.	1–2 ft.	6 ft.
G. lydia	Zones 4–9	Very flattened stems carry an abundance of bright yellow flowers in late spring on arching branches.	1½ ft.	3 ft.
G. pilosa (hairy)	Zones 4–8	In late spring yellow flowers grow in junctures of leaves and stems. Pods more than 1 in. long. Prostrate habit of growth. 'Vancouver Gold' is free flowering.	1 ft.	7 ft.
G. sagittalis (winged)	Zones 4–9	The large wings on the stems make this appear to be evergreen. Bright yellow flowers in early summer.	6 in.	3 ft.
G. tinctoria (dyer's greenweed)	Zones 3–7	Best in sunny, sandy areas. Bright yellow flowers in early June on an arching shrub.	3–4 ft.	4–5 ft.
Deciduous *Hamamelis intermedia*	Zones 5–9	Flowers are a fine copper-red shade. Many good flowering varieties have been derived from this hybrid that flowers from late winter to early spring.	20 ft.	15–18 ft.
H. mollis (Chinese)	Zones 5–8	Slightly toothed leaves are 3–7 in. long; undersides are covered with grayish hairs. Aromatic golden yellow blossoms have reddish centers more than 1 in. wide.	25 ft.	15–18 ft.
H. virginiana (common)	Zones 3–8	Many-toothed leaves are 4–6 in. long. Brilliant yellow flowers do not appear until mid to late fall. Mature specimens have attractive profile. Will grow in shade.	15 ft.	8–10 ft.
Evergreen *Hebe buxifolia*	Zones 7–9	Glossy deep green leaves less than 1 in. long overlap for dense effect. One-in. spikes bear white blooms in midsummer.	5 ft.	2–4 ft.
H. cupressoides	Zones 7–9	Scalelike leaves and tiny, pale blue or purple flowers in early summer.	6 ft.	4 ft.
Deciduous *Heptacodium miconoides*	Zones 4–9	As well as the flowers and fruit, the tan bark shreds to show a light brown inner bark adding winter interest.	15–20 ft.	8–10 ft.
Deciduous *Hibiscus syriacus* (rose of Sharon, or althaea)	Zones 5–8	Single or double flowers are rose or purple to white. Hybrid forms preferable.	12 ft.	6–8 ft.
H. s. 'Aphrodite'	Zones 5–8	Dark pink flowers with a red eye are up to 5 in. across.	9 ft.	6–8 ft.
H. s. 'Blue Bird'	Zones 5–8	Late-blooming, single blue blossoms are almost 4 in. wide.	12 ft.	6–8 ft.
H. s. 'Diana'	Zones 5–8	Large pure white flowers with a heavy texture and crimped petals.	12 ft.	6–8 ft.
H. s. 'Minerva'	Zones 5–8	Five-in.-wide flowers are lavender with a dark red eye.	8 ft.	6–8 ft.
Evergreen *H. rosa-sinensis* (rose of China)	Zones 10–11	Rose red to white flowers. Named forms are preferable.	8–15 ft.	5–10 ft.
H. r. 'Cooperi'	Zones 10–11	Variegated olive and white leaves on a compact plant with red flowers.	3–6 ft.	3–5 ft.
H. r. 'Crown of Bohemia'	Zones 10–11	Double yellow flowers with a reddish-orange center.	8–15 ft.	5–10 ft.
H. r. 'Scarlet Giant'	Zones 10–11	Huge bright red flowers 5–7 in. across.	8–15 ft.	5–10 ft.

Long-lasting, showy, golden yellow flowers with prominent gold stamens characterize Saint-John's-wort (*Hypericum*). This is an excellent plant for borders and rock gardens.

Hypericum 'Hidcote'

Hippophae rhamnoides
(sea buckthorn)

Holodiscus discolor
(creambush)

Hydrangea arborescens
'Grandiflora' (hydrangea)

Hypericum
(Saint-John's-wort)

Ilex crenata
(Japanese holly)

BOTANICAL AND COMMON NAMES, GENERAL CHARACTERISTICS	USES AND REQUIREMENTS	SOIL	LIGHT	PROPAGATION (see also p. 257)
Hippophae (sea buckthorn) A silver-leaved plant with orange berries. Plants of both sexes are needed to ensure fruit.	This species is salt tolerant and thus useful for seaside or roadside plantings where winter salt is a problem. Also makes a good hedge.	☐	●	Can be grown from seed, but layering is best to produce known male and female plants.
Holodiscus (creambush, or ocean spray) The 2- to 4-in. deeply toothed alternate leaves are grayish green. Tiny cup-shaped flowers with showy protruding stamens are displayed in large panicles.	Excellent as background plant for perennial beds. Will develop most growth in rich soil in partial shade but will also grow in dry soil and sun.	☐	● ◐	Sow seeds or increase by soil layers.
Hydrangea (hydrangea) Large leaves are usually toothed and opposite. Small- to medium-sized, normally 5-petaled flowers open in large round or oblong clusters. Flowers are generally of 2 kinds: showy sterile ray flowers without stamens or pistils, and less conspicuous fertile flowers.	Plant in full sun if near coast or partial shade if inland. Protect from strong winds. Watch out for powdery mildew on foliage of *H. macrophylla*. If it occurs, treat as recommended on p. 513. Blue-flowered type of *H. macrophylla* may turn pink in alkaline soil. Color can be restored by watering with aluminum sulfate at rate of 3 oz. per gal. of water. This makes soil acid.	☐	● ◐	Seeds can be sown when ripe or stored for up to 1 yr. in cool, dry place prior to sowing. Take firm-wood cuttings in late summer or leafless hardwood cuttings in fall.
Hypericum (hypericum, or Saint-John's-wort) Long-lasting, cup-shaped flowers appear in clusters in shades of pale to bright yellow. Leaves generally have no marginal teeth or lobes.	Makes outstanding addition to borders or rock gardens. Most kinds will live in dry, sandy soil.	■	● ●	Ripened seeds can be planted at once or stored in cool, dry place for up to 1 yr. prior to sowing. Take semi-hardwood cuttings in summer or firm-wood cuttings in late summer. Also responds to root division.
Ilex (holly) A handsome, valuable addition to any garden. Alternate leaves are often attractive. Greenish or white flowers that grow in juncture of leaf and stem are seldom noticeable. Berrylike fruits are frequently spectacular, but are borne only on female plants; so in order to assure fruits, both male and female plants must be planted in close proximity.	Excellent choice for hedges. Add plenty of peat moss or compost to planting holes. Prune heavily after transplanting to lessen shock. A slow grower and not easy to establish. Water well during first year. When plants achieve good size, they can be selectively pruned in winter to provide indoor decoration. Lower branches on older shrubs have tendency to bend to ground and root, assuming unruly appearance. To avoid this, trim off lowest branches.	☐	● ◐	Prior to planting, seeds should be stratified at room temperature for 3 to 5 mo. and then given temperature of 41°F for another 3 mo. Germination often takes from 2–5 yr. Take semi-hardwood cuttings in summer. Can also be soil-layered.

■ well drained to sandy ■ moist ■ wet ■ acidic ■ alkaline ☐ regular soil ● full sun ◐ partial shade ● shade

Hydrangea paniculata 'Grandiflora'

Hydrangea arborescens 'Annabelle'

Conical clusters of white flowers appear in late summer on *Hydrangea paniculata* 'Grandiflora'. *H. arborescens* 'Annabelle' bears rounded snow-white flowerheads from midsummer to the first frost.

SPECIES AND VARIETIES	HARDINESS	DECORATIVE CHARACTERISTICS AND REMARKS	HEIGHT	SPREAD
Deciduous *Hippophae rhamnoides* (common sea buckthorn)	Zones 5–9	Narrow silver leaves on spiny branches. Berries attract birds. Grows well on the Prairies and is useful for stabilizing dry, sandy soils.	10–15 ft.	8–10 ft.
Deciduous *Holodiscus discolor*	Zones 3–7	Branches are gracefully arching or pendulous. Undersides of oval leaves are fuzzy and whitish. White to creamy flowers open in midsummer in 9-in. clusters. As flowers fade, they turn golden brown and remain effective for many weeks. To improve bloom the following summer, shrub should be pruned immediately after flowering.	10–18 ft.	8–12 ft.
Deciduous *Hydrangea arborescens* 'Annabelle'	Zones 3–9	A more compact and neater shrub than *H. a.* 'Grandiflora'.	3 ft.	3–4 ft.
H. a. 'Grandiflora'	Zones 3–9	White flowers open in early summer in semi-flattened clusters. Habit of growth is open and rounded. Root divisions of this variety are easily made.	4 ft.	4 ft.
H. macrophylla (hortensia—florist's hydrangea)	Zones 5–9	Blue, purple, pink, or white flower clusters are rounded and often up to 10 in. wide; they begin opening in midsummer. Withstands partial shade. A good seacoast plant.	12 ft.	6–10 ft.
H. m. 'Blushing Bride'	Zones 5–9	One of an endless range of Endless Summer hydrangeas, this opens pure white and fades to a bluish-pink or blue, depending on soil acidity.	3–6 ft.	3–6 ft.
H. paniculata 'Grandiflora' (peegee)	Zones 3–8	Huge white flower clusters, appearing in late summer, are long lasting and turn pink and purple as they age. A vigorous, dependable variety.	25 ft.	6–10 ft.
H. quercifolia (oak leaf)	Zones 5–8	Reddish twigs. Red leaves in fall. Erect clusters of white blossoms in summer turn purple later. Tolerates dry soil and sun but also does well in shade.	6 ft.	4–6 ft.
Evergreen *Hypericum calycinum* (Aaron's beard)	Zones 6–8	Foliage turns purplish in autumn. Flowers are somewhat sparse but up to 2 in. across; blooms from midsummer to early fall. This species makes useful and highly decorative ground cover.	1 ft.	1–2 ft.
H. 'Hidcote'	Zones 5–9	Large yellow flowers from midsummer to frost. It will grow back from the roots if the tops are killed at the limits of its hardiness.	3 ft.	3 ft.
Evergreen *Ilex cornuta* (Chinese)	Zones 6–9	Glossy oblong leaves bear 3 spines at tips and often 2 more on sides. Bisexual plant sets red fruit clusters without need for separate male and female specimens planted close together.	9 ft.	5–8 ft.
I. c. 'Burfordii' (Burford)	Zones 6–9	Wedge-shaped leaves are brilliant green and have only 1 spine at tip. Abundant fruit.	9 ft.	5–8 ft.
I. c. rotunda (dwarf)	Zones 6–9	An excellent dwarf variety that withstands drought and considerable heat.	2–3 ft.	2–3 ft.
I. crenata (Japanese)	Zones 5–8	A highly popular species with oblong 1- to 2-in. deep green leaves resembling those of boxwood. Fruits are black and not especially noticeable. Develops dense growth that responds well to shearing.	15 ft.	4–8 ft.
I. c. 'Convexa'	Zones 5–8	Leaves are convex on upper sides and concave underneath. Handsome when sheared. Spreading habit of growth.	5 ft.	10 ft.
I. c. 'Helleri'	Zones 5–8	Attractive dark green leaves are about ½ in. long. Slow grower. Compact.	4 ft.	5 ft.
I. meserveae	Zones 4–9	A group of extra hardy hybrid hollies with spiny, dark green foliage.	8–10 ft.	8 ft.
Deciduous *I. verticillata* 'Winter Red'	Zones 3–9	Brilliant red berries, but no winter foliage. Does well in wet soil.	6 ft.	4 ft.

With full sun, pink flowers will continue to bloom amid the fernlike leaves of indigo (*Indigofera*) from summer to late fall. Evergreen mountain laurel (*Kalmia latifolia*) on the other hand prefers partially shaded locations and flowers earlier.

Indigofera heterantha

Kalmia latifolia

Indigofera heterantha
(indigo)

Itea virginiana
(sweetspire)

Jasminum nudiflorum
(jasmine)

Juniperus horizontalis
(juniper)

Kalmia latifolia
(mountain laurel)

BOTANICAL AND COMMON NAMES, GENERAL CHARACTERISTICS	USES AND REQUIREMENTS	SOIL	LIGHT	PROPAGATION (see also p. 257)
Indigofera (indigo) Alternate compound leaves and pealike blossoms develop in racemes in angles formed between leaves and stems. Tiny dry pods form in autumn.	Can be used as a specimen or trained against a wall.	◼	●	Immerse ripened seeds in very hot water, and soak for 8 hr. prior to planting. Make root divisions in early spring. Take semi-hardwood cuttings in summer, or root cuttings in late winter or early spring.
Itea (sweetspire) Native from New Jersey to Florida, it provides fragrant flowers in June and July when few other shrubs are in bloom.	Grows best in moist soils but is adaptable and quite drought tolerant.	◼	●◑	Sow seeds outside when ripe. Take softwood cuttings in late spring to early summer.
Jasminum (jasmine) Branches are viny. Opposite leaves consist of 3 leaflets 1–3 in. long. Yellow flowers are solitary and single, occasionally double.	Useful for covering walls or unsightly tree stumps. Can be planted in greenhouses in cool climates. Plant in soil fortified with plenty of humus or peat moss.	☐	●	Plant seeds as soon as ripe, or store for up to 1 yr. Make soil layers. Take semi-hardwood cuttings in summer or firm-wood cuttings in late summer.
Juniperus (juniper) Handsome foliage is of 2 distinct types: needle shaped and scalelike. Young vigorous branches usually bear the former, while both are generally seen on older plants. Females set small blue berrylike fruits that may take up to 3 yr. to mature. A particularly valuable group of plants in wide range of heights and shapes.	Good choice near buildings. Takes pruning well and can be sheared for formal hedges. Does best in hot, dry places. Plant in any soil enriched with compost or humus. Will live in slightly acid to slightly alkaline conditions. Withstands smog.	☐	●	Ripened seeds should be stratified for 3–5 mo. at room temperature and then left another 3 mo. at 41°F prior to sowing. Make soil layers. Take firm-wood cuttings in late summer.
Kalmia (mountain laurel) A handsome ornamental, especially when its flowers open in early summer. Blossoms are flat or cup shaped and form on lateral or terminal clusters. Leaves are poisonous.	Excellent companion for other evergreens and attractive when planted under tall oaks. Does best in peaty soil that retains some moisture but also drains well.	◼	◑	Plant ripened seeds immediately or store in cool, dry place for up to 1 yr. Stratify seeds—in damp sand if possible—at 41°F for 3 mo. Also by soil layering. Cuttings difficult to root.

◼ well drained to sandy ◼ moist ◼ wet ◼ acidic ◼ alkaline ☐ regular soil ● full sun ◑ partial shade ● shade

Hardy junipers enhance any garden. *Juniperus horizontalis* 'Blue Chip', admired for its year-round blue foliage, makes excellent ground cover. Jasmine is grown for its decorative foliage and fragrant flowers. In a sheltered location, the bright yellow blooms of winter jasmine (*Jasminum nudiflorum*) open in midwinter.

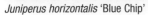

Juniperus horizontalis 'Blue Chip'

Jasminum nudiflorum

SPECIES AND VARIETIES	HARDINESS	DECORATIVE CHARACTERISTICS AND REMARKS	HEIGHT	SPREAD
Deciduous *Indigofera heterantha* (Himalayan)	Zones 4–7	Has many branches. Each leaf consists of up to 21 leaflets measuring about ½ in. each in length. Reddish-purple blooms appear in abundance in midsummer in up to 6-in.-long racemes.	4 ft.	3–4 ft.
I. kirilowii	Zones 4–8	Leaflets are up to 1½ in. long. Rose-colored blossoms open in early summer on 5-in. spikes. Excellent ground cover that suckers rapidly.	3 ft.	2–3 ft.
Deciduous *Itea virginiana* 'Henry's Garnet'	Zones 5–9	Flower spikes up to 6 in. long and bright reddish-purple fall color.	3–6 ft.	5–7 ft.
Deciduous *Jasminum nudiflorum* (winter)	Zones 6–10	Deep green leaves have 3 oval leaflets. Vivid yellow blooms open in midspring and reach width of up to 1 in. Habit of growth is upright, although branches droop. Tolerates partial shade and heavy clay soil. Prune occasionally to maintain shape.	10 ft.	10 ft.
Evergreen *Juniperus chinensis* 'Ames'	Zones 3–9	Steel-blue foliage. Pyramidal shape. A slow grower.	7 ft.	3 ft.
J. c. 'Blaauw'	Zones 3–9	Feathery blue foliage. Irregular, dense habit of growth; vase shaped.	4 ft.	3 ft.
J. c. 'Columnaris'	Zones 3–9	Narrow and columnar with dense gray-green foliage.	12–15 ft.	2 ft.
J. c. 'Echiniformis' (hedgehog)	Zones 2–8	Extremely dense, compact mound, with dark green needles. Excellent plant for containers and rock gardens.	6 in.	1 ft.
J. c. 'Pfitzeriana'	Zones 2–9	Gray-green foliage on nodding branchlets. Spreading habit of growth.	5 ft.	10 ft.
J. c. 'Pfitzeriana Aurea' (golden pfitzer)	Zones 2–9	One of the most popular of variegated junipers. New foliage is bright yellow.	4 ft.	10 ft.
J. communis 'Compressa'	Zones 4–6	Needles are blue-gray. Heavy branching and tight, upright habit of growth.	3 ft.	1½ ft.
J. horizontalis (creeping)	Zones 3–9	Grayish-blue or bluish-green foliage forms on spreading branches. Fruit is blue. Some varieties show purplish coloration in fall. Shapes and sizes vary widely.	1–2 ft.	4–10 ft.
J. h. 'Bar Harbor'	Zones 3–9	Bluish-green foliage. Spreads well.	2–3 ft.	5–6 ft.
J. h. 'Douglasii' (Waukegan)	Zones 3–9	A ground cover with bluish leaves that turn purple in winter.	2 ft.	5 ft.
J. h. 'Plumosa' (Andorra)	Zones 3–9	A flat-topped juniper with grayish needles that become plum-colored in winter.	2 ft.	5–6 ft.
J. sabina (savin)	Zones 3–7	Deep green foliage grows on spreading or ascending branches. Needles on generally low-growing varieties range in color from pale green to grayish green. Brown fruit shows a delicate blue powdery coating.	8 ft.	3–4 ft.
J. scopulorum 'Skyrocket'	Zones 3–7	An ideal accent plant. The narrow form is very distinctive.	15 ft.	4 ft.
J. squamata 'Meyeri' (Meyer)	Zones 4–7	Spreading branches turn up gracefully at tips. Bluish-green needles show whitish hue on upper surfaces. Oval fruits are purplish black. Excellent in rock gardens.	3 ft.	2–3 ft.
Evergreen *Kalmia latifolia* (mountain laurel)	Zones 4–9	Moderately glossy oval leaves are up to 4 in. long. Flowers are white to rose and extremely showy. Selections with deep red buds often available.	15 ft.	8 ft.
K. polifolia (pale, or bog, laurel)	Zones 1–6	Leaves, opposite or in threes, are 1½ in. long, glossy green above, powdery white beneath. Rose-purple flowers appear in late spring and early summer.	8 in.–2 ft.	1–1½ ft.

In choosing a spot for a beauty bush (*Kolkwitzia*), remember that this shrub can be as wide as it is tall. 'Pink Cloud' blossoms abundantly.

Kolkwitzia amabilis 'Pink Cloud'

Kerria japonica
(kerria)

Kolkwitzia amabilis
(beauty bush)

Laurus nobilis
(laurel)

Lantana
(lantana)

Lespedeza bicolor
(lespedeza)

Leucothoe
(leucothoe)

Ligustrum
(privet)

BOTANICAL AND COMMON NAMES, GENERAL CHARACTERISTICS	USES AND REQUIREMENTS	SOIL	LIGHT	PROPAGATION (see also p. 257)
Kerria (kerria) Single or double yellow flowers especially handsome in late spring. Semi-pendulous branches are green and show to particular advantage during the winter. Its bright green leaves are heavily veined and turn yellow in autumn. One form has leaves with white margins. There is only one species.	Useful for espaliering on walls, arches, and fences; also good selection for foundation plantings and border. Tolerates poor soil. Mulch roots in spring, and water thoroughly in dry weather. Prune out older wood occasionally to maintain vigor. Top growth may winter-kill in cold climates, but plants often recover.	☐	●●	Divide root clumps in spring before growth resumes. Take softwood cuttings in spring or leafless hardwood cuttings in autumn.
Kolkwitzia (beauty bush) Produces good show of flowers in early summer. Oval leaves, up to 3 in. long, turn reddish in fall. Brown, hairy fruits last into winter.	A popular accent plant that does best in dry, sandy soil but is very tolerant of most soils.	☐	●	Can be raised from seeds planted when ripe, but a particularly good shade of pink is best perpetuated by leafy semi-hardwood cuttings taken in summer.
Lantana (lantana) Rough leaves have an unpleasant odor when crushed. Small flowers in dense heads at ends of branches. May be invasive.	Good for containers or as specimen shrubs. Can be grown in sun room where not hardy.	☐	●	Softwood cuttings in spring and early summer.
Laurus (laurel, or sweet bay) Aromatic leaves are used in stew and sauces. Tiny flowers are hardly noticeable.	Excellent for tubs and topiary work. Vigorous grower.	☐	●◐	Seeds as soon as ripe or firm-wood cuttings in late summer.
Lespedeza (bushclover) Cloverlike leaves up to 2 in. long on an upright shrub. The center leaflet is the largest and all are dark green above and pale beneath.	Easy to grow in any well drained soil, but avoid those rich in nutrients or growth will be excessive and flowers few.	■	●	Sow seeds as soon as ripe or take softwood cuttings in early summer.
Leucothoe (leucothoe) Displays handsome alternate leaves and small white urn-shaped flowers. Its stems assume graceful arching habit. In late fall foliage turns red or bronze.	Blends in nicely with many other evergreens. Soil should be rich in organic matter. Occasional removal of older wood at soil level helps maintain vigor and graceful shape.	■■	◐	Seeds can be sown immediately when ripe or stored in cool, dry place for up to 1 yr. Take semi-hardwood cuttings in summer or firm-wood cuttings in late summer. Can also be increased quite easily by root divisions made during early spring.
Ligustrum (privet) Privet leaves are generally oval. White blossoms are considered by some to have unpleasant odor. Blue or black fruits are berrylike and sometimes inconspicuous.	Tolerates sand and thrives in salt spray. Withstands dust, smog, high wind, and frequent shearing. Deciduous kinds are among the least expensive plants to use as hedge. The evergreens often serve as single specimen plants in borders.	☐	●◐	Seeds can be stratified when ripe or stored in cool, dry place for up to 1 yr. prior to stratifying for 3 mo. at 41°F. Take softwood cuttings in spring or firm-wood cuttings in late summer.

■ well drained to sandy　■ moist　■ wet　▨ acidic　▨ alkaline　☐ regular soil　● full sun　◐ partial shade　● shade

Ligustrum ovalifolium 'Aureum'   *Ligustrum vicaryi*

Because of its numerous branches and thick growth, privet makes excellent hedges. *Ligustrum ovalifolium* is evergreen in warm climates. The leaves of *L. vicaryi* turn purplish bronze in fall.

SPECIES AND VARIETIES	HARDINESS	DECORATIVE CHARACTERISTICS AND REMARKS	HEIGHT	SPREAD
Deciduous *Kerria japonica* (Japanese)	Zones 4–9	Alternate leaves are up to 4 in. long, oval and toothed. Single yellow blossoms are more than 1 in. wide and form along ends of branches.	6 ft.	6 ft.
K. j. 'Pleniflora'	Zones 5–9	Rounded double flowers are brilliant yellow and long lasting. They bloom abundantly and make pleasing sight, causing branches to bend gracefully beneath their weight. An outstanding variety. Both this and *K. japonica* are good in shade; their bright green bark is attractive in winter.	8 ft.	6 ft.
Deciduous *Kolkwitzia amabilis*	Zones 4–8	Bell-shaped blossoms are light pink to lavender-pink with yellow throats. They are in clusters on erect branches that arch gracefully at ends. Since poor, washed-out pinks are sometimes sold, it is best to select and buy plants while they are in bloom.	8 ft.	8 ft.
Evergreen *Lantana camara*	Zones 10–11	Flowers for most of the summer. Many named forms with blooms that often change color as they age, giving a two-toned effect.	8 ft.	8 ft.
Evergreen *Laurus nobilis*	Zones 8–10	Dark green, fragrant, oblong leaves up to 4 in. long.	20 ft.	20 ft.
Deciduous *Lespedeza bicolor* 'Summer Beauty'	Zones 4–7	Sprays of rose-purple flowers up to 5 in. long are carried on the top 2 ft. of the stems from July until September. Cut back in early spring before growth starts if needed.	5 ft.	5 ft.
Evergreen *Leucothoe axillaris* (coast)	Zones 5–9	Leathery leaves are somewhat lance shaped and 2–4 in. long. Flower clusters in mid to late spring are up to 3 in. long, developing in junctures of leaves and stems.	6 ft.	3–5 ft.
L. fontanesiana (drooping)	Zones 5–8	Glossy, dark green leaves and waxy flower clusters in early summer. The selection 'Rainbow' has leaves variegated with white and pink.	6 ft.	3–5 ft.
Deciduous *Ligustrum amurense* (Amur)	Zones 5–7	Flowers in early to midsummer. Good choice where hardy.	15 ft.	8–10 ft.
L. obtusifolium regelianum (Regel)	Zones 4–7	Horizontal branches gracefully support oblong or elliptic leaves that are more than 2 in. long. Nodding spikes of blossoms open in midsummer.	5 ft.	3–4 ft.
L. ovalifolium (Californian)	Zones 6–8	Semi-evergreen with glossy leaves. Most widely used privet for hedges.	15 ft.	15 ft.
L. o. aureum	Zones 6–8	Looks quite similar to *L. ovalifolium*, but leaves are yellow with green spot in centers.	15 ft.	15 ft.
L. sinense (Chinese)	Zones 7–10	Showy midsummer flowers. Very graceful habit of growth.	12 ft.	9 ft.
L. vicaryi (Vicary golden)	Zones 5–8	Outer leaves are yellow but yellowish green if grown in shade.	12 ft.	9 ft.
L. vulgare 'Lodense'	Zones 4–7	Compact variety with large clusters of glossy black fruits.	4 ft.	6 ft.
Evergreen *L. japonicum* (Japanese)	Zones 7–10	Glossy, deep green, leathery foliage. Blossom panicles to 6 in. long.	12 ft.	6–10 ft.

The Oregon grape (*Mahonia aquifolium*) grows in sun and shade. Yellow spring flowers and purplish winter color make it of interest year-round.

Mahonia aquifolium

Lindera
(spicebush)

Lonicera fragrantissima
(honeysuckle)

Magnolia stellata 'Waterlily'
(magnolia)

Mahonia aquifolium
(mahonia)

Murraya panicula
(orange jessamine)

BOTANICAL AND COMMON NAMES, GENERAL CHARACTERISTICS	USES AND REQUIREMENTS	SOIL	LIGHT	PROPAGATION (see also p. 257)
Lindera (spicebush) Forms a rounded bush, all parts of which are spicy-scented when broken. Leaves are light green, becoming yellow in fall, and the yellow flowers open in spring before the leaves.	A good shrub for the border or as an understory plant in open woodland. Plant container-grown stock since roots are fibrous and slow to establish.	■	● ◐	Store seeds at 75°F for 30 days, then at 41°F for 90 days in just moist peat moss, before sowing. A small percentage of semi-hardwood cuttings will root.
Lonicera (honeysuckle) Leaves are opposite. Bell-shaped or tubular blossoms develop in terminal clusters or in pairs at junctures of leaves and stems. Often aromatic flowers are white, pink, red, or yellow. Fleshy berries in white, red, yellow, blue, or black attract and are quickly devoured by birds.	Makes excellent addition to any shrub border. Extremely easy shrub to grow and one that is seldom troubled by pests or by diseases, however, aphids may attack new growth, causing a tassel effect. Prune after flowering to shape plant. In winter cut back some of older stems at ground level to encourage vigorous young growth.	■	● ◐	Seeds can be stratified at once or stored in a cool, dry place for up to 1 yr. and then stratified for 3 mo. at 41°F. If germination does not occur within 4 mo., stratify for another 3 mo. at 41°F. Responds to soil layering and root division. Take semi-hardwood cuttings in summer or hardwood cuttings in fall. Increase deciduous kinds by taking leafless hardwood cuttings in autumn.
Magnolia (magnolia) Elegant flowers make this a valuable shrub in climates where it will grow. Blossoms are large and have 6–15 petals. They open before or at same time as alternate leaves that have smooth margins. In late summer or early fall conelike fruits split open to reveal handsome bright red seeds.	Plant in soil containing plenty of organic matter. In northern gardens transplanting is best done in spring. Buy only balled and burlapped specimens. Mulch roots in mid-spring and water freely in dry weather.	■	● ◐	Ripened seeds should be stratified for 4 mo. at 41°F prior to planting. Take softwood cuttings in spring. Can also be soil-layered in spring.
Mahonia (mahonia) Alternate, compound, green to blue-green leaves are decorative all year. In fall leaflets of some species and varieties turn purplish or bronze.	Attractive in foundation plants and shrub borders. Does best in a place with protection from winter sun and wind. Water well during droughts.	□	◐	Ripened seeds should be stratified for 3 mo. at 41°F. Take semi-hardwood cuttings in early summer or firm-wood cuttings in late summer.
Murraya (orange jessamine) Glossy, compound leaves. Perfumed clusters of bell-like flowers appear several times each year.	Makes good hedge.	□	● ◐	Easy from either seed or cuttings.

■ well drained to sandy ■ moist ■ wet ■ acidic ■ alkaline □ regular soil ● full sun ◐ partial shade ● shade

Magnolias are among the first flowers of spring. In midspring, before even the leaves appear, the pink-flushed white flowers of the star magnolia (*Magnolia stellata*) appear.

Magnolia stellata

SPECIES AND VARIETIES	HARDINESS	DECORATIVE CHARACTERISTICS AND REMARKS	HEIGHT	SPREAD
Deciduous *Lindera benzoin*	Zones 4–9	Leaves are up to 5 in. long with hairy margins. Edible fruits last well into the fall until eaten by birds. Flowers best when grown in full sun. May be killed back to snow line at northern limits of its range.	6–12 ft.	6–12 ft.
Deciduous *Lonicera fragrantissima* (winter)	Zones 4–8	Thick oval leaves are deep green and up to 2 in. long; upper surfaces are deeper green than undersides. Creamy white blossoms from midwinter to midspring offer intense aroma. Red fruits appear in late spring. Semi-evergreen where winters are mild. Tolerates clay soil.	6–10 ft.	6–10 ft.
L. korolkowii 'Zabelii' (Zabel's)	Zones 2–7	Oval leaves are 1 in. long, pointed, and hairy on undersides. Their color is handsome bluish green. Dark pink flowers in late spring and early summer are followed by red fruits in late summer.	12 ft.	6–8 ft.
L. tatarica (Tatarian)	Zones 3–8	Pointed oval leaves are more than 2 in. long. Pink to white blossoms provide fine aroma in late spring and early summer. Yellow or red fruits appear in mid to late summer. Habit of growth is erect and tidy.	9 ft.	6–8 ft.
L. xylostoides 'Clavey's Dwarf'	Zones 3–6	A small form with creamy white flowers on a dense bush. Makes a good hedge. Red fruit.	3 ft.	3–4 ft.
Evergreen *L. nitida* (boxleaf)	Zones 7–9	Dark green oval leaves are about ½ in. long. Creamy white blossoms in late spring are aromatic but not especially noticeable. Bluish-purple fruits can be seen in early to mid fall. Makes handsome hedge and withstands salt spray and wind.	6 ft.	6 ft.
Deciduous *Magnolia kobus*	Zones 4–8	Becomes a large shrub in time, but slow growing toward the limit of its range.	12–18 ft.	10–12 ft.
M. loebneri 'Merrill'	Zones 4–9	Flowers are about 3½ in. across, have 15 petals, and are abundantly produced, even on young plants. A first-rate variety.	20–25 ft.	20–25 ft.
M. soulangiana (saucer)	Zones 4–9	Flower buds may be injured by late frost, so plant in protected location. Allow plenty of room.	15–25 ft.	15–20 ft.
M. stellata (star)	Zones 4–8	Fragrant, double, white, star-shaped blossoms about 3 in. wide bloom in midspring before leaves appear. Sensitive to extreme cold or heat. Fine lawn specimen.	18 ft.	12 ft.
Evergreen *Mahonia aquifolium* (Oregon grape)	Zones 4–8	Oblong or oval leaflets are leathery and often shiny. Erect yellow flower clusters about 3 in. long open in late spring. Fruit is edible. Restrict height to about 3 ft.	3–4 ft.	3–4 ft.
M. japonica 'Bealei'	Zones 7–9	Leaves are blue-green and quite spiny. Very fragrant yellow flowers in early spring.	6–10 ft.	6–8 ft.
Evergreen *Murraya paniculata*	Zones 10–11	The waxy white flowers are about 1 in. wide. Can be a small tree.	10 ft.	5–8 ft.

Native to the Mediterranean and southeastern Europe, *Myrtus communis* produces white flowers in mid and late summer, and dark purple berries in fall.

Myrtus communis

Myrica
(bayberry)

Myrtus communis
(myrtle)

Nandina domestica
(heavenly bamboo)

Osmanthus delavayi
(osmanthus)

Philadelphus 'Snowbelle'
(mock orange)

Photinia villosa
(photinia)

BOTANICAL AND COMMON NAMES, GENERAL CHARACTERISTICS	USES AND REQUIREMENTS	SOIL	LIGHT	PROPAGATION (see also p. 257)
Myrica (bayberry) Aromatic leaves are alternate. Small green flowers are inconspicuous, but female plants produce waxy fruit.	Attractive and useful along seashore. Transplant with large soil ball. Male and female are on separate plants, so both needed for fruit. Stands shearing.	■	●	Soak seeds in warm water to remove wax. Stratify for 3 mo. at 41°F and plant.
Myrtus (myrtle) White or pink flowers in small clusters on the stems. Attractive berries in fall.	Does well in hot, dry locations and near the coast. Good hedge plant.	■	●	Seeds as soon as ripe or semi-hardwood cuttings in summer.
Nandina (heavenly bamboo) Not a bamboo, but related to barberries. Leaves have thin 1- to 2-in. leaflets.	Will grow in almost any type of soil but must have sufficient moisture. Can be invasive in some areas.	□	●	Ripened seeds should be kept moist before planting. Germination usually takes several months.
Nerium (oleander) Leaves are narrow and leathery. Clusters of single or double flowers in summer. All parts are poisonous.	Tolerates pollution. Good for tubs or indoors.	□	●	Take semi-hardwood cuttings in summer or firm-wood cuttings in late summer.
Osmanthus (osmanthus) Opposite leaves may be hollylike, finely toothed or smooth edged. Small blossoms are intensely fragrant and develop in junctures of leaves and stems or in terminal clusters. Fruits are egg shaped and fleshy.	Ideal for planting beside a window to scent indoors.	□	● ◐	Seeds can be sown when ripe but often take 2 yr. to germinate. Take firm-wood cuttings in late summer.
Philadelphus (mock orange) Habit of growth is generally upright, but branches curve or droop. Opposite leaves sometimes have marginal teeth. Attractive single or double flowers are often fragrant and make fine showing from late spring to early summer.	Excellent for borders. Prune as soon as possible after flowering, since blooms grow from wood that develops during preceding year.	□	● ◐	Sow ripened seeds at once, or store in cool, dry place for up to 1 yr. prior to planting. Make root divisions in early spring. Lower branches can be soil-layered. Take semi-hardwood cuttings in summer or leafless hardwood cuttings in fall.
Photinia (photinia) Leaves are oblong to elliptic. Attractive shrubs, some with leathery evergreen foliage, abundant white flower clusters, and handsome red fruits.	Plant in soil enriched with plenty of organic matter.	□	●	Seeds should be stratified at 41°F for 3 mo. prior to sowing. In early summer take semi-hardwood cuttings of evergreen and deciduous forms. Deciduous types can be propagated by leafless hardwood cuttings taken in fall.

■ well drained to sandy   ■ moist   ■ wet   ■ acidic   ■ alkaline   □ regular soil   ● full sun   ◐ partial shade   ● shade

Osmanthus delavayi

Photinia villosa

Clusters of white flowers appear on both osmanthus and photinia in mid to late spring and are followed by fruits— black or purple ones on osmanthus, spectacular clusters of egg-shaped red berries on photinia.

SPECIES AND VARIETIES	HARDINESS	DECORATIVE CHARACTERISTICS AND REMARKS	HEIGHT	SPREAD
Deciduous *Myrica pensylvanica*	Zones 2–7	Oblongish leaves are 3–4 in. long and remain on plant through part of winter. Small, waxy, light gray berries are borne abundantly along stem and are used in candle making.	9 ft.	8 ft.
Evergreen *Myrtus communis* (common)	Zones 8–9	Leaves are fragrant when bruised. Blooms in midsummer have fluffy stamens.	9 ft.	6–8 ft.
Evergreen *Nandina domestica*	Zones 6–9	New leaflets, bronze in spring, turn red in fall. Clusters of white flowers are up to 1 ft. long in midsummer. Red fruits attractive into early winter.	8 ft.	4–6 ft.
Evergreen *Nerium oleander*	Zones 10–11	Many named forms have flowers in a range of colors. Leaves are paler on the underside.	10–20 ft.	4–10 ft.
Evergreen *Osmanthus delavayi*	Zones 7–9	Starry white flowers bloom from early to mid spring, and blue-black fruits appear in late summer. Tolerates heavy clay soils if soil is aerated with humus and coarse sand.	8 ft.	8 ft.
O. fragrans (sweet olive)	Zones 8–11	Flowers heavily in spring but bears some flowers for most of the year. Highly perfumed, plant where the scent will carry indoors.	10 ft.	8 ft.
O. heterophyllus (holly)	Zones 7–9	Glossy oval or oblong leaves. Greenish-white blooms in early and mid summer are followed in early fall by bluish-black fruits. Tolerates clipping; so it makes good hedge.	18 ft.	6–10 ft.
Deciduous *Philadelphus* 'Buckley's Quill'	Zones 3–8	Narrow quill-like petals give this an unusual appearance when in bloom.	6 ft.	5 ft.
P. coronarius	Zones 3–8	A straggly variety. Best used at back of a shrub border, where fragrance can be appreciated without form being too conspicuous.	6–8 ft.	5–6 ft.
P. c. 'Aureus' (sweet golden)	Zones 3–8	Bright yellow foliage which lasts all summer. Flowers sweetly scented but not conspicuous.	8 ft.	5 ft.
P. lewisii 'Waterton'	Zones 2–8	A selection from Waterton Lakes, Alberta. Hardy, with a tidy form of growth.	4–6 ft.	4 ft.
P. 'Snowbelle'	Zones 3–8	A small rounded shrub with fragrant, double, slightly pendulous flowers in compact clusters.	4 ft.	4 ft.
P. virginalis 'Minnesota Snowflake'	Zones 3–8	Branches are decidedly drooping. From 3 to 7 fragrant double flowers open in each cluster and are more than 1 in. wide. Very hardy and well suited to northern gardens.	6 ft.	4–5 ft.
P. v. 'Virginal'	Zones 3–8	Double 2-in. blossoms are intensely fragrant.	4–5 ft.	5 ft.
Deciduous *Photinia villosa* (oriental)	Zones 4–7	Leaves have pointed tips and hairy undersides. In fall they turn red-bronze. In late spring and early summer flowers open in flat 2-in. clusters.	15 ft.	8–10 ft.
Evergreen *P. fraseri* (red tip)	Zones 7–9	A vigorous shrub with glossy, leathery leaves. New foliage is a coppery red. Can be planted as a hedge and kept clipped.	10–15 ft.	6–8 ft.
P. serratifolia (Chinese)	Zones 7–9	Glossy leaves to 8 in. long open with reddish hue, then turn green. Blooming from late spring to midsummer, flower clusters are often 6 in. wide.	15–35 ft.	6–12 ft.

New foliage of the lily-of-the-valley shrub (*Pieris japonica*) is coppery, turning green with age. Flower color ranges from white to deep pink.

Pieris japonica 'Valley Rose'

Physocarpus opulifolius (ninebark)

Picea glauca 'Albertiana' (spruce)

Pieris 'Forrest Flame' (andromeda)

Pinus mugo mugo (pine)

Pittosporum' (pittosporum)

BOTANICAL AND COMMON NAMES, GENERAL CHARACTERISTICS	USES AND REQUIREMENTS	SOIL	LIGHT	PROPAGATION (see also p. 257)
Physocarpus (ninebark) Resembles spirea. Leaves often have 3 lobes. Small blossoms form profusely in terminal clusters. Small fruits consist of inflated pods. Bark shreds or peels.	Good as background in shrub borders or where fast-growing plant is needed to fill space. Seldom needs attention.	☐	● ◑	Sow seeds when ripe, or store in cool, dry place for up to 1 yr. prior to planting. Take semi-hardwood cuttings in summer or leafless hardwood cuttings in fall. Root divisions are also easy to make very early in spring.
Picea (spruce) Evergreen conifers with short needlelike leaves arranged in 2 rows or spiraled. They dislike pollution and hot sites, so do not plant close to major roads or where reflected heat from walls may occur.	While most of the spruce are large trees, there are a few dwarf forms that fit in well with other shrubs, giving contrast, or are suitable for a rock garden.	■	● ◑	Seed germinates readily if sown fresh. Commercially, named varieties are produced by grafting.
Pieris (pieris, or andromeda) Generally alternate leaves are toothed. Flower buds are attractive all winter. In mid to late spring white blossoms resembling lilies of the valley and of considerable beauty are borne in terminal panicles. All kinds grow slowly.	Does best in sandy soil fortified with peat moss or humus that provides some acidity. Mulch roots with rotted oak leaves or pine needles.	■ ▨	◑	Ripened seeds can be sown at once or stored in cool, dry place for up to 1 yr. prior to planting. Lower branches can be soil-layered. Take semi-hardwood cuttings in early summer or firm-wood cuttings in late summer.
Pinus (pine) Evergreen with needles in twos, threes, or fives. Most pines develop a tap root and need regular transplanting in a nursery to move well. They are tolerant of city conditions, especially those with their needles in pairs.	As with spruce, most are large trees but there are smaller forms that make good screens, while the very dwarf ones are suitable for a rock garden. Pines can be kept smaller by removing half of the new growth (candle) in spring.	☐	●	Generally grown from seed, which often needs stratification. Named forms are grafted in commercial nurseries.
Pittosporum (pittosporum) Leaves are leathery and alternate. Flowers are creamy in spring at branch tips.	Makes a good informal hedge or border plant. Good on coast.	☐	● ◑	Use seeds, semi-hardwood or firm-wood cuttings.

■ well drained to sandy ■ moist ■ wet ▨ acidic ▨ alkaline ☐ regular soil ● full sun ◑ partial shade ● shade

Physocarpus opulifolius 'Luteus'

Pinus mugo

Ninebark (*Physocarpus*) is one of the faster-growing shrubs. As summer progresses, leaves of *P. opulifolius* 'Luteus', bright yellow when young, become olive-green and tinged with bronze. The hardy, slow-growing mountain pine (*Pinus mugo*) is not fussy. It has a bushy spread and makes a large shrub in time. The variety 'mugo' is better for a small space.

SPECIES AND VARIETIES	HARDINESS	DECORATIVE CHARACTERISTICS AND REMARKS	HEIGHT	SPREAD
Deciduous *Physocarpus opulifolius*	Zones 2–7	Rounded or ovalish leaves are more than 3 in. long. In early summer small white or pinkish flowers in clusters up to 2 in. across make a nice showing. In autumn clustered dried capsules turn from reddish to brown and cling to plant throughout winter. Habit of growth is upright or sometimes arching.	8–10 ft.	6–8 ft.
P. o. Coppertina™	Zones 3–7	Foliage opens a copper color and turns rich red at maturity.	8–10 ft.	6–8 ft.
P. o. 'Luteus' (golden)	Zones 2–7	New foliage is golden yellow, and slowly turns green in summer.	6–8 ft.	5–6 ft.
P. o. Summerwine™	Zones 3–7	Dark red-purple foliage contrasts with pink flowers.	5–6 ft.	5–6 ft.
Evergreeen: *Picea abies* 'Nidiformis' (bird's nest)	Zones 2–7	A flat top is formed by tiers of branches bearing wiry, dark green needles.	10–16 ft.	10–16 ft.
P. glauca albertiana 'Conica' (dwarf Alberta)	Zones 3–6	Soft grass-green foliage and a bushy conical shape, help make this an attractive conifer.	10–16 ft.	6–8 ft.
P. mariana 'Nana'	Zones 2–7	Delicate bluish-gray needles form on radiating shoots to produce a handsome irregular globe. Outstanding for rock gardens and troughs.	1 ft.	2 ft.
Evergreen *Pieris floribunda* (mountain)	Zones 4–6	Faintly toothed, ovalish or elliptic leaves are 1–3 in. long. Masses of semi-pendulous flowers grow in upright 2- to 4-in. panicles. Makes striking hedge.	6 ft.	6 ft.
P. 'Forest Flame'	Zone 4	An upright shrub with leaves that open red, then turn, through pink and white, to dark green. Hanging sprays of white flowers in June.	12 ft.	6 ft.
P. japonica (lily-of-the-valley shrub)	Zones 4–8	Young leaves show handsome coppery color in early spring. Mature leaves are dark green, glossy, and more than 3 in. long. Flowers droop on 5-in. panicles. Outstanding ornamental shrub with dense habit of growth and many named forms.	8 ft.	8 ft.
Evergreen *Pinus densiflora* 'Umbraculifera' (umbrella)	Zones 4–7	Globular when young, it takes on an umbrella shape with age. Red bark peels on older plants.	16–23 ft.	16–26 ft.
P. mugo mugo (mugo)	Zones 2–7	These are grown from seed and are very variable in ultimate form and size. The named forms, like 'Mops', 'Paul's Dwarf', and 'Slowmound' are more predictable.	5–6 ft.	10–16 ft.
P. strobes 'Nana' (dwarf white)	Zones 3–8	Irregular branching produces a conical shape, often with more than one leader. Growth becomes more open with age.	10–16 ft.	16–23 ft.
P. sylvestris 'Watereri' (waterer's scotch)	Zones 3–8	Greenish-blue needles are up to 1¼ in. long on semi-erect, dense branches.	10–16 ft.	10–16 ft.
Evergreen *Pittosporum tobira*	Zones 9–10	Oval leaves are up to 4 in. long. Hairy fruit in late summer. Makes a good houseplant.	10ft.	6–8 ft.

Cinquefoil (*Potentilla*) needs next to no attention, but prefers a sunny location. The orange and red varieties lose their color in strong sunlight.

Potentilla fruticosa 'Red Ace'

Potentilla fruticosa 'Coronation Triumph'

Fargesia nitida
(several genera of bamboos)

Potentilla fruticosa
(potentilla, or cinquefoil)

BOTANICAL AND COMMON NAMES, GENERAL CHARACTERISTICS	USES AND REQUIREMENTS	SOIL	LIGHT	PROPAGATION (see also p. 257)
Pleioblastus (several genera of bamboos) These members of the grass family usually have hollow jointed stems. There are several closely related genera, all with attractive, feathery foliage and slender, arching stems that often develop in clusters. Bamboos are classified as running or clump, depending on how rhizomes (underground stems) grow. If rhizomes are fast spreading and produce numerous vertical stems that may cover sizable areas, they are called running. If rhizomes are not spreading and vertical stems form close to parent plant, they are called clump bamboos. All plants mentioned here are running types except for *Bambusa multiplex* and *Fargesia nitida*. Most genera produce flowers only at long intervals, and most are rapid growing.	Running bamboos, which spread by underground rhizomes, frequently overwhelm their surroundings unless planted in tubs sunk 3 ft. into ground. Top growth should be cut back severely every 2 yr. Clump bamboos are less aggressive and slower growing.	☐	●	Increase running bamboos by root cuttings taken from midwinter to early spring. Make root divisions of clump bamboos. Take wood cuttings or make soil layers when weather is warm.
Potentilla (potentilla, or cinquefoil) Erect branched stems support compound leaves with at least 3 and sometimes 5 slightly hairy leaflets. Single roselike flowers in many clusters from early summer to midfall.	A fine coastal plant. Suitable for informal hedges. Grows well and will live even in heavy clays. Except for watering in dry spells, it needs little care once established.	☐	● ◗	Sow seeds when ripe. Make root divisions in early to mid spring or early fall. Take semi-hardwood cuttings in early summer or firm-wood cuttings in late summer. The latter cuttings root especially well.

■ well drained to sandy   ■ moist   ■ wet   ■ acidic   ■ alkaline   ☐ regular soil   ● full sun   ◗ partial shade   ● shade

Phyllostachys niger

Phyllostachys niger, with its green stems that turn shiny black when mature, can grow to a height of about 20 ft.

SPECIES AND VARIETIES	HARDINESS	DECORATIVE CHARACTERISTICS AND REMARKS	HEIGHT	SPREAD
Evergreen				
Pleioblastus pygmeus (dwarf)	Zones 6–11	Deep green, toothed leaves and a compact habit make this an excellent ground cover in areas where it can be grown.	1–1½ ft.	3 ft.
P. variegatus	Zones 6–11	Leaves show handsome white striping. Slender stems die in cold winter areas and should be cut back to ground in spring to stimulate new growth. Needs restraint, especially in fertile soil. Spreads by suckers.	3 ft.	3–6 ft.
P. viridistriatus (auricomus)	Zones 4–11	A relatively low-growing, running form with bright yellow leaves with green stripes. May not be so hardy where snow cover is uncertain.	1–5 ft.	5 ft.
Bambusa multiplex (hedge)	Zones 7–10	Reddish-green leaves to 6 in. long have silvery undersides. Among varieties are one with yellow- and green-striped shoots and another with white-striped leaves. A clump-forming species. A slow grower, good for hedging.	25 ft.	4–10 ft.
Fargesia nitida (fountain)	Zones 4–10	Forms dense clumps with purplish stems and lance-shaped green leaves about 4 in. long. Stems branch in second year, becoming more showy.	5–15 ft.	5 ft.
Phyllostachys aurea (fishpole)	Zones 6–10	Upright, rigid, straw-colored stems are edible when young. Narrow, densely growing leaves to 5 in. long look best when watered regularly.	20 ft.	4–10 ft.
P. niger (black)	Zones 6–10	Leaves are up to 5 in. long and faintly toothed at edges. Undersides are bluish green. Green stems turn black as they mature, displaying white bands beneath each joint. Needs restraint. Young shoots are edible.	20 ft.	4–10 ft.
Pseudosasa japonica (Metake)	Zones 6–10	Glossy leaves 4–12 in. long have whitish, slightly hairy undersides. Not aggressive spreader. Used as tub plant. In cold winter areas stems die back to ground, but plants produce new growth each spring.	15 ft.	3–6 ft.
Sasa palmata	Zones 7–10	Green 4- to 15-in.-long leaves have silvery undersides. Foliage may stay green in mild winters. Spreads by suckers.	8 ft.	3–6 ft.
S. veitchii (Kuma grass)	Zones 5–10	Useful where small stature is desirable. Foliage green with silver margin. Spreads moderately quickly.	2–3 ft.	3–5 ft.
Deciduous				
Potentilla fruticosa 'Abbotswood'	Zones 2–7	A tall selection with large white flowers and blue-green leaves.	3 ft.	4 ft.
P. f. 'Coronation Triumph'	Zones 2–7	Developed on the Prairies, a strain with golden yellow flowers.	2 ft.	2–3 ft.
P. f. 'Gold Drop' (or 'Farreri')	Zones 2–7	Lacy foliage and brilliant primrose-yellow blossoms are showy. Fine for border backgrounds.	2½ ft.	2½ ft.
P. f. 'Jackman's Variety'	Zones 2–7	One of the most popular forms with an upright habit. Makes an excellent hedge plant.	3 ft.	3 ft.
P. f. 'Klondike'	Zones 2–7	Similar to *P. f.* 'Gold Drop' but with larger blooms.	2½ ft.	2½ ft.
P. f. Mango Tango™	Zones 2–7	Yellow flowers overlaid with orange and red. Color is most intense in cool weather.	2 ft.	2 ft.
P. f. 'Tangerine'	Zones 2–7	Plants grown in sun produce yellow blooms; in shade, orange.	2½ ft.	2½ ft.

'Rosea', which produces double flowers in midspring, prefers a sunny location.

Prunus glandulosa 'Rosea'

Prunus cistena
(purple-leaf sand prunus)

Pyracantha coccinea
(firethorn)

Rhaphiolepis umbellata
(raphiolepis)

BOTANICAL AND COMMON NAMES, GENERAL CHARACTERISTICS	USES AND REQUIREMENTS	SOIL	LIGHT	PROPAGATION (see also p. 257)
Prunus (prunus) A vast and valuable genus with both evergreen and deciduous plants. All the flowers have 5 petals and are bisexual. Leaves are simple, alternate, and usually toothed. Deciduous kinds are grown mostly for spring flowers, and a few have edible fruits. Evergreen kinds valued for attractive foliage, flowers, and small ornamental fruits.	Protect evergreen forms from strong wind during winter and keep roots moist.	☐	● ◑	Take semi-hardwood cuttings in summer, or grow from stratified seeds.
Pseudotsuga (Douglas fir) Mostly evergreen trees with green or blue-green foliage.	Dwarf forms are good, slow-growing rock garden plants.	▪ ▪	●	Seeds germinate readily without chilling.
Pyracantha (firethorn) Valuable shrub from several standpoints. Foliage is attractive, and small white flower clusters provide fragrance. Highly ornamental fruit clusters in autumn are red, orange, or yellow and remain on plants well into winter and sometimes until spring.	Thorns help make this a useful barrier. It can be clipped or left unsheared. Also fine for espaliering. Mulch roots in spring and water freely in dry spells. Can be invasive in some areas.	☐	● ◑	Ripened seeds can be stratified at once or stored for up to 1 yr. in cool, dry place prior to stratifying. Take semi-hardwood cuttings in summer or firm-wood cuttings in late summer.
Rhaphiolepis (raphiolepis) Leaves are thick and fleshy. Pink or white blossoms develop in terminal clusters, and fruits are bluish black or purplish black.	Plant in soil fortified with peat moss or humus.	☐	● ◑	Sow ripened seeds. Take firm-wood cuttings in late summer.

■ well drained to sandy　■ moist　■ wet　■ acidic　■ alkaline　☐ regular soil　● full sun　◑ partial shade　● shade

Pyracantha coccinea 'Red Column'

Pyracantha 'Soleil d'Or'

As a hedge shrub, the firethorn (*Pyracantha*) makes a good barrier because of its sharp thorns. Its white flowers appear early in summer.

SPECIES AND VARIETIES	HARDINESS	DECORATIVE CHARACTERISTICS AND REMARKS	HEIGHT	SPREAD
Deciduous *Prunus cistena* (purple-leaf sand cherry)	Zones 3–7	Single white flowers just as the purple foliage unfurls. Followed by purple fruits.	5–7 ft	5 ft.
P. glandulosa 'Rosea' (dwarf flowering almond)	Zones 4–8	Handsome in bloom with double pink flowers in late spring.	4 ft.	4 ft.
P. g. 'Sinensis'	Zones 4–8	This variety has dark green lance-shaped leaves and double pink flowers.	4 ft.	4 ft.
P. tenella (dwarf Russian almond)	Zones 2–6	One of the earliest flowering shrubs, with rose-colored flowers.	3–4 ft.	6–8 ft.
P. tomentosa (Manchu, or Nanking, cherry)	Zones 2–7	Sometimes treelike with small pink flowers in midspring followed by edible vivid red fruits in early and mid summer. Makes good lawn specimen or hedge.	9 ft.	4–6 ft.
P. triloba 'Multiplex' (flowering almond)	Zones 3–6	Small double pink flowers bloom in midspring before foliage appears.	12 ft.	10 ft.
Evergreen *P. laurocerasus* 'Otto Luykens'	Zones 6–8	Shiny dark green leaves with white flower spikes in spring, followed by purple to black fruits. Growth is compact, and spreading.	10–20 ft.	10–20 ft.
P. l. 'Schipkaensis'	Zones 6–8	Leaves are 2–4½ in. long. An especially hardy and attractive variety.	9 ft.	2–3 ft.
P. l. 'Zabeliana'	Zones 6–8	Smaller leaves than *P. l.* 'Schipkaensis' develop on horizontal branches.	5 ft.	10 ft.
Evergreen *Pseudotsuga menziezii* 'Little Jon'	Zones 6–8	Leaves are deep green. Conical form with somewhat irregular branching. After about 10 years may reach 30 in.	5–6 ft.	4–5 ft.
Evergreen *Pyracantha angustifolia*	Zones 6–9	Occasionally seen with prostrate branches, this species flowers in late spring. Its fruit is vivid orange to brick-red and frequently clings to plant until early spring.	12 ft.	8 ft.
P. coccinea	Zones 6–9	Toothed ovalish leaves are almost 2 in. long. Blossom clusters are coated with soft hairs. Produces heavy crop of brilliant red berries.	15 ft.	15 ft.
P. c. 'Kasan'	Zones 5–9	Berries are orange-red. Hardier than *P. coccinea*.	15 ft.	15 ft.
P. c. 'Lalandii'	Zones 5–9	Fruit is orange. Excellent choice for training on walls.	15 ft.	15 ft.
P. 'Mohave'	Zones 6–9	Vigorous shrub with long-lasting bright red berries.	12 ft.	15 ft.
P. 'Rutgers'	Zones 5–9	Spreading shrub with copious orange fruits and dark green leaves.	3 ft.	9 ft.
P. 'Soleil d'Or'	Zones 8–10	An upright shrub with red-tinged shoots and bright yellow berries in fall.	10 ft.	8 ft.
Evergreen *Rhaphiolepis delacourii*	Zones 8–10	Toothed leaves and pink blossoms form on this decorative compact hybrid. Makes attractive terrace plant.	6 ft.	3–4 ft.
R. indica (Indian hawthorn)	Zones 8–10	Glossy leathery leaves are toothed and up to 3 in. long. Pinkish or white flowers are about ½ in. wide.	5 ft.	4–5 ft.
R. umbellata (Yeddo hawthorn)	Zones 8–10	Thick leathery leaves are up to 3 in. long and slightly toothed. Aromatic white blossoms are attractive in late spring.	5 ft.	4–8 ft.

The dwarf form of purple osier (*Salix purpurea*) shown here grows about half as tall as the species.

Salix purpurea 'Nana'

Rhus typhina
(staghorn sumac)

Ribes sanguineum
(flowering currant)

Robinia hispida
(rose acacia)

Rubus cockburnianus
(rubus)

Salix purpurea
(willow)

BOTANICAL AND COMMON NAMES, GENERAL CHARACTERISTICS	USES AND REQUIREMENTS	SOIL	LIGHT	PROPAGATION (see also p. 257)
Rhododendron (rhododendron) See page 370.				
Rhus (sumac) Grown for its leaves, which in autumn turn fiery red, sometimes with orange undertones. Flowers are generally greenish yellow. Also of decorative value are its brilliant red fruits, which are hairy and appear in tight vertical clusters. Plants usually bear either male or female flowers, occasionally both. If unisexual, male and female plants should be grown near each other to ensure formation of fruit that sets on female plants only.	A strong grower that spreads by underground roots; so it is best limited to informal settings with plenty of room. Autumn leaf coloration is best on plants placed in light, sandy loam.	☐	●	As soon as seeds ripen, stratify them for 5 mo. at room temperature and then at 41°F for another 3 mo. prior to sowing. Make root cuttings in early spring. Remove and plant rooted suckers in spring or fall.
Ribes (flowering currant) Once prized for their edible berries, plants are now grown mainly for decorative effects. Flowers are generally yellow or greenish yellow, but those of some kinds are red. They open early in spring and are followed by fruit in midsummer.	Good for coastal gardens. Can be sheared for hedges. Tolerates alkalinity. Must have water in dry spells. If growth is slow, feed in spring and summer. Alternate host to white pine blister rust; so never plant within 1,000 feet of white pines. Leaf spot fungus can cause foliage to become blotchy. (See p. 254 for controls.)	☐	●	Increase by seeds, soil layers, or leafless hardwood cuttings taken in fall.
Robinia (rose acacia) Pea-shaped flowers in late spring or early summer open in hanging racemes. Compound alternate leaves made up of 12 or 13 rounded leaflets give the plant interesting texture.	Useful in poor, rocky soils where few other plants will grow. Helps prevent erosion on steep banks. Can be trained as a standard (single stem). Spreads rapidly by suckers and needs plenty of room. In some locations it could become nuisance.	■	●	Sow seeds when ripe, or store in a cool, dry place for up to 1 yr. Soak seeds overnight in water at 90°F; then plant. Take root cuttings or remove and plant suckers.
Rose (rose) See page 353.				
Rubus (rubus) Usually has thorny canes and alternate leaves composed of several leaflets with smoothed edges. Flowers of some kinds are followed by red ornamental raspberries.	Ornamentals of this group, according to kind, are used for their foliage, flowers, and colorful stems; grown also for berry crop. Makes useful barrier.	☐	● ◐	Stratify seeds at 70°F for 3 mo.; then 41°F for 3 mo. Make root divisions or take root cuttings in early spring. Often soil-layers naturally.
Salix (willow) Rapid grower with brittle branches. Alternate leaves are generally lance shaped and narrow. Erect catkins, of great ornamental value on some kinds, appear before or just as leaves unfold.	Many species and varieties do best in moist soil. A few, however, grow better in poor, dry soil.	☐ ●	● ◐	Seeds must be sown as soon as they are ripe, due to brief viability. Take semi-hardwood cuttings in summer or leafless hardwood cuttings in fall.

■ well drained to sandy   ■ moist   ■ wet   ■ acidic   ■ alkaline   ☐ regular soil   ● full sun   ◐ partial shade   ● shade

Clusters of fragrant early-spring flowers make flowering currant (*Ribes sanguineum*) an attractive shrub. 'King Edward VII' is noted for its drooping bunches of deep red flowers.

Ribes sanguineum 'King Edward VII'

SPECIES AND VARIETIES	HARDINESS	DECORATIVE CHARACTERISTICS AND REMARKS	HEIGHT	SPREAD
Deciduous *Rhus aromatica* (fragrant)	Zones 3–9	Roughly toothed compound leaves emit pleasant scent. Yellowish flowers appear in early to mid spring before leaflets unfold. This species can be propagated by semi-hardwod cuttings taken in summer.	3–7 ft.	2–5 ft.
R. copallina (shining)	Zones 4–9	Oblong leaflets up to 4 in. long are a handsome glossy green and have smooth margins. Greenish blooms appear in mid to late summer.	10–18 ft.	6–10 ft.
R. glabra 'Laciniata' (smooth)	Zones 2–9	This is an extremely hardy variety with deeply cut leaves and attractive bright red fruits. Flowers are green and form in dense panicles.	10–20 ft.	6–10 ft.
R. typhina 'Dissecta' (staghorn)	Zones 3–8	Has delicately segmented leaves and greenish flower clusters in early or mid summer. It also forms handsome spires of rich red fruits.	10–30 ft.	8–12 ft.
Deciduous *Ribes alpinum* (alpine)	Zones 2–7	Used for hedges and as a specimen shrub in the shade. Propagate male plants only, by cuttings. Females are susceptible to white pine blister rust.	4–7 ft.	3–5 ft.
R. aureum (golden)	Zones 2–6	Yellow flowers in spreading or drooping clusters. Fruits are purplish to black.	8 ft.	4–6 ft.
R. odoratum (buffalo)	Zones 2–6	Deeply toothed lobed leaves turn scarlet in fall. Spicy, aromatic yellow flowers in drooping clusters. Fruits are black. Plant is susceptible to wheat stem rust.	6 ft.	3–5 ft.
R. sanguineum (pink winter)	Zones 5–7	Lobes of leaves are unevenly toothed. Pink or red flowers grow in showy hanging clusters. Fruits are bluish black. A good companion for forsythia.	10 ft.	7 ft.
Deciduous *Robinia hispida* (bristly)	Zones 5–8	Clusters of pink to purplish-pink blossoms have attractive character of wisteria. It is often trained upright as a standard to show blossoms to best effect. Fruits and brittle twigs are covered with bright red bristles. Seedpods are up to 3 in. long.	4 ft.	3–6 ft.
R. neomexicana (New Mexico)	Zones 5–8	An upright shrub or small tree with hanging clusters of pink flowers in early summer and brown seed pods.	15–20 ft.	15 ft.
Deciduous *Rubus cockburnianus* (ghost bramble)	Zones 5–9	Admired in winter for its stems that are coated with an interesting white, waxy powder. Leaves, also white coated, consist of 7–9 oblong to lance-shaped leaflets. Flowers are small and purplish in thin, 4- to 6-in.-long terminal panicles. Fruits are not palatable.	5–7 ft.	4–6 ft.
R. odoratus (flowering raspberry)	Zones 3–9	Leaves are 3–5 lobed with finely toothed margins. Undersides are hairy. Fragrant rose-purple to whitish blooms 1½–2 in. across in summer. Flat red fruits are not palatable.	5–9 ft.	4–6 ft.
Deciduous *Salix* 'Flame'	Zones 3–6	Stems are orange at base, red at tips, giving good winter color. Leaves turn yellow in fall and last well. No catkins. Cut back hard every second spring to keep good stem color.	20 ft.	15–20 ft.
S. gracilistyla (rose-gold pussy)	Zones 5–8	Bluish-green leaves are 2–4 in. long and have hairy undersides; they form on gray hairy twigs. Reddish catkins are seen in early to mid spring.	6 ft.	6 ft.
S. purpurea (purple osier)	Zones 2–6	Young twigs are purplish, changing to gray with age. Leaves are 2–4 in. long; upper surfaces are darker colored than undersides. Good where soil is moist.	8 ft.	4–5 ft.
S. sachalinense 'Sekka' (fantail)	Zones 4–7	Young flattened branches assume twisted shapes, giving this variety unusual profile, particularly in winter. Catkins are silvery and up to 2 in. long.	15 ft.	10–12 ft.

To produce their hollylike red berries, male and female shrubs of *Skimmia japonica* must be planted together.

Skimmia japonica

Salvia coccinea
(sage)

Sambucus racemosa
(elder)

Santolina chamaecyparissus
(lavender cotton)

Sarcococca
(sarcococca)

Sequoia sempervirens
'prostrata' (redwood)

Shepherdia argentea
(buffaloberry)

Skimmia japonica
(skimmia)

BOTANICAL AND COMMON NAMES, GENERAL CHARACTERISTICS	USES AND REQUIREMENTS	SOIL	LIGHT	PROPAGATION (see also p. 257)
Salvia (sage) A large genus of shrubs, perennials, and annuals, that play an important role in the garden. Leaves are mid-green, often slightly hairy, and frequently fragrant, but not always pleasantly so.	Small shrubs for the front of a border or to form a low, informal hedge.	☐	● ◑	Easy from seed (may self-sow) or named varieties can be grown from softwood cuttings at almost any time of the year.
Sambucus (elder) Large shrubs with colored foliage. Moderately showy flowers and fruits.	Varieties grown for their colored foliage should be in full sun. Others may be in shade. For brightest yellow foliage, cut almost to the ground in spring.	☐	● ●	Soft cuttings in July or hardwood with a heel in the fall. Species from seed.
Santolina (lavender cotton) Foliage is aromatic. Yellow flowers appear in late summer.	Can be clipped for small hedges.	■	●	Take softwood cuttings in spring.
Sarcococca (Sarcococca) Aromatic white blooms are petalless. Separate male and female flowers on each plant.	A good choice for shade but needs adequate moisture.	■	●	Sow ripe seeds.
Sequoia (redwood) A narrow, pyramidal tree with branches that curve downward and short needles that are dark green above, silvery-blue beneath. The giant among trees, there are a few dwarf forms that still become comparatively large at maturity.	With annual pruning, the dwarf forms make a mound of dense foliage. Redwood is unusual for a conifer in that it will produce new growth from old wood, so pruning can be quite severe.	■ ■	●	Seeds should be sown as soon as ripe. Cuttings taken in early spring root if treated with hormone. Named forms are grafted commercially.
Shepherdia (buffaloberry) Very hardy, with silver foliage. Shrub produces bright berries.	Drought- and wind-resistant. As both sexes are required for berries, several shrubs should be planted in a clump.	☐ ■	●	Sow seeds outdoors in the fall, or inside in spring.
Skimmia (skimmia) Short-stalked leaves are aromatic when crushed. Has small clusters of creamy white flowers. Male and female flowers of some kinds on separate plants; male blossoms scented. Red fruit is like that of holly.	Leaf discoloration may result if planted in hot, dry places. For good fruit production, plant 3 or 4 females in close proximity to every male.	☐	◑	Sow seeds when ripe. Take semi-hardwood cuttings in summer.

■ well drained to sandy   ■ moist   ■ wet   ■ acidic   ■ alkaline   ☐ regular soil   ● full sun   ◑ partial shade   ● shade

The colorful *Sarcococca humilis* produces bright green leaves and pink-tinged white flowers. Black fruits appear in summer.

Sarcococca humilis

SPECIES AND VARIETIES	HARDINESS	DECORATIVE CHARACTERISTICS AND REMARKS	HEIGHT	SPREAD
Evergreen *Salvia coccinea* (tropical)	Zones 9–11	A Mexican perennial with flowers ranging from light to dark pink. Cut back in early spring.	3 ft.	3 ft.
S. microphylla (desert)	Zones 7–10	A native shrub with red flowers. There are several named forms. Best in a moister soil	4 ft.	6 ft.
Deciduous *Sambucus canadensis* 'Aurea' (golden American)	Zones 3–9	A very ornamental form with bright foliage. Black fruit.	12 ft.	8–10 ft.
S. nigra 'Guincho Purple'	Zones 4–7	Dark green new foliage turns dark purple. Flowers are pink, berries purple.	8–10 ft.	8–10 ft.
S. racemosa (European red)	Zones 3–6	Large white flower heads, followed by red fruit in clusters.	10–14 ft.	10–12 ft.
S. r. 'Sutherland Gold'	Zones 3–6	Feathery golden foliage which keeps its yellow color all summer.	10 ft.	8–10 ft.
Evergreen *Santolina chamaecyparissus*	Zones 6–9	Small, fuzzy gray leaves about 1 in. long. Cut back after flowering.	2 ft.	2–3 ft.
Evergreen *Sarcococca humilis*	Zones 6–9	Dense growth with dark green elliptical leaves. Makes a good ground cover.	2 ft.	2–3 ft.
Evergreen *Sequoia sempervirens* 'Adpressa'	Zones 6–9	Needles lie close the stems. New growth is a creamy-white becoming bright green in time. Prune in spring, removing all upward growing shoots to retain dwarf habit.	6 ft.	6 ft.
S. s. 'Prostrata'	Zones 6–9	This has needles that are twice the normal width and form a low, flat plant. If one branch is staked upright, the branches will spread stiffly in layers and make a much more attractive plant.	10 ft.	10 ft.
Deciduous *Shepherdia argentea* (silver)	Zones 1–6	Small yellow flowers followed by scarlet to orange edible berries. Good hedge plant.	10–15 ft.	6–10 ft.
Evergreen *Skimmia japonica* (Japanese)	Zones 6–8	Produces numerous branches. Yellowish-green, oblong or elliptic leaves up to 5 in. long are generally bunched near ends of twigs. Usually has male and female blooms on separate plants.	4 ft.	4 ft.
S. j. reevesiana	Zones 7–8	Leaves are smaller and duller green than *S. japonica*. Since its flowers include both stamens and pistils, each specimen sets dull red fruits and can thus be planted as a single specimen.	6 ft.	4–5 ft.

Long, handsome feathery leaves make the Ural false spirea (*Sorbaria sorbifolia*) a good choice as a ground cover. From early to late summer, Spanish broom (*Spartium junceum*) bears sprays of fragrant golden yellow flowers.

Sorbaria sorbifolia

Spartium junceum

Sorbaria tomentosa
(Kashmir false spirea)

Spartium junceum
(Spanish broom)

Spiraea arguta
(spirea)

Staphylea trifolia
(bladdernut)

BOTANICAL AND COMMON NAMES, GENERAL CHARACTERISTICS	USES AND REQUIREMENTS	SOIL	LIGHT	PROPAGATION (see also p. 257)
Sorbaria (false spirea) Handsome shrub with elegant, feathery, ashlike leaves. Lance-shaped leaflets with toothed margins make up its long compound leaves. Creamy white flower plumes are up to 1 ft. long.	Use at back of borders. Does best if peat moss or other humus-forming material is mixed into soil. Rapid growth increased by fertilizing in spring and summer. Water well in dry spells. Prune in late winter to promote strong, new stems. Makes a good ground cover.	■	● ●	Sow seeds when ripe, or store in cool, dry place for up to 1 yr. before planting. Root divisions should be made in early spring. Leafy semi-hardwood cuttings may be taken in summer, or hardwood cuttings in autumn.
Spartium (Spanish broom) This shrub has showy, golden yellow flowers from early to late summer.	Fine for dry sites and most soils. Also excellent seacoast plant. Difficult to transplant; so use potted or container-grown plants.	■	●	Sow seeds as soon as they are ripe.
Spiraea (spirea) Leaves are usually toothed or lobed. Bears attractive flattish clusters or plumelike panicles of white, pinkish-purple, or red flowers. Fruit is a dry capsule.	Excellent for informal hedges and for coastal areas. Easy to transplant and requires little care. Will live in almost any soil.	□	●	Sow seeds when ripe. Take semi-hardwood cuttings in summer or firm-wood cuttings in late summer. Root divisions are easy to make.
Stachyurus (stachyurus) Yellow catkinlike trusses of flowers appear before the new leaves open. Leaves have toothed edges.	Plant where early spring display can be appreciated.	□	● ◑	Take semi-hardwood cuttings or layer branches.
Staphylea (bladdernut) Native from Quebec to Missouri this has leaves with 3 leaflets, the middle one long-stalked. Flowers are greenish-white in 2 in. sprays in spring. They give rise to inflated pods whose seeds rattle in the wind.	Plant close to a path where the noise of the seeds can be heard in winter. Makes a dense stand when established and producing suckers.	■	◑ ●	Seed needs 3 months at 70°F, followed by 3 months at 41°F. Both softwood and hardwood cuttings root readily. Suckers can be dug up and planted.

■ well drained to sandy   ■ moist   ■ wet   ■ acidic   ■ alkaline   □ regular soil   ● full sun   ◑ partial shade   ● shade

Spiraea vanhouttei

A dense growth habit makes bridal wreath (*Spiraea vanhouttei*) a good hedge plant. Clusters of white flowers that appear in early summer add to this graceful shrub's attractiveness.

SPECIES AND VARIETIES	HARDINESS	DECORATIVE CHARACTERISTICS AND REMARKS	HEIGHT	SPREAD
Deciduous *Sorbaria sorbifolia* (Ural)	Zones 2–7	Branches arch gracefully. Pinnately compound leaves consist of 13–23 coarsely textured leaflets; they are among the first to appear in spring but have no significant fall color. Very showy in midsummer when tiny white flowers open in pyramidal clusters up to 10 in. long.	6 ft.	5–7 ft.
S. tomentosa (Kashmir)	Zones 4–7	Young branches are vivid red. Bright green leaves consist of up to 21 leaflets. Flowers are borne in erect panicles up to 10 in. long during mid and late summer.	10 ft.	9 ft.
Deciduous *Spartium junceum*	Zones 8–10	Has slender green branches and few or no small, bluish-green, narrow leaves. Fragrant pealike blossoms grow in terminal clusters that are often more than 1 ft. long.	8 ft.	7 ft.
Deciduous *Spiraea arguta* (garland)	Zones 3–8	In late spring this hybrid blooms more abundantly than any other white-flowering kind. It makes a striking single specimen plant.	6 ft.	6 ft.
S. bumalda	Zones 3–8	Doubly toothed leaves are lance shaped or ovalish. White or deep pink blossoms appear in midsummer on this hybrid. A good choice for limited space.	3 ft.	4 ft.
S. b. 'Anthony Waterer'	Zones 3–8	Leaves have pinkish hue when young but turn green when they reach full size. Rose-red blossom clusters sometimes measure 6 in. across. This variety flowers in summer.	4 ft.	4 ft.
S. b. 'Goldflame'	Zones 3–8	A newer selection with young foliage red, becoming yellow, then green.	3–4 ft.	3–4 ft.
S. japonica (Japanese)	Zones 2–7	Oblong or oval leaves have wedge-shaped bases; their undersides are pale, and veins are covered with hairs. Pink blossoms form in loose, flat clusters in summer.	5 ft.	6 ft.
S. j. 'Goldmound'	Zones 2–8	A smaller selection with bright yellow foliage all summer.	2–3 ft.	2–3 ft.
S. j. 'Shirobana'	Zones 2–8	Flowers are rose, pink, and white, often in the same cluster.	3 ft.	3–4 ft.
S. nipponica 'Halward's Silver'	Zones 3–8	A dense, mound-shaped plant with abundant white flowers.	3 ft.	3 ft.
S. trichocarpa (Korean spice)	Zones 3–8	Valued because of its late-flowering characteristic.	5 ft.	5 ft.
S. t. 'Snow-white'	Zones 2–8	Similar to *S. vanhouttei* but much hardier.	4 ft.	5 ft.
S. trilobata (three-lobed)	Zones 2–7	A hardy, attractive species. One of the parents of *S. vanhouttei*.	4 ft.	3 ft.
S. vanhouttei (bridal wreath)	Zones 3–8	A hybrid with oval leaves. Pure white blossoms in late spring or early summer are borne on branches that arch gracefully. Fine as clipped or unclipped hedge and well suited to city gardens, since it tolerates smog.	6 ft.	4–5 ft.
Deciduous to semi-evergreen *Stachyurus praecox*	Zones 7–9	As well as the flowers, leaves turn red in autumn and bark is attractive. Protect from late frosts.	12 ft.	10 ft.
Deciduous *Staphylea trifolia*	Zones 3–8	An upright shrub with bright green spring foliage that turns pale yellow in fall.	10–15 ft.	15–20 ft.

The Indian currant (*Symphoricarpos orbiculatus*) has small white blossoms in summer, long-lasting red berries and good fall color in autumn.

Symphoricarpos orbiculatus

BOTANICAL AND COMMON NAMES, GENERAL CHARACTERISTICS	USES AND REQUIREMENTS	SOIL	LIGHT	PROPAGATION (see also p. 257)
Stephanandra (stephanandra) Main assets include somewhat fernlike leaves that are faintly toothed or lobed; they turn yellow, orange, or purplish in fall. Although its small whitish flower clusters somewhat resemble those of spirea, they are much less decorative. In winter bark is a handsome light brown.	Once established, it produces abundance of suckers close to its base.	☐	● ◑	Sow ripened seeds or make root divisions. Take semi-hardwood cuttings in summer. Arching branches sometimes root where they touch ground.
Symphoricarpos (symphoricarpos) Vigorously branching shrub that is grown primarily for its clusters of showy, fleshy fruits in fall.	Good shrub for city gardens, since it withstands smog. Tolerates alkalinity.	☐	● ◑	Take semi-hardwood cuttings in summer, hardwood cuttings in fall. Also propagated by root cuttings, root division, soil layering, and transplanting of rooted suckers. Difficult to grow from seeds.
Syringa (lilac) Small tubular flowers are often intensely fragrant and appear in handsome clusters. Flower color varies with kind but includes blooms of pale violet, blue-violet to deep purple, pink-violet. Flowers may also be in shades of cream to yellow-white. Bloom period for lilacs may last up to 6 wk. or longer in zones where assortment of species and varieties can be grown. Leaves are opposite, quite variable in size and shape, and usually not lobed.	Fine as single specimen plant or informal, unclipped hedge. Withstands smog in city gardens. Mulch roots in midspring. Water during dry spells. Remove most flowers from recent transplants during first year to give them good start. For optimum flowering, apply dried cow manure every second spring; remove dead blossoms to prevent seed formation. Cut back to first node where new buds can be seen. If cut beyond this point, next year's flowers will be lost. Every second or third year, prune out most suckers from base of shrub.	■	● ◑	Ripened seeds should be stratified for 2 mo. at 41°F prior to planting. Take semi-hardwood cuttings in summer. On plants grown on their own roots (not grafted), rooted suckers can be dug up from around base and replanted.

Stephanandra incisa
(stephanandra)

Symphoricarpos chenaultii
(symphoricarpos)

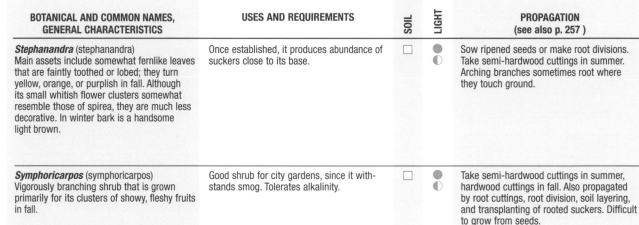

Syringa microphylla
(lilac)

■ well drained to sandy   ■ moist   ■ wet   ■ acidic   ■ alkaline   ☐ regular soil   ● full sun   ◑ partial shade   ● shade

Strong and hardy, the common lilac (*Syringa vulgaris*) produces highly scented blue-violet blooms in late spring. Fragrance from the creamy white blossoms of 'Primrose' is fainter, but equally pleasant.

Syringa vulgaris

Syringa vulgaris 'Primrose'

SPECIES AND VARIETIES	HARDINESS	DECORATIVE CHARACTERISTICS AND REMARKS	HEIGHT	SPREAD
Deciduous *Stephanandra incisa* (lace shrub)	Zones 4–7	In autumn leaves turn reddish purple. Small greenish-white blossoms are seen in early summer on arching branches. Good for border backgrounds.	7 ft.	6 ft.
S. i. 'Crispa'	Zones 4–7	Inconspicuous flowers are greenish white. Dense habit of growth makes this useful hedge plant that needs almost no pruning. Also good as a ground cover. Grows well in full sun, but bright green foliage is particularly attractive in light shade. Plant is quick to spread if branches are pegged down.	3 ft.	3 ft.
S. tanakae	Zones 6–8	In fall 2- to 4-in. leaves turn red, orange, or yellow. Greenish-brown twigs support white blossoms in early and mid summer.	6 ft.	6 ft.
Deciduous *Symphoricarpos albus laevigatus* (snowberry)	Zones 3–7	Leaves are oblong or oval. Very small, almost inconspicuous blossoms appear in early summer. White berries form in abundance in early fall, bending branches to ground. Fungus may turn berries brown.	3–4 ft.	6 ft.
S. chenaultii (Chenault coralberry)	Zones 4–7	Leaves have hairy undersides. Bears pink berries that are white on shaded side. This hybrid makes a good low hedge.	3 ft.	8 ft.
S. c. 'Hancock' (Hancock coralberry)	Zones 4–7	A Canadian introduction that is low-growing and useful as a ground cover.	2–3 ft.	6 ft.
S. orbiculatus (Indian currant)	Zones 2–8	Leaves turn a striking crimson in autumn. Inconspicuous white or yellowish-white flowers are followed by masses of bright reddish-purple berries that last well into winter and are more spectacular against snow than the white-fruited forms. Suckers freely; so it is useful on slopes.	6 ft.	4–5 ft.
Deciduous *Syringa chinensis* (Chinese, or Rouen)	Zones 2–8	A hybrid with smooth oval leaves that grow 2 in. long. Flowers are pale purple.	10 ft.	6–8 ft.
S. hyacinthiflora (American)	Zones 3–7	Flowering before the French hybrids, with looser flower trusses. 'Gertrude Leslie', white, has one of the longest flowering periods of any lilac. 'Ester Staley' has red buds and opens rose pink.	8–15 ft.	8–10 ft.
S. josikaea (Hungarian)	Zones 2–7	Violet flowers unfold in late spring or early summer.	12 ft.	12 ft.
S. microphylla (littleleaf)	Zones 5–8	Length of ovate leaves is always less than 2 in. and often under ½ in.; undersides are hairy. In late spring or early summer small, aromatic, lilac-colored blooms open.	5–7 ft.	10–12 ft.
S. persica (Persian)	Zones 3–7	Leaves are less than 3 in. long, lance shaped, and often lobed. A tidy grower that produces many perfumed, pale lilac blossoms in late spring.	6 ft.	4–5 ft.
S. prestoniae (Preston)	Zones 2–7	A later flowering group, developed at Ottawa. Most popular are 'Coral', pink; 'Donald Wyman', rose; 'Hiawatha', light pink; and 'Royalty', red.	8 ft.	6–8 ft.
S. reticulata (Japanese tree)	Zones 3–7	Leaves are hairy and 6 in. long. Yellowish-white flowers open in early summer. A late bloomer among lilacs. Habit of growth is treelike.	30 ft.	8–10 ft.
S. villosa (late)	Zones 2–7	Tubular pinkish flowers appear after other lilacs have faded.	15 ft.	10 ft.
S. vulgaris (common)	Zones 3–8	A strong, sometimes treelike species with oval- and heart-shaped leaves up to 6 in. long. Lilac-colored flowers open in late spring and are intensely fragrant. Widely grown are those varieties, often called French lilacs, having single or double flowers.	20 ft.	12 ft.

The hardy *tamarix ramosissima* 'Pink Cascade' produces beautiful pink flowers early summer into fall.

Tamarix ramosissima 'Pink Cascade'

Tamarix ramosissima
(Amur)

Taxus cuspidata
(Japanese yew)

Thuja plicata 'Stoneham Gold'
(arborvitae)

Thujopsis dolobrata
(hiba, or false, arborvitae)

Tsuga canadensis
(hemlock)

BOTANICAL AND COMMON NAMES, GENERAL CHARACTERISTICS	USES AND REQUIREMENTS	SOIL	LIGHT	PROPAGATION (see also p. 257)
Tamarix (tamarix) Twigs on supple, slender branches bear tiny scalelike leaves. In autumn both twigs and foliage drop. Small pink blossoms are displayed in conspicuous spraylike panicles or racemes.	May be considered as a noxious weed where winters are warm, but still useful in the north where it is good for hedges or screens. Since branches bend easily in winds, it will tolerate seacoast conditions, taking salt spray in stride.	▪	●	Ripened seeds can be sown at once or stored in cool, dry place for up to 1 yr. and then planted. Take semi-hardwood cuttings in summer or leafless hardwood cuttings in autumn. Both usually root readily.
Taxus (yew) Handsome deep green leaves are about 1 in. long and needlelike but fairly soft; undersides bear 2 parallel grayish-green or pale yellow lines. Red or brownish berries are fleshy and open at one end. Seeds and leaves are poisonous.	Many kinds make beautiful hedges and topiaries, since they stand shearing. Plants of both sexes must be grown near each other if females are to produce berries in fall.	☐	● ◖	Ripened seeds can be stratified at once, or stored for up to 1 yr. in cool, dry place prior to stratifying, which should be done for first 5 mo. at 70°F. Follow with another 3 mo. of stratifying at 41°F, then sow. Take semi-hardwood cuttings in summer, firm-wood cuttings in late summer.
Thuja (arborvitae) Evergreen shrubs with erect branches and a scaly bark. Juvenile foliage is needlelike, but becomes scalelike as it matures. Branchlets appear flattened. One species is widely used for hedging in the central and eastern regions, but there are many named forms that vary greatly in size and color.	Named varieties are used for foundation plantings or as specimen plants. Some of the smaller forms are suitable for the rock garden.	▪	● ◖	Hardwood cutting taken with a heel in late autumn to winter root well.
Thujopsis (hiba, or false, arborvitae) Dark green, shiny foliage with a ridge on the underside that has a row of white dots on either side. Branchlets are flattened and in opposite rows. It makes a dense, pyramidal plant.	The species is a good landscape plant but too large for most gardens. Named forms are smaller and suitable for a mixed border or foundation planting with protection from winter winds.	▪ ▪	● ◖	Hardwood cutting with a heel taken in early winter. They need to be grown in a closed environment and be misted frequently.
Tsuga (hemlock) New foliage is a light green, changing with age to a very dark, glossy green. Mature bark is deeply furrowed and a commercial source of tannin. Hemlock makes a large tree but there are many cultivars in a wide range of shapes and mature sizes	Very versatile species that can be used for hedges, screens, accent plants, or on a rock garden. In sun, it needs a soil rich in humus.	▪ ▪	● ◖	Stratify seeds for 2-4 months at 41°F. Low growing forms can be layered in spring. Take cuttings in Jan-Feb.

▪ well drained to sandy   ▪ moist   ▪ wet   ▪ acidic   ▪ alkaline   ☐ regular soil   ● full sun   ◖ partial shade   ● shade

'Compacta' produces flattened needle leaves that are dark green above with pale green bands on the underside.

Taxus baccata 'Compacta'

SPECIES AND VARIETIES	HARDINESS	DECORATIVE CHARACTERISTICS AND REMARKS	HEIGHT	SPREAD
Deciduous *Tamarix parviflora* (small-flowered)	Zones 4–8	Flowers appear in spring. Displays dark brown to purple bark. Prune immediately after flowers fade. Often sold as *T. tetrandra*.	15 ft.	15 ft.
T. ramosissima (Amur)	Zones 2–8	Leaves are purplish. Fluffy flowers open in late summer and early fall. Prune in early spring. An especially hardy species.	15 ft.	15 ft.
T. r. 'Pink Cascade'	Zones 2–8	Leaves have a bluish tinge and flowers are brighter.	15 ft.	15 ft.
Evergreen *Taxus baccata* 'Compacta' (English)	Zones 5–7	Shiny dark green foliage turns an attractive reddish-brown in winter. Ascending branches grow slowly, forming tight pattern.	5 ft.	5 ft.
Taxus cuspidata (Japanese)	Zones 4–7	Berries are scarlet. Low and spreading in habit of growth, this form is particularly valuable for hedging.	3–4 ft.	15–20 ft.
T. c. 'Aurescens'	Zones 4–7	Foliage is at first vivid yellow but gradually turns green by the following year. Erect branches develop on ascending branches.	4–5 ft.	8–10 ft.
T. c. 'Nana'	Zones 4–7	Needles are short and dark green. Branches develop horizontally.	10 ft.	12 ft.
T. media	Zones 4–7	As branches mature, they turn reddish green. This hybrid has pyramidal shape.	5–15 ft.	15–20 ft.
T. m. 'Densiformis'	Zones 4–7	Spreading habit of growth; dense foliage. No berries.	3–4 ft.	4–6 ft.
T. m. 'Hicksii'	Zones 4–7	Female is good berry bearer, but both sexes available. Columnar habit of growth.	12 ft.	10 ft.
Evergreen *Thuja occidentalis* 'Hetz Midget'	Zones 3–8	A true miniature with a rounded shape and rich green foliage. An excellent rock garden plant.	3–4 ft.	3–4 ft.
T. o. 'Holmstrup'	Zones 3–8	Very pyramidal and slow growing. The foliage is bright green and arranged in almost vertical sprays, very close together.	10 ft.	6 ft.
T. o. 'Rheingold'	Zones 3–8	Golden yellow foliage in summer, turning coppery in winter. Pyramidal habit of growth. A good specimen plant giving winter interest.	4–5 ft.	3–4 ft.
T. orientalis 'Aurea Nana' (Berckman's golden)	Zones 6–9	Yellow-green leaves in vertical sprays, and a rounded shape. Densely branching growth. Good rock garden plant, but may be too large eventually.	5 ft.	3 ft.
T. plicata 'Stoneham Gold'	Zones 6–9	A conical form with bright yellow new foliage turning dark green with age.	6 ft.	3 ft.
Evergreen *Thujopsis dolobrata* 'Nana'	Zones 5–7	Slow growing, it bears shiny ½ in. leaves on narrow branches, and makes a low, wide, mound.	3 ft.	8 ft.
T. d. 'Variegata'	Zones 5–7	Similar in form to the previous variety but with foliage marked with creamy white blotches.	3 ft.	8 ft.
Evergreen *Tsuga canadensis* 'Cole's Prostrate'	Zones 3–7	A very prostrate form that will trail over a wall or down beside steps. It does best in shade. Slow growing, it is suitable for even small gardens.	1 ft.	5–8 ft.
T. c. 'Jeddeloh'	Zones 3–7	This makes a low, spreading shrub with a nestlike top and pendulous shoots. It becomes more globelike in time.	4–5 ft.	8–10 ft.
T. c. 'Pendula'	Zones 3–7	Makes a good specimen that hugs the ground. If one shoot is trained upright to a desired height, the side shoots will cascade down with great effect.	3 ft.	10 ft.

Cowberry or cranberry (*Vaccinium vitis-idaea*), a carpet-forming shrub, thrives in acidic soil. Its bell-shaped pink or white flowers open in late spring or early summer.

Vaccinium vitis-idaea

Vaccinium corymbosum
(vaccinium)

Viburnum plicatum
(viburnum)

BOTANICAL AND COMMON NAMES, GENERAL CHARACTERISTICS	USES AND REQUIREMENTS	SOIL	LIGHT	PROPAGATION (see also p. 257)
Vaccinium (vaccinium) Short-stalked, alternate leaves frequently have tiny hairs on margins. Autumn leaf coloration is often vivid scarlet and crimson. Small flowers are relatively inconspicuous. Fruit is a berry and is sometimes edible. This genus includes blueberries, huckleberries, and cranberries.	Not easy to transplant. Buy only balled and burlapped specimens. Plant in peaty, acid soil with pH of 4–5. Must have constant moisture. Restrain weeds with mulch of wood chips or hardwood sawdust. Covering plants with cheesecloth, netting, or wire enclosure is sometimes necessary to keep birds from berries.	■	● ◐	Sow seeds when ripe. Low-growing kinds respond to root division in early spring. Take semi-hardwood cuttings in summer. Take leafless hardwood cuttings of nonevergreen kinds in fall. Shoots can be soil-layered in spring or fall.
Viburnum (viburnum) Leaves are opposite and often show handsome fall coloration. Small flowers are usually white and develop in attractive flat or ball-like terminal clusters. Fruits are frequently colorful. In some kinds these fruits remain on plants into winter. Birds are attracted to fruits of other kinds and quickly devour them. A very valuable and extensive group of landscape plants. There are many improved named varieties of the species listed.	Grows well in acid or alkaline soil with moderate moisture. In warm climates evergreen kinds may need some shade. Deciduous kinds grow rapidly, and old plants benefit from removal of some of oldest wood at ground level every few years. Evergreen kinds need less pruning except to shape and remove weak wood. If grown as hedge, prune to maintain desired height and form. When planting kinds with ornamental fruits, to ensure fruiting, it is advisable to plant nearby individuals of 2 or more clones (plants raised from different seeds or propagated from different seedlings). It is wise to buy from separate nurseries. Where fruiting types are used to attract birds, prune as little as possible. When necessary, pruning is best done in early spring rather than immediately after flowering. Earliest-flowering kinds may fail to set fruit some years if weather at blossoming time is cold, rainy, or even windless. Insects—particularly aphids, but also thrips, two-spotted mites, and scale—may need to be controlled, and in some regions powdery mildew may occur in late summer (see section on plant disorders, p. 506).	□	● ◐	Ripened seeds can be stored for up to 1 yr. in cool, dry place and then stratified for 5 mo. at room temperature. Stratify another 3 mo. at 41°F before planting. Root divisions and soil layers can be made. Take semi-hardwood cuttings in late summer. Deciduous kinds root well from leafless hardwood cuttings taken in fall.

Viburnum (viburnum)—continued p. 338

■ well drained to sandy   ■ moist   ■ wet   ▨ acidic   ▨ alkaline   □ regular soil   ● full sun   ◐ partial shade   ● shade

Among the evergreen viburnums, *Viburnum davidii* is prized for its dark blue-green leaves. Small white summer flowers are followed by bright blue berries that last all winter long. The European bush-cranberry (*Viburnum opulus*) produces a fall crop of bright red berries. Snow-white globular flowerheads on the European snowball (*V. o.* 'Roseum') turn whitish pink as they fade.

Viburnum davidii

Viburnum opulus

Viburnum opulus 'Roseum'

SPECIES AND VARIETIES	HARDINESS	DECORATIVE CHARACTERISTICS AND REMARKS	HEIGHT	SPREAD
Deciduous *Vaccinium corymbosum* (highbush blueberry)	Zones 3–7	Pale green twigs are warty. Elliptic leaves are 2–3 in. long; in autumn they turn a striking scarlet. Pinkish or white blossoms are urn shaped. They appear in late spring and are followed by profusion of edible bluish-black fruits. Makes an effective hedge.	5 ft.	5 ft.
V. parvifolium (red whortleberry)	Zones 3–7	Flowers are pinkish. Red berries are about ½ in. across and edible.	10 ft.	6–8 ft.
Evergreen *V. ovatum* (California huckleberry)	Zones 7–9	Twigs are hairy. Slightly toothed leaves have glossy bright green upper surfaces. Pink or white bell-shaped blossoms open in summer. Berries are black.	10 ft.	6–8 ft.
V. vitis-idaea (cowberry, or cranberry)	Zones 2–6	Glossy green oval leaves develop on erect shoots. Urn- or bell-shaped flowers are pink or white and open in late spring or early summer. Fruits are bright red. Once established, this creeping species makes a fine ground cover, especially for wild-flower gardens.	6 in.	8–10 ft.
Deciduous *Viburnum bodnantense* 'Dawn'	Zones 6–8	This hybrid has red fall foliage and aromatic blossoms that are rose with a white flush. Tolerates heavy clay soils.	10 ft.	10 ft.
V. burkwoodii (Burkwood)	Zones 5–8	This hybrid has shiny foliage that is semi to fully evergreen in frost-free climates. Aromatic blossoms are white. 'Mohawk' is an improved form.	6 ft.	4–5 ft.
V. carlcephalum (fragrant)	Zones 5–8	Leaves are glossy. In mid to late spring aromatic rounded flower clusters cover this hybrid. Fruits are deep blue.	7 ft.	7 ft.
V. carlesii (Korean spice)	Zones 4–7	Very fragrant pink buds open white. Parent of improved hybrids, such as 'Cayuga'.	4–5 ft.	5 ft.
V. dentatum (arrowwood)	Zones 3–8	Foliage is dark green on straight shoots and turns red in fall. Flat heads of white flowers in late spring and black fruit that brings the birds.	8–10 ft.	6–8 ft.
V. lantana (wayfaring tree)	Zones 3–8	A vigorous shrub that attracts birds. 'Mohican' is more compact.	8–15 ft.	6–8 ft.
V. lentago (nannyberry)	Zones 2–8	A large shrub with good fall color and blue-black fruit.	12 ft.	8 ft.
V. opulus 'Roseum', or *V. o. sterile* (European snowball)	Zones 3–8	Maplelike leaves turn red in fall. Flower clusters open in late spring and early summer. Does not set fruit, since flowers are sterile. Susceptible to attacks by aphids.	12 ft.	12 ft.
V. plicatum tomentosum (doublefile)	Zones 5–8	Branching habit is horizontal. Outer flowers in each cluster are sterile; fertile flowers at centers produce red fruits that later turn blue-black. Flowering period is from late spring to early summer. 'Lanarth' has larger flowers.	10 ft.	8 ft.
V. sieboldii	Zones 4–7	Glossy, oval, wrinkled leaves are up to 6 in. long. Ill-scented flowers in late spring or early summer. Deep pink or red fruits turn blue-black.	30 ft.	10–15 ft.
V. trilobum (high bush-cranberry)	Zones 2–7	Bright red fruit that lasts well into winter. Edible but not tasty.	12 ft.	10 ft.

Weigelas are among the most popular summer-flowering shrubs. 'Red Prince' bears clusters of funnel-shaped dark red flowers.

Weigela 'Red Prince'

BOTANICAL AND COMMON NAMES, GENERAL CHARACTERISTICS	USES AND REQUIREMENTS	LIGHT	SOIL	PROPAGATION (see also p. 257)
Viburnum (viburnum)—continued				
Vitex (vitex) Opposite long-stalked leaves consist of 3–7 leaflets with hairy undersides. Tiny fragrant blossoms form in terminal spikes and are followed by very small fruits.	May die back to ground at northern limits of range.	●	■	Stratify seeds for 3 mo. at 41°F prior to planting. Branches can be soil-layered. Take semi-hardwood cuttings in summer or leafless hardwood cuttings in fall.
Weigela (weigela) Leaves are opposite. Blossoms are usually funnel shaped and more than 1 in. long in clusters of up to 3, appearing in late spring and early summer.	If pruning becomes necessary, it should be done as soon as flowers fade, since blooms develop on short shoots from previous year's growth.	● ◑	□	Sow seeds when ripe. Take softwood cuttings in spring or leafless hardwood cuttings in fall.
Yucca (yucca) Valued for its handsome spikes of flowers. Blooms are generally white or yellowish and cup shaped.	Good tub plant. Seldom needs water.	●	■	Sow seeds when ripe. Make root cuttings or remove rooted offshoots from base of plant.

Vitex agnus-castus
(vitex)

Weigela florida
(weigela)

Yucca filamentosa
(yucca)

■ well drained to sandy   ■ moist   ■ wet   ■ acidic   ■ alkaline   □ regular soil   ● full sun   ◑ partial shade   ● shade

Yuccas have towering spikes of creamy white waxy bells.

Yucca filamentosa 'Bright Edge'

Yucca filamentosa

SPECIES AND VARIETIES	HARDINESS	DECORATIVE CHARACTERISTICS AND REMARKS	HEIGHT	SPREAD
Evergreen *Viburnum davidii*	Zones 8–9	Shiny leathery leaves are 2–6 in. long. White blossoms in early summer are followed by light blue fruits in early and mid fall.	3 ft.	5 ft.
V. dilatatum (linden)	Zones 4–7	In late spring and early summer flowers open in clusters up to 5 in. wide. Reddish-brown leaves and scarlet fruits appear in fall. 'Erie' is more rounded.	9 ft.	6–9 ft.
V. odoratissimum (sweet)	Zones 8–9	Has glossy leaves. Fragrant flowers show in late spring. Red fruits turn black.	10 ft.	5–6 ft.
V. rhytidophylloides 'Allegheny'	Zones 4–8	A spreading shrub with dark green crinkled leaves. Yellowish flowers in late spring and bright red fruits.	10–15 ft.	10–15 ft.
V. rhytidophyllum (leatherleaf)	Zones 5–8	Handsome crinkled leaves are up to 7 in. long; semi-evergreen in cold-winter regions. Creamy white blossoms appear in early summer. Red fruits turn black.	10 ft.	10–15 ft.
V. tinus (laurustinus)	Zones 7–10	Shiny deep green leaves are 2–3 in. long. Flowers in mid to late summer often show a pink hue. Fruits are blue-black. Makes good sheared hedge. Needs winter protection in its northernmost range.	10 ft.	8–10 ft.
Deciduous *Vitex agnus-castus* (chaste tree)	Zones 7–9	Green lance-shaped leaves are grayish beneath and exude pleasant odor when crushed. Small, fragrant, light purple to bluish blossoms in 7-in. spikes open from midsummer to early fall.	10 ft.	6–8 ft.
V. negundo	Zones 6–9	Leaflets usually display toothed edges. Dark bluish-lavender flowers are attractive to bees.	15 ft.	8–12 ft.
Deciduous *Weigela* 'Bristol Ruby'	Zones 4–8	Masses of blossoms open ruby-red and turn yellowish crimson as they mature. This hybrid flowers in late spring and again heavily in summer.	7 ft.	4–5 ft.
W. florida 'Pink Princess'	Zones 4–8	A spreading shrub with bell-like lavender-pink flowers.	5–6 ft.	4–5 ft.
W. f. 'Variegata'	Zones 4–8	Pink blossoms are especially handsome in combination with leaves that have pale yellow edges.	5 ft.	4 ft.
W. f. 'Java Red' ('Foliis Purpureis')	Zones 4–8	Purple-tinged foliage. Red buds open pink, paler inside.	3–4 ft.	4–5 ft.
W. 'Minuet'	Zones 3–8	Bright pink flowers on a dwarf hardy plant with dark foliage.	2 ft.	2–3 ft.
W. 'Red Prince'	Zones 4–8	Good red bloom on an upright shrub. Often reblooms.	5–6 ft.	4 ft.
W. 'Rumba'	Zones 3–8	Flowers are red with a yellow throat. Reblooms in late summer. Foliage is purplish.	3 ft.	3–4 ft.
W. 'Vanicek', or *W.* 'Newport Red'	Zones 4–8	A fine red bloomer with good resistance to cold winters.	5–6 ft.	3–4 ft.
Evergreen *Yucca filamentosa* (Adam's needle)	Zones 3–9	Sharply pointed leaves are more than 2 ft. long. White blossoms are often 4 in. wide and appear in 2-ft. clusters in late summer. There are several variegated varieties.	8–10 ft.	4–6 ft.
Y. glauca (Spanish bayonet)	Zones 3–8	Pointed leaves are gray-green, serrated at edges, and reach length of more than 2 ft. Four-in.-wide flowers that are greenish white, or sometimes cream, bloom in midsummer.	2–4 ft.	4–6 ft.

SHRUBS FOR SPECIFIC LOCATIONS/PURPOSES

Shrubs for Wet or Moist Soils

Clethra alnifolia

Kalmia latifolia

Salix purpurea gracilis

Aronia melanocarpa
  (black chokeberry)
Calycanthus floridus
  (Carolina allspice)
Cephalanthus occidentalis
  (buttonbush)
Clethra alnifolia (summersweet)
Cornus stolonifera
  (red osier dogwood)
Dirca palustris (leatherwood)
Hamamelis virginiana
  (common witch hazel)

Hypericum kalmianum
  (Kalm St. John's wort)
Ilex verticillata (winterberry)
Itea virginica (sweetspire)
Kalmia latifolia (mountain laurel)
Lindera benzoin (spicebush)
Salix species (willow)
Stephanandra incise
  (cut-leaved stephanandra)
Thujopsis dolobrata (false arborvitae)
Tsuga canadense
  (Canadian hemlock)

Shrubs for Dry Soil

Arctostaphylos uva-ursi

Daphne cneorum

Juniperus sabina

Amorpha fruticosa (leadplant)
Arctostaphylos uva-ursi (bearberry)
Colutea arborescens (bladder senna)
Cornus racemosa (gray dogwood)
Corylus avellana (European filbert)
Cytisus species (broom)
Daphne cneorum (February daphne)
Elaeagnus commutata (silverberry)
Elaeagnus umbellatus (autumn olive)
Genista species (woadwaxen)
Hypericum species (St. John's wort)

Juniperus communis
  (common juniper)
Juniperus sabina (savin juniper)
Myrica pensylvanica (bayberry)
Potentilla fruticosa (cinquefoil)
Prinsepia sinensis (cherry prinsepia)
Pyracantha species (firethorn)
Shepherdia argentia (buffalo berry)
Tamarix ramosissima (tamarix)
Yucca filamentosa (Adam's needle)
Yucca glauca (Spanish bayonet)

Shrubs for Acidic Soils

Calluna vulgaris

Chamaecyparis pisifera

Fothergilla gardinii

Arctostaphylos uva-ursi (bearberry)
Berberis julianae
  (wintergreen barberry)
Calluna vulgaris (heather)
Chamaecyparis pisifera
  (Sawara false cypress)
Clethra alnifolia (summersweet)
Cornus canadensis (bunchberry)
Cytisus species (broom)
Deutzia species (deutzia)
Dirca palustris (leatherwood)
Enkianthus campanulatus
  (redvein enkianthus)
Erica species (heath)
Fothergilla species (fothergilla)
Gaultheria procumbens (wintergreen)

Halesia caroliniana (silberbells)
Hamamelis mollis
  (Chinese witch hazel)
Hydrangea macrophylla (florist's
  hydrangea)
Ilex species (holly)
Kalmia latifolia (mountain laurel)
Leucothoe fontanesia (fetterbush)
Magnolia species (magnolia)
Pieris japonica (Japanese pieris)
Rhododendron
  (rhododendron and azalea)
Stephanandra incise
  (cut-leaved stephanandra)
Styrax japonicus (snowbell)
Thujopsis dolobrata (false arborvitae)

Salt-tolerant Shrubs (Road Salt or Sea Spray)

Caragana arborescens

Euonymus alatus

Hippophae rhamnoides

Arctostaphylos uva-ursi (bearberry)
Caragana species (peashrub)
Clethra alnifolia (summersweet)
Cytisus species (broom)
Elaeagnus angustifolius
  (Russian olive)
Euonymus alatus (winged euonymus)
Hippophae rhamnoides
  (sea buckthorn)

Juniperus communis
  (common juniper)
Juniperus horizontalis
  (creeping juniper)
Juniperus virginiana (red cedar)
Lonicera species (honeysuckle)
Myrica pensylvanica (bayberry)
Rhus typhina (staghorn sumac)
Syringa species (lilac)
Tamarix ramosissima (tamarix)

Salt-intolerant Shrubs

Chaenomeles 'Geisha'

Kolkwitzia amabilis

Taxus elegantissima

Amelanchier species (serviceberry)
Chaenomeles species
  (flowering quince)
Cornus stolonifera
  (red osier dogwood)
Kolkwitzia amabilis (beautybush)
Philadelphus species (mock orange)

Spiraea bumalda (bumalda spirea)
Spirea japonica (Japanese spirea)
Taxus species (yew)
Tsuga canadensis
  (Canadian hemlock)
Viburnum opulus
  (European bush cranberry)

Shrubs for Full (All-Day) Shade

Cornus alba

Kalmia latifolia

Vinca minor

Cornus alba (Tatarian dogwood)
Cornus canadensis (bunchberry)
Gaultheria procumbens (wintergreen)
Kalmia latifolia (mountain laurel)
Kerria japonica (Japanese kerria)
Leucothoe fontanesiana (fetterbush)
Pachysandra terminalis
  (pachysandra)

Ribes alpinum (alpine currant)
Staphylea trifolia (bladdernut)
Symphoricarpos albus (snowberry)
Taxus species (yew)
Viburnum lentago (nannyberry)
Vinca minor (periwinkle)

Shrubs With Fruits That Attract Birds

Amelanchier canadensis

Ligustrum vicaryi

Viburnum opulus

Amelanchier—all (serviceberry)
Aronia melanocarpa
  (black chokeberry)
Cornus—most (dogwood)
Cotoneaster—most (cotoneaster)
Elaeagnus angustifolia (Russian olive)
Euonymus fortunei (wintercreeper)
Hippophae rhamnoides
  (sea buckthorn)
Ilex verticillata (winterberry)
Ligustrum—most (privet)

Lonicera tatarica
  (Tatarian honeysuckle)
Myrica pensylvanica (bayberry)
Prinsepia sinensis (cherry prinsepia)
Prunus tomentosa (Nanking cherry)
Rhus typhina (staghorn sumac)
Ribes—most (currant)
Sambucus canadensis
  (American elder)
Viburnum—most (viburnum)

Shrubs With Interesting Winter Bark or Form

Cornus stolonifera

Corylus avellana 'Contorta'

Cotoneaster horizontalis

Buddleija alternifolia
  (fountain buddleia)
Cornus alba (Tatarian dogwood)
Cornus stolonifera 'Flaviramea'
  (yellow-twig dogwood)
Corylus avellana 'Contorta'
  (corkscrew filbert)
Cotoneaster horizontalis (rockspray)
Euonymus alatus (winged euonymus)

Forsythia viridissima
  (green-twig forsythia)
Kerria japonica (Japanese kerria)
Prunus tomentosa (Nanking cherry)
Rosa nitida (shining rose)
Salix 'Flame' (flame willow)
Salix matsudana (corkscrew willow)
Salix sachalinense 'Sekka'
  (fantail willow)

Shrubs for Fall Color (and Conspicuous Fruit*)

Cotinus coggyria

Hamamelis intermedia

Symphoricarpos orbiculatus

Acer palmatum (Japanese maple)—
  RED
Amelanchier species
  (serviceberry)—YELLOW TO CRIMSON
Arctostaphylos uva-ursi
  (bearberry)*—BRONZE
Aronia species (chokeberry)*—
  SCARLET
Berberis mentorensis
  (Mentor barberry)—CRIMSON
Calycanthus floridus
  (Carolina allspice)—YELLOW
Clethra alnifolia
  (summersweet)—YELLOW
Cornus stolonifera
  (red osier dogwood)*—DARK RED
Cotinus coggygria
  (smokebush)—YELLOW TO ORANGE
Enkianthus campanulatus
  (redvein enkianthus)—ORANGE TO RED
Euonymus species—most
  (euonymus)*—CRIMSON
Fothergilla species
  (fothergilla)—YELLOW TO SCARLET
Halesia caroliniana
  (silverbells)*—YELLOW

Hamamelis species
  (witch hazel)—YELLOW
Hydrangea quercifolia
  (oak-leaved hydrangea)—PURPLE
Magnolia stellata
  (star magnolia)—YELLOW TO BRONZE
Mahonia aquifolium
  (Oregon grape)*—PURPLE
Rhus aromatica
  (fragrant sumac)*—ORANGE TO RED
Rhus typhina
  (staghorn sumac)—YELLOW TO
  SCARLET
Ribes aureum
  (golden currant)—YELLOW
Spiraea bumalda
  (Bumalda spirea)—RED TO PURPLE
Symphoricarpos orbiculatus
  (coralberry)*—YELLOW
Viburnum dentatum
  (arrowwood)*—YELLOW TO RED
Viburnum dilatatum
  (linden viburnum)*—BRONZE
Viburnum lentago
  (nannyberry)*—PURPLE

Shrubs for Part (Dappled) Shade

Acer palmatum

Buxus sempervirens

Hydrangea arborescens

Acer palmatum (Japanese maple)
Arctostaphylos uva-ursi (bearberry)
Buxus hybrids (boxwood)
Calluna vulgaris (heather)
Calycanthus floridus
  (Carolina allspice)
Clethra alnifolia (summersweet)
Cornus stolonifera
  (red osier dogwood)
Cotoneaster dammeri
  (bearberry cotoneaster)
Erica species (heath)
Hamamelis virginiana
  (common witch hazel)
Hippophae rhamnoides
  (sea buckthorn)
Hydrangea arborescens
  (smooth hydrangea)
Hydrangea quercifolia
  (Oak-leaved hydrangea)

Hypericum 'Hidcote'
  (Hidcote St. John's wort)
Ilex verticillata (winterberry)
Lindera benzoin (spicebush)
Magnolia soulangeana
  (saucer magnolia)
Magnolia stellata (star magnolia)
Mahonia aquifolium (Oregon grape)
Myrica pensylvanica (bayberry)
Pieris japonica (Japanese pieris)
Rhododendron species and hybrids
  (rhododendron and azalea)
Rhus aromatica (fragrant sumac)
Styrax japonica (snowbell)
Thujopsis dolobrata (false arborvitae)
Tsuga canadensis
  (Canadian hemlock)
Viburnum species—most (viburnum)

Useful Vines to Grow

Vining plants take up very little ground area and have flexible stems that can be trained to provide the maximum display. Some vines are climbers that attach themselves to their support by twining tendrils, rootlets, or clinging disks. Others must be tied in order to climb. This is indicated in the first column on the charts that begin below.

Vines are listed alphabetically according to their botanical names. The deciduous and evergreen plants have been grouped on separate charts. To determine whether a vine can reasonably be expected to survive in your area, check the zone designation for that vine in the Hardiness column. Then refer to the Hardiness Zone Map at the front of the book.

Most vines can be cut back lightly at any time to keep them in bounds. For details on pruning those that are overgrown, see page 271.

Serpentine soil layering, a method of propagating vines, is illustrated on page 263. For specific information on planting vines, see page 251.

Actinidia kolomikta

Actinidia kolomikta
(actinidia)

Aristolochia durior
(aristolochia)

Campsis radicans
(trumpet creeper)

Celastrus
(bittersweet)

BOTANICAL AND COMMON NAMES	SPECIES AND VARIETIES	HARDINESS	SOIL	LIGHT	CHARACTERISTICS, REQUIREMENTS, AND REMARKS
Actinidia (actinidia) Robust plant with twining stems, numerous alternate leaves, and edible fruits. Since male and female blossoms form on separate plants, individual specimens of both sexes should be grown near each other to ensure fruiting.	*Actinidia arguta* (bower actinidia, or tara vine) *A. chinensis* (Chinese gooseberry, or kiwi vine) *A. kolomikta*	Zones 3–8 Zones 8–9 Zones 3–8	■	●	Oval leaves are up to 5 in. long. Small greenish-white flowers open in midsummer. Greenish-yellow fruits are sweet. Fast growth forms dense cover. 'Issai' is self-fertile. Velvety red hairs on new shoots; leaves to 8 in. long. White to yellow blooms appear in early summer. Male plant has large white to pinkish mark on leaf. Flowers, in spring, are white. Fruits are greenish yellow.
Aristolochia (aristolochia) Has twining stems and large, handsome leaves.	*Aristolochia macrophylla* (syn. *durior*) (Dutchman's pipe)	Zones 4–8	■	● ◐	Foul-smelling yellowish-brown flowers resemble small tobacco pipes. Rounded leaves are up to 1 ft. long.
Campsis (trumpet creeper) Fast grower has compound leaves, vivid trumpetlike blooms (which attract hummingbirds), and long seedpods. Rootlets along stems attach to supports, but vine may also require tying. Not a good choice where space is limited, but ideal for growing over roof, toolshed, or similar structure. Vine can cause damage to building siding.	*Campsis radicans* *C. tagliabuana* 'Madame Galen'	Zones 4–9 Zones 5–9	■	●	Orange to red blossoms, 2 in. in diameter, appear in midsummer. Although nearly identical to *C. radicans*, blooms of this vine are slightly larger.
Celastrus (bittersweet) Has twining stems, alternate stalked leaves, which are usually deciduous. Tiny greenish blooms. Colorful fruits split to show red-to-orange-coated seeds. Male and female flowers on separate plants, so both needed for fruit.	*C. scandens* (American)	Zones 3–8	■	● ◐	Oblong leaves are up to 5 in. long. Yellow fruits poisonous. Rampant grower that needs plenty of room but is useful for covering tops of low stone walls.

■ well drained to sandy   ■ moist   ■ wet   ■ acidic   ■ alkaline   □ regular soil   ● full sun   ◐ partial shade   ● shade

Wisteria floribunda can make a huge vine with a tortuous trunk. Make sure the trellis or arbor is strong enough to take its weight. Large-flowered clematis, such as this long-blooming variety, are especially popular.

Wisteria floribunda 'Multijuga'

Clematis 'Henryi'

Clematis 'Nelly Moser' (clematis)

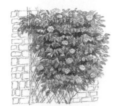

Hydrangea anomala (climbing hydrangea)

Parthenocissus quinquefolia (Virginia creeper)

Wisteria sinensis (Chinese wisteria)

BOTANICAL AND COMMON NAMES	SPECIES AND VARIETIES	HARDINESS	SOIL	LIGHT	CHARACTERISTICS, REQUIREMENTS, AND REMARKS
Clematis (clematis) Opposite leaves are compound. Twining leaf stalks cling to supports. Vine needs partial shade, alkaline soil, and loose mulch to help keep roots cool and moist.	*Clematis alpina* (alpine clematis) C. *jackmanii* C. *macropetala* (bigpetal) C. *montana* (anemone clematis) C. *tangutica* (Russian) C. *texensis* (scarlet clematis) C. *viticella* (virgin's bower) C. named hybrids (many)	Zones 4–8 Zones 3–8 Zones 2–6 Zones 5–8 Zones 1–6 Zones 4–8 Zones 2–8 Zones 3b–4	■	● ◑	Small, nodding bells, white, blue, or pink in early spring. Purple blooms as wide as 6 in. appear from midsummer to midfall. Hybrids have many large flowers in range of colors. Semi-double flowers in late spring, may rebloom. Leaves are prominently toothed. White 1- to 3-in. blossoms open in late spring. Very vigorous. Bright yellow bells from summer to fall. Attractive seed heads. Ovalish leaves are bluish green. Vine displays scarlet, urn-shaped blooms from midsummer to early fall. Summer-flowering with masses of smaller flowers. Summer flowering in a wide range of colors.
Hydrangea (climbing hydrangea) Flower clusters are white. Leaves, usually toothed, are opposite. Stem rootlets cling to support.	*Hydrangea anomala petiolaris*	Zones 4–7	■	● ◑	Side growth may reach as far as 8 ft. from main stem, forming dense screen that is useful for masking work areas.
Parthenocissus Leaves turn bright red in fall. Inconspicuous flowers are followed by dark blue to black berries. Vines climb trees if bark is rough.	*Parthenocissus quinquefolia* (Virginia creeper) P. q. *engelmannii* (Engelmann's ivy) P. *tricuspidata* (Boston ivy) P. t. 'Veitchii'	Zones 3–9 Zones 3–9 Zones 4–8 Zones 4–8	■	● ●	Large 5-parted leaves. Birds seek out deep blue to black berries. Should not be allowed to grow into treetops, since twining stems can smother them within a few seasons. Similar to P. quinquefolia but has smaller leaflets. Shiny green 3-parted leaves are up to 8 in. across. May be semi-evergreen in mild climates. Has rootlike tendrils with disklike pads. Young leaves are purplish and smaller than in the species.
Wisteria (wisteria) This genus has large compound leaves and pealike flowers in handsome pendent clusters. Long velvety seedpods develop in autumn. Wisterias are robust climbers with twining stems. There are two groups: one, the Chinese, twines from left to right; the other, Japanese, from right to left	*Wisteria floribunda* (Japanese) W. f. 'Lawrence' W. f. 'Longissima Alba' W. f. 'Rosea' W. f. 'Royal Purple' W. *sinensis* (Chinese) W. s. 'Alba'	Zones 5–9 Zones 5–9 Zones 5–9 Zones 5–9 Zones 5–9 Zones 5–8 Zones 5–8	■	● ◑	In late spring dark blue or violet blooms form clusters up to 18 in. long. Flowers may smell sweet. Blossom color is violet to bluish violet. White flowers have a rich perfume. Pale pink blooms are heavily scented. Deep purple flowers make a showy display. Aromatic bluish-violet flowers open in late spring and hang in clusters up to 1 ft. long. Pure white blooms are attractive, especially when planted together with colored wisterias.

Akebia, an evergreen vine in the South, is a deciduous vine in the North. Its inconspicuous but aromatic flowers open at night in late spring. Hummingbirds are attracted to the showy, trumpetlike flowers of the trumpet creeper (*Campsis radicans*).

Wisteria and *Clematis montana* 'Rubens' ➡

Akebia quinata

Campsis radicans 'Madame Galen'

EVERGREEN VINES

Akebia trifoliata (akebia)

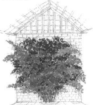
Bougainvillea (bougainvillea)

Fatshedera lizei (fatshedera)

Hedera (ivy)

Jasminum officinale (jasmine)

Passiflora caerulea (passionflower)

Solanum jasminoides (potato vine)

BOTANICAL AND COMMON NAMES	SPECIES AND VARIETIES	HARDINESS	SOIL	LIGHT	CHARACTERISTICS, REQUIREMENTS, AND REMARKS
Akebia (akebia) Compound leaves on twining stems are evergreen in the southern United States This twiner needs shade and can be invasive.	*Akebia quinata* (five-leaved)	Zones 5–8	■	●	Leaves consist of 5 leaflets. Inconspicuous but aromatic flowers open at night in late spring. Purple pods up to 3 in. long are edible.
Bougainvillea (bougainvillea) Flowerlike bracts in a range of colors. Twining stems need tying at first. Drought resistant.	*Bougainvillea buttiana*	Zones 9–11	■	●	Many named forms have large clusters of flowers from summer to fall.
Fatshedera (fatshedera) Leaves resemble English ivy's but are larger. Needs tying to supports or trellises.	*Fatshedera lizei*	Zones 7–11	■	● ◐	Shiny leaves grow to 7 in. long and 10 in. wide. Clusters of tiny light green flowers opening in early and mid fall are up to 10 in. long.
Hedera (ivy) Leaves are alternate, stalked, and toothed or lobed. This genus, popular for its decorative foliage, produces tiny greenish flowers and black fruits. Rootlets along stems cling to rough surfaces. Vine is considered invasive in some parts of the United States, particularly the Pacific Northwest.	*Hedera canariensis* (Algerian) *H. helix* (English) *H. h. baltica*	Zones 7–10 Zones 5–9 Zones 4–9	■	◐ ●	Six-in.-long leaves. Dark red twigs and leaf stalks. Leaves are 2–5 in. long, with 3–5 lobes; tops are deep green, undersides yellowish green. This small-leaved variety is especially hardy.
Jasminum (jasmine) This easily grown genus has white, yellow, or pink flower clusters that are usually fragrant. Compound leaves are either alternate or opposite. Its awkwardly climbing stems need tying to supports or walls. Most kinds are evergreen or semi-evergreen to deciduous. Usually grown in a cool greenhouse.	*Jasminum floridum* (showy) *J. humile* (Italian) *J. mesnyi* (primrose) *J. nitidum* (angel-wing) *J. officinale affine* (white)	Zones 7–11 Zones 7–10 Zones 8–10 Zones 8–11 Zones 8–10	■	● ◐	Semi-evergreen leaves; yellow blossoms in midsummer. Leaves are sometimes semi-evergreen. Sweet-scented blossoms are golden yellow. Glossy leaves are up to 2 in. long. In midspring this semi-evergreen vine bears yellow blossoms. Glossy, leathery green leaves up to 3 in. long. White flowers are very fragrant. Not reliably hardy below 32°F. Glossy leaves are semi-evergreen or deciduous. White 2-in.-wide flowers open in midsummer.
Passiflora (passionflower) Climbs with tendrils. May be semi-evergreen at the limits of range.	*Passiflora caerulea* (blue) *P. edulis* (passionfruit)	Zones 6–9 Zones 6–9	■	● ◐	White flowers are sometimes tinged with pink, and banded with blue-violet in summer. White flowers in summer become yellow. Edible fruit is purple.
Solanum (solanum) Rather floppy climber (good for window boxes) with dark green, poisonous foliage.	*Solanum jasminoides* (potato vine)	Zones 8–10	□ ■	●	Terminal clusters of blue-white flowers with yellow stamens in summer and fall.

■ well drained to sandy　■ moist　■ wet　▨ acidic　■ alkaline　□ regular soil　● full sun　◐ partial shade　● shade

HEDGES

Hedges are an essential part of most gardens. They can be clipped and formal, or they can be loosely informal, with arching branches clothed with flowers in season.

Hedges are used to provide privacy, to screen one part of the garden from another, to serve as backgrounds for flower borders and other plantings, and as windbreaks.

Evergreens can be ideal as hedging plants because they stay dense and green all winter long. Among the best are yews and boxwoods, both of which grow densely and need clipping only once a year. Where climate permits, fast-growing evergreen privets are also used; but to keep them tidy and to promote bushy growth, they must be clipped two or even three times a year.

Hedges of conifers, most of which are evergreen, are often dark green and rather somber, but there are lighter-colored conifers, such as the golden thread-leaf cypress, which will make a dense and compact hedge. A fairly common longtime favorite for hedges is the hemlock, which can be clipped without fear of shoots dying back. To create a thick, interwoven shield of branches, plant young conifers at intervals of about 2 feet.

Where the hedge is not employed as a boundary, informal flowering or berrying shrubs, such as forsythia 'Lynwood', lilac, potentilla or cinquefoil, buckthorn, and hawthorn, can be allowed to develop their individual characteristics more than clipped formal hedges can.

Many species and cultivated forms of spirea make excellent informal hedges. Some spireas are hardy in all but the coldest zones (1 and 2); others cannot survive those colder than Zone 5. Spireas range from 1½ to 7 feet high. Their flowers can be pink or white.

Trees are often grown as giant hedges to create windbreaks. They are more effective than a fence or wall in protecting a garden from wind. This is largely because they allow the air to filter through, slowing

it down gradually. A wall stops the wind completely but produces strong downdrafts.

In coastal areas, Austrian pines that are planted a few yards apart make ideal windbreaks, since they are resistant to salt spray. Hedges of linden trees afford good shelter for inland gardens.

On the following pages are illustrated listings of the deciduous and evergreen plants most frequently used for hedges. Included with each is information about height, location, and hardiness. The height indicates the sizes to which they are usually trimmed. Most of them will grow taller if allowed to.

Location indicates if a plant takes sun or shade. Those with flowers will be more floriferous in full sun.

To see if a plant can be expected to survive the lowest average temperatures in your area, check the Zone designation under Hardiness, then compare it with the Hardiness Zone Map at the front of the book.

Attractive glossy foliage that ranges from pale green shades in spring to orange browns in fall is among the attractions of the European beech (*Fagus sylvatica*).

Fagus sylvatica

Deciduous Hedge Plants

Caragana arborescens
Bright yellow, pealike blossoms appear on the Siberian peashrub in late spring. A vigorous shrub with leaves up to 3 in. long makes a fine windbreak that requires little maintenance. In fall 2-in. pods develop.
Height: 4–15 ft.
Location: sun.
Hardiness: Zones 2–7.

Carpinus caroliniana
The American hornbeam is a small, robust tree with leaves up to 5 in. long. Catkins appear in mid and late spring and are followed by pendulous clusters of winged nutlets (but not if the hedge is clipped).
Height: 3–5 ft. or more.
Location: sun or partial shade.
Hardiness: Zones 3–9.

Chaenomeles japonica
The flowering quince is an outstanding dwarf with abundant red blooms that open in late spring before the leaves unfold. *C. speciosa* has bright red flowers in early to mid spring. Varieties are available with white or pink blossoms.
Height: *C. japonica*, 3 ft. *C. speciosa*, 6 ft.
Location: sun or shade.
Hardiness: Zones 4–8.

Crataegus crus-galli
The cockspur hawthorn is a good hedge plant, as its heavy branching habit and thorns make a nearly impregnable barrier. White blooms are followed by red berries. The foliage remains on the shrub until late fall.
Height: 3–5 ft. or more.
Location: sun or partial shade.
Hardiness: Zones 3–7.

Elaeagnus angustifolia
The Russian olive has straplike leaves up to 5 in. long, which are silvery beneath. The small flowers in early summer have a fragrance similar to gardenias, and are succeeded by yellow and silvery fruits that are relished by birds. Plants withstand dry climates, sandy soils, and salt-laden ocean breezes.
Height: 3–15 ft.
Location: sun or partial shade.
Hardiness: Zones 2–7.

Fagus sylvatica
The European beech and its copper and purple varieties are useful as windbreaks. They retain their red-brown autumn leaves throughout winter and early spring. Beeches grow well in all but wet, heavy soils. Branches are a handsome gray.
Height: 6–15 ft. or more.
Location: sun or partial shade.
Hardiness: Zones (4) 5–7.

Forsythia intermedia
Of the forsythias, the border forsythia has the largest flowers. In early or mid spring it is a mass of yellow blooms. Like almost all other forsythia species, it can easily be trained to form a dense hedge. Excellent varieties include 'Lynwood', 'Spring Glory', and 'Karl Sax'.
Height: 3–8 ft.
Location: sun or shade.
Hardiness: Zones 4–8.

Fuchsia magellanica 'Riccartonii'
Hedges of fuchsia can be grown where winters are mild. The bright red blooms are delightful in summer. *F. magellanica* flourishes near the sea. Its generally solitary purple and red flowers open in early summer.
Height: 2–6 ft.
Location: sun or partial shade.
Hardiness: Zones 7–9.

Sea buckthorn (*Hippophae rhamnoides*) makes an ideal wind-break, especially for coastal areas. With summer-long flowers—colors vary with the variety—*Potentilla fruticosa* (shrubby cinquefoil) makes a good informal hedge.

Hippophae rhamnoides

Potentilla fruticosa 'Red Ace'

Deciduous Hedge Plants (*continued*)

Hippophae rhamnoides

Sea buckthorn bears narrow leaves with grayish-green upper surfaces and silvery green undersides. Orange berries appear in autumn if both male and female plants are grown together. It makes a good seaside hedge, as it tolerates salt spray.
Height: 3–15 ft.
Location: sun or partial shade.
Hardiness: Zones 3–7.

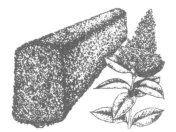

Ligustrum

Many species of privet make excellent hedges. All are rapid growers with glossy leaves. *L. amurense* withstands severe cold. *L. obtusifolium* bears black berries in fall. *L. ovalifolium* is a semi-evergreen. *L. vulgare* grows in almost any soil; its black fruits develop in heavy clusters.
Height: 2–12 ft.
Location: sun.
Hardiness: Zones 4 to 6–7 to 8.

Philadelphus

Many species and varieties of mock orange are suitable for hedging. All have fragrant white blossoms in mid-summer. *P. coronarius* offers flowers up to 1½ in. across. *P. lemoinei* is a hybrid with an upright habit of growth.
Height: *P. coronarius*, 6–8 ft. *P. lemoinei*, 4–6 ft.
Location: sun.
Hardiness: Zones 3 or 4–8.

Potentilla fruticosa 'Farreri'

This variety of cinquefoil makes an ideal informal hedge, as do several other cinquefoils. The yellow flowers appear in profusion in June, and there are scattered blooms until frost. No regular shearing required. Cut any shoots growing too long.
Height: 3 ft.
Location: sun.
Hardiness: Zones 2–7.

Prunus cerasifera

The cherry, or myrobalan, plum has dark green leaves and makes a colorful hedge if interplanted with *P. c.* 'Nigra', the purple-leaved plum. Both types have clusters of small white flowers in early spring, which are sometimes followed by striking red or yellow "cherry plums."
Height: 6–15 ft.
Location: sun.
Hardiness: Zones 4–8.

Prunus tomentosa

Clusters of pale pink blossoms appear on the branches of Manchu, or Nanking, cherry shortly after the snow melts. The blossoms are followed by tasty, bright red cherries which ripen in July. On a closely clipped hedge the fruit is almost hidden by the foliage.
Height: 3–15 ft.
Location: sun or partial shade.
Hardiness: Zones 2–7.

Rosa

Roses in any shrub form can be used as a hedge. One outstanding species is *R. harisonii*, with vivid yellow blooms. *R. rugosa* is an excellent plant. Its flowers are white, pink, or red. Floribundas also make good hedges.
Height: 3–6 ft.
Location: sun.
Hardiness: Zones 2 to 4–7 to 8.

Salix purpurea 'Nana'

Willow has attractive, soft, gray to blue-green leaves borne on slender branches. This is not an effective barrier plant but has considerable value wherever soil is heavy and wet.
Height: 2–3 ft.
Location: sun.
Hardiness: Zones 3–6.

Known for its rapid growth, Leyland cypress (*Cupressocyparis leylandii*) is ideal for tall hedging. 'Robinson's Gold' is named for foliage that ranges from golden yellow in springtime to lime-green in fall.

Cupressocyparis leylandii 'Robinson's Gold'

Evergreen Hedge Plants

Berberis stenophylla

Barberry has arching branches with clusters of golden flowers in spring. In fall purplish-black berries appear. Its leaves are up to 1 in. long. This plant stands up well to shearing. One of the hardiest, *B. julianae*, has spiny 3-in. leaves.
Height: 3–6 ft.
Location: sun or partial shade.
Hardiness: Zones 5–7.

Buxus sempervirens

Most boxwoods can be used as hedges. Boxwood has dark green leaves up to 1¼ in. long. This plant assumes a treelike habit of growth if it is not clipped. It is a fine choice for privacy screens.
Height: 1–2 ft. or more.
Location: sun or partial shade.
Hardiness: Zones (4) 5–8 (9).

Camellia

Almost any camellia species can be used for hedging. *C. japonica* is available in many varieties, with large showy flowers of white, pink, red, and variegated colors appearing from midfall to midspring. Straplike, glossy, deep green leaves are up to 5 in. long.
Height: 3–12 ft. or more.
Location: partial shade.
Hardiness: Zones 7–9.

Chamaecyparis lawsoniana

Any upright form of this genus makes a suitable hedge. False cypress has soft leaves and grows compactly. It needs a great amount of moisture. *C. thyoides* has light green, scalelike leaves and reddish brown bark. This is a good plant for wet-soil areas.
Height: 4–15 ft. or more.
Location: sun.
Hardiness: Zones 5–7.

Cotoneaster

C. lacteus has gracefully arching branches with twigs that bear whitish hairs. Specimens of this shrub form a dark-green-leaved hedge of imposing character. White flowers develop in late spring, and clusters of red berries last from fall into winter.
Height: 6–12 ft.
Location: sun or partial shade.
Hardiness: Zones 6–8.

Cupressocyparis leylandii

The Leyland cypress is an extremely vigorous conifer, ideal for tall hedges. A hybrid, it is very fast-growing and has a distinct columnar habit. Its leaves are small and scalelike. This is a good selection where rapid screening is desired.
Height: 3–15 ft. or more.
Location: sun or partial shade.
Hardiness: Zones 6–10.

Escallonia

E. rubra is identified by its reddish twigs that are up to 2 in. long. The leaves are lance shaped and have sticky surfaces. In midsummer small red blossoms form in loose, hanging clusters. Several of its varieties also make excellent hedges.
Height: 3–12 ft.
Location: sun.
Hardiness: Zones 7–9.

Euonymus

E. japonicus has glossy green leaves, handsomely variegated in many varieties, yellow flowers in spring so small as to be insignificant, and pink berries in fall. It grows in any soil with good drainage and tolerates shearing very well.
Height: 2–12 ft.
Location: sun or partial shade.
Hardiness: Zones 7–9.

Both English holly (*Ilex aquifolium*) and false holly (*Osmanthus heterophyllus*) make excellent hedges. Foliage bordered in creamy white makes 'Silver Queen' one of the more attractive of the English hollies.

Ilex aquifolium 'Silver Queen'   *Osmanthus heterophyllus*

Evergreen Hedge Plants (*continued*)

Hebe

The overlapping 1-in. leaves of *H. buxifolia* produce an interesting overall texture. In midsummer white flowers open in 1-in. spikes. This is a popular plant in West Coast gardens. It does well in sandy soil and grows best with infrequent watering and feeding.
Height: 2–4 ft.
Location: sun.
Hardiness: Zones 7–9.

Ilex aquifolium

The foliage of the English holly has long been a favorite Christmas decoration. The glossy, dark evergreen leaves and thick growth of this species make it an attractive hedge. The vivid red fruit clings to the plants well into winter. *I. opaca*, the American holly, has dull upper-leaf surfaces and yellow-green undersides. Its fruit is also red.
Height: 4–15 ft. or more.
Location: sun or partial shade.
Hardiness: Zones 6–9.

Ligustrum japonicum

The Japanese privet has shiny, deep green leaves that grow up to 4 in. long. Unless plants are clipped, 4- to 6-in. blossom clusters develop from midsummer to early fall. *L. lucidum* has longer leaves than *L. japonicum*, and its flower clusters grow to almost 10 in. long.
Height: 3–15 ft.
Location: sun or partial shade.
Hardiness: Zones 8–10.

Lonicera nitida

The shrubby honeysuckle is grown mainly for its small foliage, which forms a dense barrier. Although fragrant whitish or yellowish-green flowers open in mid and late spring, they are sparse and relatively inconspicuous. This species resists salt spray in shore gardens.
Height: 2–4 ft.
Location: sun or partial shade.
Hardiness: Zones 7–9.

Mahonia aquifolium

The Oregon grape is noted for erect clusters of deep yellow blossoms that open in late winter or early spring. They are followed by edible blue-black fruits. The hollylike leaves are glossy green. In cold areas at the limits of its range, the Oregon grape loses its leaves in winter.
Height: 2–3 ft.
Location: partial shade.
Hardiness: Zones 4–8.

Osmanthus

Most species of osmanthus will make suitable hedges. *O. heterophyllus* produces aromatic, greenish-white flowers throughout the summer. Blue-black berries develop in early fall. Glossy oblong to oval leaves grow to 2 in. or more.
Height: 3–15 ft.
Location: sun or partial shade.
Hardiness: Zones (6) 7–9.

Picea

Both the Norway spruce (*P. abies*) and the white spruce (*P. glauca*) make excellent hedges where a fairly tall growth is required. With regular trimming, they will remain good for at least 50 years. Neither species should be left to become overgrown: if they need to be cut back hard, regrowth will be slow.
Height: 5–7 ft.
Location: sun.
Hardiness: Zones 2–7 and 2–6 respectively.

Pinus strobus

Many species of pine can be used as a windbreak hedge but few will make as good a formal hedge as white pine. Trimmed regularly, it will remain soft. The light green new growth is particularly attractive. Swiss stone pine (*P. cembra*) is marginally hardier and also makes a good hedge.
Height: 5–7 ft.
Location: sun or partial shade.
Hardiness: Zones 3–8.

Santolina chamaecyparissus 'Lemon Queen'

Taxus baccata 'Elegantissima'

Aromatic leaves and tiny buttonlike lemon-yellow flowers make the cotton lavender (*Santolina chamaecyparissus*) a good choice for ornamental hedging. Among varieties of English yew, 'Elegantissima' is prized for its yellow-striped foliage.

Evergreen Hedge Plants (*continued*)

Pittosporum tobira

Japanese pittosporum has striking deep green leaves that may grow up to 4 in. long. Clusters of creamy white flowers open in late spring. Although inconspicuous, they are intensely fragrant. Suitable only for West Coast gardens, this is an especially useful shrub in seashore settings.

Height: 3–12 ft.
Location: sun or partial shade.
Hardiness: Zones 8–10.

Prunus

The Portugal laurel (*P. lusitanica*) and the cherry laurel (*P. laurocerasus*) are fine hedging plants that grow into small- or medium-sized trees if allowed to develop naturally. The leaves are shiny, toothed, and up to 5 in. long. Fragrant white flowers are followed by purplish fruits.

Height: 4–15 ft.
Location: sun.
Hardiness: Zones 6–8.

Pyracantha

Noted for its fruit clusters that appear in autumn in vivid colors, the firethorn is available in several fine species, all of which have thorns and small white blossoms. *P. coccinea* 'Lalandei' has ovalish leaves up to 1½ in. long. The leaves of *P. crenulata* are often 3 in. long. Both species bear orange-red berries.

Height: 3–12 ft.
Location: sun.
Hardiness: Zones (5) 6–9.

Santolina

Cotton lavender (*S. chamaecyparissus*) is a handsome dwarf shrub with silvery, dissected, fernlike leaves. In midsummer bright lemon-yellow, rounded flowers help make it a delightful hedge. This is a useful plant that requires no shearing. In its northernmost range it should be given a heavy winter mulch.

Height: 1–2 ft.
Location: sun.
Hardiness: Zones 6–9.

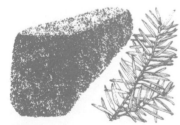

Taxus

All species of yew that attain sufficient height can be used as hedges. *Taxus baccata*, the English yew, is a slow-growing, broad-shaped conifer with dark green foliage and brownish-green fruit. The red berries on *T. cuspidata* produce an attractive contrast to the dark green leaves. *T. media*, a fine hybrid, combines good looks with hardiness.

Height: 2–15 ft.
Location: sun or shade.
Hardiness: varies with species.

Thuja occidentalis

Arborvitae, or eastern white cedar, is probably the commonest hedging plant in North America. Most of these cedars are dug up from the wild and take several years to form a dense hedge. Nursery-grown cedars will form a screen more quickly.

Height: 4 ft. or more.
Location: sun or partial shade.
Hardiness: Zones 2–8.

Thuja plicata

Giant arborvitae, or western red cedar, is a fast grower with handsome deep green leaves. In its northernmost range its leaves turn bronze from autumn through winter. This tree needs moist soil and considerable humidity.

Height: 6–15 ft. or more.
Location: sun.
Hardiness: Zones 5–7.

Tsuga canadensis

The upper surfaces of the needles on the hemlock are green, and the undersides are light gray. This conifer is a forest tree with an upright habit of growth. It requires moderate moisture and shelter from high winds. It will not thrive in heat or city conditions. Other upright-growing hemlock species also make good hedges.

Height: 6–15 ft. or more.
Location: sun or partial shade.
Hardiness: Zones 3–7.

Arborvitae or eastern white cedar (*Thuja occidentalis*) is one of the most popular hedging plants. 'Sunkist' is characterized by dense, yellow-tipped foliage.

Thuja occidentalis 'Sunkist'

How to Grow a Successful Hedge

Hedges can be planted either as a single row or as a double, staggered row. The double row will make a stronger, denser hedge.

Deciduous hedges can be planted any time in fall, late winter, or spring when the ground is not frozen. In mild regions hedges can be planted throughout the winter as well. But it is best to plant evergreens in early fall or in spring.

If bare-root plants are delivered before you are ready to plant them, set them in a shallow trench, and cover their roots with soil.

To plant, dig a trench about 2 feet wide and 1 foot deep along the length of the proposed hedge. The trench, of course, should be larger if the size of the root balls requires it.

Fork compost or peat moss into the bottom of the trench. Put in about a wheelbarrowful for every 6 feet. When replacing the topsoil, mix in some compost, peat moss, or other suitable organic material to lighten the texture of the soil. Also mix in bone meal—2–3 ounces (about 2–3 rounded tablespoons) for every 6 feet of trench.

Use a length of cord to define the location of the row or rows.

For a double row of hedging shrubs, establish the rows 18 inches apart, and stagger the plants so that no two are growing directly opposite each other.

Dig the holes big enough to give the roots plenty of space when spread out or to receive the soil ball around the roots. If you are up to it, double digging is especially useful (see p. 505). Set each shrub so that the nursery soil-mark on the stem (where the light- and dark-colored barks meet) is at ground level. Carefully work the soil into the spaces between the roots of bare-root specimens, and gently shake the stem up and down to get rid of air pockets. Fill in the rest of the hole. Finally, firm the soil by treading lightly. Then water thoroughly to settle soil about the roots.

To prevent the wind from loosening the newly set plant, firmly fix posts at the end of each row. Run a wire tightly between the posts, and tie each plant to the wire. Alternatively, individual stakes can be used to support each plant, but drive them into the ground before planting to avoid root damage.

Newly planted hedges require a few weeks to recover from transplanting. In exposed locations recently planted evergreens may be scorched by the wind. To prevent this, use a screen of burlap netting or brushwood.

To prevent excessive water loss through the leaves of evergreens after planting, spray the foliage with an antidesiccant. If the weather is dry in the months after planting, water the newly established hedge thoroughly at least once a week.

Pruning a new hedge. For informal hedges it is usually enough to clip back the newly set out plants by one-third after planting.

Formal hedges require a dense base and thick, uniform growth. To encourage this, find the shortest plant, cut this back by 10 percent, then cut the other shrubs level with this after planting.

Cut back by one-half or one-third of the new growth every year until the required height is reached. Maintain the hedge at this level by shearing back the new growth almost to its base every year.

Use a line between two stakes to mark the height, and cut to this level. Taper the sides of the hedge toward the top to encourage a thick base.

Formal hedges that grow moderately to rapidly should be pruned two or three times a year, in spring and summer. Informal hedges that bloom on the previous season's shoots should be pruned after flowering; those that bloom on the current season's shoots should be pruned in spring.

Use hedge shears to clip small-leaved shrubs, such as privet, box, or shrubby honeysuckle. Pruning shears are better for cutting back long-leaved shrubs to prevent the leaves from being cut in half.

Power trimmers work well on young, short green shoots, but they may lacerate woody branches if they are not powerful enough for the job.

Fertilize established hedges in spring, top-dressing the roots with any complete organic fertilizer. Repeat in early summer, watering after the application of fertilizer if the soil is dry; then mulch. Mulching hedges helps to keep the soil evenly moist.

PLANTING AND TRAINING A NEW HEDGE

1. Dig a 2-ft.-wide trench; put compost at bottom; refill with soil.

2. Dig individual holes at the proper spacing, and set the plants in place.

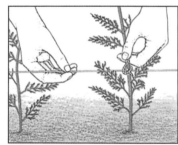

3. Prevent wind damage to plants by tying to a horizontal wire.

4. For a formal hedge, shorten shoots by one-third after planting.

5. Cut new growth by half annually until the hedge is required height.

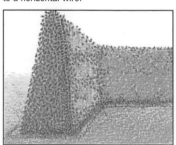

6. Trim the mature hedge so that it tapers from the base toward the top.

ROSES

Probably more than any other flower, the rose has captured the imagination of humankind and has been celebrated in song and legend since ancient times.

The rose held a prominent place in pagan and Oriental religions. The early Christians rejected it because of its pagan heritage, but by the 12th century they adopted it as the symbol of the mother of Christ. And one of the great architectural achievements of the Middle Ages reflects an appreciation of the rose—the rose windows of the great cathedrals of the period.

The species and natural hybrids of roses grow wild in most countries in the northern part of the temperate zone, and fossil remains in Europe and North America show that the rose existed long before humans.

During its evolution the rose developed various habits of growth, ranging from low-growing shrubs to robust tree climbers that reach high toward the sky from the forest floor.

The wild roses are the true species. There are at least 150 of them, the great majority having originated in Asia. With few exceptions all grow single flowers, with five petals.

Throughout the ages gardeners have cultivated the rose, developing the double flower and, eventually, the high-pointed, modern hybrids in which ancestral floral characteristics are almost totally submerged.

The French rose (*Rosa gallica*) was among the first species cultivated, and it is believed to be the plant from which all modern garden roses have descended.

At some stage a cross between *R. gallica* and another wild species produced the damask rose (*R. damascena*). This is believed to have originated in the Damascus region of Syria and was brought to Western Europe by the Crusaders.

The earliest varieties of the original species probably started as "sports"—chance offshoots that differ from the plant on which they arose. For example, a pink flower might appear on a plant that usually bears white blooms. These sports have been propagated by grafting, budding, or taking cuttings—all ancient skills—to establish new varieties.

The arrival in Europe of the China rose (*R. chinensis*) in the 18th century changed the course of rose history. By then gardeners had learned how to breed roses, and by crossing the old with the new, tea roses and hybrid perpetuals were developed. These were the most popular kinds to the end of the 19th century.

Much early hybridizing took place in France. Empress Josephine made roses fashionable with the species and varieties available at the time.

Hybrid tea roses, probably the most popular with today's gardeners—largely because they are hardier than many of their precursors—are relatively recent. They were developed in France at the end of the 19th century by crossing tea roses with hybrid perpetuals.

A little later came the polyanthas, with clusters of small roses. These were produced by hybridizing the Japanese *R. multiflora* with *R. chinensis*. Further crossbreeding in Denmark and the United States led to the popular floribundas. These in turn were crossed with hybrid teas to produce the grandifloras.

As roses became more highly bred, their use in gardens became more formal. During the 19th century, it was fashionable to grow roses by themselves in geometric beds. Often, only roses of one variety would be grown in each bed. This practice is still followed in some estate and exhibition gardens.

Nowadays roses are often grown in a more casual manner and mingled with other plants. There are probably two main reasons for this. The segregated rose bed is a dead space for several months of the year and contributes nothing to the garden when the roses are not in bloom. And in today's more limited garden spaces, the average gardener usually wants to grow a variety of plants.

Mixing roses and other plants. Roses can be combined with other shrubs or herbaceous perennials, placed individually in a particular position, or used to fill a corner, flank a doorway, or adorn a house wall. For instance, tall, arching, modern shrub roses, such as 'Nevada', 'Frühlingsgold', and the species *R. moyesii*, look splendid behind shrubs of moderate size or some lower-growing hybrid teas or floribundas.

When combining roses of different varieties, or growing them among other plants, keep in mind the size and flowering seasons of all the plants. Allow at least 2 feet of space between the plants for air circulation. Make sure that short varieties of hybrid teas and floribundas will not be hidden by tall grandifloras, such as 'Queen Elizabeth', 'Mount Shasta', 'Camelot', or 'Arizona'. Some nursery catalogs indicate the height to which each variety may grow.

Floribundas are ideal roses to mix with other plants to create an interesting visual effect or to prolong the flowering season. In general, they are hardier and smaller than hybrid teas, and can be used at the front of a mixed-shrub border. They do not usually blend well into a perennial border unless planted in a cluster at one end. Arranged like this, they will provide a spectacular splash of color during the midsummer doldrums.

Dedicated rose growers usually prefer not to mix hybrid teas with any other kind of plant. However, many gardeners will find the appearance of the garden greatly improved if they conceal the rather leggy structure of the hybrid teas by planting various other low-growing perennials or annuals at their base.

Edgings for rose beds. Miniature roses are a good choice to use as edgings. Also suitable are the low-growing annuals with a long flowering season, such as ageratums, wax begonias, pansies, and dwarf snapdragons. Perennials often used include lamb's ears and santolinas.

Roses for hedges. Several types of roses make handsome floral hedges, although they are leafless in winter. Except for the floribundas, they take up more space laterally than the usual hedging plants. Good results can be obtained by planting them only slightly closer together than they would be planted in the garden and by pruning them lightly.

Because of their dense foliage, rugosas are the best hedging roses. Most rugosas also have a long flowering period. The royal purple 'Roseraie de l'Hay', the white 'Blanc Double de Coubert', and the double, soft lavender 'Delicata' grow fairly tall. The hybrid white 'Schneezwerg' makes a good 4-foot hedge.

For lower hedges (but a shorter flowering period), the most dramatic color patterns are made by the very old gallica roses—especially the popular crimson- and white-streaked Rosa Mundi (*R. gallica* 'Versicolor').

The double blossoms of 'Stanwell Perpetual' are borne from summer to fall; those of 'Charles de Mills' open in late spring, with a repeat blooming in early autumn.

Rosa 'Stanwell Perpetual'

Rosa 'Charles de Mills'

Classes of Roses

The thorny Scotch rose, *R. pimpinellifolia*, makes a highly efficient barrier against animals and also tolerates poor soil. The variety 'Stanwell Perpetual' bears masses of scented, double light pink flowers over a long blooming period.

Another vigorous variety with large, double white flowers is 'Karl Forster'. Slightly scented, it has good green foliage and blooms intermittently during the season.

In milder climates more tender roses can be used. The white floribunda 'Iceberg' makes a fine hedge, up to 5 feet in height. 'Betty Prior' has single pink flowers throughout the growing season. Shorter is the red-blooming 'Frensham', with semidouble flowers.

The grandiflora 'Queen Elizabeth' makes a lovely prickly-stemmed hedge, which in season has pink blossoms. Planted at 2-foot intervals and trimmed in winter or early spring, it will grow 6 feet high. For a shorter, thicker hedge, cut the plants back severely in early spring.

Among climbing roses, 'New Dawn' makes an excellent dense hedge or screen. When regularly pruned, it behaves as a shrub rose. It is well branched and strong, and is covered almost continuously with sweetly scented blush-pink flowers.

The bright red-flowered 'Blaze', although not suited to making a thick, freestanding hedge, can be trained along a fence by tying its branches horizontally.

Roses to provide ground cover. A few roses that hug the ground closely are excellent for covering the bare soil and, when established, for suppressing weeds. They can also be used to cover steep banks.

The best roses for ground cover include 'Max Graf', a rugosa hybrid with scented, single, pink flowers and crimped petals. It flowers in midsummer and spreads widely, taking root as it goes. *R. wichuraiana*, called the memorial rose, grows 1–1½ feet tall and makes good cover on banks.

It produces its scented, small, creamy white flowers in late summer.

Roses in containers. For decoration, roses in tubs, pots, or boxes are a good choice. Containers about 20 by 20 by 20 inches are best. Miniature roses can go in a 1- by 1- by 1-foot container. Floribundas and polyanthas make bushy plants with many flowers. The soil must be well drained and moisture retentive. Mix garden soil with one-third peat moss and one-third perlite or coarse sand.

Never let plants dry out completely. Control insects and fungi as needed, and apply a liquid fertilizer monthly. In colder climates put containers in a garage for the winter.

All-America roses. In buying roses, one sooner or later encounters certain bushes with attached green and white tags bearing the initials AARS plus the name of the variety of rose. Some catalog varieties are designated as AARS—All-America Rose Selections.

In 1938, to combat the introduction of poor varieties, and to help the gardening public recognize superior roses, some of North America's leading rose growers organized the All-America Rose Selection. The purpose of the nonprofit organization was to test new varieties of rose to determine which ones were worthy of recommendation to the public.

Candidates for the All-America award are grown outdoors at testing stations throughout North America. During the testing period, roses receive the normal care they would receive from the average gardener. Evaluated by official AARS judges according to a prescribed point system, they are scored on vigor, hardiness, disease resistance, foliage, flower production, bud and flower form, opening and final color, fragrance, stem, and overall value and novelty. Only the top-scoring roses in each category are considered for the AARS designation.

Visit www.rose.org for more information and pictures of winners.

Hybrid tea. More roses of this class are sold than of any other.

Most of the hybrid teas produce double flowers with long-pointed buds borne one to a stem. They flower intermittently and have a wider color range than the older tea roses.

Popular varieties include 'Chrysler Imperial' (red); 'Tropicana' (reddish orange); 'Love and Peace' (yellow-edged red); Whispers™ (white); Memorial Day™ (pink); 'Crimson Bouquet' (red); and 'Peace' (pink and yellow).

Floribunda. Flowers in clusters are borne continuously and in profusion. When they were introduced early in the 20th century, the flowers were borne in large clusters, and most were single or semi-double.

Many of the newer varieties have blossoms much like the hybrid teas, although they are smaller and may be single, semi-double, or double.

Popular varieties include 'Europeana' (red); 'Nearly Wild' (single pink); 'Iceberg' (white); Eureka™ (apricot yellow); 'Marmalade Skies' (tangerine); and 'Sentimental' (burgundy and cream).

Grandiflora. The grandiflora is a tall, stately bush with great vigor, whose overall appearance is somewhere between that of the hybrid tea and the floribunda. Individual flowers resemble those of the hybrid tea, but they appear several to a stem like the floribunda.

Favorites are 'Queen Elizabeth' (pink); 'Gemini' (pink); 'Mr. Hood' (ivory); 'Cherry Parfait' (white-edged red); and About Face™ (yellow).

Polyantha. A few stalwart representatives of the once-popular polyantha class are still represented in catalogs. They are distinguished by clusters of small flowers on low plants that bloom intermittently.

Commonly grown are 'The Fairy' (semi-double pink); 'Cecile Brunner' (light pink with hybrid tea flower form); and 'Margo Koster' (coral-orange with almost round buds and cup-shaped flowers).

Miniature. The miniature plants are small in stature, generally 10-15 inches tall, with proportionately sized flowers that are mostly semi-double or double. Some bear flowers that are almost identical in form to the hybrid teas.

Miniatures are particularly suitable for growing in containers. Some favorites are 'Sun Sprinkle' (yellow); 'Gourmet Popcorn' (white); 'Green Ice' (very pale yellow-green).

Tree, or standard. The tree form has a slim, erect, bare stem on top of which the desired variety—usually a hybrid tea or floribunda—is grafted (budded). Tree roses have a formal elegance, and they provide an attractive vertical accent.

Tree roses (also called standard roses) are trained on stems about 3½ feet high. Half standards, or dwarf trees, are trained on stems about 2 feet high; miniatures, on 1½-foot stems. Weeping trees are taller, with stems up to 5 or 6 feet. The budded top is a rambler with flexible canes that hang down to the ground.

Climbers. The large-blossomed climbers that are repeat blooming or everblooming have mostly replaced the older climbers that have only one period of bloom. Most climbers have flowers quite similar to the hybrid tea, although some look more like the clustered floribundas.

Popular varieties are 'Coral Dawn' (coral-pink); 'Golden Showers' (yellow); 'Blaze' (crimson); 'New Dawn' (pink); and 'White Dawn' (white).

Shrub roses. For informal landscape use and as hedges, shrub roses are of particular value. They are available in many nurseries and from rose specialists. Included here are the true species, hybrids between the species, and man-made hybrids. The plants tend to be shrublike, and many grow 4–5 feet high and equally wide.

Many are very hardy, and are particularly suitable in cold areas. Your local nursery will offer selections for your region.

Rosa 'Polar Star'

Rosa 'La France'

Rosa 'Julia's Rose'

These three hybrid tea roses are all unique. 'Polar Star' is exceptionally free-flowering, 'La France' is probably the first hybrid tea introduced, while 'Julia's Rose' is an unusual coppery shade.

Step-by-step Guide to Planting Roses

Creating the Best Conditions for Roses

Roses will grow in a wide variety of soils and situations, and will survive with relatively little attention. But they do best in an open, sunny location that has a fairly rich, slightly acid soil. If humus is added, clay soil is excellent. Good drainage is essential, although roses need ample watering in the absence of rain. Once planted, roses will survive in the same bed for many years if the ground is regularly mulched and fed.

Moisture retention in the soil is of utmost importance. A month before planting, dig the ground to the depth of a spade, and work in about one-third by volume of humusy material, such as compost, leaf mold, or well-rotted manure. No fertilizer need be added at this time. Leave the topsoil untrampled so that it is loose and air can circulate. Level the soil for the sake of appearance if so desired.

Heavy clay and sandy soils will need even more organic matter, often as much as one-half by volume. In addition to those materials mentioned above, chopped-up turf is excellent when available, since it breaks down into humus quickly and its nutrients will not leach out of the soil rapidly. After this initial improvement of the planting site, roses in clay and sandy soils benefit greatly from yearly application of a top-dressing of well-rotted manure or garden compost.

If the soil is alkaline, spread about two buckets of peat moss and one handful of elemental sulfur per square yard, and mix it well into the top 6–10 inches of soil. Be sure to wear quality protective gloves when handling the flowers of sulfur. If the soil is too acid (below a pH of 5.5), apply ground limestone at a rate of 3–5 pounds per 100 square feet.

In areas where it is difficult to provide proper drainage, you may want to consider planting your roses in raised beds.

When to plant. The best time to plant bare-root roses in cold sections of the country is in early spring. This gives the roots time to become established before top growth begins. Fall planting is slightly riskier, and the plants must be protected through the winter. In mild regions where the soil does not freeze for long periods, roses are best planted in late fall or late winter.

If bare-root plants are purchased from a garden center or ordered by mail and arrive during a spell of hard frost, they can be kept in a garage or shed, wrapped in their packing—usually a plastic bag with damp sphagnum moss around the roots. Open the plastic to allow air to get to the roots so that they do not mold. Keep the packing damp (not soggy), and occasionally water the stems as well. If the roots are not wrapped, cover them with burlap, peat moss, newspapers, or any material that will keep them moist.

It is best to plant roses as soon as possible. If it is necessary to store the plants more than a few days, bury the roots in a shallow, slant-sided trench in a shaded spot and water them well.

Container-grown plants can be set out just about any time they are available. However, most nurseries pot bare-root plants in very early spring, and it is preferable to purchase them in spring or early summer before they become too pot-bound. Roots that are confined in a container often grow so tightly together that they have trouble growing into the surrounding soil when planted in the garden. Also, if a nursery forces its potted roses into early growth and bloom, care must be taken not to set such plants in the garden until the danger of frost is passed, as the young growth will be very tender and more subject to damage than plants already acclimated to the outdoors.

Planting distances. Plant each rose at least 15 inches from any path or lawn. The following distances between plants are recommended for the indicated varieties.

Miniature—12 inches. Tree, or standard—at least 3 feet. Hybrid tea, floribunda, hybrid perpetual, polyantha, bushes of moderate growth—at least 18 inches; bushes of stronger growth—2 feet or more. Grandiflora—minimum of 2–4 feet. Shrub—5 feet. Climber and rambler—at least 7 feet.

Preparing the Roses Before Planting

When planting, bring the roses to the garden a few at a time. Ideally, a windless, overcast day is the best time to plant. While waiting for such conditions, keep the plants shaded and the roots damp.

If bare-root plants arrive with dry, shriveled stems, immerse them in water completely for a few hours. If they do not plump up, return them to the nursery for replacement.

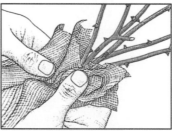
1. To prevent drying prior to planting, keep roots covered.

2. If roots seem dry, make a puddle; swirl roots in it before planting.

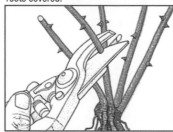
3. Cut back any dead or damaged canes to wood that is firm and live.

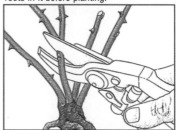
4. Cut back canes on an angle and just above an outward-facing bud.

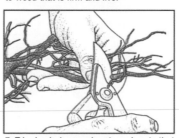
5. Trim back damaged roots and roots that are too long to fit the hole.

6. Cut out any coarse, thickened root that appears to be an old taproot.

'Eye Paint', a floribunda rose,
has dark green, glossy foliage
and single, scentless flowers
in large clusters.

Rosa 'Eye Paint'

Shaping the Hole to Fit the Roots

Dig a hole deep and wide enough to accommodate the roots without crowding them when they are spread out in the natural position in which they have been growing. Some roots grow toward one side.

Instructions often call for planting the roses on a mound of soil with the roots spread down the sides. Unless done carefully, however, this procedure can lead to planting at an improper depth.

Spread out the roots, and comb them with the fingers to keep them from crossing. They should not be coiled around the circumference of the hole.

Lay a stake across the hole to mark the prospective level of the soil in the bed, and use this to establish the correct planting depth.

Planting Bush Roses at the Proper Depth

When deciding how deep to plant a rose, it is important to understand the reasons behind what often appears to be conflicting information. The controversy has to do with the bud union and the distance above or below the ground that it should be set. The bud union is the point at which the hybrid variety has been budded to the rootstock, and this union is essential to the growth of the hybrid. In cold climates it affects the survival of the plant.

The bud union

When the bud union is above the soil level, new canes are produced more freely from the base. This is

DIGGING THE HOLE TO SUIT THE ROOTS

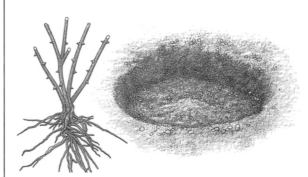

Round hole. If the roots spread out in all directions from the main stem, dig a round hole about 2 ft. in diameter and 1 ft. or more in depth. Spread the planting mixture 1 in. deep in the hole before spreading out the roots.

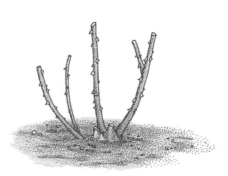

Fan-shaped hole. If roots run in one direction, make a fan-shaped hole (see center illustration, bottom of p. 357). If necessary, slant the hole to accommodate the longest roots, but keep the bud union at the proper depth for your climate.

highly desirable. Therefore, in mild climates roses are always set with the union about an inch above the soil level. In climates where temperatures drop below 20°F for much of the winter, the traditional recommendation has been to set the union 1–2 inches below the soil level to protect it from cold injury. But recently some cold-climate gardeners have found it preferable to set the union above the soil level and then to protect it with a thick mulch in winter.

All roses require firm planting. When the hole is about two-thirds filled, tread the soil around the perimeter of the roots. Then slowly add water to fill the hole, and let it soak in before adding more soil. This helps to eliminate the air pockets. Finish filling the hole, and make a catch basin around the edge of the hole to hold water in the root area.

After watering again, mound 6 inches of soil over the canes for a few weeks to prevent drying. Remove the extra soil before the buds begin to swell in spring.

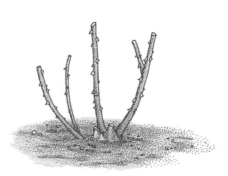

1. Mark the soil level with a cane. Hold the bud union at proper level.

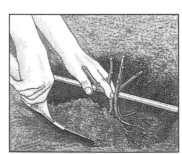

2. Add planting mixture over the roots, fill about two-thirds of hole.

3. Jiggle the plant up and down to fill spaces between roots with soil.

4. Tread the soil and water thoroughly. Fill hole, tread, and water.

Rosa gallica var. *officinalis* (syn. 'Crimson Damask')

Rosa 'Tuscany Superb'

All garden roses stem from the French or apothecary's rose (*Rosa gallica*). 'Crimson Damask' has half-double, 'Tuscany Superb' fully-double blossoms on compact shrubs that grow about 3 ft. tall.

Planting and Staking a Tree (Standard) Rose

Although tree roses are planted in much the same way as others, there are a few special considerations.

Because a standard is quite tall and is supported by a single cane, it must be firmly staked. This is best done at planting time. Use a 1- by 1-inch stake or a strong metal rod or pipe. It should be long enough to extend 2 feet into the ground and several inches into the foliage. If wood is used, sharpen the stake, and paint the underground portion with a wood preservative. Do not use creosote, which is toxic to plants.

After digging, set the stake in the center of the hole. Since the trunk of a standard rose often suffers from sunscald, especially in hot climates, shade it by putting the stake on its south side. Alternatively, the trunk may be wrapped with burlap.

Set the rose close to the stake and as nearly vertical as possible. The bud union on a tree rose is at the top of the stem, so there is no need to worry about how deep to set it. Look at the stem and find the line where the bark changes color. This line should be at ground level when you plant. In cold climates you will need to bury the entire plant over winter to protect the bud union.

Hold, or temporarily tie, the standard firmly in position against the stake while covering the roots. Wiggle the plant slightly to settle it in. Tread the soil over the roots when the hole is half full. Fill the hole with water, and let it soak in. Finish filling the hole, firm the soil again, and water. Form a catch basin with earth mounded around the plant to help hold the water.

The standard rose should be secured to the stake with at least two ties. Place one securely at the top, just beneath the head of the plant, and another midway down the main stem. Do not hesitate to use a third tie if necessary.

Plastic ties are available and convenient to use, but garden twine can also be used if the stem is well wrapped with burlap. (The burlap wrapping is often applied for protection against sun or cold.)

Keep the plant well watered. In cold climates dig up the plant in late autumn, lay horizontally, and cover with soil. Replant in early spring.

Planting Climbers Against a Wall

The basic planting method for climbers is the same as for bush roses. Before training the rose against a wall, stretch plastic-coated wire between two screw eyes, and tighten with a turnbuckle. The wire should be 4–6 inches out from the wall to allow air to circulate behind the stems.

In tying the rose canes to the wire, train the main canes to a horizontal position. Most of the large-flowered climbers produce more blooms when they are trained in this way.

There is usually more deadwood on young climbers than on bush or standard roses. This should be cut back to just above a live bud.

1. Dig hole 12–15 in. wide, and then hammer in stake.

2. Hold plant upright, spread out roots, and partially cover with soil.

3. Half-fill hole with soil, firm, and water. Then fill to ground level.

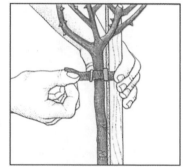

4. Secure standard to stake with several rubber or plastic ties.

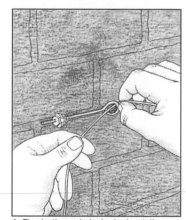

1. Fix plastic-coated wire horizontally on the wall at 15-in. intervals.

2. Plant the rose 12 in. from the wall, with the roots pointing away from it.

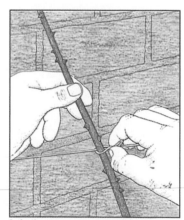

3. As the canes grow, spread them in a fan shape and attach to wires.

The floribunda rose 'Princess of Wales' has pure white, delicately scented blooms. Introduced in 1997, it was named for Princess Diana. 'Sexy Rexy', another fairly recent floribunda rose, has clusters of 3-in. flowers that last well when cut.

Rosa 'Princess of Wales'   *Rosa* 'Sexy Rexy'

Caring for Roses Throughout the Year

How to Identify and Remove Suckers

Always be on the watch for shoots that come from below ground level and from the stems of standard roses. These suckers grow from the rootstock below the point of union and can usually be identified by their leaves and thorns, which are different from those of the top growth. The sucker leaflets are narrower than those of the garden rose, and the thorns are needlelike. It is commonly thought that suckers have seven leaflets on each leaf and that the growth above the point of union has only five leaflets, but this is not always the case.

The surest test is to trace the suspect growth to its point of origin, which will be below the union of rootstock and branches if the growth is a sucker. Wrench the sucker off at its point of origin; do not cut it, because this is merely a form of pruning that will encourage additional suckers to grow.

Encouraging Roses to Produce More Flowers

As soon as hybrid tea blooms wither, cut them off with pruning shears to a point just above a strong shoot or an outward-facing leaf bud. This will encourage a second flowering.

Many rose growers simply cut back to the first leaf with five leaflets. But this may result in the loss of several potential flowering stems.

Toward the end of the season, deadhead more lightly—to the first leaf bud below the flower—as young growth that will not harden before winter should be discouraged.

In fall in cold climates, cut the flower off with a short stem. With floribundas deadheading must be ruthless. There are no leaf buds on the blossom stems; so the whole flower truss must be cut back to the first leaf bud below it. Seed heads should not be allowed to form unless they are wanted for decoration or seeds and, even then, not until the rose is two years old.

Bush roses. Dig away soil, find junction, and wrench sucker off.

Tree roses. Remove all shoots on stem below bud union.

Hybrid tea. Cut just above an outward-facing leaf bud.

Floribunda. Remove the cluster back to first leaf bud.

Encouraging Larger Blooms by Disbudding

If some of the flower buds are removed from hybrid teas, the remaining flowers will grow larger.

As new stems develop on hybrid teas, one or more side buds appear just below the central terminal bud. While they are still tiny, nip off the side buds with your fingers at a point 6 inches below the terminal bud.

Some rose exhibitors remove the larger center buds and the smallest buds from each cluster on floribunda roses to achieve the same results.

For bigger blooms pinch off buds just below the largest one.

When to Water and Spray Roses

The weather and the type of soil dictate when to water. Sandy soils need abundant water. In other kinds most roses, other than newly planted ones, will tolerate a two-week drought.

A soaker hose or some other device that provides water only around the roots is best. Overhead watering can damage roses in full flower.

When the plants are not in bloom, a soaker hose can be used to provide a continuous supply of water. To avoid wasting water, steer clear of a sprinkler with a fine mistlike spray. Do not use a coarse stream of water that will splash soil on the leaves and spread soil-borne diseases.

Keep a careful watch on your roses to identify pests and diseases as soon as they start. Treating the problem early makes it easier to keep the plants healthy. Problems left to multiply can be very difficult to control, and some pests and diseases increase at an alarming rate.

Use a fine mist sprayer: the tank-type pressure sprayer is best. Cover the upper- and lower-leaf surfaces, as well as surrounding soil.

Rosa 'Alchemist'

The climbing rose 'Alchemist' has very fragrant blooms that are paler early in the season. It will grow up to 12 ft. high and has very thorny wood.

A Simple Feeding and Mulching Routine

In the first year after planting, roses should not be fed. In subsequent years feeding can begin as soon as the frost has gone and new growth begins. Additional feedings should be given as one blooming period ends, to stimulate the next one. In cold areas roses should not be fed after August. A mix of blood and bone meal or an organic rose fertilizer should be scratched lightly into the soil around the plants.

As soon as the ground warms up in spring, apply a 2- to 4-inch cover of mulch (water first if the soil is dry) to conserve moisture, improve the soil, and keep weeds down. Well-rotted cow or horse manure is a good mulch and also adds important nutrients, but it contains weed seeds and is scarce.

Good mulches include compost, ground corncobs, shredded leaves, sawdust, salt hay, straw, shredded bark, buckwheat hulls, and cocoa hulls.

Rake the mulch aside when applying fertilizer. Liquid fertilizers can be applied directly through the mulch. Replace mulch annually to minimize pests and diseases.

Winter Protection for Roses

Winter protection greatly extends the range in which roses—particularly hybrid teas, floribundas, and grandifloras—can be grown. The principle is to insulate the crown of a plant to enable buds (which will form the following year's plant) to survive. This is done by mounding up the crown to a depth of 9–12 inches.

The commonest material for mounding is garden soil. It should be taken from a separate location: digging soil from between the plants may damage the surface feeder roots. Leaves or straw, packed into a wire collar, can also be used. It is wise, when using leaves or straw, to set rodent traps.

In Zone 4 or colder, climbing roses should be taken off their trellis each fall, laid on the ground and protected with soil, straw, and wooden boards.

Remember: snow is an excellent insulator. Anything that will cause snow to accumulate on your rose bushes is beneficial.

What Can Go Wrong With Roses

For the best results, roses require regular attention to their needs. If your plants show symptoms that are not described below, consult the section on plant disorders beginning on page 506. Look up control methods on page 542.

SYMPTOMS AND SIGNS	CAUSE	CONTROL
Shoots and flower buds are covered with greenish insects. Severe attacks cause malformation of stems, leaves, and buds.	Aphids	Spray plants with a strong stream of water or apply insecticidal soap.
Leaves are eaten, sometimes also rolled.	Caterpillars and sawfly larvae	Handpick pests. For caterpillars, apply *Bacillus thuringiensis kurstaki*. For sawfly larvae, apply neem.
Leaves have black rounded spots and may fall prematurely.	Black spot fungus	Spray with fungicidal soap or wettable sulfur.

SYMPTOMS AND SIGNS	CAUSE	CONTROL
Leaves and flower buds may be severely distorted. Leaves often have tattered or spotted appearance.	Plant bugs	Spray with summer oil or insecticidal soap.
Flowers are malformed, or buds turn brown and fail to open. Tiny insects scurry among petals.	Thrips	Spray plants with a strong stream of water. Apply *Beauveria bassiana* or spinosad.
Leaves are off-color, often bronzed, with fine silver-white dots. Leaves may be webbed.	Two-spotted mites (red spider mites)	If problem is severe, spray top and bottom of leaves with insecticidal soap weekly.
Knotted galls on roots. Plants are sickly, stunted, off-color.	Root-knot nematodes	Buy plants certified free of nematodes. Do not replant roses in infected soil for 4 yr.
Leaves show pale mottling, may yellow and fall prematurely. Small jumping and flying insects on plant	Leafhoppers	Spray plants with a strong stream of water. Apply *Beauveria bassiana*. Insecticidal soap may provide control.
Stems and crowns are attacked, causing dieback and purplish-black to brown cankers.	Cankers (fungus)	Prune affected stems back to at least 1 in. below any discolored area on stems. Do this after spring growth begins. After each cut, dip knives and pruners in a 1:10 chlorine bleach solution. Spray with lime sulfur.
Plants are attacked at soil line, causing large knotty growths.	Crown galls (Bacteria)	Remove and destroy badly affected plants. Take care not to damage stems when working around plants. Difficult to control.
Leaves and young shoots have whitish coating. They may be distorted.	Powdery mildew (fungus)	Spray with baking soda or fungicidal soap.
Shoots are twisted or malformed; covered with orange powder. Small yellow spots are visible on undersides of leaves, which may fall prematurely.	Rust (primarily on West Coast)	Not always easy to control, but spray with wettable sulfur or fungicidal soap at first sign of attack. Cut out and destroy affected shoots.
Shoot tips are blackened or purplish. Slightly discolored patches may occur on young leaves.	Frost or cold wind	If this happens regularly, make sure final pruning is delayed until spring so that young shoots are produced later.
Leaves yellow and fall early. Flowers are few and short-lived. General growth is thin and poor.	Starvation, drought, or combination of both	Usually occurs when roses are grown in thin, gravelly soil or against walls that block rain. Make sure that soil does not dry out. Mulch annually with well-decayed manure or garden compost, plus rose fertilizer.

Hybrid teas are excellent cut roses with blooms of 4–6 in. in diameter. 'Blessings' has loose double blossoms on strong stems, on an upright plant.

Rosa 'Blessings'

Growing Better Roses by Good Pruning

When to Prune and How to Do It

The best time to prune most roses is at the end of the dormant season in your area, just before new growth begins and as the buds begin to swell. In mild climates this may be as early as December or January; in colder climates it may be as late as May. Wait until you are sure that all danger of hard frost is past, or newly pruned tips may be killed.

This rule does not apply to climbers, ramblers, and weeping standards. Climbers are best given a light pruning when they finish flowering and again in the spring. Ramblers are best pruned after flowering, as are weeping standards (which are ramblers grafted onto tall stems).

Terms used in pruning roses. A stem or branch of the current year's growth is called new wood. Hybrid teas, floribundas, and other modern roses flower on these stems.

"Old wood" is a stem of some previous year's growth. Ramblers and most climbers (except the climbing sports) flower on old wood. The shoots grow one year and bear flowers the next.

An "eye" is a young or incipient growth bud, found in the axil of a leaf. In winter an eye appears as a mere pinhead on a stem, from which a shoot may grow.

There are two types of bud. One is a growth bud (or eye, as above), from which a stem will form. The other is a flower bud.

The shoots by which the main stems of roses extend themselves are known as leaders. "Laterals" are stems that grow from a leader.

A "snag" is a dead stump resulting from a pruning cut made too far above a bud or too far from the junction of one cane with another.

How to make a pruning cut. To make a pruning cut, use strong, sharp pruning shears to cut the stem cleanly, leaving no ragged edges. Cut no more than a quarter inch above

an eye or a growth bud. Angle the cut so that it slopes slightly back and away from the bud.

Correct cut (left); the others are wrong.

The bud should face outward to allow growth to spread from the center and keep the bush uncrowded. This applies to all roses except ramblers and climbers, which must be encouraged to grow along a support, and prostrate types, which are trained along the ground.

To prevent damage, do not cut too close to the bud. Alternatively, if the cut is made too high above the bud, the stem may die back.

If two growth buds develop at the same point after pruning, pinch out the weaker one. This must be done carefully with your thumbnail or the point of a clean, sharp knife.

When removing a complete stem, cut as close as possible to the parent stem with pruning shears; then trim the stump flush with the stem, using a sharp knife.

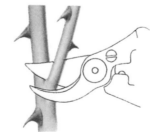

Remove stem flush with adjoining one.

Do not try to cut thick stems with pruning shears. Instead, use long-handled loppers for a good, clean cut. For old hardwood use a narrow-bladed pruning saw. Saw cuts should be pared clean with a knife.

Pruning Newly Planted Roses

Any necessary pruning of bush and tree roses that are planted in spring must be done immediately. If they are planted in fall however, prune them in spring.

The basic steps of pruning (essentially, removing dead or weak wood and stems that cross and rub) apply to all types of roses. Treat each rose according to its type, and prune as recommended.

Newly planted hybrid teas and grandifloras are pruned hard to about 4 inches from the ground.

Floribundas are pruned in the

same way except that they should be cut a little higher—about 5–6 inches from the ground. Cut short varieties, such as 'All Gold', somewhat lower.

Moderately prune newly planted species roses. They bloom on the wood produced in the previous season, and the more stems, the greater the next crop of flowers.

Climbing and rambling roses need moderate cutting back in order to compensate for the inevitable loss of roots when they are transplanted. Both old and modern shrub roses should be treated the same way.

Cut polyanthas back by one-third, and prune miniature roses back to within 2 inches of the ground.

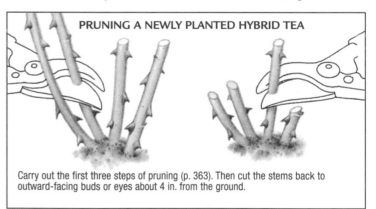

PRUNING A NEWLY PLANTED HYBRID TEA

Carry out the first three steps of pruning (p. 363). Then cut the stems back to outward-facing buds or eyes about 4 in. from the ground.

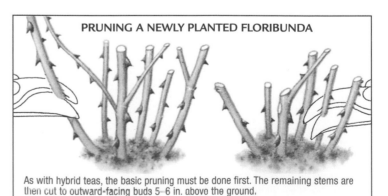

PRUNING A NEWLY PLANTED FLORIBUNDA

As with hybrid teas, the basic pruning must be done first. The remaining stems are then cut to outward-facing buds 5–6 in. above the ground.

Rosa 'Cinderella'

The exquisite white blossoms of the miniature rose 'Cinderella' have a faint tinge of pink. The tiny thornless bush grows only about 1 ft. tall.

How to Prune Bush and Tree Roses

Basically, the object of all rose pruning is to remove deadwood and crossed canes, to shape and thin for better circulation of air, and to encourage the production of the largest or the greatest number of flowers. Suckers—shoots that originate below the bud union and have different foliage—should also be removed whenever seen (p. 358).

Make all pruning cuts just above an outward-facing bud in order that new shoots will grow away from the center of the bush and minimize crowding. Begin with the three basic pruning steps described on the opposite page; then prune each one according to its type.

Hybrid teas, floribundas, and grandifloras should have their tops cut back by about one-third each year in spring, when the buds begin to grow and when there is no danger of hard frost. This is moderate pruning for garden display. Larger, but fewer, flowers of exhibition quality can be produced with harder pruning—as far back as three buds above the base of the stem.

Grandifloras and floribundas often develop new shoots more freely than do hybrid teas. For this reason, somewhat less pruning is needed to stimulate growth.

Hybrid perpetuals bloom best on one-year-old wood. Each spring remove some three- to four-year-old wood at soil level, and trim new growth back to about 3 or 4 feet. Light pruning should be done when flowers are cut for indoor use or when dead flowers are removed.

Miniatures and polyanthas need little pruning beyond trimming their tips back in spring, thinning, and removing weak shoots. In summer miniatures often send up some shoots much taller than the others; thin these back to maintain symmetry.

Tree, or standard, roses, either hybrid teas or floribundas, should be pruned in the same way as bush roses, but more severely. Shape each plant to provide a rounded head.

A bush-type rose, ready for pruning before growth commences in early spring, may have a variety of problems. There may be dead or old and unproductive stems, as well as stems that are diseased. In addition, some canes may cross and rub together, while others may be thin or weak.

The floribunda rose 'Iceberg' may have blossoms until Christmas; they appear in clusters on slender stems. Blossoms of the miniature rose 'Baby Masquerade' turn from yellow through orange to rose, and all colors may be present at the same time.

Rosa 'Iceberg' (syn. *R.* 'Schneewittchen')   *Rosa* 'Baby Masquerade'

THE THREE BASIC PRUNING STEPS

1. Cut back dead stems. Cut back any dead stem to the point where it meets a healthy stem, or, if necessary, cut it all the way back to the union between bud-wood and rootstock. Cut back any part of a stem that is diseased to just above an outward-facing bud on healthy wood.

2. Cut out thin or weak stems. To allow more nourishment to reach vigorous wood, cut out completely all very thin or weak stems. Cut them back to their point of union with a strong stem or with the rootstock. Feeble wood will merely waste the plant's strength and probably produce no flowers.

3. Cut stems that cross or rub. When two stems cross, cut back the weaker of the two to a growth bud below the point where they cross. This prevents overcrowding of new growth and allows air and light to penetrate. With climbers and ramblers this is not practical. Simply train stems so that they do not rub.

HOW MUCH SHOULD YOU PRUNE

Weak varieties and thin shoots should always be cut back harder than vigorous varieties and strong shoots. Prune tree roses harder than bushes, and hybrid teas harder than grandifloras and floribundas.

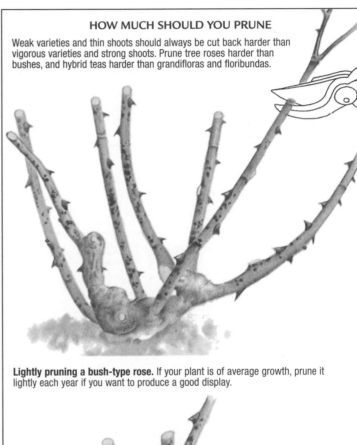

Lightly pruning a bush-type rose. If your plant is of average growth, prune it lightly each year if you want to produce a good display.

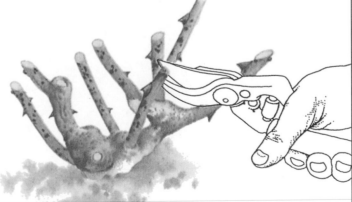

Hard pruning a bush-type rose. If you want to grow large, well-formed roses, though few in number, prune your plant back hard annually.

Both of these climbing roses have lustrous dark green leaves. 'Dortmund' grows upright; 'Bantry Bay' forms numerous side shoots and is exceptionally free-flowering.

Rosa 'Dortmund'

Rosa 'Bantry Bay'

Pruning Climbing Roses

One of the most important points to keep in mind if you have climbing roses is not to delay pruning—it will only become more difficult. Yearly attention pays dividends in improved appearance, better flowering, and easier maintenance.

Some climbers naturally produce more new canes than others and thus require heavier pruning to prevent undisciplined growth. But basically, all dead or weak wood should be removed in spring. In summer, as soon as the flowers have faded, cut back the laterals on which they were borne to within two or three buds of the main canes. Some of the older canes can be cut back to the base each spring on varieties that bloom just once, such as the 'Dr. Van Fleet'. On all other climbers, remove old canes only when necessary to shape the plant or to prevent overcrowding.

New leaders, which are larger in diameter than the laterals, may appear high up on old canes. Cut these back to just above the new growth.

Tips of laterals that are too long can be pruned back at any time.

As new leaders develop, be sure to tie them to the supports. Later on they will be less supple.

SUMMER PRUNING

After a climber has bloomed, trim back the flowered stems to the selected new buds. Do not let seedpods form, as they will deprive the rose of energy, which will be better used to produce new growth and new flowers. Discard prunings; do not add them to the compost pile. The thorns could cause injury.

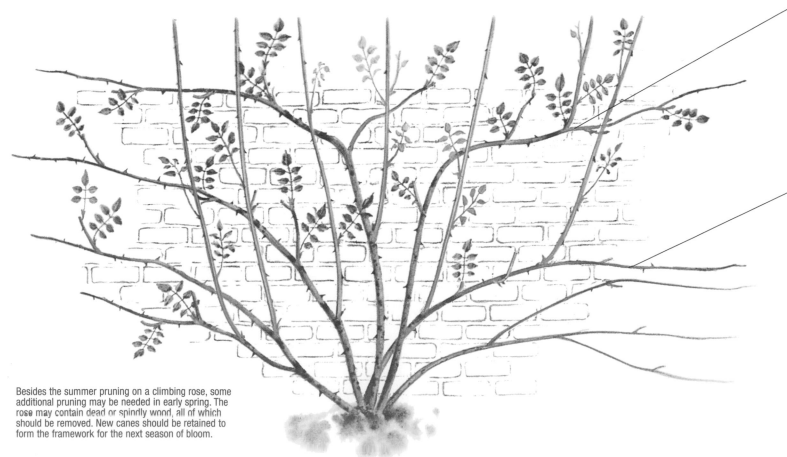

Besides the summer pruning on a climbing rose, some additional pruning may be needed in early spring. The rose may contain dead or spindly wood, all of which should be removed. New canes should be retained to form the framework for the next season of bloom.

Rosa 'Leverkusen'

Rosa 'White Cockade'

Rosa 'Golden Showers'

These three climbing roses all grow 8–10 ft. tall and flower almost continually from summer to fall.

Pruning Ramblers

True ramblers develop long, flexible canes from the base of the plant. These canes do not produce flowers until their second year.

It is best to prune ramblers soon after they have flowered. At that time it is usually much easier to tell which ones are the canes that have just borne the flowers and should therefore be removed.

Most rambler varieties develop new canes in abundance. For each new cane remove an old one at ground level. If too many new ones come up, remove the weaker ones.

Some varieties, however, produce new canes above the base, and old ones can only be cut back to that point. When there is little new basal growth, retain the strongest old canes, and cut the side shoots back to two or three buds in early spring.

Ramblers are best trained on supports that allow the air to move freely. When they are grown against a wall, the reflected heat may invite spider mites and thrips.

Weeping standards, which are ramblers budded on an upright stem, are pruned like ramblers.

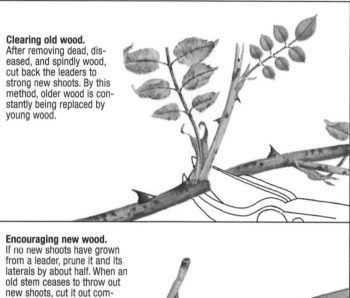

Clearing old wood.
After removing dead, diseased, and spindly wood, cut back the leaders to strong new shoots. By this method, older wood is constantly being replaced by young wood.

Encouraging new wood.
If no new shoots have grown from a leader, prune it and its laterals by about half. When an old stem ceases to throw out new shoots, cut it out completely to encourage new growth from the base.

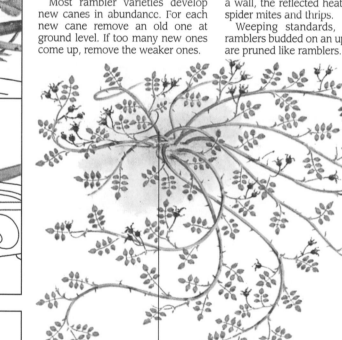

TRAINING A CLIMBING ROSE

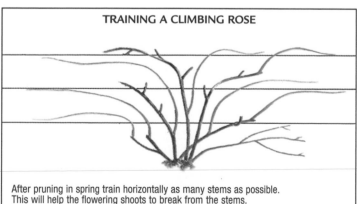

After pruning in spring train horizontally as many stems as possible. This will help the flowering shoots to break from the stems.

Where new growth sprouts liberally from the base of a rambler, cut the old flowered canes right down to the ground. Trim the cuts with a knife and leave no snags.

The hybrid musk rose 'Cornelia' has bronzy foliage and large clusters of flowers. It is particularly floriferous late in the season.

Rosa 'Cornelia'

Dwarf *Rosa* 'Red Ace' ➡

Pruning Shrub Roses—Species and Hybrids

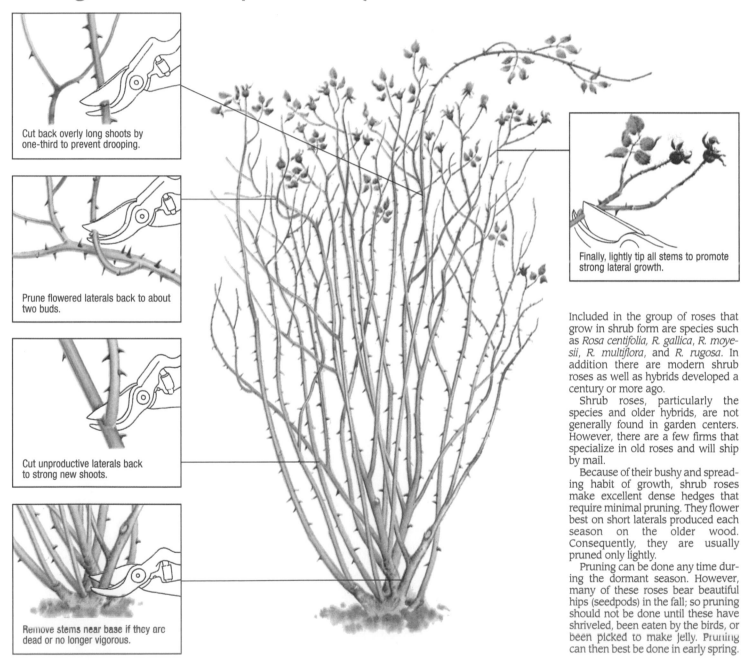

Cut back overly long shoots by one-third to prevent drooping.

Prune flowered laterals back to about two buds.

Cut unproductive laterals back to strong new shoots.

Remove stems near base if they are dead or no longer vigorous.

Finally, lightly tip all stems to promote strong lateral growth.

Included in the group of roses that grow in shrub form are species such as *Rosa centifolia, R. gallica, R. moyesii, R. multiflora,* and *R. rugosa.* In addition there are modern shrub roses as well as hybrids developed a century or more ago.

Shrub roses, particularly the species and older hybrids, are not generally found in garden centers. However, there are a few firms that specialize in old roses and will ship by mail.

Because of their bushy and spreading habit of growth, shrub roses make excellent dense hedges that require minimal pruning. They flower best on short laterals produced each season on the older wood. Consequently, they are usually pruned only lightly.

Pruning can be done any time during the dormant season. However, many of these roses bear beautiful hips (seedpods) in the fall; so pruning should not be done until these have shriveled, been eaten by the birds, or been picked to make jelly. Pruning can then best be done in early spring.

The faintly scented blossoms of 'Mary Rose' have a light lilac tint. This modern shrub rose grows to a height of about 3 ft.

Rosa 'Mary Rose'

Propagating Hybrid Teas by Budding

Preparing Rootstock and Budwood

The best way to propagate hybrid tea roses is by budding—that is, cutting a dormant growth bud, or "eye," from the desired variety and grafting it onto a vigorous rootstock.

Rootstocks can be raised from seeds (a slow process), from cuttings, or bought at nurseries that specialize in roses. Many kinds of roses can be used as rootstocks, including *R. multiflora*, *R. canina* (dog rose), and the climbing 'Dorothy Perkins'.

Before the grafts can be made, rootstocks must be well established. In late autumn or early spring plant the desired number 12 inches apart. Cover the roots and the lowest inch or so of stem with soil; water well.

The next summer cut the budwood (the stem that will provide the bud) from the variety that you want to propagate. Select a strong 12-inch length of stem on which the flowers have just faded. The dormant growth buds lie within the leaf axils.

To make the stem easier to handle, remove all thorns. Next, cut off the leaves, retaining half an inch of leaf stalk. Remove the faded flowers, severing the stem just above a bud or leaf axil. Submerge the budwood in water.

Hold the stem of the rootstock to one side with your foot. Carefully dig out the soil on the other side, making sure that the top roots are completely exposed. Remove any soil from the stem and wipe it dry.

Using a budding knife or other sharp tool, make a T-shaped cut in the bark close to the roots. Cut the top of the T first, making it about half an inch long. Do not cut into the woody tissue below the bark.

With an upward stroke, cut a slightly longer "tail" that meets the top cut. Using the blunt edge of the knife blade (or the quill of the budding knife), gently pry apart the bark and fold it outward. The rootstock is now ready for grafting.

PLANTING THE ROOTSTOCK

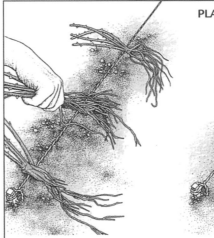

1. In late fall or early spring mark a line; lay rootstocks 12 in. apart.

2. Turn a spade sideways in the soil, making a series of V-shaped holes.

3. Plant rootstocks by sweeping roots into holes. Cover with soil.

HOW TO PREPARE BUDWOOD AND ROOTSTOCK

1. In midsummer cut a 12-in. stem from the plant to be propagated.

2. Remove thorns, or budwood, by pressing thumb sideways.

3. Clip leaves from the budwood, retaining ½ in. of leaf stalk.

4. Push aside the rootstock stem with your foot. Remove soil with a trowel.

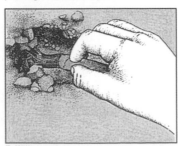

5. With your fingers or a cloth, clean rootstock just above the roots.

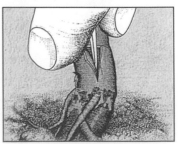

6. Make a T-shaped cut in the bark of the rootstock and open the flaps.

Rosa 'John Cabot'

'John Cabot' is a climbing or pillar type of rose with strong, arching canes that will grow 8–10 ft. tall.

Combining Bud and Rootstock

After preparing the rootstock, remove the budwood from the water. Then slice out one of the dormant growth buds.

To do this, begin the cut half an inch above the bud. Draw the blade behind the bud, coming out half an inch below. Use a shallow scooping motion, so that a sliver of wood behind the bark is also removed. The piece produced is called the shield.

Hold the shield with one hand, and peel back the strip of bark until the sliver of wood is exposed. Hold the sliver between your thumb and index finger. With a slight twist, ease it out smoothly from the bark and then discard the bark. If the sliver of wood has been satisfactorily removed, the dormant bud will be visible as a tiny

bump on the inner side of the remaining piece of shield.

Hold the shield by the stump of leafstalk, and slide it into the T cut on the rootstock. Trim off any portion of the shield that protrudes above the top of the cut. Close the flaps around the shield.

With damp raffia, soft twine, or budding rubber (which can be purchased from horticultural supply houses), tie the insert in place firmly but not too tightly. Make two turns below the stub of the leafstalk and three turns above. Do not cover the bud. Carefully replace the soil around the rootstock until the soil is level with the base of the grafted bud.

Inspect the bud several weeks after grafting. If it is plump and green, budding has been successful, and the twine can be removed. (Budding rubber need not be removed.) If the bud

has shriveled, insert and tie a second shield in a fresh T cut made on the same rootstock.

Winter treatment for budded plants is the same as for other roses, with one exception: late in the season all of the plant above the graft should be cut off.

Generally, a bud will not grow until the first spring after grafting. When the new growth is several inches long, pinch it back to two buds above the grafting point. This will encourage growth. In autumn transplant to a permanent site.

Buds can be grafted onto the main stems of established rose plants, rather than onto rootstocks. To make a graft onto a plant growing in a hedge, insert buds in the upper sides of the young side shoots, as close to the main stem as possible. Make two or three grafts on each brier.

BUDDING A STANDARD

To make a standard (tree) rose, grow a rootstock until it reaches the desired height. In summer, bud onto the main stem or, preferably, onto the upper surfaces of three shoots at the top.

GRAFTING THE BUD ONTO THE ROOTSTOCK

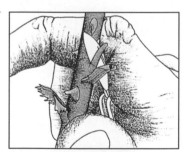

1. Scoop a bud ("eye") from budwood, cutting ½ in. above and below.

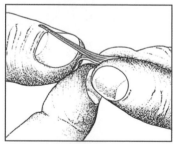

2. Peel and retain the bark from the piece of budwood (shield).

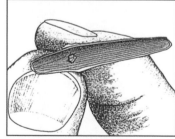

3. The growth bud is visible as a small bump on inside of the shield.

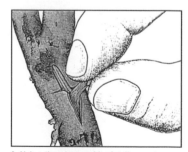

4. Using the stump of leafstalk as a handle, slide the shield into the T cut.

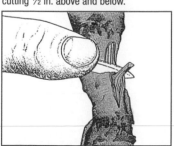

5. Carefully cut off the upper end of the shield and close the bark flaps.

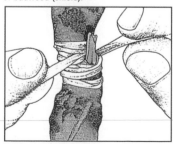

6. Using raffia or twine, keep shield tied to stem for several weeks.

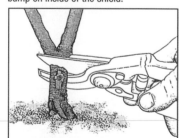

7. In late winter clip the top growth (above the bud) from the rootstock.

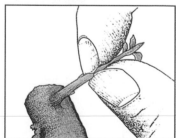

8. When new growth is 3–4 in. long, pinch it back above the second bud.

RHODODENDRONS AND AZALEAS

The vivid displays produced by rhododendrons and azaleas can last from spring into summer. There are plants to fit any size garden, but the soil must be right.

Where they can be grown, rhododendrons and azaleas make excellent additions to the home landscape. Ranging from matlike dwarf shrubs no more than a few inches high to trees more than 40 feet tall, these plants offer a remarkable variety of sizes and shapes.

Most rhododendrons have magnificent foliage, and the flowers of many varieties are among the most beautiful in the world of shrubs. Flower colors are white, lavender, violet, purple, pink, crimson, scarlet, orange, and yellow. Varying in size from ¾ to 6 inches wide and from ¾ to 4 inches long, flowers can be tubular, star-, funnel- or bowl-shaped, and bell-like. They are usually produced in rounded trusses with as many as 15 individual blossoms on each one.

Rhododendrons and azaleas grow beautifully in dappled sunlight or partial shade and in moist, acid soil. They also do quite well in full sunlight, although flowers will last longer with some shade. They will not survive in alkaline soil or in hot, dry situations.

Rhododendrons and azaleas have a remarkable range of hardiness. Gardeners in all but the coldest climates can enjoy at least a few of these attractive shrubs.

The word "rhododendron" is derived from the Greek words *rhodon* ("rose") and *dendron* ("tree"). When the traditional large-leaved rhododendrons are in bloom, they fully live up to the promise of their name.

The first species made available for garden use, in the mid-1600's, was *Rhododendron hirsutum*, native to the mountains of Europe. In 1753 the Swedish botanist Linnaeus officially established and named the genus *Rhododendron*. At the same time he created the separate genus *Azalea*. Then, in the 19th century, another botanist, George Don, discovered that there was little botanical difference between the two, and they were both classified as the genus *Rhododendron*, which they remain to this day.

Gardeners, however, still talk of rhododendrons and azaleas as separate kinds of plants, and they are so identified in nurseries and catalogs. There are deciduous and evergreen species of both kinds. The evergreens are the most popular, but there is an increasing interest in deciduous azaleas. Few deciduous rhododendrons are grown.

Rhododendrons occur in the wild all over the world. Most hybrids have been developed from species native to Burma, China, and northern India. Many of these were crossed with native North American species, particularly *R. catawbiense*, which grows wild in the mountains of the southern United States.

The varieties developed from these crosses are remarkably hardy. Most *R. catawbiense* hybrids will survive temperatures as low as -25°F. The flower buds, however, may be killed at -13°F.

Since the flowers are the major glory of the rhododendron, the degree of bud hardiness is a critical factor. The plants themselves will survive temperatures a few degrees lower. This is a valuable safety margin for the harder-than-average winters that come along every 10 years or so in most cold climates.

The more resistant a rhododendron is to cold weather, the more resistant it will also be to heat. Therefore, to grow rhododendrons in a warmer climate than is usually recommended, it is best to choose the hardiest varieties.

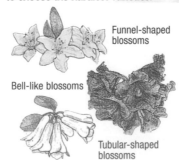

Funnel-shaped blossoms

Bell-like blossoms

Tubular-shaped blossoms

Rhododendron rubiginosum grows up to 10 ft. tall. The hybrids 'Scintillation' and 'Susan' are of medium height and spread.

Rhododendron rubiginosum   Rhododendron 'Scintillation'   Rhododendron 'Susan'

Growing Healthy Rhododendrons and Azaleas

All rhododendrons must have a well-drained soil that is rich in humus and definitely on the acid side. A pH of 4.5–5.5 is best. (Neutral is 7. For more information on acid-alkaline balance and how to control it, see p. 498.)

Azaleas are more adaptable than rhododendrons. The deciduous varieties do well in soils with a pH below 4 and as high as 6. The optimum for evergreen azaleas is about pH 5.

The soil must contain sufficient humus to hold moisture long enough for the roots to take it up. But the soil should not be soggy, or roots will die. To test drainage, dig a hole about 18 inches deep, and fill it with water. If it takes more than 10 or 15 minutes to soak in, there is not sufficient drainage.

Sometimes drainage in a planting hole can be improved by breaking the ground to a greater depth. If this does not work, spade up an area the size of the root ball, and put the plant on the surface. Then mound up around the root ball with a soil mixture that has the necessary humus and acidity. You may need three or four wheelbarrows of soil to cover the root area with a gently sloping mound that will not wash away.

These plants also lend themselves to being grown in raised beds and large containers, where the structure of the soil and the pH can be precisely controlled.

All rhododendrons and azaleas should be mulched with coarse organic material immediately after planting. The mulch should be heavy enough to stay in place and open enough to admit air and water. Wood or bark chips, pine needles, salt hay, or oak leaves are excellent. Peat moss is not; when it dries, it becomes almost impervious to water and can be blown away.

When a plant is firmly set in the planting hole, fill the hole with garden soil in the recommended pH range. Mix some humus in with the soil you are adding—about 10 percent by volume is recommended.

The humus can be peat moss, compost, rotted sawdust, or similar material available locally. The shrub should be planted at the same depth at which it grew in the nursery (you will see the soil line on the trunk).

In setting out plants that were growing in containers in a nursery, it is essential to break up the root ball before planting. The shape of the soil around the roots, as formed by the containers, must be thoroughly broken, and the outer roots should be well loosened.

If this is not done, the feeder roots may never grow out into the surrounding soil; the plant will become root-bound and die.

As for fertilizer, the common practice of putting it directly in the bottom of a planting hole can be fatal to rhododendrons and azaleas. Always bear in mind that these plants should be fertilized only moderately. Rhododendrons and azaleas respond best to moderation in all aspects of cultivation: moderate light, moderate water, and moderate pruning.

During planting, it is safe to add bone meal, but no more than one handful for each plant. Mix it thoroughly with the soil in the top 9–12 inches of the hole, which is where most of the roots will grow.

After the plant is well rooted, fertilize once early each spring and again in midfall. Scatter no more than one handful of a complete organic fertilizer evenly over the root area of each plant, and water it in. As a general rule, give rhododendrons and azaleas only one-fourth to one-half the amount of any fertilizer recommended for shrubs.

If you prefer to use a soluble fertilizer, make a manure tea by soaking a bag of manure in water. Dilute by ²⁄₃ and water into the soil around each plant. The feeding can be repeated every two or three weeks during the season of active growth.

Use an acidic fertilizer, such as cottonseed meal. Some organic fertilizers are alkaline.

Growing Rhododendrons in Alkaline Soil

Although you may live where the soil and water are alkaline, you can grow rhododendrons by providing the acid conditions they require. Plant them in a raised bed at least 18 inches high, containing a specially prepared growing medium.

The sides of the raised bed should be made of masonry or rot-resistant wood, such as redwood, cedar, or cypress. Other woods should first be treated with a nontoxic preservative.

The growing medium should have a pH of 5, and certainly no higher than 5.5. It can be made up of peat moss, leaf mold, composted oak leaves, well-rotted wood chips, or rotted sawdust, plus some of your best topsoil—about 10 percent by volume. Mix thoroughly.

Check the pH level with a reliable soil-test kit. If the pH is too high, acidity can be increased by adding elemental sulfur (see p. 498). Spread about half a cup over a circle 4 feet in diameter. Repeat six months later as needed.

REMOVING DEAD FLOWERS

To get the maximum number of flowers each year, carefully break off flower heads entirely as soon as rhododendrons have finished blooming.

Helping Rhododendrons to Flower

It is not unusual to buy a heavily budded rhododendron in early spring, to plant it and enjoy a magnificent show of flowers, only to be disappointed the following year, when you discover that few if any flower buds have developed.

In most such cases the problem is too little light. Although these plants will grow well in dappled shade, and even survive in deep shade, unless they get at least three or four hours of high-intensity light every day, they will not set many flower buds.

Flower production is also affected by feeding. Phosphate in particular

increases the number of buds. For plants 3–5 feet across, you can provide a phosphate boost by sprinkling four to six handfuls of bone meal around each plant, and scratch it lightly into the soil. It may take a year or so for the effects to show.

This topdressing can be applied for two or three successive years. Giving phosphate at this rate is safe; the same amount of a complete fertilizer would be harmful.

Some plants will establish a pattern of blooming heavily only every second year. This rhythm of alternate flowering can be broken by removing some of the buds after they are fully formed in the fall if they seem to be too crowded.

Rhododendron 'Moerheim'

Rhododendron luteum

'Moerheim', a small-leafed dwarf rhodo-dendron, has a rich display of blossoms in spring. The strong-scented blossoms of azalea (*Rhododendron luteum*) appear from late spring to early summer.

Choosing Varieties for Your Area

There are hundreds of species and varieties of rhododendron, and if you live in a region with cool but not too cold winters, you have a wide choice. Nurseries that specialize in rhodo-dendrons and azaleas will advise you on the best varieties for your area. Or you can contact the American Rhododendron Society at www.rhododendron.org for advice, information, and photographs.

The harsher your winter, the more restricted the list of suitable varieties, but even in Zone 4 there are varieties that will survive and bloom reliably.

In general, deciduous azaleas are a better choice for northern gardens.

Because they lose their foliage each year, they do not have the winter-damaged leaves that detract from the appearance of the evergreens.

The Northern Lights Series of azal-eas, developed at the University of Minnesota, are becoming increas-ingly popular. Available in a range of pastel colors, such as 'Orchid Lights', they are well adapted to cold winters.

Some small-flowered evergreens such as 'P.J.M.' (mauve) and 'Olga Mezitt' (pink) are also very tough and have survived –40°F with little dam-age. New large-flowered introduc-tions from Finland are also associated with varieties based on the native *R. catawbiense*. 'Hellikki' (dark red) and 'Peter Tigerstedt' (white flecked with purple) are worth searching for.

1. To multiply growth, remove leaves along 10 in. of lower branches in fall.

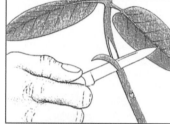

2. Release sap by making a small cut in the bark close to the branch tip.

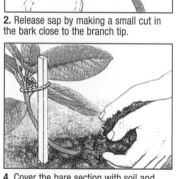

3. Peg the bare section into a mulch-filled groove in the soil.

4. Cover the bare section with soil and stake the branch tip as shown.

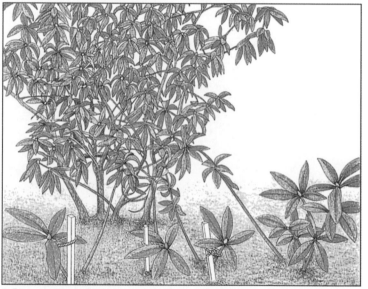

5. Because of its shallow rooting requirements, rhododendron growth can be expanded all around the tree simply by following the steps outlined here.

Rhododendron and Azalea Propagation

Once established, rhododendron and azalea plants need little attention other than watering during droughts. They are easily propagated and two popular methods are shown above and at right. Seeds germinate readily, especially when fresh in the fall.

Store seed in a closed container in the refrigerator for spring sowing. Sow onto an acidic mix, cover very thinly and germinate at 55°–65°F. Transplant seedlings when they have four true leaves and grow on. Plants raised from seeds may take four or five years to flower. Remember that seeds from garden hybrids will not come true and most seedlings will be inferior when they flower.

Commercially, many rhododen-drons are now raised by tissue cul-ture under laboratory conditions. The new plant is grown from a few cells (from a growing tip). Many more plants can be produced than by cut-tings or grafting and they can be grown to salable size faster than by conventional methods.

Rhododendrons can also be rooted in late summer from 6-in.-long cuttings. Put a small cut in the bark, and cut in half all leaves longer than 7 in.

Many azaleas shed their leaves in winter, but the Japanese or Kurume azaleas are evergreen. *Rhododendron* 'Hino-crimson', whose glowing blossoms appear from late spring to early summer, belongs to this group.

Rhododendron 'Hino-crimson'

How and When to Prune Rhododendrons

Rhododendrons seldom need pruning except to control their size and shape. Any required pruning should be done as soon as they have finished blooming. The plant grows vigorously at that time, and it is wise to keep this energy from going into unwanted growth. Simply cut the branches to the shape and size you want, making clean cuts with sharp tools. The pruning of both young and old plants is illustrated below.

If a plant outgrows its site, it can be relocated. Because of their relatively shallow and fibrous root systems, rhododendrons are among the easiest of all plants to move.

SPINDLY YOUNG PLANTS

To encourage growth, prune stems in spring. Cut just above the small green buds.

STRAGGLY OLD SHRUBS

For renewal, in early spring use a saw to cut back old shrubs to within 3 ft. of the ground.

Caring for Greenhouse-Grown Azaleas

The greenhouse-grown azaleas that florists sell in full bloom for Easter and other occasions can be planted outside, where they will continue to grow and flower each year if given proper care. When they have finished flowering indoors and the danger of frost is past, plant them in the garden. Care for them as you would any rhododendron.

Break up the sides of the root ball thoroughly, or the roots may never expand beyond the size and shape of the container and the plant will fade away after a year or two.

In frost-free climates most azaleas can be left outside all year. But in the North, where it freezes in winter, it is necessary to dig the plants up in autumn and pot them. Keep them in a light, cool, frost-free place. Flower buds are formed during the summer, to bloom next spring, so keep them well-watered or the buds will shrivel. In spring plant the azaleas in the garden as soon as there is no further danger of frost.

What Can Go Wrong With Rhododendrons and Azaleas

Some of the problems that are likely to occur in growing rhododendrons and azaleas are discussed in the chart below. If your plant should show symptoms that are not described in this chart, turn to the full-color identification section on plant disorders and diseases beginning on page 506. This illustrates symptoms that may occur on different parts of a plant—leaves, flowers, stems, or roots. To find more information on controls, turn to page 542.

SYMPTOMS AND SIGNS	CAUSE	CONTROL
Lace bug damage appears in early to midsummer and can be identified by tarry spots on undersides of leaf. Leaves lose luster and turn grayish green.	Lace bugs	Spray with insecticidal soap or pyrethrin at first sign of attack. Be certain to spray leaf undersides. Repeat three times at 10-day intervals.
Symptoms of mite damage occur primarily during hot summer and on evergreen azaleas.	Red spider mites	Spray with insecticidal soap or neem. To prevent infestation, spray leaves regularly with water.
Older branches at center of shrubs may have small holes. Leaves become pale then yellowish and wilt.	Rhododendron borers	Prune out infected branches below holes. Water and fertilize to encourage vigorous growth.
Leaf edges have semi-circular notches. Leaves may wilt, indicating that weevil larvae are feeding on roots or main stem. If stem is girdled, plant will die.	Vine weevils	Resistant to most controls. Inspect new plants carefully to avoid introducing them. Cover soil with plastic, shake adults off shrubs and tread on them. Parasitic nematodes are available commercially.
Leaves have round, dark red or brown spots late in summer.	Leafspot (fungus)	Spray with a copper fungicide before spots appear in late spring. Later applications are not effective.
Tiny spots on undersides of petals enlarge and bleach out. Flowers wilt.	Petal blight (fungus)	Spray with fungicidal soap every 5 days during bloom season. Rake up and destroy infected leaves.
Young shoots on single branch wilt in midsummer, or entire shrub may wilt. Diseased branches show brown stain under bark just below soil level.	Wilt (fungus)	Remove and destroy diseased branches; in severe cases destroy entire shrub. Mulch to avoid splashing spores from soil surface onto shrub.
Leaves show yellow patches between veins or are flushed all over; may wither.	Chlorosis	Treat with chelated compounds (sequestered iron), and mulch with pine needles.

HEATHERS AND HEATHS

Heathers and heaths offer a tremendous range of foliage, flower colors, and blooming times. Where winters are not too severe, you can have them in flower almost year-round.

The importance of heathers and heaths has been recognized for centuries. As early as 1401 there were laws in Britain governing their burning. In the Scottish Highlands they were used for building materials, brooms, and beds, and there were even recipes for heather ale. Heaths and heathers also provided grazing for sheep and deer. Heather (*Calluna*), the superior grazing, was called "he heath," while the inferior *Erica* was known as "she heath."

Even today, heathers have an economic use. Brier pipes are not made from rose briers, as you might suppose, but from the roots of a species of heath (*E. arborea*). The misnaming comes from a poor translation of *bruyère*, the French common name for this shrub.

Strictly speaking, heather is the common name for the genus *Calluna*, which has a single species, *C. vulgaris*. Heath is the name given to the genus *Erica*, which has many species, and to *Daboecia*. In practice, the two common names are often used indiscriminately.

No matter what you call them, their most important use today is as garden plants, and the many named forms available attest to their popularity. Most of these evergreen shrubs require acidic soil, while the more lime-tolerant winter-flowering heaths *E. carnea*, *E. darleyensis*, and *E. erigena* are the best choice if your garden is not acidic.

Heathers and heaths vary greatly in size from low, prostrate plants to those almost 20 feet tall—and some tender species from South Africa can get even larger. Foliage is also variable and ranges from a bright golden yellow through myriad shades of green to orange and dull reddish purple. Some varieties remain a constant color all year, while others change with the seasons. Tiny bell flowers range from white, through shades of pink and lilac, to red, crimson, and almost purple. Although

attractive individually, it is the massed effect of hundreds of blooms clothing each branch that is responsible for the popularity of these plants.

Where summers are not too hot, heaths and heathers combine well with other acid-lovers such as rhododendron, azalea, pieris, and mountain laurel. Wherever they can be combined, use them to give floral interest when the other shrubs are finished blooming.

Heathers and heaths are also used in beds on their own—with the occasional upright conifer to give height—where the tapestry effect of their foliage can be seen to best advantage. Plant them in groups of three to five of the same variety for best display. Pay careful attention to their blooming times, and foliage and flower colors, especially varieties that change through the seasons.

If your basic soil is alkaline, you can still grow heaths and heathers. Because their root systems are relatively shallow, even a low raised bed filled with an acidic soil mix will provide good growing conditions. Top dressing with oak leaves or pine needles, and the occasional sprinkle of powdered sulfur, will keep the bed acidic.

Best Varieties of Heathers and Heaths

Calluna. Heathers are dwarf evergreen shrubs with small, green, scalelike leaves that become tinged with purple in cold weather, and bloom from mid to late summer. Also known as ling, they are mostly low-spreading plants, although with about 500 named varieties, there is a range of heights, spreads, and colors.

Grow them in an open location, in full sun, and a well-drained, humus-rich, acid soil. With reliable snow cover, they are hardy to Zone 3, but where midwinter thaws can be expected, give a mulch of straw or salt hay and cover with pine boughs.

Daboecia. The Irish heath (*D. cantabrica*) is native from the West of Ireland to the Azores and is a prostrate to erect shrub, growing 6–7 feet high and wide, with lance-shaped, mid to dark green leaves. Flowers—from white, through pink, to dark purple—appear from summer to fall. Even with good snow cover, it will only survive where winter temperatures do not fall below –5°F.

Erica. There are about 700 species of heath, a great number from South Africa that are hardy only where winters are frost-free. The hardy species are a mainstay in more northern gardens where, by growing named forms of the different species, they will provide flowers for many months.

Winter-flowering heaths. These are probably the most popular of the heaths because of the bright display they give during winter's drab days.

E. carnea (winter heath): Low-spreading shrubs growing 6–8 inches tall, with dark green leaves that often turn a coppery color with cold weather. Many varieties have been selected for their colorful foliage of yellow, lime, orange, or copper, others for their flowers, which are carried on one side of the stems and are mostly in shades from white to purplish pink. It is hardy to –25°F, and probably colder under a reliable snow cover.

E. darleyensis (Darley Dale heath): A hybrid that blooms later and grows taller than the winter heath, and is therefore more subject to winter injury. New foliage is often a different color at first and the flowers are white to rose-pink to red. Hardy to –15°F.

E. erigena (Irish heath): The most tender of the winter-flowering species (hardy to 0°F), this upright shrub can reach 8 feet in height and 3 feet across, with brittle branches. Foliage is dark green to yellow, and the honey-scented flowers are pink.

Spring-flowering heaths. *E. arborea* (tree heath): A tall heath that can reach 20 feet in ideal conditions. Leaves are dark green and the flowers are a grayish white. The variety *alpina* is smaller (6 feet) and has dense spikes of white blooms. These are hardy to only about –15°F.

Summer- to fall-flowering heaths. *E. ciliaris* (Dorset heath): A spreading shrub that grows about 2 feet tall and wide. Foliage is gray-green and the pink to white flowers, which hardly open, resemble tiny elongated eggs. It is hardy to about –5°F.

E. cinerea (bell heath or bell heather): One of the most widely grown heaths with a large number of named forms that differ in flower and foliage color. It forms a compact shrub up to 24 inches high with very dark green foliage (yellow in some varieties), and has white, pink, or bright red flowers from early summer into fall. Hardy to about –15°F.

E. tetralix (cross-leaved heath): A distinctive heath with woolly, grayish foliage arranged in a cross. Flowers are white to pink, and the old flowers last over winter for added effect. Hardy to –30°F.

E. vagans (Cornish heath): This spreading shrub grows to 2½ feet, with bright green new growth, darkening later. Flowers are white to mauve in summer. Hardy to –25°F.

There are named forms of all of these species that may have colored foliage, brighter flowers, or blooms with more than one color.

Erica carnea 'Praecox Rubra'

Erica carnea 'Golden Starlet'

Winter heather (*Erica carnea*) owes its name to its early blossoms, which begin appearing in February. Some varieties, however, are grown more for their bright foliage.

Cultivating Healthy Plants

Well-drained but moisture-retentive soil is essential, although the Irish and cross-leaved heaths will grow happily in very wet conditions. Peaty and sandy soils are best, but heavy clay is acceptable providing washed river sand or fine gravel is added. Cultivate the soil to a full-spade depth, removing all perennial weeds, and work in a 3- to 4-inch layer of well-rotted manure, garden compost, or moist peat moss.

With a home soil-test kit, check the pH of your soil. The ideal range is 4.5 to 5.0. If it is higher than 6.0, add powdered sulfur at a rate of one-half cup per square yard. This will lower the pH by about one point, but the amount needed depends on the soil type, so wait a few days and test again. If your basic garden soil is alkaline, grow heaths and heathers in a raised bed, otherwise the ground water will neutralize the acidity you add.

Site them in full sun in an exposed location—remember, these are native to windswept moorlands. At the northern limits of their range, a winter windbreak of snow fence or burlap will protect them from desiccation and help collect snow, as will evergreen boughs laid over them. Spring or fall planting is best but, apart from periods of high summer heat, large, pot-grown plants can be planted any time the soil is workable.

Young plants are potted into a very peaty mixture that may fall off the roots easily, so take care when removing them from pots. Dig a hole deep enough to take the root ball and plant in the normal way, firming the soil around the plant to leave a slight depression that will collect water. Water well after planting. Keep plants watered for the first year, after which they only need watering during prolonged drought.

The distance between plants depends on what species you are growing, and can be as close as 10 inches for some varieties of the winter heath, or even up to 3 feet for tree heaths.

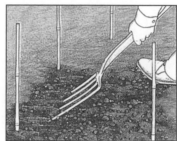
1. Prepare the bed, dig in moist peat moss, and check the pH.

2. Remove pots carefully so you do not break the root ball.

3. Plant at the same level it was in the pot, and firm into place.

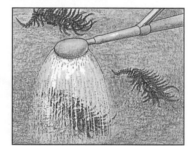
4. Water well after planting and for the first summer.

Trimming Fosters Flowers

If not trimmed after a few years, heathers and heaths will become straggly and produce fewer flowers. If allowed to continue, most species cannot be cut back hard to rejuvenate them as they will not shoot from old wood, although *Erica arborea, E. vagans,* and *Daboecia* will break out again. Snipping off old flowering shoots with scissors or pruning shears makes plants produce more side shoots, which in turn will have more flowers.

Trim winter- and spring-flowering varieties after flowering. Those that flower in summer, where the old flowers hang on over winter, are done in early spring. Varieties grown mainly for the colorful new spring foliage should be trimmed in late summer. Heathers (*Calluna*) are best trimmed every spring.

TRIMMING OLD FLOWERS

Trimming off old flower spikes helps keep the plants compact and improves blooming.

What Can Go Wrong With Heathers

If your plants show symptoms that are not described here, turn to the full-color identification drawings of pests and diseases on page 506. For more information and a list of other organic controls, turn to the section beginning on page 542.

SYMPTOMS AND SIGNS	CAUSE	CONTROL
Flowers and new foliage eaten; large shiny insects present.	Japanese beetles	Handpick or spray with insecticidal soap or neem.
Growth stunted, stems have a corky appearance.	Scale insects	Prune out infected branches if few; spray with summer oil in June to kill young stage.
Leaves become silvery; shoots wilt and eventually die.	Wilt (fungus)	Remove infected plants and surrounding soil and dispose of them. Improving the drainage may help.
Green foliage becomes yellowish in summer.	Iron chlorosis (high pH)	Spray plants with chelated iron and lower soil pH by adding sulfur.

The bell heath (*Erica cinerea*), and the cross-leaved heath (*E. tetralix*) are both summer blooming. The cross-leaved heath is prized for its silvery foliage, but the bell heath has more flowers.

Erica tetralix 'Alba Mollis'

Erica cinerea 'Steven Davis'

New Plants by Layering

Once plants are three or four years old and becoming large and bushy, it is easy to get more plants from each one by layering. This is not a commercial way of propagating, as the number of new plants is small, but it is well suited to the home garden.

In spring, decide which branches can easily be bent into contact with the soil. Then, using a sharp knife or one-sided razor blade, either make a slanting cut partway through the piece of branch that will touch the soil, or remove a section of the bark in that place. Dust the wound with hardwood rooting powder and gently push it into close contact with the soil. Keep the soil moist all summer.

By fall, the wound should have produced roots, but wait until the following spring before cutting the new plant off, digging it up, and replanting somewhere else. If the plant is upright, wound several stems close to their base and mound soil up over the lower part of the plant.

1. In spring decide which branches can easily be bent to touch the soil.

2. Cover the wound with soil and keep in place with a stone.

New Plants by Cuttings

Most heathers and heaths root easily from cuttings. This is a good way to grow a lot of a single variety for later planting, or to grow a few each of several new varieties. (Cuttings seem to root better when there are several in a pot, rather than just two or three.) The best time to root cuttings is in July and August, once the new season's growth has started to harden, or in November and December.

(Heaths and heathers do not root well indoors from softwood cuttings taken in spring.)

If using old pots, sterilize in a 10 percent bleach solution. Rinse well to remove all traces of bleach. Cuttings should be 1–1½ inches apart. Mix a batch of rooting medium using 1 part peat moss and 1 part perlite. You can substitute washed sand for perlite, but it is not as effective. Fill pots level with the medium and firm gently with the base of another pot.

Cuttings should be 2½–3 inches long, but even 1½-inch cuttings will root well. Take them from the current season's growth and remove 1 inch of leaves from the lower half. Swish the cuttings in a bath of fungicidal soap to kill any fungal spores. Shake off excess moisture and dip the bottom of the cuttings in semi-hardwood rooting hormone. They will root without it but will take longer. Using a pencil, make holes on the rooting medium and insert the cut-

tings, firming each one into place. Water, allow to drain, and cover with a plastic bag. Keep on a bright windowsill, but out of direct sunlight, or place about 6 inches from fluorescent lights. Rooting will take place in one to three months. Once new growth is showing, gradually remove the plastic bag. Pot the rooted cuttings into individual small pots with a peaty soil mix and grow on a sunny windowsill; east- or west-facing is best. Harden off before planting out.

1. In late summer select cuttings from current growth.

2. Remove all needles from the bottom inch of the cutting.

5. When well rooted, carefully remove the cuttings one by one.

3. Plant ½ in. deep in a mix of peat moss and perlite.

6. Pot the cuttings into individual small pots of peaty soil.

4. A plastic tent will speed growth, but remove when growth begins.

7. Firm soil around the cutting, water, and grow in a sunny window.

*L*imited space should not be a deterrent to growing your own bounty of fruits. Some tree fruits, such as apples, peaches, and cherries can be trained against a wall. Plums, like 'Earliblue' shown here, are best grown as a pyramid. Bush fruits, currants, cane fruits, berries, and other tasty delights can find a home in most home gardens.

FRUITS

Even a small garden has room for fruit—not only bushes, canes, and vines, but also fruit trees. These may be dwarf forms on a restricted rootstock, or full sized trees grown in place of shade trees.

Most fruits fall into two main categories—small fruits and tree fruits. Among the small fruits are the bush fruits, such as blueberries, currants, and gooseberries; cane fruits like raspberries, loganberries, and blackberries; vine fruits like grapes, and ground fruits such as strawberries. Tree fruits comprise the larger growing species, including apples, pears, cherries, avocados, citrus, and peaches. All of these respond well to organic growing methods and give the grower the satisfaction of producing a crop free from chemical residues.

Using Fruit in the Garden

Fruit bushes and trees do not have to be kept isolated in a special part of the garden, although on a large property, this can be a good idea since it enables you to plant a ground cover, such as white clover, between the trees and bushes to attract the many small predatory insects that help keep pests under control. In a smaller garden the fruits can be integrated into the general planting plan.

Bush fruits can be planted in a mixed border—remember that you will need to work all around the bush at picking time so don't plant too close to other flowers or shrubs. Low bushes, like some varieties of blueberries, can make a dwarf or informal hedge, if the soil is acidic. But don't use gooseberries for this, they are too spiny. Strawberries can be grown as an edging along the front of a border where they are easy to pick.

Cane fruits are normally grown in a row, and thus they can be used to make a divider part-way across a narrow garden, screening the rest of the garden from view and making it appear shorter. They can also be trained against a fence and can make even a chain-link fence appear attractive.

Grape vines can also be trained against a fence, but crop almost as well, and are more decorative, when trained over an arbor or archway. Just be aware that a vine laden with ripe bunches of grapes is quite heavy and needs a strong structure to support its weight.

Tree fruits can be planted in place of ornamental or shade trees. There is such a range of eventual heights in fruit trees that one can be found to suit almost every location. For example, the eventual size of apple trees depends on the rootstock they are grafted onto. Some of the dwarfing stocks give mature trees that are only 6-10 feet in height and spread, while the semi-dwarfing stocks will produce trees 15-20 feet tall; much smaller than trees growing on non-dwarfing stocks.

Before You Plant

Bush, cane, and tree fruits are a long-term project, the gardener can expect to be picking their produce for many years, so it makes sense to spend time enriching the soil before planting so the tree or bush will have a humus-rich soil in which to grow.

If you are only planting a couple of bush fruits in an existing border, enrich the soil over as large an area as possible with compost or commercial sterilized manure. Don't restrict the compost to only the planting hole, the surrounding soil needs to be enriched as well to encourage the roots to grow out.

Where larger trees are to be planted, it pays to grow a green manure crop, such as alfalfa, clover, or buckwheat, the summer before and turn it under in the fall to increase the humus content of the soil (See Green Manuring, p. 502).

Pollination

Many of the tree fruits need more than one variety to ensure pollination and a good fruit set—they are self-sterile—and this should be kept in mind when deciding what to plant. The so-called "family" apple trees have several varieties grafted onto a single stem and pollinate themselves, but care is needed in pruning so that one variety does not become dominant and cause the others to decline. When ordering trees, check out the pollination requirements from the nursery catalog, and if possible, order a self-fertile variety. Sometimes neighbors can work together and each plant a variety that will act as a pollinator for the other. Most bush fruits, with the exception of some blueberry varieties, do not need a different pollinator. Growing a range of other plants, especially those that are in flower at the same time as the fruit trees or bushes, helps entice bees and other pollinating insects into the garden, which results in a good crop of fruit.

Buying Fruit Trees

Most mail-order catalogs list some fruit trees, but when deciding on which varieties to plant, try to get catalogs from several different nurseries, so you get a wider choice of varieties. Be careful to check the hardiness zone, nurseries south of your location may sell varieties that are not hardy for you. Make sure the eventual size of the tree will fit the space available. Catalogs do not always give the rootstock information, which governs the eventual size of the tree, and you may have to call them or check online to be certain.

Some varieties have built-in disease resistance. Varieties of apples, for example, differ greatly in their susceptibility to scab and mildew, and those with good disease resistance are preferable for planting in a home garden since they will need less care. Many of the small fruits also have varieties that are resistant to one of more of the problems that may occur, so it is worth taking the time to do a thorough check before ordering.

Growing Fruit Organically

Growing fruit using organic methods can be very rewarding; you can produce fruit free of pesticides, that is picked fresh when it is full of flavor; so different from the often tasteless produce available in the stores. With many fruits, simply using good gardening practices, being alert to invading pests and diseases and dealing with them before they become major problems, is all that is required. Read through the individual "What Can Go Wrong" boxes for the fruits you are growing, so that you are aware of potential problems and can keep a sharp lookout for them.

The major tree fruits, apples, pears, cherries, etc. do have a number of potentially serious problems, but by gardening organically, encouraging natural predators, and using the most ecologically friendly control methods, these are rarely serious enough to cause concern. Apart from winter or early spring spraying with dormant oil and lime sulfur to kill off overwintering egg masses and disease spores, a regular spray program is rarely needed. Unlike commercially produced fruit, which is sprayed on a regular basis from before the flower buds open until close to picking time, the actual fruit on an organic tree may not have to be sprayed at all.

By using lures, pheromone traps, and possibly releasing some of the known parasitic insects, fruit trees can be kept almost free of the major pests. Occasional sprays of a copper- or sulfur-based fungicide may be needed to keep diseases in check, depending on the weather.

All gardeners come to accept a certain level of damage in their homegrown fruits. Similarly, an organically produced crop will not have the cosmetic perfection found in fruit purchased from a supermarket. There may be a small patch of scab on an apple, for example, which does not affect the taste, but you will know that the fruit is chemical-free and has been picked at the peak of ripeness, and not been ripened in a transport truck on its way to the market.

Do not crowd roots.

Refill the hole.

Prune evenly.

Dig a hole large enough to take the roots without crowding. Plant, using the excavated soil, and firm down. Prune to give evenly shaped branches.

Planting Fruit Trees and Bushes

In warmer zones, unless fruit trees have been supplied in containers, plant them between midfall and early spring, the earlier the better. In cold climates plant only in early spring. Trees in containers can be planted at any time the ground can be dug, as long as the roots are established.

Do not plant until the soil is in suitable condition. It must not be frozen or too wet. Ideally, a handful should hold together when squeezed but fall apart when dropped.

On the day of planting, dig a hole wide enough to accomodate the tree's outspread roots and deep enough so that the top roots will be covered with 3–4 inches of soil. Loosen the soil at the bottom of the hole with a fork so that the roots can penetrate as deeply as possible.

Ideally, fruit trees should not be grown in heavy, waterlogged soils; but if you have no option, dig the hole one-third deeper than usual and work in a wheelbarrow load of sandy soil or coarse gravel when refilling. However, even this may not help if subsoil is impervious (hard pan). Check by filling the hole with water and timing how long it takes to drain away. If the water level sinks less than 2 inches per hour (over the total depth of the hole), you should consider planting your fruit tree somewhere else.

Place a stake (tall enough to reach the point where the stem begins to branch) as deeply and firmly near the center of the hole as possible. Put 4–6 inches of well-rotted (or dehydrated) manure or compost in the hole. Work this material around thoroughly so that the roots will not come into contact with large pieces.

If the roots are dry, soak them in water for about two hours before planting. Cut out damaged roots with pruning shears, making a sloping cut. Trim off any stumps of deadwood on the top branches flush with the stem; cut back damaged tips.

Plant the tree no deeper than it was in the nursery, as indicated by the soil mark around the stem. Count on having a helper. You may need someone to hold the tree.

Fill in the topsoil first. Shake the tree from time to time to settle the soil around the roots. Once the roots are covered, firm the soil by treading.

Then add the rest of the soil, leaving it loose. Level the surface with a fork, and build a low mound around the excavation to prevent water from running off. Tie the tree to the stake (see p. 219).

Do not grow grass around the tree for two or three years. After planting, the old soil mark should be just visible, and the union between scion and rootstock should be at least 4 inches above soil level.

In areas where rabbits or mice are a nuisance, protect the tree by encircling it with a plastic collar or wire screening to a height of 1½ feet.

Cordons, espaliers, and fans. Before planting, set up supporting wires, attaching them with screw eyes and turnbuckles to a wall or posts. For cordons, stretch wires at 1 foot, 3 feet, 5 feet, and 7 feet above the ground; for horizontal espaliers, every 12–15 inches; for fans, every 9–12 inches, starting at the appropriate height aboveground.

If planting against a wall, set the stem at least 6 inches from the wall to avoid the dry soil in the sheltered area at the base. Lean the stem slightly toward the wall to make it easier to tie to the wires. Point the stems of cordons toward the north, if possible, to give them the maximum amount of light. Make sure that the scion is uppermost, to prevent it from breaking if the cordon has to be lowered. Plant the last tree in a row at least 8 feet from the end of the posts or wall so that there will be room for lowering.

Other fruits. For planting figs, grapes, raspberries, and strawberries, see the appropriate section. Blackberries, blueberries, gooseberries, loganberries, and red currants are planted like shrubs (see p. 250).

What to Do If You Cannot Plant at Once

If the trees, bushes, or canes arrive at a time when you cannot plant them, temporarily cover their roots with soil in a trench. This protective treatment is called heeling in.

Since the soil must be neither too dry nor too wet, a good site for heeling in during wet weather is against the wall of a house where the ground is not soaked. If the site is too dry, it should be watered.

To keep the site moist and to prevent it from freezing, cover it in late fall: first, with plastic sheeting; then, with dry straw, lawn clippings, or leaves; and finally, with more plastic sheeting. When the trees, bushes, or canes arrive, uncover the heeling-in site, and dig a trench as shown below.

Unfasten the bundle and lay the trees along the sloping side of the trench. Heap soil back to cover roots completely. Make sure that the stems are not covered any higher than the mark indicating the soil level in the nursery. Finally, firm the soil.

If the trees arrive at a time when neither planting nor heeling in is possible, unfasten them, place them in an unheated shed or garage, and cover their roots with moist peat moss or other light mulch. Do not keep them for too long in this way, because the roots may dry out.

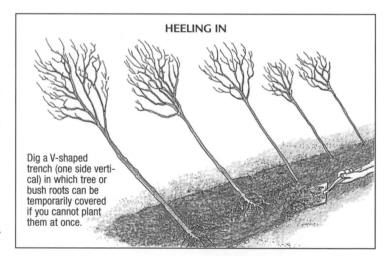

HEELING IN

Dig a V-shaped trench (one side vertical) in which tree or bush roots can be temporarily covered if you cannot plant them at once.

Tree Spacing

The planting distances given in the table at right are only a guide. Find out the recommended distances when buying trees. Keep in mind that the more vigorous the rootstock and the more fertile the soil, the farther apart trees should be planted. All of the distances given here are mainly for dwarfing or less vigorous rootstocks.

FORM OF TREE	BETWEEN TREES	BETWEEN ROWS
Dwarf	8–15 ft.	8–15 ft.
Semi-dwarf	10–12 ft.	10–12 ft.
Dwarf pyramid	3½–4 ft.	7–10 ft.
Espalier		
Cordon	2½–3 ft.	6–10 ft.
Horizontal	10–15 ft.	8–10 ft.
Fan	15–24 ft.	8–10 ft.

Supports are necessary to prevent heavily laden branches from breaking under the weight of their fruit. Nets offer the only effective protection from birds.

Support heavily laden branches.

Netting will protect from birds.

Encouraging a Reluctant Tree to Fruit

When the top growth of a tree is overvigorous—growing well but producing little or no fruit—one remedy is to reduce its supply of nitrogen. You can do this by growing grass over the root area. Keep the grass mowed during the growing season so that it will continue to grow and use up the nitrogen in the soil. One drawback to growing grass over the root area is the possibility of damaging the tree trunk with your mower. be careful to avoid this.

Another useful method is to prune the roots of the tree in winter while it is dormant. Inscribe a half-circle, at a distance from the trunk of slightly less than the spread of the branches. Dig a narrow trench along the line deep enough to expose the horizontal roots, and cut through all the roots encountered. The fine roots can be cut with a sharp spade. Use pruning shears to cut through the thick, thonglike roots. When the roots have all been cleanly cut, replace the soil in the trench and tamp it down well. The following winter treat the other half of the tree in the same way.

For apple and pear trees another remedy is bark ringing at blossom time. There is, however, a risk of killing the tree if it is not done properly, as explained below.

About 6 inches below the point where the branches begin, cut off a narrow strip of bark around half of the tree's trunk, and another around the other half, 3 inches below the first strip (so that you do not cut a complete circle around the trunk). The younger and smaller the tree, the narrower the strips should be. On even the largest trees cut strips no more than ⅛ inch wide.

Use a sharp knife, and cut carefully into the surface bark only. Peel off this layer of bark, and immediately cover the exposed portion with insulating tape. Do not cut too deep. If the cambium layer, just under the bark, is cut all the way around the trunk in a continuous strip, the tree will die.

Because of this, bark removal should be used only as a last resort.

Protecting Fruit Against Damage and Disease

Fruit buds and growing fruits can be seriously damaged by birds. The only real protection is to cover the trees or bushes with 1-inch nylon mesh or polyethylene netting.

Small fruits and trees grown on supports are most easily protected with temporary cages. Other devices include polyethylene bags, stockings, newspaper cones, or plastic sleeves put over individual fruits. Less effective are various bird-scaring devices, bird-repellent sprays, and cotton or aluminum-foil threads that have been tied among the tree's branches.

Fruit trees can also be damaged by animals; mice eating the bark in winter, raccoons breaking branches when fruit is ripe, and porcupines stripping bark at any time of the year. The bark may also be damaged by mowers; avoid growing grass near the trunk.

Fungi, bacterial and viral diseases, and insects, which can seriously damage or kill trees, are the other main problems in fruit growing.

Organic controls are now available at most garden centers.

Keep in mind that even organic fungicides should be used with restraint. For home gardeners, some spraying is advisable. Sprays should be applied carefully and not when the trees or plants are in bloom because of possible harm to pollinating insects.

Some pests can also develop resistance to organic controls. To prevent resistance, it is a good practice to vary the product that you use when repeated sprays are required.

Keep a close watch for pests, and use control measures only when the insects can be seen or if the plant was attacked the previous year. Treat only the infected tree or bush and those nearby.

Good garden hygiene also helps to keep pests and diseases under control. Never leave prunings lying around, and in autumn and winter pick off and destroy old fruit.

Commercial orchardists, including organic growers, apply regularly timed sprays because of market demand for unblemished fruit. You can make your own choice about how "perfect" you want your fruit to be, but if your goal is spot-free apples, for example, you will have to commit to expensive and time-consuming spray schedules, like this one for apples.

When buds show half an inch of green, spray for scales and mites. At least seven days later, but before blossoms open, spray for apple scab and aphids.

When 90 percent of the flower petals fall, spray for scab, curculios, caterpillars, and mites.

Fourteen days later, spray again for scab, codling moth, and cuculios.

Two weeks later, spray for scab and codling moth.

Twenty-one days later, spray for scab, fruit rot, apple maggots, and aphids. Repeat this three times at three-week intervals.

These recommendations are for one area. The sprays and the timing vary from region to region. The best source of up-to-date information on this is your county extension agent.

Branches heavily laden with fruits can be supported individually to prevent them from breaking under the weight. This can be done with loops of rope tied to a stake.

Or branches can be propped up with a forked stake. For both methods, use padding between branch and support to prevent chafing.

The apple blossom opens in spring and is often pollinated by wild bees.

Apple blossom

Apples

Apple 'Golden Delicious'

The apple is one of the most widely grown fruits. Apple trees grow in most soils but do best in well-drained, neutral or slightly alkaline soil that does not dry out in summer.

Apples do not grow well in seaside gardens because salt-laden winds can be damaging. Few apple trees grow well in areas without winter freezes. However, a few varieties are now offered for warmer regions.

Most varieties of apple trees need cross-pollinating by another variety that blossoms at the same time (see p. 400). But "family trees" are now available with three to five cross-pollinating varieties growing on a single rootstock. Using these, you need plant only a single tree.

To meet the needs of a family of four that likes apples, 6 dwarf trees (or 4 fans, 4 espaliers, 8 modified leaders, or 12 cordons) should provide ample fruit. The fruit matures from midsummer until fall, and many types can be kept in storage until the following spring.

The best time to plant is in autumn or spring; in cold climates, in spring only (see p. 381). The roots of newly planted trees need plenty of water; so make sure that the soil is kept moist.

For the first two or three years, cover the soil in spring with straw or other mulch. Keep mulch 2 feet from the trunk. Do not use cedar bark or pine needles as a mulch. They may make the soil too acid.

In late winter feed trees with a balanced organic fertilizer. This can be repeated in the spring if there is any indication that the trees lack vigor. A sensible average feeding for a mature dwarf tree with a foliage spread of 6 feet is ½–1 pound distributed over the root area. Keep in mind that most of the feeder roots are concentrated away from the trunk toward the outer ends of the branches.

Sprinkle the fertilizer over the soil, covering an area slightly larger than that overspread by the branches. Let it penetrate naturally. Do not fork it in; this can damage the roots. Remove weeds by shallow hoeing. Trees will need watering during long dry spells.

Thinning a Heavy Crop of Young Apples

The aim of thinning is to allow the remaining apples to grow to full size. Too heavy a crop will only crowd the fruits and result in small apples of poor quality.

Start thinning a heavy crop of young apples in late spring or before the natural drop occurs. If this early natural drop seems too heavy, which it may be if the soil is poor or dry, some feeding and mulching as recommended on these pages is in order to prevent further drop.

From each cluster, first remove the central fruit; if it is misshapen, remove by cutting its stalk with a pair of scissors with pointed blades. Never pull fruit off the tree when thinning, as this can damage the

Harvesting Apples According to Their Season

The best way to test if apples are ready for picking is to lift one up to the horizontal in the palm of your hand and twist it gently. It is ready for picking only if it parts easily from the tree with the stalk remaining on the fruit.

For reaching high fruit, use apple pickers—nets on bamboo poles. Push the rigid frame of the net against the stalk. If the apple is ready, it will drop into the net. Because they bruise easily, apples should be harvested with the care you would use in handling eggs. Place ripe apples in a container lined with soft material.

Early apples (ready in early fall) will not keep and are best eaten as soon as they are picked. Midseason and late varieties should be picked in midfall before they are ripe; they mature during storage.

Store midseason varieties (ready for eating from late fall to early winter) separately from late varieties (ready from midwinter onward). This is advisable because the ethylene

spur. Then cut off any inferior apples, leaving two on each cluster (one if clusters are close). Thin again in midsummer if there is a good crop.

For the best fruit, thin dessert apples to 4–6 inches apart, cooking apples to 6–9 inches apart. Leave only one apple on each spur.

In early summer thin fruits to two per cluster.

gases given off by the earlier apples may unduly hasten the ripening of the later ones.

Some late apples will keep until mid or even late spring if they are stored in suitable conditions. After picking the apples, place them in a cool, well-ventilated room or shed to sweat for two or three days. After they have sweated, sort them out for storing, placing to one side any damaged or diseased fruits (even those only slightly affected) or any without a stalk. Those that are unsuitable for storage can be used immediately.

Apples ready for picking will twist off easily, stalk attached.

In addition to aphids and other pests, apple trees are vulnerable to fungal diseases and viruses.

Apple scab   Fruit rot

How to Store Your Apple Crop

The ideal way to store apples is to wrap each one in waxed paper or in a 10-inch square of newspaper. Do not make an airtight seal; just fold one corner of the paper over the fruit, overlap this with the opposite corner, then fold over the other two corners. Apples can also be stored without wrapping, but there is a danger of excessive moisture loss, as well as spreading of rot.

Instead of wrapping your apples individually, you can store them in a strong polyethylene bag holding 4–6 pounds. Use small bags for the fruits. Respiration inside bags slows ripening, but if the bags are airtight, apples may rot. Use a nail or pencil point to make six small holes in each 24 square inches of bag.

Store apples in a dark, humid, cool place, with a temperature of 35°–40°F. Too much ventilation will cause the fruits to shrivel, but too little may cause them to rot internally. To raise the humidity, damp down the storeroom floor occasionally. Stand wrapped apples, folds underneath, in a single layer on a slatted shelf, or stack them two or three layers deep in a well-ventilated box.

Regularly remove any apples that show signs of rotting.

What Can Go Wrong With Apples

The majority of apple pests can be controlled with one dormant spray plus the controls specified in the chart, if the pest is identified. The dormant spray goes on just as buds open. When applying sprays in the spring, avoid spraying at times when pollinating insects are present. Applying a repellent garlic extract spray may deter apple pests overall. See page 506 for more information on plant disorders, including symptoms not listed in the chart. For more information on controls, look in the section beginning on page 542.

SYMPTOMS AND SIGNS	CAUSE	CONTROL
Leaves curled (sometimes flushed with red); shoots may be distorted. Many sticky insects present.	Aphids (greenfly or several other kinds)	Apply a dormant oil spray just after bud break to kill eggs. Apply insecticidal soap just before bloom. Repeat after blossoming if necessary.
Apples have small skin blemishes. Inside, mature fruits show corky brown streaks; maggots ("worms") visible.	Apple maggots (fly larvae)	Pick up and dispose of fallen fruit daily. Hang red sticky ball traps in trees.
Young fruits have small brown holes in skin, often with brown ribbonlike scars leading from them. Unpleasant odor present when fruits are cut open; "worms" visible.	Apple sawflies (larvae)	Hang white sticky cards in trees at blossom time and remove them at petal fall. Spray with neem immediately after petal fall. Apply parasitic nematodes to the soil beneath the trees shortly after petal fall.
From midsummer on fruits bear small holes; no associated scar. No noticeable odor when fruits are cut open. White caterpillars feed inside fruits.	Codling moths (larvae)	Hang traps in trees to catch male moths. Spray *Bacillus thuringiensis* about 2 weeks after petal fall starts, then apply two more sprays, 5 days apart.
Leaves finely mottled, turning yellow or rusty brown.	Two-spotted, or red spider, mites	Spray with insecticidal soap in early summer. Repeat if necessary. Plant ground covers to attract mite predators.
Eggs, deposited on twigs, hatch when flowers are deep pink. Larvae (caterpillars) chew foliage.	Leaf rollers or leaftiers (moth larvae)	Apply *Bacillus thuringiensis* at pink bud stage; spray again at petal fall if pests are still present.

SYMPTOMS AND SIGNS	CAUSE	CONTROL
Curculios puncture and lay eggs in very young fruits, leaving crescent-shaped scar. After eggs hatch, larvae (grubs) feed inside apples, causing premature drop.	Plum curculios (weevils)	Collect fruit as it drops. When petals fall, spread a sheet below the tree and hit the tree trunk with a padded stick; collect and destroy the curculios daily for 3 wks. Also, apply horticultural kaolin clay at petal fall and then weekly for 6 to 8 weeks.
Rough, scaly deposits (white, gray, or brownish) occur on twigs, bark, and fruits. Juices are sucked from trees, causing reduced growth and yellowed leaves.	Scale insects (San Jose, oyster shell, scurfy scale, or others)	Spray with dormant oil at bud break. Summer oil can be sprayed as contact control in late spring when new scales ("crawlers") appear.
Leaves and young stems distorted, covered with white powder. Premature leaf fall may occur.	Apple powdery mildew (fungus)	In late spring and early fall spray regularly with wettable sulfur.
Brown or blackish scabs on fruits, leaves, and shoots. When scabs have coalesced, they may become corky.	Apple scab (fungus)	From the time bud scales fall to midsummer, spray with sulfur. When pruning, cut out and destroy diseased parts.
Leaves turn brown and look burned, hang down from the branch, but do not fall. Cankers arise on branches.	Fire blight (fungus)	Prune out infected branches when seen. Spray with lime sulfur in late winter and with a copper fungicide as leaves unfurl.
In early summer foliage has orange rusty spots, which become dark orange, crusty, and scabby. Fruits may show sunken areas or orange spots; generally unsightly.	Rust (cedar-apple or hawthorn)	If possible, eliminate all red cedars (*Juniperus*) within ½-mi radius. Cut off overwintering fungal galls on cedars. Spray with copper fungicide when flower buds show pink. Repeat at blossom time, again at petal fall, again 10 days later, and twice more.

Pear 'Williams Bon Chrétien'

Apple 'Jonagold'

Quince 'Ronda'

Pear trees can take heavier pruning than apple trees, while quince need little pruning at all.

Pruning and Training Apple Trees

During the first four years of the life of a fruit tree, the aim of pruning is to develop a strong, regular framework of branches.

After that the aim is twofold: to keep the tree open to light and air and to maintain the right balance between growth and fruitfulness.

Winter pruning (late fall to late winter) promotes growth by directing energy to growth buds at the expense of fruit buds. Summer pruning (from mid to late summer) on the other hand reduces foliage and promotes the formation of fruit buds. In summer, prune small branches (up to 1 inch in diameter) only.

Fruit buds and growth buds. When pruning a fruit tree, you must be able to distinguish between a fruit bud (which will produce a blossom and then fruit) and a growth bud (which will produce a new shoot). They are illustrated below. Growth buds may develop into fruit buds. A heavy winter pruning promotes growth buds. A summer pruning (after new growth is made) tends to promote fruit buds.

Leaders and laterals. A leader is the leading shoot of a branch. A lateral is a side shoot from a branch.

Spurs and tips. Some apple varieties produce most of their fruit on short growths known as spurs. These varieties include 'Golden Delicious', 'McIntosh', and 'Stayman'. But some varieties also produce fruit on one-year shoots (tips), both terminally and laterally. 'Rome Beauty' and 'Jonathan' fall into this group. We now have so-called spur strains, and

these trees make about one-third less growth and are heavily laden with spurs. 'Golden Delicious', 'Red Delicious', 'McIntosh', 'Winesap', and 'Rome Beauty' are available as spur

Making a pruning cut

strains. For backyard apple trees on dwarfing stocks, the spur strains are recommended.

Making a pruning cut. Use sharp shears; otherwise damage may result and disease may enter. Cut just

above an outward-pointing bud; do not leave a stump above it, because it will die back and can harbor disease. Cut in the same direction as the bud.

Training. Trees bought from a nursery are usually partly trained and may be up to four years old. Find out the age when you buy so that you can train correctly.

Bearing. A tree should not be allowed to bear more than one or two fruits in the first year after planting. A cordon may fruit within a year after planting; a dwarf tree on a vigorous rootstock may take five years.

The time a tree takes to reach full bearing capacity can vary from 4 to 15 years, depending on the variety of tree, rootstock, and kind of pruning.

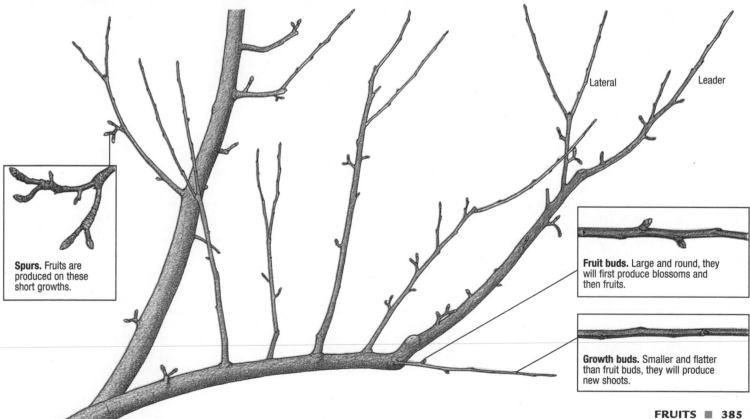

Spurs. Fruits are produced on these short growths.

Lateral

Leader

Fruit buds. Large and round, they will first produce blossoms and then fruits.

Growth buds. Smaller and flatter than fruit buds, they will produce new shoots.

Training and pruning are the same for core-fruits and stone-fruits in the first three years. But cherry and plum trees must be pruned in early spring, not in winter.

Plum 'Stanley'

Sour cherry 'Meteor'

Pruning and Training a Dwarf Tree

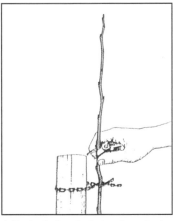

1. Plant, attach a plastic tree tie, and cut the main stem above a bud to 18–24 in.

Training a One-Year-Old Dwarf Tree

Plant dwarf trees 8–15 feet apart, depending on the rootstock (which should be either dwarfing or semi-dwarfing). Check the type and the planting distance with the nurseryperson or look in the catalog.

If you buy a one-year-old tree, cut the stem back to an 18- to 24-inch

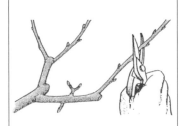

2. Leave three or four buds to form branches. Rub out unwanted buds.

height, just above a bud, after planting in autumn or spring (see p. 381). The buds or small shoots just below the cut will grow out the following summer. There may be only four or five. Choose three or four to form the first branches. They should be evenly spaced around the stem, with none pointing toward the supporting stake. Rub out with your thumb any unwanted buds or shoots.

Training a Two-Year-Old Dwarf Tree

In the winter a two-year-old dwarf tree will have the three or four branches that grew in the summer. Cut back each of the branches to an

outward-pointing bud; how far back you cut them depends on their vigor.

If the branches are thick and vigorous, cut them back by half. If they are thin and weak, cut them back by two-thirds. Rub out with your thumb any inward-pointing buds just below the cuts.

Training a Three-Year-Old Dwarf Tree

By a tree's third winter a number of lateral shoots will have grown out from the branches. Choose some of these laterals to form, with the first branches, the main structure of the tree. They should all point outward, and their tips, after pruning, should be at least 18 inches apart.

Cut all main branches back to an outward-pointing bud, shortening the new growth on each branch by one-third if the branch is growing vigorously or by one-half if it is of average growth. If it is weak, shorten the new growth by two-thirds.

Each of the laterals not chosen to form main branches should be cut back to a point that is four buds from the base of the shoot.

Cut off remaining side branches on the main stem flush with the stem.

Pruning an Established Spur-Forming Dwarf

Established dwarf trees that bear nearly all their fruit on spurs (such as 'Golden Delicious' and 'McIntosh') should be pruned each winter by the method known as the renewal system. The principle of this system is to produce new growth each season to replace some that has already borne fruit. It is based on the three-year cycle of fruiting growth.

During its first summer a growth bud sends out a shoot. During the second summer this shoot produces fruit buds. During the third summer the fruit buds form spurs and bear fruit that same summer and in succeeding summers.

During its second summer a shoot produces not only fruit buds but also new growth from its tip, so that a two-year-old shoot has one-year-old growth extending from it. In the same way, three-year-old growth has both two-year-old and one-year-old growth extending from it.

Under the renewal system several two-year-old and three-year-old shoots are cut back. This method prevents overcropping and crowding, improves fruit quality, and makes way for new growth.

There is no rule governing how many shoots to prune and how many to leave. Use your judgment to maintain a balance between growth and fruitfulness. The purpose of pruning is to prevent a tree from becoming overloaded with branches and still allow sufficient new fruit-bearing shoots to form.

Do not prune one-year-old shoots growing out from a main branch. But you cannot avoid cutting away some of the one-year-old extension growth when cutting back two-year-old and three-year-old growth. When choosing shoots for pruning, trace back to older wood from one-year-old tips.

On trees with weak growth, cut selected two-year-old growth back to two fruit buds. On stronger trees,

ONE-YEAR-OLD SHOOTS

One-year-old shoots from a main branch have only growth buds. Do not prune them.

TWO-YEAR-OLD GROWTH

Two-year-old growth has fruit buds. Cut back to two buds on weak growth; leave more buds on stronger trees.

THREE-YEAR-OLD GROWTH
Three-year-old growth has spurs. Prune some growth back to lowest spurs to encourage replacement spurs.

Apple 'Red Delicious' flowers

Quince 'Smyrna' flowers

Fruit trees are a practical addition to a kitchen garden, and when they bloom, they are beautiful, too.

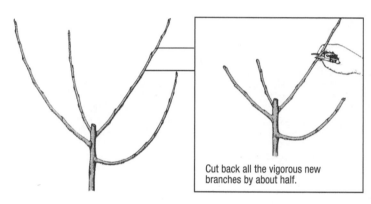

Cut back all the vigorous new branches by about half.

leave more buds. Cut back selected three-year-old growth to the lowest fruiting spur. Growth buds on the spur will produce new shoots the following season, and the cycle of growth will start again. Branch leaders should have their new growth cut by one-third if the branch is growing vigorously, by one-half if it is of average growth, by two-thirds if it is very weak. When branches are fully grown (about 8 feet long), prune them in the same way as shoots.

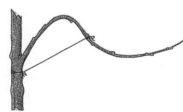

Branches arced this high are liable to break.

Aim for a smooth, even arc when inclining branches outward.

Pruning an Established Tip-Bearing Dwarf Tree

There are not as many tip-bearing varieties of dwarfs as spur-forming varieties. Tip-bearing dwarf trees, which include 'Rome Beauty', 'Jonathan', and 'Stayman', produce many of their fruit buds on the tips of shoots; the rest are produced on spurs. The cycle of growth in these dwarfs is the same as for spur-forming trees, but many one-year-old shoots produce a fruit bud at the tip.

Tip-bearing trees need comparatively little pruning. Once a year, in winter, prune back any shoot without a fruit bud at its tip. Cut just above the highest fruit bud if there is one; otherwise, cut back to four or five growth buds from the base of the shoot.

Shoots that have a fruit bud at the tip should not be pruned unless they are crowded—that is, if the tips are less than 1 foot apart. Thin them out by pruning some tips back to two buds from the base, preferably above a fruit bud if there is one.

Prune branch leaders by removing the fruit bud at the tip, cutting back to a growth bud; this induces the lower growth buds to break and produce more tip-bearing shoots. Shoots crop more when they are near horizontal, and it pays to tie down upright shoots as shown on left.

Colonnade Apple Trees

In 1962, on a McIntosh apple tree in an orchard in Kelowna, British Columbia, a branch developed that had no side shoots, only fruiting spurs. It was propagated, and the buds grew into upright trees with no branches, just fruiting spurs.

These were crossed with other eating apples and crabapples and eventually gave four varieties of this new form. They were exhibited at the Chelsea Flower Show in England in 1989 as "Ballerina Trees." In North America the name was already trademarked, so they are known here as "Colonnade apples."

They grow as a slender column, about 24 inches in diameter, eventually becoming 8 feet tall, but they can be kept smaller with careful pruning.

At present, there are four eating apples and one crab that is the pollinator. Breeding work is ongoing, and the number of varieties will increase. Available varieties are 'Emeraldspire', early with green fruit, 'Ultraspire', mid-season with red fruit, 'Crimsonspire', also mid-season, and 'Scarletspire', late with large red fruit. The crabapple, 'Maypole', has carmine-red flowers.

These are a good choice for small gardens or containers on decks and balconies where the climate is mild. But they will need extra protection, such as wrapping the trunk and insulating the container. Planters should be at least 18 inches in diameter and the trees will need to be fertilized regularly to produce fruit.

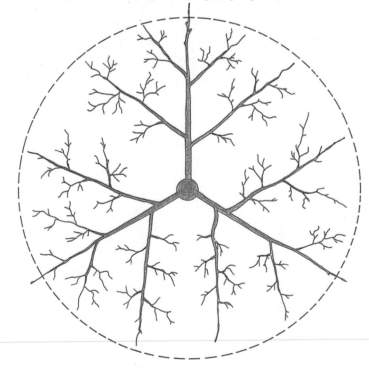

This bird's-eye view of the perfectly shaped round crown shows three branches extending at 120-degree angles from the main stem.

Apple 'Golden Delicious' ➡

These branches were cut too close to the trunk and covered with paint. They will be slow to heal. The tangle of spurs (right) needs careful pruning.

These wounds will be slow to heal.

Lack of pruning is all too evident here.

Pruning and Training a Modified Leader Tree

Training a One-Year-Old Modified Leader

Dwarf pyramids are usually trained to a height of about 7 feet, with short branches spreading out all around the stem or trunk.

Trees should be spaced 3½ feet apart (4 feet on more fertile soils) in rows from 7 to 10 feet apart. Plant them between midfall and early spring (see p. 381).

If you begin with a one-year-old (maiden) tree, cut back the stem to about 20 inches above soil level immediately after planting. Cut just above a bud or side shoot, and then rub out the bud or shoot that is second from the top; otherwise it may produce a second leading shoot.

Select three or four of the buds below the topmost bud to form the tree's first branches. Space them to grow out in different directions. Rub out unwanted buds or shoots.

The topmost bud will grow upward to form the tree's central leader, and the next two buds should form strong branches, but the lowest buds will produce weak branches unless they are stimulated.

They therefore need notching; remove a half-moon of bark from above each of these buds.

Training a Young Modified Leader in Winter

In the second winter cut back the central leader to about 18 inches from the first year's cut. To help produce a straight stem, make the cut just above a bud facing in the opposite direction from the bud chosen during the previous winter.

As in the previous winter, rub out the bud below the top one, and choose three or four buds below it that are well spaced for forming another tier of branches. With a sharp knife carefully notch above the two lower buds as before.

Repeat this training each winter until the main stem has reached a height of about 7 feet.

In the second winter only, cut back the leaders of the first tier of branches to a length of about 9 inches—above a bud on the underside of the limb. After this, cut back branch leaders in summer only.

WINTER TRAINING

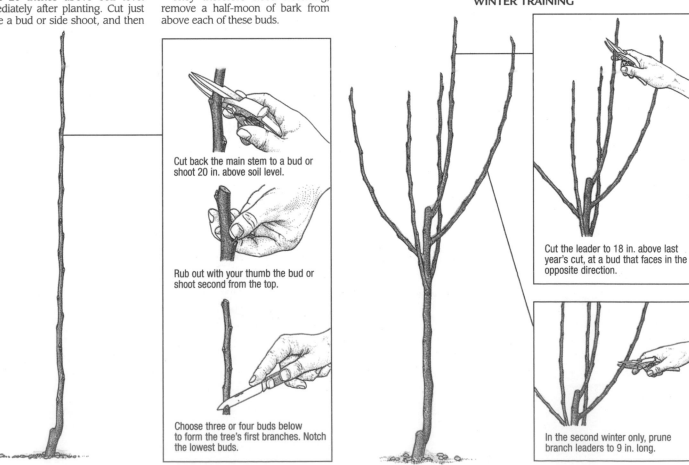

Cut back the main stem to a bud or shoot 20 in. above soil level.

Rub out with your thumb the bud or shoot second from the top.

Choose three or four buds below to form the tree's first branches. Notch the lowest buds.

Cut the leader to 18 in. above last year's cut, at a bud that faces in the opposite direction.

In the second winter only, prune branch leaders to 9 in. long.

A sun-dappled wall offers these upright cordon trees protection and support. The columnar training permits closer spacing of the plants.

Upright cordon trees

Pruning a Young Modified Leader in Summer

No pruning is needed in the summer after training a one-year-old tree. For older trees prune new growth as it matures, usually starting in mid-summer and continuing for perhaps a month.

Growth is mature when it is at least 9 inches long, woody at the base, and has dark green leaves. Cut back extension growth on branch leaders (but not the central leader) to five or six leaves beyond the basal cluster. Cut above a bud on the underside of the limb.

Cut any of the mature laterals that are growing from the branches back to three leaves from the basal cluster.

If there are any mature side shoots growing from laterals or spurs, cut them back to one leaf from the basal cluster. Until the fourth summer remove new shoots growing from the main stem.

If new growth is not mature enough for pruning in midsummer, it may be ready in late summer. If it is still not mature enough then—this may be the case in more northerly regions—wait until early fall.

If you have pruned in summer, you may find that secondary growth has sprung from the pruned shoots by fall. If it has been a rather dry summer and not much secondary growth has occurred, cut it all back to one bud from the parent stem during the fall. After a wet summer that has produced a great amount of such growth, you may have to continue pruning into early winter in order to maintain the pyramidal shape of the tree.

Training a Modified Leader to Full Height

Continue winter training and summer pruning until the central stem reaches a height of about 7 feet. (This point is likely to be reached when the tree is seven or eight years old.) By this time the tree will have at least six tiers of branches from each winter training.

Then in late spring cut back the central stem by half the previous season's growth. The shape of the modified leader is now established.

Once the tree reaches about 15 years of age, its upper branches will have grown to the same spread as the lower ones, and the Christmas-tree shape will be lost. All the branches should be kept at a length of about 18 inches.

In midsummer prune new growth on branch leaders—not the central one—to five or six leaves from the basal cluster.

Cut back mature laterals from branches to three leaves from the basal cluster.

FALL PRUNING

In early fall cut secondary growth from the earlier pruning back to one bud.

Cut back mature side shoots growing from laterals to one leaf from the basal cluster.

CUTTING THE MAIN STEM

When the central leader reaches a height of about 7 ft., in late spring, cut it back by about half the previous season's growth.

Espalier trees are trained mostly with four to five pairs of main branches and a total spread of around 12 ft. Single cordons can be trained to form archways.

Horizontal espalier

Single cordon archways

Pruning an Established Modified Leader Tree

In late spring cut back the central leader above a bud, leaving only ½ inch of the previous season's growth. When branches reach 18 inches, maintain this length.

If branch leaders begin to overlap the branches of neighboring trees, cut back half of the new growth during one spring pruning. Thereafter, cut back to only ½ inch of new growth each spring.

As in previous summers, prune growth as it becomes mature in summer. Cut back mature laterals from branches to three leaves beyond the basal cluster. Cut back mature side shoots from laterals or spurs to one leaf beyond the basal cluster.

If growth is not mature enough for pruning during midsummer, prune in late summer or early fall.

Cut any secondary growth from the summer pruning back to one bud in the fall. After a wet season that has produced a lot of such growth, you may have to continue pruning into early winter.

On older modified leader trees the fruiting spurs may become over-crowded and need thinning. Do this in winter; remove some entirely, cut-ting flush with the parent stem, and reduce the size of others.

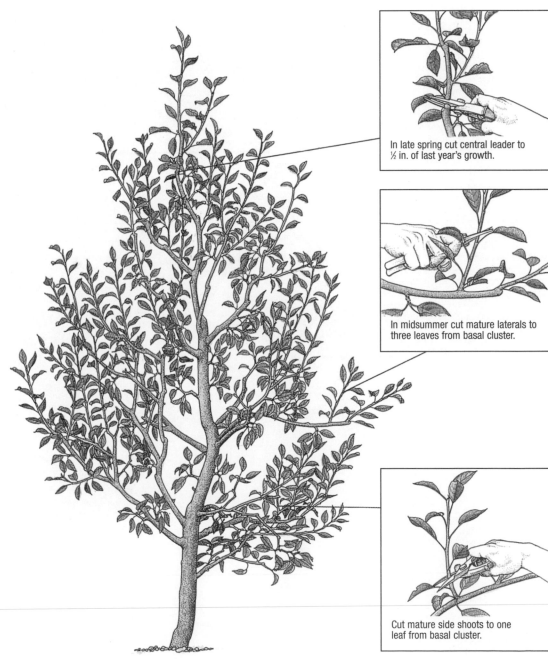

In late spring cut central leader to ½ in. of last year's growth.

In midsummer cut mature laterals to three leaves from basal cluster.

SPUR THINNING

Thin out overcrowded spurs in winter. Remove some entirely, and reduce others in size.

Cut mature side shoots to one leaf from basal cluster.

The color of an apple is not an indicator of its sweetness. Many green apples are sweet and some red ones tart.

Green apple

Pruning a Neglected Apple Tree

Neglected standard or dwarf apple trees can be renovated in winter. If the tree is making little new growth, all pruning can be done at once; otherwise, space the work over two or three years.

First, remove any dead and diseased branches. Then, let in light and air by removing enough of the large branches, particularly in the center, for those remaining to be 2–3 feet apart in the outer spread where the new growth develops. Cut out any crossed or badly placed branches. On very tall trees shorten the tallest branches back to a lateral.

When removing a whole branch, look for the raised ring of tissue (the collar) close to the branch base and cut just outside this. Do not cover with wound paint.

Thin out any complicated spur systems, reducing some in size and removing others entirely. As a general guide, spurs should be spaced 9–12 inches apart. Spread spur thinning over several seasons, whether the tree's growth is slow or vigorous.

Clear away any weeds and grass around the tree base, and lightly fork the soil in a circle about 8 feet across.

As order is restored, prune each year according to whether the tree is a spur-forming variety or a spur and tip bearer (see pp. 386–387).

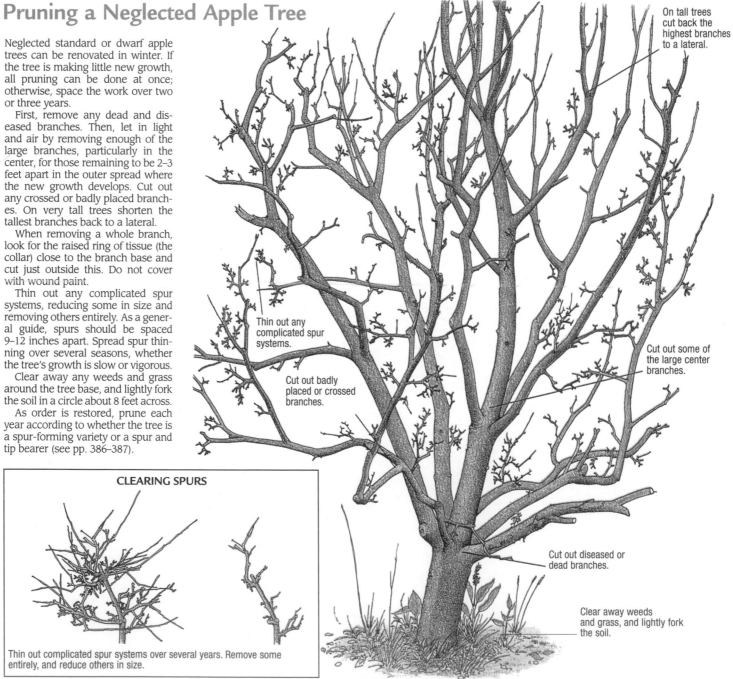

On tall trees cut back the highest branches to a lateral.

Thin out any complicated spur systems.

Cut out badly placed or crossed branches.

Cut out some of the large center branches.

Cut out diseased or dead branches.

Clear away weeds and grass, and lightly fork the soil.

CLEARING SPURS

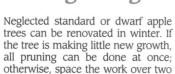

Thin out complicated spur systems over several years. Remove some entirely, and reduce others in size.

'Jonathan'

'Idared'

'Jonathan', an old apple variety, is still very popular. It is a parent of many newer varieties, including 'Idared'.

Pruning and Training a Cordon Espalier

Plant cordons 2½ feet apart—3 feet apart on fertile soil (see p. 381). Rows should be at least 6 feet apart.

After planting a tree, wire a bamboo cane, 8–10 feet long, to the horizontal wires, at the same angle as the tree (usually 45 degrees). Tie the stem to the cane with soft string. Remove the cane when the stem of the tree reaches the top wire.

No pruning is necessary at planting time. Prune in summer as growth becomes mature. This is generally in mid to late summer but may not be until early fall. Mature growth is woody at the base and at least 9 inches long.

Cut back mature laterals to three leaves from the basal cluster. Cut back the mature side shoots from laterals or spurs to one leaf from the basal cluster. Do not prune the main stem leader.

If you prune in summer, there will probably be secondary growth. If the summer is reasonably dry and not much new growth occurs, cut all growth back to one bud in the early fall; after a wet summer that produces much secondary growth, you may need to continue pruning into early winter.

If spurs become overcrowded, thin them out in the winter (see p. 392).

When a cordon grows beyond the top wire, untie it and refasten it at a more acute angle. Do not lower it to less than 35 degrees from the horizontal, however, or it will break. Once it cannot be lowered any farther, trim back new growth at the tip

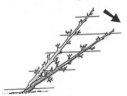
Lowering a cordon

to ½ inch, cutting above a bud. This pruning operation should be done sometime in late spring.

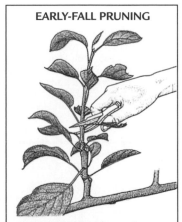

EARLY-FALL PRUNING

Cut back all the small secondary growth from the midsummer pruning. Prune it to one bud.

In midsummer prune mature laterals back to three leaves from the basal cluster.

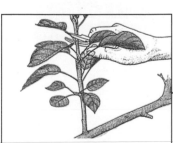
In fall, cut back the resulting new growth on this lateral to one leaf from the basal cluster.

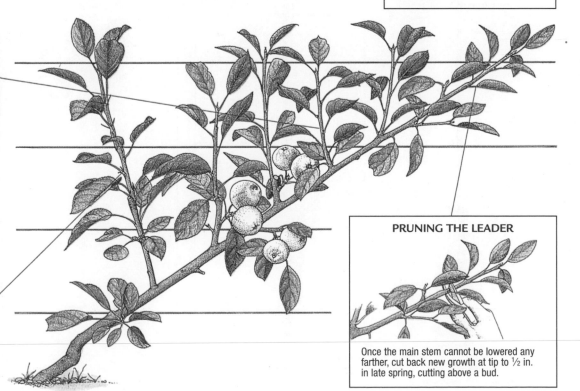

PRUNING THE LEADER

Once the main stem cannot be lowered any farther, cut back new growth at tip to ½ in. in late spring, cutting above a bud.

Apple trees that remain small can nevertheless bear several hundred fruits with proper care. Sour varieties are good for cider.

Eating apples

Cider apples

Pruning and Training a Horizontal Espalier

Training a One-Year-Old Horizontal Espalier

Depending on the rootstock, plant espaliers 10–15 feet apart (see p. 381). Ask the nurseryperson what the recommended planting distance is for the rootstock you are buying.

Shorten a young (one-year-old) tree immediately after planting. Cut it back to a bud or shoot about 14 inches above the ground—about 2 inches higher than the lowest horizontal support wire.

Choose a bud with two other buds or shoots beneath it that are pointing along the line of the wire and are located on opposite sides of the stem. The top bud will produce a shoot to grow upright as the main stem; the two lower buds will produce shoots to form the first tier of opposite horizontal branches. Rub out with your thumb all other buds or shoots.

Notch the bottom bud to stimulate growth. Although the top two buds should grow out strongly, the lowest may not. Use a sharp knife to remove

a half-moon of bark from the stem just above the bud.

The following summer, as growth develops, train the three shoots in the required directions by means of bamboo canes. The shoot from the topmost bud is trained upright, the two side shoots diagonally.

Fasten an upright cane to the wires, and use soft string to tie the shoot to it from the topmost bud. Then fasten two more canes to the wires on each side of the first cane—both at an angle of 45 degrees. Tie

the shoots from the side buds to the two canes with soft string.

You can train two branches to grow equally by adjusting the angles of the two canes. If one branch is growing more vigorously than the other, lower its cane. (This will slow its growth.) At the same time raise the other cane to which the weaker shoot is attached. (This will stimulate growth.) Adjust the canes in this way as necessary until growth is matched. Remove any other buds that grow on the stem.

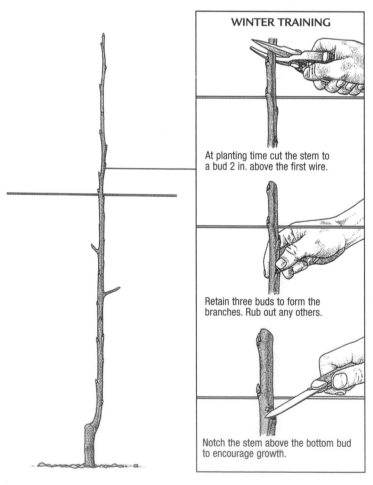

WINTER TRAINING

At planting time cut the stem to a bud 2 in. above the first wire.

Retain three buds to form the branches. Rub out any others.

Notch the stem above the bottom bud to encourage growth.

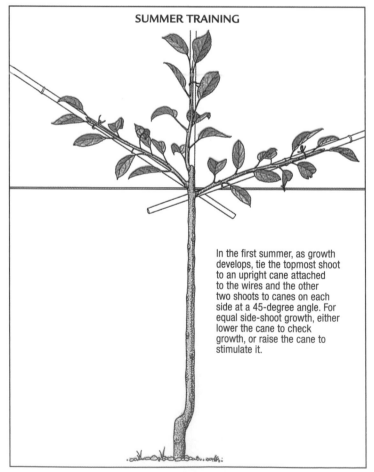

SUMMER TRAINING

In the first summer, as growth develops, tie the topmost shoot to an upright cane attached to the wires and the other two shoots to canes on each side at a 45-degree angle. For equal side-shoot growth, either lower the cane to check growth, or raise the cane to stimulate it.

For an espalier, the main branches can be trained at a slant, in a U-shape or in fan shapes. The shape is completely formed after the third winter.

Cordon espalier

Training an Espalier in Its Second and Third Years

During the espalier's second winter lower the two side branches to the horizontal wire on each side of the main stem. Remove the canes and tie the branches to the wire with soft string. This is the age at which many espaliers are bought from nurseries.

Trim back the branch leaders to stimulate the growth of fruiting spurs from them, cutting just past a bud. Strong leaders should be pruned back by less than half, weak ones by more than half. The aim is to make both branches grow to about the same length eventually.

Cut back the main stem to a bud about 2 inches above the second wire. Then select two other buds below it to form a second pair of horizontal branches. Rub out with your thumb all other buds or shoots.

As with the first tier, notch the bottom bud to encourage growth, cutting away a half-moon of bark just above it with a sharp knife.

The following summer fasten canes to the second-tier side shoots at an angle of 45 degrees to the main-stem cane. Train the branches in exactly the same way as the first-tier branches the year before. Tie the extension growth on the first-tier leaders to the wires.

Prune the current season's growth as it becomes mature. This is usually done in midsummer—but in some cases, depending on weather or area, in late summer or early fall.

Mature growth is at least 9 inches long, is woody at the base, and has dark green leaves. Cut back mature laterals to three leaves beyond the basal cluster.

If you have pruned in summer, new secondary growth may develop from the cut wood by fall. Cut it all back to one bud. After a wet summer that has produced considerable secondary growth, you may need to delay pruning into early winter.

In the third winter cut back branch leaders as before, and select buds for the third tier.

In the fourth summer train the third tier, and prune the mature growth, as was done in the third summer. Cut side shoots from spurs or laterals back to one leaf from the basal cluster.

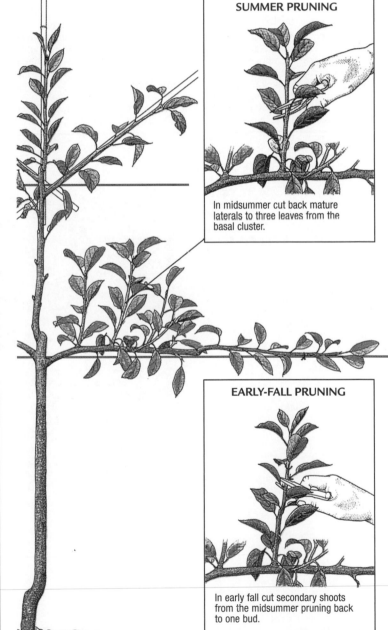

SUMMER PRUNING

In midsummer cut back mature laterals to three leaves from the basal cluster.

EARLY-FALL PRUNING

In early fall cut secondary shoots from the midsummer pruning back to one bud.

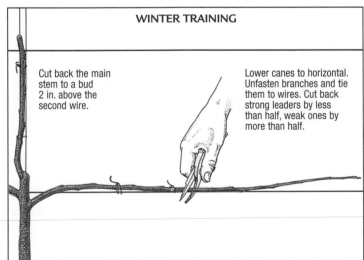

WINTER TRAINING

Cut back the main stem to a bud 2 in. above the second wire.

Lower canes to horizontal. Unfasten branches and tie them to wires. Cut back strong leaders by less than half, weak ones by more than half.

'Red Delicious' is a hardy variety. The sweet, aromatic eating apple 'Cox Orange' is more tender and suited only to the best locations.

'Red Delicious'

'Cox Orange'

Finishing Off the Top Tier of a Horizontal Espalier

The top tier of an espalier is created by pruning in winter. Cut back the main stem to just above two side buds, and rub out unwanted buds below. This effectively stops the main stem from growing upward.

Early in the following summer, when the side buds have put out their shoots, tie them to canes at an angle of 45 degrees. Train the growth of the two branches the same way you handled other tiers in previous summers—raise the cane to stimulate the growth of a weaker branch, or lower it to slow the growth of a stronger branch.

In winter lower the branches to the horizontal, remove the canes, and tie the branches to the wires.

Four or five tiers are usually the maximum to which espaliers are grown, resulting in a tree 6–8 feet high; the usual width is about 12 feet (6-foot branches on each side).

A tree can also be grown to 10 tiers if desired. In this case, for a good crop, the width is usually kept to about 6 feet. Alternatively, trees can be held to one tier in height—about 12–15 inches from the ground.

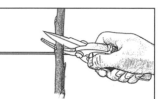

For the top tier cut the stem to leave two side-branch buds only.

Pruning a Fully Trained Horizontal Espalier

Prune the current season's growth each summer as it becomes mature, generally in late summer. Mature growth is more than 9 inches long; its greenish-brown bark has started turning brown at the base, and its leaves are dark green.

Mature laterals growing directly from branches should be cut back to three leaves beyond the basal cluster. Cut back mature side shoots from laterals or spurs to one leaf from the basal cluster.

If new growth is not mature enough in midsummer, it may be ready for pruning in late summer. In the North it may not be ready until early fall.

If you have pruned in the summer, there will probably be secondary growth in the fall. If the summer has been fairly dry and not much secondary growth has occurred, cut the growth back to one bud. After a wet summer that has produced a lot of secondary growth, you may have to delay pruning into early winter.

Apart from that, winter pruning is not usually necessary. Once branch leaders have reached a length of about 6 feet (or have filled the available space), prune them in summer as you would mature laterals.

The fruiting spurs may become overcrowded on mature trees. Thin them out in winter by cutting some flush with the parent stem and by reducing the size of others (p. 399).

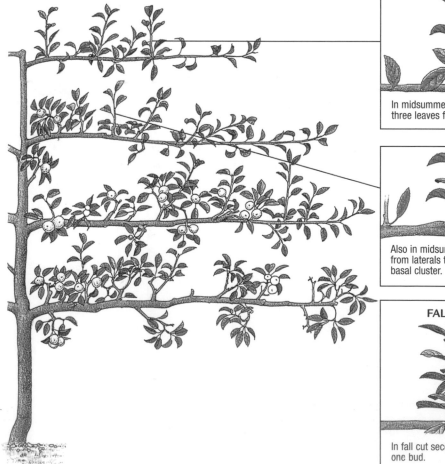

In midsummer cut laterals to three leaves from the basal cluster.

Also in midsummer cut side shoots from laterals to one leaf from the basal cluster.

FALL PRUNING

In fall cut secondary growth back to one bud.

'Melba'

'Melba', a midseason variety
hardy in Zones 5 to 9, makes
a fine dessert apple.

Pruning and Training a Fan Espalier

Training a One-Year-Old Fan-Shaped Tree

Fans should be spaced 15–20 feet apart, depending on the kind of rootstock. Plant the trees in autumn or spring (see p. 381).

If you plant a year-old tree, cut back the stem to about 2 feet from the ground after planting. Cut just above two opposite side buds.

The following summer, when shoots 9–12 inches long have grown from these buds, tie them to canes attached to the supporting wires at an angle of 45 degrees. Rub out any buds or shoots below them.

Regulate the growth of the two branches—the first ribs of the fan—by adjusting the angle of the canes. If one rib is growing more vigorously, lower its cane to slow growth, and raise the other rib cane.

When growth is matched, fix the ribs at an angle of 45 degrees. Remove the canes, and tie the ribs to the wires when stems are woody.

WINTER TRAINING

Cut back the main stem to 2 ft. from the ground, above two buds.

SUMMER TRAINING

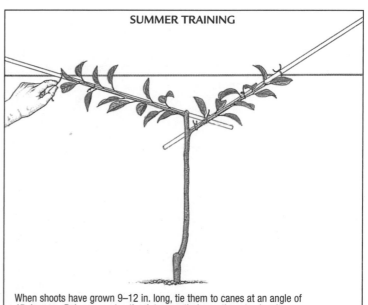

When shoots have grown 9–12 in. long, tie them to canes at an angle of 45 degrees. Raise canes to stimulate growth; lower them to slow it.

Training a Two-Year-Old Fan-Shaped Tree

During the second winter prune each of the ribs back to 1–1½ feet. Cut just above a growth bud.

During the second summer tie the extension growth from each end bud to a cane at the same angle as the rib. Then on each rib select two evenly spaced shoots on the upper side and one on the lower side. Rub out all other shoots.

As the chosen shoots grow long enough, fasten six more canes to the wires, and train the shoots to them.

WINTER TRAINING

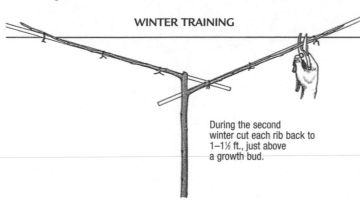

During the second winter cut each rib back to 1–1½ ft., just above a growth bud.

SUMMER TRAINING

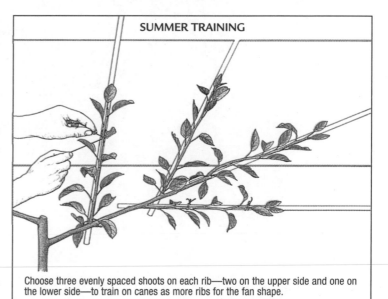

Choose three evenly spaced shoots on each rib—two on the upper side and one on the lower side—to train on canes as more ribs for the fan shape.

'Golden Delicious', a high-quality dessert and cooking apple, can be stored for up to 120 days.

'Golden Delicious'

Training a Three-Year-Old Fan-Shaped Tree

In the third winter prune each of the eight fan ribs back to 2–2½ feet, just above a growth bud.

The following summer tie the growth from the end bud of each rib onto the canes. Choose three evenly spaced shoots from each rib—two on the upper side and one on the lower—for training as additional ribs. Cut mature shoots not wanted as fan ribs back to three leaves from the basal cluster.

Tie the 24 new ribs to the canes when they are long enough. The fan will now have 32 ribs, probably enough to cover the wall. Remove the canes and tie the shoots to the wires when they become woody.

WINTER TRAINING

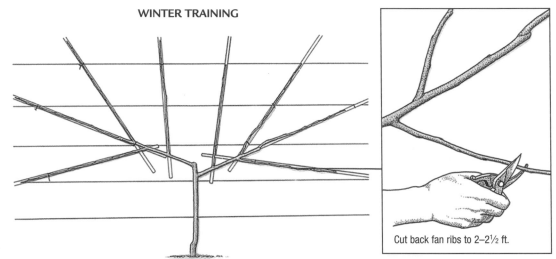

Cut back fan ribs to 2–2½ ft.

SUMMER TRAINING

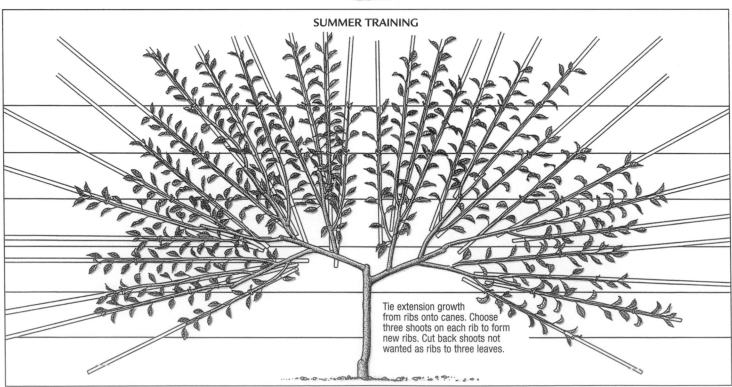

Tie extension growth from ribs onto canes. Choose three shoots on each rib to form new ribs. Cut back shoots not wanted as ribs to three leaves.

The eating apple 'Idared' is robust but susceptible to mildew. Its medium to large fruits are pale to dark red in color and sweetish and mild in taste.

'Idared'

Pruning a Fan After It Has Been Trained

Once the tree's fan shape has been established, the only pruning necessary in winter is the thinning out of overcrowded spurs. This will help the tree to produce regular crops and better-quality fruit.

Remove some of the overcrowded spurs entirely, cutting them off flush with the parent stem. Then cut back others to reduce their size and thin out the cluster of fruit buds (see p. 385).

Prune new growth in summer as it becomes mature, generally starting in midsummer and perhaps continuing for about a month.

Mature growth is at least 9 inches long, has turned woody at the base, and has dark green leaves. Cut back mature new side shoots from ribs to one leaf beyond the basal cluster, unless they are needed as replacements. Tie the replacement shoots to the wires.

New growth that is not mature enough for pruning in midsummer may be ready in late summer. If it is still not mature enough at that time— this may well be the case in the North—wait until early fall.

When you prune new growth in summer, secondary growth may develop from the cut wood by fall.

After a reasonably dry summer that has not produced much secondary growth, cut it all back to one bud in the fall.

When the summer has been wet and a great deal of secondary growth has occurred, you may need to delay pruning into early winter.

If the ribs of the fan grow beyond the space allotted, cut them back to a strong side branch, and tie it in as a replacement leader.

SUMMER PRUNING

If ribs outgrow the available space, cut them back to a strong side branch, and tie it in as a replacement leader.

In mid-summer cut back all mature new side shoots from ribs to one leaf from the basal cluster.

'Cortland', a robust medium-red variety and popular dessert and cooking apple, is ready for harvesting 125 to 130 days from bloom.

'Cortland'

Varieties of Apples to Grow

The varieties listed should be available at nurseries. They are listed in the order in which they mature.

Pollination group. No apple tree is fully self-fertile; so more than one variety should be grown. Ideally, choose trees from within the same pollination group, although pollination will usually occur between varieties in adjoining groups. The groups relate to flowering time:

1. Early to mid season
2. Midseason
3. Mid to late season

Triploids (marked T) are almost sterile varieties and therefore poor pollinators. They need to be grown with two other varieties from the same group—to pollinate both the triploid and each other.

Picking time. The days from bloom to picking time indicated below are only an average. The exact time varies according to season and locality. All the apples on a tree do not ripen at the same time; and, for the early- and mid-season varieties, more than one picking is needed.

NAMES	POLLINATION GROUP	DAYS FROM BLOOM TO PICKING	COLOR	REMARKS
'Gravenstein' (T)	1	90–95	Red striped	Good quality. High acidity. Cooking; 40–60 days' storage.
'Cortland'	2	125–130	Medium red	Good quality. Medium acidity. Dessert and cooking; 90–100 days' storage.
'Honeycrisp'	2	125–130	Red striped	High quality. Low acidity. Dessert; 90–150 days' storage.
'Liberty'*	2	125–130	Red	Good quality. Medium acidity. Dessert and cooking; 90–120 days' storage.
'McIntosh' (S)	1	125–130	Medium red	Good quality. Medium acidity. Dessert and cooking; 60–90 days' storage.
'Jonagold' (T)	2	125–130	Red over yellow	Good quality. Medium acidity. Dessert; 90–120 days' storage.
'Golden Delicious' (S)	2	140–145	Yellow	High quality. Medium acidity. Dessert and cooking; 90–120 days' storage.
'Jonathan'	2	140–145	Bright red	Good quality. Medium-high acidity. Dessert and cooking; 60–90 days' storage.
'Red Delicious'* (S)	2	140–150	Medium red	Popular. Low acidity. Dessert and cooking; 90–100 days' storage.
'Northern Spy'	3	145–155	Red striped	Good quality. Medium acidity. Dessert and cooking; 120–150 days' storage.
'Empire'*	3	155–165	Red	High quality. Medium acidity. Dessert and cooking; 90–120 days' storage.
'Mutsu' (or Crispin)	3	155–165	Green	High quality. Medium acidity. Dessert; 90–120 days' storage.

(T) *Indicates triploid number of chromosomes and the need for 2 other varieties nearby for cross-pollination.* (S) *Indicates that spur strains on dwarfing rootstocks are available.*
* *Indicates disease-resistant varieties.*

Varieties of Hardy Apples to Grow

The apple varieties listed above are hardy in Zones 4 to 9. The following varieties are hardier, and grow well in the upper Midwest. Consult your local nursery to determine picking time and which varieties are best suited to your area. To ensure pollination, plant more than one variety. Or, you can grow a crab apple. These make good pollinators for eating apples and are often planted in commercial orchards. It need not be very close, bees will still find both.

NAMES	COLOR	REMARKS
'Breakey'	Yellowish green	Eating and cooking.
'Carroll'	Creamy green	Eating and cooking.
'Collet'	Greenish yellow	Dessert and cooking.
'Edith Smith'	Greenish yellow	Eating.
'Glenorchie'	Pale yellow	Eating and cooking.
'Haralson'	Green	Eating.
'Harcourt'	Yellow with splashes of red	Eating.
'Luke'	Yellow and red	Dessert and cooking.

Varieties of Apple Crabs to Grow

Apple crabs are crosses between regular apples and crab apples. They are extremely hardy and can be grown in exposed locations where regular apples might not fruit well. The following varieties are the most widely available.

NAMES	COLOR	REMARKS
'Kerr'	Dark red	Eating; also for canning and jelly.
'Renown'	Yellow and red	Eating; sweet in mid-September.
'Rescue'	Yellow and red	Eating; also for canning.
'Trail'	Striped red and yellow	Eating; also for canning.

Starting a Spray Program

It is almost impossible to produce pest-free fruit in a home garden unless a spray program is followed. See page 384 when symptoms occur during the growing season. If your goal is blemish-free fruit, follow a spray schedule throughout the early part of the year, the time when most of the damage usually occurs, but do not spray while the tree is in bloom and bees are active. Consult your county extension agent or nurseryperson for problems specific to your area.

The European apricot is comparatively fussy about climate and location. Apricots with Manchurian and Siberian genes are much tougher.

'Moorpark', a European variety

Apricots

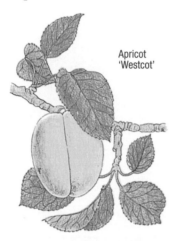

Apricot 'Westcot'

There are two strains of apricots: the traditional European varieties that are relatively tender and need a sheltered site, and new varieties that have been developed using hardy species from Manchuria and Siberia. Although the fruit of these is not of a very high quality, they are much hardier and can be grown successfully on the Great Plains. They are still very early flowering and should never be planted in a frost pocket.

European strains of apricots are best grown as fan trees against a south-facing wall. In milder areas they can be grown as dwarf trees if they are sheltered from cold winds.

One tree should be enough for an average family. The fruiting time is from midsummer to early fall, depending on the variety.

Soil and feeding requirements are the same as for plums (see p. 426). Trees bear fruit on one-year-old and older wood. Train dwarf and fan trees like apple trees (see pp. 386, 397) until the framework is built, but prune in early spring as growth begins. Then prune fans like plum trees, (see p. 427), dwarf trees like tart cherries (see p. 407).

Apricots are self-fertile, but they flower when few pollinating insects are about; so artificial pollination is advisable to ensure a good crop. Dab a small, soft paintbrush on the open flowers every two or three days.

Thinning is necessary only if the branches are very heavy with fruit. Wait until the stones are formed (check by cutting a fruit), as there is often a natural drop of fruit just before this. Fruits should be spaced about 5 inches apart on the branch.

Varieties of Apricots to Grow

Always plant named varieties. Nursery catalogs will sometimes offer plants as just apricot, or Manchurian apricot, but these are seedlings whose performance is unknown.

They could be satisfactory and give good-tasting fruit, but there is an equal chance that the fruit could be inedible.

NAMES	SEASON	REMARKS
European apricots		
'Goldcot'	Mid	Medium sized with good quality.
'Harlayne'	Late	One of the hardiest Europeans.
'Harglow'	Mid	Juicy fruit on a dwarf plant.
'Skaha'	Early-mid	Not self-fertile. Good on West Coast.
'Veecot'	Late	Good for canning.
Hardy apricots		
'Brookcot'	Mid	1½-in. fruit with good flavor.
'Sungold'	Mid	Plant with 'Moongold' for pollination.
'Moongold'	Mid	Plant with 'Sungold' for pollination.
'Westcot'	Mid	The most bud-hardy, with good flavor.

Avocados

Avocado
(*Persea americana*)

Avocado trees are large, broad-leaved evergreens, varying in form from upright to broadly spreading. They make magnificent display plants, resembling in general appearance the evergreen magnolias of the South.

The individual flowers are inconspicuous, but the blooming period itself is impressive because of the long clusters of flowers borne on the tree over a span of several months. Bloom may begin as early as December and continue into April. This extends the harvest.

If early bloom should be damaged by frost, the later bloom will still produce fruit.

The fruits are attractive, varying in color from bright green to a glossy purplish black. They can be round or pear shaped.

The peel, or skin, of the fruit may be smooth and thin, or it may be rough, thick, and woody. It sticks tightly to the flesh of some varieties but slips off easily from others. Most trees bear heavily one year and lightly the next, although a few varieties produce fruit fairly consistently from year to year.

Avocado fruit is low in sugar content, so it is generally used in salads and in sauces, such as *guacamole*, rather than in desserts. It is high in calories and its protein content (1–4 percent) is higher than most other tree fruits. Avocados are a good source of vitamins A, B_1, B_2, and C.

Avocado trees are native to tropical and subtropical regions of North and Central America, where three groups, or "races," have developed: the Mexican, Guatemalan, and West Indian. The fruits of these groups vary considerably in their characteristics. Most current avocado varieties are hybrids of two or all three races, but only those with some Mexican heritage have any appreciable hardiness to cold.

Some pure Mexican types will tolerate temperatures slightly below 20°F, but the West Indian types will be damaged at temperatures below 28°–30°F. The Guatemalan types are generally hardy to temperatures as low as 25°F.

Harvest avocados—by clipping, not pulling—while they are still hard, and allow to ripen at room temperature.

Avocado (*Persea americana*)

Blackberries

Taking Care of Avocado Trees

Thoroughly soak the soil around young trees every two weeks. Allow it to dry out somewhat between waterings, to protect the shallow roots from rot. Avocados do well in both slightly acid and slightly alkaline soils, but chlorosis may develop in trees grown in very alkaline soils. It can usually be corrected with applications of iron chelates to the soil.

Little if any pruning is required, other than to keep trees to the desired shape. All frost-damaged branches are best removed after new growth matures. If large areas of dead bark appear on branches well below the new growth, however, the affected branches should be removed promptly, or they may break under the stress of crops or wind.

Varieties of Avocados to Grow

The pollination cycle of avocado trees differs by variety. Type A have flowers that are receptive to pollen in the morning, but their pollen is not

Because avocado fruits often fall off the tree before ripening fully, they must be harvested when still hard. (They ripen readily at room temperature.) Fruits should be harvested on the basis of season and size—that is, a given variety attains its mature size during certain months and will ripen satisfactorily off the tree if harvested at the appropriate time. The purplish-black varieties can be harvested at any time after more than half their peel has darkened.

The Mexican varieties crack badly if exposed to hot, humid conditions in summer. But the fruit usually ripens satisfactorily if it is harvested before cracking and placed in a cool, dry room.

Avocados should not be pulled off the tree, as fruit rots if the stem is pulled out. Clip off with the stem attached.

shed until afternoon, when flowers are no longer receptive. Other varieties, type B, have the reverse pattern. In theory, neither type will set fruit if planted alone. However, in practice, all varieties are usually self-pollinating.

Blackberry 'Thornless Evergreen'

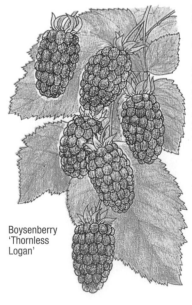

Boysenberry 'Thornless Logan'

Blackberries can be erect or trailing. Among the trailing types are the loganberry and the boysenberry. These are hybrids from crossing blackberries with other species of *Rubus*. All require essentially the same care. The average family will need three to five plants.

Blackberries, loganberries, and boysenberries are used for desserts, jams, and wines. They also adapt themselves well to freezing.

They do best in sun but will take partial shade. Provide a well-drained but moisture-retentive soil, with a pH of about 5.5. Adequate moisture all season is essential.

Rooted canes are best planted in early fall (see p. 250), but they can be put in at any time until early spring if the soil is not frozen. Install supports (see p. 403) before planting. Position erect varieties 5 feet apart in rows 8 feet apart; vigorous, thornless, trailing plants, such as 'Thornless Evergreen', 8–12 feet apart in rows 10 feet apart; others, 4–6 feet apart in rows 8 feet apart, depending on soil fertility and training system. Immediately after planting, cut the canes back (just above a bud) to 9–15 inches above ground level.

Diseases and insects can be kept to a minimum by using ground that has been cultivated for several years, choosing disease-resistant varieties, buying stock free of nematodes and diseases, removing old canes after harvest, and keeping plants free of weeds and fallen leaves.

The diseases that can attack are verticillium wilt, cane gall, anthracnose (spots on canes, leaves), and orange rust. Troublesome insects include aphids, leafhoppers, mites, fruitworms, scales, leaf rollers, beetles, weevils, cane borers, and white grubs (on roots).

Controls for many of these diseases are given in the section beginning on page 506. For control of other disease and insect problems, contact your regional county extension agent for the latest recommendations.

NAMES	HARDINESS	SEASON	REMARKS
California			
'Bacon'	25°–27°F	Fall	Green, medium. Flower type B.
'Duke'	20°–24°F	Fall	Green, medium. Flower type A.
'Fuerte'	28°–30°F	Winter	Green, medium. Fruit type B.
'Gwen'	28°–30°F	Spring-Summer	Green, medium. Flower type A.
'Hass'	28°–30°F	Winter	Dark purple, medium. Flower type B.
'Pinkerton'	28°–30°F	Winter	Green, medium-large. Flower type A.
Florida			
'Booth 8'	28°–30°F	Early winter	Green, medium-large. Flower type B.
'Brogdon'	20°–24°F	Late summer	Dark purple, medium. Flower type B.
'Choquette'	28°–30°F	Winter	Green, very large. Flower type A.
'Duke'	20°–24°F	Midsummer	Green, medium. Flower type A.
'Simmonds'	28°–30°F	Late summer	Green, very large. Flower type A.
'Waldin'	28°–30°F	Early fall	Green, large. Flower type A.

Many blackberry blossoms are quite fragrant. The berries, which are used for desserts, jams, and wines, are readily frozen.

Blackberry flowers

Wild blackberries

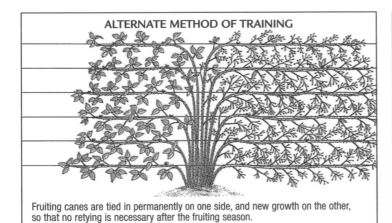

ALTERNATE METHOD OF TRAINING

Fruiting canes are tied in permanently on one side, and new growth on the other, so that no retying is necessary after the fruiting season.

AFTER FRUITING

Once fruit has been picked, cut canes back to ground level.

Raising New Blackberry Plants

Trailing blackberries root easily. One way is to layer the tips of shoots. In midsummer bend a new season's shoot to the ground. Dig a 6-inch-deep hole and plant the tip of the shoot. By early fall the tips will have rooted. Sever each new plant from its parent just above a bud. In late fall transfer each new cane to its permanent bed. It will fruit in its second or third year.

For erect blackberries, dig up roots of established plants in early spring, cut them into 3-inch lengths, and bury them in trenches 2 or 3 inches deep.

Cultivating and Training the Plants

Erect blackberries can be grown without supports, but it is best to use them. For a trellis arrangement, set posts in a row 15 feet apart, and stretch a wire between them 30 inches from the ground.

Train trailing blackberries up a post or wires, so that the growing shoots are kept away from the two-year-old shoots, which bear the fruit. This prevents disease from spreading. Use 9–10 feet of 4- by 4-inch timber for each post, leaving 7 feet above the ground. Train fruiting canes up the post, and tie loosely together to one side the new shoots growing from the ground. For fruiting canes on wires, use 10- to 12-gauge wire stretched between posts to a height of 6 feet. Place wires 12 inches apart; fasten to posts with staples.

There are several ways of training the canes. With the fan method the fruiting canes are fanned out on each side, and the new growth is temporarily tied to the top wire. Weaving is similar, except that the fruiting canes are woven around the wires. With a third method, fruiting canes are tied permanently on one side of the wires,

new growth on the other side. Or just tie the canes loosely to a stake.

Watering and feeding. Water only during dry spells in summer. One to two months before growth starts in spring, apply about 5 pounds of a 10–10–10 fertilizer or a similar mix per 100-foot row. For the first year or two, apply 3–4 ounces of fertilizer in a 12-inch radius at the base of each plant. Mulch with compost.

Cutting Out the Old Canes

After the fruit is picked, cut out the fruited canes at ground level. In the case of post training and fan and weaving systems, untie the current year's shoots from their temporary positions, and tie them so as to replace the old, cut-down shoots.

Hybrid Berries

There are several hybrid berries now appearing in nursery catalogs. Most have been grown for many years, but are only now becoming readily available. Boysenberry and loganberry are the best known, but the rampant Sunberry, Tayberry, and Jostaberry are also popular. Their culture is the same as for blackberry.

Varieties of Blackberries to Grow

Buy blackberry plants that have been certified to be free from virus.

Blackberries—including loganberries and dewberries—need no cross-pollination (with the exception of 'Flordagrand'). Thornless varieties are the easiest to pick.

NAMES	SEASON	USUAL AREA	REMARKS
Erect			
'Arapaho'	Very early	Pacific Coast	Excellent flavor.
'Brazos'	Early	Gulf states	Thorny.
'Darrow'	Early	Northeast, Central	Thorny. Cold hardy.
'Illini Hardy'	Mid-late	Cooler areas	Very hardy.
'Marion'	Late	West	Thorny.
'Navaho'	Very late	Not for South	Disease resistant.
Trailing			
'Black Satin'	Mid	Cooler areas	Thornless. Disease resistant.
'Chester'	Mid	Pacific Northwest	Thornless. Sweet flavor.
'Hull'	Late	Not for extreme South	Thornless. Large fruit.
'Lucretia'	Early	Cooler areas	Dewberry. Hardy if protected against severe cold.
'Thornless Young'	Mid	West	Thornless. Suckers from roots are thorny.

The midseason blueberry 'Bluecrop' is a good choice. It is erect and robust, and the large fruits have a good aroma.

'Bluecrop'

Blueberries

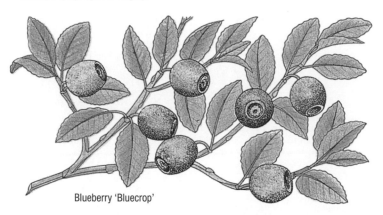

Blueberry 'Bluecrop'

There are many blueberries native to North America. For best results, choose the cultivated forms recommended by your regional county extension agent.

The berries, fresh or frozen, are suitable for desserts and jam making, and, of course, make excellent pies.

Blueberries need a moisture-retentive, acid soil—with a pH value between 5 and 6 (see pp. 496–497). They do best in an open, sunny area, but they can be grown in partial shade. In northern regions the bushes should be given protection from cold winds.

It is useless to try to grow blueberries in alkaline soil. When only alkaline soil is available, blueberries can be grown in containers, though these need special winter protection. Fill the containers with an acid- or a peat-based compost, with no lime added.

From four to six bushes should provide a good supply of blueberries for the average family. Berries are generally ready for picking in mid and late summer. Each of the plants will bear fruit over a period of several weeks.

Blueberries are not completely self-fertile; to ensure a good yield, plant at least two varieties.

Plants can be propagated by layering in fall or spring or by taking semihardwood cuttings in late summer.

How to Prune Blueberries

Blueberries need no pruning for the first three years after planting. After that, prune each winter.

Fruit is borne on the previous year's wood. To promote new shoots that will fruit the following year, cut from one to four of the oldest shoots from each bush.

Either cut them back hard to a strong new shoot, or if there are plenty of young basal shoots, cut them down to soil level.

Cut from one to four of the oldest shoots back hard to a strong new shoot or down to soil level.

Planting and Tending Blueberries

Plant blueberry bushes in fall or spring when soil is workable. Set the bushes 3–4 feet apart and about 1 inch deeper in the soil than they were in the nursery.

Before planting, test the soil. If the pH is higher than 5.5, seek recommendations for how much sulfur to add to adjust the pH to between 4.0 and 5.5. Fertilize plants yearly with soybean meal or alfalfa meal (¼ to 2 cups per plant). Recheck every 3 years and add more sulfur if needed.

Early each summer mulch with well-rotted manure, garden compost, or leaf mold. Protect plants from birds with netting.

Plants may suffer from chlorosis, which can be caused by soil that is not sufficiently acidic. Yellow mottling or patches occur on the leaves, growth is poor, and few blueberries are produced. To decrease the pH, dig in acidic material, such as peat moss, and apply sulfur to the soil as directed on the container.

For other symptoms and more information on pest and disease control, see Plant Disorders on page 506.

Varieties of Blueberries to Grow

The season of ripening given below is for most major blueberry areas; ripening will occur later in the North. However, since ripening time is an estimate only, it will vary according to the growing conditions prevailing during the season.

NAMES	SEASON	REMARKS
'Northland'	Early (mid to late summer)	Small, medium berries. Small spreading bush, only 4 ft. at maturity. Good hardiness.
'Berkeley'	Midseason (late summer)	Very large berry. Medium quality. Bush is medium hardy.
'Bluecrop'	Midseason (late summer)	Large, good berries. Average-vigor bush; quite hardy and drought resistant.

Although it has been on the market for over 100 years, the sweet cherry 'Bing' is still widely grown. It ripens mid-season, and is one of the main commercial varieties, especially in the west.

Sweet cherry 'Bing'

Cherries

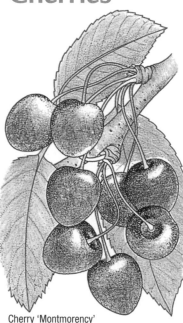

Cherry 'Montmorency'

There are two kinds of cherries: sweet, which are eaten fresh; and tart, which are used mainly for cooking, canning, jam making, and pie baking. Tart cherries are hardier than sweet cherries and will grow in northern Zone 4.

Both of these kinds of cherries need deep, well-drained soil, around pH 6.5. Tart cherries will do better in somewhat poorer soils than sweet cherries.

Train sweet cherries to a modified leader form. Many varieties are not self-fertile and you will need to plant two varieties for good fruit set. If you have a small yard, your best option is to train your two sweet cherry trees as fan-trained trees.

Tart cherries are definitely less vigorous, but they are easier to grow than sweet cherries. Be sure to grow them as bush trees or as fans. They are self-pollinating; so a single tree will bear fruit.

Two trees of either type will bear enough fruit for an average family.

How to Grow Fan-Trained Sweet Cherries

Even when grafted onto the dwarfing rootstock 'Colt', sweet cherries make good-sized trees. Train them to a modified leader or as fans. Fan trees will span 15–20 feet. Plant them 18–24 feet apart (see p. 381) against a wall facing either south or west.

Modified leader trees will not need heavy pruning once they're established. Remove dead, damaged and crossing limbs yearly. After trees reach 7 years of age, remove some old wood each year as well as to maintain good air circulation.

Cherry trees do not need much fertilizing, and too much fertilizer can cause succulent growth that is susceptible to fire blight. Spreading a thin layer of compost over the root zone in the spring should be sufficient. Water during prolonged dry spells.

In early summer drape the entire tree with netting to protect the fruit from birds.

Do not pick sweet cherries until they are completely ripe; then pull them off by hand with an upward twist. The fruit does not keep well; put it in a plastic bag and refrigerate. **Training and pruning.** For the first three years after planting a one-year-old, train and prune it like a fan apple (see p. 393). Prune it in early spring before growth begins, not in winter. After the framework is established, treatment differs; sweet cherries have more spurs and fewer laterals, and heavy pruning is not necessary.

In early summer rub out the current year's shoots that are growing directly toward or directly away from the wall. Pinch out the tips of the others in early or middle summer when they have four to six leaves.

When ribs reach the top of the wall, cut back to a weak lateral. Otherwise, bend the shoot to the horizontal, and tie to the wire. This slows the growth rate and encourages new shoots to break out. The shoot can then be cut back to a weak lateral.

In early fall cut back shoots pinched out in summer to three or four flower buds (large, plump ones).

Also cut away any deadwood. Make the cuts flush with the parent stem. On older trees tie new shoots into the fan shape when there is room in early or mid summer. Some may be needed to replace old shoots.

Protection. Sweet cherries bloom early in spring and are liable to have their flowers damaged by late frosts and cold winds. Where winds are a problem, grow deciduous or evergreen hedges to form a windbreak, or erect temporary windbreaks with burlap-covered frames or open-weave fencing. Remember, a slightly open fence that slows wind speed is better than a solid fence that causes turbulence on the lee side.

If late frosts are liable to cause problems, flowers can be protected with a burlap-covered frame that stands in front of the tree. It should be braced against the wall so that it does not touch the flowers and must be removed during the day to allow access to pollinating insects. Trunks are prone to sunscald in summer and should be shaded with a burlap wrap.

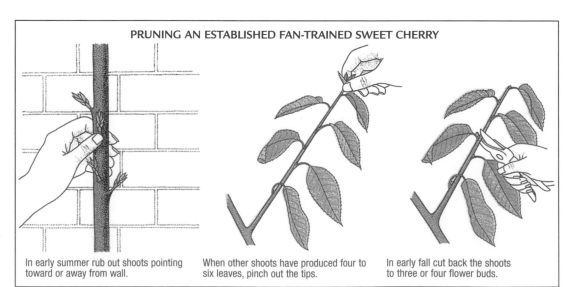

PRUNING AN ESTABLISHED FAN-TRAINED SWEET CHERRY

In early summer rub out shoots pointing toward or away from wall.

When other shoots have produced four to six leaves, pinch out the tips.

In early fall cut back the shoots to three or four flower buds.

Tart cherry 'Montmorency'

Tart cherry 'North Star'

Sour cherries demand less of the soil than sweet cherries and are slightly hardier.

How to Care for Tart Cherries

Tart cherries can be grown either as bush trees or as fans. (The latter type can be grown against any wall, even one facing north.) Plant both forms of tree 15–18 feet apart (see p. 381). Plant trees upon receiving them.

Weed control by shallow cultivation or mulching is essential around young trees. Later, a cover of closely mowed grass can be used.

Care for tart cherry trees in the same way as sweet cherry trees. Harvesting, however, is different. Cut off the ripe fruit with scissors; otherwise you may break the spurs.

Bush trees can be planted between other fruit trees, like apples and pears. Their fruit ripens earlier and is eaten by birds. Bush trees are easier to protect with netting attached to surrounding fruit trees.

Pruning dwarf trees. For the first three years, train and prune your dwarf cherry trees like dwarf apples (see p. 386), but prune in spring as growth begins.

Trees bear the most fruit on the previous year's growth. The aim of pruning an established tree is to constantly stimulate new wood.

Once a tree has started to fruit, thin it out to let in light and air, cutting back older shoots to just above one-year-old laterals. Thin out the outer spread occasionally, where new growth develops.

Pruning fan-trained trees. Prune and train fan tart cherries in early spring like fan apples (see p. 397). Thin fans like tart cherry trees.

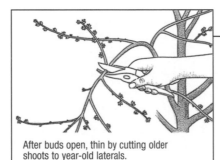
After buds open, thin by cutting older shoots to year-old laterals.

PRUNING CHERRY TREES

What Can Go Wrong With Sweet and Tart Cherries

The commonest problems in cherry growing are aphids and leaf spot.

If plants show symptoms that are not described here, turn to the section on pests and diseases on page 504. Look up controls in the section beginning on page 542.

SYMPTOMS AND SIGNS	CAUSE	CONTROL
Shoots and leaves distorted, covered with black insects.	Aphids	Immediately after flowering, spray with insecticidal soap.
Eggs laid in fruits, which show scars. Young insects ("worms") destroy fruits.	Plum curculios (weevils)	Spray with insecticidal soap at petal fall, and repeat at least 3 times at 7- to 14-day intervals. Collect fallen fruit.
Serious disease of fruits, which are covered with powdery brown spore masses. Also causes twig dieback.	Brown rot (fungus)	Apply first spray at preblossom stage (buds just beginning to open). Repeat 5 or 6 times at 7- to 10-day intervals. Use wettable sulfur.
Minute spots, dark blue at first, later reddish brown and black, on flowers, fruits, and leaves.	Cherry leaf spot (fungus)	When petals fall, spray with Bordeaux mixture. Repeat every 7–10 days except when very dry. Destroy infected leaves.

Varieties of Sweet and Tart Cherries to Grow

Sweet cherries need a partner to cross-pollinate at blossom time; so two trees must be grown. Not all varieties flowering at the same time will pollinate each other. Therefore, at least two different varieties must be grown in close proximity to ensure pollination. When selecting varieties, follow the catalog recommendations for suitable pollenizers, or check with your local county extension agent.

Tart cherries are self-fertile and therefore do not need a pollination partner planted nearby.

NAMES	SEASON**	REMARKS
Sweet cherries*		
'Bing'	Midseason	Dark red, but cracks badly.
'Stella'	Midseason	Self-fertile, black fruit.
'Black Tatarian'	Early	Black, soon goes soft.
'Rainier'	Early	Yellow, disease resistant.
Tart cherries		
'Montmorency'	Midseason	Scarlet, yellow flesh.
'North Star'	Early	Red skin, yellow flesh.
* Plant more than one variety of sweet cherry to ensure pollination.		
** Cherries ripen from early to mid summer in most regions.		

'Washington Navel', a virtually
seedless variety, bears fruits up
to 4 in. in diameter.

Citrus sinensis 'Washington Navel'

Citrus

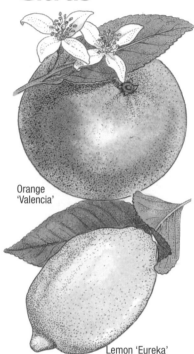

Orange
'Valencia'

Lemon 'Eureka'

Although best known for their fruit, citrus trees are handsome, glossy-leaved evergreens that, in warm climates, can be used to great advantage in the landscape. Some will grow to 30 feet but can be kept smaller by pruning. Others can be considered large shrubs, and some are suited to growing in containers.

The many closely related groups of citrus trees include the sweet orange, tangerine (or mandarin), grapefruit, lemon, and lime. Not only are there several varieties of each species, but there are ornamental species and distantly related kinds, such as the deciduous, inedible trifoliate orange (*Poncirus trifoliata*) that can be grown as far north as Washington, D.C.

The various species have been hybridized with each other and with more distant relatives. Some hybrids of tangerines and grapefruits, known as tangelos, are fine dessert fruits.

Citranges are hybrids of trifoliate and sweet oranges. They are resistant to frost and produce juicy, orangelike fruits. However, these are

inedible, and so citranges are only used as rootstocks.

There are red-fleshed, or blood, oranges, red-fleshed grapefruits, and pink-fleshed lemons, as well as those with the commoner yellow and orange flesh. There are also variegated forms of several kinds of citrus in which the fruit peel and leaves are a mixture of green and white.

Citrus trees grow well in a range of soils but will not tolerate saline conditions or poor drainage. Citrus is very sensitive to climate. Freezing temperatures ruin the quality of the fruit and, if too low, will kill the tree. This varies with the kind of citrus. Lemons and limes are restricted to the warmest locations, while satsuma mandarins are much tougher and grow well along the Gulf Coast from Florida to Texas, where temperatures can drop to 15°F.

The deepest orange color of both peel and juice is produced in the cooler areas. The thickest peel develops in dry regions and the juiciest fruit under wet, humid conditions.

Grapefruit is acid in cool climates and sweet in hot ones. The flesh of blood oranges turns red in cool climates, but in warmer regions it is often mottled or lacking in red. Lemon and lime trees bloom periodically throughout the year and continue bearing fruit in all seasons. Other citrus trees flower in the spring, but the ripened fruit will last on the tree for several months.

Three or four mature trees will keep a family of four in citrus fruit much of the year. Few gardens can support four large trees, but even small trees furnish a considerable amount of fruit. For varieties of citrus trees suitable to your region, consult your local county extension agent.

Many people grow the various citrus as house plants, often starting them from seeds taken from store-bought fruit. While this is fun to do, the resulting plant may not be true, since some citrus cross-breed easily. However, since citrus seeds grown from seed indoors rarely produce usable fruit, this is not very important.

How to Care for Citrus Trees

In Florida citrus trees are protected from the cold by banking soil approximately 2 feet high around the trunks in winter. In parts of Texas and the Southwest, special insulating material is often wrapped around the tree trunks.

The soil from 3 to 6 feet around the trunks of young trees should be kept free of weeds for the first four years. Mature citrus trees can be grown in lawn grass if extra water and fertilizer are added, but it is best to keep the soil bare beneath the canopy of foliage.

Young trees should be watered once a week during the first year after planting, but allow clay soil to dry between waterings. In Florida, mature trees do not require irrigation, though it increases yields.

Citrus trees require irrigation in Texas and the Southwest. One thorough soaking in January may last until March; then water every two to four weeks, depending on how soon the soil dries out.

Before planting citrus on infertile soils in Florida, enrich the soil with organic matter, and top-dress the soil around the trees four times a year with compost or alfalfa meal.

Only nitrogen is needed on the more fertile soils of other regions. Alfalfa meal, soybean meal, and blood meal are satisfactory sources of nitrogen. Overfeeding can reduce the quality of the fruit and decrease the hardiness of the plant.

Deficiencies in trace elements, revealed by leaves mottled yellow or white, may need correcting. Yellow mottling indicates zinc deficiency. If veins are green and the rest of the leaf is pale, more iron is needed.

Pruning Citrus

There are two types of pruning. "Heading back" means shortening a branch. This encourages the development of buds just behind the cut. This response is local. Heading back a branch on one side will force buds on that branch but does little to stimulate growth on other parts of the tree. "Thinning out" means completely removing a branch, regardless of size, at the point where it is attached to another. This does not stimulate growth except where removal of large limbs lets in enough light to stimulate development of dormant buds on interior branches.

The best way to keep a tree at a given size is to thin it out so that it will not get much larger than desired. Thinning out is preferred to heading back. Heading back tends to develop a canopy, with the entire interior of

the tree shaded. Thinning also requires fewer cuts and promotes a more balanced production of fruit.

Neglected trees can be reduced in size and rejuvenated by cutting them back to whatever height is desired. If the tree is sound, a smaller framework can be created by cutting back selected branches as large as 1 or 2 inches in diameter. Prune in early spring before new growth starts but after danger of frost has passed. In one year a vigorous new fruiting top will develop on the framework you have structured in this way.

The top growth of citrus trees is sometimes killed by frost. When this happens, it is best to wait until leaves of the first flush of spring growth mature before removing damaged large limbs, or further dieback may occur. Plants in containers should be kept to the desired size largely with thinning out cuts.

'Jonkheer van Tets'

'White Pearl'

'Jonkheer van Tets' is a good early variety of red currant. 'White Pearl' is an early white variety with small, sweet berries.

Currants

Black currant 'Consort'

Red currants are widely available in the U.S. White currants are rarely seen. Black currants cannot be legally grown in some areas of the country, as they can spread white pine blister rust. Check local regulations with your county extension agent. Red currants do best in the cooler humid regions and are used for desserts, preserves, or wine.

Almost any water-retaining but well-drained soil is suitable, though red currants do best in lighter soils. They will thrive in either sun or partial shade. Because they flower early in the year, take care not to plant in frost pockets.

For a good, regular fruit supply, the average family needs 4 to 6 bushes or 12 to 15 cordons. Harvest time is usually in early summer. Before planting, dig the bed over, and thoroughly work in a rich compost or a balanced organic fertilizer. The plants are especially susceptible to potash deficiency, which causes leaf edges to appear scorched.

Plant in early spring or autumn. Place bushes 5 feet apart; single cordons, 15 inches apart; double, 30 inches apart; and triple, 45 inches apart. Cordon rows should be about 4 feet apart.

Cordons need 2- by 2-inch stakes for each stem. Use stakes 8 feet long with 5–6 feet above ground level. Another method is to grow rows against three or four horizontal wires at 2-foot intervals and tie them to vertical canes fastened to the wires.

In late winter or early spring, feed with alfalfa meal or blood meal, ringed a foot away from the plant base. Add a 2-inch mulch of well-rotted manure or garden compost.

Control weeds by mulching or hand pulling. Do not hoe. This can cut shallow roots.

Water only during prolonged dry spells. Take out any suckers that spring from the main stem or the roots. If frost lifts young plants, firm them in with your feet. Strong winds may break off shoots. On young bushes stake those shoots that are important to maintain the shape.

Birds are one of the main problems for currant growers. They can damage buds and strip the plant of its fruit. Bird netting is a good means of protection. Pick fruit as soon as it is ripe.

How to Raise Your Own Currant Bushes

Currants are best propagated from cuttings that are about 15 inches long. In midfall select the straightest shoots from the current year's growth, and cut them off low, just above a bud.

Trim off any softwood at the tip (there should not be more than an inch or so), cutting just above a bud; do not cut if it is brown to the tip. Trim the lower end just below a bud for a 15-inch cutting.

Rub off all but the top four or five buds on the cutting. Buds left on lower down will produce suckers that may prevent the formation of a leg. Black currants are grown as multi-stemmed bushes and should have the buds left on. Dip the lower end of each cutting in hormone rooting powder.

Cut an 8-inch deep V-shaped slit with one side vertical and the other at a 45-degree angle. Sprinkle sand in the bottom for drainage. Set cuttings upright, about 6 inches apart, leaving 9 inches above soil level. Fill trench and firm.

Cuttings will root by late fall. Lift them with a fork, and replant them where they are to go.

Set the plants in the ground 2 inches deeper than they were as cuttings, and immediately after replanting, shorten branches by one-half.

Varieties of Currants to Grow

The varieties sold at local nurseries are tried and true in that area. Such varieties are quite likely to perform well in your garden. If there are no currants available locally, they can be purchased from mail-order sources.

While currants are self-fertile, if you plant more than one variety, you can extend the cropping season and not have the fruit all ripening in a few days. Bushes will be productive for at least 20 years, so it will pay to search for varieties not available locally.

Red currants. *Early:* 'Cascade' has large berries, originated in Minnesota and so is a good choice for gardens in cold climates. 'Jonkheer van Tets' is an older European variety. *Midseason:* 'Red Lake' is the most widely grown of all red currants and is very hardy. It produces large crops of lightish red berries in long clusters that are easy to pick. 'Diploma' has medium-long clusters of dark red fruit. *Late:* 'Cherry' makes a vigorous, dense plant with medium-sized fruit.

White currants (a form of red and not as widely grown). *Midseason:* 'White Imperial' and 'White Pearl' are the most widely available. Both have medium-sized fruit; that of 'White Pearl' has a slight pink tinge.

Black currants. *Early:* 'Boskoop Giant', a European variety that is very hardy. 'Topsy' is the first to ripen and has good-quality fruit. *Midseason:* 'Consort' has small fruit but is resistant to white pine blister rust. 'Wellington XXX', another old variety that is still popular. *Late:* 'Champion' has short clusters of fruit, but is the last to ripen. 'Raven' has extra-large berries and crops well.

Red currant 'Red Lake'

Currants develop their best fruits on wood two to three years old. Proper pruning will provide for a rich harvest with splendid berries. 'Boskoop Giant' is an early black currant.

'Boskoop Giant'

Pruning Bushes and Cordons in Winter

Red currants bear most of their fruit on spurs that develop on older wood. On planting a one-year-old bush, cut each branch back to four buds from the main stem above an outward-pointing bud.

In the second winter cut out any branches that ruin the overall bush shape. Shorten branch leaders by two-thirds if growth is weak or by one-half if growth is strong, cutting to an outward-pointing bud. Prune laterals back to one bud from their bases so that they will form spurs.

In the third and fourth years, let some laterals grow into branches, so that the bush has 8 to 10 main branches on a 6- to 9-inch leg. Cut other laterals back to spurs yearly.

Cut back branch leaders by one-half their new growth in the third winter, regardless of vigor. In the fourth winter remove about one-quarter of new growth. After that, prune back about 1 inch yearly.

On cordons cut back laterals to one bud to form spurs. Until the leader is 6 feet high, cut back new growth by about 9 inches. When the leader reaches 6 feet, remove all new growth each winter—cutting just above a bud.

Black currants fruit on the previous season's wood and are not grown on a leg. At planting, cut all stems back to one bud aboveground. Next winter, remove all weak and down-pointing shoots. In following winters cut to their bases one-quarter to one-third of all two-year-old wood that has borne fruit and any weak shoots.

From early summer on, cut back laterals to three or five leaves.

Pruning Bushes and Cordons in Summer

Bushes and cordons that are two years old or more are pruned similarly every summer. Start pruning in early summer, when new stems start to turn brown. Cut the laterals back to three or five leaves, just above a leaf joint.

Once a cordon is 6 feet high, cut back new leader growth to four leaves—preparatory to removing it entirely the next winter.

What Can Go Wrong With Currants

Aphids and birds are the commonest problems confronted in growing cur-rants. If plants show symptoms that are not described here, turn to the section on pests and diseases on page 506. Look up controls in the section beginning on page 542.

PRUNING IN THE SECOND WINTER

Shorten new growth on leaders by one-half if growth is strong, by two-thirds if growth is weak.

Cut back laterals to one bud from their bases to form spurs.

Cut flush to the stem any shoots that spoil bush shape.

SYMPTOMS AND SIGNS	CAUSE	CONTROL
Leaves are curled or blistered, often with reddish tinge. Shoot tips may be distorted.	Currant aphids	Spray with dormant oil in midwinter to kill eggs. Insecticidal soap, applied as a cover spray, gives good control.
Smooth, spotted, greenish worms eating leaves.	Currant sawfly	Hand pick and destroy larvae. They will quickly defoliate a bush.
Leaves are distorted and off-color, with very small silver dots.	Two-spotted mites	Use insecticidal soap weekly as needed.
Fruit fail to develop and fall early.	Currant fruit fly	Cover soil under the bush with plastic sheeting to prevent adults from emerging from the soil to lay eggs on the fruit. Hang sticky traps in the bushes.
White powdery masses on plant; later, masses turn brown. Shoots may become distorted.	Powdery mildew (fungus)	Cut off affected shoots in autumn. Spray with wettable sulfur or potassium bicarbonate product.
Small brown spots on leaves in summer. Leaves turn yellow and fall early, weakening plant.	Anthracnose (fungus)	Remove and destroy infected foliage. Spray with copper-based fungicide in early spring as leaves start to unfurl, again when half open and again when fully open.
Fruits covered in a gray mold.	Botrytis (fungus)	Allow good air circulation by not growing other plants nearby, and by pruning to keep the center of the plant open.

'Oregon Champion'

'Poorman'

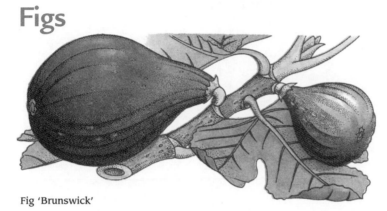

Gooseberries ask little of soil and climate. Like many fruit trees and bushes, they are nevertheless vulnerable to late frost at blossom time.

Figs

Fig 'Brunswick'

Since figs require copious sunshine, they do best in the southern half of the country but can survive in cooler areas with protection. Figs need well-drained but moisture-retaining soil. They bear two crops: one in midsummer; another in late fall. Varieties include 'Brown Turkey', 'Celeste', 'Hunt', and 'Kadota'.

Restrict roots to limit growth. Dig a hole 3 feet wide and 3 feet deep, and line it with bricks or concrete, leaving drainage holes in the base. Fill with good topsoil and plant in early spring. Mulch with a 1- to 2-inch layer of rotted manure or garden compost. Repeat in mid to late spring. Water well when dry.

Propagate figs by layering (p. 262); or take semi-hard cuttings (p. 258).

Pruning and training. Fig trees grow fine without formal training. Prune each year in the spring to maintain good air circulation and control the tree's size, following the general principles on page 385. To protect figs in cold-winter areas, you can cut back the tree in fall, wrap the branches with twine and insulating material, and then cover the top with a tarp to keep the insulation dry. Alternatively, you can cut through some of the roots so that you can tip the tree into a trench dug beside it (line the trench with boards and cushion the branches with leaves. Cover the trench with soil. Unbury and place the tree upright in spring once freeze danger has passed.

Thinning and harvesting. Take away immature figs larger than peas at the end of the season. The embryo fruits carried in the leaf axils at the tops of new shoots will develop the next spring and ripen in late summer. Pick figs when soft to the touch.

What Can Go Wrong With Figs

Fig trees in home gardens are usually trouble-free and suffer from few serious problems. Mealybugs can be controlled by spraying with insecticidal soap, or using summer oil. Follow label directions.

Flat or rounded scales on leaves and stems are insects. In late spring spray with 1–1½ percent oil emulsion.

Yellow or rusty leaves, leaf drop, or spotting of fruit may be caused by mites. Spray insecticidal soap on new leaves and shoots.

Yellow wilted plants may have root-knot nematodes; diseased roots may show knots or tiny lesions. Be sure to destroy any diseased plants, and do not replant in this location.

As a final precaution, cover trees with netting to protect the fruit from bird damage.

Gooseberries

Gooseberries are good for dessert or for making jam. They grow best in areas of the country that have well-drained but moisture-retaining soil, and they thrive in full sun or partial shade. Do not plant gooseberries in frost pockets; frost may prevent fruit formation.

They are grown mainly as bushes. For the average family six to nine bushes should provide enough fruit. Gooseberries are self-fertile. Fruit is available from early summer (for cooking) to mid to late summer and can be green, yellow, red, or white, depending on the variety.

Tending and Feeding Gooseberries

Each spring apply a mulch of mature compost topped with 2 inches of wood chips or bark mulch to prevent the soil from drying out and to keep down weeds. To prevent root damage, do not remove weeds with a hoe or a fork. Pull away any suckers that grow from the stem or roots. Water the bushes only in dry summer spells.

Gooseberries growing in well-prepared soil may not need additional feeding beyond the spring application of compost. If plants seem to need a boost, try watering them with a fish emulsion solution or compost tea. In winter firm in any plants lifted by frost. Birds feed on buds; so protect bushes with netting or cotton threads. At blossom time shield bushes from frost at night with heavy netting, but remove it during the day to allow access to pollinating insects.

Buy plants two or three years old, and plant between midfall and early spring. Double-dig the soil (p. 503), and work in plenty of rotted manure or garden compost. Plant bushes 5–6 feet apart. Support them upright with 2- by 2-inch stakes about 5 feet high.

Among the best varieties, 'Pixwell' can be grown throughout most of the North (down to Zone 2), but it is thick-skinned. 'Hinnomaeki' (red) and 'Hinnomaeki Yellow' are flavorsome and hardy (Zone 3). 'Captivator' is thornless with small red fruit. 'Poorman' has very sweet fruit. 'Oregon Champion' is a heavy cropper.

Thinning and Harvesting Gooseberries

Start picking gooseberries for cooking when they are the size of large peas. Thin out on each branch so that remaining berries will reach a good size for eating fresh or for using in pies. The thinned fruits should be at least 3 inches apart. Do not pick any fruit for dessert until it is fully ripe.

Gooseberry 'Pixwell'

Beware of sharp spines when picking gooseberries, and watch for diseases and pests.

Gooseberry thorns

Botrytis or gray mold

A branch defoliated by sawflies

Pruning a One-Year-Old Gooseberry Bush

Fruit is borne on new wood and on old-wood spurs. Prune during autumn or winter or as late as, but no later than, bud burst if birds are likely to damage the buds.

The aim of pruning is to keep the center of the bush open to light and air. Varieties range from spreading bushes on which branches tend to droop (this can spoil fruit) to very upright bushes. Cut back spreading bushes to an upward- or inward-pointing bud, upright varieties to an outward-pointing bud. For in-between varieties, or if in doubt, prune to an outward-pointing bud.

On a one-year-old bush (see below), choose the best three or four shoots, and cut them back, above a bud, to a quarter of their length. Cut other shoots flush with the stem.

Pruning a Two-Year-Old Gooseberry Bush

On a two-year-old bush (see right), choose from six to eight of the strongest shoots. Cut the new growth on these shoots by one-half if they are growing well, or by two-thirds if growth is weak. Cut back other shoots to one bud from their bases.

Gooseberries can also be grown as cordons—especially fan cordons. Pruning is the same as for bush form, but shoots are tied back to wires in a single plane.

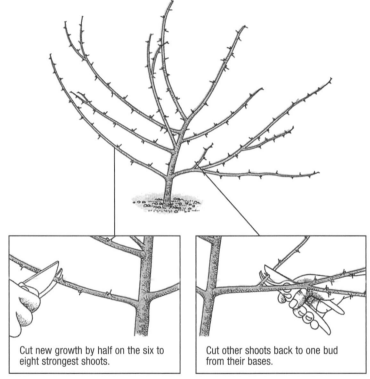

Cut new growth by half on the six to eight strongest shoots.

Cut other shoots back to one bud from their bases.

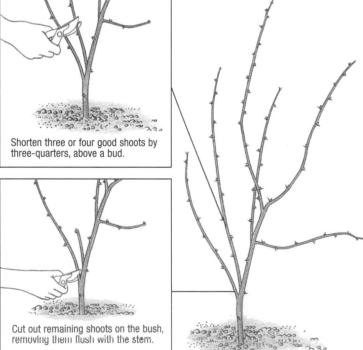

Shorten three or four good shoots by three-quarters, above a bud.

Cut out remaining shoots on the bush, removing them flush with the stem.

What Can Go Wrong With Gooseberries

The most important problems are gooseberry sawfly and mildew. If plants show symptoms that are not described here, turn to the section on pests and diseases on page 506. Look up controls in the section beginning on page 542.

SYMPTOMS AND SIGNS	CAUSE	CONTROL
Leaves curled or blistered, often with reddish tinge; shoot tips may be distorted.	Aphids	Spray with 60-sec. miscible oil in mid-winter to kill eggs. Use insecticidal soap for heavy infestations.
Leaf tissues are eaten.	Larvae of gooseberry sawfly	Handpick and crush larvae. For severe infestations, spray with pyrethrins.
Fruits have gray moldy deposits. Leaves often show brownish to black areas. In severe cases twigs die back.	Botrytis (fungus)	Use Bordeaux mixture. Spray before blossoms open; repeat after flowers open and until fruits mature.
White powdery masses on leaves, shoots, fruits; later, masses turn brown, shoots become distorted.	Powdery mildew (fungus)	Cut off affected shoots in autumn. Spray regularly with a potassium bicarbonate product or wettable sulfur.

'Phoenix'

'Boskoop Glory'

'Phoenix' and 'Boskoop Glory' are among the newer, problem-free table grapes now available to the hobby gardener.

Grapes

Pruning an Established Gooseberry Bush

In winter cut back branch leaders of established bushes by half their new growth. To encourage spur formation, prune the strongest side shoots to 3 inches of new growth and the weaker ones to 1 inch. Remove the weakest shoots completely, cutting them flush with the branch.

If a branch has drooped to the ground, choose a new shoot as a replacement, and cut back the drooping branch to the source of the new shoot. Prune the new branch by at least half to ensure sturdy growth. Keep the bush's center open.

In midsummer shorten all of the side shoots to five leaves, cutting just above a leaf joint. Do not prune the branch leaders.

WINTER PRUNING

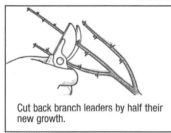

Cut back branch leaders by half their new growth.

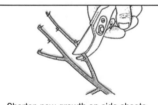

Shorten new growth on side shoots to 3 in. (if strong) or 1 in.

Propagating Gooseberries

The easiest way to grow more plants of a favorite variety is by layering. In spring, bend a low branch down to touch the soil a little way back from the tip. Work humus and sand into the soil. Wound the underside of the branch by removing a sliver of bark, and dust with a semi-hardwood rooting powder. Push the wound into good contact with the soil and hold in place with a rock. As the branch grows during the summer, tie the shoot to a cane to develop the upright stem base. The new plant will

be rooted by fall, but leave until spring before cutting it free and replanting it in a new location.

Gooseberries can also be raised from hardwood cuttings. In early fall, take 12- to 15-inch shoots of that year's growth. Trim the tops off these just above a bud to leave cuttings 10–12 inches long. Insert to half their depth in a trench with a layer of sand in the bottom. Most varieties will root in a year, but those with European ancestry—such as 'Hinnomaeki'—take two years.

Before planting out, rub off all the buds to 4 inches above ground level.

Grape 'Concord'

A favorite fruit and source of wine throughout the ages, grapes can be eaten fresh, dried to make raisins, or converted into juice and wine.

With a few exceptions, all grape varieties are cultivated in much the same way.

In the United States the European types (*Vitis vinifera*), such as 'Thompson Seedless' and 'Flame Tokay', are characterized by skins that adhere to the flesh. They are grown mostly in the western portion of the country.

The native American types derived from *V. labrusca* or its hybrids, such as the 'Concord' grape, have skins that slip free from the flesh. The slip-skin grapes do best east of the Rocky Mountains and north of the Gulf states.

Finally, there are the muscadine types (*V. rotundifolia*), which are not noted for their hardiness. These include the 'Southland' variety. They are cultivated in the southeast and especially in the Gulf states.

The main stem of a grapevine is called the trunk. The trunk sends off

laterals, which if allowed to grow, develop into arms, spurs, and canes. It is the cane that bears the fruit.

There is perhaps no plant more amenable to training than the grapevine. Depending on your purpose and skill, a single vine can be trained to produce one trunk or two or three.

Training to a single trunk saves space, allowing you to grow additional varieties in a given area. If you are growing grapes only for fresh fruit, two single-trunk vines should yield enough for the average family. If juice or wine is your goal, you will need more vines.

Any type of grapevine can be trained to grow on a trellis, a fence, an arbor, or on a pergola. European-type grapes can also be head trained to grow in the form of small trees, only waist high, supported by individual stakes.

Soils and planting. Good drainage and at least moderately fertile soil are essential for grape cultivation.

A fertile loam of medium texture is best. And if the fruit is to have a sugar content high enough for juice or wine and for good eating, the vines must have full sunlight.

Grapevines can be planted in early spring or fall in a hole slightly deeper and wider than their root systems. Plant the vines in rows.

The distance between plants in a row should be about 6 feet. Make sure you allow at least 8 feet between rows for easy access.

If you buy a rooted cutting, plant it with the top bud level with the ground; then mound some soil over it. The developing shoots will push their way through the mound.

Grapes require a lot of moisture, but they will not tolerate wet soil, so good drainage is essential. They also use up nutrients quickly.

Grapes respond well to mulching early in spring, particularly to the use of well-rotted manure mixed with straw. In humid areas extra nutrients are required.

Spread a cupful of general fertilizer on the ground in a ring 6 inches wide, a few inches from the base of the vine. In arid areas additional nitrogen compounds may be needed. Apply about ⅓ cup per plant. Stop feeding when fruits start to ripen.

For information about exact feeding instructions consult your local county extension agent.

Training Young European Grapevines

It takes three or four years to train a European grapevine. After that it needs pruning only to improve or maintain grape production. Vines can be encouraged to develop canes. They can be trained as cordons. Or they can be allowed to grow more freely on arbors or pergolas.

Young vines. To encourage a good root system on a rooted cutting, let the vine grow one season without pruning. Water well but not excessively, and mist the foliage from time to time, particularly on hot days. During the next dormant season remove all but the strongest cane, and prune it back to two or three buds. When growth resumes, remove all but the best-shaped and strongest single shoot. Tie this loosely to a stake, and permit it to develop side shoots. Remove suckers from the base, and pinch off all of the low-growing lateral shoots. If a head- or cane-trained vine is desired, allow the leader to grow about a foot above its supporting stake; then pinch it back.

The second summer. With a cordon-trained vine, early in the second summer prune back all growth except two of the strongest-growing laterals, or work with the leader shoot and one lateral. Tie the chosen shoots along a trellis wire so that they will grow in opposite directions. Let them grow about 18 inches; then pinch back the tips.

For a head-trained vine, cut off the topmost fruit-bearing cane at a node, just above the point where you want the head to form. Be sure to cut completely through the node. By cutting through the node, you effectively destroy the bud. Remove all laterals below the middle of the trunk as well as the weakest laterals above this point. Two to four laterals should be allowed to remain; cut each back to one to four buds. As a general rule, leave one bud on a cane that is as thick as a pencil, two on a cane that is as big around as your little finger, three on a cane the size of your index finger, and leave four buds on a thumb-sized cane.

A cane-pruned vine may have only a single cane with 8 to 10 buds at the end of the second summer. If the cane is weak, cut it back to a spur with only two buds.

The third summer. The next year, on both head- and cane-trained vines, rub off all suckers from the lower half of the trunk.

For cordon-trained vines, trim back the most vigorous shoots to 15–18 inches long. This allows weaker shoots to keep pace with the faster-growing ones. Remove all shoots from the bottom of the arms.

To keep the arms growing straight, tie the strong terminal growths to an upper training wire. If they are allowed to grow without training, they will probably twist around the trellis wire. Remove some clusters early so that they do not crowd together, as this can slow formation of the vine.

By the third season's end, the vines will have achieved their permanent shape and should thereafter be treated as mature vines.

Pruning Mature European Vines

Head-pruned vines. Head pruning is used on many wine grapes and a few table varieties, such as 'Flame Tokay'. Vines trained in this way must be cut back every year if they are to be productive in limited space.

In the winter remove all but three to six of the best canes, leaving those that are evenly placed around the top of the trunk. Cut these back to two to four buds each. Most of the buds will become fruiting spurs the next growing season; some will grow into new canes. Each year select a few new canes that have grown from spurs or that have appeared directly from the trunk, and repeat the pruning process. As the vine gets older, you can allow more spurs to develop.

Cane-pruned vines. Cane pruning, used mainly for raisin grapes and a few wine varieties, also involves heavy annual pruning. Each winter remove canes that have borne fruit. Leave two to four new canes per vine. Prune them back to 6 to 10 buds each. They will bear fruit during the upcoming season. At the same time, prune back two to four other new canes to spurs, as with head-pruned vines. From the several shoots that form at the top of the trunk during the growing season, select the two strongest and tie them to a training wire, facing in opposite directions. These will produce more fruiting canes in years to come.

As each vine ages, you will be able to increase its number of canes to six. If you are training a plant to grow against a wall or over a pergola, the number can be increased to fill any blank spaces. The new canes selected each year should be as close to the trunk as possible.

Cordon-pruned vines. Vines trained to form a cordon need considerable attention. Spurs on the arms must be kept 8–10 inches apart, with only two or three buds allowed on each. As the arms increase in girth, they will sag if not straightened frequently; young shoots must be tied to a wire above the arms.

During the growing season pinch back all vigorous growth to permit weaker shoots to keep pace. Make sure the vines do not overbear. Thin by removing some of the clusters as they appear; if uncrowded, they will yield better bunches of larger grapes.

Arbor-trained vines. Vines that are to grow over an arbor are handled much as cordon-pruned grapes are, except that the trunks are allowed to become longer and the arms, rather than being trained to grow along a horizontal wire, are directed to fill in the spaces on the arbor. After the supporting structure has been covered, a combination of cane and spur pruning is used to maintain the vine's productiveness (see p. 416).

Maintain about 3 feet between the canes that are to develop into arms. When their development is complete, spur-prune for fruit. On arbors and pergolas the horizontal growth will produce most of the grapes. For training on walls, the multiple-cordon system is best. Space the cordons 3 feet apart, and tie arms to the supports (see Kniffin system, p. 416).

'Seedless Concord', one of the most popular grape varieties, produces medium-size berries and fruit clusters. 'Muscat Hamburg' is relatively frost-resistant and not susceptible to pests and fungal infection.

'Seedless Concord'

'Muscat Hamburg'

How to Prune American Grapes

American grapes, such as the 'Concord' and its hybrids, are trained in much the way as their cane-pruned European cousins. The difference is that they are supported in the manner of the four-arm Kniffin system, as shown on the right.

Set posts 24–30 feet apart. The top wire (9 gauge galvanized) should be 5½–6 feet from the ground and the lower wire (10 gauge), about 3 feet from the ground. Plant three vines between posts.

The rooted cutting is planted and pruned back so that a single cane bears two buds. During the vine's first summer, pinch back all shoots except the strongest one, which will become the trunk. Tie this shoot to a stake. The next dormant season cut off all new canes except the central one, and with a soft string tie it to the uppermost wire. Tie the lower cane loosely to the bottom wire.

After the second growing season remove all side branches from the trunk except for two at each wire level. Tie these canes to the wires, one to the left and one to the right on each level. These canes will bear fruiting shoots the next summer. If, not counting the basal bud, more than four to eight buds develop on each shoot, remove them.

Shoots will also be produced near the base of these canes. Cut these back to two buds to form the spurs for the next season's growth.

In the years that follow, keep removing old fruited canes each winter so that the new canes of the previous summer can initiate the buds to fruit in the next growing season. Cut the new canes back to 6 to 10 buds, depending on their vigor. The spurs, with their two buds apiece, will bear bunches of fruit on their shoots, but most of their strength will go into forming fruiting canes for the next year. All of these steps must be repeated annually. Keep in mind, however, that removing too much foliage will reduce the amount and quality of the fruit by limiting the food produced.

American grapes can also be trained on arbors, pergolas, and walls, like the European types. On an arbor extend the trunk to the desired height, and allow well-spaced canes and spurs to grow from it. Prune the vine as described for the Kniffin system.

KNIFFIN TRAINING SYSTEM

In winter cut back to four new canes and tie as shown. Cut back four to six other new canes to two-bud spurs for next year.

Cultivating American Grapes

As a rule, selected varieties of American grapes (see Varieties of Grapes to Grow, p. 417) can be successfully cultivated down to Zone 4. With care and attention, however, and by protecting the vines during winter, it may even be possible to grow them in sheltered locations of Zone 3. Be sure to choose a south-facing slope with protection fom wind. Ideally, choose a spot with a body of water at the base of the slope.

In poorly drained soils—fine silts or clay loams, for example—increase the humus content of the soil by addition of manure, or by green manuring with cover crops such as clover, alfalfa, or ryegrass. On sandy soils with a greater leaching effect it will be necessary to increase the amount of fertilizer (particularly nitrogen) used during the growing season.

In areas at the edge of the grape-growing range, make certain that the vines enter winter in a fully dormant state by not fertilizing later than mid-summer.

Cultivating Muscadine Grapes

Muscadine grapes can be grown throughout the Southeast and Gulf states. Plant the vines where they will receive at least half a day of sun. Allow 20 running feet of space per vine on a one- or two-wire trellis, a fence, or an arbor.

Muscadines can be male, female, or bisexual and self-fertile. Plant one male for every 6–10 females.

While dormant, prune all new growth back to two- to four-bud spurs on the long arms. Clusters of grapes will appear on the third to sixth nodes of that seasons growth. Prune after the first hard freeze, but before the beginning of the new year.

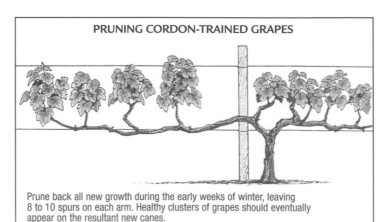

PRUNING CORDON-TRAINED GRAPES

Prune back all new growth during the early weeks of winter, leaving 8 to 10 spurs on each arm. Healthy clusters of grapes should eventually appear on the resultant new canes.

When to Harvest Your Grapes

Tasting is the best test for maturity. If grapes are sweet and flavorful, they are ready to pick. The next best guide is color. Green varieties, such as 'Romulus' and 'Thompson Seedless', turn whitish or yellowish; black and red varieties take on an added depth of color. The presence of birds on the vines is usually a good guide to ripeness.

Once grapes have been picked, they will not ripen further. Therefore, wait until your crop is fully mature; then harvest by clipping off the bunches with scissors or a sharp knife. Discard overripe, withered, or diseased grapes soon after picking before they spoil the bunch.

Grapes that are intended for raisins, such as 'Thompson Seedless', should be left on the vine somewhat longer than wine or table varieties in order to increase the sugar content.

Grapes can be stored for several weeks at a temperature of about 32°F and a humidity of 90 percent.

Canada's specialty Icewines begin with the hand-harvesting of grapes that have frozen on the vine. During crushing and pressing, most of the grapes' natural water content is removed as ice crystals, leaving a highly concentrated grape juice behind.

'Vidal'

Tending the Vine While Grapes Are Maturing

You can improve the yield of your grape vines by giving them extra care during the summer, such as thinning the flowers and fruit, pruning extraneous foliage, and girdling the trunk and branches (as explained in the final paragraph of this segment).

Grapes can be thinned by three methods: removing flower clusters in spring; removing fruit clusters when they have set; or thinning the grapes within a cluster.

Removing some flower clusters as they appear is the simplest way of ensuring that those remaining will develop into larger, more compact bunches. More selectively, you can wait for fruit to set before thinning out the smaller clusters.

Thinning grapes within a cluster is tedious, but combined with flower- or fruit-cluster thinning, it enables you to produce excellent bunches of grapes. Shortly after fruit has set, use scissors to remove the lower tip of each bunch and one or more weaker stems within the cluster.

While fruit is developing, leaves shield it from the hot midsummer sun. Later on, too much shade inhibits ripening. In late summer, therefore, pinch foliage-bearing side shoots back to one leaf.

Girdling is a means of interfering with the flow of sugar back to the roots of the vine, thus making more nourishment available to the fruit. To girdle, simply remove a 3/16-inch-wide band of bark from the trunk, an arm, or a cane. The bark should heal in three to six weeks.

Making New Vines

Grapes are easy to propagate using the winter prunings. Use ripe wood from the bottom of year-old shoots and make cuttings 8 inches long, trimming just above and below a bud. Wrap the cuttings in plastic sheeting and store in the refrigerator until the garden soil is workable. Inspect cuttings occasionally and if mildew occurs, remove the infected cuttings, then rewrap.

In the garden choose a spot where the soil is well-drained, or work in some sand. Make a 6-inch-deep trench, and line the base with sand. Stand the cuttings in the trench, 6 inches apart, push the soil back, and firm it down.

In a greenhouse you can root two-bud cuttings in autumn. At leaf drop, cut lengths of vine from the current growth into pieces with a bud at each end, making an angled cut above the top bud and a straight cut under the lower one. Remove a sliver of bark opposite the lower bud. Pot these.

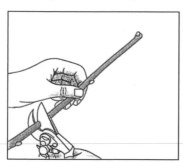

1. Make cuttings of last year's wood about 8 in. long.

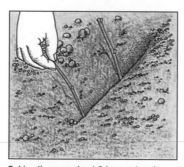

2. Line them up about 6 in. apart and deep, in well-drained soil.

Varieties of Grapes to Grow

Select grapes that are suitable for your climate and intended use. All are self-pollinating, so a single plant is sufficient. Your chances of producing better crops, however, will be greatly increased if you plant two or more vines.

NAMES*	COLOR	SIZE Berry	SIZE Cluster	REMARKS
American grapes and hybrids				(Grown east of Rockies and north of Gulf states.)
'Canadice' (seedless)	Red	Med.	Large	Similar to 'Delaware', but hardier.
'Fredonia'	Black	Med.	Med.	Productive; good for arbors. Hardy. Good table grape.
'Himrod' (seedless)	White	Small	Large	Susceptible to black rot. Eaten fresh.
"Delaware'	Red	Small	Small	For juice, wine; eaten fresh.
'Suffolk Red' (seedless)	Red	Large	Med.	Excellent quality, but not as hardy as 'Canadice.'
'Beta'	Black	Med.	Small	Very hardy. For wine, dessert.
'Niagara'	Yellow-white	Med.	Med.	Popular. Hardy.
'Concord'	Blue-black	Med.	Med.	Widely planted. Hardy. For juice, wine.
European grapes				(Grown in Southwestern U.S. and Calif.)
'Thompson Seedless'	Greenish white	Med.	Large	Cane-prune. Popular. Tolerates hot valleys. Good table variety.
'Baco Noir'	Red	Med.	Small	Needs heavy soil to fruit well.
'Aurore'	White	Med.	Large	Head-prune. For juice. Warmer areas only.
'Seyval'	White	Med.	Large	Good for wine, but needs bunches thinned.
'Muscat Hamburg'	Black	Med.	Med.	Head-prune. Highly recommended, but suited to warmer areas only.
Muscadine grapes				(Grown in Southeastern and Gulf states.)
'Carlos'	Bronze	Med.	Large	Very productive. For wine.
'Cowart'	Black	Large	Large	Low acidity. Eaten fresh.
'Higgins'	Bronze	Large	Large	Very productive. Needs male or self-fertile.
'Hunt'	Black to pink	Large	Large	Old variety but still good.

*Each group listed in approximate order of ripening.

The European hazel (shown here) has larger fruit, but is not as hardy as the American hazel. Walnuts are large shade trees, not suitable for small yards.

Hazelnuts   Walnuts

Hazelnuts and Walnuts

What Can Go Wrong With Grapes

Grapes are subject to attack by many diseases and insects. If plants show symptoms that are not described here, turn to the section on pests and diseases on page 506. Look up controls in the section beginning on page 542.

SYMPTOMS AND SIGNS	CAUSE	CONTROL
Adult beetles come into vineyards when new shoots are 12–15 in. long. Eggs are laid inside shoots about 6 in. from tips. Larvae tunnel inside shoots, destroying them.	Cane girdlers	As insects appear, Inspect canes and cut off about 4 in. below girdling area.
Moth larvae feed inside fruits. Grapes are often webbed together. Wormy fruits result.	Grape berry moths	Set out pheromone traps to know when to spray with *Bacillus thuringiensis kurstaki*.
Larvae of moths feed on foliage of new shoots, chewing them badly. They may also feed on fruits.	Leaf rollers; leaf tiers	Spray with neem in early summer. Repeat 2 wk. later.
Adult beetles feed heavily on foliage during day, causing severe skeletonizing of leaves.	Rose chafers, Japanese beetles, and oriental beetles	Handpick adult beetles. Spray vines with neem to deter beetles from feeding. Place pheromone traps downwind and at least 25 feet away from the vines.
Fungus attacks leaves in early summer and later appears on fruits that are half grown. Entire grape shrivels to dry, black, raisinlike fruit.	Black rot	Infection occurs during bloom period. Apply copper sprays just before bloom, after bloom, and every 10–14 days thereafter up to early fall. Remove and destroy mummified fruit.
Fungus, one of most destructive of all grape diseases, first attacks leaves and canes; later it infects young shoots. Dead arm phase results from infection through wounds caused by pruning or winterkill.	Dead arm	Remove infected vine at ground level during winter pruning. Spray with Bordeaux mixture when new shoots are about 1 in. long and again when they are 5 in. long.
First appears as small yellow spots on top of leaves. Later, downy white mats appear on lower surfaces. Complete defoliation may occur. Grapes are attacked, harden, and turn off-color.	Downy mildew	Same program as for black rot (above). Varieties such as 'Concord' are resistant to this disease.
Mildew occurs on foliage in early summer and fall, producing white powdery growth on leaves and fruits.	Powdery mildew	Sulfur sprays should be applied as needed. Plant resistant varieties, such as 'Canadice', 'Ives', and 'Steuben'.

The deciduous shrubs and small trees known as hazelnuts or filberts (*Corylus*) produce edible fruits in clusters of egg-shaped nuts. Smooth shells are covered by a leafy growth.

Hazelnuts thrive in partial shade in any well-drained soil, but they can also live in heavy wet clay. Grow several specimens for adequate cross-pollination. The hazelnut's double-toothed alternate leaves are usually hairy. Tiny flowers precede the leaves: the male flowers grow into pendulous yellow catkins; the red-tasseled female buds grow in clusters and develop into nuts.

Layering in late summer is the best propagation method, since hazelnuts have stems that tend to arch downward and take root. Propagation may also be accomplished by sowing seeds in late summer or by planting rooted suckers in late autumn or early spring. Trees are usually trouble-free. Nuts, borne after three or four years' growth, should be harvested as soon as the husks take on a yellowish tint.

The largest fruit is obtained from the European hazel (*C. avellana*). This is hardy to Zone 4, and grows well where summers are not too hot. The varieties 'Barcelona' and 'Daviana' do well in the Pacific Northwest. In the eastern states the varieties 'Bixby', 'Italian Red', and 'Royal' are worth a try.

The American filbert (*C. americana*) is hardier, but the round fruit, which grows in clusters, is much smaller and surrounded by a prickly coat. 'Rush' and 'Winkler' are two selections with larger fruit.

Hybrids between the European hazel and the American filbert have reasonably sized fruit, much of the hardiness (Zone 4) of the filbert, and they also fruit well in the North. Depending on the specific cross, the fruits produced are sometimes called hazelburts or filazels.

Look for 'Laroka' (a cross between the European and Turkish hazels), 'Graham', and 'Gellatley's Earliest.'

Hybrid hazelnut

Persian walnut

Growing Walnuts

The Persian or English walnut (*Juglans regia*) is not as hardy (Zones 5–7) but has nuts that are easier to crack and meatier than the native black walnut (*J. nigra*, Zones 3–7). They make good shade trees, growing to 40 feet tall and wide at maturity, and do well in dryish soils. Newly planted trees will start to fruit in about eight years and can live for 100 or more.

Roots of walnuts give off a toxic chemical that stunts or even kills some plants. Do not plant close to existing flower beds, but grass is not affected. Nuts are ready for harvest when they start to fall. Shake the trees to make them drop or squirrels will gather most of the crop.

Good varieties of Persian walnuts are 'Broadview', 'Hansen', and 'Lake.' 'Carpathian' is the hardiest variety (Zones 3–7). For black walnuts, try 'Hare' and 'Thomas.'

Melons

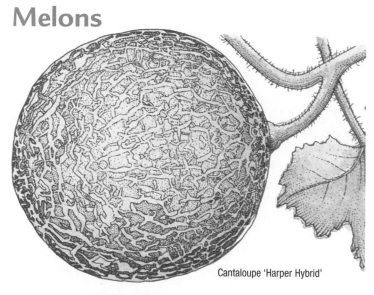

Cantaloupe 'Harper Hybrid'

Although they are fruits, melons are usually grown in the vegetable garden. While they are growing, in fact, it is often difficult to distinguish them from their close relatives, cucumbers and squashes.

Like those plants, melons are vines and need a lot of room, warm weather, and plenty of moisture to grow properly.

Melons take a long time to mature, usually from three to four months. For this reason, most varieties of melon—watermelon, honeydew, Crenshaw, Persian, and casaba—are grown in gardens in warm areas. Only the cantaloupe, properly called the muskmelon, matures fast enough—in 75 to 85 days—to be suitable for planting in areas with shorter growing seasons.

More recently, however, horticulturists have developed hybrid varieties of honeydew, Crenshaw melons, and miniature watermelons that

How to Grow Melons

If you live in an area with a short growing season and are determined to grow melons, start them indoors in pots, sowing them three seeds to a

mature in 80 to 90 days and so can be grown in many cooler regions.

Melons will not flourish in areas where temperatures fall below 55°F at night and below 80°F during the day. Unless you can count on these temperatures for three months, grow quick-maturing varieties.

Gardeners in areas with short growing seasons have a bagful of tricks for encouraging melon growth. They usually start the melon seeds indoors, in pots, to get the longest possible growing season. They also plant their melons against a south-facing wall or fence that will reflect the sun's warmth, grow them in cold frames, or set them out in large tubs in warm, sheltered spots. Gardeners often use black plastic mulch on the soil in which the melons grow. Plastic mulch warms the soil with the heat it absorbs, and by acting as insulation also helps keep soil temperatures from dropping at night.

pot. Use 3-inch peat pots or large paper cups that you can tear away when the seedlings are set out, because melons will not tolerate root disturbance when transplanted.

Do not use compressed peat

cubes, however; they hold too much moisture and may cause the seeds to rot before they germinate. Sow the seeds about four weeks before the date of the last expected frost, and leave the pots in a warm place. Melon seeds need constant soil temperatures of about 70°F in order to germinate.

When the seedlings are about 2 inches high, thin them to the single strongest plant. Set them out when you can be sure of the required minimum daytime and nighttime temperatures, and preferably before they have started to grow vinelike tendrils. If melon seedlings are exposed to temperatures below 50°F, they will continue to grow, but they may never bear fruit. Before you transplant melons into the garden, be sure to harden them off by exposing them gradually to outdoor conditions.

Planting melons. Melons are usually planted in enriched earth mounds called hills. To prepare a hill, dig a hole 1 foot deep and 2 feet wide, piling the excavated soil to one side. Fill the bottom of the hole with 4–6 inches of compost or well-rotted manure. Return the excavated soil to the hole until it forms a slight mound, about 4 inches high. Space the hills 4–6 feet apart, except for those intended for large watermelons, which should be spaced approximately 10 feet apart.

Cover the mounds with black plastic mulch. If you do not want to use plastic, you can spread on an organic mulch. It will add nutrients to your soil, but it will not trap heat as well as plastic mulch. Let the mounds settle for a few days before planting the seedlings in them.

Seedlings grown in peat pots are transplanted in their containers. Be sure the rims are set well below the ground surface so that the entire pot will remain moist and decompose. Just before setting the plants into the garden, slit the pots down the sides so that the melon roots can grow through the sides more easily. Paper-

cup containers should be carefully cut away from the root ball.

If you have used clay pots, rap each pot sharply on the bottom to loosen the entire root ball; then slip the plant out as gently as possible, to avoid disturbing the roots.

Make two planting slits in the plastic mulch covering each mound. Plant no more than two seedlings in each one. Overcrowding will inhibit, rather than increase, yields.

Immediately after transplanting the seedlings, cover each one with a plant protector. You can make your own from ½ gallon milk cartons by cutting off their tops and punching a few holes in the sides for ventilation, or cut the bottoms of 1 gallon plastic juice bottles to make mini-greenhouses. Plant protectors help retain warmth in the soil and shield the tender seedlings from chill winds and voracious insects. Remove the coverings in a few days when the plants have become established.

Water each hill thoroughly. If you are using a plastic mulch, water the mounds through the slits in the mulch.

Starting melons in warm climates. If you live in a warm-weather region, you can start melons from seeds sown directly into the garden. Prepare the soil as described above; then plant six to eight seeds in each hill. When the seedlings appear, choose the two strongest in each hill and cut off the others. Do not keep more; two plants will amply fill the space provided for them.

Caring for melons. When the runners are about a foot long, feed the plants with a mix of 1 part blood meal to 2 parts bone meal—about ⅓ cup scattered around each hill. Fertilize again after the first fruits appear. In dry weather, be sure to keep the soil moist with a good soaking through the mulch.

If weeds start to grow, pull them by hand, or hoe no more than 1 inch deep to avoid injuring the melons' root systems.

If you have not laid down a mulch, when the melons form, lift each one gently and place under it a pad of straw or hay. By pillowing it in this way you will prevent the rotting that may occur when the fruit rests directly on the ground. Like cucumbers, melons can be trained to grow up a trellis or fence. Melons are much heavier than cucumbers, however, and will need support.

You can devise a sling from old sheeting; slip a strip of cloth under the melon, and tie each end to the trellis. Or use net bags, such as those onions are sold in. Place a bag over each melon, tying the ends to the trellis. Start training the vines while they are still young—melon vines grow more brittle as they mature. As the vines grow more upward, be sure to keep tying the new growth securely to your fence or trellis.

What Can Go Wrong With Melons

Striped cucumber beetles attack melon stems, leaves, and fruit, and may spread bacterial wilt, a disease that causes plants to wilt and die. Deter these pests by spraying young plants with horticultural kaolin clay up to twice a week.

Wilting leaves may also indicate the presence of squash vine borers, which hatch from eggs laid at the base of the plant, and tunnel into the

Varieties of Melons to Grow

Recommended cantaloupe varieties include the green-fleshed 'Burpee Hybrid' (72 days to maturity from seed); the orange-fleshed 'Pulsar' (80 days); and the fast-maturing, salmon-fleshed 'Earlisweet' (68 days), all of which are resistant to fusarium wilt.

Popular watermelon varieties include the rosy-fleshed 'You Sweet Thing' (70 days); the crisp, red-

Harvesting melons. Cantaloupes should be picked at the "slip" stage: when you press at the point where the melon joins the stem, the melon will slip off the vine.

Crenshaw and Persian melons are ripe when they give off a sweet, fruity odor, and casabas and honeydews are ripe when they turn yellow.

The surest sign of a ripe watermelon is a hollow sound as you give it a thump. A yellowing of the skin on the side that rests on the ground is another indication that the watermelon is fully ripe.

A word of caution: if melons start to form after midsummer, pick them off the vine.

In view of their late start, they will not have time to ripen fully and so they will merely draw nourishment away from the other developing fruits.

stalks. Search for and crush these reddish-brown egg custers. Slit vines near entry holes and remove and kill any borers you find.

The major disease of melons, fusarium wilt, can be avoided by planting disease-resistant varieties. If plants show signs of this disease—brown coloration of the stems followed by wilt—destroy them.

White floury powder on the leaves is a sign of powdery mildew. Cut out affected shoots, and spray regularly with potassium bicarbonate.

fleshed 'Sugar Baby' (72 days); the deep-red-fleshed 'Sweet Beauty' (79 days); and the crisp, yellow-fleshed 'Yellow Baby' (72 days).

If you want to try another type of melon, choose from the white fleshed Casaba 'Golden Beauty' (120 days); yellow-skinned Casaba 'Amy' (75 days) with very sweet white flesh; hardy 'Angel' (60 days), a Mediterranean type; or the honeydew 'Earlidew' (75 days) with pale green flesh that is also disease tolerant.

Peaches and Nectarines

Peach 'Redhaven'

How to Care for Peach and Nectarine Trees

Any good, well-drained soil is suitable for both trees. Plant in the same way as other fruit trees.

Peach trees should grow 12 to 18 inches yearly. If your trees are growing sluggishly or if the leaves are yellow-green, apply compost in the spring, spreading it across the entire root zone, or apply 1 to 2 pounds of a balanced organic fertilizer per tree. Periodic foliar applications of seaweed will also improve tree growth and health. If the soil is acid, apply 5 pounds of lime every other year in humid regions. Peaches need more nitrogen when growing in sod than in cultivated soil. After a few years of fertilizing and mulching, they may need relatively little fertilizer if mulched annually.

Water the soil liberally whenever there is danger that it might dry out.

Peaches and nectarines can be grown throughout the country except where winter temperatures drop below –10°F.

Trees that are trained as espaliers, as well as the upright dwarf forms, will grow in any location other than a frost pocket or a site exposed to cold winds, but they will, of course, do best in a warm, sunny position. Those that are trained as espaliers have the best chance of success, especially when they are grown against a wall facing south or southwest to catch the sun.

Nectarines are smooth-skinned peaches, and they are becoming increasingly popular in home gardens. Peach and nectarine trees are self-fertile—that is, each flower fertilizes itself—so only one tree is needed to obtain fruit.

One mature tree should provide enough fruit for the average family. Fruit that is grown outdoors will usually be ripe and ready to eat from midsummer on.

Nectarines need more frequent watering and a little more fertilizing than peaches while the fruits are swelling. Weed by shallow hoeing, or keep weeds down with a mulch.

To ensure a good crop, it pays to assist pollination by lightly dabbing every blossom with a camel's hair paintbrush about every third day. This is best done on warm, dry days at about noon.

When the peaches are the size of marbles, start thinning them out, reducing all clusters to a single fruit. Remove fruits that have no room to develop properly.

When the peaches are the size of Ping-Pong balls, thin them out so that they are spaced 9 inches apart.

Fruit is ready for picking when the flesh around the stalk yields to gentle pressure from the fingers.

Store peaches in a cool place, not touching one another, in containers lined with soft material.

Peaches and nectarines do not need cross-pollinating to produce fruit. An espalier on a south-facing wall is a good way to grow them.

Nectarine 'Redgold'

Training and Pruning a Dwarf Peach Tree

Training a One-Year-Old Peach Tree

In spring, when growth buds have appeared on a one-year-old tree planted in very early spring or the previous autumn, cut back the central leader to about 2 feet above the ground. Cut just above a bud.

Leave the top three or four buds or side shoots below the cut to form the first branches.

Remove all the side shoots lower down the stem.

Pruning the Tree in Succeeding Years

All pruning in the following years is done in late winter. Remove any branch that crosses over another, cutting it off flush with its parent branch. Cut back damaged branches to just above a healthy shoot.

Remove any shoots that remain attached to the main stem beneath the lowest branch; cut them off flush with the stem. Any branch that is dying at the tip should be cut back to a good side shoot or outward-pointing branch. If the cut wood shows brown discoloration, it is affected by dieback; so cut it back to healthy wood.

On a well-established tree, cut off any branches that droop to the ground due to heavy fruit bearing. Also remove the older branches as they become unfruitful. This will encourage new wood to develop from the center.

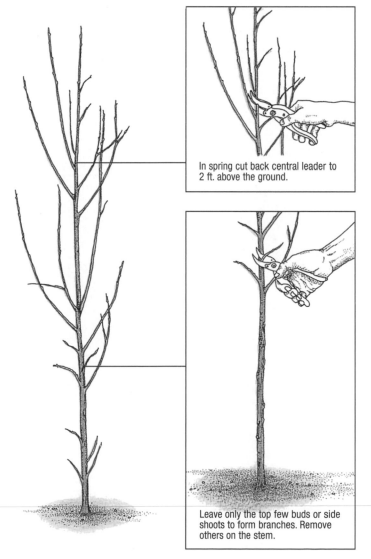

In spring cut back central leader to 2 ft. above the ground.

Leave only the top few buds or side shoots to form branches. Remove others on the stem.

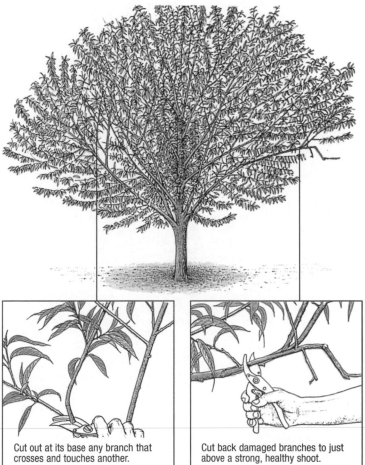

Cut out at its base any branch that crosses and touches another.

Cut back damaged branches to just above a strong, healthy shoot.

Training and Pruning a Fan-Shaped Peach Tree

Train a young fan peach like a fan apple (p. 397), but prune in early spring, not in winter. Unlike apple trees, peach trees produce side shoots off the current year's growth. Pinch out side shoots one bud from their base.

From the fourth spring after planting (when a tree has 24 to 32 ribs), pruning differs, as peaches fruit mainly on the last year's shoots. When the fourth spring's growth starts, rub or pinch out buds or shoots that point toward or away from the wall. From the buds remaining, select good ones on each side of a rib, at 6-inch intervals, and rub out all others except the bud at the tip.

During the fourth summer these buds will produce laterals that will bear fruit the following summer, and the bud at the tip will grow on as a rib leader. Toward the end of the summer, tie both laterals and leaders to the wires. If a lateral grows more than 18 inches long, pinch off its tip.

The fifth spring let the tips of fruit-bearing laterals grow to help develop fruit. Pinch off side shoots.

In fall, after picking fruit, cut back each lateral that has borne fruit.

Repeat this process of removing buds, pinching back, cutting old shoots, and tying in replacements every year. On the extension growth from each rib, choose buds to grow out as new laterals, as in the fourth spring. Treat rib leaders reaching the top wire as laterals.

Varieties of Peaches and Nectarines to Grow

Peaches and nectarines are self-pollinating; so only one variety need be planted. Each variety's ripening time is based on that of the popular 'Elberta' peach, and the figures given in the Ripens column below is the number of days before this time.

NAMES Peach (P) Nectarine (N)	DAYS THEY RIPEN BEFORE 'ELBERTA'	FLESH COLOR	REMARKS
'Candor' (P)	59	Yellow	Freezes well.
'Reliance' (P)	36	Yellow	Very bud-hardy.
'Golden Jubilee' (P)	35	Yellow	Crops heavily.
'Redhaven' (P)	30	Yellow	Dependable. Very popular.
'Mericrest' (N)	25	Yellow	Hardy.
'Fantasia' (N)	13	Yellow	Needs warmth to crop well.
'Loring' (P)	11	Yellow	Excellent all round.
'Redgold' (N)	3	Yellow	Widely grown. One of best.
'Elberta' (P)	0	Yellow	Widely grown. Ripens in late summer.

Each spring there will be at least two growth buds at the base of each fruiting lateral. Keep one as a replacement, and remove the other one when it is 2–3 in. long.

Leave fruiting shoots to grow on. If space is limited, pinch them back to four leaves once they have six.

After fruit picking, cut back each lateral that has borne fruit to its replacement, and tie in the replacement.

Not just the blossoms but the peach tree itself is vulnerable to frost. As is the case with the even more sensitive nectarine, it needs a warm location.

Peach 'Suncrest' blossom

Pears

What Can Go Wrong With Peaches and Nectarines

If your peach or nectarine trees show any symptoms or signs that are not described here, turn to the section on pests and diseases on page 506. For more information, look up controls in the section beginning on page 542.

SYMPTOMS AND SIGNS	CAUSE	CONTROL
Orange-brown gum oozes from base of tree. Borers tunnel under bark, destroying tree.	Peach tree borers	Squirt a solution of *Steinernema carpocapsae* nematodes into borer holes; seal the holes with grafting wax. Spray with horticultural oil in autumn after leaves fall.
Older leaves gradually turn bronzy yellow and dry out.	Mites	Spray dormant oil at the pink bud stage. Apply insecticidal soap for severe infestations. Plant ground covers to attract mite predators.
Leaves are eaten or spun together with strands of silk.	Moth larvae	Spray with *Bacillus thuringiensis kurstaki* as soon as damage is noticed.
Shoots wilt; fruits exude gummy liquid.	Oriental fruit moths (caterpillars)	Plant early-maturing varieties to prevent damage. Prune and destroy infected shoots. Apply horticultural kaolin clay at petal fall, then weekly for 6 to 8 wks.
Small green peaches drop prematurely.	Plum curculios (weevils)	Collect fruit as it drops. Once petals start to fall, each day spread a sheet below the tree and hit the tree trunk with a padded stick; destroy the curculios that fall onto the sheet. Continue for 3 wks.
Young growth twisted, foliage and fruit shiny and sticky with white flecks, becoming black and dull later.	Peach aphids (black or green)	Spray dormant oil just after bud break to kill eggs. Make spot applications of insecticidal soap just before bloom. Repeat after blossoming if necessary.
Growth weak, foliage yellowish, bark warty with brown, gray, or whitish deposits.	Scale insects (various)	Spray with dormant oil at bud break. Summer oil can be sprayed as contact control in late spring when new scales ("crawlers") appear.
Brown powdery masses on fruits. Later, fruits shrivel and form hard "mummies."	Brown rot (fungus)	Prune trees to encourage air circulation. Destroy dropped fruit. Spray with sulfur at preblossom. Repeat when flower shucks split, then weekly for 2 wks.
Large reddish blisters on foliage. Leaves become whitish, then brown, then fall prematurely.	Leaf curl (fungus)	Choose varieties that are tolerant of the disease. Spray lime sulfur in autumn as leaves fall and in early spring before buds swell.
Gummy twigs and bark. Leaves have purplish spots and holes.	Perennial canker (fungus)	Prune out cankered branches 4 in. below the canker. Use a sharp knife to cut out infected areas of large cankers.

Pear 'Bartlett'

Pears—which can be used for fresh eating desserts, cooking, or canning—are as easy to grow as apples. But in cold climates, because they blossom earlier, they are more liable to injury by late spring frosts. The trees will do best if planted in a sunny position, sheltered from cold winds.

Being less tolerant than apple trees of dry conditions at their roots, pear trees prefer a deep, loamy soil that will keep its moisture in summer. Like apples, they do not grow well on or near a seacoast because of damage from salt-laden winds, and should not be planted close to roads salted in winter.

Pear trees can be trained to the same forms as apple trees. Only one or two varieties are tip bearers. At least two varieties must be grown for cross-pollination. See Varieties of Pears to Grow (p. 425) for more about this. The trees grown on dwarfing rootstocks are preferred by most home gardeners.

As with apples, "family" trees (those with three or more varieties on one rootstock) are available.

An average family should get as many pears as it needs from four dwarf trees (three fans, three espaliers, six dwarf pyramids, or eight cordons).

Overfertilizing pears can lead to fire blight problems. Do not fertilize trees unless growth seems sluggish (less than 1 foot of new growth yearly). If needed, apply compost in the spring, spreading it across the root zone.

There is some natural fall of fruit in early summer, but dry, poor soil can cause an entire crop to drop.

Harvesting the fruit. The time of picking is critical. Pears should not be allowed to ripen fully on the tree. If this happens, they will become soft and mealy inside.

Harvest early varieties by cutting the stalk when the fruit is mature but still hard—before it will twist easily from the stalk by hand. Pick midseason and late pears as soon as they will part easily from the tree after a gentle lifting and twisting motion.

After picking, place the pears, not touching, in a single layer on a shelf in a cool room, at a temperature of about 38°–40°F. The atmosphere should be a little drier than for apples. Inspect pears regularly and remove fruit that shows signs of rot.

To finish ripening, place the fruits in a warm room at about 65°F for two or three days. If properly stored, they should keep well for several months. Use the small fruits first.

Pruning and training pear trees. Pruning and training are done the same way as for apple trees (see p. 385). Pear trees, however, should be pruned less severely to avoid forcing the development of soft, new growth susceptible to fire blight.

Pear trees also produce fruiting spurs more easily, and these will need more thinning out. Summer pruning should be done in midsummer, earlier than for apples.

If you have a garden where there is a neglected standard or dwarf pear tree, treat it in the same way as an apple tree that has been neglected.

Cedar apple rust

Cedar apple rust can strike pear foliage, but does not cause severe damage.

What Can Go Wrong With Pears

Aphids and fire blight are the major problems. If your pear trees show symptoms that are not described here, turn to the section on pests and diseases on page 506. Look up controls in the section beginning on page 542.

SYMPTOMS AND SIGNS	CAUSE	CONTROL
Shoots and young leaves are crippled or stunted. Small sticky insects are present.	Aphids	Spray dormant oil just after bud break to kill eggs. Make spot applications of insecticidal soap just before bloom. Repeat after blossoming if necessary.
Numerous tiny dark brown bumps appear on both sides of leaves.	Leaf blister mites	Destroy infected leaves and fruits. Spray with lime sulfur in early spring. Plant ground covers to attract mite predators.
Young fruits become deformed, often elongated or rounded. Later, fruits may crack, decay, and fall.	Pear midges	As a preventative, spray with insecticidal soap when petals fall. Destroy all fallen fruits.
Leaf surfaces eaten; later, exposed veins brown and die. Small black caterpillars are visible.	Pear or cherry sawflies	Sprinkling dusty soil on tree leaves may kill larvae. Spray with neem immediately after petal fall. Apply parasitic nematodes to the soil beneath the trees shortly after petal fall.
Eggs are laid in young fruits. Larvae feed on and destroy fruits.	Plum curculios (weevils)	Collect fruit as it drops. Once petals start to fall, each day spread a sheet below the tree and hit the tree trunk with a padded stick; collect and destroy the curculios that fall onto the sheet. Continue this for 3 wks. Also, apply horticultural kaolin clay when petal fall starts and then weekly for 6 to 8 wks.
Full-sized fruits, on tree or in storage, show pale brown areas with concentric rings of small whitish or yellowish bumps. Sometimes fruits dry up on tree.	Brown rot (fungus)	Keep trees well pruned to encourage air circulation, and cut out and destroy dead shoots. Destroy all rotten and withered fruits on tree, on ground, and in storage. Spray with sulfur in late summer to reduce rotting of stored fruits.
Leaves turn brown and look burned, hang down from the branch, but do not fall. Cankers arise on branches.	Fire blight (fungus)	Plant resistant varieties. Apply streptomycin spray at early bloom stage. Prune out infected branches as soon as seen, cutting well into healthy wood. Apply Bordeaux mixture at the green-tip stage.
Brownish or blackish spots appear on leaves and fruits; blisters and cracks develop on shoots in spring.	Pear scab (fungus)	Spray with sulfur when flower buds are nearly open, when petals fall, and 3 wks. later.

Varieties of Pears to Grow

Except 'Kieffer', all the varieties listed below are considered to be dessert pears because they are sweet and juicy. Other than the variety 'Seckel', they are all of good size.

Apart from the variety 'Duchess' (not listed), which is self-pollinating, pears must have a pollination partner in order to set fruit.

To ensure the pollination of all the other kinds, three or more varieties should be planted near one another, or three different varieties can be grafted on one rootstock to make, in effect, a self-pollinating tree. Some nurseries offer pears that are grafted on dwarfing rootstock.

NAMES	USUAL AREA	REMARKS
Early		
'Clapp's Favourite'	All areas	Fruits heavily, every year.
'Harrow Delight'	North Central	Yellowish green, blight resistant.
'Moonglow'	All areas	A blight-resistant 'Bartlett.'
'Summercrisp'	All areas	Good flavor, stores well.
Midseason		
'Bartlett'	All areas	High-quality fruit. Easy to grow, but blight susceptible.
'Bosc'	North Central	A much-grown variety.
'Harvest Queen'	North Central	Do not use 'Bartlett' as a pollinator.
'Patten'	All areas	Very hardy, excellent taste.
'Ure'	North	Extra hardy, good for cooking.
Late		
'Anjou'	North Central	Widely grown by home gardeners.
'Highland'	All areas	Sweet and juicy, blight susceptible.
'Kieffer'	South	Medium-sized fruit, need care to store well. Blight resistant.
'Orient'	West Coast	Heavy cropper, very blight resistant.
'Seckel'	All areas	Small, sweet fruit, blight resistant.

Asian Pears

Also known as apple pear, crunch pear, and sand pear, Asian pears are round rather than pear-shaped, and have a higher content of stone cells, the little crunchy bits in pear flesh. Asian pears are highly resistant to fire blight and are one parent of hybrids such as 'Kieffer' and 'Orient.' They crop very heavily; a mature tree can produce up to 400 pounds of fruit. However, it must be allowed to ripen on the tree before picking and, as a result, bruises easily.

'Housi' has large golden-brown fruit that store well; 'Kousi', early small fruit with bronzy russet skin. 'Nijisseiki' (may be called 'Twentieth Century') has thin skin, but stores well. 'Seuri' has the largest fruit, but does not store well.

'Stanley', a European plum, and 'Shiro', a Japanese variety, are both very popular.

'Shiro'

'Stanley'

Plums and Damsons

Plum 'Toka'

Plums and damsons are stone-fruit trees of the genus *Prunus;* their culture is essentially the same.

Plums are eaten fresh or used for canning, cooking, or jams and jellies. Greengages are a very flavorful type of plum. Damsons are small and tart. Prunes are plums with a sugar content high enough that they can be dried without fermentation around the pit. If the fruit is eaten canned or fresh, it is a plum; dried, it is a prune.

All these fruit trees will succeed in most well-drained soils. Plums and greengages flower early and should not be planted in areas where spring frosts are likely.

Greengages give best results if grown against a wall. Damsons can stand more rain and less sun than plums and greengages can, and they usually flower a little later.

Plum and damson trees tend to grow too large for the average-size garden unless they are on semi-dwarfing rootstock. Fans and pyramids are the most suitable espaliered forms for home gardens. All damsons are self-fertile, but some varieties of plums need to be grown with another variety as a pollenizer.

Two or three trees can provide enough fruit for the average family. Plums ripen from midsummer to fall; damsons, late summer to fall.

In mild regions plant trees in early spring or autumn (p. 381). If the weather is dry, make sure the soil is well watered beforehand. On very acid soils (pH 5 and below), add 1 pound of lime per square yard.

In early spring mulch with a 2-inch layer of straw or well-rotted garden compost to keep the soil moist. Repeat each year. Control weeds by shallow hoeing or by hand pulling.

Pull out suckers as soon as they form—remove enough soil to reveal the root, and tear the suckers from the root. Do not cut them off.

Types of Plums

Two distinct types of plums are commonly grown, European and Japanese. European plums are sweet, and their high sugar content enables them to be dried as prunes. The fruits are oval, and most varieties have blue skins, although they may also be green, yellow, or reddish. Damsons, a form of European plum, are usually blue or purple, but are not as sweet as plums and are used mostly for cooking and making preserves. Damson trees are smaller than plums, making them more suitable for city gardens.

If regular pears grow well in your region, and not just the hardy hybrids such as 'Kieffer', you can probably grow European plums and damsons. These do not grow well in the South or Southwest.

Japanese plums originated in China and have been cultivated for centuries. They ripen earlier than the European varieties, and the fruits are predominantly red, but may also be green, yellow, or purple. Ripe fruits are softer and juicier than those of European plums, but are not as sweet and do not make good prunes.

Japanese plum trees are a bit smaller at maturity and can be spaced closer together, 18–20 feet rather than 20–22 feet. They are better suited to warm climates, such as in the West, but there are also hardy strains that will grow well in the Northeast and Mid-Atlantic regions. If you can grow peaches, you can certainly grow Japanese plums.

Hybrid plums are crosses between native North American species and Japanese plums. They are even hardier and will survive and fruit most years on the Great Plains. Some varieties flower very early and may be caught by late frosts. They are not self-fertile, so plant more than one variety. With late-flowering varieties such as 'Brookred', 'Brookgold', and 'Pembina', plant a sand cherry (*Prunus besseyi*) as a pollinator.

Feeding Plum and Damson Trees

In late winter or early spring in humid regions, apply 1–3 pounds of a balanced organic fertilizer. In arid regions only nitrogen may be needed; alfalfa meal or blood meal are very good organic nitrogen sources.

Sprinkle the fertilizer evenly over the soil, covering an area a little larger than the spread of the tree's branches. Do not fork it in, as this might damage the roots; allow the fertilizer to work its way into the root area naturally.

Thinning and Harvesting the Crop

Tree branches are often brittle, and if they snap, there is a danger that rot or other diseases will enter and infect the wound.

Start thinning a heavy crop in late spring to take some weight off the branches. Curl a finger around the stalk, and snap off the fruit with your thumbnail, leaving the stalk attached to the tree.

Complete thinning later, after the natural drop of the fruit. Thin dessert plums to 2–3 inches apart; thin cooking plums to 2 inches. This usually means leaving one plum to each cluster.

Pick ripe fruit by the stalk to avoid bruising. The stalk will snap and come away with the fruit.

Allow the plums that you intend to eat raw to ripen on the tree as long as possible. Pick those that will be used for cooking or canning just before they are ripe.

Plums can be kept in good condition for a few weeks if they are picked just before they are ripe, wrapped in paper, and placed in a cool, well-ventilated room or shed. Remove any rotting fruit regularly, as it may spread disease. The wrapping paper will discolor if fruit rots.

'Mirabelle' blossom

'Mirabelle'

'Mirabelle', a European plum, can be harvested after mid-August. Early-ripening plums provide fresh fruit in July; the last plums come at the end of October.

Training and Pruning a Modified Leader Tree

Training a One-Year-Old Plum Tree

Modified leader plum trees are similar in shape to modified leader apple trees (p. 397), but slightly taller (about 9 feet) and wider (8–10 feet). Plums are more irregular in outline; they generally grow vigorously, making it difficult to maintain their shape. After the basic framework has been established, plum trees need less restrictive pruning than apple trees do.

If you decide to train a one-year-old tree to modified leader form, cut the stem back to 5 feet above the ground in early spring after planting. Cut just above a bud. Cut off flush with the stem any young branches lower than 18 inches from the ground.

If the tree is much less than 5 feet high, let it continue growing for another year before training it.

Training a Two-Year-Old Pyramid Tree

On a two-year-old tree cut back the main leader in early spring to about 18 inches from the previous year's cut. Make the cut just above a bud.

Cut back from three to five of the strongest side shoots at the top of the stem to 9 inches, pruning to an outward-pointing bud. Cut back all other side shoots to 6 inches. Since lower growth is likely to be weaker, cut it back harder to encourage even growth. All these side shoots will now grow to form the tree's first main branches.

Training From Three Years Old to Full Height

Early each spring cut back the central leader to 18 inches above the previous year's cut and just above a bud. Cut back branch leaders by one-third of new growth if growing well, by one-half if growth is average, or by two-thirds if weak. Cut the strongest laterals from main branches back to 9 inches and the remaining ones to 6 inches; always make the cut above an outward-pointing bud.

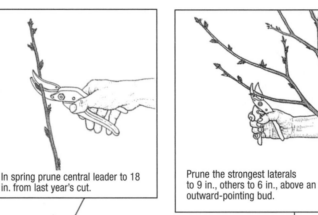

In spring prune central leader to 18 in. from last year's cut.

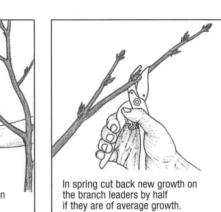

Prune the strongest laterals to 9 in., others to 6 in., above an outward-pointing bud.

In spring cut back new growth on the branch leaders by half if they are of average growth.

Cut from three to five strong shoots at the top of the stem to 9 in., and all others to 6 in.

Virus diseases are hard to control. The best method is good sanitation in the fall (collecting leaves as they fall).

Ring spot virus

Pruning an Established Pyramid Tree

Once the tree has reached about 9 feet (when it is about six years old), keep it at this height by cutting back the central leader to a strong lateral in the summer. You may need to do this every second or third winter, depending on growth.

Plum trees bear fruit on the previous season's shoots as well as on spurs on old wood. If the tree is fruiting regularly, prune as little as possible—just pinch vigorous new side shoots back to six or seven leaves from the parent stem.

Thin out overcrowded branches as necessary, cutting flush with the parent stem.

If branch leaders grow exceptionally long, cut them back to a strong main lateral.

If the tree grows vigorously but does not fruit regularly, root pruning (see p. 382) may be required.

In summer cut back central leader to a 9-ft.-high lateral.

Pinch vigorous new side shoots back to six or seven leaves.

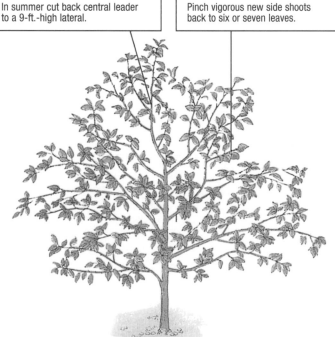

What Can Go Wrong With Plums

The fungal diseases black knot and brown rot are fairly common on plums. If your plums show symptoms that are not described here, turn to the section on plant disorders on page 506. Look up controls in the section beginning on page 542.

SYMPTOMS AND SIGNS	CAUSE	CONTROL
Fruits have small skin blemishes; insides may show corky brown streaks. Maggots ("worms") are visible.	Apple maggots (fly larvae)	Pick up and dispose of fallen fruit daily. Hang red sticky ball traps in trees.
Leaves have pale or reddish mottling and may fall prematurely.	Spider mites	To kill eggs, spray with dormant oil while trees are dormant in winter. Plant ground covers to attract mite predators. Spray with insecticidal soap in summer.
Leaves and young shoots are twisted and stunted. Tiny, sticky insects are present.	Leaf curl plum aphids	Carefully timed sprays of horticultural oil will kill these aphids as they hatch. Or, apply neem when aphids are seen on leaves
Leaves are eaten or spun together. Green caterpillars are usually present.	Moth larvae	Spray with *Bacillus thuringiensis kurstaki* as soon as damage is noticed.
Small crescent-shaped scars on fruit, which drop early.	Plum curculios (weevils)	Pick up fallen fruits frequently. Once petals start to fall, each day spread a sheet below the tree and hit the tree trunk with a padded stick; collect and destroy the curculios that fall onto the sheet. Continue for 3 wks.
Brown corky areas are visible on twigs and leaves.	Scale insects	Spray with dormant oil at bud break. Also, summer oil can be sprayed as contact control in late spring when new scales ("crawlers") appear. Be sure to prune out badly infected branches.
Fruits have brown powdery masses. Fruits shrivel and form "mummies."	Brown rot (fungus)	Keep trees well pruned to encourage air circulation. Remove and destroy dropped fruit. Spray with sulfur at preblossom stage. Repeat when flower shucks split, then weekly for 2 wk.
Smoky black knots (galls) on twigs and limbs, which range in size from ½ in. to 1 ft.	Black knot (fungus)	Plant resistant cultivars, such as 'President' and 'Shiro'. Prune off galls. Make sure to cut at least 4 in. below swellings.

Aphids are relatively easy to control, but controlling viruses can be difficult.

Leaves distorted by aphids

SYMPTOMS AND SIGNS	CAUSE	CONTROL
(Continued from previous page)		
Leaves have silvery sheen. Branches die back after 1 or more yr. When infected branches are cut out, wood shows dark brown staining. Small fungi appear on deadwood.	Silver leaf (fungus) (mostly on West Coast)	Cut out affected branches to 6 in. below point where brown stain ceases. Paint all wounds with Bordeaux mixture. Feed, mulch, water, and/or drain as necessary to encourage vigor. A foliar feed may hasten recovery.
Leaves turn brown and look burned, hang down from the branch, but do not fall. Cankers arise on branches.	Fire blight (fungus)	Plant resistant varieties. Apply streptomycin spray at early bloom stage. Prune out infected branches as soon as seen, cutting well into healthy wood. Apply Bordeaux mixture at the green-tip stage.
Small purple spots on leaves become brown and leaves may fall early.	Pear leaf blight (fungus)	Spray with copper or fungicidal soap as soon as seen. Collect and dispose of fallen leaves.
Large protuberances at soil line may girdle and kill entire tree.	Crown gall (bacteria)	Root out and destroy infected plants. Disinfect all pruning tools with rubbing alcohol or diluted bleach solution (1 part bleach, 10 parts water).
Brown spots may appear on leaves, eventually becoming holes. Flat cankers develop on stems and smaller branches; branches die back.	Bacterial canker	Cut out infected branches in midsummer. Spray foliage with Bordeaux mixture in midsummer, late summer, and midautumn.
Leaves, twigs, and fruits develop small spots that range in color from pale green to deep purple or brown. Fruits may crack; twig cankers may develop.	Bacterial leaf spot	Applications of Bordeaux mixture at and after leaf fall are beneficial. Prune and destroy badly cankered twigs. Destroy infected leaves.
Narrow strap-shaped leaves are brittle, thick, and coarsely wrinkled.	Prune dwarf (virus)	Plant virus-free stock. Destroy affected plants.
Leaves have yellow rings and spots. Fruits develop surface bumps and may drop from tree.	Ring spot (virus)	No effective control. Infected plant material must be destroyed. Control of insects tends to reduce spread of disease.
Stems and sometimes small branches die back. Plant lacks vigor.	Unsatisfactory soil conditions	Improve drainage. Test soil to determine whether addition of lime is necessary.

Varieties of Plums and Damsons to Grow

Although most varieties listed are self-fertile, it is a good idea to plant another tree, as indicated, to ensure pollination. Select pollenizers of the same major type as the tree to be pollinated; thus, a European variety with another European variety.

Varieties that may be hardy enough to grow in cooler areas are so indicated in the Remarks column. Japanese types are most subject to frost damage.

Greengages need a warm, sunny position. If grown in a cold area, they should be planted against a building or garden wall that is oriented toward the south or west.

NAMES	COLOR	REMARKS
European types		
'Earliblue'	Blue	Prune. Very early ripening. May be slow to produce fruit. Good quality. Hardy tree.
'Italian'	Blue	Prune. Widely planted. Good fresh and for canning. 'Brook's Giant' good strain where available.
'Mount Royal'	Blue	Prune. Extra hardy (Zone 4). Fruit will stay on tree when ripe without spoiling. Self-fertile.
'Pipestone'	Red (gold blush)	Plum. Fine quality. Hardy tree for colder climates. 'Toka' a good pollenizer.
'President'	Blue	Prune. Late season. Widely planted; fruitful. Fine textured. Cross-pollination advisable.
'Reine Claude'	Yellowish green	Greengage. Good for canning. Some improved strains available.
'Shropshire'	Purple	Damson. Hardy tree. Very good for preserves.
'Stanley'	Blue	Prune. Crops prolifically every year. Self-fertile.
'Toka'	Orange	Plum. Very hardy tree for colder climates. Rich flavor.
'Valor'	Blue	Prune. Large, early fruit of excellent quality. 'Stanley' will pollinate this. Susceptible to black knot.
Japanese types		
'Burbank'	Red-purple	Plum. Low tree. Necessary to thin fruit.
'Early Golden'	Yellow (red blush)	Plum. Freestone. Early season. Necessary to thin fruit; several pickings.
'Methley'	Purple	Small plums that ripen over several weeks. Self-fertile and good pollinator.
'Ozark Premier'	Yellow	Plum. Large, delicious fruit. Hardy tree.
'Santa Rosa'	Red	Plum. A standard variety. Delicious flavor.
'Shiro'	Yellow	Plum. Early season. Productive. 'Burbank' will not pollenize it.
'Tecumseh'	Red	Large plums of good flavor. Very hardy.

This vigorous variety produces two crops of fruit each year.

'Heritage'

Raspberries

Raspberry 'Heritage'

Raspberries can be used for fresh eating, desserts, cooking, or jam making; they can also be frozen. Some varieties bear fruit in midsummer on the previous season's shoots; others fruit in early or mid fall on the current season's shoots. Canes that have produced fruit die and are replaced year by year by new canes that grow from the roots.

There are three types of raspberries grown in this country. The reds, which are the most popular, have erect canes and are propagated by suckers from the roots. The blacks and the purples also grow upright, but they have arched canes that take root at the tips. These are dug up and set for new plants. The purples are hybrids of reds and blacks and are more vigorous. Yellow varieties are variations of the reds. All kinds of raspberries are self-fertile.

Buy one-year-old canes for planting in early spring. Raspberries are prone to viral diseases; it is advisable to get them from a reputable nursery to ensure that they are free of disease. To avoid the risk of spreading viral diseases, it is best not to replenish your stock by raising new plants from those you already have; always try to buy new canes of certified virus-free stock.

Raspberries generally do best in full sun but will grow in partial shade. Do not plant them in positions exposed to frost or strong winds and avoid planting them on steep slopes, which drain too quickly. Raspberries do well in any well-drained but moisture-retaining, slightly acidic soil. They will also grow in alkaline soil if it is enriched with compost or decayed manure. The average family should obtain a plentiful fruit supply with 18 to 24 raspberry canes.

Supporting the Long, Flexible Shoots

During summer, when the canes are producing fresh growth, sink an 8-foot wooden post 2 feet into the ground at each end of the row. Then

Preparing the Bed and Planting the Canes

Raspberries grow best in a row, with the canes trained against wires. First, clear the site of perennial weeds—either dig them up or, (if time permits), smother them with black plastic.

In late summer or early fall, prepare the ground by digging a spade-deep trench about 2½ feet wide. Fork in compost or well-rotted manure at the rate of about two 2-gallon buckets per square yard. Then fill in the trench with soil.

Planting is usually done in early spring, unless you buy plants produced by tissue culture methods. Wait until after frost danger has passed. Dig a shallow trench about 3 inches deep and 6–9 inches wide. Place the young plants upright in it,

stretch two galvanized wires between the posts 3 feet and 5½ feet above the ground; or stretch two parallel wires, 1 foot apart, from crosspieces fixed at right angles to the posts about 4 feet above the ground. Keep the wires parallel with strong

18 inches apart and with roots spread out. Cover the roots with 3 inches of soil, and then firm it gently with your feet. Leave 6 feet of space between rows.

Immediately after planting, cut each cane to just above a good bud, 9–12 inches above ground level. Well-rotted manure is ideal fertilizer, applied in the fall each year. In spring, one month before growth starts, apply ¼ pound of bone meal per square yard. Allow these fertilizers to be washed into the soil naturally.

In early spring mulch with a 2-inch layer of shredded leaves, bark mulch, or wood chips. Water well in warm, dry spells. Control weeds by pulling them up by hand. Do not hoe between the canes, as this can damage the shallow surface roots.

Protect ripening fruit from birds, preferably with netting.

S-shaped hooks. For both methods use 12–13 gauge galvanized wire.

The first midsummer after planting, tie canes individually with soft string to the two-wire system. With parallel wires, simply ensure that all canes are inside them.

Two-wire system. Between posts, stretch wires 3 ft. and 5½ ft. above the ground; tie the canes to them.

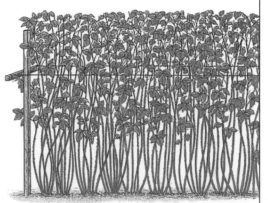

Parallel-wire system. Stretch two parallel wires between 4-ft.-high crosspieces; train canes inside them.

'Fall Gold'

Hardy and vigorous, 'Fall Gold' is an excellent choice for the home garden.

1. In late summer cut down to soil level all canes that have borne fruit.

2. Choose up to eight of the strongest new canes per plant; cut out the rest.

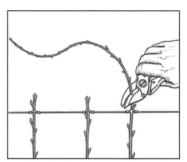

3. After supporting the new canes, pull out suckers springing from roots.

4. In winter trim canes growing beyond top wire to a bud just above it.

Replacing Old Canes With New

Raspberry varieties that bear one midsummer crop are biennial. The canes grow the first summer, fruit the next, then die. In late summer, when summer-fruiting raspberries have been picked, untie canes that have borne fruit, and cut them off just above soil level. Do not cut canes of the current year's growth.

Train eight of the strongest new canes on each plant. Cut out weak new canes at soil level. Also cut out all the canes that spring up between rows in order to reduce crowding.

In late winter cut back each cane growing above the top wire to a bud just a few inches above the wire.

To obtain early-summer *and* fall fruits from everbearing varieties, such as 'Heritage', prune the canes back to live wood, and thin out the weaker canes in the winter after fruiting in the fall. But, if you also have a summer-bearing one-crop variety, such as 'Sodus', prune the 'Heritage' type by cutting all canes to ground level in winter. This forfeits the early crop but produces larger and better berries in the fall.

Varieties of Raspberries and What Can Go Wrong

Select raspberry varieties that are certified to be virus-free. If your raspberries show symptoms that are not described here, turn to the section on plant disorders on page 506. Look up controls in the section beginning on page 542.

NAMES	SEASON	REMARKS
'Boyne'	Early-mid	Medium red. Large, firm berries.
'Brandywine'	Late	Purple. Very large fruit, good for jam.
'Bristol'	Mid	Black. Large berries.
'Canby'	Mid	Red. Thornless canes.
'Cumberland'	Mid	Black. Vigorous, but susceptible to disease.
'Fall Gold'	Early and late	Yellow. Vigorous, hardy.
'Heritage'	Early and late	Red. Productive. Good berries. Vigorous.
'Latham'	Early	Red. Fair-quality berries. Quite hardy.
'Redwing'	Mid	Red. Large fruit with good flavor.
'Royalty'	Late	Purple. Thorny, but excellent sweet berries.
'September'	Early and late	Red. Medium-sized berries.
'Sodus'	Mid	Purple. Large, good-quality berries. Vigorous, quite hardy.

SYMPTOMS AND SIGNS	CAUSE	CONTROL
Leaves rolled and/or distorted; sticky insects.	Aphids	Spray with a strong stream of water or insecticidal soap.
Tips of canes wilt soon after leaves unfurl.	Cane borers	Cut tops of canes off 6 in. below wilted section and destroy.
Berries eaten, small worms present.	Fruit worms or sawfly larvae	Spray with neem when blossom buds appear and just as blossoms open. Spray worms with *Bacillus thuringiensis*.
Fruits distorted and eaten; insects present.	Plant bugs (tarnished, harlequin)	Spray young nymphs with neem or *Beauveria bassiana*.
Foliage distorted, off-color. Plant fruits poorly.	Two-spotted mites	Spray with insecticidal soap several times at 5-day intervals.
Canes have large brown dead areas. Leaves on fruiting canes wilt and wither in summer.	Cane blight (fungus)	Cut back diseased canes to below-ground. Disinfect knife immediately. Spray with Bordeaux mixture as new canes develop.
Canes show purple circular spots, which become cankers. Fruits often misshapen.	Cane spot or anthracnose (fungus)	Same as for cane blight except lime sulfur spray can be used also.

The strawberry 'Tribute' has comparatively large fruits. This variety blossoms repeatedly, which means it is everbearing, and it yields a good harvest.

'Tribute'

Strawberries

Strawberry 'Veestar'

There are three types of strawberries: those that bear one crop (Junebearer) in early summer; the everbearing kind that gives a crop in summer and another in fall; and the day-neutrals that fruit in early summer, take a short rest, then crop again until frost. These outproduce the rest.

An average family will need 24 to 36 plants. Buy stock that has been certified free of any viral disease.

Strawberries grow in fertile, well-drained soil that is somewhat acid (pH 5.5–6). It should contain enough organic matter to retain moisture. Plant in spring or fall in an open, sunny bed, preferably facing south. Avoid planting in frost pockets.

Preparing the Ground and Planting

For Junebearer varieties the best time to plant is in early spring—in mild climates, also in early fall. Plant everbearing varieties in spring.

Clear the bed of weeds, especially perennial weeds, that could compete with your crop. Spread 2 inches of well-rotted manure or compost over the bed and dig it in. Or, sprinkle a balanced organic fertilizer blend at the rate recommended on the package. Strawberries do not have a deep root system; so you do not need the fertilizer worked deeply into the soil.

Place plants 18 inches apart in rows 30 inches apart. Soak those that are in peat pots for an hour first; plant the pots so that they are just covered with soil. Plant unpotted strawberries in moist soil. Dig a hole 1 or 2 inches deeper than the roots, and put the plant on a mound in the hole with roots spread out.

Position the upper part of the roots (the crown) level with the surface. If it is buried, the crown bud can rot; if its base is exposed, the roots can dry out. Fill in and firm around carefully. Water in dry weather.

Spread roots on a mound so the crown is level with the surface.

Strawberries—From Planting to Harvesting

Water regularly in dry weather for the first few weeks after planting. Lack of water at this time can retard growth or kill the plants.

In autumn, to conserve the plants' energy, cut off any runners that have grown. In late winter apply a balanced organic fertilizer blend according to the directions on the package. If growth is generally poor, spread more complete fertilizer along rows in midspring. In spring control weeds with shallow hoeing.

In their first season remove the blooms from Junebearer strawberries that were planted in late autumn or spring. On everbearing varieties, remove flowers in early spring to encourage more and better berries later on.

In subsequent years, when the developing fruits of the Junebearer varieties are heavy enough to almost reach the ground, tuck clean straw beneath the berries and around the plants.

An alternative is to use plastic sheeting to keep the berries off the ground. Be sure the soil is moist before putting it down.

One good way to keep fruit off the ground—particularly useful for plants grown in pots or in a greenhouse—is to use loops made of galvanized wire. Insert them in the soil beside the plants. Hang one stem over each support. Attach carefully—not too tightly—with plastic-covered ties.

Water during dry spells, particularly when ripening begins, in order to swell the fruit. But be careful not to overdo it; too much water during the ripening process can encourage a fungal disease known as gray mold. To ensure good flavor, pick strawberries with their stems attached, when the berries are fully ripe all around. Be sure to avoid excessive handling, since the fruits bruise easily.

PROTECTING YOUNG PLANTS AND FRUIT

To keep fruits clean and away from soil, use fresh straw or plastic sheeting.

Supports can be made with loops of galvanized wire. Hang one stem over each.

Watering is essential during budding.

Plenty of watering is needed after planting, during budding, and before ripening. There should be a straw bed beneath ripening fruits.

Straw bed keeps fruit off ground.

Clearing Out the Strawberry Bed

On Junebearer varieties, as soon as all the fruit has been picked, fork the straw well up to the plants, and set fire to it to burn off the leaves. This will not harm the plants but will destroy old, diseased leaves and kill off any pests. New leaves will soon show through and will have plenty of air and light.

If burning in your area is illegal, cut down plants with shears, or with a lawn mower set on high, to about 3 inches above the crown. Pull off any unwanted runners and old, diseased leaves, and remove plastic sheeting. Rake off litter and destroy it.

Renew strawberry plants every two or three years. After this time they will not crop so heavily, and disease is more likely. New plants can be raised easily from existing plants.

Everbearing varieties will keep on bearing fruit until autumn frosts. Cover with clear plastic early in the fall to ensure fruit for picking.

Do not remove leaves from everbearers or day neutrals, as this will destroy new growth, but clear away

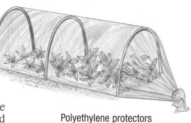

Polyethylene protectors against frost

some of the old leaves. Renew plants after one or two seasons of fruiting.

It pays to have two beds of strawberries, one you are picking and one that has just been planted. If you work on a three-year rotation, every third year you will get fruit from both.

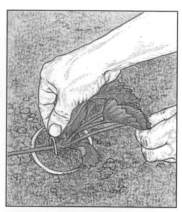

1. In summer extend four runners from a strong, healthy plant.

2. Pin an embryo plant on each runner to a pot of loam buried beneath.

3. Nip the runner beyond the new plant, but do not cut from its parent.

4. Four to six weeks later, sever from its parent; transplant one week later.

CUTTING DOWN JUNEBEARER STRAWBERRIES

When all fruits are picked, fork straw up to the plant, and set fire to it to burn leaves and kill pests.

Where burning is prohibited, cut plants to 3 in. above the crown. Pull off old leaves and unwanted runners.

Raising New Plants From Runners

In summer choose four strong runners from each healthy plant that has been cropping well, and extend the runners out from the parent plants. Runners rooted in pots are easier to transplant. Fill 3-inch pots with good loam, potting mix, or a mixture of the two. On each runner choose the embryo plant—a strong tuft of leaves—nearest to the parent, and with a trowel dig a hole beneath it big

enough for the pot. Sink the pot to its rim in the hole; then pin the runner to the rooting media in the pot. Use a 6-inch piece of galvanized wire bent into a U-shape, as shown above. Do not sever the runner between the parent and the young plant, but pinch off the extra growth just beyond the pot. Keep the rooting media moist.

Runners are rooted and can be severed from parent in four to six weeks. A week later, move to permanent positions. Then tend as you would newly planted strawberries.

'Ogallala' is an everbearing variety. 'Temptation'—an alpine strawberry—can be raised from seed, and will produce its small fruits from June to frost. 'Redcoat', an older variety, is still widely grown.

'Ogallala'

'Temptation'

'Redcoat'

A STRAWBERRY BARREL

Bore six 1-in. drainage holes in a barrel bottom, and several 2-in. holes 9 in. apart in its walls. Fill barrel with 2 parts good soil, 1 part mature-compost, 1 part coarse sand. Set plants in place as barrel is filled.

Varieties of Strawberries and What Can Go Wrong

The indicated bearing season (see chart, top right) will vary with the weather. If your strawberries show symptoms not described here, turn to the section on plant disorders on page 506. Look up controls in the section beginning on page 542.

NAMES	USUAL AREA	SEASON
Junebearer		
'Earliglow'	East Central	Early
'Guardian'	North Central, Northeast	Early
'Honeoye'	Northeast	Mid
'Pocahontas'	South Central	Mid
'Redchief'	East Central	Mid
'Sparkle'	North Central, Northeast	Late
Everbearing		
'Ogallala'	Northern areas	
'Ozark Beauty'	Southern areas	
Day neutral		
'Tribute'	Most areas	
'Tristar'	Most areas	

SYMPTOMS AND SIGNS	CAUSE	CONTROL
Leaves are crippled or stunted; turn yellow.	Leaf aphids	Spray plants with a strong stream of water or alternatively apply insecticidal soap.
Berries are small with sunken areas caused by bugs sucking sap from the fruit.	Tarnished plant bugs	Cover bed with floating row cover. Plant ground covers to encourage predatory insects. Spray young nymphs with *Beauveria bassiana*.
Small insects feed on foliage and roots.	Root weevils	Spread parasitic nematodes on the soil for larvae. Dust plants with neem for adults.
Grubs (rootworms) damage roots, adults eat leaves.	Strawberry leaf beetles	Apply neem to soil around plants.
Plants weak, off-color. Mites feed on undersides of buds and new leaves.	Two-spotted mites	Every 7–10 days throughout season spray with insecticidal soap
Fruits rot, become covered with grayish velvety mold.	Gray mold (fungus)	Destroy diseased fruits. Keep fruit up, away from contact with the soil.
Leaves turn purple and curl upward, exposing undersides.	Powdery mildew (fungus)	Spray just before blossoming with 1 ½ % lime sulfur. Repeat every 10–14 days until 1–2 wk. before picking time.
Leaves are small, yellow margined, and in flattened tufts; plants stunted and distorted. Poor crops.	Virus disease	No cure. Dig up and destroy plants. Keep aphids that spread virus under control. Purchase virus-free plants.

SYMPTOMS AND SIGNS	CAUSE	CONTROL
Chewed flowers and fruits. Leaves generally chewed, rolled, or tied together.	Caterpillars	Spray with *Bacillus thuringiensis kurstaki*.
Distortion of crown, leaves, blossoms, and fruits. Most serious pests in many areas.	Cyclamen mites	Dig up plants and destroy. Replant with fresh stock in a different area.
Insects feed on fruits and hide under plants by day.	Earwigs	Trap them in straw-filled pots—empty daily.

Homegrown vegetables are guaranteed pesticide-free and can be picked at the peak of flavor. A large range of vegetables and their varieties are available, including broccoli 'Premium Crop'.

VEGETABLES

Homegrown vegetables have a flavor rarely matched by those you buy. And even a small garden can produce enough to be well worthwhile.

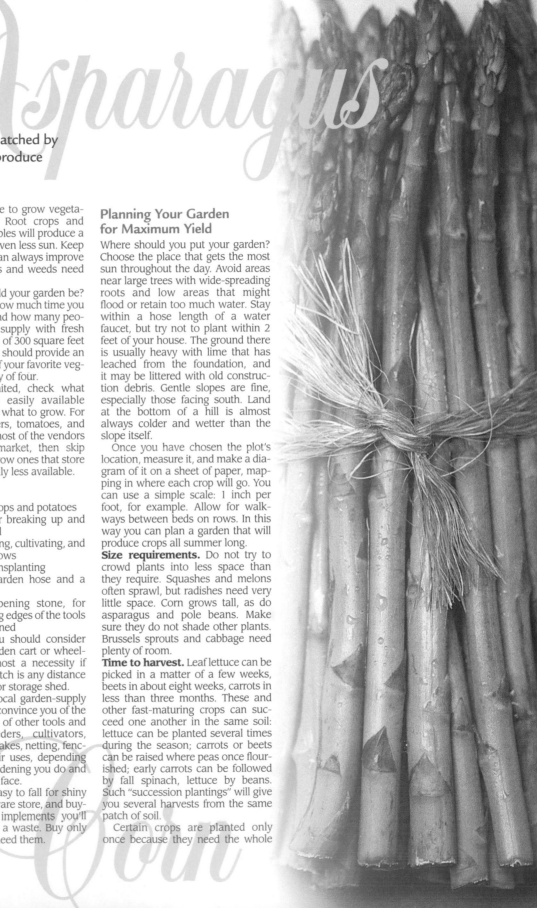

Here's a truism that more and more people are rediscovering: Nothing tastes quite as good as the vegetables you grow yourself in your own home garden. Millions of folks are adding food gardens large and small to their landscapes and reaping the benefits of fresh, organic, vitamin-rich vegetables. While it takes a bit more effort and advance planning to grow vegetables than flowers, the results are well worth it.

Before you decide to start a vegetable garden, size up your yard to make sure you have an appropriate site. Vegetable crops need well-drained soil and plenty of sunlight, and it's best to have a convenient water source nearby. If you have a spot that receives at least six hours of sun daily and is well away from trees and shrubs whose roots might compete for moisture and nutrients, then

you should be able to grow vegetables successfully. Root crops and some leafy vegetables will produce a decent crop with even less sun. Keep in mind that you can always improve your soil, so rocks and weeds need not be a deterrent.

How large should your garden be? That depends on how much time you can devote to it and how many people you want to supply with fresh produce. A garden of 300 square feet (15 feet by 20 feet) should provide an adequate supply of your favorite vegetables for a family of four.

If space is limited, check what local produce is easily available before you decide what to grow. For example, if peppers, tomatoes, and corn are sold by most of the vendors at the farmer's market, then skip those crops and grow ones that store well, but are usually less available.

Tools for the Vegetable Gardener

Basic vegetable-gardening tools have not changed for centuries, and if you do any gardening at all, you probably own most of them already. But because vegetable gardens require a great deal more digging and cultivating than flower gardens, it is a good idea to make certain that your tools adequately suit your height, weight, and strength.

Long-handled spades, for example, are difficult for short people to use; and if you are tall, doubling over a short hoe will almost surely give you a backache.

Before you buy any gardening tool, try it for size—it should feel well balanced when you pick it up; the working end should not weigh too much; and the handle should fit your grip comfortably.

Do not buy everything at once, but start with the essentials:
• A square-ended spade and a round-ended shovel, for digging
• A garden fork, for light digging and

harvesting root crops and potatoes
• A steel rake, for breaking up and smoothing the soil
• A hoe, for weeding, cultivating, and opening seed furrows
• A trowel, for transplanting
• A good long garden hose and a watering can
• A file or sharpening stone, for keeping the cutting edges of the tools clean and well honed

In addition, you should consider investing in a garden cart or wheelbarrow—it is almost a necessity if your vegetable patch is any distance from your house or storage shed.

A visit to the local garden-supply center can easily convince you of the need for a variety of other tools and equipment: weeders, cultivators, tillers, sprayers, stakes, netting, fencing. All have their uses, depending on how much gardening you do and the problems you face.

However, it's easy to fall for shiny tools at the hardware store, and buying a bunch of implements you'll never use can be a waste. Buy only when you really need them.

Planning Your Garden for Maximum Yield

Where should you put your garden? Choose the place that gets the most sun throughout the day. Avoid areas near large trees with wide-spreading roots and low areas that might flood or retain too much water. Stay within a hose length of a water faucet, but try not to plant within 2 feet of your house. The ground there is usually heavy with lime that has leached from the foundation, and it may be littered with old construction debris. Gentle slopes are fine, especially those facing south. Land at the bottom of a hill is almost always colder and wetter than the slope itself.

Once you have chosen the plot's location, measure it, and make a diagram of it on a sheet of paper, mapping in where each crop will go. You can use a simple scale: 1 inch per foot, for example. Allow for walkways between beds on rows. In this way you can plan a garden that will produce crops all summer long.

Size requirements. Do not try to crowd plants into less space than they require. Squashes and melons often sprawl, but radishes need very little space. Corn grows tall, as do asparagus and pole beans. Make sure they do not shade other plants. Brussels sprouts and cabbage need plenty of room.

Time to harvest. Leaf lettuce can be picked in a matter of a few weeks, beets in about eight weeks, carrots in less than three months. These and other fast-maturing crops can succeed one another in the same soil: lettuce can be planted several times during the season; carrots or beets can be raised where peas once flourished; early carrots can be followed by fall spinach, lettuce by beans. Such "succession plantings" will give you several harvests from the same patch of soil.

Certain crops are planted only once because they need the whole

Sandy soil

Clay soil

Loam

Clay is wet and cold in spring and bakes hard in summer. Sandy soil dries out quickly; loam is the ideal soil that warms early but holds moisture.

summer to mature. Tomatoes, eggplants, and winter squashes need up to three months to ripen. They also require plenty of nutrients and ample space. Allot them a large, sunny area.

Sunlight. Spinach and lettuce will grow very well in partially shaded spots or between the rows of such taller crops as broccoli or Brussels sprouts.

How to Improve Your Soil

The quality of a tomato, an eggplant, or a crisp green pepper depends first on the variety; it also reflects soil conditions. Vegetables may grow to maturity in poor, uncultivated ground—but they will not produce their best crops. Neither will the soil continue to produce summer after summer if its essential nutrients are diminished or if it is allowed to become dense and hard packed.

What can you do to improve your soil? First, determine the soil texture. If it is heavy and dense, it may contain too much clay; if it is loose and light, it probably has an overabundance of sand. The perfect garden soil is loamy and friable: it is dark and rich in color, and when you work a handful into a ball, it molds easily and keeps its shape but crumbles at a touch. Clay soil forms into a dense ball, which will break up into large, solid clods when you give it a poke. Sandy soil will not hold together at all. Both clay and sandy soils may be deficient in organic matter, which, as it decays, separates and lightens clay particles, while it binds sandy particles together and increases their water-holding capacity. Thus, adding quantities of composted leaves, grass clippings, straw, or well-rotted manure will eventually change the soil consistency, making it loose enough for seedlings to thrust their way through but dense enough to support their roots. By adding organic matter you will also enrich the soil

Interplanting. Fast-maturing vegetables—leaf lettuce, mustard greens, or spinach—may be planted among the seedlings of slow-growing vegetables, such as peppers, eggplants, or tomatoes. Radishes are often planted in the rows of slower-growing carrots or parsley. They sprout quickly, and can be picked and eaten while the other vegetables are still small.

with nutrients that all plants must have in order to grow and flourish.

The key to soil improvement, then, is the addition of organic matter, and one of the best sources of organic matter is a compost pile (see p. 500). But to begin, almost any soft vegetable matter will do. You can use dried leaves (shredded and bagged with a lawn mower, if you have one), vegetable wastes from the kitchen, hay from a local farmer, or well-rotted manure. All of these improve the soil. Add a nitrogen source, such as alfalfa meal, to aid in decomposition, and spread to a depth of 2–3 inches. Then dig the additions in by hand or with a rotary tiller if you have access to one.

Soil cultivation is best done in fall when the ground is warm and dry and when you have the winter months ahead to break down the materials into humus. By spring the additions will be blended in, making the soil richer and more friable.

All plants need a proper balance of nutrients—the major three are nitrogen, phosphorus, and potassium. Soils deficient in any one of these elements will not produce healthy plants. One way to ensure proper nutrient balance is to spread on a complete organic fertilizer. Or you can have your soil tested: your local nursery or garden center may be able to do this, and if not, they can recommend someone qualified to do so. (For more information on fertilizers and on soil testing, see p. 498.)

Perennials. Rhubarb, asparagus, and strawberries need considerable space. Rhubarb and asparagus will not produce a crop until, at the earliest, two years after planting.

Harvest yields. A long row of lettuce planted all at once will produce more salad than you can possibly eat. It is more practical to plant short rows of fast-maturing crops and to make succession plantings at two- or

The mysteries of pH. If your soil, enriched and fertilized as it is, still does not nurture healthy plants, it may be a matter of pH—the term for the degree of acidity or alkalinity of the soil. This is measured on a scale of 1 (totally acid) to 14 (totally alkaline). Acidity is a common problem, especially in the eastern portion of North America. Sandy or clay soil, or ground where pines, oaks, or rhododendrons thrive,

three-week intervals. If you have storage space, plant more winter squashes, onions, and potatoes. If you have a freezer, grow more Brussels sprouts, carrots, beets, and okra. For home canning, raise extra tomato plants.

Planting times. Peas and spinach require cool spring weather. Tomatoes cannot be put out until it is certain that there will be no more frost.

will probably measure on the lower, acidic end of the pH scale. Vegetables grow best in a soil that has a pH reading of between 6 and 7. If your soil is too acid, the imbalance can be corrected with a dressing of finely ground limestone. Extremely alkaline soil can be treated with peat moss or powdered sulfur. (For a more detailed discussion of pH, see pp. 498–499.)

1. Cut down tall weeds and fork them out.

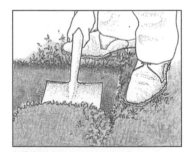

2. If the area was previously lawn, skim off the sod.

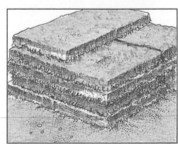

3. Stack the lifted sod, grass side down, to decompose.

4. Dig the area, turning the soil a full-spade depth.

To make optimal use of available ground, divide it into sections and plant different kinds of vegetables in a three-year cycle. Rotating crops in this way will prevent a buildup of soil-borne pests and diseases.

Intensive gardening in a small space

Traditional row crop system

KEEP YOUR GARDEN GROWING—PLANT FROM SPRING TO FALL

EARLY SPRING		MIDSPRING			EARLY SUMMER		MIDSUMMER TO FALL		
Plant as soon as the ground can be worked:		Plant 2 wk. before the average last frost date:		Plant 1 wk. later:	Plant when soil and sun are warm:		Plant in late June:	Plant in early August:	Plant 10 wk. before first killing frost:
PLANTS	**SEEDS**	**PLANTS**	**SEEDS**	**SEEDS**	**PLANTS**	**SEEDS**	**SEEDS**	**PLANTS**	**SEEDS**
Broccoli	Endives	Cauliflower	Beets	Beans	Eggplant	Cucumbers	Beets	Broccoli*	Beets
Cabbage	Lettuce		Carrots	Corn	Peppers	Lima beans	Broccoli	Cabbage*	Carrots
Fava beans	Onion sets		Onion sets	Early potatoes	Tomatoes	Melons	Cabbage	Cauliflower*	
Leeks	Peas		Parsnips			Okra	Carrots		
Onions	Radish		Swiss chard			Pumpkins	Cauliflower	**SEEDS**	
	Spinach					Squash	Lettuce	Lettuce	
	Turnips					Winter potatoes	Radish	Spinach	
								Turnips	

* Plants are set out later than seeds are sown because hot weather is not favorable to good growth.

Know Your Region's Frost Dates

American winters vary enormously in length: a gardener in Minnesota can be sure of only about 100 growing days, while a Georgia gardener may have 300. The length of the growing season is defined by the customary dates of the last frost in spring and the first killing frost in fall. Gardeners use these dates to judge when planting should begin and how long the growing season can be stretched. To find out the frost dates in your area, check with your local gardening center or county extension agent, and set up your planting calendar accordingly.

Keep in mind that frost dates are dependent on such factors as elevation and proximity to large bodies of water. If you live in a valley, your planting season will be shorter than that of someone in your region who lives on a slope.

"As soon as the ground can be worked" is printed on many seed packets. Vegetables that withstand frost (spinach, onions, and peas) can be planted as soon as the soil has lost its sogginess. To test whether your soil is workable, squeeze a bit of it into a ball in your hand. If the ball crumbles easily, you can begin gardening. If it holds its shape, the soil is still too moist; wait another few days.

Buying Vegetable Seedlings and Seeds

Some vegetables, including root crops such as carrots and parsnips, must be sown directly into the ground as seeds. Others can be started in flats or pots and then set in the garden as seedlings.

Buying seedlings. In spring most garden centers are overflowing with cell packs (usually small divided containers with six or eight plants growing in each) and single pots containing seedlings of a variety of vegetables: broccoli, cabbage, lettuce, tomatoes. Such commercially grown plants are convenient. They save time and eliminate the often risky effort of starting seeds indoors at home. For those who lack sunny window space, they are essential.

When you buy seedlings, however, you are limited to a small number of varieties. And if you buy them at a supermarket, you may not be able to get the facts you need—whether a particular tomato plant is a late or an early bearer, for example, or what variety it is. Small growers usually give you this information.

The advantage of single plants in their own pots is that they do not require separating, which might cause root damage. But if you need larger quantities, cell packs are cheaper.

Check the plant stems. They should be short and thick; tall, spindly plants probably have weak root systems and may never recover from the shock of transplanting. Take a close look at the foliage; if it is yellowish or discolored, the plant may be diseased or poorly nourished. A purplish hue on cabbage, broccoli, and cauliflower plants, however, indicates that they have been "hardened off" to make them ready for early planting. (For instructions on setting out seedlings, see p. 440.)

Buying seeds. If you have enough sunny space in your house, or if you have a greenhouse or cold frame, you can grow your own seedlings.

How do you choose among the enormous variety of types, colors, shapes, and sizes available for each vegetable? First, obtain a seed catalog. Ask your local garden center to recommend one or more reputable seed companies that specialize in seeds for your area. Then send an e-mail to the company requesting a catalog.

Evaluate each catalog entry according to disease resistance (if it is resistant to diseases that commonly attack the plant, the catalog will say so), size of plant, yield (heavy yielders will be indicated), and the number of days to harvest. A variety that has won an All-America Award has performed well in trial plots throughout the continent—an important indication of quality. In the vegetable descriptions that follow (see pp. 442–482), All-America Award winners are marked with an asterisk (*).

New varieties are often improvements over older varieties. They may be more disease-resistant or have a larger yield. The plant may need less room for growth, or its produce may have a better flavor.

In deciding how much seed you should buy, choose the smallest packet. It usually provides adequate seeds for a 25-foot row, and 25 feet will grow up to 20 pounds of beets, 25 pounds of carrots, or 20 pounds of lettuce.

Although most seeds will remain viable when kept in a cool, dry place, it is usually safer to buy only as much as you need each year. Catalogs also offer some vegetable seeds in easy-to-handle forms—either "pelleted" (coated with a claylike material to make each seed larger and easier to plant) or secured to a water-soluble tape. The seeds on tapes are spaced at the proper distances; all you have to do is lay the strip in a shallow furrow and cover it with soil.

Tapes eliminate the need for thinning; but if some of the seeds fail to germinate, you will have empty spaces in your row. Both pellets and tapes are considerably more expensive than plain seeds.

Ready for planting

Laying down seed tapes

Young plants, removed from the fibrous pots in which they have been raised, are ready for planting. Seed tapes are lightly covered with soil.

Planting Seeds

Indoors

You can gain up to 10 weeks extra growing time if you start certain vegetables indoors. Peppers, eggplant, cauliflower, and tomatoes are among the vegetables seldom sown directly in the garden; they are usually started indoors and transplanted.

Some basic techniques for indoor seed planting of annual flowers are discussed on page 193. These same techniques can also be used to start vegetables indoors—with the following additional tips.

Potting soils. Do not use plain garden soil. It harbors weed seeds and fungi that can prevent your vegetable seeds from growing properly. Buy sterilized potting soil, or use a mixture of peat moss and sand or vermiculite. Milled sphagnum moss is often recommended for small seeds. Soilless mixtures must be given a liquid fertilizer solution, because they contain no nutrients themselves.

Seeding containers. Depending on the size of the seed, and the number of plants you require, there is a wide range of containers for seeding. A pinch of lettuce seed for plants to set out early could go in a 3-inch pot, but leek or onion seed to provide a winter's supply of vegetable may need a small flat. Larger seeds can be sown in individual pots of clay, plastic, or peat. Peat pots can be put directly

into the ground, where they will decompose; thus, the seedlings suffer less shock from transplanting.

Schedule indoor plantings with an eye to how long each vegetable takes to grow and when it can be set out. Peppers, for instance, need 8 to 10 weeks indoors and should be planted outside well after the last frost. Leek seedlings should be set out in early spring, at the age of 12 weeks. Sow cabbage seeds five to seven weeks before setting plants out, cucumbers three to four weeks beforehand.

Most seeds need fairly warm soil to germinate; so keep flats or pots in a warm spot. Cover until seeds sprout, to keep out light and retain moisture.

Keep track of expected germinating times. If, for instance, no eggplant sprouts appear by three weeks after sowing, something has gone wrong, and you had better buy a few plants to replace them. After the seeds sprout, place them where they will get maximum light.

The "damping off" problem. The warmth and humidity that encourage seed germination also encourage the fungi that can prevent germination or cause seedlings to collapse. You can prevent this "damping off" disease by purchasing sterile potting soil, by not overwatering or overfertilizing seedlings, and by keeping a watchful eye on your seed trays for signs of too much moisture. If water

NAMES	WEEKS TO SOW INDOORS BEFORE LAST FROST	WEEKS TO GERMINATE	SET OUT TRANSPLANTS
Broccoli	5–7	1–2	After frost, late summer
Brussels sprouts	4–6	1–2	After frost, late summer
Cabbage	5–8	1–2	After frost, late summer
Cauliflower	5–8	1–2	After frost, late summer
Cucumbers	2–3	1–2	2 wk. after frost
Eggplant	8–9	2–3	Late spring-early summer
Leeks	10–12	2–3	Midspring
Head lettuce	3–5	2–3	Around last frost
Onions (globe)	6–8	2–3	When soil dries
Peppers	8–10	1–2	Late spring-early summer
Tomatoes	6–8	2–3	Mid to late spring

drops collect on the insides of the plastic or glass coverings, remove them and wipe or shake the water out before replacing them. You can also apply commercial products containing beneficial microbes that fight damping-off fungi. If you notice seedlings falling over, with a black zone near the soil, remove the diseased seedlings and increase air circulation to remainder, with a fan if possible, before fungus can spread.

Thinning and potting. When seeds have sprouted and young plants

have their first set of true leaves, thin them out, removing smaller specimens so that the stronger ones will have room to grow. Snip stems with a small scissors; do not pull or you may disturb root systems. Later on, when seedlings are established and the pot is crowded again, prick out the seedlings. Very delicately, take a label stake or fork, and use the pointed end to separate the seedlings and transplant them into individual 2½- to 3-inch pots. If they have been growing in soilless mix, transplant

STARTING YOUR SEEDS OFF THE RIGHT WAY

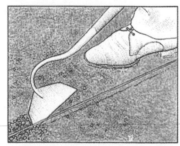

1. Using a line as a guide, make a shallow furrow with a hoe.

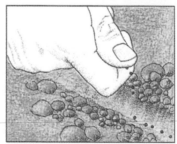

2. Distribute seeds evenly in the furrow with your fingers.

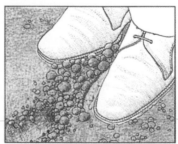

3. Close the furrow with your feet, but avoid treading too firmly.

TRANSPLANTING SEEDLINGS

Carefully lift the seedlings out of the ground with a small stick.

Slugs, aphids, earwigs, and caterpillars are among the most common pests in a vegetable garden.

Caterpillars

Aphids

them into a compost-based mix in the new pot, which will provide nutrients for continued growth. Water transplants immediately with a weak solution of manure tea to reduce the shock of transplanting.

Hardening off. Seedlings grown indoors have been treated with tender loving care far beyond anything they will experience in ordinary garden conditions. They must be toughened—that is, conditioned to lower and more variable temperatures and to far less water—before being transplanted. The easiest and safest hardening-off method is to use a cold frame (see p. 195).

When the spring sun begins to warm, and certainly no later than one week before you plan to set out your seedlings, put them inside the frame. If the weather is bright and sunny, protect the tender plants from too much sun by anchoring newspapers over the glass cover.

Prop open the lid of the frame a little more each day as the weather warms, making certain the temperature inside the frame never rises above 70°F. Close the frame at night if temperatures drop below 55°F. If a cold snap occurs, cover the frame with a blanket. By the time you are ready to plant them in the garden, the seedlings should have had two or three nights uncovered. If nights are too cold for this, delay planting.

PUTTING IN YOUNG PLANTS

1. Press down firmly on the soil, so that the plant will take hold.

2. If the plant comes up with a slight tug, it was not firm enough.

Outdoors

You have dug up your garden plot, enriched it with organic material, and fertilized it. You have raked out the stones. Now you are ready to plant. Check your garden plan to see that rows run from east to west if this is practical; that tall plants will be on the northern and eastern sides of the plot; and that you have planned to grow early crops (lettuce, peas, spinach) as well as hot-weather vegetables (tomatoes, eggplant, peppers). Remember to design succession plantings: early lettuce followed by late carrots, or radishes followed by beets. Remember, too, that you need not plant entire rows of quick-maturing or very productive plants, such as lettuce or Swiss chard. Plant partial rows and follow up with more plantings later.

Sowing the seeds. Mark your row with stakes at each end, and stretch a garden line between them. Make furrows, also known as drills, barely ½ inch deep for small seeds, approximately 1 inch deep for the larger ones. Scatter small seeds evenly and close together.

Larger seeds can be planted about an inch apart, but for exact distances see the instructions beginning on page 442 on how to raise specific vegetables. Especially where soil tends to crust over, cover small seeds with a thin layer of potting mix, compost, or of soil mixed with sand or fine peat moss. Tamp down over the seeds and water gently. Mark the row with a plant label on which you have written—in indelible ink—the name of the vegetable, the variety, and the planting date.

Seeds must have continuously moist soil around them until they sprout. Check for moisture every day, and if the soil seems too dry, water it lightly. Do not overwater: soggy soil can cause the larger seeds to rot—the soil should be damp, but never waterlogged.

Watch for germination. Cold soil and cool weather both impede seed sprouting. Lettuce will germinate in about 10 days in early spring, but in only 4 or 5 days when it is warmer. Carrots and parsnips are slow to sprout; so you should not despair if, after two weeks, nothing has happened. After three weeks, though, you should put in a new row; something has prevented germination. Perhaps the soil was too dry or too cold, the furrow was too deep, or the surface had a crust too hard for seedlings to push through.

Many home gardeners sow seeds of salad greens and some other crops in wide rows or by broadcasting them lightly across the full width of a bed.

Thinning. For beginning gardeners especially, thinning can be a painful process. It seems wasteful to destroy perfectly good seedlings. But it must be done. If unthinned, radishes will not form bulbs. Carrots will not grow or will twist grotesquely. Lettuce will form puny heads.

You should begin thinning when the seedlings are about 1 or 2 inches high. (For the optimum separation between plants, see the discussion of individual vegetables beginning on p. 442.) Do not try to thin out seedlings all at once. A thick row of leaf lettuce can be thinned at first by removing every other plant. You can remove more plants in later thinnings, when the lettuce will be large enough to eat. When thinning a thickly seeded row, pull each plant out carefully, lifting straight up, to avoid disturbing the roots of neighboring plants.

It is possible to transplant well-grown seedlings from a thinned row if you take steps to avoid damaging their roots or stems. Use a small trowel or label stake to dig them up along with a small clump of soil surrounding their roots, and handle them gently.

Setting plants out. When your indoor-grown seedlings have been sufficiently hardened off, wait for a cloudy day to set them out. (Don't rely on commercially grown seedlings being hardened off when you buy them.) Remember that too much heat can wither a plant as quickly as dry soil.

If no clouds are imminent, plant the seedlings in the late afternoon, and shade them with newspapers, bushel baskets, or anything that will shield them from the sun's rays but still let in a little air.

When you are ready to set out your plants, dig evenly spaced holes according to the directions for each vegetable. (See discussions of individual vegetables in the section beginning on p. 442.) Fill the holes with water, and let it soak into the soil—this will give the roots of each plant sufficient moisture to make a good beginning.

If you are using peat pots, the plant can be set out in the pot, but be sure to slit its sides in two or three places to allow for root growth. Bury the pot completely in the ground, so that it will remain moist and disintegrate.

Plants grown in plastic pots or flats must be handled carefully. Remove or cut out each plant along with the soil that surrounds its roots. When setting these in the holes you have dug, make sure that the garden soil is pushed firmly but gently around the root balls. Leave a slight soil depression around each plant to collect and hold moisture. Then water well.

Preparing the garden

A healthy summer garden

Although spring and summer are the gardener's most intensive work seasons, a lot of clearing up and preparation has to be done in autumn and winter.

Taking Care of Your Garden

The vegetables you have carefully planted in soil that you have improved and enriched will thrive if they get plenty of water and lots of sun and if weeds are eliminated. The weeds compete with the vegetables for whatever moisture and nutrients are available and will grow rampant in rich, well-cultivated soil. And if you allow weeds to grow undisturbed at the beginning, when you pull them up later, you may injure the roots of plants you want to keep.

Work out a weeding program, a once- or twice-weekly trip between your garden rows with a hoe. When weeds are small, you can simply scrape them away. But if you dig your hoe more than half an inch or so into the ground, you run the risk of cutting into vegetable roots. Large weeds and those growing within the rows have to be pulled out by hand. Weed pulling is easier if the soil is moist; try to weed after a rainstorm, or schedule weedings for the day after waterings.

Watering. During hot, rainless weather, or whenever the garden soil becomes powdery and dry, you will have to water your garden. Watering is particularly important for young plants with shallow roots. As plants grow larger, their roots thrust deeper into the soil, where moisture remains even when the surface soil is dry. Thorough, deep waterings are far more effective than brief, shallow ones. Sprinkling encourages plant roots to stay on the surface where they are susceptible to hoeing damage and to the drying heat of the sun.

A garden hose is a basic watering implement. Use an oscillating or rotary sprinkler for efficient use of water. Keep the droplet size as large as possible to reduce evaporation. Fine sprays can lose up to 50 percent in hot weather. Soaker hoses (perforated plastic tubes) laid with their holes down are an efficient way to water. The water soaks into the soil in a fan shape, soaking the root zone. As a general rule, schedule your waterings for the morning or early afternoon, so that leaves can dry off before nightfall. Wet leaves are more susceptible to fungal diseases. Water evaporates less quickly on overcast days than on sunny days.

Plants need between 1 and 1½ inches of water each week. You can keep track of the amount yours are getting simply by leaving an open container in your garden, marked off in half inches. During dry midsummers especially, be sure to water your garden well once a week.

Mulching. A mulch is a soil cover composed, usually, of organic materials, such as leaves, hay, or grass clippings. Mulch is made in nature every year by the dead leaves, twigs, and plants that fall to the ground and decompose there. Gardeners who use mulch do not have as much weeding to do and find that a layer of mulch around their plants helps to conserve moisture in the soil. It may also help to prevent the spread of various soil-borne diseases.

Organic mulch decomposes slowly and is incorporated into the soil. It adds nutrients, making the soil looser and more friable, and provides good living conditions for earthworms, which aerate the soil, and many beneficial microorganisms.

Some good mulching materials include hay, especially "spoiled hay," which has already begun to decompose; grass clippings after they have begun to dry and turn gray; shredded or composted leaves; well-rotted manure mixed with straw; peat moss mixed with sawdust or wood chips (peat moss alone will pack down and dry, and water will not penetrate it). Sawdust and pine needles are also good mulching materials, but they may need an addition of lime, to counteract their acidity, and of nitrogenous fertilizer, to compensate for the nitrogen used by the microorganisms that cause decay. Garden-supply stores sell black plastic strips (some types are biodegradable) for use as mulching material. They provide quick soil protection and also boost soil temperature, which helps promote fast growth of crops, such as melons that do best in warm soil.

When seedlings are about 4 inches high, spread a thick layer of mulching material among the plants and between the rows. As summer progresses and the mulch breaks down, add more. Sprinkle mulch with blood meal to hasten the decomposing process.

If you keep a perpetual cover of mulch on your garden, the soil will take longer to warm up and dry in spring than will unmulched soil. For early planting, therefore, push aside the mulch where you intend to make seed furrows, and wait for the ground to warm up and dry.

Hints for a healthy garden. To protect vegetables from diseases and discourage pest infestations, here are a few simple rules to follow.
• Choose seeds of disease-resistant varieties whenever you can.
• Inspect store-bought plants carefully. Spotty or discolored leaves may be signs of damage, insufficient nutrients, or disease.
• Pull up and throw away any diseased plant. Do not compost it.
• Rotate crops, especially cabbage and its many relatives, to prevent the spread of soil-borne diseases.
• Weed often and dispose of any weeds that harbor plant-eating pests.
• Do not work in your garden immediately after a rainstorm. Wet leaves are more vulnerable to damage and disease, and walking over rain-soaked soil will harden it.
• After harvesting each crop, destroy what remains of the plants. If they were healthy, compost them.

Whatever precautions you take, diseases and pests will occur. In the discussions that follow, you will learn what can go wrong with each vegetable and how to prevent or treat the disorder.

Crop rotation. All vegetables need the complete range of soil nutrients, both the big three—nitrogen, potassium, and phosphorus—and the minor nutrients. However, different crops use them at different rates.

If you grow the same crop in the same patch of soil for several years, it will deplete some of the nutrients essential to that plant and the yields will decrease. In addition, pests and diseases that attack that particular plant will build up in the soil and the crop will be under constant attack.

Crop rotation takes these factors into account. Vegetables are grouped by family or habit of growth. Generally, plants in the same family, for example, eggplant, tomato, and pepper, have the same nutritional needs and the same pests—replacing peppers with tomatoes would not solve anything. But by planting the brassicas on land that was used by legumes the previous year, you reap the benefit of the nitrogen left behind in the pea and bean roots.

The diversity of crops grown in vegetable gardens can make rotation a little more complicated. It is best to rotate on a five-year system. Plot 1 is the cabbage group—cabbage, broccoli, cauliflower, Brussels sprout, kohlrabi—all of the Asian greens, like bok choy, kale, and turnip, and is given compost and fertilizer. Plot 2 (which will move to Plot 1 the next year) is the tomato group—tomatoes, potatoes, peppers, and eggplant—and the root crop group—carrots, beets, Swiss chard, parsnips, parsley (and celeriac), sweet potatoes, and celery. Plot 3 is the squash group: summer and winter squash, melons, watermelons, cucumbers, and zucchini. Plot 4 is the onion group: onions, shallots, leeks, and garlic. The various peas and beans, both bush and pole, are in the pea group, as is okra, and make up Plot 5. Corn is best considered as a group by itself, since the shade it casts may limit where it can be planted. Lettuce can be tucked in odd spots as fillers.

If there is not enough space in the vegetable garden, artichoke plants can be quite an adornment in a flower bed.

Artichoke 'Green Globe'

Artichokes

Artichoke 'Green Globe'

There are two unrelated artichoke plants that the gardener is likely to try and grow. Globe artichokes, native to the southern Mediterranean, are related to the thistle. Jerusalem artichokes, relatives of the sunflower, are native to North America.

Globe artichokes grow best in a warm climate, and most varieties need at least 100 frost-free days to produce their edible flower buds. In the North newer short-season varieties are treated as annuals and raised from seed each spring. Where winters are mild they are perennial and will give good crops for years.

Ten weeks before the average last frost, chill the seeds in damp sphagnum moss in the refrigerator for two weeks before sowing. Pot seedlings individually in small pots, moving them into 5-inch pots later.

Prepare the bed by digging in plen-ty of compost or old manure. Nurseries sometimes have plants or, where it is warm, dormant root divisions. Plant potted plants at soil level, root divisions 4 inches deep. Existing plants can be propagated by cutting off suckers in spring and planting these individually. Space 4–6 feet apart; they form large plants.

Jerusalem artichokes (sunchokes) are rather like knobby potatoes but are hardy. They grow 8–10 feet tall and have small yellow flowers in fall. They prefer a well-drained soil and will still give a crop even if the soil is poor. They do crop better on a rich soil as long as it is well drained. They are not wide-spreading plants and should be planted about 4 inches deep and 2 feet apart. One tuber planted in spring will produce a cluster that can be dug in fall and stored over winter in a frost-free place.

1. With a sharp knife, carefully detach a sucker.

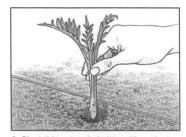

2. Plant this out and shelter with a plant protector for a few days.

Taking Care of Your Artichokes

Instructions here are for globe artichokes as Jerusalem artichokes will crop no matter how neglected they are. Where they will overwinter, globe artichokes should be given a permanent location. If treated as annuals, they should be fitted into the crop-rotation scheme. (Jerusalem artichokes will cast considerable shade and should be sited with care for this reason.) As the weather warms, mulch to keep the soil cool and water during periods of drought. Cut the flower bud when it is about the size of an orange. Cut just below

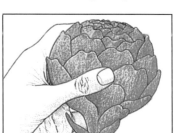

1. The flower bud is ready for cutting when it is the size of an orange.

3. After frost, cut the main stems down to the ground.

Varieties to Grow

Globe artichoke. 'Imperial Star' is the best choice for an annual. Buds are round, thornless, freely produced, and average 4 inches. 'Green Globe Improved' does well in the West, will also crop in other regions, but does

the bud and then remove the stem down to the top side shoot. These side shoots will produce more buds. In late fall, once cold stops further development, cut the main stem down to the ground. Where winters are not too harsh, protect the crown with straw. Remove the protection in early spring or the crowns will rot. Where winters are long and cold, treat the plants as annuals and plant again the following spring.

Globe artichokes can be attacked and badly deformed by aphids. Spray with insecticidal soap at the first sign. Slugs and snails also feed on the foliage, and earwigs hide under the flower-bud scales during the day.

2. Cut just below the bud with about an inch of the stem.

4. Mulch around the crown with straw, or mound over with soil.

not produce heavily the first year. Purple-tinged 'Violetto' heads are longer and more oval than 'Green Globe'.
Jerusalem artichoke. The tubers of 'Stampede' are not as knobby. The plant does not grow as tall and flowers earlier with chocolate-scented blooms.

Green asparagus must not be allowed to grow more than 8 in. high, or the stalk will become woody.

Ready to cut

Mature plants

Asparagus

Asparagus is one of the few perennials in the vegetable and fruit garden—the others being rhubarb and strawberries. Like them, asparagus offers the pleasure of a crop to enjoy year after year.

Asparagus 'Mary Washington'

A well-cultivated asparagus bed can produce for 20 seasons or more. Bed preparation is extensive, and the asparagus will not be ready for harvesting until the third year after you plant it. But if you have the time and the space, there are few more rewarding crops, for asparagus is an expensive vegetable to buy at the market. If you decide to grow your own, remember that asparagus retains its delicate flavor when frozen.

How to Grow Asparagus

Gardeners usually start their asparagus beds with roots, not seeds, because a seed-planted bed requires another year's growing time. You can buy roots from a nursery or mail-order house. Allow 25 feet of row for every 12 plants, with rows spaced 2 feet apart.

Asparagus can be grown in any well-drained, fertile soil. Test for pH—the soil should be slightly acid but not below pH 6. As soon as the ground can be worked, dig a trench 18 inches wide and 10 inches deep. Backfill the trench with 4 inches of compost and sprinkle in 1 pound of bone meal per 20 feet of row. Fill the trench with this mixture to about 6 inches below ground level. Tamp it down and place the roots on top, 2 feet apart. For the best results, cover with 2–3 inches of soil. As the plants sprout, be sure to add more soil until the trench is full.

Feed the stand each spring and fall by spreading ½ inch of compost around and between the crowns. Top that with a 1-inch layer of shredded leaves or pine needles. Watch for weeds. Hoe them out shallowly to avoid injuring the underground stems. Mulching around the plants will help keep weeds down and moisture in. In fall, when the leaves have been killed by frost, cut off the top growth to ground level and mulch the bed again.

Over the first two years an extensive root system will grow to feed and support the stalks. The second spring after planting, you can pick a few shoots when they are about 7 inches high—but make sure that you restrict the harvesting to a month at most. From the third year after planting, cut all shoots except the very thin ones. Harvest shoots when they are about 5–8 inches tall and buds are still tight; when buds begin to open, the spears are past their prime.

What Can Go Wrong With Asparagus

Properly grown, asparagus has few problems. Rust, which used to be a major cause of failure, is now almost unknown in newer plantings, thanks to rust-resistant varieties. Crown rot can be serious, and if plants become infected, it is best to remove them and start a new asparagus patch elsewhere in the garden.

If small beetles are feeding on foliage or berries, spray with insecticidal soap. The spotted asparagus beetle feeds mainly on berries, so plant an all-male variety.

Varieties of Asparagus to Grow

The rust-resistant variety 'Mary Washington' remains available. 'Viking', an improved 'Mary Washington', was developed at Ontario's Vineland Research Station. As well, ask about new productive all-male cultivars at your local nursery.

Modern research has given rise to rust-resistant, all-male varieties that crop more heavily, have thicker spears, and have fewer of the very thin spears. Because they do not have fruit, they are unlikely to be at-

Being a perennial vegetable, asparagus should always be planted to one side of the garden so that it will not be disturbed by the care and cropping of the annual vegetables.

Harvest by cutting about 1 inch below the soil surface. If you cannot use the asparagus immediately, keep the stalks upright in water until you are ready to cook them.

The harvest season lasts six to eight weeks. After this, the stalks will grow into tall, fernlike branches that will feed the roots.

If growth is stunted and the ends of branchlets are blue-green, the plants have asparagus aphid. Sanitation is a good control; clean up dead foliage in fall to remove winter hibernation sites. If plants are badly attacked and severely stunted, next year's crop could be reduced, so spray with insecticidal soap.

Where summers are humid, plants may be infected with purple spot. Small, sunken purple spots appear on spears, stems, or branches. If purple spot attacks in spring, while the spears are being cut, the crop may be unusable. Use good sanitation to prevent reoccurrence.

tacked by the spotted asparagus beetle, but may still get the regular asparagus beetle. Of these varieties, 'Jersey Giant' and 'Jersey Knight' are the most popular, but 'Jersey Centennial', 'Jersey General', 'Jersey King', and 'Supermale' are also available. 'UC-157' is the best variety for areas with mild winters and dry summers.

All-male varieties are raised from seed and may contain the occasional female, which should be weeded out during the first couple of years, before plants are set out in their permanent location. This should have been done to any such plants you buy.

The lima bean is also known as the fat or butter bean and the vetch. Depending on the variety, it ripens from late May to August.

Lima beans

Beans, Lima

Pole lima bean
'King of the Garden'

Like all beans, lima beans and baby lima beans (the small-seeded varieties called butter beans) belong to the highly nutritious legume family. Besides being good for you, limas have a delicious nutlike flavor and are relatively easy to grow. However, they do need a long, warm summer to mature and for this reason are grown mainly in warmer regions. (If your climate is not right for limas, you may want to grow fava, or broad, beans, which need a long, cool grow-ing season and have the added advantage of producing well with little care. See Decorative Beans, p. 446.)

Limas, like the snap beans that are discussed on the following pages, can be grown as either bushy plants or pole plants. Pole beans give larger yields in a smaller space than do the bush varieties, but they take somewhat longer to ripen. Pole lima beans mature in about three months—about two weeks after the bush varieties begin to yield.

How to Grow Lima Beans

When preparing the soil for lima beans, work in a ½ inch layer of compost. Sow the seeds at about the same time that you set out such warmth-loving plants as tomatoes, peppers, and cucumbers.

Plant bush lima seeds 1–1½ inches deep, spacing the seeds 2–3 inches apart, in rows 2 feet apart. Bush beans require only about 4 inches between plants; so unless each seed germinates, thinning is not needed.

The illustration on page 446 shows three different methods to support pole beans, both limas and snap beans. Build the supports before you sow the seeds. Supports for limas should be sturdier than those for snap beans (because lima plants are heavier) and taller (limas grow up to 8 feet high, compared to 6 feet for snap beans).

If you are growing pole beans along a fence, sow single seeds 3–5 inches apart. Thin seedlings to a spacing of 6–10 inches. To grow plants on poles, stake out the supports 2 feet apart in rows 3 feet apart. Sow about six seeds around each pole, and thin to three or four plants.

When the pod is round and firm, and the shape of the beans is visible inside, it is time to harvest. Pick steadily as beans ripen, as mature beans on the plant will discourage the growth of new ones.

At season's end you can let the remaining beans dry before picking. Sterilize them in a very low oven for about an hour, and seal them in jars. Home-dried limas can be stored for several months.

What Can Go Wrong With Lima Beans

If limas blossom in extremely hot weather, they may not set. In some areas the lima-bean pod borer may devour the seeds inside the pods. Early plantings are less vulnerable, and cleaning up leaves removes the insects' nesting places.

Because limas are very sensitive to mildew and other diseases, cultivate them shallowly and only during dry weather. Water them at soil level (never from above), and always do it in the morning so that the sun will have a chance to dry off moisture that falls on the plants. Mulch to conserve moisture in the soil and to keep weeds down. Fertilize sparingly.

Varieties of Lima Beans to Grow

Most seed catalogs carry at least one variety of lima bean, but you may have to search a little to find some of those listed.

Seed racks in small garden centers may not contain lima beans at all; they are not as popular as snap beans but nevertheless are well worth searching for.

For bush-lima-bean plants, select 'Fordhook 242', which resists high temperatures at pod-setting time. For pole varieties, take advantage of that dependable old favorite, 'King of the Garden'.

NAMES	DAYS TO MATURE	REMARKS
Bush type		
'Eastland'	70	Mildew- and cold-tolerant; dwarf plant.
'Fordhook 242'	70	The most popular variety; heat-tolerant.
'Henderson'	65	Smaller than 'Fordhook', with a good flavor.
Pole type		
'King of the Garden'	85	The most popular pole type.
'Prizetaker'	90	Large beans with good flavor.
'Christmas'	90	Large, flat bean with chestnutlike flavor.

'Blue Hilda'

Snap-bean vines need stake or frame supports.

Tall string-bean varieties must be cultivated on long runners or frames. The stringless variety 'Blue Hilda' has purple pods.

Beans, Snap

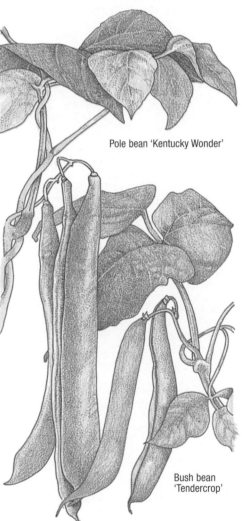

Pole bean 'Kentucky Wonder'

Bush bean 'Tendercrop'

A favorite with vegetable gardeners, the snap bean is easy to grow, prolific, and nutritious. Both the green and yellow (wax) beans that you buy in the market are snap beans and can be grown in any good soil either as bushy plants or as pole beans, climbing vinelike upon a tall support. Bush beans are usually smaller and more tender than the pole variety, but many people consider pole beans more flavorful. If you have enough space, try both kinds.

Bush-bean plants, which grow to about 1½ feet, mature in about 60 days (or sooner when planted in

How to Grow Snap Beans

Beans, like peas, are legumes, and with all other legumes they share the ability to absorb nitrogen from the atmosphere and add it to the soil. Because soil bacteria help in this nitrogen accumulation, you may want to dust your bean seeds with a commercial preparation containing these bacteria—called a soil inoculant—before you plant them.

In preparing your soil, simply work in a ½ inch layer of compost. Do not apply a fertilizer with a high nitrogen count, or you will grow enormously leafy plants with few beans.

Bean seeds are susceptible to fungal infections that cause the seeds to rot. The best way to avoid rot is to be sure the soil has warmed well before planting, and to plant only in well-drained soil. You can also treat the planting area with a product containing beneficial microbes that help fight against rot fungi. Avoid using seeds treated with chemical fungicides.

Planting bush beans. Make sure that the soil has become thoroughly warm and is no longer soaked from winter rains and snows. Seed catalogs generally recommend soil temperatures of at least 60°F, which is usually attained a week or two before the average date of the last spring frost. If you want to be on the safe side, delay planting until the time of the last expected frost.

Space your rows approximately 2 feet apart, with furrows 1 inch deep. Plant a seed every 2–3 inches. Because bush beans need only about 4 inches of space between plants, thinning will not be necessary unless

midsummer) and yield for two or three weeks. Because they mature in such a short time, you can make succession plantings for a constant supply during the summer. Pole-bean plants, which grow to a height of 6 feet or more, take about two weeks

every seed germinates. Furrows for midsummer sowings should be 2 inches deep, thus putting the seeds closer to the soil moisture. Whether you are sowing in spring or midsummer, however, never cover the seeds with more than an inch of soil. Too much overlay may prevent seedlings from pushing through.

As bush beans have a fairly short harvest period, plan to make succession plantings every three weeks, until about eight weeks before the first fall frost is expected. If possible, do not plant later crops of beans in the same place you grew them earlier in the year.

Cultivating bush beans. When plants are 6 inches tall, water them with a seaweed solution to supply a range of micronutrients. Keep the soil well moistened, but never water from above—and never touch the plants when the leaves are wet, as this may spread any diseases that the beans may have. Mulch to conserve moisture and to keep down weeds.

Harvesting bush beans. Pick bush beans before they are mature—while they will still snap when you bend them, and before the seeds inside the pod swell visibly. To keep each plant productive for two to three weeks, be sure to remove any pods that have grown large and tough. Ripe beans left on the vine will definitely cause the plant to slow down production.

You have to be gentle when harvesting the beans. Hold the fruiting stem with one hand while you carefully pull off the bean with the other; otherwise, you may pull away some of the plant as well.

longer to mature than bush varieties do, but they bear for a much longer time—about six to eight weeks—and they produce a larger crop. Per square foot of garden plot, pole beans are a more productive crop than bush beans.

Planting pole beans. Pole-bean plants will produce for much of the summer if you provide sufficient nutrients. Before planting, work in a 1 inch layer of rich compost or well-rotted manure. Plant pole beans later than bush beans—when the last frost is due.

You will need to build a solid support system for your pole beans—one that can bear the weight of the plants and hold up in a high wind. (For illustrations of supports, see p. 446.)

Most gardeners use lumberyard stakes or rough wood poles with the bark left on them to provide a grip for the vines. Set the poles 3 feet apart in rows 3–4 feet apart, and drive them 2 feet into the soil. If you are planting the beans in a corner of the garden, drive three poles into the ground in the shape of a triangle, and tie them securely at the top, tepee fashion.

A tall chicken-wire trellis or solid fence can also be used as a support for pole beans. Be sure that the trellis or fence is on the north side of your garden, where it will cast the least shade. Anchor the trellis solidly in the ground so that it will be able to withstand winds after it has become laden with vines.

Once you have built your support, sow the seeds 1–1½ inches deep. Along a fence or trellis, sow seeds 2 inches apart and thin the seedlings later to 4–6 inches. For pole growing, sow six seeds around each pole. Thin to the four strongest seedlings.

Cultivating pole beans. When the pole-bean plants begin to climb, help them up their support by winding the curly, climbing stem onto its pole or wire fencing. Always wind the stem in the same direction that it curls.

Although low-growing shrub beans get along without support, some form of support system can be advantageous in rainy years. Harvesting is also easier with supports.

Supports make harvesting easier.

Bush beans mature in 60 days.

Add compost or a balanced organic fertilizer blend in midseason in a band 6 inches from the plants or in a ring around the poles. Water well at ground level, being careful not to wet the plants. A thick mulch will help keep moisture in the soil and discourage weeds.

Harvesting pole beans. If your plants have received plenty of moisture and food, and if the weather has been warm, you can expect to start harvesting pole beans about 2 months after planting. Do not pick them when they are small, as you do with the bush varieties. For the best flavor, pole beans should be large and thick when you harvest them.

To ensure a continuous crop, harvest all the pods as soon as they seem mature. The more you pick, the more you will harvest. As with bush beans, pick carefully. Hold the fruiting stems with one hand as you pluck a pod with the other. If you pull off the beans roughly, you risk injuring the vine.

The harvesting season should last until the first frost. If at that time there are too many beans for immediate use on the vine, wait until the pods become dry and beige colored before picking. Then shell the beans, and heat them for an hour in an oven set at its lowest temperature. This will kill any weevils that may have infested them.

Dried pole beans are good for use in soups and stews, and they can be kept stored in sealed jars for several months.

METHODS OF SUPPORTING BEANS

One good way is to set stakes on both sides of a double row. Or use wire, or nylon, netting, or a pole with string and pegs in a tepee shape.

Varieties of Snap Beans to Grow

Bush beans. There are several good bush varieties of snap beans.

'Provider' and 'Jade' are top-quality green beans.

'Royal Burgundy' is a purple bean that turns dark green when it is cooked.

'Carson' and 'Rocdor' are yellow, or wax, beans. 'Romano Gold' grows flat pods.

Pole beans. 'Kentucky Wonder' and the smaller-seeded 'Blue Lake' are two of the most popular green pole beans.

'Romano', also called Italian pole bean, is a broad, flat bean that matures somewhat earlier than most other pole varieties.

'Fortex' grow extremely long, and 'Blauhilde' grows purple beans that turn green when they are boiled. If you want pole beans for shelling and drying, 'Oregon Giant' is a popular variety.

See also the discussion on various varieties under the heading Decorative Beans at right.

What Can Go Wrong With Snap Beans

In some areas Japanese beetles may become a major pest. If there are not too many beetles, knock them off the leaves into a pail of water covered with a film of dishwasing liquid. This method must be continued every day until there is a significant reduction in the number of beetles. If the beetles are too numerous to knock off in this fashion, spray the plants with insecticidal soap, carefully following label instructions. You can also take steps to prevent next year's crop from being attacked by Japanese beetles. Ask your local garden center about milky spore disease. This is, in effect, a bacterial soil treatment that introduces a disease harmful only to Japanese beetle grubs, which live in the ground through the winter.

Mexican bean beetles—copper-colored, black-spotted insects that look like ladybugs but are larger and yellower—and their spiny yellow larvae are also major pests of beans. Usually found on the undersides of the leaves, they chew the foliage and eat the beans as well. Several generations may reproduce in one season. Search for beetles and larvae on plants and destroy them (wear gloves when you handpick these pests.) Spray *Beauveria bassiana* to kill the larvae. For a serious infestation, apply neem.

Aphids, especially the black bean aphid, also attack snap beans. Wash these pests off with a strong stream of water from the garden hose, or spray with insecticidal soap.

Beans are particularly sensitive to mildews and blights, especially during cool, wet weather. The best preventive measures are to avoid brushing against bean leaves when they are wet, to allow plants to dry thoroughly before picking, and to water during sunny hours so that leaves can dry before evening. If bean leaves show whitish, moldy patches (powdery mildew), apply a potassium bicarbonate spray.

Decorative Beans

Runner beans are a type of pole bean that is sometimes grown purely for its decorative effect. The most common variety has bright scarlet flowers that are freely produced for much of the summer in the North. Where summers are hot, the plants go out of flower in midsummer and resume blooming when the weather cools. Beans should be picked often; any that have gone hard should be discarded. When eaten young, this bean probably has the most flavor of any. At the end of the season, old beans can be picked and shelled, and stored for use in soups and stews.

'Scarlet Runner' is the most commonly listed variety; 'Emperor', 'Prize Winner', and 'Red Knight' are other red-flowered varieties. 'Painted Lady' produces red and white flowers; 'Aztec White', white flowers.

Showy and productive, fava or broad beans grow best in cooler climates. Sow them as soon as the ground is workable in spring, or where soil does not freeze in winter, on the shortest day. They can be picked young—when the beans are 3–4 inches long—and cooked entire, or allowed to develop fully and podded. These beans are extremely susceptible to attack from the black bean aphid. 'Windsor Long Pod' is an old variety still widely available.

With purple-tinged foliage, bright purple flowers, and reddish-purple pods, the hyacinth, or dolichos, bean is also grown for its ornamental value. Like the runner bean, this rampant grower needs a strong support; unlike the runner bean, it grows best in a warm climate. The young seed pods, picked before the beans develop, are eaten in Asia, but the dry beans, uncooked, can be toxic.

Red beets cultivated early can be picked in June. By August, the early growth is mature; beets should be taken up for storage in October.

'Rote Kugel'

Beets

Beet 'Early Wonder'

Beets have a double attraction for vegetable gardeners: they are easy to grow, and practically the whole plant can be eaten. Although they are fairly tolerant of heat, they do best in cool climates, and they can withstand cold weather short of severe freezing. Beets mature quickly (55 to 70 days), take up little room, and require minimum care.

One caution, however—they will not do well if soil is extremely acid.

Beets are a root crop whose tops are also edible. When the plants are young and the leaves are tender, beet greens are excellent in salads. As the plant matures, you can cook the greens as you would spinach. Beet roots are even more versatile. You can cook them fresh from the garden, store them in a cool place for winter use, pickle them, or can them.

How to Grow Beets

To prepare your soil for beets, spade it well, to a depth of about 8 inches, and rake it to remove stones. If your soil is very acid (beets do best in a soil with a pH of 6.0 to 7.5), work in lime at least a week before planting. (For details on liming soil, see pp. 498–499.) Wood ashes, which contain lime and potash, are useful in reducing acidity just before sowing, applied at a rate of no more than 2 pounds per 100 square feet.

Because beets germinate best and grow fastest in cool weather, plant the seeds as soon as the ground can be worked. In areas where summers remain relatively cool, make succession plantings at three-week intervals to ensure a continuous crop throughout the season. If you live where midsummers are long and hot, time your plantings so that the beets mature either before or after the period when daytime temperatures consistently exceed 80°F.

Seed rows for beets should be spaced at least 14 inches apart, and furrows should be ½ inch deep. Sow the seeds, which are actually clusters of three or four seeds within a casing, at 1-inch intervals.

The plants will emerge in little clumps, which you should thin to one plant per inch when the seedlings are about 2 inches tall. When they reach 4 inches, thin to four to six plants per foot.

For midsummer plantings, make the furrows about an inch deep, to reach the soil moisture, and cover the seeds with compost, vermiculite, or some other material that will not form a crust and will allow water to run through.

Rapid growth and timely harvesting are the key factors in producing tender, juicy beets. Too little water, too few nutrients, or heavy weed infestation slows growth and results in roots that are tough and woody. If you have fertilized your beet rows before planting, you need apply only one more dressing before harvesting.

When the seedlings are about 3 inches high, scatter a band of bone meal along each side of the row—about 5 ounces for every 10 feet. Then lay down a light mulch of straw, chopped leaves, or lawn clippings to help conserve soil moisture and keep down weeds. If weeds persist, remove them by hand within each row, and hoe shallowly between the rows to avoid injuring the beets' roots. Water regularly.

You can enjoy the produce of your beet crop early if you harvest the young, tender leaves for salad greens. But take only a few leaves at a time from each plant. The plant needs foliage to produce nourishment and maintain growth.

Beet roots mature within 55 to 70 days, depending on the variety. When the root tops begin to push up above the ground, carefully remove the soil from around one of them to check its size.

The best harvest size is between 1½ and 2 inches in diameter. Do not let beets grow much larger than this, since they tend to become fibrous as their size increases.

In harvesting, *pull* the roots out of the ground—do not dig them up. As you separate the greens from the root, leave an inch of stem on each root to prevent the root from "bleeding" (losing some of its color) when it is cooked.

Beets usually store well in a cool, dark cellar. To maintain their crispness, bury them in moist sand or peat moss, or put them in plastic bags into which you have cut a few small holes for ventilation.

What Can Go Wrong With Beets

Very early beet sowings may "bolt"—run to seed rather than form edible roots—if temperatures remain below 40°F for several weeks. If this happens, pick the leaves for use as salad greens, and sow the row again. If the beet leaves become stunted or yellowish, and you have already limed the soil, there may be a phosphorus deficiency. In this case apply a dressing of bone meal.

Beets are prey to few pests, especially where winter freeze kills bugs and larvae in the soil. In warm areas beets may be attacked by tiny yellow leaf miners, which can be controlled with neem or by protecting plants with floating row cover.

If you grow beets exactly where you planted them the year before, leaf spot may develop. Grow beets in a different location each year (see crop rotation on page 441).

If beet roots develop black areas, it is an indication that the soil may be deficient in boron. You can increase soil boron content by adding compost or growing green manure crops in areas where you plan to plant beets in the future. You can also spray young plants with liquid seaweed extract to supply boron directly.

Varieties of Beets to Grow

Beets may have red, yellow, or white roots. Recommended red beets are 'Early Wonder', which matures in about 55 days, and 'Scarlet Supreme', grown for its greens and its baby boots. 'Formanova' has a long cylindrical root for easy, uniform slicing. For yellow and white varieties, try 'Burpee's Golden' and 'Albina Venduna', respectively.

Broccoli 'Arcadia'

Broccoli 'Violet Queen'

Broccoli flowers should be cut when they are well formed, but before they begin to open.

Broccoli

Broccoli 'Green Comet'

Broccoli belongs to a large and varied genus, *Brassica,* that includes Brussels sprouts, cabbage, and cauliflower, and that has the ability to grow in cool weather. Not only is broccoli extremely hardy in cold weather but it requires a long, cool season for growth. It will be one of the earliest vegetables you plant in the garden each year, and it will produce its delicate flower heads in late spring and early summer. A second planting made in late summer will be ready for harvest in fall.

or vermiculite on top, and water well. Keep the flats in a dark, cool place until the seeds sprout, or cover them with newspaper.

The seedlings should stand about ½–1 inch apart. If necessary, clip out the overly crowded ones with scissors. When the plants are about 1½ inches tall, transplant them into individual pots or into flats where they will have more room. Keep the seedlings in a sunny but cool place in your house; they will not grow well in warm temperatures.

At least two weeks before it is time to set out the seedlings (earlier if the weather is not too cold), place them in a cold frame or in a sunny, sheltered spot outdoors, to harden them off. (See Hardening Off the Young Plants, p. 195.)

In choosing a planting location, remember that broccoli and its *Brassica* relatives are affected by several soil-borne diseases; so never plant broccoli where *Brassica* members were grown the year before.

Prepare the soil about two weeks before transplanting time by working in a 2-inch layer of compost or 1 inch of well-rotted manure. Lime the soil now if it is strongly acid and if you did not lime it the previous fall.

About two weeks before the last expected frost, set out your hardened seedlings. Place them 1½–2 feet apart in rows 3 feet apart. Protect the plants against cutworms by

surrounding them with paper collars, which you can make by cutting the bottoms out of paper cups. Push each collar 1 inch into the soil. Water well, and mulch the soil thoroughly.

For a fall crop start growing seedlings in late May or in June in a cold frame or in a garden row. Sow the seeds ½ inch deep; cover with a thin layer of soil mixed with sand or peat moss to prevent crusting. Thin the seedlings to stand 1 inch apart. When they reach 5 inches, transplant them into an area where you have harvested a root crop, such as carrots. Before transplanting the seedlings, fertilize the soil.

To raise a good broccoli crop, you need abundant water and rich soil. Ensure moist soil with a thick mulch and deep, slow waterings during dry periods. At least once during the growing season, pull aside the mulch, and apply ½ pound of a balanced organic fertilizer or a cup of fish meal or alfalfa meal along every 10 feet of row. Replace the mulch, and water to soak the fertilizer into the soil.

A thickened cluster growing at the top of a broccoli stalk will tell you that the plant is nearing maturity. The cluster is the plant's main head and should be harvested before the flowerets begin to open. Slice off the stem 5 or 6 inches below the head. Side shoots should produce smaller clusters for two months or more.

How to Grow Broccoli

Broccoli plantings must be timed so that the clusters of small flower buds the plant produces can be harvested while the days remain cool. To accomplish this, it is usually best to start the seeds indoors, especially in areas with short growing seasons. Seed catalogs list the number of days to harvest from the time the seedlings are planted in the garden. In addition to the 60 to 80 days indicated for outdoor growing, you

should allow another four to six weeks for starting the seeds indoors. (In warm climates sow seeds directly outdoors as soon as the soil can be worked.)

Start broccoli indoors at least four weeks before the time to set out the seedlings—which you should calculate as two weeks before the date of the last expected frost. If you have a short growing season, six weeks will give you larger plants to set out. Sow the seed ½ inch deep in flats, sprinkle a thin layer of sterile sphagnum moss

What Can Go Wrong With Broccoli

Clubroot is a serious disease and is best avoided by crop rotation. Weak, yellow plants with malformed roots indicate clubroot. To combat the disease, raise the soil pH to at least 6.8 by adding ground limestone. Destroy infected plants and do not plant members of the cabbage family in that location for several years.

Flea beetles, small black insects that hop away when disturbed, make

small, pale spots on the leaves and can kill young plants. Cover small plants with a floating row cover or spray them with kaolin clay.

If cabbage worms attack, apply *Bacillus thuringiensis.*

Varieties of Broccoli to Grow

Good early varieties of broccoli include 'Green Comet'*, 'Premium Crop'*, and 'Packman'. 'Arcadia' is recommended for fall crops.

'Oliver'

With compact rosettes of mostly uniform size evenly distributed on the stalk, 'Oliver' is among the top varieties of Brussels sprouts.

Sprouts taste better after a hard frost.

Brussels sprouts 'Long Island Improved' ➡

Brussels Sprouts

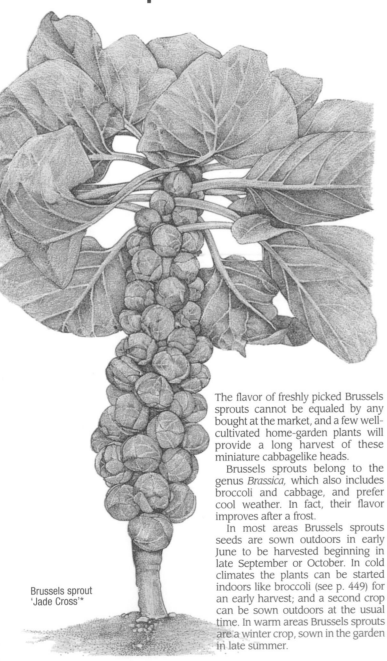

The flavor of freshly picked Brussels sprouts cannot be equaled by any bought at the market, and a few well-cultivated home-garden plants will provide a long harvest of these miniature cabbagelike heads.

Brussels sprouts belong to the genus *Brassica,* which also includes broccoli and cabbage, and prefer cool weather. In fact, their flavor improves after a frost.

In most areas Brussels sprouts seeds are sown outdoors in early June to be harvested beginning in late September or October. In cold climates the plants can be started indoors like broccoli (see p. 449) for an early harvest; and a second crop can be sown outdoors at the usual time. In warm areas Brussels sprouts are a winter crop, sown in the garden in late summer.

Brussels sprout 'Jade Cross'*

How to Grow Brussels Sprouts

Prepare the soil carefully. To avoid the diseases and pests common to *Brassica* relatives, choose a plot of land on which no *Brassica* vegetable was grown the previous year. Two weeks before sowing, dig in a 2–4-inch layer of organic matter—compost, well-rotted manure, or leaf mold—into the soil, or simply add a shovelful to each planting hole that you dig. If the soil tends to be acid, add a sprinkling of lime.

Sow the seeds in groups of three or four, leaving 2 feet between clusters and 3 feet between rows.

When the seedlings are about 1½ inches tall, clip out all but the strongest plant in each group. Immediately protect these seedlings against cutworms by slipping over each plant a paper cup with its bottom removed. Set the cutworm collars about an inch deep into the soil.

Given rich, well-prepared soil, Brussels sprouts grow splendidly with little more attention, providing the soil has been well firmed. Be sure the plants get plenty of water, especially when they are young. A thick mulch around them will help the soil to retain moisture and will also keep down weeds.

When the first tiny sprouts begin to form around the bottom of the stem (10 to 12 weeks after sowing), scatter a 6-inch band of fish meal or alfalfa

What Can Go Wrong With Brussels Sprouts

Avoid clubroot and other soil-borne diseases by not planting Brussels sprouts where they or any *Brassica* relative had been growing the previous year. Treat the soil for clubroot by applying ground limestone.

If green cabbage worms appear on your plants, spray the plants with *Bacillus thuringiensis.* Cabbage maggots feed on the roots of Brussels

meal around each plant, and water it into the ground.

Because Brussels sprouts grow slowly, their rows make excellent areas for intercropping. If you plant radishes or lettuce between the Brussels sprouts plants, you will harvest these quick-maturing vegetables long before your sprouts grow large enough to shade the area.

Brussels sprouts form all along the main stalk, growing in the spaces between the leafstalks. When the sprouts are hard and firm and at least ½ inch in diameter, they can be harvested. The best harvest size is from ½ inch to 1½ inches.

Properly harvested, one plant can produce for six to eight weeks. The sprouts at the bottom of the stalk will be ready first. To harvest, pull off the lower leaves by snapping them sharply downward. Remove the leaves gradually, from the bottom up, as you progressively harvest the sprouts. With the leaves gone, the sprouts have more room to grow; so take off the leaves slightly in advance of sprout harvesting. Do not remove the top tuft of leaves; if this is removed, the stem will stop growing and sprouts will stop forming.

If you want an early crop, pinch off the growing tip of the plant in September. The sprouts will mature three weeks ahead of schedule—and all at the same time—but the plant will not yield as much as when allowed to produce normally.

sprouts, causing the plants to collapse. The most effective way to kill the maggots is by applying parasitic nematodes to the soil—if this is a serious problem.

Varieties of Brussels Sprouts to Grow

'Jade Cross'* matures in about 100 days and grows to 22 inches. 'Oliver' matures in 90 days and can be sown in summer for fall.

Because it has so many varieties, cabbage can be picked fresh from late May until December. Late varieties can be readily stored.

Common green cabbage   Red cabbage

Cabbage

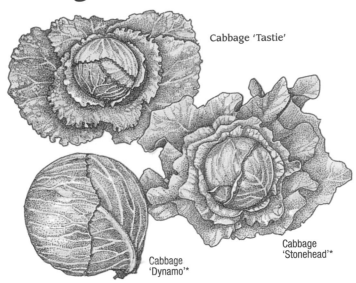

Cabbage 'Tastie'

Cabbage 'Dynamo'*

Cabbage 'Stonehead'*

Cabbage is a hardy vegetable that grows well almost anywhere, provided the soil is fertile and not too acid. You can choose among red, savoy, green, and Chinese varieties, and by planting early, midsummer, and late varieties you can harvest cabbage from summer through fall. But cabbage takes up a considerable amount of space; so if you have a small garden, only plant one or two of each variety.

Varieties to Grow

In warm climates you can have cabbages year-round. In harsher climates varieties sown in fall to overwinter may not survive. Cabbage mature fast. To avoid a glut, sow or plant only a few at any one time.

VARIETIES	SEASON	SOW IN	SPACING
Cabbage			
'Dynamo'*	Early	Early spring (indoors)	14 in.
'Early Jersey Wakefield'	Early	Early spring	14 in.
'Golden Acre'	Early	Early spring	14 in.
'Stonehead'*	Summer	Early spring	14 in.
'Copenhagen Market'	Summer	Spring	14 in.
'Danish Ballhead'	Fall	Late spring	20 in.
'Princeton'	Winter	Spring	20 in.
'Roulette'	Winter	Spring	20 in.
'Vantage Point'	Late	Spring	20 in.
Red cabbage			
'Cairo'	Early	Early spring	14 in.
'Super Red 80'	Summer	Early spring	14 in.
'Ruby Perfection'*	Summer	Early spring	14 in.
Savoy			
'Savoy Ace'*	Fall	Late spring	20 in.
'Savoy Express'*	Summer	Early spring	14 in.

How to Grow Cabbage

To avoid soil-borne diseases, choose a place for cabbage where neither it nor any of its *Brassica* relatives (including broccoli, cauliflower, turnips, and kale) were grown the previous year. If your soil is strongly acid, lime it well ahead of planting time—preferably in the fall before your spring planting. Cabbage grows best where the pH factor is from 6.0 to 7.5.

Cabbage matures faster—and will taste better—if it is grown in heavily fertilized soil. Well-rotted manure, if you can obtain it, is the perfect additive because it enriches the soil while improving its texture and its water-holding capacity.

Whether or not you use manure, it is generally advisable to add a balanced organic fertilizer blend, as well. Apply according to label directions. Like all brassicas, cabbage grows best in a well-firmed soil. Before planting, firm the soil by treading all over to fill air pockets and compact it slightly.

Early cabbage varieties should be sown indoors, five to eight weeks before the last expected frost. (For details on starting seeds indoors, see Broccoli, p. 449.) You can also grow early cabbage from seedlings bought at a nursery.

Look for young plants that have short, thick stems—an indication of strong, well-started seedlings.

Set out the seedlings two or three weeks before the last expected frost, placing them at least 1 foot apart in rows 2–3 feet apart. Protect each cabbage plant against cutworms with a collar made from a paper cup with its bottom removed. Set the collar around the stem, 1 inch into the ground.

Sow midsummer cabbage directly outdoors at about the time of the last expected frost. Plant three or four seeds together about ¼ inch deep, and space each group of seeds according to the chart at left.

When the seedlings emerge, thin them to the single strongest one in each group.

Unless your soil is very rich, fertilize cabbage regularly. Once a month put a 6-inch-wide band of a nutrient-rich supplement, such as fish meal or alfalfa meal around each plant.

Cabbage plants have shallow roots. For this reason it is advisable to mulch the soil around them to retain the moisture in the upper layers. Mulching also discourages weeds from growing; but if some manage to push through the mulch cover, pull them out by hand. If you use a hoe, be careful not to disturb the cabbages' shallow root systems.

Large cabbage heads sometimes split during hot weather. You can avoid this (and slow down growth if too many heads are nearing harvest at one time) by cutting the roots on one side of the plant with a spade.

It is time to harvest when the cabbage feels solid. The length of time to maturity depends on the variety. The range is about 60 to 110 days from the time young plants are set out in the garden, plus 30 to 50 days for starting seedlings indoors. To harvest cabbage, cut the stalk just beneath the head.

What Can Go Wrong

While plants are small they are likely to be attacked by flea beetles. These small black pests, who hop back onto the soil when disturbed, feed on the upper surface of the leaf and leave small pale spots. Cover plants with a floating row cover or spray them with kaolin clay or a garlic repellent spray.

Green cabbage worms, the larvae of white butterflies, will eat holes in the leaves of larger plants and can make mature cabbages inedible. Spray with *Bacillus thuringiensis* at first signs of damage, especially the undersides of the leaves.

Keep carrot flies away with netting or by planting a row of onions, leeks, or chives between carrot rows.

Harvest when carrot crowns are ¾ in. in diameter.   Alternate rows of onions may keep carrot flies at bay.

Carrots

The carrot, a domesticated relative of the weed Queen Anne's lace, not only is flavorful, crisp, and rich in vitamin A but is easy to grow and stores well. With judicious planning, you can have a homegrown supply of this healthful vegetable for much of the year.

Because carrots are cold resistant and need a relatively short time to mature (50 to 85 days), you can sow your first crop early and make several succession plantings. Although carrots prefer cool weather, midsummer plantings in all but the hottest areas will produce a good crop if you keep the soil well watered. And where winters are not too severe, a crop planted in September and kept well mulched may produce carrots through Christmas.

Carrots are grown for their roots, which may be short, long, or medium length, tapering or stump shaped. Before you decide which types to plant, determine what kind of soil you have. With a 10- to 12-inch depth of porous, sandy, stone-free soil, you can grow the long, slender varieties, such as 'Imperator' or 'Gold Pak'. In clayey or rocky soils, plant stubbier types, such as 'Danvers 126', which grows to 6 or 7 inches; 'Short 'n Sweet', which is round and thick and grows only 4–5 inches long; or 'Minicor', which is only 3 inches.

How to Grow Carrots

As soon as the ground can be worked, spade the soil to a depth of at least 8 inches, raking it well to remove stones. If you have a heavy clay soil, which discourages carrot growth, be sure to work in quantities of humus or sand.

Mark a row with a garden line, and dig a shallow furrow. Carrot seeds germinate slowly, and the row may be well defined by weeds long before the carrot tops appear.

It is a good idea, therefore, to mix a few radish or leaf-lettuce seeds with the carrot seeds. The radishes and lettuce will sprout quickly and will mark the row. Because they will be ready long before the carrots are, they will not interfere with the growth of the carrots, and you will also be making more efficient use of your garden space.

Sow carrot seeds ¼ inch deep in rows 6–8 inches apart. (For hot-weather plantings, sow the seeds ½ inch deep.) To prevent crusting, cover the seeds with a thin layer of fine compost or sieved soil, firm the soil well, and water. Be sure to keep the soil fairly moist until the seedlings have emerged. Thin them first to stand 1 inch apart; then, as the tops of the carrots grow thicker, thin again to 2–3 inches apart. Plant carrots at about three-week intervals during the season, making your last planting 40 to 60 days before the first killing frost is expected in the fall.

Carrots require minimum care. Once you have spaded and worked the soil and removed any rocks that might impede their downward growth, they require only regular watering and weeding. Mulching will help to retain moisture in the soil and to keep weeds from growing.

Although moist soil is essential for germination, do not make the mistake of keeping the soil soaked as your crop matures. Too much moisture toward the end of the growing period can cause roots to crack.

If you are concerned about your soil's fertility level, water with a fish emulsion solution when the tops are 3–4 inches tall, and again when they reach 6–8 inches. Watch for the appearance of the orange root crowns just at the soil's surface, and keep them covered with soil; sunlight will turn them green.

Carrots mature fully within 50 to 85 days as mentioned, but they may be juicier and tenderer if you pull them earlier. Check each crown, and if it seems sufficiently thick—about

Carrot 'Short 'n Sweet'

¾ inch in diameter—pull the carrot. There is no need to harvest your crop all at once. Carrots can be left in the ground for a few weeks without

What Can Go Wrong With Carrots

The larvae of the carrot rust fly hatch in warm weather and tunnel into carrot roots; to avoid damage, plant early and late crops. The carrot weevil, a small brown beetle, may destroy a crop that it infests. To control it, apply parasitic nematodes to the soil.

If carrot roots are misshapen or forked, the cause may be either rocky ground or overcrowding. Dig deeper for your next crop, and thin carrot seedlings earlier.

Varieties of Carrots to Grow

Besides the types mentioned earlier, 'Nantes' is a quality medium-length carrot. 'Purple Haze'* has a purple exterior and orange interior, and a sweet flavor. The carrots are particularly delicious when small.

growing tough. If late crops are well mulched, you may be able to continue harvesting through a blanket of snow.

Cauliflower cultivation demands special care. In choosing plants, select some varieties that will sprout in hot weather.

Cauliflower roots need water to form heads.

Cauliflower

Cauliflower 'Snow Crown'*

Of all *Brassica* genus vegetables (broccoli, Brussels sprouts, turnips, kale, and cabbage), cauliflower is the most difficult to grow. It needs cool temperatures, a lot of moisture, and fertile soil. It does not withstand frost as well as its *Brassica* relatives; yet it will not form a head in hot weather. Although often planted as a spring crop, cauliflower is easiest to grow for fall harvesting. Early cauliflower requires 55 to 80 days to mature from the time seedlings are set out. Fall crops are grown outdoors from seed and take about 10 weeks to mature.

The pure white color of cauliflower that you are used to seeing is achieved by blanching—covering the head to shut out light that would turn the flower buds (called curds) to green. Blanching also preserves the cauliflower's delicate flavor. "Self-blanching" varieties have tall leaves to shade the curd. Although most cauliflower is white, there are purple varieties that do not have to be blanched and are often recommended for home gardeners. They turn green when cooked and taste somewhat like broccoli.

How to Grow Cauliflower

Soil requirements for cauliflower are much the same as for cabbage. If your soil is strongly acid, give it an application of lime as far ahead of planting time as possible, preferably in the fall. Because a fertile soil is an absolute necessity, work in a 2- to 4-inch layer of mature compost or a 1-inch layer of well-rotted manure.

For spring plantings in most areas, start cauliflower seeds indoors, six to eight weeks before the last expected frost. Sow the seeds in individual pots, three or four seeds to a pot. When the seedlings emerge, snip off all but the single strongest plant. Keep the seedlings in a sunny, cool spot. Two weeks before planting them outside, harden them off in a cold frame. (For more details on starting seeds indoors, see the instructions in Broccoli, p. 449)

Set out the seedlings at about the time of the last expected frost. Space the plants 16–24 inches apart, in rows 2–3 feet apart. To protect the young plants against cutworms, slip a cutworm collar around each plant. You can make the collars from paper cups with the bottoms removed.

For a fall crop, you can sow seeds directly outdoors in June. Prepare the soil and sow the seeds ½ inch deep, in groups of three or four, spacing the groups 18–24 inches apart. When the seedlings are about 1 inch tall, thin them to the single strongest in each group. To save garden space, sow the seeds in a cold frame or seedbed and transplant the seedlings to the cauliflower row when they are 4–5 inches tall.

Cauliflower grows better in soil that is enriched regularly. Every three or four weeks, scatter a 3-inch band

of complete fertilizer along each side of the row, being careful not to let it fall on the plants. Water thoroughly to soak the fertilizer into the soil.

Soil enrichment alone, however, will not ensure a good crop. If cauliflower roots are deprived of water for even a short time, the plants will probably not form heads. Be sure that the bed receives a good soaking at least once a week, and mulch the ground with a thick layer of hay or half-rotted compost.

As mentioned earlier, the head must be protected from the sun's rays to grow white. Watch for a small bud to appear at the center of the plant. When the bud is 4–6 inches in diameter, it is time to blanch the head. Draw the lower leaves of the plant loosely over the bud, and fasten them together with a piece of soft twine or a rubber band. Leave enough room inside this leafy bag for the head to grow to full size—about 8–12 inches across.

The cauliflower head is ready to harvest when it is firm and compact. New colored varieties are appearing in catalogs. 'Cheddar' is orange-yellow, 'Graffiti' is purple, and 'Veronica' is green with spiky florets.

There are also hybrids between broccoli and cauliflower that have pale green curds. It is best grown for late-fall or early-spring harvest.

Varieties of Cauliflower to Grow

Recommended early varieties of cauliflower include 'Snow Crown'*, which is ready for harvest about 50 days after the plants are set out, and 'Early Snowball', which averages 60 days. 'Violet Queen' matures in 70 to 75 days and can be grown as either an early or a late crop. For late crops, 'Snowball' is a good choice; or you may want to try 'Self-Blanch Snowball', whose leaves grow naturally over the head, eliminating the need for blanching.

What Can Go Wrong With Cauliflower

Cauliflower is subject to the same diseases and pests as its *Brassica* relatives. You can avoid the diseases by shifting the location of *Brassica* crops—do not plant cauliflower, Brussels sprouts, cabbage, or turnips in the same soil where any one of these plants grew the year before.

If cabbage worms are a problem, apply *Bacillus thuringiensis*. Wash off aphids with a strong stream of water from the garden hose, or spray plants with a garlic-based repellent.

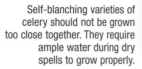

Self-blanching varieties of celery should not be grown too close together. They require ample water during dry spells to grow properly.

Self-blanching celery

Celery

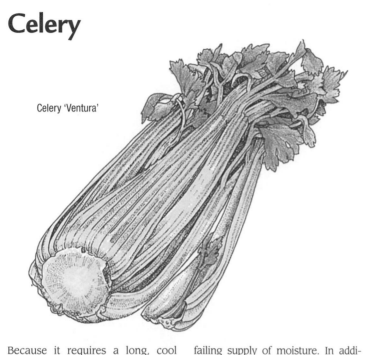

Celery 'Ventura'

Because it requires a long, cool growing season (five to six months from seed) and special care in its cultivation, celery is not an easy vegetable to grow. It needs more than the usual quantities of soil nutrients, a particularly well-prepared soil, and an abundant and never-failing supply of moisture. In addition, its tiny seeds are difficult to nurture into seedlings, even under ideal indoor conditions. So if you do raise a crop of this crisp and succulent vegetable, you will have won the right to consider yourself an accomplished horticulturist.

How to Grow Celery

Celery is usually started indoors in flats. Before sowing the seeds, which are small and hard, soak them in water overnight to soften the seed coat. Use a light soil-and-sand mixture or sterile sphagnum moss as a growing medium, sprinkle the seeds into the pots, and cover with ¼ inch of sphagnum moss. Keep the soil moist, and be patient—celery seeds take up to three weeks to sprout.

When the seedlings are about an inch tall, transplant them to individual pots. Do not transplant seedlings into the garden until they are at least 3 inches tall—a height they will reach 10 to 12 weeks after sowing.

You can also buy seedlings from a local garden center, which should have sturdy 6-inch plants available in time for early planting.

Set out the seedlings when all danger of frost is past, or the plants may bolt. Count on at least 120 days of outdoor growing time for home-grown seedlings, 115 days for nursery plants. Because celery grows best in cool temperatures, much of that growing time should be in spring, when the weather is moderate. Although celery is planted in early spring in most areas, the seedlings are set out in the fall in parts of the West Coast, where springs are warm and winters mild.

For years the classical method of planting celery was to dig a trench, set the seedlings at the bottom, and then heap earth around the stems as they grew. The earth helped conserve soil moisture and blanched the celery—that is, kept the stems white and tender by protecting them from the sun's rays. In recent times, however, celery strains have been developed whose sun-greened stalks remain tender and are also more nutritious than blanched stalks. "Self-blanching" varieties, with yellowish stalks, have also been developed. Because blanching is no longer essential, most gardeners now plant celery in ordinary furrows.

But trenching offers advantages even though blanching is not necessary: it protects late crops against frost, makes fertilizing easier, and eliminates the need for weeding. If you decide to use this method, dig a trench 15 inches wide and 10 inches deep, fertilizing it as described below, and filling with topsoil to a depth of 5 inches.

Whether or not you employ the trench method, you must enrich the soil with plenty of organic matter—either compost or well-rotted manure. Prepare the soil at least two weeks before setting out your plants.

Choose a cloudy day for transplanting. Set the seedlings 6–8 inches apart in rows at least 2 feet apart, and water them in well with a compost tea solution. To protect against sun shock, cover the plants for the first few days with some form of shading, such as a floating row cover.

Because celery is an exceptionally thirsty plant, mulch the soil heavily to conserve moisture and prevent weed growth. Keep the soil rich by watering around each plant with compost tea diluted to half strength, every two or three weeks. Or apply a balanced organic fertilizer blend every two weeks, at the amount recommended on the product label.

If you would like to experiment with blanching but have not trenched your celery, you can still produce white stalks by placing 12-inch-wide boards on either side of the row, holding them upright with stakes driven into the ground. Or blanch each plant separately by wrapping heavy paper around the stalk cluster, leaving the leafy tops exposed to the sun. Begin blanching two weeks before harvest time.

Celery will be ready for harvest about four months from the time they were planted outdoors. But you can begin nibbling at your crop two or three weeks before maturity by cutting off a single stalk from the outside of each plant. To harvest the whole plant, pull or dig it up and cut off the root base.

What Can Go Wrong With Celery

Fungal diseases, which cause yellow or brown spots on leaves and stalks, are a major problem with celery. You can prevent them by drenching the soil with compost tea; by not planting celery in soil where it was previously grown; by not touching the celery plants when they are wet; and by keeping the bed free of weeds.

If spots nevertheless appear, spray or dust the celery plants with copper fungicide.

Varieties of Celery to Grow

'Ventura' is a popular early green celery variety. Other recommended green types include 'Florida 683' and 'Tendercrisp'. One of the most popular early yellow varieties is 'Golden Self-Blanching'.

If you can count on a long, cool summer, you may want to try 'Utah 52–70', a dark green, thick-stalked celery that will not run to seed—produce a tough, flowering stalk—as readily as most celery varieties do.

Chinese and Other Asian Vegetables

Chinese celery
cabbage
Bok choy

Japanese
shungiku

Napa
cabbage

There is a tremendous appetite for Asian vegetables across the United States today, and most catalogs now include some of the more popular forms, either in a separate section, or added to the North American varieties. There are also seed houses that specialize in these vegetables, and carry a large selection. Check out the Kitazawa Seed Company's website at www.kitazawaseed.com to discover how many different Asian vegetables can be grown from seed.

Like most other vegetables, Asian ones grow best in a soil that has been rough dug the previous fall and allowed to overwinter in large lumps. The action of frost helps to break the soil down into a crumblike structure and also kills many of the pests that overwinter in the soil. The addition of compost, either homemade or commercial, before digging will help to improve soil structure, and provide some nutrients the following summer. The good gardening practices apply to all vegetables.

Leafy Vegetables

Most of these are shallow rooting so they need to be watered frequently and benefit from a mulch to help keep the soil moist. In general, they are fast growing and need plenty of additional nitrogen if they are to develop properly; side-dress with blood meal, giving a light application every two weeks. They are subject to a variety of pests and diseases, especially aphids and flea beetles.

Amaranth (yin choi). Usually listed in the flower section of seed catalogs, *Amaranthus tricolour*, or Joseph's coat is known as Chinese spinach in Asian seed lists. Leaves are marked or colored with red areas and the flower spikes are brightly colored with yellow and red. Amaranth is rich in iron, calcium, and vitamins A and C. It can be used raw in salads (the colored leaves are particularly attractive); in cooked dishes, it can be used in place of spinach, but it takes less time to cook. It can also be

added to soups. If plants run to seed, the seed can be ground to made into a high-protein flour.

Sowing time varies with the variety and use: Early spring for seed production, late spring to early summer for leaves, picked as you would spinach. Sow seeds ¼ inch deep and ½ inch apart in rows 18 inches apart. Cropping time is up to 50 days. Amaranth will tolerate dryer conditions and poorer soil than most other Chinese vegetables.

Good varieties to grow: 'All Red Leaf', 'White Leaf'.

Mustard greens (gai choi). American mustard greens tend to be very strong flavoured, almost bitter, but the Chinese varieties are mild and can be used raw or cooked and have a peppery taste. There are several different varieties which differ in their form and intensity of flavor. Some have curly foliage, some form heads like a cabbage, while others have red or purple colored leaves. Use the mild ones raw in salads, the more pungent ones in stir fries, soups, or pickles. Even the roots on these versatile vegetables can be boiled, peeled, and sliced. The seeds can be ground and used to make a mustard with vinegar and spices.

They thrive in cool weather and should be sown outdoors in spring, and again in autumn where winters are mild, sowing the seeds ½ inch deep, ¾ inch apart in rows 12 inches apart. Thin to 4 inches apart and start to pick the leaves when the plants are about 6–8 inches tall. Plants will be mature between 35 and 50 days, depending on the variety.

Good varieties to grow: 'Red Giant', 'Mike Giant', 'Bamboo Gai Choi'.

Chrysanthemum greens (shungiku). This is a plant that is often grown in the flower garden, but the regular garden mums are too bitter to be used as food. Even the edible chrysanthemums leaves are rarely eaten raw, but are used cooked in

soups, stir fries, and mixed with other leafy crops like spinach or beet greens. The flower petals can be used as a garnish on salads. There are several varieties which differ in the shape of their leaves; from slightly lobed to deeply serrated.

Chrysanthemum is a cool weather plant that matures in 30–40 days, so sow in early spring and again in late summer. Sowings made during the heat of summer tend to be bitter. Sow ¼–½ inch deep, 2 inches apart in rows 18 inches apart. Thin to 6 inches apart, eating the thinnings.

Good varieties to grow: 'Garland Round Leaved', 'Garland Serrate Leaved'. It may be listed in catalogs as "Chop suey greens."

Chinese cabbage. These come in several different forms, each with its own name. The main shapes are barrel (napa or wong bok), cylindrical (michihli), and loose- or semi-headed. The first two are well known and widely available in many seed catalogs. It can be grown as a mature crop or can be cut semi-mature. Sow crops to be left to mature in summer or early fall, those to be cut semi-mature from spring to autumn. In cool climates, mature crops can also be sown in spring.

Sow outside ½–¾ inch deep and about 1 inch apart in rows 12 inches apart. Thin in stages to 12 inches apart. Seeds can also be started indoors but are best sown in individual peat pots so they can be planted out without root disturbance.

Good varieties to grow: Napa type—'Blues', 'Tenderheart', and 'China Pride' are all suitable for spring sowing. Michihli type—'Greenwich', 'Green Rocket', and 'Jade Pagoda' should all be sown in late summer.

Loose-headed type—'Kaisin Hakusai', and 'Lettucy' sow from late spring through summer.

Chinese celery cabbage (pak choi or bok choi). Also known as celery cabbage and mustard cabbage, this is

Unlike the regular type of radish, Asian varieties are much larger and take longer to mature.

Radish 'White Chinese'

probably the most widely available of all the Chinese vegetables, available in most grocery stores year-round. Pak choi grows best in cool weather so plant it in early spring and again after the heat of summer. It will mature in about 8 weeks and spring sown crops should be cut

Beans

Beans are eaten cooked, added to soups, sown thickly for bean sprouts, or dried for later use.

Adzuki bean is a dwarf bean with a slightly sweet taste. It grows like a French bean and should be sown like regular bush beans (see page 445). They can be dried for later use, needing only a couple of hours of soaking to be ready to cook.

In cold climates, sow them in cellpaks indoors and plant out once all danger of frost is gone and the soil temperature has reached 60°F. They take about 4 months from sowing to harvest, so where summers are long enough they can be sown outside once the soil is warm. Sow the beans 1 inch deep, 3 inches apart in rows 18 inches apart.

Good varieties to grow: 'Express' and 'Tamba'.

Soybean is the basis for a great range of products from soy milk and soy curd (tofu), to soy sauce in several different guises, miso paste, and black bean sauce. All this and there are still the beans that can be eaten fresh or dried and roasted and eaten as a snack. Depending on the variety, the actual beans may be green, tan, yellow, white, or black; the variety depends on the length of the growing season, so check carefully that you grow one suitable for your climate.

Soybeans should be grown like the Adzuki bean, above, either starting them indoors in pots or directly into the soil outdoors, depending on the length of your growing season. Space them 3 inches apart

as mature plants. Those sown for fall use can be treated like Swiss chard or spinach and have a few outer leaves removed for use, leaving the heart to produce more foliage. Cook the leaves like spinach and the stems like asparagus. Both green stemmed and white

in rows 12–14 inches apart. They prefer a slightly acidic soil and are rich in protein.

Good varieties to grow: 'Beer Friend' (70 days), 'Envy' (75 days), 'Butterbeans' (90 days), and 'Black Jet' (105 days).

Yard-long bean is actually misnamed. Most varieties grow only half this size at best. They produce long, slender pods, about the diameter of a pencil. The young pods can be used like snap beans, cooked after being broken into short pieces, either on their own, as part of a stir-fry or added to soups. Being slender, they cook very rapidly. They are reputed to taste like asparagus and are sometimes listed as asparagus bean. The leaves and young stems can also be picked, steamed, and served with olive oil. The actual beans vary in color, depending on the variety.

Yard-long beans are heat lovers and should not be planted out or sown until the night temperatures generally remain above 65°F. However, they are quick growing and will be cropping within 3 months. They grow on a vine similar to pole beans, but more aggressive, especially in hot summers; they will need a strong support. Sow them in the same way as Adzuka beans and plant them 6 inches apart in rows 2 feet apart.

Good varieties to grow: 'Mosaic' with multicoloured pods, 'Akasanjaku' has light green pods with red seeds, and 'Kurojuroku' has dark green pods and black seeds.

stemmed varieties are available in catalogs.

Sow ¼–½ inch deep and 2 inches apart in rows 18 inches apart. When the seedlings are about 4 inches tall, thin to 6 inches apart, eating the thinnings. Pak choi is really a biennial and in warm climates will come into

Radishes

Asian radishes are a far cry from the small, generally round, radish commonly grown. They can be white, have red or green flesh, and are frequently served cooked, like turnips. There are two main types of Asian radish: the white "mooli" or daikon type, often called Japanese radish, and the Chinese ones with colored flesh or skins.

Mooli radish have a crisp texture and vary in flavor from sweet to very hot, although this can depend, in part, on soil and growing conditions. Most of the pungent taste is in the skin, so these radishes are usually peeled. Raw, they can be grated, cubed, or cut into thin slices for use in salads or with cooked meats. Cooked, they can be used in place of turnips, stir-fried, grated into sauces, or added to soups. They are a cool weather crop and are sown either in early spring to mature in early summer or in summer for a fall crop, depending on the variety. In very mild regions, a late fall sowing can be made to overwinter for cropping the following spring.

Sow seeds ½–¾ inch deep and sow thinly to make thinning easier. Spacing will depend on the variety, but seedlings should be thinned in stages, starting when they are large enough to handle. Space the rows 18 inches apart.

Good varieties to grow: For early spring sowing—'Omni', 'April Cross', and 'Mino Early'.

For late summer sowing—'Karaine', 'Resist Riso', and 'Wakayama White'.

flower the second year, the young flowering shoots being especially tasty.

Good varieties to grow: Green stemmed—'Mei Qing Choi' and 'Shanghai'.

White stemmed—'Joi Choi', 'Taisai', and the miniature 'Toy Choi'.

Chinese radish comes in several forms, often having the flesh colored in shades of pink, green, or purple. Great variation in size and spacing is because there are so many varieties available. This makes it absolutely necessary to follow the sowing and cultivation instructions on individual packets.

The "Beauty Heart" radishes have a rough green exterior, but the inside is white with rays of pink to red radiating from the center. They definitely need to be grown in a warm climate and should not be sown until the temperature is above 60°F. They usually take upward of 90 days to mature and can weigh up to 2 pounds when mature.

Green fleshed radishes are more cold tolerant and can be sown in spring or late summer. They mature in about 60 days. Depending on the variety, the flesh may be dark green at the top becoming lighter, or pale green shading to white. They grow with much of the radish exposed above the soil and can weigh up to 1 pound.

Red skinned radishes are very much similar to those normally grown in North America, except they weigh up to 1 pound. Sow in early summer for fall use, and, where winters are mild, in midsummer for winter use. They can be left in the soil and be lifted as needed if given a covering of straw.

Good varieties to grow: Beauty Heart—'Mantanghong', and 'Red Meat'. Green fleshed—'Green Meat' and 'Misato Green'. Red skinned—'China Rose' and 'Cherokee'.

Corn

Corn 'Golden Cross Bantam'

There is only one way to truly enjoy the flavor of fresh corn: grow it yourself—for corn loses much of its sweetness within minutes after picking. True corn lovers start water boiling on the stove before they pick, so that they can rush the tender ears straight from the garden into the pot.

The earliest corn matures in about two months, the latest in three. Many gardeners plant early, midseason, and late varieties at the same time to give themselves a longer harvesting season. Some catalogs offer a package of three varieties that will ripen in succession.

Another way to reap corn longer is to make succession plantings of an early, fast-maturing variety every 10 days or so until midsummer.

How to Grow Corn

You must have considerable garden space to grow corn, since each stalk takes up a surprising amount of room and produces only one or two ears. Because corn is wind pollinated, it must be planted in such a way that adjacent stalks can pollinate one another. For this reason, corn is not planted in a single, long row. Instead, several short rows are sown in a block so that pollen from the corn tassels needs to travel only a short distance between plants. Allow space for a block that is at least 6 feet wide by 8 feet long—a total area of 48 square feet. This will allow you to plant four rows of corn 2 feet apart.

Prepare the soil by incorporating well-rotted manure or compost. Apply as much as 30 pounds per 100 square feet of garden bed.

Two weeks before the last expected frost, sow the corn seeds 3–4 inches apart and about 1 inch deep. Before you plant use a soil thermometer to confirm that the soil temperature is at least 60°F. You can warm the soil by spreading clear or black plastic over the planting area for a week before planting. (For summer plantings, sow 2 inches deep, to reach the deeper soil moisture.) Space rows for early corn about 2 feet apart. Later corn, which grows taller, should be planted in rows about 3 feet apart. When the seedlings are 3 inches tall, thin out the weaker ones, for a final spacing of 1 foot between plants.

To plant corn in hills, sow six seeds along the perimeter of a 12-inch-diameter circle (called a hill, although it is not mounded). Each hill should be 3 feet from neighboring hills. When the seedlings are 3 inches tall, cut off all but the three strongest plants in each circle.

Corn needs moisture. To retain it (and to hold down weeds), spread on a heavy mulch of rotted straw or hay.

Once corn has sprouted, it grows rapidly. When stalks are 6–10 inches

Extrasweet corn varieties should be cultivated alone, as they lose their sweetness through cross-pollination. Harvest cucumbers when their sides are parallel and they are 6–8 in. long.

Se and Se+ corn has high sugar content.   Cucumbers 'Tanja'

Cucumbers

1. Pinch off any side shoots from base of stem when about 6 in. long.

2. Mound soil around stems to encourage rooting for support.

high, spread a band of fish meal or alfalfa meal on both sides of each row. If you have covered the ground with mulch, pull it aside before applying the fertilizer, or use a water-soluble fertilizer, such as fish emulsion, that you can pour over the mulch. Weeds will flourish, but be careful not to disturb the plants' shallow roots.

Harvest corn while it is young, or it will lose its sweetness, as the sugar turns to starch. Test each ear for ripeness: when an ear feels firm and full and the tips of the silks are dry and dark brown, it is ready to be picked. To remove an ear, pull it

What Can Go Wrong With Corn

If you find small holes in the base or sides of the ears, the corn has probably been invaded by corn borers—inch-long grubs that feed in the stalks and then attack the ears and sometimes the tassels. Prevent borers by spraying with *Bacillus thuringiensis kurstaki*. Cover the leaves surrounding the ears and the silks with spray. Respray at five-day intervals at least three times. To protect your

Varieties of Corn to Grow

Recommended early varieties include 'Earlivee' (SU) and 'Sugar Buns' (Se+). Good midseason corn includes 'Delectable' (Se+), yellow

downward by hand and twist it off the stalk. Harvest only as much corn as you can eat at one meal.

New Sugar-Enhanced varieties keep their sweet taste longer after picking. Many catalogs use the following abbreviations to denote sweetness: SU, for Normal Sugary with traditional corn flavor; Se and Se+, for Sugar Enhanced with increased tenderness and a higher sugar content; those marked Sh2 have shrunken kernels when dry and a "Super Sweet" taste. These must be grown in isolation from regular varieties, or poor-quality corn will result.

next year's crop, destroy old cornstalks and stubble, which can harbor corn borer larvae over the winter.

Ears that are enlarged, bursting open, often with swollen brown or gray kernels visible, have smut, a seed-borne disease. Discard.

The worst problem affecting corn is often raccoons. These night raiders spoil the ears. To prevent raccoon damage, try taping each individual ear to the stalk, wrapping the tape around the ear and stalk about 1 inch below the tip of the ear.

and white; 'Brocade' (Se+), yellow; and 'Indian Summer'* (Sh2), with multicolor kernels. Popular late varieties are yellow 'Golden Cross Bantam' (SU) and white 'Avalon' (Sh2).

Cucumbers need a lot of attention, but given the proper care, they are very prolific—four or five plants will supply a family of four through the summer. And even though the plants require warm weather, they mature so quickly (55 to 60 days) that they can be grown almost everywhere.

Before planting cucumbers, make sure that you have either plenty of garden space to give them or something that they can climb on. A cucumber plant is a vine that, when grown on the ground, will sprawl for over 6 feet in length.

If your garden is too small to accommodate such long, trailing vines, however, you can train cucumbers to climb up a fence or a trellis. Besides saving valuable ground space, trellis-trained plants often produce better-formed cucumbers.

In selecting cucumber varieties, you will find a wide choice. There are large, narrow, slicing cucumbers for eating fresh from the garden, and short, fat, pickling types. But note that you can pickle slicing kinds and eat the pickling ones raw.

An important fact to look for in seed descriptions on packages or in catalogs is disease-resistance. Cucumbers are vulnerable to scab, mosaic, and downy and powdery mildew, but horticulturists have bred varieties that are resistant to these diseases. Ask the staff at your local nursery about which varieties will withstand the diseases that are prevalent in your area.

You will be sure to notice that some varieties are described as "parthenocarpic." Normally, a cucumber vine bears both male and female flowers, with the fruits forming from pollinated females. Parthenocarpic varieties produce solely female flowers, so that the vine will bear a larger crop. The female flowers do not need to be pollinated, and they produce cucumbers with very few seeds.

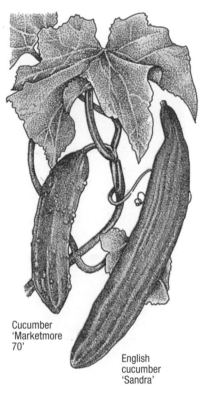

Cucumber 'Marketmore 70'

English cucumber 'Sandra'

How to Grow Cucumbers

Cucumbers can be grown in hills (clusters of two or three plants) or in rows. Hills are to many gardeners the traditional way to plant cucumbers, but rows are particularly well suited for growing cucumbers up a fence or beside a trellis.

Rows should be spaced 6 feet apart; make hills 1 foot in diameter, spacing the perimeters 6 feet apart.

Soil preparation is particularly important; cucumbers need fertile soil with good drainage. Dig up the earth to a depth of about 1 foot, and work in 1 wheelbarrowful of well-rotted manure or rich compost for every 10 feet of row or for every two hills you plan to plant.

Eggplant generally crop well unless planted out while the soil is still cold.

Eggplant

TRIM SHOOTS

Trim fruit-bearing lateral shoots back to one or two leaves above the first cucumber.

In most areas cucumber seeds are sown indoors in individual peat pots two to three weeks before the last expected frost. (Pots are recommended rather than flats because cucumbers will not tolerate the root disturbance that is inevitable when you separate plants grown in flats.)

Sow three seeds ½ inch deep in each pot, and when the seedlings are about 1½ inches tall, thin them to the strongest one. If you choose a gynoecious variety (which produces plants with female flowers only), be sure to sow a couple of the dyed seeds in the packet, too. These are a separate variety that will produce plants with male flowers.

Seedlings will be ready for transplanting outdoors in three or four weeks. Space them 1 foot apart in rows, or place two or three seedlings in the center of each hill.

In regions with long growing seasons, sow the seeds directly in the garden at about the time of the last expected frost. Label the pollinating plants so that you do not later thin them out unwittingly.

For rows plant seeds ½ inch deep and 4–6 inches apart. When the seedlings are about 1½–2 inches tall, thin them to stand 1 foot apart.

For hills plant six to eight seeds per hill, ½ inch deep, and later thin the seedlings to two to three per hill.

Young cucumber plants are often set back by spring rain and cold. You can protect them against the elements by covering them with translucent caps, which are available at most garden centers.

Cucumbers need a lot of moisture; so water the soil frequently, and spread a thick layer of organic mulch or lay a black plastic mulch before planting to help the soil remain damp. A plastic mulch has the added advantage of warming the soil for early plantings.

If weeds manage to grow despite the mulch, pull them out by hand to avoid injuring the cucumbers' shallow root systems.

Slicing-type cucumbers are fully ripe when 6–8 inches long; pickling cucumbers, when they are 1½–3 inches long. But either type of cucumber may be picked before it reaches full size. Strip your vines of mature cucumbers every two or three days, or the plants will stop producing.

Pick the cucumbers while they are still dark green; yellow ones are overripe. To pick the fruit off the vine, hold the vine firmly in one hand while you twist off the cucumber with the other hand.

What Can Go Wrong With Cucumbers

Cucumber beetles feed on the plants and spread bacterial wilt. If such beetles are endemic in your area, protect young plants with protective caps or floating row covers. Or spray plants with kaolin clay to deter beetles.

Varieties of Cucumbers to Grow

Popular slicing varieties include 'Sweet Success'* (a parthenocarpic type) and 'Marketmore 76'. Recommended pickling cucumbers are 'Eureka' and 'Cool Breeze'. For a "burpless" type, try 'Diva'* (also parthenocarpic).

Eggplant

Eggplant 'Burpee Hybrid'

Eggplant, peppers, and tomatoes have much in common. They form the basis of the Mediterranean vegetable stew called ratatouille. All three are related, members of the nightshade family. All need warm, rich soil and a long growing season.

Eggplants are particularly tricky to grow. The seeds must be sown indoors at least eight weeks before the plants are set out, and the seedlings require sunshine and warm, moist soil. To encourage germination, soak the seeds in warm water for 24 hours before sowing.

Because starting eggplants can be difficult, you may want to buy them from a garden center. In selecting seedlings, look for individual pots (for minimal root disturbance in transplanting), and check the stems (woody-stemmed plants will not produce as well as green, pliable stems).

Eggplants require 100 to 120 days to mature from seeds. The number of days given on seed packets or in catalogs can be misleading, because the days are counted from the time the seedlings are planted outside.

Seedlings should not be transplanted into the garden before daytime temperatures reach 70°F. In areas where summer arrives late, plant early, or fast-maturing, varieties.

How to Grow Eggplant

If you decide to raise the seedlings yourself, start them eight weeks before the last expected frost. Plant in pots in which you have placed a layer of vermiculite or sphagnum moss over the potting soil. Sow three seeds in each pot, ¼ inch deep, and water thoroughly. Keep the pots in a warm place: a

As a winter vegetable, kale can withstand considerable cold. Where winters are not too severe, it can be harvested from fall to late March.

Kale 'Winterbor'

Kales and Collards

Kale 'Green Curled Scotch'

temperature of 75°F is needed for germination, which may take three weeks.

When the seedlings reach 1½–2 inches, clip off the two weakest ones, leaving the best plant in each pot. Reduce the temperature as the seedlings grow, but be especially careful when you harden off the plants—that is, when you expose them to outdoor conditions to prepare them for transplanting into the garden. Temperatures below 50°F will set back eggplant.

When you choose a spot for eggplant, try to avoid the vicinity of tomatoes or peppers, and, if possible, do not plant in soil where eggplants, tomatoes, peppers, or potatoes previously grew. Because these plants are related, they are all susceptible to the same soil-borne diseases.

To prepare the soil, dig in about 1 bushel of compost or well-rotted manure for every 10 feet of row. Set out the eggplants on an overcast day or in the evening so that the sun will not wilt the tender seedlings. Dig shallow holes about 2 feet apart, in rows 3 feet apart, and fill these with water. When the water has drained out, plant the seedlings, leaving a slight depression around each plant to hold water. Water again as soon as you have planted the seedlings.

To protect eggplants from cutworms, make a collar of stiff paper (or use a paper cup with its bottom removed) and set this around the stem and into the ground an inch or more deep. If the leaves droop or seem wilted, cover the plants for a few days with newspaper tents.

To help your eggplants flourish, keep the ground well watered and weed free. Mulch around the plants to conserve soil moisture and prevent weed growth. Black plastic mulch is preferable because it also warms the soil, but you can use any available mulching material.

If weeding becomes necessary, do it by hand.

When the blossoms set and the fruits begin to form, count the number of fruits on each plant. For a healthy crop, each plant should bear no more than six fruits, so pinch off any extra blossoms.

Between 55 and 80 days from the day you planted the eggplant seedlings in the garden, the fruits will be 5–6 inches long and 4–5 inches in diameter, and will have glossy, dark purple, pink, or white skins. At this point they are ready to pick. Once the sheen on the skin fades, the fruit is past its prime. Never try to pull the fruit off the plant—you may take some of the stalk with it. Instead, use a sharp knife to sever the stem about an inch from the fruit.

Place the harvested eggplants in a cool place and use them as soon as possible. Eggplants do not store well.

What Can Go Wrong With Eggplant

Verticillium wilt, a soil-borne disease that affects eggplants can also affect tomatoes and potatoes. The best prevention is crop rotation: do not plant eggplant where it, or either of the other two vegetables, has been grown within the last three years.

Colorado potato beetles, flea beetles, and aphids feast on eggplant. Control adult Colorado beetles by hand picking. Spray with spinosad or *Beauveria bassiana* to control the larvae. Apply kaolin clay to deter flea beetles.

Varieties of Eggplant to Grow

Among varieties recommended for short growing seasons are 'Dusky', 'Fairy Tale'*, 'Hansel'*, and 'Black Bell'.

For longer seasons, 'Black Beauty', 'Ghostbuster' (White), and 'Italian Pink Bicolor' are worth trying.

Kale and collards are among the oldest of cultivated vegetables and among the most nutritious; yet many people have never tasted either one. Leafy green vegetables related to the cabbage, they can be used cooked or, when young and tender, eaten raw as salad greens.

Both vegetables are easy to grow and productive, and for gardeners in areas with a short growing season, have the added advantage of improving in cold weather. A touch of frost sharpens their flavor, and kale, especially, thrives well into winter.

Kale grows about 2 feet high and takes 2 months to mature; collards reach about 3 feet in 2½ months.

Boston lettuce 'Marion' ➡

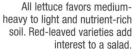

All lettuce favors medium-heavy to light and nutrient-rich soil. Red-leaved varieties add interest to a salad.

Green and red-leaved lettuce

How to Grow Kale and Collards

Both kale and collards require fertile soil that is not too acid. If acidity is a problem, lime the soil (to a pH of 6.5 or above) well ahead of planting. Enrich it with organic matter. Spread a 1- to 2-inch layer of compost or well-rotted manure over the planting area and work it into the top few inches of soil.

Plant kale and collards outdoors in early spring, as soon as the ground can be worked. Sow the seeds an inch apart in 1-inch-deep furrows 2–3 feet apart, and cover with half an inch of soil. The seeds should germinate in 7 to 10 days.

If you have the space, sow a second collards or kale crop in June for harvesting in fall. Kale withstands cold better than collards and can be harvested long after other leafy green vegetables have disappeared. In areas where the ground does not freeze, you can sow kale in late summer for harvesting in winter.

When the seedlings are 3 inches high, start thinning them gradually until the plants stand 2 feet apart. (You can use the thinnings for salads.) Because the plants grow fairly tall and have heavy leaves, they should be supported against strong winds. When staking, be careful not to injure the shallow, spreading roots: set the stakes along the row during the thinning process, and tie on the plants when they reach about 1 foot in height.

Because kale and collards have roots that grow close to the surface of the soil, be careful in weeding. Hoe no deeper than an inch or so, to avoid cutting the roots. A thick mulch will deter weed growth.

Fertilize these vegetables at least once during the growing season, scattering a band of complete fish meal or alfalfa meal on each side of the row at the rate of 1 cup per 10 row feet.

You can begin harvesting kale in about a month, when the leaves have turned a rich green. If the leaves become too dark, however, they will be tough and bitter. Do not take too many leaves from a single plant, or it will stop growing. To maintain kale in cold weather, mulch each plant heavily with straw, salt hay, or leaf mulch; or hill earth up around the bottom of the stem for a few inches.

Collards are fully mature two to three months after planting, but you can begin eating them much sooner. You can harvest the whole plant or cut off some leaves from the bottom of the stem. But in cutting, be careful not to injure the central growing bud because new leaves are formed only as the stem grows.

What Can Go Wrong With Kale and Collards

To avoid diseases of the *Brassica* genus—to which kale, collards, cabbage, broccoli, and Brussels sprouts belong—do not plant kale or collards where any of these plants were grown in the past year or two.

Kale and collards are prey for cabbage worms. If you see these pests, the most effective way to control them is by spraying the plants with the microbial insecticide *Bacillus thuringiensis kurstaki.*

Varieties of Kale and Collards to Grow

'Green Curled Scotch' is a recommended kale variety. 'Winterbor' is extrahardy for overwintering. 'Flowering Kale' is so attractive that gardeners sometimes cultivate it as an ornamental plant.

One of the most popular and widely used collard varieties is called 'Vates'. This is a low-growing, thick-leaved selection. Other popular varieties include 'Champion', 'Top Bunch', and 'Morris Heading'.

Lettuce and Endive

Boston lettuce 'Escort'

The number of lettuce varieties available at the grocery store is great, as it is at vegetable stands at the market, but even so, the range of varieties available to the home gardener is even greater. Who can resist trying 'Lollo Rossa', a loose-leaf type with curly pale green leaves edged in pink, or the old favorite romaine 'Winter Density', that will withstand frost and cold weather?

There are four major types of lettuce: true head lettuce (of which 'Iceberg' is the most familiar variety), whose leaves come together to form a tight head, somewhat like a cabbage in shape; butterhead, which also forms a head, but one that is much looser; cos, or romaine, whose tall oval heads may stand almost a foot high; and loose-leaf lettuce, which produces a summer-long harvest of leaves to be cut and replaced by new ones. True head lettuce is seldom grown in home gardens in most parts of the country because of its exacting climatic requirements. The three other types of lettuce, however, are easy to grow almost anywhere—loose-leaf grows the fastest and produces the largest crops.

Most types of lettuce grow best before midsummer heat. When temperatures reach a fairly consistent 70°F, lettuce has the habit of bolting—sending up a stem that bears flowers and then seeds—and when it bolts, it becomes too tough to eat. Loose-leaf lettuce is the least likely to bolt during hot spells and also takes the least time to mature. So it can be planted in late June or July in cool areas where it would be too late to plant the other types of lettuce.

Leaf lettuce matures 6 to 7 weeks after sowing; butterhead, 9 to 10

Loose-leaf 'Lollo Rossa'

Head lettuce 'Buttercrunch'

Leaf lettuce forms either very loose heads or none at all. Leaf lettuce, such as 'Lollo Rossa', should be picked leaf by leaf as needed; head lettuce, such as 'Buttercrunch', should be cut off in its entirety at ground level.

weeks; cos, 11 to 12 weeks. (Leaves of all types are edible at any stage of growth.) To keep a constant supply of lettuce on your table, make succession sowings, planting a row of about 5 or 6 feet every two weeks. Stop making succession plantings before the hottest weeks and start again after midsummer for fall crops.

You can also plant lettuce between slow-maturing vegetables, such as peppers or cabbage. By the time peppers or cabbage are large enough to need all the surrounding space, you will have harvested the lettuce.

Endive grows like lettuce, looks like lettuce, and is used as salad greens. Being more tolerant of hot weather, it will flourish when temperatures soar too high for lettuce to grow. Endive is also more cold resist-ant and can be planted for a later harvest than lettuce.

The two most popular types of endive are the slender, wavy-leaved curly endive and the flatter-leaved escarole. Both varieties have tougher leaves and a sharper flavor than lettuce and need to be blanched (shielded from sunlight) when growing, so that their leaves will become milder and more tender.

Mesclun Mix

With mesclun, a mix of lettuce and small salad greens, such as arugula and cress, even a small garden can produce the ideal salad. Sow as soon as soil is dry enough to work and every three weeks afterward. Sow short rows about 4 inches wide. Harvest when plants are 4 inches tall, cutting 1 inch above soil. You should get four cuttings from each sowing.

How to Grow Lettuce and Endive

Lettuce and endive grow best in soil that is rich in humus. To prepare the soil, dig in substantial amounts of organic matter, such as compost or well-rotted manure. One bushel per 25 feet of row should do the job. Lacking this, add a balanced organic fertilizer according to instructions.

Planting and tending lettuce. Loose-leaf lettuce is usually sown directly into the garden as soon as the ground can be worked and is no longer soggy from winter snow and spring rains. Butterhead and cos varieties can be started indoors in flats about six weeks before the ground can be worked, or they can be sown outdoors at the same time as loose-leaf lettuce.

When sowing seeds in flats, plant them ½ inch deep and about 1 inch apart. Keep the flats in a cool place; lettuce will germinate at 60°F. When the seedlings are 1 inch high, thin them to stand about 2 inches apart, or transplant them into individual pots. Place the seedlings in a cool, sunny spot.

Flat-grown seedlings can be transplanted outside when they reach 2–3 inches in height and the ground can be worked. Give them a week of hardening off—gradual exposure to outside weather conditions—before you transfer them to the garden. When transplanting, place the seedlings 6–8 inches apart, in rows 1–1½ feet apart.

Sow seeds outdoors ½ inch deep, 1 inch apart, and in rows 1–1½ feet apart. When the seedlings are 2 inches high, thin them to stand about 2 inches apart. Thin them again when the plants are almost touching one another. (You can eat these thinnings, or you can transplant them to another row if you are careful not to disturb the roots unduly.) You will probably have to thin the seedlings again to achieve the proper spacing of 6–8 inches between plants.

Although lettuce will grow in crowded rows, the heads will be smaller, and the plants will have a tendency to bolt.

Lettuce needs to be fertilized at least once during the growing season. Options include watering the plants with compost tea or a liquid fish fertilizer solution weekly or every two weeks. Or you can use compost as a sidedressing alongside the plants a week after planting.

Weed lettuce gently and water it frequently. Because the plants need constant moisture, a light mulch is helpful in retaining it. In a small garden with only a few plants, pick leaves off the outside of each plant, and allow it to mature.

Planting and tending endive. You can plant endive directly into the garden. Or if space is a problem, you can sow seeds in a seedbed, and when seedlings are 2–3 inches high, transplant them into rows from which you have harvested an earlier crop.

Endive grows best when the seeds are sown in midsummer for a fall harvest. Sow the seeds ½ inch deep, 1 inch apart, in rows 2 feet apart. Thin, as with lettuce, until the plants stand 14–16 inches apart.

Fertilize, weed, and water endive as you do lettuce. In addition, in the final two or three weeks of growth, blanch the heads to mellow the rather harsh natural flavor of the endive leaves.

To blanch, gather the long outer leaves together over the top of the plant and secure them with a rubber band. Another way to blanch is simply to place a wide board directly on the tops of the plants. Because the foliage grows low to the ground, you will not crush it.

Harvesting lettuce and endive. Loose-leaf lettuce is harvested by picking the outer leaves, leaving the center of the vegetable intact to grow new leaves. For butterhead and cos lettuce and endive, cut the entire plant at ground level. Harvest frequently. If you leave lettuce unharvested after the heads reach maturity, they begin to lose their nutritive value as well as their flavor.

What Can Go Wrong With Lettuce and Endive

Lettuce and endive suffer from a few predators. Slugs may be a problem in wet areas. Dispose of them by setting out sunken saucers of stale beer, in which these slimy creatures will drown themselves; or look for them at night with a flashlight, and pick them up by hand. Iron phosphate slug baits are also acceptable for organic gardens. Read and follow label directions. Aphids can be controlled by spraying the plants with insecticidal soap. Leafhoppers may feed on the undersides of leaves and can be controlled with neem. Should pale green worms chew on your lettuce, pick them off by hand, or spray with *Bacillus thuringiensis*. Always follow product labels exactly.

Varieties of Lettuce and Endive to Grow

Recommended loose-leaf lettuce varieties include 'Grand Rapids', 'Black-Seeded Simpson', and the red-leaved 'Red Sails'*. Although these mature in 40 to 45 days, you can start harvesting in a month.

'Esmarelda', 'Buttercrunch'*, 'Bibb', 'Ithaca', and 'Deertongue' are green varieties. 'Sangria' has rosy red leaves and good flavor.

Among cos, or romaine, lettuces, 'Parris Island Cos', which grows about 10 inches high, and 'Cimmaron', with dark red-ringed leaves, are favored varieties.

'Green Curled' is a popular curly endive variety. 'Full Heart Batavian' is an escarole that has proved to be succulent in salads over the years.

Okra

Okra 'Perkins Mammoth Long Pod'

A relative of the tropical flower hibiscus, okra was brought to the Americas from Africa in the 1600's. Also called gumbo in many parts of the world, okra became a staple of the cuisine of the South. Its sticky consistency makes it a good thickener for "gumbo" soups and stews, and it is also fried or cooked with tomatoes.

Although okra grows best where the summers are long and hot, it will flourish wherever corn grows. By starting its seed indoors and thus getting a jump on summer, northern gardeners can enjoy this vegetable. It can be raised in ordinary garden soil, although like most vegetables, it will do better in rich, loamy ground.

Okra grows up to 5 feet tall and needs a lot of room. (Some people grow it as a hedge or garden border.) Because the plants are sensitive to cold winds, in cool regions they are often planted in a protected area.

The okra plant grows rapidly, producing large, pale yellow flowers, behind which slender, pointed seedpods soon develop. These pods are the edible fruit of okra and are ready to be picked about 60 days after the seeds are sown. Although the pods may grow up to 9 inches long, they are best when they are small—no longer than a finger.

How to Grow Okra

In cool areas—in fact, in any region where frost is common in winter—it is advisable to start okra indoors. Allow the seedlings about a month of indoor growing time.

To speed germination, soak the seeds for 24 hours before planting. Then, sow them in peat pots, two seeds to a pot, and after the seeds sprout, place the pots in a warm, sunny place. When the seedlings are about 1 inch tall, clip off the weaker plant. When nighttime temperatures remain above 55°F, set out the okra plants in their peat pots. Slit the sides of the pots so that the roots can push through easily, and bury the pots well belowground so that they will disintegrate. Space the plants 18 inches apart, in rows 3 feet apart.

In warm regions sow okra seeds directly in the garden. Sow the seeds in clusters of three or four—1 inch deep, 18 inches apart, in rows 3 feet apart. When the seedlings are about 1 inch tall, be sure to cut off all but the strongest plant in each one of the clusters.

Feed the plants twice with a compost tea—first when the plants are about 10 inches tall, and again when they start to blossom. As an alternative, apply sidedressings of a balanced organic fertilizer according to label instructions.

Okra needs very little attention beyond regular watering and weeding. A 2- to 3-inch layer of mulch will help keep weeds down and maintain soil moisture. Okra pods are at their peak when they are 2–3 inches long. Once they appear, they grow rapidly and become wild and stringy in a few days; keep a sharp eye on the pods from the time they start maturing.

To harvest okra, cut off the pods with a sharp knife. Do not leave ripe pods on the plant, because their presence causes the plant to stop production. Harvest daily, and store what you cannot eat in the refrigerator for a few days. If you harvest regularly, your plants should keep producing until the first frost

What Can Go Wrong With Okra

Okra seldom succumbs to pests or diseases. If borers should infest a crop, spray the ground with *Bacillus thuringiensis kurstaki* and pick the borers off the plants. Control aphids, Japanese beetles, and corn earworms with neem.

Varieties of Okra to Grow

Most modern varieties of okra are "spineless"—they are without the prickly spines that once forced okra

In hot areas, fusarium wilt, a soil disease, can destroy a crop; if it does, do not plant okra (or annual hibiscus) in the area for at least three years.

Plants started indoors and then put out are often attacked by cutworm. Protect them by ringing young plants with a collar set ½ inch in the soil. Frozen-juice cans cut in half are excellent for this purpose.

harvesters to wear gloves. 'Annie Oakley II' and 'Cajun Delight'* are suitable for short-season areas. 'Burgundy'*, which produces red pods on a red-stemmed bush, is both decorative and edible.

To prevent their long stems from becoming green, leeks should be planted in a trench, and soil heaped around the lengthening stems as they grow.

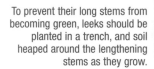

Leek 'Titan'

Onions, Leeks, and Garlic

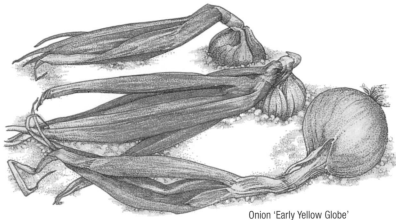

Onion 'Early Yellow Globe'

The common "globe" onion is grown for its bulb, but because the home-grown version is not noticeably superior to the commercially raised product, home gardeners often do not plant them.

Scallions, or green onions (the young, green form of the onion), are more flavorful straight from the garden than when they come from the store—and they take up less space in the garden than globe onions.

Although any onion can be picked at its scallion stage, certain varieties have been bred to be eaten solely as small-bulbed scallions. Because they are usually sold at the market in bunches, seed catalogs very often describe them as bunching onions.

The leek is a close relative of the onion. It resembles a giant scallion but has flat, broader leaves and different growing requirements. It does not store well out of the ground.

The time to maturity for onions and leeks is considerable—three to five months from seed for onions, and about four and a half months for leeks, although scallions can be harvested as early as two months after sowing.

Garlic, related to onions and leeks, has a different growing schedule, and is covered separately at the end of this section. Chives, also related to onions and leeks, are considered herbs and are covered in the section on herbs, which begins on page 483.

How to Grow Onions and Leeks

Onions and leeks need fertile, carefully worked, moist soil with good drainage. Because they can be replanted for several years in the same spot, it is worth the effort to prepare a good bed for them. Work in 2 pounds or more of well-rotted manure or compost for every 5 feet of row. If your soil is heavy clay or slow to drain, make raised planting beds.

Planting globe onions. Globe onions are hardy, and their seeds can be planted in the garden in early spring. Most home gardeners plant onion "sets," or small bulbs, because this shortens the time to maturity by four to six weeks and is more reliable than starting the plants from seeds. Where the ground freezes no more than ½ inch deep, onions can be planted in the fall for spring harvest.

Onion sets are sold by the pound; ½ pound will fill a 25-foot row. The bulbs should be no larger than ½ inch in diameter, or they may run to seed (flower prematurely) before producing edible onions.

Plant onion sets as soon as the ground can be worked. Place them 4 inches apart, 1 inch deep, in rows 12 inches apart. (Garden centers also carry onion seedlings; plant them in the same way as sets.)

If you are starting globe onions from seeds, sow the seeds as soon as the ground can be worked. Sow them about 1 inch apart and about ½ inch deep. When the seedlings are 3–4 inches tall, thin them to stand 2 inches apart. When the seedlings reach 6 inches, thin them to stand 4 inches apart.

Planting scallions (bunching onions). One way to grow scallions is to plant globe-onion seeds close together in clusters—about six to a cluster. Because you restrict their growing space by doing this, the plants will form long, white stems rather than globes. They can be harvested within two to three months.

Another way to raise scallions is from the seeds of specially bred bunching varieties. There are two main types: one is planted in early spring for summer harvest; the other can be sown either in late spring for harvesting in early fall, or in fall for harvesting the following spring. In cold areas provide a thick mulch cover for fall planting.

To start scallions from seeds, follow the directions given earlier for starting globe onions from seeds—but do not thin out the seedlings.

Tending onions and scallions. Globe onions and scallions have shallow root systems, and therefore they need frequent watering and careful weeding. To keep the weeds down, hoe shallowly between rows; within the rows pull out the weeds by hand.

The plants will also need additional fertilizer while they are growing. When they are 8–10 inches tall, spread a band of compost along both sides of each row. You can also apply a liquid fish fertilizer solution once a month.

Harvesting onions and scallions. Globe onions are ready for harvest about five months after seeds have been sown or three and a half months after planting out sets or seedlings. The onion tops wither as the bulbs reach maturity, turning yellow and then brown. You can speed up the maturation process—and produce larger bulbs—by bending the tops over when the outer leaves turn yellow. Two weeks later loosen the bulbs by pushing a spading fork beneath them and lifting them slightly. In another two weeks lift out the bulbs with the fork. You can either cut the tops off an inch from the bulb or leave them on for braiding after the onions have dried. Spread the bulbs in a warm, airy place for a few days until they are completely dry. Then braid them and hang them up; or hang them up in mesh bags.

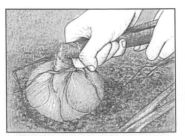

1. When the outer leaves of onions begin to turn yellow, bend over the tops.

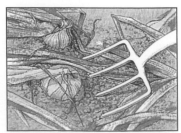

2. Two weeks later, lift the onions with a fork; spread them out to dry.

The 'Early Yellow Globe' onion is well suited for sowing outdoors. It is easier to plant onion sets.

Onion 'Early Yellow Globe'

Or store them loosely in shallow, open boxes. The storage area should be cool and moderately humid.

You can begin harvesting scallions when the bulbs have reached ¼–½ inch in diameter. The only way to determine the size is to pull up a green onion and examine it. Once bunching onions start maturing, pull them up only as you need them—they can be stored for no more than about two weeks. Like onions, scallions should be completely dried before storage.

Planting leeks. Leeks need fertile soil, so spread 2–4 inches of compost over the soil and work it in well, or plant a green manure crop. Prepare the soil during the fall before planting so that the organic matter will be fully incorporated into the soil by spring planting time. Because the leek is grown for its long white bulb end, and the bulb will turn green and grow tough if exposed to sun, leeks are customarily planted in a trench so that the bulbs can be kept covered with earth. To prepare the trench, dig a furrow about 6 inches deep and 9 inches across. If you dig more than one trench, leave 1–2 feet between trenches. Clear the trench bottom of stones and clods.

Because of the time leeks take to mature (130 days), the seeds are sown indoors in most areas, 10 to 12 weeks before the date of the last expected frost. Sow the seeds 1 inch apart and ⅛ inch deep. When sprouts appear, thin them with clippers so that the remaining plants stand about 2 inches apart. When the seedlings are about 4 inches tall, drop them into holes made 4–6 inches apart in the bottom of the trench, so that only the upper leaves stick partly out. As the leeks grow, heap the soil that you previously excavated for the trench around the lengthening bulbs.

Leek seeds can also be sown directly into the garden as soon as the soil can be worked. Garden-sown leeks may not be fully mature by the fall, but they can be mulched to remain in the soil through the winter, then harvested the next spring.

Plant leek seeds in a seedbed ½ inch deep in rows 6 inches apart, and when the seedlings are 6–8 inches tall, transplant them to a trench (described previously). Cut half the leaf portion of each plant before transplanting; this lessens the shock in moving them.

Tending and harvesting leeks. Cultivate leeks as you do onions, fertilizing them in midseason with compost tea or a fish fertilizer solution. Weed assiduously and carefully, as with onions.

Leeks can be harvested long before full maturity. Dig up the plant with a spading fork. Store leeks in soil in your cellar, or leave heavily mulched in the garden for harvesting. Side shoots can be removed and transplanted to yield another crop.

What Can Go Wrong With Onions and Leeks

Onion maggots feed on onions and leek bulbs. Once they infest a crop, nothing will save it. But you can protect your crop with floating row covers when the plants are young. Thrips feed on the leaves, causing them to mottle and wither. Choose varieties with round leaves and an open habit. Use water sprays, garlic repellent sprays, or neem.

Varieties of Onions and Leeks to Grow

Popular varieties of globe onions include 'Walla Walla', 'Southport Red Globe', 'Super Star', 'Candy', and 'Early Yellow Globe'. Among bunching onions, 'White Lisbon', 'Evergreen White', and 'Southport White' are recommended.

Popular varieties of leek are 'American Flag', 'King Richard', and 'Tadorna'.

How to Grow Garlic

Garlic will grow in most types of soil, but does best in a deep, sandy loam. In poorly drained soils grow them on ridges. It needs a sunny location and will not crop properly with less than 6 hours sunlight a day. The soil should be reasonably fertile, but adding manure before planting is not recommended, although well-rotted compost will help to improve the soil structure. On poor soils, apply a light dressing of blood meal before planting. Since garlic is subject to the same pests and diseases that attack onions, do not grow them in soil that grew onions the previous year.

Garlic is a biennial, but will act like a perennial since the new cloves will grow the following year. Commercially it is divided into soft-neck and hard-neck types. Soft-neck produces many smaller cloves around a soft central stalk while hard-neck has fewer, larger cloves and a stiffer central stem. Most of the garlic sold in stores are soft-neck grown in China or California. Hard-neck is the better type for growing in cooler regions. The individual cloves of either type are planted and will grow to form complete bulbs.

When planting for the first time, it is advisable to get locally grown garlic bulbs to divide. Garlic grown in a different climatic region will not produce as well as that grown locally. Some varieties are better suited to warm climates, others to cool. Visit www.thegarlicstore.com for a list of varieties and information on where they grow best. Garlic is normally planted in the fall and is a crop for regions that have a cool winter since it needs a cold period of at least one month when the temperature is around or below freezing to grow properly. In regions where winters are cold and there is little snow cover, or where the soil is very heavy, plant in spring, as soon as the soil can be worked. Where the growing season is short, the cloves can be started indoors in individual pots or in cell packs. They should be placed outdoors in a sheltered location to receive the necessary cold period and planted in spring.

Planting Garlic

Break the bulbs into individual cloves, discarding any diseased or soft ones. The cloves generally have a flattened region at the base where they were attached to the mother bulb, and are pointed at the top, although with some varieties it may be hard to tell. The bulbs tend to move up in the soil, so it is best to plant them several inches deep. Space them 8 inches apart in both directions for the highest yield, or plant in rows 10–12 inches apart with 3–4 inches between the cloves. In cold regions, cover the garlic with a layer of straw or salt hay about 6 inches deep. This can stay on as mulch the following spring.

Tending and Harvesting Garlic

Garlic has a shallow root system and weeds should be pulled by hand, rather than being hoed out, although with a good straw mulch there should not be many weeds. Water during prolonged droughts. Pick off the flower spikes as they develop; they can be cooked and eaten. The flavor is that of a mild onion.

In late summer, when the garlic foliage starts to turn yellow, lift the bulbs, handling them gently to avoid bruising. Trim off the roots with a sharp knife and peel off the outside, dirty layer of leaves to show a clean, white layer. Lay the bulbs out in an airy location—but out of direct sunlight—to dry for a few days. Store them under cover while the stems and leaves dry, allowing the nutrients in the foliage to help fatten the bulb. Once the tops are dry, cut them off a little above the bulb and store in a cool, but frost-free, dry location.

Because they are less hardy than smooth-seeded peas, wrinkle-seeded peas should not be sown outdoors before mid-April. Wrinkled peas are tender and taste better than the smooth-seeded variety.

Early pea 'Maestro'

Parsnips

The parsnip is a root vegetable that takes four months to mature. But because frost enhances its sweet, delicate flavor, it is a favorite with gardeners in areas with short growing seasons. In fact, if the soil is mulched well enough so that it does not freeze, parsnips can be left in the ground and harvested all winter. If the ground does freeze, they can be dug up the following spring.

In regions where winters are mild, parsnips can be planted in the fall for use as a winter crop.

How to Grow Parsnips

Parsnips are raised in much the same way as carrots. The edible root may grow to a depth of 15 inches, and any obstruction will cause it to fork or twist. So the soil where parsnips are to grow must be deeply spaded and raked clear of stones.

The seeds are sown directly into the garden about two weeks before the date of the last expected frost. Sow them thickly, ½ inch deep, in rows 12 inches apart. Cover the seeds lightly with soil or with a combination of soil and sand or soil and peat moss; then tamp the soil down firmly. Because parsnip seeds germinate slowly, it is a good idea to sow radish seeds among them. The radishes will come up quickly and mark the row long before the parsnips sprout. When the parsnip seedlings are about an inch high, thin them to stand 3–4 inches apart.

Parsnips planted in well-prepared soil do not need any fertilizing during the growing season. Once the seedlings are up and growing, mulch them with compost topped with shredded leaves to suppress weeds.

You can begin harvesting parsnips when the tops of the roots are 1½–2 inches in diameter. Dig them up carefully to avoid breaking them. Parsnips left in the ground for spring harvesting should be taken up before the plants begin to sprout new leaves. Stored in a cool place, parsnips remain sweet for weeks.

What Can Go Wrong With Parsnips

Do not plant parsnips near carrots or celery, for the same pests attack all three. The chief pest is the carrot fly. To protect plants, cover them with floating row covers from seeding until harvest.

Varieties of Parsnips to Grow

Recommended varieties of parsnips include 'Andover', 'Harris Model', and 'Hollow Crown'. 'All-America' is a high-quality parsnip that matures earlier than most other parsnips (in about 100 days).

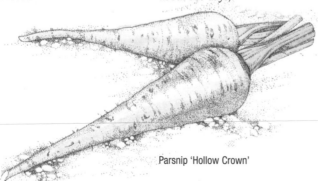

Parsnip 'Hollow Crown'

Peas

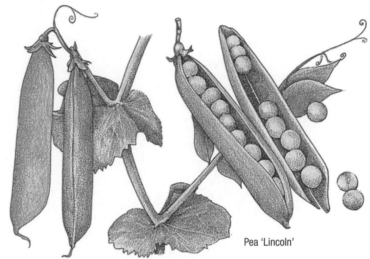

Pea 'Lincoln'

Homegrown peas cooked fresh from the garden are so much better than store-bought ones that a place for them should be found in even the smallest garden. Because peas are a cool-weather crop, planted in early spring, and because they mature quickly—about 55 days for very early peas—you can start another vegetable in their place after they have been harvested.

There are two major pea types: green peas (or English peas) and the edible-pod varieties (called sugar peas or snow peas), which are cooked and eaten with their pods. Although the yield for the edible-pod varieties is smaller, they are well worth growing for their delicate flavor and crisp texture.

Both green peas and edible-pod peas come in tall-vined and dwarf varieties. Dwarf peas usually require no support. The tall varieties need some support on which to climb, but they repay the extra effort with larger harvests.

Peas are extremely susceptible to heat and will stop maturing when the temperature regularly climbs above 70°F. When buying seeds, check the length of time each variety takes to mature. Choose early types if you live in an area with a short, cool spring. If cool weather lasts into summer, buy both an early and a late variety, and plant the two at the same time for a continuous crop.

Peas planted in cold, wet soil may succumb to rot. To avoid this problem, add compost to the soil to boost beneficial microbes that protect against rot. Do not sow too early. You can also apply a beneficial fungal product (*Trichoderma harzianum*) to protect seedlings from rot.

How to Grow Peas

Dig your pea patch as early in the spring as the ground can be worked. In turning the soil, work in generous amounts of organic material—rotted manure, compost, leaf mold, or old hay. For dwarf peas, dig a flat-bottomed furrow about 2 inches deep, 3–4 inches wide. For tall varieties, which need a trellis for support, be sure to make the furrow

Sugar-snap peas are popular because they do not have a tough shell, and so can be eaten with their tender pods.

Sugar-snap 'Sugar Sprint'

10 inches wide, set the support in its center, and plant a row on each side. Tall peas can also be grown on a fence.

If you do not want to bother with a trellis, you can plant a double row of peas, which will support each other as the vines grow. This method works best with moderately tall plants that grow to about 18 inches. The high climbers—2½–3 feet tall—need extra support.

If you use a trellis, set it up before planting. Almost any form of support will serve: chicken wire, the lightweight plastic mesh available at garden centers, or rows of string drawn between two posts. You can also make a rough trellis from several tall, sticks staked close together down the length of the row.

Just before sowing the seeds, cover the bottom of the trench with a ½-inch layer of mature compost or leaf mold and work it into the soil before sowing the seeds.

Before sowing, you may want to dust pea seeds with a soil inoculant, a nitrogen-fixing bacterial culture that increases the plants' ability to add nitrogen to the soil. Soil inoculants are available from seed-catalog companies or garden centers.

Sow the pea seeds about 1 inch apart and 2 inches deep. To prevent birds from eating the newly planted

seeds, cover the rows with bird netting until the peas have sprouted.

When the seedlings reach about 3 inches in height, mound a bit of soil around the stems for support. As plants grow taller, hook their climbing tendrils around the trellis or other support you have provided.

Peas need a good deal of moisture; so mulch the rows to maintain moisture and hold down weeds. Check the soil occasionally, and water when necessary. Because peas are especially vulnerable to fungal disease, water the plants at soil level so that the leaves will not get wet.

When plants are 6–8 inches tall, spread a band of compost or a balanced organic fertilizer blend on both sides of each row.

If your pea vines should start to trail away from their support as they grow taller, tie them against it with a few pieces of soft twine.

Peas taste best if they are picked while young and tender. One or two days too long on the vine can turn tender peas tough. If you harvest regularly, you will be able to pick the peas when they are just at their prime. Check the lowest pods often, for they mature first. Pods left on the vine serve as a sort of signal to the plant to halt production.

Green peas should be picked when the pods are well filled but the peas

inside are not yet hard. Edible-pod, or snow, peas are ready when the pods are just beginning to swell. If you wait until the pea shapes showing through the pod are noticeably round, the pods may be too tough to eat. (If you let snow peas remain on the vine too long, shell and cook as you would green peas.) Sugar-snap peas are like edible pod peas but are allowed to fill out. Pods snap like green beans, and pod and peas are eaten together. Pods will develop "strings" down their spines if overmature, but can still be shelled to cook the peas.

Harvest peas with care, holding the vine with one hand while you pick off the pod with the other. Otherwise you may remove part of the plant along with the pod.

If you are planning a succession crop in your pea patch, you should

bear in mind that peas are heavy feeders and that what they take from the soil should be replaced. When the harvest is over, cut off the plants, and put them in the compost. The nitrogen nodules on their roots will feed the next crop. Fertilize the soil again, and add compost before you plant another crop in the pea patch.

If, as the end of the harvesting season draws near, there is a superabundance of peas on the vines, you may want to dry those you cannot use immediately. Simply leave the pods on the vine until the peas are completely hard. Then pick and shell them, and dry them for half an hour in an oven set on "low." Store the dried peas in jars. If you plan to keep them over the winter, place jars in a dry place to prevent mold forming.

What Can Go Wrong With Peas

Aphids spread pea mosaic, a serious virus disease for which there is no treatment. If aphids appear on the stems or undersides of pea leaves, wash them off with water or spray with insecticidal soap. Spider mites may attack peas in hot weather, causing white speckling on leaves and webbing between leaves. Spray plants with a strong stream of water.

Powdery mildew is a common problem during cold, wet springs. Treat the plants by dusting or spraying with a potassium bicarbonate spray.

Root rot is also common. It can attack the plants at flowering time, turning the leaves yellow and darkening the stems and roots. There is no treatment, but you can avoid the disease the following season by planting peas in well-drained soil, preferably where they have not been grown before.

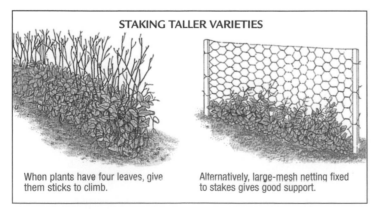

STAKING TALLER VARIETIES

When plants have four leaves, give them sticks to climb.

Alternatively, large-mesh netting fixed to stakes gives good support.

Varieties of Peas to Grow

Popular dwarf varieties of green peas include 'Little Marvel', which grows 15–20 inches tall; the smooth-seeded 'Maestro' and 'Improved Laxton's Progress'. Probably the best early main-crop variety, 'Improved Laxton's Progress' matures in about 55 days. Among recommended tall types are 'Wando', 30 inches tall, a heavy-yielding variety that will tolerate hot weather; 'Mr. Big'*,

30 inches tall, with 5-inch pods containing 8–10 very sweet peas. Good for late sowings; and 'Lincoln', which grows to 30 inches tall. Many rank this variety among the tastiest of peas. Good edible-pod peas are 'Oregon Giant', an early (60 days to maturity) variety that needs no staking; and 'Super Sugar Pod', a taller vine that needs support. Increasingly popular, the sugar-snap peas include 'Sugar Snap'*, a tall variety, and the dwarfs 'Sugar Ann'* and 'Sugar Sprint'.

Peppers

Pepper 'Ace'

There are two kinds of peppers: sweet and hot. Sweet peppers—also called bell peppers (for one of their characteristic shapes) or green peppers—may turn red, yellow, purple, or white when fully ripe. Hot peppers also are green at first, turning red, chocolate, or yellow as they mature. Like tomatoes and eggplants, peppers are warmth-loving vegetables; all three are similarly cultivated.

Seed catalogs list a dizzying variety of shapes and sizes for both sweet and hot peppers. Gardeners in areas with short growing seasons find it advisable to choose the early varieties, for even the earliest types need at least two months from the time young plants are set out to the time when peppers are mature enough to be harvested—and this does not include the eight weeks necessary to produce seedlings ready for transplanting outdoors.

How to Grow Peppers

Peppers can be started indoors from seeds about eight weeks before the date of the last expected frost. Sow the seeds in individual pots, placing three seeds, ¼ inch deep, in each pot. Keep the containers in a warm location—about 75°F.

When seedlings appear, move the pots to a place that is sunny as well as warm. When the plants are about an inch tall, remove all but the strongest one in each container.

Be especially careful in "hardening off" pepper plants—exposing them gradually to outdoor conditions. Do not plant outside until all risk of frost has passed and the nights are warm. Cold will slow the plants' growth and cause any flowers to abort.

Pepper seedlings are available at garden centers if you do not want to raise them yourself. Make certain that the plants you buy have short, sturdy stems and deep green leaves.

In planting peppers, avoid areas where you have previously grown tomatoes or eggplants, for all three vegetables are susceptible to similar diseases. Enrich the planting area with a 3- to 4-inch layer of organic matter, and work it into the top several inches of the soil. Space the rows 2 feet apart.

You can also prepare individual planting areas for the seedlings. Dig holes 6 inches deep and 6 inches in diameter. Put in a 2-inch layer of compost or rotted manure mixed with a handful of bone meal. Then fill the hole with soil.

Allow at least 2 feet in all directions between holes. Although it is not absolutely necessary, staking the plants will help keep them from toppling in strong winds. Set the stakes in position before you plant the seedlings.

When all danger of frost is past and daytime temperatures stay above 70°F, it is time to transplant your seedlings. Set them out on a cloudy day or in the evening, so that the sun will not scorch them. Allow 18 inches between seedlings in rows.

After planting, water the soil well, and immediately provide the plants with protection against insects and the elements.

Keep cutworms away by placing around each plant a collar made from a paper cup with its bottom removed. Shield the young plants against chilly rains or too much sun by covering them with translucent paper cups, which are available at most garden stores.

Peppers are not heavy feeders. If you have provided sufficient fertilizer before planting, you should not need to fertilize the soil again during the growing season.

Pepper plants require a moist soil for fruit formation; so cover the ground surrounding the plants with a mulch, and water regularly in dry weather. If weeds manage to grow through the mulch cover, pull them up carefully by hand.

Sweet peppers can be eaten at any stage of their growth. Full-size green peppers left on the plant will turn color and become slightly sweeter. Harvest them as you like or as you need them—but do not leave fully ripe peppers on the plant. Their presence will reduce its subsequent yield.

When harvesting peppers, always *cut* the fruit off its branch. If you try to pull off the pepper, you may break the branch.

Because peppers mature late in the season, frost may occur before you have harvested all the fruits. If cold weather threatens, protect the plants by covering them with plastic sheeting anchored to the ground with rocks or soil.

If the frost is not too severe, this measure may save the plants. Or, if the plants are nearing the end of fruit production, pull them up by the roots and hang them in a cool spot indoors. In this case, the peppers on the plant will continue to ripen for a few more days.

Hot peppers should be allowed to achieve full growth and flavor before harvesting. They will keep well if you thread a string through their stems and hang them indoors.

What Can Go Wrong With Peppers

Few pests attack peppers. If aphids appear, wash them away with a stream of water from the garden hose, or if necessary, spray the plants with insecticidal soap. If you see whiteflies, hang sticky traps, or spray with insecticidal soap.

Varieties of Peppers to Grow

'Ace' and 'Carmen'* are early sweet peppers. Later types include 'Big Bertha', 'Gypsy'* (yellow), 'Sweet Banana'* (yellow), and 'Sweet Chocolate' (brown). Popular hot peppers include 'Holy Molé'*, 'Habanero', 'Mariachi'*, and 'Hungarian Wax'.

Young potato foliage seldom survives freezing temperatures; so do not rush to plant unless your winter is very mild.

Potato flowers

Potatoes

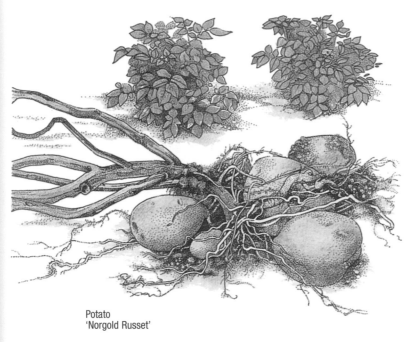

Potato
'Norgold Russet'

It takes quite a bit of garden space—and no small effort—to grow potatoes. But if you have lately sorted through soft, wrinkled potatoes in the market to find a few firm ones, you may be eager to try your hand at cultivating your own potato patch.

Potatoes will grow almost anywhere if they have plenty of sunshine and well-drained, fertile soil, rich in organic matter. In most parts of the country, three potato types can be planted: early, mid-season, and late. The former, for summer harvest and use, is generally lower yielding than the latter, which can be harvested in the fall and stored for winter use. In areas where winters are frost free and summers are very hot, only one crop is planted in fall or early winter.

How to Grow Potatoes

Potatoes are grown from those pieces of the tuber that contain the "eyes," the tiny depressions from which sprouts grow. These "seed" pieces, when planted, will produce leafy vines aboveground and clusters of potatoes below.

Do not use store-bought potatoes for seed, since they are often treated with a chemical that inhibits sprouting. You will be much surer of getting a good crop if you order certified disease-free seed potatoes from a seed company or buy them at a farm supply center.

Use the seed potatoes as they are, or cut them into 2-ounce pieces, each approximately the size of a large walnut. Make sure that each piece contains at least one eye (but preferably two). You will get best results if sprouts from the eyes are about ¾ inch long.

Cure the seed pieces by spreading them out in a bright, airy place until they dry slightly and their cut surfaces harden. Some gardeners dust the pieces with sulfur to prevent rot. If the eyes are properly dried and not stored in a humid place, however, the sulfur dusting will not be necessary.

Potatoes require acidic soil, tolerating soil with a pH as low as 4.8. Do not plant them in areas that have recently been limed.

An excellent way to prepare the soil for potatoes is to spread a 3- to 5-inch layer of well-rotted manure or rich compost over the area to be planted; this will serve to enrich the soil and to improve drainage. You can also supplement this by adding fish meal at a rate of 3 pounds per 100 square feet of planting area. Mix the amendments thoroughly into the top several inches of soil for best results.

As soon as the ground can be worked, plant the seed pieces in furrows 4 inches deep, 3 inches wide, and 3 feet apart. Set the pieces 12 inches apart, with eyes facing upward, and cover with about 3 inches of soil.

About three weeks after the seeds are planted, sprouts will push up through the ground. As the vines grow, mound up over them with earth, leaves, straw, or compost to keep the developing tubers covered. Potatoes that are exposed to sunlight turn green and develop a toxic substance called solanine. If there is any risk of night frost, cover with a layer of straw or newspapers.

It is not necessary to fertilize the plants again during the growing period, but be sure that the soil around them remains loose and free of weeds. To do this, cultivate with a hoe—shallowly because the tubers grow close to the surface.

You can start harvesting tubers at about the time the potato flowers bloom, seven to eight weeks after planting. Push aside the earth at the base of the plant, and carefully pick off some of the small potatoes.

These are the highly valued "new" potatoes, which you can boil and eat in their skins. Leave some potatoes to grow to full size.

When the plant foliage begins to wither and die down, the potatoes are full-grown. At this time, dig the tubers from the soil with a spading fork. Although you can leave potatoes in the ground for a time after the foliage has died, you should dig them up before the first heavy frost.

If you want to store potatoes, gently brush off any soil and put them loosely in a ventilated, covered container to dry for a few hours. (Never expose potatoes directly to sunlight.) Store them in a dark, cool (37°–40°F) place.

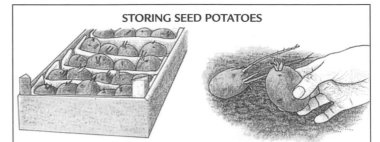

STORING SEED POTATOES

Set a single layer of seed potatoes, eyes uppermost, in a box. Store in a cool, bright place for about six weeks until they sprout.

New potatoes

New potatoes should be ready for harvesting in July.

Potatoes, Sweet

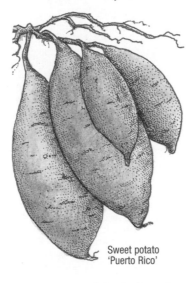

Sweet potato 'Puerto Rico'

Sweet potatoes thrive in long, hot summers, but they can be raised wherever they will have 150 frost-free days to grow in. Once planted, sweet potatoes produce their nutritious, flavorful roots with little further attention.

How to Grow Sweet Potatoes

Sweet potato vines are raised from the sprouts, or slips, that their tubers send out. One potato suspended on toothpicks in a container and half-covered with water will produce several sprouts. Larger quantities can be grown by placing several potatoes on a bed of sand and covering them with a 2-inch layer of moist sand or soil. Keep sprouting tubers at 75°F. Buy slips at a garden center if starting your own is not feasible.

Start the slips a month before warm weather settles in, when nights get no colder than 60°F. During that month the sprouts will grow to 8–10 inches, and each will bear several leaves. Remove the slips for planting by giving them a twist.

Sweet potatoes do best in loose, sandy soil. To prepare the soil, spread a 1- to 2-inch layer of compost and work it into the soil. Then push the soil into a foot-wide, flat-topped mound 6 inches high.

Plant the slips 15 inches apart in the center of the mound, and set them 6 inches into the ground, leaving at least two leaves aboveground. Water well.

Sweet potatoes require very little care. A bit of weeding, done carefully so as not to injure the shallow roots, is usually all that is needed.

When the tops of the plants turn black after the first frost, the sweet potatoes are ready to harvest. (In frost-free areas, harvest four months after planting the slips.) In areas with less than four months' growing time, tubers can be dug out before they reach mature size.

Dig sweet potatoes carefully, for their skins bruise easily. Let the tubers dry for several hours, and then spread them in newspaper-lined boxes. Leave them in a dry, warm area for about two weeks; then store in a cool, dry place (50°–55°F).

What Can Go Wrong With Sweet Potatoes

The sweet potato weevil feeds on the leaves of the vine, and its larvae tunnel into the tuber. To get rid of this pest, keep the ground clear of leaves and other debris when possible. Treat the soil with parasitic nematodes, and destroy infested potatoes.

Varieties of Sweet Potatoes to Grow

There are two types of sweet potato: dry-fleshed and moist-fleshed. In cool areas dry-fleshed varieties, such as 'Nemagold', 'Jersey Orange', and 'Nugget', are recommended. 'Centennial', 'Puerto Rico', 'Vardaman', and 'Beauregard' are popular moist-fleshed types.

What Can Go Wrong With Potatoes

You gain much protection against many of the diseases that infect potatoes when you use certified seed potatoes. You must keep in mind, however, that potatoes are susceptible to several soil-borne pests and diseases, so crop rotation is also essential.

Even then, your potatoes may fall victim to blight, a dry rot that first appears as purplish blotches on the leaves, which then turn brown and rot as do the tubers. To prevent blight, plant a resistant variety, such as 'Kennebec', or spray the potatoes with a copper-based fungicide at the first sign of infection.

Another common potato disease is scab. This is caused by an organism often present in sandy soils that have a high lime content. Prevent it by planting a scab-resistant variety such as 'Norland', and by keeping the soil acid.

The potato's worst insect enemy is the Colorado potato beetle. Both the adult beetle and its red larvae defoliate and destroy potato plants. Pick off the pests and remove egg masses by hand, or spray the plants with spinosad or *Beauveria bassiana*.

For battling aphids and leafhoppers, which can spread potato virus diseases, insecticidal soap is effective.

Varieties of Potatoes to Grow

Check with a garden center for the best varieties to grow in your area. Of the early potatoes, 'Caribe', 'Norgold Russet', and 'Norland' do well in most areas. 'Yukon Gold', an early to mid variety, stores well. Of the late potatoes, 'Desiree', 'Kennebec', and 'Russet Burbank' are popular. Try some of the varieties you do not find in the stores: 'Russian Banana', with slender tubers; and 'All Blue', with a pale lilac flesh.

Radishes

There are two distinct types of radish: the popular bright-red or white fast-maturing summer radish, and the slower-maturing, sharper-flavored winter radish, which has either a black or a white skin.

Children like to grow red radishes because the time between planting and eating them is so short—only three weeks for many varieties. Plant short rows—5 or 6 feet will produce all that the average family can consume during one crop's brief harvesting period. To ensure a supply all season long, however, make succession plantings every week or 10 days—except in midsummer, for radishes will not grow well when temperatures go above 80°F. In most areas a few succession crops can be planted in late summer for harvest before the ground freezes.

Winter radish varieties mature in 50 days or more, and they are planted in midsummer for fall use.

How to Grow Radishes

To prepare the soil for radishes, dig it to a depth of about 6 inches, and work in a 1- or 2-inch layer of compost or well-rotted manure. Or, the preceding fall, work some chopped leaves into the soil.

Sow the radish seeds directly into the garden as soon as the ground can be worked. The seeds are just large enough so that you can space them by hand when planting, and thus avoid much time-consuming thinning later on. In a ½-inch-deep furrow, put down one seed every ½ inch. Tamp the soil firmly over the seeds, and water gently.

You can save garden space by interplanting radishes in rows with slower-growing vegetables, such as carrots and parsnips.

The prime requirements for healthy radishes are water (a good soaking at least once a week, and more often during dry spells) and adequate growing space. Over-

For radishes to stay crisp and tender, the soil must always be kept uniformly moist.

Radish 'Cherry Belle'*

Radish 'Champion'*

Rhubarb

Although rhubarb is generally classified as a vegetable, its long, red, tart-flavored stalks are traditionally used as a fruit—in pies, cobblers, jams, and jellies, or simply stewed and served as a compote. Rhubarb lovers will want to allot space for this vegetable, whose foliage is as attractive as the stems are tasty.

Rhubarb is a long-lived perennial plant, and its cultivation is similar in many respects to that of another prized perennial vegetable, asparagus. Like asparagus, rhubarb is planted in beds that require a lot of preparation, but once the plants are established, they need a minimum of care and will produce for many years. Like asparagus, rhubarb needs a dormant period and grows best in areas where winters are cold enough to freeze the ground to a depth of at least 2 or 3 inches.

Rhubarb, like asparagus, grows well in almost any type of soil, but it is a heavy feeder and should not be planted in poor soil unless you are able to add copious quantities of organic material and fertilizer.

Rhubarb is seldom started from seeds. Instead, it is propagated by planting "crowns"—root divisions that carry the buds from which new plants will grow. Rhubarb crowns can be ordered from seed catalog companies, or you can buy the crowns from your local nursery or garden center.

Because rhubarb is a perennial plant, which inhabits the same piece of ground for many years, it should be given an isolated spot in your vegetable garden—in a corner, for example, or along one side—where it will not interfere with, or be damaged by, your work on annual crops.

crowded radish plants will not form the thick roots for which they are grown. No matter how carefully you have sown your seeds, you will probably have to thin the plants to achieve the optimum spacing of 1–2 inches between plants.

Weed often and carefully, remembering that radish roots grow close to the soil surface.

Depending on the variety, summer radishes mature in 20 to 30 days, and winter varieties in 50 to 75 days. The seed packet will tell you the best harvesting size for the variety you are growing. If radishes grow too large, they become tough and sharp-flavored. A cracked or split root means the vegetable is overage.

What Can Go Wrong With Radishes

Insects rarely attack the pungent radish. The main pest is a root maggot, which tunnels into the radish roots and is often in the soil where cabbage has previously grown. To combat this pest, sprinkle hot pepper over the soil surface. Or, cover the planting area with a floating row cover right after planting and leave it in place until harvest.

Flea beetles often attack radishes, feeding on the leaves, and can kill plants. Protect with a floating row cover.

Varieties of Radishes to Grow

Popular red summer radishes are 'Cherry Belle'* (matures in 22 days, and is ¾ inch in diameter), 'Comet'* (25 days, 1 inch), and 'Champion'* (28 days, 2 inches). 'White Icicle' (28 days, 5 inches long) is a mild, white summer radish, best eaten when young. 'French Breakfast' (25 days, 2 inches long) is red with a white tip. Good winter types are 'Round Black Spanish' (55 days, 3¼–4 inches in diameter) and 'White Chinese', also called 'Celestial' (60 days, 6–8 inches long).

Rhubarb 'Valentine'

Rhubarb

Rhubarb does best in productive soil improved with well-decayed compost or stable manure.

Spinach

How to Grow Rhubarb

Rhubarb plants need well-drained, fertile soil, and the ground has to be worked quite deeply. But rather than having to dig a row or trench, you need only make a hole for planting each crown.

Dig the holes 2 feet deep and 2 feet wide, and space them about 3 feet apart in all directions. Then fill the bottom of each hole with a 6-inch layer of compost or rotted manure. Mix the soil you have dug up with an equal amount of compost or rotted manure. Fill the hole with the enriched soil mixture to a depth of 1 foot.

In early spring place one rhubarb crown in each hole so that the top, where the plant buds are located, sits 3–4 inches below the soil surface. Tamp the soil firmly around the roots, and fill each hole with the compost and topsoil mixture until level with the surrounding soil.

When the first growth appears—and every succeeding spring as well—spread a ½-inch layer of compost around the shoots, and scratch it into the soil with a hand cultivator. Maintain a permanent mulch around each plant to help keep the soil moist and to prevent winter frost from setting in too hard around the roots. Remove the mulch before fertilizing, and afterward push it back in place.

Rhubarb plants produce seed stalks which, if allowed to flower, will reduce production of edible stalks. So, cut off seed stalks as soon as you see them.

What Can Go Wrong With Rhubarb

Rhubarb is relatively free from pests or diseases. The rhubarb curculio—a short, yellow, juice-sucking beetle—thrives in weedy patches, however. Keep the land weed free; pick any curculios off plants.

After several years, rhubarb plants tend to become crowded and the stalks grow noticeably thinner. At this point, dig up the plants and divide their roots. Do this in the spring when the new shoots are just beginning to emerge, or in early fall. Cut the roots into several parts, each of which should have one to three buds. Treat these sections as though they were new crowns, and plant them in another part of your garden. If you plant the crowns in the fall, mulch heavily.

Rhubarb stalks grow to 18 inches or taller. If your plants are of mature size, harvest a few stalks in spring the second year after planting. Beginning the third year, harvest about half the stalks, leaving the thinner ones, which will grow and nourish the roots.

Harvest rhubarb by holding the stalk near the base and twisting it off. Do not eat the rhubarb leaves; they are mildly poisonous.

Forcing rhubarb in winter. If you would like to enjoy rhubarb in winter, try this easy forcing method: In the fall, after the tops have died down, dig up a whole plant and place it in a tub 18 inches in diameter, which you have filled with topsoil, compost, and well-rotted manure. Leave the tub outside for several weeks of freezing weather, and then move it to a dark, cool place. Keep the soil moist. About a month before you plan to harvest, move the tub into a warm area (60°F is best), still in the dark. The dormant roots will begin to sprout, and you can harvest when the stalks are about 18 inches tall.

Varieties of Rhubarb to Grow

'Canada Red' and 'Valentine' are standard red-stemmed rhubarb varieties. 'Victoria' has green, rather than red, stalks. For areas where the winters are relatively mild, 'Cherry Red' is recommended.

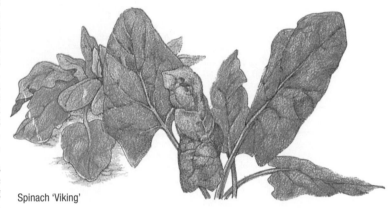

Spinach 'Viking'

Spinach, chard, and mustard greens belong to a group of vegetables loosely referred to as greens because they are grown for their tender, vitamin-rich leaves and stems. (Greens also include kale and collards, discussed on pp. 461–462, and turnip greens, discussed on p. 482.)

Spinach grows well only in cool regions. In warmer areas gardeners often substitute Malabar spinach or New Zealand spinach, both of which are unrelated to true spinach but taste somewhat like it and are used like it. Chard (or Swiss chard) is a relative of the beet but is grown for its tops only. It is easy to grow and prolific. Mustard greens have a piquant flavor and mature quickly.

Spinach, Swiss chard, and mustard greens have the same soil and nutrient needs: a nonacid soil (with a pH of 6.0–7.5) enriched with organic matter and high in nitrogen. With the exception of Swiss chard and Malabar and New Zealand spinach, greens are cool-weather crops; in hot weather they will "bolt" (produce seeds and stop growing). Greens are resistant to cold and, if they are given a thick mulch cover, will thrive through a few light frosts.

How to Grow Spinach, Chard, and Mustard Greens

To prepare beds, dig the soil as soon as the ground can be worked, adding 1 bushel of rotted manure or compost for every 50 square feet, plus a few handfuls of fish meal.

Planting and tending spinach. Sow spinach seeds in furrows ½ inch deep, spacing the rows about 15 inches apart. Because spinach matures quickly—in 40 to 50 days—and bolts easily, plant short rows, and make succession sowings every 10 days until daytime temperatures reach a consistent 70°F. Start succession plantings again in late August for harvesting through the fall.

Thin the newly emerged seedlings to stand 3 inches apart. When the leaves of plants touch, pull up every other plant, and use it for salad. The final thinning should leave the plants about 10 inches apart.

When the plants are 6–8 inches high, water them well with a fish fertilizer solution. Weed regularly, and keep the plants thoroughly watered.

Begin culling the outside leaves as soon as they reach edible size. Harvest the entire plant when buds start to form in its center.

In order to stimulate further growth, pluck the leaves of spinach as soon as they are big enough.

Spinach 'Tyee'

Squash and Pumpkins

Squash 'Zucchini Select'

Planting and tending Malabar and New Zealand spinach. Malabar spinach is a glossy-leaved vine that does well in extremely hot weather. Trained to grow up a fence or trellis, it takes very little space and produces edible leaves in about 70 days. When all danger of frost is past, sow the seeds ½ inch deep and about 3 inches apart.

New Zealand spinach also does well in warm weather. Sow the seeds in pots indoors, first soaking the seeds overnight. Leave them in a cool place, and when sprouts appear, clip off all but the single strongest seedling in each pot. Set the plants out about two weeks before the last expected frost.

New Zealand spinach can spread 3–4 feet across; so give it plenty of room—18 inches between plants in rows 3 feet apart. About 60 to 70 days after planting outdoors, the leaves nearest the growing tips, and the tips themselves, can be cut off and eaten. The more you cut, the more the plant will grow.

Planting and tending chard. Beginning about 60 days after sowing, Swiss chard will produce greens generously all summer long. Around the time of the last frost, sow the

seeds (which are actually clusters of several seeds) in furrows ½ inch deep and 30 inches apart. Space these seedballs about 3 inches apart, and when the seedlings appear, thin the young plants to stand 6 inches apart. When the leaves of plants touch, pull out every other plant; you can eat the plants you remove.

Mulch the ground and fertilize at least once during the season by watering the plants thoroughly with a fish fertilizer solution.

To harvest Swiss chard, cut off the outer leaves near the base of the plant; new leaves will develop at the center. Pick often while chard leaves are young.

Planting and tending mustard greens. Plant mustard greens in prepared soil early in the spring and, in areas with mild winters, in September or October. Sow the seeds 1–1½ inches apart, in furrows ½ inch deep and about 15 inches apart. When seedlings appear, thin them to stand 6 inches apart. Make several succession sowings in the early spring and one or two in late summer. Mustard greens should be harvested in 35 to 40 days, before the plants are full-grown, or they may go to seed.

What Can Go Wrong With Spinach

Spinach is often afflicted with a mosaic virus, or blight, that causes the leaves to yellow; to avoid it, buy

resistant varieties. If aphids attack, it is best to spray the plant with insecticidal soap. Handpick and destroy the leaves attacked by leaf miners. Leaf miners also sometimes infest chard.

Varieties of Greens to Grow

Popular varieties of spring spinach include 'Bloomsdale Longstanding' and 'America'*, both crinkly leaved ("savoyed") types, and 'Melody'*, a smooth-leaved variety. 'Tyee' and 'Winter Bloomsdale' can be planted either in spring or in fall. Look for New Zealand and Malabar spinach under "Spinach" in seed catalogs.

Among Swiss chard varieties, 'Fordhook Giant', with dark green leaves, and 'Lucullus', with lighter ones, are popular. 'Bright Lights'* is multicolored with stalks of gold, pink, orange, purple, and white. Leaves may be green or bronze. Of the mustard greens, 'Savanna' is the fastest growing—about 35 days to harvest. 'Green Wave' matures in 45 days and has frilly leaves, deeply cut.

Despite their difference in taste and appearance, the two main types of squash, summer and winter, are closely related botanically and are grown and cultivated in the same way. Along with melons and cucumbers, they belong to the gourd family, all members of which need a lot of room to grow.

Summer squashes usually grow as sprawling bush plants. Their fruits are harvested long before they reach maturity, while their skins, which may be green, yellow, white, or striped, are still tender and edible. Many summer squashes are cylindrical in shape.

Most winter squashes grow as vines, requiring even more space than summer squashes. They are left on the vine until fully mature; by then, their rinds are tough and generally inedible. Fruits come in several colors that may change with maturity, and may be squat, long, round, or onion shaped. Skin may be smooth or ridged. Properly stored, winter squashes can be kept throughout the winter.

Pumpkins and inedible ornamental gourds fall into the winter squash category.

Pumpkins are simply a kind of squash—some of them growing as bushes, others as vines. Like winter squashes, they are allowed to mature before harvesting.

The types of squash seem infinite. Summer squashes include yellow squash, either "crookneck" or "straightneck"; zucchini, or green squash; and the white or pale green scallop squash. Most summer varieties can be picked within 50 to 60 days after planting.

The earliest-maturing winter squashes are acorn and butternut, which are ready to be picked in 75 to 85 days. The turban-shaped buttercup squash matures in about 100 days. Slate-gray or green Hubbard squash, which can grow to enormous size, is ready for harvest in about 110 days. Pumpkins ripen in 90 to 120 days.

All squashes need a rich, loamy soil that will retain moisture, and grow best when nutrients are added in the form of humus or fertilizer. Regular watering is essential for summer squash after transplanting and during flowering and fruiting. The deeper-rooted winter squash needs watering only in dry weather.

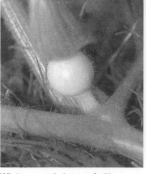

Zucchini and pumpkins are harvested when they are still immature. Pumpkins must be allowed to ripen before storage, however.

Winter squash (young fruit) Pumpkin 'Baby Bear' Zucchinis 'Seneca'

Pumpkin 'Baby Bear'*

How to Grow Squash and Pumpkin

Squash is usually planted in mounds of earth called hills. To prepare a hill, dig a hole 12–18 inches deep and about 2 feet in diameter.

Fill the bottom of the hole with compost or well-rotted manure to a depth of 4–6 inches. Then shovel the excavated soil back into the hole, piling it in until it forms a soil mound about 6–8 inches high. Space the hills 4–6 feet apart for bush varieties and 8–10 feet apart for vine plants, including pumpkins.

Squash can be sown outdoors at the same time that tomato and eggplant seedlings are set out—when night temperatures remain above 55°F. Hasten germination by soaking the seeds overnight before planting.

Sow six seeds per hill, about 1 inch deep. When the seedlings are approximately 6 inches tall, thin them to the two or three strongest plants in each hill.

Squash seeds can also be sown indoors, about three to four weeks earlier. Simply place two or three seeds on their sides in small pots of soil mix, cover, and water well. Choose the strongest seedlings for transplanting. Seedlings can be set back by transplanting, however, and you must be very careful not to disturb their roots.

If you have provided sufficient compost or manure during soil preparation, you should not have to add fertilizer. But if you are not sure that your squash has enough nutrients, sidedress with a balanced organic fertilizer around each plant when it has put out a few leaves.

Like other gourd family members, squash needs a lot of moisture. Water the plants slowly and deeply during dry spells, but resist the temptation to soak them constantly.

Mulching is especially beneficial; besides keeping the soil moist and weeds down, a layer of mulch under the vines protects the fruits against insects and keeps them from rotting.

Squash vines can be pruned if you find that they are invading other areas of your garden. At the time that you see small fruits on the vines, cut off the ends of the long runners, making sure that you have left sufficient leaves to nourish the plant. Remove any foliage that might deprive the fruits of sunlight.

To harvest squash, cut off the fruits with a small knife. A summer squash should be cut when it is still small and when you can easily pierce its skin with a fingernail. Pick elongated squashes when they are 1½–2 inches in diameter; pick scallops when they are 3–4 inches across.

Winter varieties should be left on the vine until their rinds are hard. Cure them in the sun or in a warm, ventilated area for a week or so; then store them in a dry place where the temperature is 55°–60°F.

What Can Go Wrong With Squash and Pumpkin

Squash and pumpkin are subject to the same diseases that attack cucumbers and melons.

Striped cucumber beetles feed on the leaves and roots and can spread a bacterial disease that causes the plants to wilt and die. Cover young plants with floating row covers. Destroy the adult beetles by spraying unprotected plants with pyrethrins.

Squash vine borers hatch from eggs laid at the plants' base and tunnel into the stalks. The most effective treatment is to wrap nylon stockings around the base, but if the borers hatch and tunnel into the plants, cut them out with a knife.

There is no treatment for fusarium wilt, a fungal disease, but it can be prevented by crop rotation.

If powdery mildew should appear on the leaves, cut off the affected shoots, and spray regularly with a potassium bicarbonate spray.

HARVESTING TIPS

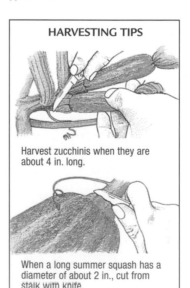

Harvest zucchinis when they are about 4 in. long.

When a long summer squash has a diameter of about 2 in., cut from stalk with knife.

Varieties of Squash and Pumpkin to Grow

Popular summer squashes include yellow 'Goldrush'* and 'Black Beauty' (both zucchini types); and 'Peter Pan'*. All are bush types.

Recommended winter squash vine varieties include 'Blue Hubbard' (15 pounds); 'Table Queen' (1–2 pounds); 'Sunshine'* (2–4 pounds); and 'Bonbon'* (4–5 pounds). Bush types include 'Gold Nugget' (2 pounds) and 'Sweet Dumpling', with 4-inch fruit on short vines.

Among pumpkins, 'Baby Bear'* grows to an 8-inch diameter and is especially good for pies. 'Sorcerer'*, a semi-vine type can reach up to 25 pounds in weight, and can be carved or used for pies.

A good semi-bush variety is 'Orange Smoothie'*, ideal for carving, painting, or decoration.

Leaf curl

Late blight

Poor growing conditions can cause leaf curl, which is often only temporary. Late blight is a fungal disease.

Tomatoes

Tomato 'Small Fry Hybrid'

The tomato has for some time been the most popular plant in the home vegetable garden, and seed catalogs devote more space to it than any other vegetable.

The popularity of this easy-to-grow plant has encouraged seed developers to come up with hundreds of new varieties—in shapes, sizes, and colors that the early Mexican Indians (who grew *tomatl* long before Europeans set foot on their soil) would have difficulty recognizing. More important than the look or taste of the new tomatoes, however, is the fact that a large number of them are hybrid varieties, bred to resist the soil-borne diseases to which tomatoes are particularly vulnerable.

Seed catalog listings always include information about the disease or pest resistance of each variety: the letter V means the tomato plant is resistant to verticillium wilt; F stands for fusarium wilt resistance; N, for nematode resistance. Both verticillium and fusarium cause wilting of the tomato leaves. Nematodes are microscopic worms that destroy the plant's root system. Buying resistant seeds will not guarantee healthy tomato plants, but it will give your plants a far better chance to grow until harvest time.

Tomato varieties are divided into two broad groups—early and main season. Early tomatoes are usually determinate: that is, they grow to a certain size, produce a crop, and then die. They do not have to be supported. Main-season tomatoes are almost always indeterminate: they will continue to grow and bear indefinitely, until frost kills them. And although they will produce if left to sprawl along the ground, the crop will be more vulnerable to diseases and insects, and it will not ripen as fast as it does when the plants are properly staked and firmly supported.

Because tomatoes are highly sensitive to cold, gardeners in areas with short growing seasons should plant a few early tomatoes, as well as a main crop. In all but the warmest areas of the country, tomatoes are set out as seedlings; and the number of days to maturity given in seed catalogs is always counted from the time plants are set out in the garden.

How to Grow Tomatoes

Tomato seeds should be sown indoors about eight weeks before the date of the last expected frost in your area. Sow them $\frac{1}{8}$ inch deep in flats or pots, and when the seedlings are about 1 inch tall, transplant them to individual 3- or 4-inch pots.

Keep the seedlings moist and set them in a warm, sunny spot. Be sure to harden them off before transplanting them outdoors.

If you do not want to start your own tomato plants, seedlings are available at garden centers. Ask your nurseryperson which types would grow best in your area, and choose sturdy plants in uncrowded flats.

Find out, too, whether the tomatoes have been hardened off. If they have not, you will have to do the job.

Soil preparation is important for a good tomato crop. The fall before you plant, dig your tomato plot, and work it several inches deep, incorporating a 2-inch layer of compost or organic matter into the soil. In early spring, rake in a balanced organic fertilizer at the suggested label rate.

If you have not prepared the soil this way, dig a hole for each plant— 6 inches deep and 2 feet in diameter for early tomatoes, 3 feet for later ones. In the bottom of each hole place a 2-inch layer of compost mixed with a handful of balanced organic fertilizer and some of the topsoil you have dug up.

Supporting tomatoes. If you plan to use a trellis or stakes, set them into the ground before planting. The most popular form of support is a tall stake driven into the ground next to each plant. As the plant grows, the stem is tied loosely to the stake with soft twine or cloth strips. Tall-growing tomato plants will have to be tied several times.

There are other methods of supporting tomatoes: try a 6-foot-high trellis made of chicken wire, running the length of the row; or set posts at the ends of the row, run a wire between them, or use tomato cages available at garden centers. All these techniques serve the same aims: to support the plants as they grow and to keep the tomatoes off the ground and exposed to the sun so that they ripen faster.

Smaller, determinate varieties need not be staked, but it is advisable to keep them off the ground. One way to do this is to place a 36-inch-high, 18-inch-diameter wire-mesh cage around each plant after setting it into the ground. Make sure the mesh cage has at least 6-inch openings so that the branches can grow through them. Secure the enclosure with a stout stake driven about 6 inches into the ground.

Another way to keep low-growing tomatoes off the ground is to spread mulch around each plant (black plastic sheeting serves well, too) while it is still small, to protect the fruits from soil pests.

Planting and tending tomatoes. Set out your tomato seedlings when nighttime temperatures are fairly

The range of varieties available at garden centers is usually restricted. To get more unusual ones, grow them from seed.

'Gardener's Delight'   'Sweet Million'   'Husky Gold'

sure to remain above 55°F. Seedlings should be spaced 2 feet apart for early tomatoes and 3 feet apart for main-season types, in rows at least 3 feet apart. Alternatively, plant the seedlings in holes prepared as described above.

Set each plant deeply in the ground, burying most of the stem; the stem will produce roots and anchor the plant firmly. Plant tall, lanky seedlings on their sides, placing the entire stem up to the top leaves underground.

Immediately after planting, do the following: (1) give the seedlings a boost with 1 cupful of compost; (2) protect each plant with a cutworm collar, which you can make by removing the bottom from a paper cup, and set the collar into the soil about 1 inch deep; (3) listen for cold-weather warnings, and if a late frost seems imminent, cover the plants at night.

If you do not enrich the soil before planting, feed tomatoes weekly by spraying foliage with a seaweed solution.

Cover the ground with a thick mulch of grass clippings mixed with straw or chopped leaves to help keep the soil moist and prevent weed growth.

To keep indeterminate plants from making too much leafy growth, prune them to a single main stem by breaking off side shoots as soon as they appear.

You will notice these side "suckers" growing between the main stem and the leaf stem. Cut them out while they are small. And if you see additional suckers growing from the base of the stem, remove them too.

Tomato plants need at least an inch of water per week; so water them well, especially during dry spells. Continue looking for and eliminating sucker growth and tying staked tomatoes as they grow taller.

Harvesting tomatoes. Given warm weather and abundant rainfall, tomatoes ripen in 60 to 85 days from the time seedlings are set out. When the fruits begin to turn red, check the plants every day, and pick those tomatoes that are fully red (or yellow, if you are growing a yellow variety) and are firm but not hard. Overripe tomatoes will fall off and rot quickly.

A very light frost will usually kill a few leaves, but the plant itself will continue to grow and produce. However, anything more severe than a touch of frost is likely to kill the entire plant. If you hear that frost is coming, protect each plant by draping it in plastic sheeting or old bed sheets; or you can pull up each plant by its roots and hang it upside down in your cellar until the fruit ripens.

Neither method is guaranteed to work, and in cool areas an early frost almost always means the end of tomato harvesting.

Unripened tomatoes need not go to waste, however. Pick them and ripen them quickly in a warm place, or wrap them individually in newspaper, and store in a cool, dark place for slower ripening. Also, check your cookbooks for ways to use green tomatoes.

PRUNING TOMATOES

Cut out or twist off suckers while they are small.

When six trusses of fruit have formed, cut off the growing point.

STAKING PLANTS

Tie tomato stems to stakes with soft twine or cloth.

Or as plants grow, twist them around string attached to an overhead wire.

What Can Go Wrong With Tomatoes

Tomatoes are prey to many insects and diseases, but if you raise your crop in rich, properly prepared soil (preferably where no tomatoes were grown the year before), you may reduce the damage.

Look for green tomato hornworms in areas where the leaves are tattered, and pick them off by hand. If aphids attack, spray the plants with a strong stream of water from the hose or with insecticidal soap.

Tomato blight is a fungal disease that first manifests itself in large, dark green wet spots on the leaves. A whitish growth appears on the undersides of leaves and on the petioles and stems. The fungus spreads rapidly and can kill the plant. Prevent it by spraying with a copper-based fungicide every 10 to 14 days from the time that fruits first appear. Blossom-end rot shows itself as a leathery scar or a patch of rot on the blossom end of the fruit. It is usually related to a lack of soil calcium and moisture and can be prevented by liming and watering.

Tomato Varieties to Grow

Many varieties have inbred resistance to certain diseases. Seed catalogs show this with letters after the name—A, alternaria fungus (early blight); C, cladiosporum (leaf mold); F, fusarium wilt, race 1; FF, fusarium wilt, races 1 and 2; N, nematodes; S, stemphylium (leaf spot); T, tobacco mosaic virus; V, verticillium wilt. Days to maturity are in parentheses.

Some good early varieties include 'Early Girl' VFF (52), indeterminate; 'First Lady' VFFNT (60), indeterminate; 'Oregon Spring' V (58), determinate. Next to ripen are 'Betterboy' VFN (70), indeterminate.

Main-season varieties generally have larger fruit and include 'Big Beef' VFFNTSA (73), indeterminate; 'Celebrity'* VFFNTA (72), determinate; and 'Golden Boy' A (80), indeterminate with yellow flesh.

Other popular varieties include the paste tomato 'Roma' and cherry tomatoes 'Sweet Million'. Heirloom varieties without the built-in disease resistance are becoming increasingly available. Check with local growers or farmers' markets.

Turnips and Rutabagas

Turnips 'Just Right'
'Tokyo Cross'

Rutabaga
'Laurentian'

Turnips are small-rooted vegetables, closely related to the large-rooted rutabagas (also known as swede turnips). Turnip roots taste best when they are about 2 inches in diameter and are good for cooking straight from the garden. Turnips are also grown for their nutritious leaves. The roots of the rutabaga can reach 5 or 6 inches in diameter and will keep for months in storage.

Both turnips and rutabagas are cool-weather vegetables and are commonly grown as fall crops. Turnips can also be planted in early spring, but they tend to "bolt," or produce seeds, and turn woody during hot weather.

Because they are planted in summer, turnips and rutabagas have the advantage of being suitable as succession crops in the space, for example, where you have finished

How to Grow
Turnips and Rutabagas

To prepare the soil for turnips and rutabagas, dig it up and rake it thor-

harvesting spinach, peas, or early potatoes. If you fertilized the soil heavily for the earlier crop, you will need to add very little additional fertilizer. Neither turnips nor rutabagas do well in acid soil, however; so if you find that the pH of your soil is less than 5.5, rake in a scattering of ground limestone as long before planting time as possible.

Depending on the variety, turnips need six to eight weeks to grow to maturity; rutabagas, about three months. Turnips are usually planted in midsummer for harvesting in midfall. There are several turnip varieties that withstand some warm weather and can be planted in early spring. Rutabagas can be planted only once, in early summer. Turnip varieties grown for greens alone are planted in early spring, but can also be grown for roots where summers are cool.

oughly. If the soil has not been fertilized for a previous crop, spread a 1-inch layer of compost over the planting area, and rake it in.

Sow the seeds in shallow furrows,

about ½ inch deep, in rows 1–2 feet apart. To prevent the soil from crusting, which makes it difficult for seedlings to break through, cover the seeds with a mixture of sand and soil.

As soon as the seedlings germinate, thin them to stand about 1 inch apart. A later, second thinning when the plants are 3–4 inches tall should leave turnips standing 4 inches apart, rutabagas 5 inches apart.

Feeding turnips during their growing period is not usually necessary; but if you have not fertilized, or if the plants are not thriving, try watering them with a solution of fish emulsion or compost tea, or apply a foliar spray of seaweed solution.

As with all root crops, turnips and rutabagas must be kept weed free so that their roots can develop normally. A light mulch will help smother weeds as well as retain moisture in the soil. Weeds should be pulled by hand or hoed out carefully to avoid disturbing the tops of the roots, which grow close to the surface and sometimes push through it.

What Can Go Wrong With
Turnips and Rutabagas

The maggots that attack cabbage sometimes infest the roots of turnips and rutabagas. To avoid maggot problems, cover areas planted with turnips or rutabagas immediately after sowing seeds and keep plants covered until harvest. If plants are uncovered, try dusting hot pepper on the soil surface around them to repel the flies.

Look for aphids on the undersides of the leaves. If you see them feasting there, blast them off with a hard stream of water. Insecticidal soap will kill the aphids.

Striped flea beetles can eat hundreds of tiny holes in leaves. To combat them, spray leaves with kaolin clay. Another option is to introduce some repellent plants, such as garlic.

Turnips are at their tenderest when they are 2–3 inches in diameter. If left to grow much beyond this size, they become hard and lose their flavor. Although turnips grow sweeter with a slight touch of frost, they must be harvested before hard frost sets into the ground. Store the turnips that you cannot use right away by burying them in moist sand and keeping them in a cool place.

Turnip leaves, or tops, can be harvested whenever they reach edible size. You can use the tops from thinnings or cut larger leaves from more mature plants. If you want a root harvest as well, cut only a few leaves from each plant.

Rutabagas are ready to eat when they reach a 3-inch diameter, but they can be left to grow until they are much larger. Their flesh coarsens, however, if they grow beyond 5 or 6 inches in diameter. They keep well in storage, placed in moist sand in a cool place. They can also be left, well mulched, in the ground in freezing weather and dug up later.

Varieties of Turnips
and Rutabagas to Grow

Popular turnip varieties include 'Purple-Top White Globe', which has a purplish-red root top and matures in about 55 days; 'Tokyo Cross'*, a pure white turnip that matures in about 35 days; 'Just Right'*, which is mature in 60 days when grown for its roots, in 30 days when grown for its tops. 'Purple-Top White Globe' and 'Tokyo Cross' are slow to bolt and good for early planting.

Turnips grown primarily for greens include 'Foliage' ('Shogoin'), whose tops mature in 30 days, and 'Seven Top', ready in 45 days.

Among the most popular rutabagas are the yellow-fleshed 'Laurentian' and 'Altasweet' and the white-fleshed 'Macomber'. All of these should be ready to harvest in about three months.

Nature's bounty of herbs provides wonderful accents to meats, vegetables, oils, and vinegars. Any dwelling, rural or urban, large or small, can be home to an herb garden—preferably close to the kitchen for easy access.

HERBS

Growing herbs is a practical pleasure—
they are handsome and fragrant in the
garden, indispensable in the kitchen,
easy to grow, and fascinating to study.

The gardening of herbs is as old as civilization.
The earliest known writings of nearly every culture include references to herbs used for preparing
and preserving food, scenting the air, or treating
wounds and illness. The roots of modern medicine—
in fact, of modern science itself—can be traced back
to the herb gardens of medicine men, witches, and
sorcerers and were nurtured through the ages by the
systematic studies of herbalists. Some of the plants
prescribed nearly 2,000 years ago are used in drugs
prescribed by modern doctors for the same ills—
although they are no longer boiled in wine or infused
with honey, as was once recommended.

Most herbs are tough, wild plants that have
changed remarkably little despite centuries of cultivation. Almost all of them do best in sunny
locations and fertile, well-drained soil, but some will
survive in partial shade and poor soil.

Herbs can occupy their own part of the garden—by
tradition near the kitchen door—or they can be
grown with other plants. Herb gardens are often
arranged in intricate patterns to accentuate the contrasting colors and textures of their foliage.

To avoid confusion when sprouts come up, label
each bed carefully. Better still, draw a precise map
of your planting pattern. Plan the beds so that
the taller plants do not cast shade on the low-growing ones.

Companion planting. Many aromatic herbs, such
as mint, parsley, sage, and rosemary, tend to repel
certain insect pests and are thus valuable garden
companions for vulnerable plants. Hyssop, balm, dill,
and thyme, on the other hand, are among the herbs
that attract bees—which serve to pollinate other
plants. Also, the leaves or roots of several herbs
exude substances that tend to promote, or sometimes to inhibit, the development of various nearby
plants. Green beans, for example, are improved by
the proximity of summer savory but are inhibited by
chives or any other allium. Dill is said to be a good
companion to members of the cabbage family; but if
it is allowed to flower close to carrots, it is reputed to
release a substance into the soil that may reduce the
size of the carrot crop.

Winter supplies. Many herbs can be grown indoors
during the winter, in pots or boxes near a sunny window. Grow such perennials as marjoram, chives,
mint, and winter savory from divisions or cuttings
taken in the fall. Basil, dill, parsley, and other annuals
can be started from seeds sown in pots outdoors in
late summer and brought inside in autumn. Use light,
freely draining potting soil, and water as needed.

The lemony taste of balm blends well with fish. It attracts bees to the garden to pollinate other plants.

Balm

Herbs You Can Grow

Angelica
(*Angelica archangelica*)

Spectacular tall border plant, particularly if allowed to reach its full height and to bear clusters of greenish-white flowers in late spring of its second year. Yellowish-green leaves grow to 2 ft. long. If flower heads are removed, plant will grow on as perennial; if not, it will die back after flowering.
Uses: Cut and candy young stems to decorate cakes and pastry. Blanch midribs of leaves for use in salads, as you would celery. Chopped leaves can replace some of sugar in fruit pies. Brew seeds into sweetish tea.
Type: Biennial or perennial.
Height: 4–7 ft. **Spread:** 3 ft.
Location: Partial shade, in moist, rich soil.
Planting: In late summer sow groups of 3 or 4 fresh seeds 2 ft. apart. When seedlings have 3 or 4 leaves, thin each group to only 1 strong young plant.

Harvesting: Cut young stems in spring of second year, before flowering. Take leaves all summer, seeds when ripe in late summer.
Preserving: Crystallize stems in saturated sugar syrup.
Propagation: Sowing fresh seeds is essential for good germination. Plant self-sows abundantly if allowed to set seed and die back as biennial.

Anise
(*Pimpinella anisum*)

Originated in the Middle East, where it is grown today as a commercial crop. Small white flowers bloom in midsummer, followed by tiny licorice-flavored fruits called aniseed. A favorite spice of ancient Romans, who collected it from their colonies in payment of taxes and who ate cakes flavored with aniseed to cure indigestion. Common constituent of cough medicines and of ointments that relieve itching.
Uses: Aniseed adds rich flavor to cookies, cakes, candies, bread, and applesauce. Widely used in Indian curries and stews. Flavors the liqueurs anisette and absinthe. Use fresh leaves in salads.
Type: Hardy annual.
Height: 18 in. **Spread:** 9–12 in.
Location: Warmth and sun, in light, well-drained soil.
Planting: Sow seeds in midspring, ½ in. deep in rows 12–18 in. apart. Thin established seedlings to 9 in.

Harvesting: About 1 mo. after flowering, when seeds are ripe but have not fallen, cut flower heads into paper bag. Thresh by hand over sheet of paper.
Preserving: Allow seeds to dry, and store in closed, dry container.
Propagation: From seeds.

Balm
(*Melissa officinalis*)

Often called lemon balm because of fragrance of its light green leaves. Small white or pale yellow flowers appear in late summer and early fall, and are highly attractive to bees—thus the generic name, *Melissa,* from the Greek for "honeybees."
Uses: Leaves lend gentle lemonish flavor to puddings, soups, stuffings, punch, and other summer drinks. Pleasant garnish for fish and shellfish. Brew leaves to make excellent mild tea, which acts as gentle sedative. Like angelica, can replace some of sugar in fruit pies.
Type: Hardy perennial.
Height: 2–4 ft. **Spread:** 12–18 in.
Location: Sun or partial shade, in any soil having good drainage.
Planting: Sow tiny seeds in pot in late spring. Thin established seedlings to 2 in. apart. When they are about 4 in. tall, plant in garden, 1 ft. apart. Set out nursery-grown plants in midspring.

Harvesting: Cut shoots individually as soon as flowers appear, continuing until midfall.
Preserving: Dry or freeze leaves.
Propagation: Divide in spring. Cut root clumps into several pieces, each with 3 or 4 buds, and plant 12 in. apart in rows spaced 18 in. apart.

Basil
(*Ocimum basilicum*)

Perennial in its native tropics; grows as annual in temperate climates. Shiny green leaves, 1–2 in. long, have scent like cloves and are attractive in herb gardens or borders. Repellent to mosquitoes; good companion for tomato plants. White or purplish flower spikes in late summer. Miniature variety, *O. basilicum minimum*, only 1 ft. high, makes good pot plant.
Uses: Leaves have warm, spicy flavor. Use sparingly in soups, sauces, salads, omelets, and with meat, poultry, and fish. Basis for pesto.
Type: Tender annual.
Height: 1–2 ft. **Spread:** 1 ft.
Location: Sun, in light, rich soil.
Planting: Sow seeds near sunny window or in greenhouse in early spring. Transplant to garden in early summer. Or sow seeds directly in garden in late spring.

Harvesting: For immediate use, take as needed all but 2 or 3 leaves at base of each branch before flowers bloom. Remove flower buds to encourage leaf growth. To obtain larger sections for preserving, cut plants to 6 in. once or twice.
Preserving: Dry or freeze. Leaves can also be puréed with olive oil, kept refrigerated in jars, or frozen with oil topping.
Propagation: From seeds.

Bay leaves have a stronger flavor when dried, so use them in moderation.

Sweet bay

Bay, Sweet
(Laurus nobilis)

This is the laurel tree of ancient Greece, whose leaves were woven into wreaths to honor heroes; do not confuse it with the native American mountain laurel (*Kalmia latifolia*), whose leaves are toxic. On its native Mediterranean shores it grows to 60 ft. tall; in North America it is often only a shrub. Where hardy (Zone 8), an attractive lawn or background plant, with dark, glossy foliage. Elsewhere, can be grown in pot or tub and taken indoors in winter; trim 2 or 3 times during growing season.
Uses: Powerful seasoning. Use 1 leaf, whole, in stews, casseroles, or meat sauces. Put leaves in stored grain or flour to repel insects.
Type: Shrub.
Height: 14 ft. **Spread:** 14 ft.
Location: Sun or partial shade, sheltered, in well-drained soil.
Planting: Where hardy, put out young plants in early autumn or mid-spring.

Harvesting: Pick leaves as needed.
Preserving: Dry in dark. Spread leaves between sheets of absorbent paper, using board on top as press. Or dry quickly in warm oven.
Propagation: Take semi-hard cuttings in late summer (see p. 259).

Borage
(Borago officinalis)

Produces pendent, star-shaped flowers of sky-blue, lavender, or pink, with pleasant odor; attractive to bees. Medieval herbals prescribed tea brewed from plant's large, blue-green leaves as source of courage. (One said that syrup concocted from its flowers "purgeth melancholy and quieteth the lunatick person.") Good companion plant for strawberries and in fruit orchards. Repellent to tomato worms.
Uses: Pick young leaves to use in salads for their cool cucumber flavor. Candy flowers for pastry decoration, or float in wine or punch.
Type: Hardy annual.
Height: 1–3 ft. **Spread:** 2 ft.
Location: Full sun or partial shade, in any well-drained soil.
Planting: Sow seeds in late fall or early spring, ½ in. deep in rows 18 in. apart. Thin established seedlings to 12 in. apart.

Harvesting: First leaves can be picked about 6 wk. after seeds germinate. Pick flowers as they appear or just before they open.
Preserving: No satisfactory method for leaves. To candy flowers, dip in beaten egg white, then in sugar, and dry them.
Propagation: From seeds. If flowers are left on, will self-sow.

Burnet
(Sanguisorba minor)

Attractive bedding or container plant, also known as salad burnet. Tiny reddish flowers open in thimble-shaped heads from late spring to fall. Remove them to encourage growth of young leaves. Prescribed by early herbalists to stop bleeding and to cure gout.
Uses: Fresh leaves impart mild cucumberlike flavor. Use them whole in fruit cups and iced drinks, or chop into salads, soups, and green vegetables. Mix into cream cheese or melted butter, or use as garnish.
Type: Hardy perennial.
Height: 1 ft. **Spread:** 9–12 in.
Location: Full sun, in light, well-drained soil.
Planting: For year-round supply of young leaves, sow seeds outdoors in early spring, and again in mid-summer and fall where practical. During winter, transplant into pots by south-facing window and keep well watered. Plant ½ in. deep in rows 12 in. apart. Thin established seedlings to 9 in. apart.

Harvesting: Young, tender leaves are best. Cut as needed.
Preserving: No good method.
Propagation: From seeds, or divide in midspring (see p. 40). Self sows freely if allowed to flower.

Caraway
(Carum carvi)

Finely cut leaves and flat, greenish-white flower heads resemble those of carrots. Seeds have been reputed to aid digestion, strengthen vision, improve memory, cure baldness, stop a lover's fickleness, and prevent theft of any objects containing them.
Uses: Seeds add tangy flavor to baked goods. Sprinkle over pork, lamb, or veal before roasting, and on baked apples. Add to cheese dishes, applesauce, and apple pie. To reduce cooking odor of cabbage, place a few seeds in muslin bag, tie, and add to cooking water. Use young leaves in salads and soups; cook old leaves like spinach.
Type: Hardy biennial.
Height: 1–2 ft. **Spread:** 9–12 in.
Location: Full sun, in ordinary well-drained soil.
Planting: Sow seeds in spring or late summer, ¼ in. deep in rows 1 ft. apart. As soon as the seedlings are established, thin to 1 ft. apart.

Harvesting: Flowers appear in mid-summer of following year. Cut heads as seeds begin to ripen. Pick leaves as needed.
Preserving: Place seed heads in brown paper bag to finish ripening; seeds will fall to the bottom. Store in jars.
Propagation: From seeds.

Coriander

Chive blooms

Seedpods of the coriander should be cut off and dried, and the seeds knocked out by hand. The young leaves are also usable. Chives should be divided every other year. In winter some can be put in a pot and placed in a window.

Chervil
(*Anthriscus cerefolium*)

Also known as French parsley. Spreading, fernlike foliage makes it attractive garden plant. To improve leaf production, pinch out flower buds as they appear. Said to give radishes a hotter taste when used as companion plant.

Uses: Fresh leaves are used in French cooking in much the same way as parsley; has slight anise flavor. Chop with equal parts chives, parsley, and tarragon for omelets, soups, and tartar sauce. Shred fresh leaves into potatoes, tuna, or green salads; add to poultry, egg, cheese, and fish dishes. Serve as garnish with red meat and oysters. Include dried leaves in stuffings.
Type: Hardy annual.
Height: 1–2 ft. **Spread:** 9–12 in.
Location: Partial shade, in moist, well-drained soil.
Planting: Sow seeds ¼ in. deep in rows 12 in. apart. Thin established seedlings to 9 in. apart. Sow every 4–6 wk. from early spring to fall for succession of plants. Raise as house plant or in cold frame for winter use.

Harvesting: Leaves are ready 6–8 wk. after sowing. Cut plant back to ground.
Preserving: Fresh leaves are best, but they can be dried (see p. 494).
Propagation: From seeds only.

Chives
(*Allium schoenoprasum*)

Thin, tubular, grasslike foliage and cloverlike lavender flower heads that bloom in midsummer make this an attractive border and edging plant. Bulbs exude substance that may discourage a fungus that is harmful to carrots.
Uses: Leaves have mild onion flavor. Chop them and add to salads, egg and cheese dishes, cream cheese, mashed potatoes, sandwich spreads, and sauces. Use flowers in salads.
Type: Perennial.
Height: 6–10 in. **Spread:** 12 in.
Location: Full sun or slight shade, in rich, well-drained soil.
Planting: Sow seeds in spring or fall, ½ in. deep in rows 12 in. apart. As soon as seedlings are established, thin to 6 in. apart. Or set out nursery-grown plants in early spring, 9–12 in. apart.

Harvesting: Leaves can be cut 4–6 mo. after sowing; then cut often and close to ground.
Preserving: Leaves lose color in drying. Grow winter supplies indoors by potting clumps in fall. Chill outside 4 wk., then grow in sunny window. Can also be preserved by deep freezing (see p. 494).
Propagation: Lift and divide clumps every 3 or 4 yr.

Cicely, sweet
(*Myrrhis odorata*)

Delicate fernlike foliage is attractive in borders. Frothy clusters of small white flowers appear midspring to midsummer. Old herbals prescribed mix of wine and cicely roots for bites of snakes and mad dogs; ointment from seeds was thought to ease skin eruptions.
Uses: Use sweetish leaves for anise-like flavor in salads, soups, and stews. Chop them fine to substitute for some of sugar in fruit pies or to sprinkle over strawberries. Seeds are spicy; use them fresh and green in soups and salad dressings. Roots can be eaten raw or boiled, like fennel.
Type: Perennial.
Height: 2–3 ft. **Spread:** 18 in.
Location: Shade or partial shade, in moist, well-drained soil.
Planting: Sow seeds in early autumn for germination the following spring. Plant ½ in. deep in rows 18 in. apart. Thin established seedlings to 12 in. apart. Set out nursery-grown plants in spring.

Harvesting: Gather seeds while still green; use fresh. Pick leaves as needed in summer; cut back to ground in autumn.
Preserving: Dry or freeze leaves.
Propagation: From seeds. Or divide roots in fall or spring (see p. 40).

Coriander
(*Coriandrum sativum*)

Ancient spice whose seeds have been found in Egyptian tombs and were used in Rome to preserve meat. Mentioned in *The 1001 Nights* as aphrodisiac and means of summoning spirits. Parsleylike leaves and rosy white flowers are attractive, but their odor is unpleasant until aromatic seeds ripen.
Uses: Grind dry seeds to powder, and dust over veal, pork, or ham before cooking. Sprinkle on cakes, pastries, cookies, or sweet dishes. Use in ground meat, sausage, and stews. Constituent of curry powder. Young leaves are known as cilantro or Chinese parsley. The roots, which can be frozen, are used to flavor soups; serve chopped with avocado pears.
Type: Hardy annual.
Height: 18 in. **Spread:** 6–9 in.
Location: Full sun, in soil with good drainage.
Planting: Sow seeds in early spring, ¼ in. deep in rows 12 in. apart. Thin established seedlings to 6 in. apart.

Harvesting: Pick young leaves as cilantro. Cut seed heads when ripe.
Preserving: Spread seed heads on trays to dry in sun or mild artificial heat. Thresh by hand. Store in jars when completely dry.
Propagation: From seeds.

Both fennel and dill need full sun and well-drained soil. Once established, they grow best from self-sown seeds.

Fennel

Dill

Costmary
(*Chrysanthemum balsamita*)

Also known as alecost because leaves were once used in brewing ale and beer, and as Bible leaf because the aromatic 6- to 8-in. leaves were used as bookmarks in church by American colonists. Somewhat weedy looking in garden, but leaves have pungent, minty odor. Small, pale yellow flowers bloom in buttonlike heads; pinch them back as soon as they appear in midsummer to encourage leaf growth. Roots are rampant and persistent; they creep freely unless kept in check.
Uses: Leaves taste minty and slightly bitter. Use sparingly in green salads or to flavor iced drinks. Brew leaves fresh or dry to make pleasant tea. Place in drawers and closets for fragrance and to repel moths.
Type: Hardy perennial.
Height: 2–3 ft. **Spread:** 3 ft.
Location: Full sun or partial shade, in rich, well-drained soil.
Planting: Not grown from seeds. Set out nursery-grown plants in early spring, 2 ft. apart.

Harvesting: Pick young leaves as needed. Cut plants back in fall.
Preserving: Dry or freeze leaves.
Propagation: Divide roots in early spring every third year (see p. 40).

Dill
(*Anethum graveolens*)

Light green plumelike foliage stands out against blue-green stems. Yellow umbrella-shaped flower heads, developing in midsummer, attract honeybees. Highly aromatic plant. Good companion plant for cabbage, but root secretions are said to damage carrots.
Uses: Both seeds and leaves have sharp, slightly bitter taste. Use dried or fresh leaves, known as dillweed, to flavor fish, soups, salads, meat, poultry, omelets, and potatoes. Seeds can be used in same way, but remember that they are much stronger. Sprinkle dill on sliced cucumber to make sandwich filling.
Type: Hardy annual.
Height: 2–3 ft. **Spread:** 9–12 in.
Location: Full sun, in moist, well-drained soil.
Planting: Sow seeds in early spring, ¼ in. deep in rows 9 in. apart. Thin established seedlings to 9 in. apart.

Harvesting: For best flavor pick leaves just as flowers open. Cut stems in dry weather as seeds ripen.
Preserving: Dry leaves slowly or chop and freeze. Hang mature flower heads in a brown paper bag until seeds fall, then dry in sun or slightly warm oven.
Propagation: From seeds (self-sows).

Fennel
(*Foeniculum vulgare*)

Plant resembles dill but is taller and coarser. Some varieties have copper-colored foliage. In ancient times regarded as all-purpose medicine.
Uses: Leaves have sweetish flavor, particularly good in sauces for fish; also useful with pork or veal, in soups, and in salads. Seeds have sharper taste; use sparingly in sauerkraut, spaghetti sauce, chili, hearty soups, and as condiment on baked goods. One variety, Florence fennel (*F. vulgare dulce*), has enlarged leaf base that is cooked and eaten as vegetable called anise. Stems of Sicilian fennel (*F. vulgare piperitum*) are blanched and eaten like celery.
Type: Perennial.
Height: 3–4 ft. **Spread:** 2 ft.
Location: Full sun, in ordinary well-drained soil.
Planting: Sow groups of 3 or 4 seeds in midspring, ¼ in. deep and 18 in. apart. Thin established seedlings to strongest of each group.

Harvesting: Pick leaves as needed; the best appear just as flowers bloom. To use stems, cut young flower stalks just before blooming. To grow for seeds, cut stems in autumn, and treat flower heads in same way as those of dill.
Preserving: Dry or freeze leaves.
Propagation: From seeds every 2 or 3 yr.

Garlic chives
(*Allium tuberosum*)

Cultivated for centuries in China, Japan, and other Asian countries, garlic chives are also known as Chinese chives and flowering leek. They are similar to regular chives but have flat leaves, and white flowers in late summer. Do not allow to set seed since they tend to become invasive.
Uses: They have a mild garlic flavor and all parts are edible, flowers and buds, stems and leaves, either raw or cooked. They are used as a seasoning in salads, soups, and fish and egg dishes. Bunches of flowers can be dried for use as a garnish in winter. Pot some in fall, give them a few weeks outside in the cold, then bring them indoors to force for winter use.
Type: Perennial.
Height: 12–18 in. **Spread:** 6–8 in.
Location: Full sun in moist soil.
Planting: Sow indoors in early spring and transplant outside when about 4 in. tall. Divide established clumps in spring or fall.

Harvesting: Do not harvest seed-raised plants for the first year. After this cut as needed but never more than half a single plant at a time.
Preserving: Dry bunches of flowering stems in a sun-free location.
Propagation: From seed in spring or summer, or by division.

Leaves of lovage and marjoram can be picked fresh as needed. Marjoram can also be dried; to do this, cut the leaves just before the flower buds open. The semi-shrub hyssop makes a good border for herb beds.

Lovage

Marjoram

Hyssop

Horseradish
(*Armoracia rusticana*)

Member of cabbage and mustard family, raised for its tough white roots; sometimes found growing wild. Leaves are large and coarse. Roots are voracious and incursive; will invade and choke out other plants if not removed completely every fall. (In any case, young, first-year roots are preferable for culinary use.) When planted near potatoes, horseradish discourages fungal diseases. Also said to repel blister beetles, but not potato beetles. Do not interplant; set in corners.

Uses: Shred roots fine to make piquant hot sauce for beef, fish, game, and other dishes.
Type: Perennial.
Height: 2 ft. **Spread:** 12–18 in.
Location: Full sun or partial shade, in deep, moist soil.
Planting: In early spring plant 3-in. root cuttings 1 ft. apart, and barely cover with soil.

Harvesting: Lift roots in late autumn; be sure to leave no broken pieces.
Preserving: Trim away and discard small side roots. Store cylindrical main roots in sand in dark, cool, dry place.
Propagation: By root cuttings in early spring (see p. 42).

Hyssop
(*Hyssopus officinalis*)

Attractive perennial; evergreen in warm climates. Amenable to trimming; useful as border or low hedge. Glossy dark green foliage has musky odor. Bright blue, pink, or white flower spikes appear from midsummer well into autumn, attracting bees and butterflies. Leaves long used medicinally as purgative and antiseptic.

Uses: Leaves have resinous, bitter flavor, not for everyone's taste. Brew to make invigorating tea, best sweetened with honey. Use sparingly in soups, stews, and salads.
Type: Partly woody perennial.
Height: 2 ft. **Spread:** 9–12 in.
Location: Full sun, in light, well-drained soil.
Planting: Sow seeds ¼ in. deep in seedbed in early spring. As soon as seedlings are established, thin to 3 in. apart. When weather is warm enough, transplant seedlings to garden, 12 in. apart.

Harvesting: Pick leaves as needed, choosing only youngest for use fresh in salads.
Preserving: Dry or freeze leaves.
Propagation: From seeds, or divide roots in spring (see p. 40). Take tip cuttings in late summer (see p. 41).

Lovage
(*Levisticum officinale*)

Vigorous, nearly shrub-sized perennial that looks, smells, and tastes much like celery but is larger, stronger, and sweeter. Valuable as background planting in garden. Greenish-yellow flowers appear in late summer in flat-topped clusters above foliage. Unless seeds are desired, pinch flowers off as they appear to prevent entire plant from yellowing. Ancient herbalists recommended lovage as cure for fever and intestinal disorders.

Uses: Tender young leaves add rich celerylike flavor to soups, stews, salads, and sauces. Dried seeds, whole or ground, can be used in same way. Blanch stem bases and eat as you would celery.
Type: Perennial.
Height: 3–4 ft. **Spread:** 2–3 ft.
Location: Sun or partial shade, in rich, deep, moist soil.
Planting: Sow seeds in autumn when ripe. Cover lightly with soil. In spring thin seedlings to about 2 ft. apart.

Harvesting: Gather young leaves as needed. Cut seed heads when ripe.
Preserving: Dry or freeze leaves. Treat seeds in same way as dill.
Propagation: From seeds or by root division in spring (see p. 40).

Marjoram, pot
(*Origanum onites*)

Either green stemmed with white flowers or purplish stemmed with pale purple flowers. Valued in gardens for its fragrance. Differs from sweet marjoram in that it is only about half as tall, has larger flowers, and is hardier; nevertheless, it requires warm location in northern areas if it is to flourish.

Uses: Sprinkle chopped leaves fresh or dried over lamb, pork, and veal before roasting. Use to flavor soups, stews, stuffings, egg and cheese dishes, and fish sauces. Flavor is similar to sweet marjoram but is slightly bitter and thymelike.
Type: Perennial.
Height: 1 ft. **Spread:** 1 ft.
Location: Full sun, warm and sheltered, in rich, well-drained soil.
Planting: Sow seeds in autumn or early spring, ¼ in. deep in rows 1 ft. apart. Thin established seedlings to 1 ft. apart. Set out nursery-grown plants in spring, 1 ft. apart.

Harvesting: Pick leaves as needed. For drying, cut leaves just before flowers open in midsummer.
Preserving: Dry leaves.
Propagation: Divide plants in midspring (see p. 40). Tip cuttings can be taken in summer (see p. 41).

Parsley is very suitable for drying and freezing. The crinkled-leaf variety is good for garnish.

Parsley

Marjoram, sweet
(*Origanum majorana*)

The marjoram species most often grown in gardens for fragrance and flavor of its leaves. Also known as knotted marjoram, from the form of its flower heads. Makes a good border planting. Oval, gray-green leaves feel soft and velvety. In ancient Rome they were strewn on floors to sweeten air. Medieval herbalists brewed them into tea to relieve chest congestion.
Uses: Same as for pot marjoram; flavor is much the same but not bitter. Use leaves fresh in salads or dried in sachets.
Type: Tender perennial.
Height: 2 ft. **Spread:** 12–18 in.
Location: Full sun, in rich, well-drained soil.
Planting: Sow seeds in early to mid spring, ¼ in. deep in rows 12 in. apart. Thin established seedlings to 12-in. spacings. In cooler areas sow under glass in very early spring; after hardening off, plant out in early summer.

Harvesting: Encourage foliage by removing flowers as they appear. Pick leaves as needed. For drying, cut before flowers open in midsummer.
Preserving: Dry leaves.
Propagation: From seeds. By root division in warm areas, where plant grows as perennial (see p. 40).

Mint
(*Mentha* species)

The most popular mints are apple mint (*M. rotundifolia*), peppermint (*M. piperita*), and spearmint (*M. spicata*). White or purple flower spikes are attractive, but pinch them off to encourage leaves. Mints are repellent to white-cabbage butterflies.
Uses: Brew leaves into tea, or use to garnish cold drinks. Spearmint is generally used to make mint sauce or jelly. Sprinkle dried or fresh leaves over lamb before cooking.
Type: Perennial.
Height: 2–3 ft. **Spread:** 12–18 in.
Location: Partial shade, in rich, moist, well-drained soil.
Planting: In autumn or spring, plant 4- to 6-in. pieces of root 2 in. deep and 12 in. apart. Water well. Check roots' incursive tendency by sinking boards or bricks 1 ft. deep around bed or by planting in a large bottomless plastic bucket sunken into a garden bed.

Harvesting: Pick leaves as needed. For double crop, cut plant to ground in midsummer.
Preserving: Dry or freeze leaves.
Propagation: Divide roots in autumn or spring.

Oregano
(*Origanum vulgare*)

Also called wild marjoram. Plant is similar to sweet marjoram but shrubbier and more spreading; leaves are darker green, with sharper fragrance and flavor. Prescribed by ancient herbalists to aid digestion, stimulate appetite, and act as purgative. Roots tend to be incursive. Small white, pink, or purple flowers are fragrant, but pinch them back to encourage leaf production.
Uses: Dried leaves frequently used in Italian, Spanish, and Mexican cooking—especially in meat and tomato sauces, where they blend well with garlic and hot spices. Use in salads, stews, stuffings, egg and cheese dishes, and with fish.
Type: Perennial.
Height: 2 ft. **Spread:** 18–24 in.
Location: Full sun, in almost any well-drained soil.
Planting: Sow seeds in spring or autumn, ¼ in. deep in rows 18 in. apart. Thin established seedlings to 12 in. apart. Set out nursery-grown plants in midspring, spacing them 12–18 in. apart.

Harvesting: Pick leaves as needed. For drying, cut top 6 in. off stems just before flowers open.
Preserving: Dry leaves.
Propagation: From seeds, or divide in midspring (see p. 40).

Parsley
(*Petroselinum crispum*)

Bright green, crinkly leaves and compact growth habit make this good plant for edging or low borders. Interplant with roses and tomatoes to enhance vigor of both. Used since antiquity to sweeten breath after eating onions, garlic, or red meat and after drinking alcoholic beverages.
Uses: Mix leaves into salads, soups, stews, casseroles, and omelets. Serve fresh as garnish with meat, fish, and onion dishes.
Type: Biennial; grown as annual.
Height: 1 ft. **Spread:** 1 ft.
Location: Sun or partial shade, in rich, moist, deep soil.
Planting: Sow seeds in midspring for summer cutting, midsummer for autumn and winter harvests. Soak seeds overnight and broadcast thinly. Thin established seedlings to 9–10 in. apart.

Harvesting: Cut stems as required—no more than 2 or 3 at a time from any one plant. Pick leaves before flowering in second year; later, they turn bitter.
Preserving: Freeze (see p. 494). Can also be dried, but, comparatively, the dried form has a very poor flavor.
Propagation: From seeds as annual. Plant will self-sow its second season if allowed to flower.

Rosemary makes a good pot plant for a sunny windowsill in winter and will flower for several months.

Rosemary

Rosemary
(Rosmarinus officinalis)

Shrublike evergreen valuable as a landscape feature where ground does not freeze solid in winter. Glossy, needlelike leaves have piny scent. Abundant lavender or blue flowers bloom in early summer. Repellent to cabbage butterflies, carrot flies, and mosquitoes.

Uses: Insert a sprig or two into lamb, pork, veal, or poultry before roasting; or toss some onto charcoal over which beef, chicken, or ribs are cooking. Sprinkle chopped leaves over beef or fish before broiling. Use sparingly in soups, stews, sauces, and vegetables. Add to boiling water when cooking rice. Brews into a tasty tea.
Type: Tender perennial.
Height: 2–6 ft. **Spread:** 2–6 ft.
Location: Full sun or partial shade, in light, well-drained soil.
Planting: Can be grown from seeds, but buying young plants is generally more satisfactory. Set out young plants in late spring about 2 ft. apart.

Harvesting: Cut sprigs as needed.
Preserving: Dry or freeze leaves.
Propagation: By hardwood cuttings in fall or spring (see p. 257), or semi-hard cuttings of 6-in. shoots in mid-summer (see p. 258).

Sage
(Salvia officinalis)

Evergreen subshrub, good as low background planting or border, or in its own bed. Narrow gray-green leaves sometimes have white, purple, or yellow variegations. Used as medicinal herb since antiquity; was prescribed for ailments of blood, brain, heart, liver, and stomach, as cure for epilepsy and fever, and as preventive of plague. Repellent to white-cabbage butterflies, carrot flies, and ticks. Do not grow sage near annual seedbeds, as it inhibits root production.

Uses: Dried leaves are traditional constituent of poultry stuffing. Use also with lamb, pork, sausage, and in cheese dishes and omelets.
Type: Perennial.
Height: 2 ft. **Spread:** 18 in.
Location: Full sun, in almost any well-drained soil. Fairly drought resistant; avoid overwatering.
Planting: Can be grown from seeds sown in early spring. Set out nursery-grown plants in midspring approximately 1 ft. apart.

Harvesting: Pick leaves as needed. For drying, cut top 5–6 in. of stalks before flowering in early summer; repeat as new growth develops.
Preserving: Dry leaves.
Propagation: Make softwood cuttings in early summer (see p. 260). Divide in spring or early fall every 2nd or 3rd yr. (see p. 40).

Savory, summer
(Satureja hortensis)

Small aromatic leaves are shiny green. Tiny lavender or pinkish-white flowers cover plant in midsummer. Attractive to bees; makes flavorsome honey. Interplant with green beans and onions for increased yield and better flavor. Applying bruised savory leaves to skin is folk remedy for discomfort of bee and wasp stings.

Uses: Leaves have peppery, somewhat mintlike flavor. Traditional seasoning with beans. Use in sausages, stuffings, meat pies, soups, stews, bean dishes, rice, and sauces for pork, lamb, veal, and poultry. Add fresh leaves to salads, fish dishes, omelets. Brew into fragrant, tangy tea; or add to vinegar for use in salad dressing.
Type: Annual.
Height: 12–18 in. **Spread:** 6–12 in.
Location: Full sun, in rich, light, well-drained soil.
Planting: Broadcast seeds in early to mid spring, in rows 12 in. apart. Allow 4 wk. for germination. Thin established seedlings to 6–9 in. apart.

Harvesting: Leaves are most flavorful before flowers form in midsummer. Cut plant partially back for 2nd crop.
Preserving: Dry leaves.
Propagation: From seeds.

Savory, winter
(Satureja montana)

Lower, more spreading than summer savory. Glossy, dark green leaves are stiffer, less aromatic, with larger flowers. Makes good border. Dwarf form (*S. montana pygmaea*), about 4 in. tall, is ideal for edging.

Uses: Flavor is less delicate than summer savory's and somewhat bitter as well as peppery. Use much the same way in cooking; also, fresh leaves make good dressing for trout. Combine dried leaves with basil to substitute for salt and pepper in salt-free diets.
Type: Partly woody perennial.
Height: 6–12 in. **Spread:** 12–18 in.
Location: Full sun, in sandy, well-drained soil.
Planting: Seeds germinate slowly. Sow in fall or early spring, ¼ in. deep in rows 1 ft. apart. When seedlings are established, thin to 1 ft. apart. Or set out nursery-grown plants 1 ft. apart in midspring.

Harvesting: Pick leaves as needed. Cut plants halfway back before flowering for 2nd crop.
Preserving: Dry leaves.
Propagation: Divide established plants in early spring (see p. 264). Take softwood cuttings in late spring (see p. 260). Replace plants every 2 or 3 yr.

Lemon thyme, a perennial, creeps over the ground. Tarragon needs full sun and well-drained soil.

Lemon thyme

Tarragon

Sorrel
(*Rumex* species)

Two species are commonly grown: garden sorrel (*R. acetosa*) and French sorrel (*R. scutatus*). Both are valued for large, light green leaves—heart shaped in French sorrel, spade shaped in garden sorrel. In early to mid summer, both species bear long, reddish-brown flower spikes, popular for dried arrangements.

Uses: Leaves give sharp, acidic taste to stews, soups, and sauces that is more pronounced with French sorrel. Use fresh young leaves sparingly in salads. Cook with spinach, cabbage, or other greens; or cook in place of spinach. Make into purée to serve with fish and meat.

Type: Perennial.

Height: 2 ft. **Spread:** 12–15 in.

Location: Full sun or partial shade, in rich, well-drained, moist soil (slightly drier for French sorrel).

Planting: Sow seeds in early spring, ¼ in. deep in rows 12 in. apart. When seedlings are 3 in. tall, thin to 12 in. apart. Or set out nursery-grown plants in fall or early spring.

Harvesting: Cut shoots before flowers open. Cut plant to ground after harvest to encourage fall crop.

Preserving: Freeze cooked, puréed leaves.

Propagation: Divide roots in early spring (see p. 40), or sow seeds.

Tarragon, French
(*Artemisia dracunculus*)

Has fragrant, shiny, dark green leaves on woody stems. Creeping rhizomatous roots are not completely resistant to severe cold; more likely to be damaged in damp soil than in dry. Hardy to Zone 4. Similar, but less flavorsome, is Russian tarragon (*A. dracunculoides*). This can be raised from seed available at many seed houses.

Uses: Chop the anise-flavored leaves for use in soups, salads, egg dishes, stews, and soft cheeses. Excellent with lamb. Serve in melted butter with fish, steak, or vegetables. Constituent of tartar sauce and many chutneys. Makes good flavoring for vinegar when leaves are steeped for 2 or 3 wk.

Type: Perennial.

Height: 2 ft. **Spread:** 15 in.

Location: Full sun, in dry, not too rich, well-drained soil.

Planting: Does not grow true from seeds. Set out nursery-grown plants in early spring, 18 in. apart.

Harvesting: Pick leaves as needed. Cut plant to ground in autumn.

Preserving: Dry or freeze leaves.

Propagation: Divide roots of established plants in early spring (see p. 40).

Thyme, common
(*Thymus vulgaris*)

Shrubby and low growing, with aromatic, gray-green foliage; good as edging plant or low border, or in its own bed. Small, lilac-colored flowers appear in late spring to midsummer; attract bees and make excellent honey. Valued for centuries as medicinal herb, thyme yields an oil—thymol—used today in antiseptics, deodorants, and cough drops. Possibly repellent to the cabbage butterfly.

Uses: Rub chopped leaves (fresh or dried) into beef, lamb, veal, or pork before roasting. Sprinkle over eggs, cheese dishes, vegetables, fish, or poultry. Add to soups, stews, stuffings, and rice. Brew into tea with a little rosemary and mint.

Type: Partly woody perennial.

Height: 8 in. **Spread:** 9–12 in.

Location: Full sun, in almost any well-drained soil.

Planting: Set out nursery-grown plants in early spring, 6–9 in. apart. Sow seeds in midspring in shallow rows 1 ft. apart. When seedlings are established, thin to 6-in. spacings.

Harvesting: Pick leaves as needed. For drying, cut plants just before flowers open in early summer.

Preserving: Dry leaves.

Propagation: Every 3 or 4 yr. divide established plants in spring (see p. 264).

Thyme, lemon
(*Thymus citriodorus*)

This hybrid between *T. vulgaris* and a procumbent relative, *T. pulegioides*, looks much like common thyme but grows lower and spreads by creeping along ground. Purple flowers attractive to bees.

Uses: Can be used in cooking in same way as common thyme; flavor is less pungent and distinctly lemony, particularly tasty in stuffing for veal and poultry. Mix chopped leaves into custards, puddings, and whipped-cream toppings. Sprinkle lightly over fresh strawberries and other acidic fruits.

Type: Partly woody perennial.

Height: 6 in. **Spread:** 1 ft.

Location: Full sun, in almost any well-drained soil.

Planting: Cannot be raised from seeds. Set out nursery-grown plants in early to mid spring, 9 in. apart.

Harvesting: Pick fresh leaves as needed. Cut leaves for drying just before flowers open in early summer.

Preserving: Dry leaves.

Propagation: Divide established plants in spring (see p. 264). Layer in spring by mounding soil on center of each plant, causing branches to produce roots along their length. Each branch can then be severed and planted.

Almost all herbs can be dried for winter use. Those with fleshy leaves can also be frozen.

Herb garden

Preserving Herbs for Winter

How to Dry Homegrown Herbs

The leaves of most herbs should be harvested for drying before the flowers open, when the plants are in bud. Gather on a dry day—early in the morning, once the dew has dried, but before the day's heat starts evaporating the essential oils. If the leaves are dirty, or have soil splashed on them, swish the stems briefly in cold water, roll in a towel, and pat dry.

Large-leaved herbs, such as mint, basil, or marjoram, can be dried in two ways. Individual leaves can be picked off—discarding any that are damaged—and spread on wire racks or sheets of paper towel to dry in a warm dark place. They should be turned frequently for the first two days to dry them rapidly and retain the flavor. Alternatively, they can be tied in small bunches and hung to dry on coat hangers, or in brown paper bags, in an airy place.

Small-leaved herbs, such as rosemary, tarragon, or thyme, can also be hung in bunches in the open, but dry better if placed in brown paper bags. Leave the tops open for the first few days to let most of the moisture escape, then tie loosely closed to keep the herbs clean.

Do not put different herbs in the same bag, or close together in bunches. Strong-flavored herbs may overpower more delicate ones.

Oven drying. If no suitable room is available for drying herbs, the job can be done in or on the kitchen oven. But exercise care; the object is simply to dehydrate the herbs, not to cook them.

Set the oven to its minimum temperature (some ovens start at 195°F, but appliances vary) with the door open; spread the herbs on wire racks or baking trays. Put the racks or screens in the oven, and leave them there until the herbs are crisp—probably about an hour.

Microwave drying. Many herbs can also be dried in the microwave oven, but put a small cup of water in with the herbs. Power rating of microwave ovens varies; so it is impossible to give exact timings. Small-leaved herbs, such as rosemary and thyme, however, should take about one minute, while those with larger leaves may take up to three. You will have to experiment to find the proper timing for your particular oven.

A note of caution: if you dry the leaves too much, they may catch fire, especially those such as sage, which have a high oil content.

Crushing and storing. Once the leaves are fully dry, pick them off the stems, but do not crush them yet. Whole leaves keep their flavor better and they are easy to crumble into small pieces with the fingers when you need to use them.

Do not powder an herb until it is needed in powder form, or the flavor will be lost. When powder is needed, push the bits of leaves through a sieve, or use a mortar and pestle.

Store in airtight containers and keep in a dark place. If left in the light, dried herbs bleach to a pale color and lose some of their flavor.

Label each jar with the name of its contents and the date of storage. Dried herb leaves seldom keep their flavor for longer than a year.

DRYING LARGE-LEAVED HERBS

Strip leaves from stems, and spread leaves on wire racks, mesh screening, or paper towels to dry in a dark, airy room.

DRYING SMALL-LEAVED HERBS

Before hanging to air dry, roll washed branches of small-leaved herbs in a towel (or paper toweling) to remove surplus water.

Preserving Herbs in the Freezer

Many soft-leaved herbs can be preserved by deep freezing. The most satisfactory are balm, basil, chives, fennel, lovage, mint, parsley, sorrel, sweet cicely, and tarragon. Young shoots or leaves are preferable; cut them early in the morning, and process them without delay. Do not mix different types of herbs; deal with each kind separately.

Chop the herbs, pack loosely into small jars, and label with the type of herb and date before putting them in the freezer. When you need the herb, remove the jar from the freezer and, without thawing, scrape out the required amount with a spoon. Return the jar to the freezer.

Alternatively, chop the herbs and put a small amount in each section of an ice-cube tray. Fill the tray with water and freeze. Once frozen, the cubes can be put into a plastic bag for storage. Frozen herbs are for use in recipes, not salads. Add while still frozen; they turn to mush if thawed.

Freezing parsley. Individual leaves can be frozen as described, or parsley can also be frozen as sprigs. Cut off small sprigs and lay on a baking sheet. Place the sheet in the freezer and flash-freeze. Frozen, it can be put into a plastic bag, where the sprigs will remain separate, rather than freezing together.

Oils and vinegars. Flavored oils and vinegars are easy to make at home. Classic examples are tarragon and chive flower vinegars, and rosemary and basil oils, but combinations are limited only by your imagination.

Fill a clean, wide-mouthed jar with one or more fresh herbs and cover completely with a good-quality olive oil, or a white- or red-wine vinegar and seal. Because of the risk of *Clostridium botulinum* bacteria, keep home-prepared products stored in oil in the refrigerator, and discard after one week. For vinegars, allow to steep, tasting every few weeks. Once the flavor is to your liking, strain out the herb and pour the vinegar into a container. Store in the dark.

CRUSHING FROZEN PARSLEY

If frozen parsley is needed in small pieces, break up frozen and brittle leaves by rubbing the plastic bag gently between your hands before you open it.

Taking Care of Your Garden

Your garden must be well prepared and adequately fertilized if you are to have good growth and a rich harvest. Many different nutrients are needed if plant roots, foliage, flowers, and fruits are to develop properly. Weeds, pests, and diseases must also be controlled. The following pages show how to accomplish all these things, enabling you to avoid most garden problems and plant ailments altogether, and to identify and quickly correct those that do occur.

WHAT YOU SHOULD KNOW ABOUT THE SOIL

Before planting your garden, take stock of your soil. Whether it is clayey or sandy, acid or alkaline determines what you can grow and what improvements are needed.

Soil is a complex mixture of diverse ingredients, containing all the nutrients that sustain life on earth. Plants are uniquely adapted to extract these nutrients through their roots and to convert them to forms usable by the plant, and by mankind and other animals. The gardener's job is to keep the soil in the best possible condition and to replace the nutrients that plants have taken up.

Soil has five main components—inorganic particles of rocks and minerals; dead and decaying organic matter (humus); water; air; and a teeming community of living creatures, ranging from insects, earthworms, and fungi to microscopic bacteria and protozoa. Soil is defined by the quality and proportions of these components.

The nature of soil varies a great deal, not only from place to place but also at different depths in the same location. Dig down 3 feet or more, and you will uncover a series of definite layers, differing in color, texture, and composition. Taken together, these layers constitute what is known as the soil profile.

The upper layer, or topsoil, is generally darker than the deeper layers because it is richer in humus. It is in this layer that life is most abundant, and it is here that the majority of plants develop the roots that take up their nutrients. Topsoil may be only an inch or two deep, or it may be a foot or more. It is usually thin on steep slopes and deeper in flat lowlands, where humus and silt are carried by rainwater runoff. Although many plants will grow in shallow topsoil, most will need frequent fertilizing and watering to flourish in it.

Beneath the topsoil is the subsoil layer. It is harder to dig and is stickier when wet because of its high clay content, most of which is washed down from the topsoil. Also washed down are oxides of iron and other minerals, often giving subsoil a reddish color. These minerals may collect at a given depth and cement the soil particles into a layer called hardpan, which often blocks the penetration of roots and interferes with drainage.

Beneath the subsoil lies the geologic base, mineral matter that is often the parent material of the soil above. It may be solid bedrock; or it may be loose and porous to great depths, in which case the roots of trees and some shrubs may reach well into it.

Texture. The stablest soil component is its framework of rock particles; it is according to the size of these that soil is classified as sand, silt, or clay. Most soil is a mixture of all three. Its texture is defined by the proportions in which they are present. Laboratory analysis will determine the exact composition of any soil, but you can form a rough judgment of texture simply by rubbing a pinch of moist soil lightly between your thumb and forefinger.

Sand feels harsh and gritty, and its grains scarcely hold together. They are the largest soil particles—if they were any larger, they would be called gravel. Sandy, or coarse-textured, soil is easy to work. It came to be called light soil because it could be plowed with only a light team of horses. It drains easily, and with the water that filters through it go many nutrients. To grow most garden plants in light soil, therefore, requires constant replenishment of water, humus, and nutrients.

Silt particles are smaller than sand and larger than clay. They feel smooth and floury between the fingers. Silt packs together with fewer air spaces than sand, which makes for slower drainage, but it does not hold together well, becoming light and powdery when it dries out.

Clay soil was termed "heavy," as opposed to the light, sandy soil, because it took a heavy team to plow it. A particle of clay is at least 1,000 times finer than a grain of coarse sand. Clay particles pack into compact lumps that dry as stony clods. When you rub a bit of moist clay between your thumb and finger, it rolls into a wormlike cylinder. Clay particles swell up when exposed to moisture, closing pores in the soil,

compacting it, and impeding drainage. The soil shrinks again when it dries but remains hard-packed, sometimes forming deep cracks on the surface. Though it can be difficult to get plants started in clay soil, most will to do well once established.

Although the best way to improve a clay soil is by the addition of humus, on a heavy clay it can take several years to have an appreciable effect. Until the soil becomes more workable, dig it over in the fall, leaving the soil in large clods. Do not break these down since the action of winter winds, frost, and cold breaks the clay into small crumbs, a process known as flocculation. In spring, once the winter wet has drained through the soil, it can be forked over and will retain this crumb structure. Do not work on the soil while it is wet, since this will squeeze the crumbs together and you will be back to a sticky clay that will bake hard in the sun.

Loam is the name given to medium-textured soil containing sand, silt, and clay in well-balanced proportions. The term is a bit vague, including such imprecisions as sandy loam, clay loam, and silty loam, but essentially it means "good soil." It is friable, which is to say that large clods break down easily into smaller particles. A pinch of moist loam rubbed between your fingers will be reduced to a rough smear. Once you have dealt with good loam, you are not likely to mistake it for anything else. It holds moisture well and encourages the organic activity that makes most nutrients available to plant roots. With proper management almost any crop can be grown in loam, but humus and other organic matter must be added regularly to maintain desirable levels, and liming may be occasionally needed to correct acidity.

Tilth and structure. Tilth refers to the soil's fitness for cultivation. This is largely a matter of structure—that is, the way in which particles of sand, silt, clay, and humus clump together into granules or crumbs.

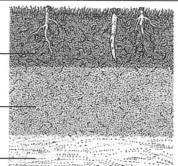

Topsoil: rich in humus and minerals, this is the zone where most root growth takes place.

Subsoil: usually poor in essential nutrients, this layer serves to anchor the roots of trees and shrubs.

Geologic-base: this may be a few inches or many feet deep. Only large tree roots reach this zone.

Dig a spadeful of moist loam, and let it drop onto a hard surface. If it comes apart in porous crumbs that are up to half an inch in diameter, the structure is good. Each crumb will retain moisture; air spaces between them will allow excess water to drain. If soil breaks into blocky clods with flat surfaces, it is too heavily compacted and you have work to do.

Nature's method of bringing soil into good tilth is to grow cover crops year after year. The roots of these plants break up compacted soil, the foliage protects the surface from the bombardment of heavy rain, and the plants eventually break down into basic organic matter, which is pulled into the soil by earthworms and other soil-dwelling animals or insects. Microorganisms in the soil break this organic matter down into usable nutrients. In the process, polysaccharides are produced—useful by-products that bind soil particles into crumbs. For ways to put this method to work in your garden, see green manuring on page 502.

For quicker results, in the fall dig in a 2- to 4-inch-thick layer of dehydrated manure, compost, or similar organic material, double digging if the subsoil is extremely heavy.

Humus. Organic material, derived from animals and plants, breaks down in the soil to a dark, gummy substance called humus. Not only is this rich in nutrients but it is the agent by which faulty texture and structure are best remedied. In light soil, humus binds sand particles together; in heavy soil it keeps clay particles apart, allowing room for air and water. Soil containing a great deal of humus is termed "rich," whereas "lean" soil is humus-deficient.

Any bulky organic waste materials—manure, fallen leaves, grass clippings, kitchen scraps—are useful as sources of humus. You can compost them first, if desired. If added directly to soil, it takes time for the material to break down, and few nutrients are available to plants until their form has been altered by decomposition. Moreover, the microorganisms that cause decay use up a great deal of nitrogen in the first stages of the process; so the addition of carbon-rich organic waste can cause temporary nitrogen deficiency in the soil. (This is why it is a good idea to mix in a little nitrogen-rich fertilizer when using sawdust, bark chips, or similar organic material as a summer mulch.)

You can obtain humus-forming materials, such as well-rotted manure or leaf mold in ready-to-use form from garden supply centers, or you can process your own by composting. Either way, it should be worked well into the soil. A good application would be a 6-inch layer of loose organic material worked into the soil to a depth of at least 12 inches.

Dig up a soil sample with a spade. Throw aside the first cut, then remove a smooth slice of earth.

Selecting a soil sample

Improving Soil Quality

Taking Samples for a Soil Test

To make the best use of the soil in your garden, you should know its properties; before you can improve it, you must know its deficiencies.

Some states will do a complete soil analysis for free, usually through the land grant university. This test will tell you the texture and pH of your soil, and provide an analysis of its nutritional content and requirements. Some county extension agents will provide a pH analysis of your soil, but the availability of this varies. Where soil tests are not available from the state, look for commercial laboratories online under "Soil Testing."

Soil-test kits are available if you wish to do the job yourself. With the exception of pH-test kits, however, they can be tricky to use, and the results are meaningless without knowledgeable interpretation.

Either way, the reliability of the test depends upon the care with which the soil sample is taken. Avoid contaminating it with fireplace ashes, residue from tools or containers, or any other foreign substance.

It is also important that the small sample you send is representative of an entire area where similar plants, such as roses or vegetables, are to be grown. This means gathering soil from several places and mixing it together to form a composite, from which you need take no more than a pint of soil for analysis. Do not, however, mix together soil from clearly different areas. Have each area analyzed separately.

When feasible, take samples in midfall, when the growing season is over. Certain corrective materials, such as bone meal and elemental sulfur, take several months to become effective; so they are best applied in fall.

There are special tools for sampling, but the job can easily be done with a sharp spade or trowel. For each sample make a steep vertical

1. With some soil-testing kits, a reagent solution is added to soil.

cut 6–8 inches deep. From this vertical face take a ½-inch-thick slice to the full depth of the cut. Remove stones and other debris. Mix all the samples from an area thoroughly in a clean container, and take about a pint of soil for analysis.

Put it in a container that will stand the rigors of shipping, such as an ice cream container or a plastic (not glass) food storage container. Attach to each sample a letter, including your name and address; the date the sample was taken; the place it was taken (front lawn, garden, etc.); whether fertilizer or lime was used the previous year; what type of crop you plan to grow (grass, shrubs, flowers, vegetables, etc.); and as much information as possible about how the land has been used in the recent past. Enclose the containers and letters in a durable cardboard box. Be sure your name and address are clearly marked on the outside before shipping.

The pH Level: Acid or Alkaline

Acidity and alkalinity are measured on the pH scale, which runs from 0 (pure acid) to 14 (pure lye). From the neutral point, 7, the numbers increase or decrease in geometric progression: thus, pH 5 is 10 times more acid than pH 6; pH 4, 100 times more acid; and so forth.

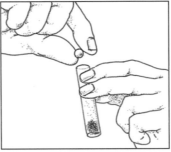

2. In other kits you mix the supplied pellets with some soil and water.

Slightly acid soil—about pH 6.5—is best for most plants, but there are exceptions. Rhododendrons, for example, require pH 4–5.5 in order to thrive. Cabbage does best in slightly alkaline soil, about pH 7.5, partly because the clubroot fungus that can afflict it thrives in acidity. Few plants will survive in soil more acid than pH 4 or more alkaline than pH 8.

For more information on optimal pH levels for specific flowers and vegetables, turn to the charts on page 499. But remember that most annuals, perennials, and vegetables will grow well with a soil that is near neutral pH or very slightly acid.

If you do want to increase the alkalinity of the soil, use finely ground limestone, which is available from most garden-supply centers. In fall dig the soil to a depth of 8–12 inches. Spread the lime evenly over the surface, and rake it in. The rate of application depends on the texture of the soil. In sandy loam 50 pounds per 1,000 square feet will raise pH a point; in medium loam use 70 pounds. In heavy soil 80 pounds of limestone is required for the same pH change. These quantities are to change the soil's pH from 5.5 to 6.5. The more acid the soil, the more lime is needed to raise its pH by one point. Quantities should be increased by about one-fifth if the pH is lower than 5.5.

To increase the acidity of the soil

3. The mixtures are matched to a chart showing different pH levels.

drastically, use elemental sulfur, which over a few months will turn to sulfuric acid in the soil. This, too, is available from most garden-supply centers. Like limestone, the amount to use depends on the soil texture: in sand 8 pounds per 1,000 square feet will lower pH by about a point; in heavy loam 25 pounds is needed. For the most effective and long-lasting treatment, work the sulfur in to a depth of about 12 inches, along with large amounts of leaf mold.

Leaf mold can also be acidic, depending on the trees it is made from (oak especially), and incorporating pine needles into the soil will also reduce the alkalinity. Both work more slowly than sulfur but have the added advantage of improving the tilth of soil that is too light or too heavy.

Whether you are raising or lowering pH, there is always the danger of overdoing it. Use only as much corrective material as you are sure you need, based on reliable soil tests.

Supplying Nutrients With Fertilizers

Of the 16 elements known to be necessary to plant growth, 3—carbon, hydrogen, and oxygen—come from the air and water. The rest are taken from the soil. Most of these are trace elements, needed in such minute quantities that they

Sand

Clay

Humus-rich soil

Before preparation and cultivation, examine the soil to get an idea of its condition. Clay soil forms hard lumps when dry; sandy soil feels gritty on the fingers. The humus content of soil is a measure of its fertility. It helps open heavy soils and retain moisture in sandy ones.

are not likely to be depleted. The others must be replaced to keep the soil productive.

Nitrogen, phosphorus, and potassium are needed in the largest amounts, are used up the fastest, and are therefore the chief ingredients of the so-called all-purpose fertilizers, which are meant to maintain nutrient levels for most plants in average soil. These fertilizers are available in solid form (as powders or granules) and in liquid form. Liquids have the advantage of being easily applied and quickly absorbed. They are generally more expensive, however, and they do not remain in the soil as long as solid fertilizers; so they must be applied oftener, in smaller doses.

When you buy a bag or bottle of fertilizer, you will find at least three numbers on the label (3–4–3, for example). This is the NPK rating. The first number represents the percentage of nitrogen (N); the second

stands for the percentage of phosphorus (P); and the third, the percentage of potassium (K) in the form of potash. If one of these nutrients is missing, a zero indicates its absence. Thus, to apply 1 pound of N, 1 pound of P, and 1 pound of K requires 20 pounds of a fertilizer rated 5-5-5 or about 33 pounds of one rated 3-3-3. The proportions of nutrients are the same, but the quantity of each nutrient is greater in the fertilizer with the higher rating.

Nitrogen is one of the building blocks of plant cells and is needed continually all the time a plant is growing. Some forms of nitrogen are soluble and wash through the soil with rain or watering. Phosphorous aids in root, flower, and fruit development but is not soluble so needs to be worked into the soil where it can be absorbed by the roots. Potassium is needed for the movement of sugars and nutrients within the plant.

OPTIMAL pH LEVELS TO MAKE YOUR VEGETABLES GROW

VEGETABLES	BEST pH LEVEL	VEGETABLES	BEST pH LEVEL
Artichokes	5.5–7.5	Lettuce and endive	6–7
Asparagus	6–8	Okra	6–7.5
Beans	6–7.5	Onions and leeks	5.8–7
Beets	6–7.5	Parsnips	5.5–7
Broccoli	6–7	Peas	6–7.5
Brussels sprouts	6–7.5	Peppers	5.5–7
Cabbage	6–7.5	Potatoes	4.8–6.5
Carrots	5.5–7	Potatoes, sweet	5.2–6.0
Cauliflower	5.5–7.5	Radishes	6–7
Celery	5.8–7	Rhubarb	5.5–7
Corn	5.5–7.5	Spinach	6–7.5
Cucumber	5.5–7	Squash and pumpkin	5.5–7
Eggplant	5.5–6.5	Tomatoes	5.5–7
Kale and collards	6–7.5	Turnips and rutabagas	5.5–6.8

OPTIMAL pH LEVELS TO MAKE YOUR PLANTS THRIVE, YOUR FLOWERS BLOOM

FLOWERS	BEST pH LEVEL	FLOWERS	BEST pH LEVEL	FLOWERS	BEST pH LEVEL	FLOWERS	BEST pH LEVEL
Aconitum (aconite)	5–6	*Corylus* (filbert)	6–7	*Hemerocallis* (day lily)	6–7	*Petunia* (petunia)	6–7.5
Adiantum (maidenhair fern)	5–6	*Cotoneaster* (cotoneaster)	6–8	*Hepatica* (hepatica)	6–8	*Philadelphus* (mock orange)	6–8
Adonis vernalis (spring adonis)	6–8	*Crataegus* (hawthorn)	6–7.5	*Heuchera* (coralbells)	5–7	*Phlox* (phlox)	6–8
Ageratum (ageratum)	6–7.5	*Crocus* (crocus)	6–8	*Hydrangea* (hydrangea)	4–6.5	*Primula* (primrose)	5–7
Amaranthus (amaranthus)	6–6.5	*Cyclamen* (cyclamen)	6–7	*Ilex* (holly)	5–6	*Ranunculus* (buttercup)	6–8
Antirrhinum (snapdragon)	6–7.5	*Dahlia* (dahlia)	6–7.5	*Impatiens* (impatiens)	5.5–6.5	*Rhododendron* (rhododendron)	4.5–6
Aquilegia (columbine)	6–7	*Daphne* (daphne)	6–7	*Iris* (iris)	5–7	*Rosa* (rose)	5.5–7.5
Aster (aster)	6–7	*Deutzia* (deutzia)	6–7.5	*Lathyrus odoratus* (sweet pea)	6–7.5	*Sambucus* (elder)	6–8
Begonia semperflorens (wax begonia)	5–7	*Dianthus* (dianthus)	6–7.5	*Ligustrum* (privet)	6–7	*Saxifraga* (saxifrage)	6–8
Bellis perennis (English daisy)	5–6	*Dicentra* (dicentra)	5–6	*Lilium* (lily)	5–6	*Solidago* (goldenrod)	5–6
Buxus (boxwood)	6–7.5	*Digitalis purpurea* (foxglove)	6–7.5	*Lonicera* (honeysuckle)	6–8	*Spiraea* (spirea)	6–7.5
Calceolaria (calceolaria)	6–7	*Erica* (heath)	4–4.5	*Magnolia* (magnolia)	5–6	*Syringa* (lilac)	6–7.5
Calendula officinalis (calendula)	6.5–7.5	*Forsythia* (forsythia)	6–8	*Matthiola* (stock)	6–7.5	*Tagetes* (marigold)	5.5–7
Callistephus (China aster)	6–8	*Fuchsia* (fuchsia)	5.5–6.5	*Myosotis* (forget-me-not)	6–8	*Tamarix* (tamarix)	6.5–8
Calluna (Scotch heather)	4–6	*Gentiana* (gentian)	5–7	*Narcissus* (narcissus)	5.5–7.5	*Trollius* (trollius)	5.5–6.5
Campanula (campanula)	5.5–7	*Gladiolus* (gladiolus)	6–7	*Nerium* (oleander)	6–7.5	*Tropaeolum majus* (nasturtium)	5.5–7.5
Canna (canna)	6–8	*Hamamelis* (witch hazel)	6–7	*Nicotiana* (nicotiana)	5.5–6.5	*Tulipa* (tulip)	6–7
Chrysanthemum (chrysanthemum)	6–7.5	*Hedera* (ivy)	6–8	*Nymphaea* (water lily)	5.5–6.5	*Veronica* (veronica)	5–6
Clematis (clematis)	5–6.5	*Helenium* (sneezeweed)	5–7.5	*Oenothera* (oenothera)	6–8	*Viburnum* (viburnum)	5–7
Coleus (coleus)	6–7	*Helianthus* (helianthus)	5–7	*Paeonia* (peony)	6–7.5	*Viola* (pansy)	5.5–6.5
Convalaria (lily of the valley)	4.5–6	*Helleborus niger* (Christmas rose)	6–8	*Papaver* (poppy)	6–8	*Zinnia* (zinnia)	5.5–7.5

When preparing to plant a tree or a shrub, fresh compost is the ideal soil fertilizer.

Fresh compost

Composting

It is also soluble and will wash out of the soil slowly after rain.

All-purpose organic fertilizers, in a variety of formulations, are available commercially. They contain nutrients that derive from natural sources. Because of their organic origins, the nutrients are not immediately available and the ingredients must be broken down by the microbes and bacteria in the soil to release them. This results in the fertilizers being active for a longer period. (Plant damage due to overfeeding, which can occur with chemical fertilizers, is rare when organic fertilizers are used.)

Dried blood and finely ground hoof and horn meal both contain 7–15 percent N. Fish meal and fish emulsion are 5–10 percent N and 2–6 percent P. Finely ground bone meal is 3–5 percent N and 20–35 percent P. Cottonseed meal provides 6–9 percent slow-acting N, 2–3 percent P, and about 2 percent K. Thoroughly burned wood ashes, especially those of hardwoods, are another source of K—they contain about 8 percent, but are also very alkaline and should never be used fresh around plants.

Sometimes in alkaline soil, trace elements, though present, are not broken down into usable forms. Iron deficiency, for example, results in chlorosis, or loss of green color. It can be corrected by applying iron chelates to the soil or the foliage, in the amount recommended by the manufacturer. Manganese deficiency, common in vegetables, can be treated by spraying foliage in spring with a weak solution of Epsom salts in water.

Foliar feeding can be valuable in other ways as well—not as a substitute for root feeding but as a supplement. Spraying the leaves of shrubs, for example, with a fish emulsion solution can give a boost to growth during dry spells. Plants with poor or diseased root systems can also benefit from sprayings of fish emulsion or kelp fertilizer.

The Gardener's Black Gold

Composting is a way to recycle house and garden vegetable waste into a useful additive that will improve the texture and fertility of almost any soil. It also improves the drainage of heavy, clay soils by making small channels through which the water can flow, and improves the water-holding capacity of light sandy soils by acting as a sponge and retaining water that otherwise would drain away. Making compost is simple, the labor is minimal, and, if you follow certain guidelines, there is no smell.

During composting, microorganisms and bacteria break down vegetable matter into a form where the nutrients contained are made available again. In nature, trees in woodlands shed their leaves in the fall, these decompose and feed the growing trees in subsequent years. In the garden, it is impractical to spread garden waste directly on the soil, and so we compost it first.

Composting can be done in a pile, in a homemade bin or in a commercial container. A pile is probably the least satisfactory as it is hard to keep it tidy, and it is slow to decompose since it looses a lot of heat and moisture through the open sides. It needs to be turned at least once to ensure that the outside decomposes.

You can build an open compost pile in a hidden corner of the garden. Start with a 1-foot-thick layer of grass clippings, hay, or leaves laid out in a square at least 2 feet by 2 feet. Tread it down and water well. Sprinkle on a handful of blood meal or organic compost accelerator, or add a 1-inch-thick layer of manure. Cover with a 2-inch layer of soil.

Continue to build the pile, adding vegetable waste as it becomes available. Tread down and water each 1-foot layer, and cover with enriched soil, until the pile is several feet high.

Make the top slightly concave to catch rainwater. Cover the finished pile with a soil layer. Water well and keep moist, but not soggy; in a dry summer, it should be watered every two weeks.

Commercial composts, while expensive initially, are efficient, long lasting, and very suitable for small townhouse gardens or apartment balconies where space is limited. Their cost is often subsidized by municipalities to encourage composting and reduce the amount of waste going into landfill. There are also compost makers like small cement mixers, which tumble the contents and produce the finished produce in a matter of weeks. Their capacity, however, is quite limited.

Homemade Compost Bins

If properly made, homemade compost bins are cheap, durable and produce good compost. A bin about 1 yard square will be large enough to hold the compostable waste from an average-sized city family. In rural areas, or if you have a large vegetable garden, increase the size accordingly, or make multiple bins (see illustration page 501). You can make the compost bin in many forms and of almost any material that will withstand the pressure of the compost. Use whatever is available at reasonable cost. If you can get straight logs from a wood lot, you can notch these and build the sides log-cabin style. You can also use 2 x 6 inch lumber, ½-inch exterior-grade plywood, or strong construction sheeting; make sure the wood is not treated with a preservative as this can make the compost toxic. If solid material is used, drill holes to allow air circulation. 1 inch holes spaced 6-8 inches apart should be sufficient. Cracks between logs or boards will normally admit enough air.

Plywood panels can be held together with hooks and eyes bolted

BUILDING A COMPOST PILE

Start with a 1-ft.-thick layer of soft vegetable matter, 2 ft. square. Tread down and water. Cover with 2–3 in. of enriched soil. Build the pile layer by layer, as garden and kitchen waste becomes available.

The wooden slatted sides allow air into the compost, while the front can be added piece by piece as the compost builds up.

Wooden homemade compost bin

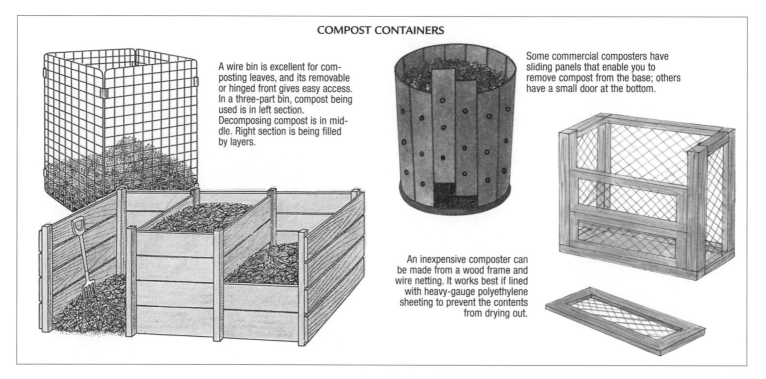

COMPOST CONTAINERS

A wire bin is excellent for composting leaves, and its removable or hinged front gives easy access. In a three-part bin, compost being used is in left section. Decomposing compost is in middle. Right section is being filled by layers.

Some commercial composters have sliding panels that enable you to remove compost from the base; others have a small door at the bottom.

An inexpensive composter can be made from a wood frame and wire netting. It works best if lined with heavy-gauge polyethylene sheeting to prevent the contents from drying out.

through and bent around each corner, while boards can be screwed to corner posts or slotted inside angle irons driven into the soil at each corner. Try to make the front in sections that can be added as the depth of the contents increases. If the soil under the composter is very heavy and slow to drain, place some paving slabs in the base of the composter, leaving gaps between them to act as drainage channels, so that following heavy rain, the bottom layer won't be sitting in water.

Another form of construction is to make a frame of lumber covered with heavy-duty wire netting. The disadvantage is that, like a compost pile, the outside dries out and doesn't decompose. If lined with heavy-duty polyethylene sheeting (such as used potting soil bags) this problem is overcome (be sure to make slits in

the bags to allow excess moisture to escape). This makes a very good container for leaves, which all arrive over a short time period, but which break down fairly rapidly. They are often ready for use, even if not completely decomposed, before the leaves fall the following year.

What to Compost

Virtually any vegetable material can be added to the compost, although diseased plants and weeds that have gone to seed are best disposed of in the garbage. Most kitchen wastes are easy to compost, but don't add meat or dairy products as they will attract vermin. You can also add hair and vacuum cleaner contents (synthetic fibers won't break down but small amounts still help to open the soil). Pet litter should go into the garbage as it could contain parasites. From

the garden, add lawn clippings, weeds not in seed, and flower heads.

More difficult to compost are the woody stems of perennials, cabbage stems, corn stalks, small branch prunings, etc. Unless you can cut them into small pieces, they take a lot longer to decompose. They will break down in time but may have to be recycled through the compost twice to fully decompose. The use of a shredder, which chops these woody stems into very small pieces, speeds decomposition greatly.

The bacteria that break down the compost material need energy to do their job. This comes from the carbohydrates in the raw compost, which contain carbon. They also need nitrogen and phosphorus to make proteins. All the waste material you add to the compost bin contains both carbon and nitrogen, but in different

proportions. In general, green material, such as soft weeds, lettuce leaves, flower petals, is rich in nitrogen, while more woody material, such as flower stems, thin twigs, and potato peelings, is higher in carbon. As a rough guide, add three times as much green stuff as woody to produce good compost. The presence of woody material also helps to hold the material open, allowing essential air to permeate the heap. Too much green material at one time, a thick layer of lawn clippings for example, will pack down and exclude the air. Decomposition still takes place but it involves different bacteria, known as anaerobic bacteria, and one by-product is a foul-smelling gas. Grass clipping should always be mixed with more coarse material as they are added. Maintaining this ratio may be difficult during the summer months

Spread compost as a mulch after planting container-grown shrubs.

Adding compost

when the bulk of the waste is soft growth and weeds, but you can always add shredded newspaper to supply the required carbon.

Using the Compost

If, when you dig down below the surface layer, you discover a dark-brown to black, sweet smelling material that resembles soil, the compost is ready for use. The time needed to make usable compost varies with the climate. In warm regions that have very little winter, it could be as quickly as three months, but in northern climates, with long, cold winters, a full year may be needed. In a commercial container with sliding panels, it is possible to take small amounts from the base when you need them. With a large heap or container, the most convenient time to use the compost is usually in the fall. At this time the garden is being cleaned up, vegetable beds are being dug ready for the following spring, and the compost can be dug in where needed, used as a mulch around trees and shrubs, or spread between perennials.

Lift off the top undecomposed layer with a garden fork and set it to one side. This layer will be about 6 inches deep and makes the base for the next pile. If you have a double composter, it can go directly into the other side. As you shovel out the

compost, separate out any undecomposed woody material that you find and add it to the top layer for further time in the composter. The best way to remove the finished compost is to slice it downward, like cutting a block of cheese, so that you get material from every level mixed together. This evens out the different nutritional levels that may occur in the compost.

Green Manuring

You can improve the texture of your soil, even without adding compost or buying ready-made humus by the process known as green manuring. It is particularly useful if you are in the garden-planning stage but not ready to make permanent plantings. Any area that will not be needed for a couple of months can be improved by green manuring. It adds organic matter to the soil which helps increase the nutrient level, and improves the drainage on heavy soils or the water-holding capacity on light ones.

Green manuring involves growing a crop of a quick-maturing plant and digging it into the soil just before it flowers. The best crops for green manuring are legumes. Members of the pea family, they use bacteria present in the soil that has the ability to extract nitrogen from the air. The legumes can store nitrogen in nodules on their roots in a form that can

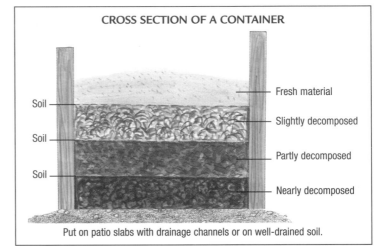

CROSS SECTION OF A CONTAINER

Soil — Fresh material

Soil — Slightly decomposed

Soil — Partly decomposed

Nearly decomposed

Put on patio slabs with drainage channels or on well-drained soil.

be used by plants. When the plants are dug under, the nitrogen is released and made available for the following crop.

Dig over the area to be sown to break up any surface crust and remove perennial weeds. Then sow with clover, alfalfa, cow peas, lupines, or beans. The first time you do this, add a legume inoculant to ensure the necessary bacteria are present in the soil. Other, non-legume crops that can be used for green manuring include buckwheat, ryegrass, mustard, alfalfa, millet, and most other cereals. All these can usu-

ally be obtained from a farm supply store if they are not listed in your regular seed catalog. Any time before the crop starts to set seed, it can be dug into the ground to provide humus. Depending on the length of the growing season, it is possible to turn under three crops of buckwheat in a single summer. In warm climates, green manure crops are often sown in fall to turn under in spring. As the green crop breaks down in the soil it causes a temporary nitrogen shortage, so it helps to add blood meal or fish meal to counteract this. Apply at half a cup per square yard.

An easily made leaf composter. Fork over the area to improve the drainage.

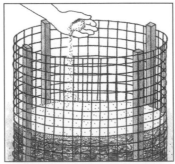

Make a wire cage around wooden stakes, add compost accelerator to each layer.

When full, cover with a layer of soil to prevent them from blowing away.

By next fall they will be decomposed and can be forked out for use in the garden.

Crumbly soil is ideal for a garden, so begin by improving it with humus to make the soil friable.

A friable soil is easy to hoe

Working the Soil

Tools for Working the Soil

However small your plot of land, when you set about turning it into a garden you will find that some tools are basic necessities. It is important to have a sharp spade to open the soil, a garden fork to break it up, a shovel to dig holes in it, and a garden rake to level its surface.

Then you will need a trowel for small-scale digging, a garden hoe and a scuffle hoe to keep down weeds, and a long-handled and short-handled cultivator to keep the surface loose and friable. You will also need a high-quality garden hose, equipped with an adjustable nozzle, and a garden line to ensure you have straight rows.

If your garden space is larger than 500 square feet, a rotary tiller may be a worthwhile investment; it makes deep cultivation a quick and relatively effortless job. A wheelbarrow is in order, as well as a light roller. Other tools that may come in handy include a crowbar for lifting large rocks, and a mattock or pick for breaking hard-packed surfaces.

When buying tools, look for the best—cheap tools are always more expensive in the long run. Lift each one to be sure the handle fits your hands comfortably and the tool is well balanced. Carefully examine the way the handle is joined to the working end; this is the weak point. Round handles should be fitted into long metal shanks and riveted firmly in place. Make sure all cutting edges are solid, sharp, and well aligned.

Good tools deserve good care. Clean them off after use. Remove rust spots with a solvent and steel wool. Use a file to smooth out nicks as soon as they occur. Tighten anything that is loose, and occasionally apply a drop of oil to moving parts. At the end of the season, rub down all metal parts with an oily rag and wooden handles with boiled linseed oil before storing tools for the winter.

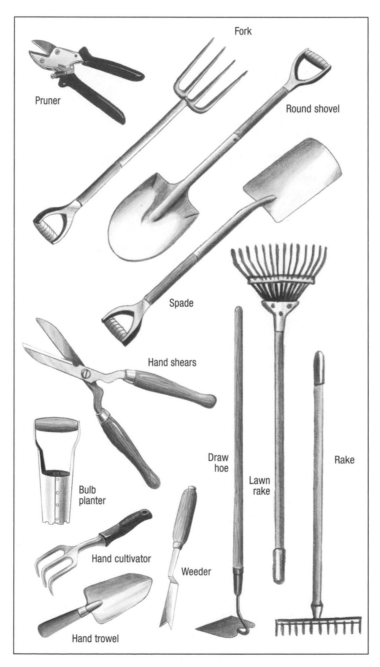

Pruner
Fork
Round shovel
Spade
Hand shears
Bulb planter
Draw hoe
Lawn rake
Rake
Hand cultivator
Weeder
Hand trowel

Correcting Poor Drainage

Dig a hole 2 feet deep, and fill it with water. If water remains after 24 hours, drainage is poor. Root growth will be limited even with sandy topsoil.

Poor drainage may simply be the result of compacted subsoil or a hardpan. In either case, the problem is easily solved by double digging to break through the hardpan and then working in porous material to lighten the subsoil. If this has no effect, it means that the water table is high. You will have to choose between growing shallow-rooted plants, raising the garden, or lowering the water table.

The water table should be about 4 feet down, where it can provide a reservoir for the deep roots of trees and shrubs.

In low-lying areas it may be possible to lower the water table by digging trenches across slopes above your garden to divert water as it runs down. Or you may need to install a drainage system.

In the latter case the first step is to decide where excess water will go. It must drain to a point lower than the lowest point of the system. The obvious choices are a nearby pond, stream, ditch, or downward slope.

Dig a trench 2–3 feet deep, running downward from the highest point of your garden to such an outlet. On the bottom, place lengths of earthenware or concrete pipe, 4–6 inches in diameter. Leave $1/8$-inch gaps between them. Cover with 8–10 inches of coarse gravel; then replace the soil.

If no simple outlets exist, the alternatives are to connect with a storm drain or to build a dry well, which is a deep, gravel-filled pit. Both jobs are best left to experts.

There are also many trees, shrubs, and perennials that will grow in such conditions, and the easiest solution may be to plant these.

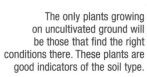

The only plants growing on uncultivated ground will be those that find the right conditions there. These plants are good indicators of the soil type.

Wild mustard—sandy

Chamomile—slightly acid

1. Insert the spade upright, driving it in deeply with the weight of the body.

2. Slide one hand down the handle, and bend both knees slightly.

3. Lift the loaded spade by straightening the legs.

How to Dig the Garden

If you create a garden with permanent pathways and do not walk on the beds, you should have to dig the soil only once. In subsequent years, you can simply loosen the soil slightly with a digging fork and work compost into the first few inches of soil.

First, divide the plot down the middle, and mark the centerline. Dig out a 1-foot-wide trench to the depth of the spade blade, running from one side of the plot to the middle. Put the soil in a pile just outside the plot near the centerline. It will be used later to fill the last trench.

There is a technique to digging, illustrated above, that lightens the strain on your back. Also, avoid overloading each spadeful; it just makes the work more difficult.

If you are adding compost or other humus, spread it evenly over the ground. Hold some aside with the soil for the final trench. Push the humus from the next strip of ground into the trench you have dug, spreading it evenly.

Now, dig the second strip across the half plot, turning each spadeful upside down into the first trench, so that what was on the surface is now about 10 inches deep.

Continue in this way, one strip of soil at a time, to the end of the plot; then work back along the other half. Fill the final trench with the soil from the first one.

Sterilizing Infested Soil

When the same soil is used repeatedly in the greenhouse, cold frame, or even with potted plants, eventually it is almost certain to become infested with nematodes, fungi, and other soil-borne pests and diseases. They can be destroyed by sterilizing the soil with heat.

The simplest and most effective method of heat sterilization is with steam. There are high-pressure units available for steaming large amounts of soil at a time, but unless yours is a big greenhouse operation, it is hardly practical to buy one. If a source of steam is available, however, you can attach a piece of garden hose to the outlet and insert the end into a flat basket or box of soil. Maintain steam for 45 minutes to 1 hour.

You can accomplish the same end in another way. First, bring ½ pint of water to a boil in a large saucepan. Then put 3-4 quarts of dry soil in the pan, cover tightly, and return to boil. After 5 to 6 minutes, turn off the heat, but keep tightly covered for another 8 to 10 minutes.

There are some other ways of sterilizing small quantities of soil using kitchen equipment. In a regular oven, fill a shallow ovenproof dish with soil, cover with tinfoil and insert a meat thermometer. Preheat the oven to 200°F and put the dish of soil in the oven. When the soil temperature reaches 140°F start a timer set for 30 minutes. Be sure to keep a check on the soil temperature, which should not be allowed to rise above 180°F. If necessary, remove the soil from the oven and allow to cool slightly.

You can also sterilize soil in the microwave. Make sure the soil is moist and free of stones and foreign matter. Put the soil in a microwave-safe bowl or a baking bag but do not seal. Two pounds of soil will take 10-15 minutes to heat at 30-40 percent power, or 2½ minutes at full power. Watch out for sparks which indicate that there is metal in the soil. Stop immediately if this occurs and carefully remove the metal if possible. Sterilizing the soil by heating can produce a very strong odor. Be sure to keep windows open.

Watering: How Much and How Often

Nutrients are useless to plants until they have been dissolved in water. They are equally useless to ordinary land plants if they are in waterlogged soil. The main day-to-day problem facing the gardener, therefore, is likely to be too much or too little water in the soil.

The problem of too little water is easier to solve, provided there is a source from which to augment nature's gift of rain. In general, the time to water is when about half the moisture that the soil is capable of holding has dried out. Determine this point by picking up a handful of topsoil and squeezing it into a ball: if it holds its shape, moisture is probably sufficient; if it crumbles easily, more water is probably needed.

When watering, soak the soil to at least a foot deep. Mere surface sprinkling encourages shallow roots, which are vulnerable to scorching in the hot sun. (Seedlings, however, including young lawn grass, may need as many as two light sprinklings a day until their short roots have grown deeper.)

How often you should water depends on the condition of your soil, the weather, the kinds of plants you are growing, and their location. Vegetables, on the average, need twice as much water as flowers. Newly planted trees and shrubs require frequent watering in dry weather. Plants sheltered by walls or hedges may need watering even after a rainstorm, but they are not likely to dry out as fast as plants in the open. Plants high on a slope will dry out faster than those at the bottom. Plants growing in light, sandy soil need watering oftener than those growing in heavier soil.

Prevent moisture loss by mulching the soil surface. The kind and amount of mulch to use varies with different plants; consult appropriate sections of this book, and the facing page.

After digging out perennial weeds, fork compost into the soil to prepare a bed for planting.

Preparing a bed

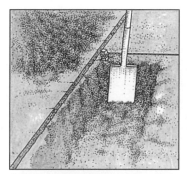

1. Pile soil from first trench at the end of the plot near the centerline.

2. Use a fork to break up the trench bottom, and work in some humus.

3. Dig second 2-ft. trench, turning the soil upside down into the first.

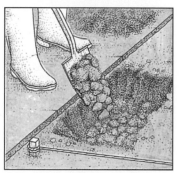

4. Use the pile of soil from the first trench to fill the final trench.

Preparing a Bed by Double Digging

Sometimes, to improve drainage or to prepare a bed for deep-rooted plants, it is useful to work the soil more deeply than single digging allows. This is done by double digging.

Divide the plot to be dug, and mark the centerline, as with single digging (see facing page). Dig the first trench 2 feet wide and to the depth of the spade blade, running from the side of the plot to the middle. Pile the soil near the centerline. Spread humus over the ground still to be dug.

Then use a garden fork to thoroughly break up the bottom of the trench. Push in the humus from the top of the next 2-foot strip, and work

it in evenly with the fork. Then dig the next 2-foot strip, turning each spadeful of soil upside down into the open trench. Break up the bottom of this trench with the fork, and work in the humus from the next strip. Continue in this manner around the two half plots until the final trench is filled with soil from the first.

If humus is in short supply, dig what you have in with the topsoil and use undecomposed material in the trench base. This could be garden waste from the compost that has not yet broken down, leaves, straw, manure, or any other potential source of humus. The material will decompose slowly underground, but even in the rough state will help improve the structure of the soil.

Mulching

Mulches have three main functions; they regulate soil temperature, reduce water loss, and help with weed control. They may be organic, inorganic, or a combination of both.

Sheets of plastic laid on the soil in early spring will warm the soil quickly and enable it to dry out faster. They can be used to prepare a site for an early crop of lettuce, or to warm the soil for sowing melon seeds. Black plastic has the advantage that it smothers any weed seedlings that germinate beneath it and can be used to control perennial weeds.

Loose mulches laid between the plants or around trees and shrubs insulate the soil from extremes of temperature, but they also work in reverse and hold high or low temperatures in the soil. This is important where winters are cold. Trees planted in fall should not be mulched until the following summer. A mulch applied at planting time keeps the soil frozen until late spring. The tree's roots are only under the mulched area, while the tops, in warm air, start to grow before the soil thaws

and the roots can take up moisture, often killing the tree.

Where winters alternate between freeze and thaw, heaving can be a problem. A loose mulch applied in early winter after the soil has cooled, or even frozen, will help prevent this.

By protecting the surface of the soil from the sun and wind, loose mulches help reduce water evaporation. If applied 4–6 inches deep, they cut off the light to weed seeds so they do not germinate. If laid around trees and shrubs, the mulch should not be put close to the trunk, and should extend to the end of the branches.
Organic mulches. These should be large enough to resist being blown or washed away, but must allow the passage of water and air. Coarse bark chips and shredded cedar bark are the most commonly available, but cocoa husks or spent hops are also good mulches.
Inorganic mulches. In addition to plastic sheeting, landscape fabric, or geotextile cloth, is used. It allows water to pass through, stops weeds from growing, but will break down in sunlight and has to be covered with a thin layer of organic mulch.

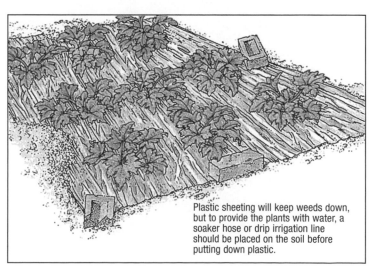

Plastic sheeting will keep weeds down, but to provide the plants with water, a soaker hose or drip irrigation line should be placed on the soil before putting down plastic.

PLANT DISORDERS

Most plant ailments can be treated successfully. First, identify the problem from the pictures and descriptions; then, apply the remedy recommended.

This section will enable you to recognize and control the pests, diseases, and physiological disorders that most commonly strike cultivated plants.

Although these problems present a formidable picture when viewed together, only a few are likely to afflict a single garden.

Check the plants in your garden every couple of days to see whether the leaves, stems, or flowers appear in any way unhealthy. For example, are they distorted or discolored?

It is best to take remedial action as quickly as possible.

Warning: do not spray when blossoms are open; you may kill the pollinating insects.

Plants that have been regularly attacked in the past by certain pests and diseases should be protected against them in advance. Soils that are known to harbor pests should be cultivated frequently with a fork or hoe, or treated with a suitable control for the specific problem. Crop rotation also helps.

How to identify plant disorders. On the left is an ailing dahlia. The leaves have tattered holes; the shoots are rotting and covered in places with a gray fungus; the roots have been damaged by larvae.

In the ensuing pages, the illustrations of symptoms are set out in the following order: leaves, shoots, flower buds, flowers in bloom, fruits, vegetables, root structures, and lawns. The picture may not show the plant affected in your garden, but each caption lists the plants most commonly affected, the symptoms and signs, the danger period, as well as the treatment.

To discover what is wrong with the dahlia's leaves, look through the illustrations under the heading Leaves With Holes (starting on p. 507) until you find the one that most closely resembles the damage. In this instance it is plant-bug damage, as described on page 508, together with the proper control. (This illustration is also shown top right, this page.)

By turning to the section Shoots Discolored, you will find that the shoots of the dahlia may be suffering from gray mold (see p. 523).

When a plant is obviously ailing but no damage is visible aboveground, dig it up. Perhaps its roots, like those of the dahlia are being attacked by wireworms (see p. 536).

Treatments recommended for various disorders use environment-friendly methods. Consult the section on biological controls and other organic controls, that begins on page 542. There you will discover what all-natural forms are available and what treatments are best for your garden.

Leaves with tattered holes (by plant bugs, or leaf bugs)

Shoots rotting and disfigured (by botrytis)

Roots attacked (by wireworms)

Plant bug, or leaf bug

Botrytis, or gray mold

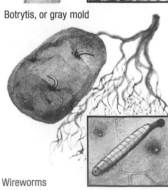

Wireworms

Depending on where you live, snails may be quite small, or very large. They all eat plants.

Snails

Leaves With Pests Visible

Scale insects
Plants affected: Camellias, foliage plants, and many others.
Symptoms and signs: Flat or rounded scales.
Danger period: Spring, early summer outdoors; any time indoors.
Treatment: On dormant deciduous trees and shrubs, apply dormant oil in late winter. In late spring, spray with neem or summer oil. Apply insecticidal soap on greenhouse plants. Rub scales off houseplants. Move houseplants and greenhouse plants outdoors when warm so natural predators can attack scales.

Aphids
Plants affected: Nearly all cultivated plants.
Symptoms and signs: Colonies of small insects.
Danger period: Spring and early summer outdoors; any time of year indoors.
Treatment: Wash aphids off plants with strong stream of water. Encourage predators such as lacewings and lady beetles. Apply repellent sprays such as garlic. Spray infested plants with insecticidal soap or neem.

Whiteflies
Plants affected: Ageratums, azaleas, Brussels sprouts, cabbage, chrysanthemums, cucumbers, fuchsias, gerberas, lantanas, tomatoes, and many other plants.
Symptoms and signs: White insects beneath leaves. Leaves off-color.
Danger period: Late spring to early fall outdoors; all year in heated greenhouse or indoors.
Treatment: Spray plants with insecticidal soap. Trap adults on yellow sticky boards. Destroy old plants.

Leaves With Holes

Caterpillars (including inchworms, gypsy moth larvae, and tent caterpillars)
Plants affected: Many different plants, especially shrubs and trees.
Symptoms and signs: Irregular pieces eaten from foliage, often leaving large holes.
Danger period: From early spring onward.
Treatment: If possible, remove caterpillars by hand picking or pruning. Or spray thoroughly with *Bacillus thuringiensis kurstaki* when symptoms appear.

Colorado potato beetles
Plants affected: Eggplants, peppers, tomatoes, white potatoes.
Symptoms and signs: Large pieces of leaves chewed out by larvae (grubs).
Danger period: Late spring to fall.
Treatment: Surround plants with a deep layer of straw. Crush egg masses with your fingers, handpick and destroy larvae and adults. Apply *Beauveria bassiana* or spinosad to kill young larvae.

Mealybugs
Plants affected: Annuals, grapes, citrus.
Symptoms and signs: Small pink insects on leaves. Masses of white "cotton" at leaf nodes.
Danger period: Any time.
Treatment: Spray thoroughly with insecticidal soap. Introduce mealybug destroyer in the West. Another solution is to paint small colonies with 50% rubbing alcohol.

Japanese beetles
Plants affected: Grapes, lindens, roses, and many other plants.
Symptoms and signs: Petals frayed and leaves skeletonized. Green beetles may be visible.
Danger period: Early summer to midfall.
Treatment: Handpick and destroy beetles. When possible, cover plants with row cover. Apply neem to deter feeding, or spray insecticidal soap or pyrethrins.

Earwigs
Plants affected: Clematises, dahlias, gladioli, and some other plants, especially young vegetables.
Symptoms and signs: Irregular, tattered holes in leaves.
Danger period: Late spring to midfall.
Treatment: Trap by providing daytime hiding places, such as pots filled with straw or short pieces of old hose pipe. Empty daily.

Slugs are hostas' worst enemy but some varieties are eaten more than others.

Hosta eaten by slugs

Leaves With Holes (*continued*)

Leaftiers and leaf rollers, or tortrix caterpillars

Plants affected: Shrubs, trees, and herbaceous plants, especially apples, chrysanthemums, heleniums, perennial phlox.
Symptoms and signs: Small holes eaten in leaves; later, leaves are drawn together with silk webbing.
Danger period: Late spring to early summer outdoors; any time of year in greenhouse.
Treatment: Spray thoroughly with *Bacillus thuringiensis* as soon as larvae hatch; or remove caterpillars by hand.

Vine and flower weevils

Plants affected: Camellias, clematises, primroses, rhododendrons, yews, various vines.
Symptoms and signs: Small, irregular notches eaten from leaf edges. Roots chewed by larvae.
Danger period: Spring and summer outdoors; any time of year in greenhouse.
Treatment: Remove accumulations of plant debris where weevils rest by day; drench soil with parasitic nematodes.

Plant bugs, or leaf bugs
(four-lined, harlequin, tarnished)

Plants affected: Apples, beans, buddleias, currants, dahlias, forsythias, and many other plants.
Symptoms and signs: Tattered holes in young leaves.
Danger period: Midspring to late summer.
Treatment: Good garden hygiene and weed control can reduce damage. Protect plants with a floating row cover. Apply *Beauveria bassiana* or neem.

Shot-hole disease

Plants affected: Cherries, peaches, plums, and other *Prunus* species.
Symptoms and signs: Brown patches on leaves drop out and leave irregularly shaped holes.
Danger period: Growing season.
Treatment: First, determine whether the disease is bacterial or fungal—more than one pathogen can cause these symptoms. For fungal infection, prune off and destroy infected plant parts. Spraying Bordeaux mixture or copper may help. For bacterial infection, feed trees annually and prune to improve air circulation.

Rose slugs (sawfly larvae)

Plants affected: Roses.
Symptoms and signs: Irregular areas in leaves eaten partly through, leaving transparent membranes.
Danger period: Early summer to early fall.
Treatment: Spray thoroughly with neem or horticultural oil.

Pea leaf weevils

Plants affected: Beans, peas.
Symptoms and signs: Leaf edges eaten in scalloped pattern.
Danger period: Early spring to early summer.
Treatment: Cover young seedlings with row covers until they become established. Damage to established plants is not significant.

Gooseberry sawflies (larvae)

Plants affected: Gooseberries.
Symptoms and signs: Leaf tissues eaten away, with many leaves reduced to skeleton of veins.
Danger period: Midspring to late summer.
Treatment: Spray thoroughly with insecticidal soap or neem in midspring or when symptoms first appear.

Leaf-cutting bees use the pieces they remove to make their nests.

Damage by leaf-cutting bees

Leaves With Altered Color

Slugs and snails

Plants affected: Delphiniums, lettuce, lilies, tulips, sweet peas, hostas, and many other plants.
Symptoms and signs: Irregular holes in leaves; slime trails visible.
Danger period: Spring to midfall.
Treatment: Cultivate thoroughly, and dispose of decaying plant material. Avoid heavy mulches. Beer placed in shallow pans or saucers will drown slugs. Apply iron phosphate baits.

Flea beetles

Plants affected: Cabbage, radishes, tomatoes, turnips, and related plants.
Symptoms and signs: Youngest leaves pitted with tiny holes.
Danger period: Dry spells in late spring.
Treatment: Cover young plants with a floating row-cover fabric. Good garden hygiene will reduce the risk of attack. Deter flea beetles by spraying plants with garlic sprays or kaolin clay.

Tar spot

Plants affected: Maples.
Symptoms and signs: Large, raised black spots with bright yellow edges.
Danger period: Summer.
Treatment: Rake up and destroy affected leaves. This disease is seldom serious enough to cause lasting harm to a tree.

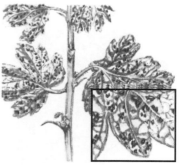

Anthracnose and other dark leaf spots

Plants affected: Many types.
Symptoms and signs: Brown, round or oval spots, often with definite margins and sometimes showing small black pinpoints.
Danger period: Growing season.
Treatment: Remove and destroy affected leaves. Choose resistant varieties when available. Stake and prune plants to improve air circulation. Sulfur sprays may help prevent spread.

Leaf-cutting ants and bees

Plants affected: Golden chains, lilacs, privets, and roses.
Symptoms and signs: Semi-circular pieces eaten out of leaf edges.
Danger period: Early to late summer.
Treatment: Leaf-cutting bees are useful pollinators, so do not take measures to kill them; tolerate the damage. For leaf-cutting ants, spray plants with garlic sprays or neem to repel the ants.

Water-lily beetles

Plants affected: Water lilies (both species and hybrids).
Symptoms and signs: Surface tissue of leaves eaten away in furrows. Flowers may also be damaged.
Danger period: Early to late summer.
Treatment: Spray or hose plants forcibly with water to knock adult beetles and larvae off leaves so that fish can feed on them.

Willow anthracnose, or leaf spot

Plants affected: Weeping willows.
Symptoms and signs: Small brown spots on leaves.
Danger period: As leaves unfold in spring; sometimes in wet summers.
Treatment: Spray small trees as leaves unfold with fungicide, such as Bordeaux mixture.

Use a strong stream of water
to rinse aphids off plants.

Spray water

Leaves With Altered Color (*continued*)

Leaf spot

Plants affected: Most trees and shrubs, perennials, annuals, vegetables, and house plants. Note, however, that "leaf spot" is a very general term that can apply to many diseases, some fungal, some bacterial. As such, there is no way to recommend effective spray treatment without first getting a specific diagnosis of the type of disease.
Symptoms and signs: Small black, brown, purple, or gray spots, often with a yellow halo, but may appear water-soaked.
Danger period: Growing season.
Treatment: Remove and destroy infected foliage. Keep plants healthy, but avoid over-fertilizing. If problem is severe, identify the specific pathogen causing the problem and seek appropriate controls.

Yellow mottle

Plants affected: Camellias.
Symptoms and signs: Some leaves have white blotches; other leaves turn completely white; can be caused by a virus. Mutation or genetic variegation can also cause these symptoms.
Danger period: Any time after a cutting (scion) from infected plant is used for graft.
Treatment: Destroy badly affected plants. Isolate those with mottle from healthy ones. No infected plant should be used as source of propagating material.

Scab

Plants affected: Apples, flowering crab apples, firethorns, pears.
Symptoms and signs: Olive-green blotches of fungal growth on leaves, which fall prematurely.
Danger period: Growing season.
Treatment: Cut out cracked and scabby shoots when pruning. Spray with sulfur when flower buds are nearly open, when petals fall, and 3 wk. later.

For illustration of scab on fruit, see p. 532.

Rusts

Plants affected: Many types, but particularly apples, flowering quinces, hawthorns, red cedars, white pines, asparagus, barberries, beans, carnations, geraniums (*Pelargonium*), hollyhocks, Saint-John's-worts, snapdragons, sweet Williams, wheat.
Symptoms and signs: Brown, orange, or yellow powdery masses of spores develop on affected leaves and stems, and occasionally on flowers, fruits, and seedpods. Irregularly round galls are found on twigs.
Danger period: Growing season. Late summer for roses; autumn for sweet Williams.
Treatment: Rusts are of 2 types—1 host and 2 host. Two-host rusts have an alternate host; for instance, apple rust attacks red cedars as well as apples. This is true of barberries and wheat, cedars and hawthorns, white pines and currants. For 2-host rusts, it is a good idea to locate and destroy the alternate hosts. This will break the cycle and stop the disease.

To avoid rust problems, plant resistant cultivars when available. Remove and destroy diseased leaves for all types of plants; also prune off rusted twigs and galls when found. For plants in greenhouses, reduce humidity by ventilating. For outdoor plants such as asparagus and annual and perennial flowers, space plants more widely to improve air circulation. Sulfur sprays can be effective at preventing the disease, but timing of sprays depends on the specific plants to be protected. Seek crop-specific advice before spraying, because frequent sulfur sprays can lead to mite infestations on many plants.

Hosta virus X

Plants affected: Hosta
Symptoms and signs: Leaves develop thin and wrinkled areas, variegation tends to flow along veins from darker areas into lighter.
Danger period: Any part of the growing season.
Treatment: Destroy infected plants immediately. This is very contagious and can spread on hands, boots, equipment. Buy plants only from a local source after inspecting them and plant in a separate location, away from other hostas. It may take several years to become obvious.

Water roses by soaking the soil, rather than overhead, to avoid splashing the black spot spores onto uninfected leaves.

Rose black spot disease

Leaf mold

Plants affected: Tomatoes in greenhouses.

Symptoms and signs: Purple-brown mold on undersides of leaves; on upper surfaces whitish spots appear first and develop into yellow blotches.

Danger period: From early summer onward and sometimes in mid to late spring.

Treatment: Grow resistant varieties. Keep humidity below 85 percent and increase air circulation. Take care to avoid wetting leaves when watering, since spores are spread by splashing water. Avoid overfertilizing with nitrogen. When harvest is complete remove and destroy all crop residue and disinfect the greenhouse.

Pear leaf blister mites

Plants affected: Pears, mountain ashes.

Symptoms and signs: Numerous dark brown pustules appear on both sides of leaves.

Danger period: Midspring to late summer.

Treatment: Grow russet pears, which do not show mite damage. Pick off affected leaves and destroy. To control mites, spray with lime sulfur after harvest or with dormant oil while dormant.

Botrytis, or gray mold

Plants affected: All types, but particularly chrysanthemums, lettuce, and tomatoes in greenhouses, as well as many outdoor crops; also, dogwoods, hydrangeas, lilacs, peonies.

Symptoms and signs: Gray velvety mold on rotting leaves.

Danger period: Entire growing season, especially following wet weather.

Treatment: Remove infected foliage if possible, improve air circulation.

Rose black spot

Plants affected: Roses.

Symptoms and signs: Distinct black or dark brown spots, either small and diffuse or up to $\frac{1}{2}$ in. across. Leaves soon turn yellow and fall prematurely.

Danger period: Growing season; worst from early summer on.

Treatment: Rake up and destroy diseased leaves. Avoid overhead watering because this may splash spores onto uninfected leaves. Encourage plant vigor by spraying bushes with compost tea and giving them good general care throughout the growing season. Prune previously infected plants back hard to allow uninfected regrowth. Spray plants with a potassium bicarbonate fungicide to prevent symptoms; sulfur sprays can also be effective.

Edema

Plants affected: Mainly camellias, zonal geraniums (*Pelargonium*), and vines.

Symptoms and signs: Small, water-soaked spots that break out into corky growths.

Danger period: Growing season indoors.

Treatment: Ventilate greenhouse to reduce humidity, and be sure that plants are not waterlogged.

Lace bugs

Plants affected: Mountain laurels, pierises, rhododendrons (including azaleas), and many other deciduous trees and shrubs.

Symptoms and signs: Silvery gray spots on leaves. Hard black spots and tiny lace bugs on undersides.

Danger period: Late spring to early fall.

Treatment: Spray leaf undersides thoroughly with superior oil or insecticidal soap in early summer; repeat 2 wk. later.

A late spring frost can damage tender young foliage. Protect plants with a floating row cover if frost is forecast.

Plant affected by frost

Leaves With Altered Color (*continued*)

Two-spotted, or red spider, mites

Plants affected: Many plants. Cucumbers, dahlias, fuchsias, peaches, roses, strawberries, and violets are particularly susceptible.

Symptoms and signs: Very fine, light mottling of upper leaf surfaces, followed by general yellow discoloration and sometimes death. Severely infested plants may be covered with silk webbing.

Danger period: Almost any time of year in greenhouses, early spring to late fall outdoors.

Treatment: Maintain humid atmosphere in greenhouse, spraying plants with water if necessary. Outdoors, mist daily with water early in the day. Thorough spraying with insecticidal soap may check infestations, but mites become resistant relatively quickly. Release commercially available mite predators. There are several different ones for greeenhouse or garden use (see p. 542).

White rust

Plants affected: Aubrietas, cabbage, candytufts, honesties, radishes, sweet alyssums.

Symptoms and signs: Blisters or swellings, full of white powdery spores and often glistening, develop on leaves and sometimes on stems.

Danger period: Growing season.

Treatment: Cut off and destroy diseased leaves. Eradicate shepherd's purse, a common weed of the cabbage family that is important overwinter host for white rust fungus.

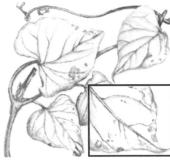

Cold damage

Plants affected: Magnolias, morning glories (*Ipomoea*), sweet peas, bedding plants, and others.

Symptoms and signs: Young, soft leaves become white or pale yellow.

Danger period: Seedling stage.

Treatment: None, but applications of foliar fertilizer can help restore green color to foliage.

Gall aphids

Plants affected: Common and serious on spruces. Can also appear on firs, larches, pines, and other conifers.

Symptoms and signs: Green swelling occurs on new growth in late spring. Colonies of small, dark aphids partially covered by tufts of white woolly wax infest undersides of leaves and leaf axils.

Danger period: Spring, but symptoms may not be noticed until browning appears in summer.

Treatment: For spruces and Douglas firs, spray dormant oil before midspring, and follow with contact spray of insecticidal soap in late spring. Be sure to spray bark crevices on twig tips and bases of buds. Do not use dormant oil sprays on blue-needled evergreens.

Spittlebugs, or froghoppers

Plants affected: Chrysanthemums, clovers, lavenders, perennial asters, pines, roses, and many other plants.

Symptoms and signs: Frothy masses of "frog spit" covering small pink or green insects.

Danger period: Early to mid summer.

Treatment: Wash off "frog spit" with water from garden hose. Then spray exposed insects with insecticidal soap.

Powdery mildew

Powdery mildew attacks many plants and is difficult to control, especially on trees and shrubs.

Silver leaf

Plants affected: Cherries, peaches, plums, and other *Prunus* species; apples, lilacs, pears; other trees and shrubs.

Symptoms and signs: Leaves become silvered, and upper surfaces peel off easily. When cross section of affected branch 1 in. or more across is moistened, brown or purple stain appears. Flat, purple fungus eventually develops on deadwood. Affected branches ultimately die back.

Danger period: Early fall to late spring. Symptoms may not appear until sometime after infection has taken place.

Treatment: Cut out affected branches to 6 in. below point where stain in wood stops. Feed, mulch, water, and/or drain soil as necessary to encourage vigor. Foliar applications of fertilizer may hasten recovery.

Conifer mites

Plants affected: Cypresses, junipers, pines, spruces, and some other conifers.

Symptoms and signs: Needles turn bronze and fall prematurely. Needles frequently covered with webbing spun by nearly microscopic mites.

Danger period: Early summer to early fall.

Treatment: Spray thoroughly with insecticidal soap in early summer; repeat as needed.

Leafhoppers

Plants affected: Geraniums (*Pelargonium*), primroses, roses, and other plants.

Symptoms and signs: Small white spots appear on leaves, caused by hoppers feeding on undersides. Molted insect skins can often be seen on undersides.

Danger period: Midspring to midfall outdoors, but any time of year indoors.

Treatment: Cover plants with row covers. Repel leafhoppers by applying garlic sprays or kaolin clay. As a last resort, spray insecticidal soap.

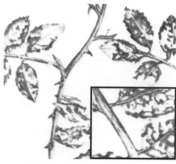

Powdery mildew

Plants affected: Many types, but especially begonias, euonymus, lilacs, perennial asters, phlox, roses, apples, gooseberries, strawberries, lawn grasses.

Symptoms and signs: White, floury coating on leaves and shoots, and sometimes on flowers. Strawberry leaves turn purple and curl.

Danger period: Growing season.

Treatment: Pick off affected leaves on herbaceous plants and cut out severely affected shoots on trees and shrubs. When feasible, spray plants with a milk spray (1 part milk mixed with 9 parts water), or apply *Bacillus subtilis* or compost tea. Potassium bicarbonate and fungicidal soap sprays can help prevent and reduce mildew. For strawberries, at early blossoming stage, spray 3 times at 2-wk. intervals with potassium bicarbonate. For apples, spraying sulfur weekly as new leaves develop provides control.

Frost damage

Plants affected: Cucumbers, snapdragons, tomatoes, and nearly all tender herbaceous plants.

Symptoms and signs: All leaves on seedlings or young plants are silvered.

Danger period: Seedlings and new-growth stage in spring, mature-plant stage in fall.

Treatment: To prevent frost damage, cover plants with floating row covers or light blankets.

Thrips

Plants affected: Gladioli, day lilies, peas, privets, and many other plants.

Symptoms and signs: Leaves finely mottled, with general silvery appearance. Flowers become deformed and discolored with pale streaks.

Danger period: Early summer to early fall, especially during hot, dry weather.

Treatment: Keep plants well watered. Spray or dust with spinosad or neem when signs are first seen.

Leaves With Altered Color (*continued*)

Lime-induced chlorosis
Plants affected: Many different types, but particularly ceanothus, hydrangeas, raspberries; also acid-soil plants, such as rhododendrons, growing in insufficiently acid soils.
Symptoms and signs: Yellowing between veins, which remain green.
Danger period: Growing season.
Treatment: Dig in acidifying materials, such as peat moss or sulfur. Apply foliar spray of kelp fertilizer.

Manganese deficiency
Plants affected: Many types.
Symptoms and signs: Yellowing between veins of older leaves.
Danger period: Growing season.
Treatment: Apply a foliar spray of kelp or compost tea. Test soil pH, and if soil is alkaline, add lime as directed to reduce pH. To boost manganese content in soil for the long term, add dried poultry manure and compost to soil.

Magnesium deficiency
Plants affected: All types, particularly apples and tomatoes.
Symptoms and signs: Orange bands between veins, which later become brown. Affected leaves may wither.
Danger period: Growing season or after applications of high-potassium fertilizer, which tends to hold magnesium in soil.
Treatment: Spray with solution of magnesium sulfate (Epsom salts): 8 rounded tbsp. to 2½ gal. of water, plus a few drops of liquid detergent.

Scorch
Plants affected: Woody plants, especially those growing close to buildings, particularly beeches, horse chestnuts, maples.
Symptoms and signs: Pale brown spots appear on leaves; entire leaves may become dry and papery.
Danger period: Spring for most trees and shrubs, summer for house plants and greenhouse plants.
Treatment: Shade greenhouse. Make sure that no plant suffers from dry soil (especially trees, during cold, drying spring winds). Spray affected plants with foliar applications of fertilizer.

Virus disease
Plants affected: All types, but particularly daffodils, lilies, raspberries, squash.
Symptoms and signs: Yellow striping (on daffodils and lilies) and blotching or mottling of leaves (on raspberries and squash).
Danger period: Growing season.
Treatment: Dig up and destroy. In the case of small fruits, plant only stocks certified to be free of virus. Spraying insects that carry virus can help prevent it; use insecticidal soap.

Leaf nematodes, or leaf eelworms and bud eelworms
Plants affected: Begonias, chrysanthemums, ferns, and some other plants.
Symptoms and signs: Brown or yellow mottling on leaves.
Danger period: Midsummer to early winter outdoors; year-round in greenhouses.
Treatment: Keep foliage and stems of plants reasonably dry if possible. Remove and destroy affected leaves and severely affected plants.

Lilac MLO (mycoplasma-like-organism)
Plants affected: Lilacs
Symptoms and signs: New foliage is pale green with darker streaks and may be twisted. Plant lacks vigor.
Danger period: Spring and summer.
Treatment: Dig up and destroy plant. Control aphids and leafhoppers that can spread this organism. Research is still taking place to determine the exact nature of this problem.

The Brussels sprouts have lost most of their foliage, probably to cabbage white caterpillars.

Brussels sprouts

Nitrogen deficiency

Plants affected: All types, but it is commonest on broad-leaved evergreens, fruit trees, and vegetables.
Symptoms and signs: Leaves yellow-green, later becoming yellow, red, or purple. Plants weak.
Danger period: Growing season.
Treatment: Apply nitrogenous fertilizer, such as blood meal, on trees and shrubs the following spring. Foliar applications of fish emulsion may help during growing season; on vegetables, side-dress with blood meal or alfalfa meal.

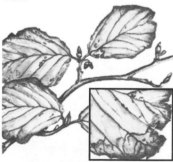

Nutrient deficiency

Plants affected: All types.
Symptoms and signs: Many leaves turn yellow and may fall prematurely.
Danger period: Growing season.
Treatment: Feed as necessary, mulch, and make sure soil never dries out. Drain if soil is waterlogged. Spray with foliar fertilizer, such as liquid seaweed.

Late blight

Plants affected: Potatoes, tomatoes.
Symptoms and signs: Purplish blotches on leaves, with white furry coating on undersides. Leaves quickly turn completely brown and then rot.
Danger period: Midsummer until end of season.
Treatment: Plant only certified disease-free seed potatoes. Few resistant varieties of tomatoes are available. Keep plant foliage dry as much as possible. Apply preventive sprays of compost tea. Remove and destroy infected plants. Clear out all crop debris after harvest. Repeated copper sprays can prevent infection, but can also lead to other pest problems. For illustration of potato tuber affected by late blight disease, turn to p. 537; for tomato fruit, see p. 533.

Dutch elm disease

Plants affected: American elms (*Ulmus americana*).
Symptoms and signs: Leaves turn yellow; then they turn brown and hang on dead branches. Brown discoloration of internal wood visible, as well as beetles' "feeding galleries" under bark. Wilting and dying of branches and leaves is caused by fungus, which is spread from tree to tree by elm bark beetles.
Danger period: Late spring to early fall.
Treatment: Destroy dead or badly damaged trees, including stumps; send to local incinerator. Isolate root system to prevent spread of fungus to other trees. Remove bark from logs before storing for firewood. In less severe cases, there may be a chance of saving tree if you remove diseased branches. For prevention it is important to keep trees well watered. Feed in spring and fall to maintain vigor. Prune infected limbs. To control *Scolytus* beetle that carries this disease, apply dormant oil spray in early spring. Use hydraulic sprayer or mist blower for tall trees. Call in professional tree expert. Plant resistant elm varieties. See also Elm Bark Beetles, p. 521

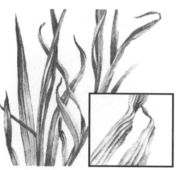

Fusarium yellows

Plants affected: Carnations, freesias, gladioli.
Symptoms and signs: Yellowing of leaves. Affected leaves eventually die.
Danger period: Growing season.
Treatment: Dig up and destroy affected plants. At end of season, dip remaining corms of freesias and gladioli in 10% household bleach before storing; plant them in different part of garden the following year.

Downy mildew

Plants affected: Cabbage, cucumbers, grapes, lettuce, onions, wallflowers.
Symptoms and signs: Yellow spots developing on upper leaf surfaces, gray or white furry patches on undersides.
Danger period: Fall and spring.
Treatment: Choose resistant varieties. Avoid growing crops during cool, wet weather. Promote good air circulation. Apply compost tea or potassium bicarbonate sprays to prevent symptoms, or neem when symptoms first appear. Copper-based fungicide is a last resort.

Leaves With Altered Color (*continued*)

Sooty mold

Plants affected: Many types, especially birches, camellias, citrus, lindens, oaks, plums, roses, willows.
Symptoms and signs: Black sooty deposits appear on upper leaf surfaces, and young leaves are sticky.
Danger period: Summer and autumn.
Treatment: Sooty molds develop on plants infested by such pests as aphids, mealybugs, and scale insects. Control pests with a strong stream of water or insecticidal soap.

European red mites

Plants affected: Apples, pears, plums, and some related ornamentals.
Symptoms and signs: Older leaves gradually turn bronze-yellow, dry out, and die. Webbing often present.
Danger period: Midspring to late fall.
Treatment: Plant flowering plants near your fruit trees to attract natural predators of mites. Spray dormant oil shortly after bud break. For severe infestations, spray insecticidal soap or horticultural oil.

Botrytis, or gray mold

Plants affected: Lilies.
Symptoms and signs: Oval spots, at first water soaked and then brown, eventually spread until entire leaf is affected.
Danger period: Until flowering time.
Treatment: Avoid overhead watering. Space plants widely for good air circulation. Remove and destroy infected leaves as soon as noticed.

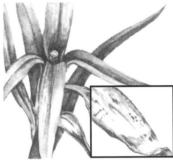

Fusarium wilt

Plants affected: Many types, particularly beans, carnations and other *Dianthus* species, peas, sweet peas, tomatoes.
Symptoms and signs: Leaves become discolored and plants wilt. Stem bases may also be discolored.
Danger period: Growing season.
Treatment: Remove and destroy affected plants. Select resistant varieties when possible. Grow susceptible plants on fresh site each year.

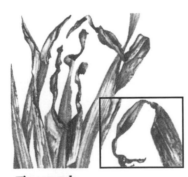

Tip scorch

Plants affected: Amaryllises (*Hippeastrum*), crinums, narcissi.
Symptoms and signs: Scorched or burned appearance at tips of leaves.
Danger period: Spring.
Treatment: Cut off affected leaf tips, and spray with fungicidal soap to prevent further fungal infection on leaves.

Heather dieback

Plants affected: Scotch heathers.
Symptoms and signs: Dieback of shoots following gray discoloration of foliage. Entire plant may be killed.
Danger period: Any time of year.
Treatment: Dig up and destroy. Do not plant another heather in same site unless soil is first changed completely.

Drought

Plants affected: All types, but symptoms and signs are most obvious on trees.
Symptoms and signs: Many leaves turn orange, sometimes with other tints. Leaves fall prematurely.
Danger period: Growing season.
Treatment: Mulch to conserve moisture; never allow soil to dry out. Affected plants sometimes benefit from foliar applications of compost tea or kelp.

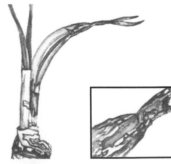

Smolder

Plants affected: Narcissi.
Symptoms and signs: Leaves rotting and covered with gray velvety mold.
Danger period: Spring, especially during cold, wet periods, and during winter storage.
Treatment: Destroy affected plants during growing season when symptoms appear on foliage. Destroy affected bulbs.

Scale insects can be removed with a cotton swab dipped in 50% rubbing alcohol.

Scale Insects

Leaves Distorted or Disfigured

Boxwood leaf miners

Plants affected: Boxwood.
Symptoms and signs: Leaves puffed with yellow blotches. Orange maggots visible if leaves are cut open.
Danger period: Late spring.
Treatment: Use sticky traps to see when adults emerge. Spray with superior oil. Spraying neem may be effective against larvae.

Chrysanthemum leaf miners

Plants affected: Chrysanthemums, cinerarias, columbines, sweet peas.
Symptoms and signs: Narrow, sinuous white mines eaten in leaf tissues; often many mines in 1 leaf.
Danger period: Midsummer to early winter.
Treatment: Remove and burn severely affected leaves. Spray with insecticidal soap whenever pests are active. In greenhouses, release parasitic wasps to kill adult leaf miner flies.

Holly leaf miners

Plants affected: Hollies.
Symptoms and signs: Blotchy yellow snakelike mines in leaves.
Danger period: Late spring to early winter, but symptoms persist throughout year.
Treatment: Remove and destroy affected leaves. Spray with insecticidal soap when pests are active in late spring; coat both sides of leaves thoroughly.

Lilac leaf miners

Plants affected: Lilacs, as well as ashes and privets.
Symptoms and signs: Tissues of leaves almost completely eaten out; leaves distorted and rolled. Two generations per year.
Danger period: Early summer to early fall.
Treatment: Pick off and destroy affected leaves. Spray with insecticidal soap in late spring, repeating if necessary.

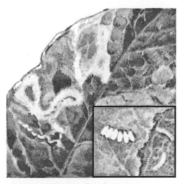

Vegetable leaf miners

Plants affected: Beets, corn, eggplant, spinach, Swiss chard.
Symptoms and signs: Leaves show large white puffy blotches or snakelike trails.
Danger period: Spring and early summer.
Treatment: Cover seedlings with row cover. Handpick and destroy damaged leaves. Remove weeds that host leaf miners.

Cyclamen and broad mites

Plants affected: Begonias, cyclamens, dahlias, delphiniums, English ivies, ferns, fuchsias, gerberas, and many greenhouse plants.
Symptoms and signs: Leaves distorted in severe infestations, slightly curled at edges, and brittle.
Danger period: Any time of year.
Treatment: Wash plants well with water and place in direct sun for at least 2 hr. Dip plants in solution of half-strength insecticidal soap.

Leaf-curling plum aphids

Plants affected: Damson and other varieties of plums.
Symptoms and signs: Young leaves puckered and curled.
Danger period: Midspring to midsummer.
Treatment: Spray thoroughly with insecticidal soap in early spring, before trees blossom, and again after blossoming. Repeat as necessary.

Rose leaf rollers

Plants affected: Bush and climbing roses.
Symptoms and signs: Leaves tightly rolled along their entire length. Holes in leaves and buds.
Danger period: Late spring to midsummer.
Treatment: Spray with dormant oil in late winter. Remove and destroy affected leaves in late spring.

Leaves Distorted or Disfigured (*continued*)

Black cherry aphids
Plants affected: Cherries, both ornamental and those grown for fruit.
Symptoms and signs: Leaves at tips of young shoots curled.
Danger period: Late spring to mid-summer.
Treatment: Spray with insecticidal soap at first sign of attack. Spray with dormant oil in late winter to kill over-wintering adults.

Violet leaf gall midges
Plants affected: *Viola* species.
Symptoms and signs: Young leaves curled upward at edges and greatly thickened. Small galls develop on leaves.
Danger period: Early summer to early winter.
Treatment: Remove and destroy affected leaves as soon as they appear.

Azalea gall
Plants affected: Small-leaved rhodo-dendrons, including azaleas.
Symptoms and signs: Leaves greatly thickened; at first pale green or pink, then white, finally brown.
Danger period: Any time of year, but symptoms may not appear until months after fungal infection.
Treatment: Avoid planting rhododen-drons in poorly drained soil. Cut off and destroy galls before they turn white.

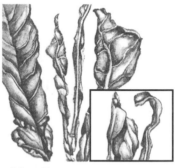

Whiptail
Plants affected: Broccoli, cauliflower.
Symptoms and signs: Leaves ruffled, thin, and straplike.
Danger period: Growing period.
Treatment: Since it is caused by nutri-ent deficiency and low pH (acid), feed plants, add lime, then water with seaweed solution.

Stem and bulb nematodes, or stem and bulb eelworms
Plants affected: Hyacinths, narcissi, tulips, and some other bulbs.
Symptoms and signs: Leaves stunt-ed and distorted, with small yellow bumps.
Danger period: Midwinter to late spring.
Treatment: Destroy affected plants. Do not plant bulbs in that site for three years.

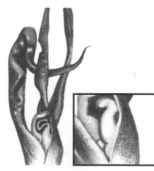

Onion nematodes, or onion eelworms
Plants affected: Onions, as well as chives and garlic.
Symptoms and signs: Leaves swollen and bloated.
Danger period: Early to late summer.
Treatment: Remove and destroy affected plants. Keep to 3-yr. rotation, and grow from seeds rather than from sets if possible.

Russian aphids
Plants affected: Honeysuckles, especially Tatarian honeysuckle.
Symptoms and signs: New leaves are small, twisted, and form a tassel-like growth. Few flowers or berries.
Danger period: Early spring.
Treatment: Spray with dormant oil in winter to kill overwintering eggs. Spray with insecticidal soap in early spring when growth begins, and repeat 7–10 days later if needed.

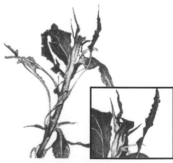

Phlox nematodes, or phlox eelworms
Plants affected: Perennial phlox.
Symptoms and signs: Leaves become threadlike, wrinkled, swollen, and curled. Younger leaves unusually narrow and die off prematurely.
Danger period: Early spring to early summer.
Treatment: Remove and destroy severely affected plants. Clean stock can be raised by taking root cuttings, but do not replant in infected soil.

When watering a plant, avoid wetting the foliage because disease spores can be spread by water on plant leaves.

Overhead watering

Virus disease

Plants affected: Many types, but particularly geraniums (*Pelargonium*), lilies, squash, and strawberries.
Symptoms and signs: Leaves crinkled, small, and sometimes irregularly shaped.
Danger period: Growing season.
Treatment: Destroy diseased plants. Spray with insecticidal soap to control aphids and other insects that carry virus.

Willow redgall sawflies

Plants affected: Willows.
Symptoms and signs: Small green, yellow, or red, bean-shaped galls growing out of both sides of leaves.
Danger period: Early to late summer.
Treatment: Damage is seldom severe. Pick off and destroy galls if possible. Call a professional arborist if problem is severe.

Clubroot

Plants affected: Brassicas (broccoli, cabbage, cauliflower), stocks, wall-flowers.
Symptoms and signs: Leaves wilted and sometimes discolored from galls on roots.
Danger period: Growing season.
Treatment: If possible, do not plant brassicas in areas where clubroot has been a past problem. Test soil pH and add ground limestone at least 6 wk. before planting to raise pH to 6.8 to 7.5. Clean all debris from garden after harvest.

Frost damage

Plants affected: Apples, camellias, chrysanthemums, rhododendrons, and many other plants.
Symptoms and signs: On camellias and rhododendrons, leaves look distorted, particularly at tips. On other plants, leaves pucker; undersides blister and often split and peel.
Danger period: Spring and fall.
Treatment: None. Prevent when possible.

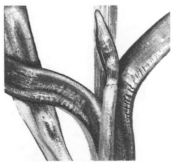

Snowball viburnum aphids

Plants affected: European snow-ball (*Viburnum opulus* 'Sterile').
Symptoms and signs: Leaves are puckered, twisted, and curled into a ball.
Danger period: Spring, just before flowering.
Treatment: Spray with a strong stream of water or insecticidal soap as the leaves start to unfurl; repeat if aphids persist.

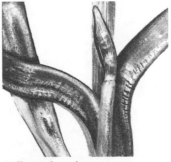

Bulb scale mites

Plants affected: Amaryllises (*Hippeastrum*), narcissi.
Symptoms and signs: Leaves twisted and malformed, with rusty brown or red scars.
Danger period: Midwinter to mid-spring for narcissi, especially when bulbs are forced. Any time of year for amaryllises in greenhouses.
Treatment: Destroy severely affected plants and bulbs. Expose dormant bulbs to frost for 2 or 3 nights, or immerse them for 1 or 2 hr. in water heated to 110°F.

Asparagus beetles

Plants affected: Asparagus.
Symptoms and signs: Leaves eaten and may turn brown above stem damage. Yellow larvae and/or yellow and black adults may be present.
Danger period: Late spring to early fall.
Treatment: Handpick beetles and larvae. Cut down fronds early in fall; burn or shred. Cover emerging spears with row cover, check underneath often for beetles. For a severe infestation, spray pyrethrins.

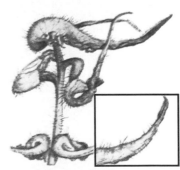

Hormone weed-killer damage

Plants affected: All types, particularly tomatoes and vines.
Symptoms and signs: Leaves are nar-rowed, curled, fan-shaped, and fre-quently cupped. Caused by drift of hormone weed killers, such as Silvex and 2,4–D.
Danger period: Growing season.
Treatment: None once damage has occurred, but plants usually recover unless badly hit by spray drift.

Sink beer traps flush with the soil level so that slugs can crawl in easily. The cover prevents dilution by rain.

Beer trap

Leaves Distorted or Disfigured (*continued*)

Verticillium wilt

Plants affected: Asters (perennial), carnations, chrysanthemums, snapdragons, maples, smoke trees, sumacs, tomatoes.
Symptoms and signs: Progressive wilting of leaves on several shoots, affected branches eventually dying back. On tomato plants all leaves are affected, but they recover at night.
Danger period: Growing season.
Treatment: On trees and shrubs, cut affected branches back to living tissue. If trouble persists, dig up plant, destroy it, and grow less susceptible plant in that location. Destroy diseased plants in greenhouse, isolate infected soil from adjacent healthy plants, and sterilize greenhouse at end of season. If necessary to propagate plant affected by verticillium wilt, use tip cuttings with vigorous growth. The likelihood of disease having affected tips of plant is less than on portions of plant nearer roots.

Willow anthracnose

Plants affected: Willows.
Symptoms and signs: Leaves curl, become spotted, and fall prematurely.
Danger period: As leaves unfold in spring, sometimes in wet summer.
Treatment: Destroy any fallen leaves. Spray small trees as leaves unfold with Bordeaux mixture or copper. Repeat at least twice at 10-day intervals.

Gall mites

Plants affected: Maples, willows.
Symptoms and signs: Rashes of small, elongated or spherical red galls on upper leaf surfaces.
Danger period: Early summer to midfall.
Treatment: Remove and destroy affected leaves if possible, and spray small trees thoroughly with lime sulfur in early spring. They are rarely serious enough to need spraying later.

Gall wasps

Plants affected: Oaks, some species of roses and willows.
Symptoms and signs: Many different galls, which resemble peas, cherries, silk buttons, or apples growing out of leaves. Sometimes solitary, often numerous.
Danger period: Growing season.
Treatment: Remove and destroy if possible, but gall wasps seldom cause serious damage. Dormant sprays of oil will help.

Red currant blister aphids

Plants affected: Red currants.
Symptoms and signs: Leaves with raised, irregular, red or green blisters.
Danger period: Late spring to early summer.
Treatment: Encourage natural predators of aphids. Apply dormant oil in midwinter to kill eggs. If aphids are severe, apply insecticidal soap, especially on underside of foliage, in spring, just before flowering. Repeat after flowering if necessary.

Apple aphids

Plants affected: Apples.
Symptoms and signs: Leaves puckered and distorted, sometimes with curled, thickened red edges.
Danger period: Late spring to midsummer.
Treatment: Apply a dormant oil spray just after bud break to kill eggs. Make spot applications of insecticidal soap just before bloom. Repeat after blossoming if necessary.

Peach leaf curl

Plants affected: Peaches, nectarines, almonds, including flowering types.
Symptoms and signs: Leaves with large red blisters become white, then brown, and fall prematurely.
Danger period: Before buds open.
Treatment: Spray trees with lime sulfur just before buds swell. If the problem has been serious in the past, also apply lime sulfur just before leaf fall. Remove and destroy disease leaves before they whiten.

Aphids

Aphids multiply very rapidly and can severely weaken a plant if not controlled.

Shoots Eaten or With Pests Visible

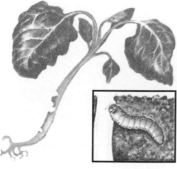

Cutworms

Plants affected: Lettuce, other vegetables, young ornamental annuals.
Symptoms and signs: Shoots eaten through at soil level; fat caterpillars in soil. Daily digging around plants with fingers will usually reveal cutworms, which are gray-brown to black and form a C shape when disturbed.
Danger period: Early spring and late summer.
Treatment: Control weeds, which encourage cutworms. Collars of cardboard (½ a frozen-juice container) or tinfoil pushed 1 in. deep into the soil will also protect transplants. or use bran moistened with *Bacillus thuringiensis kurstaki* spread on soil before planting.

Aphids

Plants affected: Many different types, but especially roses and snap beans.
Symptoms and signs: Colonies of aphids on young shoots.
Danger period: Late spring to midsummer outdoors, almost any time of year in greenhouses.
Treatment: Spray with a strong stream of water or spray with insecticidal soap. See also Aphids, p. 507.

Leopard moths (larvae)

Plants affected: Apples and pears (both fruiting and flowering), ashes, birches, cherries, cotoneasters, hawthorns, and other trees.
Symptoms and signs: Branches tunneled by 3-in. borers (larvae), causing wilting of leaves.
Danger period: Any time of year.
Treatment: Prune off infected shoots well below problem area.

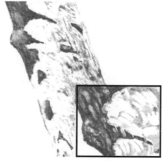

Deer, rabbits, and other animals

Plants affected: Many.
Symptoms and signs: Bark stripped from woody shoots at or slightly above soil level or snow line. Soft growth eaten to soil level.
Danger period: Almost any time, but especially winter and early spring.
Treatment: Protect shoots of young trees by winding spiral tree protectors around them or by using small-mesh wire netting.

Dried blood, bags of hair, and bars of deodorant soap have been used successfully to repel deer.

Commercial repellents are also available; choose one with organic ingredients. Protect flowers and vegetables with a chicken wire fence buried 4 in. in the soil. Repellents are also useful for control of these common pests.

Tent caterpillars/Fall webworms

Plants affected: Many trees and shrubs, especially cherries.
Symptoms and signs: Webs form nestlike structure in cleft of branches in spring (tent caterpillars), or on ends of branches in late summer (fall webworms). Branch is stripped of foliage.
Danger period: Spring or summer.
Treatment: Spray with dormant oil to kill overwintering eggs. Spray young larvae with *Bacillus thuringiensis*.

Scale insects

Plants affected: Many different types, but especially beeches, ceanothuses, cotoneasters, horse chestnuts, magnolias.
Symptoms and signs: Colonies of black, brown, yellow, or white scales on older shoots.
Danger period: Most times of year, but active in late spring and summer.
Treatment: Spray shrubs and young trees with dormant oil in winter, with insecticidal soap in summer. See also Scale Insects, p. 507.

Elm bark beetles

Plants affected: Elms.
Symptoms and signs: Intricate galleries eaten out under bark.
Danger period: Growing season.
Treatment: Remove affected deadwood, including stumps and roots, during winter and send to local incinerator. Keep trees growing well by regular feeding and watering. See also Dutch Elm Disease, p. 515.

Red lily beetles

Plants affected: Lilies and fritillaries.
Symptoms and signs: Leaves and flowers eaten. Bright red beetles and/or brownish larvae present.
Danger period: Spring to fall.
Treatment: Handpick and destroy the beetles. Spray with neem; reapply after rain.

Mealybugs look similar to woolly aphids; they are protected by their cottony covering and are not as easy to control.

Powdery mildew

Shoots Discolored

Spur blight
Plants affected: Loganberries, raspberries.
Symptoms and signs: Canes bear purple blotches that later become silver, spotted with black. Spurs on these die back.
Danger period: Spring and summer.
Treatment: Promote good air circulation. Use drip irrigation to avoid wetting foliage. Avoid overfertilizing. Remove old and infected canes after harvest. Apply lime sulfur when buds begin to swell.

Woolly aphids
Plants affected: Apples, cotoneasters, hawthorns, mountain ashes.
Symptoms and signs: Woody swellings and tufts of white wool on trunks and branches.
Danger period: Midspring to early fall.
Treatment: Apply a dormant oil spray just after bud break to kill eggs. Make spot applications of insecticidal soap just before bloom. Repeat after blossoming if necessary.

Mealybugs
Plants affected: Greenhouse and house plants, especially when put outside for the summer.
Symptoms and signs: Colonies of mealybugs covered with white mealy or waxy wool that is usually concentrated around buds and leaf axils.
Danger period: Most times of year, but particularly late summer and fall.
Treatment: See Mealybugs, p. 507.

Two-spotted mites and European red mites on fruit trees
Plants affected: Apples, peaches, plums.
Symptoms and signs: Tiny red mites may be seen on shoots or red-brown eggs may be visible with a strong lens. Leaves become dull, with many tiny yellow dots. May have a purplish tinge and turn yellow. Very fine webs run from leafstalk to shoot.
Danger period: Late fall to midspring.
Treatment: Plant flowering plants near your fruit trees to attract natural predators of mites. Spray dormant oil shortly after bud break. For severe infestations in spring, spray insecticidal soap or horticultural oil.

Powdery mildew
Plants affected: Apples, euonymus, gooseberries, perennial asters, roses, and many other plants.
Symptoms and signs: White powdery coating on shoots.
Danger period: Growing season.
Treatment: Cut off affected shoots at end of season. Spray as for Powdery Mildew on p. 513.

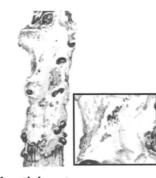

Sclerotinia rot
Plants affected: Many types, but in particular dahlias.
Symptoms and signs: Stems affected by white, fluffy fungal growth with large black areas. Stems decay rapidly and collapse.
Danger period: Spring and summer.
Treatment: Destroy all rotting material.

Viburnum leaf beetles
Plants affected: Viburnums.
Symptoms and signs: Holes in leaves which may be reduced to only the veins. Plants stunted and shoots distorted from lack of leaves.
Danger period: Early to late summer.
Treatment: Prune off and destroy infested twigs in fall and winter. Spray young larvae in spring with spinosad or insecticidal soap.

Botrytis, or gray mold

Plants affected: All types, but particularly clarkias, gooseberries, magnolias, roses, zinnias.
Symptoms and signs: Rotting stems covered with gray fungus.
Danger period: Growing season in wet weather.
Treatment: Cut out affected shoots. Ensure good air circulation around the plants. For botrytis on leaves, see p. 511; on lettuce, see p. 528; on peonies, see Peony Blight, p. 529; on chrysanthemums, see p. 530; on small fruits, see p. 533; on tomatoes, see p. 534.

Bacterial canker of stone fruits

Plants affected: Cherries, pears, plums, flowering *Prunus* species.
Symptoms and signs: Elongated, flattened canker-bearing exudations of gum on shoots that die back; leaves yellow and wither prematurely.
Danger period: Fall and winter, but symptoms do not appear until following spring or summer.
Treatment: Keep trees well-fed and watered. Cut out infected branches in summer. Apply copper sprays in fall and early spring, but note that some strains of the bacteria are resistant. Spraying during the growing season is not effective.

Witches'-broom

Plants affected: Birches, hackberries, *Prunus* species, and many other trees and shrubs.
Symptoms and signs: Several shoots, sometimes bearing blistered foliage, growing from single point and crowded together on infected branches.
Danger period: Throughout life of plant.
Treatment: Cut out affected branch to point 6 in. below broom.

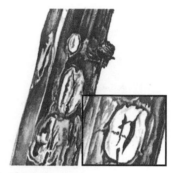

Anthracnose

Plants affected: Loganberries, raspberries, and other cane fruits.
Symptoms and signs: Small circular, purple spots enlarge to become elliptic white blotches with purple border, about ¼ in. long. These eventually split to form small pits, which give canes rough, cracked appearance. Leaves may also be spotted and fruits distorted.
Danger period: Late spring to midfall.
Treatment: Thin canes to promote good air circulation. Use drip irrigation to avoid wetting leaves. Avoid overfertilizing. Cut out and destroy infected canes. Apply lime sulfur just before buds open.

Willow anthracnose

Plants affected: Weeping willows.
Symptoms and signs: Small brown cankers on shoots, which may die back.
Danger period: Growing season.
Treatment: Cut out as many cankered shoots as possible, together with all deadwood. Spray small trees with fungicide (Bordeaux mixture or copper), and repeat at least twice in summer.

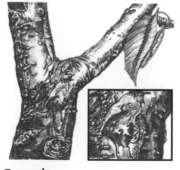

Gumming

Plants affected: Cherries and other *Prunus* species.
Symptoms and signs: Gum exudes on branches and trunks and gradually hardens.
Danger period: Any time of year.
Treatment: Feed, mulch, and water to stop gumming. Gum may have to be removed so that deadwood beneath can be cut out.

Shoots Distorted or Wilted (*continued*)

Rose rust
Plants affected: Roses.
Symptoms and signs: Early infection, indicated by tiny $1/25$-in. bright orange spots on undersides of leaves and light yellow areas on uppersides. Swellings on stems burst open to reveal bright orange, powdery spores.
Danger period: Spring and summer.
Treatment: Cut out and destroy affected shoots. Spray with sulfur. See also Rusts, p. 510.

Clematis wilt, or leaf and stem spot
Plants affected: Clematis.
Symptoms and signs: One or more shoots wilt and die rapidly.
Danger period: Growing season.
Treatment: Choose resistant types of clematis. If plants develop symptoms, cut out affected shoots, even if they are below soil level. Keep plants well-watered and mulch the area around the roots.

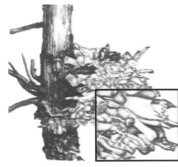

Leafy gall
Plants affected: Many types, but in particular chrysanthemums, dahlias, dianthuses, geraniums (*Pelargonium*), gladioli, strawberries, sweet peas.
Symptoms and signs: Abortive, often flattened shoots with thickened, distorted leaves develop at ground level.
Danger period: During propagation and growing season.
Treatment: Prune infected parts where feasible. Or destroy infected plants. When replanting, grow a non-susceptible type of plant.

Petunia wilt (verticillium wilt)
Plants affected: Petunias, salpiglossises, zinnias, and other bedding plants.
Symptoms and signs: Plants wilt, often as they are about to flower. Stem bases may be discolored.
Danger period: Growing season.
Treatment: Choose resistant varieties if available. Keep plants well fed and watered to prevent stress. Destroy diseased plants. Try solarizing the soil where infected plants grew to kill the fungus that persists there.

Mint rust
Plants affected: Mints.
Symptoms and signs: Swollen, distorted shoots bear orange-colored spore pustules.
Danger period: Symptoms appear in spring, but affected plants are permanently diseased.
Treatment: Cut out and destroy affected shoots. Burn over mint bed at end of season where permissible. See also Rusts, p. 510.

Normal

Stunted

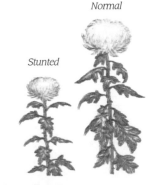

Virus disease
Plants affected: All types, but particularly blackberries, chrysanthemums, dahlias, lilies, strawberries, tomatoes.
Symptoms and signs: Plants are very stunted and may produce discolored leaves and poor flowers. Small fruits may fail to mature.
Danger period: Growing season.
Treatment: Dig up and destroy infected plants. Control insects, such as leafhoppers and aphids. They transmit virus to other plants.

Fasciation
Plants affected: Many types, but in particular delphiniums, forsythias, lilies, *Prunus* species.
Symptoms and signs: Shoots are flattened but may branch and bear normal leaves and flowers.
Danger period: Usually spring, but symptoms appear months later.
Treatment: Cut out affected shoots on woody plants to below flattening. No treatment is required for herbaceous plants.

China aster wilt
Plants affected: China asters.
Symptoms and signs: Plant wilts, usually as it is about to flower. Pink fungal growth may be seen on stems just above ground level.
Danger period: Summer.
Treatment: Destroy diseased plants as they appear. Grow resistant varieties on new site.

Canker can be serious, but generally attacks only older trees. Prune infected branches well inside diseased area.

Apple tree with canker disease

Apple canker

Plants affected: Apples, and less commonly ashes, beeches, mountain ashes, pears, poplars.
Symptoms and signs: Elliptical cankers, with bark shrinking in concentric rings until inner tissues are exposed. Girdling of shoot or branch by canker causes dieback.
Danger period: Any time of year.
Treatment: Cut out and destroy infected spurs and small branches. On larger branches and main trunks, pare away all diseased material (which should be destroyed) until clean wound is left. In severe cases, spray with Bordeaux mixture just before leaf fall, when half of leaves have fallen, and at budbreak. Improve drainage if waterlogging occurs, since this can aggravate trouble.

Nectria canker, or coral spot

Plants affected: Many trees and shrubs, particularly figs, magnolias, maples, red currants.
Symptoms and signs: Coral-red, spore-filled pustules on deadwood. Usually secondary, on wood killed by other agent. Entire plant may die.
Danger period: Any time of year.
Treatment: Cut out all dead shoots to 2–4 in. below diseased area, and destroy. Feed, mulch, water, and/or drain soil to encourage vigor.

Fire blight

Plants affected: Apples, cotoneasters, hawthorns, mountain ashes, pears, and other related ornamentals.
Symptoms and signs: Shoots die, particularly flowering spurs; and cankers develop at their base, leaves wither but do not fall.
Danger period: Flowering time.
Treatment: Prune and destroy all infected material. Cut at least 8 in. below injury. Disinfect pruning shears between each cut with 10% liquid chlorine bleach. Disease is bacterial and difficult to control.

Poplar canker

Plants affected: Poplars.
Symptoms and signs: Unsightly cankers ¼–6 in. long, erupt on shoots, branches, and sometimes trunk. Dieback of young shoots occurs in early summer.
Danger period: Any time of year.
Treatment: Destroy badly diseased trees. On less severely affected trees cut out and destroy cankered shoots.

Bark splitting

Plants affected: Many types of trees, including fruit trees.
Symptoms and signs: Bark splits, and cracks open up.
Danger period: Any time of year.
Treatment: Cut out any deadwood, and remove loose bark until clean wound is left. If tree is then fed, mulched, and watered properly, wound should heal naturally. In cold climates, shield split from winter sun by wrapping or with a plank.

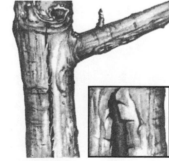

Scab

Plants affected: Apples, pears.
Symptoms and signs: Small blister-like pimples develop on young shoots, later burst bark and then show as ringlike cracks or scabs.
Danger period: Growing season.
Treatment: Cut out cracked and scab-by shoots when pruning. Spray with sulfur when flower buds are nearly open, when petals fall, and 3 wk. later. See also Scab, p. 510.

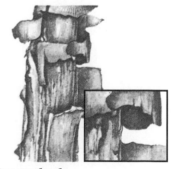

Papery bark

Plants affected: Many types, but particularly apples, mountain ashes, viburnums.
Symptoms and signs: Bark becomes paper-thin and peels off. Dieback follows girdling of shoots.
Danger period: Any time of year.
Treatment: See Faulty Root Action, p. 526. If bark has peeled on shoots not yet dead and that have not been girdled, remove loose bark.

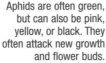

Aphids are often green, but can also be pink, yellow, or black. They often attack new growth and flower buds.

Aphid infestation

Shoots Distorted or Wilted (*continued*)

Forsythia gall
Plants affected: Forsythias.
Symptoms and signs: Pea- to tennis-ball-size nodules on stems.
Danger period: When shrubs are at least 5 yr. old, but usually on even older plants.
Treatment: Cut out and destroy affected shoots. Disinfect pruning shears with a 10% chlorine bleach solution after each cut.

Crown gall
Plants affected: Blackberries, raspberries, roses.
Symptoms and signs: Walnut-size galls, sometimes in chains, develop on aerial shoots or at soil level.
Danger period: Growing season.
Treatment: Cut out shoots bearing galls. Disinfect tools after each cut. Control on roses is difficult. See also Crown Gall, p. 539.

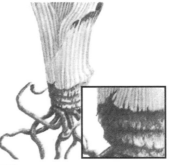

Rhizome rot
Plants affected: Bearded and other rhizomatous irises.
Symptoms and signs: Soft, yellow, foul-smelling rot of rhizome at growing point; leaves collapse.
Danger period: Any time of year, but particularly in wet weather.
Treatment: Improve drainage if necessary, and control slugs and other pests. Destroy badly affected plants; on others cut out rotting parts.

Blackleg
Plants affected: Geraniums (*Pelargonium*), potatoes.
Symptoms and signs: Black rot develops at base of cuttings or at stem base, and affected tissues become soft. Leaves yellow, and entire cutting or stem dies.
Danger period: For geraniums, soon after cuttings are taken; for potatoes, early summer.
Treatment: Destroy badly affected plants. No other treatment is required for potatoes, apart from planting healthy seed tubers. Prevent disease on geraniums by using sterilized soil, maintaining strict greenhouse hygiene, and watering carefully. If valuable cuttings become affected, remove diseased parts with a knife dipped in weak disinfectant (10% liquid chlorine bleach) and repot cuttings in clean pots of fresh soil. Allow geranium cuttings to dry and callus for 24 hr. before potting.

Faulty root action
Plants affected: Trees (particularly fruit trees and poplars) and shrubs.
Symptoms and signs: Shoots bearing discolored leaves turn brown and die back at random.
Danger period: Any time of year.
Treatment: Cut out deadwood until living tissues are reached. Feed, mulch, water, and/or drain as necessary. Applications of foliar fertilizer may hasten recovery. Determine cause if possible, and correct.

Stem rot
Plants affected: Carnations, clarkias, lobelias, tomatoes; each is affected by different form of this disease.
Symptoms and signs: Rotting of stems, but no very obvious fungal growth is visible on affected areas.
Danger period: Growing season.
Treatment: Where possible, cut out affected parts. Alternatively, destroy diseased plants. Do not plant susceptible plants in soil known to be infected.

Lilac blight
Plants affected: Lilacs.
Symptoms and signs: Young shoots blacken and wither away (but similar symptoms can be due to frost damage or flooding).
Danger period: Spring.
Treatment: Plant resistant cultivars. Increase air circulation and avoid wetting leaves. Improve drainage if soil stays wet in spring. In dry weather, cut out infected shoots 10 in. below the diseased tissue. Spray *Bacillus subtilis* or a copper-based fungicide in early spring.

Tulip fire (botrytis)
Plants affected: Tulips (base of stem).
Symptoms and signs: Shoots rot at ground level and become covered with gray velvety fungus.
Danger period: Spring.
Treatment: See Tulip Fire, p. 535. See also illustration at right. Remove and destroy diseased bulbs. Apply preventive sprays of *Bacillus subtilis*. Clean up and destroy all tulip debris after flowering.

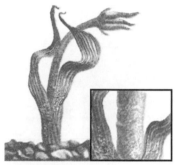

Tulip fire (botrytis)
Plants affected: Tulips (young shoots).
Symptoms and signs: Young shoots are crippled; they rot aboveground and become covered with gray velvety mold. Flowers become distorted and show streaks.
Danger period: Spring.
Treatment: See Tulip Fire, p. 535. See also illustration at left.

Crown rot
Plants affected: Delphiniums, peonies, rhubarb, and many other herbaceous crown-type perennials.
Symptoms and signs: Rotting of terminal bud, followed by progressive rotting of crown. Leaves are spindly and discolored, and die down early.
Danger period: Growing season.
Treatment: Dig up and destroy. Do not plant this type of plant again in same location.

Dry rot
Plants affected: Primarily gladioli, but crocuses and freesias are also susceptible to infection.
Symptoms and signs: Dry rot of leaf sheaths at soil level makes top growth topple over. Affected tissues are covered with minute black forms, just visible to naked eye.
Danger period: Growing season.
Treatment: See Dry Rot, p. 536.

Foot rot
Plants affected: Beans, bedding plants, sweet peas, tomatoes.
Symptoms and signs: Stem bases, which may be discolored, rot. Roots usually die.
Danger period: Growing season.
Treatment: Rotate vegetables and bedding plants, and always use sterile soil for pot plants. In the garden, solarize infected beds. Drench soil with a biological fungicide effective against Fusarium fungi.

Peony wilt
Plants affected: Peonies.
Symptoms and signs: Affected shoots collapse at ground level.
Danger period: Growing season.
Treatment: Cut out affected shoots to below ground level, and dust crowns with dry Bordeaux mixture. Spray with Bordeaux mixture soon after leaves appear.

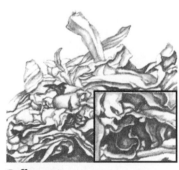

Collar rot
Plants affected: Cinerarias, primroses, and other pot plants.
Symptoms and signs: Tissues rot at or just above soil level, and plants collapse.
Danger period: Growing season.
Treatment: Prevent by using sterilized soil and watering carefully. If trouble occurs, remove all affected tissue, and dust infected areas with dry Bordeaux mixture. Repot plant in lighter soil, and reduce amount of watering.

Pansy wilt
Plants affected: Pansies and other *Viola* species.
Symptoms and signs: Wilted plants with rotten crowns. Plants can be lifted easily.
Danger period: Growing season.
Treatment: Rotate bedding plants so Viola species are not grown in the same position every year. Plant only in well-drained soil, raised beds, or containers with good drainage. Allow soil to dry between watering. Keep surface mulch away from plants. Lift affected plants, together with all roots, and destroy.

Damping-off disease can strike very quickly and kill almost every seedling in just a few days. Inspect seedlings regularly to catch it in the early stages.

Damping-off disease

Shoots Distorted or Wilted (*continued*)

Botrytis, or gray mold, on lettuce

Plants affected: Lettuce.
Symptoms and signs: Wilted plants are rotten at ground level, where tissues are covered with gray velvety mold. Top growth separates easily from roots.
Danger period: Growing season.
Treatment: Remove and destroy diseased plants and leaves. Enrich soil with compost. Plant only in well-drained soil. Use raised beds if necessary.

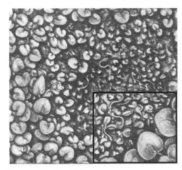

Damping-off

Plants affected: All seedlings can be affected, but lettuce, snapdragons, and zinnias are particularly susceptible.
Symptoms and signs: Seedlings rot and collapse at ground level.
Danger period: As seeds germinate.
Treatment: Use fresh seed. Provide high light for indoor seedlings. Top off seeded containers with a thin layer of peat moss. Water containers from the bottom, but do not let containers sit in water for long periods. Run a small fan to promote good air circulation. If the disease appears, remove all affected seedlings and increase light levels and air circulation. If problems continue, compost all soil mix, wash containers thoroughly with 10% bleach solution, and replant using fresh mix. Apply a beneficial fungal product according to label directions.

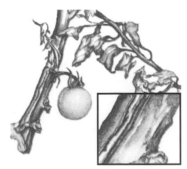

Virus disease

Plants affected: Sweet peas, tomatoes, and many other plants.
Symptoms and signs: Wilting of plants that show streaks on stems and leaf stalks.
Danger period: Growing season.
Treatment: Dig up and destroy affected plants.

Flower-Bud Disorders

Rose chafers

Plants affected: Peonies, roses, and many other plants.
Symptoms and signs: Petals eaten.
Danger period: Early summer to early fall.
Treatment: Handpick and destroy the ½-in.-long yellow-tan beetles. In the spring, set up a barrier of cheesecloth or floating row cover around vulnerable plants (the beetles won't fly over it). Remove the barrier in early summer. Cultivate soil around plants in spring, summer, and fall to destroy eggs, larvae, and pupae.

Caterpillars and sawfly larvae ("slugs")

Plants affected: Apples, chrysanthemums, roses, and other plants.
Symptoms and signs: Holes eaten into buds and leaves.
Danger period: Early spring to early summer outdoors, but almost any time of year in greenhouses.
Treatment: Handpick and destroy caterpillars and sawfly larvae when practical. When caterpillars are present, spray with *Bacillus thuringiensis*. For sawflies, spray with neem to kill larvae.

Rhododendron leafhoppers

Plants affected: Rhododendrons.
Symptoms and signs: Buds killed by bud-blast disease, which is spread by leafhoppers.
Danger period: Late summer, when flower buds are developing.
Treatment: Try to prevent disease by spraying plant with insecticidal soap if pests are seen. If disease occurs, remove and destroy infected buds.

Rhododendron bud blast

Plants affected: Rhododendrons.
Symptoms and signs: Buds die and become covered with black heads of fungal spores.
Danger period: Late summer, when flower buds are beginning to develop, but symptoms are not seen until following spring, when buds fail to open.
Treatment: Cut off and destroy infected buds. Apply garlic spray to deter leafhoppers, which spread the disease.

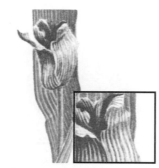

Blindness

Plants affected: Narcissi, tulips, when forced indoors.
Symptoms and signs: Withering of flowers before opening.
Danger period: During storage or growing season.
Treatment: To prevent blindness, store bulbs in cool, dry place. Plant at correct time, and make sure that soil never dries out once growth has started. Do not force bulbs at too high a temperature. Affected bulbs can be replanted outdoors.

Peony blight, or botrytis, or gray mold

Plants affected: Peonies.
Symptoms and signs: Flower buds rot and become covered with gray velvety mold.
Danger period: Flowering time.
Treatment: Avoid overhead watering. Space plants widely for good air circulation. Remove and destroy all infected shoots at or below ground level as soon as symptoms are noticed. Spray *Bacillus subtilis* as a preventive measure.

Pedicel necrosis

Plants affected: Poppies, pyrethrums, roses.
Symptoms and signs: Discolored patch develops on flower stalk, immediately below rosebuds or slightly lower on herbaceous plants. Stalks collapse at that point. Buds on affected stalks fail to open. Cause is unknown.
Danger period: Flowering time.
Treatment: Mulch, never allow soil to dry out, and feed only at appropriate time with appropriate fertilizers. Once disease appears, little can be done apart from cutting out affected flowers—although applications of foliar fertilizer may encourage development of second crop of flowers on roses.

Virus disease

Plants affected: Lilies.
Symptoms and signs: Flower buds are distorted and fail to open properly.
Danger period: Any time of year, but not apparent until flowering.
Treatment: Destroy affected plants. Aphids spread lily viruses. Encourage native aphid predators, spray plants with a strong stream of water to remove aphids, or apply insecticidal soap.

Bud drop

Plants affected: Camellias, gardenias, sweet peas, wisterias.
Symptoms and signs: Buds or partly open flowers fall without opening properly.
Danger period: When flower buds begin to develop, although symptoms will not appear until flowering time.
Treatment: Once bud drop starts, nothing can stop it. Try to prevent trouble by mulching and never allowing soil to dry out. Maintain fairly even temperature for gardenias. Nothing, however, can prevent bud drop of sweet peas and wisterias when it is caused by cold nights.

Flowers Attacked After Opening

Caterpillars

Plants affected: Carnations, chrysanthemums, and other plants.
Symptoms and signs: Petals eaten; caterpillars often inside blooms.
Danger period: Any time of year indoors, late spring to midfall outdoors.
Treatment: If relatively few blooms are affected, remove caterpillars by hand. Alternatively, spray with *Bacillus Thurigiensis* —preferably before plants are in full bloom, since flowers may be marred by spraying.

Earwigs

Plants affected: Chrysanthemums, clematis, dahlias, and some other plants.
Symptoms and signs: Ragged pieces eaten out of petals.
Danger period: Late spring to midfall.
Treatment: Earwigs can be trapped in rolls of corrugated cardboard, in old burlap, or in flowerpots stuffed with straw. Empty daily.

Ray blight, or petal blight

Plants affected: Chrysanthemums, rhododendrons, dahlias.
Symptoms and signs: Dark, water-soaked spots spread on petals until flowers rot.
Danger period: Flowering time, particularly in cold, wet summers.
Treatment: Destroy affected flowers. Prevent disease in greenhouses by keeping humidity low. Spray plants with copper just before flowers open. Repeat every 7 days as necessary.

Virus disease

Plants affected: Chrysanthemums, dahlias, lilies, tulips, *Viola* species, wallflowers, and many other types of herbaceous plants.
Symptoms and signs: Flowers distorted or flower color broken (white streaks, or stripes in lighter or darker shade of background color).
Danger period: Growing season.
Treatment: Destroy affected plants. Many virus diseases are spread by insects and mites; so take steps to minimize insect feeding on plants.

Mycoplasma

Plants affected: Heleniums, *Primula* species, strawberries; occasionally chrysanthemums and narcissi.
Symptoms and signs: Flowers are green, instead of their normal color.
Danger period: Growing season.
Treatment: With heleniums, cut out that part of clump bearing affected blooms. With the others, destroy entire plant.

Plant bugs, or leaf bugs
(four-lined, harlequin, tarnished)

Plants affected: Chrysanthemums, dahlias, and many other ornamental annuals and perennials.
Symptoms and signs: Flowers distorted.
Danger period: Early summer to mid-fall outdoors, but continuing later in greenhouses.
Treatment: Hand pick if possible.

Tulip fire (botrytis)

Plants affected: Tulips.
Symptoms and signs: Small brown spots on petals. These may rot and become covered with gray velvety mold.
Danger period: Flowering time.
Treatment: See Tulip Fire, p. 535.

Botrytis, or gray mold

Plants affected: Chrysanthemums.
Symptoms and signs: Spotting followed by rotting of flowers, which are covered with gray mold.
Danger period: Flowering time.
Treatment: Avoid overhead watering. Space plants widely for good air circulation. Remove and destroy all infected plant parts as soon as symptoms are noticed. Spray *Bacillus subtilis* as a preventive measure.

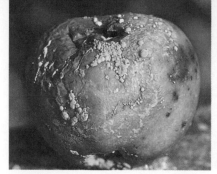

Apples that are even slightly bruised will rot in storage and can then affect healthy fruit nearby.

Fruit rot

Tree-Fruit and Small-Fruit Disorders

Gladiolus thrips

Plants affected: Gladioli and some related plants.
Symptoms and signs: Silvery flecks appear on petals and leaves. In severe infestations flowers become completely discolored and may die.
Danger period: Any time of year.
Treatment: Spray with insecticidal soap. Encourage natural predators, such as lacewings.

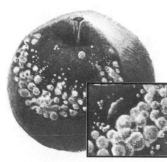

Brown rot

Plants affected: All stone fruits, especially cherries, nectarines, peaches, plums.
Symptoms and signs: Fruit turns brownish white; concentric rings of powdery fungal spores often cover it; fruit withers, shrinks, and often falls.
Danger period: During storage and in summer.
Treatment: Remove infected fruit, pick up fallen fruit and discard. Control insects that damage fruit, allowing fungus to enter.

Codling moths

Plants affected: Mainly apples, but also pears.
Symptoms and signs: Caterpillars eat into calyx end of ripening fruit and destroy it.
Danger period: Early to late summer.
Treatment: Cover developing fruits with nylon barriers early in the growing season. Or, place one hormone attractant trap per tree. Spray *Bacillus thuringiensis* three times, beginning 15 days after petals fall.

Bitter pit

Plants affected: Apples.
Symptoms and signs: Slightly sunken brown spots beneath skin and throughout flesh.
Danger period: Growing season, but not seen until harvesting or in storage.
Treatment: Fertilize and mulch; never allow soil to dry out.

Japanese beetles

Plants affected: Roses and other garden flowers, grapes, lindens, and many other plants.
Symptoms and signs: Flowers and leaves are heavily chewed by beetles, leaving petals frayed and leaves skeletonized.
Danger period: Early summer to midfall.
Treatment: For control, see Beetle Grubs, p. 540. As a last resort, spray infected plants with insecticidal soap.

Fruit drop

Plants affected: All tree fruits.
Symptoms and signs: Fruit drops prematurely while still very small.
Danger period: During and just after flowering time.
Treatment: See that suitable pollinators, such as bees, are present in garden. Feed, mulch, and water. Do not spray while trees are flowering. Nothing can be done in cold seasons when fruit drop is due to poor pollination. If dropped fruit shows small crescent-shaped scars, cause could be plum curculio (see p. 533).

Apple red bugs and tarnished plant bugs

Plants affected: Mainly apples, but also pears.
Symptoms and signs: Bumps and corky patches on ripening fruit.
Danger period: Midspring to late summer.
Treatment: Spray with dormant oil during dormant period to kill overwintering eggs.

Apple sawflies

Plants affected: Apples.
Symptoms and signs: Caterpillar form of sawfly eats into cores of young fruits, which then drop prematurely. This pest also causes superficial scarring of mature fruits.
Danger period: Late spring to early summer.
Treatment: Hang white sticky cards in trees at blossom time and remove them at petal fall. Spray trees with neem and apply parasitic nematodes to the soil beneath the trees after petal fall.

In addition to aphids and other pests, apple trees are vulnerable to fungal diseases and viruses.

Apple scab

Tree-Fruit and Small-Fruit Disorders (*continued*)

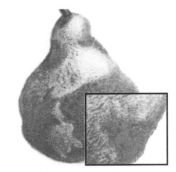

Cracking
Plants affected: Apples, pears, plums.
Symptoms and signs: Skin of fruit splits.
Danger period: Growing season.
Treatment: Try to avoid irregular growth by mulching (to conserve moisture) and by never allowing soil to dry out. Overwatering coupled with poor drainage or long, heavy rains can also cause cracking.

Stony pit
Plants affected: Old pear trees.
Symptoms and signs: Fruit pitted and deformed, with patches of dead, stony cells in flesh that make fruit inedible. Symptoms appear on single branch and over the years gradually spread until all fruit on tree is affected.
Danger period: Growing season.
Treatment: Pruning back old wood severely and feeding trees may help. If not, remove the infected tree.

Faulty root action
Plants affected: Tree fruits and, to a lesser extent, small fruits.
Symptoms and signs: Gradual diminishing of crop over several years, usually accompanied by discolored foliage and perhaps dieback of shoots.
Danger period: Growing season.
Treatment: Apply appropriate fertilizers at correct time. Feed, water, and mulch. Drain if waterlogging occurs. Applications of foliar fertilizer may hasten recovery.

or Poor pollination
Plants affected: Small fruits, tree fruits, tomatoes.
Symptoms and signs: Very little fruit is produced, and that which is formed may be distorted.
Danger period: Flowering time.
Treatment: Since trouble is usually caused by cold weather at flowering time, little can be done for fruit other than to ensure that suitable pollinators for tree fruit are present. For tomatoes, provide good cultural treatment, and spray in dry weather to supply moist atmosphere.

or Virus disease
Plants affected: Small fruits.
Symptoms and signs: Gradual diminishing of crop over several years, usually accompanied by other symptoms, such as stunting of plants and distortion or yellow blotching of leaves.
Danger period: Growing season.
Treatment: Destroy infected plants. Replant on fresh site with stocks certified to be free of virus disease.

Raspberry fruitworms
Plants affected: Raspberries.
Symptoms and signs: Adults lay eggs in developing fruit, which the larvae feed on.
Danger period: Late spring to early fall.
Treatment: Cultivate lightly around canes in late summer to expose the adult beetles and pupae to predatory birds. Handpick adults and spray spinosad on fruit buds to kill larvae.

Powdery mildew
Plants affected: Apples, gooseberries, grapes, strawberries, and many other fruits.
Symptoms and signs: White powder turns brown on gooseberries but may show as loss of color on strawberries. Grapes may split. Apples show powdery leaves.
Danger period: Growing season.
Treatment: Take steps as for Powdery Mildew, p. 513.

Split stone
Plants affected: Nectarines, peaches.
Symptoms and signs: Kernel rots within stone, which splits and causes fruit to crack at stalk end. Also, cleft in fruit is deeper than normal.
Danger period: Growing season.
Treatment: Fertilize and mulch. Never allow soil to dry out, in order to keep growth even while fruit is swelling.

Scab
Plants affected: Apples, pears (and sometimes firethorn berries).
Symptoms and signs: Brown or black scabs on fruit, which may, in severe cases, crack when scabs have merged and become corky.
Danger period: Growing season.
Treatment: See Scab, p. 510.

Scald

Plants affected: Grapes, sometimes gooseberries and tree fruits in hot weather.
Symptoms and signs: Discolored sunken patches on fruit.
Danger period: In hot weather.
Treatment: If plants are in greenhouse, shade and ventilate it well. Cut out any affected fruit before it rots.

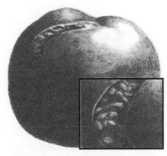

Botrytis, or gray mold

Plants affected: All small fruits.
Symptoms and signs: Fruit rots and becomes covered with gray mold.
Danger period: Flowering time, but symptoms appear when fruit matures.
Treatment: For strawberry, use plastic mulch to prevent berries from contacting soil. Remove and destroy infected leaves and fruit. Pick all ripe fruit. Clean up all crop debris after harvest. Apply beneficial fungal product to soil, and apply sprays of *Bacillus subtilis*.

Tomato and Pea- or Bean-Pod Disorders

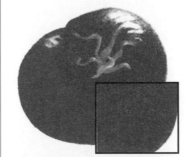

Cracking

Plants affected: Tomatoes.
Symptoms and signs: Skin splits near shoulder, often in form of ring, sometimes vertically.
Danger period: As fruit develops.
Treatment: Try to maintain even growth by never allowing soil to dry out. Avoid giving too much or too little water.

Greenback and blotchy ripening

Plants affected: Tomatoes.
Symptoms and signs: Hard green or yellow patch develops on shoulder of fruit near stalk; similar patches may develop on other parts.
Danger period: As fruit develops.
Treatment: Grow resistant varieties; keep soil moist to maintain even fruit growth. Shade greenhouse in hot weather. Nutrient deficiency may be cause; maintain potassium level in soil.

Plum curculios

Plants affected: Apples, apricots, cherries, peaches, plums.
Symptoms and signs: Crescent- and T-shaped punctures in young fruit. Larvae feed on developing fruit, destroying it. Small fruit may drop.
Danger period: After petals fall; in some areas again later on.
Treatment: Collect fruit as it drops. Once petals start to fall, each day hit the tree trunk with a padded stick; collect and destroy the curculios that fall. Continue this for 3 wk. Also, apply horticultural kaolin clay when petal fall starts and then weekly for 6 to 8 wk.

Shanking

Plants affected: Grapes.
Symptoms and signs: Dark spot develops along stalk of berry and eventually rings it. Berry fails to ripen— it becomes red in case of black varieties and remains green in white varieties.
Danger period: Growing season.
Treatment: Feed, mulch, and never allow soil to dry out. Do not overcrop vine. If trouble occurs, cut out affected berries before they rot.

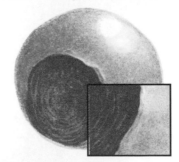

Early blight and late blight

Plants affected: Tomatoes outdoors.
Symptoms and signs: In wet weather dark green water-soaked spots on leaves enlarge, become dark brown to black. Undersides of leaves, stems, and petioles have whitish growth (late blight only). Fungus develops rapidly.
Danger period: Mid and late summer when weather is very wet.
Treatment: Choose resistant varieties. Provide good air circulation. For early blight, use preventive sprays of potassium bicarbonate. Remove and destroy infected plants. For late blight, repeated copper sprays can prevent infection.

Blossom-end rot

Plants affected: Tomatoes.
Symptoms and signs: Circular brown or black patch at blossom end of fruit, which, despite disease's name, does not usually rot. Nonparasitic disease.
Danger period: As fruit develops.
Treatment: Prevent trouble by never allowing soil to dry out; this maintains even growth. Also, avoid irregular watering. Do not cultivate close to plants. Lime acidic soils to ensure sufficient calcium is available.

Tomato and Pea- or Bean-Pod Disorders (*continued*)

Tomato wilt (fusarium and verticillium wilt)

Plants affected: Tomatoes.
Symptoms and signs: As first fruit begins to ripen, lower leaves yellow and droop on one side of plant. One shoot often dies first. Fungus enters from soil into roots, goes up stems, and plugs them, so that they wilt.
Danger period: Midsummer to midfall.
Treatment: Plant wilt-resistant varieties, marked F or FF in catalogs. Rotate crops.

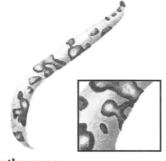

Anthracnose

Plants affected: Many kinds of beans.
Symptoms and signs: Sunken brown-black areas on pods, brown spots on leaves and stems. Leaves may fall.
Danger period: Growing season—particularly cool, wet summers.
Treatment: Remove and destroy affected plant parts. Choose resistant varieties when available. Stake and prune plants to improve air circulation. Sulfur sprays may help prevent spread.

Botrytis, or gray mold

Plants affected: Tomatoes, occasionally bean and pea pods in wet weather.
Symptoms and signs: Gray velvety mold develops on rotting fruit.
Danger period: Growing season.
Treatment: Remove and destroy diseased fruits or pods. Indoors and outdoors, apply preventative sprays of *Bacillus subtilis.*

Bulb, Corm, Tuber, and Root Disorders

Stem and bulb nematodes, or stem and bulb eelworms

Plants affected: Hyacinths, narcissi, tulips, and some others.
Symptoms and signs: Bulbs discolor internally and eventually rot away. Poor and distorted growth.
Danger period: Dormant bulbs in late summer and autumn; growing plants in spring.
Treatment: Destroy affected plants. Do not replant bulbs in affected areas of soil for at least 3 yr. Solarize areas infested with nematodes.

Narcissus bulb flies

Plants affected: Narcissus bulbs.
Symptoms and signs: Bulbs soft and rotten, brownish maggots inside.
Danger period: Between early spring and early summer; symptoms apparent in dormant bulbs in fall or spring.
Treatment: Discard soft bulbs at planting time. Cultivate soil around plants as leaves die, to block holes in soil that would allow flies to get down to bulbs to lay eggs. Dust at this time and at planting time with pyrethrins.

Gray bulb rot (rhizoctonia)

Plants affected: Hyacinths, tulips, and similar plants.
Symptoms and signs: Dry gray rot at neck of bulb, which soon becomes covered with black fungus and disintegrates.
Danger period: Soon after planting.
Treatment: Remove and destroy debris from diseased plants; replace surrounding soil.

Iris borers

Plants affected: Iris, mainly tall bearded and Siberian.
Symptoms and signs: Foliage yellows and may eventually fall over as borers feed inside rhizomes.
Danger period: Early summer to fall.
Treatment: Clean plants in fall to remove eggs. Destroy infested leaves in spring. Crush borers inside leaves between your fingers. When soil temperature has risen above 50°F in spring, drench plants and surrounding soil with a solution of parasitic nematodes, following package directions. Reapply one month later. When dividing irises, destroy infested rhizomes.

Basal rot

Plants affected: Many bulbs, such as crocuses, lilies, and narcissi.
Symptoms and signs: Rotting of roots and base of corm or bulb, which, if cut longitudinally, shows dark strands spreading from base or chocolate-brown rot spreading upward through inner scales. Affected corms or bulbs eventually rot completely.
Danger period: Any time, including during storage.
Treatment: Destroy severely affected corms and bulbs. In early stages, lily bulbs may be saved by cutting out diseased roots and scales. As a preventive, dust bulbs with sulfur fungicide before storing.

Ink disease

Plants affected: Bulbous irises, red-hot pokers.
Symptoms and signs: Black crusts on outer scales of bulb, followed by decay within, leaving small pockets of black powder.
Danger period: Any time of year.
Treatment: Destroy affected bulbs or corms. Destroy foliage at end of season. Replant healthy bulbs or corms in fresh site after dipping them in solution of bleach.

Neck rot, or smolder

Plants affected: Narcissi.
Symptoms and signs: Bulbs decay and small, black, flat fungus develops.
Danger period: During storage.
Treatment: After digging bulbs, remove all yellowed foliage. Store them in a cool, dry area with good air circulation. Be sure storage bins or bags are clean before placing bulbs in them. Inspect stored bulbs periodically and destroy affected bulbs.

Tulip-bulb aphids

Plants affected: Crocuses, gladioli, irises, tulips.
Symptoms and signs: Colonies of dark green aphids develop on dormant bulbs and corms in storage.
Danger period: Late fall to late winter.
Treatment: Sprays of insecticidal soap can be used, but make sure that treated bulbs and corms dry thoroughly afterward.

Carrot rust flies

Plants affected: Carrots, celery, parsley, parsnips.
Symptoms and signs: Fly maggots tunnel into roots.
Danger period: Early summer to midfall.
Treatment: Cover sown areas with row covers so adult flies can not reach plants to lay eggs. Drench soil with parasitic nematodes to kill maggots in soil. Do not put infested roots into compost piles.

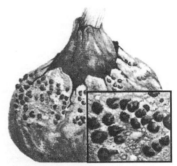

Tulip fire (botrytis)

Plants affected: Tulips.
Symptoms and signs: Bulbs rot; small black fungus develops.
Danger period: Shortly before or after planting.
Treatment: Buy and plant large, disease-free bulbs only. Rotate the location of your tulips from year to year (3 yr. is desirable). Plant in well-drained soil, and avoid overwatering and overfertilizing. Dig bulbs within 3 wk. of petal fall, when conditions are dry. Store only healthy bulbs; destroy rotten or infected bulbs. After replanting, remove and destroy any diseased plants as they appear during growing season. Remove and destroy all tulip debris after flowering. Apply preventive sprays of *Bacillus subtitlis*.

Iris soft rot

Plants affected: Iris.
Symptoms and signs: Foliage yellows, flowers are small, rhizomes, when lifted, are soft and foul-smelling.
Danger period: Summer.
Treatment: Avoid damaging rhizomes by close hoeing. Control iris borers. When replanting, be careful to use only rot-free rhizomes and plant in a fresh location.

Commercial slug traps have a raised lid, which lets slugs get in, and protects its content of beer from rain.

Commercial slug pot

Bulb, Corm, Tuber, and Root Disorders (*continued*)

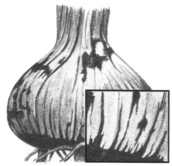

Dry rot

Plants affected: Crocuses, freesias, gladioli, potatoes, and some other tubers.

Symptoms and signs: Many small dark lesions develop on corms or tubers and merge to produce larger black areas before dry rot shrivels corm or tuber completely.

Danger period: During storage.

Treatment: Remove and destroy affected corms or tubers as soon as first symptoms appear. Before storing or replanting healthy ones, dust with sulfur fungicide. Dry thoroughly before storing. Grow corms or tubers in fresh site each year.

Potato mop-top

Plants affected: Potatoes.

Symptoms and signs: Brown arclike marks in flesh of tuber. Might be caused by virus.

Danger period: Growing season.

Treatment: Destroy badly affected tubers, and do not plant potatoes in same site for several years.

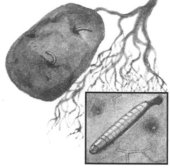

Wireworms

Plants affected: Carrots, lettuce, potatoes, tomatoes, and other vegetables; chrysanthemums and other ornamentals.

Symptoms and signs: Underground parts are invaded by larvae.

Danger period: Early spring to early fall.

Treatment: Cultivate infested soil thoroughly and frequently before planting. Control weeds.

Powdery scab

Plants affected: Potatoes.

Symptoms and signs: Uniform round scabs, raised at first, later bursting open to release powdery mass of spores. Affected tubers may be deformed and have earthy taste.

Danger period: Growing season.

Treatment: Destroy diseased tubers and do not plant potatoes in same site for several years. Provide good drainage; use no lime on soil.

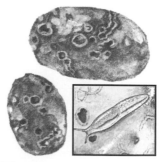

Slugs

Plants affected: Narcissi, potatoes, tulips, and many other plants.

Symptoms and signs: Irregular holes and tunnels eaten into bulbs, corms, and tubers. Slugs often present; slime residue left on plant.

Danger period: Most of the year.

Treatment: Lift potatoes as early as possible to minimize damage. Stale beer in shallow dish is useful as slug trap.

Look carefully at iris roots and rhizomes when transplanting, and cut off any that have been attacked by borers.

Root examination

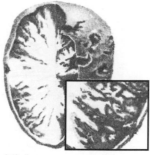

Late blight

Plants affected: Potatoes.
Symptoms and signs: Red-brown discoloration appears under skin but shows through as gray patch on surface of potato. Fungal disease spreads inward, and affected areas are often entered by bacteria, which cause foul smelling soft rot.
Danger period: Midsummer until end of potato-growing season.
Treatment: Plant only certified disease-free seed potatoes. Hill soil around uninfected plants to keep spores from reaching tubers. Remove and destroy infected plants. Clear out all crop debris after harvest. Repeated copper sprays can prevent infection, but can also lead to other pest problems.

Common scab

Plants affected: Potatoes.
Symptoms and signs: Ragged-edged scabs on tubers.
Danger period: Growing season.
Treatment: Do not apply lime before planting potatoes. Give soil plenty of humus, and keep growth even by watering before soil dries. If trouble persists, grow resistant varieties, such as 'Norchip', 'Norland', or 'Superior'. Destroy debris and infected peelings.

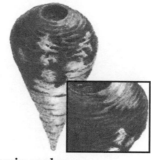

Parsnip canker

Plants affected: Parsnips.
Symptoms and signs: Red-brown or black rotting canker on shoulder of root.
Danger period: Growing season.
Treatment: Grow parsnips in deep, loamy soil, with lime added if necessary. Use balanced fertilizer. Sow seeds early and thin seedlings to about 3 in. apart. Grow resistant varieties or rotate crops if trouble persists. Begin harvesting in midsummer.

Vine weevils

Plants affected: Tuberous begonias, pot cyclamens, primroses, saxifrages, and some other plants. Much damage is done to greenhouse plants, but these pests also appear outdoors and are particularly serious on rhododendrons and azaleas, and on yews.
Symptoms and signs: Small, white, fat, legless grubs that live in soil eat roots, tubers, and corms.
Danger period: Most times of year. Grubs are usually noticed in winter and early spring.
Treatment: Remove and destroy any grubs found when plants are repotted. On outdoor shrubs, inspect plants carefully for chewed bark around base of stem and reject any showing signs. Add parasitic nematodes to the soil.

Cracking

Plants affected: All kinds of root vegetables.
Symptoms and signs: Lengthwise splitting.
Danger period: Growing season.
Treatment: Try to avoid irregular growth by watering before soil dries out completely.

Boron deficiency

Plants affected: Beets, rutabagas, turnips.
Symptoms and signs: Gray or brown patches in flesh of lower half edible root, or browning—and sometimes eventual blackening—of interior of root.
Danger period: Growing season.
Treatment: Apply 1 rounded tbsp. of borax (mixed with fine sand for easier distribution) to every 20 sq. yd. of soil.

Bulb, Corm, Tuber, and Root Disorders (*continued*)

Root and Stem Disorders

Corm rot
Plants affected: Acidantheras, freesias, gladioli.
Symptoms and signs: Rotting from center outward, corm becomes spongy and dark brown or black.
Danger period: During storage.
Treatment: Store corms in dry atmosphere at 45°–50°F. Before storage, dust corms with sulfur. Destroy affected corms.

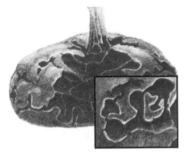

Hard rot (Septoria)
Plants affected: Gladioli, but corms of other kinds can also be affected.
Symptoms and signs: Large, black-brown, clearly outlined, somewhat sunken spots develop on corms, which may become hard and shriveled.
Danger period: Infection occurs during summer, but symptoms show during storage.
Treatment: See Dry Rot, p. 536.

Onion maggots
Plants affected: Leeks, garlic, onions.
Symptoms and signs: Bulbs turn mushy. Small maggots are visible feeding on rotting tissue.
Danger period: Late spring to late summer.
Treatment: Cover seedlings with a floating row cover to keep flies from laying eggs. Onion sets are less likely to be attacked than seedlings.

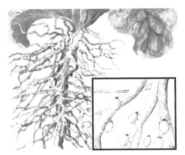

Root aphids and root mealybugs
Plants affected: Primroses, lettuce; and some other ornamentals.
Symptoms and signs: Colonies of white, wax-covered aphids or mealybugs infest roots.
Danger period: Late summer and fall outdoors; any time of year in greenhouse.
Treatment: Choose resistant varieties. Keep plants growing quickly and avoid stressing plants.

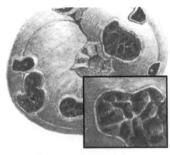

Gladiolus scab
Plants affected: Gladioli.
Symptoms and signs: Round craters develop toward base of corm. Each crater has prominent raised rim and often varnishlike coating.
Danger period: Infection occurs during summer, but symptoms may not show until corms are lifted and put in storage.
Treatment: See Dry Rot, p. 536.

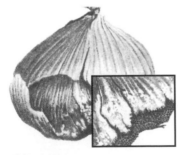

White rot
Plants affected: Onions, especially spring onions; occasionally garlic and leeks.
Symptoms and signs: Base of bulbs and roots are covered with white fungus and rot.
Danger period: Growing season.
Treatment: Grow onions on new site each year if possible; disease contaminates soil for at least 8 yr. Destroy diseased plants.

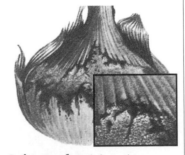

Onion neck rot (botrytis)
Plants affected: Onions.
Symptoms and signs: Gray velvety mold develops near neck of stored onions, which rot rapidly.
Danger period: Growing season, but symptoms do not show until storage.
Treatment: If possible, buy treated seeds. Store only well-ripened hard onions; put them in dry, cool, airy place. Destroy diseased onions.

Cabbage maggots
Plants affected: Recently transplanted brassicas, especially Brussels sprouts, cabbages, cauliflower; also wallflowers.
Symptoms and signs: Maggots in soil feed on roots, causing complete collapse of young plants.
Danger period: Midspring to early fall.
Treatment: Protect transplants by planting through individual maggot barriers. Or, cover transplants with row covers.

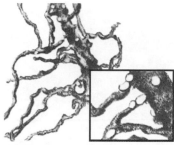

Golden potato cyst nematodes

Plants affected: Potatoes, tomatoes.
Symptoms and signs: Pinhead-size yellow or brown cysts on roots. Plants wilt and die.
Danger period: Midsummer to early fall.
Treatment: If crop is severely affected, wait 17 yr. before replanting. This is the worst nematode, and when it occurs, quarantine regulations prevent the movement of plants and soil from the area. Plant certified seed potatoes.

Clubroot

Plants affected: Brussels sprouts, cabbages, cauliflowers, stocks (*Matthiola* and *Malcolmia*), and other members of cabbage family.
Symptoms and signs: Roots become swollen and distorted by slime mold. Plants look weak and yellow.
Danger period: Growing season.
Treatment: If possible, do not plant brassicas in areas where clubroot has been a past problem. Test soil pH and add ground limestone at least 6 wk. before planting to raise pH to 6.8 to 7.5. Clean all debris from garden after harvest.

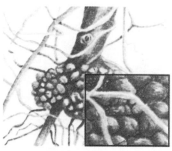

Armillaria root rot, or honey fungus

Plants affected: All kinds of woody plants, especially on the West Coast.
Symptoms and signs: White fan-shaped sheets of fungal growth beneath bark at ground level. Dark threads may appear on roots.
Danger period: Any time of year.
Treatment: This disease does not seem to be as devastating in North America as it is in Europe. No control is known here, but plants fed and watered properly generally seem to survive.

Crown gall

Plants affected: Many plants in rose family.
Symptoms and signs: Walnut- to football-size galls develop on roots and occasionally on stems.
Danger period: Growing season.
Treatment: Avoid injuries to roots. Prevent waterlogging by adequate drainage. Do not plants roses in crown-gall-infested soil. Destroy severely diseased plants. Prune and destroy aerial galls.

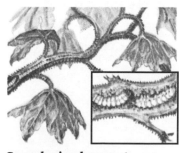

Squash vine borers (larvae)

Plants affected: All squashes, pumpkins, cucumbers, muskmelons.
Symptoms and signs: Wilting of plant; greenish excrement near holes at base of stems. Adult borers—metallic brown moths with red, black, and white markings—may be visible.
Danger period: Late spring and early summer.
Treatment: Slit vine and remove borer.

Tree and shrub borers (larvae)

Plants affected: Fruit trees, especially cherries and peaches; also dogwoods, lilacs, rhododendrons.
Symptoms and signs: Stem and tree bases exude jellylike material. Shoots wilt. Branches or entire tree may die.
Danger period: Growing season.
Treatment: Difficult to control as borers are inside shoots. Prune off small infected branches and destroy.

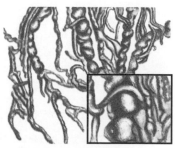

Root-knot nematodes, or root-knot eelworms

Plants affected: Mainly commercial crops, especially cucumbers, cyclamens, tomatoes, begonias, coleuses.
Symptoms and signs: Irregular, lumpy galls or swellings on roots. Foliage yellowed, plants stunted.
Danger period: Any time of year.
Treatment: Remove severely infested plants; destroy them to limit possible infection of healthy plants. Plant only in sterilized soil or soilless mix.

White grubs eat the roots of lawn grasses, and cause yellow patches. The grass can then be pulled up easily.

Lawn disorder

Lawn Disorders

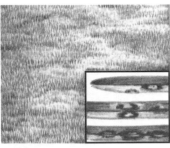

Leaf spot (helminthosporium)

Plants affected: Bent, blue, fescue, and rye grasses.
Symptoms and signs: Small, brown, irregularly oval spots generally appear in pairs on grass blades. Blades shrivel and bend over; stems, crowns, and roots may rot.
Danger period: Early summer to midfall.
Treatment: Do not mow too closely. Resow with resistant cultivars. Avoid giving excess nitrogen in spring.

Pink snow mold

Plants affected: Nearly all types of grasses.
Symptoms and signs: Large dead patches of lawn covered with white fungus, which is most obvious in moist weather and after snow melts.
Danger period: Winter to early spring.
Treatment: Do not apply too much nitrogen fertilizer, especially after late summer. Keep grass short in fall; long grass is more susceptible to mold. Use a fan rake to break up fungus threads.

Bluegrass rust

Plants affected: Many kinds of grasses, but primarily 'Merion' Kentucky blue-grass.
Symptoms and signs: Yellow-orange or red-brown powdery spots on leaves.
Danger period: Late summer and early fall (until frost).
Treatment: Lawns well fed with nitrogen resist rust. Resistant grass varieties include 'Adelphi', 'Fylking', 'Pennstar', 'Windsor'.

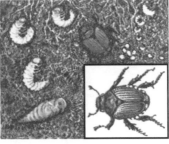

Beetle grubs (larvae of Japanese, Asiatic, and June beetles, rose chafer and others)

Plants affected: Primarily roots of lawn grasses, but also roots of corn and many garden perennials.
Symptoms and signs: Turf shows irregular yellow and brown patches that vary in size. Turf can be rolled up like carpet because grubs have severed roots. In such conditions there may be 35 to 60 grubs per square foot of lawn. On other plants grubs chew off roots, causing wilting, drying, and ultimate death of plants.
Danger period: Spring and fall for most beetles and chafers. For white grubs (May-June beetle larvae), midspring to late fall.
Treatment: Apply milky spore disease in spring or fall when soil temperature is above 70°F. Or, apply *Heterorhabditis* nematodes according to package instructions.

Red thread, or Corticium disease

Plants affected: Nearly all types of grasses.
Symptoms and signs: Dead patches of lawn; blades show red fungal growth.
Danger period: After rain in fall.
Treatment: Keep soil pH between 6.5 and 7.0. Water deeply to promote strong roots and avoid frequently wetting of the turf. Do not overapply nitrogen fertilizers. Collect infected clippings when mowing and destroy them.

Fairy ring

Plants affected: Nearly all types of grasses.
Symptoms and signs: Large brown ring with dark green center on lawn. In late summer, fruiting bodies (mushrooms) appear in outer area of ring.
Danger period: Summer.
Treatment: Aerate the soil in the area of the rings. Keep the area well-watered to stimulate grass growth. Feed lawn overall so that it remains green. Mow regularly to prevent mushroom growth.

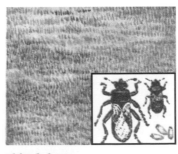

Chinch bugs

Plants affected: Lawn and golf-course turf.
Symptoms and signs: Turf is off-color, dying in irregular pattern. Dead grass does not pull up easily.
Danger period: Warm, sunny weather from early summer to midfall.
Treatment: Water lawn heavily, then keep very moist for 3–4 weeks. A natural fungus will control the chinch bugs

Holes in lawn

Plants affected: Most lawn grasses.
Symptoms and signs: Holes, tea-cup size or larger, appear in lawn overnight.
Danger period: Late summer to fall, but occasionally at other times.
Treatment: Control grubs. Holes are made by animals (mostly skunks) digging for the grubs as food.

Organic Pest and Disease Control

A plant's main enemies are pests (such as rabbits, insects, slugs and snails, and nematodes) and diseases (like fungi, bacteria, and virus). Most can be controlled using ecologically friendly methods. Rather than setting a goal of a pest-free garden, learn how to work with nature to keep problems at an acceptable level. Vigilance is the key to growing good plants; paying close attention to how the plants are growing will pay off. Finding a pest or disease problem in the early stages, when it is relatively easy to deal with, is preferable to suddenly discovering that the crop or plant in question is seriously infected with some problem.

Pest control This can be approached in stages, depending on the problem. Animals (rabbits, gophers, etc.) can be kept away from food crops by surrounding the area with a wire fence with the base buried in the soil. In the flower garden, plant species they do not like to eat. Protect the stems of trees with a wire guard for the winter (make it high enough to allow for snow) and spray shrub stems with a hot pepper spray after the last rain in fall. Deer and elk are difficult to repel without enclosing the entire garden with a high fence, but there are plants that they are less likely to eat (see list on p. 68).

Large insects, such as caterpillars and beetles, can be picked off by hand and dropped into a bucket of soapy water. When larger plants, like trees, are attacked, the soil directly under their foliage can be covered with drop sheets and the plant shaken to dislodge the pests. The drop sheets can then be carefully lifted and the pests destroyed. Caterpillars that congregate in webbing "nests," like tent caterpillars and fall webworms, should be controlled during the day, when the young larvae have left the nest, by spraying them with *Bacillus thuringiensis*. Another alternative is to wait until evening when the caterpillars have returned to the nest. Prune off the nests and immerse them in a bucket of soapy water to kill the larvae.

Plants can be protected from damage by soil-dwelling caterpillars, like cutworms, by enclosing them in a barrier made from half a frozen juice can or a circle of heavy-grade tinfoil pushed slightly into the soil. Wireworms (orange and curl into a half circle) and millipedes (dark brown and curl into a spiral) both live in the soil and feed on plant roots or burrow into root crops. They are seldom numerous, except in reclaimed pastureland, but destroy them when digging.

Quick-moving small pests, such as flea beetles, carrot flies, and leafhoppers, can be kept away from young plants—the most vulnerable—by covering them with a floating row cover supported on wire hoops made from cut-down clothes hangers. This also gives protection against late frost and against sunscald on newly planted plants.

Slow-moving small pests, like aphids and mites, can be washed off many plants with a strong stream of water, however, this should not be used on plants with large, soft foliage, or on the fragile growing tips of plants. Mites can also be kept to a minimum by spraying frequently with water, using a hand sprayer, and soaking the undersides of the foliage. Planting flowers that attract native predators also helps to control aphids and mites.

Insects can be lured to bright yellow or red traps coated with a nondrying sticky substance, which holds them. There are also traps baited with scent lures called pheromones. These are scents released by insects to attract others of their species. When used in a trap, they may imitate a female scent and entice many of the males to enter. The unbalanced population results in a large reduction in the number of eggs laid, and young hatching.

Many natural predators can be used to help solve a pest problem. They can be released into the garden and will target a specific pest or range of pests (see p. 546). Naturally, it takes time for the predator population to build up sufficiently to bring the problem under control, so there is always a lag between introducing the predator and solving the problem. They rarely completely kill off all the problem pests, but they will bring the population down to acceptable levels. Remember, spraying for pest control will often wipe out the beneficial insects as well.

Nematodes are microscopic wormlike creatures, some of which attack plants, but others are beneficial and attack plant pests. They are especially useful for controlling some lawn pests and are simply mixed with water and applied with a watering can. In warmer parts of the country, one application will give several years control, but in the North, the cold kills them and they need to be reapplied if the problem occurs again.

Bacteria are also weapons in the fight against plant pests. *Bacillus thuringiensis kurstaki*, commonly known as BT or Dipel, was the original strain that attacks the caterpillars of certain species of moths and butterflies. There are now several other strains of this bacteria that can control Japanese beetle larvae, mosquito larvae, Colorado beetle larvae, and more. A large range of these predators and lures are available by mail or through your local nursery.

If none of the above methods control the problem to your satisfaction, you may have to resort to spraying with one of the organic controls listed on pp. 544–545.

Disease control. This is more difficult than pest control because the disease has usually got a hold on the plant before any symptoms appear. Many fungal diseases are spread by very small spores that float on the breeze and land on a plant leaf. They "germinate" and insert a small thread (called a hyphae) into the plant tissue. This feeds on the plant and grows, forming a network of hyphae between the cells inside the leaf. It is not until this point that the plant begins to show signs of stress—different colored spots, wilting, or fungal tissue visible (as in mildew). Such leaves should be picked off as soon as noticed and put in the garbage—not in the compost. If caught in time, this may be enough to stop the further spread of the disease.

Many plants, providing they are not under stress from poor growing conditions, can emit defensive secretions that can either kill fungal spores or limit the damage they can cause. It therefore makes sense to grow plants properly, giving them the soil conditions, acidity or alkalinity, and moisture they grow best in. In addition, allow good air circulation through plants, especially those, like phlox and bergamot, that are prone to mildew. Stagnant air in the middle of a large clump of stems is a mildew heaven.

Other fungi are great opportunists. Although they are not able to directly infect a plant, they can gain entry through stem and leaf wounds. Many cankers fall into this category. They can attack a plant only when it has been damaged by careless hoeing or gain entry through a wound caused by mower damage.

Fungi are important agents in plant decay, and most work in the gardener's favor. They help break down compost and are responsible for rotting wood in forests and returning the nutrients to the soil. Without them, the woods would be choked with dead trees. Some, such as coral spot, will also attack living material that is under stress from another cause. The appearance of small, bright coral-pink fungi on a branch indicates a problem.

Mixed cultivation can keep certain kinds of pests at bay. Tomatoes, for example, protect various varieties of cabbage from cabbage flies and butterflies.

A mixed bed of cabbage, lettuce, and tomatoes

Homemade Organic Controls

Most of the fungicides listed in the chart on pp. 544–545 are preventative, rather than curative. They should be applied before the disease strikes to form a protective layer on the foliage that kills the fungal spores on contact.

Bacteria are minute organisms that can be rod-shaped, spherical, or spiral, and there are several million in a typical teaspoon of soil. They are important in breaking down dead plant material, but a few attack living plants, generally causing plant tissue to disintegrate. Soft rot of iris is a typical bacterial disease. They are difficult to control and long-lived in the soil, but generally specific to one species or group of plants. Avoid replanting the same species in soil where a bacterial disease has been diagnosed. Some bacteria attack certain insects and are used as insecticides.

Virus are submicroscopic primitive life-forms that live inside cells of plants and animals. They tend to be very specific, limiting their attack to a single genus or plant family. Some virus are used as insecticides but others attack plants. There is no cure and infected plants should be dug up and disposed of in the garbage. Infected plants usually have foliage with strange mottling or streaks, and are often puckering as well. The recently discovered virus attacking hostas is typical in this way. Plant infections can be spread by hand, shears, and other gardening tools. Newly infected plants may take several years to show symptoms, during which time the virus can be spread to other plants. Virus are also spread by sap-sucking insects, such as leafhoppers, so controlling these insects is very important. Many modern varieties of vegetables, especially tomatoes, have built-in resistance to some of the virus and other diseases that attack them. This information is usually indicated by a series of code letters in seed catalogs.

Compost Tea

Homemade compost or special compost preparations available from garden suppliers are the basis of this tea. Simply put a shovelful of finished compost in a burlap sack and immerse it in a bucket of water for about a week. Strain the resulting tea through cheesecloth or some other material to remove all solids. Use the tea full-strength to water any and all plants in your garden. Compost tea not only provides a wide range of nutrients, but it also boosts plants' natural defenses against disease. Spraying plants with aerated compost tea can convey even greater benefits. To make aerated compost tea, follow the instructions that come with the compost preparations procured from a garden supplier.

Herbal Sprays

While herbal sprays do not appear to actually kill insects, they do seem to act as an effective repellent, and spraying plants with a tea made of garden herbs may help to keep them pest-free. Sage, thyme, rosemary, and white clover seem to help ward off attacks from leaf-eating caterpillars. To make, either soak 1 cup of fresh leaves overnight in 2 cups of water or pour 2 cups of boiling water over 2 cups of fresh leaves. To use, strain, dilute with an equal amount of water, and add a few drops of liquid soap (not detergent) to act as a spreader.

Stinging Nettle Spray

Stinging nettles grow as weeds in the eastern parts of the country but they can be used to make a spray that helps plants resist disease attacks.

When collecting nettles to make the spray, wear long pants, cover the arms, and wear good work gloves. Place about 1 pound of nettle leaves and young stalks in a bag and soak it in 1 gallon of chlorine-free water (tap water that has stood uncovered for 48 hours). Cover the bucket and leave it in a warm place for a week. The mixture will have a strong smell when uncovered and may need straining through a cheesecloth. Dilute with five times its volume of chlorine-free water and spray plants that are known to be susceptible to fungus diseases. Spray every 2 weeks for continued coverage. It also helps deter aphids and acts as a foliar feed. Store any unused spray concentrate in a glass jar, it will keep for a month.

Starch Spray

This forms a sticky coating on the leaf surface, which traps the pests and holds them until they die. It works best on small pests like aphids and thrips, rather than on large beetles and caterpillars. Mix 2–4 tablespoons of potato flour (available in health food stores) in one quart of water and add a few drops of liquid soap as a sticker. Shake well and spray onto the plants, covering the entire leaves. It will wash off in rain or can be hosed off after a few days.

Garlic Oil Spray

A mix of garlic, mineral oil, and soap gives very good results against many sucking and chewing insects. These include aphids, cabbageworms, leaf-hoppers, larval mosquitoes, squash bugs, and whiteflies.

Some plants are sensitive, so try it on a single shoot first. If there is no damage after 48 hours, spray the entire plant. Soak 3 ounces of finely chopped garlic in 2 teaspoons of mineral oil for 24 hours. Dissolve 1 teaspoon of insecticidal soap in 2 cups of water and add it to the garlic and oil. Stir well and strain. To use, add 1–2 tablespoons to 2 cups of water and spray on the pests. Store the remainder in a glass container for future use.

Hot Pepper Dust

Grow your own hot peppers to provide the source for a repellent dust that will help protect plants from cabbage maggots, carrot root flies, ants, and other pests. Dry the harvested pepper first, and then grind them with a mortar and pestle (always wear protective eye gear and gloves when working with hot peppers because the dust can be very irritating to your eyes). Sprinkle the dust along plant rows just after seeding or around the base of young plants. Apply more dust after rainfall or watering.

Beer can be put out as bait for slugs, which come out in particularly large numbers in wet weather. So-called slug fences will preserve beds from insects.

Slug infestations increase with rain.

CONTROL	APPLICATION AND TRADE NAMES	DESCRIPTION
BACILLUS SUBTILIS	**Spray:** Serenade; Sonata	A naturally occurring bacterium that helps protect plants from some fungal diseases by outcompeting the pathogens. Applied as a foliar spray to help prevent powdery mildew, anthracnose, blight and other diseases.
BACILLUS THURINGIENSIS	**Spray or dust:** Dipel	Biological control for bagworms, cankerworms, gypsy moth and tent caterpillars, loopers. Considered harmless to humans and animals.
Var. TENEBRIONIS	Novodor	For the control of Colorado beetle larvae and elm leaf beetle.
BEAUVERIA BASSIANA	**Spray:** Serenade; Sonata	Biological control for a broad range of leaf-feeding insects, including aphids, caterpillars, mealybugs, leafhoppers, thrips, and whiteflies. *Beauveria* is a fungus that occurs naturally in many soils. The fungus invades the pest insects' bodies and kills them, and then can spread naturally to continue killing more pests. May also harm beneficial insects.
BENEFICIAL BACTERIA AND FUNGI	**Soil drench or spray:** Mycostop; RootShield	Formulations of bacteria (*Streptomyces*) or fungi (*Trichoderma*) that help protect plant roots from diseases such as damping-off by outcompeting the pathogens. Generally applied to soil as a drench or spray.
BORAX	**Spray or bait:** Pyrobor	Insecticide that is used on ants. It is poisonous to the larvae when taken back to the nest and fed to them.
BORDEAUX MIXTURE	**Spray or dust:** Bordeaux mixture sold under various trade names, such as Bordo-Mix	Fungicide mixture of copper sulfate and hydrated lime. This and other pesticides containing lime should not be mixed with other organic controls. Bordeaux mixture should always be used alone. If mixed spray is required, use a low-soluble copper. Used for many different plant disorders. Harmful to fish.
COPPER HYDROXIDE	**Spray:** Kocide	Controls bacterial blights and leaf spots of tomatoes, beans, cucumbers, and peppers.
COPPER SULFATE	**Spray or dust:** Basicop Tri-Basic Copper Sulfate	Fungicide that can be used as alternative to Bordeaux mixture. Toxic to livestock and fish.

CONTROL	APPLICATION AND TRADE NAMES	DESCRIPTION
FERROUS (IRON) PHOSPHATE	**Bait:** Sluggo; Escar-Go!	Slugs that eat these baits containing iron phosphate stop eating plants and die within several days. Also effective against snails. Applied to soil surface. Remaining bait breaks down naturally in soil to supply nutrients for plants.
KAOLIN CLAY	**Spray:** Surround	A fine clay that is mixed in suspension with water and sprayed on plant foliage. Deters feeding and egg-laying by a wide range of pests, including Japanese beetles, flea beetles, other leaf-eating beetles, leafhoppers, and thrips. Must be reapplied after rain.
LIME SULFUR	**Spray:** Lime Sulfur	Fungicidal spray for trees, shrubs, and fruit. Used at full strength during dormancy and at half strength after the leaves have opened.
NEEM	**Spray or drench:** Neem	An oil extracted from the seeds of the tropical neem tree, which upsets the growth pattern of insects. When diluted, it can be used to control a large range of insects pests and is best against chewing insects like Japanese beetle. It is not very effective for sucking insects like aphids.
OIL EMULSIONS and MISCIBLE OILS	**Spray:** Dormant oils available under various brand names	Superior and supreme miscible spray oils and oil emulsions are insecticides used as dormant sprays to control eggs of mites, tent caterpillars, gypsy moths, and other insects. Apply as dormant spray before buds break on deciduous trees and shrubs. Temperature should be above 45°F but not over 70°F. Use as spray to control mealybugs and two-spotted mites on greenhouse and house plants. Some oils may be used in summer; see directions on label.
PYRETHRINS or PYRETHRUM	**Spray:** Content of most home and garden sprays	Nonpersistent insecticide. Used against aphids, small caterpillars, and whiteflies.
SOAP	**Spray:** Insecticidal Soap	Nonpersistent insecticide. Selected fatty acids that control a wide range of pests on contact. They are environmentally safe and have low toxicity to humans and pets.

Ladybug

Hover fly

Spider and its web

Aphids are eaten by ladybugs, and larvae of many pests by hover flies, while spiders eliminate a variety of garden pests.

CONTROL	APPLICATION AND TRADE NAMES	DESCRIPTION
SPINOSAD	**Spray:** Monterey Garden Insect Spray; Entrust; Bulls-Eye	Natural insecticide containing toxins produced by an actinomycete (form of bacteria). Kills a wide range of pests including many caterpillars, Colorado potato beetles, fire ants, sawflies, and thrips.
SULFUR	**Dust:** Available from many manufacturers	Finely ground sulfur can be dusted onto plants to control some diseases. Added to the soil, it slowly lowers the acidity.

HOME RECIPES AND NATURAL PRODUCTS

The controls listed on pages 544-545 are from naturally occurring sources and are widely used by organic gardeners. The following home recipes and natural products may also be of interest.

BAKING SODA	A 5% solution of baking soda sprayed onto plants will prevent the spores of many fungi from germinating. It will not kill fungi once they are attacking the plant. Dissolve 1 tsp. baking soda in 1 qt. of water, and add a few drops of dishwashing liquid. You will need to reapply after rain.
GARDEN FRIENDS	The small black ground beetles you find scurrying about prey on many garden pests. Do not tread on them. Millipedes feed on plant roots and curl up into a spring when disturbed. Kill these. Centipedes feed on other soil creatures, including many that attack plants. They run away when disturbed. Do not kill these. Encourage birds into the garden by feeding them in the winter, providing nest boxes and growing plants that give food and shelter. Birds eat insects and seeds, pests and weeds.
PARASITIC NEMATODES	While some nematodes attack plants, others are parasitic on soil-dwelling plant pests, such as wireworms. These beneficial nematodes can be purchased commercially and added to the soil. Where winters are cold, they will not survive, but by then most of the harmful soil pests will have been destroyed.
SOLARIZING SOIL	While commercial soil sterilants are too dangerous to use in the average garden, soil that is badly infested with pests or weed seeds can be partially cleaned by heat. In midsummer, prepare the soil by cleaning off plant debris and raking it smooth. Water the area well, then stretch a sheet of 2–4 mil clear plastic to keep it tight. Leave it in place for several weeks. The higher the temperature you achieve, the better pest and weed control you will get. However, you will also kill beneficial insects in the soil.

Although generally considered pests, earwigs also eat aphids. A pot filled with straw hung in a tree will provide daytime shelter so they can feed on aphids at night.

Earwig shelter

Honeybee on a *Gaillardia* ➡

Little Helpers in the Fight Against Pests

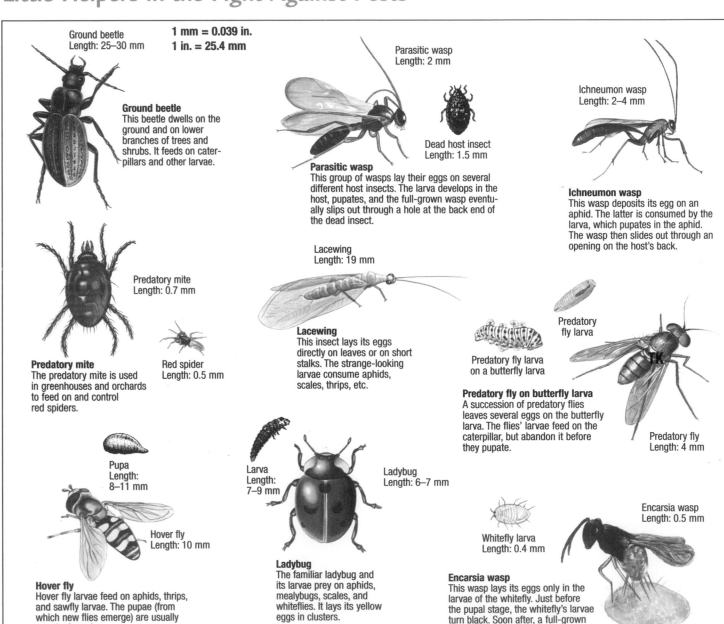

1 mm = 0.039 in.
1 in. = 25.4 mm

Ground beetle
Length: 25–30 mm

Ground beetle
This beetle dwells on the ground and on lower branches of trees and shrubs. It feeds on caterpillars and other larvae.

Parasitic wasp
Length: 2 mm

Dead host insect
Length: 1.5 mm

Parasitic wasp
This group of wasps lay their eggs on several different host insects. The larva develops in the host, pupates, and the full-grown wasp eventually slips out through a hole at the back end of the dead insect.

Ichneumon wasp
Length: 2–4 mm

Ichneumon wasp
This wasp deposits its egg on an aphid. The latter is consumed by the larva, which pupates in the aphid. The wasp then slides out through an opening on the host's back.

Predatory mite
Length: 0.7 mm

Red spider
Length: 0.5 mm

Predatory mite
The predatory mite is used in greenhouses and orchards to feed on and control red spiders.

Lacewing
Length: 19 mm

Lacewing
This insect lays its eggs directly on leaves or on short stalks. The strange-looking larvae consume aphids, scales, thrips, etc.

Predatory fly larva

Predatory fly larva on a butterfly larva

Predatory fly on butterfly larva
A succession of predatory flies leaves several eggs on the butterfly larva. The flies' larvae feed on the caterpillar, but abandon it before they pupate.

Predatory fly
Length: 4 mm

Pupa
Length: 8–11 mm

Hover fly
Length: 10 mm

Hover fly
Hover fly larvae feed on aphids, thrips, and sawfly larvae. The pupae (from which new flies emerge) are usually on a leaf nearby.

Larva
Length: 7–9 mm

Ladybug
Length: 6–7 mm

Ladybug
The familiar ladybug and its larvae prey on aphids, mealybugs, scales, and whiteflies. It lays its yellow eggs in clusters.

Whitefly larva
Length: 0.4 mm

Encarsia wasp
Length: 0.5 mm

Encarsia wasp
This wasp lays its eggs only in the larvae of the whitefly. Just before the pupal stage, the whitefly's larvae turn black. Soon after, a full-grown wasp emerges.

WEEDS

The illustrations in this section show some of the commonest weeds that are likely to be found in flower beds and lawns.

To help you identify the weeds in your garden, the illustrations are arranged according to the most readily identifiable characteristics: those with similar leaf shapes or habits of growth are grouped together.

For each weed the common and botanical names are given. The captions indicate whether the weed is an annual or a perennial and how it reproduces. Recommended organic controls are also listed (generally hand weeding or hoeing). Providing the weeds are small and not in flower, they can often be left on the bed to wither and die although some may root again.

Color illustrations of some weeds are accompanied by black-and-white line drawings that show the weeds at their seedling stage. Recognizing a weed at a young stage will help you deal with it as early as possible. If no such drawing is included, this indicates that the seedling has leaves that are similar in general outline to those of the mature plant. The sooner you attack a weed, the easier it is to control.

Weeds in flower beds or borders are best controlled by hoeing. This is quite simple if the weeds are killed at the seedling stage. Regular hoeing every two or three weeks during spring and early summer will eliminate the need for other forms of control.

Weeds in seed should be dug up before the seeds have fallen. Once removed from the soil, they should not be placed on a compost heap, but disposed of with the garbage.

Soil will be greatly disturbed by deep hoeing. This will result in a significant loss of moisture and also brings up more weed seeds, which will germinate and need hoeing in turn. Always hoe as shallowly as possible to disturb the soil a minimal amount.

Grasslike Leaves

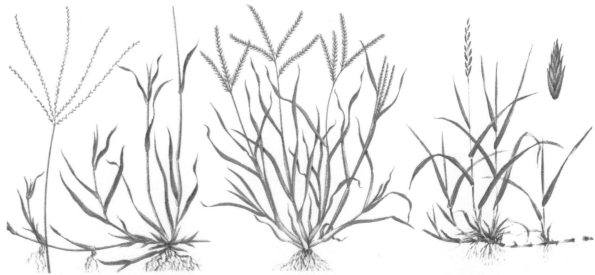

Yellow foxtail *(Setaria glauca)*
Annual. Common in gardens. Spreads by seeds. Control: Hand weed while still small, they set seed while young.

Wild garlic and wild onion
(Allium vineale and A. canadense)
Perennial. Spreads by bulbs, bulblets, and seeds. Control: Difficult. Dig up and destroy. Do not allow to flower.

Annual bluegrass *(Poa annua)*
Annual or winter annual. Spreads by seeds. Control: Collect seed heads in grass catcher while mowing.

Large crabgrass and smooth crabgrass
(Digitaria sanguinalis and D. ischaemum)
Annual. Spreads by seeds. Control: Apply corn gluten before seeds germinate.

Goose grass *(Eleusine indica)*
Annual. Often confused with crabgrass. Spreads by seeds. Control: Apply corn gluten before seeds germinate.

Quack grass *(Agropyron repens)*
Perennial. Spreads mainly by portions of rhizome. Control: Dig out with a fork. Look again a week or two later for new shoots and remove.

Weeds between paving slabs are easier to remove while small. Kill off seedlings by scraping the joints with a pointed trowel.

Hand weeding

Johnson grass (*Sorghum halepense*)
Perennial. Spreads by seeds and rootstocks.
Control: Dig out with a fork. Remove flower spikes as they appear.

Yellow nut sedge (*Cyperus esculentus*)
Perennial. Spreads by seeds and nutletlike tubers.
Control: Difficult. Dig up and destroy. Identify when small by triangular leaves and dig out.

Common reed (*Phragmites australis*, or *P. communis*)
Perennial. Found in wet areas. Spreads by seeds and pieces of rhizome.
Control: If possible, drain the area. If not, dig out when soil is dryish.

Compound Leaves

Bracken (*Pteridium aquilinum*)
Perennial. Spreads by spores and rootstocks. Control: Dig out or smother with a black plastic cover for 1 year.

Creeping buttercup (*Ranunculus repens*)
Perennial. Found in lawns. Spreads by seeds and creeping stems. Control: Rake out with a fan-type lawn rake, hand weed.

Carpetweed (*Mollugo verticillata*)
Annual. Spreads by seeds. Control: Hoe or hand pull as soon as seen. Remove plants if in flower. Mulch heavily.

Some weeds, like goutweed, are almost impossible to dig out. Instead, smother them with black plastic.

Goutweed

Compound Leaves *(continued)*

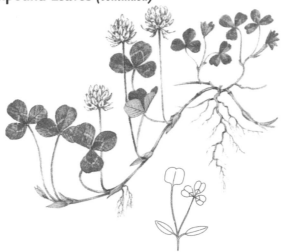

White clover (*Trifolium repens*)
Perennial. Spreads by seeds and creeping stems. Control: Dig out in beds, difficult to control in a lawn but stays green in drought.

Goutweed (*Aegopodium podograria*)
Perennial. Spreads by sections of rhizome. Control: Dig small areas, smother with black plastic for large areas.

Pineapple weed
(*Matricaria matricarioides*)
Annual. Spreads by seeds. Control: Hand weed or hoe. Do not allow to flower. Apply mulch.

Poison ivy (*Rhus radicans*)
Perennial woody vine. Spreads by seeds and creeping rootstocks. Control: Wear protective clothing and dig or smother with black plastic.

Common ragweed (*Ambrosia artemisiifolia*)
Annual. Spreads by seeds. Control: Hoe or hand weed before it flowers. Mulch area.

Common yellow wood sorrel
(*Oxalis stricta*) Perennial. Spreads by seeds and by bits of root (left when weeding). Control: Hand weed using a small fork to lift the thin, brittle roots.

Common yarrow
(*Achillea millefolium*)
Perennial. Spreads by seeds and rootstocks. Control: Dig before it flowers.

Dandelions

Dig up dandelions in the lawn in spring. They are easier to pull before they put out side roots.

Simple Leaves—Plants Close to Ground

Field bindweed (*Convolvulus arvensis*)
Perennial. Spreads by seeds and deep, rootlike rhizomes. Control: Dig out roots, repeat if it regrows.

Common chickweed (*Stellaria media*)
Annual. Spreads by seeds. Control: in lawns, rake up runners to find crown and pull out.

Mouse-ear chickweed
(*Cerastium vulgatum*)
Perennial. Spreads by seeds.
Control: As for common chickweed.

English daisy (*Bellis perennis*)
Perennial. Spreads by seeds.
Control: Dig out with daisy grubber.

Dandelion (*Taraxacum officinale*)
Perennial. Spreads by windblown seeds and divisions of deep, fleshy taproot.
Control: Dig out taproot, easiest in spring.

Heal-all (*Prunella vulgaris*)
Perennial. Spreads by seeds and rootstocks. Control: Dig up and remove, it roots again easily.

Henbit (*Lamium amplexicaule*)
Annual or biennial. Spreads by seeds and rooting stems. Control: Dig out. Cover large areas with black plastic.

Simple Leaves—Plants Close to Ground *(continued)*

Ground ivy, or creeping Charlie (*Glechoma hederacea*)
Perennial. Spreads by seeds and creeping stems. Flourishes in damp, shaded areas with rich soil; found in lawns. Control: Frequently rake out of lawns, remove raked-up stems.

Prostrate knotweed
(*Polygonum aviculare*)
Annual. Spreads by seeds. Control: Hoe or hand weed. Aerate lawns and add humus.

Liverwort (several species)
Perennial. Spreads by spores. Control: Shallow rooted, scrape off soil and add lime.

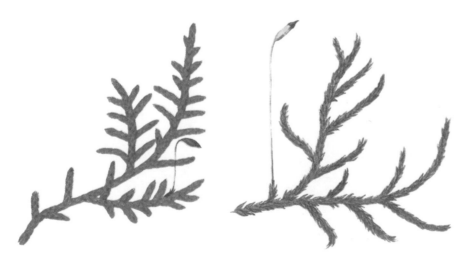

Moss on lawns (several species)
Perennial. Appearance on lawn usually indicates poor drainage, low fertility, or excessive soil acidity. Spreads by spores. Control: improve drainage, fertilize regularly, and add lime.

Bird's-eye pearlwort (*Sagina procumbens*)
Perennial. Common in lawns and golf greens. Spreads by seeds. Control: Difficult. Fertilize in spring. Do not mow closely.

Plantago major

Plantains have a fibrous root system and are not difficult to pull up. In the lawn, they set seed below mowing level.

Broad-leaved plantain
(*Plantago major*) Perennial. Found in lawns, roadsides, and uncultivated areas. Spreads by seeds. Control: Dig out. Aerate lawns and fertilize.

Buckhorn plantain
(*Plantago lanceolata*)
Perennial. Also called narrow-leaved plantain. Spreads by seeds. Control: As for broad-leaved plantain.

Common purslane
(*Portulaca oleracea*)
Annual. Spreads by seeds. Control: Hand weed or hoe. Edible—use in salads.

Shepherd's purse
(*Capsella bursa-pastoris*)
Annual. Spreads by seeds. Control: Hand weed or hoe. This sets seed while still small.

Red sorrel (*Rumex acetosella*)
Perennial. Spreads by seeds and creeping roots. Control: Fork out and remove. Watch for regrowth from brittle roots.

Creeping speedwell (*Veronica filiformis*)
Perennial. Spreads by creeping stems. Control: frequent raking; or resod small areas. Control is difficult.

Spotted spurge (*Euphorbia maculata*)
Annual. Found in lawns, gardens, cultivated fields, and waste places. Spreads by seeds. Control: Hoe or hand weed. Apply deep mulch.

Simple Leaves—Upright Plants More Than 6 Inches Tall

Curled dock (*Rumex crispus*)
Perennial. Spreads by seeds. Control:
Dig out while young, old plants difficult
to remove.

Small-flowered galinsoga (*Galinsoga parviflora*)
Annual. Common in fields and gardens. Spreads by seeds.
Control: Hoe or hand weed before flowering.

Common groundsel
(*Senecio vulgaris*)
Annual. Spreads by seeds. Control:
Hand weed and mulch area.

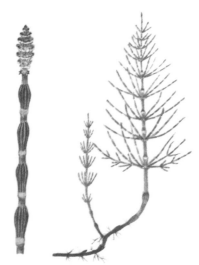

Field horsetail
(*Equisetum arvense*)
Perennial. Spreads by spores and
rhizomes. Control. Difficult as it very
deep rooted. Repeated hoeing or
smother with plastic.

Japanese knotweed
(*Polygonum cuspidatum*)
Perennial. Spreads by seeds and
rhizomes. Control: Invasive. Dig out
then cover area with plastic.

Lady's thumb
(*Polygonum persicaria*)
Annual. Spreads by seeds
Control: Hoe or pull out. Aerate
lawns to reduce compaction.

Common lamb's-quarters
(*Chenopodium album*)
Annual. Spreads by seeds. Control:
Hoe while still small. Mulch infect-
ed areas.

The yellow waterlily, or spatterdock, spreads by underground runners and can be quite invasive.

Nuphar luteum

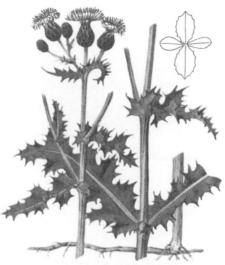

Virginia pepperweed
(*Lepidium virginicum*)
Annual or biennial. Common in fields and in roadsides. Spreads by seeds. Control: Hoe or pull out. Mulch heavily.

Redroot pigweed
(*Amaranthus retroflexus*)
Annual. Spreads by seeds. Control: Pull-up when young and remove — roots again easily.

Canada thistle (*Cirsium arvense*)
Perennial. Spreads by seeds and creeping rootstocks. Control: Dig out, but deep rooted. Lay black plastic mulch over area

Annual sow thistle
(*Sonchus oleraceus*)
Annual. Spreads by seeds. Control: Hand weed or hoe. Spread mulch over area.

Water Weeds

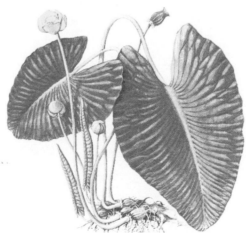

Duckweed (*Lemna minor*)
Floating plants with minute leaves $1/16$–$3/16$ in. across. Multiplies rapidly from new plants on leaf edges or from water-borne seeds. Can be a pest. Control: scoop off surface.

Eurasian water milfoil
(*Myriophyllum spicatum*)
Perennial. Weed is submerged. Spreads by seeds and rooting stems. Control: Rake out and compost.

Spatterdock (*Nuphar lutea* and *N. advena*)
Perennial. Spreads by creeping rhizomes. Control: Drain pool and dig out.

Types of Weeds and Their Control

Any plant growing where it is unwanted—a petunia in a cabbage patch, a lettuce in a flower border, a nasturtium in an onion bed—can be considered a weed. In practice, however, the term "weed" is used for any plant that grows rapidly, thrives in a wide range of conditions and soils, competes successfully with surrounding plants, and reproduces itself with ease.

Although weeds often have colorful flowers and can be attractive in a field or on vacant land, they are usually unsightly in a garden. But there are several more practical reasons for removing them from the garden.

Weeds compete with cultivated plants for water, nutrients, and heat—to the disadvantage of the cultivated plants. For example, weeds check the early growth of such vegetables as onions and carrots, both of which are extremely slow to germinate and to develop.

Weeds can also be hosts to insects and diseases that attack several garden and greenhouse plants. For example, the shepherd's purse harbors flea beetles and cabbage-root flies, both of which infest many types of green vegetables.

Weeds can carry over such pests from season to season, thus causing the infestation of any new crops planted nearby.

All-natural Weed and Grass Herbicides

There are a number of reliable weed and grass herbicides that contain natural ingredients only. These sprays are very effective in killing weeds using citric acid, garlic, yucca extracts, vinegar, and clove oil, among other ingredients. They are also biodegradable, breaking down into inert materials when in the soil. Ask about them at your local nursery or garden supply center.

Invasive Plants

Depending on the climate and soil, plants that are well behaved in one part of the country, can be invasive pests in another. In addition, many of the plants we grow as ornamentals are native to other parts of the world, and, if they escape from our gardens, can displace native flora. The damage they cause is increased by them not providing the food and habitat required by indigenous species of insects, mammals, and birds, so these in turn are placed under stress.

The following list of plants contains some that are considered invasive in parts of the continent. Check with a local garden club or conservation society, if you should avoid planting any of these in your locality.

Two Types of Weeds: Annuals and Perennials

Annuals complete their cycle of growth—from seeds to mature, seed-producing plants—within a few months; then they die. Examples include the prostrate knotweed, common ragweed, goose grass, and common chickweed. Some weeds can be either annual or biennial, and some annuals can have several generations in a single growing season.

Perennial weeds can be herbaceous or woody. Herbaceous weeds are soft-stemmed plants that store food in fleshy roots, tubers, or bulbs, survive the winter in a dormant condition, and resume growth the following spring.

These plants usually have deep root systems, which make them difficult to control. Examples are the goutweed, curled dock, and quack grass.

Woody perennial weeds, such as poison ivy, store most of their food in woody stems. Since they do not have extensive root systems, they are comparatively easy to control. However, dead plants remain toxic for about a year.

Keeping Down Weeds by Cultural Methods

Weed control is an ongoing process. Weeds are relatively easy to control when small, but can become a major problem if allowed to grow to flowering size. A few minutes' work with a hoe on a dry day, repeated as often as new weeds appear, is the best way of dealing with weeds growing near ornamentals.

When first cultivating a weedy area, remove as many roots or rhizomes of perennial weeds as possible. Sites that are particularly weedy, but not immediately required for crops, can be sown with grass. Close mowing of the grass for two consecutive growing seasons will usually eliminate most perennial weeds; then the area can be planted.

A weed-infested lawn may take some time to become weed-free, but it *is* possible. Feeding and topdressing are required to develop the vigor of the grass and to reduce the chance that weeds will reappear. Some weeds, such as red sorrel, can be discouraged from growing in lawns by liming the soil to reduce the acidity on which the weed thrives.

INVASIVE TREES

SPECIES NAMES	COMMON NAMES
Acer platanoides	Norway maple
Albizia julibrissin	mimosa
Ailanthus altissima	tree-of-heaven
Alnus glutinosa	black alder
Betula pendula	European white birch
Elaeagnus angustifolia	Russian olive
Elaeagnus umbellata	autumn olive
Melaleuca quinquenervia	cajeput tree
Morus alba	white mulberry
Paulownia tomentosa	princess tree
Picea abies	Norway spruce
Pinus sylvestris	Scots pine
Phellodendron amurensis	Amur corktree
Populus alba	white poplar
Populus nigra var. *italica*	Lombardy poplar
Rhamnus cathartica	European buckthorn, common buckthorn
Rhamnus frangula	glossy buckthorn
Robinia pseudoacacia	black locust
Ulmus pumila	Siberian elm

Acer platanoides

Albizia julibrissin

Phellodendron amurensis

Morus alba

Syringa vulgaris

Tanacetum vulgare

Although widely grown, both lilacs and the common tansy can become invasive and spread into woodlands and meadows, displacing native flora.

INVASIVE SHRUBS AND CLIMBERS

SPECIES NAMES	COMMON NAMES
Berberis thunbergii	Japanese barberry
Buddleja davidii	butterfly bush
Caragana arborescens	Siberian pea tree
Celastrus orbiculatus	Asiatic bittersweet, Oriental bittersweet
Euonymus fortunei	wintercreeper
Fallopia baldschuanicum	mile-a-minute vine
Ligustrum vulgare	common privet
Lonicera japonica	Japanese honeysuckle
Lonicera tatarica	Tartarian honeysuckle
Nandina domestica	heavenly bamboo
Pueraria lobata	kudzu vine
Pyracantha coccinea	firethorn
Rosa eglanteria	sweetbriar, eglantine
Rosa multiflora	multiflowered rose
Rosa rugosa	Japanese rose
Spiraea japonica	Japanese spirea
Syringa vulgaris	lilac
Tamarix ramosissima	tamarix
Viburnum lantana	wayfaring tree
Viburnum opulus	European highbush cranberry
Wisteria floribunda	Japanese wisteria
Wisteria sinensis	Chinese wisteria

Caragana arborescens

Pyracantha coccinea

Viburnum opulus

INVASIVE AQUATICS

SPECIES NAMES	COMMON NAMES
Butomus umbellatus	flowering rush
Eichhornia crassipes	water hyacinth
Hydrocharis morsus-ranae	European frog-bit
Myriophyllum spicatum	Eurasian water milfoil, spiked water milfoil
Nymphoides peltatum	floating heart
Pistia stratiotes	water lettuce

Nymphoides peltatum

INVASIVE PERENNIALS

SPECIES NAMES	COMMON NAMES
Aegopodium podagraria	goutweed
Ajuga reptans	bugleweed
Angelica sylvestris	angelica
Artemisia absinthium	absinth, wormwood
Asperula odorata	sweet woodruff
Campanula ranunculoides	creeping bellflower
Convallaria majalis	lily-of-the-valley
Coronilla varia	crown vetch
Cytisus scoparius	Scotch broom
Dennstaedtia punctiloba	hay-scented fern
Fallopia japonica	Japanese knotweed, Mexican bamboo
Hedera helix	English ivy
Hemerocallis fulva	orange daylily
Hesperis matronalis	dame's rocket
Hypericum perforatum	St. John's Wort
Impatiens glandifera	Himalayan balsam
Imperata cylindrica	cogon grass
Iris pseudacorus	yellow flag
Lamium maculatum	spotted deadnettle
Lathyrus latifolius	perennial sweet pea
Lathyrus tuberosus	fyfield pea
Liriope muscari	lilyturf
Lunaria annua	silver dollar, honesty
Lysimachia nummularia	moneywort, creeping Charlie
Lythrum salicaria	purple loosestrife, swamp loosestrife
Matteuccia struthiopteris	ostrich fern
Miscanthus sinensis	eulalia grass, Japanese silver grass
Origanum vulgare	oregano
Persicaria virginiana	jumpseed
Phalaris arundinacea	reed canary grass, gardener's garters
Tanacetum vulgare	common tansy
Thelypteris novaboracensis	New York fern
Vinca minor	periwinkle

Ajuga reptans

Convallaria majalis

Hedera helix

Iris pseudocarus

Lysimachia nummularia

Lythrum salicaria

INDEX

Note: Page numbers in **bold** indicate main references; those in *italic* are photographs. Plants are listed by botanical names (in italics) and by common name (regular type).

bog rosmary (*Andromeda polifolia*), **157**

bok choi (Chinese celery cabbage), *456*, **456–457**

Boltonia (boltonia), **47**

borage (*Borago officinalis*), **486**

Borago officinalis (borage), **486**

borax, 544

bordeaux mixture, 544

borers, 534, 539

boron deficiency, 537

Boston ivy (*Parthenocissus tricuspidata*), *271*, **343**

botrytis (gray mold)
    flowers attacked after opening, 530
    on gooseberries, 412, *412*
    leaves with altered color, 511, 516
    on lettuce, 528
    on peonies, 529
    shoots discolored, 523
    on shrub cuttings, 261
    small-fruit disorders, 533
    tomato and pea- or bean-pod disorder, 534
    tulip fire, 527, 530, 535

bottlebrush buckeye (*Aesculus parviflora*), **288–289,** *289*

bottlebrush (*Callistemon*), **292–293**

Bougainvillea (bougainvillea), *271*, **344**

Bouteloua gracilis (blue grama, or mosquito grass), *97*, *98*, **99**

boxwood (*Buxus*), 249, **292–293,** *293*, 341, **349**

boxwood leaf miners, 517

boysenberries. *See* blackberries

Brachyscome iberidifolia (Swan River daisy), **198**

bracken (*Pteridium aquilinum*), **549**

braconid wasps, 17

Brassica oleracea acephala (ornamental cabbage, and kale), **199**

Braun's holly fern (*Polystichum braunii*), **108**

Briza (quaking grass), **98**

broad-leaved plantain (*Plantago major*), 25, **553,** *553*

broad mites, 517

broccoli, 449, **449**

Brodiaea (brodiaea), **122**

Brodiaea uniflora (spring starflower), **126**

broom. *See Cytisus* (broom)

broom, Spanish (*Spartium*), 269, *330*, **330–331**

broom (*Genista*), **163,** *308*, **308–309,** 340

Broussonetia (paper mulberry), **227**

Browallia (browallia spp.), **199**, 214

brown rot, 531

Bruckenthalia (bruckenthalia, or spike heath), **159**

Brunnera (brunnera, or Siberian bugloss), **47**

Brussels sprouts, 450, **450,** 451

buckeye, bottlebrush (*Aesculus parviflora*), **288–289,** *289*

buckeye (*Aesculus*), *226*, **226,** 245

buckhorn plantain (*Plantago lanceolata*), **553**

buckthorn, sea (*Hippophae*), *252*, **310–311,** 340, 341, **348,** *348*

buckthorn (*Rhamnus* spp.), 556

bud blast, rhododendron, 529

Buddleja (buddleia), 249, *253*, 269, 270, 272, *292*, **292–293,** 341, 557

bud drop, 529

bud eelworms, 514

buffaloberry (*Shepherdia*), **328–329,** 340

bugbane (*Cimicifuga*), 48, **48,** 67, 68

bugleweed (*Ajuga*), *28*, **28,** 68, **156,** 557

bugs
    apple red, 531
    chinch, 540
    four-lined plant, 508
    harlequin, 508
    lace, 511
    leaf, 508, 530
    mealybugs, 507, 522, *522*, 538
    plant, 508, 530
    root mealybugs, 538
    spittlebugs, 512
    tarnished plant, 531

bulb eelworms, 518, 534

bulb nematodes, 518, 534

Bulbocodium (bulbocodium), **122**

bulbs, **109–150**
    alphabetical listing, **121–131**
    autumn flowering, 111, 114
    bulb, corm, tuber, and root disorders, **534–538**
    bulblets and cormels, 117
    buying, 115
    care, 116
    categories, 110–111
    deadheading blooms, 116
    for under deciduous trees, 132
    dividing, 116–117
    favorite flowers, 112–113
    feeding and watering, 114, 116
    forcing, 119–120
    with fragrant flowers, 132
    frost protection, 116
    group planting, 114
    for indoor flowering, 119–120
    interplanted with perennials, 38
    late-winter/early-spring flowering, 111, 124
    lifting, transferring, drying, storing, 117
    mulching, 116
    naturalizing, 110, 111, 114, 115, 132
    offsets, 116–117
    pH levels, optimal, 499
    planning process, 110
    planting, 114–115
    problems, 117
    to produce cut flowers, 114, 116, 132
    in rock gardens, 114
    with seed heads to dry, 132

sites for, 110, 114
soil preparation, 114
spring flowering, 110, 111, 114, 115
summer flowering, 111
supports for, 116
in temperature extremes, 115
weed control, 116
See also individual plants, e.g. Crocus; Narcissus

bulb scale mites, 519

Bulgarian onion (*Nectaroscordum*), **128,** 132

bulrush (*Typha*), *185*, **188**

bunchberry (*Cornus canadensis*), **160**

burnet (*Sanguisorba minor*), **486**

burning bush (*Dictamnus*), 50, **50,** 67

bush anemone (*Carpenteria*), 294, **294–295**

bushclover (*Lespedeza*), **314–315**

busy Lizzie (*Impatiens walleriana*), **205,** 214

Butomus (flowering rush), *183*, **185,** 557

buttercup. *See Ranunculus* (ranunculus, or buttercup)

butterflies, attracting, 14–17, 68, 214

butterfly bush (*Buddleja davidii*), 249, *253*, 269, 272, *292*, **292–293,** 557

butterfly flower (*Schizanthus pinnatus*), *211*, **211,** 214

butterfly weed (*Asclepias*), *18*, **46,** 67, 68

butternut (*Juglans cinerea*), **231**

buttonbush (*Cephalanthus*), **294–295,** 340

Buxus (boxwood), 249, **292–293,** *293*, 341, **349**

C

cabbage, *452*, **452**

cabbage, ornamental (*Brassica oleracea acephala*), **199**

cabbage maggots, 538

cabbage white caterpillars, *515*

Cabomba (fanwort), 177, **184**

cactus (*Opuntia humifusa*), 20

Caesalpinia (poinciana), **227**

cajeput tree (*Melaleuca quinquenervia*), 556

Caladium (caladium), **122**

Calamagrostis acutiflora (feather reed grass), *97*, *97*, 98, **99**

Calendula officinalis (calendula, or pot marigold), *192*, **199,** *199*, 214

Calibrachoa hybrida (many bells), **199**

California bluebell (*Phacelia campanularia*), **209**

California fan (*Washingtonia filifera*), **238**

California huckleberry (*Vaccinium ovatum*), **336–337**

California lilac (*Ceanothus*), 268, 269, 273, **294–295**

California nutmeg (*Torreya californica*), **244**

California poppy (*Eschscholzia californica*), **203,** *213*

Calla (bog, or water, arum), 177, 182, **185**

calla (*Zantedeschia*), *131*, **131,** 132, **188**

Callicarpa (beauty-berry), *257*, **292–293,** *293*

calliopsis (*Coreopsis tinctoria*), **201,** 214

Callistemon (bottlebrush), **292–293**

Callistephus chinensis (China aster), **199,** 214

Calluna (heather), 249, *303*, 340, 341, **375–378**

Calocedrus (incense cedar), **240**

Caltha (marsh marigold, or kingcup), 177, 184, **185**

Calycanthus (Carolina allspice), **292–293,** 340, 341

Camassia (camassia, or camass), *122*, **123,** 132

Camellia (camellia), **292–293, 349**

Campanula (bellflower), *40*, *48*, *48*, 67, *153*, **159,** 557

Campanula medium (Canterbury bell), **199**

campion (*Lychnis*), *58*, 67, 68, **165**

campion (*Silene*), **168,** *168*

Campsis (trumpet creeper), 271, **342,** *344*

Canada thistle (*Cirsium arvense*), **555**

Canadian pondweed (*Elodea*), 177, 182, **184**

canary creeper (*Tropaeolum peregrinum*), **212**

candytuft (*Iberis* spp.), *164*, **164,** *189*, **204,** *204*

cane fruits. *See* fruit canes

cane girdlers, 418

canker
    apple, 525, *525*
    bacterial, of stone fruits, 523
    nectria, 525
    parsnip, 537
    poplar, 525

canna, water (*Thalia*), **188**

Canna (canna), 111, **123,** *123*, 132

Canterbury bell (*Campanula medium*), **199**

Cape figwort (*Phygelius aequalis*), **209**

Cape fuschia (*Phygelius*), **61, 209**

Cape marigold (*Osteospermum* hybrids), **208**

Capsella bursa-pastoris (shepherd's purse), **553**

Capsicum annuum (ornamental pepper), **199**

Caragana (pea shrub), 267, 340, **347,** 557

caraway (*Carum carvi*), **486**

marigold, French (*Tagetes patula*), **211,** 214

marigold; pot (*Calendula officinalis*), *192,* **199,** *199,* 214

marigold, signet (*Tagetes tenuifolia*), **211,** 214

marjoram (*Origanum onites, O. majorana*), *489,* **489, 490**

marshmallow (*Althaea*), **45**

marsh marigold (*Caltha*), *177, 184,* **185**

masterwort (*Astrantia*), 68

Matricaria matricarioides (pineapple weed), **550**

matricaria (*Tanacetum parthenium*), *193,* **212**

Matteuccia struthiopteris (ostrich fern), *102, 102,* **107,** 557

Matthiola bicornis, M. incana annua (stock), **207,** 214

mayapple (*Podophyllum*), **61**

Mayday (*Prunus padus*), *234,* **234**

mayflower (*Epigaea*), **162**

meadow rue (*Thalictrum*), **65,** 68, **169**

meadow saffron (*Colchicum autumnale*), 111, **123**

meadow sweet (*Filipendula*), **52,** 67

mealybugs, 507, 522, *522,* 538

mealy cup sage (*Salvia farinacea*), **210,** 214

Melaleuca quinquenervia (cajeput tree), 556

Melissa officinalis (balm), *485,* **485**

melons, **419–420**

Mentha spp. (mint), **165, 490**

merrybells (*Uvularia*), *169,* **169**

Mertensia maritima (oyster plant), **58,** 67, **165**

Mertensia (mertensia, or Virginia bluebell), **58,** 67, **165**

Mesembryanthemum criniflorum (Livingston daisy), **202**

Metake bamboo (*Pseudosasa japonica*), **322–323**

Metasequoia (dawn redwood), **242,** 245, 246

Mexican bamboo (*Fallopia japonica*), 557

Mexican orange (*Choisya*), **296–297**

Mexican sunflower (*Tithonia rotundifolia*), **212**

Michaelmas daisy (*Aster novi-belgii*), *38,* **47,** *47,* 68

Microbiota decussata (Russian arborvitae), **30**

midges, violet leaf gall, 518

mignonette (*Reseda odorata*), **210,** 214

mildew
   downy, 515
   powdery, 513, *513,* 522, 532

milfoil, water (*Myriophyllum*), **184, 555,** 557

milfoil (*Achillea*), *34,* **44,** 67, 68

milkwort (*Polygala*), **166**

millipedes, 545

mimosa (*Albizia*), **226,** 556

Mimulus (monkey flower, or mimulus), **186, 207,** *207,* 214

miners. *See* leaf miners

mint (*Mentha* spp.), **165, 490**

mint rust, 524

Mirabilis jalapa (four o'clock), *207,* **207**

Miscanthus sinensis (Japanese silver grass, eulalia), *96, 97,* **100,** *100,* **188,** 557

miscible oils, 544

mites
   broad, 517
   bulb scale, 519
   conifer, 513
   cyclamen, 517
   European red, 516, 522
   gall, 520
   organic controls, 542–543
   pear leaf blister, 511
   predatory, 546
   red spider, 512
   two-spotted, 512, 522

mock orange. *See Philadelphus* (mock orange)

mold, 511, 516, 540
   See also botrytis (gray mold)

Molina caerulea (purple moor grass), *97,* **100**

Mollugo verticillata (carpetweed), **549**

Molucella laevis (bells of Ireland), **207,** 214

Monarda didyma (bergamot, or bee balm), *35,* **59,** *59,* 67, 68

Monarda fistulosa (wild bergamot), *42,* **59**

mondo grass (*Ophiopogon*), **59**

money plant (*Lunaria annua*), **206,** 214, 557

moneywort (*Lysimachia nummularia*), **30, 186,** 557

monkey flower (*Mimulus*), **186, 207,** *207,* 214

monkey puzzle (*Araucaria araucana*), **240**

monkshood (*Aconitum*), *36,* **44,** *44,* 67, 68

montbretia (*Crocosmia* hybrids), 111, 132

morning glory, dwarf (*Convolvulus tricolor*), **201**

morning glory (*Ipomoea purpurea,* or *I. tricolor,* vine), *205,* **205**

Morus (mulberry), **233,** 245, 246, 556

mosquito grass (*Bouteloua gracilis*), *97, 98,* **99**

moss on lawns, 26, 552

moss phlox (*Phlox subulata*), **30, 166**

moss rose (*Portulaca grandiflora*), *20, 195,* **209**

moths, 521, 531, *539*

mountain ash (*Sorbus*), **237,** 246

mountain avens (*Dryas octopetala*), *155,* **162**

mountain bluet (*Centaurea montana*), *40,* **48**

mountain laurel (*Kalmia latifolia*), *249, 312,* **312–313,** 340, 341

mouse-ear (*Cerastium*), **160, 551**

mowers and mowing, 22, 24

mugo pine (*Pinus mugo mugo*), **320–321,** *321*

Mukdenia rossii (red-leaved mukdenia), **30**

mulberry, paper (*Broussonetia*), **227**

mulberry (*Morus*), **233,** 245, 246, 556

mulches and mulching
   organic and inorganic, 441, 505
   See also individual plants, or categories of plants

mullein (*Verbascum*), *66,* **66**

Murraya (orange jessamine), **316–317**

Musa (banana), **59**

Muscari (muscari, or grape hyacinth), **127,** 132

mycoplasma, 530

Myosotis spp. (myositis, or forget-me-not), **166, 207,** 214

Myrica (bayberry), *249,* 267, **318–319,** 340, 341

Myriophyllum aquaticum (parrot feather), **184**

Myriophyllum (water milfoil), **184, 555,** 557

Myrrhis odorata (sweet cicely), **487**

Myrtis (myrtle), *318,* **318–319**

N

naked ladies (*Amaryllis belladonna*), 111, **121,** *121*

Nandina (heavenly bamboo), **318–319,** 557

Nanking cherry (*Prunus tomentosa*), **324–325,** 341, **348**

nannyberry (*Viburnum lentago*), 268, **336–337,** 341

narcissus bulb flies, 534

Narcissus (narcissus and daffodils)
   deadheading, 116
   dividing bulbs, 116
   flowering period, 111, 112
   forcing, *116,* 119
   interplanting, 38, 101
   jonquils, *112,* **112, 127**
   naturalizing, 111, 112, 115
   planting, 114–115
   for specific locations/purposes, 132
   types, **112,** *116, 119,* **127–128**
   See also bulbs

narrow beech fern (*Thelypteris phegopteris*), **108**

nasturtium (*Tropaeolum majus*), **212**

Nasturtium (watercress), **186**

Natal plum (*Carissa*), **292–293**

naturalizing bulbs, 110, 111, 114, 115, 132

neck rot, 535

necrosis, pedicel, 529

nectarines. *See* peach trees

Nectaroscordum (Bulgarian onion), **128,** 132

nectria canker, 525

neem, 544

Nelumbo (lotus), **187**

nematodes
   bulb and stem, 518, 534
   golden potato cyst, 539
   leaf, 514
   onion, 518
   organic controls, 542–543
   parasitic (natural predator), 545
   phlox, 518
   root-knot, 539

Nemesia strumosa (nemesia), **207,** 214

Nemophila (five spot, and baby blue-eyes), **208**

Nepeta (nepeta, or catmint), **59,** 67, 68

Nerine (nerine), *128,* **128,** 132

Nerium (oleander), **318–319**

netted chain fern (*Woodwardia*), *108,* **108**

New York fern (*Thelypteris noveboracensis*), **108,** 557

New Zealand flax (*Phormium tenax*), 67

Nicotiana (nicotiana, or ornamental tobacco), *208,* **208,** 214

Nierembergia spp. and hybrids (nierembergia, or cupflower), **208**

Nigella damascena (nigella, or love-in-a-mist), *192,* **208,** 214

night flowering jasmine (*Cestrum nocturnum*), **294–295**

ninebark (*Physocarpus*), **320–321,** *321*

Nippon bells (*Shortia uniflora*), **168,** *168*

nitrogen
   dahlias and, 138
   fruiting of trees and, 382
   nutrient for plants, 24, 437, 498–499

nitrogen deficiency, 515

nodding star of Bethlehem (*Ornithogalum nutans*), *128,* **128**

Norfolk Island pine (*Araucaria heterophylla*), **240**

Nuphar advena (spatterdock), **555**

Nuphar lutea (yellow pond lily, or spatterdock), *176,* **555,** *555*

nutmeg, California (*Torreya californica*), **244**

nutrient deficiency, 515

Nymphaea (water lily)
   fertilizing, 176
   problems, 178, 509
   propagation, 180
   soil and planting, 176
   varieties, *174, 175, 176, 179, 180,* **183**

Nymphoides (floating heart), *177,* **183,** 557

Nyssa (sour or black gum, or tupelo), **233,** 245, 246

Credits and Acknowledgments

GARDENING CONSULTANTS

FERN MARSHALL BRADLEY

Fern Marshall Bradley is a freelance writer and editor whose favorite topics are organic gardening and sustainable living. She is the co-author of Reader's Digest's *Vegetable Gardening*. During the 1990s, Fern conceived and edited several top-selling garden titles, including *Rodale's All-New Encyclopedia of Organic Gardening*, *The Organic Gardener's Handbook of Natural Insect and Disease Control*, *The Experts Book of Garden Hints*, and *Gardening with Perennials*.

Fern's education and experience ideally support her passion for gardening and garden writing. She has degrees in plant science and horticulture from Cornell and Rutgers universities, and she honed her organic gardening skills while managing a 1-hectare market garden in western New Jersey. Fern now lives in the Cambridge Valley of New York State, where she is revitalizing a neglected garden.

TREVOR COLE

Trevor Cole received his early training in horticulture at London's famed Royal Botanic Gardens, Kew. He joined Agriculture Canada in 1967. In 1972 Trevor became the curator of the Dominion Arboretum in Ottawa, Ontario, a post he held for 23 years.

Trevor has authored and co-authored a number of books and served as consultant or editor-in-chief on many others. His writing has earned him an Award of Merit from the Garden Writers Association of America and the Carlton R. Worth Award from the North American Rock Garden Society. For generously donating his time and expertise to gardening organizations, he has received the Ontario District Association Service Award and been twice honored with the international Lilac Society's Award of Merit. A past president of the Ottawa Horticultural Society, he has also served as director of the Rhododendron Society of Canada.

Trevor lives outside Ottawa with his wife, Brenda, also a horticulturist and garden writer. The couple met when they were students together at Kew.

OTHER ADVISERS AND CONSULTANTS

Technical Adviser
Kenneth A. Beckett

Special Consultants
Cornelius Ackerson
Harvey E. Barké, Ph.D.
Henry O. Beracha
Arthur Bing, Ph.D.
Norman F. Childers, Ph.D.
August DeHertogh, Ph.D.
Marjorie J. Dietz
James E. Dwyer
Jerome A. Eaton

Eleanor Brown Gambee
Myron Kimnach
A. H. Krezdorn, Ph.D.
Donald Maynard, Ph.D.
John T. Mickel, Ph.D.
Margaret C. Ohlander
Donald Richardson
Brigitte Roy
Robert Schery, Ph.D.
James S. Wells
Helen M. Whitman

Translator
Alex Farrell

ILLUSTRATIONS

Tegra Premedia Private Limited, India

p. 501, green bin, p. 502 bottom: Christine Hart-Davies/ Eaglemoss Publications Ltd.

Norman Barber
David Baxter
Howard Berelson
Leonora Box
George Buctel
Pam Carroll
Helen Cowcher
Cyril David
Brian Delf
Jean-Claude Gagnon
Ian Garrard
Tony Graham, LSIA
Roy Grubb
Vana Haggerty
Nicolas Hall
Gary Hincks

David Hutter
Richard Jacobs
Gillian Kenny
Sarah Kensington
Yves Lachance
Patricia Ann Lenander
Richard Lewington
Carlos Lillo
Donald A. Mackay
Edward Malsberg
Noel Malsberg
Constance Marshall
Sean Milne
Thea Nockels
Charles Pickard
Charles Raymond

Ken Rice
John Rignall
John Roberts
Allianora Rosse
Anne Savage
Jim Silks
Ray Skibinski
Kathleen Smith, MSIA
Les Smith
Joyce Tuhill
Joan Berg Victor
Michael Vivo
John Western
Michael J. Woods
Elsie Wrigley

PHOTO CREDITS

Photos: Reader's Digest
Except
Agrar Service:
  Nigel Cattlin/Holt: 443L, 455
  Nigel Cattlin: 467
  Rosemary/Mayer/Holt: 381L
Louise Bilodeau: 7, 14-15R-L
BipFloral.com: 13L, 17TR
Dr. Helga Butcher-Weissbrodt: 379, 380TR, 381M, 381R, 382L, 382R, 384L, 384R, 385L, 385M, 385R, 386L, 387L, 387R, 388L, 388R, 389, 390TL, 391L, 391R, 393L, 393R, 394L, 394R, 395, 396L, 396R, 399, 401, 403, 404L, 405, 406, 407L, 407R, 408L, 409L, 409R, 411L, 411R, 412L, 412M, 412R, 413L, 413R, 415, 416R, 418L, 418R, 421, 423, 424, 425, 426L, 426R, 426R, 427L, 427R, 428, 429, 430, 432, 433L, 433R,

434L, 434M, 434R, 435, 440L, 445L, 446R, 459L, 461, 462, 472, 475, 478L, 478M, 479L, 479R, 480R, 481, 487L, 487R, 488L, 488R, 489L, 489M, 489R, 490, 491, 492, 493L, 493R, 495, 504L, 504R, 531, 532, 545L, 545M, 545R, 546, 550, 551
Janet Davis/beautifulbounty.com: 11MT, 18BL, 18BR, 483
Monique Dumas: 12BM, 13TR, 15BR, 16TM
Elizabeth Eastman: 81
Florastar Bildarchiv: 386R
Ann Gordon Images: 12L, 17B, 18TR, 20ML
Garden Picture Library/Photolibrary: 19TR
Hild Samen: 445R, 446L, 447, 459R, 460L, 460R, 480M

Saxon Holt photography: 19TL
André Hébert: 77, 368
Michelle Lafontaine, designer/courtesy Andryves.com: 10-11
Harald Lange: 499L, 499R
Emanuel Lowi: 416
Allan Mandel: 9, 11R, 1MB, 12TR, 13BR, 16, 170-171
Montreal Botanical Garden: 397, 398, 400, 402, 404R, 410, 414L
Okapia:
  G. Büttner: 444
  Hans Reinhard: 441R
  G. Synatzschke: 443R
Patricia Pennell/West Michigan Environmental Action Council: 19BL
PhotoDisc: 15TR, 22TR, 133, 152, 353, 436, 441L, 458, 496-497R-L, 541, 547

Suzanne Puech: 32-33R-L, 247, 277L, 283R, 329, 334, 340TML
Eberhard Raiser: 544
Rosen Union: 358L, 358R
Bildarchiv Sammer: 543
Silvestris Fotoservice:
  Daniel Bühler: 437L, 437M, 437R
Edith Smeesters: 20TR, 20BL, 20BR
Julius Wagner: 442, 448, 449L, 452L, 453L, 454, 457, 463, 466, 468, 469, 474, 476, 480L
Werner Kost: 438L, 438R, 439L, 439R, 440R, 449R, 450L, 450R, 451, 452R, 453R, 470, 473, 478R
Wolfgang Redeleit: 23L, 25L, 25R, 26L, 26R, 27, 499M
Wolf-Garten: 21, 23R, 25M